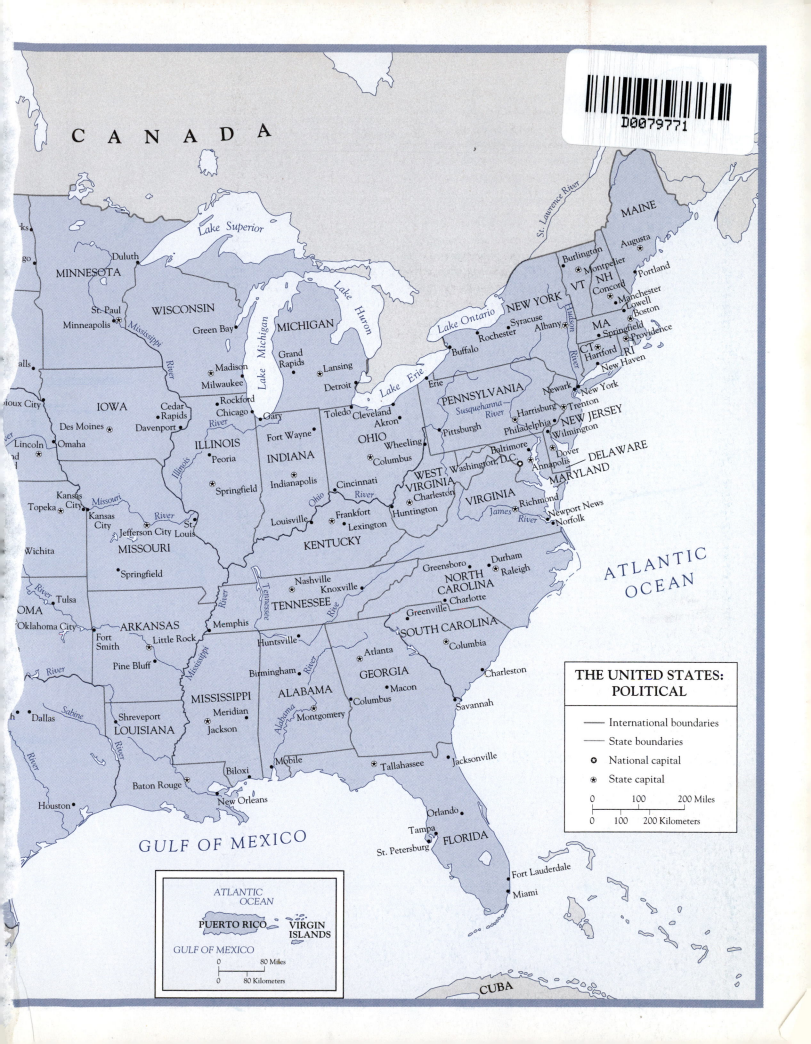

THE AMERICAN PAST

A Survey of American History

THE AMERICAN PAST

A Survey of American History

Volume I: To 1877

NINTH EDITION

Joseph R. Conlin

WADSWORTH
CENGAGE Learning™

Australia • Brazil • Japan • Korea • Mexico • Singapore • Spain • United Kingdom • United States

WADSWORTH
CENGAGE Learning™

The American Past: A Survey of American History Volume I: To 1877, Ninth Edition
Joseph R. Conlin

Publishers: Clark Baxter and Suzanne Jeans

Senior Sponsoring Editor: Ann West

Senior Development Editor: Margaret McAndrew Beasley

Assistant Editor: Megan Curry

Editorial Assistant: Megan Chrisman

Senior Media Editor: Lisa Ciccolo

Media Editor: Yevgeny Ioffe

Senior Marketing Managers: Diane Wenckebach and Katherine Bates

Marketing Communications Managers: Heather Baxley and Christine Dobberpuhl

Production Manager: Samantha Ross

Senior Content Project Manager: Lauren Wheelock

Senior Art Director: Cate Rickard Barr

Manufacturing Manager: Marcia Locke

Senior Rights Acquisition Account Manager — Text: Margaret Chamberlain-Gaston

Production Service: Macmillan Publishing Solutions

Text Designer: Dutton & Sherman Design

Permissions Account Manager, Images/Media: Mandy Groszko

Photo Researcher: PrePress PMG

Cover Designer: Dutton & Sherman Design

Cover Image: © Stapleton Collection/ Corbis, *Photograph of Leather Workers Preparing Skins at Bevingtons and Sons*

Compositor: Macmillan Publishing Solutions

© 2010, 2009 Wadsworth, Cengage Learning

ALL RIGHTS RESERVED. No part of this work covered by the copyright herein may be reproduced, transmitted, stored, or used in any form or by any means graphic, electronic, or mechanical, including but not limited to photocopying, recording, scanning, digitizing, taping, Web distribution, information networks, or information storage and retrieval systems, except as permitted under Section 107 or 108 of the 1976 United States Copyright Act, without the prior written permission of the publisher.

For product information and technology assistance, contact us at **Cengage Learning Customer & Sales Support, 1-800-354-9706**

For permission to use material from this text or product, submit all requests online at **www.cengage.com/permissions**

Further permissions questions can be e-mailed to **permissionrequest@cengage.com**

Library of Congress Control Number: 2008943443

ISBN-13: 978-0-495-57288-6

ISBN-10: 0-495-57288-8

Wadsworth
20 Channel Center Street
Boston, MA 02210
USA

Cengage Learning products are represented in Canada by Nelson Education, Ltd.

For your course and learning solutions, visit **www.cengage.com**

Purchase any of our products at your local college store or at our preferred online store **www.ichapters.com**

Printed in the United States of America
1 2 3 4 5 6 7 13 12 11 10 09

To the memory of
J.R.C. (1917–1985)
L.V.C. (1920–2001)

Brief Contents

List of Maps   xv
How They Lived   xvii
Preface   xix

CHAPTER 1

Discoveries
Indians, Europeans, and the Americas About
15,000 B.C. to A.D. 1550   1

CHAPTER 2

Settlements Across the Sea
Motives, Failures, and Finally, a Colony
1550–1624   20

CHAPTER 3

Thirteen Colonies
England's North American Empire
1620–1732   39

CHAPTER 4

English Designs, American Facts of Life
Colonial Society in the 1600s   55

CHAPTER 5

Other Americans
Indians and Africans in the Colonies   71

CHAPTER 6

Contest for a Continent
French America and British America
1608–1763   91

CHAPTER 7

Family Quarrels
Dissension in the Colonies 1763–1770   112

CHAPTER 8

From Riot to Rebellion
The Road to Independence 1770–1776   126

CHAPTER 9

The War for Independence
The Rebels Victorious 1776–1781   143

CHAPTER 10

Inventing a Country
American Constitutions 1781–1789   160

CHAPTER 11

We the People
Putting the Constitution to Work
1789–1800   178

CHAPTER 12

The Age of Jefferson
Frustration Abroad 1800–1815   196

CHAPTER 13

Nationalism: Culture, Politics, Diplomacy
1815–1824   216

CHAPTER 14

Machines, Cotton, Land
Economy and Society 1790–1824   234

CHAPTER 15

The People's Hero
Andrew Jackson and a New Era
1824–1830   252

CHAPTER 16

In the Shadow of Old Hickory
Personalities and Politics 1830–1842   269

CHAPTER 17

Religion and Reform
Evangelicals and Enthusiasts 1800–1850   284

CHAPTER 18

The Peculiar Institution
Southern Slavery   301

CHAPTER 19

From Sea to Shining Sea
Expansion 1820–1848   319

CHAPTER 20

Apples of Discord
Western Lands and Immigration
1844–1856   334

CHAPTER 21

The Collapse of the Union
From Debate to Violence 1854–1861   347

CHAPTER 22

Tidy Plans, Ugly Realities
The Civil War through 1862   364

CHAPTER 23

Driving Dixie Down
General Grant's War of Attrition
1863–1865   382

CHAPTER 24

Aftermath
The Era of Reconstruction 1863–1877   399

Appendix   A-1
Credits   C-1
Index   I-1

Table of Contents

List of Maps   xv
How They Lived   xvii
Preface   xix

CHAPTER 1

Discoveries
**Indians, Europeans, and the Americas
About 15,000 B.C. to A.D. 1550**   1

THE FIRST COLONIZATION   2
WESTERN EUROPE: ENERGETIC AND
   EXPANSIVE   6
PORTUGAL AND SPAIN: THE VAN OF
   EXPLORATION   10
THE SPANISH EMPIRE   13
   How They Lived: Big City Life   15
THE COLUMBIAN EXCHANGE   16
Further Reading   19
Key Terms   19
Online Resources   19

CHAPTER 2

Settlements Across the Sea
**Motives, Failures, and Finally,
a Colony 1550–1624**   20

THE ENGLISH REFORMATION   21
ELIZABETHAN ENGLAND: THE SEEDBED
   OF ENGLISH AMERICA   24
BEGINNINGS OF AN EMPIRE   26
JAMESTOWN   30
OTHER BEGINNINGS   35
   How They Lived: Common Seamen   36
Further Reading   37
Key Terms   38
Online Resources   38

CHAPTER 3

Thirteen Colonies
**England's North American Empire
1620–1732**   39

THE NEW ENGLAND COLONIES   39
RHODE ISLAND, CONNECTICUT, AND NEW
   HAMPSHIRE   45
PROPRIETARY COLONIES   47
   How They Lived: Puritan Sunday   53
Further Reading   53
Key Terms   54

Online Resources   54
Discovery   54-A

CHAPTER 4

English Designs, American Facts of Life
Colonial Society in the 1600s   55

TRADE   55
MERCANTILISM IN THE SOUTH   58
NEW ENGLAND   63
THE MIDDLE COLONIES   67
   How They Lived: Finding the Way   69
Further Reading   70
Key Terms   70
Online Resources   70

CHAPTER 5

Other Americans
Indians and Africans in the Colonies   71

THE EASTERN WOODLANDS INDIANS   71
A WORLD TURNED UPSIDE DOWN   76
AMERICANS FROM AFRICA   80
THE TRANS-ATLANTIC SLAVE TRADE   85
   How They Lived: Slave Stations   88
Further Reading   89
Key Terms   90
Online Resources   90

CHAPTER 6

Contest for a Continent
**French America and British America
1608–1763**   91

NEW FRANCE AND LOUISIANA   91
A CENTURY OF CONFLICT   95
A CHANGING SOCIETY   97
   How They Lived: Piracy's Golden Age   98
POLITICS: IMPERIAL AND COLONIAL   103
RELIGION: DECLINE AND REVIVAL   105
BRITAIN'S GLORIOUS TRIUMPH   107
Further Reading   110
Key Terms   111
Online Resources   111
Discovery   111-A

CHAPTER 7

Family Quarrels
Dissension in the Colonies 1763–1770   112

IMPERIAL PROBLEMS 112
THE CRISIS OF 1765 119
How They Lived: Colonial Politicians 122
ACT TWO 123
Further Reading 125
Key Terms 125
Online Resources 125

CHAPTER 8

From Riot to Rebellion
The Road to Independence 1770–1776   126

STORMS WITHIN THE LULL 126
How They Lived: The Hated Redcoats 130
THE MARCH TOWARD WAR 132
REBELLION 134
CUTTING THE TIE 139
Further Reading 141
Key Terms 142
Online Resources 142

CHAPTER 9

The War for Independence
The Rebels Victorious 1776–1781   143

AN IMBALANCE OF POWER 143
BOSTON GAINED, NEW YORK LOST 147
THE TIDE TURNS 152
How They Lived: Ignoring the Revolution 156
Further Reading 158
Key Terms 159
Online Resources 159
Discovery 159-A

CHAPTER 10

Inventing a Country
American Constitutions 1781–1789   160

STATE CONSTITUTIONS 160
AMERICA UNDER THE ARTICLES OF
    CONFEDERATION 164
How They Lived: Laying Out the Land 166
DIFFICULTIES AND ANXIETIES 169
THE CONSTITUTION 171
RATIFICATION 175
Further Reading 176
Key Terms 177
Online Resources 177

CHAPTER 11

We the People
**Putting the Constitution to Work
1789–1800**   178

THE FIRST PRESIDENCY 178

TROUBLES ABROAD 184
How They Lived: Turning Forests into Farms 186
THE TUMULTUOUS NORTHWEST 189
THE PRESIDENCY OF JOHN ADAMS 191
Further Reading 194
Key Terms 195
Online Resources 195

CHAPTER 12

The Age of Jefferson
Frustration Abroad 1800–1815   196

THE ELECTION OF 1800 196
THE LOUISIANA PURCHASE 202
How They Lived: White Americans in Slavery 206
FOREIGN WOES 207
JEMMY APPLEJOHN AND THE WAR
OF 1812 209
Further Reading 214
Key Terms 215
Online Resources 215
Discovery 215-A

CHAPTER 13

Nationalism: Culture, Politics, Diplomacy
1815–1824   216

TWO SECTIONS, ONE COUNTRY 216
THE TRANSPORTATION REVOLUTION 221
How They Lived: Funding and Digging the Erie
    Canal 224
THE HAPPY PRESIDENCY OF JAMES MONROE 229
MISSOURI 231
Further Readings 232
Key Terms 233
Online Resources 233

CHAPTER 14

Machines, Cotton, Land
Economy and Society 1790–1824   234

THE INDUSTRIAL REVOLUTION 234
THE INDUSTRIAL NORTHEAST 237
How They Lived: New England Mill Girls 240
THE SOUTH AT THE CROSSROADS 242
THE TRANS-APPALACHIAN FRONTIER 244
FEDERAL LAND POLICY 248
Further Reading 250
Key Terms 251
Online Resources 251

CHAPTER 15

The People's Hero
**Andrew Jackson and a New Era
1824–1830**   252

THE ELECTION OF 1824 252
THE AGE OF THE COMMON MAN 256
THE REVOLUTION OF 1828 258

How They Lived: Pistols at Twenty Paces   260
ISSUES OF JACKSON'S FIRST
   TERM   263
Further Reading   268
Key Terms   268
Online Resources   268

CHAPTER 16

In the Shadow of Old Hickory
Personalities and Politics 1830–1842   **269**

VAN BUREN VERSUS CALHOUN   269
JOHN C. CALHOUN   269
THE WAR WITH THE BANK   272
THE SECOND PARTY SYSTEM   275
How They Lived: Alma Mater   278
Further Reading   282
Key Terms   283
Online Resources   283
Discovery   283-A

CHAPTER 17

Religion and Reform
**Evangelicals and Enthusiasts
1800–1850**   **284**

AGE OF REASON, AGE OF FAITH   284
THE BURNED-OVER DISTRICT   288
EVANGELICAL REFORM   292
How They Lived: Secular Sensations   294
THE ABOLITIONISTS   296
Further Reading   299
Key Terms   300
Online Resources   300

CHAPTER 18

The Peculiar Institution
Southern Slavery   **301**

SOUTHERN ANTISLAVERY   301
THREATS TO THE SOUTHERN
   ORDER   304
THE SOUTH CLOSES RANKS   306
How They Lived: Fugitive Slaves   306
WHAT WAS SLAVERY LIKE?   310
LIFE IN THE QUARTERS   316
RESISTANCE   316
Further Reading   318
Key Terms   318
Online Resources   318

CHAPTER 19

From Sea to Shining Sea
Expansion 1820–1848   **319**

MEXICO'S BORDERLANDS   319
THE OREGON COUNTRY   324
How They Lived: The Patricios   325

Further Reading   333
Key Terms   333
Online Resources   333

CHAPTER 20

Apples of Discord
**Western Lands and Immigration
1844–1856**   **334**

SLAVERY AND THE WEST   334
THE CRISIS OF 1850   337
How They Lived: How They
   Mined for Gold   340
THE COMPROMISE   341
THE KANSAS-NEBRASKA ACT   343
Further Reading   346
Key Terms   346
Online Resources   346
Discovery   346-A

CHAPTER 21

The Collapse of the Union
**From Debate to Violence
1854–1861**   **347**

BLEEDING KANSAS   347
A HARDENING OF LINES   350
How They Lived: Defying the Law:
   Importers of Slaves   355
THE ELECTION OF 1860   356
THE CONFEDERACY   359
Further Reading   362
Key Terms   363
Online Resources   363

CHAPTER 22

Tidy Plans, Ugly Realities
The Civil War through 1862   **364**

THE ART OF WAR   364
THE SOBERING CAMPAIGN
   OF 1861   368
How They Lived: Facing Battle   372
1862 AND STALEMATE   373
Further Reading   380
Key Terms   381
Online Resources   381

CHAPTER 23

Driving Dixie Down
**General Grant's War of Attrition
1863–1865**   **382**

THE CAMPAIGNS OF 1863   382
THE FORTRESS AT VICKSBURG   383
How They Lived:
   The Anti-Draft Riots   387

TOTAL WAR   389
THE AMERICAN TRAGEDY   394
CONSEQUENCES OF THE
   CIVIL WAR   395
Further Reading   397
Key Terms   398
Online Resources   398

CHAPTER 24
Aftermath
The Era of Reconstruction 1863–1877   399

THE RECONSTRUCTION CRISIS   399
1866: THE CRITICAL YEAR   404
RADICAL RECONSTRUCTION   406

How They Lived: Gullah   408
GRANT'S TROUBLED ADMINISTRATION   410
THE TWILIGHT OF RECONSTRUCTION   412
Further Reading   413
Key Terms   414
Online Resources   414
Discovery   414-A

Appendix   A-1
Credits   C-1
Index   I-1

List of Maps

Map 1:1	Mesoamerican Cities	4
Map 1:2	Aztec Mexico	6
Map 1:3	Trade Routes Before the 1500s	8
Map 2:1	The Virginia and Plymouth Companies, 1607	30
Map 3:1	The New England Colonies	46, 54-B
Map 3:2	The Middle Colonies	49, 54-B
Map 3:3	The Southern Colonies	51, 54-B
Map 4:1	The Chesapeake Estuary	60
Map 4:2	Two Triangular Trade Routes	65
Map 5:1	Major Eastern Woodlands Tribes	74
Map 5:2	The Atlantic Slave Trade	86
Map 5:3	West African Slave Stations	89
Map 6:1	French and British Empires in North America	107
Map 6:2	The Atlantic Slave Trade	111-A
Map 7:1	The Proclamation of 1763 and Pontiac's Uprising	114
Map 8:1	The First Battles, April–June 1775	137
Map 9:1	Stalemate at Boston, June 1775–March 1776	148
Map 9:2	Years of Defeat and Discouragement, 1776–1777	149
Map 9:3	Victory at Saratoga, October 17, 1777	150
Map 9:4	The Battle of Yorktown, May–October 1781	154
Map 10:1	The Western Lands Mess	165
Map 10:2	The Northwest Terrritory and the Rectangular Survey	168
Map 11:1	The Federalist Treaties	188
Map 11:2	Indian Wars in the Northwest Territory	189
Map 12:1	Louisiana and the Expeditions of Discovery, 1804–1807	203
Map 12:2	The War of 1812	212
Map 13:1	Rivers, Roads, and Canals 1820–1860	223
Map 13:2	Railroads 1850–1860	227
Map 14:1	Cotton Mills, 1820	238
Map 14:2	The Spread of Cotton Cultivation	244
Map 14:3	Population Density, 1790–1820	245
Map 14:4	Cities of at Least 5000 Inhabitants, 1800–1840	247
Map 15:1	Presidential Election of 1824	254
Map 15:2	Presidential Election of 1828	256
Map 15:3	Removal of the Southeastern Tribes 1820–1840	265
Map 16:1	Van Buren's Victory in 1836	277
Map 16:2	The Whig Victory of 1840	281
Map 18:1	Liberia	303
Map 18:2	Major Southern Crops, 1860	313
Map 19:1	Americans in the Mexican Borderlands, 1819–1848	321
Map 19:2	Americans in the West to 1849	326
Map 19:3	Campaigns of the Mexican War, 1846–1847	331
Map 20:1	The Gold Rush	337
Map 20:2	Gold Rush California	338
Map 21:1	The Legal Status of Slavery 1787–1861	352
Map 21:2	Presidential Election of 1860 and Southern Secession	357
Map 21:3	Crittenden's Compromise Plan of 1861	360
Map 22:1	The Battle of Bull Run, July 21, 1861	369
Map 22:2	The War in the West, 1862	374
Map 22:3	The Peninsula Campaign and the Seven Days Battle, March 17–July 2, 1862	377
Map 22:4	Stalemate in the East, 1862	379
Map 23:1	Grant's Vicksburg Campaign	385
Map 23:2	Chancellorsville and Gettysburg	386
Map 23:3	Grant Before Richmond, 1864–1865	390
Map 23:4	The Campaign for Atlanta	393
Map 24:1	Radical Reconstruction	406

How They Lived

Big City Life	15	Funding and Digging the Erie Canal	224
Common Seamen	36	New England Mill Girls	240
Puritan Sunday	53	Pistols at Twenty Paces	260
Finding the Way	69	Alma Mater	278
Slave Stations	88	Secular Sensations	294
Piracy's Golden Age	98	Fugitive Slaves	306
Colonial Politicians	122	The Patricios	325
The Hated Redcoats	130	How They Mined for Gold	340
Ignoring the Revolution	156	Defying the Law: Importers of Slaves	355
Laying Out the Land	166	Facing Battle	372
Turning Forests into Farms	186	The Anti-Draft Riots	387
White Americans in Slavery	206	Gullah	408

Preface

This is the eighth time I have revised *The American Past*. My take on so many of the topics I deal with in the book has undergone such heels over head changes from edition to edition that, thumbing through one of the older versions, I sometimes wonder what in the world I could possibly have been thinking when I dispatched it to the publisher.

In one matter, however, I look at *The American Past* today with precisely the same aspirations with which, almost three decades ago, I typed out the first page of the first chapter of the first edition. My ambition is that *The American Past* be enjoyable as well as educational reading. Like other professors who have taught a United States history survey course for many years, I long ago recognized that a large proportion of my students found it onerous to plow through a textbook on a subject that did not particularly interest them. A majority of survey course students are captives. They are treated better than galley slaves but they are seated at their oars only because American history is a required course or because a section of the survey was the only offering in a time slot they had to fill before their semester schedule was stamped "OK." They are accounting or botany or mathematics or physics majors for whom history has few charms, particularly if their textbook is a dry-as-dust recitation of facts, essential as they are to the course, and full of historical interpretations that only readers already well-schooled in the facts can appreciate.

So, here in the ninth edition, as in the first, I have reminded myself while revising and often writing each page from scratch that my students, with all their innumerable interests and with the tantalizing diversions that surround them on campus and beyond, have to be seduced into reading the book—*simply reading it!*—because it is a pleasant experience to do so—illuminating, interesting, and even, here and there, amusing.

I am too old and battered to worry about a 100 percent success rate. But I am gratified to be able to say that from the start until just a few months ago, I have regularly opened letters from dozens of history instructors who, in addition to criticisms of my take on various topics, added compliments to the effects that "for me, nevertheless, *The American Past* is indispensable. My students actually read it. They take me aside to tell me how much they *like* the book."

That is more than good enough for me. If students are reading *The American Past* and they like it, they must be learning some American history, which is what the survey course and textbooks are all about.

New to This Edition

There is a great deal of material that is brand new to this edition of *The American Past*. I have added fresh corroborative evidence in every chapter and rewritten several lengthy multichapter sections of the book to take into account historians' findings in recently published studies. For example, the wars between colonials and native populations during the eighteenth and early nineteenth centuries, especially the French and Indian War, have attracted the attention of half a dozen perceptive historians since the eighth edition was published. So, I have restructured and written anew large parts of Chapters 6 through 10 to reflect this recent scholarship. There is also a good deal that is conceptually new with this edition about Indians and Indian-settler relations in Chapters 2, 5, and 30. Several chapters have been reorganized so fundamentally that, although they deal with the same topics as the equivalent chapters of the eighth edition, they may be described as "completely redone": Chapters 5, 6, 7, 13, 17, and, of course, the final two chapters.

I have reorganized the subjects dealt with in Chapters 13 and 14 of the eighth edition in the interests of clearer presentations. Some instructors will want to modify their syllabuses. Chapter 17 includes expanded treatment of religious beliefs and the Protestant denominations during the early nineteenth century. I have combined the material in the eighth edition Chapters 18 and 19 (slavery and the South) into a single chapter in this edition—Chapter 18. As a result, the chapter enumeration from Chapter 19 to Chapter 47 differs from that in the previous edition. The equivalent of Chapter 20 in the eighth edition (American Expansion 1920–1848) is, in this edition, Chapter 19 and so on through Chapter 46.

The accounts of the War with Mexico (Chapter 19) and of the Irish famine immigrants of the 1840s and 1850s, and the Know Nothing movement that rose in response to them have been redone. I have moved my discussion of urban political machines from Chapter 26 (late nineteenth century politics) to Chapter 29 (urban America). I have expanded the discussion of urban development in the late nineteenth century (Chapter 29), adding new anecdotal and statistical evidence as well as insights new to me. I have recast coverage of American interventionism in the Caribbean and Central America based on recent scholarship (Chapters 34 and 35). Financial booms and busts of the early twenty-first century provided the inspiration to re-do my discussions of the land speculations of the early nineteenth century and the Florida land boom and Coolidge Bull Market of the 1920s (Chapters 14, 38, and 39).

Chapter 47 is new; there was no equivalent in the eighth edition. Chapter 47 brings together the story of race in twentieth-century America and the African American struggle for equality that culminated in the civil rights movement of the 1950s and 1960s.

The eighth edition Chapter 51 (1992–present) has been divided into two topically organized chapters. The revised Chapter 51 deals with the social and cultural history of the

final third of the twentieth century, including an almost entirely new discussion of late twentieth-century religion. Chapter 52 treats political and economic history from 1992 to 2009.

In addition, I've made the following general updates: Ten of the popular "How They Lived" features are new to this edition (Chapters 1, 12, 14, 19, 21, 23, 25, 32, 33, and 35). I have updated the "Further Readings," adding important titles published since the eighth edition. In response to a request by an instructor who has long assigned the text, I have added a new category to the "Further Readings"—"Classics"—books the value of which has not decreased with the years because of their literary quality or historiographical importance. After every third or fourth chapter, I have inserted a pedagogical tool, "Discovery" that defines problems for, and asks questions of, students based on primary source excerpts, images, and maps.

ACKNOWLEDGEMENTS

I will list those persons to whom I owe thanks for the contributions they made to this book in the order that I contracted my debts to them.

One's first task in revising a textbook is to review criticisms of the previous edition. The reviewers this time around were particularly helpful. I have not agreed with every one of their criticisms. In some cases limitations of space prevented me from fully responding to some suggestions for improvement with which I was in agreement. In most instances, however, I adjusted the discussion according to their advice, and I am grateful for every suggestion provided by the professors of history who gave parts of the book a close once-over.

List of Reviewers

Caroline Barton, *Holmes Community College*
B. R. Burg, *Arizona State University*
Richard A. Dobbs, *Gadsden State Community College*
David Long, *East Carolina University*
Karen Markoe, *SUNY Maritime College*
James Mills, *University of Texas—Brownsville*
Lex Renda, *University of Wisconsin—Milwaukee*
Delilah Ryan, *West Virginia Northern Community College*
Scott E. White, *Scottsdale Community College*
Mark R. Wilson, *University of North Carolina—Charlotte*

Task number two, of course, was a chapter by chapter, page by page rewrite, which meant researching problems the reviewers pointed out or were obvious to me after several years away from the book.

Every day revising *The American Past* generated up to a dozen questions of fact that needed confirmation and every week the titles of up to a dozen books I needed to read or re-read. Occasionally I needed to consult hard-to-find books and for this I had the astonishingly good fortune to be acquainted with librarian Susan M. Kling of Bandon, Oregon. Ms. Kling cheerfully designed and administered a massive interlibrary loan operation that put hundreds of titles on my desk at no more inconvenience to me than typing out lists for her. I am grateful beyond graceful expression.

For the fourth time, Wadsworth/Cengage Learning assigned Margaret McAndrew Beasley as the Developmental Editor for this text. She conveyed Wadsworth's guidelines to me, selected reviewers for every chapter, provided useful wrap-ups of the reviewer comments, and—much appreciated—communicated with me, sometimes several times daily to resolve questions as they came up, thus avoiding traffic jams further on. I have long since come to think of Margaret's efficiency as just normal which, when I think about it a bit, I know is singular indeed. There cannot be many people in the business as good at her job as she is. After doing four revisions of the book under her guidance and supervision, I am still astonished by her calm and courteous demeanor as well as by her fine suggestions for improvement throughout the process.

After Margaret Beasley's review, my material was put into the hands of Lauren Wheelock, Content Project Manager. Lauren ably oversaw and coordinated the many hands responsible for milling my ruminations into a big, handsome book while keeping the entire project on schedule. Project Manager Teresa Christie of Macmillan Publishing Solutions saw *The American Past* through copyediting, proofreading, design, art, map making, composition, and indexing. Martha Williams fixed up my worst sentences; Heather Mann did the proofreading.

I worked directly with Catherine Schnurr, photo researcher with Pre-Press PMG. Catherine is a master of pictorial resources. Repeatedly she found illustrations that I did not believe existed but asked for them anyway. And in most cases, Ms. Schnurr gave me a choice of two or more illustrations of subjects I thought would be beyond graphic depiction.

Assistant Editor Megan Curry has managed the team of supplements authors to make sure that each of the ancillaries accompanying this text stays true to the approach and revised content in *The American Past*.

And a Word to Students ...

This is a textbook history of the United States written for you—many of you may be women and men just setting out on your college educations.

"Textbook" means that the author is careful to stick close to the tried and true essentials—to sidestep the slippery spots on the trail where the specifics are uncertain and it is too easy for everyone to take a spill.

"History" means that our subject is the people and events of the past that have made us what we are today. Not just "the facts." They are usually easy. What happened to our country at Pearl Harbor, Hawaii, on December 7, 1941, is well known and easily documented. The facts do not change. But in retelling them, historians discover new ways

in which American society was changed by the Japanese attack that day. The facts remain the same. History changes all the time.

History changes when documents believed to be lost forever turn up, sometimes in dusty corners of farmhouse attics. (It really does happen.) Or, documents we never knew existed are discovered, sometimes in the archives where they belonged, but on the wrong shelf. The diaries of important men and women that were legally sealed for thirty or forty years by the terms of their wills are opened. Governments release memoranda that had been stamped "Top Secret." With fresh sources like these, historians quite often change their own and our collective understanding of past events.

History can change when documents long in full view but indecipherable are suddenly comprehensible. Just since the first edition of *The American Past* was published, scholars who, for a century, had scratched their heads in bewilderment at the carvings on ruined Maya temples in Central America decoded what were also hieroglyphics. Almost in an instant they were able to draw a new portrait of the Maya civilization that was quite at odds with what they had previously suspected (and had been describing in textbooks like this one).

New technologies can also change history. The computer's capacity to crunch huge numbers meant that data that had been too vast for historians to do much with (for example, the handwritten reports that armies of census takers turned into the Census Bureau every ten years) became founts of a rich social history that, before the Cyber Age, was unimaginable. Moldering baptismal and marriage registries in thousands of churches became historical goldmines.

Fresh perspectives, new vantages from which to look at past events, have changed history. In the second half of the twentieth century, demands for better treatment by African Americans, Native Americans, Mexican Americans, women, and other groups with special interests led not only to political and social reforms, but also to research in African American history, American Indian history, and so on from the perspective of those groups. Environmental history, a rich and imaginative field of study today, came into being quite recently as a side effect of the recognition that our own environment has problems.

Finally, individual historians of genius change history when, poring over documents that hundreds of people had read before them, see something that none of their predecessors had noticed or thought much of. It does not happen often, but every now and then there comes along a book that, written from long familiar sources, without employing any new technology, and inspired by nothing outside the historian's mind, is so compelling in its insights that history—our understanding of the past—is radically changed.

Because American history is constantly changing, textbooks like this one must be revised every three or so years.

All of this is old hat to research historians, to history instructors, and to graduate students. I have run through it here because *The American Past* has not been revised for them, but for first- and second-year college and university students who, happily or under duress, are enrolled in a United States history survey course. *The American Past* is written for men and women who are majoring in accounting, botany, mathematics, psychology, zoology, or any of five dozen other fields. The idea that history is eternally in flux may be an idea new to them.

My goal, through nine editions now, has been to produce and improve a book that, even for reluctant readers, will be a pleasure to read. It has made my day (on quite a few days) when I open a letter or an e-mail from a history instructor that says, "my students really like your book." That is my purpose and, of course, to present the history of the United States as I have understood it at a moment in time not too long before your instructor's first lecture.

Using the "Discovery" Sections in This Textbook to Analyze Historical Sources: Documents, Photos, and Maps

Astronomers investigate the universe through telescopes. Biologists study the natural world by collecting plants and animals in the field and then examining them with microscopes. Sociologists and psychologists study human behavior through observation and controlled laboratory experiments.

Historians study the past by examining historical "evidence" or "source" materials—government documents; the records of private institutions ranging from religious and charitable organizations to labor unions, corporations, and lobbying groups; letters, advertisements, paintings, music, literature, movies, and cartoons; buildings, clothing, farm implements, industrial machinery, and landscapes—anything and everything written or created by our ancestors that give clues about their lives and the times in which they lived.

Historians refer to written material as "documents." Brief excerpts of documents appear throughout the textbook—within the chapters and in the "Discovery" sections. Each chapter also includes many visual representations of the American past in the form of photographs of buildings, paintings, murals, individuals, cartoons, sculptures, and other kinds of historical evidence. As you read each chapter, the more you examine all this "evidence," the more you will understand the main ideas of this book and of the course you are taking. The better you become at reading evidence, the better historian you will become.

"Discovery" sections, appearing every three to four chapters, assist you in practicing these skills by taking a closer look at specific pieces of evidence—documents, images, or maps—which will help you to connect the various threads of American history and to excel in your course.

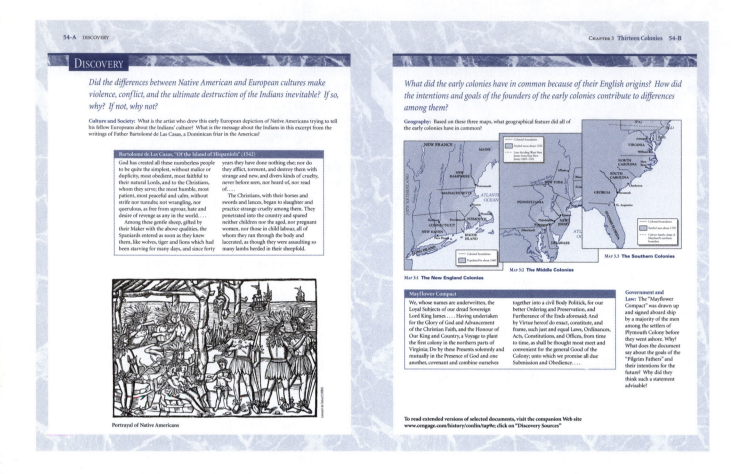

Online and Instructor Resources

Instructor's Manual with Test Bank. Prepared by Stephen Armes, this manual has many features, including chapter outlines, chapter summaries, suggested lecture topics, and discussion questions maps and artwork as well as the documents in the text. World Wide Web sites and resources, video collections, a Resource Integration Guide, and suggested student activities are also included. Exam questions include essays, true-false, identifications, and multiple-choice questions.

PowerLectures. This resource includes the Instructor's Manual, Resource Integration Grid, ExamView testing, and PowerPoint slides with lecture outlines and images that can be used as offered or customized by importing personal lecture slides or other material. ExamView allows instructors to create, deliver, and customize tests and study guides (both print and online) in minutes via an easy-to-use assessment and tutorial system. Instructors can build tests with as many as 250 questions using up to twelve question types. Using ExamView's complete word processing capabilities, they can enter an unlimited number of new questions or edit existing ones.

Transparency Acetates for U.S. History. This set contains more than 150 four color map images from all of Wadsworth's U.S. History texts. Packages are three-hole punched and shrink-wrapped.

Wadsworth American History Resource Center. http://ushistory.wadsworth.com. Organized chronologically with a user-friendly time line navigation bar, this Web site acts as a primary source e-reader with more than 350 primary source documents. It also includes time lines, photos, interactive maps, exercises, and numerous other materials you can assign in class. Contact your representative for information about providing your students with access to this resource.

Book Companion Web site. The Book Companion Web site includes learning objectives, tutorial quizzes, essay questions, Internet activities, and glossary flashcards for each text chapter to support what students read about in the book and learn in class.

THE AMERICAN PAST

A Survey of American History

Chapter 1

Discoveries

Indians, Europeans, and the Americas
About 15,000 B.C. to A.D. 1550

The Art Archive/Picture Desk

I feel a wonderful exultation of spirits when I converse with intelligent men who have returned from these regions. It is like an accession of wealth to a miser. Our minds, soiled and debased by the common concerns of life and the vices of society, become elevated and ameliorated by contemplating such glorious events.

—Peter Martyr d'Anghiera

Broken spears lie in the roads;
We have torn our hair in our grief.
The houses are roofless now,
And their walls are red with blood....
We are crushed to the ground;
We lie in ruins.
There is nothing but grief and suffering
in Mexico and Tlateloco.

—Anonymous Aztec poet

North and South America were the last of the world's great landmasses to be populated. Even isolated Australia was peopled 20,000 years before a human being first impressed a footprint in American mud.

Exactly when the Americas were first discovered is disputed, but the best bet is that, about 15,000 B.C., bands of Stone Age hunters began to wander from Siberia to Alaska on a "land bridge" that, for the last 10,000 years, has been drowned 180 feet beneath the frigid waters of the Bering Strait. Thus, the name geologists have given the land bridge, Beringia.

Beringia was high and dry in 15,000 because the earth was locked in an ice age. Much of the world's water was frozen in the polar ice caps and in glaciers larger than most nations today. Consequently, sea level was about 400 feet lower than it is today. Our beaches were miles inland from the surf. Vast tracts of what is now sea bottom were dry; Beringia was not really a bridge, it was hundreds of miles wide.

The people who crossed to America had no idea they were entering a "New World" empty of human beings. They were Stone Age nomads—hunters. They were checking out the range, as nomads do. They were following after dinner—herds of caribou, perhaps mastodons—or they were fleeing enemies. In just a thousand years, however, these Paleo-Indians (old Indians, ancestors of American Indians) explored and colonized much of two continents, advancing on average a mile a month.

Endangered Species

Mastodons, hairy elephants larger than elephants today, lived in North America. The species went extinct several thousand years after the arrival of the Paleo-Indians. Did the first Americans wipe them out? Despite the primitiveness of their weapons, it is likely they did. We know that they hunted mastodons; spear points have been found in fossilized mastodon skeletons. Elsewhere in the world, Stone Age peoples destroyed entire species, saber-toothed tigers in Europe, any number of brightly plumed birds in New Zealand. Zoologists have determined that if hunters kill only slightly more of a species each year than are born, the species will disappear in a few centuries.

THE FIRST COLONIZATION

The Paleo-Indians were a prehistoric people. Knowledge of them is beyond the jurisdiction of historians, who study the past in written records. To learn about people who lived, loved, hated, begat, and died before there was writing, we must turn to archaeologists, linguists, and folklorists who sift particles of information, like gold dust from gravel, by analyzing artifacts, by studying the structures of languages, and by delving for the meaning in tales passed word of mouth from one generation to the next and then to the next.

The pictures these scholars sketch are fuzzier than the portraits historians can draw using their written documents. As a Chinese saying has it, "the palest ink is clearer than the best memory." Still, fuzzy is better than blank. Without folk tales and language analysis, without artifacts, the American past would not begin until A.D. 1492, when Europeans, who scribbled endlessly of their achievements and follies, made their own discovery of America. Thanks to archaeology, linguistics, and folklore—and a few fragmentary written Indian records that have only recently been decoded—we can pencil in a more ancient past.

Diversity

The Paleo-Indians knew no more of agriculture than of alphabets. When they crossed Beringia, there was not a farmer on the planet. The first Americans lived by hunting, fishing, and gathering edible seeds, nuts, berries, leaves, and roots. Nature also provided the makings for their clothing, shelter, tools, and weapons. They did not remain in one place for long. For thousands of years, they were nomads, wanderers. They lived on the move, because, in all but the lushest environments, as few as a hundred people quickly exhaust the game and plant food in their neighborhood. "Home" was where the food was. That, sooner rather than later, was somewhere else. The Paleo-Indians were campers.

By the time the mysteries of agriculture were unlocked in the Middle East, about 8000 B.C., the Americas and the "Old World" (the Eurasian land mass and Africa) were unknown to one another. A global warming had melted the glaciers and polar ice caps of the last ice age to a size not much larger than they are today. As the ice melted, the sea level rose. The oceans submerged Beringia and "land bridges" elsewhere in the world. Emigration from Asia ceased.

In the two Americas, the Paleo-Indians' cultures—their ways of life—diversified rapidly. The Americas were uncrowded, to say the least. Wandering communities split up when they grew too numerous for the range they could exploit or when, human nature being what it is, bigwigs with their separate followings had a falling out. Soon enough, the vastness of the continents and the diversity of its climates and land forms isolated Paleo-Indian tribes from one another. The result was a dizzying variety of cultures.

Languages, for example, probably just a handful of them at first, multiplied until there were at least 500 on the two continents. Tribes living in harsh environments continued to survive precariously into historic times on what they could hunt, snare, net, gather, and grub. Other Indians learned how to farm. Mesoamerica (meaning between the Americas: Mexico and Central America) may be the only place other than the Middle East where agriculture was discovered—invented—and not learned from others. The greater abundance of food

The Age of Exploration 1400–1550

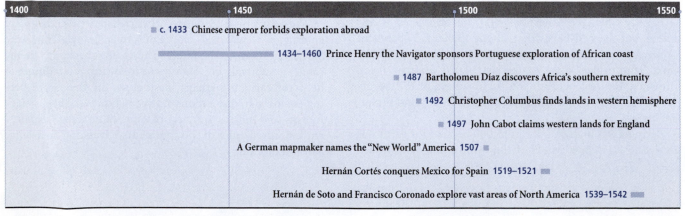

1400	1450	1500	1550

- c. 1433 Chinese emperor forbids exploration abroad
- 1434–1460 Prince Henry the Navigator sponsors Portuguese exploration of African coast
- 1487 Bartholomeu Díaz discovers Africa's southern extremity
- 1492 Christopher Columbus finds lands in western hemisphere
- 1497 John Cabot claims western lands for England
- A German mapmaker names the "New World" America 1507
- Hernán Cortés conquers Mexico for Spain 1519–1521
- Hernán de Soto and Francisco Coronado explore vast areas of North America 1539–1542

The Maya and Aztec built pyramidal temples as large as the ziggurats of ancient Mesopotamia. This one is on the small side, but perfectly preserved. Its walls are built of precisely cut stones, and filled in with rubble.

from farming made possible a population explosion and, for some Indians, a sedentary life (living in one place). In Mesoamerica and in Ecuador and Peru, where agriculture was most productive, sophisticated civilizations developed.

Many Indian peoples had mastered only primitive tool making when, after 1492, they were dazzled (and crushed) by European technology. Others perfected handicrafts to a degree of refinement not then achieved in Africa, Asia, and Europe. Some Indians still sheltered in rude piles of brush as late as the 1800s. By way of contrast, by about 1000 the Anasazi of present-day New Mexico were building apartment houses of five and six stories. In the 1300s, the "mound builders" of the upper Mississippi valley were numerous enough, well-enough fed, and sufficiently disciplined to undertake massive feats of cooperative labor. They heaped up dozens of earthen structures that survive today. One mound complex near Cahokia, Illinois, stretched over five square miles with a central platform 100 feet high and a sculpted bird 70 feet in height. In Ohio, two parallel "walls" extended sixty miles from Chillicothe to Newark.

Mesoamerican Civilization

The most advanced American culture evolved in Guatemala, Belize, and southern Mexico. A succession of dominant peoples—Olmecs, Maya, Aztecs—produced enough surplus food that large numbers of them could quit farming and congregate in cities where they specialized in numerous crafts, trading the goods they made for their eats. Urban life and the "division of labor" are two of the components of what historians call civilization. A third is a hierarchical social system, superior and inferior social classes, some giving the orders, others doing the work. A fourth component of civilizations is writing. Like the people of ancient Iraq, Egyptians, the Harappans of Pakistan's Indus River Valley, and the Chinese—the founders of the Old World's civilizations—the Maya developed a system of writing using 8,000-character hieroglyphics (like picture-writing in ancient Egypt). They carved them into stone (prayers, myths, puffed-up praises of their rulers) and composed "books" on flattened bark or processed strips of cactus fiber.

Sadly, after 1500 a zealous Spanish bishop, Diego de Landa, condemned the books as "superstition and lies of the devil" and ordered hundreds of them destroyed. Only four Maya literary works survive. Inscribed rock, however, was too tough for the censors, and most Maya cities were unknown to the Spanish, already smothered by vegetation when they arrived. Inscriptions carved in stone are abundant in Guatemala and Belize today, and scholars have learned, although just recently, to read many of them. They provide a chapter of the American past long thought unknowable.

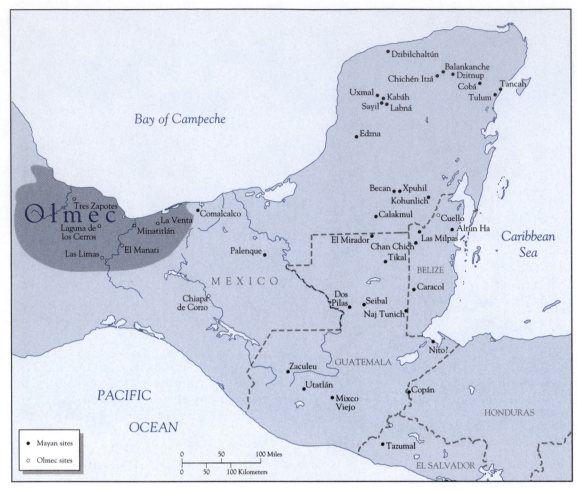

MAP 1:1 **Mesoamerican Cities.** The Olmecs, among whom most of the finer points of Mesoamerican civilization originated, lived in southern Mexico. Their centers were disintegrating, perhaps under pressure from the Maya, about 200 B.C. when, to the East in Yucatan, Guatemala, and Belize, the first of perhaps hundreds of Maya cities were built. Those cities too rose and fell. By 1520, when Spaniards subdued their homeland, only sixteen very small Maya cities in the remote highlands, survived. The greatest Maya centers like Chichen-Itza and Palenque were already swallowed up by jungle.

At one time or another, about forty large cities, several housing more than 20,000 people, plus smaller ones, dotted Guatemala. The northernmost, Teotihuacan, founded near present-day Mexico City about the time of Christ, may, by A.D. 500, have been home to more than 100,000. The cities were governed by a tight-knit aristocracy of priests and warriors intermarried with their relatives. This elite directed the construction of at least one pyramid-shaped earth and stone temple in each city. The pyramid at Chichén Itzá, probably the greatest of the Maya cities, rose eighteen stories.

The Maya were superb mathematicians and astronomers. They discovered the use of the zero, a breakthrough achieved in only one other world culture, India. They timed the earth's orbit around the sun as accurately as any other people of the time, applying their findings to an accurate calendar.

War and Religion

Each Maya city-state was independent, governing a rather modest agricultural hinterland. The Maya did not attempt to build empires, an obsession of Old World civilizations. Not that they were peace loving. Far from it. Cities fought chronically with neighbors, for their religion compelled war. Maya gods (jaguarlike beings, eagles, serpents, the sun) thirsted for human blood.

In solemn public rituals, noblewomen made symbolic blood sacrifices by drawing strings of thorns through punctures in their tongues. Their brothers and husbands drew the barbs through their foreskins. The blood from their wounds was sopped up by strips of fiber that were then burned, dispatching the sacrifice in smoke to the heavens.

But symbolic blood sacrifice was not enough for the Mesoamerican deities. They also demanded that priests throw virgins into pits and drag men to the tops of the pyramids where, using razor-sharp stone knives, the priests tore their hearts, still beating when the operation was correctly performed, from their breasts. Thus the chronic war (or, more accurately, raids): The Maya needed captives to sacrifice.

© Copyright The British Museum

A Maya sculpture depicting a priest and a kneeling woman who is making a blood sacrifice by drawing a thong of thorns through a hole in her tongue. These were public ceremonies performed by women and men of the aristocracy. They demonstrated the gods' approval of their right to rule by such rituals. Then they, unlike captives who had their hearts torn out, went home.

Cultural Cul-de-Sac?

Elsewhere in the world, states made war in order to exploit those they conquered. Along with the misery they caused, the wealth their conquests brought them made possible further breakthroughs in the evolution of civilization. The blood lust of the Mesoamerican gods, however, meant that the Maya and others made war for the unprogressive purpose of rounding up people to kill. They expended their energies in a direction that, in material and intellectual terms, led nowhere. Their culture centered on staying on the right side of terrifying gods, avoiding worse problems than those with which they had to contend when heaven was in a good mood. Mesoamerican culture was pathologically conservative.

Conservatism did not save them. The Olmec cities disappeared by about A.D. 900. The Maya cities also disintegrated dramatically, albeit at different times. In one area, a population that may have reached several million was, by 1500, 30,000. Once great cities—Tikal, Chichen-Itza, Palenque—had been overgrown by tropical vegetation, swallowed up by jungle and not rediscovered until the nineteenth century. By 1520, most Maya were simple villagers. A few were still literate but in a far less sophisticated language than their ancestors had used. They could read only fragments of the ancient inscriptions on their temples. Bishop de Landa was beating a dead horse when he burned the Maya books. Nobody was going to get any dangerous ideas from them.

What happened? Probably a combination of factors. The Maya destroyed vast expanses of forest for the fuel they needed to make the plaster with which they surfaced their buildings. The consequence was soil erosion and a reduced food supply. A long period of serious droughts beginning about A.D. 800 further devastated agriculture. And with widespread hunger came social instability within cities and an increase of warfare between them.

The civilization itself did not die. But by 1500 its center had shifted several hundred miles northwest of its Central America birthplace to the valley of Mexico. The cultural heirs of the Olmecs and Maya were a variety of Mexican peoples, most notably latecomers to the area from the north whom we call the Aztec.

The Aztec

The Aztec (they called themselves "the Mexica," thus Mexico) had emigrated to the vicinity of Mexico's Lake Texcoco during the 1200s. By 1325, they had carved out an enclave on the lake among longtime residents, the Toltecs, Texcocans, Tlaxcalans, and others. The Aztec embraced their neighbors' civilization and, by 1400, defeated them in a series of wars. Unlike the Maya, the Aztec were empire builders. Their armies struck east and west, subduing almost every people from the Gulf of Mexico to the Pacific Ocean.

Rebellions were frequent. But Tenochtitlán, the Aztec capital on Lake Texcoco, was impregnable. Combat in Mexico was hand to hand. Surrounded by water, Tenochtitlán could be entered on only three narrow, easily defended causeways. If a rebel army threatened them, the Aztec raised drawbridges that spanned gaps in the viaducts, sat back, and waited for the moment that favored them to retaliate. Thirty-foot granite walls could not have made a city more secure.

The Aztec were uninterested in the daily doings of the peoples they conquered. They left local customs, religion, and the enforcement to native kings and nobles. All the Aztec wanted from their provinces were submission and tribute. On appointed days (access to Tenochtitlán was closely regulated), each subject people was required to bring to the capital minutely prescribed quantities of bulk goods (maize, beans, salt, cloth, lumber), luxuries (jade and gold and—as precious as gold in Mexico—colorful feathers), and last but not least, people to sacrifice, for the Aztec adopted that old Mesoamerican tradition too. Failure to pay tribute on time meant an Aztec military assault. The Aztec stationed military garrisons at key points throughout the empire for just such occasions.

Tenochtitlán was a splendid city by anyone's standards. By 1519 (the fatal year for the Aztec), much of it was brand new, recently rebuilt in a massive urban renewal project. A catastrophic flood in 1499 had destroyed thousands of buildings that were replaced within a few years. The emperor's palace of 100 rooms, covering six acres, was new. (It was the empire's administrative center as well as a residence.) There were pyramidal temples (which had survived the flood) in every quarter of the city.

MAP 1:2 **Aztec Mexico.** The Aztec directly governed only Tenochtitlan and its hinterland, not a large area. Their empire (shaded area) consisted of thirty-eight provinces that made their own laws but which paid tribute in the form of bulk goods and luxuries to the Aztec. The alternative was an almost always successful Aztec attack.

Blood and Gore

Tenochtitlán's main temple was huge: 200 feet square at the base. Two dizzyingly steep staircases climbed to altars 200 feet above the street. The steps were black with the dried blood of sacrificial victims whose bodies, minus hearts, the priests threw down to the streets to be butchered; the Aztec practiced ritual cannibalism.

The scale of Aztec human sacrifice seems to have exceeded that of any other Mesoamerican people. One important god, Huitzilopochtli, was said to have demanded 10,000 hearts in an ordinary year. In 1478, a year Huitzilopochtli was especially agitated, so the records said, priests dressed in cloaks of human skin and stinking of gore (they were forbidden to wash or cut their hair) sent 20,000 volunteers to their doom in four days. The emperor Ahuitzotl, so it was said, slaughtered 80,000 to dedicate a new temple.

These astronomical figures are not be taken as gospel truth. All ancient chroniclers (and more than a few historians today) inflated their statistics into the realm of absurdity. But the point of the implausibly large numbers of victims is clear enough: Lots of people were ritually slaughtered in ancient Mexico.

The Aztec empire was powerful, but its culture trembled with insecurities. Mesoamerican civilization was ancient, but Aztec power was not. Moctezuma II, who became emperor in 1503, was only the fifth of his line; the first emperor assumed power only in 1440, within the living memory of the oldest inhabitants. The Aztec never enjoyed an untroubled era. Droughts were frequent, slashing the food supply. A freak snowstorm sunk the Aztec *chinampas*, floating vegetable gardens on Lake Texcoco. There was the flood of 1499 and comets in the sky in 1499, 1502, and 1506. (Comets made people uneasy everywhere in the world.) There was a total eclipse of the sun in 1496. Common people and nobles alike told one another stories of female spirits who wandered Tenochtitlán at night, wailing in grief. In 1514, the king of neighboring Texcoco died; his last words were that Mexico would soon be ruled by strangers.

The Aztec were a people on edge in 1519 and none was edgier than Moctezuma II. It has been suggested that, psychologically, he was ready prey for an enemy that was obsessed not with staying on the right side of demanding gods, but to exploring and exploiting the new, strange, and the vulnerable wherever in the world it could be found.

WESTERN EUROPE: ENERGETIC AND EXPANSIVE

On October 12, 1492, on a beach in the Bahamas, a thousand miles from Tenochtitlán, a group of rugged, ragged men, mostly Spaniards, rowed ashore from three ships. They named their island landfall San Salvador, Holy Savior. Their leader was a graying but still ruddy Italian about 40 years of age. To his Spanish crew he was Cristóbal Colón, to us Christopher Columbus. To the Arawaks, the Bahamians who welcomed him warmly, he and his men were like nothing they had ever imagined.

Reproduced from the Collections of the Library of Congress

A charming but fanciful depiction of Columbus about to step ashore on San Salvador. There is no surf; the painter shows the ocean as a pond. Columbus probably did not wear a beard. The friar sitting in the back of the boat is the artist's invention; there were no priests with Columbus. The warm, welcoming character of the Arawaks is accurate, but they fled into the interior at their first sight of Columbus, emerging only later.

Other Discoverers

There are many legends of outsiders visiting the Americas between the Paleo-Indians' discovery of the "New World" and Columbus's arrival in 1492. The Olmecs told of black skinned people; some anthropologists have seen negroid features in the huge stone heads the Olmecs carved and then buried. A Chinese document of 200 B.C. tells of Hee Li, who visited a land across the Pacific he called Fu-Sang. About A.D. 700, Irish bards began to sing of St. Brendan, a monk who had sojourned far to the west of the Emerald Isle in a land "without grief, without sorrow, without death."

There is nothing legendary about Vikings from Greenland who, about A.D. 1000, visited Newfoundland and—they made about five voyages in all—may have sailed as far south as Nova Scotia. They called the country Vinland and built what they intended to be a permanent settlement at L'Anse aux Meadows on Newfoundland's northwestern coast. For a time, they traded with the locals whom they called "skraelings" (wretches): their cows' milk for the natives' furs.

The Vinland colony did not last. The Greenlanders were glad to trade for the lumber the Vinlanders brought back, but they had little to offer in return. And, for good reason or bad, the skraelings grew hostile. Their fierce attacks paralyzed the Vinlanders with fear. One assault was repulsed only when a pregnant woman, Freydis, disgusted by her trembling menfolk, seized a sword and chased the skraelings off by slapping it on her breasts and, no doubt, having an unpleasant word or two to say to the locals. Freydis then had the cowards of the colony killed; the survivors returned to Greenland.

Christopher Columbus

Falling to his knees, for he was as pious as any Aztec priest, Columbus proclaimed San Salvador the possession of the woman who had financed his voyage, Queen Isabella of Castille, and her husband, King Ferdinand of Aragon. Columbus wrote in his report to them that the trees of the island were "the most beautiful I have ever seen." He "found no human monstrosities, as many expected; on the contrary, among all these peoples good looks are esteemed." The Arawaks were "very generous. They do not know what it is to be wicked, or to kill others, or to steal." Unsettling to us, he added that because their weapons were primitive, it would be easy to enslave them. There was no irony in this juxtaposition for Columbus (or Isabella). In their world, owning slaves was one of the perquisites of wealth and power; being a slave was one of the misfortunes suffered by the unlucky.

For the moment, Columbus enslaved no one. He enquired politely of the whereabouts of Japan and China. Those fabulous lands, not the balmy but poor Bahamas, were the places for which he was looking.

The evolution of the America we know—the history that runs on a line of causes and effects to our own world—begins with Columbus's arrival in the Bahamas. No matter what our genetic inheritance, the origins of our culture and society—our historical legacy—lay not on the pyramids of Mexico but in the churches, state chambers, and counting houses of Western Europe, a civilization that had already, by 1492, begun to impress itself throughout the world.

Motives

Columbus believed that San Salvador and the much larger islands he visited, Hispaniola and Cuba, lay on the fringes of "the Indies," the name Europeans gave collectively to mysterious, distant Cipango (Japan), Cathay (China), the Spice Islands (Indonesia), and India itself. Thus did Columbus bestow upon the Arawaks and other Native Americans he met the name by which their descendants are known to this day—Indians.

Columbus had sailed from Spain to find a practical sea lane to the Indies. In part, he was motivated by religion. A zealous Roman Catholic, Columbus sincerely believed God had selected him to carry Christ's gospel to the lost souls of Asia. He had worldly motives too. Columbus longed for personal glory. Like the artists and architects of the Renaissance, he craved recognition as a great individual. If obsession with the self has become tawdry and repellent in our own day, ambitious individualism was once one of the forces that made Western civilization dynamic.

Another such force was greed. Columbus wanted wealth. He meant to get rich doing business with (or conquering) the peoples he encountered. Gold and silver were always in season. "Gold is most excellent," Columbus wrote, "He who has it does all he wants in the world, and can even lift souls up to Paradise." European gold and silver paid for the Asian gems and porcelains that rich Europeans coveted, the fine cotton cloth of Syria and silks of China, and tapestries and carpets that were beyond the craft of European weavers.

Prester John and Marco Polo

Western civilization's fascination with the world beyond Europe dates from its very origins. Plato wrote, "I believe that the earth is very vast, and that we . . . inhabit a small portion only about the sea, like ants or frogs about a marsh, and that there are other inhabitants of many other like places." By Roman times, educated Europeans knew of the existence of India, China, and Japan, if not much else. In the Middle Ages, books purporting to be descriptions of the lands of the mysterious East were "best sellers."

The Letter of Prester John began to circulate about 1150. The ostensible author, John, a Christian king and priest, claimed to "reign supreme and to exceed in riches, virtue, and power all creatures who dwell under heaven." He wanted to form an alliance with Christian Europe in order to "wage war against and chastise" their common enemies, the Muslims. The prospect of a powerful Christian friend with whom to catch the Muslims in a pincers (and from whom to buy the goods of the Indies) was enough to overcome skepticism about the red and green lions in John's kingdom, and a pebble that made men invisible. The early Portugese explorers asked every people they met if they were acquainted with John.

The letter was, of course, a fraud, as was the *Travels of Sir John Mandeville*, published in the mid-1300s. It told even taller tales about the wonders to be found in far-off lands but it too whetted the appetites of men like Prince Henry the Navigator and Columbus to see for themselves.

The Voyages of Ser Marco Polo also included absurdities such as snakes wearing eyeglasses, but while some scholars today doubt that Polo, from Venice, lived in China for twenty years, as he claimed, much about China that he described was plausible and accurate and enticing. He revealed that the Asian porcelains, silks, tapestries, and spices for which Europeans paid high prices cost a pittance in China. No document, more than Polo's *Voyages,* convinced the explorers of the fifteenth century that betting their lives on voyages to the East would mean fabulous riches as well as titillating sights.

Then there were the exotic drugs, dyes, perfumes, and especially the spices of the Indies: cinnamon from Ceylon, Indonesian nutmeg and cloves, Chinese ginger, and cardamom and peppercorns (black pepper, not chili peppers) from India. These were luxuries that made life pleasanter for the Europeans who could afford them, something more than a struggle for survival on earth and salvation after death.

High Overhead

The goods of the Indies had trickled into Europe since the Caesars ruled Rome. They were expensive; only the very rich enjoyed them. But the European market was enlarged to include the merely well-to-do by the era of the Crusades. The crusaders, European knights and noblemen who, for a century, ruled much of present-day Syria, Lebanon, and Israel, learned

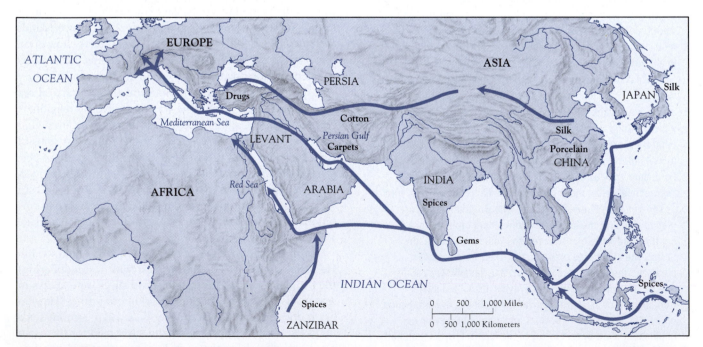

MAP 1:3 Trade Routes Before the 1500s. All Asian and East African trade goods came to Europe via the 8,000-mile "Silk Road" in caravans or in ships, manned mostly by Arabs, via the Red Sea and Persian Gulf. Few merchants accompanied the overland caravans the entire distance; the goods were sold and resold several, even many times. There were plenty of middlemen, each taking a profit, to add to the costs of the luxuries Europeans coveted.

to enjoy first hand the opulent lifestyle of their enemies, the Muslim Arabs who had long enjoyed a regular trade with the Indies. When the Muslims drove the crusaders back to Europe, they returned with a taste for the luxuries of the East.

The Arabs of the Levant (present-day Israel, Lebanon, and Syria) were happy, as middlemen, to sell to them. They brought the goods by ship via the Indian Ocean and Persian Gulf or Red Sea. Or, they bought them from caravaners of Central Asia who had carried them on donkeyback to the Mediterranean. The coveted goods were then transported in the vessels of Venice and Genoa, powerful Italian city-states. Merchants in those cities were wholesale distributors who sold the spices and the rest to retailers from all over Europe.

By the time the goods of the Indies reached the castles of Spain and the market towns of France, they were expensive indeed. The cost of transport was alone prodigious. The silk that clothed an English lady may have been carried eight thousand miles in a caravan. The "Silk Road" passed through the domains of Central Asian tribesmen who lived by preying on the trade. Caravaners paid tolls ("bribes") to pass safely through, or they hired thugs to beat back the toll collectors. Either way, operating expenses swelled. If the pepper and cloves that enlivened a German bishop's stew came by sea, Arab sailors had to deal with East African pirates— "tolls" again—or pay armed escorts. All costs, of course, were passed on to buyers each time the products changed hands.

Nobody Likes a Middleman

Then there was profit. The merchants of Christian Constantinople, Genoese huddled in fortified trading posts on the Black Sea, and the Muslims of Egypt, Syria, and Lebanon were not in business to serve human kind. The took their cut when they sold to the Italians. The Italian wholesalers added their markup, shrugging off complaints that they were gougers. Today, the magnificent cathedrals and palaces the Italian merchant princes built are world treasures, admired by all. In Columbus's day, the glories of Italy were more likely to arouse the bitter resentment of Europeans who paid exortionate prices for Asian imports. It was their money that paid for the fact that Renaissance Italy glowed so splendidly.

The grotesque prices were particularly grating because educated Europeans knew from travelers' accounts, first of all the widely circulated book, *The Voyages of Ser Marco Polo,* that the goods of the Indies were cheap, even dirt cheap, in the Indies. The Western European prince whose navigator discovered a route to the Indies that bypassed the Italians and the Muslim Middle East would stanch the flow of his country's wealth to the middlemen. Indeed, that prince's own subjects might displace the Venetians and Genoese as Europe's wholesalers of Asia's products.

The castle at Elmina in present-day Ghana. The Portugese founded West Africa's first European trading colony here in 1482. The castle was designed to defend against seagoing rivals as well as local peoples. At first, gold was the commodity for which the Portugese traded. Before long, however, the value of slaves seized in the interior by the powerful Ashanti people outstripped gold in value. In 1637, the Dutch seized Elmina from the Portugese.

Ariadne Van Zandbergen/africanpictures.net/Image Works

PORTUGAL AND SPAIN: THE VAN OF EXPLORATION

Portugal was first to look for new trade routes. Unlike any other European natives, Portugal faces west, the Atlantic Ocean. Its mountainous back is to Europe. Portugal's lifeblood was the sea fishing and trade with northern Europe. Lisbon was the major way station for Italian exports to Europe's north. But at first it was the goods of Africa, not of Asia, that pulled Portugal into the van of exploration and discovery.

To the south of Portugal was Morocco, Portugal's ancient enemy, and south of Morocco the Sahara and a coast that was, until the 1400s, a mystery. Arab explorers had sailed as far south as Cape Bojador, but their vessels, designed for the usually placid Mediterranean, were savaged by the constant, powerful winds off the cape. The Arabs called the Atlantic "the green sea of darkness" and gave up on it. They brought the slaves, gold, and ivory they purchased in black Africa across the Sahara on foot and camelback.

Cheng Ho

The sea route between Europe and Asia might easily have been opened not by the Portuguese but by a Chinese, Cheng Ho (Zheng He). Beginning in 1405, he commanded six voyages to the Indian Ocean. One of his fleets consisted of sixty-two vessels, some of them gigantic five-masted junks, one described as 400 feet long. Cheng discovered (for China) Borneo, India, and in Africa, Zanzibar and Kenya.

He wanted to round Africa from east to west. Had he done so, it is not far-fetched to imagine him reaching Europe although, unlike Portugal's nimble caravels, Cheng Ho's junks did not sail well against the wind; he depended on the seasonal monsoons in the Indian Ocean to sail between China and India. Cheng died in 1433 and the emperor ordered his fleet disassembled, proclaiming the death penalty for any Chinese who traveled abroad. The emperor had concluded that there was nothing China wanted from distant lands except silver, and it dependably flowed in over land.

Portugese Discoveries

A son and brother of Portugese kings, Prince Henry, believed that the green sea of darkness could be mastered. Known to history as Henry the Navigator (although he personally made but one short sea voyage), Henry was fascinated by the Atlantic and by the lands, both real and imagined, that bordered it. He knew of the big profits the Arabs enjoyed from their trans-Saharan trade. Why should Portugal not bypass the Sahara and bring African gold, ivory, and slaves home by sea? Henry also believed that Prester John, a great Christian king who was looking for allies to fight against the Muslims, was a black African. (Prester John was a myth.) And Henry knew that in the Indies the trade goods that all Europe coveted cost little. Surely the Indies could be reached by finding and rounding Africa's southern tip.

The prince funded an informal "research and development" operation at Sagres in southern Portugal. He lured mariners there to share their experiences with mapmakers and scholars (many of them Genoese like Columbus) who also pored over narratives written by travelers in Asia. Henry organized fifteen expeditions to explore the African coast. Sailors blown out into the Atlantic by the winds that had discouraged the Arabs discovered and colonized the island of Madeira, 350 miles from Africa, and the Azores, 900 miles west of Portugal.

Shipwrights at Sagres and Lisbon perfected a vessel that could cope with ocean waves and winds, the caravel. Very sturdy, caravels could be rigged at sea with either the swiveling triangular lateen sails of the Mediterranean for sailing into the wind or with the large square sheets of northern Europe which pushed a vessel at high speed when the wind was behind. Caravels had bulging holds so they could be provisioned for voyages far longer than any other craft of the era, but they required relatively small crews to sail. "The best ships in the world and able to sail anywhere," wrote Luigi da Cadamosto, an Italian in Prince Henry's service. Less dramatically but also important, Portugese coopers improved casks for drinking water and wine so that the leakage and evaporation that had discouraged long ocean voyages was radically reduced.

Portugal's Route to Asia

Henry the Navigator died in 1460, but Portuguese explorers carried on. Every few years, one of them mapped a few more miles of African coast, returning with slaves, gold, and ivory. The Portuguese built forts at strategic points along the way to serve both as trading centers and as rest stops for Portugese explorers bound farther south. In 1488, Bartholomeu Díaz returned with the news that he had reached Africa's southern extremity, which he called the Cape of Storms. The king promptly renamed it the Cape of Good Hope because, from there, surely, it would be clear sailing to the Indies.

Not for another decade, however, would Vasco da Gama reach the Indian port of Calicut and return with a 2,000-percent profit. That was quite profitable enough to prompt the Portuguese to pump resources into extending their commercial empire. Their "colonies" were, in fact, not territorial but strongly fortified trading posts. The Portuguese were not interested in making homes in Africa or Asia; they wanted to trade.

The string of forts stretched the length of Africa's western coast and up east Africa as far as Mombasa (in present-day Kenya); across the Indian Ocean to Goa (India); and to Macau (China). The Portuguese even had a nonfortified presence in Japan. In 1500, Pedro Cabral staked a Portuguese claim in South America when, bound for India, his ship was blown across the Atlantic to what is now Brazil. (Even more important than Brazil at first, Cabral discovered that ships reached the Cape of Good Hope more quickly by sailing south in the mid-Atlantic, rather than by hugging the coast.)

The African and Asian trade enriched Portugal. Its merchants easily undersold the Italians. Pepper in Lisbon sold for half the price charged in Venice and, at that, the cost was twenty times what the Portuguese had paid for it in India.

Columbus: The Downside

Columbus was a virtuoso navigator. He was a master of the Atlantic's currents and winds. He crossed the Atlantic in just four weeks, as quickly as anyone would make the trip for centuries to come, and his return to Europe was almost as fast. Columbus was an able mapmaker too, but he was not much of a geographer. The Portugese and Spanish scholars who advised against his Enterprise of the Indies were correct in saying that Japan was 9,000 miles away and not 2,500 as Columbus insisted.

Columbus clung to his discredited measurement because, lifelong, he simply ignored or distorted information that contradicted what he had decided to believe. Pierre D'Ailly, the author of *Imago Mundi,* an authoritative geography of the the era, warned readers not to regard theories he described as proven facts. Some say this, some say that, d'Ailly wrote, take them for what they're worth. In the margins of his copy of the book, Columbus wrote of those of d'Ailly's speculations that suited him as facts. At the mouth of the Orinoco River, the ocean was brown from the thousands of tons of soil the river carried with it daily. That meant the Orinoco drained a large continent. But Columbus wanted to believe Venezuela was an island. He ignored the contrary evidence and refused to explore the river.

Columbus was also a disaster as a colonizer. He sited his first American town, Isabela, in a marsh three miles from fresh water! What was he thinking? As governor, he proclaimed that Indians who failed to bring him gold each day would have their hands amputated, a law he could not enforce without destroying his colony.

Having little gold to bring back to Spain, Columbus brought enslaved Indians instead, another colossal blunder. Church authorities advised Queen Isabella that American Indians could not morally be enslaved. Columbus's captives, with whom he thought he would please the queen, were freed (those who were still alive). One may lament that the great navigator spent his final years in disgrace, but Queen Isabella had good reason to be sick of him.

The Santa Maria, the largest of Columbus's vessels, and his flagship. Columbus did not much like it; it was a carrack, slow and difficult to handle, but because it held large quantities of provisions, it was invaluable.

The Art Archive/Picture Desk

Spain Goes West

Christopher Columbus witnessed the growth of Portugal's empire up close. He settled in Portugal in 1476, earning his living by drawing nautical charts. He made a number of ocean voyages to as far north as England and as far south as the Canary Islands where he observed that the prevailing winds blew strongly to the west, across the Atlantic. Although his brother, Bartholomew, may have sailed with Diaz, Columbus took little interest in the African trade. His goal was the Indies and in 1484, he asked the king to fund an "Enterprise of the Indies" by which he would make a short, speedy crossing of the Atlantic from the Canaries. Japan, Columbus argued, was only 2,500 miles from Portugal.

Trying to reach the Indies by rounding Africa, as the Portugese were doing, was a waste of resources. Portugese navigators had explored far more than 2,500 miles of African coast and had no indication they were anywhere near the continent's southern reach. (Diaz's discovery of the Cape was three years in the future.) Moreover, hugging the African coast meant struggling with uncooperative winds. Columbus would have easy sailing west and, by returning a few degrees of latitude farther north, he would return to Portugal with the winds behind him.

He got nowhere with his scheme. If the size of Africa was frustrating, the African trade was lucrative. There would be no slaves, gold, and ivory along Columbus's route. And King John II's university advisors told him that Japan was not 2,500 miles away but 9,000 (they were right) with no string of Portugese forts in which to take refuge and replenish supplies. Columbus and the king's money would vanish at sea. The king agreed; he called Columbus "a big talker, full of fancy and imagination."

Why America? Why not Columbia?

Why was the New World not named Columbia? In part, the fault was Columbus's. He never claimed that he had discovered a place that needed a name. He had sailed to "the Indies."

Amerigo Vespucci was an Italian who twice crossed the Atlantic. Where Columbus was a medieval man, Vespucci was a modern. He wrote of his voyages, "Rationally, let it be said in a whisper, experience is worth more than theory"—meaning the writings of the ancients, including the Bible. Marvelling at American animals unknown in Europe, Vespucci noted: "so many species could not have entered Noah's ark," a heresy of which the pious Columbus was incapable.

It was Vespucci who first declared in print that it was a "New World" across the Atlantic. In 1507, a German cartographer, drawing the first map to show the Americas separate from Asia, named this new world for Amerigo in the Latin form of his name, feminine—ending in "a"—because the Latin names for the continents of Europe, Africa, and Asia were of feminine gender.

In the late nineteenth century, a descendant of Amerigo, Signora America Vespucci, petitioned the United States Congress for compensation for 400 year's unauthorized use of her name. She did not collect.

Columbus took his plan to Queen Isabella in neighboring Castille. Her experts from the University of Salamanca repeated what the Portugese scholars had said: it was 9,000 miles across the Atlantic to Japan; no ship could be provisioned for so long a voyage; the "Enterprise of the Indies" was "vain, impracticable, and resting on grounds too weak to merit the support of the government."

But Columbus had some influential friends at Isabella's court. They persuaded the queen to pay him a modest annuity just to keep him around. Who knew? When, in 1492, Isabella learned that Columbus was planning to present his proposal to the kings of France and England, she decided to take a chance.

Actually, Isabella's financial risk was piddling. Outfitting Columbus cost no more than the annual salary of one of her innumerable officials or entertaining a visiting dignitary's entourage. The title Columbus demanded, "Admiral of the Ocean Sea," was a pretty exalted one, but it did not cost the queen a ducat. Nor did the authority over any lands he might discover (another demand) nor his big cut of purely hypothetical profits. A town that owed the queen money and friends of Columbus picked up the cost of two caravels, the *Niña* and *Pinta,* and the clumsy but larger carrack, *Santa Maria.*

Frustration

Four times Christopher Columbus would sail the ocean blue carrying letters of introduction from Isabella and her husband addressed to the emperors of China and Japan. Four times he returned to Spain after Indians told him that no, sorry, they had never heard of such illustrious persons. Four times, Columbus told Isabella and Ferdinand that, next time for sure, he would "give them as much gold as they need, . . . and I will also give them all the spices and cotton they need."

To the day he died in 1506, Columbus insisted he had reached some of the 7,448 islands that Marco Polo said ringed East Asia. Sustained for half a lifetime by a vision, he could not face up to what, by 1506, knowing Spaniards understood. Columbus had not reached the Indies; he had discovered islands previously unknown to Europe.

Until 1521, knowing Spaniards considered Columbus's islands of little value. While the Portugese were raking in money by selling the goods from their African and Asian trading posts, Cuba and Hispaniola produced little of commercial value. A few hundred Spaniards had carved out comfortable lives for themselves in the West Indies by exploiting Indian labor. But most of the Spaniards in the New World, soldiers who had crossed the ocean to march on rich Asian cities, languished with "burnyng agues [fevers], . . . blysters, noysome sweates, aches in the body, byles, yellowe jaundyse, inflammations of the eyes," and fought among themselves.

It seemed as if no news from Cuba and Hispaniola was good news. In 1513, Vasco Núñez de Balboa crossed the Isthmus of Panama and discovered another great ocean, the Pacific. The implication was painful to face: The real Indies were as distant as the scholars of Salamanca had said they

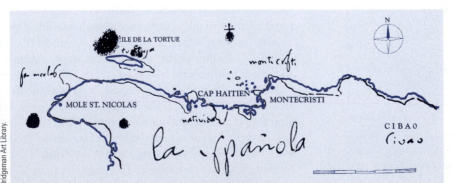

Sketch of the coast of Española, drawn by Columbus on the first voyage, from the original in the possession of the Duque de Barwick y de Alba, 1492 (ink on paper), Columbus, Christopher (1451-1506) (attr.to)/Private Collection/The Bridgeman Art Library.

Columbus's skills as a navigator are famous. Not so well known was his expertise as a maker of charts, as maritime maps are called. The black outline of the northwest coast of what is now Haiti was drawn by Columbus from shipboard. The broader blue line is from a modern map based on satellite images. The Admiral was close to perfect.

were. In 1519, a flotilla commanded by Ferdinand Magellan confirmed the awful truth. Sailing with five ships and 265 men, Magellan found an all-water route to the Pacific by rounding South America. But it was hardly a plausible trade route. Passing from the Atlantic to the Pacific in the face of adverse currents and winds was an extremely difficult feat of sailing. Distances in the Pacific were boundless. Native peoples were poor and hostile. Magellan was killed in the Philippines. Only one of his vessels, the Victoria, commanded by Juan Sebastián de Elcaño, manned by just eighteen half-year sailors, struggled back to Spain by sailing around the world.

In any case, the Spanish were barred from trading anywhere in the Pacific except the Philippines. In 1493, to avert a conflict between Spain and Portugal, the pope, in a proclamation, *Inter Caetera,* divided the world's lands not "in the actual possession of any Christian king or prince" between the two nations. His line of demarcation ran from pole to pole through a point 100 leagues (about 300 miles) west of the Portugese Azores. The next year, in the Treaty of Tordesillas, the Portuguese persuaded Isabella and Ferdinand to move the line a bit farther west (thus laying the legal grounds for Portuguese settlement of Brazil after its discovery in 1500). Africa and the East Indies were Portugal's.

THE SPANISH EMPIRE

In 1519, Hernán Cortés, a soldier and hustler living on Hispaniola led an expedition of eleven ships, 508 Spanish soldiers, about 200 Indians, and several Africans, along with seven cannon, sixteen horses, and dozens of war dogs—gigantic mastiffs trained to kill—to Mexico. What Cortés found and did there ended Spain's envy of Portugal's commercial empire.

Cortés in Mexico

Cortés was not the first Spaniard to set foot in Mexico. In 1511, Gonzalo Guerrero was shipwrecked on the Yucatan peninsula and actually became a military leader of the Maya. Another castaway who had learned the Maya language joined up with Cortés. He worked as an interpretor in tandem with an Indian girl, Malinche (Doña Marina, Cortés called her) who spoke both Mayan and Nahuatl, the Aztec language.

But Cortés's arrival made a difference—overnight. He soon learned of the riches of Tenochtitlán, founded the town of Vera Cruz as a base, and sent word to Cuba and Hispaniola that (rather a violation of his commission) he was marching his army there. He hoped for a peaceable takeover of the Aztec but was prepared to fight. He called for reinforcements, tempting recruits with the fabulous stories of Aztec riches he had been told.

The Tabascans of the coast attacked Cortés, but they were no match for cannon, horses, war dogs, and steel swords. After the Spanish victory, Cortés shrewdly offered the Tabascans an alliance against the Aztec. They, like almost all Mexicans, resented the Aztec because of the tribute they extorted from them. By comparison, Cortés and his men must have seemed benificent. Several times on the long march to Tenochtitlán, the scenario

was repeated: Spanish victory in battle, generous peace terms, alliance. Totomacs, Tlaxcalans, Tolucans, and Cholulans all joined up. By the time Cortés reached Lake Texcoco, he commanded at least ten Mexican warriors for each of his Spaniards.

The news about Cortés bewildered the Aztec emperor, Moctezuma II. He rejected the advice of some of his nobles to attack the invaders outside the city. Moctezuma may have worried that Cortés was the god, Quetzalcoatl, a deity who—uncanny good luck for Cortés—was fair-skinned, had tried to forbid human sacrifice (as Cortés did), and who, in the legend, had disappeared from Mexico in the direction from which Cortés came. To top things off, 1519 was Quetzalcoatl's year in the Aztec calendar. According to one of Moctezuma's advisors, the emperor "enjoyed no sleep, no food. . . . Whatsoever he did, it was as if he were in torment." Cortés did not have to battle his way over the causeways. On November 8, 1519, he and his army were welcomed into the city.

It did not take the Aztec long to discover that Cortés and his men were not gods. When some soldiers stumbled on a store of jewels, silver, and gold in Moctezuma's palace, "as if they were monkeys, the Spanish lifted up the gold banners and gold necklaces . . . . Like hungry pigs they craved that gold." Always on top of developments, Cortés quickly made Moctezuma his hostage. Masterfully, he cultivated, cozened, and threatened the emperor. Cortés still thought he could have Mexico peacefully. For more than six months, Moctezuma did what he was told to do.

Outside the palace, however, dissident nobles organized the increasingly hostile common people, who had been forced to provide the Spanish and their allies with huge quantitites of food every day. In June 1520, a mob assaulted the palace. When Cortés marched Moctezuma out to quiet the rioters, the emperor was struck by a rock and, a short time later, died.

Conquest

Without their hostage, the Spanish had problems. Tenochtitlán erupted behind the new emperor, Cuitláhuac, and the Aztec came close to wiping out the invaders. Half of Cortés's men and perhaps 4,000 Tlaxcalans were killed on what the Spanish called *la noche triste,* the sad night, July 1, 1520. Nevertheless, even with their lives in the balance, the Spaniards insisted on carrying eight tons of gold and other treasure on their retreat. They really did suffer, as Cortés had told Moctezuma, "from a disease of the heart which can be cured only with gold."

But it was the Aztec, not the Spanish, who were doomed. Cortés mobilized his Indian allies and Spanish reinforcements. He returned to Tenochtitlán with 700 Spanish infantry, 120 crossbowmen, 90 cavalry, a "navy" of boats he built to take control of the lake, and, so Cortés estimated, 50,000 Tlaxcalans and Texcocans. (Again, such figures are not to be taken as gospel.) For eighty days they assaulted a much smaller Aztec army led by yet another emperor, Cuauhtémoc. (Cuitláhuac had died of smallpox.) Cortés took Tenochtitlán, but hardly intact. When the battle ended on August 13, 1521, much of the city had been leveled.

Hernán Cortés had won a turnkey empire. He and his lieutenants inserted themselves at the top of Aztec society in place of the nobility they had effectively exterminated (15,000 Aztec were killed on the final day of fighting). They carved out great estates and lived off the labor of the masses as the Aztec nobles and priests had done. The traditional submissiveness of the common people made it possible for the Spanish to rule with minimal resistance. Mexicans took quickly to the wheel, pulley, iron tools, and beasts of burden. Within fifty years, most had embraced the Roman Catholic religion while not abandoning all traditional practices.

The *Conquistadores*

The Spanish king—best known to history as Emperor Charles V—took little interest in his American empire. He spent the gold sent to him alright, but he never mentioned Mexico (now called New Spain) in his memoirs. Spanish adventurers, however, were electrified. There was a rush to the Americas by thousands of mostly young men who braved hideous conditions shipboard to search for Mexicos of their own. They called themselves *conquistadores* (conquistadors in English)—conquerors within a generation's life span, they subdued a territory larger than Europe.

Rarely has history shaped a people for conquest as Spain's history shaped the conquistadors. Much of Spain is arid or mountainous; agriculture never attracted the ambitious. Because the Christian Spanish associated trade—business—with the despised Jews they had driven out of the country, the upper classes shunned commerce. The worldly role of the *hidalgo*, the Spanish male with pretensions to social standing, was to fight. He was a *caballero*, a knight. The bravery and fortitude of the conquistadors under daunting conditions awe us. The other side of their military character, their ruthlessness and cruelty, has also been remembered.

Spain's zealous Roman Catholicism factored into the conquistadors' achievement. Because the ancestral national

The Discoverer of the United States

The discoverer of what is now the United States was Juan Ponce de León. In 1513, aged 53, ancient for such gallivanting, Ponce sailed to Florida to find Bimini where, Indians said, there was "a particular spring which restores old men to youth"—the fountain of youth. In 1521, Ponce de León returned to Florida to live. Instead of enjoying his retirement paddling about in rejuvenating waters, he was killed by Indians.

Bibliotheque Nationale, Paris

An Aztec artist's depiction of Moctezuma II, Cortés, and Spanish soldiers proceeding through Tenochtitlan. Curiously, a Spaniard altered the painting, depicting Cortés and Malinche in a European style. Malinche (or Doña Marina) was Cortés's invaluable interpreter to whom he often turned for advice. She was also his mistress and bore his child.

Big City Life

As Catholics, Cortés and his men were appalled by the Aztec eagle and serpent gods and disgusted by human sacrifice. But they were pleasantly astonished by the city of Tenochtitlán. They admired more about Aztec lifestyle than they deplored.

Unlike the streets of European cities, which were filthy with refuse and human waste, Tenochtitlán's streets were tidy and clean. They were swept daily and there were public toilets—unheard of in Europe—at regular intervals. The Aztec themselves were a fastidious people who bathed regularly (and cooled off) in Lake Texcoco and the canals that reached into the city. They must have found the odor of the Spaniards, sweating in their armor and not keen on bathing to begin with, hard to stomach.

Tenochtitlán's streets were safe (before the Aztec rebelled, that is). The numbers of potentially hostile subject people bringing tribute were strictly regulated and closely guarded. At night, the main thoroughfares were illuminated by fires in raised braziers (made of clay, not brass) where people paused to warm their hands and converse. In Europe's cities, every building was a minifortress, sealed tight at sundown for protection from thugs. Few dared to walk far after dark except skilled swordsmen—and then in groups.

There were no very broad avenues in Tenochtitlán (the Aztec didn't need them; they had neither vehicles nor beasts of burden) and the narrowest residential alleys were narrow indeed, just wide enough for two people to squeeze past one another. But there was an air of openness in the city not to be found in Europe where cities were hemmed in by towering walls. Tenochtitlán's defense was broad Lake Texcoco.

Street life was lively, even frenetic. There were plenty of open workshops and retail stores, almost as varied in their offerings as shops back home. (Not quite: There were no blacksmiths or, curiously, cabinet makers.) Cortés's soldiers were bemused by the lack of furniture in Aztec houses. In humble homes, there was nothing but sleeping mats and even the rooms of Moctezuma's palace were all but empty.

The buildings were constructed of adobe brick; the better homes were plastered with a mud stucco. All roofs were flat, made of pine boards or maguey leaves. When the war between the Aztec and the Spanish erupted, Spanish soldiers discovered that every building was a platform from which they were pelted with large stones and bricks. Ordinary people lived in tiny apartments: one or two small rooms. They were smoky; there were no chimneys. However, with a refreshing candor unusual when Europeans described Indians, several Spaniards wrote that the homes of the Aztec poor were superior to the homes of humble Castilians (which did not have chimneys either). Wealthy Aztec lived in large, well-built homes built around open courtyards, like grand residences in Spain.

Tenochtitlán's day began at sunrise when priests blew on horns from the tops of the temples. The city was a beehive of activity all day. There was a lot to be done and every burden was carried. A feature of life in Tenochtitlán mentioned in the writings of several Spaniards was the ubiquity of vendors of ready-to-eat meals —"fast food, like" tacos and hot chocolate sweetened with honey.

How big a city was Tenochtitlán? One has to be cautious; estimates made at the time were all over the place. Bartolome de las Casas, a Dominican friar, said the city was home to a million people. But he had an axe to grind and is often unreliable. In order to maximize the evil his fellow Spaniards did, he exaggerated, sometimes wildly, the numbers of Indians who suffered from Spanish depredations.

Nevertheless, other Spaniards suggested figures approaching De Las Casas's, but not Cortés. He said that Tenochtitlán was about the size of Seville or Cordoba or about 50,000 to 60,000. The most responsible students of the Aztec today seem to have settled on a figure in the neighborhood of 200,000, counting outlying suburbs. Preconquest Tenochtitlán was far larger than any city in Europe.

---

enemy had been of another faith, Islam, Spanish nationalism and Roman Catholicism were of a piece. Like their Muslim foes, the Spaniards believed that a war even nominally for the purpose of spreading true religion was holy. Death in such a war was a first-class ticket to paradise. It was a belief that made for soldiers nonchalant about death and, for that, chillingly brave.

Exploration South and North

Spain's rulers encouraged conquest by granting conquistadors the lion's share of the gold and silver they won. (The king got a fifth of it.) Conquistadors were granted land and *encomiendas*, the legal right to force the Indians who lived on their land to work for them. They were not slaves—enslaving Indians was forbidden—but, in practice, the distinction was fine.

Only one conquistador was as fortunate as Cortés. In 1531, an aging illiterate, Francisco Pizarro, led 168 soldiers and 62 horses high into the Andes mountains of South America. There he found the empire of the Incas, 3,000 miles in extent, tied together by 12,000 miles of roads Pizarro called unmatched in Christendom. Inca highways were narrow, trails really. Like the Aztec, the Incas had no wheeled vehicles; their roads needed to accomodate only foot traffic. Nonetheless, some stretches were magnificently engineered: One traversed a pass 16,700 feet above sea level; a suspension bridge spanned 250 feet; its weight-bearing cable made of twisted fibers was a foot in diameter.

Pizarro was bolder than Cortés, for reinforcement was out of the question. He was such an artist of deceit as to make Cortés look saintly. When he captured the Inca emperor, Athualpa, 80,000 Inca soldiers were paralyzed. For eight months, they brought Pizarro a ransom of gold that filled a room twenty-two feet long by seventeen feet wide. Then—so much for the honor of the Castilian *caballero*—Pizarro murdered Athualpa.

That was it for American treasure troves although the search for them continued. In 1541, Francisco Orellana with sixty men searched for El Dorado, a king who was said to be sprinkled daily with gold dust which he washed off nightly in a pool. It certainly sounded as if it were worth dredging. Orellana and forty-six survivors crossed tropical South America, a distance of 2,500 miles, on the Amazon river.

Between 1539 and 1542, Hernando de Soto's army wandered what is now the southeastern United States in another fantasy-based quest for riches. Viciously cruel with the Indians he battled, De Soto was buried in the Mississippi River. Only half the mourners at his funeral got back alive to the West Indies. During the same years, Francisco Coronado trekked extraordinary distances in the Southwest. With about 300 conquistadors ("vicious young men with nothing to do"), a few blacks, and 800 Indians, Coronado was looking for the "Seven Cities of Cíbola," said to have been founded by seven Spanish bishops who, centuries earlier, had fled from the Moors to the "blessed Isles." One of these conurbations, according to an imaginative priest, Fray Marcos de Niza, was "the greatest city in the world . . . larger than the city of Mexico." Coronado's men found only dusty adobe villages. "Such were our curses that some hurled at Fray Marcos," wrote one soldier, "that I pray God may protect him."

Spanish America

For more than a century Mexican and Peruvian gold and silver made Spain the richest and most powerful nation of Europe. By 1550, $4.5 million in precious metals crossed the Atlantic each year, by 1600, $12 million. Not for another century would the flow of riches wither to a trickle. American wealth financed the cultural blossoming of Spain and great armies to do the king's bidding.

By 1700, Spain's empire stretched from Florida and New Mexico to the Rio de la Plata in South America. In so vast a realm, economy and social structure varied immensely. Generally, however, land ownership was concentrated in the hands of a small group of *encomenderos* who lived off the labor of Indians and slaves imported from Africa. Government was centralized in the hands of several viceroys (vice kings). The Roman Catholic church exercised great power, generally for the good: Many—not all—priests and friars took seriously their mission to protect the Indians from rapacious fellow Spaniards.

At a time when only a few hundred French and English had slept overnight on American soil, Spanish America boasted two hundred towns and cities, twenty printing presses, and six universities. The fate of the Indians of Mexico and the West Indies, however, was not so bright a story. It has been estimated that there were at least five million Mexicans in 1500. In 1600, there were a million. In 1492, the Indian population of Hispaniola was about 200,000; in 1508 it was 60,000, in 1514, 14,000. By 1570, only two small native villages survived on the island.

The Black Legend

It can seem a wonder that any Native Americans survived. Indeed, the horrors they suffered was the lifetime message of a few priests who took up their cause. "I am the voice of Christ," Father Antonio de Montesinos told conquistadors who had come to church to doze, "saying that you are all in a state of mortal sin for your cruelty and oppression in your treatment of this innocent people."

A Dominican friar, Bartolomé de las Casas, devoted his life to lobbying the Spanish king for laws protecting the Indians. The Spaniards treated them, De las Casas said, "not as beasts, for beasts are treated properly at times, but like the excrement in a plaza." His scorching description of conquistador cruelty, *A Brief Relation of the Destruction of the Indians,* was overblown. De las Casas was a propagandist; propagandists exaggerate. But the picture he drew was not fantasy; the *leyenda nera,* the "black legend" of Spanish cruelty, was true enough in its essence.

Still, the *encomenderos* must not be thought unique. In the context of the sixteenth century, the atrocities they perpetrated were close to the norm. It was an era of indifference to suffering, and callousness was neither a Spanish nor a European monopoly. It was Asian, African, and Native American too, and exercised not only on those of different race. Warfare in Europe meant terror for peasants caught in the paths of marauding armies. The goriness of Mesoamerican religion has been noted. Chinese techniques of torture were particularly exquisite. Africans needed no tutoring by outsiders in savagery.

THE COLUMBIAN EXCHANGE

More Indians died of pick and shovel than at sword point. And more died of disease than from forced labor. Columbus's voyage established a biological pipeline between land masses that had drifted apart 150 million years before human beings appeared on earth. Some species had flourished in both worlds: oaks, dogs, deer, mosquitoes, the virus that causes the common cold. There were, however, many animals and plants in the Americas that were new to Europeans. And Europeans brought with them flora, fauna, and microbes unknown to the Indians.

The Impact on America

Native American mammals were generally smaller and less suited for food and draft than Old World livestock. The Aztec

Leonard de Selva/Corbis.

This portrayal of Native Americans, a woodcut, was carved in Germany about 1500, so the artist surely never saw an Indian. Note the European facial features. Of all the tribes known to Europeans by 1500, only the Caribs of the West Indies ate human flesh. But, as today, sensationalism sold.

had only five domesticates: the turkey, muscovy duck, dog, bee, and a cochineal insect. So, the Spanish were quick to import hogs, cattle, sheep, goats, and chickens along with European grasses to feed them (plus about 70 percent of the plants we call "weeds"). Indians were soon dependent on the newcomers. Even those native peoples who escaped Spanish conquest were glad to raid Spanish flocks and herds for food. The weaving art identified with the Navajo of the American Southwest was refined when the Navajo adopted European sheep.

The people of Mexico were initially terrified by the sight of a man mounted on a horse. It reinforced their briefly held delusion that the Spaniards were divine. Even after the Mexicans recognized that horses were ordinary beasts, the Spaniards' equestrian monopoly gave them an immense advantage in battle. Within two centuries, runaway horses gone feral had migrated as far as the Great Plains of North America. There they became the foundation of several cultures that had never heard of Spain. The Sioux, Commanche, Pawnee, Nez Percé, Blackfoot, Crow, and other tribes of the plains, who had previously done their hunting on foot, captured mustangs and became peerless horsemen independent of European example.

Among the valuable "green immigrants" from the Old World were grains such as wheat and barley, citrus fruits, and sugar cane. Mexico was exporting wheat to the West Indies by 1535. It is difficult to imagine the West Indies without sugar cane, but it too was an import. Columbus himself introduced lettuce, cauliflower, citrus fruits, figs, and pome-

granates to America. Within a few decades of his death, bananas (from Asia) and watermelons (from West Africa) were being cultivated in the New World.

Feeding the World

America contributed few food animals to world larders, but American plant foods revolutionized the European, African, and Asian diet. Maize (Indian corn), an American native, astonished Europeans by the height of its stalks and the size of its grains. Cultivation of the crop spread to every continent, increasing the food supply and contributing to the runaway increase in population that characterizes the last five hundred years of human history.

The sweet potato became a staple in West Africa, where it was introduced by slave traders. (Yams, superficially similar to sweet potatos, were already established there.) Beans, squash and pumpkins, peppers, strawberries (there was a European strawberry, but it was inferior to the American), vanilla and chocolate, wild rice, and tomatoes are American natives unknown in Europe, Africa, and Asia before 1492.

Of 640 food crops grown in Africa today, almost 600 originated in the Americas. Manioc (tapioca), also of American origin, is today a staple for 200 million people in the tropics. The white ("Irish") potato, a native of the Andes, provides basic subsistence for even greater numbers, from Ireland to China.

Many national cuisines today depend on foods of American origin for their zest, notably the tomato and the extraordinary variety of chili peppers that have been developed from

Taters and Tomaters

Europeans took slowly to potatoes and tomatoes. Some believed that the former was an aphrodisiac and the latter poisonous. Some 300 years passed before the white potato became a staple in the country with which we most associate it, Ireland.

Tomatoes were grown in Europe as ornamentals by 1500. A Jesuit gourmet pronounced them excellent eating as early as 1590 when southern Italians were already growing them for the kitchen. By the eighteenth century, they were central in Mediterranean cuisine. In the United States, President Thomas Jefferson, a gourmet, served them at White House dinners. Which is not to say that every guest partook, for some medical authorities continued to warn of the dire effects of eating them. As late as 1820, Robert G. Johnson of Salem, New Jersey, was able to gather a large crowd expecting to see him collapse in agony when he announced he would consume an entire tomato on the steps of the county courthouse.

VD

It has been suggested that syphillis was not carried from America to Europe but was a mutation of yaws, a disease long endemic in hot climates in the Old World. If so, the timing and place of the mutation—1493 in Cadiz, the port to which Columbus returned—is a coincidence without rival. The case for an Old World origin of syphillis is next to no case at all. The only evidence for it is an anatomical similarity of the yaws microbe and the syphillis spirochete. The argument amounts to "it could have been."

The evidence for an American origin is mostly circumstantial—when and where syphillis first appeared in Europe—but powerfully so. And there is more than circumstance: The Indians in Hispaneola told de las Casas that the disease had been around long before Columbus. Half of the buried bodies of moundbuilders which archaeologists have exhumed were syphillitic. Signs of syphillis have been found in human bones in America dating to 4000 B.C., but none in African, Asian, and European bones before 1493.

Mexican forebears. Think of Hungarian paprika, of Italian sauces. These, as well as tobacco, were contributed to the Old World by New.

Disease

The most tragic of the intercontinental transactions was in microscopic forms of life. Many diseases for which Europeans, Africans, and Asians had developed resistance, even immunity, were unknown to Native Americans before Columbus. Smallpox, measles, influenza, bubonic and pneumonic plague, tuberculosis, typhoid fever, typhus, and cholera were as foreign to the Americas as horses and Spaniards. Biologically, the Indians had not learned "to live with" these killer diseases.

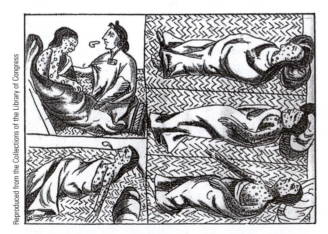

An Aztec depiction of smallpox victims. The disease killed plenty of Europeans and Africans, but it devastated Indian populations. Native Americans had inherited no resistance to the disease (and others!) as Europeans and Africans had.

Why were they absent from America? Probably because all of these diseases first spread to human beings from domesticated animals that live in herds and flocks—sheep, goats, cattle, pigs, and fowl. Native Americans had few such domesticates. The Indians of the Great Plains hunted herd animals—the bison—but they did not, like Europeans, Africans, and Asians, live in close daily proximity to them. The rarity of large cities in the Americas also explains the absence of virulent epidemics in the pre-Columbian era. Smallpox, measles, and the other terrible ailments Europeans brought on their ships are "crowd diseases." Highly infectious once among a dense population, they rage and kill massively. If, before Columbus, similar afflictions appeared in the Americas, they died out for the lack of "crowds" in which to do their work.

Old World diseases were catastrophic in America. While transplanted Europeans and Africans suffered badly enough when smallpox or measles swept through a population, Indians died in heartrending numbers.

America's microbic revenge was venereal disease. Europeans first identified syphillis as a new disease in 1493, in Cadiz, Spain, the port to which, in that year, Columbus returned and dismissed his crew. Syphillis was next noticed in Naples, where several of Columbus's crewmen went as soldiers. It spread at terrifying speed throughout the world, following the trade routes. What better agents for spreading a sexually transmitted disease than seamen and the prostitutes who were their usual sexual partners?

Europeans, Africans, and Asians reacted to syphillis as Indians reacted to diseases previously unknown to them. Symptoms were severe and death came quickly. About 10 million people died of syphillis within fifteen years of Columbus's voyage. Only later did the disease take on the slower-acting form in which it is known today.

Reproduced from the Collections of the Library of Congress

FURTHER READING

Classics   William H. Prescott, *History of the Conquest of Mexico*, 1873; Samuel Eliot Morison, *Admiral of the Ocean Sea*, 1942.

General   D. W. Meinig, *Atlantic America 1492–1800*, Volume I of *The Shaping of America: A Geographical Perspective on 500 Years of History*, 1986; Alvin M. Josephy Jr., *America in 1492: The World of the Indian People Before the Arrival of Columbus*, 1991.

Paleo-Indians   Brian M. Fagan, *The Great Journey: The Peopling of Ancient America*, 1987 and *Ancient North America*, 2000; Stuart J. Fiedel, *Prehistory of the Americas*, 1991; Helen R. Sattler, *The Earliest Americans*, 1993; Francis Jennings, *Prehistory of America*, 1993.

Mesoamerican Civilization   Norman Hammond, *Ancient Maya Civilization*, 1982; Linda Sechele and David Freidel, *A Forest of Kings: The Untold Story of the Ancient Maya*, 1990; Brian M. Fagan, *Kingdoms of Gold, Kingdoms of Jade: The Americas Before Columbus*, 1991; Charles C. Mann, *New Revelations of the America Before Columbus*, 2005; Linda Sechele and Mary Ellen Miller, *The Blood of Kings*, 1986; Jared Diamond, *Guns, Germs, and Steel: The Fates of Human Societies*, 1997, and *Collapse: How Societies Choose to Fail or Succeed*, 2005.

European Exploration   Daniel J. Boorstin, *The Discoverers: A History of Man's Search to Know His World and Himself*, 1985; Steven Frimmer, *Neverland: Fabled Places and Fabulous Voyages of History and Legend*, 1976; Jorge Magasich-Airola and Jean-Marie de Beer, *America Magica: When Renaisssance Europe Thought It Had Conquered Paradise*, 2006; Peter Russell, *Prince Henry "The Navigator": A Life*, 2000; Hugh Thomas, *The Slave Trade: The Story of the Atlantic Slave Trade: 1440–1870*, 1997; Giles Milton, *Nathaniel's Nutmeg: The True and Incredible Adventures of the Spice Trader Who Changed the Course of History*, 1999; William D. Phillips Jr. and Carla Rahn Phillips, *The Worlds of Christopher Columbus*, 1992; James Reston Jr., *Dogs of War: Columbus, The Inquisition, and the Defeat of the Moors*, 2005.

Conquerors and the Conquered   Hugh Thomas, *Conquest: Montezuma, Cortés, and the Fall of Old Mexico*, 1993; Leon Lopez-Portilla, *The Broken Spears*, 1962; Thomas C. Patterson, *The Inca Empire: The Formation and Disintegration of a Pre-Capitalist State*, 1991; John Logan Allen, *North American Exploration*, vol. I, 1997; J. C. H. King, *First Peoples, First Contacts: Native People of North America*, 1999; James Lockhart and Stuart B. Schwartz, *Early Latin America*, 1983; Mark A. Burknolder and Lyman L. Johnson, *Colonial Latin America*, 1990; Donald J. Weber, *The Spanish Empire in North America*, 1990; J. H. Elliott, *Empires of the Atlantic World: Britain and Spain in America, 1492–1830*, 2006.

Biological Exchange   Alfred W. Crosby, *The Columbian Exchange: Biological and Cultural Consequences of 1492*, 30th Anniversary Edition, 2003, and *Ecological Imperialism: The Biological Expansion of Europe*, 1986.

KEY TERMS

Use the following listing of key terms to review important figures, events, locations, and concepts covered in this chapter. A glossary of these terms is available on *The American Past* companion Web site: www.cengage.com/history/conlin/tap9e

Beringia, p. 1

Paleo-Indians, p. 1

Mesoamerica, p. 2

Moctezuma II, p. 6

Columbus, Christopher, p. 6

Hispaniola, p. 7

Henry the Navigator, p. 10

Vespucci, Amerigo, p. 12

Inter Caetera, p. 13

Cortés, Hernán, p. 13

conquistadors, p. 14

Columbian Exchange, p. 16

ONLINE RESOURCES

Find additional resources, including primary source documents, images, interactive maps, simulations, chapter review exercises, and Internet links at

***The American Past* companion Web site**
www.cengage.com/history/conlin/tap9e

American History Resource Center
http://ushistory.wadsworth.com/

Collection of The New-York Historical Society. #1049 C

Chapter 2

Settlements Across the Sea

Motives, Failures, and Finally, a Colony 1550–1624

Where every wind that rises blows perfume,
And every breath of air is like an incense.
— *Francis Beaumont and John Fletcher, English poets*

The nature of the Country is such that it Causeth much sickness, and the scurvy
and the bloody flux, and divers other diseases, which maketh the body very poor,
and Weak.... We are in great danger, for our Plantation is very weak, by reason of
the death, and sickness.... I have nothing to Comfort me, nor is there nothing to be
gotten here but sickness, and death.
— *Richard Frethorne, early settler in Virginia*

Columbus's story was known all over Europe within months. It was the most sensational news since the fall of Constantinople forty years earlier. Isabella published his report even before he arrived at her court. In Rome, it was published in Latin, making it accessible to every educated European (and in the hands of the continent's best distribution network, the Pope's). By the time the now celebrated Admiral of the Ocean Sea weighed anchor on his second voyage to "the Indies" in September 1493, his account of the first crossing was circulating in half a dozen editions.

England's King Henry VII, who had brushed off Columbus's brother, ruminated for a few more years (he was a tightwad), then decided to fund an Italian navigator living in Bristol, John Cabot (Giovanni Caboto). Cabot had a pretty good sales pitch. Columbus, he said, found only poor islands peopled by half-naked savages because he crossed the Atlantic too far to the south. Japan, Cabot pointed out quite correctly, lay just a few degrees below England's latitude. In 1497, he sailed due west. Cabot had a far more difficult crossing than Columbus's because of adverse winds. Instead of Japan, however, Cabot found Newfoundland and Nova

Scotia. Like Columbus, Cabot believed they were the fringes of the Indies. He was lost at sea on his second try.

The French king took no interest in overseas exploration until 1523 when it was known that America was not the Indies. A French captain captured three Spanish caravels—the two nations were at war—carrying an eye-catching cargo: 500 pounds of gold dust and three large crates of gold ingots. It was booty from Mexico that Cortés had shipped to Spain. King Francis I promptly dispatched his Italian navigator (they were everywhere), Giovanni Verrazano, across the ocean. He explored, mostly from shipboard, pretty much the entire Atlantic shore of what is now the United States. Verrazano infused new life into the fading belief there was an easy sea route to the Indies when he reported that only a narrow sandy island separated the Atlantic from the "Indian Sea" or, as some mapmakers were soon calling it, "Verrazano's Sea." (Probably, he mistook Pamlico Sound, inside North Carolina's Outer Banks, for ocean.)

The pope scolded Francis I, reminding him that the world's non-Christian real estate had been divided between Portugal and Spain. Francis dipped his pen in sarcasm and asked to see the part of Adam's will that authorized the pope

THE ENGLISH REFORMATION

© Corbis

John Cabot may have been arguing that the Indies could be reached by sailing west before Columbus's voyage. Only in 1497, however, did England's Henry VII finance the voyage of discovery that established England's legal claims to North America. The king rewarded Cabot with an income of £20 a year for life. Cabot collected his annuity only once. He and his ship were lost on a second voyage in 1498.

to distribute such gifts. (When a conquistador told a Cenú Indian what the pope had done, the Indian remarked that "the pope must have been drunk.")

Drunk or sober, Adam's will or no Adam's will, the Americas remained (except for Portuguese Brazil) a Spanish monopoly for a century. Other nations envied Spain's Aztec and Inca riches; they made the 1500s Spain's *siglo de oro*, its "golden century" of prosperity and culture. But they also feared the huge armies Spain's silver financed.

There were plenty of transatlantic voyages. French, English, and Dutch fishermen spent winters on Newfoundland, Nova Scotia, and even New England maintaining camps for drying and salting the codfish netted on the Grand Banks. The French made a half-hearted attempt to establish a base in Canada after Verrazano's voyage. In 1536, an Englishman, Richard Hore, sailed to Labrador with the crackbrained scheme of seizing an Indian to exhibit for an admission fee in London. But no nation made a serious attempt to found a colony until late in the century.

Europe Divided

The delay owed only in part to fear of Spanish retaliation. More important was the turmoil all over Europe in the era of the Protestant Reformation. When Cortés was shattering the Aztec, a German monk, Martin Luther, was shattering the religious monopoly of the Roman Church. When Coronado was looking for the seven cities of Cibola in the scorching southwest, a French lawyer in rainy Geneva, John Calvin, was laying the foundations of a dynamic new religious faith that would profoundly shape American history.

In 1517, Luther denied the truth of several doctrines of the Roman Catholic Church. Called to account by the Holy Roman Emperor Charles V (who was also king of Spain), Luther denied the pope's religious authority. The only source of God's word, he declared, was the Bible. In a short time, large parts of Germany and the Netherlands and all of Scandinavia embraced the Evangelical Lutheran faith. Many ordinary folk had long been disgusted by the moral laxity common among Catholic priests. German princes, no paragons of morality themselves, were attracted to Lutheranism because, if they

The Background of English Colonization 1550–1603

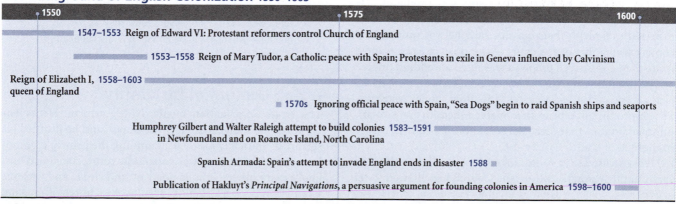

	1550	1575	1600
	1547–1553 Reign of Edward VI: Protestant reformers control Church of England		
	1553–1558 Reign of Mary Tudor, a Catholic: peace with Spain; Protestants in exile in Geneva influenced by Calvinism		
Reign of Elizabeth I, 1558–1603 queen of England			
	1570s Ignoring official peace with Spain, "Sea Dogs" begin to raid Spanish ships and seaports		
Humphrey Gilbert and Walter Raleigh attempt to build colonies 1583–1591 in Newfoundland and on Roanoke Island, North Carolina			
Spanish Armada: Spain's attempt to invade England ends in disaster 1588			
Publication of Hakluyt's *Principal Navigations*, a persuasive argument for founding colonies in America 1598–1600			

cut their ties to the Roman Church, they could seize Church lands, a fourth to a third of all the acreage in Europe.

Spain, Portugal, Italy, and most of France remained Catholic. In England, King Henry VIII condemned Lutheranism in a book, *Defense of the Seven Sacraments,* which so pleased Pope Leo X he named Henry "Defender of the Faith."

Henry's Bad Reputation

The best known portraits of Henry VIII, painted when he was middle-aged and corpulent, have saddled him with a reputation for gluttony. Indeed, he was a glutton when he was older. As a young man, however, he was quite handsome and athletic.

The fact that Henry ran through six wives has implied that he was as sexually abandoned as other kings who surrounded themselves with willing women. However (again except when he was quite young), Henry was no lecher nor even particularly sexual. Wife five (Catherine Howard) and very likely wife two (Anne Boleyn) looked elsewhere for their satisfaction. Henry could not bring himself to consummate his marriage with wife four (Anne of Cleves). By the time he married wife six (Catharine Parr), Henry was morbidly obese and assailed by half a dozen health problems. It is difficult to imagine that he and Catharine indulged in a sex life anywhere near half as wanton as society demands of couples today.

Henry VIII's Reformation

Just a few years later, the Defender of the Faith broke with the Church. Henry had no quarrel with most Catholic beliefs and rituals. His problem was domestic, marital, and dynastic. Henry had no male heir and his wife of twenty years, a Spanish princess, Catherine of Aragon, was at the end of her childbearing years (she was 45 in 1530). There was a daughter, Mary. But kings still rode to battlefields in the 1500s. (Francis I was captured and held prisoner by the Spanish.) Henry believed that if his dynasty, the Tudors, was to be secure, he must have a son to succeed him, a king who could suit up in armor. For that he needed a new, young wife.

And then there was Cupid, for Henry was a romantic. He had been far more loving with Catherine than kings were expected to be with their queens. Now he was smitten by a comely young flirt of the court, Anne Boleyn. Anne wanted more than a mistress's pillow; she wanted a wedding ring.

The Catholic Church forbade divorce. However, when the rich and powerful had marital difficulties, popes were usually able to find fine print that enabled them to grant an annulment; that is, that there never had been a valid marriage in the eyes of God.

Henry's case for an annulment was as good as those of many another notable whom the Church had allowed to set a wife aside. The professors at nine European universities endorsed his case; the faculty at six, three of them in Spain, rejected it. But Pope Clement VII was in no position to help

out the Defender of the Faith. He was at odds with a far more powerful figure than Henry VIII, the Emperor Charles V, who happened to be Catherine of Aragon's nephew. And he was not doing very well in the dispute. In 1527, the emperor allowed his army to run amok in the city of Rome.

While the pope hemmed and hawed, Anne Boleyn announced that she was pregnant. If her son—for surely the child would be a boy—were to succeed Henry as king, he had to be legitimate, born within marriage. Henry directed his bishops to grant an annulment and marry him to Anne. A compliant Parliament outlawed the pope's authority in England and named Henry head of the Church of England. Henry then emulated the Lutheran German princes he had denounced; he dissolved England's 400 monasteries and nunneries and seized their lands. Beginning in 1538, Henry sold these prime properties to ambitious subjects. Simultaneously he filled his treasury and created a class of landowners whose wealth and social position depended on defending the Church of England against the Church of Rome.

A Good Catholic Boy

Henry VIII continued to hear mass in Latin, the core of Catholic worship, until the end of his life. (He died in 1547.) Although he avoided the words, he retained the doctrines of transubstantiation and purgatory, which every Protestant reformer denounced.

Transubstantiation held that, in the mass, bread and wine were transformed into the actual body and blood of Christ; *purgatory* was a real place where the dead whose sins were minor did penance for them until, by their suffering and thanks to the prayers of those still on earth, they were admitted to heaven. It was the doctrine over which Martin Luther began the Protestant Reformation. In his will, Henry set aside money to pay for masses said for his soul.

He insisted that Church of England priests not marry (another practice Protestants condemned) and he rejected a proposal that churches be stripped of "papist" statues, saying "it is very laudable to pray to saints." He continued to denounce Lutheran doctrines and to burn Lutherans at the stake.

Henry was a Protestant? Not really. He was a good Catholic boy whom the pope had driven into rebellion.

A Half Century of Instability

The king's Reformation involved little reform. Henry encouraged his subjects to vilify the popes, and he justified his seizure of church lands by condemning the principle of monasticism. But the king was personally comfortable with just about every other Catholic doctrine and ritual, and with the Church's episcopal structure. That is, the Church of England was governed from the top down by bishops whom the king appointed.

Elizabeth Regina

Queen Elizabeth enjoyed a good time. She was witty and enjoyed bantering. She had a romantic streak, but the politician in her decided early on she would not marry. A husband meant political complications. No sixteenth-century prince would hover quietly in the shadows as Elizabeth II's Prince Philip has done for more than fifty years. Elizabeth I flirted with young men and enjoyed bawdy humor, but she really was a virgin queen. A pregnancy would have been the end of her.

Elizabeth was ridiculously vain. Far from beautiful, she was a sucker for flattery. Walter Raleigh was just one of her "favorites" who knew there was no such thing as laying it on too thick. The Earl of Essex was another. When Elizabeth was 56, shriveled, balding, half her teeth missing, half of them black, he told her, "I do confess that, as a man, I have been more subject to your natural beauty, than as a subject to the power of the king." And she lapped it up.

Portraits of the queen as an old woman (she died at age 69) show her so heavily made up she is clownlike: no eyebrows—every hair had been plucked—her face starkly white, caked with lard dusted with chalk, then splotched with bright rouge. Her white hair was dyed a brilliant red.

But was the makeup nothing but vanity? With no eyebrows to arch involuntarily and her face encased in a plaster, Elizabeth presented those who approached her throne with a face that could not be read. She betrayed no emotion behind her mask, neither surprise nor curiosity nor approval nor anger, no matter what a courtier or ambassador said. She was a politician to the end.

Queen Elizabeth I (1530–1603) knighting Francis Drake (1540-96) from 'Illustrations of English and Scottish History' Volume I (engraving), Gilbert, Sir John (1817-97) (after)/ Private Collection, Ken Welsh/Bridgeman Art Library

Until 1580, Queen Elizabeth responded to Spanish complaints about Francis Drake by saying that he acted without her permission. When, in 1580, Drake returned from his voyage around the world with his ship packed to the gunwhales with Spanish treasure, the queen had to choose between returning it and punishing Drake or accept responsilbity for him, collect her share of his loot, and face the consequences of war with Spain. She boarded Drake's ship and knighted him.

For ordinary Englishmen and women, the "English Reformation" meant little. The rhythms of their religious lives remained the same. Pope or king: What was the difference to a baker or a milkmaid? Church services and readings from the Bible were now in English rather than in Latin. That made them less mysterious, but they were familiar prayers and rituals in all other ways. Compared to the violence and psychic dislocations of the Reformation on the European continent, Henry VIII's Reformation was easy not to notice.

However, as people with power have discovered before and since, tinkering even a little with an established order of things can set loose a wild spirit of innovation. A true Protestantism germinated within the Church of England during the brief reign of Henry's son, Edward VI (1547–1553). Reformers abolished the mass. Parish priests too Catholic in their styles were dismissed. Churches were stripped of statues and other Catholic paraphernalia (not least among them chalices and candle holders made of versatile gold). The Protestant *Book of Common Prayer* replaced Catholic devotionals.

Alas for the reformers surrounding Edward—he died at age 16. His successor, his half-sister, Mary, was the intensely Catholic daughter of Catherine of Aragon. For two decades, Mary had seethed over her mother's humiliation and the break with Rome. Now queen, she repealed Edward's reforms and appointed Catholics as bishops. Then she married Prince Philip of Spain, a zealous Catholic. Even he, Philip, was alarmed by the ardor with which Mary persecuted English Protestants. Three hundred people were executed for their religion during her reign (also brief: 1553–1558), earning the queen the unattractive nickname, "Bloody Mary."

If Mary had been as sly as she was devout, if she had delivered a son or daughter around whom English Catholics could have rallied, England might well have been eased back into the Roman Church. Quite a few powerful nobles and many of the gentry were still Catholics at heart. As is always the case, a much larger proportion of people of wealth and social position leaned in the direction the wind blew. Except in London and southern England, the evidence seems to say that, in the mid-1500s, the common people were more Catholic than Protestant.

ELIZABETHAN ENGLAND: THE SEEDBED OF ENGLISH AMERICA

But Bloody Mary was a fanatic. She would not hear talk of politics, tactics, and long-term plans when religion was the issue. Her successor, her half-sister, Elizabeth, was the precisely opposite type. She had been raised a Protestant, but she was no zealot. Indeed, religion did not much interest her. She described the Reformation as "a dispute over trifles" and said she did not care to make "windows into men's souls," investigating their religious beliefs. Elizabeth was a politician. In a country religiously divided, Elizabeth cleverly had herself crowned in a hybrid ceremony, part Catholic, part Anglican, partly in Latin, partly in English.

She comforted Protestants by naming a Church of England man Archbishop of Canterbury and by agreeing to bring back

the *Book of Common Prayer*. But when approval of the prayer book squeaked through Parliament by a mere three votes, Elizabeth backed off. She refused to persecute Catholics as militant Protestant advisors urged her to do. A foreign envoy wrote home that the queen "has treated all religious questions with so much caution and incredible prudence that she seems both to protect the Catholic religion and at the same time not entirely to condemn or outwardly reject the new Reformation."

Elizabeth's Church of England, like her coronation, was a hybrid. Its rites were in English, which was enough for all Protestants but the most radical. The mass was abandoned, but the Catholic sign of the cross with holy water was retained. Church of England services were so similar to the old rites that Catholics did not "discern any great fault, novelty, or difference from the former religion . . . save only change of language . . . and so easily accomodated themselves thereto." Only after 1570, when one pope excommunicated her, and in 1580, when another effectively called for her assassination, did Elizabeth begin to execute Catholic leaders, and then she did not burn them as heretics but hanged them as traitors.

The Sea Dogs

Hostility to Spain at Elizabeth's court also moved the queen from neutrality in religious issues to the Protestant side. When she was crowned, Spain and England were allies. Hoping to save the alliance, Philip II of Spain proposed marriage to Elizabeth. She knew better than to accept. Her sister's marriage to Philip had been the stupidest of Mary's blunders. However, Elizabeth did not want a war with Spain that England could not possibly win. Rather than insult Philip with an abrupt refusal, she waffled like a coquette; hinting she might accept him, then avoiding him, killing time until Philip was worn down and left the country.

Elizabeth played a devious game in other theaters of Anglo-Spanish relations. When Jean Ribault, who had built a French Protestant fort in Florida, tried to buy supplies in England, Elizabeth threw him into prison for violating Spain's claim to Florida. At the same time, she winked at attacks on Spanish ships and towns ("singeing King Philip's beard") by a restless, swashbuckling fraternity of sea captains known as "sea dogs" after a shark common in English waters.

The most daring and successful of the sea dogs was a sometime slave trader who aspired to cleaner work, Francis Drake. In 1577, Drake set sail in the *Golden Hind*, rounded South America by the Strait of Magellan, and looted Spanish ports on the Pacific. It was a cakewalk. Spain's Pacific ports were unfortified. No ship of any other nation had ever plied those waters.

Drake correctly reckoned that Spanish warships lay in wait for him in the Atlantic. Instead of returning to England the way he had come, Drake sailed north to California, reconditioned the *Golden Hind*—no one knows exactly where—and struck west across the Pacific. His expedition was only the second to circumnavigate the globe.

While Drake was at sea, another sea dog, Martin Frobisher, sailed three times to Newfoundland looking for a "northwest passage" through North America to the Pacific. While ashore, his men found what Frobisher thought was a gold mine. He loaded his ships with a thousand tons of ore and sped back to England where it turned out to be worthless rock. In 1578, Elizabeth licensed another sea dog, Sir Humphrey Gilbert, to establish a "plantation" in America on land "not in the actual possession of any Christian prince." Elizabeth was playing cute with Spain's claim to all of North America.

In 1580, Elizabeth's game was up. Drake had returned, the *Golden Hind* so overloaded with £600,000 in Spanish treasure that it was close to capsizing. Investors collected £47 for every pound they had put into the project. As queen, Elizabeth was entitled to £160,000, but to collect meant dropping the pretense of friendship with Spain and going to war. Elizabeth boarded the *Golden Hind* and knighted Drake.

Spanish Virginia

The Spanish did not entirely ignore America north of Florida. In 1526, about 500 colonists, including 100 slaves, began to build a town at the mouth of the Pee Dee River in what is now South Carolina. But the slaves rebelled and many escaped to the forests; only 150 Spaniards limped back to the Caribbean.

In 1571, two Jesuit priests established a mission in Virginia, not far from where, thirty-five years later, the English founded Jamestown. They converted several high-ranking Powhatans to Catholicism, or so they thought. The Powhatans killed them.

Spain recognized England's rights to its North American colonies only in 1670.

John White, later the governor of Roanoke, painted the Indians of North Carolina so that Raleigh could use them when courting investors. In this watercolor White depicted a man and woman in the village of Secotan dining on boiled corn kernels. Indians boiled food by dropping heated rocks into watertight baskets or clay pots. Understandably, they coveted European iron pots, which could be set directly on a fire.

From the Collections of the Library of Congress

Walter Raleigh and Roanoke

Between 1577 and 1580, Drake relieved the Spanish of £600,000 in silver and gold bullion. Some 236 other captains set sail in hopes of emulating his success. (None came close.) In 1583, with five ships and 260 men, Sir Humphrey Gilbert sailed to Newfoundland with the intention of founding a permanent base from which English raiders could sally forth. There he found thirty-six ships of half a dozen nations fishing for cod. With so much company, the living there was so pleasant that Gilbert dawdled until winter. He then headed south to be caught in a ferocious storm. Bold old dog to the end, Gilbert's last recorded words, shouted across the waves to another ship were: "We are as near to heaven by sea as by land." He was: He was drowned.

Gilbert's half-brother, Walter Raleigh, inherited his license to found a colony. Quite on his own, he charmed his way into Queen Elizabeth's favor. In return for his flattery, she lavished properties and incomes on him. An ambassador there commented sourly, "two years ago he was scarcely able to keep a single servant, and she has bestowed so much upon him that he is able to keep five hundred."

That was an exaggeration, but Raleigh was riding high and his life's ambition was to found England's first American colony. With so much at stake at Elizabeth's court—a favorite had to be constantly on guard against envious rivals—he did not dare to voyage to America himself. Instead, in 1584, he dispatched an expedition to select a site for his colony. The men returned singing the praises of the Chesapeake Bay and, a bit farther south, Roanoke island in what is now North Carolina.

Roanoke appealed to Raleigh for several reasons. Manteo, an Indian who returned with the reconnaisance party, was from nearby Croatoan Island. His tribe would be an ally. Roanoke was closer to Spanish sea routes than the Chesapeake. However, a colony on Roanoke would not easily be seen from the Atlantic because it was obscured by barrier islands—huge sandbars, actually—now called the Outer Banks. (A Spanish ship later sent to destroy Roanoke came within two miles of the colony and never saw it.) Finally, Raleigh's maps showed him that "Verrazano's Sea"—free sailing to the Indies, so he thought—was somewhere in the neighborhood of Roanoke.

In 1585, Raleigh assembled five ships filled mostly with soldiers. Unfortunately, he named a hothead (who might have been quite mad) to command the expedition. He made enemies of Indians living a few miles from Roanoke by burning their village because of a petty theft. The soldiers left behind to hold the fort through the winter barely survived. When Francis Drake (fresh from another round of robbing Spaniards) arrived with supplies, they begged to be taken home. Drake took them.

In 1587—he was spending a lot of money!— Raleigh sent ninety-one men, seventeen women, and nine children with instructions to found his colony on the Chesapeake where, it was hoped, the natives would be friendlier. However, one of his captains (another ill-advised appointment) dumped the settlers on Roanoke. The governor of the colony, a sometime artist named John White, was so ineffective as a governor that

Portrait of Sir Walter Raleigh (1554–1618) 1588 (oil on panel), English School, (16th century)/Private Collection/Bridgeman Art Library.

Sir Walter Raleigh was a favorite of Queen Elizabeth. That is, she kept him around for his conversation and "favored" him by giving him property, paying positions at court, a knighthood, and a license to plant a colony. Artful flattery was a favorite's favorite tool. Raleigh named Virginia for Elizabeth, "the Virgin Queen."

he was virtually forced to return to England. White expected to return the following spring with supplies and more colonists; he left his daughter and infant granddaughter on the island.

Three years passed before White returned to find Roanoke's buildings abandoned. The word "CROATOAN" was carved on one of the structures in "fayre Capitall letters." This was a good sign. White had instructed the colonists that, if they left the island, they were to leave the name of their destination in just such a manner. If they were *forced* to leave for any reason, they were to punctuate their message by carving a cross. There was no cross "or signe of distress" and Croatoan Island made sense as a refuge; it was Manteo's home.

But the Roanoke colonists were never found. There are many theories of what happened to them based on fleeting glimpses of Indians with blond hair or speaking English. None has been proved. What happened to the "Lost Colony" remains a mystery.

BEGINNINGS OF AN EMPIRE

Raleigh and White failed to resupply Roanoke on time because, in 1587, Queen Elizabeth proclaimed a "stay of shipping": No vessel could leave English ports without special license. Philip II had assembled a fleet of 130 ships with which to invade England in retaliation for Drake's pillaging and to put Elizabeth's Catholic heir, Mary Stuart, on the throne. The queen wanted all her sea dogs at home. (And, after dithering in agony for years, she had Mary Stuart beheaded.)

The Spanish Armada

In the end, there was no invasion. The Invincible Armada of 1588 (the "Spanish Armada") was a disaster. Indeed, except for the king, just about every high-ranking Spaniard involved in the enterprise knew that it would be. When Philip answered the rational objections of the Duke of Parma, the commander of the invasion army, by saying that God would work a miracle, the Duke replied, "God will tire of working miracles for us."

The naval commander, the Duke of Medina Sidona, pointed out that only thirty-five of his ships were first-rate warships; the rest were transport vessels carrying the army. The Spanish would be overwhelmingly outgunned by the sea dogs waiting for the Armada. Which was true: The Armada carried 172 cannon, the English vessels waiting in the channel had 497. So the English would refuse to close and grapple with the large Spanish galleons—the only kind of naval battle that favored the Armada. They would, instead, harass the fleet from a distance. Everyone agreed that if the 30,000 troops in the Armada and another Spanish army waiting in the Netherlands could be landed in England, they would roll over the opposition. But only the king believed they could be landed and that the English would fight an all-or-nothing war rather than retreat, fighting the Spanish to an expensive draw that would exhaust Philip's treasury. The fact was, the mighty Armada was not up to its assigned task; it was a cut-rate project.

As expected, the sea dogs harassed the Armada in the English Channel but the tight Spanish formation did not break. The only vessel lost, the *Rosario*, was incapacitated not by English guns but by a collision with another Spanish ship. When the Armada regrouped in Calais in France, the English sent eight fireships—old tubs lathered with tar, stuffed with gunpowder, and set afire—into its midst. (The crews of the fireships jumped off at the last minute to be rescued by speedy boats.) No Spanish ship caught fire, but the atttack was a success in causing a panic as the Spanish captains cut loose of their anchors and fled to deep waters.

Returning home by rounding the British Isles to the north, the Armada was cursed by violent weather, losing twenty-eight ships. Twenty ships went aground in Ireland; 6,000 men lost their lives. Only half of the great fleet made it back to Spain, only a third of Philip's soldiers. The Elizabethans may be excused for assuming that God had lined up on their side. They called the storms that battered the Armada "the Protestant Wind" and told one another that "God himselfe hath stricken the stroke, and ye have but looked on." There was truth in that: English cannon did not sink a single Spanish ship.

Whatever the cause, the Armada's debacle demonstrated that Spain was not invincible. As the *siglo de oro* drew to a close, the English, the French, and the Dutch were able to ponder the possibility of planting their own colonies in America.

Promoters

The sea dogs showed that the English could challenge Spain. Other Elizabethan worthies promoted the idea that England *should* establish colonies as Spain had done. Raleigh was the most energetic of the propagandists, but Richard Hakluyt was more influential. Hakluyt was a bookish but by no means parochial minister of the Church of England. He rummaged tirelessly through the libraries of Oxford and London, collecting hundreds of explorers' accounts of the geography, resources, and attractions of America. His masterwork, *The Principal Navigations, Voyages, Traffiques, and Discoveries of the English Nation,* was published between 1598 and 1600.

In his books and in uncountable conversations with men of money, Hakluyt argued that investment in American colonies would infallibly produce profit, add to England's prestige, and "enlarge the glory of the gospel." He lived until 1616, long enough to be a shareholder in the first successful English settlement in America.

Despite his losses, Raleigh continued to promote colonization. He told the queen he would make her "lord of more gold, and of a more beautiful empire, and of more cities and people, than either the King of Spain or the grand Turk." But his day ended not long after the failure of the Roanoke colony. He fell out of Elizabeth's favor, and her successor in 1603, James I, stripped him of everything Elizabeth had bestowed on him. Raleigh was imprisoned for a decade in the Tower of London. He emerged to have one last colonial adventure in South America (another failure), returned to England, and was beheaded.

The promoters, like advertisers of every era, played down the risks of living in America, puffed up the attractions beyond anything the Indians would have recognized, and simply lied through their teeth. Virginia, they said, rivaled "Tyrus for colours, Balsan for woods, Persia for oils, Arabia for spices, Spain for silks, Narcis for shipping, the Netherlands for fish, Pomona for fruit and by tillage, Babylon for corn, besides the abundance of mulberries, minerals, rubies, pearls, gems, grapes, deer."

Hard Economic Facts

Every promoter of American colonies promised the possibility of English Mexicos and Perus. Because the Spanish had not found the all-water passage to the Indies, it had to be in the north, which the Spanish had hardly explored. Maps of the era showed "Verrazano's Sea" (his grandson claimed that just six miles of land separated it from the Atlantic) or the "Strait of the Three Brothers" (three Portugese brothers claimed to have sailed through the passage *west* to *east!*). Belief in the existence of a "Northwest Passage" would survive for more than 200 years. Promoters also envisioned colonies as havens from which sea dogs would sally forth to seize Spanish treasure ships. Hakluyt identified dozens of harbors and coves he said were suitable to such enterprises.

Few English investors had moral qualms about stealing from the Spanish. After 1600, however, capturing treasure ships was much more difficult. The Spanish began to convoy them. It was expensive—twenty warships to defend twenty merchantmen—but it was effective.

More compelling for sober English capitalists were signs by 1600 that Spain's American gold and silver mines were not unmitigated blessings. Spain's fabulous wealth had enabled her grandees to purchase whatever they desired, to enjoy a luxurious life that was the envy of Europe, and to field huge armies that terrorized the continent. It was also evident, however, that the blizzard of riches blew out of Spain with as much force as it blew in. The Spanish purchased food abroad, impoverishing their own farmers. Fisheries were neglected in favor of buying salted fish from others. The king's attempt to encourage the manufacture of textiles, leather, and iron goods was thwarted by the cheapness of imports. Even the majority of Spain's dreaded armies were German and Italian mercenaries who spent none of their wages in Spain.

Mexican and Peruvian gold and silver ended up in countries with no mines, but with a class of canny, grasping merchants and manufacturers. Other nations did the final count of the Spanish doubloons, including Spain's enemies, for the English and the Dutch were happy to make and transport whatever the Spanish would buy. (Many of the cannon of the Armada and the guns the soldiers carried had been shipped from England during the two years before 1588.) Every transaction left Spain poorer and her enemies richer. Hakluyt's projection of colonies buying English manufactures shipped by English merchants had more appeal to investors than the gold mines that might or might not lie under Virginia's forests.

Northeast Passage

The Northwest Passage to the Indies was not the only geographical delusion of the sixteenth and seventeenth centuries. Some explorers, among them Henry Hudson, believed that the quickest route to the Indies lay *northeast* around the practically unknown far reaches of Norway. Hudson's first attempt to find this waterway in 1607 was—no surprise—foiled by sea ice. On his second voyage in 1608, Hudson had an even more fantastic scheme: He would sail directly over the North Pole. He persuaded his backers that the polar ice cap melted during the long days of the arctic summer.

Hudson's second fiasco killed his reputation among English investors. However, some Dutch speculators were intrigued by his theories and, in 1610, provided him with a small ship, the *Half Moon*, and instructions to search again for the Northeast Passage. Hudson ignored his orders and, instead, sailed west. He rediscovered New York harbor (and the Hudson River) and, with high hopes, sailed into Hudson's Bay. He never sailed out. His crew mutinied and put Hudson and his son adrift in a small boat.

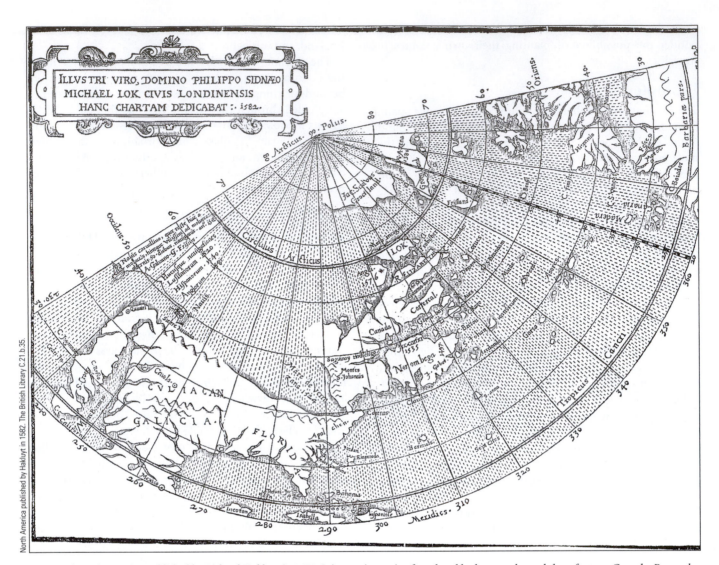

North America published by Hakluyt in 1582. The British Library C.21.b.35.

A map of North America published by Richard Hakluyt in 1682. It is a curious mix of good and bad geography and sheer fantasy. Canada, Bermuda, Florida, and Cuba (here called Isabella) are well positioned. Most of North America, however, is pure imagination, most notably "Verrazano's Sea" (Mare de Verrazana) which is a short hop across the continent and provides clear sailing to the Pacific and the Indies. The proximity of Verrazano's Sea was one of the factors that attracted Raleigh to Roanoke.

Surplus Population

The Crown (the king, his advisors, and Parliament—the government) was interested in colonies because of the anxiety that there were just too many Englishmen and women. The population of England had soared during the 1500s, particularly the numbers of those with little or no means of feeding and sheltering themselves. Many people blamed the "enclosure movement." That is, purchasers of monastery lands often expelled the peasants who had worked them as tenants and turned the fields into pastures for sheep, *enclosing* the fields with hedges. Areas that had grown crops that fed a hundred villagers plus some income for the landlord returned a much larger income when converted to wool production. But tending sheep provided work for a mere handful of shepherds.

Former tenant farmers were sent on their way to wander the countryside in gangs, worrying villagers and gentry alike with their begging, bullying, and theft. The boldest and

most desperate waylaid travelers on lonely stretches of highway. Most of the refugees flocked into the cities, especially London, to form a half-starved underclass that, like the poor of all ages, was a source of disease, disorder, and crime. By 1600, there were an estimated 12,000 beggars in the capital. Many gathered at Cripplegate, outside the city walls to the north, "a surcharge of people, specially of the worst sort, as can hardly be either fed or sustained or governed."

"Yea many thousands of idle persons," Hakluyt wrote, "having no way to be set on work . . . often fall to pilfering and thieving and other lewdness, whereby all the prisons of the land are daily pestered and stuffed full of them."

His solution was the alchemy of a sea voyage. Colonies would be social safety valves. People who were economically superfluous and socially dangerous at home would become cheerful consumers of English manufactures, paying for them by producing the raw materials that England needed. "The fry

Public Domain

The "pestering poor": A beggar asks for alms from an elegantly dressed Elizabethan gentleman. Elizabethans believed that the growing population of destitute people unable to find work were a threat to domestic peace (they were; note that the gentleman carries a sword with which to defend himself) but also a source of colonists to extend England's presence to North America.

of the wandering beggars of England that grow up idly, and hurtful and burdenous to this realm, may there be unladen, better bred up, and may people waste countries to the home and foreign benefit, and to their own more happy state."

Private Enterprise

The first colonies were not, however, financed and organized by the government but by private companies that were forerunners of the modern corporation. These merchants-adventurers companies ("adventurer" refers to the adventuring or risking of money) had developed as a response to the considerable expense and high risks involved in overseas trade.

That is, it was neither cheap nor a sure thing to send a ship laden with trade goods out to sea and bring other goods back to sell at home. Pirates, warships of hostile nations, and storms and shoals waited to do vessels in. A rich man betting a large part of his fortune on the fate of a single voyage was flirting with ruin. Instead, investors joined with others, each buying "shares" in the enterprise. The odds their ship would simply disappear were the same. But if it did, a dozen (or three dozen) shareholders shared the loss; nobody was ruined. And some voyages in which they invested would return at considerable profit.

Trading companies made themselves attractive to investors by winning privileges from the Crown. Thus, in 1555, the Muscovy Company agreed to enter the risky business of buying furs in semisavage Russia in return for a monopoly on the sale of Russian furs in England. The biggest, most famous, and longest lived of these privileged corporations was the East India Company. Chartered in 1600 to trade in India, its powers were so broad that it governed much of the Indian subcontinent for a century and a half.

When James I was persuaded that North American colonies would be beneficial to the nation, he issued two charters patterned on the charters of the the Muscovy and East India companies. In 1606, the king authorized a company

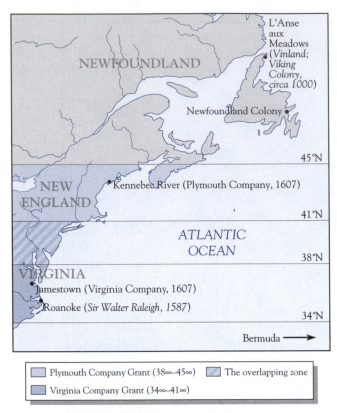

MAP 2:1 The Virginia and Plymouth Companies, 1607
The Virginia and Plymouth Companies both attempted to plant colonies in 1607. Only the London Company's Jamestown succeeded. Note the zone between 38° and 41° north latitude. Both the Plymouth and Virginia companies were permitted to settle in that area. However, once one had done so (neither did), the other company was obligated to build at least 100 miles away.

headquartered in the port of Plymouth to found a colony on the American coast between 38° and 45° north latitude. The Virginia Company of London was granted the same privilege between 34° and 41°.

The zones overlapped so as to encourage both companies to hasten along. Because they were forbidden to set up shop within a hundred miles of one another (so they would not compete in trading with the Indians), the first to get going had the pick of sites.

JAMESTOWN

Both companies sent expeditions to North America in 1607. The Plymouth Company established Fort St. George on a bluff above Maine's Kennebec River. The forty-five settlers found the northern winter disagreeable, but when Raleigh Gilbert arrived with a supply ship in the spring, he insisted that "all things were in great forwardness." Then, at summer's end, another relief ship informed Gilbert that his childless older brother back in England had died; he had inherited the family fortune! Who needed Fort St. George? Everyone returned home with the happy heir.

The First Families of Virginia

The London Company had better luck in Virginia, if a decade of wholesale suffering and death may be described as lucky. In May 1607, Captain Christopher Newport brought the *Susan Constant* and two other ships into Chesapeake Bay, landing his passengers on the James River (named for the king). Barely connected to the mainland, the site could be defended against Indians but the Spanish could discover its whereabouts only by lucky accident. (Many believed that the Spanish had destroyed Roanoke.) Captain John Smith, a soldier who remained in Jamestown, as the fortified village they built was called, said that Newport's choice was "a verie fit place for the erecting of a great citie."

It was nothing of the kind: Jamestown was surrounded by brackish marshes. Indians told the English that the river water was undrinkable for several months each year. Two centuries later, when the town ceased to be Virginia's capital, just about everyone who lived in the place moved out.

Who were the first settlers? The leaders, company officials, were gentlemen. There were soldiers like John Smith. The others, several hundred of whom arrived each spring, were a mixed bag—"of all sortes"—some of them farmers and artisans (including several Polish glassmakers, Protestant refugees). But the large majority of recruits were probably drawn from England's most wretched and desperate poor. "None but those of the meanest quality and corruptest lives went there," one observer wrote. Sir Thomas Dale, Virginia's governor in 1611, sighed that even after four years "Oh sir my heart bleeds when I thinke what men we have here."

Recruiters for the company were competing with court favorites who needed tenant farmers for the "plantations" they had been granted in Ireland, a much more attractive destination than Virginia. The industrious and ambitious were inclined to sign up with the East India Company that promised big money. In the year that Jamestown was founded, the East India Company dispatched an expedition carrying £17,000 in gold bullion and £7,000 in trade goods. By comparison, Virginia was a shoestring operation.

Surviving

Tropical Asia was already notorious as an Englishman's graveyard. Of the 1,200 who had gone there since 1600, 800 were already dead. But Virginia proved even deadlier. Christopher Newport left 144 colonists in 1607. There were enough provisions to keep them until spring but, in January 1608, the storehouse burned. The English proved inept at hunting and foraging so that, seizing authority, John Smith persuaded the Powhatans to sell them corn and, when that failed, he raided their stores. Still the Virginians died from malnutrition, amoebic dysentery, scurvy, and typhoid fever. When relief arrived in the spring of 1608, just thirty-eight were alive.

The "starving times" continued for several years, drought adding to other problems. No crop was planted in 1608 and a drought ruined the crop of 1609. During those two years, 500 new colonists arrived. In 1610, Jamestown's population was down to sixty. Most of the survivors were living with the Indians or huddling downriver near the bay, living on little more than oysters. The Powhatans may have tolerated Jamestown when it was so vulnerable because they expected nature to eliminate the newcomers for them.

John Smith credited his dictatorship with saving the colony during its first years. Thomas West, Baron de la Warr, named governor in 1610, also enforced a rigorous discipline. Hoping to make the colony self-sufficient in food, de la Warr marched the settlers to the fields like soldiers. Troublemakers and the merely idle were punished swiftly and harshly. Even then, a third of the colony perished. De la Warr's successor, Thomas Dale, was tougher yet. He prescribed the death penalty for dozens of offenses, including individual trading with the Indians and killing a domestic animal without permission. Virginians were whipped for throwing washwater into the streets or carrying out "the necessities of nature" within a quarter mile of the fort.

Authoritarian rule worked. Fields were expanded and adequate "earth-fast" houses (what we call pole buildings; no foundations) were erected. Virginia expanded along the banks of the James; outlying villages were constructed. Mortality remained high. Between 1610 and 1618, 3,000 new recruits arrived. In 1619, the population of Virginia was just 1,000. Between 1619 and 1623, there were 4,000 newcomers. In 1624, the population of Virginia was 1,300. Other emigrants died before they ever saw Virginia. In 1618, a ship that left England with 180 aboard managed to land only 50 of them alive. The Virginia Company was able to keep apace with the deaths only by throwing hordes of England's wretched poor into the American maw.

Thank You for Not Smoking

James I called smoking "a custom loathesome to the eye, harmful to the brain, dangerous to the lungs, and in the black stinking fume thereof, nearest resembling the Stygian smoke of the pit that is bottomless." Charles I felt the same way. He said that smoking caused "enervation of the body and of courage."

Neither king was willing to take a cut in income in order to discourage the habit. When a big hike in the tobacco duty caused a sharp reduction in imports (and, therefore, taxes on tobacco), James I reduced the tax.

Two colonies enacted anti-smoking ordinances. Connecticut tried to license smokers; only those prescribed tobacco for reasons of health could apply. Massachusetts briefly forbade smoking *out of doors*, not for reasons of health or morality or to gratify "thank you for not smoking" crusaders, but to prevent fires.

North Wind Picture Archives

When tobacco proved to be a boom crop during the 1610s, the inhabitants of Jamestown planted every available square inch of the available soil in the weed.

The "Stinking Custom"

Had the Virginians not found a way to make money, the Company would surely have gone broke. But they did—in a native American plant that Columbus had brought back to Europe on his first voyage: tobacco.

Many Indians, including the Powhatans, cultivated tobacco, dried the leaves, and "drank" the smoke of the burning leaves for religious, social, and diplomatic reasons. (The custom of beginning a negotiation by "smoking the peace pipe" was real.) In the Old World, smoking got off to a bad start. The Spanish Inquisition jailed an early nicotine addict, Rodrigo de Jerez, for seven years. James I loathed smoking, calling it a "stinking custom." The Russian Czar slit smokers' noses. The Turkish Sultan and the Shah of Persia decreed the death penalty for lighting up.

To no avail. Addictions are powerful adversaries. Inexorably, the smoking habit spread throughout the Old World. Russian explorers found the natives of remote northern Siberia smoking before 1600. The lure of the exotic—the "trendy"—is always potent among the leisured classes and, if they can afford it, the unleisured ape them. Some European physicians seized on tobacco as a miracle drug, prescribing "the holy, healing herb" as "a sovereign remedy to all diseases." About 1580, Thomas Harriot said of regular smokers: "their bodies are notably preserved in health, and know not many greevous diseases wherewithall wee in England are oftentimes afflicted."

At the time Jamestown was founded, the Spanish West Indies were providing tobacco for the European market. John Rolfe, a smoker who arrived in Virginia in 1609, brought a pouch of West Indian seeds with him. This proved to be a lucky decision because the Powhatans' tobacco (a different species) he found "poore and weak and of a byting taste." Rolfe experimented in his garden in 1612. In 1614, he had more than he needed for his own pipe and shipped four barrels of tobacco to England. The reception was sensational. It sold in a trice at a huge profit. In 1617, Virginia exported 10 tons of tobacco at a profit of 3 s. (shillings) per pound! In 1618, the shipment topped twenty-five tons, by 1628, 250 tons.

Who Shall Till the Fields?

Virginia had a reason to exist. Emigrants with skills and ambitions and some with money crossed the Atlantic. They planted the very streets of Jamestown in tobacco and founded new villages up river. A colony recently starving now neglected grain and gardens in order to cultivate a weed to be burned. Company agents lamented that the settlers' "greediness after great quantities of tobacco causeth them [neither to] build good homes, fence their grounds, or plant any orchards." As late as 1632 in "An Acte for Tradesmen to Worke on Theire Trades," the Virginia Assembly commanded "gunsmiths and naylers, brickmakers, carpenters, joyners, sawyers and turners to worke at theire trades and not plant tobacco."

It was a losing effort. A carpenter could make a living in Jamestown. If he turned farmer he could tend a thousand tobacco plants plus four acres of maize, beans, and squash—enough to support a household of five. It did not require a gift for higher mathematics to calculate what the income from 10,000 tobacco plants was.

But where was the planter of 10,000 plants to find people to work for him? Land was endless. Who would work for wages for someone else when a five- or ten-mile hike took one to lands that, planted in tobacco, could make a carpenter or brickmaker rich?

One source of labor presented itself in 1619 when a Dutch ship with about twenty African aboard—probably seized in the Spanish West Indies—tied up on the James. The Virginians bought them with tobacco and ships' supplies. Periodically, other human cargos arrived. By 1660 there were 900 black Virginians in a white population of 25,000.

But Africans and their children remained a minority of the agricultural work force until after 1700. Most of Virginia's laborers were white Englishmen and women. They were not free. Some were convicts, sold to planters to serve out their sentences as servants. Other servants—*not* employees but bound by law to serve and obey their masters—were voluntary emigrants, poor people persuaded to sign "indentures." These documents bound them to work as servants for four, five, or seven years in return for their passage to Virginia and the chance, when their time was served, to set up as free men and women.

Virginia's headright system, instituted in 1618, employed the abundant land to encourage planters to import servants. Each head of household who came to Virginia was granted 50 acres for each person whose trans-Atlantic fare he paid. Thus, a family of five secured 250 acres upon disembarking. If the family had the means to bring ten indentured servants with them, they were granted another 500 acres. Thus was Virginia peopled, thus the tobacco grown, thus were the beginnings of a society in which some planters put together great estates.

Pocahontas

Shortly after landing in Virginia, John Smith was captured by the Powhatans. According to Smith—and he was more than capable of inventing a story—he was seconds away from having his skull crushed when Powhatan's 12-year-old daughter, Matoaka, also known as Pocahontas, "the playful one," begged the chief to spare Smith's life.

Maybe. Pocahontas was playful. Naked, she visited Jamestown and turned cartwheels in the tracks that passed for streets. In 1614, Pocahontas became a Christian and married John Rolfe. She bore a son, but both she and Rolfe died when he was still a lad, Pocahontas in 1617 while visiting England, Rolfe in 1622 when Pocohantas's uncle attacked Jamestown.

Courtesy of John Carter Brown Library at Brown University

The Jamestown Massacre of 1622 was unexpected, sudden, terrifying, and devastating: Three hundred Virginians were killed, including several of the Africans who had been sold to tobacco growers three years earlier. The start of it in Martin's Hundred, an outlying village, probably looked much as this contemporary artist rendered it.

The Powhatans

The native peoples of Virginia were called Powhatans. Historians disagree radically as to just how many Powhatans there were when Jamestown was founded; two recent writers on the subject say 75,000 and 15,000 respectively. They lived in about thirty villages, each with its chief, and were uneasily confederated under a paramount chief whom the English called Powhatan. He maintained his position by politics and diplomacy but was prepared to use force when defied. The English heard of a massacre of dissidents shortly before they arrived and, in 1608, Powhatan leveled a village called Plankatanks when its chief agreed to plant extra corn for the Jamestowners.

The Virginians' relations with the Indians were erratic from the start. Some of them held the Indians in contempt, comparing them to the "savage Irish" whom the English had long despised. Others preferred living with the Indians to staying in Jamestown and had to be forced to return. The whites and Indians skirmished regularly during the colony's first

years, but fatalities were few. The aging chief Powhatan did not much like the newcomers, but he coveted the cloth, iron pots and pans, firearms, and novelties such as glass beads and mirrors that they offered as gifts or in trade. In 1614, when John Rolfe married Powhatan's favorite daughter, the famous Pocahontas, something of a détente was inaugurated. The Virginians and the Powhatans coexisted.

Then Powhatan died and his successor as paramount chief was his brother Opechancanough. He had consistently called for war against the colony. John Smith had captured and humiliated him in 1609, and Opechancanough grasped something that Powhatan seems not quite to have understood. Opechancanough saw that a once starving English enclave was pushing further annually into the Indians' ancestral hunting grounds, mowing down the trees, and chasing away the game. By 1622, a number of Powhatan hamlets on the James and Chickahominy rivers had been forced to move to make room for tobacco.

The Massacre of 1622

In March 1622, Opechancanough and between 500 and 600 warriors entered Martin's Hundred, a hamlet seven miles from Jamestown. They made as if to trade or chat when suddenly, they attacked, killing all seventy-five people there. They marched rapidly on Jamestown, wiping out other villages on the way. Had Jamestown not been warned everyone there might have been killed. As it was the death toll was 347 Virginians (including the founding father of the tobacco business, John Rolfe).

It was a catastrophe, but it was not enough when fortunes were being made. The survivors bandaged their wounds and regrouped; the Virginia Company sent 1,500 muskets and pistols along with reinforcements. Over two years, they gained the upper hand, some calling for what we know as genocide: "a perpetuall warre without peace or truce [to] roote out from being any longer a people, so cursed a nation,

Courtesy of Maryland Department, Enoch Pratt Free Library, Baltimore

Cecilius Calvert, Lord Baltimore, intended Maryland as a refuge for English Catholics like himself. Catholic nobles were required to pay an annual tax and were forbidden to hold public office and to attend university, but their wealth insulated them from harassment. Catholics of humble social station were vulnerable to hostile mobs. Some went to Maryland during the colony's early years, but they were outnumbered by Protestants from the start. After 1692, Maryland's Catholics were permitted to worship only privately in their homes; no parish churches were permitted.

ungratefull to all benefitte, and incapable of all goodnesse." In one incident, about 200 Powhatans were invited to a peace parley and were poisoned.

By 1625, the Powhatans' numbers had been drastically reduced, but they were able to launch another offensive in 1644 when they killed 500—one Virginian in 12. What was left of the tribe was driven into the interior. In 1669, they numbered 2,000. By 1685, the Powhatans were extinct. The pattern of white–Indian relations that would be repeated for more than two and a half centuries had been drawn.

The Virginia Company was another casualty of the 1622 massacre. Although tobacco planters were prospering, the Company itself never recorded a profit. In 1624, citing economic failure and the massacre, King James I revoked the Company's charter and took direct control of Virginia. The House of Burgesses—a legislative assembly established in Jamestown 1619, made up of twenty-two members elected by landowners—continued to meet. However, the Crown appointed a royal governor with the power to veto laws the Burgesses enacted.

Maryland: A Second Tobacco Colony

George Calvert—Lord Baltimore—was a Catholic nobleman who had long been interested in colonies. He had owned shares in the Virginia Company and purchased land in Newfoundland where, he thought, English Catholics might find a refuge from harassment and persecution at home. The harsh Newfoundland winter dismayed him, but, in 1628, he visited Virginia and liked what he saw. In 1632, Calvert persuaded King Charles I to detach the land north of the Potomac River from Virginia and give it to him.

Calvert died shortly, but his son, Cecilius, the second Lord Baltimore, was also devoted to the idea of a refuge for English Catholics. In 1634, he sent 200 settlers to the colony he called Maryland where they founded the town of St. Mary's. Maryland prospered from growing tobacco but the two lords' dream of a Catholic colony was dashed from the start. Catholics were never a majority in Maryland. When Calvinist Protestants, intensely hostile to Catholicism poured into the colony, Calvert had to act quickly simply to prevent violence against his co-religionists. His Act of Toleration of 1649 provided that "noe person or persons whatsoever within this province . . . professing to believe in Jesus Christ, shall from henceforth bee any waies troubled, Molested or discountenanced for or in respect of his or her religion."

Reminiscent of "speech codes" in colleges today, Calvert even tried to outlaw verbal abuse. He prescribed the whipping post for "persons reproaching any other within the Province by the Name or Denomination of Heretic, Schismatic, Idolater, Puritan, Independent, Presbyterian, Popish Priest, Jesuit, Jesuited Papist, Lutheran, Calvinist, Anabaptist, Brownist, Antinomian, Barrowist, Round-Head, Separatist, or any other Name or Term, in a reproachful Manner, relating to matters of Religion."

It was all to no avail. Protestants repealed the Act of Toleration in 1654, inflicting double taxation and other disabilities on Roman Catholics. In 1689, John Coode led a rebellion of Protestants who, three years later, forbade Catholics to worship publically. (Oddly, three of Coode's four lieutenants were married to Catholic women.)

OTHER BEGINNINGS

England was not the only European nation to found North American colonies in the late 1500s and early 1600s: French, Dutch, and Swedish adventurers also ignored Spain's claim to the entire continent—with varied results.

The French in North America

In 1562, the French sea dog, Jean Ribault founded Charlesfort near what is now Port Royal, South Carolina. Like Roanoke, the colony simply evaporated. Two years later, René Goulaine de Laudonnière took 300 colonists to the St. John's River in Florida. Most of the settlers were Huguenots, French Protestants.

The colony was vexed by conflict with the Indians, the refusal of the self-proclaimed aristocrats among them to labor (the same thing happened in Jamestown), and the desertion of men who stole the colony's boat in order to raid Spanish shipping. But a problem-free French colony in Florida would have been doomed. Florida was too close to Spanish Cuba. In 1565, Pedro Menéndez de Avilés set out to destroy the French colony. He was dismayed to discover five French warships anchored in the mouth of the St. John's. It was a relief expedition commanded by the ubiquitous Ribault. Menéndez withdrew a few miles to the south. When Ribault's ships, bent on destroying Menéndez, were blown far beyond his camp and wrecked in a storm, Menéndez led 500 soldiers overland to Fort Caroline and easily captured it. With only one casualty, the Spaniards killed 142 during the attack. Learnng that most of the survivors were Protestants, they murdered them.

Sensibly, French interest shifted north. In 1608, an extraordinary sailor, Samuel de Champlain (he made twelve voyages to the New World) founded Quebec on the St. Lawrence River. New France, the St. Lawrence River basin, grew slowly. In 1627, there were but 100 French there, in 1650, 657, and in 1663, 3,000. (There were 3,000 Europeans just in New Netherlands—New York—at that time; 50,000 whites and 2,000 blacks in the English colonies.) Rude as it was, Quebec was a religious and cultural as well as an administrative center. A college was founded there in 1635 (a year before Harvard, the first English college in America) as well as an Ursuline convent school for Indian girls. But mostly, Quebec was a rude, uncomfortable trading post where Indians exchanged hides and furs for decorative trinkets, blankets, other textiles, iron tools and implements, guns, and brandy.

Hispanic Beginnings

In 1565, before marching on Fort Caroline, Pedro Menéndez de Avilés established St. Augustine, Florida, between the Matanzas and San Sebastian Rivers. In 1586, Sir Francis Drake sacked the town, but St. Augustine recovered. It is the oldest surviving European settlement in what is now the United States.

In 1609, two years after the founding of Jamestown, a party of Spaniards walked and rode the banks of the Rio Grande almost to its source in the Sangre de Cristo Mountains of New Mexico. There they founded Santa Fe, from which traders tapped the numerous Indians of the country for furs, hides, and small quantities of precious metals. Franciscan missionaries sallied out to win the Indians' souls. By 1630, the padres claimed to have baptized 86,000 mostly Pueblo Indians.

Santa Fe is the oldest seat of government in the United States. (St. Augustine was administered from Cuba.) Its history, however, is not continuous. During the 1670s, the Pueblo Indians were ravaged by disease, hunger, and assaults by Apaches and Navajos, whom the small Spanish military garrison was unable to beat back. When some Pueblos reverted to their old religion, the Spanish hanged several and whipped dozens.

In the summer of 1680, led by a chief whom the Spanish had imprisoned, Popé, nearly all the Pueblos around Santa Fe rebelled, killing half the priests in New Mexico and about 350 other Spaniards and Mexicans. The survivors fled south to El Paso. Popé's Rebellion was the Indians' most effective violent resistance to Europeans since the *skraelings* drove the Vikings out of Vinland. Only after ten years elapsed were the Spanish able to restore their power in Santa Fe.

New Netherlands and New Sweden

In 1624, the Dutch West India Company (organized much like the Virginia company) established New Netherlands, claiming as its borders the Connecticut and the south (Delaware) Rivers. Its capital was New Amsterdam, at the southern tip of Manhattan Island. New Amsterdam defended what the Dutch hoped would be both a fur-trading center and a colony of farmers. A fort where furs and hides were purchased from Indians was built at Fort Orange on the upper Hudson River, present-day Albany. Fort Orange was perfectly located to attract Indian traders from the east (present-day Connecticut), from the north, and via the Mohawk River from the west.

New Amsterdam grew slowly but steadily. It was a small but bustling commerical center. The colony exported more than 60,000 pelts during its first year. Annually thereafter, as many as a hundred Dutch ships tied up in the best harbor on the Atlantic seaboard.

Along the Hudson between New Amsterdam and Fort Orange, the West India Company tried to promote settlement by granting huge "patroonships" to rich Hollanders. These were vast tracts of land with 18 miles of river frontage. The

Common Seamen

By our standards, sailors of the age of discovery and colonization were small men; few seamen topped five and a half feet. Most were teenagers or men in their twenties. It was an unhealthy and dangerous life. Privateers like Francis Drake weighed anchor with three times as many men as they needed to sail their vessels, in part because they were looking for fights, in part because their men would die off of sickness and accidents. In addition to the diseases that afflicted landlubbers, common seamen ran a high risk of contracting scurvy, a vitamin C deficiency. Scurvy can be prevented and even reversed by a diet of fruits and vegetables. At sea, however, the menu did not include such foods because they were perishable. Meals consisted of salt beef, rock-life biscuit called hardtack, water, and wine. Officers did better. The onions, garlic, and dried fruit in their larders doubtless explains the lower incidence of scurvy among them.

Seamen faced shipwreck, death in an attack, and the hazards of living on a ship: a fall from a yardarm, being crushed by a dropped spar, slipping oveboard and drowning. (Few of them could swim.) They might be killed or maimed by a crewmate in a fight over a triviality. They might die being punished for picking a fight. Discipline on the high seas was immediate and brutal. Floggings were as regular as rain. Keelhauling (dragging a man under the hull from one side of the ship to another) was unusual but far from unknown. After a mutiny, Magellan beheaded one ringleader, quartered another alive, and marooned a third on a desert island. When he pardoned the other mutineers, they were so grateful that they became Magellan's most devoted followers.

A sailor's labor was heavy. Seamen hauled heavy canvas up and down masts, pulleys their only mechanical aid. Merely holding the ship on course left a man's arms weary. The crude tiller pitted his strength against the power of the wind and ocean currents. Every ship leaked and had to be pumped by hand, frantically so during storms.

Ships on long voyages had to be serviced regularly—"refitted." Barnacles reproduced to a point where they were heavy enough to cut a vessel's speed by half. If far from a friendly port, the crew sailed to a beach where, at high tide, the ship was "careened," grounded, and eased on its side. The men then scraped the barnacles—horrible work—and recaulked the hull with rope and pitch. When the captain ordered that the sails needed to be rearranged—rigged differently—seamen virtually rebuilt the ship above deck. On the easiest of days, crews were kept hopping, repairing sails and lines, scrubbing the decks with vinegar and salt water, smoking out their quarters to kill vermin. Officers knew that idleness and boredom were more likely to cause discontent than overwork.

Criminals (the Portugese called them *degredados*) were pardoned if they signed on long voyages when no other recruits were available. (Columbus's crew was rounded out with convicts.) They did not raise the moral tone of the crew. But most seamen of the age were willing volunteers. Many were born in seaports, bred to aspire to nothing more. And, for all its dangers and discomforts, the sea offered a remote chance for social and economic improvement. While some of the great captains of the era were born into the upper classes, others, like Columbus, worked their way up from the bottom. Columbus first shipped out as a boy, perhaps only 10 years old. Yet he stood before kings and queens. Many *conquistadores* first came to the New World as common seamen and lived to be wealthy landowners.

---

patroon's part of the bargain was to transport and settle fifty families on his land, where they would be beholden to him almost as serfs. Only one patroonship succeeded, 700,000-acre Van Renssaelerwyck, just south of Fort Orange. Dutch immigrants preferred to find land in western Long Island, on Staten Island, and in what is now New Jersey. There they did not have to tip their hats to a patroon.

New Netherlands had trouble finding a good governor. The founder of New Amsterdam, Peter Minuit, who purchased Manhattan Island from the Indians (or so he thought), was quarrelsome. Governor Willem Kieft was as incompetent an official as ever breathed American air. His soldiers slaughtered peaceful Indians who had actually taken refuge with the Dutch. Several Algonkian tribes retaliated with results as

devastating as the Jamestown Massacre, reducing the population of the colony to 700.

In 1638, Peter Minuit was back in New Netherlands, but not with the West India Company's approval. Now employed by a Swedish colonial company, he founded a string of tiny settlements along the lower Delaware River and Delaware Bay, mostly on the western bank so as to avoid conflict with the Dutch. Only Christiana (in present-day Delaware) amounted to much. The Swedes and Finns (Finland was then part of Sweden) who emigrated spread out along the Delaware from the future site of Philadelphia to the southern end of the bay. There were as many Dutch and English farmers eking out a living in New Sweden as there were Swedes and Finns.

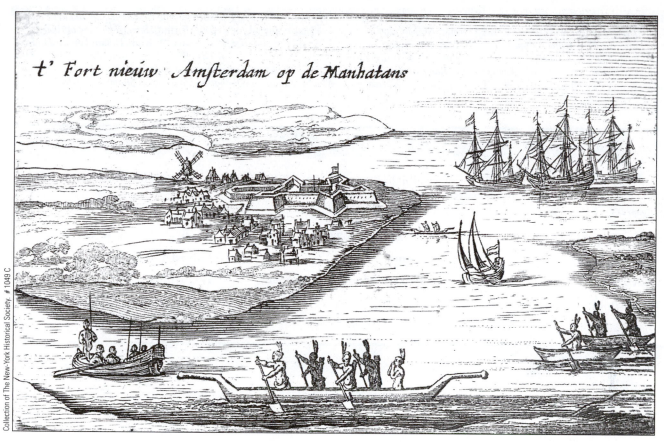

t' Fort nieuw Amsterdam op de Manhatans

Collection of The New-York Historical Society, # 1049 C

New Amsterdam when only two or three years from its founding. The Dutch (and the English) always built a protective fort before they built houses. New Amsterdam's fort was far more formidable than the stockades that surrounded Jamestown and Plymouth. The artist makes it clear what the colony was all about: the fur trade. Indians are bringing furs by canoe; Dutch ships are waiting to haul them to Holland.

FURTHER READING

Classics Wesley F. Craven, *The Southern Colonies in the Seventeenth Century*, 1949; Daniel Boorstin, *The Americans: The Colonial Experience*, 1958.

General D. W. Meinig, *The Shaping of America: A Geographical Perspective on 500 Years of History*, Volume 1, *Atlantic America 1492–1800*, 1986; Jack P. Greene and J. R. Pole, eds., *Colonial British America*, 1984.

English Background Keith Wright, *English Society, 1580–1680*, 1982; Peter Laslett, *The World We Have Lost*, 1965; Carl Bridenbaugh, *Vexed and Troubled Englishmen*, 1968; G. W. Bernard, *The King's Reformation: Henry VIII and the Remaking of the English Church*, 2005; Paul Johnson, *Elizabeth I*, 1974; James A. Williamson, *Sir Francis Drake*, 1975; Stephen J. Greenblatt, *Sir Walter Raleigh*; P. L. Barbour, *The Three Worlds of Captain John Smith*, 1964; Roger Lockyer, *James VI and I*, 1998; Thomas E. Roche, *The Golden Hind*, 1973; John Cummins, *Francis Drake: The Lives of a Hero*, 1995; Neil Hanson, *The Confident Hope of a Miracle: The True History of the Spanish Armada*, 2005.

Roanoke David Stick, *Roanoke Island: The Beginnings of English America*, 1983; Karen Ordahl Kupperman, *Roanoke: The Abandoned Colony*, 1984; David B. Quinn, *Set Fair for Roanoke*, 1985; Giles Milton, *Big Chief Elizabeth: The Adventures and Fate of the First English Colonists in America*, 2000; Glyn Williams, *Voyages of Delusion: The Quest for the Northwest Passage*, 2002.

Jamestown Carl Bridenbaugh, *Jamestown, 1544–1699*, 1980; Alden Vaughan, *Captain John Smith and the Founding of Virginia*, 1975; Thad W. Tate and David W. Ammerman, eds., *The Chesapeake in the Seventeenth Century*, 1979; R. Menard, *The Economy of British North America 1607–1789*, 1985; James Horn, *Adapting to a New World: English Society in the Seventeenth Century Chesapeake*, 1994; William M. Kelso, *Jamestown: The Buried Truth*, 2001; Robert Appelbaum and John Wood Sweet, *Envisioning an English Empire: Jamestown and the Making of the North Atlantic World*, 2005; James Horn, *A Land as God Made It*, 2006.

Colonists and Indians Peter Wood et al., *Powhatan's Mantle: Indians in the Colonial Southeast*, 1989; Helen L. Rountree, *The Powhatan Indians of Virginia*, 1988 and *Pocohontas, Powhatan, Opechancanough: Three Indian Lives Changed by Jamestown*, 2005; Karen O. Ordahl, *Indians and English: Facing Off in Early America*, 2000; Peter C. Mancall and James H. Merrell, eds., *American Encounters: Natives and Newcomers From European Contact to Indian Removal, 1500–1850*, 2000; Russell Bourne, *Gods of War, Gods of Peace: How the Meeting of Native and Colonial Religions Shaped Early America*, 2002.

Maryland See Tate and Ammerman, *The Chesapeake* and James Horn, *Adapting to a New World* (above, "Jamestown"); John T. Ellis, *Catholics in Colonial America*, 1965; Lois Green Carr, ed., *Colonial Chesapeake Society*, 1988 and *Robert Cole's World: Agriculture and Society in Early Maryland*, 1991.

Spanish, French, and Dutch Beginnings David J. Weber, *The Spanish Frontier in North America*, 1992; Jerald T. Milanich, *Florida Indians and the Invasion from Europe*, 1995; John T. McGrath, *The French in Early Florida: In the Eyes of the Hurricane*, 2000; Andrew L. Knaut, *The Pueblo Revolt of 1680: Conquest and Resistance in Seventeenth Century New Mexico*, 1997; W. C. Eccles, *France in America*, 1972; Bruce G. Trigger, *Natives and Newcomers: Canada's "Heroic Age" Reconsidered*, 1985; John Ferling, *Struggle for a Continent: The Wars of Early America*, 1993; Oliver A. Rink, *Holland on the Hudson: An Economic and Social History of Dutch New York*, 1986; Russell Shorto, *The Island at the Center of the World: The Epic Story of Dutch Manhattan and the Forgotten Colony that Shapes America*, 2004.

Key Terms

Use the following listing of key terms to review important figures, events, locations, and concepts covered in this chapter. A glossary of these terms is available on *The American Past* companion Web site: www.cengage.com/history/conlin/tap9e

Siglo de oro, p. 21

annulment, p. 22

Elizabeth I, p. 24

Sea dogs, p. 24

Drake, Francis, p. 24

enclosure, p. 28

merchants-adventurers company, p. 29

headright system, p. 32

Calvert, George, p. 34

Huguenots, p. 35

Online Resources

Find additional resources, including primary source documents, images, interactive maps, simulations, chapter review exercises, and Internet links at

***The American Past* companion Web site**
www.cengage.com/history/conlin/tap9e

American History Resource Center
http://ushistory.wadsworth.com/

Chapter 3

Thirteen Colonies

England's North American Empire
1620–1732

The Art Archive/Picture Desk

We must be knit together in this work as one man; we must entertain each other in brotherly affection; . . . we must uphold a familiar commerce together in all meekness, gentleness, patience and liberality; we must delight in each other, make other's conditions our own, rejoice together, mourn together, labor and suffer together.

—John Winthrop

They differ from us in the manner of praying, for they winke [close their eyes] when they pray because they thinke themselves so perfect in the highe way to heaven that they can find it blindfold.

—Thomas Morton

In 1608, 125 men, women, and children left the village of Scrooby in the middle of England and made their way to the port of Hull. There they took ship to the "fair and beautifull citie" of Leiden in Holland, which they intended to make their lifelong home.

They traveled furtively because they were breaking the law. Going abroad without the Crown's permission was forbidden. The Scrooby villagers were willing to risk arrest because they were already being harassed for their religious practices, even imprisoned in "noisome and vile dungeons." They belonged to a sect called "Separatists" because they believed that Christians who were "saved" should not worship together with the unsaved multitude but should, according to the Bible, "come out from among them, and bee yee separate." This belief guaranteed trouble for all Englishmen and women were obligated to attend Church of England services.

The Separatists are better known as the "Pilgrims." One of their leaders, William Bradford, gave them the name because they wandered, as if on a pilgrimage, in search of a place where they could live godly lives unmolested.

THE NEW ENGLAND COLONIES

The Pilgrims were not molested in Leiden. Because the Dutch were splintered into a variety of religious denominations—Calvinists much like the Pilgrims, Catholics, Lutherans, Anabaptists—the great merchants who ran the country adopted a policy of freedom of conscience as the only alternative to social instability.

Increasing and Multiplying

Nearly half of Plymouth's settlers died during the colony's first winter. Just four of the survivors more than made up for the losses within their own lifetimes. John and Eliza Howland raised ten children and had 88 grandchildren. John Alden and Priscilla Mullins, who married soon after arriving on the *Mayflower* both lived into their eighties. They had 12 children of whom 10 survived to adulthood. Eight of the Aldens married and, together, had at least 68 children. Alden's and Mullins's great-grandchildren, a few of whom they lived to see born, numbered 400, four times the original population of the colony.

Plimouth Plantation, Inc., Photographer, Gary Andrashko

A contemporary reconstruction of Plymouth when the settlement was several years old. This "street" was broad enough for an ox or horse to pass, but not a wagon. Others were wider. Dooryards were fenced not for privacy but to keep hogs our of gardens. Although Plymouth had good relations with nearby Indians, the town was surrounded by a palisade of logs half a mile in length.

Still, the Pilgrims were unhappy. The presence of so many Catholics disturbed them. Strict with their children, they were shocked by the notorious indulgence of Dutch parents. The Pilgrims fretted that their own offspring were "getting the reins off their necks," picking up loose behavior from Dutch companions. And the Pilgrims were unhappy, as foreigners living abroad often are, that their sons and daughters were growing up more Dutch than English. They may have fled English laws hostile to them. They were still English to the core, as ethnocentric as any Chinese, Ghanian, or Powhatan Indian.

Plymouth Plantation

Some returned to England in trickles. Others, unhappy as they were, stayed on until 1620 when a stroke of luck (God's intervention so far as the Pilgrims were concerned) provided a way out of their quandary. The old Plymouth Company had been reorganized as the Council for New England but was having trouble recruiting settlers for a new colony. The tobacco boom in Virginia was attracting most Englishmen and women willing to go to America. So, a prominent shareholder in the company, Sir Edwin Sandys (himself with Calvinist leanings) persuaded King James I to tolerate the Pilgrims' religious practices if they relocated across the Atlantic.

The exiles in Leiden were delighted. In 1620, they returned to England just long enough to board two small ships in the harbor at Plymouth, the *Mayflower* and the *Speedwell*. The *Speedwell* leaked so badly it turned back immediately.

The English Colonies 1600–1700

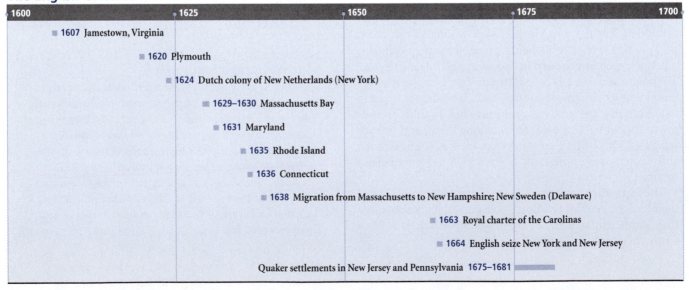

1600	**1625**	**1650**	**1675**	**1700**

■ 1607 Jamestown, Virginia

■ 1620 Plymouth

■ 1624 Dutch colony of New Netherlands (New York)

■ 1629–1630 Massachusetts Bay

■ 1631 Maryland

■ 1635 Rhode Island

■ 1636 Connecticut

■ 1638 Migration from Massachusetts to New Hampshire; New Sweden (Delaware)

■ 1663 Royal charter of the Carolinas

■ 1664 English seize New York and New Jersey

Quaker settlements in New Jersey and Pennsylvania 1675–1681 ■■■■

The *Mayflower* was none too seaworthy herself but, well skippered, she survived a rough passage longer than Columbus's a century earlier.

A hundred settlers, mostly Separatists, disembarked at the southern end of Massachusetts Bay. They built "Plimouth Plantation" on the site of Pawtuxet, an abandoned Wampanoag village. Pawtuxet had been wiped out three years earlier by disease contracted from English fishermen. To the Pilgrims, the sight of open fields ready to be plowed was a sign of God's approval. He had "cleared" the land of people (Wampanoag bones still littered the area) to make room for his Saints.

God did not, however, see to it that the *Mayflower* left enough provisions behind and the winter of 1620–1621 was a hard one. Half of Plymouth's settlers died of malnutrition or disease before a relief ship arrived in the spring. God then, having tested them—the Pilgrims saw God's hand at work at every turning—blessed them again. "A special instrument sent of God," Tisquantum, or Squanto, an Indian speaking English well, joined them.

Squanto was a native of Pawtuxet. He had gone to England with fishermen in 1605, was in Jamestown briefly in 1614, and was captured by Spaniards. Escaping from Spain, he made his way to England. Just six months before the Pilgrims arrived in Massachusetts, he had worked his way home on a fishing vessel and found Pawtuxet deserted.

The well-traveled Squanto was a good deal more cosmopolitan than any Pilgrim. When he adopted the newcomers as his tribe, he became, surely, the most valuable member of the community. He schooled the Pilgrims in Indian methods of hunting, fishing, and cultivation, and he guided them about the Massachusetts woods. According to Bradford, now governor of the colony, he asked for prayers so that "he might goe to the Englishmen's God in Heaven."

Self-Government

Squanto was a better citizen than many who arrived on the *Mayflower*. Even before stepping ashore, Bradford and other leaders worried that some of the "strangers" among them (non-Separatists) would defy their authority. Several had boasted as much; they meant to go their own way once off the ship. Because Plymouth Plantation lay outside the boundaries the company charter allowed them, Bradford and his military commander Miles Standish worried that their authority might have no legal standing.

In order to assert it, forty-one passengers signed the "Mayflower Compact" while still aboard ship. The document began by asserting everyone's enduring loyalty to "our dread Sovereign Lord King James"; This was standard fare. The Compact then declared settlers bound together in a "Civil Body Politik" for the purpose of enacting and enforcing laws. The Mayflower Compact is memorable because of its implicit principle that a government's authority was based on the consent of those who are governed.

Not that it occured to the Pilgrims to create a democracy. They would have shuddered at the suggestion. *Democracy* was a dirty word; in the seventeenth century it meant "mob rule." Nevertheless, in practice, Plymouth was a rather democratic place. Almost every male Separatist head of household voted to elect the governor. (They reelected Bradford annually for thirty years.) Many community questions were resolved by vote. Women could not vote even if they were heads of household. Nor could adult unmarried males who owned no land, nor "strangers." Still, so broad a popular participation in government was found in few places elsewhere in the world.

Subsistence Economy

The Pilgrims experienced little interference from England. The Crown took no interest in the colony after chartering a company to run it. The major shareholders in the Plymouth Company, who remained in England, would have dispatched reams of directives and a new governor (the Mayflower Compact meant nothing to them) had Plymouth stumbled on a moneymaker like Virginia's tobacco. But the Pilgrims never did. Furs and hides purchased from Indians provided some income with which to buy English goods. Fishing helped; there was a market for salted codfish in Europe.

But that was about it. Plymouth was largely a community of subsistence farmers. The Pilgrims raised enough food to feed themselves, but they were quite poor. When the governor of New Netherlands, Peter Minuit, sent Governor Bradford "two Holland cheeses"—a rather modest gift, it would seem—Bradford had to apologize for "not having any thing to send you for the present that may be acceptable." Plymouth's population remained small. There was no repetition of the terrible mortality of the first winter, but epidemic disease was a regular visitor: In 1628, eighteen women arrived in Plymouth to find husbands; fourteen died within a year.

Plymouth's poverty discouraged the shareholders back in England. In 1627 they agreed to sell out to the colonists. Even then it took the Pilgrims fifteen years to pay them off. Nonetheless, the sale transferred legal control of Plymouth Plantation to its inhabitants. Plymouth was effectively a self-governing commonwealth until 1691 when it was absorbed into its younger but much larger neighbor to the north, Massachusetts Bay.

Massachusetts Bay

Self-government was half accidental in Plymouth. Had a plowman turned up a vein of gold ore in his corn field, the Company would have exercised its charter prerogatives and the Crown might have royalized Plymouth as it did Virginia in 1624.

In Massachusetts Bay, by way of contrast, self-government was part of well-laid plans from the start. Massachusetts was a bigger and better-organized operation than either Jamestown or Plymouth. The first wave of settlers in 1630 totaled a thousand people in seventeen ships. Such an operation required massive stores of provisions. There were no starving times in Massachusetts Bay (located about forty miles north of Plymouth). The founders of the Bay Colony worked out the details before they weighed anchor. In just a few months,

Merrymount

"Merrymount" (later Quincy) was a few miles from Plymouth. In 1623, an eccentric character named Thomas Morton persuaded several other settlers (in the words of Governor Bradford) to found a town where they would be "free from service, and . . . trade, plante, & live togeather as equalls."

According to Bradford, Merrymount was a riotous place. Its inhabitants were frequently drunk and "set up a May-pole, drinking and dancing aboute it many days togeather, inviting the Indean women, for their consorts, dancing and frisking together, (like so many fairies, or furies rather,) and worse practices."

Bradford had economic as well as moral reasons for wanting to close down

The Art Archive/Picture Desk

Merrymount. Morton was stealing the Indian trade from Plymouth by offering firearms in return for furs and hides. This worried Bradford because the Indians were better hunters than the whites "by reason of ther swiftnes of foote, & nimblnes of body," and because their guns might easily be turned against Plymouth. He sent Captain Miles Standish and a few soldiers to arrest Morton. There was no battle because, according to Bradford, Morton and his friends were too drunk to resist. The only casualty was a Merrymounter who staggered into a sword and split his nose.

Morton was put on an island to await a ship bound for England. Indian friends brought him food and liquor and helped him escape, whence he returned to England on his own and denounced the Pilgrims. Neither he nor the Pilgrim Fathers were punished. If the authorities had been familiar with the phrase "can of worms," they would surely have applied it to the squabble.

---

seven towns were under construction. And colonists kept coming. In the "Great Migration" of 1630–1640, 20,000 people arrived in Massachusetts.

They were a pretty solid lot. By design, the settlers were a fair cross section of English society. They were of both sexes, evenly divided. (The ratio of emigrants to Virginia was four men for each woman, in Spanish Mexico ten to one.) They were of all age groups and social classes up to the rank of lady and gentleman. There was even one noblewoman in the first wave, but she had come just to have a look and returned to England. Most settlers were farmers and laborers, but there were skilled artisans of many trades, and professionals, notably university-educated ministers.

The founders of Massachusetts Bay meant to create a *New* England, a society like that they had always known. Except in one particular: Although they insisted that they were members of England's established church, the founders of Massachusetts abhorred the Church of England's structure and rituals and none too politely, they called bishops "the excrement of Antichrist." They denounced Anglican ceremonies as Catholic. England had embraced sinful ways in its hybrid church; New England would be a truly godly commonwealth.

To ensure that they would shape their Zion without interference, the colonists brought the Massachusetts Bay Company charter with them. It provided the shareholders (all of them emigrants; shareholders who chose to remain in England sold out to those who went) with self-government. What

took Plymouth twenty years to accomplish, Massachusetts Bay had from the start.

Puritan Beliefs

These cautious, calculating people were the Puritans. Like the Pilgrims, they were Calvinists. They believed that human nature was inherently depraved, that all men and women bore the stain of Adam's and Eve's original sin. In the words of Massachusetts poet, Anne Bradstreet, man was a "lump of wretchedness, of sin and sorrow."

It was a harsh doctrine: If God were just, and nothing more, every son and daughter of Eve would be damned to hell for eternity because of their sinful nature. God was all good; there was nothing that a man or woman could do—no "good works," no act of charity, no sacrifice, no performance of a ritual, not even a statement of faith—to earn salvation. Everybody deserved damnation.

Fortunately, God was not merely just. He was also loving and merciful. He chose some people—elected them—and bestowed grace upon them. They were his "Saints."

Having been so abundantly and undeservedly blessed—for they were as inherently sinful as anyone—the Elect bound themselves in a covenant (contract) with God. They would enforce God's law in their community. If they failed to do so, they understood, if they tolerated sinning, God would punish their community as surely as he had punished his covenanted people of the Old Testament, the Hebrews, when they tolerated sin.

The Puritan covenant is central to understanding the society and culture of Massachusetts, which differs so significantly from our own that it can be difficult to realize that the Puritans are culturally our ancestors.

Errand in the Wilderness

Schoolchildren were once taught that the Puritans fled to America so that "they could worship as they pleased." Not really: Unlike the handful of Pilgrims, the Puritans were numerous in old England, and they included among them quite a few people of high station. In regions where they were few, they were harassed. But where the big landowners, even the nobles, were Puritans, they took over Church of England parishes. Puritans were particularly powerful in England's eastern counties—Norfolk, Suffolk, Cambridgeshire, Lincolnshire—from which most of Massachusetts's early settlers came. Massachusetts Bay's most prominent minister, John Cotton, had held the pulpit at St. Botolph's in old Boston, said to have been the largest parish church in England. He was a man of high status and great influence. Cotton did not hide in hedges to escape persecution. When church authorities finally called him to task for his Calvinist preaching, he simply resigned, packed up, and went to Massachusetts.

Far from suffering because of their religious beliefs, most of the 20,000 Puritans who removed to Massachusetts in the "Great Migration" left England because they lacked the authority to prevent others from worshiping as they pleased. All around them they saw with dismay a "multitude of irreligious, lascivious, and popish persons." In tolerating this sinfulness, old England was flagrantly violating God's law and courting his wrath. "I am verily persuaded," wrote John Winthrop, who became governor of Massachusetts Bay, that "God will bring some heavy affliction upon this land."

The Saints did not want to be around for the payoff. In Massachusetts, they would escape old England's punishment because their church and colony would be purified of Catholic blasphemies (thus the name Puritan) and the covenant honored.

The Puritans said that they were on an "errand into the wilderness." For years, some of them nursed the illusion that old England would look across the ocean, see by the Puritan's example the error of their ways, and invite the Puritan fathers home to escort England into righteousness. "We shall be as a citty on a hill," Winthrop wrote, a beacon of inspiration visible from afar.

Community

The Puritans believed in a *community* of a kind that little resembles what we mean by the word. Every member of the Puritan community was (in theory) bound to every other by a network of ties as intricate as a spider's web. People had rights, but their obligations to others—religious, economic, social—preoccupied the Puritans. In Winthrop's words, "every man might have need of [every] other, and from hence they might be knit more nearly together in the bond of brotherly affection."

The Puritans were suspicious of individualism; they had no time for eccentricity. The covenant made it all-important to be ever on the lookout for sin and to punish it promptly. Even behavior that was mildly dubious attracted the notice of Puritan zealots, and a brotherly word or two. Judge Samuel Sewall heard that his cousin had taken to wearing a wig, then the height of fashion. The troubled judge crossed town to tell his kinsman that artificial hair was sinful; God had selected each person's hair; was one to question his choice? To the Puritans, Sewall was not a busybody. He was being charitable; he was looking after his cousin's soul. The cousin liked his wig too well to give it up, but it never occurred to him to tell Sewall to go mind his own business. He argued only as to whether wigs really were sinful.

Sin was not just an individual sinner's business. If the community knew of a sin and failed to punish it, in that case, the entire community was subject to God's wrath. Simple people understood this principle so alien to us. In 1656, a teenager named Tryal Pore was caught in the sin of fornication; she told her congregation in her confession that "by this my sinn I have not only done what I can to Poull Judgement from the Lord on my selve but allso upon the place where I live."

Never on Sunday

Husband and wife were not to have sexual intercourse on Sunday. Because a common superstition had it that a child was born on the same day of the week on which it was conceived, the parents of an infant delivered on Sunday (one in seven, one has to guess) were at least the subject of gossip. The Rev. Israel Loring of Sudbury refused to baptize children born on Sunday. Then, one Sunday, his wife presented him with twins.

Blue Laws

The statutes of Massachusetts (and other colonies) brimmed with regulations of behavior that would today be considered outrageous or ridiculous blue laws. The blue laws applied to everyone, visitor as well as resident, the unregenerate as well as the elect, nonchurch members as well as church members.

God commanded that the sabbath be devoted to him. Therefore, the Puritans forbade, on Sundays, activities that,

Messages from On High

Almost every happening out of the ordinary was likely to strike some Puritans as a sign from God. After a series of earthquakes in New England, Michael Wigglesworth observed that "these notable Winks of God do very often betoken his Anger toward Mankind." God's signs could be quite personal. When the Rev. Cotton Mather's small daughter tottered into a fire and severely burned herself, Mather, in painful anguish wrote in his journal: "Alas, for my sins the just God throws my child into the fire."

Public Domain

A few hours sitting in the stocks—public humiliation—was a common punishment for minor offenses in early New England. A variation on the stocks was the pillory, in which the offender stood, head and hands locked in place. Laughter and mockery of the offender were accepted; physical abuse was not.

on Wednesday or Thursday, were perfectly in order: working, tossing quoits or wrestling, whistling a tune, "idle chatter," "dancing and frisking," even "walking in a garden." Some things appropriate in private were forbidden in public. In 1659, a sea captain named Kemble returned from a three-year voyage and warmly kissed his wife on the threshold of their home. He was sentenced to sit in the stocks for two hours for "lewd and unseemly behaviour."

A woman who was a "scold" (given to "Exorbitancy of the Tongue in Raling and Scolding") was humiliated on the ducking stool. She was strapped to a chair on a plank mounted like a see-saw, and dunked in a pond to her humiliation and everyone else's amusement. Church attendance was mandatory. In Maine (then part of Massachusetts) in 1682, Andrew Searle was fined 5 shillings "for not frequenting the publique worship of god" and for "wandering from place to place upon the Lords days." More serious offenders—thieves, arsonists, assaulters, wife beaters—were flogged, branded, had their ears cropped, or their nostrils slit.

However, so far as capital crimes were concerned, Massachusetts was positively liberal. In England during the seventeenth and eighteenth centuries, the number of capital crimes rose steadily until, in time, there were more than a hundred of them. A wretch could be hanged for snaring a rabbit on a gentleman's land. But the Puritans reserved hanging or burning at the stake for those offenses that were

punished by death in the Bible: blasphemy, witchcraft, treason, murder, rape, adultery, incest, sodomy (homosexuality), and buggery (bestiality in the Puritan lexicon).

Even then, the Puritans were not bloodthirsty. Many people convicted of capital crimes were let off with lesser sentences. Between 1630 and 1660, fewer than twenty people were executed in Massachusetts: four murderers, two infanticides, three sexual offenders, two witches, and four Quakers, members of a religious sect believed to "undermine & ruine" authority.

Cases of adultery during the sixty years the Puritans governed Massachusetts are beyond counting, but there were only three executions for the crime. Most adulterers were let off with a whipping or branding or, although clearly guilty, they were acquitted by juries which did not care to see the offenders executed. Connecticut proclaimed the death penalty for a child who struck or cursed his parents, but the law was never enforced. When Joseph Porter was brought to court for calling his father "a thief, liar, and simple ape shittabed," his conviction was thrown out on appeal. New Haven made masturbation a capital offense, but while offenders were surely multitudinous, none was hanged.

It is important to understand about societies past that what the law said and what the articulate voiced do not always describe everyday practice. On paper, Massachusetts was a police state. But not every Puritan was a fanatic. When authorities stripped two Quaker women to the waist and whipped then until blood ran down their breasts, villagers were so disgusted that they mobbed the authorities and set the women free.

Puritan Names

Many Puritans named their children from the Old Testament, after the great figures, of course—*Adam, Noah, Deborah, Judith*—but also after obscure ones: *Ahab, Zerubbabel, Abednego,* and so on.

Some Puritans used their children's names to make a statement. *Increase* Mather, a prominent minister, got his name from the Biblical injunction, "Increase, multiply, and subdue the earth." Records have not revealed anyone called *Multiply* or *Subdue,* but there was a *Fight the Good Fight of Faith Wilson,* a *Be Courteous Cole,* a *Kill-Sin* Pemble, and a *Mene Mene Tekal Upharsin* Pond. Other notable names: *The Lord is Near, Fear-Not, Flee Fornication,* and *Job-Raked-Out-of-the-Ashes.*

A couple named Cheeseman was told their infant would die during childbirth. Not knowing the child's sex, they baptized it *Creature.* Creature Cheeseman fooled the midwife and lived a long life bearing her unusual monicker.

Too much must not be made of these names. Only 4 percent of Puritans were saddled with them. Half of the girls in records of Massachusetts Bay baptisms were bestowed just three rock-solid English names: *Sarah, Elizabeth,* and *Mary.* Almost half the boys were *John, Joseph, Samuel,* or *Josiah.*

Assumptions

Little as they liked James I and Charles I, the Puritans assumed that monarchy was sacred. Democracy—known to them only in the abstract—was a horrifying concept. They were nationalists too; English customs, they believed, were superior to those of every other people. Children were born full of sin, "vipers and infinitely worse than vipers," and were to be rigorously bent to godliness and their parents' will. "Better whipped than damned." Wives were subordinate to their husbands, women to men, although not to male servants. (Once again, these were ideals: Puritans did not routinely brutalize their children, and many a wife, albeit privately, told her lord and master what to do whence he did it.)

The Puritans assumed that clear social distinctions were God's will. "Some must be rich, some poore," said John Winthrop, *not* some happen to be rich, some happen to be poor. It was an offense when people dressed themselves in a way inappropriate to their social class. In Connecticut in 1675, thirty-eight women were arrested for wearing silk. Obviously, they could afford such finery, but their social standing did not entitle them to wear it. Another law forbade people of humble station—farmers, laborers—to wear silver buckles on their shoes. Silver was "fit" only for magistrates and ministers.

The magistrates who governed the New England colonies, which, at the start, legally owned all the land, closely regulated where people could acquire it. That is, a family could not pick up, move into the forest, select land for a farm, pay for it, and have a home. New arrivals and people of an overpopulated township for whom there was no land were, in

New Englanders did not live in log cabins. That durable American institution was introduced by Swedes and Finns living along the Delaware River. New Englanders erected frames of hewn timbers a foot and more square and sided the frame with overlapping clapboards. Frame construction required a sawmill and skilled carpenters and joiners, both of which the well-organized Puritans had from the start. This substantial home—much larger than the norm—was constructed in Dedham, Massachusetts, in 1637.

Photograph by Wilfred French, Courtesy of the Society for the Preservation of New England Antiquities

groups of 50 to 100 families, alloted land for a new township usually abutting on an existing township at the edge of settlement. Within the new township, each family was assigned a homesite in a compact village, fields for tillage, a woodlot for fuel, and the right to keep livestock on the town common.

Social control enabled the Puritans to create the most literate population in the world. In 1642, Massachusetts required parents to teach their children how to read. In 1647, townships of fifty families were required to support an elementary school, towns of a thousand a Latin School (a secondary school for boys only). A college to train ministers, Harvard, was founded in 1636.

RHODE ISLAND, CONNECTICUT, AND NEW HAMPSHIRE

In 1630, there were two colonies in New England: Plymouth and Massachusetts. Within ten years there were seven, four of which were to become states. The rapid multiplication of New England's colonies was a direct consequence of the Massachusetts Puritans' intolerance of diverse religious views and the General Court's (the governing assembly's) tight control of land grants.

Troublesome Roger Williams

Rhode Island and Providence Plantations (still the long official name of the smallest state) was founded by a brilliant but cranky minister named Roger Williams who had differences with the governors of Massachusetts from the start. Williams was a strict Puritan and impeccable in his personal behavior. But he came to conclusions at odds with Governor Winthrop, the General Court, and "establishment" ministers like John Cotton; and he insisted on expressing them.

Williams agreed that most people were damned, that God bestowed his grace on very few. But just who were the Elect? Massachusetts ministers had procedures for determining who were "visible saints" and, therefore, who were admitted to church membership and the right to vote. Williams insisted that no one could be certain of anyone's election but his own. To underscore his point, he said that while he prayed with his wife, he did not know for certain if she was truly saved. She knew; God knew; no one else could know.

Therefore, Williams concluded, religion and government—church and state in our terms—must be separate. If the elect could not be known, there must be no religious test, as there was in Massachusetts, to determine who could vote to choose magistrates or, at a town meeting, who could vote whether to spend public money to bridge a stream or to use it for something else. Every male head of household should have that right, Williams insisted.

This was a dangerous doctrine. Church members were a minority in Massachusetts. Williams's teaching threatened the Puritans' control of the commonwealth—the very reason they had come to America, to be in charge. If the majority of the people, the unregenerate as well as the saints, made laws and elected officials, the covenant would soon lay in tatters and God would "surely break out in wrath" against the colony.

Williams also rattled the Winthrop oligarchy by preaching that their royal charter did not give them legal and moral ownership of the land. The Indians owned the land by right of occupation. Colonists must purchase land from the natives if they were to dwell on it. In fact, Massachusetts Bay did pay the Indians for much of the land they occupied. But when Williams called the Massachusetts charter "a solemn public lie," he was attacking a document that was sacrosanct. The charter was the foundation of Massachusetts's virtual independence.

Rhode Island: "The Sewer of New England"

John Winthrop admired Roger Williams. He turned to him often for advice. But after several years of Williams's subversive preaching, the top Puritans had their fill: Williams was ordered to return to England. Instead, he fled to the forest, spent

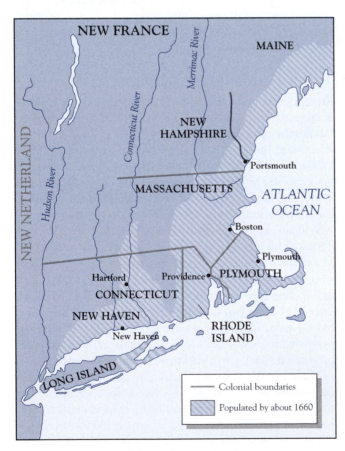

MAP 3:1 **The New England Colonies.** The Crown recognized seven colonial entities in New England: Plymouth (founded 1620), Massachusetts (1630), Connecticut (1636), Rhode Island (1636, chartered 1644), New Haven (1638), New Hampshire (chartered 1622, first real settlement 1638), Maine (first settled 1623). Connecticut absorbed New Haven in 1622. Massachusetts acquired Maine in 1677. Plymouth was joined to Massachusetts in 1691. Eastern Long Island was settled by New Englanders but was incorporated into New York in 1664.

the winter with the Narragansett Indians, and then established a farm and trading post, Providence, on Narragansett Bay, which was beyond the boundaries of Massachusetts Bay. He soon had neighbors, Puritans who shared his beliefs or were attracted by the prime land of what became Rhode Island.

Williams may have believed the king had no right to give away lands the Indians owned. However, he also knew that he needed the Crown's recognition of Rhode Isand if the colony were to be safe from a takeover by Massachusetts Bay. In 1644, he sailed to London where he won a charter for his colony. Massachusetts, reverential toward its own charter, would not violate Rhode Island's.

In fact, the Massachusetts Puritans had good reasons to leave Rhode Island alone. It was useful as a place to which to banish dissenters. So long as problem settlers took their blasphemies beyond the colony's borders, the Puritan fathers did not have to fear God's anger. But shipping colonists back to England was risky: They might appeal to the Crown and win their case. Rhode Island was a better alternative. Dissenters banished there were likely to stay there. The Puritans called Rhode Island the "sewer of New England." Quite like us, they shuddered to think about sewers. Quite like us, they understood their usefulness.

Anne Hutchinson

The first important dissenter to be banished to Rhode Island was Anne Hutchinson, in 1638. Hutchinson was a devout member of the Massachusetts elite. (She was Winthrop's neighbor.) Taking seriously the admonition that saints should study the word of God, she invited people into her home on Sundays to discuss the morning's sermon. Hutchinson's analysis of it was often critical and sometimes acerbic. When her meetings grew in popularity, it raised the hackles of the preachers who were the targets of her intelligence and wit.

They shook their heads that a woman should be a theologian. "You have stept out of your place," Winthrop told Hutchinson, "you have rather bine a Husband than a Wife and a preacher than a Hearer." Such behavior was not "fitting for your sex." Indeed, Winthrop believed that a woman jeopardized her mental balance by thinking about difficult theological questions.

Had Hutchinson's offense been no greater than crowing, she might have gotten off with a reprimand. She had influential supporters. But Hutchinson taught that some people—her, for instance—were divinely inspired. This was antinomianism, a grave heresy. The word's two Greek roots mean *against* and *the law.* That is, antinomians believed that people specially blessed by God were above the rules and regulations of human governments. As Winthrop put it, Hutchinson said that she was not "subject to controll of the rule of the Word or of the State" and therefore, she was "a woman not fit for our society." Another of her judges, the Rev. John Wilson, used stronger language. Hutchinson was "a dangerous instrument of the Devil raised up by Satan amongst us."

To ensure that Anne Hutchinson was convicted, she was charged with eighty heresies! Something would stick and it

North Wind Pictures.

This representation of Anne Hutchinson being questioned by Governor Winthrop nicely captures the atmosphere of the occasion. Records of the trial reveal that Hutchinson was confident, unyielding, and witty. She several times bested Governor Winthrop and the other magistrates who judged her, but they had the power and Hutchinson was banished.

did. She was banished to Rhode Island; some of her disciples followed.

New Hampshire, Maine, and Connecticut

As early as 1622, the Crown had given what are now the states of New Hampshire and Maine to two courtiers, granting them the same powers Lord Baltimore had in Maryland. John Mason and Fernando Gorges had no high-flown projects in mind, like Baltimore's Catholic refuge. They wanted to make money selling land to settlers. Fishermen founded villages in Gorgas's Maine and a few farmers drifted over the border from Massachusetts to Mason's New Hampshire, but not until a disciple of Anne Hutchinson, Rev. John Wheelwright, led a group north was there a noticeable English presence above Massachusetts.

Neither Maine nor New Hampshire made much money for their proprietors, and Massachusetts Bay disputed their rights to the land. In 1680, to end the squabble, the Crown took control of New Hampshire, making it a royal colony. In the meantime, Massachusetts gained Maine by subterfuge. In 1677, a Boston merchant, John Usher, purchased the white elephant from Gorgas's heirs for £1,250. Usher immediately

deeded the land to Massachusetts Bay. The "Maine District" remained a part of Massachusetts for almost fifty years after the American Revolution.

The Puritans knew that the bottomlands of the Connecticut River valley were fertile. Moreover, Connecticut was a rich source of beaver pelts that the Mohawks were selling to the Dutch in New Netherlands. In 1636, with both farming and the fur trade in mind, the Rev. Thomas Hooker, an ultrastrict Puritan, led a contingent of his followers to the river, where they founded Hartford.

Hartford was forty miles from Long Island Sound, in the heart of the hunting grounds of the Pequots, a tribe then suffering from Mohawk incursions. Now pressed from the East too, the Pequots tried to form an anti-Mohawk alliance with Massachusetts. But when the Puritans dithered, they concluded they had to neutralize the whites, whom they considered weaker than the Mohawks. In May 1637, the Pequots attacked Wethersfield, not far from Hartford.

After Roger Williams, at Winthrop's request, convinced the Narraganset Indians to remain neutral, Massachusetts Bay, Connecticut, a few men from Plymouth, and several Indian tribes sent an army into Connecticut. By night, they surrounded a town the Pequots thought was secretly located and set it afire. As the Pequots fled, the invaders shot and killed more than 400 of them, women and children as well as warriors. After a few more battles, an attack by the Mohawks, and more than a little treachery, the Pequots were for practical purposes annihilated. (But not quite. It was a part-Pequot who founded the first and richist Indian casino on the tribe's old hunting grounds.)

During the Pequot War, two Massachusetts ministers founded New Haven on Long Island Sound on land claimed by New Netherlands. New Haven is best known for having more rigorous blue laws than even Massachusetts. It remained small and, in 1662, was absorbed into Connecticut.

PROPRIETARY COLONIES

Plymouth, Massachusetts Bay, Rhode Island, and Connecticut were *corporate colonies*. Their charters from the king were their constitutions. While acknowledging the king's sovereignty they were, in practice, self-governing commonwealths. They were governed by officials elected by heads of household who (except in Rhode Island) were members of the established church—what came to be known as the Congregationalist Church.

Virginia was a corporate colony until 1624 when James I revoked its charter and took direct control of it. As a *royal* colony, Virginia was governed by the king through an appointed governor. Royal colonies had elected assemblies with considerable say in how money was spent. But the royal governor could veto any law the assemblies enacted and he controlled the patronage: who was appointed to offices paying salaries. By the time of the American Revolution in 1776, nine of the thirteen colonies were royal colonies.

Proprietary colonies, like Maryland and early New Hampshire, had yet another kind of government. The king gave all the powers he exercised in royal colonies to highly placed men who, for one reason or another, he wished to benefit. Proprietary colonies were governed much as royal colonies were governed except that lords proprietors, rather than the king, appointed the governor.

Making Money

Lord Baltimore hoped that Maryland would be a refuge for Catholics. But he, like Mason and Gorgas, hoped to profit from his colony too. One of his (and other lords proprietors') methods of making money was feudal, hearkening back to the Middle Ages. Settlers were given land by headright, so many acres (50 to 100) for each member of the colonist's household—himself, his wife and children, and other dependents, including servants.

They were then obligated to pay the proprietor (or king) an annual quitrent. This was not rent as we understand it. The settlers owned the land; they were not tenants. Nor was a quitrent quite a tax. The quitrent principle dated from the era when the feudal system was breaking up in England (around 1300) and landowners commuted, or changed, their tenants' obligation to labor for them so many days each year into an annual cash payment in perpetuity. People owning land in "free and common socage" were "quit" of their old obligations to serve their lord as a soldier, to shear sheep, to repair the castle moat, or whatever. But there was an annual payment in recognition of what they had been granted.

Colonial quitrents were small: The idea was to attract people to America, not to discourage them with extortionate demands. Thus, for each acre freeholders in Maryland owned, they paid an annual quitrent of 2d. (pence) worth of tobacco. The quitrent for a hundred acres in New York was a bushel of wheat each year. In Georgia, the quitrent was 2s. per 50 acres.

Not much: but for the proprietor of a vast domain, thousands of pittances added up to a handsome income while the quitrents the lords proprietors owed the king were purely symbolic: two Indian arrowheads a year for Maryland; two beaver pelts a year for Pennsylvania.

New Netherlands Becomes New York

In 1646, the Dutch West India company named Peter Stuyvesant governor of New Netherlands. He was dictatorial, ill-tempered, bigoted, and cantankerous. ("His head is troubled," people said, not to his face, "he has a screw loose.") If

---

Double Dutch

The Dutch of New Netherlands coined the word *Yankee*. "Jan Kies" (John Cheese) was their collective term for New Englanders. The English retaliated with a host of insulting uses of *Dutch*. A one-sided deal was a "Dutch bargain," a potluck dinner a "Dutch lunch." Liquor was "Dutch courage," a frog was a "Dutch nightingale," and a prostitute was a "Dutch widow."

---

not personable, Stuyvesant was a superb governor. When he took over, New Netherlands' future was doubtful. Stuyvesant brought prosperity, maintained good relations with both Algonkian and Iroquois Indians, promoted immigration so the population increased from 700 to 6,000, and added New Sweden to the colony.

Most New Netherlanders were Dutch, but the colony's population was far more diverse than the population of the English colonies. There were Swedes and Finns on the Delaware River, a large English population everywhere, a substantial black population, most of them slaves but many free, and even a Jewish community. (The Jews were not to Stuyvesant's liking; he wanted to expel them but was overruled by his bosses in the West India Company.)

Stuyvesant had two problems he could not overcome: his personal unpopularity and England's unease with the Dutch wedge between New England colonies and the tobacco colonies. After seventeen years as governor, Stuyvesant had offended just about everyone in the town of New Amsterdam, including his council. In 1664, four warships sailing for the Duke of York (Charles I's brother) threatened to bombard New Amsterdam if it did not accept English rule. However, the commmander, James Nichols, offered generous terms if the Dutch did not resist: The Dutch language and the Dutch Reformed Church would have official status and Dutch inheritance laws, which differed significantly from England's, would be enforced.

Stuyvesant wanted to fight. In a rage, he ripped to pieces the letter from Nichols. But New Netherlands' number two man, Nicholas De Sille, pieced the document together and the Council unanimously overruled the sputtering governor. Without a shot, New Netherlands became New York, New Amsterdam the city of New York.

A Successful Transition

New York was the Duke of York's proprietary colony until, in 1685, he was crowned King James II, whence it became a royal colony. James II, extremely unpopular at home because he was a Roman Catholic who heaped favors on Catholic nobles, was welcomed in New York, at first, because his policies were more liberal than the crusty Stuyvesant. Few Dutch departed. De Sille stayed as, indeed, did Stuyvesant, who owned a good deal of property. And Dutch immigrants continued to come to the colony.

In 1689, after King James II was dethroned back home, a German merchant, Jacob Leisler, led a somewhat ragtag group to seize control of New York City. He proclaimed his loyalty to England's new rulers, William (a Dutchman) and Mary (James II's daughter). But when their troops arrived to restore order, Leisler's men fired on them. They were arrested and eight were sentenced to hang; just two were; six were pardoned. Leisler and one other man were hang; the six were pardoned. William and Mary restored James II's policies of tolerance.

The Carolina Grant

In 1663 (a year before the takeover of New York), Charles II granted the land lying between 36° and 31° north latitude

A Bizarre Constitution

The Carolina proprietors had bizarre plans for their colony. The scheme was outlined in The Fundamental Constitutions of Carolina, the brainchild of Anthony Ashley Cooper (later the Earl of Shaftesbury). Its 120 painfully detailed articles were written by his secretary, John Locke, who must have found them absurd for he is known to history as a philosopher of political liberty.

The Fundamental Constitutions divided Carolina into square counties, in each of which the proprietors (the "seigneurs") owned 96,000 acres. Other contrived ranks of nobility called "caciques" (an Indian title) and "landgraves" (European) had smaller, but still ample tracts. Humble "leetmen" (a medieval term) and even humbler African slaves, over whom their owners had "absolute power and authority" would contribute the labor.

Was it all a promotional device designed to attract buyers of land with the promise of a puffed-up title? Maybe. But in 1671, Sir John Yeamans claimed the right to be governor because he was a landgrave and the appointed governor a mere cacique. In any case, with land so abundant, the constitution was unworkable and repeatedly revised. It did not much affect the actual development of the Carolinas.

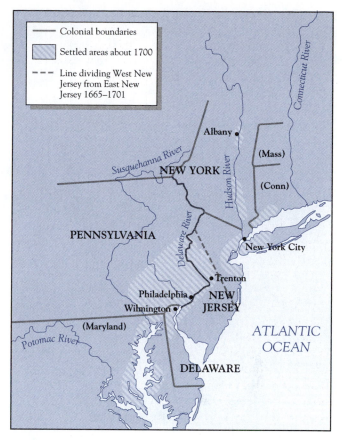

MAP 3:2 **The Middle Colonies.** All the middle colonies except Pennsylvania were carved out of Dutch New Netherlands, which claimed as its borders the Delaware and Connecticut Rivers. (In fact, a number of Dutch farmers had settled in Pennsylvania before it was granted to William Penn in 1681 and New Sweden, which the Dutch seized, was west of Delaware Bay.) New Netherlands surrendered to an English fleet in 1664. All the middle colonies (New York, New Jersey, Pennsylvania, and Delaware) were originally proprietary colonies under the English. Pennsylvania remained a Penn family property. New York, New Jersey, and Delaware all became royal colonies.

(the northern boundary of the state of North Carolina and the southern boundary of South Carolina) to eight nobles and gentlemen, including Virginia's governor, Sir Wiliam Berkeley. There were already a few colonists living on Albemarle Sound within the new colony of Carolina (named for the king; *Carolus* is Latin for Charles). They had been sent there by Berkeley a decade earlier to defend Virginia's southernmost plantations from the Tuscarora Indians. Even after the eight proprietors took over, however, population grew slowly. Most settlers were rather poor, small-scale farmers who dribbled down from Virginia.

Carolina's first significant settlement was farther south, Charleston (more flattery of the king), founded in 1669. Many of the first white settlers were planters from the West Indian island of Barbados, where land had become exorbitantly expensive. Barbados was England's most lucrative colony. It grew sugar, for which all Europe had developed a craving. The cane was planted and harvested by African slaves who worked far harder and were treated far worse than blacks in Virginia, Maryland, and New York. The Barbadans brought both their slaves and their harsh slavery laws to southern Carolina.

At first, the economy of Charleston and its hinterlands was diversified. The whites bought hides and furs from the Muskohegan tribes which reached as far into the interior as present day Alabama. Timber (and other naval stores) were harvested from Carolina's pine forests. Some tobacco was grown and, on the sandy "sea islands" that rimmed the coastline, cotton. All except the fur trade depended on slave labor, and the African population increased faster than the white population. By 1700, half of Carolina's 5,000 people

were African or African Americans, a far greater proportion than in any other English colony.

Indeed, African slaves introduced the crop that made South Carolina rich. They had grown rice in Africa and discovered that the marshy lowlands along the Ashley and Cooper Rivers made ideal rice fields. As an export, rice was less lucrative than sugar but more profitable than tobacco. The slaves found themselves raising not their food on a small scale but rice by the hundreds of tons on large plantations.

Two Carolinas

The settlements of northern and southern Carolina were separated by 300 miles of sandy beaches, islands, pinewoods, swamps, and meandering waterways. Overland connections barely existed; communication was by sea. The two regions differed economically and socially. The northerners grew tobacco, mostly on farms rather than large plantations. Few whites owned slaves, none in large numbers. Charleston, the colonial capital virtually ignored the northern settlements.

Colonial Williamsburg Foundation

Charleston, South Carolina, was the only real city south of Philadelphia. Built between the Ashley and Cooper Rivers, it had a superb harbor from which to export rice, cotton, furs and hides, and, later, indigo. More African slaves were imported into Charleston than into any other port.

The rice planters of southern Carolina prospered, the biggest landowners became fabulously rich. Unlike Virginia tobacco planters, however, Carolina rice growers did not live on their lands. The low country that produced their wealth was, due to mosquito-borne diseases like malaria and yellow fever and waterborne sickness, an unhealthy place. It was, a resident said, "in the spring a paradise, in the summer a hell, and in the autumn a hospital." Carolina's elite built town houses in Charleston, which was open to sea breezes, and left the sickness and death of the pestilential rice plantations to white overseers poor enough to risk their lives and slaves, who had no choice in the matter. If the rice grandees visited their plantations at all (and many did not for years at a time), it was for a month or two in winter and spring. Thus, unlike in Virginia, where planters lived among their servants and

slaves, southern Carolina's elite was urban, interested in the land only in that it enriched them.

For administrative purposes, the increasingly unpopular proprietors divided the colony into North and South Carolina with separate assemblies. It was not enough. The proprietors' ineffective defense against Indian attacks and a raid by the Spanish and French caused an ongoing, sometimes violent unrest among the whites of Albemarle Sound. In 1729, the Crown revoked the proprietors' charter and established North and South Carolina as separate royal colonies.

New Jersey and the Quakers

New Jersey began as two colonies and ended up as one. In 1665, the Duke of York gave Lord John Berkeley and Sir George Carteret the part of his Dutch conquest west of

Thou, Thy, and Thee

Like French, Spanish, Italian, and German, the English language once had two forms of the pronoun with which to address a person. *Thou* (like *tu* in French) was used when speaking to family members, intimate friends, children, social inferiors, and God in prayer—it survives in the Christian Lord's Prayer: "hallowed be thy name." *You* (like *vous* in French) was for formal conversation, with casual acquaintances, strangers, and when addressing social superiors.

Thou, thy, and *thee* were going out of style in the late 1600s in favor of using *you* in all cases, as we do today. However, the rules were well known. When Quakers expressed their belief in the spiritual equality of all by addressing strangers, judges, and even nobles as *thou, thy,* and *thee,* it was taken as profoundly ill-mannered, an insult. Not, however, by Charles II when his favorite Quaker, William Penn, called him *thee.* The king thought it was great fun.

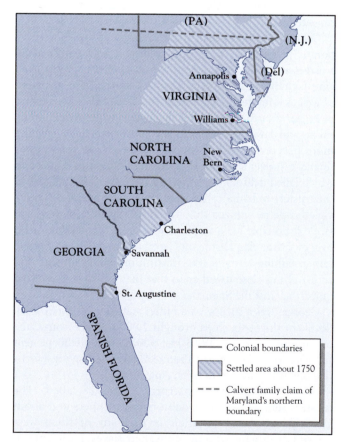

MAP 3:3 **The Southern Colonies.** The Carolina colony was chartered in 1663, a year before the English seized New York from the Dutch. But it developed slowly except around Charleston in the south and the two rivers, the Ashley and the Cooper, between which Charleston was built. Georgia was chartered in 1713 to serve as a buffer between the Spanish in Florida and valuable Charleston.

the Hudson River. The two proprietors divided their grant roughly north to south, Carteret taking East New Jersey facing New York harbor and the Atlantic, Berkeley the western half facing the Delaware River. In 1674, West New Jersey was sold to two members of a fringe religious sect, the Society of Friends, or "Quakers." (Members trembled with emotion at their religious services.)

The Quakers were ridiculed, harassed, and sometimes brutally persecuted in old England and in Massachusetts. Masachusetts hanged several of them when, after they were banished to Rhode Island, they returned and resumed preaching their belief that God communicated directly with all men and women. Their doctrine was more obnoxious to the Puritans than Anne Hutchinson's. She had said that God directly inspired some people; the Quakers said God inspired everyone.

The Friends worried authorities in old England because they were pacifists. Friends were forbidden to take up arms, even in self-defense. Armies of the era were not made up of draftees, but pacifism was still bothersome because war was a routine way of effecting national policy. Then, the Quakers said that because of every person's divine "inner light," there was no need for priests, ministers, or bishops. They challenged the Church of England more radically than Puritans did.

When hauled into court, Quakers refused to take oaths—to swear on the Bible. Some refused to remove their hats in the presence of social superiors, a pointed insult to magistrates because most Quakers were of the lowest ranks of English society.

Finally, the doctrine of the equality of all before God meant that women participated in Quaker services and preached in the streets. It was an affront to one of society's most basic assumptions, that women were subordinate to men and played no role in public life.

The proprietors of West New Jersey hoped that their coreligionists would flee persecution at home, go to their colony for religious freedom, and, of course, purchase land from them. They did. Beginning in 1675, Quakers by the thousand crossed the ocean, mostly, at first, to West New Jersey. It was a "great migration" almost as carefully orchestrated as the Puritan migration a generation earlier. In 1682, 2,000 Quakers came to America in twenty-three ships. Between 1682 and 1685, ninety ships brought more Quakers

Eccentrics Welcome

William Penn's toleration extended to eccentrics. In 1694, a German, Johannes Kelpius, and about forty followers who called themselves "The Woman in the Wilderness," built a 40-foot by 40-foot "monastery" outside Philadelphia. They had individual cells but gathered in a common room to eat, pray, study, and perform chemistry experiments. Kelpius kept a telescope on the roof; it was attended around the clock. Suffering no interference, Woman in the Wilderness survived for fifty years. Its third leader, affectionately known as *Der alte Matthai* (Old Matthew) wandered benignly around Philadelphia carrying an alpenstock.

King Charles II receiving William Penn. Royal protocol held that no one wore a hat in the king's presence. Quakers taught that no man took off his hat for another because all were equal before God. Penn's behavior was so outrageous that it amused rather than offended the good-natured king.

Reproduced from the Collections of the Library of Congress, Prints and Photographs Division, Washington, D.C.

to America than remained in England. By 1750, the Society of Friends was the third largest religious denomination in English America. By 1683, however, most headed not for New Jersey, but for a new colony on the western bank of the Delaware.

Pennsylvania: "The Holy Experiment"

Charles II had a lot of courtiers and creditors clamoring for favors. Proprietary colonies were a cheap way to oblige them. They cost the king nothing.

The most unusual of the king's beneficiaries, and the most successful proprietor he created, was William Penn, the wealthiest and most influential Quaker in England, and the most visionary. That so highly placed a gentleman should worship with cobblers and housemaids amused the good-natured king. When Penn, hat on head, was ushered into the his presence, Charles removed his own headgear, remarking that it was customary, when the king was present, for only one man to wear a hat.

Charles owed Penn £16,000 for services Penn's dead father, an admiral in the navy, had rendered. In 1681, to cancel the debt, he carved what is now the state of Pennsylvania out of the Duke of York's property and chartered the land to Penn as Pennsylvania—"Penn's Woods." The king picked the name, not Penn, in honor of Penn's father. For Charles II, it was a bargain: He disposed of a £16,000 debt with distant woodland when other proprietorships were changing hands for £1,000. The next year, Penn purchased what is now Delaware from the Duke of York, annexing it to Pennsylvania as the "three lower counties." (Delaware was detached from Pennsylvania in 1701 and became a royal colony. New Jersey, where William Penn also was a proprietor, became a royal colony the same year.)

Penn envisioned his colony not only as a refuge for Quakers but as a "Holy Experiment" governed on Quaker principles. All religious faiths were tolerated. Penn paid the Indians higher prices for land than the governments of other colonies and insisted that the natives be treated justly. Early Pennsylvania suffered no Indian wars. And he sold land at bargain prices, a shilling to 3s. an acre at a time when a carpenter made 3s. a day in wages.

Philadelphia (like Charleston) was a planned city. The streets of the "greene countrie towne" were laid out on a gridiron, making possible a tidiness that even the well-ordered Puritans had been unable to command of Boston. Philadelphia became the largest and most prosperous city in English North America, partly because of Quaker liberality. By the mid-1700s, it was "the second city of the British empire," smaller only than London in the English-speaking world.

Georgia: A Philanthropic Experiment

Georgia was the thirteenth colony. It was chartered in 1732, with Savannah established the next year, as a military buffer state protecting valuable South Carolina from the Spanish in Florida. Spanish forces had seriously threatened Charleston during a war between 1702 and 1713. A tough, battle-hardened soldier, James Oglethorpe, was put in command of Georgia to ensure the threat was not repeated.

Command is the proper word. Georgia was neither a corporate, proprietary, nor royal colony. It was governed by trustees who met in England. Most of them sympathized with Oglethorpe's vision of Georgia as a social experiment as well as a fortress. Oglethorpe was troubled by the misery of England's urban poor, the alcoholism widespread among them, and laws that imprisoned people for debt, creating more poverty as well as convicts guilty of, at worst, poor financial judgement. He thought of Georgia as a place in which jailed debtors might have a fresh start. He persuaded the trustees to ban alcohol from the colony and also slavery. Oglethorpe recognized that, in South Carolina, slavery had made it possible for a small elite of great planters to lord it over everyone else. He meant Georgia to be a colony of small, self-sustaining farmers (the maximum land grant was fifty acres), living close together so that they could be mobilized quickly against the Spanish.

Georgia was a success as a buffer state. In 1742, a Spanish flotilla of thirty-six ships brought 2,000 soldiers from Cuba to capture Savannah. With just 900 men, Oglethorpe sent them packing. Oglethorpe then retaliated, destroying a fortified Spanish town north of St. Augustine.

As a philanthropic enterprise, Georgia failed. The trustees sent about 1,800 debtors and paupers and about 1,000 people came on their own. Many of them were South Carolinians who brought their slaves in defiance of Georgia law. Oglethorpe, although as tyrannical a personality as Peter Stuyvesant, could not stop them. Nor could he keep Georgians away from their rum. He returned to England disgusted. In 1752 the trustees surrendered control of the colony to the king, a year earlier than the charter required.

Puritan Sunday

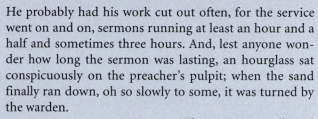

On Sunday mornings, before sunrise in winter, Puritan families bundled up and walked to the meeting house. Few skipped services, even during a blizzard; absence meant a fine. The walk was usually short; most New Englanders lived in villages, their homes clustered around the meetinghouse. The compactness was deliberate, to reinforce the feeling of community. In 1652, Plymouth called Joseph Ramsden on the carpet for locating his house off by itself. He was admonished "to bring his wife and family with all convenient speed near into some neighborhood."

It was a *meetinghouse,* not a *church.* To call the simple, unpainted clapboard structure a church would have been "popish." The Puritans shunned every emblem hinting of Catholicism. There were no statues or other embellishments such as adorned Catholic and Anglican churches. If there was a steeple (called a belfry), it was crowned by a weathercock, not a cross. That reminded the congregation that St. Peter denied that he knew Christ three times before the cock crowed. The sinfulness of all was a theme on which the Puritans constantly harped.

In winter, the meetinghouse was scarcely warmer than the snowy fields outside. There may have been a fireplace, but the heat did not reach those sitting more than ten feet from it. The congregation bundled in fur envelopes—*not* sleeping bags; there was a fine for nodding off. People rested their feet on brass or iron footwarmers holding coals brought from home. If footwarmers were prohibited as a fire hazard, worshipers might bring a well-trained dog to lie on their feet.

Women sat on the left side of the meetinghouse with their daughters. Men sat on the right, but boys, apt to be mischievous, were placed around the pulpit where a warden could lash out at the fidgety ones with a switch.

He probably had his work cut out often, for the service went on and on, sermons running at least an hour and a half and sometimes three hours. And, lest anyone wonder how long the sermon was lasting, an hourglass sat conspicuously on the preacher's pulpit; when the sand finally ran down, oh so slowly to some, it was turned by the warden.

The Puritans allowed no instrumental music in the meetinghouses, but they sang psalms from the *Bay Psalm Book,* published in Massachusetts. It was composed with accuracy of translation in mind, not poetry. Psalms exquisitely beautiful in the King James version of the Bible (which the Puritans did not use, preferring the William Tyndale translation) were awkward and strained. For example, in the Puritan translation, the magnificent Psalm 100 is barely comprehensible.

> The rivers on of Babylon, there when we did sit downe; Yes even then we mourned, when we remembered Sion. Our harp we did hang it amid upon the willow tree, Because there they thus away led in captivitie, Required of us a song, thus asks mirth; us waste who laid Sing us among a Sion's song unto us then they said.

Puritan singing appalled outsiders; it was a "horrid medley of confused and disorderly noises."

Services ended about noon. Families returned home for a meal that had been prepared before sundown the previous day. Like Jews on the sabbath, the Puritans took the Lord's Day seriously: no cooking, no work, certainly no play. Conversation was spare. It was no more proper to talk about workaday tasks than to perform them. Pious families discussed the morning's sermon or other religious subjects. In the afternoon, they returned to the meetinghouse to hear community announcements and another sermon.

FURTHER READING

Classics Charles M. Andrews in *The Colonial Period of American History,* 1934–1938; Daniel Boorstin, *The Americans: The Colonial Experience,* 1958; William Bradford, *History of Plimmoth Plantation* (numerous editions); Perry Miller, *Orthodoxy in Massachusetts, 1630–1650,* 1933; *The New England Mind: The Seventeenth Century,* 1939; Edmund S. Morgan, *The Puritan Dilemma,* 1958.

General David Hackett Fisher's *Albion's Seed: Four British Folkways in America,* 1989; Alan Taylor, *American Colonies,* 2001; Jack P. Greene, *Pursuits of Happiness: The Social Development of Early Modern British Colonies and the Formation of American Culture,* 1988 and Jack P. Greene and J. R. Pole, eds., *Colonial British America, 1607–1789,* 1984; John J. McCusker and Russell Menard, *The Economy of British North America,* 1985; Stanley Katz, *Colonial America:*

Essays in Political and Social Development, 1992; John E. Pomfret and Floyd Shumway, *Founding the American Colonies,* 1970; Alison Games, *Migration and the Origins of the English Atlantic World,* 1999; John Ferling, *Struggle for a Continent: The Wars of Early America,* 1993.

New England George Langdon, *Pilgrim Colony: A History of New Plymouth, 1620–1691,* 1966, and John Demos, *A Little Commonwealth: Family Life in Plymouth Colony,* 1970; Nathaniel Philbrick, *Mayflower: A Story of Courage, Community, and War,* 2006; Colin G. Calloway, *Dawnland Encounters: Indians and Europeans in Northern New England,* 1991 and *New Worlds for All: Indians, Europeans, and the Remaking of Early America,* 1997; David Cressy, *Coming Over: Migration and Communication Between England and New England in the Seventeenth Century,* 1987; Harry Stout, *The New England Soul: Preaching and Culture in Colonial New England,* 1986; Charles Hambrick-Stowe, *The Practice of Piety,* 1982; David Hall, *Worlds of Wonder, Days of Judgment: Popular Religious Belief in Early New England,* 1989; Andrew Delbanco, *The Puritan Ordeal,* 1989. Emery Battis, *Saints and Sectarians: Anne Hutchinson and the Antinomian Controversy in Massachusetts,* 1962 and Sydney V. James, *Colonial Rhode Island: A History,* 1975.

The Middle Colonies Edwin B. Bronner, *William Penn's "Holy Experiment,"* 1962; Gary Nash, *Quakers and Politics: Pennsylvania, 1681–1726,* 1971; James T. Lemon, *The Best Poor Man's Country: A Geographical Study of Early Southeastern Pennsylvania,* 1972; Richard and Mary Dunn, *The World of William Penn,* 1986; Michael Kammen, *Colonial New York,* 1975; Robert C. Ritchie, *The Duke's Province,* 1977; Joyce D. Goodfriend, *Before the Melting Pot: Society and Culture in Colonial New York City, 1664–1730,* 1992; Russell Shorto, *The Island at the Center of the World: The Epic Story of Dutch Manhattan,* 2004; Edwin G. Burrows and Mike Wallace, *Gotham: A History of New York City to 1898,* 1999; J. E. Pomfret, *The Province of East and West New Jersey,* 1956; Brendan McConville, *These Daring Disturbers of the Public Peace: The Struggle for Property and Power in Early New Jersey,* 1999.

The Carolinas and Georgia William S. Powell, *Colonial North Carolina,* 1973; Eugene Sirmans, *Colonial South Carolina,* 1966; Robert M. Weir, *Colonial South Carolina: A History,* 1983; Robert Orwell, *Masters, Slaves, and Subjects: The Culture of Power in the South Carolina Low Country,* 1998; Phinizy Spalding, *Oglethorpe in America,* 1977.

KEY TERMS

Use the following listing of key terms to review important figures, events, locations, and concepts covered in this chapter. A glossary of these terms is available on *The American Past* companion Web site: www.cengage.com/history/conlin/tap9e

Pilgrims, p. 39

Puritans, p. 42

Winthrop, John, p. 43

blue laws, p. 43

Williams, Roger, p. 45

Hutchinson, Anne, p. 46

corporate colony, p. 47

royal colony, p. 47

proprietary colony, p. 47

Penn, William, p. 52

ONLINE RESOURCES

Find additional resources, including primary source documents, images, interactive maps, simulations, chapter review exercises, and Internet links at

The American Past **companion Web site**
www.cengage.com/history/conlin/tap9e

American History Resource Center
http://ushistory.wadsworth.com/

DISCOVERY

Did the differences between Native American and European cultures make violence, conflict, and the ultimate destruction of the Indians inevitable? If so, why? If not, why not?

Culture and Society: What is the artist who drew this early European depiction of Native Americans trying to tell his fellow Europeans about the Indians' culture? What is the message about the Indians in this excerpt from the writings of Father Bartolomé de Las Casas, a Dominican friar in the Americas?

Bartolomé de Las Casas, "Of the Island of Hispaniola" (1542)

God has created all these numberless people to be quite the simplest, without malice or duplicity, most obedient, most faithful to their natural Lords, and to the Christians, whom they serve; the most humble, most patient, most peaceful and calm, without strife nor tumults; not wrangling, nor querulous, as free from uproar, hate and desire of revenge as any in the world....

Among these gentle sheep, gifted by their Maker with the above qualities, the Spaniards entered as soon as they knew them, like wolves, tiger and lions which had been starving for many days, and since forty years they have done nothing else; nor do they afflict, torment, and destroy them with strange and new, and divers kinds of cruelty, never before seen, nor heard of, nor read of....

The Christians, with their horses and swords and lances, began to slaughter and practice strange cruelty among them. They penetrated into the country and spared neither children nor the aged, nor pregnant women, nor those in child labour, all of whom they ran through the body and lacerated, as though they were assaulting so many lambs herded in their sheepfold.

Leonard de Selva/CORBIS

Portrayal of Native Americans

What did the early colonies have in common because of their English origins? How did the intentions and goals of the founders of the early colonies contribute to differences among them?

Geography: Based on these three maps, what geographical feature did all of the early colonies have in common?

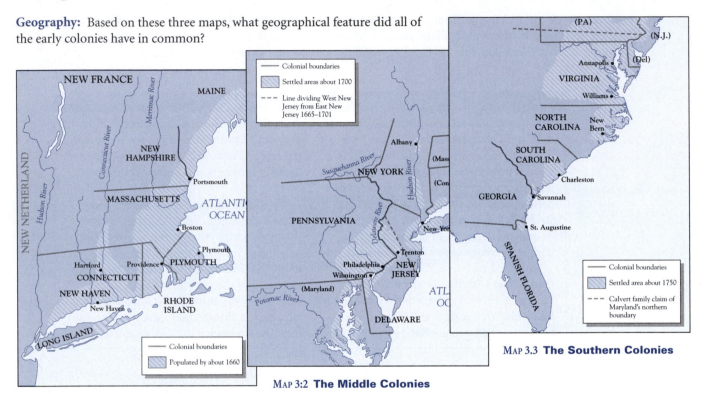

MAP 3.3 **The Southern Colonies**

MAP 3.2 **The Middle Colonies**

MAP 3.1 **The New England Colonies**

Mayflower Compact

We, whose names are underwritten, the Loyal Subjects of our dread Sovereign Lord King James . . . . Having undertaken for the Glory of God and Advancement of the Christian Faith, and the Honour of Our King and Country, a Voyage to plant the first colony in the northern parts of Virginia; Do by these Presents solemnly and mutually in the Presence of God and one another, covenant and combine ourselves together into a civil Body Politick, for our better Ordering and Preservation, and Furtherance of the Ends aforesaid; And by Virtue hereof do enact, constitute, and frame, such just and equal Laws, Ordinances, Acts, Constitutions, and Offices, from time to time, as shall be thought most meet and convenient for the general Good of the Colony; unto which we promise all due Submission and Obedience. . . .

Government and Law: The "Mayflower Compact" was drawn up and signed aboard ship by a majority of the men among the settlers of Plymouth Colony before they went ashore. Why? What does the document say about the goals of the "Pilgrim Fathers" and their intentions for the future? Why did they think such a statement advisable?

To read extended versions of selected documents, visit the companion Web site www.cengage.com/history/conlin/tap9e; click on "Discovery Sources"

Reproduced from the Collections of the Library of Congress

Chapter 4

English Designs, American Facts of Life

Colonial Society in the 1600s

And those that came were resolved to be Englishmen,
Gone to the world's end but English every one,
And they ate the white corn kernels, parched in the sun
And they knew it not but they'd not be English again

—*Stephen Vincent Benét*

In 1660, King Charles II was an exile. He had fled England when a Parliamentary army defeated his father in battle, then beheaded him. For a decade, the "Commonwealth of England" was governed by a military dictator, a Puritan, Oliver Cromwell.

Cromwell died in 1658 and England's experiment with republican government was over. People generally were weary of Cromwell's Massachusetts-like blue laws: no theater, no games on Sunday, and so on. Powerful nobles, men never comfortable without a king, invited Charles II to return.

Charles executed the men who had signed his father's death warrant, and he scrapped the blue laws. However, he endorsed other legislation enacted by the Commonwealth, among them a series of "Navigation Acts" that set down the rules governing colonial trade. Charles II was not the wisest of kings, but he understood, as he said in 1668, "the thing that is nearest the heart of the nation is trade." The Navigation Acts of the 1660s defined England's and, later, Great Britain's colonial policy—laws regulating the colonies' trade—for more than a century.

TRADE

A nation's overseas trade was central to a theory of national wealth and greatness later called mercantilism. It was first described systematically by Thomas Mun, a shareholder in the greatest trading venture of all, the East India Company.

English and British

Even today the terms *English* and *British* are often confused. *English* refers to a language, of course, and to a nationality. Henry VII, John Cabot's patron, was king of England, so the colonies founded on the basis of Cabot's discoveries were *English* colonies. In 1603, the king of Scotland became King James I of England. Scotland and England never again had different monarchs. However, the two countries retained their own parliaments, laws—and possessions. There was a Scots colony in Central America, but it collapsed almost immediately; the colonies that existed were England's.

Until 1707: In that year, England and Scotland were united under one Parliament as the United Kingdom of Great Britain. Nationally, Scots remained Scots and English English, but both were also now British, and the American colonies became British colonies.

Mun's book, *England's Treasure by Foreign Trade*, was published during Charles II's reign, in 1664.

Mercantilism

The object of mercantilism was to strengthen England (or France or Spain or the Netherlands) by increasing the nation's hoard of coin: gold and silver—the gold and silver in

55

Boundary Dispute

One of several border disputes resulting from the Crown's carelessness in granting American lands pitted Maryland against Pennsylvania. In the Maryland charter of 1632, the colony's northern line was set vaguely at "under the Fortieth Degree of North Latitude." William Penn's charter, granted fifty years later, set Pennsylvania's southern line at 40° north latitude.

So what was the problem?

The problem was that William Penn, misinformed by an incompetent surveyor that the 40th parallel was forty miles farther south than it actually is, located his capital, Philadelphia, just below 40°. The city was thriving when Penn's mistake was discovered so he was not about to abandon his "greene countrie towne" to the Calverts of Maryland.

Luckily for Penn, there was that vague phrase "under the Fortieth Degree" in Maryland's charter. And the Penn family was in better odor at court than the Calverts were. Pennsylvania kept Philadelphia.

Exactly where the Pennsylvania-Maryland line ran, however, was disputed until 1763 when two surveyors employed by both colonies, Charles Mason and Jeremiah Dixon, began to mark it at 39°, 43′, 18″, the "Mason-Dixon Line."

Victoria and Albert Museum, V & A Picture Library

An English merchant's warehouse and wharf. His "counting room"—office—was inside and often his family's residence too. Vessels were unloaded and loaded on wharfs like this one stretching for miles on the Thames, London's river, and in Plymouth, Bristol, and other ports.

the possession of all the realm's subjects, not just what was in the royal treasury. The key to accumulating coin, Mun said, was a favorable balance of trade, that is, for the English "to sell more to strangers yearly"—to foreigners—"than wee consume of theirs in value." Thus the word *mercantilism* (*mercator* is Latin for merchant) for merchants engaged in overseas trade were the country's moneymakers and merchants were mercantilism's chief proponents and beneficiaries.

So, the argument ran, when a merchant dispatched a ship from Bristol to West Africa with a cargo of woolen cloth, traded the cloth for slaves, transported the slaves to Spanish Cuba where they were exchanged for sugar which was sold in Italy or Denmark for gold, the profit on each transaction increased "England's treasure" at the expense of every other party involved. African chiefs, Cuba, Denmark, and Italy were expending wealth in order to consume; English merchants were bringing gold home.

The merchants' success depended on the government—the Crown—acting aggressively to nurture, protect, encourage, and favor them with subsidies, special privileges such as monopolies, and naval protection. To a mercantilist, there was no better reason for a nation to go to war than to protect or to expand foreign trade, and no issue more important when writing peace treaties than winning control of overseas ports or concessions for England's merchants. In 1713, in a treaty ending a successful war with Spain, Great Britain took

Colonial Society and Economy 1600–1700

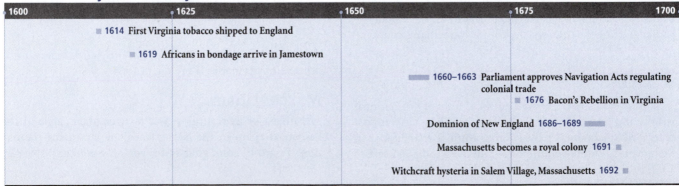

1600	1625	1650	1675	1700

■ 1614 First Virginia tobacco shipped to England

■ 1619 Africans in bondage arrive in Jamestown

1660–1663 Parliament approves Navigation Acts regulating colonial trade

■ 1676 Bacon's Rebellion in Virginia

Dominion of New England 1686–1689

Massachusetts becomes a royal colony 1691 ■

Witchcraft hysteria in Salem Village, Massachusetts 1692 ■

as its prize the *Assiento,* the privilege of selling 4,800 African slaves each year in Spain's colonies.

Manufacturing was important to mercantilists. Manufacturing added cash value to raw materials at no cash expense. Even in the Middle Ages, England's kings concluded that it was economic lunacy to export raw wool to the low countries (present-day Belguim and Holland) and then buy it back in the form of cloth. The cloth, having been spun into yarn, woven, and dyed in the low countries, commanded a considerably higher price than the sacks of English wool from which it was made. The difference in value was gold and silver drained out of the England.

So the Crown banned the export of raw wool. Through subsidies and other favors, kings and Parliaments encouraged the spinners, weavers, and dyers whose skills and labor added to the value of English cloth to be sold abroad. In treaties with other states, forced on them by the mouths of cannon, if necessary, the Crown secured markets for the nation's clothmakers. Seventeenth-century mercantilists urged the Crown to promote other kinds of manufacturing—of finished iron goods, for example—with similar inducements.

The Colonial Connection

In a perfect world, England would be self-sufficient. Its people would produce everything they consumed and buy nothing abroad. Gold and silver earned from exports would roll in; none would depart.

In the real world, self-sufficiency was impossible. An island nation in a northerly latitude, England imported any number of tropical products. Cotton came from Egypt and the Middle East; silk from Italy and East Asia; spices (of course; always spices) came from the Indies, and by the end of the seventeenth century, the tea of Ceylon and China had made its appearance, soon to become the national beverage.

The English produced little wine but they drank a good deal of it. It was imported from France, Portugal, and the German states of the Rhineland. Sugar was still a luxury but getting cheaper; those who could afford it bought lots of it, increasingly from the West Indies. The English purchased furs both for luxurious adornment and for the manufacture of felt for hats. The finest furs came from Muscovy, as Russia was known.

As a maritime nation, Britain consumed vast quantities of timber just to build ships. A full-size warship consumed 2,000 oak trees, some of them 1½ feet in diameter. But the country's forests had been thinned by centuries of harvesting; over much of the country they had disappeared. "Good old English oak" was not plentiful enough to meet the planking needs of the nation's many shipyards. Virtually all the long straight-grained trees from which masts were made had to be purchased in Scandinavia. Teak, to become invaluable to ship builders because of its resistance to rot, and luxurious woods like mahogany and black, iron-hard ebony were tropical. Then there were the other naval stores, tar, pitch, and turpentine manufactured from pine, and fiber for the manufacture of rope.

This is where colonies entered the mercantilist equation. Colonies reduced England's dependence on foreign lands for both essential imports and luxuries. By seizing islands in the West Indies like Barbados (in 1627) and Jamaica (1655), the English created dependable sources of sugar both to sate its own people's sweet tooth and to sell to other countries. A shaky English enclave in Central America (present-day Belize) shipped mahogany and logwood (source of a precious dye) back home. The North American colonies were almost entirely forested with both hardwoods like oak and maple and, in New England, with towering, straight-grained pines. The woods teemed with beaver, mink, otter, and other furred animals, and with deer, the hides of which made a leather more versatile than leather from cattle and sheep. And, of course, there was tobacco, which had almost as hungry a world market as sugar's.

Money spent in the colonies had to be subtracted from the national store of gold and silver but not so much as had to be paid to foreign suppliers. Few imports from

Courtesy Murray Harbour, Prince Edward Island, Canada

Shipbuilders lined every navigable river in England. They needed prodigious quantities of lumber, particularly well-seasoned ("winter-cut"), flawless oak for the ribs of vessels. Scholars estimate that the largest naval vessels consumed parts of 2,000 oak trees! North America—one sprawling forest—was a major source of supply. New England's pineries also provided long, straight-grained "mast trees."

the colonies were paid for with coin. Mercantilists—the Crown—defined colonies as producers of (cheap) raw materials and colonials as consumers of (costly) manufactures. The balance of trade was favorable to the mother country—exceedingly favorable—as long as the mother country made the rules.

The Navigation Acts

The Navigation Acts of 1660–1663 minced no words in defining the purpose of the American colonies as the enrichment of the mother country. The welfare of the colonies was not entirely ignored. However, when the economic interests of colonials clashed with the economic interests of the English, the latter were the ones who counted. Colonies were tributaries of empire; they were not partners with the mother country.

So, the Navigation Acts stipulated that all colonial trade had be carried in vessels built and owned by English or colonial merchants. These ships were to be manned by crews in which at least three seamen in four were English or colonials. Not even lowly seamen's wages were to be paid to foreigners who might take their meager earnings home with them.

Next, the Navigation Acts required that European goods intended for sale in the colonies be carried first to certain English ports designated as entrepôts (places from which goods are distributed: clearing houses). There they were monitored, taxed, and only then shipped to America. The purpose of this law was to ensure a precise record of colonial trade, to collect taxes on, for example, French, Spanish, and Portugese wines (which were coveted in the colonies), and to see to it that English merchants and even port laborers benefited from transactions that involved foreign products.

The Navigation Acts designated some colonial exports—the most valuable—enumerated articles. These could be shipped only to English ports, even if they were destined for sale elsewhere. Once again, the object was to ensure that part of the profit in the colonies' sales in Europe or Africa went into English purses. Enumerated articles bound for France or Poland or Italy were taxed. These duties were an important source of government revenue. Charles II collected a fabulous £100,000 a year just from the tax on tobacco.

The enumerated articles included most colonial products that readily sold on the world market: sugar and the molasses made from sugar, furs and hides, naval stores, rice, cotton, and tobacco. Foodstuffs—grain, livestock, salted fish, lumber not suited to shipbuilding—"bulk goods"—were less profitable and not enumerated. Rum, because it was so cheap, was overlooked. Colonials could ship these products directly to foreign ports, and they did. The North American colonies fed the sugar islands of the West Indies—French, Spanish, Dutch, and Danish (when they would buy) as well as English—and New England annually shipped thousands of tons of salted cod to Portugal, Spain, and Italy.

MERCANTILISM IN THE SOUTH

The Navigation Acts applied to every colony, to Barbados and Bermuda as well as to Rhode Island and Virginia. However, the colonies' widely varying climates and landforms meant that they had sharply differing economies. These and different social structures meant that England's commercial code affected colonials in sharply differing ways.

Well before 1700, the North American colonies were defined geographically: the New England colonies, the southern colonies, and the middle colonies. New England was New Hampshire, Massachusetts (including Maine), Rhode Island, and Connecticut. The southern colonies were Maryland, Virginia, North Carolina, South Carolina, and, after 1732, Georgia. In between were what had been New Netherlands, the middle colonies: New York, New Jersey, Pennsylvania, and Delaware.

English merchants prized the southern colonies. Like the sugar islands of the West Indies, they grew two profitable enumerated articles: tobacco and rice. Like the West Indies, the southern colonies were home to a large, bonded labor force, mostly white servants in the 1600s, black slaves after 1700. Their masters had to clothe and shoe these laborers with English manufactures and provide them with tools manufactured in the mother country. On top of that, by 1700, the planter elite of Maryland, Virginia, and South Carolina was rich enough to covet and consume every luxury that ever a merchant thought to load on a sailing ship.

Tobacco's Luster Lost

American colonists were given a monopoly of tobacco production in England's empire; English farmers were forbidden to grow the crop. But it was not so great a favor by the 1660s. The heady days of 3 shillings per pound tobacco were long gone. As more and more acres of Maryland and Virginia (and, on a smaller scale, North Carolina) were planted in tobacco, the wholesale price of tobacco (the price at which the planters sold to tobacco factors, as merchants were sometimes called) declined to 3d. (three pence) a pound, and then to 1d. and, in some years, less. So much leaf was being grown that the world's smokers, chewers, and snorters no longer demanded it at any price. It was cheap.

Complaining about the forces of a world marketplace was like complaining about the weather. Tobacco planters could do nothing about either. They could, however, blame hard times on the Navigation Acts. The Dutch reached markets the English did not, planters argued, but the Navigation Acts forbade selling tobacco (an enumerated article) to the Dutch. Planters complained: "If the Hollanders must not trade to

The Tobacco God
When Edward Seymour was asked to support the creation of a college in Virginia because the ministers trained there would save souls, he replied, "Souls! Damn your souls! Make tobacco!"

Colonial Williamsburg

A tobacco factor and a planter (said to be Peter Jefferson, father of Thomas Jefferson) negotiating the sale of the year's crop at a planter's wharf. Tobacco was packed in hogsheads, large barrels. Most goods transported by ship were packed in barrels. No matter how heavy, barrels could be rolled; good ones were watertight; and, properly stacked in the hold on their sides, they did not shift in rough seas.

Virginia, how shall the planters dispose of their tobacco? . . . The tobacco will not vend in England, the Hollanders will not fetch it from England. What must become thereof?"

One thing that became thereof was evasion of the Navigation Acts. Smuggling (which is illegal trade) was common and by no means an unrespectable practice. Dutch tobacco buyers illegally tying up at wharves on the Chesapeake rarely had to listen to lectures about the sanctity of English trade law. If they paid a farthing more per pound than the going English rate, they did not sail off in ballast. Widespread evasion of the Navigation Acts was not difficult because of the topography of the Chesapeake region.

The Tidewater

The Chesapeake Bay is the estuary of not one but many streams. Among countless briny creeks flowing into the bay are several sizable rivers: the Choptank, Nanticoke, and Wicomico in Maryland, the Potomac (bigger than the Seine), Rappahannock, York, and James (larger than the Thames) in Virginia.

They are broad, slow-moving rivers for miles inland so high tides reach far beyond the open bay. The vessels of the seventeenth and eighteenth centuries could sail as far as salt water reached. Ships anchoring there might careen in sticky black mud at low tide. But twice a day salt water returned to float them and their cargos.

The most desirable land in the Chesapeake region was on the "necks" between the navigable rivers. There, in the words of a Virginia planter, Robert Beverley, ships could tie up "before the gentleman's door where they find the best reception or where 'tis most suitable to their Business." By 1700, most land with river frontage, known as the "tidewater," had been consolidated into large tobacco plantations worked by white servants and black slaves, but owned by just a few hundred great planter families, the tidewater aristocrats. Not only did they sell their tobacco and receive English goods they had ordered on their own wharves, they also hosted the small-scale tobacco growers whose farms were inland.

They were exhilarating days when the tobacco factors arrived. Indians and landless, poor whites hired themselves out to roll hogsheads (large barrels) of tobacco to the dock alongside servants and slaves. Middling land owners and their wives, called the "yeomanry," danced, drank, raced on foot and horseback, shot targets, and bought what they thought they could afford from the visiting merchants. Tobacco ships were variety shops. There would be spades, shovels, axes, and saws; household items such as kettles, pots, pans, sieves, funnels, pewter tankards, and tableware; oddments such as buttons, needles, thread, pins, and ribbons. There were textiles for both the planter families' fine clothing and rough wraps for poor farmers, servants, and slaves; shoes and boots; bricks, nails, and paint; goods to trade with the Indians (all of the above plus trinkets, mirrors, and the like); and firearms, shot, and gunpowder. For the wealthy few there were luxuries: silver candlesticks, chests and other fine furniture, wine, brandy, spices, books, even violins and harpsichords with which to grace a parlor and cheer an evening.

Everyone discussed the news of battles and kings that the ships brought. Some received letters from old country family,

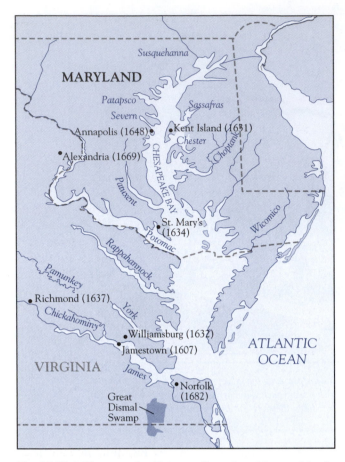

MAP 4:1 **The Chesapeake Estuary** Seagoing ships could sail many miles up the broad rivers of the Virginia and Maryland tidewater and transact their business on the premises of large plantations, all of which had wharves. The few towns of the region were centers of government that were nearly deserted when the colonial assemblies and courts were not in session. They were not commerical centers.

friends, and business agents. The sailors enlivened the carnival with their giddiness at being ashore after a couple of months at sea, spending their wages, as tradition required, on games and rum and the favors of women of three races. For the women of the yeomanry, whose only chance to socialize the rest of the year might be an hour after church on Sunday, the arrival of a tobacco ship was the high point of the year.

The First Families of Virginia

The excitement of the tobacco factor's annual visit briefly masked a potential conflict within tobacco colony society and a potential for resentment of the mother country. Because ships had easy access at plantations throughout the Chesapeake, no cities developed in Virginia and Maryland, no urban ports. The colonial capitals, Jamestown (Williamsburg after 1699) and St. Mary's (Annapolis after 1695) were ghost towns when the assembly was not meeting and the courts not in session, which was most of the year.

No cities meant there were no urban merchants (who doubled as bankers) nor a class of artisans that, elsewhere—in old England, in New England, in the middle colonies—had interests different from those of farmers, and often at odds with them. As the only wealthy people in the tobacco colonies, the great planters of the tidewater had no opposition with which to contend for political power.

Servants, slaves, and the poor were numerous—six Virginians in seven were "Poor, Indebted, Discontented" according to the royal governor—and therefore worrisome. But they did not vote. Yeoman farmers, owners of small tracts of land, did vote, but dependably for tidewater aristocrats whom they admired and whose circle they aspired to join.

The "first families of Virginia" were conscious of themselves as an elite with common social and political interests. With each passing year, they grew more tightly knit by intermarrying, creating a social class of cousins. In 1724, all twelve members of Virginia's Royal Council and half of the members of the House of Burgesses were related to one another by blood or marriage.

Few of the first families traced their ancestry to Jamestown's first years (as prominent New Englanders enjoy tracing their American origins to the *Mayflower*). Little pioneer blood survived by the late 1600s. The "starving times" of 1607–1610 and two devastating Indian massacres had snuffed out many a bloodline in the making. High mortality from disease interrupted other lines of descent. Well into the 1600s, life expectancy in Virginia was ten years shorter than it was in old England, twenty years shorter than in New England. Virginia's population remained an immigrant population for decades.

The founders of the first families (and Virginians of lower station) came to America beginning in the late 1640s. Sir William Berkeley, royal governor from 1646, called them "distressed cavaliers." That is, they were royalists (known as cavaliers) who had supported Charles I in the Civil War that ended with the king's execution. Under Oliver Cromwell they fell on hard times.

Those who fled to Virginia were generally not destitute. They were the offspring of established merchant and artisan families, of the landowning yeomanry and gentry, and a few, like Berkeley himself, were from noble families. Out of favor in Cromwell's England, they had good reason to remove to the end of the world and they brought money with which to acquire and expand tidewater lands, and to buy servants and slaves to work their fields. William Randolph, founder of one of Virginia's most aristocratic families, owned 10,000 acres when he died in 1711. Many were educated; Berkeley had a university degree. They were genteel, on the well-mannered side, and they often had "connections" back home.

In recruiting such settlers, Governor Berkeley was doing something new in Virginia: seeking people able to buy large parcels of land (Berkeley had plenty to sell) rather than people to labor. Berkeley favored the distressed cavaliers and organized them into a clique that maintained him in power. Berkeley himself became quite rich in land and servants, and not just in Virginia: He was also one of the lords proprietors of North Carolina. If the governor slipped into corruption (by our definition of the word), he was also constructive.

Under his sometimes dictatorial supervision, Virginia's population increased fivefold, from 8,000 to 40,000.

Conflict in the Piedmont

After 1670, Berkeley and his tidewater cronies confronted a crisis that undid the once untouchable governor, rattled the planter elite, and when the crisis passed, left the great planters chronically in debt to English merchants, generation after generation.

Virginia's high mortality and the collapse of tobacco prices favored the richest tidewater planters at the expense of smaller scale landowners. The planter with twenty-five or thirty servants or slaves could absorb the loss of some of them from disease. The farmer who had plunged everything he had into buying two or three laborers was wiped out by an epidemic. Low tobacco prices meant a collapse in the cost of land. The great planters increased their acreage by buying small bankrupt properties at bargain basement prices. With Berkeley a leading participant, they compensated for their own loss of income from tobacco by investing in the fur and hide trade with the Indians to the west.

The trouble was that the farmers the tidewater planters bought out, and recent immigrants to Virginia were moving west, pushing into Indian lands in the Piedmont, the foothills of the Appalachians, where land was cheap. They were joined on the frontier by hardscrabble dirt farmers, many of them freed servants, all of them in a desperate way. They were a rude and boisterous lot who dealt roughly with the Indians and suffered when the Indians retaliated. The Piedmonters demanded that Berkeley order a massive attack on the tribes and drive them away from the white settlements. The Indians, notably the Susquehannocks, who were selling hides and furs to the tidewater planters, complained about white incursions into their hunting grounds.

Berkeley devised a compromise. He began to build a line of nine defensive stockades on the headwaters of Virginia's rivers. Each was to be manned by 50 soldiers, with a cavalry of 125 patroling between the forts. Even before the defensive line was completed, however, it was obvious it was not going to work. Indian marauders had no trouble slipping between the forts to raid isolated white settlements, then disappearing. Moreover, like American frontiersmen for two centuries to come, Virginia's backcountry settlers did not think in terms of holding a line against the Indians. Ever increasing in numbers, they meant to clear the land they wanted of the natives.

Bacon's Rebellion

When the death toll of backcountry whites reached 300, with dozens of women and children kidnapped, the Piedmonters rebelled. Nathaniel Bacon, a recent immigrant become planter, himself a distressed cavalier of some means, set himself up as the commander of a force of 500 "tag, rag and bobtayle" frontiersmen who decimated the Oconeechee tribe. The Oconeechees had not attacked any whites; indeed, the tribe had expressed interest in an alliance with the

Virginians against the Susquehannocks! No matter: They were Indians. Bacon crushed them and turned his army toward Jamestown.

Intemperate words in the streets led the governor to arrest Bacon as a rebel. When Bacon's frightening followers milled about, threatening to lay the little town waste, Berkeley released him. Bacon was shaken and departed, but after an uneasy spell of stalemate, he returned to Jamestown with a larger force, blustered that he would hang the governor, and declared that he was in charge "by the consent of the people." Berkeley fled across the Chesapeake and sent a ship to England with the alarming story.

For several months, Nathaniel Bacon governed Virginia. Then, in October 1676, he fell ill and died, his age just 29. He must have been a charismatic figure. With him gone, the rebels scattered into the forests. Berkeley returned with a squadron of three warships and 1,100 troops. Their commander signed treaties with the Indians, tacitly admitting that frontier whites were the cause of the violence. In the meantime, Berkeley rounded up and hanged several dozen of Bacon's men.

But the governor was finished. Charles II was disgusted by Berkeley's blunders and vindictiveness. He remarked that "the old fool has hanged more men in that naked country than I have done for the murder of my father." He fired Berkeley and recalled him to England where he died within a few months.

Ill feeling between Tidewater and Piedmont Virginians did not die. The tidewater aristocracy continued to dominate Virginia's economy, government, and culture, and the people of the backcountry continued to resent them.

Big Spenders

After 1700, the great planters of Virginia and Maryland cultivated a gracious style of life modeled after the life of the English country gentry. They copied as best they were able the manners, fashions, and quirks of English squires and their ladies. When tobacco was returning a decent price (never again was it the bonanza crop), they built fine homes in the style of English manor houses and filled them with good English-made furniture. They stocked their cellars with port and Madeira, hock from the Rhineland, and claret from France, which they generously poured for one another at dinners, parties, balls, and simple unannounced visits that marked the origins of the famous "southern hospitality." Travelers looked to plantation houses for food and drink. The poorer sort, including blacks, were provided a roof over their heads and simple but adequate meals. Gentlemen and the occasional lady on the road were taken into the big house, dined with the master of the plantation, and often enough were urged to stay for several days. (It was a lonely life on many plantations; a good conversationalist was very welcome.)

Some tidewater families educated their sons at Oxford, Cambridge, or the Inns of Court, the law schools of England. If they feared the effects of English miasmas on innocent American bodies (smallpox, a deadly scourge in Europe, did not spread so easily in rural America), they schooled

Reproduced from the Collections of the Library of Congress

BACON'S REBELLION.

Nathaniel Bacon confronting Governor Berkeley. The artist's sympathies are obvious: Bacon is a dashing cavalier, as are his backup men; Berkeley and his cohorts are cringing, terrified. To the artist, Bacon was fighting against a tyrant. A tidewater planter's pictorial interpretation of Bacon's Rebellion would more likely depict Bacon' and his followers as a mob of frontier hooligans.

their heirs at the College of William and Mary, founded at Williamsburg in 1693.

The grandeur of the great planters' social and cultural life must not be overstated. William Byrd of Westover (one of the richest of the tidewater elite; he owned 179,000 acres when he died in 1744), was very well educated and cultured: he preferred the high life in London to Virginia. When his first wife, Lucy Park, died, Byrd sailed to England to find the daughter of a wealthy nobleman to succeed her and bring him a fat dowry. When Byrd found just the lady he was looking for and proposed, her father sent Byrd packing. His daughter had an annual income equal to Byrd's entire fortune; she could do much better than him. William Byrd looks like a duke in a portrait he commisioned in London. The fact was, even the grandest of tobacco planters was too poor to be a poor relation among the English upper classes.

Like many poor relations with pretensions, tidewater planters were constantly in debt. When income from tobacco drooped, Virginians and Marylanders could not or would not break the habits of consumption they had cultivated. They continued their annual orders of luxuries from England. To pay the bills, they mortgaged future crops—at a discount, of course—to the merchants who took their tobacco and who were to deliver their goods. It was not unusual that, by the time the tobacco went into the ground in spring, the imports it was to pay for had already been purchased and, in the case of wine, consumed.

Planter debt gratified English merchants. It meant yet more money for them in the form of interest and discounts flowing from colony to mother country. In time, chronic indebtedness would make anti-British rebels of practically the entire tidewater aristocracy.

South Carolina

The social structure of South Carolina was similar to that of Virginia and Maryland: A small, wealthy, intermarried elite, living on the labor of white servants and black slaves, governed a struggling class of small farmers gone west into the foothills. The rhythms of life in South Carolina were, however, quite different from those in the Chesapeake. The cash crops were rice, some cotton, and by the mid-1700s, indigo, a plant that yielded a precious blue pigment for dying cloth. Indigo was developed as a crop by Eliza Lucas of Barbados, on her father's South Carolina plantation, which she managed for him.

Rice and indigo nicely complemented one another. They required intensive labor at different seasons, so South Carolina's slaves produced wealth for their masters twelve

Reproduced from the Collections of the Library of Congress, Prints and Photographs Division, Washington, D.C. [LC-USF34-045219-D]

A New England stone fence. The first farmers of the rocky soil had little time to attend to such picturesque constructions. They piled those stones they could dig out in piles and plowed around others. They confirmed property lines by walking them in a group each year. Only later, as more and more stones were removed from fields and there was some free time, were New England's famous stone fences built.

months a year. However, because the marshy rice lands were breeding grounds for mosquitoes and mosquito-borne diseases—malaria and the dreaded yellow fever—the slaves and white overseers who tended the crops were left to be bitten, sicken, and die while South Carolina's planters lived in airy Charleston.

By congregating in a genuine city, South Carolina's elite was all the more conscious of its privileged position, all the more united in its determination to preserve it. No colony (or state) was dominated by so small and all-powerful a ruling elite as the one that ran South Carolina for 200 years.

New England

The European populations of Virginia, Maryland, and New England were almost entirely English. (There was a sprinkling of Huguenots, French Protestants, in South Carolina.) However, while most of the "distressed cavaliers" of the Chesapeake came from the southern counties of the old country, New England Puritans were overwhelmingly from the East. The sharp distinction between the flat New England accent and the "southern drawl," already noticeable in the 1700s, reflect the distinct regional origins of southerners and New Englanders.

However, the culture and social structure peculiar to colonial New England was largely the product of the northern colonies' religious heritage—Puritanism—and New England's climate and the land itself.

Geography and Society

The preeminent geographic facts of life in New England were the long, cold winters, which meant a short growing season—two months shorter than Virginia's—and the rocky character of much of the soil.

How do You Deal with a 10-Ton Boulder?

Clearing New England's soil of rocks was not simply a matter of hauling 50- and 100-pound stones to the edge of the woods. Granite boulders could weigh many tons. Farmers let some of the largest outcroppings go, to become highlights of suburban landscaping today. Other big ones had to be broken up. Sledge hammers were usless. There was no dynamite, and gunpowder was too expensive. The solution was water. Cracks in boulders were filled with water in winter. Falling temperatures froze the water into ice, which is greater in volume than water, and split the rocks or, at least, widened the crack for another go the next year. In time, a 10-ton boulder was broken into manageable pieces.

Health Food

The staples of the New England diet were corn boiled into mush or baked into a crumbly bread; wheat bread (whole grain, of course); apples raw, dried, baked in pies, or in the form of vinegar and cider; maple syrup or molasses for a sweetener; and large quantities of meat and fish.

In the late twentieth century, when health food devotees discovered that colonial New Englanders had a life expectancy exceeding that of any other people of their era, they fastened on the whole grains, apples and vinegar, and unrefined sweeteners as the secret (while overlooking New England's large meat consumption). One of the countless "miracle" diets of the era was based on Puritan grub.

Winter and summer, temperatures in New England were 10°F to 30°F cooler than they were in Virginia. The lethal diseases that plagued life the South—subtropical in origins—were less threatening in New England; some were unknown. Consequently, New Englanders lived longer than southerners. Twice as many children in Massachusetts survived infancy than survived in Virginia. One result of this godsend was larger families and a more rapid natural increase in population. Indeed, colonial New England was the world's first society in which it was commonplace for people to have personally known their grandparents.

In its soil, New England was less fortunate. Geologically, the entire region is a glacial moraine. It was there that the continental glaciers of the last ice age halted their advance. When they receded—melted—they left behind the rocks and gravel they had scooped from the earth on their journey from the Arctic.

Before New England's farmers could plow effectively, they had to clear rocks by the thousands from their fields, breaking up the large boulders, and hauling off what were not needed for construction to wasteland or, in time, to stack them in the stone fences that are so picturesque to those of us who did not have to build them. This back-wrenching toil went on for generations, for each winter's freeze heaved more rocks to the surface.

The intensive labor required to clear the land reinforced the Puritans' commitment to a society of small family farmers. The demanding New England countryside produced a variety of foods so that the population of the closely regulated townships was fairly dense. But there were no grand plantations in New England. A household might well take in a servant or two—usually the adolescent children of relatives or neighbors, and there were African slaves in every sizable New England town, usually domestic servants. But the small size of farms meant that families grew enough food to feed themselves and, at most, a small surplus to sell in the towns. Quite unlike Marylanders and Virginians, no New Englanders grew rich farming.

The Need for Coin

The crops New Englanders produced in no plenitude were much the same as those that the mother country grew: grain, squash, beans, orchard nuts, apples, livestock. So English mercantilists looked at New England with less interest than they looked at the South.

Indeed, the mother country's merchants, shipbuilders, and fishermen saw New Englanders as competitors. Boston was sending ships down the ways before 1640. The shipwright's craft flourished in every town with a harbor. Whaling, a calling New Englanders would come to dominate, began as early as 1649. Nantucket and New Bedford, Massachusetts, became synonymous with whalers. Fishermen sailed out of Portsmouth, Salem, Marblehead, New London, and dozens of other ports to harvest more than their share of the codfish of the North Atlantic. It was a short trip from New England to the Grand Banks of Newfoundland, the world's richest fishery, compared to the transatlantic voyage European fishermen had to make. New Englanders undersold European fishermen in European markets. Newport, Rhode Island, was a center of the African slave trade, another profitable business the English would have preferred to reserve for themselves.

New Englanders had no choice but to compete with the mother country. It took money—gold and silver—to purchase English manufactures. With no cash crop like tobacco or rice, whaling, fishing, and trade were the obvious solutions to the colonies' balance of payments problem.

Yankee Traders

Where did New England merchants sail? By the time of the American Revolution, just about everywhere in the world, even to China. The term "yankee trader" was universally known to signify a shrewd deal maker, even one who was not above chicanery.

During the 1600s and early 1700s, however, the New Englanders were Atlantic traders. There were several triangular routes, voyages of three legs, which their ships regularly plied at least in part. They carried rum distilled in New England to West Africa, traded it for captives, transported them to the West Indies, usually Barbados or Jamaica but, illegally, to Cuba too, where they were exchanged for sugar or molasses, itself a salable commodity back home and the raw material from which rum was made.

Or, a New Englander carried provisions from the middle colonies—wheat and livestock, plentiful in New York and Pennsylvania—to the West Indies where just about all foodstuffs except garden produce had to be imported. West Indian sugar and molasses were carried to England; and English manufactures—from cloth and tools to luxuries—were transported back home.

Other merchants carried Maryland and Virginia tobacco to England; manufactures to the West Indies; and West Indian slaves, mostly of African birth, to South Carolina, Virginia, and Maryland. Before 1700, very few enslaved blacks came directly from Africa to the North American colonies. Even after 1700, most slaves sold in North America spent some time in Barbados or Jamaica where they were "seasoned," that is, restored to something resembling health and fitness after their harrowing voyage across the Atlantic.

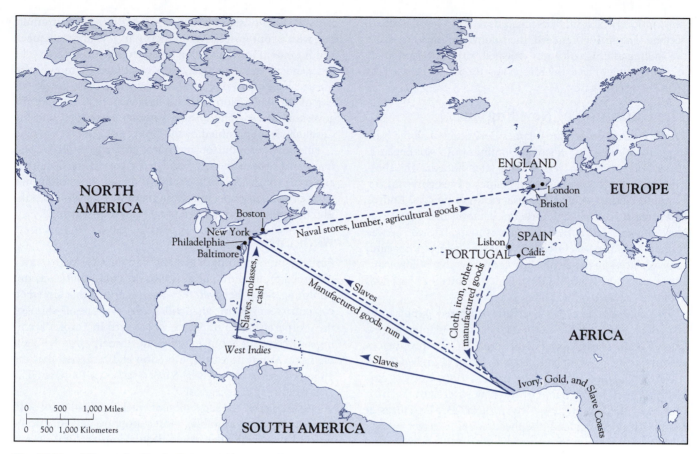

MAP 4:2 **Two Triangular Trade Routes.** Not every British and colonial ship plied one of the triangular routes year after year, but they were popular because profitable. Merchants were required by law to carry enumerated articles to England. Some returned to the colonies with manufactured goods; others added a transaction to their voyage by carrying trade goods to West Africa to exchange for slaves. Seafaring merchants were opportunists, taking on profitable cargos (and destinations) that presented themselves.

Most New England merchant vessels never crossed the Atlantic. They were "coasters," transporting whatever wanted moving from one colonial port to another in sloops and schooners. The harbors of Portsmouth, Boston, Newport, New Haven, New York, Philadelphia, and Charleston teemed with them. Long-distance overland travel was difficult for a man or woman on a horse to almost the end of the colonial era. Shipping freight overland was unheard of. Everything moved on water.

In a word, New England merchants were themselves mercantilists. They competed with the English in the same carrying trade on the same routes. Unsurprisingly, British mercantilists looked on New England with, at best, indifference. The northernmost colonies produced nothing profitable; New England merchants competed with the traders of the mother country.

An Independent Spirit

Indeed, the charters of Plymouth, Massachusetts; Rhode Island; and Connecticut gave those colonies such extensive powers of self-government that they functioned much like independent commonwealths. New Englanders (most of them) drank toasts to the king. A few of the grandchildren of the Puritans still entertained the fiction that they were members of the Church of England. But these were little more than pieties during a century when two English kings were dethroned, one of them decapitated, and when it often took two months for a message from the mother country to reach her American daughters.

During the decade Oliver Cromwell ruled England, the New England colonies ignored almost every directive he issued. In 1652, Massachusetts minted its own coin, the "pine tree Shilling." This was assuming a right reserved to sovereigns

And the Award for Incompetence in Colonial Government Goes to ...

By far the most foolish act of the Dominion of New England was a law invalidating all titles to land held under the abrogated Massachusetts charter. *Every* land title in the colony dated prior to 1685 had been granted under the charter!

Sir Edmund Andros did not intend to evict everyone in Massachusetts. The idea was to enrich the treasury by collecting fees for the paperwork of revalidating the titles, and to provide opportunities for graft among Sir Edmund's cronies who, for a consideration, could expedite the process.

since antiquity. Nor did Massachusetts retreat when Charles II became king in 1660. Indeed, the colony continued to strike the shilling after Charles was crowned. He was forced to go to court, suing to have the Massachusetts charter revoked. In 1684, he won his case.

The Dominion of New England

The next year, the new king, James II, combined all the New England colonies into a single Dominion of New England. (New York and New Jersey were later added.) He abolished the colonial assemblies and endowed his governor, Sir Edmund Andros, with a Spanish viceroy's powers. Andros had some success in New York, but he never had a prayer in New England. James II, unpopular at home because he was Roman Catholic, was forced, in 1688, to flee from England, to be replaced on the throne by joint monarchs, William and Mary. Mary was James II's Protestant daughter, her husband, William, the head of the Dutch state.

The news of James II's overthrow inspired popular uprisings in several colonies. In Maryland, a planter named John Coode seized power from the Catholic proprietors whom Coode assumed had fled with James II. In New York, a German named Jacob Leisler gained control of the city, claiming that, in the name of the new sovereigns, William and Mary, he was ridding New York of "Popish Doggs & Divells." In New England, the merchant elite, never subservient to Andros, simply resumed acting as it always had—independently. Prudently, Andros put to sea.

However, the Calverts of Maryland had played safe; they never unreservedly committed to James II. They eventually regained their proprietary rights. In New York, Leisler, dizzied by his power, ordered a volley fired at newly arrived troops who really did act for William and Mary. He and an aide were sentenced to be "hanged by the Neck and being Alive their bodys be Cutt Downe to the Earth that their Bowells be taken out." On second thought, the judge decided that hanging would be enough.

As for the Dominion of New England, William and Mary knew better than to revive it. Colonial opposition had been too emphatic for that. They restored the charters of Connecticut and Rhode Island (where there had been little tumult) but, with a court's decision on their side, the king and queen had no intention of allowing Massachusetts to return to its independent ways. In 1691, they combined Plymouth and Massachusetts into one royal colony. After 1691, the governor of the Bay Colony was no longer elected. He, like the governors of New Hampshire, Virginia, New York, and the Carolinas, was appointed by the Crown.

This was no easy pill for latter-day Puritans to swallow. Their forebears had been divinely mandated to govern Massachusetts as a godly commonwealth. That God should allow the Crown to take their "citty on a hill" from them was a profound punishment calling for anguished prayer and soul-searching.

Witchcraft

Puritan soul-searching when the community was severely disturbed focused on vile sins that the community was not punishing. Some believed they had identified that sin when two pubescent girls in Salem Village, a downscale off-shoot of the prosperous town of Salem, were seized in fits of screaming and crawling about making odd throaty sounds. Their physician found no earthly affliction and reckoned that the girls were being tortured by Satan's servants—witches. The girls confirmed his diagnosis.

Few laughed at the suggestion of witchcraft, and fewer with any sense laughed in public. Most Europeans and Americans believed that individuals could acquire supernatural powers (like the capacity to torture little girls) by promising to serve Satan, a bargain sometimes sealed by having sexual intercourse with him (or, for men, with satanic spirits called *succubi*). It was a serious business. Witchcraft was a capital crime; the Bible said, "thou shalt not suffer a witch to live." Since the Reformation, tens of thousands of Europeans had been executed for witchcraft. In the 1640s in East Anglia, the heartland of the Massachusetts emigration, as many as 200 witches were executed. A few people had been hanged as witches in the colonies, one in Boston in 1691. (None, contrary to a common belief, was burned at the stake. That was a European specialty.)

Just what set off the girls who started the witchcraft hysteria in Salem in 1692 is a mystery. Perhaps mental illness? Maybe the spooky tales told them by Tituba, a West Indian slave in the home of the Reverend Samuel Parish? In any case, the girls seem to have enjoyed being the center of attention and began to accuse specific villagers of bewitching them. Their targets could not have been better chosen for their vulnerability by a committee of sociologists. Most were women (as were, when it was all over, almost all the accusers). Some of the victims were eccentrics (conformist New England still looked askance at non-standard behavior); others were unpopular in the village for good reason and bad; several were loners without friends to defend them. Only a few of the accused women had husbands or adult sons—freeholder voters— to speak up on their behalf. Another Salem witch was an impoverished hag who may have been senile; yet another was deaf and probably never understood the charges against her. An 88-year-old male witch was notorious as a crank and, in his younger years, he had been an unabashed open adulterer.

Put on More Weight

Salem's witches were hanged except one man who was "pressed" to death. That is, he was held prostrate under a heavy plank. Stones were piled one by one on the plank until he expired of suffocation.

Why the special treatment? He refused to plead either innocent or guilty. To plead not guilty and then to be convicted (which he knew was in the cards) meant that his heirs would forfeit their rights to his property. The magistrates were not happy with his stubborness. After each stone was added, they begged him to plead. They would have been delighted with a "not guilty." A trial would follow and their consciences would be clear. Even a guilty plea would end the torture (and might have saved his life), but he refused. His final words were, "Put on more weight."

Accusers and accusations multiplied. Of some 130 people who were fingered as witches, 114 were charged. Of those who were found guilty, 19 were hanged. Although some of Massachusetts's most distinguished men were caught up in the hysteria, including Judge Samuel Sewall and the eminent minister, Cotton Mather, the authorities called a halt to the frenzy when people of their own eminence (notably the wife of the governor) were named as witches. Of the 19 witches executed, only one was a male of respectable social station.

THE MIDDLE COLONIES

William Penn did not believe in witchcraft. When, during the Salem hysteria, he was asked if there might not be witches in Pennsylvania too, he replied that settlers in his colony were free to fly about on broomsticks if they liked. The liberality of the middle colonies—religious tolerance first and foremost—was rooted in Quaker principles in Pennsylvania, New Jersey, and Delaware. In New York it was the consequence of a population that was too diverse for regimentation.

Liberality and an abundance of good land cheap made the middle colonies the preferred destination of immigrants who were able to pay the trans-Atlantic fare and even the poor who had to sign on as servants. Just two years after Penn selected the site of Philadelphia, it was a city of 300 houses and 2,500 people. When Pennsylvania was 20 years old, its population was the third largest in the colonies.

Philadelphia was never the "greene countrie towne" Penn had envisioned, every house having "room enough for House, Garden and small Orchard." Laid out on a tidy gridiron, it was quite compact. New York City, contained behind a wall (present-day Wall Street) out of fear of Indians, was even more densely populated.

Balanced Economies

The growing season in the middle colonies was longer than it was in New England. The soil in the alluvial valleys of the Hudson, Delaware, Schuylkill, and Susquehannna Rivers was rich and deep (and without glacial rocks). Outside Philadelphia the soil was mildly alkaline, enriched by eroded limestone, perfect for growing wheat. Almost from the start, middle colonies farmers produced a surplus they could sell. Because individual landholdings were much larger than the New England colonies had apportioned to families, all but the poorest middle colonies farmers could pasture more animals than they needed for their own meat, something else to

Courtesy Peabody Essex Museum, Salem, Massachusetts neg.#14,272

A woman (or girl) accuses another of witchcraft. This victim of the Salem hysteria is more fortunate than most. She lives in a substantial house and has a male defender. She has a good chance of surviving persecution. All but a few of the witches hanged at Salem were poor and friendless. Many were unpopular in the village for good reason or bad; they were easy targets.

Reproduced from the Collections of the Library of Congress Prints and Photographs Division, Washington, D.C. [LC-USZC4-12538]

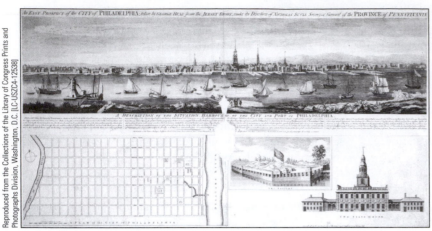

A view of Philadelphia from the New Jersey of the Delaware river, during the early eighteenth century, William Penn's "green countrie towne" outstripped Boston and Philadelphia in size. Streets were laid out in an orderly gridiron pattern (although only the eastern half of the city was actually built-up when this engraving was made). Visitors found Philadelphia a cleaner and more agreeable city than any other in the colonies. Its port was also the busiest, exporting the products of Pennsylvania's and New Jersey's rich farmlands.

sell. Most farmers, on however small a scale, were commercial, not subsistence farmers. Pennsylvania's surpluses were so great it was called the "breadbasket of the colonies."

There were great estates along New York's Hudson river, but there were few such agribusinesses in New Jersey and Pennsylvania. It was the proprietors' policy in the Quaker colonies to sell lands in family-size parcels. Those farmers who made some money took in servants to improve their productivity or purchased slaves. New York, New Jersey, and Delaware all had large African and African American populations. But familes owning slaves by the dozen, common in the South, were rare. The common pattern was for a well-off but working farm family to own two, four, maybe six slaves, often a family, the adult men working the fields, the women and girls helping to run the home.

Middle colonies farmers did not themselves export their grain, cattle, hogs, and horses, as tidewater planters exported their tobacco. They sold to "middlemen," merchants headquartered in New York and Philadelphia who had markets overseas, mostly in the sugar islands of the West Indies. The wealthiest merchants, intermarried Dutch and English families in New York, Quakers in Philadelphia, dominated the colonial assemblies and sat in the governors' councils. Farmers were not without political power; they voted. But the merchant aristocracy of the cities, allied with the governors, ensured that farmers were underrepresented in the assemblies. Until the 1750s, between 70 and 80 percent of Pennsylvania's assemblymen were Quakers, the majority from Philadelphia.

Diverse Populations

New Jersey and Pennsylvania (including Delaware until 1701) officially tolerated all religious denominations. In New York, the Church of England and the Dutch Reformed Church had privileges not enjoyed by other denominations. However, the laws proscribing other forms of worship were ignored except when, for example, anti-Catholic feelings boiled over (and Catholics were few). Indeed, a Roman Catholic, Thomas Dongan, was briefly governor of the colony. A visiting Virginian marveled that New Yorkers "seem not concerned what religion their neighbor is, or whether hee hath any or none."

The populations of New England and the South (always excepting black slaves) were ethnically homogenous. Almost all white people were of English ancestry. Not so in the middle colonies; their populations were diverse from the beginning. The Dutch remained a large minority in New York. Outside of Manhattan, they clustered in Dutch villages, preserving their language and customs. Even in the city, most married other Dutch. (Except for the upper class Dutch, which freely intermarried with upper-class English and often became members of the Church of England.)

The city of New York was, even in colonial times, an ethnic jumble of whites and blacks (many of them free), people of mixed European and African blood, and pockets of just about every Western European people. Isaac Jogues, a French priest passing through the city, heard eigthteen languages spoken on New York's streets.

There were numerous Dutch, Swedes, and Finns in New Jersey, Delaware, and Pennsylvania before the English colonies were chartered. William Penn advertised for immigrants in the German and Swiss states along the war-torn Rhine River. The first to respond belonged to persecuted religious sects known as "Anabaptists," a name they did not like, or "Mennonites," which they accepted. Like the Quakers, they were pacifists. They wanted to farm and developed the rich rolling land west of Philadelphia into model farms. Some of their descendants, still observing some seventeenth-century customs, are the "Pennsylvania Dutch." Other Germans, mostly Lutherans but a few Catholics too, founded Germantown near Philadelphia, now just a neighborhood within the city.

FINDING THE WAY

Public Domain

Sailors in the African trade found their way out and home by the ancient expedient of keeping the coastline in sight. They sailed the way the pilot of a small airplane flies, by following landmarks. Deepwater seamen—transatlantic sailors beginning with Columbus and Cabot—depended on the compass and the cross-staff, backstaff, or astrolabe when out of sight of land.

The Chinese first discovered that magnetized iron pointed north. Italians adapted this knowledge into a navigational instrument. By the seventeenth century, the ship's compass was a magnetic needle delicately balanced on a brass bowl with a flat top marked with sixteen directions (north, east, south, and west, of course, plus NE, SE, and so on, and NNE, ENE, ESE, SSE). The compass was within sight of the helmsman and mounted on pivots so that it remained level when the vessel pitched and rolled.

The cross-staff, astrolabe, and backstaff (left to right above) enabled navigators to measure the angle between the horizon and the sun by day and, by night, the horizon and the North Star (the Southern Cross below the Equator). With this information, a navigator could determine his ship's latitude, that is, the distance of its position from the equator. With one or another of these instruments, sailors knew on which east–west line they were sailing.

So, a captain who was headed for Cape Cod, which he knew was located at about 42° north latitude, sailed southerly out of England until his instruments told him his vessel was at 42°. Then, using the compass, and checking the astrolabe or cross-staff for corrections at least daily, he sailed due west.

What sailors could not determine with any accuracy was longitude—their position on the imaginary arcs than run north-south from pole to pole. On an east to west voyage such as across the Atlantic, navigators had only a reckoner's notion of how far they had sailed from their port of departure and, therefore, how far they were from their destination.

There were ways of determining—very roughly—a ship's speed and, therefore, *approximate* longitude on an east-west voyage. The log line was a rope knotted every forty-eight feet with a wooden float tied to the end. It was thrown overboard and, measuring minutes with a sandglass, the navigator counted the number of knots that passed over the stern in a given period of time. Since the log was not blown as the ship was, the speed of the wind and therefore the ship could be estimated. (Measuring a ship's speed in knots, as is still done today, dates from the day of the knotted log line; so does the custom of calling the captain's written records the ship's log.)

No one trusted too much to a log line. It did not take account of ocean currents which could radically increase or decrease a ship's progress. (The log was in the grip of the current, just as the ship was.)

Not until the mid-eighteenth century, near the end of the colonial period, was the problem of determining longitude systematically attacked. In 1752, a German astronomer, Tobias Mayer, devised a set of tables and a mathematical formula for determining longitude from the position of the moon. His method worked, but it was far from practical. A skilled mathematician needed four hours to complete the calculation. Few ship's captains were so skilled. None had four hours to spare from other duties very often. In 1767, the Royal Observatory at Greenwich, England (which in time became 0° longitude) issued the *Mariner's Almanac*, a volume of tables that simplified Mayer's formulas, but the streamlining diluted their accuracy.

Not until the invention of the "chronometer," a highly accurate clock undisturbed by the ocean's rough handling of it, was longitude mastered. Set at the beginning of a voyage at the time in Greenwich on the River Thames, which was designated 0° longitude (or Paris aboard French ships, Amsterdam aboard Dutch), the chronometer informed a navigator what the time was at 0° longitude wherever in the world he was, which he then compared with the time aboard ship (determined from the position of the sun), and thus, with simple arithmetic established his ship's position.

FURTHER READING

Classics Charles M. Andrews, *The Colonial Period of American History*, 1934–1938; Daniel Boorstin, *The Americans: The Colonial Experience*, 1958; Bernard Bailyn, *The New England Merchants in the Seventeenth Century*, 1955; Marion G. Starkey, *The Devil in Massachusetts*, 1969.

General D. W. Meinig, *Atlantic America 1492–1800*, volume I of *The Shaping of America: A Geographical Perspective on 500 Years of History*, 1986; Jack P. Greene and J. R. Pole, eds., *Colonial British America*, 1984; Alan Taylor, *American Colonies*, 2001; Jack P. Greene, *Pursuits of Happiness: The Social Development of Early Modern British Colonies and the Formation of American Culture*, 1988; John J. McCusker and Russell Menard, *The Economy of British North America*, 1985; David Hackett Fisher's *Albion's Seed: Four British Folkways in America*, 1989.

Trade Ralph Davis, *The Rise of the Atlantic Economies*, 1973; Kenneth R. Andrews, *Trade, Plunder, and Settlement: Maritime Enterprise and the Genesis of the British Empire, 1480–1630*, 1984

The Southern Colonies David L. Ammerman, ed., *The Cheasapeake in the Seventeenth Century*, 1979; Gloria Main, *The Tobacco Colony: Life in Early Maryland, 1650–1719*, 1982; William S. Powell, *Colonial North Carolina*, 1973; Robert M. Weir, *Colonial South Carolina: A History*, 1983; Robert Orwell, *Masters, Slaves, and Subjects: The Culture of Power in the South Carolina Low Country*, 1998. The standard work on Bacon's Rebellion is Wilcomb E. Washburn, *The Governor and the Rebel*, 1957.

The Middle Colonies Gary Nash, *Quakers and Politics: Pennsylvania, 1681–1726*, 1971; James T. Lemon, *The Best Poor Man's Country: A Geographical Study of Early Southeastern Pennsylvania*, 1972; Richard and Mary Dunn, *The World of William Penn*, 1986; Michael Kammen, *Colonial New York*, 1975; Robert C. Ritchie, *The Duke's Province*, 1977; Joyce D. Goodfriend, *Before the Melting Pot: Society and Culture in Colonial New York City, 1664–1730*, 1992; Russell Shorto, *The Island at the Center of the World: The Epic Story of Dutch Manhattan* 2004; and the appropriate chapters of the superb Edwin G. Burrows and Mike Wallace, *Gotham: A History of New York City to 1898*, 1999. On New Jersey: J. E. Pomfret, *The Province of East and West New Jersey*, 1956; Brendan McConville, *These Daring Disturbers of the Public Peace: The Struggle for Property and Power in Early New Jersey*, 1999.

New England Stephen Foster, *The Long Argument: English Puritanism and New England Culture, 1570–1700*, 1991; Philip J. Greven Jr., *Four Generations: Population, Land, and Family in Colonial Andover, Massachusetts*, 1970; Howard S. Russell, *A Long, Deep Furrow: Three Centuries of Farming in New England*, 1976.

Witchcraft Paul Boyer and Stephen Nissenbaum, *Salem Possessed*, 1974; John Demos, *Entertaining Satan: Witchcraft and the Culture of Early New England*, 1982; Carol Karlsen, *The Devil in the Shape of a Woman*, 1987; Frances Hill, *The Salem Witch Trials*, 2000; Mary Beth Norton, *In the Devil's Snare: The Salem Witchcraft Crisis of 1692*, 2002.

Trade and Navigation Daniel Vickers, *Young Men and the Sea: Yankee Seafarers in the Age of Sail*, 2005; Dana Sobel, *Longitude: The True Story of a Lone Genius Who Solved the Greatest Scientific Problem of His Time*, 1995.

KEY TERMS

Use the following listing of key terms to review important figures, events, locations, and concepts covered in this chapter. A glossary of these terms is available on *The American Past* companion Web site: www.cengage.com/history/conlin/tap9e

mercantilism, p. 55	enumerated articles, p. 58	tidewater, p. 60
Navigation Acts, p. 58	cavaliers, p. 60	Berkeley, Sir William, p. 60

ONLINE RESOURCES

Find additional resources, including primary source documents, images, interactive maps, simulations, chapter review exercises, and Internet links at

The American Past companion Web site
www.cengage.com/history/conlin/tap9e

American History Resource Center
http://ushistory.wadsworth.com/

Chapter 5

Other Americans

Indians and Africans in the Colonies

Roberta Wilson, New York State Museum

Why will you take by force what you may obtain by love? Why will you destroy us who supply you with food? What can you get by war?

—*Powhatan*

Is it not enough that we are torn from our country and friends to toil for your luxury and lust of gain? Must every tender feeling be likewise sacrificed to your avarice?

—*Olaudah Equiano*

The eastern slope of North America, between the Appalachians and the Atlantic, the most densely populated region of the United States, was probably the most populous part of North America when the colonization era began.

How many Indians lived on the "Eastern Seaboard" in 1600? We do not know. The natives built no cities for archaeologists to excavate, measure, and calculate a reliable estimate of the number of people that inhabited them. The Eastern Indians' towns and villages were constructed of wood and other organic material that rapidly decayed when the sites were abandoned.

The first colonists rarely counted their neighbors and, in any case, they knew only of villages nearest to their own settlements. When Chief Powhatan felt threatened by the Jamestowners, he was able to disappear entirely from their purview for ten years by moving his capital a few miles inland. Modern estimates of the Indian population in about 1600 are so heavily based on guesswork that some are twenty times larger than others. Perhaps the most persuasive guess is that about 150,000 Indians lived between the Appalachians and the ocean.

One demographic observation is beyond doubt. Whatever the Eastern Indians' numbers in 1600, they suffered a catastrophic decline thanks to epidemics of European diseases to which Native Americans had no inherited immunities. The deserted village of Pawtuxet, where the Pilgrims founded Plymouth, was just one of several Wampanoag communities that had simply died out. Massasoit, chief of the Wampanoags, claimed he had been able to muster 3,000 warriors in 1600. Even if he was exaggerating, it is noteworthy that, by 1630, he had only a few hundred. It was a rare coastal tribe that, by 1650, was more than half the size it had been in 1600. In the Carolinas at the time of the first English incursions in the 1660s, the native population was about 20,000. In 1715, colonial authorities counted only 8,000 Carolina Indians. The Lenni Lenape of the Delaware River valley suffered a similar devastation.

THE EASTERN WOODLANDS INDIANS

The economies of the many tribes who lived in what is now the eastern third of the United States were much the same, shaped by the forest that was their home. From the Atlantic Ocean to beyond the Mississippi River, North America was woods. Seamen approaching New England smelled the fragrance of pine trees days before they sighted land. Dozens of species of hardwoods dominated other forests. There were gaps in the woods, natural prairies or "oak openings," some of them sizable. The Indians cleared large tracts both to create farmland and to improve hunting by encouraging the growth of the sun-loving grasses, berries, and shrubs on which moose, elk, deer, and bear fed.

Some man-made landscapes in New England were park-like, gigantic hardwoods towering over ground that was not quite a lawn but was without brush. Much of Virginia's Shenandoah Valley was a checkerboard of alternating open land and groves of trees. Mostly, however, the eastern third of the continent was forest. The canopy of the oaks and maples was so dense in places that, except in winter, it blocked out the sun. Virgin forest could be a gloomy place. Underbrush could grow so thickly as to make the forest floor impenetrable, especially when the brush was canebrake, an American bamboo.

Bow and Arrow

The bow of most Eastern Woodlands Indians were made from a single piece of wood like the famous English longbow, but it was shorter: Five feet was typical. Different tribes preferred different woods: hickory, ash, or elm. A few tribes made composite bows, laminating animal sinews to willow for increased pull and power.

Lethality at short range was important to the Indians; accuracy at distances less so. Indians hunted and battled in forests; if a target was visible, it was rarely further than fifty yards away. At that range, an arrow shot from a New England Algonkian bow could pass entirely through a deer . . . or an enemy.

Hunters

All Eastern Woodlands Indians depended on hunting for much of their food. Men and adolescent boys using bows and arrows with flaked stone heads harvested meat for sustenance and for furs and hides from which clothing, mats, and blankets were made. They did not usually range far from their villages. They had to be able to carry their venison or birds home before they had eaten it themselves and before, in summer, the meat spoiled. Fortunately, the woods teemed with game to a degree unimaginable in the United States today. Tribes could overhunt their range, of course, and they

did. Scarcity of game was a major reason why tribes relocated, sometimes over a considerable distance.

To the Indians, no one *owned* land. The idea of private or even tribal property land was alien to them, as was the idea of "boundaries" between tribal hunting grounds. "They range rather than inhabite," a Virginian wrote. A Dutchman in New York elaborated: "wind, stream, bush, field, sea, beach, and riverside are open and free to everyone of every nation with which the Indians are not embroiled in open conflict."

This did not mean that hunting parties from different tribes waved cordially if they happened upon one another in the forest. If the Indians were not territorial, they were tribal. While two distinct peoples might be friendly with one another, trading partners or even allies, hostility—even between villages within a tribal culture—was a common state of affairs. Hunting parties had to be wary of the whereabouts of enemies, an added incentive for hunters from small tribes not to wander too far from home. The Wampanoag and Massachusetts Indians had been contesting hunting grounds with the Narragansetts of Rhode Island long before the Puritans introduced them to the concept of "this land is mine." The Narragansetts skirmished with the Pequots of Connecticut to the west of them. The Pequots contended with Mohicans, Mohegans, and Mohawks to the west of their homeland.

Farmers

All the Eastern Woodlands Indians farmed. They cleared fields by the slash-and-burn method, a technique still employed in tropical forests today. Slash-and-burn is well suited to a people whose numbers are few and whose tools are simple. (There were none made of iron in North America.) First, the Indians girdled the trees in future fields. That is, they stripped the trunk of bark and hacked a gash into the exposed wood around the circumference of the tree. This prevented the circulation of sap, and the slashed trees died. When they were leafless, admitting sunlight, the underbrush was burned.

Women did the farming (and the gathering, seasonally collecting fruits, berries, nuts, roots, and reeds and grasses for

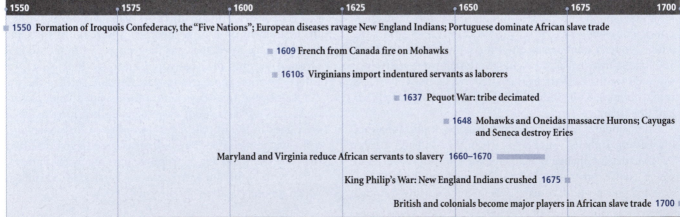

Indians and Africans in Early Colonial History 1550–1700

1550	1575	1600	1625	1650	1675	1700

1550 Formation of Iroquois Confederacy, the "Five Nations"; European diseases ravage New England Indians; Portuguese dominate African slave trade

1609 French from Canada fire on Mohawks

1610s Virginians import indentured servants as laborers

1637 Pequot War: tribe decimated

1648 Mohawks and Oneidas massacre Hurons; Cayugas and Seneca destroy Eries

Maryland and Virginia reduce African servants to slavery **1660–1670**

King Philip's War: New England Indians crushed **1675**

British and colonials become major players in African slave trade **1700**

From the Collections of the Library of Congress

This watercolor of the village of Secotan in North Carolina was painted in 1585 by John White, the governor of the Roanoke colony. It reveals an orderly society and the fact that the villagers planted two crops of corn each year in order to maximize their food supply. The logs in the village palisade were actually positioned next to one another with apertures cut through some of them for bowmen. White took the liberty of spacing them apart in his painting so that the interior of the village was visible. Many Eastern tribes built such fortifications. They were effective if an attack was not a complete surprise.

women with other chores that took them from the fields. (An Indian woman's work was literally never done.) Among the Powhatans of Virginia, the corn ran out so regularly that the women were set to digging for tuckahoe, an edible although not very appetizing root. They hated the job; it was cold, wet work. If Powhatan women had decided how many acres to plant in the three sisters each year, there would have been no shortages.

"Starving times" were regular among many tribes long before the hunger Jamestown suffered. John Smith observed that the Powhatans gorged and fattened up each fall and were scrawny in the spring. Analysis of bones in the Indian burial sites of pre-colonial New England show a high incidence of malnutrition and anemia. Indians living along the St. Lawrence River were familiar with scurvy, a vitamin C deficiency; when the first French explorers began to suffer from the disease, Indians showed them their cure for it: a spruce tea. Frequent shortages and occasional famines help explain why, unlike in Mesoamerica, Eastern Woodlands communities were small. The Powhatans gathered in camps of a thousand in the late summer when food was abundant, but broke up into small, scattered camps the rest of the year. Only the Iroquois nations, which planted cornfields of more than 100 acres, lived in such large concentrations year round.

Colonists sometimes described the Indians as nomads. But they were not; none of the Eastern peoples were full-time wanderers. *Seminomadic* (a term unknown to seventeenth-century English) would have been more accurate. Except for the Iroquois, Creeks, and Cherokees, whose town sites remained fixed for up to ten years, the woodlands tribes relocated every two or three years when the men had overhunted the range, the women had exhausted the soil, the flimsy huts of bent saplings covered with mats were falling to pieces, and when everyone was sick and tired of the accumulated human filth and the rats, mice, and lice that had taken up residence.

making baskets and mats). In the ghostly forests—the lifeless trees that were not used for firewood stood for years—the women planted maize ("Indian corn"), squash of uncountable varieties, beans, melons, cabbages, gourds to serve as vessels, and a little tobacco. Maize, beans, and squash were the staples. The Iroquois of New York called them the "three sisters" because they were planted together in mounds. The corn stalks served as poles for the climbing beans; the large leaves of squash plants acted as a mulch, stifling weeds for lack of sun and preserving moisture.

Maize and beans, kept dry and cool, lasted a year. With the supply of meat so often problematical, avoiding hunger in the spring depended on a village's store of corn. The Mohawks of New York maintained vast fields and huge corn reserves; they were large-scale growers. Many other tribes, however, neglected agriculture. The men loaded their

What's in a Name?

The name many Indian tribes gave themselves translates as "the people" or "the human beings." The terms they used for the people of other tribes, however, were often unflattering. "The other things" was mild. More common were insults like "Mohawk," which is Narragansett for "blood sucker." "Sioux" is Chippewa for "snake."

Sometimes the colonists gave tribes an entirely irrelevant European name that stuck. They called the Lenni Lenape "Delawares" because their heartland spanned the river the English called the Delaware. The tribe, soon pushed to the Ohio River Valley, adopted it. A Canadian Iroquois band that refused to ally with either the French or the English became known as "Neutrals," and they accepted that name.

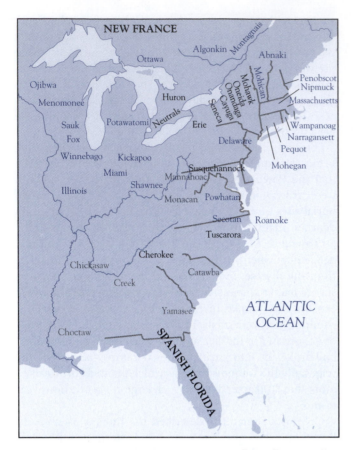

NEW FRANCE

Ottawa

Algonkin

Montagnais

Abnaki

Ojibwa

Menomonee

Huron

Mohawk

Oneida

Onandaga

Cayuga

Seneca

Mohican

Penobscot

Nipmuck

Massachusetts

Sauk

Fox

Potawatomi

Neutrals

Erie

Wampanoag

Narragansett

Pequot

Winnebago

Kickapoo

Delaware

Miami

Mannahoac

Susquehannock

Mohegan

Illinois

Shawnee

Monacan

Powhatan

Secotan

Roanoke

Tuscarora

Cherokee

Chickasaw

Catawba

Creek

ATLANTIC OCEAN

Yamasee

Choctaw

SPANISH FLORIDA

MAP 5:1 Major Eastern Woodlands Tribes. Every Eastern tribe, often every band within a tribe, was effectively independent. The numerous Creek towns periodically formed confederations, but they were unstable and did not last long. In 1607, most Chesapeake Indian villages acknowledged Powhatan as "Paramount Chief," but that coalition too was shaky with outlying villages restive. Only the Five Nations—the Iroquois Confederacy—of New York, founded about 1550, preserved political unity.

Language

Languages were more numerous in North America than they were in Europe. In the Eastern Woodlands, however, all the languages fell into one of four linguistic families. That is, within each family, the languages had evolved from a single root language as Spanish, French, and Italian all evolved from Latin. Siouan- and Muskohegan-speaking peoples were found mostly in the southern interior. However, just about every tribe with which the early English colonists interacted spoke an Algonkian (Algonquin) or Iroquoian tongue.

The first Native American words the settlers of Virginia and New England heard spoken were Algonkian: Powhatan in Virginia, Wampanoag in Massachusetts. Other Algonkian-speaking tribes were the Mohegans, Massachusetts, Narragansett, Abnaki, and Pequots in New England; the Lenni Lenape (Delawares) in the middle colonies; and south of the Great Lakes, the Miami, Shawnee, Potowatomi, Illinois, Kickapoo, Fox, Sauk, and Chippeway (Ojibwa).

Quite a few Algonkian words and place names are now fixtures of American English: *hickory, hominy, moccasin, succotash, tomahawk, totem,* and *wigwam; Massachusetts, Connecticut,* and *Chesapeake.*

By no means could all Algonkian speakers understand one another, anymore than a Sicilian can understand a Parisian. The greater the distance between two tribes, the further back in time their common ancestors, the greater the differences between their languages. Neighboring Algonkian tribes like the Wampanoags and Massachusetts conversed easily, but in one corner of North Carolina, several small tribes that resided within ten miles of one another for at least half a century could trade (or squabble) only by means of sign language.

One of the largest southern tribes, the Cherokee, spoke an Iroquoian language, as did the Tuscarora of North Carolina. Most Iroquoian speakers lived farther north: the Susquehannocks in Virginia; the Erie south of Lake Erie; and the Seneca, Cayuga, Onandaga, Oneida, and Mohawk tribes of New York.

Warriors

Two tribes having a mutually beneficial trade (or a frightening common enemy) might be allies for decades. Wariness of outsiders is, however, the essence of tribal culture everywhere. While most Eastern peoples' name for themselves translates as something like "the human beings," they called the people of other tribes "the other things" or worse, "bloodsuckers," "man-eaters."

Warfare was chronic in the Indians' world because males aspired, above all else, to bravery. A man's reputation for courage was the key to his status in the tribe. Consequently, when a gang of young men on a hunt happened on young men from another tribe, reckless belligerence was common. A New Englander who lived among Indians wrote that they battled "for a pastime."

Oral tradition told of massacres of entire villages, but wholesale bloodshed was not typical of Indian warfare. Neither their military technology nor the object of wars nor the Indians' manner of fighting was adapted to mass slaughter. Their weapons were made of wood and stone, which meant fighting at close quarters, with bow and arrow or hand-to-hand. Palisaded villages—surrounded by a wall of upright logs—were usually secure against such "low-tech" assaults (as long as there were sentinels). And bravery meant boldness, not necessarily killing an enemy (counting coup, striking him, was just as prestigious); splitting a baby's head open with a tomahawk was not (although it was done often enough). The object of assaults that were planned, as opposed to accidental confrontations, was to steal corn or meat or to seize women and children to adopt.

Finally, casualties were usually low because Indian warriors did not fight in disciplined, coordinated units as Europeans did. They cooperated in ambushing enemies but then battled one on one in chaotic melees. When things got too hot, they fled, one by one. Roger Williams observed that "the Indians' Warres are far less bloudy and devouring than the cruell warres of Europe." When, in 1637, soldiers from Massachusetts and

The Iroquois longhouse (this one is Mohawk) was a physical expression of the clan structure of Iroquois tribes. Families belonging to a clan were closely related to one another through the clan's women: mothers, daughters, sisters. Husbands were drawn from other clans in order to avoid inbreeding and became members of their wives' clan. (For as long as she could stomach having him around. If she divorced him, he returned to his mother's longhouse and clan.) Each nuclear family in a clan had its own apartment, separated from others by a partition, but open to the central aisle.

Roberta Wilson, New York State Museum

Connecticut shot down Pequots who were attempting to flee their burning village, their Narragansett allies, incredulous and perhaps disgusted, shouted at them to stop.

The Iroquois Confederacy

The most powerful Eastern tribes were the five Iroquois Nations that occupied most of what is now upstate New York. Until about 1550, the Seneca, Cayuga, Onandaga, Oneida, and Mohawk fought as fiercely among themselves as any other tribes. They were notorious for torturing the prisoners they took.

Torture, like farming, was woman's work. Captives were forced to "run the gauntlet"—to race between two lines of shrieking women swinging clubs and thrusting with spears. From among the survivors, the women selected those they would adopt into their clans (subdivisions of the tribe that shared the same longhouse). The leftovers were tied to trees and slowly roasted by small fires built at their feet, skinned, dismembered finger by finger and limb by limb, and blinded with firebrands, not necessarily in that order. When a victim passed out, torture was suspended until he regained consciousness. The fun was in the captive's agony, not his death.

About 1550, a visionary known to history as Hiawatha, set out to end warfare among the five tribes. He traveled tirelessly from one nation to another preaching the advantages of cooperation. Astonishingly, Hiawatha succeeded. All five tribes retained their independence—their *sovereignty* in Europeans terms. Each tribe governed itself and was free to make war on tribes outside the Confederation without consulting the others.

However, the leaders of the Five Nations vowed not to make war on one another. Inevitable problems—if, for example, a Seneca killed a Cayuga—were resolved without further bloodshed at an annual meeting of delegates from all five tribes at the chief town of the Onandagas, the central-most of the Nations. It worked. Hiawatha's Confederation kept the peace among the New York Iroquois for more than two centuries.

"Empowered Women"

A tribe's delegates at the annual meetings were men. However, they were selected by women. Indeed, among the Iroquois, descent was matrilineal, traced from mother to daughter, not from father to son as among Europeans. Women governed the clans within the tribes for they were the only permanent clan members. When a couple married, the groom left his mother's longhouse and moved to his wife's. He became a member of her clan, socializing, hunting, wandering, and warring alongside his wife's unmarried brothers and her sisters' and cousins' husbands. If his wife tired of him—divorce was easy—he moved out of her longhouse and returned to his mother's. The children stayed.

Iroquois social stability depended on matrilineal clans. The Iroquois had a lackadaisical attitude about who had sexual relations with whom. The paternity of a child, therefore, could not be reliably known. So, father-son relationships counted for little, clan membership a lot.

Iroquois women also held extensive political power within tribes because Iroquois men were endlessly on the move. With their own towns secure from attack thanks to the Confederation, the young men could range far into the hunting grounds of other tribes itching for a fight.

A consequential fight occurred in 1609. About 200 Mohawks on the shores of Lake Champlain ran into a party of Montaignais and Hurons from the north. They were accompanied by a few oddly dressed white men. They were French soldiers from newly founded Quebec; the Hurons and Montaignais were showing them the north–south trade route of which the lake was a part. Among the French was the governor of the colony (and the namesake of the lake), Samuel de Champlain. When the Mohawks advanced, Champlain and two others opened fire with arquebuses (matchlock muskets). Loaded with shrapnel—odd bits of iron—each shot felled several Mohawks. Bewildered and terrified—it was their introduction to firearms—the survivors fled. They would have their revenge.

A WORLD TURNED UPSIDE DOWN

Battling with strange newcomers was not new to the Indians. Tribes regularly moved a hundred miles and more. The diseases the whites brought with them, however, were a devastating novelty. As early as 1550, European fishermen holed up for the winter on New England shores, trading and carousing with the coastal tribes. The fishermen infected the natives with highly contagious Old World diseases to which they had little resistance—diphtheria, cholera, typhus at first, later measles and smallpox. Infected coastal Indians, in turn, spread the devastating sicknesses to inland tribes who had never seen a white man.

A Fate Worse than Death

Colonial women captured by Indians and not rescued immediately often decided to remain with their captors when, later, they were given the choice of returning. If they had borne children, they knew that their offspring could live as equals among the Indians but would be outcast "half-breeds" in white society. Indeed, having coupled with Indian men, the women themselves would be considered defiled back home.

As much as the stories of "white squaws" disturbed the colonists, no tale was more terrible than Esther Wheelwright's. In 1704, Abenakis kidnapped and took her to the French in Quebec. There, she converted to Roman Catholicism, became a nun, and, in time, Mother Superior of the Ursuline order. That made her the highest ranking churchwoman in North America. New Englanders, for whom the Catholic Church was the Whore of Babylon, were appalled.

Separate Spheres

Aside from the curse of new diseases, which did their work everywhere in the Americas, the experience of the Eastern Woodlands Indians was quite unlike that of Native Americans who lived in lands the Spanish conquered. First, there were not as many of them. More Indians lived within 50 miles of Lake Texcoco than lived in the forests of North America that the English penetrated during the 1600s.

Nevertheless, the English had a more difficult time dominating the Indians than the Spanish did. In part, this was because English colonization was not primarily military as Spanish colonization was. The English were uninterested in conquering the Indians, ruling them, and living off their labor. They meant to build English communities on land from which they cleared the Indians.

The sexual ratio among the English in New England and the middle colonies made segregation by race plausible. The Spanish conquerors of Santo Domingo (which Columbus had called Hispaneola), Cuba, Mexico, and Peru were soldiers—all males; decades passed before more than a handful of Spanish women came to America. But, except in Virginia, the English colonies were settled by families, and single English women of marrying age. Colonial men did not look to the tribes for wives and mistresses as the extent the conquistadors did. One scholar has identified only three Indian-white marriages

North Wind/North Wind Pictures

Native culture in transition. The bark-covered wigwams and the log stockade were traditional; many tribes of the woodlands fortified their villages with palisades long before they had contact with English and French colonials. As long as there were sentinels and enough men present, the walls were effective defenses against enemies. The cabins indicate the permanent presence of white trappers and traders or the partial Europeanization of some members of the tribal band. from the first, some Indians preferred the colonial's housing.

in Virginia (where white men vastly outnumbered white women) during the colony's first century, including John Rolfe and Pocahontas!

There was plenty of extramarital miscegenation, of course: English-Indian, English-African, and African-Indian. Some Virginians thought that Indian-white marriages were a solution to white-Indian conflict. As late as the 1770s, Patrick Henry and John Marshall urged the Virginia Assembly to enact a law encouraging interracial marriages. But theirs was a minority view. "Half-breeds" were consigned to the Indians, perhaps in part because they were illegitimate, but mostly because of the consciousness of race that steadily grew in intensity in colonial society.

The Indians and Christianity

Like the Spanish (and the French in Canada), the early English colonists said that they meant to convert the Indians to true religion: Protestant Christianity in their case. Looking to the Bible to explain who the natives were, the Puritans concluded that they were descendants of the "ten lost tribes of Israel" whom they would win "to the knowledge and obedience of the true God and Saviour of Mankind." The Great Seal of Massachusetts depicted an Indian pleading "Come over and help us."

However, the creation of a replica of old England—where there were no Indians—was much more important to Puritans than Indian souls. A few ministers, most famously John Eliot, "the Apostle to the Indians," devoted their lives to christianizing Indians. But John Cotton, the most prestigious preacher in Massachusetts, better represented the colonial mind when he called the Indians "children of Satan" who should be "blasted in all their green groves and arbours."

Few Indians converted to Puritan Protestantism. In 1675, after half a century of the English presence, there were only thirteen villages of "praying Indians" in all of New England. By way of contrast, Spanish priests commonly converted almost all the Indians in a region to Roman Catholicism within a few decades. The French had similar successes in Canada and among the Indians of the Anglo-French borderlands. Why such different results?

It was a central tenet of Roman Catholicism that every human being, saint and sinner alike, should belong to the "One True Church." (The word *catholic* means "universal.") The Puritans believed that only a minority of their own people were saved. It was not easy to convince Indians to embrace a religion that taught that all but a few of them were damned to hellsfire.

For a millennium Catholic missionaries had preached to peoples of diverse cultures. Accepting baptism in the Church was what mattered to Catholic missionaries. They took little interest in changing cultural practices if they did not clash with Church teachings. Indeed—anything to baptize—they tailored their message and even their own behavior to the cultures of the peoples among whom they worked. They emphasized similarities between Roman Catholicism and the beliefs of Mexicans, Chinese, and Iroquois in order make baptism more congenial to them. The Roman Church was comfortably "multicultural."

English colonists, by way of contrast, were intensely nationalistic. Their religion—Puritan or Anglican—was inextricably tangled with English ways of eating, dressing, working, looking at the world. Even John Eliot insisted that Christian Indian men farm and women weave, that they live not in wigwams but in English houses, that they barber their hair as the Puritans did, even that they stop using bear grease to ward off mosquitoes. Small wonder his successes were so modest.

Finally, Catholicism had long been the religion of people who, like the Indians, could not read or write. Catholic worship was ritualistic, ceremonial, theatrical, and mysterious. Protestants, especially Puritans, were a "people of the Book," the Bible. Religious services consisted of long sermons by learned preachers who minutely dissected biblical passages which were well known to English listeners because the pious among them read the Good Book daily. A religion that began and ended with a book was, if not incomprehensible to Indians, without much appeal. The only interest North Carolina tribe Indians took in the Bible, an appalled visitor reported, was in rubbing its soft vellum binding on their bellies.

Land Hunger

It is often said that the colonists simply stole the land they wanted from the Indians. This was rarely the case—in the eyes of the settlers. When they assumed possession of lands that had been vacated, like the site of Plymouth, their justification was an ancient legal principle that unoccupied land is anybody's pickings. Colonials acknowledged the legal and moral right of the tribes to own the land they occupied and purchased what they could of it. Roger Williams purchased Providence, Rhode Island, from the Narragansetts. William Penn and the Quakers conscientiously paid reasonable prices for the land they settled.

The problem was that when Indians sold land to newcomers, the two parties to the deal had two entirely different assumptions as to what had transpired. Thus, the Dutch in New Netherlands complained that they had paid for Manhattan three times over. Indeed they did because the sellers, three different tribes, believed that, in return for goods the Dutch gave them, they were accepting the Hollanders' presence on the island. They were saying that they were willing to share their hunting grounds with the whites in peace, just as they shared them with the other two tribes. The Dutch assumed they were purchasing exclusive right to Manhattan, as they might purchase a canal house in Amsterdam, and they took it unkindly that the sellers did not move out. The Indians were bewildered, and not only by the alien concept of ownership. Jasper Danckhaerts wrote of a land purchase in New York in 1679 that "the Indians hate the precipitancy of comprehension and judgement [of the whites], the excited chatterings, . . . the haste and rashness to do something, whereby a mess is often made of one's good intentions."

The almost inevitable consequence of the misunderstandings was conflict ignited by Indian trespass (in the colonials' eyes), Indians shot or insultingly handled, their tribes retaliating, and then outright war. The wars inevitably ended in victory for the more numerous, better armed colonials and were settled by the further dispossession of the Indians. Possession of territory by right of conquest in a just war had a long pedigree and compelling recommendations to the party with the military edge.

Even if there been no cultural misunderstanding of what was involved in a land sale, the nature of European agriculture made it impossible for the Indians to survive where the English lived. The Indians farmed by borrowing fields from the forest; they rudely cultivated the soil for a few years, and moved somewhere else. Their fields reverted to hunting grounds. The colonials destroyed the forest, removing the trees, roots and all, from hundreds of acres. When the soil of their farms was depleted, they did not move elsewhere. They converted the tired fields into pasture for their horses, cattle, and sheep, who manured and revived it, while the settlers converted more forest nearby into arable land. Their decisive destruction of the forest meant the flight of the game that was vital to Eastern Indian survival. "Our fathers had plenty of deer and skins, our plains as also our woods, and of turkeys," a Narrgansett sachem said, "but these English . . . , with their scythes cut down the grass, and with axes fell the trees; their cows and horses eat the grass, and their hogs spoil our clam banks, and we shall all be starved."

Scalping

In the 1870s, a crusader for Indian causes, Susette La Flesche, told audiences all over the United States that scalping—a gory practice that gave her listeners the shivers—had been taught the Indians by the English and French. Her evidence was the fact that several colonial assemblies paid their Indian allies a bounty for each enemy scalp they delivered. La Flesche's contention was revived in the 1980s and 1990s when it was fashionable to look on Indian-white relationships as all virtuous on one side (the Indians') and all vile on the other (the whites').

But it was nonsense. Seventeenth-century Europeans had a large repertory of gory practices—drawing and quartering was a good one—but there is no record of scalping among Europeans. There was not even a word for the practice in the English, French, and Dutch languages until 1535 when Jacques Cartier observed Indians along the St. Lawrence River taking their dead enemies' hair as trophies.

Furs and a New Kind of War

The Indians enjoyed a nice beef, mutton, or pork dinner but no Eastern tribes became herders. The pastoral life was as alien to them as the colonists' laborious intensive farming with oxen and plow. (Not to mention that fact that colonial men, not women, did the farming. The Indians were appalled.) There was, however, nothing alien to the Indians about trade. They were anxious to buy what the colonials had, from beef to baubles (the famous beads); anything made of iron, copper, or brass—vessels, tools, iron tomahawks; woven woolen blankets (which were far more serviceable than hides); and other textiles. The Indians also took tragically to intoxication, craving liquor, usually cheap brandy in New France, rum in the English colonies. Most of all, Indian braves wanted muskets, which improved hunting

Culver Pictures

A HURON—TYPE.

A Huron warrior. The Hurons, who lived north of the St. Lawrence River (in Canada) befriended the French as soon as they arrived. Their choice is understandable: The Hurons badly needed an ally against the Iroquois Confederation, which regularly savaged them. But the Hurons' closeness to The French helped to doom them. Their numbers were reduced radically by European diseases, especially smallpox. A devastating epidemic caused some to abandon the Christianity to which the French had converted them. Then, in 1648, a surprise attack by thousands of Mohawks and Oneidas—the army's size was unheard of in Indian warfare—wiped out nearly all the Hurons who were still alive.

and gave them a leg up on old tribal enemies who had no firearms.

In return for European products, the Indians hunted and trapped for the hides of deer and the furs that the colonials coveted. The immediate consequence of the fur trade was a leap in the Indians' standard of living. But competition for furs between tribes introduced a vicious kind of war that had been virtually unknown to the Indians. And in time the fur trade resulted in the destruction of the ecology of which the Eastern Indians been a part far beyond colonial farmlands.

Before the arrival of Europeans, the Woodlands tribes killed only the moose, deer, beaver, and other animals for which had an immediate need. Why kill more? Because the Indians were few, their needs had a minimal impact on the overall animal population. Indeed, their harvests of game probably had a healthy effect on wildlife by preventing overpopulation and disease.

Europeans could not get too many skins and pelts, however. The European upper classes coveted the furs of the beaver, otter, marten, and weasel. Inferior furs were chopped and pressed to make felt for hats. Leather made from deerskins

was superior, for many purposes, to leather made from cattle and hogs. In order to buy the goods the Europeans offered, the Eastern tribes soon virtually exterminated the deer and beaver in hunting grounds that had been adequate to their needs for centuries. This forced the tribes that supplied the Europeans to expand their operations into the hunting grounds of other peoples. Indian warfare, once highly formalized and not very bloody by European standards, became savage with the extermination of rivals—for the fur trade— the major object.

Thus, the Dutch in Fort Orange (Albany, New York) first bought furs from the Mohicans, an Algonkian tribe. When the Mohican hunting grounds were trapped out, the Dutch turned to the neighboring Mohawks. Powerful and aggressive, the Mohawks (and their allies in the Iroquois Confederacy) began to range farther in all directions. In 1637, they helped New Englanders in their war against the Pequots. Between 1643 and 1646, they cooperated with the Dutch in nearly destroying the Mohicans and other Algonkian tribes. In March 1648, a thousand Mohawk and Seneca warriors— a number unprecedented in Indian warfare—marched to north of the Great Lakes and swooped down on several Huron villages. They killed (according to estimates to be entertained with caution) 10,000 men, women, and children. The next year, below the Great Lakes, Cayugas and Senecas destroyed the Eries as a functioning tribe and then drove other peoples out of their ancestral homes in western Pennsylvania.

King Philip's War

After a few minor skirmishes with the Massachusetts Indians, the Puritans maintained strained but peaceful relations with them and with Massasoit's Wampanoags for forty years. Thanks largely to Roger Williams, there was peace with the powerful Narragansetts. Indeed, the Narragansetts cooperated with a combined Plymouth, Massachusetts, and Connecticut attack on the Pequots in 1637.

The Pequot War was the last significant conflict in New England until 1675. In that year, Plymouth hanged three Wampanoags for murdering Sassamon, a "praying Indian." The new Wampanoag chief, Metacomet (whom New Englanders called "King Philip") was already hostile to the colonials, in part because of a personal insult, in part because he understood that the colonials were not just another tribe but, with their ever-increasing numbers, destroying the Indian way of life. Quietly, he persuaded two other chiefs, Pomham of the Nipmucks and Canonchet of the Narragansetts (formerly enemies of the Wampanoags) to join the Wampanoags in a coordinated attack on outlying colonial towns. It was the first pan-Indian (that is, intertribal) attempt to preserve traditional culture and, briefly, it was quite successful.

Through most of 1675, the alliance was unstoppable. The Indians attacked fifty-two of New England's ninety towns, wiping twelve of them off the map. About 500 soldiers were killed and as many as 1,000 other New Englanders—one in 35. It was a devastating blow, but King Philip's alliance was unable to follow up on it. His own warriors ran short of provisions, and other tribal leaders began to quarrel among themselves. Most of the "praying Indians" allied with the whites. The Mohicans and the remnants of the Pequots declared neutrality. The opportunistic and ever-expansive Mohawks attacked King Philip's followers from the rear. And the New Englanders regrouped and counterattacked. They killed 2,000 to 3,000 Narragansetts, the most powerful tribe in southern New England. (The total death toll among the natives is unknown.) King Philip was killed, his head mounted on a stake in Boston in best seventeenth-century fashion. Canonchet's head was exhibited in Hartford, Connecticut.

Mixed Feelings

The aftermath of King Philip's War dramatized the difference between white and Indian conceptions of race. The Indians were quintessentially tribal: They thought in terms of us-versus-them; members of the tribe were in an entirely different category of people than all those who were not part of the tribe. However, there was no racism in their mindset. Captives adopted into the tribe—white prisoners as well as Indians born into another tribe—were fully accepted as "brothers" and "sisters." Indeed, tribes that lost population because of disease or war raided other tribes and white settlements specifically to increase their numbers.

Among the colonists, however, what began as a disdain for Indian culture—morals, manners, and religion—the English compared Indians to the long-despised Irish—became a contempt based on race. The Indians were "savage" not because of a blighted culture that education and conversion could overcome, but because they were racially inferior. Therefore, all Indians were enemies. After King Philip's War, Massachusetts banished most of the "praying Indians" (who had supported the colonials against King Philip!) to an island; they were "interned" because they were Indians. Only four Christian Indian villages were rebuilt.

Not every colonial was what we would call a racist. Benjamin Franklin, the Pennsylvanian who sanctified hard work and the squirreling away of money, betrayed a wistfulness when he wrote of the Indians: "Having few artificial wants, they have abundance of leisure for improvement by conversation. Our laborious manner of life, compared with theirs, they esteem slavish and base." To condemn all Indians for what some did, he said, was like launching a vendetta against all people with red hair because a man with red hair did one an injury. Whites captured and adopted by Indians commonly refused to return to white society when they had the chance. However, a Pennsylvanian wrote, "we have no examples of one of these Aborigines having free choice becoming European."

That was overstating it. Indians chose European ways only to discover that their race still excluded them from white society. In general, however, it is striking how few Eastern Indians found the ways colonials lived to be appealing. In 1744, Virginia invited the Iroquois to send six boys to the College of William and Mary. The Iroquois replied that they had had bad luck with Indian lads educated at New England colleges. "When they came back to us, they were bad runners, ignorant of every means of living in the woods, unable to bear either cold or hunger, knew neither how to build a cabin, take a deer, or kill an enemy; they were totally good for nothing."

The Iroquois understood that the Virginians meant well: "If the gentlemen of Virginia will send us a dozen of their sons, we will take great care of their education, instruct them in all we know, and make men of them."

AMERICANS FROM AFRICA

To colonials, the Indians were in the way. They had to be cleared from the land, preferably by peaceful means agreeable to both parties. White colonials looked on America's third race rather differently, particularly in the plantation regions of the South. Africans—blacks—most of them from West Africa, were highly desirable immigrants as domestic servants in the homes of the rich, as extra hands whose labor made a small farmer's life easier, and in gangs on plantations where the master's wealth and social standing were built atop their brawn and brains.

Africans were involuntary immigrants; they were brought to America against their will. This in itself did not set them apart from many poor whites. A sizable minority of British emigrants during the seventeenth and eighteenth centuries were forced to go to the colonies, including Scots rebels captured in battle. The Africans were not free, but neither were about half of European immigrants during their first years in America. Nor—at first—were Africans set apart from whites before the law. By the 1660s, however, the race of the Africans—the fact that they were identifiable as Africans at a glance, made it possible for the people in charge to reduce them to a lifelong slavery that no white men or women experienced.

Slavery and the English

Enslaved Africans and their descendants had been the backbone of the plantation labor force in the West Indies and in Portuguese Brazil for a century before the founding of Jamestown. So, on the face of it, the planters of Virginia and Maryland had an obvious example to which to look to meet their need for cheap labor.

They did not, however, turn to African slavery to bring their crops in. The English, unlike the Spanish and Portuguese, had no tradition of owning human beings as property. Slaves, even serfs, had vanished from English society centuries before the era of colonization. As for Africa, the English, again unlike the Spanish and Portuguese, had little experience of trade or war with the black peoples who occupied the continent south of the Sahara.

By the later 1500s, a few English seafarers, notably John Hawkins and Francis Drake, were selling blacks in the Caribbean to augment their income but, mostly, they were slaves the sea dogs had stolen from Spaniards on one island to sell to Spaniards on another. As late as 1618, when an African merchant on the Senegal River offered slaves to Richard Jobson in payment for English trade goods, Jobson replied indignantly that "we were a people who did not deal in any such commodities, neither did wee buy or sell one another, or any that had our owne shapes." The African was astonished, telling Jobson that the other white men who came to the Senegal wanted nothing but slaves. The English captain answered that "they were another kinde of people different from us."

Had this goodly mariner's principles prevailed, North America would have been spared its greatest historical injustice, the enslavement on a grand scale of Africans and their descendants.

New Uses for an Old Institution

During the 1600s, the tobacco growers of the Chesapeake brought their crops in using mostly fellow Englishmen and women bound by law to work for them as indentured servants. The institution of indentured servitude was an adaptation of the well-established English means of training boys to be artisans and caring for orphans who were, under the law, the responsibility of the parish in which they lived.

Thus, if a man wanted his son to learn a skilled trade, to be a blacksmith or a baker or a carpenter or a cooper (a man who made barrels), he signed a legal agreement called an indenture with a master of that craft. The boy was tied to the master; he was bound in the law to labor for him for a period of years, customarily seven, from age 14 (old enough to work a long day) to age 21. In return for the lad's labor, the master agreed to shelter, clothe, and feed his apprentice and to teach him the "mysteries" of his craft. An apprentice was not free. He was a servant, obligated to obey his master as if the master were his father. He was subject to corporal punishment if he disobeyed. If he ran away, his master could call on the authorities to force his return.

The English also used the institution of indentured servitude—bondage to another for a period of years—to provide for orphans. Children whose parents died or abandoned them were farmed out as menial servants (there was no education involved) to families who agreed to bear the expense of raising them. The parish was spared the expense of feeding, clothing, and housing orphans; the families who took them in got a menial laborer bound to them for the cost of meals, clothing, and a corner for sleeping.

Apprentices and servants were not slaves; their masters did not own them. They had personal rights their masters were required to respect. There are many cases of servants who proved they were abused and because of the abuse won their freedom. The term of their servitude was written down in black and white on their indentures. The day arrived when the apprentice and the maidservant walked off as free man and free woman. While they were servants, however, under the Statute of Artificers of 1562, masters had the same broad authority over them that parents exercised over their children

Seven Years

People ordered into indentured servitude by courts were bound for seven years. Seven years was the traditional term of apprenticeship and there was a biblical justification. Deuteronomy 15:12 said of a servant that "in the seventh year thou shalt let him go free from thee." In Genesis 29, Jacob labored seven years for Laban in order to win the hand of Laban's daughter, Rachel. The seven years "seemed unto him but a few days, for the love he had for her," which was surely not the way indentured servants in the colonies looked upon their term of servitude. They would have found more familiar the fact that Laban tricked Jacob. He married Jacob to his elder daughter, Leah, who was veiled. Jacob had to sign on for another seven years to get Rachel.

Kidnapped

Our word *kidnapped* was first used to refer to people seized in England and sold as servants in the colonies. In a seventeeth-century book, *New World of Words*, Edward Phillips defined kidnappers as "those that make a trade of decoying and spiriting away young Children to ship them to foreign plantations." In a dictionary of 1724, Nathan Bailey defined the word as "a Person who makes it his Business to decoy either Children or young Persons to send them to the *English* plantations in *America.*"

(which was considerably more authority than the law allows natural parents today).

Indentured Servants

Indentured servitude well suited great planters (and more modestly fixed farmers) who needed laborers in their fields. Their agents in England recruited impoverished adults and adolescents to sign indentures to work in the colonies as servants for an agreed upon number of years. (Terms varied from three to seven years depending on how badly masters needed workers.) In return for signing away several years of freedom, the servants' passage across the Atlantic was paid. When they were freed, servants were given clothing (usually two changes, one for work, one for church), perhaps some tools, a little money, sometimes land (50 acres in Maryland, less elsewhere).

Not every servant signed indentures voluntarily. English courts sentenced convicts to "transportation" to the colonies; that is, they served their sentences as bound servants. Crimps kidnapped boys off the streets of seaports and men foolish enough to get too drunk too near to the docks when a servant ship only half-filled lay at anchor in the harbor. In

Mary Evans Picture Library/Arthur Rackman/The Image Works

A highly romanticized depiction of a village "goose girl." In reality, tending geese was among the most menial tasks in rural England, inevitably assigned to orphan girls many years younger than this young lady and certainly not so tidy and clean nor dressed so attractively. Goose girls were bound servants and objects of contempt. They were of the social class from which indentured servants dispatched to the colonies were drawn.

1659, the Venetian ambassador in London saw 1,200 people openly rounded up against their will to be shipped to Barbados.

Redemptioners

After 1700, however, British indentured servants were less attractive to colonial masters than they had been. Parliament enacted laws protecting British subjects from the worst abuses to which colonial servants were subjected. Law enforcement authorities in England and courts in the colonies cracked down on kidnapping. The law required that very specific terms of servitude be approved by a magistrate in Great Britain; indentures not bearing a magistrate's seal were unenforceable in the colonies.

These protections did not, however, extend to Europeans (mostly Germans) who were not British subjects. And an institution had developed among the Germans of Pennsylvania that was quickly perverted to provide American farmers with a new kind of servant. German families already in Pennsylvania made agreements with shipping companies that if they transported their relatives to Philadelphia, they—the German-American families—would *redeem* them upon their arrival by paying the cost of their passage. Thus, the newcomers were called redemptioners.

Shippers soon realized that they could increase their business by recruiting impoverished Germans (and Dutch and Swiss) who had no relatives in the colonies waiting to redeem them. "Spirits" and "soul sellers," usually men who had been in the colonies, persuaded would-be emigrants that they could bind themselves to the shipper (on terms far inferior to those by which British servants were protected) and, once arrived in the colonies, negotiate a term of service with a farmer or planter who would then pay their passage.

It was a dirty business. The cost of a transatlantic crossing after 1700 was as high as £20. The soul sellers lied about how long a redemptioner would have to work as a servant to make his labor worth £10–£20. To keep costs down, servant ships were overcrowded. The holds were "full of pitiful signs of distress—smells, fumes, horrors, vomiting, various kinds of sea sickness, fever, dysentery, headaches, heat, constipation, boils, scurvy, cancer, mouth-rot, and similar afflictions." Mortality was often so high as to sicken even people of that harder-hearted age. In 1720, the *Honour* left England for Annapolis, Maryland, with 61 convicts; 20 survived. The *Love and Unity* left Rotterdam in 1731 with 150 German redemptioners aboard; it arrived in Philadelphia with 34. In 1741, the *Sea Flower* sailed out of Belfast with 100 Irish passengers; 60 survived. In 1751, the *Good Intent* ran into adverse weather and was at sea for twenty-four weeks. Not a single servant who had embarked on a new life in America was still alive.

Black Servants

The first Africans in the colonies were servants, albeit without indentures. They arrived in 1619 when a Dutch vessel sailed into the Chesapeake Bay and offered about twenty "negars" for sale in Jamestown. The Dutch were probably privateers who had seized the Africans from a slave trader in the Spanish West Indies. The Netherlands was at war with Spain; Dutch commerce raiders had taken up where the sea dogs left off. Virginia was in the midst of the tobacco boom, and the Africans were snapped up.

Other ships carrying African captives arrived periodically in Virginia, but not many. Sugar planters in the West Indies paid better prices for slaves, and the tobacco growers do not seem to have encouraged the trade. European servants were getting the job done. Blacks did not become an important part of the labor force in the tobacco colonies for more than fifty years. In 1660, African Americans were just 4 percent of the population in Virginia and Maryland. New Netherlands, still Dutch in 1660, had much a higher proportion of blacks in its population, 15 percent.

The first Africans arrived in New Netherlands by 1624. They were defined as slaves but, within a few years, some of their number successfully petitioned the company that governed the colony to grant "half freedom" to married males. That is, married men were permitted to work for themselves part-time and to use the proceeds to purchase their wives' and children's freedom.

Even under English rule, slavery was never the onerous institution it was in the South. There was no plantation slavery in New York, simply because there were no plantations—no commercial agriculture on a grand scale. Few if any New Yorkers owned as many as fifty blacks as late as 1750, when many Virginians did. Most slaves in New York worked for householders in New York City or were farmhands, belonging to small-scale family farmers who owned only a few. New York had a higher proportion of white slave owners than any colony, 40 percent in New York City and adjoining counties in the late 1700s. With the master-slave relationship so often intimate, manumission was common in the colony.

Until the 1660s, the legal status of black Virginians and Marylanders seems to have been identical to the status of white servants. If they survived in the disease-ridden region, Africans were freed after a term of service comparable to what whites served. A few actually enjoyed American success stories. One African who arrived in Jamestown in 1619

Stranger than Fiction

In 1756, Hamet, a Moroccan seaman, was seized by a Portuguese captain but, in port, he escaped to a British ship. It was a bad choice; the vessel was Carolina-bound where there was always a good market for slaves. Hamet was sold in Charleston. At a remote plantation 150 miles inland, he worked for fifteen years grinding corn for the field hands. When his master went bankrupt in 1771, Hamet approached the creditors who came to liquidate his property and told his story. The creditors (to their credit) were shocked. They freed Hamet and helped him find passage to Morocco.

adopted the name Anthony Johnson and became a prosperous planter with several white servants bound to him. By 1650, there was a substantial population of free blacks in the Chesapeake colonies. There were free blacks among Nathaniel Bacon's rebels.

The Emergence of Slavery

By Bacon's time, however, social acceptance of blacks, both free and in bondage, had largely disappeared. Beginning in the 1660s and probably earlier, the legal status of black servants in Virginia and Maryland was radically redefined. They ceased to be indentured servants with the same rights as white servants, and were defined as the property of their masters—slaves serving *durante vita,* throughout their lives.

The transformation was effected not by the adoption of a comprehensive code, but piecemeal; or, at least, we know of it only from a scattering of laws and court cases that have survived. In 1662, Virginia's House of Burgesses enacted a law punishing fornication involving a black and a white more severely than fornication by two blacks or two whites was punished. This act may be a reflection of increased racism among Virginia's whites; it applied to free blacks as well as servants. Or, it may tell us that black servants were already in a bondage different from that of white servants.

Race was not mentioned when the Burgesses declared that "all children born in this country shall be held bond or free according to the condition of the mother." But the law makes no sense applied to an infant born to a white servant because she and her child would be legally free before the child was old enough to work.

In several court rulings punishing runaways, the slave status of blacks was obvious. In one instance, a black and a white servant ran away together and were captured together. Their offenses were identical. However, two years were added to the white runaway's service. The black runaway was flogged. Obviously, he was already a "servant" for life. In a similar case, a white runaway was branded, shackled on the leg for a year, and ordered to work seven years for the colony. The black man, named Emmanuel, suffered the same penalty except that no time was added to his bondage.

In 1682, the colony proclaimed that conversion to Christianity was not grounds for freeing a slave, even if the slave's master wished to do so. Masters who did free their slaves were required to transport them out of the colony.

The Role of Race

Why did Virginia and Maryland (and, eventually, all the colonies) reduce Africans and their children to the status of property? First of all, they realized that they *could* do so. They had become familiar with the fact that Africans in the West Indies were chattels, not servants. They traded with Barbados, England's sugar producer since 1627, and Jamaica, seized from the Spanish in 1655. Moreover, South Carolina's first settlers came not from Europe but from Barbados, and they brought their slaves and a comprehensive slave code with them.

It was, of course, to the economic interest of the Virginia and Maryland elite, which made the laws, to force their fieldhands to labor for them their entire lives rather than for three or four years. They could not make white servants slaves *durante vita.* As the king's subjects, they had certain personal rights, and they were aware of them. Africans in bondage had no such rights. They were fair game.

Finally, if it was universally assumed that blacks were somebody's slave unless they could prove they were free, planters took a giant step toward stabilizing their labor force. Runaways were a chronic, nagging problem for tobacco planters. Even in the oldest tobacco-growing areas of Virginia and Maryland, the country was mostly woods. Cleared fields were mere gaps in the forest. Roads were mere tracks, some of them so narrow two horsemen could not pass without jostling one another.

It was not easy for a white servant to make a permanent escape, but it was possible. By lying low in the forests by day and stealing food and moving by night, they could make it to a city like Philadelphia and lose themselves in the crowds of strangers. Immigrants known to no one streamed through colonial ports daily. The few law enforcement officers could not practicably ask every white stranger to prove he was not a runaway.

A runaway black, because of his race, stood out in the throngs of immigrants. Black strangers were so few that it was worth a constable's time to ask them to show their papers. An unknown black trudging along a country road was immediately suspect. A black woman or man without freedom documents—free blacks, such as seamen, took good care of their papers—was assumed to be a runaway slave and jailed until his or her master—masters advertised runaways and could be contacted—showed up and paid the costs of keeping the runaway plus a fee. Such fees were an important parts of sheriffs' income.

But there was more to it than imitation. The Chesapeake's rich tobacco planters, who made the colony's laws, *could* reclassify blacks to their own benefit. It was obviously in their interest that their field hands labor for them for life rather than for a few years. Enslaving white servants was out of the question; their rights as persons were sacrosanct. African servants, however, had no claim on the "rights of Englishmen." English law and tradition did not protect them.

An increase in the supply of captive Africans after 1700 encouraged tobacco planters to make the most of them as laborers. The English were latecomers in the business of buying slaves in Africa but, by 1660, English slavers were making up for lost time. In 1663, the Crown created the Royal African Company to ensure that the big profits to be made selling slaves in the colonies went into English rather than foreign purses—mercantilism again!

A Better Buy

Nevertheless, except in South Carolina, white indentured servants were far more numerous than African slaves until after 1700. They were the "better buy." Slaves had to be purchased

A SLAVE-SHED.

North Wind Picture Archives

These captives, tied by their necks in a village in the West African interior, were fated to be slaves somewhere in the Americas, if they survived the deadly march to the coast and the trans-Atlantic voyage. Contrary to a widespread assumption, almost all Africans bound for American slavery were made captive not by Europeans but by other Africans. The economy of some powerful tribes was based on the seizure of others for delivery to Europeans on the coast.

in Africa; white servants were free in Europe. Transportation costs from Africa were higher than the costs of the shorter voyage from Europe. The asking price of a lifetime worker was higher than the price of a white servant who would win freedom within a few years. As a rule, a slave cost three times as much as a servant of the same age and sex.

The high mortality rate in the Chesapeake colonies favored the purchase of white servants. Every new arrival, black and white, stood a dismayingly good chance of contracting a fatal disease within a year—smallpox, influenza, dysentery, typhoid fever, typhus, malaria, yellow fever. Life expectancy for male immigrants to Maryland was 43. Governor Berkeley of Virginia estimated that four out of five servants (black and white) died within two years of arriving. When *durante vita* translated as "probably two years," it did not mean very much. It made better financial sense for planters to buy the cheaper white servants than the expensive black slaves.

After 1700, however, the mortality rate on the Chesapeake steadily improved. And planters noticed that Africans were more likely to survive yellow fever and malaria, the big killers, than whites were. (Yellow fever and the most dangerous form of malaria, *plasmodium,* originated in Africa. Blacks were more likely to have inherited immunities to them.) With everyone living longer and blacks more resistant to two of the worst diseases of the country, after 1700, planters had an incentive to save money on the *annual* cost of a bound laborer rather than on the *initial outlay*—the purchase price. It now made sense to buy workers who served longer and whose offspring were also their mothers' owners' property.

British laws protecting the rights of British servants—the same laws that encouraged the turn toward redemption-

ers in the northern colonies—encouraged the turn toward African slaves in the South. In 1670, there were 20,000 blacks in Virginia, a large majority of them slaves. After 1700, the colony's slave population grew rapidly until, by the time of the Revolution, it approached 300,000. By 1720, 67 percent of South Carolina's population was black, almost all were slaves. A British officer observed, "They sell the servants here as they do their horses, and advertise them as they do their beef and oatmeal."

THE TRANS-ATLANTIC SLAVE TRADE

Buying and selling slaves was an ancient institution in West Africa. Since early in the Middle Ages, Muslim Arabs and Berbers of present-day Morocco and Algeria crossed the Sahara in caravans to Timbuctoo, where they purchased black Africans, gold, and ivory brought from the south. Some caravans paused for a rest in towns near Cape Branco (Mauritania) where, in the 1440s, the Portuguese founded Arguin, the first European slave trading station in Africa. At first, the Portuguese purchased slaves from the caravaners, but they soon realized that they could bypass these middlemen and their profits by setting up farther south. The Portuguese soon had "slave stations" at regular intervals around the Gulf of Guinea, then in Angola, and eventually in East Africa. By 1600, when the Dutch, French and others began to horn in on the Portuguese slave trade, as many as 200,000 West Africans had already been torn from their homeland. About 50,000 were taken to Europe, 25,000 to Portugal's island colonies in the Atlantic, the rest to Brazil and to Spanish colonies in the New World.

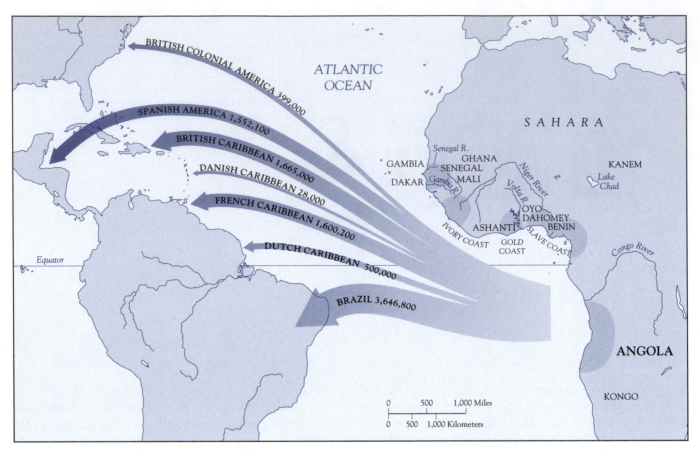

MAP 5:2 **The Atlantic Slave Trade.** Slavery looms large in American history, but in the context of the Western Hemisphere, the colonies and, later, the United States were minor players in the African slave trade. Even the tiny Dutch sugar islands of the West Indies imported more Africans than colonial Americans did. Slaves producing sugar were worked so hard they did not reproduce. Sugar planters constantly imported new workers to replace those who died. In the mainland colonies, African Americans had children at a normal rate.

Dutch and French slave traders sometimes built their own coastal forts, sometimes seized slave stations from the overextended Portuguese. Then came the English and, soon enough, Swedes, Danes, German Brandenburgers, and a few American colonials, notably from Newport, Rhode Island, a city that was built on the profits from the African slave trade.

A Collaborative Enterprise

Some whites ventured up the rivers of West Africa and seized or "panyared" villagers themselves. An English trader explained: "In the night we broke into the villages and, rushing into the huts of the inhabitants, seized men, women, and children promiscuously." But such expeditions were rare; they were too dangerous. Europeans died in great numbers from tropical diseases and native African slave stealers, who held the power in the interior, did not take kindly to whites competing at their end of the business.

So, the slave trade was a collaboration between African suppliers and white buyers with, in some areas, people of mixed blood (*lançado* in Portugese, *tapoeijers* in Dutch, *mulattos* to the English) acting as brokers. The African slave trade was never race versus race; it was a multiracial business.

Tribal kings and lesser chiefs sold off their criminals, both garden variety troublemakers and ugly hardened criminals, and prisoners they had taken in war. As the European demand for slaves grew—and it was insatiable during the 1700s—aggressive peoples like the Mandingos, Wolofs, Yoruba, and, later, the Ashanti sent raiding parties far inland for the purpose of capturing merchandise. The economy and power of the great Ashanti Confederation were founded on the commerce in slaves. By 1750, King Tegbesu of Dahomey annually pocketed £250,000 selling slaves destined for the Americas.

Captives were marched to the coast in coffles (tied or chained together neck to neck) or by boat down the great rivers of West Africa: the Senegal, Gambia, Volta, Niger, and Congo. The major dealers sold them immediately, often through *lançado* middlemen, at European forts where they were held in stockades or dungeons until a ship arrived. Free-lance slave traders, who had no access to the stations, literally cruised the shoreline looking for slaves for sale.

Unknown numbers died between capture and the day they were put aboard ship. Slaves in coffles who faltered, delaying the march, were routinely killed or abandoned. The ocean crossing, called the "middle passage," was deadlier than the overland march. Rather than providing the most healthful conditions possible for their human cargos to keep mortality low, the Atlantic slave traders crammed as many as they could in the hold "like herrings in a barrel."

A Deadly Business

The Atlantic slave trade was drenched in death. It is the ultimate testimony to human greed and, in the case of the crews of ships, of desperation that so many people were engaged in it for so long. The number of Africans who died in the coffles cannot be estimated. Four of five Europeans posted to coastal slave stations were buried there. If only one in twenty slaves crossing the Atlantic died aboard ship, the voyage was celebrated as a success. If one slave in five on the Middle Passage died—high mortality but far from unknown—there was still a big profit. A slave for whom a *lançado* charged £5–£10 sold in the New World for £25 and more. In 1779, the master of the *Hawke* spent £3000 in West Africa for nearly 400 slaves; the survivors sold in the colonies for 17,000. Only as the eighteenth century progressed did mortality on the Middle Passage decline. Proportionally, more crewmen on slavers died than the slaves they carried. One seaman in five sailing the Middle Passage failed to complete the voyage compared to 1 in 100 sailors on North Atlantic crossings.

Africans did not die because the slave ships were sailed by sadists (although some surely were). Transporting slaves was a business and it was calculated early on in the trade that it was more profitable to pack captives in and absorb large losses caused by the greater filth and disease than it was to provide the slaves with enough room that they could live with a minimum of decency. Indeed, the mortality rate on the European servant ships, which were also packed solid, was as high as on the Middle Passage.

West African Roots

Only a small proportion of the Africans torn from their homelands were destined for the North American colonies. Excluding the uncountable numbers of black Africans marched across the Sahara to be sold in Muslim lands, as many as 10 million Africans were enslaved over 400 years. By far the largest part of them—those who survived—became Brazilians, 3.6 million. About 1.6 million ended up in Spanish colonies, approximately the same number in the French Caribbean (especially Haiti) and on Britain's West Indian islands. The North American colonies were a minor market. One historian has identified 1,222 voyages from Africa's Gold Coast to British colonies between 1650 and 1807. More than half went to Jamaica, almost 20 percent to Barbados, and just 10.8 percent to the mainland colonies.

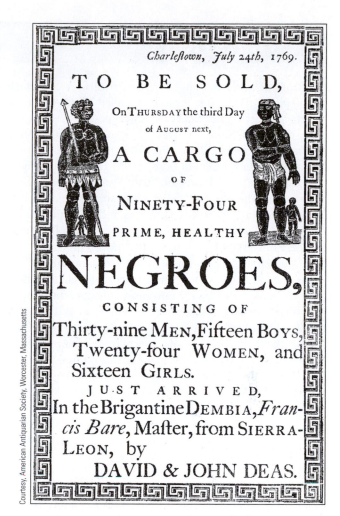

Courtesy, American Antiquarian Society, Worcester, Massachusetts

An advertisement for an auction of enslaved Africans in Charleston, South Carolina, the most important mainland destination for Atlantic slave traders. This slave auction was atypical in one respect: The wretches to be sold appear to have been brought directly from Africa. Most Africans imported into the mainland colonies spent some time in the West Indies— Barbados or Jamaica—even if just long enough to "season" them before the short voyage to North America. The origin of these slaves in Sierra Leone—they were probably purchased at Sherbro Island—was a big selling point in South Carolina. Slaves from that part of West Africa were skilled rice growers.

The Gold Coast was one region of the Gulf of Guinea coast; others were called the Slave Coast and the Ivory Coast. (They are now the nations of Gambia, Senegal, Guineau, Liberia, Sierra Leone, Ivory Coast, Ghana, Togo, Benin, and Nigeria.) Toward the end of the colonial period and after the United States gained its independence, increasing numbers of Angolans (from what is now the Congo as well as Angola), many of them warriors captured in the region's unending tribal wars, were imported. So, most African Americans today (who are not recent immigrants) have West African roots.

Linguistically, most slave ships were Babels. Ships' captains deliberately purchased slaves from as many language groups

SLAVE STATIONS

European "slave stations" in West Africa were both forts and places of business. Some, including the first, Arguin, an octagonal structure built by the Portuguese on Cape Blanco in the 1440s, were constructed of stone brought from Portugal as ballast. Elmina on the Gold Coast (Ghana), also Portuguese built but seized by the Dutch in 1637, was, according to a French visitor, "justly famous for beauty and strength." The walls of other stations were pounded earth, built by slaves. (Some slave stations, including Elmina between 1480 and 1520, actually *imported* slaves from elsewhere in West Africa for such construction projects.)

Mainland stations, usually built at the mouths of rivers, were walled to protect the European merchants within from both Africans and Europeans of different nations. The slave trade was as competitive a business as it was ugly. A weakly defended station was an invitation to Africans to seize the slaves there for sale elsewhere, and the gold, ivory, and European trade goods that were also stored there.

The stations' cannon were usually trained on the sea. Europeans of other nations in ships were a greater threat than native Africans, the most powerful of whom were trading partners and friendly: the Mandingos at Goreé, the Yoruba at Whydah, the Wolofs at Fort James. But the often undermanned stations were vulnerable to well-armed ships; several slave stations changed owners several times. Arguin was Spanish between 1580 and 1638 when the French seized it. Brandenburgers (Prussian Germans) took it over at the end of the century. The Dutch bought Arguin from the Portuguese in 1721, only to lose it to the French. Cabo Corso, built by Swedes in 1655, fell to the Dutch, the Danes, and the English in just ten years.

The most desirable location for a slave station was an island off the coast. Island forts were healthier than stations on the mainland. The Portuguese, the first Europeans in the slave trade, had and held São Tomé and Principe, strategically located midway between the Slave Coast and Angola, the two most important sources of enslaved Africans.

São Tomé and Principe were described by visitors as "stunningly beautiful." Life at Goreé, the preferred market for slave traders out of Newport, Rhode Island, was said to be "pleasant." It is difficult to understand how those adjectives occurred to anyone. The forts were places of horror, routine brutality, filth, disease, and death. Courtyards were filled with slaves tied to posts and penned in stockades while their captors waited for buyers. In the stone forts, slaves were packed into pitch-black dungeons. They died wholesale, as did the European merchants and soldiers posted to the forts: Their mortality rate reached 80 percent.

Because of the Europeans' susceptibility to tropical diseases, most "middle managers" at the stations—who negotiated directly with African suppliers—were people of mixed blood, mostly Portuguese-African *lançados*. The Portuguese had been in West Africa for more than two centuries by 1700; the *lançado* population was large. Not quite accepted by either Portuguese or Africans, they carved a niche for themselves as go-betweens. On the Guinea Coast, *lançados* dominated the slave trade for almost a century.

Stations had churches within the walls, Roman Catholic in the Portuguese and French forts, Protestant in the others, but there was little missionary work, particularly in the Catholic stations. Catholics were forbidden to enslave other Catholics. This prohibition worked to the advantage of the *lançado*, who were Catholic, but it meant nothing to Protestant Dutch and English slavers. The leaders of the Stono Rebellion in South Carolina claimed to be Catholics, and many of the first Africans in New Amsterdam had Portugese names.

Besides religious services, the only relief for Europeans from their ugly business (and the fact that their chances of seeing Europe again were one in five) was alcohol. So, the slave trading companies poured generously. Ships that came to carry slaves to the Americas brought immense quantities of cheap wine and liquors. Some was for trade, of course, but much of it was for their employees' rest and relaxation.

as were available so that few could understand one another. The idea was to minimize the threat of mutiny. There were plenty of uprisings, but most of the successful mutinies occurred within sight of the African coast. Slaves on the high seas sometimes succeeded in capturing the ship, but if they killed all the seamen, the rebels discovered they did not know how to sail the ships and they died of hunger or thirst. Slave traders sometimes returned to port with tales of finding ships adrift, their decks littered with corpses.

Relatively few Africans destined to be sold in North America were transported directly from Africa. A glance at a map

reveals why. Every week at sea increased the death toll. Because most slave traders rode the same favorable westerly winds Columbus had followed from the Canary Islands, their first landfall was in the West Indies. Even when the cargo was destined for Virginia or South Carolina, prudent slaver captains paused at a West Indian island to refit their vessels, replenish water and stores, and to put the slaves ashore for "seasoning."

Seasoning had little to do with adjusting to a new climate. West Africa and the West Indies were tropical; the climate of the colonies was more benign than either. Seasoning meant

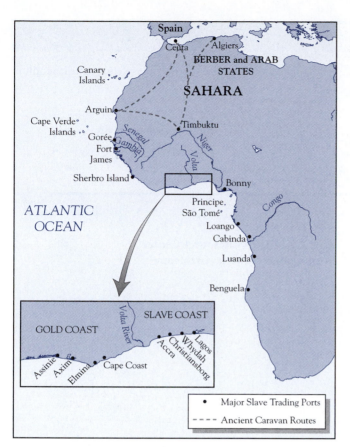

West African Slave Stations. This map shows only the most important and longest lasting slave stations from which most of the Africans taken to the Americas were sold and shipped. There were many others; at one time, on a 12-mile stretch of the Guinea Coast (the mainland opposite Sherbro Island) there were five forts representing five European nations. On the Gold Coast (present-day Ghana), freelancer slave catchers held their captives on beaches and, like hucksters at a modern tourist resort, hailed passing ships. Some "independents" maintained permanent headquarters. Betsy Heard, an English woman married to an African, ran a major operation for several years (and was famous for her ruthlessness).

recovering from the ordeal of the crossing: rest, fresh air, and a few weeks of decent food. With healthier merchandise to sell, slavers then proceeded to Savannah, Charleston, the Chesapeake, or a northern port. Most American slave traders—during the 1700s, some 900 ships from Newport, Rhode Island engaged in the trade—never laid eyes on Africa. They carried grain and livestock to the West Indies and traded their cargos for slaves recently brought across the Atlantic.

FURTHER READING

Classics Alvin M. Josephy, *The Indian Heritage of America,* 1968; Harold E. Driver, *Indians of North America,* 1970; Wilcomb E. Washburn, *The Indian in America,* 1975; Kenneth Stampp, *The Peculiar Institution,* 1956; David B. Davis, *The Problem of Slavery in Western Culture,* 1966; Edmund S. Morgan, *American Slavery, American Freedom,* 1975

General Robert F. Spencer and Jesse Jennings et al., *The Native Americans: Ethnology and Background of the North American Indians,* 1977; and *The Cambridge History of the Natives of the World.* vol. 3, *North America,* 1993.

People of the Eastern Woodlands James Axtell, *The European and the Indian: Essays in the Ethnohistory of Colonial North America,* 1981; *The Invasion Within: The Contest of Cultures in Colonial America,* 1985, and *Beyond 1492: Encounters in Colonial America,* 1988; Colin G. Calloway, *War, Migration, and the Survival of Indians,* 1990; *Dawnland Encounters: Indians and Europeans in Northern New England,* 1991; *New Worlds for All: Indians, Europeans, and the Remaking of Early America,* 1997; and *The World Turned Upside Down: Indian Voices from Early America,* 1994; William Cronon, *Changes in the Land: Indians, Colonists, and the Ecology of New England,* 1983; Neal Salisbury, *Manitou and Providence: Indians, Europeans, and the Making of New England,* 1982; Richard White, *The Middle Ground: Indians, Empires, and Republics in the Great Lakes Region 1650–1815,* 1991; Karen O. Ordahl, *Indians and English: Facing Off in Early America,* 2000; Peter C. Mancall and James H. Morrell, eds., *American Encounters: Natives and Newcomers from European Contact to Indian Removal,* 2000; Russell Bourne, *Gods of War, Gods of Peace: How the Meeting of Native and Colonial Religions Shaped Early America,* 2002; Laura M. Stevens, *The Poor Indians: British Missionaries, Native Americans, and Colonial Sensibilities,* 2005; Francis Jennings, *The Ambiguous Iroquois Empire: The Covenant Chain Confederation of Indian Tribes with English Colonies,* 1984; Daniel K. Richter, *The Ordeal of the Longhouse: The People of the Iroquois League in the Era of European Civilization,* 1992.

Servants and Slaves Ira Berlin, *Many Thousands Gone: The First Two Centuries of Slavery in North America,* 1998; David W. Galenson, *White Servitude in Colonial America,* 1981; Philip D. Curtin, *The Atlantic Slave Trade,* 1969. Hugh Thomas, *The Slave Trade: The Story of the Atlantic Slave Trade, 1440–1870,* 1997.

KEY TERMS

Use the following listing of key terms to review important figures, events, locations, and concepts covered in this chapter. A glossary of these terms is available on *The American*

Past companion Web site: www.cengage.com/history/conlin/tap9e

Hiawatha, p. 75

Five Nations, p. 76

Metacomet, p. 79

Serfs, p. 80

Redemptioners, p. 83

durante vita, p. 84

ONLINE RESOURCES

Find additional resources, including primary source documents, images, interactive maps, simulations, chapter review exercises, and Internet links at

The American Past **companion Web site**
www.cengage.com/history/conlin/tap9e

American History Resource Center
http://ushistory.wadsworth.com/

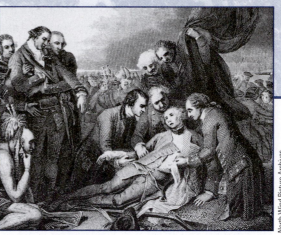

North Wind Picture Archives

Chapter 6

Contest for a Continent

French America and British America 1608–1763

This country has twice the population of New France, but the people there are astonishingly cowardly, completely undisciplined, and without any experience in war....It is not at all like that in Canada. The Canadians are brave, much inured to war, and untiring in travel. Two thousand of them will at all times and in all places thrash the people of New England.

—French Officer, Troupes de la Marine

A perfidious enemy, who have dared to exasperate you by their cruelties, but not to oppose you on equal ground, are now constrained to face you....A few regular troops from old France, ...those numerous companies of Canadians, insolent, mutinous, unsteady, and ill-disciplined.... As for those savage tribes of Indians, whose horrid yells in the forest have struck many a bold heart with affright, terrible as they are with a tomahawk and scalping-knife to a flying and prostrate foe, you have experienced how little their ferocity is to be dreaded by resolute men upon fair and open ground ....

I have led you up these steep and dangerous rocks...and, believe me, my friends, if your conquest could be bought with the blood of your general, he would most cheerfully resign a life which he has long devoted to his country.

—General James Wolfe to his troops before Quebec

In 1603, a remarkable French soldier and seafarer, Samuel de Champlain, sailed to North America searching for the Northwest Passage to the Indies that Europeans were positive existed. Champlain also had colonization in mind. He explored Acadia (now Nova Scotia) and the massive St. Lawrence River to above the site of present-day Montreal. On a second voyage in 1605, he left a few men on the western shore of Acadia to lay the foundations of Port Royal. But New France, as he named Canada (an Indian word) had its real beginnings in 1608, a few months after Jamestown was founded. In that year, Champlain's men started to build Quebec (an Algonkian word mean-

ing "the narrows") on a steep cliff on the north bank of the St. Lawrence. It was during this expedition that Champlain introduced the Mohawks to the power of firearms on Lake Champlain.

New France and Louisiana

French ambitions for their North American colony were similar to those of the English. In two respects they were more successful than the English. They established a more lucrative trade in furs with the Indians, and they were far more successful in converting the natives to Christianity. French hopes of finding an easy, mostly water route to East Asia were, however, doomed to disappointment.

Not Enough People

The fatal failure of the French was their inability to populate New France. By 1640, English men and women were crossing the Atlantic in droves. French men and women were not. Between 1630 and 1640, 30,000 Puritans emigrated to just one English colony, Massachusetts. During Quebec's first thirty years, just 300 emigrants settled along the St. Lawrence and stayed.

It was not that the French masses led such enviable lives. They did not. The problem was that the climate and soil of New France were unappealing to peasants who owned even tiny patches of "sweet France." Canada's growing season was shorter than New England's; winters were colder; the soil at least as stony. Two-thirds of those who tried to farm in New France gave up and returned home where their horror stories fed the anti-Canadian prejudice. Strikingly—for four Europeans in five were farmers—a high proportion of those who stayed in Canada came from cities and towns.

The French kings could have populated Canada with religious dissenters as the English King had. France had its troublesome dissenters, too: Calvinist Protestants similar to the Puritans called Huguenots. In areas where they were numerous, zealous Huguenots bullied Catholics, burned their churches, and cocked a snoot at the monarchy. Over most of France, however, the Huguenots were a minority and themselves victims of persecution.

Many Huguenots were willing, even anxious to move abroad. The failed French colonies of the 1500s in Carolina and Florida were Huguenot projects. The population of Champlain's Port Royal was mostly Huguenot.

But the king forbade any but Catholics in New France. Better to prevent the export of France's religious problems than to ease them at home by reducing the Huguenot population. After 1685, when the Huguenots lost the limited toleration they had enjoyed in France, they left the country by the tens of thousands. But they went not to Canada. They fled to Holland, England—*and to the English colonies!* They proved to be valuable colonists: A few were quite wealthy; many others were solidly middle class, skilled, energetic, and industrious. They would have been an animating yeast among the peasant and military population of New France.

Encouraging Settlement

Louis XIV, king for seventy years, tried to induce French Catholics to go to Canada. The bondage of indentured servants was legally limited to three years, the shortest term servants in the English colonies could hope for. When they were freed, servants in Canada were granted land and other benefits far more generous than the "freedom dues" the English colonies offered.

When positive inducements failed, Louis pressured his subjects to emigrate. Entire villages in impoverished Brittany were shipped to Quebec on the flimsiest of justifications. Soldiers posted in Canada were commanded to remain as civilians when the army discharged them. Orphan girls and the daughters of peasants who got into trouble with the tax collector were loaded aboard ships to provide wives for Canada's bachelors. The king forbade the conscription of prostitutes for removal to Canada but, in practice, *filles du roi* ("the king's daughters") were sometimes rounded up in Paris and French seaports and dispatched in "whore ships."

Savages

The Spanish, Portugese, English, Dutch, Swedes, Danes— every European people with colonies in the Americas— called the native inhabitants *Indians*—except the French. They had the word, *les Indes*. But in New France, natives, both friends and enemies, were *les sauvages*, the savages. In French, the word is not complimentary, but neither is it as derogatory as it is in English.

Colonial Wars 1688–1763

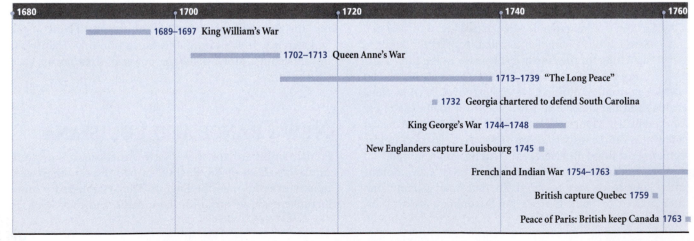

| 1680 | 1700 | 1720 | 1740 | 1760 |

1689–1697 King William's War

1702–1713 Queen Anne's War

1713–1739 "The Long Peace"

1732 Georgia chartered to defend South Carolina

King George's War 1744–1748

New Englanders capture Louisbourg 1745

French and Indian War 1754–1763

British capture Quebec 1759

Peace of Paris: British keep Canada 1763

Public Domain

The Jesuit priests of New France were zealously dedicated to converting the Indians to Roman Catholicism. Some would say they were fanatical. When the Mohawks tortured and killed Jesuits during the 1640s, the religious order was swamped by dozens of Jesuits begging to go to New France in their place. They wanted to be martyrs.

These policies helped but only a little. New France simply would not grow. By 1713, after a century of French presence, the French population in all of North America was 25,000, about the same number of Europeans as lived in the single English colony of Pennsylvania, which was only 30 years old.

Indian Friends

The French had their share of Indian troubles. After thirty years of bullying by Hurons armed with French muskets, the Iroquois Confederacy of New York had its revenge, killing Hurons by the thousands. In 1683, the Iroquois soundly defeated professional French troops in battle and came within an ace of overrunning Quebec. French fur trappers so feared the Iroquois that they detoured hundreds of miles around the Confederation's stamping ground. Better to add months of arduous travel to an expedition than to risk the agonies of Iroquois torture. As late as 1684, the Algonquins (a Canadian tribe), the first friends of the French in 1608 and their next door neighbors for seventy-five years, erupted in fury at French mistreatment and killed thirty settlers.

In general, however, the French had far better relations with Indians than the English did. Their numbers were too few to threaten the tribes with inundation as the English did. Farming was feasible in New France only in a narrow belt along the St. Lawrence; agriculture did not expand constantly into Indian hunting grounds as it did in New England and in the South. The fur trade, into which Indians plunged enthusiastically, for it provided them with the European goods they coveted, was virtually the whole of New France's economy.

While the English colonials remained aloof and apart from Indians on racial grounds, the governors of New France encouraged intermarriage. "Our sons shall wed your daughters," Champlain said, "and we shall be but one people." With French women in short supply, intermarriage was common. Their children, the *métis* (half-bloods), suffered few disabilities under French rule. The French won friendship, respect, and loyalty from the tribes with which they dealt while, at their best, Anglo-Indian relations were characterized by suspicion.

New England ministers who devoted their lives to Indians can be counted on the fingers of one hand. (There were fewer in the southern colonies.) The French flooded New France with priests whose assignment was to baptize and educate *les sauvages*. Ursuline nuns operated schools for Indian girls, whom they converted to Roman Catholicism. When the graduates returned to their villages as wives, they were themselves effective missionaries.

Most of the priests in New France were Jesuits, members of the Society of Jesus. Jesuits were the Roman Church's elite—spiritual shock troops. They were well educated, disciplined, and dedicated to spreading their religion; they were ready, even eager, to die for it. They learned the language of every tribe they targeted for conversion and lived among them. Unlike New England's ministers, they took no interest in changing anything in the Indians' culture except their religion. Unlike John Eliot in Massachusetts, the Jesuits saw nothing ungodly in wearing breechcloths, tattooing faces, sitting on the ground, or slathering on bear's grease to ward off mosquitos. They were even indulgent of Indian

Slaves in Canada

The French in Louisiana owned slaves. There were some Indian slaves in Canada despite the fact that the pope and King Louis XIV forbade the practice. Indian slavery was forced on the Canadians by Indian custom. Enslaving captives taken in war was a well-established practice. So, the Indian allies of the French presented some of them as gifts. To have insulted their allies' generosity by freeing the captives and providing a free lecture was not the French (or the Jesuit) way. So the French shrugged, made sure the king and the pope were not around, and put their slaves to work.

Their allies gave the French white captives too. They were not enslaved but held as hostages, exchanged for French the Americans had captured.

Brown Brothers

In 1673, a French priest living in what is now Michigan, Jacques Marquette, and Louis Joliet, a coureur de bois who was educated, led the greatest expedition devoted to discovery since Coronado's. The small party covered 2,500 miles in four months. Marquette was taken seriously ill on the return trip and died a short time later at age 38. Joliet was named Royal Hydographer and lived on a large land grant in Quebec until 1700. (Marquette's and Joliet's canoes were three times the size of the canoe pictured here, which would not suffice for much more than a Sunday paddle.)

---

practices that they believed immoral on the principle: better a baptized sinner who could repent, than a sinner doomed to hell because he was outside the Church.

Jesuit missionaries were a success story. When hostilities between New France and the Iroquois nations were ended after 1700, the Jesuits made more converts in the Confederacy in a decade than the English colonials had in half a century.

Intrepid Explorers

Good relations with Indians made it possible for the French to become the most accomplished explorers in North America. Trappers, traders, and priests plunged deep into the forests around the Great Lakes while the much more numerous English huddled close to the ocean. Unlike the English, clinging tenaciously to their European culture, French *coureurs de bois*, young men building up a nest-egg by trapping before settling down with their Indian wives, adopted Indian garb and Indian ways of surviving in the wilderness. When a party led by the governor of Virginia reached the crest of the Appalachians, the men celebrated by covering a table with pressed linen and setting it with china, silver, and crystalware. *Coureurs de bois* were already exploring the Missouri River

700 miles farther west. At dinnertime, they hunkered in the dirt with their Indian companions, roasted a slab of venison, and ate it with their hands.

French explorers charted what is now the central third of the United States, from the Appalachian ridges to within sight of the Rockies. In 1673—a decade before William Penn arrived in Pennsylvania—Louis Joliet, a tough but educated trapper, and Jacques Marquette, a Jesuit priest, crossed Wisconsin to the Mississippi River and, with Indian companions, paddled canoes to the mouth of the Arkansas River. They turned back only because local Indians told them of white people farther south whom Marquette and Joliet correctly reckoned to be Spaniards who would imprison them. They clocked 2,500 miles in four months, informing Quebec that the Mississippi River of rumor did indeed exist and that it flowed into the Gulf of Mexico. (The great river was not discovered from the Gulf because, in its delta, it broke up into dozens of unimpressive streams.)

In 1682—half a century before the founding of Georgia— Robert Cavelier, the Sieur de La Salle, reached the mouth of the great river. In 1699, Pierre le Moyne, the Sieur d'Iberville, founded New Orleans. To put the Spanish in Florida on notice that France was on the Gulf of Mexico to stay (in its second American province, Louisiana), the French established Biloxi and Mobile, which had the best harbor on the Gulf.

French America—New France and Louisiana—was a sprawling flimsy empire. Once beyond Quebec city and smaller Montreal, French America was, like Portugal's commercial empire, a string of isolated, more-or-less fortified trading posts at long intervals along the Great Lakes and the Mississippi River. Kaskaskia and Cahokia in the Illinois country and St. Louis, where the Missouri River meets the Mississippi, were dots on a map, manned by only a few traders and soldiers. Portugal's dots had been connected by seas and ships, French America's by lakes, rivers, creeks, portages, and freight-carrying canoes up to 40 feet long.

Imperial Standoff

The Dutch, English, and French had picked apart the overextended Portuguese empire, fort by fort, until only remnants remained. New France, with its modest population base, was overextended too, but it remained intact for more than fifty years thanks to Indian allies, highly professional military garrisons, and the English colonists' preoccupation with their own development. The English and the French skirmished, but mostly through Indian proxies. The Iroquois destroyed a small French town not far from Montreal; the Abenakis, French allies, attacked Pemaquid (now Bristol) and other towns on the coast of Maine.

Louisiana's security was, on the face of it, more precarious. Spain, also France's longtime rival, had pushed from Mexico to what is now the Texas-Louisiana border, within striking distance of New Orleans. Pensacola, in Florida, threatened Mobile and Biloxi from the east. But the Spanish were also overextended. When, in 1693, mission Indians in Texas were hit by an outbreak of smallpox and (correctly) blamed it on the Spanish, the friars packed up and fled rather than be killed as priests in New Mexico had been. Spain's hold on northern Florida was firmer, but there too, disease reduced their once numerous Temucuan allies to a fraction of their original numbers.

Moreover, Spanish Florida faced another enemy to the north, South Carolina. In 1688, South Carolinians destroyed the Spanish mission at Guale, in present-day Georgia. The same year, the undeclared little wars in North America were absorbed into a big war formally declared in Europe (with England and Spain allies). With one brief interruption, the colonies—some of them, some of the time—battled the French for twenty-four years.

A CENTURY OF CONFLICT

In 1688, an alliance led by the Dutch king of England, William III, went to war with France. The issues were control of the Rhineland and the security of the Netherlands. Neither meant much to colonial Americans. They called the conflict "King William's War" as if to say that the European War of the League of Augsburg was the king's personal project (which it was). Nevertheless, the New England colonies seized on the declaration of war to resolve their grievances with French Canada: commerce raiders sallying out of Port Royal to harass New England fishermen and seize colonial merchant ships; and the French practice of arming the Indians on the New England frontier with iron tomahawks and muskets.

Between 1688 and 1763, there were four major European wars pitting France against Great Britain. Colonials never took more than an academic interest in the issues at stake in Europe. Their concerns were French threats to commerce on the seas and the cooperation between New France and almost every Eastern Woodlands tribe from Maine to the Ohio River.

Indeed, it is more accurate to see the colonies' four wars on land between 1688 and 1763 as wars with the Indians with the French in a supporting role. French support of the Indians was critical; they supplied the modern arms. For seventy years, however, Indian warriors were more numerous than their French allies in all but a few engagements with colonials and the British army.

European War

The nature of European warfare was changing in basic ways at the end of the 1600s. Previously, in the wars of religion in the 1500s, in the Thirty Years' War (1618–1648), and in Oliver Cromwell's ravaging of Ireland in the 1650s, European warfare plumbed unprecedented depths of cruelty toward anyone who fell in the way of largely mercenary soldiers. Rootless thugs who fought for the highest bidder pillaged cities and the hovels of peasants, raped women and girls, and murdered for sport. Even the princes who hired the mercenaries recoiled in disgust. During the Thirty Years War, a Dutch jurist, Hugo Grotius, published *De Jure Belli et Pacis* (*On the Law of War and Peace*) in which, among other things, he called on rulers to protect ordinary people from their armies. By 1700, Europe's major military powers—France, Spain, Austria, Prussia, Britain—were bringing soldiers under the control of officers loyal not to money but to their prince. Armies were professionalized; warfare was "civilized."

Soldiers were recruited from among the poor into standing armies commanded and disciplined by professionally trained officers. In order to reduce foraging among the peasantry, as mercenary armies did, governments created supply units specializing in providing quarters for armies and (when things were going according to plan) a steady supply of food and forage for horses and oxen. And clothing: The military uniform became standard in European armies.

North Wind/North Wind Pictures

During the eighteenth century, opposing infantries formed three lines and advanced in order in open country toward the enemy. Typically on the order of a junior officer, the formation halted. Again on order, the men in the first line fired simultaneously. The soldiers in the second and third lines immediately stepped between those men whence the first line of soldiers, now in the rear, reloaded their muskets. and so on. Well-drilled soldiers could reload in less than a minute so that, as long as the army did not disintegrate in a panic, it maintained a continuous series of volleys. The battle line that held together longer was victorious. With sabers and lances, cavalrymen galloped after the enemy foot soldiers who had broken and run.

An innovation in weaponry helped to advance the development of professional armies. Muskets with an attachable bayonet replaced pikes and swords as the foot soldier's standard armament. To make the most of musket fire, armies formed lines and fired volleys rather than, like mercenaries, advancing in "a brute mass" and fighting in a melee, a seething mass of face-to-face, one-on-one hacking, stabbing, and slashing. The new style of warfare required long, intensive training. Soldiers had to be taught to march to a batttlefield in close formation and then, in unison in intricate maneuvers, to deploy into a line of battle. They had to be trained to shoot and reload their muskets in unison and quickly according to a "manual of arms." Reloading was a complicated procedure of twelve or more steps:

> Stand straight, head right, shoulders square, stomach in, chest out, heels close, toes turned out a little
> Holding the weapon: on the left shoulder, forefinger and thumb to the side of the stock, the other three holding the butt
> Timing: each motion to be done on a count of "one, two"

And so on. Mastering these skills meant months of exhausting practice: drill, drill, drill—and no-nonsense discipline.

Training and maintaining a professional army was expensive. So the rulers who footed the bills made it clear to their officers that they were not to waste the lives of soldiers in whom so much money was invested. Generals were to do battle only when, by maneuvering into a superior position, the odds of victory were stacked in their favor. Generals who found their army outmaneuvered and facing defeat were to retreat in an orderly fashion and "live to fight another day."

The maxims of war, wrote the English novelist Daniel Defoe, were "never fight without a manifest advantage, and always encamp so as not to be forced to it." He added sarcastically that armies "spend a whole campaign in dodging, or, as it is genteely called, observing one another, and then march off into winter quarters."

Which, often enough, was the truth. But the new professional warfare minimized casualties and almost—if never entirely—ended the indiscriminate slaughter of noncombatants. During the Thirty Years War, 3 to 4 million of Germany's 20 million people were killed. By comparison, Europe's new kind of warfare was civilized indeed.

"The American Style"

The new warfare made little impression on Americans. Very few trained British soldiers were stationed in the colonies. The French army in Canada was larger, but it stayed close to the cities of Quebec, Montreal, and Trois Rivieres. Before 1688, its job was to maintain order within the colony, not to fight foreign enemies.

Colonial militias, part-time soldiers called up in emergencies—always Indian troubles—underwent virtually no training. Farmers and tradesmen commanded by self-styled gentlemen, they had long since adopted Indian ways of combat: ambush and surprise raids, doing battle not as a unit in formation, but shooting—individually—from behind boulders, trees, or whatever other shelter the terrain afforded. French and British officers called ambush and raid the "American style of war." Most were contemptuous of it as cowardly. Indians and colonials "crept on their bellies," the antithesis of the disciplined European march. Like the Indians, they were "bellicose individuals" in battle, incapable of disciplined maneuvering.

Nonetheless, both French and British had little choice but to tolerate and even embrace warfare Indian style. French officers accompanied their Indian allies on sneak attacks on outlying New England towns of no military value, slaughtering the men, making captives of the women and children. The French called these raids *petite guerre*, "little war." Pierre de Rigaud de Vaudrouil argued in favor of it because it was war on the cheap and, by throwing the British frontier into a panic, *petite guerre* saddled the colonials with the burden of providing for thousands of refugees. Best of all, Vaudrouil pointed out, the only way the British could defend against Indians raiding at random was to build a line of forts, a project that was much too expensive for penny-pinching colonial assemblies. Every regiment assigned to garrison forts in the forest was a regiment unavailable to attack Louisbourg and Quebec.

The British and colonials were quite as nasty. Colonial militias adopted the grisly practice of scalping those they killed. The assemblies of several colonies paid bounties for scalps, and not just the scalps of enemy warriors. During Queen Anne's War (1702–1713), Massachusetts paid £40 for every Abenaki scalp that was turned in. During King George's War (1744–1748), the bounty was raised to £105 for the scalp of an Indian male older than 12—and, so much for decency toward noncombatants—£50 each for the scalps of women and children. In 1756, Pennsylvania paid 150 Spanish dollars for an adult male's hair—less for a live prisoner!

Inconclusive Conflicts

Little but atrocity was accomplished in the forest fighting of King William's War and Queen Anne's War. In 1689, Abenaki Indians leveled several towns on the Maine Coast. In 1690, Indians accompanied by a few French officers attacked Schenectady in New York and Casco in Maine. When a hundred Casco villagers tried to surrender, the Indians slaughtered them. In 1693, a French and Indian force devastated the Mohawks and Onandagas, demoralizing the Iroquois Confederacy.

There were conventional battles in the colonies. New Englanders, led by Massachusetts, organized two amphibious forces, one to attack Quebec, the other Port Royal. The Quebec expedition was incompetently commanded and got nowhere. However, in 1689, the New Englanders attacked and occupied Port Royal. When, in the Peace of Ryswick of 1697, Port Royal was returned to the French, it left a sour taste in many a New Englander's mouth.

In Queen Anne's War, which began in 1701, Spain was an ally of France. This meant that South Carolina and Spanish Florida, where King William's War had been ignored, were engaged. Their war was an exercise in ineptitude. In 1702,

BURNING OF DEERFIELD, MASSACHUSETTS.

Deerfield, Massachusetts, was on the frontier, but it was a substantial and comfortable village and—so its inhabitants thought—secure. However, in the dead of winter, 1704, Indians and French soldiers burned it to the ground. Deerfield's destruction put the whole of New England on edge.

about 500 Carolinians and 300 Indians on fourteen ships besieged St. Augustine. It was a ramshackle town; most of the population lived in huts made of sticks and reeds. But the attackers could not take it, and when two Spanish warships arrived from Cuba, they fled. A French and Spanish attack on Charleston was also a fiasco.

Deerfield and Port Royal

In New England, the French and Indians renewed *petite guerre*. The most dramatic raid on a frontier settlement was the attack on Deerfield, Massachusetts, in February 1704. Deerfield was no cluster of cabins. It was a substantial village of more than forty structures with a population of about 270. For a year, the town had been prepared for an assault. But winter in New England, the ground deep in snow, meant security, or so everyone assumed. At four in the morning, after a long march on snowshoes (an Indian invention), 47 Frenchmen and about 200 Indians, mostly Abenakis, rampaged through the town. Before the sun rose, they killed between 44 and 56, including 9 women and 25 children, and took 109 captives. Only 133 Deerfielders managed to escape and only 59 of the captives later returned.

In 1707, Massachusetts again sent a force against Port Royal. Two assaults failed, with the New Englanders suffering high casualties. However, when British warships arrived

with a force of professional soldiers, Port Royal surrendered. In the Treaty of Utrecht in 1713, Britain took Acadia from France, giving the new colony the name of Nova Scotia. But when the French built a new fortress, Louisbourg, on Cape Breton Island, the threat to New England shipping was revived.

The Treaty of Utrecht had significant consequences in Europe. French defeats at the hands of two great generals, the British Duke of Marlborough and Prince Eugene of Savoy, ended a generation of fear that France would dominate all of Western Europe. The "balance of power" in Europe—two blocs of nations of equal military strength—ushered in a "long peace" of almost thirty years. For Americans, the long peace was a time of astonishing growth and profound social and cultural developments that created a mature and confident society where there had been precariously established outposts of England.

A CHANGING SOCIETY

Between 1700 and 1776, the population of the colonies increased tenfold, from about 250,000 people to 2.5 million. With its rich and ever-expanding agricultural hinterland, Philadelphia bypassed the older cities of Boston, New York, and Charleston to become North America's metropolis; indeed, Philadelphia was the second largest city in the British empire; only London was larger.

Except for African Americans, who formed a caste submerged by prejudice and force, even when they were free, colonial Americans enjoyed the personal freedoms of which the British were so proud. Ordinary colonials participated more in government than Britons (or anybody in the world) did, and enjoyed a "standard of living" (not an eighteenth-century term) unmatched anywhere.

A Fruitful Population

Large families and longer life expectancy accounted for much of the population's astonishing growth. In New England, those who survived childhood diseases (which were a scourge) enjoyed a life expectancy nearly as high as Americans do today. Eighteenth-century New Englanders were the first people in history to know their grandparents as a matter of routine.

Their grandfathers, anyway. Unlike today, when women outlive men by half a dozen years, men (and spinsters) usually survived longer than married women in the eighteenth-century. The reason was the dangers of childbirth. Puerperal fever, an infection due to poor sanitation during birth—no one suspected that dirty hands caused problems—snuffed out the lives of many young women. However, a New England male who reached 20 was apt to die nearer 70 years of age than 60, a man of the middle colonies at least 60. Life expectancy was no longer a toss of the dice in the South, but it was lower than in the northern colonies, 45 in Virginia and Maryland, 42 in the Carolinas and Georgia. (Life expectancy for a white man of 20 in the British West Indies was 40; West

Piracy's Golden Age

There have been pirates as long as ships have been loaded with cargos worth stealing. Between 1660 and 1725, piracy was a major problem in American waters. The buccaneers (as they were called in their "golden age") were seafaring armed robbers. Most were murderers; it went with the job. They were not rapists only because they preyed on merchant vessels, which rarely had women aboard.

Why the sudden explosion in the pirate population? Mainly because the commercial wars of midcentury attracted riffraff and respected ships' masters alike to legalized maritime robbery when, to save money, France, Holland, Spain, and England commissioned privateers. These were privately owned vessels that were well armed and, for a percentage of the take, were licensed to attack the enemy's merchantmen. Privateering could be very lucrative. So, when peace treaties were signed, some captains and crews found it difficult to give up the business. They continued to hunt ships and steal from them without regard to the flag they were flying.

What kind of men became pirates? In the early 1720s, 98 percent of those who were captured said they had started life as "honest seamen." A large number said that liquor led them to choose a life of crime. Indeed, piracy was a

Reproduced from the Collections of the Library of Congress, Prints and Photographs Division, Washington, D.C. [LC-D416-43720]

good occupation for a drinking man. Life aboard a pirate vessel can seem, in the records we have, to have been one long drunken revel.

There was more to it than partying, however. An honest seaman's life was dull and laborious. The work was hard; the pay was poor. Piracy offered excitement, eternally alluring to young men agitated by bubbling hormones. Pirates risked their lives during robberies, and the gallows was their fate if they were caught. But each successful job filled their purses and, whether or not they were nonstop drunk between hits, they did not work very much. A merchant sloop of 100 tons was sailed by a crew of no more than a dozen men; the same vessel under the black flag of piracy divided the chores among eighty. If they captured slaves, they were put to work while the pirates looked for buyers. The famous Captain Kidd told of stealing "twelve slaves of whom we intended to make good use of to do the drudgery of our ship."

Pirate crews were large because numbers was one key to their success. Pirates were robbers; they did not want to sink the ships they attacked. (The cannon they carried were for defense). They wanted their victims' vessels undamaged so they could strip them of everything worth

Indian slaves died so soon after arriving to work on the murderous sugar plantations that there was virtually no natural increase of the black population during the 1700s.)

North American families were large, some of them very large. Benjamin Franklin, born in 1706, was the tenth child in his family and several siblings followed him. Patrick Henry, like Franklin to be a leader of the American War for Independence, was born in Virginia in 1736. He was one of nineteen children. John Marshall, to become the greatest Chief Justice of the Supreme Court, was born in 1755. He had fourteen brothers and sisters. The reproduction champion was the mother of a governor of Massachusetts, William Phipps. She delivered twenty-seven children.

German Immigrants

Immigration also fed the colonial population explosion. Enslaved Africans were imported in annually increasing num-

bers, up to 20,000 a year by 1770. Many were brought to the colonies in the Britain-based ships of the Royal African Company, but colonial merchants were in the business too. Newport, Rhode Island, was the colonial capital of the slave trade; at one time or another, 900 different ships based in the city were engaged in it. Ironically, more than a few of the Newport slavers were Quakers.

About 800,000 Europeans emigrated to the mainland colonies between 1700 and 1776. About half of them came as indentured servants; they were poor people. A transatlantic passage cost between £5 and £10 (a £5 ticket meant accommodations only marginally better than on a slave ship) and a new emigrant needed an additional £10 to get started in the colonies. That was a year's income for a common laborer, too much for the most frugal to hope to save. For those who could afford to pay their way, cheap American land was the taking. Thus the numbers: The captain of a merchant-man with twelve seamen (who were not fighting men) was foolish to resist eighty vicious pirates armed with cutlasses, knives, and pistols. Few did. Merchants knew that if they gave up without a fight they were more likely to be spared the cruelties of which pirates were capable. The principle was the same as the advice given today to people confronted on a dark street by a thug with a knife: give him the wallet.

Speed was the second key to successful piracy. Pirates had to catch their victims in order to intimidate them with their numbers and ferocity. A few famous pirates like Bartholomew "Black Bart" Roberts and Edward "Blackbeard" Teach had large forty gun ships. But most pirates sailed sloops, large enough to accommodate a hundred cut-throats, but speedy.

Treasure—"pieces of eight!"—was the most desirable booty. When pirates tortured captive crews or captains, it was usually to learn where any money had been hidden. If there was none, pirates took the food and drink they wanted for their own use and had to be satisfied with whatever cargo was aboard, even low-cost bulk items such as hogsheads of molasses or tobacco.

Selling such contraband presented problems. Pirates could not weigh anchor in a port and advertise for buyers. There were a few "wide-open" pirate towns in the Bahamas and Belize where merchants of dubious integrity would come for the bargains available. The governor of Jamaica encouraged pirates to make their base in Port Royal; armed pirate ships in the harbor discouraged attacks by the Spanish and French. Blackbeard was scouting Ocracoke Inlet in North Carolina for the site of a new pirate entrepôt when, in 1718, he was cornered and killed. None of the sanctuaries lasted for long. The wildest of them, Port Royal, was leveled by an earthquake in 1692, much to the satisfaction of moralists.

Pirate vessels were as democratic as New England town meetings. Where to hunt prey, from Newfoundland to the West Indies, was determined by majority vote, as was the decision whether or not to attack a vessel they had sighted. The captain (who was elected and could be voted out) claimed a far smaller share of booty than the master of a privateer did. His allowance of food and drink was the same as that of the crewmen. Only when "fighting, chasing, or being chased" did he have the absolute authority of a naval commander.

During piracy's golden age, most buccaneers were British or colonials, both black and white. At his last stand, Blackbeard had thirteen whites and six blacks with him. In 1722, Black Bart's force of 268 included seventy-seven black men. Black pirates actually had a better chance, if captured, of escaping the noose. They could and did argue—with mixed success—that they were slaves, contraband, not crew.

The golden age came abruptly to an end during the "Long Peace" when Britain and France directed their warships to hunt down pirates. In 1720, between 1,500 and 2,000 pirates in about twenty-five vessels were working the Caribbean and the North American coast. By 1723, their numbers were down to 1,000, by 1726 to 200. In 1718, there were fifty attacks on merchant vessels in North American waters but just six in 1726. Relentless pursuit was effective. So were pardons for those who turned themselves in. Many pirates had, they claimed, been forced into the life when, as "honest seamen," they were captured by pirates. The large number of men who immediately applied for the pardons seems to say that many were telling the truth.

---

chief attraction. Developed land could be had for £1–£2 per acre; each acre of raw forest land on the frontier sold for a shilling, or even less.

During the 1700s, the numbers of German immigrants, many paying their own way, rivaled the numbers of newcomers from England. Sailing from Hamburg or Rotterdam, most came to Philadelphia. (In just one week in August 1773, 3,500 immigrants arrived in the city.) Pennsylvania was still the most welcoming colony and already had a German community, a compelling attraction for people setting out on an adventure rife with anxieties. The "Pennsylvania Dutch" living on the rich farmland southwest of Philadelphia were adherents of Quaker-like pacifistic sects like the Mennonites who had been actively recruited by William Penn's agents. Most of the eighteenth-century German immigrants were Lutherans. Some came to farm—nearly all the redemptioners were destined for farm labor—but many of the Germans were shopkeepers or skilled artisans who settled in Philadelphia and nearby Germantown (now a neighborhood of Philadelphia).

Germans were so numerous in Pennsylvania (a third of the population in 1776) that some other Philadelphians were uneasy. Among them was the city's most famous citizen, Benjamin Franklin. Calling the immigrants "the most stupid of their nation," Franklin feared that the Germans would "never adopt our Language or Customs" and will "Germanize us instead of us Anglifying them." Franklin's eye for the future was usually keen, but he looked at Philadelphia's Germans through the wrong lens of the bifocals he invented. By the third generation, as with other immigrant groups, Pennsylvania's Germans were thoroughly "Anglifed."

From the Collections of the Library of Congress

One of several German language newspapers published in colonial Philadelphia. In 1776, the Declaration of Independence was published in German before it appeared in English. It was seriously suggested that the newly independent United States make German its official language. Then again, someone else seriously suggested that the country's official language be Greek.

Woman Suffrage

Oddly enough, only Virginia specifically barred women heads of household from voting. Elsewhere in the colonies there were no laws about woman suffrage because the very idea was inconceivable. Women and men alike assumed that government was a masculine affair.

Almost. Here and there, records reveal, eccentric or very bold women showed up at the polls and successfully insisted on casting a vote. In New Amsterdam in 1655, Lady Deborah Moody voted and no one said "boo." In New York in 1737, "two old Widdows" cast ballots. A few Massachusetts townships seem to have allowed propertied widows to vote.

The Scotch-Irish

Protestant immigrants from the north of Ireland outnumbered even the Germans. Between 1717 and 1776, as many as 250,000 Scotch-Irish, as they were commonly called, came to America. Again, Philadelphia was the chief port of entry but, unlike the Germans, most of the Scotch-Irish, encouraged by James Logan, the Penn family's land agent in the colony, tended to head west to the frontier. There the flood of people flowed south through upland Virginia to the Carolinas. The Scotch-Irish were the dominant ethnic element in the Appalachians (and, later, beyond). Their peculiar accent was the basis of what Americans would come to call "hillbilly" English; the day they arrived they said "whar" for *where*, "thar" for *there*, "critter" for *creature*, and "nekkid" for *naked*.

They were called Scotch-Irish because they were the grandchildren and great-grandchildren of lowlands Scots Presbyterians whom King James I had attracted to northern Ireland by giving them land taken from the native Irish, who were mostly Catholics. In Scotland, the Scotch-Irish had been a combative people, raiding villages and rustling cattle in northern England. In Ireland they brawled more or less constantly with the Catholic Irish and, in the 1690s, joined

in a war to suppress Irish rebels. When, after 1700, economic difficulties drove many of them (a third of Ireland's Protestants!) to North America, they were notoriously clannish, rude, crude, and quick to resort to violence, "a pernicious and pugnacious people" in the words of a Pennsylvania Quaker.

Few immigrant groups have been so intensely despised as the Scotch-Irish were in the 1700s. When, in 1718, 300 families petitioned the governor of Massachusetts to permit them to settle in the colony, he turned them down. Cotton Mather, New England's most respected minister, denounced the Scotch-Irish emigration as "formidable attempts of Satan and his Sons to unsettle us." In Worcester, a mob burned down a Presbyterian church Scotch-Irish newcomers were building.

At first, James Logan welcomed them to Pennsylvania precisely because of their combativeness, so that they would be "hard neighbors to the Indians." Within a few years, however, he was wringing his hands: "I must own, from my experience in the land office, that the settlement of five families from Ireland gives me more trouble than fifty of any other people." Another observer said that they huddle "together like brutes without regard to age or sex or sense of decency." A Church of England minister called them "ignorant, mean, worthless, beggarly." Another churchman said that "they delight in their present low, lazy, sluttish, heathenish, hellish life, and seem not desirous of changing it."

For all their unpopularity, the Scotch-Irish were the tough-bitten frontiersmen who, for a century, did the dirty work of encroaching on Indian lands, fighting the natives mercilessly, and making the wild West safe for the easterners who despised them.

Family and Property

The family had a standing in colonial law and custom that, today, can be difficult to comprehend. Families, not individuals, were society's political unit. Only the male head of a household owning property could vote, no matter that there were two or three adult sons and perhaps a brother at home. (Unmarried women who inherited land could be heads of household in the law but they could not vote.)

How much property was required for a man to participate in elections varied from colony to colony, but it was generally not a great deal: A farm that produced an income of 40s. in Massachusetts and Connecticut; a "competent estate" in Rhode Island, 50 acres in six of the colonies, 25 improved acres in Virginia.

Actual participation in elections was, as it is today, well below the number of eligible voters. Farmers living some miles from county seats had other things to do on election days and, before the 1760s, candidates for public office rarely differed on "the issues." Why bother? Only about 40 percent of eligible Pennsylvanians and New Yorkers voted. But it was not just inconvenient travel. Only one of four eligible voters in compact Boston bothered to turn out on election day.

Colonial property laws were written by propertied men and, therefore, they were designed to preserve the social integrity and privileges of the propertied class. Virginia, Maryland, and South Carolina adopted laws of primogeniture and entail from England. Primogeniture (meaning "first-born") held that if a head of household died intestate (without leaving a will), his entire estate passed to his eldest son. In Virginia, wealthy planters who thought to write wills still had little choice but to bequeath their real estate to their eldest sons because the land was "entailed." That is, the law required that entailed estates be passed on to a single heir in a direct line of descent. In tidewater Virginia in 1760, 80 percent of the cultivated land was entailed. (If there were no sons, the eldest daughter inherited entailed estates.)

The purpose of these laws was to preserve the social standing of the landowning elite—in a sense, to protect great estates against human nature. That is, if a planter owning a thousand acres and thirty slaves, enough to support a family in grand style, was legally able to divide his estate among four or five children and did so (as many would have done), the consequence would be four or five households of middling means. If these properties were subdivided among the children of his children, the result, from grandfather to grandchildren, was a gaggle of struggling subsistence farmers where once there had been a grandee.

Social Mobility

Propertied men were not insensitive to the futures of their younger sons and their daughters. They could and did bequeath them money (*personal* as opposed to *real* property) or they could acquire land for them that was not entailed, especially in the West. "Second sons" (a term referring to all younger sons) were educated in a profession: the ministry, medicine, the law, or the military. As professionals, they retained their status as gentlemen and the possibility of making an advantageous marriage.

For example, George Washington was a second son. His older brother, Lawrence, inherited the family lands. He helped George train as a surveyor (which meant the opportunity to acquire the best western lands) and took him along on a naval campaign in the West Indies. Washington did invest in land and he parlayed his "military experience" (it did not amount to much) to a commission in the Virginia militia. And he kept an eye trained down that other avenue to acquiring property: marrying a wealthy widow. Washington found his widow in Martha Custis. In 1771, William Carter found and married the Widow Ellison, described by the *Virginia Gazette* as "aged eighty-five; a sprightly old tit, with three thousand pounds fortune."

Wealthy men attended to their daughters' futures by providing dowries (money and slaves) that were handsome enough to attract wealthy or, at least, well-placed husbands. Fortune hunters and lovestruck but poor suitors were shown the door.

An even more attractive match for a gentleman social climber was a young woman who was an heiress, that is, a woman who had no brothers and who had inherited, or would inherit, the family estate. Women heads of household were protected in their property rights. But there was immense social pressure on them to marry; they were surrounded, sometimes virtually harassed by would-be husbands. Thomas Jefferson doubled his wealth in acreage and slaves by marrying a widow who was an heiress. Eliza Lucas, who inherited three plantations in South Carolina (she had managed them from the age of 16!) had her pick of the colony's swains. She chose Charles Pinckney, a widower richer than she was. She was still young when Pinckney died, but she had other interests—she had developed indigo as South Carolina's second cash crop—and resisted all proposals.

Coverture

The woman who wished to retain control of her fortune had to remain, in the law, *feme sole*, a single woman. If she married, she became *feme couverte*, subject to the principle of coverture which held that "husband and wife are one and

---

Dutch Women's Rights

Married women in New Netherlands had significantly different property rights than married women in the English colonies. They owned family property *jointly* with their husbands. There was no coverture. If a woman's husband died, she inherited the whole. If she remarried, her property from her previous marriage remained hers independently of her second husband. He had no say in how she used it. When she died, the property from her first marriage was divided equally among the sons *and daughters* from the first marriage. The English promised to respect this very different property code when New Netherlands surrendered in 1664. Only gradually during the 1700s did the Dutch laws fall into disuse.

Even then, ethnically Dutch women in New York clung to another Dutch custom at odds with English ways. As late as the mid-nineteenth-century, they continued to use their maiden names throughout their lives, not their husbands' surnames. Thus, Annetje Krygier, married to Jans van Arsdale, remained Annetje Krygier until she died. In sharp contrast, many English church registries did not ever note a woman's surname even in the record of her marriage.

that one the husband." A married woman's person before the law was submerged into the person of her husband. As defined by the great eighteenth-century legal codifier, Sir William Blackstone, "the very being or legal existence of the woman is suspended during the marriage, or at least is incorporated and consolidated into that of the husband."

The husband did not *own* the property his wife brought to the marriage. He could not turn land held in coverture into cash by selling it. If he died before his wife did, her estate reverted to her, not to his designated heirs. However, the husband had the *use* of his wife's land and slaves during the marriage, including the right to dispose, as he wished, of the income they produced from crops, labor, or rents.

The law provided married women with other protections. When her husband died, his widow was entitled to one-third of the income from the estate that passed (via primogeniture) to the eldest son. Her husband, no matter how nasty he (or his wife) had been, could not deny the widow her "widow's third." This entitlement was called a dower, a reference to the dowry the woman had brought to the marriage; a widow living on her third was known as a dowager. If husband and wife had signed a legal instrument called jointures, as was often the case in prenuptial agreements, the widow might be entitled to a greater income by surrendering her dower rights. Nonetheless, so long as a woman was defined by coverture, she could not buy or sell property, sue or be sued, write a will, or make a contract. She had no legal identity.

If colonial women's status was inferior to that of men, they enjoyed more favorable circumstances than women in England or other European countries. Nicholas Creswell, an English visitor in 1774, overstated it a bit when he said that the colonies were "a paradise on Earth for Women," but he was not hallucinating. In most colonies, husbands were severely punished if they beat their wives, in some colonies just for striking them. A Massachusetts man was fined when,

in public, he referred to his wife as "my servant." European visitors almost always commented on the deference colonial men paid women. In the New England colonies, a woman could sue for divorce on the grounds of adultery, bigamy, desertion, impotence, incest, or her husband's absence for seven years. (In other colonies, divorce required a special act of the assembly and was quite rare.)

In Pennsylvania, women's relatively high status owed to the prominence of the Quakers who, in their early years, treated women as almost the equals of men. In the Chesapeake colonies and the Carolinas, the deference toward women that Europeans observed may have been a legacy of the fact that, well into the 1700s, white men outnumbered white women by a ratio of three to two. When potential wives are scarce, men are apt to be more solicitous of what women there are. The phenomenon was to be repeated in the western states during the late nineteenth-century.

The Lower Orders

The intricacies of property law were of no interest to people near the bottom of colonial society: laborers in towns and cities and even hardscrabble, marginal farmers who may have owned their land. (There was no interest in enforcing primogeniture and entail among them.).

All the large northern cities—Boston, New York, Philadelphia—had their throngs of the impoverished: servants and ex-servants, apprentices, slaves and most free blacks, sailors on leave, waterfront roustabouts, and other common laborers. They usually found enough work to keep themselves alive, but little more. Their lives were too insecure for them to feel a sense of belonging to the community or to concern themselves over much with the morals of the genteel. Cotton Mather complained in a dither of the "Knotts of riotous young Men" who defiled holy Boston.

Even small sea ports like Salem, Massachusetts, had their disreputable quarters where drunkenness and brawls were endemic and the makings of a mob were ever present. The patterns of underclass crime were much as they are today. In New York, 95 percent of violent crimes were committed by men, 74 percent of thefts. Rape must have been common but it was rarely prosecuted because of respectable society's disdain for the lower orders and, possibly, the fact that convictions were difficult. The victim was unlikely to be a "woman of virtue" by the standards of decent society and, unlike today, when many states prohibit evidence concerning an alleged rape victim's personal morality, that was of decisive pertinence to colonial judges and juries. Statutory rape cases were virtually unknown. The traditional English age of consent was 10! Colonial assemblies upped this, but to no higher than 14.

With witchcraft prosecutions in bad odor after the Salem hysteria, the only major crime associated with women was infanticide. And, with high infant mortality a fact of life, even among the upper classes, the murder of an infant was rarely alleged, if often enough a subject of gossip. It was a difficult crime to prove in court. In New York between 1730 and 1780, twenty women were charged with killing their newborns, but only one was convicted. (In Virginia, the most notorious infanticide

---

Coverture in the Graveyard

The submersion of the married woman's person into the person of her husband continued after death in a cemetery in Germantown, Pennsylvania. Almost no married women buried there before 1800 are listed in the cemetery's records under their own names. Instead, their burials are recorded as "Johannes Koch's wife" and so on. A few unmarried women were buried under their own names but widows were not. Their burials were entered as "Widow Hoess" or "Alois Miller's widow."

Children—there are plenty of them in the graveyard—are identified as their father's, not their mother's. A poignant series of burials in 1769 reminds us of how different life was 250 years ago:

Oct 26 Johannes Kehrbach's child
Nov 1 Johannes Kehrbach's child
Nov 4 Johannes Kehrbach's third child

Yet another Kehrbach child was buried on May 31, 1773.

case—it occurred after independence—involved not the lower orders but a member of the elite Randolph family, and he had to demand he be charged and tried so as—he thought—to clear his name. He never lived down the suspicion.)

Illegitimate births were common. On the frontier, where the settlers "lived in comfortable fornication," as many mothers were unwed as not. A third of the brides in New England were pregnant when they took their vows. Benjamin Franklin fathered an illegitimate son by a woman unknown to us, and he never legally married Deborah Read, his wife of forty-four years.

Slave Rebellions

The lowliest of the lower orders were the slaves. Except in New York and New Jersey, where even modestly fixed Dutch farmers owned one or a few black "servants," they were not numerous north of the Mason-Dixon line, the boundary between Pennsylvania and Maryland that was surveyed in 1769. Slaves were only 8 percent of the population in Pennsylvania, 3 percent in Massachusetts.

In the southern colonies, slavery grew in importance during the eighteenth-century. The number of blacks in Virginia, most of whom were slaves, rose from about 4,000 in 1700 to 42,000 in 1743, and to more than 200,000 at the time of the American Revolution—a quantum leap! In some Virginia counties and over most of South Carolina, blacks outnumbered whites.

Where blacks were numerous, occasional rebellions unnerved whites. Reaction to disturbances was immediate and ruthless with, no doubt, many innocent blacks severely punished. In 1712, some slaves in New York City staged a demonstration that was treated as an uprising. In 1741, New York authorities blamed a series of fires on a cabal of slaves, free blacks, and poor whites. There was no evidence of a conspiracy—it was not conclusively proved that all the fires were the work of arsonists. Nevertheless, eighteen blacks and four whites were hanged; thirteen blacks were burned alive (the punishment for arson); seventy were sold to the West Indies.

In 1730, about 300 Christian slaves in Virginia fled into the Great Dismal Swamp, a then uncharted tangle of marshes, canebrakes, and woods on the Virginia-North Carlina line. Indians were hired to track them down and most were captured. (Virginia hanged twenty-nine described as the leaders.) Still, the Great Dismal Swamp remained a refuge for runaway slaves, tribeless Indians, and alienated poor whites for decades.

In 1739, about 20 slaves from a plantation near Charleston called Stono seized guns, killed several planter families, and almost captured the colony's lieutenant governor. About 150 other slaves joined them. "With Colours displayed, and two Drums beating," they began to march toward Florida where, they had learned through an astonishingly efficient slave grapevine, the governor of the Spanish colony would grant them freedom. Judging from their names, some of the rebels were Catholics, probably converted in Angola or the Congo before they were enslaved. They would have been favorably disposed toward the Spanish for religious reasons.

Most of the Stono rebels were captured within a week, but a few managed to reach St. Augustine. They settled to the north of the town with runaways from Georgia in a fortified African American village, Santa Teresa de Mose. They swore to "shed their last drop of blood in defense of the Great Crown of Spain, and to be the most cruel enemies of the English." The attraction Santa Teresa held out to slaves in South Carolina and Georgia was sufficient that, in 1740, Georgia's Governor Oglethorpe led an expedition to destroy the settlement.

POLITICS: IMPERIAL AND COLONIAL

Between 1713 and 1739, while France and Britain were at peace, the colonies prospered. Tobacco was no longer a bonanza crop, but it was profitable. Exporting rice, naval stores, hides and furs, and livestock (to the West Indies) continued to be lucrative. The middle colonies, especially Pennsylvania, fed the West Indies where sugar cultivation was so intensive that slaves had no time to grow their own food. The colonial merchant marine grew in size until there was almost as much tonnage registered in American as in British ports. In troubled times to come, Americans would look back on the "long peace" of 1713–1739 as a golden age.

Salutary Neglect

They associated the good times not so much with international peace as with the policies of the British prime minister, Robert Walpole. Lazy and easygoing, fancying his daily outsized bottle of port, Walpole believed that the best way to manage the colonies was to govern them as little as possible. He had a point: As long as colonial trade was enriching British merchants and manufacturers—which was the whole idea of mercantilism—why worry? Why do anything that will likely cause trouble?

Walpole's nonpolicy was known as "salutary neglect," beneficial neglect. Inaction was the best action, even if it meant overlooking colonial violations of the Navigation Acts, which were common.

There were critics, of course. In 1732, London hatmakers complained that the growth of that industry in the northern colonies was cutting into their North American sales. The prime minister calmed them by forbidding Americans to sell hats outside the colony where they were made and to cease training slaves in the craft. London's hatters were mollified. American hatmakers ignored the easily ignored restrictions. Walpole dined with his friends.

The Molasses Act of 1733 was Parliament's response to complaints by sugar planters in the British West Indies that Americans were buying molasses from French islands where it was cheaper. Mercantilism, they argued, entitled them to a monopoly of the molasses market in New England where it was distilled into rum, the poor man's intoxicant and a valuable commodity in the African slave trade.

The Molasses Act levied a 6d. per gallon duty on French molasses, enough to price it out of the colonial market. When importers presented customs officials with obviously

And the Governor Wore Organdy

Edward Hyde, Viscount Cornbury, was governor of New York and New Jersey from 1701 to 1709. He was a disaster. Cornbury aggravated political tensions that had been fading and harassed the Dutch Reformed Church. Within a few years, even Lord Cornbury sensed he had made a mess of things. He lamented that "a Porter in the streets of London is a happier man than a Governor in America" and begged Queen Anne to relieve him. When she finally did, he was clapped into New York's debtors' prison. He was released only when he inherited his father's title, Earl of Clarendon, and, more important at the moment, his father's money.

It was whispered (and said aloud after Cornbury went home) that he dressed up in women's clothing and sashayed on the ramparts surrounding the governor's palace and that he invited the men at a banquet to fondle his wife's ears, which he claimed were the finest ears in the world. (Lady Cornbury was herself accused of stealing jewelry—earrings?—from homes she visited.)

The evidence the governor was a cross-dresser is not reliable. There is this portrait, said to be of him, but only years after he left New York. The contemporary allegations of the governor's irregular wardrobe were all made by political enemies or were hearsay, remarks in letters of what the writer had been told but had not himself seen. Skeptics have no evidence to discredit the accusation, but they have established a reasonable doubt, which is all that is asked of defense attorneys.

Collection of the New-York Historical Society. #1952.80

---

fraudulent invoices declaring that the French molasses they were bringing in originated on a British island—along with a bribe—Walpole was looking the other way. His own associates in London were knee-deep in boodle. Why begrudge low-level customs agents a little pocket money?

In 1750, at the behest of English ironmakers, Parliament forbade colonists to engage in many forms of iron manufacture. Not only did colonial forges continue to operate with impunity, several colonial governments also openly subsidized the iron industry within their borders. Salutary neglect was a wonderful way to run an empire—as long as times were good.

Assemblies and Governors

The trouble was that Walpole's indulgent oversight of colonial affairs contributed to a steady erosion of Britain's's authority over her American daughters. Piecemeal during the eighteenth-century, in increments sometimes unnoticeable, colonial assemblies increased their power at the expense of royal governors (proprietors' governors in Maryland and Pennsylvania) and became more confident in their ability—and "right"—to govern themselves.

The key to this shift in the balance of power between royal authority (the executive) and colonial assemblies (the legislative) was the British political principle that the consent of the people's elected representatives was essential to legitimate tax laws. In Great Britain, Parliament had won this power of the purse in a century of conflict featuring the execution of one king, the banishment of another, and the signed agreement of a third. In the colonies, the thirteen elected assemblies—whether called the House of Burgesses or the House of Delegates or the Assembly—made this important prerogative their own by less dramatic means.

Thus, royal governors were authorized to veto any colonial act of which they disapproved, including budget bills. However, political and social realities required them to be cautious in exercising their power. If a governor's dispute with a colonial assembly turned nasty, the assembly could refuse to vote the governor the funds he needed for day-to-day operations, even the money he needed to maintain his personal household. A colonial assembly could, as a royal governor of New York put it, "starve him into compliance."

The power of the purse was a formidable weapon. Few men who served as governors in America (most of them ex-army officers) were as rich as they wanted to be when they took their overseas jobs. If they had been, they would have lived opulently in Great Britain, and not roughed it in Portsmouth, Williamsburg, or Charleston. The governors were men on the make; they went to the colonies "to repair a shattered fortune, or to acquire an estate." It was expected that royal governors would use their office to enrich themselves. To make money, however, usually from land speculation, governors needed to get along with wealthy and influential colonials. Constructing the core of a "court party"—the governor's party—was easy. Governors appointed the cream of the colonial elite to their Councils, the upper house in a colony's legislature. But they also needed the collaboration of the men who were elected to the assemblies.

This called for a deft touch. It was possible to get along too well with assemblies, to yield too freely to their demands, especially in the proprietary colonies. The Penns in Pennsylvania and the Calverts in Maryland wanted to see maximum income from their colonial properties. The Crown, even when Walpole was the king's first minister, expected colonial governments to pay their own expenses. The governor who became the assembly's rubber stamp would find himself recalled long before he had made his bundle.

RELIGION: DECLINE AND REVIVAL

Except in New York's Dutch villages and in Pennsylvania's German community, colonial culture was British culture. Educated Americans imported their books and periodicals from England along with fabrics for their clothing and furniture for their homes. Colonial ladies and gentlemen—particularly in the South—patterned their manners and avocations on those of the English country gentry. Young George Washington's mania for fox hunting—riding to the hounds, an exhilarating but dangerous sport—was so avid that a number of observers mentioned it, and Washington never lacked for company on his gallops. Although New Englanders sent their brighter sons to Harvard or Yale Colleges, and

Virginia had the College of William and Mary, some planters shipped their sons to Britain to be educated, particularly at the law schools in London. A few colonials were unreserved Anglophiles like Willliam Byrd of Virginia or Pennsylvania's Benjamin Franklin. Both preferred living in London to the ruder society and culture of the colonies. Except among the Scotch-Irish and some Dutch and German Americans, however, there were few colonial Anglophobes.

The Mellowing of the Churches

Church was less important to educated colonials than it had been to their parents and grandparents. There were exceptions: The father and son Boston ministers, Increase and Cotton Mather were among the most intellectual of Americans, and they were Calvinists as stern as their Puritan forebears. By the 1720s, however, when both Mathers died, their old time religion was losing its hold on New England's merchant princes. Most continued to rent pews in Congregational churches (as Puritan meetinghouses were now called). Increasingly, however, they expected their ministers (whom the congregations hired and fired) to preach sermons that were inspirational and reassuring, not reeking of hellfire, sin, and damnation.

Harvard College, New England's training school for ministers, obliged the changing tastes by mellowing the religion it taught. Harvard went so far in what we would call liberalization that, in 1701, hard-shelled Calvinists founded Yale College in New Haven, Connecticut, as an alternative seminary. Only twenty years later, however, Yale was rocked when its rector, Timothy Cutler, and most of the faculty (all ministers) resigned and announced that they were sailing to England to be ordained in the Church of England—by bishops, churchmen whom the Puritans had called "the Excrement of Anti-Christ"!

THE HANCOCK MANSION.

The splendid home of the wealthy Boston merchant John Hancock. His luxurious lifestyle bore little resemblance to the spartan simplicity in which Puritan forebears took pride. Nor did his liberal religious beliefs resemble the Calvinism of seventeenth-century Boston. In 1776, Hancock, who would otherwise be quite forgotten, ensured the immortality of his name by signing it to the Declaration of Independence in an outsized hand.

North Wind Picture Archives

Indeed, some of New England's wealthiest merchants became Anglicans. The Church of England was the church of the royal governors of Massachusetts and New Hampshire (and the proprietors' governors of Pennsylvania and Maryland after the Penn and Calvert families returned to the Anglican communion). The Church of England was the established church in New York and the southern colonies. It was the socially prestigious denomination almost everywhere in the colonies. It was almost a prerequisite to political preferment to be an Anglican.

The Church of England was an undemanding church with none of the community-enforced conformism of the seventeenth-century Congregationalists, Quakers, and Dutch Reformed Church. It was, by the 1700s, a latitudinarian denomination, tolerant of a variety of beliefs and lifestyles among its members. Educated colonials whose worldview had been shaped by revolutionary scientific discoveries like William Harvey's explanation of the circulation of blood in the body and Sir Isaac Newton's explanation of the movement of the planets and the nature of light, understood natural phenomena through observation and reason—not supernatural forces. Belonging to the easy-going Church of England was a comfortable way of retaining religious ties.

Religious Excitement

What appealed to worldly colonials, left many ordinary people cold. They looked to religion for simple certainties, moral strictures, reassurances, and emotional satisfaction. The formal liturgy of the Anglicans and the rational and restrained sermons of Harvard- and Yale-educated ministers did not meet their needs. Church membership dropped steadily during the 1700s except, in some colonies, for a burst of excitement, a "revival," during the 1730s and 1740s.

A century later, in 1841, another generation of revivalist preachers called the religious upheavals of the 1730s and 1740s "The Great Awakening," as if a divine fire had swept over the colonies from Georgia to New Hampshire, returning an entire generation to God. In fact, the eighteenth-century revival of religious zeal was a spotty phenomenon. It burned fiercely in some areas but never sparked in others. Massachusetts was the Great Awakening's ground zero; fully 43 percent of the colony's townships were swept by religious excitement. But only 2.5 percent of the towns in neighboring Rhode Island experienced revivals. In the middle colonies, New Jersey and Pennsylvania were hotbeds of the Awakening with 14 percent of towns touched by massive return to the churches; but in New York, there were only two revivals. In the South there was no Great Awakening. There was one local revival in South Carolina and none in Virginia, North Carolina, and Georgia.

Where it was hot, the revival of religion was very hot. In 1734, Jonathan Edwards, the minister of the Congregational church in Northampton, Massachusetts, began to preach sermons emphasizing the sinfulness of humanity, the torment all deserved to suffer in hell, and the doctrine that men and women could be saved only through divine grace, which God visited on individuals in the form of an intensely emotional conversion experience. Edwards did not honey his message. "The God who holds you over the pit of hell," he said in his most famous sermon, "much as one holds a spider or some loathsome insect over the fire, abhors you, and is dreadfully provoked."

Northampton was a fertile field for Edwards's kind of preaching. Excited revivals were part of local culture. There had been tumultuous religious excitements in the town in 1679, 1683, 1696, 1712, and 1718. Edwards was able to repeat his success in arousing congregations to mass conversions in few other towns.

A revivalist who made the whole of colonial North America his congregation was the Englishman George Whitefield, who made five extensive preaching tours through the colonies. Whitefield was inexhaustible. He spoke sixty hours most weeks, often to thousands of people at a time. During one spell of seventy-eight days, he delivered more than a hundred lengthy sermons calling on people to accept Jesus as their personal saviour. Whitefield prepared for his sermons with publicity campaigns well ahead of his time. His "advance men" planted stories about his miraculous conversions in newspapers in towns he planned to visit and plastered posters on walls and fences just before his arrival. His advertising worked. When Whitefield spoke in Philadelphia, the city's population doubled. Benjamin Franklin was unmoved by Whitefield's message but awed by the power of his voice; Franklin called it "an excellent piece of music". He methodically backed away from Whitefield's platform to determine the distance at which he could still understand the preacher's words. Franklin then hurried home to calculate just how many people, in theory, Whitefield could preach to at one time.

A few revivalists were lunatics or, like today, frauds. James Davenport ranted and raved, whooped and hollered, pranced and flounced about the stage, tore his clothing, rolled his eyes, and fell frothing and twitching to the floor. "Strike them, Lord, strike them!," Davenport cried when a sheriff, believing him insane, tried to restrain him.

"New Lights" versus "Old Lights"

The revivalists preached that salvation was available to all, but every individual had to accept God's grace personally "as if there was no other human Creature upon Earth." There was nothing wrong with the ordinary people, they said (always a popular message). The problem was with spiritually dead ministers. Their boasted education was spiritually worthless. They were not themselves saved and that was why their sermons were dull and uninspiring. God did not speak through ministers with Harvard and Yale degrees; he spoke through those whom he had personally touched with the lightning of his grace, no matter if they had not spent a day in a schoolroom. Their holiness was demonstrated by the excitement they aroused.

Traditional ministers, known as "Old Lights," responded to attacks on them by denouncing the "New Light" revivalists as deluded. Charles Chauncy, a Boston Congregationalist, wrote that a revivalist in the city "mistakes the working of his own passions for divine communications, and fancies himself immediately inspired by the spirit of God, when all the while, he is under no other influence than that of an overheated imagination." Others described "New Light" sermons as "wild extempore Jargon, nauseous to any chaste or refin'd Ear." Chauncy sardonically observed that people who were saved with great "out-Cries, Faintings and Fits" exhibited, after the revival was over, "the same Pride and Vanity, the same Luxury and Intemperance, the same lying and tricking and cheating, as before."

With Old Light and New Light ministers at loggerheads, the Congregationalists and Presbyterians split into two (and often additional) churches. They "Divide and Sub-divide," a North Carolina minister wrote, "Split into Parties—Rail at and excommunicate one another—Turn out of Meeting, and receive into another." Thus were born two sturdy American religious traditions: the periodic revival and the bewildering multiplicity of denominations.

The Great Awakening also marked the beginnings of what a historian has called "the feminization of American Protestantism." In 1700, religion and church affairs were the affairs of menfolk. By 1800, 75 percent of Protestant church members in the United States were women. The religious

profile of colonial Americans was also turned on its head. Before the revivals, the three largest religious groups in the colonies were the Anglicans, Congregationalists, and Quakers. By the end of the century, the three largest were the Baptists, New Light Presbyterians, and Methodists, a denomination taking shape in Great Britain during the same years as the Great Awakening in the colonies.

BRITAIN'S GLORIOUS TRIUMPH

Europe's "long peace" ended in 1739 when Parliament declared war on Spain. Ostensibly, all Britain was enraged when a merchant, Robert Jenkins, carrying one of his ears in a display case, told everyone who asked (and some who did not) that it had been cut off by a Spanish customs agent. Actually, more significant conflicts with Spain had been piling up for several years. In the colonies, Spanish Florida had been fighting a miniwar with British South Carolina and newly founded Georgia. In the north, French freebooters were raiding New England shipping again, then taking refuge in the fortress of Louisbourg on Cape Breton Island.

King George's War

The War of Jenkin's Ear merged into the War of the Austrian Succession when Prussia (then a French ally) attacked Austria (backed by Great Britain after 1743). Americans again had their own name for the conflict: King George's War.

Georgia and South Carolina exchanged attacks with Florida with Indians fighting on both sides. *Petite guerre* flickered on the New England frontier. The great event in the north was when, in 1745, a force of 4,000 militia, mostly from Massachusetts, besieged and captured Louisbourg Never had colonial soldiers won such a victory. Louisbourg was a state-of-the-art fortress; the French boasted that it was impregnable, "the Gibraltar of North America." New Englanders had a right to exult.

But their joy was short-lived. Three years later, in the Treaty of Aix-la-Chapelle, the British returned Louisbourg to France in return for French concessions elsewhere. Parliament reimbursed Massachusetts for the expenses of the Louisbourg campaign, but there was no way to restore the 500 lives lost at the fortress, nor to compensate for the fact that Louisbourg-based French ships resumed harassment of New England merchants and fishermen.

The peace lasted eight years. And the war between France and Britain that erupted in 1756 (called the Seven Years' War in Europe) differed significantly from the three Anglo-French conflicts that preceded it. First, it was a worldwide war; the British and French faced off on the high seas, in the West Indies, and in India, as well as in Europe and North America. Second, the war began in North America. It was not a European war into which the colonies were sucked; it was an American war that, within a few years, involved all of Europe's military powers. And, after a false start, Parliament proclaimed the North American theater the most important of all, with the object being the expulsion of the French from North America.

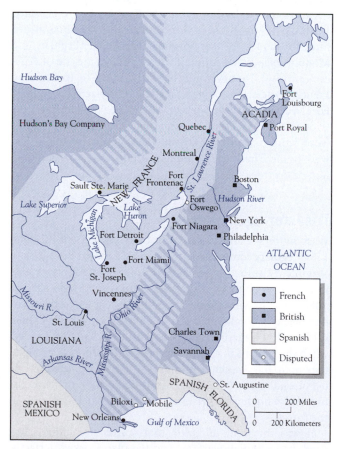

MAP 6:1 **French and British Empires in North America**
France claimed much more American acreage than Britain did. However, beyond an agricultural belt along the St. Lawrence River and in the Mississippi Delta, the cities of Montreal and Quebec and the towns of New Orleans, Biloxi, and Mobile, French America was little more than trading posts and forts scattered in wilderness that was, in reality, the Indians' country.

American Fighting Men: An Opinion Poll

George Washington claimed that his Virginians fought much better at Braddock's defeat than the British regulars. If so, it was an aberration according to the British commanders in the French and Indian War. A sampling of their opinions of American militiamen:

General Braddock: "slothful and languid"
General Abercromby: "vagabonds"
Lord Loudoun: "the lowest dregs"
General Wolfe: "contemptible cowards"
General Forbes: "the scum of the worst of people . . . a bad collection of broken Innkeepers, Horse Jockeys, and Indian traders"

Embarrassing Atrocities

The new "civilized" European warfare of the eighteenth-century provided that soldiers who surrendered be treated decently and permitted to depart. This "rule of war" was, however, at odds with Indian attitudes toward those (other Indians or whites) who lost a battle. Usually, most of the men were killed and most of the women and children adopted into the victorious tribe or enslaved.

This cultural clash led to a number of (from the French and British perspectives) unintended atrocities. On one of George Washington's western expeditions, his Indian allies killed several French prisoners before he could stop them. In 1756, the French and Indians captured 1,600 British and colonial prisoners at Fort Oswego on Lake Ontario. The Indians massacred 50 soldiers before the French called them off by promising them twenty women and children for adoption. In 1757, General Montcalm urged the British garrison at Fort William Henry to surrender while "I have it yet in my power to restrain the Savages." After destroying all the liquor in the fort, the British commander agreed. But Montcalm was unable to restrain his allies until they had killed about 270 mostly sick and wounded soldiers.

Enter George Washington

On the face of it, the British position in North America was stronger than France's and Spain's. The population of the British colonies was 1.2 million. There were only about 50,000 whites in French America, fewer than 20,000 Spanish north of Mexico. For the first time, Britain sent a large force of professsional soldiers to America. They soon outnumbered French troops stationed there.

However, the balance of military power was not that simple. The French had won the goodwill of the Indian tribes west of the Appalachians between the Ohio River and the Great Lakes. Virginia claimed this region, the "Ohio Country." Wealthy Virginians, among them a 22-year-old planter named George Washington, were already speculating in land there. The speculators held title to vast tracts of forest that they intended to survey and subdivide into farms to sell or rent to settlers. But their plans were delusions—their titles were worthless—as long as the Ohio Country remained the domain of the Indians who occupied it.

The Indians—Shawnees, Delawares, Miamis—aligned themselves with New France because the French had no thoughts of populating the Ohio Country with farmers; indeed, thinly populated New France lacked the capability of doing so. But the French supported Indian determination to hold the Ohio Country because they purchased French goods with hides and furs. The French and the Indians of the Ohio Country needed one another. Without their Indian allies, the French could not have stopped British settlement. Without French arms and forest forts to which to retreat, the Indians would, in time, lose their lands to the Virginians.

In 1753, the French began to lay out a string of forts in what is now western Pennsylvania. An alarmed Governor Robert Dinwiddie of Virginia sent George Washington west to inform the French that they were trespassing. French officers received Washington cordially but rejected Virginia's claims to the land. Although he had no military experience, Washington was sent back west with an absurdly small armed force to build a fort for Virginia where the Allegheny and Monongahela Rivers join to form the Ohio (the site of Pittsburgh today). He never got that far. Run off by Indians and French soldiers, Washington holed up in appropriately named Fort Necessity; it was nothing more than a palisade, hurriedly slapped together. He was "soundly defeated" (Washington's words) in a skirmish he sensibly kept almost bloodless and went home. The French built Fort Duquesne at the conjunction of the three rivers.

Disaster in the Forest

Washington's humiliation prompted Parliament to send 1,400 regulars commanded by General Edward Braddock to Virginia. Washington was named Braddock's American aide in charge of about 450 Virginia volunteers. Braddock was a famously brave soldier, and he had the men to take Fort Duquesne in a cakewalk. It was manned by just 72 French soldiers, 150 Canadian volunteers, and 600 Indians. Indeed, when the Indians in the fort learned of Braddock's strength, they told the French commander they were leaving. He persuaded them to stay by devising a plan to leave the fort and launch a surprise attack on Braddock's column in the forest.

It was the kind of battle that suited the Indians; indeed, it was Indian warfare. And the plan worked perfectly. Washington had warned Braddock of the possibility of an ambush, urging him to send scouting parties far in advance of the column. But the "American style" of war was alien to Braddock; he waved his aide off. The French and Indians hit the British and Virginians in a stretch of woods cleared of underbrush by burning. They were hidden, but they had clear shots to the narrow road Braddock's army was building. They hit the British vanguard with a devastating volley; fifteen of eighteen British officers were killed within ten minutes. The soldiers in the van ran to the rear in a panic just as the main body of troops was rushing forward to support them. In the confusion—the British tried to form a battle line on a front just 100 feet wide—the Indians could hardly miss. Braddock himself was shot and died a short time later. Washington managed to organize the remnant of the army, and a remnant is what it was. Two-thirds of the British and Virginians were killed or captured. The French and Indians lost only twenty-three killed and twenty wounded.

Pitt, Amherst, and Wolfe

Braddock's disaster was just the beginning. The overall commander of British troops in the colonies, John Campbell, Lord Loudoun (whose personal baggage filled an entire ship) was ineffective. General James Abercromby was utterly incompetent; with 12,000 troops he was soundly defeated by 3,000 French and Indians under Louis de Montcalm near New York's Lake George. The war seemed to be heading for a conclusion like the endings of King William's, Queen Anne's, and King George's wars, with a negotiated peace that left New France and their Indian allies dominant in the West.

Then, a remarkable politician, energetic and imaginative, took charge of the war in Parliament. William Pitt insisted that, whatever happened elsewhere, France had to be driven out of North America once and for all. He sent only a token army to Europe and, with borrowed money, paid huge subsidies to Prussia to tie down the French army, preventing France from matching the massive force Pitt sent to North America: more than 20,000 soldiers. Pitt also recruited about 11,000 Americans into the regular army and won the enthusiastic support of colonial militias by, for the first time, recognizing the ranks colonial assemblies had bestowed on American officers.

Pitt also picked the right generals. He put the able Jeffery Amherst in overall command with instructions to strike at New France's strongpoints, Louisbourg and Quebec. Amherst commanded the Louisbourg campaign, but the assault that captured the fortress was led by the young General James Wolfe. Actually, Wolfe was very lucky. He was trying to call off the attack on the fortress but could not get his orders to the front lines and the French panicked. Amherst was impressed. He put Wolfe in charge of an advance on Quebec via the St. Lawrence River while Amherst, after returning to New York, would lead a second army to the city overland via the Hudson River and Lake Champlain.

North Wind Picture Archives.

General James Wolfe died in the climactic battle for Quebec, but not before he learned of his unlikely victory. A difficult, eccentric man in life, the dead Wolfe was immortalized as a national hero without an equal until Horatio Nelson's great naval victory at Trafalgar half a century later. The pensive Indian is an Iroquois. Indians were unimportant in the fight for Quebec—it was a classic European battle—but vital to the British and French in other confrontations.

The Fall of an Empire

Amherst was delayed and Wolfe found himself alone below Quebec's cliffs. Artillery on his ships battered the city, but several frontal attacks were easily repulsed. Wolfe then tried to draw the French commmander, Montcalm, out of Quebec by laying waste to a thousand French farms, but Montcalm sat tight. It was September 1759. The leaves were turning; the Canadian winter was weeks away. Montcalm reasoned correctly that Wolfe would soon have to retire to winter quarters in Louisbourg.

Wolfe also felt the temperature dropping and gambled. Under cover of night on September 12, he led 4,000 men and a few cannon up Quebec's 250-foot cliffs on a steep, narrow trail that the French had left virtually unguarded. When the sun rose next day, Montcalm was stunned to see a British army in battle formation on open ground called the Plains of Abraham.

Montcalm's situation was from from desperate. His troops outnumbered Wolfe's, and he had the artillery with which to bombard Wolfe's exposed army. Wolfe's line of supply was vulnerable. Montcalm could have sat tight or ordered a force of 3,000 French troops nearby to attack Wolfe from the rear. Instead, he did the one thing that gave the British army tactical equality. He marched his army out of Quebec to battle Wolfe in a classic eighteenth-century European battle. At 130 yards—too distant for the muskets of the day to be effective—the French battle line fired a volley. The British did not respond. At 100 yards—just about the muskets' maximum range—the French volleyed again. Again, the British guns were silent. Again at 70 yards the French fired and, this time, British soldiers crumpled to the ground. But—and here one wonders how—Wolfe's line remained intact. Only when the French had closed to 40 yards—slaughtering range—did the British fire, literally mowing the French soldiers down like grass. The battle lasted fifteen minutes. Both Montcalm and Wolfe were killed, but the British occupied Quebec.

There was fighting elsewhere; and bickering over the terms of the peace dragged on for three years. In terms of consequences, however, the fall of Quebec was one of the half dozen most important battles ever fought in North America. In the Peace of Paris of 1763, the map of the continent was redrawn. Great Britain took Florida from Spain and all of Canada from France. To compensate Spain for the loss of Florida, France was forced to surrender Louisiana, the central third of what is now the United States, to Spain. The sprawling French American empire in the Western Hemisphere was reduced to its possessions in the West Indies and two tiny, rocky islands in the North Atlantic useful only as shelters for French fishermen.

FURTHER READING

Classics Francis Parkman, *France and England in North America*, 8 vols., 1851–1892; Charles M. Andrews, *The Colonial Period of American History*, 1934–1938; Louis B. Wright, *Cultural Life of the American Colonies*, 1957; Daniel Boorstin, *The Americans: The Colonial Experience*, 1958; Richard Hofstadter, *America at 1750*, 1971; William J. Eccles, *The French in North America, 1500–1783*, 3rd ed., 1998; Alan Heimert and Perry Miller, eds., *The Great Awakening*, 1967; Perry Miller, *Jonathan Edwards*, 1958; Edwin S. Gaustad, *The Great Awakening in New England*, 1957.

New France Bruce G. Trigger, *Natives and Newcomers: Canada's "Heroic Age" Reconsidered*, 1985; Gordon M. Sayre, *Les Sauvages Americains: Representations of Native Americans in French and English Colonial Literature*, 1997; Allen Greer ed., *The Jesuit Relations: Natives and Missionaries in Seventeenth Century North America*, 2000; James Pritchard, *In Search of Empire: The French in the Americas, 1670–1730*, 2004.

Colonial Warfare Howard H. Peckham, *The Colonial Wars, 1689–1762*, 1964; Douglas E. Leach, *Arms for Empire: A Military History of the British Colonies in North America*, 1973; Francis Jennings, *The Ambiguous Iroquois Empire: The Covenant Chain Confederation of Indian Tribes with English Colonies*, 1984, and *Empire of Fortune*, 1990; John E. Ferling, *A Wilderness of Miseries: War and Warriors in Early America*, 1980, and *Struggle for a Continent: The Wars of Early America*, 1993; John Keegan and Richard Holmes, *Soldiers: A History of Men in Battle*, 1986; James Merrell, *Beyond the Covenant Chain: The Iroquois and Their Neighbors*, 1987; Colin G. Calloway, *War, Migration, and the Survival of Indian Peoples*, 1990; Linda Colley, *Captives*, 2002.

Colonial Society Bernard Bailyn, *Voyagers to the West: A Passage in the Peopling of America on the Eve of the Revolution*, 1986, and Bailyn and Philip D. Morgan, eds., *Strangers Within the Realm: Cultural Margins of the First British Empire*, 1991; T. J. Davis, *A Rumor of Revolt: The "Great Negro Plot" in Colonial New York*, 1985; James G. Leyburn, *The Scotch-Irish: A Social History*, 1962; David Hackett Fisher, *Albion's Seed: Four British Folkways in America*, 1989. On pirates: David Cordingly, *Under the Black Flag: The Romance and Reality of Life Among the Pirates*, 1995.

Political Developments Bernard Bailyn, *The Origins of American Politics*, 1968; Robert J. Dinkin, *Voting in Provincial America: A Study of Elections in the Thirteen Colonies, 1689–1776*, 1977; Stephen Webb, *The Governors-General*, 1979; James Henretta, *Salutary Neglect*, 1972; Daniel J. Hulsebasch, *Constituting Empire: New York and the Transformation of Constitutionalism in the Atlantic World, 1664–1830*, 2005.

Religion and Culture Jack P. Greene, *Pursuits of Happiness: The Social Development of Early Modern British Colonies and the Frontier of American Culture*, 1988; Henry F. May, *The Enlightenment in America*, 1976; Jon Butler, *Awash in a Sea of Faith: Christianizing the American People*, 1990; Ned Landsman, *From Colonials to Provincials: Thought and Culture in America 1680–1760*, 1994; Frank Lambert, *Inventing the "Great Awakening*," 1999.

The French and Indian War Fred Anderson, *A People's Army: Massachusetts Soldiers and Society in the Seven Years' War*, 1984, *Crucible of War: The Seven Years War and the Fate of Empire in British North America*, 2001, and *The War That Made America: A Short History of the French and Indian War*, 2005; Francis Jennings, *Empire of Fortune: Crowns, Colonies, and Tribes in the Seven Years War*, 1988; Ian K. Steele, *Warpaths: Invasions of North America*, 1994.

KEY TERMS

Use the following listing of key terms to review important figures, events, locations, and concepts covered in this chapter. A glossary of these terms is available on *The American* *Past* companion Web site: www.cengage.com/history/conlin/tap9e

Jesuits, p. 93	**Scotch-Irish**, p. 100	**Great Awakening**, p. 107
coureur de bois, p. 94	**coverture**, p. 101	**Louisbourg**, p. 107
Marquette, Jacques, p. 94	**Stono**, p. 103	**Pitt, William (the elder)**, p. 109
petite guerre, p. 96	**salutary neglect**, p. 103	**Amherst, Sir Jeffery**, p. 109

ONLINE RESOURCES

Find additional resources, including primary source documents, images, interactive maps, simulations, chapter review exercises, and Internet links at

The American Past **companion Web site**
www.cengage.com/history/conlin/tap9e

American History Resource Center
http://ushistory.wadsworth.com/

DISCOVERY

What were the motives of the various companies and proprietors who founded colonies in North America? Why did the English king and the Parliament encourage them to do so?

Economics and Technology: Thomas Mun's "English Treasure by Foreign Trade" was a systematic presentation of the principles of "mercantilism," the dominant economic philosophy in Europe during the 1600s and 1700s. Why did Mun make exports central to the economic health of the nation? In what ways did the African slave trade, as illustrated in these figures, fit into the mercantilist scheme of things?

English Mercantilism

Although a Kingdom may be enriched by gifts received, or by purchase taken from some other Nations, yet these are things uncertain and of small consideration when they happen. The ordinary means therefore to increase our wealth and treasure is by Forraign Trade, wherein wee must ever observe this rule; to sell more to strangers yearly than wee consume of theirs in value. For suppose that when this Kingdom is plentifully served with the Cloth, Lead, Tin, Iron, Fish and other native commodities, we doe yearly export the overplus to forraign Countreys to the value of twenty-two hundred thousand pounds; by which means we are enabled beyond the Seas to buy and bring in forraign wares for our use and Consumptions, to the value of twenty hundred thousand pounds: By this order duly kept in our trading, we may rest assured that the kingdom shall be enriched yearly two hundred thousand pounds, which must be brought to us in so much Treasure; because that part of our stock which is not returned to us in wares must necessarily be brought home in treasure . . .

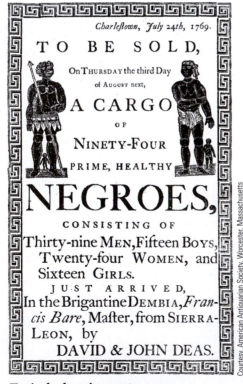

Courtesy, American Antiquarian Society, Worcester, Massachusetts

Typical advertisement

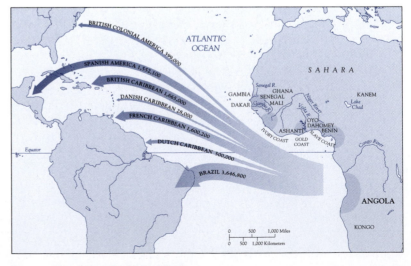

MAP 6:2 **The Atlantic Slave Trade**

Why was there so widespread a religious revival in the colonies in the 1730s? Had Americans become irreligious? What was missing in the largest churches so that so many people were open to a new religious enthusiasm?

Religion and Philosophy: Jonathan Edwards of Northampton in Massachusetts was the most brilliant of the preachers of the Great Awakening, a widespread religious revival in the 1730s and 1740s. What is the nature of Edwards's religion as reflected in his greatest sermon, "Sinners in the Hands of an Angry God" and his account of "The Great Awakening in New Hampshire"?

"Jonathan Edwards, 'Sinners in the Hands of an Angry God'"

That world of misery, that lake of burning brimstone, is extended abroad under you. There is the dreadful pit of the glowing flames of the wrath of God; there is hell's wide gaping mouth open; and you have nothing to stand upon, nor any thing to take hold of: there is nothing between you and hell but the air; it is only the power and mere pleasure of God that holds you up.

Your wickedness makes you as it were heavy as lead, and to tend downwards with great weight and pressure towards hell; and if God should let you go, you would immediately sink and swiftly descend and plunge into the bottomless gulf, and your healthy constitution, and your own care and prudence, and best contrivance, and all your righteousness, would have no more influence to uphold you and keep you out of hell, than a spider's web would have to stop a fallen rock. Were it not for the sovereign pleasure of God, the earth would not bear you one moment; for you are a burden to it. . . . There are black clouds of God's wrath now hanging directly over your heads, full of the dreadful storm, and big with thunder; and were it not for the restraining hand of God, it would immediately burst forth upon you. The sovereign pleasure of God, for the present, stays his rough wind; otherwise it would come with fury, and your destruction would come like a whirlwind, and you would be like the chaff of the summer threshing floor.

"Jonathan Edwards, 'The Great Awakening in New Hampshire ca. 1735'"

Particularly, I was surprized with the relation of a young woman, who had been one of the greatest company-keepers in the whole town. When she came to me, I had never heard that she was become in any wise serious, but by the conversation I then had with her, it appeared to me, that what she gave an account of, was a *glorious* work of God's infinite power and sovereign grace; and that God had given her a *new* heart, truly broken and sanctified. I could not then doubt of it, and have seen much in my acquaintance with her since to confirm it.

Though the work was *glorious*, yet I was filled with concern about the *effect* it might have upon others. I was ready to conclude, (though too rashly) that some would be hardened by it, in carelessness and looseness of life; and would take occasion from it to open their mouths in *reproaches* of religion. But the *event* was the *reverse*, to a wonderful degree. God made it, I suppose, the *greatest occasion of awakening* to others, of any thing that ever came to pass in the town. . . . The news of it seemed to be almost like a *flash of lightning*, upon the hearts of young people, all over the town, and upon many others. Those persons amongst us, who used to be farthest from seriousness, and that I most feared would make an ill improvement of it, seemed greatly to be *awakened* with it. . . .

Presently upon this, a great and earnest concern about the great things of religion, and the eternal world, became *universal* in all parts of the town, and among persons of all degrees, and all ages. . . . all other talk but about spiritual and eternal things, was soon thrown by. . . . Other discourse than of the things of religion, would scarcely be tolerated in any company. The minds of people were wonderfully taken off from the *world*, it was treated amongst us as a thing of very little consequence. They seemed to follow their worldly business, more as a part of their duty, than from any disposition they had to it; the *temptation* now seemed to lie on that hand, to *neglect* worldly affairs too much, and to spend too much time in the immediate exercise of religion. This was exceedingly misrepresented by reports that were spread in distant parts of the land, as though the people here had wholly thrown by all worldly business, and betook themselves entirely to reading and praying, and such like religious exercises.

To read extended versions of selected documents, visit the companion Web site www.cengage.com/history/conlin/tap9e; click on "Discovery Sources"

The Metropolitan Museum of Art, Bequest of Charles Allen Munn, 1924. (24.90.1556a) © The Metropolitan Museum of Art

Chapter 7

Family Quarrels

Dissension in the Colonies 1763–1770

Magnanimity in politics is not seldom the truest wisdom; and a great Empire and little minds go ill together.

—Edmund Burke

1 763, the year of the Peace of Paris, was an *annus mirabilis*, a year of miracles, for the British Empire. Great Britain had defeated France in India, the West Indies, and North America. Britain's ally, Prussia, had fought the French to a standstill in Europe. In the colonies, news of the terms of the treaty was greeted with the ringing of church bells from New Hampshire to Georgia. Americans were exultant. It was good to be British, to be a part of the empire that had humbled Europe's richest and most powerful nation. The Reverend Thomas Barnard of Massachusetts, preaching to the governor and assembly, proclaimed that "Now commences the Era of our quiet Enjoyment of Liberties." He called on Americans to serve and honor "Our indulgent Mother, who has most generously rescued and protected us . . . with all Duty, Love and Gratitude, til time shall be no more."

It was not to be quite like that. In 1775, a brief twelve years later, the same Americans who celebrated in 1763—a good many of them—were oiling their muskets and learning how to be soldiers—to fight the British army.

One of those men, Oliver Wolcott of Connecticut, wondered what had gone wrong. "So strong had been the Attachment" of Americans to Great Britain, he wrote, that "the Abilities of a Child might have governed this Country."

Wolcott blamed the colonial rebellion on British folly, incompetence, and tyranny. He had a point about folly and incompetence. Parliament's colonial policy was marked by blunders after stupidities upon miscalculations. But it would be a mistake, given the education in tyranny that the twentieth century has provided, to entertain Wolcott's claim that British rule was tyrannical. Always excepting the slaves, whose tyrants were closer to home than King George III, colonial Americans enjoyed more political and personal freedom than any people on the continent of Europe, in Africa, Asia, or South America.

What turned conservative men like Oliver Wolcott into rebels was the Crown's mismanagement of a reform of the administration of the British Empire combined with the refusal of colonial politicians to accept any deviation from the beneficent old policy of "salutary neglect." As the British saw it, the Americans refused to shoulder the responsibilities along with the privileges of being British. The sequence of events that led from 1763 to the War for Independence is not a story of American righteousness versus British villainy; it is merely history.

IMPERIAL PROBLEMS

Wolfe's capture of Quebec put Canada in British hands. Even before negotiators gathered in Paris to write a treaty, however, there was a debate as to whether the British should keep Canada as the spoils of war or give the colony back to France and keep the French West Indian islands of Martinique and Guadaloupe (also in British hands) as their reward.

Canada or Sugar?

The debate was heated. At least sixty-five pamphlets arguing the point were published. In the House of Lords, the Duke of Bedford argued that Britain should return Canada to France. Endless forest was not so grand a trophy. (The French philosopher Voltaire called Canada "a few acres of snow.") The Indians of Canada and the Ohio Valley—former French allies—were numerous, powerful, and hostile. Canada's 50,000 *habitants*, the French Canadians—all Roman Catholics!—would be nothing but trouble. The British had deported a few thousand Acadians out of fear of a rebellion. The Catholic Irish had been a headache for two centuries. What sense did it make to take another alien people into the empire?

Martinique and Guadaloupe, by way of contrast, could be managed by small military garrisons. They were tiny. The

White Gold, Black Death

Sugar was the most profitable crop grown in the British and French empires. In Great Britain, per capita consumption of sugar doubled every twenty years as people with a few shillings to spare became addicted to sweet coffee, tea, chocolate, candies, and cakes. Even the poorest Londoners smeared molasses on their bread.

There was little art in cultivating and processing sugar cane. Cuttings were planted in holes dug with hoes. There was no plowing, no need for livestock except to pull wagons. Cane is ready to harvest after fifteen months, but in the tropics, it can be planted almost any time, so the work for African slaves was constant. Nor was it just fieldwork. Once cut, the cane was crushed to extract a juice that was boiled, skimmed, and cooled in hellish "boiler houses" like this one. This process separated the sugar crystals from the molasses, much of which was distilled into rum in New England.

Sugar production was "labor intensive" almost beyond belief. An astonishing 150

Public Domain

slaves were needed to tend 100 acres of cane, three or four times as many as were needed to grow tobacco. The labor was heavier than tending tobacco and the West Indies were less healthy than the mainland colonies. Sugar devoured African lives. Unlike North American slave owners, sugar planters found it cheaper to work their slaves to death all the while they imported new ones. Between 1700 and 1775, 1.2 million Africans were brought to just the British West Indies. Women were worked as hard as men; their fertility was low and miscarriages were common. Indeed, slave women were known to smother their newborns rather than raise them to the life of misery they knew.

French planters who lived on the islands cared less about the design of the flag flying over the harbor forts than the fact that the soldiers there were primed to keep the masses of mistreated slaves in check and the profits from growing sugar rolling in. Sugar was white gold. Each year, Guadaloupe alone would send sugar worth £6 million to Great Britain; Canada's annual exports were a mere £14,000. Before the war, two-thirds of France's exports had gone to the West Indies: luxuries for the planters, cheap clothing and shoes for

the slaves, and, every year, more slaves from Africa. Now that lucrative market would be Britain's.

There was yet another argument in favor of keeping the sugar islands and giving Canada back. By 1763, the thirteen Atlantic colonies constituted a substantial country. Was it not possible?—was it not likely?— that the Americans had been loyal to Great Britain only because they feared the French and their Indian allies? Remove the French from Canada, thus choking off the Indians' supply of arms, and

Quarrels with the Mother Country 1760–1770

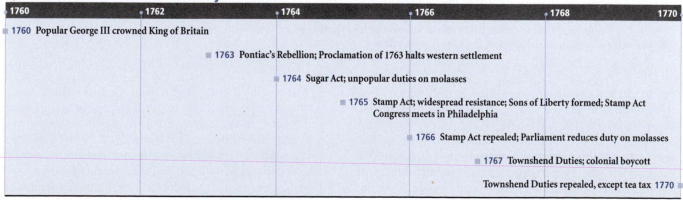

1760	1762	1764	1766	1768	1770

- 1760 Popular George III crowned King of Britain
- 1763 Pontiac's Rebellion; Proclamation of 1763 halts western settlement
- 1764 Sugar Act; unpopular duties on molasses
- 1765 Stamp Act; widespread resistance; Sons of Liberty formed; Stamp Act Congress meets in Philadelphia
- 1766 Stamp Act repealed; Parliament reduces duty on molasses
- 1767 Townshend Duties; colonial boycott
- Townshend Duties repealed, except tea tax 1770

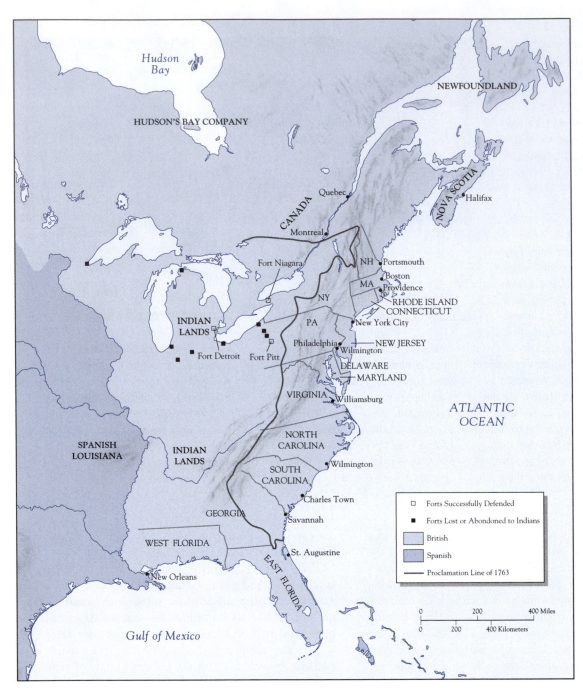

MAP 7:1 **The Proclamation of 1763 and Pontiac's Uprising.** Pontiac's well-coordinated warriors either captured or forced the abandonment of all the forts the British had inherited from France except Fort Niagara, Fort Detroit, and Fort Pitt (Pittsburgh). The multitribal assault was devastating. For a brief moment, as in King Philip's War eighty-eight years earlier, the Indians seemed to have halted white incursions into their lands. Like Metacomet before him, however, Pontiac was defeated.

the Americans would no longer need British military protection. They might well unite, in the words of a Swedish observer, Peter Kalm, and "shake off the yoke of the English monarchy." The French Foreign Minister, the Duc de Choiseul, agreed—although he did not publish his opinion. Privately, to the other French negotiators, he predicted that with Canada in British hands, the Americans would soon find British rule a burden and rebel.

In the end, Great Britain kept Canada. There was a £140 million national debt to pay. If Canada (and Louisiana) remained French, another expensive North American war was inevitable. Influential colonials like former Governor William Shirley of Massachusetts and Benjamin Franklin, who was living in London as Pennsylvania's lobbyist, warbled lyrically of the potential of the Canadian landmass. Americans generally were overjoyed.

Habitants and Indians

In the Peace of Paris, "His Britannick Majesty" agreed "to grant the liberty of the Catholick religion to the inhabitants of Canada." It was—with the Canadian population totally Catholic—a necessary concesssion but, given English anti-Catholicism, no less significant. English Catholics, few as they were in 1763, were saddled with disabilities under the "penal laws." They could not attend university or sit in Parliament, and they had to pay an annual tax. The few Catholics in the thirteen colonies were generally unmolested but, except in Rhode Island and Pennsylvania, their civil rights were restricted too. And there was a big difference between tolerating a Catholic minority in Maryland and the odd Romish church in Philadelphia and New York and coming to terms with sprawling Canada where almost everyone, Indians included, was Catholic.

Still, as in Ireland, the British held the power in Canada and the *habitants* had no background in representative government nor in making demands of authorities except in humble petitions. New France had been governed by the military. To French Canadians, taking orders from army officers in red uniforms was not much different in day-to-day terms than taking orders from French officers in white, blue, and buff. By dealing diplomatically with the testy but realistic bishop and priests of the Canadian Church, the British generals in Canada were able to govern the new province without significant resistance.

The Indians of the Ohio Valley presented a far more difficult problem. Unlike the French army, the warriors of the Ohio Country had not been decisively defeated in battle. The Treaty of Paris might tell them they were now subjects of King George. In reality, they were still securely in possession of the forests west of the Appalachians and comfortable in a way of life that was nearly intact.

The army blundered immediately in dealing with the Indians. General Jeffery Amherst looked on them as "wretched people" whose proper condition was subjection. He informed the western tribes that they would not receive the regular gifts of blankets, iron and brass tools, and vessels, firearms, and liquor that the French had provided as part of their alliance.

Neolin, a religious leader of the Delawares, a tribe that had been driven west by colonial expansion, preached that "if you suffer the English among you, you are dead men." An Ottawa chieftain, Pontiac ("I am a Frenchman and will die a Frenchman.") took action, attacking the fort at Detroit, an Indian refuge under the French, now a hostile British outpost. Pontiac was joined by eighteen tribes on a thousand-mile front. Detroit and Fort Pitt (formerly Fort Duquesne) held out but, in little more than a month, ten other western forts were overrun; 500 soldiers and perhaps 2,000 colonials were killed, more than were lost in any battle of the French and Indian War. An unnerved Amherst spoke of germ warfare—"Try to innoculate the Indians by means of Blankets, as well as to try Every other Method than can serve to Extirpate this Execrable Race"—although his instructions

were not carried out. Militarily, however, the British forces quickly regrouped and defeated Pontiac at Bushy Run near Pittsburgh. Even then, they had only stunned the Indians, not "extirpated" them. Amherst resumed the gift giving in October 1763.

The Proclamation of 1763

In order to let tempers cool, the Crown drew an imaginary line on the Appalachian divide, the crest between the sources of the rivers that emptied into the Atlantic and those that flowed into the Ohio–Mississippi River system. The king proclaimed, "We do strictly forbid, on pain of our displeasure, all our loving subjects from making any purchases or settlements whatever" west of the line. Frontiersmen and women already living west of the mountains were ordered to return east of the divide. Impatient emigrants were urged to settle in northern New England, Upper Canada (Ontario), Georgia, and Florida. Land sales west of the Appalachians ceased.

The Proclamation Line was, as one land speculator, George Washington, put it, "a temporary expedient to quiet the minds of the Indians." No one considered the Proclamation Line permanent. Indeed, royal superintendents of Indian affairs began to purchase land west of the line from Indians even before news of the proclamation had reached the more remote tribes. In the south, the Line of 1763 was redrawn—farther west— within a few months. Regularly over the next decade, trans-Appalachian lands were opened to speculation and settlement.

Nevertheless, by interfering temporarily, even on paper, with the colonial lust for land, British policy touched a tender nerve. A few years later, Americans would remember the Proclamation of 1763 as an early example of King George III's campaign to throttle their "liberties."

Money, Money, Money

Rattled by Pontiac's rebellion, General Amherst asked London for a permanent American garrison of 5,000 to

£/s/d

The British monetary unit was (and is) the pound sterling, designated by a stylized capital L with a horizontal slash: £. ("L" is the first letter of the Latin word for pound.) Since 1970, British money has been decimalized: there are 100 New Pence (p) to the pound. Before 1970—and in the eighteenth century—British coinage was more complex. The pound was divided into 20 shillings, designated "s". The shilling was divided into 20 pence ("d" for the Latin word for penny, *denarius*).

So, prices, debts, and other values were expressed in pounds, shillings, and pence: £/s/d. The smallest British coin was the farthing: one-fourth of a penny; there was also a half penny, pronounced "ha'penny." The guinea, only briefly a coin but often used in stating prices, particularly in shops specializing in expensive goods, was 21s. (£1/1s).

A View of the House of Commons, engraved by B. Cole (fl.1748-75) (engraving). English School. (18th century)/Stapleton Collection, UK./The Bridgeman Art Library.

Parliament consisted of two houses: the House of Lords in which seats were held by some 200 peers, nobles who inherited their titles, and the bishops of the Church of England; and the House of Commons, pictured here, to which 588 members were elected. In fact, noble families dominated the House of Commons, too. The small numbers of voters dependably chose the candidate the local lord selected, often the lord's younger sons or other relatives.

war had been gloriously expensive, and Pitt had financed it by borrowing. In 1763, the national debt of £122.6 million was almost twice what it had been before the war; annual interest alone was £4.4 million. The running costs of governing the empire were up. Not only were there the new acquisitions, annual administrative expenses in the thirteen mainland colonies had quintupled during the war from £70,000 to £350,000.

Whigs and Tories

Both *Whig* and *Tory*, names of political tendencies in the eighteenth century and genuine political parties in the nineteenth, were originally insults. *Whig* was a derogatory term for anti-Catholic Scottish cattle rustlers—thieves, *Tory* an insulting name applied to Irish Catholic robbers in Ulster, northern Ireland.

Just what the terms meant in politics changed over time. In the early eighteenth century, Tories believed in a powerful monarchy and hoped to restore the Stuart dynasty to the throne. England's dwindling numbers of Catholic landowners were Tories, but most Tories were good Anglicans. The original Whigs were those who had driven the last Stuart king, James II, into exile in 1688 and who, in 1714, imported the German George I to be king in order to keep the Stuart pretender to the throne in exile. These Whigs believed in the supremacy of Parliament with the king little more than a ceremonial figurehead.

By the 1760s, realistic Tories had given up on restoring the Stuarts. (The last military attempt to do so was crushed in 1746.) And George III, unlike his two predecessors, generally preferred Tory ministers to Whigs. Consequently, after 1776, American rebels called colonials who remained loyal to Britain Tories. A few called themselves Whigs, but "patriots" was a more popular name.

6,000 troops. Parliament surprised everyone by sending him 10,000. Although—several years later—Americans would say that so many redcoats—far more than had ever been stationed in the colonies in peacetime—were sent to police them, Parliament's motives were more innocent. The Crown was faced with thousands of French and Indian War veterans in Britain, and the British had never been comfortable with a standing army at home. To discharge so many men at a stroke would have led to social tumult that would cost far more to address than the soldiers' wages, not to mention acrimonious political debates.

Posting the veterans to North America seemed to be a win-win solution to the problem. American duty was popular with the redcoats. The possibility of a renewed Indian threat was real enough, but with the French gone, there would be no large battles. And the colonials were, after all, patriotic Britons, not a subject people to be kept down like the Irish. In the Quartering Act of 1765, Parliament freed itself of supporting the "pensioners" by requiring each colony to provide food, drink, and shelter for the soldiers stationed within their borders, a savings to Britain of about £200,000 a year.

The cost of supporting 10,000 soldiers was, however, the least of Parliament's financial woes. William Pitt's glorious

Parliament and King

Parliament cut some expenditures sharply: The Royal Navy's budget was slashed from £7 million in 1762 (the last year of actual fighting) to £2.8 million in 1766, and to £1.5 million in 1769. Parliament might have economized further by cleaning up waste and corruption: bribes and kickbacks in awarding padded government contracts; parasites drawing big salaries for jobs with few or no duties; others drawing pensions for rendering no particular services.

But corruption and patronage were at the heart of eighteenth century-government. Most of the men who sat in Parliament were of the same, small social class of landowning families connected by intermarriage. The heads of these noble families, just 200 of them—dukes, marquesses, earls, and viscounts—sat in the House of Lords; they inherited their titles and seats in Parliament. Moreover, most members of the House of Commons, who were elected by a small electorate (300,000 men, 3 percent of the population) were members of

Colonial Williamsburg Foundation

George III was popular in the colonies during the 1760s. Streets and taverns were named for him by the dozens. New Yorkers erected a splendid equestrian statue of the king (which was melted down to cast cannon after the Declaration of Independence). In England, the affable king remained popular after American independence.

the same families, younger sons or cousins of peers, or gentlemen who had married women of the nobility. Lords and commoners alike had yet other relations and friends looking to live off a bit of the patronage at Parliament's disposal.

Although some members of Parliament called themselves "Whigs" and others "Tories," there were no organized political parties like those we know today. Rather, Parliament was a menage of factions, some of them held together by a principle, some by blood and marriage, some just to comprise a bloc of votes to trade for patronage.

Britain's kings could no longer govern by proclamation without Parliament's approval. However, George III, crowned in 1760 at the age of 22, was an active and powerful politician. Some royal prerogatives survived; many members of Parliament believed in deferring to the king; and George had a considerable royal patronage at his disposal that he used to bind together his own faction in Parliament known as "the king's friends."

In 1776, rebellious Americans would denounce George III as a tyrant and a "royal brute," blaming him for dozens of oppressions. In fact, the king had the support of a comfortable majority in Parliament for every one of his actions. He was no tyrant. Ironically, George was a decent, sociable, and unaffected person. He rarely wore a wig, even on state occasions. His "common touch" was authentic. Interested in agriculture, he could converse comfortably for hours with rude farmers, even pitch in to fork hay or try his hand guiding a plow. He was a faithful, loving husband and a doting father (he had fifteen children.), a rarity among kings, especially in his dynasty. In his job, he was conscientious, hard working, and well meaning.

Alas—it has run in the family ever since—he was not very bright and, in colonial matters, he shared the tunnel vision of the English upper class. His inability to conceive of the Americans as anything but ignorant, rustic yokels who should do as their betters told them to do was to prove disastrous. But he was far from alone in that prejudice.

George Grenville

The unenviable job of resolving Britain's financial crisis fell to George Grenville, who, in 1763, was named First Lord of the Treasury (Secretary of the Treasury, we would say) over the objections of King George, who disliked him intensely, in part because he was highly intelligent and paraded his abilities in front of the less talented, including the king. Grenville was an expert in finance and—by the standards of his times—something of a visionary.

Grenville understood that the empire had become too vast and the colonies too scattered to be managed by the old policy of "salutary neglect." There were twenty colonies just in the Western Hemisphere. If each of them, from populous Massachusetts and Virginia to newly acquired Canada and Barbados, Jamaica, and other islands in the West Indies, was allowed to go its own way as in the past, the result would be chaos. It had been all very well before the French and Indian War to wink at colonials playing fast and loose with trade laws. British merchants did £2 million in trade with Americans yearly. But the huge national debt demanded an increase in revenue.

Grenville could not reduce the debt by raising taxes at home. Landowners were already paying 20 percent of their annual income in taxes. It seemed an easier task to list commodities that were not saddled with an excise than those that were. A foreigner living in London wrote

> The English are taxed in the morning for the soap that washes their hands; at 9 for the coffee, the tea and the sugar they use at breakfast; at noon for the starch that powders their hair; at dinner for the salt that savours their meat; in the evening for the porter that cheers their spirits; all day long for the light that enters their windows [each window in a house was taxed annually]; and at night for the candles that light them to bed.

Ordinary people were taxed more heavily than the common people of France, who thought they were mercilessly exploited. When Parliament levied a small tax on apple cider, the daily beverage in southwestern England, there were riots.

Harcourt Picture Collection

George Grenville was an aristocrat who climbed to the top of the slippery pole of British politics. He might have been remembered as a visionary who brought some order to the administration of the chaotic British Empire had colonials not resisted his Sugar Act of 1764 and Stamp Act of 1765. Instead, he is remembered (in patriotic American history) as a minister who attempted to destroy American liberties.

Not lost on Grenville nor on Parliament, while the per capita tax in Britain was 26s. a year, a British subject living in Massachusetts paid annual taxes of 1s, the average Virginian a mere 5d. And colonials had gained a great deal from the French and Indian War: the elimination of the French threat in the north and Spanish Florida in the south. Grenville concluded that the colonials had to shoulder a heavier financial burden.

There was no faulting Grenville's reasoning. Indeed, none of the Americans who protested British tax policies after 1763 denied that the colonies had a moral obligation to contribute financially to the empire. Unhappily, if the thirteen colonial assemblies had been willing to vote Grenville the money he said the Exchequer had to have, they never got the chance to do so. Grenville did not request grants from each colony as his predecessors, including his brother-in-law, William Pitt, had done. He bundled his money problem together with his intention to bring order to the administration of the empire with Parliament in charge. Grenville expected that Parliament would tell the Americans how much they would pay in taxes and what kind of taxes they would pay, and that the Americans would do so.

The Sugar Act

The Molasses Act of 1733 was the kind of law that, Grenville believed, had to be overhauled. Its 6d. per gallon tax on molasses imported from the French West Indies was so high that, merchants claimed, they could not pay it and still make a profit. Many importers presented customs collectors with fraudulent documents certifying that their cargos of French molasses came from British sugar islands. If the phoney papers were accompanied by a bribe of a penny or two per gallon, many customs agents accepted them. If bribery failed and importers were arrested as smugglers, they could usually count on local juries (their neighbors) to acquit them regardless of the evidence against them and, perhaps, to join them afterwards for a tot of rum. John Hancock of Boston, the richest man in Massachusetts and later a vociferous advocate of American independence, made his bundle smuggling French molasses.

Grenville's Sugar Act of 1764 was intended both to clean up customs collection and to generate revenue to reduce the national debt. The Sugar Act enlarged the colonial customs service and provided that accused smugglers be tried in vice admiralty courts in which judges, many of them British, and not local juries, decided innocence or guilt. To make obeying the law more palatable to American merchants, Grenville reduced the duty on molassses to 3d. a gallon, not much more than the traditional bribe. He estimated that the Sugar Act would bring in between £40,000 and £100,000 a year. (The act also levied duties on some wines, coffee, silks, and other luxury items.)

There were protests in New England and New York, where molasses was a major import. (It was distilled into rum, the poor man's tipple and a lucrative export.) The Boston town meeting declared that citizens would buy no British goods of any kind until Parliament repealed the law. New York followed suit. Even "the young Gentlemen of Yale College" announced that they would not "make use of any foreign spirituous liquors" until Grenville backed down. Their sacrifice, apparently heroic for college students, was really not much; there were oceans of domestic beer and cider for sale locally.

Grenville shrugged. He assumed that the Americans simply did not want to pay any taxes, not an unreasonable judgment: Massachusetts in particular had contributed little money to fighting the French and Indian War. However, there were also principles at stake that Grenville and Parliament refused to recognize.

The Rights of British Subjects

One of the "rights of British subjects" was the principle that the king's subjects, through their elected representatives in Parliament, *consented* to all taxes levied upon them. The king alone could not tax them as kings had in the distant past, and the king of France was still proclaiming taxes. Without majority approval in the House of Commons, no money bill was valid. Colonials did not elect men to Parliament. Therefore, Parliament had no authority to tax them. Only the thirteen colonial assemblies, their own little parliaments, could do that.

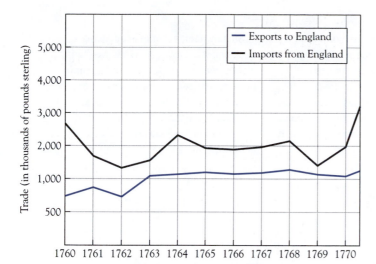

CHART 7:1 Value of Colonial Trade with Great Britain (in British Pounds). The boycott of British imports called by the Sugar Act protesters had some effect, but not much. Only with the more broadly supported boycott following the Townshend Acts of 1767 was there a decline in imports that British merchants felt sorely.

In fact, Parliament had long collected money from colonials. Under the terms of the Molasses Act of 1733, customs agents collected (or tried to collect) a tax in colonial ports without the consent of colonial assemblies. However, argued Daniel Dulany of Maryland, the Sugar Act differed in essentials from the old Molasses Act. The purpose of Molasses Act duties was to regulate trade; it was designed to price French molasses out of the American market. The purpose of the Sugar Act, on the other hand, was to raise money. The official name of the Sugar Act was the American Revenue Act.

It was within Parliament's power to regulate commerce by levying a duty on imports, Dulany and others said. But Parliament could raise money through taxation only from those who elected representatives to the House of Commons, the people of England and Scotland.

The Sugar Act raised other "rights" issues: the right of a British subject accused of a crime to be tried by a jury of his peers and the right of an accused criminal to be assumed innocent until proved guilty. They were these treasured rights, colonials believed, that set British subjects apart from—made them freer than—the French, Spanish, Poles, Chinese, Hottentots, and Shawnees of the world. By denying accused smugglers a jury trial and assuming their guilt until they proved their innocence, the procedure in vice admiralty courts, George Grenville and Parliament were tampering with the essence of Britishness.

It is impossible to know what would have happened if Grenville's program had ended with the Sugar Act. The protest against the law was peaceful, the debate conducted on a high level. Daniel Dulany had a point, but so did his critics, who said that the intention of a law was irrelevant to its validity. The Sugar Act duties and the obnoxiousness of some of the vice-admiralty courts' procedures affected very few people: men in the molasses business and—the taxes—

consumers of rum. The boycott was a failure; it made hardly a blip in colonial imports from Great Britain. And when, in 1766, the tax on molasses was reduced to a penny a gallon, the protests evaporated while "the principle of the thing" remained intact.

THE CRISIS OF 1765

But Grenville did not stop with the Sugar Act. In 1765, he proposed and Parliament enacted the Stamp Act. This was a tax on colonials that touched a great many people and violated the principle of "no taxation without representation" without the ambiguity arising from the issue of regulating trade.

The English had been paying a stamp tax since 1694. In order to be binding, some legal documents had to be written on stamped (embossed) paper purchased from the government. Massachusetts had experimented with a stamp tax in 1755. Purchase of the paper constituted the payment of a tax that could not be evaded without the possibility of the evader doing harm to himself. A sale of land not recorded on stamped paper was not a legal transaction; the buyer did not, in the law, own what he had purchased. Contracts written on ordinary foolscap were, if taken to court, thrown out as invalid.

The Stamp Act

Grenville's Stamp Act of 1765, which applied only to the North American colonies, went further than the British or short-lived Massachusetts laws. In addition to legal documents such as wills, bills of sale, licenses, deeds, insurance policies, and contracts, the act required that newspapers, pamphlets, handbills, posters, even playing cards be printed on the embossed government paper. And it was expensive. Each copy of a newspaper was taxed 2s. A license to sell liquor cost £4 in addition to the fee for the license. A license to practice law was taxed £10. The tax varied from a halfpenny on a handbill announcing a sale of taffeta to £10 for a tavern keeper's license to sell liquor. Grenville expected to make a great deal of money; to ensure that he did, he entrusted violations of the Stamp Act to the vice admiralty courts.

Grenville tried to curry favor in the colonies by offering generously paid collectorships to prominent Americans and pledging that all money raised by the Stamp Act would be spent solely in "defending, protecting, and securing the colonies." Not a farthing would go to Great Britain.

A few prominent Americans were dazzled by the opportunity, much to their later regret. Living in London, Benjamin Franklin tried to get a collectorship for a crony back in Pennsylvania. Richard Henry Lee of Virginia who, eleven years later, would propose the resolution declaring American independence, applied for a stamp tax collectorship.

But the proviso that all revenues from the act would be spent in the colonies meant nothing to those who had protested against the Sugar Act on the principle of "no taxation without

Stamps

What we call a postage stamp was unknown in the eighteenth century. The adhesive-backed paper—proof that postage has been paid on a letter—was introduced only in 1834. (The perforations between stamps arrived in 1854.) When the postal stickers appeared, the speakers of no European language except English chose the word *stamp* as the name of the novelty. To them, and to the British and the American colonials, a stamp was an image that was impressed—stamped into—paper, not something stuck on it. It was what we call embossing.

So, the stamps that caused all the excitement in 1765—shown here—were embossments, pressed into the paper to be used for licenses, newspapers, and the rest. Very few Americans ever saw a Stamp Act embossment. Only a few sheets of troublesome stamps were sold in Georgia, none in any other colony.

Tax stamp
Not so popular with colonial collectors.

Stamps.

Culver Pictures, Inc.

representation," and a great many Americans who had been indifferent to the Sugar Act. Not only was the Stamp Act designed to raise money with no pretense of being a regulation of trade, it was also a direct tax on transactions within a colony. Clearly, only a colonial assembly, in which the people of the colony were represented, could enact such a tax. Parliament had no more authority to enact such a tax on Georgians and Marylanders than the New York assembly had.

Some members of Parliament made these points during the debate over Grenville's proposal, but they were few. The Stamp Act sailed through Parliament by a vote of 204 to 49.

A Stupid Law

Parliament's nonchalance in passing the Stamp Act was remarkable because, constitutional niceties aside, it was a sloppily conceived, politically stupid law. Not only could a vice admiralty judge invalidate a bill of sale not printed on stamped paper but he could also order that a will hastily written by a dying man be ignored. Were constables to interrupt card games in taverns to examine the deck for stamps? Were authorities to devote time to tracking down the source of an unstamped handbill blowing down the street?

Moreover, the burden of Stamp Act taxes fell heavily on just those people who were in the best positions to stir up a fuss. Newspaper editors, with their influence on public opinion, would be hard hit by the act. Advertisements, a newspaper's bread and butter, were taxed 2s. Printers, who made a living by putting out broadsides (posters announcing goods for sale and public meetings—including protest meetings!) saw their business taxed at every turn of the press.

How Many Lawyers Does It Take To …

Colonials went to court often enough; the dockets were crowded with disputes over land ownership. But litigants pleaded their own cases. Professional lawyers were few until the middle of the eighteenth century. There were only three lawyers in New York City in 1692, seven in 1700. As late as 1720, Boston had only three.

In part this was because there were no law schools in the colonies. The first college to offer lectures in law was William and Mary in 1779 (although the lecturer, George Wythe, had privately trained a number of lawyers, Thomas Jefferson among them). The first permanent school of law was founded in 1812 at the University of Maryland.

Also in part, lawyers had a bad reputation for getting in the way of justice with their hairsplitting and for being chiefly concerned with diverting as much of the money in their clients' purses to their own. Massachusetts enacted a law fobidding the practice of law in 1641, Virginia in 1658.

By the end of the colonial period, this prejudice was beyond memory. Of the fifty-six signers of the Declaration of Independence in 1776, twenty-four were lawyers. Of the fifty-five delegates to the Constitutional Convention of 1787, thirty-one were lawyers.

Lawyers, persuaders by profession, had to pay a tax on every document with which they dealt. Keepers of taverns, to be saddled with more expensive licenses, were influential figures in every town and city neighborhood. Their inns

The Metropolitan Museum of Art, Bequest of Charles Allen Munn, 1924. (24.90.1566a) © The Metropolitan Museum of Art

A New Hampshire man who applied for a license to sell Stamp Act paper is tortured in effigy, possibly just outside his home. He was lucky. Mobs like this one, made up of riffraff, but substantial working men too, harassed and otherwise abused other men who took the job, forcing some to flee for their lives.

and ordinaries were the gathering places where, over rum, brandy, coffee, and tea, locals gathered to read newspapers and discuss public affairs, such as taxes.

Worse, these groups were concentrated in cities where they could easily meet with one another, cooperate, organize, and have an impact out of proportion to their numbers. It was one thing to upset such people one group at a time, as the Sugar Act riled shippers and distillers. The Stamp Act hit all of these key elements of the population at once, and the protestors won the support of large numbers of working people and even the tumultuous urban underclass.

Protest: Spontaneous and Deliberative

Parliament approved the Stamp Act in February 1765; it was to go into effect in November. As soon as the news of the tax reached the colonies, however, they erupted in anger. Local organizations called Sons of Liberty (a phrase used to describe Americans by one of their supporters in Parliament, Isaac Barré) condemned the law and called for another boycott of British imports.

Some Sons turned to violence. When the stamped paper was delivered to warehouses in port cities, mobs broke in and made bonfires of it. Men appointed stamp masters were shunned or hanged in effigy if they were lucky; others were roughed up; a few were stripped, daubed with hot tar, rolled in chicken feathers, and carried, straddling a fence rail, about town. In Norfolk, Virginia, "all the principal gentlemen in town" were present when an informer was tarred and feathered.

A tax collector in Maryland fled for his life to New York. That was a mistake; the New York's Sons of Liberty were the most volatile of all. They located the Marylander and forced him to write a letter of resignation. Led by Isaac Sears, the captain of a merchant vessel, the New Yorkers frightened

their own lieutenant governor so that he went into hiding. When they could not find him, they burned his carriages. In Boston, the crowd looted and burned the homes of several British officials. When the governor told the commander of the colonial militia to sound the alarm to muster the troops, he was told that all the militia's drummers were in the mob.

Rowdies are seldom popular and among those taken aback by the widespread rioting were wealthy colonials who opposed the Stamp Act but shuddered when they heard the sounds of a mob. They knew that a mob was a beast that, in a twinkling, could shift its depredations from one target to another when the exhilaration of hell-raising obscured the initial excuse for it. The urban colonial elite—merchants, lawyers—were men with something to lose. They wanted the Stamp Act repealed, but they feared social disorder. John Dickinson, a cautious and conservative Pennsylvanian, hoped to co-opt the mobs and bring pressure on Parliament through influential British merchants who were involved in the colonial trade. In October 1765, Dickinson and thirty-six other delegates from nine of the colonies assembled in New York City at what they called the Stamp Act Congress. They adopted fourteen resolutions and a "Declaration of Rights and Grievances" addressed to the king. It condemned the Sugar Act and Stamp Act on the grounds that they violated the British constitution. At the same time, the delegates carefully and prominently made it clear they acknowledged "all due subordination" to the Crown.

What did "all due subordination" mean? Loyalty to the king? Unquestionably: Just about everyone in 1765 agreed on the importance of the monarch as the symbol that unified a people. *Lèse-majesté*—"injuring the king"—was the gravest of political crimes. It was punished by hanging followed by disembowelment and quartering—harnessing four horses to

Colonial Politicians   *How They Lived*

Candidates in colonial elections *stood* for public office; they did not *run*. The very idea of grinning endlessly and frantically toadying to voters for the sake of personal advancement, as our politicians do as a matter of course, would have disgusted colonial candidates (and voters). They valued personal dignity. Nevertheless, colonials seeking office had to be adept at winning popular approval because far more men were eligible to vote in the colonies than there were in Great Britain.

In about half the colonies, including the most populous, Virginia, elections to the assembly were by voice vote; half the colonies used paper ballots. In none of the latter, however, were ballots secret. In colonial elections, the candidates and a voter's neighbors knew how he voted.

Elections in Virginia were particularly personal. Candidates for a seat in the House of Burgesses were present at the county seat on election day. They stood behind the table—out of doors, weather permitting—at which the roll of voters and a tally sheet were kept. When a voter announced his choice, that candidate thanked him. Often enough, he knew the voter's name. Virginia's voters certainly knew the candidates by sight. They were almost always among the largest landowners in the county. Some working farmers were eligible to stand for office, but few had time to spare to travel to Williamsburg for legislative sessions. Public office was a luxury accesible only to men of leisure.

In northern cities—Philadelphia, New York, and Boston were the only large ones—most candidates for public office were likewise of the upper crust: well-to-do merchants and lawyers. However, artisans beyond the struggling phase, entered and won elections. Benjamin Franklin of Philadelphia was a printer, a tradesman who worked with his hands; he was also among the city's most active public citizens.

In Boston and other New England towns, politicians won followings by their eloquence at town meetings, which men sufficiently interested to cast a vote on election day were apt to attend regularly. Voter participation, however, was no greater than it is today. Recent immigrants had rarely been eligible to vote in Great Britain, Ireland, or Germany; hard-working farmers were likely to consider a day in their fields better spent than a day at the polls.

There were no formal organizations resembling our political parties in any of the colonies. From Maryland south, there were hardly any factions. Candidates for seats in southern assemblies stood for election as eminent individuals and won or lost largely on the personal respect they commanded. In the northern colonies, there were political differences between candidates roughly analagous to the Tory-Whig division in Parliament. The governors of Pennsylvania, New York, and Massachusetts used their patronage to build a "court party" to support them in the assemblies. The Whiggish opposition was dedicated to keeping the governor's power in check, and reducing it when they were presented with an oppportunity to do so.

Debates in the colonial assemblies, usually reported in newspapers in the North, with some speeches printed word for word, were usually decorous and well mannered. Most members of assemblies were of the colonial elite, personally and socially acquainted with their opponents and often related. But there were exceptions to the rule, more numerous as the break with Great Britain neared. In a speech attacking the Stamp Act in Virginia's House of Burgesses in 1765, a newly elected Burgess, Patrick Henry, concluded a speech by saying, "Caesar had his Brutus, Charles the First his Cromwell, and George III . . . may profit by their example." He was shouted down with cries of "Treason!," which, indeed, Henry's reference to monarchs who were killed was. Not incidentally, Henry was not a rich planter but a self-taught trial lawyer born the son of tavern keepers. Socially, he stood far below his colleagues.

---

each of the traitor's limbs and cracking the whip. However, the loyal subjects of the Stamp Act Congress insisted that colonials were not subordinate to Parliament.

What Is Representation?
The Colonial Case

Colonials did not elect members of the House of Commons; therefore, Parliament could not tax them. To American protesters, it was that simple. Their own assemblies, which they did elect, represented them. They alone, under the British Constitution, were empowered to tax them.

The colonial case is easy to understand because our own understanding of representation reflects it. In order to be represented in government, a citizen must be entitled to vote for a city council member, county supervisor, state legislator, representative, or senator. Senators from Kentucky do not represent Iowans, who have no voice in electing them. Every significant liberalization of voting requirements in United States history—extension of the suffrage to propertyless men, to African American men, to women, and to adolescents between the ages of 18 and 21—was based on the principle that people must have the right to vote to be represented in government.

James Otis, a Massachusetts lawyer, spoke for this way of thinking at the Stamp Act Congress. He proposed that Parliament put an end to the problem of "no taxation without representation" by allowing colonials to elect members of Parliament. Benjamin Franklin, in London, also toyed with this idea. But few colonials and fewer members of Parliament

Courtesy Peabody Essex Museum, Salem, Massachusetts neg #16,507

A souvenir teapot commemorating the repeal of the Stamp Act. It was made in Great Britain for the colonial market. The potteries of Staffordshire were among the first mass-production industries. The potteries were also pioneers in identifying and exploiting short-lived sensations—"hot topics"—like the Stamp Act excitement. After American independence, the potteries produced thousands of statuettes of George Washington; some but not all shipped to the United States.

supported Otis's proposal. The Americans did not want to send representatives to Parliament. They were happy with their own assemblies, which they controlled. And they knew that any bloc of colonials in the House of Commons would be small, outvoted on every colonial issue by the British members.

Parliament rejected the idea of American members of the House of Commons because, by British lights, colonials were already represented.

What Is Representation? The British Case

In an eighteenth-century context, Parliament was correct. The British concept of representation differed (and differs) from our own. As George Grenville replied to the colonial protesters, each member of the House of Commons represented not only the borough or county that elected him; he virtually represented the people of the entire country and, in Grenville's telling, all the people of the empire.

For example, it was not (and is not) required that a member of the House of Commons reside in the electoral district that sends him or her to the House of Commons. While it is unlikely to happen today, a member of Parliament may never set foot in the district that elected him. British electoral districts are, by definition, for the sake of convenience in counting votes; each member of Parliament is regarded as virtually representing all of them. Edmund Burke, an outspoken friend of the Americans, put the point to his own constituents in the city of Bristol (and to Americans): "You choose a member . . . but when you have chosen him, he is not a member of Bristol, but he is a member of Parliament."

Only 3 percent of the British population voted. But the members of Parliament they elected represented everyone.

Indeed, in the 1760s, a dozen or so members of the House of Commons were elected from districts where, because of shifts of population, voters numbered only a dozen or so. Several of these "rotten boroughs" (they had their critics) had a single voter. One rotten borough had been under water for two centuries. Several cities did not elect members of Parliament because they had not existed when seats in the House of Commons had been assigned. But, according to the principle of virtual representation, Parliament represented them.

Colonials practiced virtual representation too. George Washington and other Virginians were elected to the House of Burgesses from counties in which they did not reside. On occasion, individuals stood as candidates in more than one county so that, if they were defeated in one of the elections, they might win in the other. Our laws today would not allow a person to run for senator in Kentucky and Iowa, or even in elections for different congressional seats in Kentucky. But few objected to the practice in Virginia. It was assumed—or, at least, said—that those who were elected would act with the interests of all Virginians in mind.

The colonists also practiced virtual representation in their restriction of the suffrage to free, white, adult male heads of household who owned property. The number of actual voters in colonial elections amounted to a small proportion of the inhabitants of the colony. Nevertheless, the colonists considered propertyless white men and women and children to be *virtually represented* in their elected assemblies. The assumption was that assemblymen acted on behalf of all, not just on behalf of those who voted for them.

ACT TWO

The Stamp Act crisis was not resolved by adding up debaters' points. The violence of the colonial protesters alarmed Parliament as much as it alarmed the men of the Stamp Act Congress. Nor could Parliament ignore the fact that many respectable, well-to-do, and conservative colonial political leaders were sufficiently concerned about the Stamp Act to make the trip to New York and write a remonstrance of their grievances. Never before had such a statement issued from the colonies.

Repeal but Not Victory

Members of Parliament who had voted against the Stamp Act praised the New York gathering. William Pitt, now in the House of Lords as the Earl of Chatham, rejoiced "that America has resisted. Three millions of people so dead to all the feelings of liberty," he said, "so voluntarily to submit to be slaves, would have been fit instruments to make slaves of the rest." Edmund Burke, a conservative traditionalist, viewed the colonists as defenders of British tradition, Grenville's backers as dangerous innovators. The radical John Wilkes egged on the colonials as his natural allies in his agitations on behalf of a free press. Charles Fox, a future cabinet minister, part cynical opportunist and part man of high principle, praised the Americans, as did Isaac Barré, a former soldier who had fought with Wolfe at Quebec.

The majority found no merit in the colonial argument that Parliament could not constitutionally tax them but, in 1766, they repealed the Stamp Act. George III was not unhappy to see Grenville fall on his face; even "the king's friends" voted for repeal. When the news reached the colonies, the celebrations were so giddy that few paid attention to the fact that Parliament had not yielded on principle. On the same day the Stamp Act was repealed, Parliament enacted the Declaratory Act, which stated that Parliament "had, hath, and of right ought to have, full power and authority to make laws and statutes of sufficient force and validity to bind the colonies and people of America, subjects of the Crown of Great Britain, in all cases whatsoever."

Not only did the Declaratory Act repudiate American claims for the authority of their own assemblies; the word-

ing of the bill also was lifted from a 1719 law that made Ireland completely subject to Great Britain despite the fact that Ireland, like the colonies, had its own parliament. That should have given colonial protesters pause, for the status of the despised Irish was precisely what they were determined to avoid. But few noticed. Their friend, Lord Chatham, was installed as prime minister and he ignored the Declaratory Act. Chatham also reduced the Sugar Act's duty on molasses from 3d. to a penny per gallon.

Then, in one of those accidents of history that has grave consequences: Chatham was taken seriously ill and ceased to play an active part in government. The man who stepped into the vacuum his illness created was as bad a stroke of luck for the colonials as Grenville had been.

Champagne Charley and the Townshend Duties

Charles Townshend lacked Grenville's breadth of vision, but he was cleverer. Townshend was personable, convivial, and jolly. He was nicknamed "Champagne Charley" because he frequently arrived at the House of Commons unsteady of his feet and even giggling. (In fairness to Townshend, Parliament convened in the evening. The daylight hours were for socializing or, for a few members, making a living. They dined before they convened. On a given night, any number of the members of Parliament were at less than their best.)

Townshend was Chancellor of the Exchequer, and he hoped to be prime minister. To earn that prize, he intended to cut taxes at home and make up for the shortfall in revenue by taxing the colonies. Townshed examined the distinctions Americans drew between external taxes regulating trade and internal taxes for the purpose of raising money. He thought the distinction nonsense but (so he thought) he accommodated colonial sensibilities by designing a series of duties that were clearly external. The Townshend Duties taxed paper, paint, lead, glass, and tea—all goods that the colonies imported. He had no trouble persuading Parliament to enact the duties in 1767.

Townshend thought he had solved the problem. Instead, his design for collecting revenues from the colonies was seriously flawed. If none of the goods Townshend taxed were produced in more than dribbles in the colonies, all except tea could be; paint, glass, and paper-making technologies were not top secret. Moreover, they could in the short run, be done without. Townshend invited a boycott, and he got one. British-American trade fell off by 25 percent and then by 50 percent. Townshend had told Parliament that his duties would bring in £40,000 annually. The actual take in 1768 was £13,000 and, in 1769, less than £3,000. That was not enough to operate a few frontier forts.

There was little violence. The boycott was organized and controlled by conservative merchants still nervous about the Stamp Act riots. They argued that when the British merchants who sold to the colonies felt the pinch of the boycott, they would collectively pressure Parliament for repeal. The

Rare Books Division, The New York Public Library, Astor, Lenox and Tilden Foundations

A LIST of the Names of *those*
who AUDACIOUSLY continue to counteract the UNITED SENTIMENTS of the BODY of Merchants thro'out NORTH-AMERICA; by importing British Goods contrary to the Agreement.

John Bernard,
(In King-Street, almost opposite Vernon's Head.
James McMasters,
(On Treat's Wharf.
Patrick McMasters,
(Opposite the Sign of the Lamb.
John Mein,
(Opposite the White-Horse, and in King-Street.
Nathaniel Rogers,
(Opposite Mr. Henderson Inches Store lower End King-Street.
William Jackson,
At the Brazen Head, Cornhill, near the Town-House.
Theophilus Lillie,
(Near Mr. Pemberton's Meeting-House, North-End.
John Taylor,
(Nearly opposite the Heart and Crown in Cornhill.
Ame & Elizabeth Cummings,
(Opposite the Old Brick Meeting House, all of Boston.
Israel Williams, Esq; & Son,
(Traders in the Town of Hatfield.
And, **Henry Barnes,**
(Trader in the Town of Marlboro'.

The following Names should have been inserted in the List of Justices.

County of Middlesex.	County of Lincoln.
Samuel Hendley	
John Borland	John Kingsbury
Henry Barnes	
Richard Cary	County of Berkshire.
County of Bristol.	Mark Hopkins
George Brightman	Elijah Dwight
County of Worcester.	Israel Stoddard
Daniel Blifs	

By 1770, when protesters published this handout calling for a boycott of merchants who were selling goods imported from Britain, the furor over the Townshend Acts was already abating.

boycott, although never close to total, was effective enough. In 1770, Parliament repealed the Townshend Duties except for a 3d. per pound duty on tea. The tea tax was a mini-Declaratory Act, Parliament's restatement of its right to tax the colonies. As far as principle was concerned, six years of wordy debate, sometimes violent protest, a momentous congress of prominent colonials, and a costly boycott had settled nothing.

FURTHER READING

Classics Olivert M. Dickerson, *The Navigation Acts and the American Revolution,* 1951; J. R. Alden, *A History of the American Revolution,* 1969; Bernard Bailyn, *The Ideological Origins of the American Revolution,* 1967, and *British Politics and the American Revolution,* 1965; Jack P. Greene, *The Reinterpretation of the American Revolution,* 1968; Merrill Jensen, *The Founding of a Nation,* 1968; Howard H. Peckham, *Pontiac and the Indian Uprising,* 1947.

General Don Higginbotham, *The War of American Independence, 1763–1789,* 1971; Alfred T. Young, *The American Revolution: A Radical Interpretation,* 1976; Pauline Maier, *From Resistance to Revolution, 1765–1776,* 1972; Robert Middlekauff, *The Glorious Cause: The American Revolution, 1763–1789,* 1982; Edward A. Countryman, *The American Revolution,* 1987; Edmund S. Morgan, *The Genuine Article: A Historian Looks at Early America,* 2004.

Problems of 1763 Wilbur R. Jacobs, *Wilderness Politics and Indian Gifts,* 1966; Gregory E. Dowd, *A Spirited Resistance: The North American Indian Struggle for Unity, 1745–1815,* 1992; Evans Dowd, *War Under Heaven: Pontiac, the Indian Nations, and the British Empire,* 2002; Philip Lawson, *The Imperial Challenge: Quebec and Britain in the Age of the American Revolution,* 1989.

Parliament, King, Taxation, and Protest John Brook, *King George III,* 1972; John L. Bullion, *A Great and Necessary Measure: George Grenville and the Genesis of the Stamp Act, 1763–1765,* 1982; Edmund S. Morgan and Helen M. Morgan, *The Stamp Act Crisis,* 3rd ed., 1995; Mary Beth Norton, *Liberty's Daughters: The Revolutionary Experience of American Women 1750–1800,* 1980; Jay Fliegelman, *Prodigals and Pilgrims: The American Revolution Against Patriarchal Authority, 1750–1800,* 1982; Peter D. Thomas, *British Politics and the Stamp Act Crisis,* 1975, and *The Townshend Duties Crisis: The Second Phase of the American Revolution, 1767–1773,* 1987; Philip Reid, *Constitutional History of the American Revolution: The Authority of Rights,* 1987; John W. Tyler, *Smugglers and Patriots: Boston Merchants and the Advent of the American Revolution,* 1986; Gordon S. Wood, *The Americanization of Benjamin Franklin,* 2004, and *Revolutionary Characters: What Made the Founders Different,* 2006.

KEY TERMS

Use the following listing of key terms to review important figures, events, locations, and concepts covered in this chapter. A glossary of these terms is available on *The American Past* companion Web site: www.cengage.com/history/conlin/tap9e

Pontiac, p. 115

Proclamation of 1763, p. 115

Grenville, George, p. 117

Sugar Act, p. 118

Vice-admiralty courts , p. 118

Stamp Act, p. 119

Virtual representation, p. 123

"King's Friends," p. 124

Declaratory Act, p. 124

Townshend Duties, p. 124

ONLINE RESOURCES

Find additional resources, including primary source documents, images, interactive maps, simulations, chapter review exercises, and Internet links at

***The American Past* companion Web site**
www.cengage.com/history/conlin/tap9e

American History Resource Center
http://ushistory.wadsworth.com/

Reproduced from the Collections of the Library of Congress

Chapter 8

From Riot to Rebellion

The Road to Independence 1770–1776

He has dissolved Representative Houses … He has obstructed the Administration of Justice … He has kept among us, in times of peace, Standing Armies … He has plundered our seas, ravaged our Coasts, burnt our towns, and destroyed the lives of our people.

—The Declaration of Independence

I can have no other Object but to protect the true Interests of all My Subjects. No People ever enjoyed more Happiness, or lived under a milder Government, than those now revolted Provinces.… My Desire is to restore to them the Blessings of Law and Liberty … which they have fatally and desperately exchanged for the Calamities of War, and the arbitrary Tyranny of their Chiefs.

—George III

The repeal of the Townshend Duties did not touch the question of Parliament's right to tax the colonies. Nevertheless, almost everyone who had been involved in the debate considered repeal to be a victory. They were relieved to see an end to confrontation and boycott. For three years after 1770, Parliament avoided provocations. In the colonies, anti-British protests were few and muted.

In fact, tensions may have been easing before mid-1770 when news of the repeal reached the colonies. A door-to-door survey of New Yorkers revealed that a majority was willing to buy all the Townshend items except tea, which could be had more cheaply from Dutch smugglers. Imports into New England, the most obstreperous colonies, began a steady rise from £330,000 a year at the peak of the boycott to £1.2 million. As, perhaps, most people usually do, Americans wanted calm, a resumption of daily life unaggravated by the folderol of politics, agitators, and authorities flexing their muscles.

STORMS WITHIN THE LULL

Still, several incidents between 1770 and 1773 indicated that not all was well in British North America. On the streets of Boston, a bloody brawl between workingmen and British soldiers dramatized a sullen hostility toward the redcoats stationed in the city. In North Carolina, frontier settlers took up arms against the elite of the eastern counties who governed the colony. And in Rhode Island, persons unknown burned a British patrol boat that was incapable of doing anyone harm.

The Boston Massacre

On March 5, 1770, the weather in Boston was frigid. The streets were icy; heaps of gritty snow blocked the gutters. Aggravated by the severity of the winter, which brought unemployment as well as discomfort, a knot of men and boys exchanged words with British soldiers who were patrolling the streets. A handful of hecklers became a crowd cursing

Reproduced from the Collections of the Library of Congress, Prints and Photographs Division, Washington, D.C. [LC-US262-35522]

This engraving of the Boston Massacre by silversmith Paul Revere was meant to be propaganda, not an accurate portrayal of the incident. The redcoats were actually backed against a wall and were, had it not been for their muskets, in some danger. The mob was large and menacing, not the handful of victims shown here. Revere never claimed his picture was factual. Giving testimony in court, he drew a map of the massacre that depicted the incident quite differently and, presumably, accurately.

active in the Stamp Act protest tried to revive anti-British feelings. A silversmith, Paul Revere, engraved a picture of the "Boston Massacre" that misrepresented what happened (as Revere conceded in court). His print depicted soldiers aggressively advancing on innocent people. Samuel Adams, an Anglophobic former brewer, circulated Revere's prints and tried to arouse tempers. Joseph Warren, a physician, embroidered passionately on the theme. "Take heed, ye orphan babes," he told a public meeting, "lest, whilst your streaming eyes are fixed upon the ghastly corpse, your feet slide on the stones bespattered with your father's brains."

But their agitation got nowhere. Most Bostonians seemed to blame the incident on the mob. John Adams, cousin of Samuel and a friend of Warren, represented the soldiers in court. Adams was nobody's stooge, least of all a stooge of the British. He was strong-headed to the point of self-righteousness and a critic of British policies. Indeed, in arguing the redcoats' case, Adams criticized the policy of stationing professional soldiers in cities like Boston. "Soldiers quartered in a populous town will always occasion two mobs where they prevent one," he said. "They are wretched conservators of the peace."

Nevertheless, Adams blamed the unsavory mob, not the accused redcoats, for the incident. The jury agreed, acquitting all the defendants but two and sentencing them only to branding on the thumb, a slap on the wrist by eighteenth-century standards.

A Dangerous Relationship

The significance of the Boston Massacre and the Battle of Golden Hill in New York in January (another brawl with soldiers) was that the vast majority of colonials let them pass. Nevertheless, they dramatized a sore spot in colonial city life: Americans did not much like having soldiers in their midst. Property owners resented paying for their keep. Working people disliked rubbing shoulders with men who, in the eighteenth century, commanded no one's respect. Others were hostile to the redcoats for the time-honored reason that they were outsiders.

and throwing snowballs at the redcoats. A few dared the soldiers to use their muskets. It was not a political incident so much as an example of the troubles young men in crowds have caused since the days of Sumer.

When the mob pressed close on King Street, backing the redcoats against a wall, the soldiers fired. Five Bostonians, one a boy, another an African American named Crispus Attucks, fell dead. Boston, a city of just 15,000 people, was shocked; it was not a violent town. A few men who had been

The Road to Independence 1770–1776

1770	1772	1774	1776

1770 Boston Massacre

1772 Rhode Islanders burn *Gaspée*

1773 Parliament passed Tea Act; "Boston Tea Party"

1774 Coercive or Intolerable Acts
Continental Congress meets in Philadelphia

British troops battle Massachusetts militia at Lexington and Concord **1775**
Rebels win moral victory at Bunker Hill
Second Continental Congress sends George Washington to take command outside Boston

Thomas Paine published *Common Sense* **1776**
Second Continental Congress declares Independence

© Bettmann/Corbis

An upscale colonial tavern, the Blue Anchor in Philadelphia. The diners are well-dressed and well-mannered gentlemen, more likely travelers than locals. Upper-class men dined out when they were in all-male circumstances such as during the continental congresses in Philadelphia. Couples living at home rarely did; they entertained at their homes. Workingmen's taverns and ordinaries were not as genteel as the Blue Anchor. Some were decent enough neighborhood pubs; others were "holes in the wall" avoided by the squeamish.

Eighteenth-century soldiers were tough and lusty young men isolated from society. Some had been pressed into military service from Britain's poorest class; a few were convicted criminals (although rarely for serious crimes) who were in the army because enlistment was offered to them as an alternative to prison. The majority of the redcoats were honest workingmen who had voluntarily signed, but they were stereotyped as "scum" along with the others.

As long as the soldiers were posted at frontier forts or lived in isolated bases like Castle Island in Boston harbor, there was little conflict. However, after the Stamp Act riots, the Crown stationed large detachments of redcoats within cities and towns. Some 4,000 soldiers were camped on Boston Common at the time of the massacre. Others, under the terms of the Quartering Act of 1765, were billeted in vacant buildings.

This brought the tightly knit redcoats into intimate daily contact with working-class colonials. Some found girlfriends, stirring up resentment on that primeval count. Others coarsely accosted young women. Redcoats off-duty (trained veterans had plenty of free time) competed with local men for casual work. There had been a fistfight over jobs at a Boston rope maker's a few days before the massacre. Redcoats also passed idle hours in taverns where colonials gathered.

Inns and taverns were not just places where travelers supped and bedded down. They were a focal point of urban social life, neighborhood social centers like contemporary English pubs. Workingmen popped in throughout the day for a cup of tea or coffee or a shot of rum, a mug of mulled cider, a pipe of tobacco, and a chat about work, family, and politics. With plenty of time on their hands, unemployed men and seamen between voyages fairly lived at ordinaries, taverns that provided cheap meals, if only to stand before the fire. The intrusion into this world by uniformed strangers laughing loudly and carrying on by themselves caused resentments even when, as between 1770 and 1773, relations with the mother country were good.

Street People

The redcoats had more to do with the anti-British feelings of lower-class colonials than Parliamentary taxation did. Poor people did not worry the fine points of the British constitution, but they were central to the protest that boiled over into riot in 1765 and rebellion after 1773. Day laborers, employed and unemployed, apprentices, boisterous street boys, and the disreputable fringe elements of the cities and towns did the dirty work in the Stamp Act crisis. They were the ones who taunted the soldiers and were killed in the Boston Massacre. John Adams described them as "Negroes and mulattoes, Irish teagues and outlandish jack-tars."

The colonial "street people" were themselves social outcasts by virtue of their poverty and their race. Seamen, suspect because they came and went, belonging to no community but their own and tending to heavy drinking in port, were prominent in colonial crowds. Crispus Attucks was an out-of-work seaman. Free blacks like him and even some slaves congregated in the mostly white crowds, frequenting cheap taverns that catered to mixed-race customers. They commanded no respect from most shopkeepers, master craftsmen, and journeymen, certainly none of the well-off. And yet, the revolution on the horizon, soon to be sainted by patriotic history, owed much to their boldness.

Waters The role of alcohol in the colonial agitations should be noted. Soldiers were a bibulous lot. It was standard military practice, before battle, to pass around just enough strong drink to settle the troops' nerves. And they did not abstain between battles. The royal governor of New York dissolved the colonial assembly in 1766 when its members refused to provide the redcoats with their accustomed ration of 5 pints of beer or 4 ounces of rum a day.

Colonials were hard drinking too, consuming far more alcohol than Americans today, even more than students. People on the bottom, with more to forget, were the thirstiest of all. Many signal episodes on the road to independence seem to have been carried out by men in their cups. "The minds of the freeholders were inflamed," wrote an observer of the Stamp Act protest in South Carolina, "by many a hearty damn . . . over bottles, bowls, and glasses." The crowd that precipitated the Boston Massacre had emptied out of the taverns. The Sons of Liberty, who ignited the last phase of the revolutionary movement with the Boston Tea Party of 1773, assembled over a barrel of rum.

Upper-crust protest leaders had mixed feelings about this kind of support. They were more than willing to exploit angry, inebriated crowds by stirring up resentment of the British, then winking at the mobs' mockeries of the law. John Adams, so scornful of the massacre mob in 1770, called the equally lawless men at the Boston Tea Party of 1773 "so bold, so daring, so intrepid." But many more cautious upper-class colonials, and not just those who remained loyal to Great Britain, worried about "the rabble."

The Regulators

Not all the tensions in the colonies pitted Americans against British officials. Westerners, living on the frontier, nursed resentments against the colonial elites, who lived in the oldest, eastern parts of the colonies. In the South, the ill-feelings

Reproduced from the Collections of the Library of Congress

Rhode Islanders burning the grounded British customs schooner, Gaspée, in Narragansett Bay in 1772. It was a gravely serious incident, legally a rebellion punishable by death, the Gaspée being a royal vessel. That an intensive investigation could not turn up one person to identify the perpetrators was a good example of community solidarity or, perhaps, fear of violent retribution.

The Hated Redcoats

British officers rarely spoke well of their troops. They are "men fit to kill and be killed," one said, and that was mild. The word "scum" recurs so often in officers' written reports that it must have been a conversational staple. Colonials described the redcoats as the off-scourings of British streets and jails.

In fact, a majority of enlistees were, though from humble backgrounds, not dregs of society. Most had been laborers from English, Scottish, and Irish farms, villages, and towns; fewer from the cities. Their pay, when they found work, was just enough to survive. Enlisting in the army could seem quite attractive to a laborer who had not worked in a month. Men enlisted for the sometimes generous bounties towns offered to fill the quotas the army assigned them, others because the army offered a security casual laborers did not know, or simply because they were fed up with stultifying lives. There were criminals in the army, young men convicted of petty crimes given a choice between the army and jail, but it was not a criminal army.

There were "draftees" too, men pressed into service in the language of the day. Under the "poor laws," regiments

dated to Bacon's Rebellion in 1676. However, they were exacerbated after 1700 by the huge influx of Scotch-Irish who, by the 1760s, were the most conspicuous ethnic element on the frontier. Like Bacon's followers, they wanted to drive the Indians even farther west, and their demands for assistance from colonial assemblies were usually customarily brushed off. The Easterners, who controlled the assemblies, did not want an expensive Indian war. Influential people in almost every colony did a lucrative trade with the natives.

In 1763, after the Pennsylvania assembly ignored the requests of Scotch-Irish settlers in Paxton on the Susquehanna River to protect them from raiding Susquehannocks, the settlers themselves launched a devastating attack on the tribe.

The assembly ordered the leaders of the assault arrested. Instead, the "Paxton Boys," fully armed, marched on Philadelphia. Much of the city was near panic when Benjamin Franklin persuaded the Irishmen to leave, promising to use his influence to cancel the arrest warrants and increase western representation in the assembly. Which he did.

In the backcountry of South Carolina between 1767 and 1769, frontiersmen actually rebelled against the colonial assembly. Dominated by low-country planters, the assembly had refused to set up county governments in the West that the settlers had demanded. Instead, they created their own counties—illegal, of course—to which they paid taxes that were supposed to go to Charleston. The rebels called unable to fill their ranks with willing enlistees were empowered to send out press-gangs to identify young men living on what we call "welfare" and force them into uniform. Many pressed soldiers were unsavory types, but such men were not numerous in the armies that fought in America. Enlistments during the war were high. Before the war, the British army signed up, on average, 2,000 men each year. There were 15,000 enlistees in 1778, about 9,000 in 1779. Two-thirds of them were Scots.

Because "draftees" were the most likely to desert, the army preferred to send them to posts where desertion was next to impossible, like Gibraltar, or where it was very difficult, such as on the West Indian islands.

A good many enlistees found army life congenial. Of 485 men in the 29th Regiment of Foot when it was sent to fight the Americans, 273 had more than six years of service. Pay was low, just 8d. a day, but when the men were not marching or in battle, they were given two twenty-day leaves of absence a year (far more vacation than Americans today). The famous red uniforms were, when fairly new, the best clothing most soldiers had ever worn. They ate better than they had as laborers; a week's rations included 7 pounds of bread, 7 pounds of beef (or 4 pounds of pork), 3 pints of peas, plus some butter and oatmeal. There was a daily rum ration; it varied although some allotments would be enough to knock most people today unconscious. When in camp, the army enforced surprisingly high sanitary standards although that was not to be so in Boston in 1775 to 1776. There, the besieged redcoats were soon "dirty as hogs" and suffered from "camp fever" probably typhus (contracted from flea bites) or typhoid (from drinking contaminated water).

Training—drilling—was rigorous for it was the essence of eighteenth-century armies. The workday for trainees was nine hours. Experienced redcoats had more time off, thus the competition with Bostonians for jobs. The men were kept in good condition for marching by running

carrying musket and a full pack. Redcoats marched at 75 steps a minute—pretty brisk—and were expected to sustain 120 steps a minute in a pinch.

The infantryman's weapon was the "Brown Bess," a 78-caliber flintlock musket little modified since its introduction in 1703. It was about 5 feet long with a 17-inch bayonet inserted into a socket for hand-to-hand fighting. To fire, the soldier removed a paper-wrapped cartridge of gunpowder from a pouch, bit off the end, poured a few grains in the firing pan where the hammer would throw a spark, pour the rest down the muzzle, then the wadded paper, and a ball, all of which was pounded home with a wooden ramrod. A well-trained soldier could load and fire five times a minute. The musket was accurate at 60 yards, lethal at 100; farther than that a hit was luck and, if not hit in a vital organ, the enemy was likely to survive. Nobody aimed, anyway; they "pointed" and fired in volleys.

Generally, the redcoats were well disciplined. The casualties Major Pitcairn's column sustained on the retreat from Concord were not high because, as a myth has it, they marched in tight "European" formation while the Minutemen intelligently sniped at them from cover. Casualties would have been greater if the British soldiers had panicked and run. On either side of the road, the column was protected by flanking parties that picked their way through fields and woods. Americans who were killed or captured during Pitcairn's retreat had inevitably been surprised when a detachment of redcoats attacked them from behind.

Until the last two years of fighting, the redcoats were much better trained than Washington's Continentals. Officers did sometimes lose control of their men when a battle had been particularly savage and a unit had suffered heavy casualties. Then, enraged soldiers, having seen friends killed, lost control of themselves and murdered prisoners. On a few occasions, officers encouraged looting and even atrocities in violation of the "rules of war" and at the risk of being unable to restore discipline.

themselves Regulators because they said they would regulate their own affairs. It was almost a small-scale version of the resistance of the colonies to Parliamentary authority.

In North Carolina, a similar dispute led to an actual battle. A band of westerners rode east to demonstrate their resentment of the colony's penny-pinching, and there was no Ben Franklin to mediate. In May 1771, the frontiersmen were met and defeated by a smaller but better trained militia at the Battle of Alamance. Only nine men were killed. (Six Regulators were later hanged.) And the West–East clash was not sweetened. When the War for Independence began, back country Carolinians, unlike westerners elsewhere, often aligned themselves with the British.

The *Gaspée*

In June 1772, the *Gaspée*, a British customs schooner patrolling Narragansett Bay spotted a vessel suspected of smuggling and chased it toward Providence. About 7 miles from the city, the *Gaspée* ran aground. That night, men from eight boats boarded the schooner, roughly set the crew ashore, and burned it to the waterline.

Because the *Gaspée* was a royal vessel, this was an act of rebellion. The authorities had good reason to believe that the ringleader of the gang was a merchant named John Brown, who had had several run-ins with customs collectors. However, neither a £500 reward nor the fact that Rhode Island's elected governor led the investigation persuaded anyone to provide evidence against him or anyone else. The Commission of Inquiry disbanded only in June 1773. By then, the three-year lull in British–colonial relations was drawing to a close.

THE MARCH TOWARD WAR

In the spring of 1773, Parliament again enacted a law that angered Americans. This time, however, instead of spontaneous protests under the control of no one in particular, resistance to British policy was organized by a number of able, deliberate men.

They may be described as professional agitators. Some were orators ("rabble rousers" to the British), others propagandists of the pen. Several were able organizers willing to devote their time to the humdrum tasks of shaping anger into rebellion. There can be no revolutions without revolutionaries, only riot and tumult. Men like James Otis and Samuel Adams of Massachusetts and Patrick Henry of Virginia made the difference between spontaneous incidents that led nowhere, like the burning of the *Gaspée*, and

Reproduced from the Collections of the Library of Congress, Prints and Photographs Division, Washington, D.C. [LC-D416-256]

Samuel Adams was unique among American protest leaders. His origins were respectable, although modest; his father was a brewer, an artisan. He was no orator: Adams was visibly nervous when addressing a crowd. Why he was so hostile to the British so early on cannot be persuasively explained. But the respect he commanded among both wealthy merchants and Boston's "street people" made him a central figure in Massachusetts's rebellion.

calculated provocations that led directly to the War for Independence: the Boston Tea Party.

Troublemakers

James Otis was a Boston attorney from a well-to-do and socially prominent family. For a time, he had been an effective prosecutor before the unpopular vice admiralty courts. (Many revolutionaries are "born again" after "a life of sin.") Like celebrated criminal attorneys today, Otis was a showman; he was excitable and theatrical, a practitioner of "anything-to-win-a-case" argumentation. His rhetoric was often excessive, even ugly. He described one group of courtroom adversaries as a "dirty, drinking, drabbing, contaminated knot of thieves," and, what's more, they were "Turks, Jews, and other infidels, with a few renegade Christians and Catholics." This sort of thing always has its enthusiasts. Otis could fire up the passions of a jury or a town meeting.

In 1761, Otis led Boston's fight against "writs of assistance." These were broad search warrants empowering customs agents to enter warehouses and homes to search for any evidence of smuggling; they did not have to specify the evidence for which they were looking. Arguing against the Writs, Otis made them an issue of the sacred, basic rights of British subjects. John Adams would later say of Otis that "then and there the child Independence was born."

For inflammatory language, Patrick Henry of Virginia was Otis's equal. Not very well read and no deep thinker, Henry was a sharp-tongued Scotch-Irish shopkeeper who became one the colony's most effective trial lawyers and, on that reputation, was elected to the House of Burgesses, a station to which few of his social class rose. He first won notice in the assembly when he denounced the king for reversing a law passed by the Burgesses, something monarchs had been doing since 1624—but in vivid, quotable language. During the Stamp Act excitement, Henry made his "Caesar had his Brutus" speech. He was one of the first colonials to call for the establishment of an army to fight the British and, in May 1775, won fame from New Hampshire to Georgia by concluding a speech with the words "Give me liberty or give me death." With his sure-fire "sound bites," Henry would have been a television talk show regular today.

Less excitable than Otis and Henry, and no orator (he was nervous at a podium, trembling and stumbling over his words), Samuel Adams of Massachusetts was the most substantial revolutionary of the early agitators. A brewer, a tax collector between 1756 and 1764 (another convert like Otis!), Adams thereafter devoted himself to moral censorship and anti-British agitation. Personal morality and civic virtue were fundamental to his dislike of British rule. He was obsessed by the concept of republican virtue the educated people of the era found in the ancient Greeks and Romans. Adams said that Boston should reconstitute itself as a "Christian Sparta." Humorless, bored by socializing, he believed that political power was legitimate only when in the hands of men who lived austerely and were ever vigilant to preserve liberty.

Adams was at the center of every major protest in Boston: against the Sugar Act, the Stamp Act, the Townshend Duties. He was the primary figure in the unsuccessful attempt to exploit the Boston Massacre. Samuel Adams was indispensable in the drift from resentment in Massachusetts to armed rebellion to independence. Amongst oratorical prima donnas like Otis and his brother-in-law, James Warren, he was a sober organizer. He was the man who handled the tasks that transform protest into politics. He also served as a liaison between protestors from the Boston elite, men like John Hancock, and the Sons of Liberty, men of Adams's own artisan class.

Fatal Turn: The Tea Act

Samuel Adams may have been thinking independence from Great Britain as early as the mid-1760s. If so, he shared his thoughts with few comrades. He was capable of unrealistic propositions (an American Sparta?) but knew that to espouse an extreme cause by himself was to be written off as a crank. His cousin John Adams to the contrary, "the child Independence" was born not when James Otis challenged the Writs of Assistance, nor when Patrick Henry threatened George III with executioners. The baby was delivered on May 10, 1773, when Parliament's Tea Act became law and Samuel Adams quietly took control of Boston's rebels.

Ironically, the Tea Act was not, like the Stamp Act and the Townshend Duties, motivated by Parliament's need to raise money. Indeed, the Tea Act was enacted without reference to North American policy. Parliament's purpose was to save the East India Company, a huge corporation invaluable to the Crown because, in return for a monopoly of trade with India, the company governed much of the subcontinent, even maintaining its own army; the East India Company was empire on the cheap. In 1773, however, it was on the verge of bankruptcy. In just a few months, East India shares plummeted on the London stock market from £280 to £160.

The company had one asset in England: 17 million pounds of tea stored in warehouses. So, the directors proposed to a friendly Parliament (many members owned shares in the tottering corporation) that the company be given a monopoly on tea sales in the colonies rather than, as it was then doing, auctioning it to merchants involved in the colonial trade. Because of what was left of the Townshend Duties boycott, tea merchants were not selling much tea in North America anyway. Boycotters were buying what they could not do without from Dutch smugglers. However, the directors of the company pointed out, they would be dumping the warehoused tea to raise whatever cash could be had. Their tea would sell for substantially less than the Dutch prices. Shrewdly—very wisely, it would turn out—the company asked Parliament to repeal the Townshend tax on colonial tea imports.

Had Parliament acted sensibly and adopted the proposal in its entirety, the East Indian Company would have had its cash, Americans would have had cheap tea, and the last point of contention between colonies and Mother Country would have been removed. Instead, the prime minister, Lord (Frederick) North, urged on by George III in one of his most foolish acts of meddling, saw a chance to finesse the colonials into paying a tax enacted by Parliament. Surely, the colonials would not shun tea priced lower than anywhere in the world west of Ceylon.

Tea Parties

The colonials did not boycott the East India Company tea. They destroyed as much of it as they could lay their hands on and sent the rest back to Great Britain. When a dozen ships carrying 1,700 chests of tea sailed into American ports, they were greeted almost everywhere by angry crowds. The tea was landed in Charleston and hastily locked up in a warehouse—surrounded by a rowdy mob. For fear of riots, the governors of New York and Pennsylvania nervously ordered the tea ships to turn around and sail back to England. In Annapolis, Maryland, a tea ship was burned. But it was a more moderate action in Boston that triggered the crisis.

The American-born governor of Massachusetts, Thomas Hutchinson, would not permit the tea ships to sail back home without unloading. Instead, while sparks flew at a series of public meetings, he hatched a plan to get the cargo under his control—that is, under royal control—rather than the Company's. He would seize the tea for failure to pay port taxes; any violence once the tea was ashore would be an act of rebellion. Even Samuel Adams would hesitate before committing a capital crime.

It was an ingenious plan, but Samuel Adams was cleverer and quicker. On December 16, 1773, the day before Hutchinson would gain custody of the tea, Adams presided over a protest meeting attended by a third of Boston's population. Some sixty hard-core Sons of Liberty slipped out of the meeting, downed a few drinks, dressed up as Mohawk Indians, and boarded the East India Company ships. To the cheers of a crowd on the docks, they dumped 342 chests worth £10,000 into Boston harbor.

The Indian costumes were a touch of political genius. They disguised the perpetrators but also lent the air of a prank to an act of gross vandalism and theft: thus the name immediately tagged on the incident, the Boston Tea Party. Adams and his collaborators knew that Britain could not let the incident pass and they guessed that Parliament would overreact. Parliament did. Instead of flushing out the individuals involved in the party and trying them as vandals, Lord North decided to punish the city of Boston and the colony of Massachusetts. It was a terrible mistake.

The Intolerable Acts

A few voices in Parliament, like reliable Lord Chatham's, warned that the Coercive Acts of 1774—Americans called them the Intolerable Acts—would not resolve the crisis but worsen it. But Lord North easily pushed them through Parliament. The first act closed down the port of Boston to all trade until such time as the city (not the culprits) paid for the spoiled tea. Second, the new governor (General Thomas

© Corbis

Americans throwing the Cargoes of the Tea Ships into the River, at Boston.

The Boston Tea Party in a woodcut cut hurriedly soon after the event. The destruction of the East India Company's tea was well organized and flawlessly executed by the Sons of Liberty led by Samuel Adams.

Salt in the Wound: The Quebec Act

Parliament did not consider the Quebec Act of 1774 a coercive act. It was not intended to punish the colonials and had been in the works before the Boston Tea Party. But the act agitated New Englanders by granting official status to the Catholic religion in Quebec. Colonial anti-Catholicism was not universal as it had been, but it was far from dead.

Colonials were also angered by a provision of the Quebec Act that extended the borders of the province of Quebec into the Ohio Valley. This was provocative. Virginians had fought the French and Indian War to win these very lands. Speculators with claims to Ohio Valley land and farmers eyeing the possibility of moving there were alarmed.

Finally, the Quebec Act did not provide for an elective assembly in Canada. This omission after a decade of debate revolving around the sacredness of elective assemblies was particularly disturbing because of Parliament's recent suppression of elected bodies in Massachusetts.

Gage) was authorized to transfer out of the colony the trials of soldiers or other British officials accused of killing protesters. (It was not unreasonable of colonials to interpret this as an invitation to the redcoats to shoot on the slightest of

pretexts.) Third, the Massachusetts colonial government was overhauled with elected bodies losing powers to the king's appointed officials. Fourth, a new Quartering Act further aggravated civilian–soldier relations. It authorized the army to house redcoats in occupied private homes. It was a gratuitous provocation.

Lord North hoped that by coming down hard on Massachusetts, he would not only intimidate protest leaders in other colonies but also isolate the Bay Colony, which had never been popular elsewhere in North America. Instead, the Coercive Acts proved to be intolerable everywhere. Several cities shipped food to paralyzed Boston. More ominous than charity, when Massachusetts called for a "continental congress" to meet in centrally located Philadelphia to discuss a united response to the Intolerable Acts, every colony except Georgia sent delegates.

REBELLION

The Tea Act marks the beginning of an inexorable march toward rebellion; the Intolerable Acts mark the beginning of a coordinated colonial resistance. Before 1774, only the informal Committees of Correspondence, groups exchanging news and views among the colonies via the mails, connected one colony's protestors to protesters elsewhere.

Now, while the delegates to the Continental Congress who trickled into Philadelphia during the summer came as New Hampshiremen and New Yorkers and Carolinians, they acted in concert—"continentally." The congress had no formal authority. But the colonial mood was such, and the prestige of the delegates so great, that its proceedings were followed as if it were a legislative body.

The First Continental Congress

The fifty-six delegates to the First Continental Congress began their discussions on September 5, 1774. One of them, hometowner Benjamin Franklin, was already famous in Europe for his experiments with electricity. The names of Samuel Adams and Patrick Henry were known throughout the colonies thanks to newspapers. The others were men of only local renown, but that was enough to legitimate the congress in their colonies. Since every colony had closer relations with Great Britain than with the other American provinces, few of the delegates had met their colleagues from other colonies.

They differed in temperament, in their sentiments toward Great Britain, and in their opinions as to what should be done, could be done, and ought not be done. But they got along remarkably well. The heritage they were soon to rebel against gave them much in common. They were all gentlemen in the English mold: planters and professionals, particularly lawyers, and merchants whose wealth was enough to make them gentle. They prized education and civility. They knew how to keep debates decorous and impersonal. In the evening, they recessed to a round of festive dinners and parties with Philadelphia high society. George Washington of Virginia rarely dined in his own chambers. John Adams gushed in letters to his wife, Abigail, about the lavishness of the meals he was served. Only Samuel Adams, nurturing his ideal of republican frugality, shunned the social whirl and won the reputation of being a gradgrind. His enemy, Joseph Galloway, wrote that Adams "eats little, drinks little, sleeps little, thinks much, and is most decisive and indefatigable in the pursuit of his objects."

None of the delegates had an "ideology"; only a few, like Samuel Adams, had an agenda. They were troubled and angry, even those who, in the end, would remain loyal to Great Britain. But they were uncertain in 1774, even vacillating. The congress was on the verge of adopting a series of conciliatory resolutions written by Galloway when Paul Revere of Boston arrived in Philadelphia after a frantic ride with a set of defiant declarations called the Suffolk Resolves. (Boston was in Suffolk County.) The aggressive tenor of the Suffolk Resolves was utterly at odds with Galloway's resolutions, but the congress adopted them.

Still, there was no king-baiting in the style of Patrick Henry. Indeed, the delegates toasted themselves tipsy every evening raising glasses to King George. George III, unfortunately, was not in a conciliatory mood. His gravest shortcomings, his disdain for colonials, and the simplicity of his mind, came to the fore. "Blows must decide whether they are to be subject to the country or independent," he told Lord North at a time when no colonial leader of consequence had publicly mentioned force as a means of resistance or independence as a conceivable alternative to colonial status. The king's intransigence left the delegates the option of submission or responding in kind. One of the Congress's last actions before adjourning was to call on Americans to organize and train militias.

Militias

Little encouragement was needed in the Massachusetts countryside. With tempers aflame, men had already oiled their guns and begun to drill with some seriousness. The law in every colony required townships and counties to support a militia unit and train regularly; four musters a year was customary. Typically, all men were obligated to serve except the very old, the disabled, clergymen, college students and professors, and, in some colonies, Quakers. In 1774, Massachusetts militiamen ranged in age from sixteen to fifty with men fifty to seventy on an emergency "alarm list." Since 1711, thirty picked men were supposed to be ready to march with "a minute's warning"—the so-called "Minutemen."

One problem was the fact that many militiamen did not own a musket, and penny-pinching colonial assemblies refused to buy them. A New Hampshire captain said that half of his soldiers were unarmed. The image of early Americans as armed to the teeth is a myth. A study of western New England, where Indians were still something of a threat, revealed that few men had guns. In the secure eastern counties of every colony, there was little reason to keep a musket. At the first real battle of the Revolution, at Concord, many of the Americans were unarmed, hoping to scavenge the musket of a fallen redcoat.

Militiamen were poorly trained, if trained at all. The men looked on the musters mainly as social occasions, which appears to have been what most were. Officers were elected on the basis of their popularity. If any of them had any knowledge of drill, they lacked the authority to force their soldiers to it. A British drill officer punished soldiers who dragged their feet with a flogging. That certainly did not happppen at musters of American militia.

Professional soldiers scorned militia men. During the French and Indian War, General John Forbes had said "there is no faith or trust to be put in them." George Washington, himself soon to command thouands of militiamen, would use almost identical words to describe them.

In one area, colonial militiamen were the redcoats' superiors. They were more likely to be marksmen because they used their muskets primarily for hunting. In Pennsylvania, many people had adopted the *Jaeger,* a rifle introduced by German immigrants. Americans extended the length of the European rifle's barrel for greater accuracy at long distances. A British officer observed, "provided an American rifleman were to get a perfect aim at 300 yards at me, standing still, he most undoubtedly would hit me unless it was a very windy day." But marksmanship won no eighteenth-century battles. Rapid volleys did, and rifles were slow to load.

The British Are Not Coming

Paul Revere (and William Dawes and Samuel Prescott) did not rouse every Middlesex village and town by shouting, as legend has it, "The British are coming! The British are coming!" In April 1775, Revere and other colonials thought themselves as British as soldiers from Yorkshire and Ayrshire (or South Carolina). They may have shouted that "the redcoats" were on the march, possibly that "the lobsters" were on the way. Those were derogatory American terms for British soldiers. Most likely, it was "The Regulars are coming." Massachusetts militiamen thought of themselves as soldiers too, but as citizen soldiers; the redcoats were professionals, members of the regular army.

Lexington and Concord

General Gage was not concerned about the Massachusetts militia when he decided to seize rebel supplies stored at Concord, 21 miles from his headquarters in Boston. He expected the British foray, commanded by Major John Pitcairn, to be a complete surprise. Not even the British troops knew of his plan. Early on the morning of April 19, 1775, 800 to 900 redcoats were awakened, given a single day's rations, thirty-six rounds of powder and ball each, and marched toward Concord. They carried no knapsacks; it was to be a one-day operation. Howe advised Major Pitcairn that if Samuel Adams and John Hancock were in Concord, as they were believed to be, he was to arrest them.

Gage did not realize that Boston's Sons of Liberty were watching. Paul Revere and two others galloped off ahead of the troops in different directions to arouse the militias. Revere was the most effective of the riders. He not only awakened every house he passed by shouting "The regulars are coming," but, at the homes of Sons of Liberty known to him, he also made sure that riders were dispatched along the roads he could not cover.

When Major Pitcairn arrived at Lexington, a few miles shy of Concord, he found seventy mostly armed but obviously uneasy militiamen drawn up in a semblance of battle formation. (But no "minutemen"; Lexington had ignored the requirement to maintain the special unit.) Pitcairn detached several companies from his column—the Concord Road bypassed the village green—and quickly formed a professional battle line of tough, grim men.

Twice Pitcairn ordered the colonials to disperse. Some witnesses said that they were beginning to do so when a shot rang out. No one knew who fired it, a colonial hothead determined to force the issue or a British soldier mishandling his musket. It did not matter. Although not ordered to respond to the single shot, the redcoats volleyed, clearing the green in minutes.

Pitcairn marched on to Concord, where a much larger force of Americans mobilized by Revere met them at a

John Carter Brown Library

One of numerous depictions of the "battle" at Lexington, each one portraying the incident in a different light. This one conveys an image of (on the left) disciplined "minutemen" in a battle line. They are actually driving off jackals in redcoats who have burned the village. In fact, the militiamen gathered on Lexington Green understood as soon as they saw the British regulars that they could not stand up to them. At least a few of them were probably dispersing when the firing began.

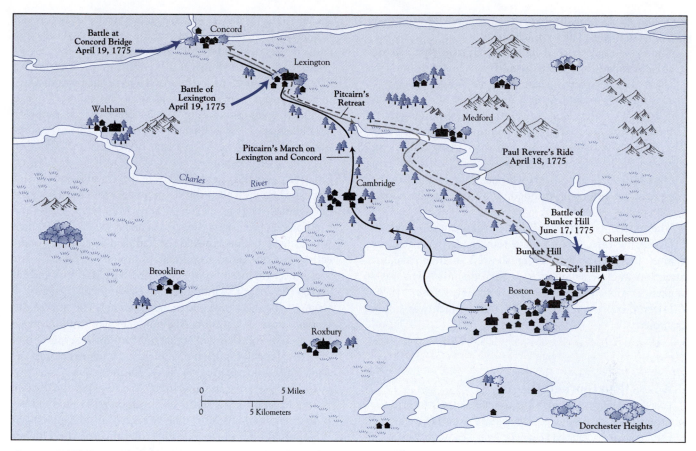

MAP 8:1 **The First Battles, April–June 1775.** The British march to Lexington and Concord, and their retreat to Boston, was through farmland interrupted by stone fences and extensive woodlots which provided cover for "minutemen" from which they inflicted numerous casualties on the retreating column. The militia surrounded Boston, but that presented the British in the city with no supply problems. The Royal Navy controlled the harbor. However, American occupation of high ground north of the city was threatening—if the Americans brought in artillery. In June, in what has misleadingly been known as the Battle of Bunker Hill, the British assaulted Breed's Hill, capturing it but at terrible cost.

bridge inside the town. Surprised by the size of the resistance and worried by the Americans' superior position, Pitcairn ordered a retreat to Boston. All the way back, militiamen sniped at the British soldiers from behind trees and stone fences, inflicting serious casualties. By the time the redcoats reached the city, 73 were dead and 174 were wounded. The casualties owed nothing to American marksmanship; the militiamen had fired, according to one calculation, 75,000 rounds. Elated nonetheless, the militia, joined by thousands more from all over Massachusetts and Rhode Island, set up camps surrounding Boston. Within two weeks, the besiegers numbered 16,000.

Bunker Hill

In London, Edmund Burke pleaded with Parliament to evacuate Boston so that tempers could cool. As always, the most thoughtful politician of the age was heard for his eloquence, then ignored. Lord North dispatched an additional thousand troops to Boston along with three more generals: Henry Clinton, John "Gentleman Johnny" Burgoyne, and William Howe. All three, as well as Gage, had been personally sympathetic to the Americans.

The British in Boston could be supplied by sea, and were protected by a land attack by the waterways that almost surrounded Boston. However, the city was vulnerable to bombardment from high ground north and south: Breed's Hill and Bunker Hill to the north across the Charles River, Dorchester Heights to the south overlooking Boston Harbor. (Unknown to the British at the time, the Americans had only about a half dozen cannon.) General Clinton asked Gage to allow him to occupy Dorchester Heights. Howe asked to be sent to seize Breed's Hill. The day before Howe was to move, 1,600 Americans dug in on Breed's Hill.

Howe sent 2,000 crack troops up the slopes. Puzzlingly, no one returned their fire. Then, when the Americans could "see the whites of their eyes" (in other words, when they could aim rather than volley), they let loose. The redcoats staggered and retreated. They regrouped and again advanced, and again they were thrown back. Now, however, Howe correctly calculated that the Americans were short of powder and shot. Reinforcing his badly mauled line with fresh men, Howe took Breed's Hill with bayonets.

The British had won, or had they? Hearing that 200 men had been killed and 1,000 wounded, General Clinton remarked that too many such victories would destroy the army's capacity to fight. Several units were utterly destroyed. The Royal Welsh Fusiliers, three officers commanding thirty-five men, were reduced to one corporal and eleven privates. The King's Own Grenadiers, with forty-three officers and men before Lexington, listed twelve men "effective" after Bunker Hill. Half the officers who had marched to Concord were dead or seriously wounded; ninety-two had been lost, a terrible toll.

The misnamed Battle of Bunker Hill was a moral victory for the Americans. General Gage remarked, "in all their wars against the French they never showed so much conduct, attention and perserverance as they do now." He was so shaken he missed a golden opportunity. He refused to allow Clinton to move on Dorchester Heights which was still not occupied.

A Less than Glorious History

Fort Ticonderoga still stands at a beautiful site between Lake Champlain and Lake George. Constructed by the French as Fort Carillon to command the ancient route between New York and Quebec, it was successfuly defended only once, by the French against an incompetent British general in July 1758.

In 1759, the British under General Jeffrey Amherst captured the "impregnable" fortress from the French.

In 1775, American militia captured it from the British without firing a shot.

In 1777, the Americans abandoned it when the British General Edward Braddock ordered artillery hauled to a high hill nearby.

In 1780, the British abandoned Fort Ticonderoga because there was no sense holdng on to it.

Ticonderoga and Quebec

American morale had a second boost in the spring of 1775. Soon after Lexington and Concord, the Massachusetts Committee of Safety instructed Benedict Arnold of Connecticut, a proven soldier, to raise an army and attack Fort Ticonderoga on Lake Champlain. Before he started, Arnold learned that backwoodsmen from what is now Vermont, the Green Mountain Boys, were preparing to march on the same fort, led by an eccentric land speculator named Ethan Allen.

Arnold caught up with the Vermonters but he was unable to get the headstrong Allen to recognize his authority. Quarreling all the way to the fort, the two shut up long enough to capture Ticonderoga on May 10. There was no battle. The fort was manned by only twenty-two soldiers and the gate was unlocked. Arnold and Allen walked in and demanded that

the first officer they met surrender. Having heard nothing of Lexington, Concord, or rebellion, the officer asked in whose name he was being addressed. According to legend, Allen replied, "in the name of the great Jehovah and the Continental Congress." Memorable as the words were, Allen was unlikely to have spoken them since he was a militant atheist.

After helping to capture several other British outposts, Arnold returned to New England where, in the fall, he was commissioned to cross the dense forests of Maine with 1,100 men. His orders were to rendezvous outside Quebec with General Philip Schuyler and about 2,000 New Yorkers and seize the city. The expedition was absurdly ill-equipped. Arnold did not even have enough tents to shelter the men from heavy snows and most of their provisions were lost in an accident. The 600 men who made it to Quebec—the rest had died or deserted—were eating raw flour, candles, and soap to survive.

Schuyler captured poorly defended Fort St. John's and his successor, Richard Montgomery, took Montreal, then a small town. Quebec also looked to be easy pickings. The city was defended by only 1,150 Scots Highlanders when Arnold arrived and, at first, French-speaking farmers in thirty-seven of fifty parishes along the St. Lawrence sheltered and provisioned the Americans, some signing on as raiders and scouts.

Unlike the French army in 1759, however, the British blocked access to the Plains of Abraham and remained behind their fortifications. The French Catholic priests of the countryside, preferring the tolerance of the Quebec Act to notoriously anti-Catholic New Englanders, put an end to local assistance. Arnold's assault on Quebec at the end of December was repelled. By spring, the combined American force numbered 8,000 troops, but General John Burgoyne arrived with a fresh British army and the rebels withdrew.

The Second Continental Congress

The delegates to the Second Continental Congress were less cautious than those of the First. Joseph Galloway, who opposed anything smacking of confrontation, was not present; Thomas Jefferson, a 32-year-old Virginian who had written several scorching anti-British polemics, was.

The situation had changed since the First Congress. Armed rebellion, barely imagined a year earlier, was a reality. Without bloodshed, royal authority was disintegrating everywhere as governors fled to the safety of British warships and self-appointed committees of rebels took over the functions of government The Congress was in danger of being left behind by events. To assert its authority, the delegates sent George Washington of Virginia (who showed up wearing a military uniform) to take command of the troops around Boston in the Congress's name.

In its "Declaration of the Cause and Necessity of Taking up Arms," published in July 1775, Congress insisted that the rebels sought only their rights as British subjects. But the inconsistency of shooting at George III's soldiers while swearing loyalty to the king was preying on many minds. With Lord North failing to propose any kind of compromise, congress

CUTTING THE TIE 139

held back only because of a thread of sentiment—the sense that monarchy was essential to good government.

CUTTING THE TIE

The man who snipped this thread was the unlikeliest of characters. Thomas Paine was a 38-year-old Englishman, only recently arrived in the colonies. He had been a corsetmaker, much lower in social class than almost all other prominent American protesters. He had failed as a businessman and as a tax collector. He drank too much—"like a fish." His appearance was "loathesome." He was "so neglectful in his person that he is generally the most abominably dirty being upon the face of the earth." And his egotism was bottomless.

Common Sense

And yet, with letters of introduction to Philadelphia printers from Benjamin Franklin, Paine was able, immediately, to demonstrate that his talents as a propagandist were greater than any native colonial's. In January 1776, he published a pamphlet that ranks with Luther's ninety-five theses and the *Communist Manifesto* as works of few words that shaped the course of history. In *Common Sense*, Paine argued that it was foolish for Americans to risk everything for the purpose of winning British approval. He shredded Americans' attachment to King George III, whom he called a "Royal Brute." Indeed, Paine attacked the idea of hereditary monarchy. Kingship was "an office any child or idiot may fill, . . . to be a king requires only the animal figure of a man."

With a gift for finding the right words that would produce many stirring calls on behalf of democracy and liberty over the next twenty years, Paine made converts by the thousands. Within a year, a population of 2.5 million bought 150,000 copies of *Common Sense;* within a decade, half a million copies. Every American who could read must have at least skimmed it; many others must have heard it read aloud. Paine boasted that it was "the greatest sale that any performance ever had since the use of letters."

Paine's unflattering depiction of the king seemed to come to life with every dispatch from London. George III refused even to listen to American suggestions for peace, and he backed Lord North's proposal to hire German mercenaries to crush the rebels. As the spring of 1776 wore on, colony after colony formally nullified the king's authority within its boundaries. Some instructed their delegates in Philadelphia to vote for independence.

Independence

On June 7, Richard Henry Lee of Virginia introduced the resolution that "these United Colonies are, and of right ought to be, free and independent states." For three weeks the delegates debated the issue. New England and the southern colonies were solidly for independence. The middle colonies were divided. New York never did vote for independence, but Pennsylvania, the large, prosperous, strategically located "keystone" of the colonies, gave in when the pacifistic John

Dickinson, a Quaker, and the cautious financier, Robert Morris, agreed to absent themselves so that the deadlock in the delegation could be broken in favor of the resolution. (Both men later supported the patriot cause.)

Delaware, also divided, swung to the side of independence when Caesar Rodney galloped full tilt from Dover to Philadelphia, casting the majority vote in his delegation. On July 2, the maneuvers concluded, Congress broke America's legal ties with England. "The second day of July 1776," an excited John Adams wrote to Abigail, "will be the most memorable epoch in the history of America." He was two days off. The "Glorious Fourth" became the national holiday when, on that day, the Congress gathered to adopt its official statement to Americans and to the world of why it chose to dissolve the political bands that tied America to Great Britain.

The Funny "S"

In documents of the revolutionary era, including the Declaration of Independence, the letter s is often written *f*. This not a lowercase F. Note that the character has only half a crossbar, and sometimes not that. The *f* is an s, pronounced the same as any other. The unfamiliar *f* originated in German handwriting and was adopted by printers in the German printed alphabet. It made its way to England when the movable type used by the earliest English printers was imported from Germany.

The use of the f was governed by strict rules. It was a lowercase letter, never a capital at the beginning of a proper noun or sentence; the familiar S served that purpose. The *f* appeared only at the beginning or in the middle of a word in lowercase, never at the end. Thus, *business* was *bufinefs* and *sassiness* was *faffinefs*. Printers abandoned this form of the letter early in the nineteenth century.

The Declaration

Officially, the Declaration of Independence was the work of a committee consisting of Thomas Jefferson, Roger Sherman of Connecticut, John Adams, Benjamin Franklin, and Robert Livingston of New York. In fact, appreciating better than we do that a committee cannot write coherently, the work of composition was assigned to Jefferson because of his "peculiar felicity of style." The lanky Virginian, nearly as careless of his personal appearance as Tom Paine, holed up in his rooms and emerged with a masterpiece.

Franklin and Adams changed a few words, and the Congress made other alterations, reducing Jefferson's original by a fourth. Most of the deletions were justified: Jefferson blamed George III for a number of crimes of which he was not remotely guilty. The most important of the erasures involved

John Trumbull's classic painting of the signing of the Declaration of Independence depicts an assembly that never existed. By the time the document was ready for signing, most of the delegates had left for home. They signed without ceremony, singly or in twos and threes, later in the summer or fall of 1776. However, Trumbull went to great lengths to capture accurate likenesses of every signer.

an issue in which the king was blameless, but that was not the reason for its removal. Jefferson took a backhanded slap at the institution of slavery when he wrote that George III "has waged cruel war against human nature itself, violating its most sacred right of life and liberty in the persons of a distant people who never offended him, capitvating them into slavery in another hemisphere." Southern delegates generally did not like the clause; delegates from South Carolina and Georgia said they would not sign the Declaration if it included a criticism of slavery.

Why did Jefferson heap all the blame on George III when the king could do little and did little without the consent of Parliament, usually on Parliament's initiative? When, in October 1775, Parliament voted on using troops to suppress the colonial rebellion, the House of Commons voted aye 278–108 and the House of Lords 69–29. Two explanations are plausible. First, the Congress had learned from Thomas Paine that personalizing an enemy was the best way to arouse emotional support for a cause. Second, the men of the Second Continental Congress had made a sacred talisman of the supreme authority of their elected assemblies. To

Common Knowledge

Jefferson did not try to be original in writing the Declaration of Independence. His purpose was to bring together ideas that were in the air, familiar to all, so as to sell the American cause. His famous restatement of the natural rights of man, for example, was taken from a speech that Samuel Adams made in Boston in November 1772: "Among the natural rights of the colonists are these: first, a right to life; secondly, a right to liberty; thirdly, to property; together with the right to support and defend them in the best manner they can." Which itself was an elaboration of philosopher John Locke, with whose writings every educated colonial was familiar.

Jefferson made the point explicit. His purpose, he wrote, was "not to find out new principles, or new arguments, never before thought of, not merely to say things which had never been said before; but to place before mankind the common sense of the subject, and to justify ourselves in the independent stand we are compelled to take."

The Art Archive/Picture Desk

King George's Spectacles

John Hancock, as president of the Second Continental Congress, was the first to sign the Declaration of Independence. He inscribed his name in an elegant hand, outsized so that, as Hancock said, King George could read his name without his glasses. In fact, Hancock often signed his name flamboyantly, including to the Olive Branch Petition, an earlier, conciliatory message to King George. And he was risking nothing in making his name clear to the king. He already had a price on his head because of his role in organizing the Boston Tea Party. Many of the other signers were, in fact, bolder, for they had previously been unknown to the king.

have demonized Britain's elected assembly—the "Mother of Parliaments"—would have been, at best, awkward.

Universal Human Rights

The Declaration of Independence is not remembered for its catalog of George III's high crimes and misdemeanors. That part of the document is hardly read, except by historians. The Declaration has a place in world history because, in his introductory sentences, Jefferson penned a stirring statement of universal human rights. Jefferson did not write solely of the rights of American colonials. He put their case for independence in terms of the rights of all human beings: "We hold these truths to be self-evident, that all men are created equal, that they are endowed by their Creator with certain unalienable Rights, that among these are Life, Liberty and the pursuit of Happiness." And he tersely codified the principle that government drew all of its authority—not just the authority to tax—from the consent of the people governed. When the people withdrew that consent and were faced with coercion, they had the right to take up arms.

Wording from the Declaration of Independence would, over two centuries, be borrowed by many peoples asserting their right to freedom, from the republics of Central and South America early in the 1800s to the Vietnamese in September 1945. In the United States, groups making demands on society—from African Americans to feminists and labor unions to organizations lobbying against smoking tobacco in bar rooms—have based their program on their "inalienable rights." In the summer of 1776, however, Americans were not thinking of the Declaration's future. The job was to win independence on the battlefield.

FURTHER READING

Classics Carl Becker, *The Declaration of Independence,* 1922; Bernard Bailyn, *The Ideological Origins of the American Revolution,* 1967; Benjamin W. Labaree, *The Boston Tea Party,* 1964; John Shy, *Toward Lexington: The Role of the British Army on the Coming of the Revolution,* 1965.

General Don Higginbotham, *The War of American Independence, 1763–1789,* 1971; Alfred T. Young, *The American Revolution: A Radical Interpretation,* 1976; Pauline Maier, *From Resistance to Revolution, 1765–1776,* 1972; Robert Middlekauff, *The Glorious Cause: The American Revolution 1763–1789,* 1982; Edward Countryman, *The American Revolution,* 1985; Baernard Bailyn, *Voyagers to the West: A Passage in the Peopling of America on the Eve of the Revolution,* 1986; Stephen Conway, *The War of American Independence 1775–1783,* 1995; Jon Butler, *Becoming American: The Revolution Before 1776,* 2000; John Ferling, *A Leap in the Dark: The Struggle to Create the American Republic,* 2003; Carol Berkin, *Revolutionary Americans: Women in the Struggle for Independence,* 2005; David McCullough, *1776,* 2005.

Landmarks Hiller B. Zobel, *The Boston Massacre,* 1970; Marjoleine Kars, *Breaking Loose Together: The Regulator Rebellion in Pre-Revolutionary North Carolina,* 2002; A. Roger Ekirch, *Poor Carolina: Politics and Society in North Carolina, 1729–1776,* 1981; David Ammerman, *In the Common Cause: American Response to the Coercive Acts of 1774,* 1974; Philip Lawson, *The Imperial Challenge: Quebec and Britain in the Age of the American Revolution,* 1989; David Hackett Fischer, *Paul Revere's Ride,* 1994.

Soldiers John E. Ferling, *A Wilderness of Miseries: War and Warriors in Early America,* 1980; Sylvia R. Frey, *The British Soldier in America: A Social History of Military Life in the Revolutionary Period,* 1984; Robert A. Gross, *The Minutemen and Their World,* 1976; Charles Royster, *A Revolutionary People at War: The Continental Army and American Character 1775–1783,* 1980; Stephen Brumwell, *Redcoats: The British Soldier and War in the Americas, 1755–1763,* 2002.

The First Battles John Shy, *Toward Lexington: The Role of the British Army in the Coming of the Revolution,* 1965; Robert L. O'Connell, *Of Arms and Men: A History of War, Weapons, and Aggression,* 1989; Peter D. Thomas, *Tea Party to Independence: The Third Phase of the American Revolution, 1773–1776,* 1991; Mark V. Kwasny, *Washington's Partisan War, 1775–1783,* 1996.

Declaring Independence Garry Wills, *Inventing America: Jefferson's Declaration of Independence,* 1978; Pauline Maier, *American Scripture: The Making of the Declaration of Independence,* 1998.

Biographies Bernard Bailyn, *The Ordeal of Thomas Hutchinson,* 1974; Richard R. Beeman, *Patrick Henry: A Biography,* 1974; Noel B. Gerson, *The Grand Incendiary: A Biography of Samuel Adams,* 1973; Ira D. Gruber, *The Howe Brothers and the American Revolution,* 1972; Pauline Maier, *The Old Revolutionaries: Political Lives in the Age of Samuel Adams,* 1980; John K. Alexander, *Samuel Adams: America's Revolutionary Politician,* 2002; Willard Sterne Randall, *Benedict Arnold: Patriot and Traitor,* 1990; Richard Brookhiser, *Founding Father: Rediscovering George Washington,* 1996; Edmund Morgan, *Benjamin Franklin,* 2002; Harvey J. Kaye, *Thomas Paine and the Promise of America,* 2005; Gordon S. Wood, *The Americanization of Benjamin Franklin,* 2004 and *Revolutionary Characters: What Made the Founders Different,* 2006.

KEY TERMS

Use the following listing of key terms to review important figures, events, locations, and concepts covered in this chapter. A glossary of these terms is available on *The American* *Past* companion Web site: www.cengage.com/history/conlin/tap9e

Revere, Paul, p. 127

Regulators, p. 129

Gaspée, p. 131

Henry, Patrick, p. 132

East India Company, p. 133

Gage, Sir Thomas, p. 134

Quebec Act, p. 134

Suffolk Resolves, p. 135

Green Mountain Boys, p. 138

Common Sense, p. 139

ONLINE RESOURCES

Find additional resources, including primary source documents, images, interactive maps, simulations, chapter review exercises, and Internet links at

The American Past **companion Web site**
www.cengage.com/history/conlin/tap9e

American History Resource Center
http://ushistory.wadsworth.com/

North Wind Picture Archives

Chapter 9

The War for Independence

The Rebels Victorious 1776–1781

The history of our Revolution will be one continual lie from one end to the other. The essence of the whole will be that Dr. Franklin's electrical rod smote the earth and out sprang George Washington. That Franklin electrified him with his rod—and thenceforward these two constructed all the policy, negotiations, legislatures, and war.

—John Adams

The signers of the Declaration of Independence pledged their lives, their fortunes, and their sacred honor to their rebellion. They were not posturing. Had George III won the quick victory he expected, the delegates to the Second Continental Congress would have been punished severely. There would likely have been hangings. The noose had been the fate of Irish rebels and would be again. The Americans might see themselves as freedom fighters. To the king they were traitors.

AN IMBALANCE OF POWER

Other Europeans—especially the French—followed the news from America with great interest. The overwhelming victory Great Britain had won in 1763 disturbed every major European power. There was little sentiment on the continent for a British victory. However, few observers gave the rebels much of a chance of prevailing. Their victories in 1775 were in skirmishes, and the year would end with Benedict Arnold's debacle at Quebec.

Opposing Armies

After Bunker Hill, Lord North's military advisor, Lord George Germain, organized an army of 32,000 to join the redcoats already in America. It was largest military operation in British history. However, a majority of the troops were not British but well-trained mercenaries rented out to Great Britain by several German princes. This was expensive. The charges were £7 a head, double if the man was killed. The German soldiers came from six different principalities, but Americans, who were enraged that mercenaries were sent against them, lumped all the Germans together as "Hessians." (Two of the suppliers were the states of Hesse-Cassell and Hesse-Hanau.) During much of the war, Britain never had fewer than 50,000 troops ready for battle. In 1781, there were 92,000 redcoats and Hessians in Canada, the thirteen colonies, Florida, and the West Indies.

At first, the Americans could field only their hastily mobilized militias. George Washington's opinion of the soldiers surrounding Boston was as negative as the assessment of them by British officers. He wrote of the "unaccountable kind of stupidity" of New England militiamen, calling them "a mixed multitude of people . . . under very little discipline, order, or government."

A few militia units were first-rate, including the "Rhode Island Army of Observation" led to Boston in 1775 by General Nathanael Greene. Later in the war, South Carolina's militia stood alone against a crack British army, avoiding a pitched battle but harassing the redcoats to distraction and retreat. Even the militias no one trusted in battle played an important part in the war effort. By policing areas the British did not occupy, which was almost the entire American countryside, they freed the soldiers of the Continental Army for battle.

The Continental Army, created by the Congress, was, by 1778, pretty well trained and usually effective. But it was an

Culver Pictures, Inc.

After the French and Indian War, New Yorkers erected a much admired equestrian statue of George III. It represented no small expenditure for a small provincial city. In the excitement following the Declaration of Independence, a mob pulled the statue down. The bronze was melted and recast into cannon for Washington's army.

army with a problem the British and Hessians did not face. "Continentals" (as the soldiers were known) enlisted for a year at a time. When they were free to leave, the majority usually did. Washington never had more than 18,500 Continentals under his command and, on several occasions, his regular army dwindled to 5,000.

The British navy was without an equal in the world in both size and quality. By the end of 1777, eighty-nine British warships carrying 2,576 guns were stationed in American waters. The patriot navy was a cipher at the start of the war and never amounted to much. Washington had to pay out of his own pocket for the first American warship, the *Hannah*,

The War for Independence 1776–1783

1776	1777	1778	1779	1780	1781	1782	1783

■ July 1776 **British troops land in New York**

▬ Aug–Oct 1776 **Washington's army repeatedly defeated around New York**

■ Sept 1776 **Benjamin Franklin in Paris to request French aid**

▬ Dec–Jan 1776 **Washington wins victories at Trenton and Princeton**

▬ Sept–Oct 1777 **Washington defeated outside Philadelphia**

■ Oct 1777 **Major American victory at Saratoga**

▬ Feb 1778 **France enters war as American ally**

1778–1781 American defeats and demoralization

■ 1781 **British army surrenders to Washington and Rochambeau at Yorktown**

Treaty of Paris: American independence; British evacuate New York 1783 ■

a schooner with only four guns. (Some merchant vessels were better armed.) The Continental Congress appropriated funds to build thirteen frigates, one for each state, but the eleven that were actually completed fared poorly. One was destroyed in battle, seven were captured, two were scuttled to keep them out of British hands, and one was accidentally set afire by its own crew. All told, the British destroyed or captured thirty-four of thirty-five vessels Congress built and lost only five of their own.

Privateers, however, did terrific damage to British shipping. The Continental Congress issued Letters of Marque to 1,697 vessels. Several states commisioned others. Some privateers preyed on British ships carrying supplies to the redcoats. Others, operating out of French ports, worked British waters, looking for merchant vessels. They captured about 15 percent of Britain's commercial fleet.

Loyalist Fears

The Reverend Mather Byles was an oddity, a Massachusetts Congregationalist minister who opposed the Revolution. His colleagues were, almost all of them, militant patriots. In a sermon in 1776 Byles explained his fear that the Revolution would liberate an undesirable trend toward democracy. "Which is better," he asked, "to be ruled by one tyrant three thousand miles away, or by three thousand tyrants not a mile away?" The question has not yet been definitively answered.

After the War

After the war, wealthy white loyalists usually went to England where, compensated for their losses, they did fine among their own social class. Whites of middling status who settled in Upper Canada (Ontario) generally prospered. Black loyalists fared less well, particularly those taken to Nova Scotia and New Brunswick. Most were compensated less than whites were. (Was not their freedom reward enough? they were asked.) Many did not receive the land they had been promised. In order to survive they had to sign indentures on whatever terms they were offered. They lived in fear of being kidnapped by slave catchers from the independent United States or, indeed, from Nova Scotia, where slavery was legal. When, in 1792, black loyalists were invited to settle Sierra Leone in West Africa, several thousand signed up; 1,200 departed on the first fifteen-vessel expedition.

Loyalists: White, Black, and Red

By no means did every American support the war. John Adams estimated that a third of the white population remained loyal to the king. That may have been overstating it but not by much. When the British evacuated Boston, 1,000

Joseph Brant, painted by Gilbert Stuart several years after the War for Independence. Brant, whose Mohawk name was Thayendanegea under whom the Cherry Valley massacre of settlers of 1778 took place, but the murderers were Senecas whom he tried to control and failed. He settled in Ontario with other Loyalist Mohawks after the war.

Americans went with them. When General Howe established his headquarters in New York, his redocats were received more as liberators than as occupiers. By the end of the war, about 19,000 Americans had enlisted in ninety-eight Loyalist regiments in the British army. One American in thirty left the country to live in England, the West Indies, or Canada. As late as 1812, 80 percent of the population of Upper Canada (Ontario) was American-born.

In the North, most Anglicans were Loyalists or, as the patriots called them, Tories. So were many merchants with close commercial ties to Britain. Imperial officials supported the Crown, of course, as did some rich South Carolina and Georgia planters.

The British won support among southern slaves by offering freedom in return for military service. Some 50,000 African Americans fled their masters during the war. Both George Washington and Thomas Jefferson lost slaves to the British. When the war ended, Britain evacuated about 20,000 black loyalists to Nova Scotia, England, Jamaica, and Sierra Leone in West Africa.

Alexander Hamilton, Washington's aide-de-camp, urged southern patriots to free slaves who agreed to take up arms in the cause of independence. "I have no doubt," he wrote, "that the Negroes will make excellent soldiers." His proposal got nowhere. Indeed, when Washington first arrived outside Boston and discovered that some Massachusetts militiamen were black, he discharged them. He later countermanded the order because free blacks in New England were pro-independence and were indignant that they were denied the chance to fight. Chronically short of troops, Washington had to suppress his slave owner's reflexive opposition to arming black men. About 5,000 African Americans, almost all northerners, fought in militias or the Continental army.

Indians lined up on both sides. The Revolution split the 200-year-old Iroquois Confederacy in two. At first, the Six Nations (the Tuscarora had joined the original five) tried to be neutral. However, a well-educated Mohawk, Thayendanega, who took the name Joseph Brant when he converted to Anglicanism, convinced most Mohawk, Seneca, and Cayuga warriors to side with the British. In 1777, the Oneida and Tuscarora aligned with the patriots. The war shattered the individual tribes as well as the Confederacy; some Iroquois of every tribe fought with the Americans and some with the British.

The Revolution was, in part, a chapter of the 150-year war of whites against Indians. George Washington's single biggest operation before the Battle of Yorktown was directed not against the British but was a 1779 assault on the Mohawks in New York.

American Hopes

For all the bad news, the patriot cause was far from hopeless. The Americans were fighting a defensive war in their homeland, the kind of conflict that bestows considerable advantages on rebels, no matter what the other handicaps. They did not have to destroy the larger British and Hessian armies. Rebels on their own ground need only hold on and hold out until weariness, demoralization, dissension, and a painful defeat here and there take their toll on the enemy.

An army attempting to suppress a rebellion, by way of contrast, must wipe out the enemy's military capacity and then occupy and pacify the entire country, never a mission that promotes goodwill. One the Americans' friends in Parliament, Edmund Burke, pointed out the immensity of this challenge as early as 1775. "The use of force alone is but temporary," he said. "It may subdue for a moment; but it does not remove the necessity of subduing again; and a nation is not governed which is perpetually to be conquered."

The British would never be able to crush the patriot military. (They came close once, in New York in 1776.) Redcoats occupied most port cities for much of the war; as late as 1780, they captured Charleston. But only one American in twenty lived in the seaports. From first to last, the countryside was largely under patriot control, providing sanctuary for their armies where they could not be pinned down. The large British garrisons in the cities had to be provisioned in large part from abroad. Even in a grain rich land, oats for horses were carried by ship from England and Ireland. At one point, British commanders believed that they would have to import hay!

Reproduced from the Collections of the Library of Congress

Benjamin Franklin in France during the War for Independence, lionized by aristocrats. His diplomatic methods, highly social and indirect in the European manner, worked superbly although they disgusted brusque and tactless John Adams, who joined him in Paris. He was ambivalent about ever returning to the United States, as he had been during his long residence in Great Britain. Had his proposal of marriage to an eccentric widow, Mme. Helvetius, been accepted he would probably have stayed. Abigail Adams was "highly disgusted" when, at dinner, Mme. Helvetius sat in Franklin's lap.

The patriots had friends in Britain like Burke, speaking and politicking on their behalf. Charles Fox, the radical John Wilkes, and the prominent Marquis of Rockingham sniped at Lord North's ministry throughout the war. They believed that the Americans were more right than wrong. Indeed, albeit privately, Lord North had doubts about the justice of the British cause.

The patriots also had reason to hope for help from Europe. They were encouraged in their rebellion from the start. From Spanish Louisiana, Governor Bernardo de Gálvez surreptitiously provided arms to American militias. France, so painfully humiliated by the British in 1763, was even more helpful. In May 1776, Louis XVI's ministers began to funnel money and arms to the rebels through a not-so-secret agent, Pierre de Beaumarchais, who also provided money to the Americans from his own purse. During the first two years of the war, 80 percent of patriot gunpowder came from France.

BOSTON GAINED, NEW YORK LOST

In September 1776, Congress sent Benjamin Franklin to Paris to seek a formal French alliance. Franklin was 70 years old but just slightly creaky. He was a social sensation among the French nobility. Already famous for his experiments with electricity, Franklin exploited a "noble savage" craze in which many of the smart set were wrapped up, enamored of primitives as they imagined Americans to be. Franklin played along. He wore rough homespun wool clothing to fashionable affairs, no wig on his bald head, and the rimless bifocal spectacles he had invented. (In real life, Franklin loved luxury. During his years in France he lived in a suburban mansion—loaned to him gratis—with servants, a fine chef, and a wine cellar.)

Conquering French high society was one thing. The foreign minister, Charles, Count Vergennes, although hoping for American success, was a tougher nut. By the fall of 1776 when Franklin arrived, the Continental Army had suffered an almost fatal series of defeats. Vergennes told Franklin that the Americans had to demonstrate that their chances of winning were plausible before he would consider committing France to open military assistance.

Pimp

General Howe's American mistress, Elizabeth Loring, was married, the wife of a Loyalist, Joshua Loring. He did not mind being cuckolded so openly that all Boston sang about it. Actually, Loring was less a cuckold than Elizabeth's pimp. Howe rewarded his good sportsmanship by showering Loring with lucrative army contracts. It is interesting to note that while Mrs. Loring was the object of ribald ridicule, her sleazy husband was hardly noticed.

Stalemate at Boston

Given the condition of the army George Washington found outside Boston in the summer of 1776—untrained, undisciplined men; only nine rounds of gunpowder per soldier; just six artillery pieces total—he did well just to hang on. General William Howe, who succeeded General Gage as British commander, may have missed an opportunity to trounce Washington's army and end the rebellion before Franklin reached Paris.

But Howe sat tight in Boston, and he had good reasons for doing so. He was justifiably haunted by the terrible casualties the British had sustained at Bunker Hill against an even rawer American force. And he disliked Boston as a base of operations. Boston was the most anti-British city in the colonies. Howe recognized immediately that he should evacuate the city and establish British headquarters in friendlier New York. For that he needed permission from London. It was granted, but because of the slow exchange of messages—an Atlantic crossing could still take two months, even longer—it was impossible to organize so massive an operation before winter.

Personally, Howe was content to see the winter out where he was. He had an opulent residence and was having a good time with a beautiful American mistress, Elizabeth Loring. Bostonians sang:

> Sir William Howe, he, snug as a flea,
> Lay all this time a-snoring;
> Nor dreamed of harm, as he lay warm
> In bed with Mrs. Loring

Washington had no mistress in his quarters across the river in Cambridge. He faithfully wrote weekly to his wife about, among other things, the dislike he had taken to New Englanders. He made an exception of Nathanael Greene of Rhode Island and Henry Knox of Massachusetts who, like Greene, had taught himself the military arts—and very well—by reading books. With some effort, Greene talked Washington out of launching a winter assault on Boston across frozen Back Bay. The ice was too thin, he pointed out, and every square foot of the bay was covered by British artillery. (Washington knew enough to defer to a New Englander when it came to frozen bays.)

Knox persuaded Washington (who, for all the combat he had seen, was not an imaginative general) to order an operation he had conceived. Knox would lead a party 300 miles west to Fort Ticonderoga where Allen and Arnold had captured dozens of cannon and mortars along with the fort. They were rusting at Ticonderoga and sorely needed at Boston. Knox believed he could bring the artillery the breadth of Massachusetts despite the rigors of the New England winter.

Dorchester Heights

Knox's feat was next to miraculous. (Washington never forgot it.) Just to cross snowbound Massachusetts was a chore. To cross the state with eighty yoke of oxen (which had to be fed) and fifty-eight mortars and cannon was a herculean

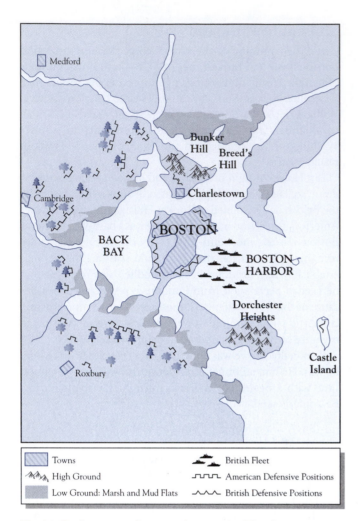

Towns		British Fleet	
High Ground		American Defensive Positions	
Low Ground: Marsh and Mud Flats		British Defensive Positions	

MAP 9:1 **Stalemate at Boston, June 1775–March 1776.**
After the shocking casualties of the Battle of Bunker Hill, the
British troops in Boston dug in and sat. General Howe wanted
to evacuate the city in 1775, but permission arrived so late
in the year that he postponed leaving to the spring of 1776.
The delay was a blessing for anti-British Boston; Howe would
have burned the city had Washington not been able to mount
artillery on Dorchester Heights that would have played havoc
with the evacuation fleet. The two generals tacitly agreed that if
Washington's cannon were silent, Howe would not torch Boston.

labor. (Three of the mortars weighed a ton each; one cannon
weighed 5,000 pounds.)

In the meantime, the redcoats in Boston had a bad winter.
Bad weather at sea disorganized their supply line. At least seventy ships carrying men, provisions, and arms from Britain
were blown south and passed the winter in the West Indies.
Common soldiers in Boston were put on short rations and
ran out of firewood. Foraging out of the surrounded city was
impossible, so the redcoats pulled down a hundred buildings, including Old North Church, for the sake of warmth.
Disease was rife. The winter in Boston was the only period of
the year when the Americans enjoyed better sanitation than
the British.

Unaware that Howe intended to evacuate Boston in the
spring, Washington set about improving his army's de-

fenses. The key position in any battle was high ground,
Dorchester Heights, a mile and a half south of the British
front lines. Neither Howe nor Washington had attempted
to occupy the Heights because the high ground was accessible only by a narrow spit of land and, therefore, easy for
the enemy to cut off. Dorchester Heights remained a no
man's land.

When Knox arrived with the Ticonderoga artillery,
Washington was emboldened to risk an exposed movement to the high ground. On the night of March 5, 1776,
as unnoticed as Wolfe's ascent to the Plains of Abraham, the
Americans moved the cannon and mortars and several thousand men to Dorchester Heights. Sunrise revealed to Howe
that the Americans were now capable of levelling Boston
at will. A British barrage revealed that their guns could
not be sufficiently elevated to reach Washington's position.
American soldiers gathered 700 cannonballs that landed
harmlessly on the hillside below their fortifications.

Worse than threatening the city, Washington's artillery
commanded much of Boston Harbor where Howe's lifeline,
the British fleet, was anchored. Howe sent a message through
the lines that, if the Americans did not interfere with his
evacuation, he would not destroy Boston (common practice
for an army evacuating a city). Washington faced a dilemma.
Knox's cannon were capable of savaging the British ships,
but not destroying the entire fleet. If he opened fire, Howe
would still escape with most of his army, but he would burn
Boston, patriot country, to the ground. Americans in other
cities might well blame the Continentals for the devastation
and think twice about where their loyalties lay. Beginning
on March 10, with the American artillery silent, about 120
British ships took aboard 9,000 troops, 1,200 soldiers' wives
and children, 1,100 loyalists, Howe and Mrs. Loring, and
sailed for Halifax in Nova Scotia.

Military Music

Drum, fife, and trumpet were essential to armies on the
move. Boys of 12 and 13 beat snare drums to set the
cadence for marching soldiers. If his men stepped off
96 paces of 30 inches each in a minute, a commander
knew that the army was covering 3 miles in fifty minutes,
allowing ten minutes every hour for a breather and a
drink.

Fifers tootled not only to entertain the men but also to
communicate orders: the *Pioneers' March* was the signal
for road-clearing crews to get started ahead of the infantry.
Roast Beef meant it was time to eat. Fifes were also vital in
battle. The men could hear their shrill voices above the roar
of firearms when they could not hear an officer's shouts.

Cavalry also used musical instruments for communication,
but kettle drums instead of snare drums, so as not to be
confused with infantry, and valveless trumpets (bugles)
instead of fifes. Requiring only one hand, they could be played
on horseback.

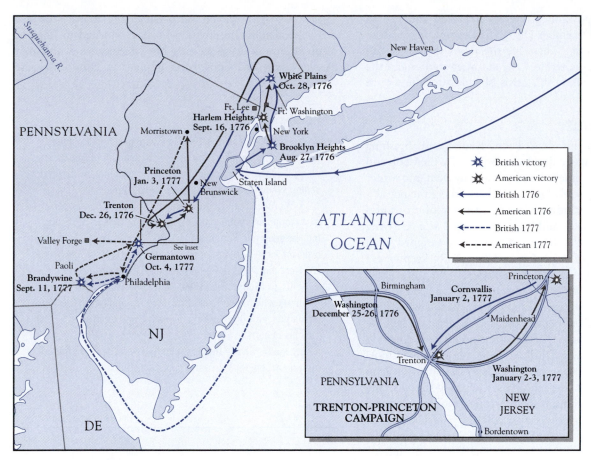

MAP 9:2 **Years of Defeat and Discouragement, 1776–1777.** American armies had a bad year in 1776. They were trounced everywhere. For George Washington, 1777 was no better. Having averted total disaster by victories at Trenton and Princeton in the winter of 1776–1777, he was defeated twice, if narrowly, outside Philadelphia.

Humiliation in New York

Halifax was for regrouping and reinforcement. Howe intended to establish his headquarters in New York, then a city of 20,000, larger than Boston and centrally located. Washington got there first, occupying Manhatttan Island and the western end of Long Island, present-day Brooklyn. (In 1776, Brooklyn was a village.) He had between 8,000 and 10,000 troops in the vicinity or on the way.

On June 29, the first British ships arrived in New York harbor, 100 of them by sunset. (One monster carried sixty guns; two carried fifty.) More arrived daily from Halifax, the West Indies, and England until 400 vessels were anchored in the harbor, most within sight of the city. About 32,000 soldiers, half British, half Hessians mustered on Staten Island. Surveying the long odds the Americans faced, one of Washington's aides wrote in his journal, "it is a mere point of honor that keeps us here."

Late in August, Howe invaded Long Island. Washington's right flank was incomplete, and the British and Hessians almost surrounded his army. If they had, it could have been the end of the war, two months after the Declaration of Independence was signed. However, in the first instance of Washington's slipperiness in escape, most of the American troops were able to regroup on Brooklyn Heights, high

ground on the East River across from Manhattan. In a skillfully executed overnight maneuver, Massachusetts fishermen ferried about 5,000 soldiers to Manhattan.

Howe was, however, right behind them. The British captured 3,000 Americans at Fort Washington and forced General Greene to abandon Fort Lee, directly across the Hudson River in New Jersey. Once again Washington and his bedraggled troops escaped within hours of capture north to White Plains where the Americans were defeated in a brief battle, then across the Hudson into New Jersey whence they fled to the south. When Washington was able to count heads in New Brunswick, he had only 3,500 soldiers under his personal command; half of them were marking time until their enlistments expired a few weeks later.

Howe and his generals enjoyed the New York campaign. It was mostly chase, reminding them of a fox hunt. When British buglers sounded tally-ho, Washington, himself an avid hunter and always super-sensitive about his dignity, was infuriated.

The remnants of the Continental army that fled across yet another river, the Delaware, into Pennsylvania, were hopelessly demoralized. Thousands of captured patriot soldiers in New York and New Jersey had taken an oath of allegiance to the Crown. In Philadelphia, a day's march to the south of Washington's position, Congress panicked and fled to Baltimore. It was December 1776. The Revolution was close to being snuffed out. "These are the times that try men's souls," Thomas Paine wrote. "The summer soldier and the sunshine patriot will, in this crisis, shrink from the service of his country."

Saving the Cause

Howe considered invading Pennsylvania and finishing Washington off. But he decided to soldier by the book and the book said that, come December, an army went into winter quarters. His army settled into New York where the population was friendly, including a large contingent of prostitutes whom both Americans and British described as a terrifying lot of "bitch foxy jades, hogs, strums." Howe assigned small advance garrisons to Princeton and Trenton to keep an eye on what was left of Washington's army.

Washington was no more an innovator than Howe was. Had his army not been near disintegration, he too would have followed the book into winter quarters. But would he have an army come spring? On Christmas night, Washington's trusty fishermen rowed Durham boats, lumbering 40-foot-long vessels used to transport pig iron from Pennsylvania to New Jersey, forty men in each, across a deserted stretch of the Delaware River. At eight in the morning (two hours behind schedule), the Americans surprised the 1,500 Hessians in Trenton and, in a fifteen-minute battle, killed and wounded over 100 and made prisoners of 900. The Americans suffered only five casualties.

It was the morale booster Washington needed, but not quite enough for him. After withdrawing across the Delaware, the Americans returned to New Jersey, eluded a large army under General Charles Cornwallis, and attacked the British garrison at Princeton, taking 300 more prisoners. Howe was forced to withdraw his forward line to New Brunswick. Washington made his winter quarters in Morristown, New Jersey.

Trenton and Princeton were small battles. Given the size of his army in New York, Howe's losses were minor. But Washington had saved the patriot cause when its prospects could not have been lower. Reading of the campaign in Prussia, the military genius, King Frederick the Great, described it as brilliant.

British Strategy

The British were still thinking New England, where the Revolution began, in 1777. The plan was for Howe's army to move north up the Hudson River, joining forces with Iroquois warriors led east on the Mohawk River by Joseph Brant and Barry St. Leger, and another large British army coming south out of Montreal. The three-part pincers maneuver would isolate New England from the rest of the colonies. With the the Royal Navy blockading New England's ports, the British army could easily subdue Massachusetts, Connecticut, and Rhode Island from the west. If the loss of New England was not enough to persuade Washington to ask for terms, the British would then move against his army.

Lord George Germain was persuaded to approve the plan by General John Burgoyne, who had returned to England from Boston and was betting his career on the campaign. A playwright and bon vivant popular in London society,

War Crimes

Soldiers and Indians on both sides were guilty of atrocities. Colonel Henry Hamilton, the British commander of Fort Detroit, was called the "hair buyer" because he paid Indians for patriot scalps, women's and children's as well as adult males'. In 1776, Cherokees ravaged the Virginia and Carolina frontiers, massacring everyone in their path. In July 1778, loyalists and Indians scourged Pennsylvania's Wyoming Valley; in November, a similar force swept through Cherry Valley in New York. About 200 were murdered in Pennsylvania, 40 in Cherry Valley.

At King's Mountain in 1780, American troops shot down redcoats who had surrendered. Virginia and North Carolina militia burned 1,000 Cherokee villages and destroyed 50,000 bushels of corn. In March 1782, Pennsylvania militia murdered ninety-six Delaware Indians who had carefully maintained their neutrality for six years.

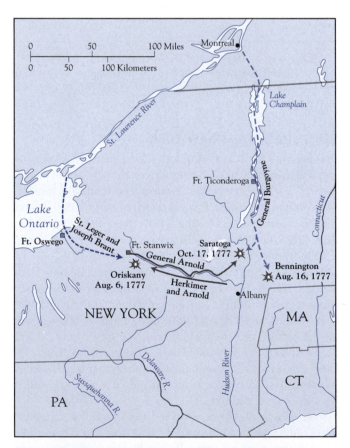

MAP 9:3 **Victory at Saratoga, October 17, 1777.** While Washington's army was setting up winter quarters in Valley Forge in October 1777, the British suffered a total defeat at Saratoga, New York. The surrender of the British army there heartened the French to sign an alliance with the United States.

The Continental Insurance Companies

Burgoyne's march from Montreal to Saratoga suffered mishaps at every turn. Nothing went right. When his army was encircled in October 1777, he surrendered to General Horatio Gates at Saratoga. The news of the major American victory was enough to bring France into the war.

Burgoyne would command the 8,000-strong army and more than 100 cannon coming from Montreal. But Howe, in New York City, sabotaged Burgoyne's bright idea. In part, perhaps, because he believed Burgoyne would get the credit for victory, in part because he was persuaded by Joseph Galloway, Pennsylvania's leading loyalist, that Philadelphia, the largest American city, was ripe for plucking, Howe took his troops south instead of north. He left only 3,000 men under General Henry Clinton in New York, not enough to hold the city and help Burgoyne upon the Hudson.

Saratoga: A Watershed

Howe moved to Pennsylvania by sea, Washington overland. On September 11, their armies met at Brandywine Creek southwest of Philadelphia. The British drove Washington from the field but without—again—destroying his army. On September 26, after another victory at Paoli, Howe occupied Philadelphia. On October 4, Washington attacked at Germantown, north of the city. While coming close to victory, in the end he was repulsed. His army fell back to winter quarters at Valley Forge, not even a town but rolling farmland. Washington found comfortable farmhouses for himself and his staff, but the soldiers had to build rude cabins. Howe was again ensconced in a comfortable and friendly city.

Alas for glory, Howe's success in 1777 was tarnished by events in the forests of New York. In June, Burgoyne had left Montreal with 4,000 redcoats, 3,200 Hessians, several hundred Canadians, some loyalists and Indians, and 138 cannon. The 3,500 Americans at Fort Ticonderoga fled without a fight. (No one, it seems, ever held Fort Ticonderoga.) But Burgoyne's progress was slow. For three weeks, the column advanced just a mile a day. Americans, proud of their ability to cope with wilderness conditions, delighted in blaming Burgoyne's personal baggage for the lack of progress. On a road that was little more than an Indian trail, his "luggage" filled thirty ox carts and included living and dining suites, a bed and linens, china, and crystal fit for a London party. But all British generals traveled with such luxuries. Mostly, Burgoyne was slow because he saw no need to rush and his pioneers (as axeman were called) had to clear the way of hundreds of trees that the Americans had felled across the road.

Then bad news began to arrive from every direction. St. Leger's and Brant's army of Mohawks, which Burgoyne expected to join him, disintegrated after a series of battles with Nicholas Herkimer and Benedict Arnold around Fort Stanwix, halfway across New York. Burgoyne sent the Hessians east on a routine foraging mission—they were to seize supplies in Bennington, Vermont—and they were wiped out by militia. And Burgoyne learned that Howe was en route to Philadelphia not north on the Hudson River. His plan, brilliant on paper, had fallen to pieces in the woods.

The occupation of New England was out of the question. The best Burgoyne could hope for was to preserve his army by retreating to Canada. Instead, he dug in near Saratoga and hoped for help from General Clinton. American General Horatio Gates jumped on Burgoyne's blunder and surrounded his army. On October 17, he accepted the surrender of 5,700 soldiers. The Battle of Saratoga was the most important event of the year, perhaps of the war. Not only did New England remain under patriot control, the major American victory was also precisely the news for which Franklin was waiting in Paris.

THE TIDE TURNS

The Battle of Saratoga allayed Vergennes's doubts about American chances of winning the war. The rout of an army of 8,000 crack redcoats and German mercenaries was no skirmish. Indeed, when Lord North heard of the British defeat, he wrote to Franklin that King George would end the war on the terms demanded by Americans up to July 1776. The Intolerable Acts and other obnoxious laws enacted between 1763 and 1775 would be repealed. Great Britain would concede the colonies' control of their internal affairs in return for them swearing loyalty to the king. In retrospect, we can see that Lord North proposed to organize the empire (the North American colonies, anyway) as a commonwealth of autonomous dominions, the status Britain accorded Canada, Australia, and New Zealand in the nineteenth century.

But victory is a tonic, and American blood was up. By the end of 1777, American animosity toward the mother country had intensified. Patriot propagandists made hay of Hessian troops, many of whom went into battle pledged to take no prisoners, and the murder and scalping of a young woman, Jane McCrea (a loyalist, ironically), by Indians under Burgoyne's command. In New Jersey, redcoats and Hessians brutally bullied farmers, raping women and girls. The old rallying cry, the "rights of British subjects," had lost its magic. The French offered a military alliance that was more attractive in the wake of Saratoga than returning, however victoriously, to the British Empire.

Foreign Intervention

In December 1777, France formally recognized the independence of the United States. In February 1778, Vergennes signed a treaty of alliance to go into effect if France and Britain went to war (which they did in June 1778). It provided for close commercial ties between France and the United States and stated that France would assert no claims to Canada after the war. France's reward at the peace table would be in the West Indies.

The war could not have been won without the French alliance. Not only did "America's oldest friend" pour money and men into the conflict, France also provided a fleet, which the Americans lacked and could not hope to create. Individual patriot seamen like John Paul Jones ("I have not yet begun to fight") and John Barry (no particularly memorable sayings) won morale-boosting victories over single British ships. But the superiority of the Royal Navy enabled the British to hold Philadelphia and New York for most of the war, and

to capture Charleston, Savannah, and Newport near the end. Without the French navy, the entire American coastline might have been blockaded.

In fact, patriot merchantmen had little difficulty moving goods in and out of the many small ports on the Atlantic. Until 1781, when the British occupied the island, Dutch St. Eustatius in the West Indies was, along with French Martinique, the major destination of American merchants. Holland was neutral, but well disposed to the Americans. Ships of all nations brought cargos destined for America to St. Eustatius where American sloops and schooners collected them for trans-shipment to the continent. When the British fleet finally seized St. Eustatius with a surprise attack, they found fifty American merchantmen in the harbor, 2,000 American seamen carousing in the port.

Spain sent Bernardo de Gálvez into British Florida, where he occupied every fort. Vergennes averted a war brewing between Prussia and Austria that would have tied down French troops in Europe, always a British objective. He persuaded both countries, as well as Russia, to declare their neutrality, denying Britain the allies the country sorely needed.

Woman Warriors

During the Revolution, an unknown number of women sheared their hair, bound their breasts, donned men's clothing, and signed up in the army. A few were discovered. Robert Shurtleff's (Deborah Sampson's) sex was discovered by a surgeon when she was badly wounded. The army took Sampson's masquerade with good grace. She was granted a pension and she lectured widely on how she pulled her trick off.

Molly Hays was carrying water to troops at the Battle of Monmouth in 1778 (she was nicknamed Molly Pitcher) when her husband, an artilleryman, collapsed from exhaustion. She took his place in the gun crew. As did Margaret Corbin at the battle of Fort Washington two years earlier.

In 1777, with the menfolk gone, women from Pepperell and Groton in northern Massachusetts mobilized to defend a bridge at the news a British army was approaching. It proved to be a false rumor, but they were as ready as Minutemen.

Mercenaries for Liberty

A Europe at peace meant that many military professionals were unhappily unemployed. Aristocratic officers, hungry for commissions with salaries attached, flocked to the United States. There was plenty of deadwood in the bunch—Washington knew it—but others were able officers—whom Washington needed—and some were motivated by more than the money.

Commodore John Barry was an Irishman, John Paul Jones a Scot—traitors like the Americans. Marie Joseph, the Marquis de Lafayette, was a 19-year-old noble (the British called him "the boy") who proved to be an excellent field commander. He accepted no salary from the army. On the contrary, he spent generously from his persional fortune on the American cause. Although he was 25 years younger than Washington, the two men became true friends on a basis of something close to equality.

Another idealist was Casimir Pulaski, a Pole who had fought Russia for his country's independence. Recruited in Paris by Benjamin Franklin, Pulaski was a romantic figure, a cavalry commander bedecked in the waxed mustache and gaudy uniforms cavalrymen favored. Pulaski was a valuable acquisition; the Continental Army had virtuallly no cavalry arm. He was killed leading a charge at the Battle of Savannah late in the war. Johann Kalb, a Bavarian who affected the title of Baron de Kalb, also lost his life during the war, at the Battle of Camden. (He was probably not a baron. Then, as now, titleless Americans slavered over Europeans who claimed them.)

Jean Baptiste, the Comte de Rochambeau (a real Count!) arrived in Newport, Rhode Island with 5,500 crack troops in 1780 and played a key role in the decisive American victory at Yorktown, Virginia, the next year. Even more valuable than combat commanders (American officers were not short on boldness and bravery) were specialists like Thaddeus Kosciusko, a Polish engineer expert in building fortifications, a military field in which few Americans were trained. Friedrich Wilhelm von Steuben, a Prussian who also styled himself a baron, was an expert in drill, another American deficiency. He wrote a drill manual the Continental Army adopted and personally supervised the training at Valley Forge in the winter of 1777–1778 that transformed Washington's men into a disciplined army. By 1781, fully one patriot officer in five was a foreigner.

The War Drags On

Steuben arrived at the right time. Washington lost 2,500 men to disease and exposure during the winter at Valley Forge and, by the spring of 1778, it was obvious that the war would go on for years. Badly outnumbered, the Americans could not force the question in a do-or-die battle. Washington's strategy, conveyed to all his subordinates, was to hold on, fighting only when circumstances were favorable. Lord Germain and General Clinton (who took over from Howe in May 1778) could hope only to throttle the American economy with a naval blockade and to concentrate land operations in the South, which had not felt the war.

North Wind Picture Archives

Washington and "the boy," the French general Lafayette, at Valley Forge during the dismal winter of 1777–1778. Lafayette was 25 years younger than Washington, but they became close friends and remained so until Washington's death. Lafayette regarded Washington as the giant of the age.

Beginning with the occupation of Savannah, Georgia, in December 1778, the redcoats won a series of victories in the South, but even there (Washington remained in the North) they could not break the stalemate. For each British victory, the Americans won another, or, in losing ground, they cost the British so heavily that the redcoats had to return to the coast, within reach of supply ships.

Washington effectively knocked the Mohawks out of the war in 1779, reducing the tribe to famine by destroying thousands of acres of corn. Nevertheless, the war was wearing heavily on the American side too. Prices of necessities soared. Imports were available only at exorbitant costs. When Congress failed to pay and provision troops in 1780 and 1781, mutinies

erupted on the Connecticut, Pennsylvania, and New Jersey lines. In September 1780, Washington learned that Benedict Arnold, commanding the important fortress at West Point in New York, sold it and his services to the British for £20,000. (He was exposed and West Point was not lost.)

The campaign of 1781 opened with American spirits lower than they had been since before the battle of Trenton. Washington was outside New York, but idle. The most active British army, led by one of the best British commanders, Lord Charles Cornwallis, lost a battle at Cowpens, South Carolina, but then repeatedly pummeled Nathanael Greene the breadth of North Carolina. Cornwallis then joined with other officers and amased 7,500 men in Virginia.

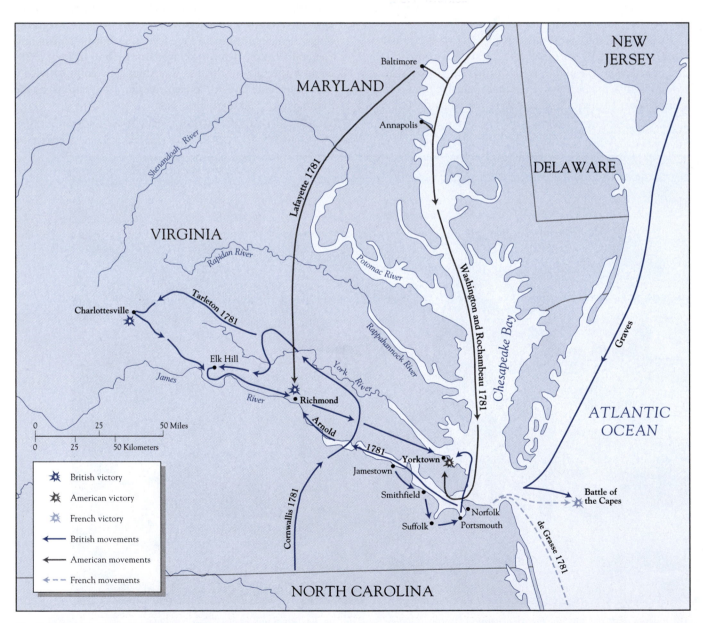

MAP 9:4 **The Battle of Yorktown, May–October 1781.** After meandering fruitlessly through Virginia, Lord Charles Cornwallis set up quarters in Yorktown and waited for a British fleet to evacuate his army. Thanks to a frantic march from the north, American and French troops commanded by Washington managed to trap him there when, in a miracle of coordination, a French fleet arrived to prevent the British evacuation ships from completing their mission. The Battle of Yorktown ended the war.

Opportunity

Cornwallis faced no American army large enough to challenge him to batttle. But he had his problems. Anywhere away from navigable waters was dangerous ground. The most rag-tag of militias could cut his overland supply line. On August 1, 1781, he set up an encampment at Yorktown, Virginia, on the same neck of land as the first permanent English settlement in America. Cornwallis requested supplies and instructions from General Clinton in New York. With Clinton dawdling, Washington wanted to attack New York. Then Rochambeau, commanding the French forces, learned that a French admiral, Count François de Grasse, was sailing from the West Indies to the Chesapeake Bay with 3,000 more troops aboard twenty-five warships.

Yorktown was George Washington's backyard. He knew the terrain intimately; he knew that if de Grasse could cut Cornwallis off by sea, the British were trapped. Nevertheless, he was reluctant to march south. He had to be persuaded by Rochambeau that surrounding and forcing the surrender of Cornwallis's army was a better bet than driving Clinton out of Tory New York. Maneuvering around the city so that a confused Clinton would sit tight, Washington raced the best of his army across New Jersey to the Chesapeake. In September, his troops joined with the French under Lafayette, Rochambeau, Steuben, and the reinforcements de Grasse had landed. The combined army of 17,000 outnumbered Cornwallis's 8,000. It was almost the first time in the war that the patriots enjoyed numerical superiority. Less often mentioned is the fact that a majority of the "American army" spoke French.

Yorktown

Cornwallis did not panic. His men were well dug in, and he expected to move them out by sea. But between September 5 and 10, de Grasse prevented the British evacuation fleet from reaching Yorktown whence it sailed off empty to New York. After that, defense was futile as the Americans reduced the British pocket around Yorktown and bombarded the British at close range. On October 17, Cornwallis asked for terms; on October 19, he surrendered.

Cornwallis was no America basher. He had been one of only four lords in Parliament to vote against the Declaratory Act. But he found his defeat at Yorktown humiliating. Claiming sickness, he sent an aide to the field to surrender his sword. The aide tried to hand it to Rochambeau, but the French general gestured him to Washington. Rather than accept the symbol of capitulation from an inferior officer, Washington delegated the honors to General Benjamin Lincoln, whom the British had similarly humiliated at Charleston. During the surrender ceremonies, the British army band played the hymn, "The World Turn'd Upside Down."

Anne S. K. Brown Military Collection, Brown University, Providence, RI

There are dozens of artists' depictions of the British surrender of Yorktown. This one makes a point that most others ignore, the key role played by the French fleet. Indeed, Washington had more French than American soldiers under his command at Yorktown.

John Adams said that one American in three was a patriot, one in three a loyalist, and one in three was not particularly interested in the war. Whether or not he had his fractions right, Adams was being honest, with himself as well as with others. He was admitting that a good many Americans simply did not care about a cause that he thought sacred.

Americans who tried to ignore the war were found in every part of the country. They were most likely to be harassed for their indifference—and they were bullied, as loyalists were—if they lived in a vociferously patriot area. New Jersey's Francis Hopkinson, a poet-politician, categorized Americans as "birds" (patriots), "beasts" (loyalists), and "bats," who claimed to be birds around birds and beasts around beasts. There was no minding one's own business in Hopkinson's War for Independence; one was either with the patriots or against them.

It was easier to sit out the war west of the Appalachians. There were battles on the frontier, but they were mostly with Indians, episodes in a conflict that began long before 1775 and would continue when the Revolutionary War was over. In fact, the most famous frontiersman and Indian fighter of the era, Daniel Boone, avoided involvement in the war even though he was a major in the Virginia militia. He continued to hunt, build roads, and dream of getting rich speculating in land. His reputation suffered because he sat the war out. He was accused of collaborating with the Shawnee, who were British allies, of being, in other words, a loyalist or one of Hopkinson's "bats."

Boone was born in Pennsylvania in 1734 and emigrated with much of his family to western North Carolina. In 1755, he was a teamster on the disastrous Braddock march to Fort Duquesne. (Given his lowly job, he did not make the acquaintance of Braddock's aide, George Washington.) Boone hated farming. He took a variety of jobs, including driving a team, to avoid it; he most enjoyed hunting deer and selling the venison. Boone spent much of the 1760s and 1770s in the forests of what is now Kentucky and saw the land there (as George Washington saw the land north of the Ohio River) as a commodity on which a man could get rich. In one way, Kentucky was a better bet for a land speculator than Ohio because the Indian population was

sparse. Both the Cherokee from the south and the Shawnee from the north hunted in Kentucky and traded with one another—Boone had run-ins with both tribes—but neither people lived there in great numbers.

In 1775, when the fighting began back East, Boone was supervising thirty axemen building the "Wilderness Road" through the Cumberland Gap into Kentucky where he intended to connect it to the ancient "Warrior's Path," a north–south route. Just when news of the Declaration of Independence and the all-out war with the British reached him is not clear, but he did sign on as a scout for the Virginia militia. Almost immediately he was captured by Shawnees and taken by them to be questioned by British officers north of the Ohio River. Boone was gone for a year and said little about his captivity when he returned. When accused of being a Tory, he denied it, but he refused to elaborate. Had he been "back East," he might not have gotten off with mere remarks.

Boone returned to developing his townsite at Boonesboro and several other frontier settlements where he claimed land. His fame as a woodsman—Boone engineered a spectacular and well-publicized rescue of his daughter, who had been kidnapped by Indians—made him Kentucky's most effective promoter, but his land speculations all failed. In part, Boone's undoing was having a sense of personal honor in a business in which ethics did not work. He sold thousands of acres cheaply to compensate associates for losses for which he felt responsible. He spent thousands on lawyers but had no stomach for going to court himself; land speculation was a profession which was half litigation, and Boone lost almost all of his courtroom contests.

In 1799, Boone moved to Missouri and never returned to Kentucky. He was broke and bitter. When, in 1815, a Kentucky creditor showed up to ask for his money, Boone's son told him, "You have come a great distance to suck a bull and, I reckon, you will have to go home dry."

Boone was nationally famous most of his life. After he died, he was installed in the American pantheon as the first and even the greatest of frontiersmen. But, if he was no Tory during the Revolution, he was no patriot either. He was simply not interested.

The Treaty of Paris

The British could have fought on. Their 44,000 troops in North America far outnumbered the French and American armies and there were 30,000 reserves in the West Indies. Despite the French naval victory at Yorktown, the Royal Navy still ruled the western Atlantic. Newport, New York, and Charleston were still occupied. Sentiment for continuing to

fight was still strong in Britain. When the House of Commons voted to negotiate with the Americans, the vote was just 234–215. By pulling a few strings and distributing patronage, George III and Lord North might have reversed the decision.

But eighteenth-century wars were fought with limited, practical objectives. When those objectives no longer seemed worth the costs of achieving them, governments made peace.

Kings did not, like dictators and self-appointed leaders of sacred movements in our own era, burrow into bunkers or mountain fastnesses and tell their subjects to fight nobly on until the last of them was dead. Early in 1782, Lord North resigned as prime minister and was succeeded by the Marquis of Rockingham, who had brokered the repeal of the Stamp Act in 1766 and had sympathized with the Americans during the war.

It took more than a year for negotiators in Paris (Franklin and John Adams heading the American team) to put a mutually satisfactory treaty together. France played no part in drafting the treaty. The American war aim was British recognition of the independence of the United States. The French had additional aspirations. Rather than be distracted by complicated diplomatic and possible endless bickering—there were those 40,000 British soldiers back home—the American legation came to terms with the British without inviting the French to the table. The Treaty of Paris, signed in September 1783, recognized American independence with the Mississippi River as the new country's western boundary. Americans were granted fishing rights off British Newfoundland and Nova Scotia (which New Englander Adams made his personal project). Adams and Franklin pledged Congress not to molest Loyalists and to urge the states to compensate Tories for property that had already been seized from them.

The Father of His Country

American independence made a celebrity of George Washington in Europe as well as in the infant United States. Adulation was heaped on the "father of his country" in every European capital, London included. There was a heated market in portraits of him and his image on, among other objects, porcelain pitchers and tableware. It was an astonishing rise in fame for a man who was a Virginia planter in 1775 with a dubious military record and no record in the heady political debates that led to the Revolution when Congress put him in command of an army that, for practical purposes, did not exist.

John Adams was catty—he often was—when he said that Washington was "too illiterate, unlearned, unread for his station and reputation." Washington was, in fact, well read. He had a large personal library and subscribed to as many as ten newspapers. He wrote (on concrete subjects, his voluminous letters and commands) with admirable clarity. He was hardheaded and shrewd in his assessments of human behavior, as when he commented at the time of the alliance with France that "men are very apt to run into extremes; hatred to England may carry some into excessive Confidence in France."

But Adams was correct in saying that Washington was no intellectual, as many political leaders of the era were. He had no formal education. He knew no Latin, a prerequisite of the educated, and did not speak French, almost as mandatory. He sat silently during debates and was, at least according to Thomas Jefferson, a dull conversationalist, "not above mediocrity, possessing neither copiousness of ideas, nor fluency of words."

Reproduced from the Collections of the Library of Congress [LC-D43-T01-50236]

General George Washington, painted by John Trumbull a few months after the battle of Yorktown. The portrait captures Washington's heroic image in Europe as well as in the United States. Washington was quartered with his army north of New York City, which was still occupied by the British, when Trumbull painted his portrait.

His record as a strategist and battlefield commander was mixed. He had to be talked out of an assault on Boston in 1775 that would have been a disaster. In retrospect, at least, it is obvious that fighting for New York City in 1776 was a mistake. Rochambeau and Lafayette had to hammer on him to abandon his plan to attack New York in 1781 and rush south to trap Cornwallis at Yorktown. Any number of his subordinates were quicker witted in the thick of a battle, although tactical mistakes do not explain Washington's many defeats.

For all that, the American victory owed as much to Washington as to French regulars. Even during the dismal days of late 1776, he kept an army in the field, the indispensable priority of the leader of a rebellion. He repeatedly extricated the Continentals from defeats by British forces superior in every way. He struggled on what seems a daily basis with inadequate provisions, poor shelter, epidemic disease

George Washington

George Washington was a fourth-generation Virginian. His great grandfather, John Washington, emgrated in 1657, one of the "distressed cavaliers" recruited by Governor Berkeley. George's father, Augustine Washington, was a prosperous planter; in addition to seven children, he left 10,000 acres of mostly prime tidewater land and forty-nine slaves to work it. When George's elder brother, Lawrence, died without children in 1752, the estate, including Mount Vernon, was his. By 1775, he held title to 60,000 acres, mostly in the Ohio Country.

Washington was tall—6'2" to 6'4"—" straight as an Indian," trim, and athletic. His face was scarred from smallpox and, famously, he had few teeth and wore dentures more for the sake of appearance than chewing; they were painful.

Washington was a superb horseman. When people complimented Thomas Jefferson for his skills with a horse, he said that Washington was far better. Washington was a fanatic fox hunter, spending up to seven hours in the saddle chasing his hounds. Less often mentioned about Washington's equestrian feats, his personal servant, a slave, Billy Lee, was always on his own horse right behind the general.

---

among his men, and Congress's frequent failure to support him. If delegates complained that he was always retreating, and some plotted to remove him from command, Washington knew exactly what he was doing and he, not malcontents in Congress, was right. "We should on all occasions avoid a general action," he wrote to a complaining Congress, "when the fate of America may be at stake on the issue." He would not fight a battle which, if lost, meant the end of the war.

In order to understand Washington's greatness, it is necessary to fall back on the intangibles that transfixed most of his contemporaries. Radicals like Samuel Adams, conservatives like Alexander Hamilton, intellectuals like Thomas Jefferson, warriors like Israel Putnam, and cultivated Europeans like Lafayette and Rochambeau—all deferred to the Virginian. Washington's deportment, integrity, his personal dignity, and his disdain for petty squabbles set him a head taller than his contemporaries as, indeed, his height of at least 6 feet 2 inches made him a very tall eighteenth-century man. He held the Revolution together with that not quite definable quality known as "character." If the very notion—character—is sappy nowadays, the shame is not on Washington's era.

FURTHER READING

General Robert Middlekauff, *The Glorious Cause: The American Revolution 1763–1789*, 1982; Edward Countryman, *The American Revolution*, 1985; Stephen Conway, *The War of American Independence 1775–1783*, 1995; John Ferling, *A Leap in the Dark: The Struggle to Create the American Republic*, 2003; David Hackett Fischer, *Washington's Crossing*, 2004; David *McCullough, 1776*, 2005.

Loyalists Paul H. Smith, *Loyalists and Redcoats: A Study in British Revolutionary Policy*, 1964; William Nelson, *The American Tory*, 1967; Mary Beth Norton, *The British-Americans: The Loyalist Exiles in England, 1774–1789*, 1972; Robert M. Calhoon, *The Loyalists in Revolutionary America*, 1973; Judith Van Buskirk, *Generous Enemies: Patriots and Loyalists in Revolutionary New York*, 2002.

Military Don Higginbotham, *The War of American Independence: Military Attitudes, Policies, and Practice*, 1971; Philip Lawson, *The Imperial Challenge: Quebec and Britain in the Age of the American Revolution*, 1989; Sylvia R. Frey, *The British Soldier in America: A Social History of Military Life in the Revolutionary Period*, 1984; Charles Royster, *A Revolutionary People at War: The Continental Army and American Character 1775–1783*, 1980; Robert L. O'Connell, *Of Arms and Men: A History of War, Weapons, and Aggression*, 1989; Mark Kwasny, *Washington's Partisan War, 1775–1783*, 1996; Peter D. Thomas, *Tea Party to Independence: The Third Phase of the American Revolution, 1773–1776*, 1991; Mark V. Kwasny, *Washington's Partisan War, 1775–1783*, 1996; Walter Edgar, *Partisans and Redcoats: The Southern Conflict that Turned the Tide of the American Revolution*, 2001.

Special Topics Richard B. Morris, *The Peacemakers*, 1965; Barbara Graymont, *The Iroquois in the American Revolution*, 1972; Mary Beth Norton, *Liberty's Daughters*, 1980; Barbara W. Tuchman, *The First Salute: A View of the American Revolution*, 1988; Colin G. Calloway, *The American Revolution in Indian Country*, 1995; Sylvia R. Frey, *Water from the Rock: Black Resistance in a Revolutionary America*, 1991; Simon Schama, *Rough Crossings: Britain, the Slaves, and the American Revolution*, 2006.

People Ira D. Gruber, *The Howe Brothers and the American Revolution*, 1972; Pauline Maier, *The Old Revolutionaries: Political Lives in the Age of Samuel Adams*, 1980; Willard Sterne Randall, *Benedict Arnold: Patriot and Traitor*, 1990; Joseph J. Ellis, *Founding Brothers: The Revolutionary Generation*, 2000; Richard Brookhiser, *Founding Father: Rediscovering George Washington*, 1996; Gordon S. Wood, *The Americanization of Benjamin Franklin*, 2004, and *Revolutionary Characters: What Made the Founders Different*, 2006; Harvey J. Kaye, *Thomas Paine and the Promise of America*, 2005.

KEY TERMS

Use the following listing of key terms to review important figures, events, locations, and concepts covered in this chapter. A glossary of these terms is available on *The American*

Past companion Web site: www.cengage.com/history/conlin/tap9e

Brant, Joseph, p. 146

Arnold, Benedict, p. 147

Saratoga, p. 151

Yorktown, p. 155

ONLINE RESOURCES

Find additional resources, including primary source documents, images, interactive maps, simulations, chapter review exercises, and Internet links at

The American Past **companion Web site**
www.cengage.com/history/conlin/tap9e

American History Resource Center
http://ushistory.wadsworth.com/

DISCOVERY

How are words and images, such as these representations used to justify actions in time of war, especially in the case of the American Revolution?

Government and Law: What was the political philosophy that Thomas Jefferson expressed in the preamble to the Declaration of Independence? When, in his view, was violent revolution justified? Implicit in what he wrote, when was insurrection not justified?

Declaration of Independence

"We hold these Truths to be self-evident, that all Men are created equal, that they are endowed by their Creator with certain unalienable Rights, that among these are Life, Liberty and the Pursuit of Happiness—That to secure these Rights, Governments are instituted among Men, deriving their just Powers from the Consent of the Governed, that whenever any Form of Government becomes destructive of these Ends, it is the Right of the People to alter or to abolish it, and to institute new Government, laying its Foundation on such Principles, and organizing its Powers in such Form, as to them shall seem most likely to effect their Safety and Happiness. Prudence, indeed, will dictate that Governments long established should not be changed for light and transient Causes; and accordingly all Experience hath shewn, that Mankind are more disposed to suffer, while Evils are sufferable, than to right themselves by abolishing the Forms to which they are accustomed. But when a long Train of Abuses and Usurpations, pursuing invariably the same Object, evinces a Design to reduce them under absolute Despotism, it is their Right, it is their Duty, to throw off such Government, and to provide new Guards for their future Security. Such has been the patient Sufferance of these Colonies; and such is now the Necessity which constrains them to alter their former Systems of Government. The History of the present King of Great-Britain is a History of repeated Injuries and Usurpations, all having in direct Object the Establishment of an absolute Tyranny over these States."

Culture and Society: How were images such as these representations of the "Boston Massacre," the "Boston Tea Party," and the Battle of Lexington employed to influence opinion? How are the British depicted? How are the Americans depicted? Are all of these accurate depictions of what happened? If any of them are not, why did the artists distort events?

The Boston Massacre

Americans throwing the Cargoes of the Tea Ships into the River, at Boston

The Boston Tea Party

The 'Battle' at Lexington

John Carter Brown Library

How did the patriots of the Revolution move from complaining about taxes to risking everything they had for the sake of winning independence from Great Britain?

Warfare: How important were women like Esther Reed in the prosecution of the War for Independence? How did she differ in her contributions to the war effort from Deborah Sampson and Molly Hays? What do those differences say about the social class of the three?

"Letter from Esther Reed to General Washington"

Philadelphia, July 4th, 1780.

Sir,

The subscription set on foot by the ladies of this City for the use of the soldiery, is so far completed as to induce me to transmit to your Excellency an account of the money I have received, and which, although it has answered our expectations, it does not equal our wishes, but I am persuaded will be received as a proof of our zeal for the great cause of America and our esteem and gratitude for those who so bravely defend it.

The amount of the subscription is 200,580 dollars, and £625 6s. 8d. in specie, which makes in the whole in paper money 300,634 dollars.

The ladies are anxious for the soldiers to receive the benefit of it, and wait your directions how it can best be disposed of. We expect some considerable additions from the country and have also wrote to the other States in hopes the ladies there will adopt similar plans, to render it more general and beneficial.

With the utmost pleasure I offer any farther attention and care in my power to complete the execution of the design, and shall be happy to accomplish it agreeable to the intention of the donors and your wishes on the subject. The ladies of my family join me in their respectful compliments and sincerest prayer for your health, safety, and success.

I have the honour to be, With the highest respect, Your obedient humble servants,

E. Reed.

To read extended versions of selected documents, visit the companion Web site www.cengage.com/history/conlin/tap9e; click on "Discovery Sources"

Chapter 10

Inventing a Country
American Constitutions 1781–1789

The National Archives

Without some alteration in our political creed, the superstructure we have been seven years raising at the expense of so much blood and treasure, must fall. We are fast verging to anarchy and confusion.

—George Washington

The American war for independence was not historically unique. From the dawn of civilization in Mesopotamia, the history of empires has been a story of subordinate peoples rising up to free themselves from the rule of imperial masters. However, the American Revolution was singular in the fact that the patriots had to re-invent themselves as Americans. They were not already "a people" as, for example, the Dutch were when, in the 1600s, they fought for and won their independence from Spain. Nor had the colonials been conquered by a foreign power as the Irish were. Most colonials were British by descent and, until 1775, they defined themselves as British first and secondly as New Hampshiremen or Virginians or Georgians.

The Articles of Confederation, which the Continental Congress wrote early in the war, created the "United States," but the first American Constitution—for that is what the Articles were—did not create a nation or a nationality. Each of the thirteen states that joined together to fight the British remained emphatically sovereign. New Hampshiremen were still New Hampshiremen, Virginians still Virginians. Their state constitutions were more important to political leaders than the Articles.

STATE CONSTITUTIONS

Connecticut and Rhode Island, as corporate colonies, had been largely self-governing since their inception. They merely converted their colonial charters into state constitutions by jiggling the wording, deleting references to the king

and the like. The constitutions the other eleven states wrote from scratch were more telling in that, to varying degrees, they institutionalized the patriots' hostility to many things British.

The fact that the state constitutions were written and aimed at covering every contingency their governments might face was a break with British practice. The "British constitution" includes written documents such as the Magna Carta of 1215 and the Bill of Rights of 1688. But most of it, especially government procedures, was unwritten, a generally recognized and accepted framework within which the king, Parliament, and the courts of law operated.

The unwritten character of the British constitution had been a big part of the problem that led to the Revolution: Just what was the extent of the king's and Parliament's legitimate authority over the colonies? The patriots believed that king and Parliament had violated the British constitution in trying to tax the colonies. But they could win the point only by taking up arms and winning the war.

Written constitutions can be violated, too, of course. However, as Thomas Jefferson wrote, "they furnish a text to which those who are watchful may again rally and recall the people." Americans wanted their constitutions in that kind of black and white.

Limiting Power, Striking Down Privilege

In Great Britain, aside from a few royal prerogatives that King George was cautious about exercising, Parliament was the government. There was no appealing Parliament's actions, as the Americans discovered. Parliament was supreme. The Americans' state constitutions, however, were written

And They're Off ...

Popular reaction against things British found form in more than written constitutions. When the United States adopted the dollar as its monetary unit, it was in part a patriotic statement. British currency was based on the pound sterling (£). *Dollar* was one of several names given to a Spanish silver coin that, as the *thaler*, dated back to medieval Germany. Adopting the dollar was something of a declaration of financial independence from Britain. It was also, however, commonsensical: There were far more Spanish dollars circulating in the infant United States than there were British pounds.

It was also during the Confederation period that Americans began to run their horse races counterclockwise around a track rather than clockwise as they were run in Britain and had been run in the colonies. No one has identified the element of common sense in that innovation.

not by their parliaments, the thirteen state assemblies, but by conventions elected specifically for the purpose of constitution making. A convention superior in authority to a state assembly was "the only proper body" to write a constitution. The state assemblies' function was "to make Laws agreeable to that Constitution." The point was that sovereignty (ultimate government power) rested with "the people" (as the word was then defined). Constitution making called for a special expression of the people's will.

The patriots had resented royal officials as arbitrary and beholden to the king, not to "the people." So, they guarded against creating a homegrown elite entrenched in public office by requiring that just about all state officials stand for election every year. Even then, executive officers had little power. State governors were empowered to administer laws and to dress up and act dignified on ceremonial occasions. Pennsylvania's 1776 constitution abolished the office of governor. (Nor did the Articles of Confederation provide for a chief executive.).

Another anti-British resentment was reflected in the disestablishment of the Church of England in every colony where it had been the official church, funded by taxes everyone paid no matter what church they attended. No longer. The Church of England lost its privileges with independence. The Protestant Episcopal Church (the new name of the church Anglicans formed) became just another private denomination legally on a par with the Quakers, Presbyterians, Baptists, and, for that matter, the handful of Catholic missions and Jewish synagogues. Like them, the Protestant Episcopal Church depended on its members to pay its ministers and patch leaky roofs.

In New Hampshire, Connecticut, and Massachusetts, the Congregationalist church had been established and was to remain so for forty years after independence. (The Constitution of 1787 forbade the federal government to establish a religion, but not the states.) Five other state constitutions expressed a "preference" for Protestant Christianity. Roman Catholics were not permitted to vote in North Carolina until 1835. Jews could vote in only the states of Pennsylvania, Rhode Island, and New York.

Democratic Drift

Every state extended the franchise to more people than had enjoyed the right to vote under colonial law. However, every state except Georgia, Pennsylvania, and Vermont (a state in fact although not in name until 1791) required that voters own property—not very much in most states; only the very poor had no say in government. Women who met the property test could vote in New Jersey. New Jersey, Massachusetts, and New Hampshire made no distinctions between free blacks and whites at the polls. Five other states (including North

An Infant Government 1777–1791

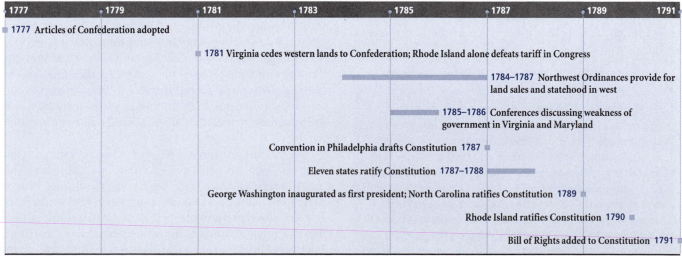

1777   1779   1781   1783   1785   1787   1789   1791

1777 Articles of Confederation adopted

1781 Virginia cedes western lands to Confederation; Rhode Island alone defeats tariff in Congress

1784–1787 Northwest Ordinances provide for land sales and statehood in west

1785–1786 Conferences discussing weakness of government in Virginia and Maryland

Convention in Philadelphia drafts Constitution 1787

Eleven states ratify Constitution 1787–1788

George Washington inaugurated as first president; North Carolina ratifies Constitution 1789

Rhode Island ratifies Constitution 1790

Bill of Rights added to Constitution 1791

North Wind Picture Archives

New Jersey's state constitution of 1776 allowed "all free inhabitants" who met the state's residency and property requirements to vote. For twenty years, a few free blacks and women took advantage of the rare privilege and protest was minimal. Indeed, a 1790 law referred to voters as "he or she." Then, in Elizabeth in 1797, seventy-five Federalist women showed up at the polls en masse. The Federalists lost the election but narrowly. The victorious Jefferson Republicans noticed. Firmly in control of the state in 1807, they disenfranchised women and blacks and eliminated the property requirement for white males.

Carolina) allowed property-owning blacks to vote for several years, but then cancelled the African American franchise.

Eight states specified rights that were guaranteed to every citizen, beginning with Virginia's constitution in 1776. After the experiences with the vice admiralty courts, the quartering acts, and the arbitrary actions of the British army, Americans heady with independence were determined that there be no vagueness in the matter of the government's

power over individuals. The rights later listed in the first ten amendments to the United States Constitution—the Bill of Rights—were found in one or another of the state consitutions written during the Revolution.

Liberty's Limits: Women

In 1777, when the air was thick with talk of liberties, Abigail Adams wrote a letter to her husband, John, who was engaged in writing the Articles of Confederation. She asked him that "in the new code of laws" to "remember the ladies and be more generous and more favorable to them than your ancestors. Do not put such unlimited power into the hands of husbands. Remember, all men would be tyrants if they could."

She was too perceptive a woman to hope for much. (Abigail and John discussed public affairs constantly and Abigail's correspondence with her friend Mercy Otis Warren was heavy with politics.) Still, she was not alone in hoping that the expansion of liberties and rights would extend beyond men. A woman describing herself as a "matrimonial republican" wrote to a newspaper, "Marriage ought never to be considered a contract between a superior and an inferior, but a reciprocal union of interest, an implied

Peace Through Marriage

Virginia Governor Patrick Henry made a novel proposal to put an end to the chronic hostilities between Indians and whites, the amalgamation of the two races. He proposed that the state pay £10 to every free white person who married an Indian plus £5 for every child born of such unions. The Virginia assembly was uninterested. Some years later, Supreme Court Chief Justice, John Marshall commented that Henry's idea "would have been advantageous to this country. . . . Our prejudices, however, opposed themselves to our interests, and operated too powerfully for them."

partnership of interests,where all differences are accomodated by conference."

She was describing a "companionate marriage" of equals, something only eccentric couples would openly practice fifty years in the future. (The term "companionate marriage" would not be coined for a century.) But devoted and doting a husband as John Adams was—in his eyes *because* he was a loving husband—neither he nor any other political mover and shaker of the era thought twice about altering a married woman's subordination to her husband. The idea of an equality of the sexes was beyond the comprehension of the era. When the first feminist manifesto, *Vindication of the Rights of Women,* was published in 1792 by an English woman, Mary Wollstencroft, it was not even thought worth the time to ridicule it, or even read it, by prominent men on both sides of the Atlantic.

Manumission in the South

If a revision of the status of women was not on the table, African American slavery was. None of the southern state assemblies seriously considered the abolition of slavery. However, several of them enacted laws indicating the hope that the institution's days were numbered. Most southern states forbade, at least temporarily, the further importation of slaves from Africa and the West Indies.

Several southern state assemblies made manumission (a master voluntarily freeing an individual slave) easier, and many slaveowners took advantage of the liberalization. Between 1776 and 1810, Marylanders freed a fifth of the slaves in the state. Delaware's slave owners came close to eliminating slavery without state action. In 1790, 70 percent of the state's black population was enslaved. By 1810, almost 80 percent of Delaware's African Americans were free.

In part, southern antislavery—and its extent should not be exaggerated—had moral and religious foundations. Most southern Quakers, quite numerous in North Carolina, freed their slaves, even if it meant moving north to do so. John Payne (father of future first lady, Dolley Madison) freed his slaves in 1783 and relocated in Philadelphia. Southern Methodists were antislavery in their early days. In 1781, the Methodist church forbade ministers to be slave owners. Impelled by an intense personal conversion experience, Robert Carter of Nomini Hall, the titular head of one of Virginia's leading families, freed 500 slaves at one stroke.

Some southerners' antislavery had political and philosophical origins. "All men are created equal," Jefferson had written in the Declaration of Independence, and he tried to take a slap at the Atlantic slave trade and, therefore, slavery itself, in the document. "Oh the shocking, the intolerable inconsistence" of owning slaves, a pamphleteer, Samuel Hopkins wrote. Wealthy tobacco planters, who still dominated the states of the upper South, were particularly troubled to own slaves while uttering (in the sardonic words of England's Samuel Johnson) "the loudest yelps for liberty."

When Richard Randolph, a wealthy planter, died at age 26 in 1796, his will liberated 200 slaves and gave some of them acreage on, "Israel Hill," so they they could get a start as freemen. Randolph explicitly explained the emancipation in terms of the ideals of the Revolution. When he freed his slaves, he wrote,

> to make retribution, as far as I am able, to an unfortunate race of bondmen, over whom my ancestors have usurped and exercised the most lawless and monstrous tyranny, and in whom my countrymen (by iniquitous laws, in contradiction of their own declaration of rights, and in violation of every sacred law of nature . . .) have vested me with absolute property. . . .

A Pennsylvania Slave Owner

There were plenty of slaves in the North, but few northerners owned large numbers of Africans. Most commonly, northern farmers (and city people) owned only two, three, perhaps five slaves. The absence of an influential social class with a great deal of money invested in slaves was a major reason why abolition was easy in the northern states.

Simon Vanarsdalen of Bucks County, Pennsylvania, a prosperous farmer but by no means a wealthy grandee, owned a large number of slaves by northern standards. Exactly how many is unknown but, when he died in 1770, he bequeathed "Black Eve," "Black Cuff," "Black Henry," and "my negro wench called Poll or Mary" to his children with instructions that they inherit "the remainder of my negroes" after the death of my wife.

Ten years later, any of Vanarsdalen's slaves who were 28 years of age were freed by Pennsylvania's emancipation law.

Abolishing Slavery in the North

The northern states went further. They abolished slavery or set in motion mechanisms by which slavery would gradually but inexorably disappear. Quasi-independent Vermont (which became a state in 1791) forbade slavery as early as 1777. In Massachusetts, slavery was abolished at one blow in 1783. Elizabeth Freeman, a slave, sued her master for her freedom on the basis of a paraphrase of the Declaration of Independence written into the recently adopted state constitution: "all men are born free and equal." If so, then how could someone own her? The judges agreed, ruling slavery unconstitutional in the state.

Pennnsylvania, where antislavery Quakers were still a potent political force, was the first state to adopt a program of gradual emancipation. In 1780 the assembly provided that all persons henceforth born in the state, no matter the status of their parents, were free. Slaves born in Pennsylvania before 1780 were to be free at age 28. Buying and selling slaves were forbidden, an inducement to masters to manumit them. And owners of slaves were forbidden to take them out of the state to sell them elsewhere. Slaves brought into Pennsylvania were legally free after residing in the state for six months. With Quakers such as a tireless tailor, Isaac Hopper, helping

African Americans in the courts, Pennsylvania's combination of laws was highly effective. Slave owners found the legal restrictions on the use of their property (and social pressures) so burdensome that most of them freed their slaves before the law did. By 1800, there were only 1,700 slaves in Pennsylvania.

Most northern states patterned their gradual abolition schemes on Pennsylvania's. Even Rhode Island, where several hundred influential merchants had been engaged in the African slave trade, adopted an emancipation program. By 1800, there were only 1,300 slaves in the five New England states.

AMERICA UNDER THE ARTICLES OF CONFEDERATION

The collective affairs of the thirteen states were governed by the Articles of Confederation, which reflected the same principles as the state constitutions. Drafted during the heady years 1776 and 1777, the Articles created no president, indeed, no executive power independent of the Congress. Congress alone was the government. Members were elected annually and could serve only three years out of every six. That is, a man elected to Congress three years in a row was ineligible to serve again until he stayed home for three years. Americans would have no permanently seated office holders.

Divided Authority

Under the Articles, the United States was explicitly *not* a nation. It was—a bit vaguely—"a firm league of friendship." Georgia, North Carolina, and the rest retained their "sovereignty, freedom, and independence." Each state, no matter how large or small its population (there were twelve Virginians for every citizen of Delaware) was the equal in Congress of every other. Delegates voted not as individuals, but as members of their state's delegation. If three of five of a state's delegates voted "nay" on an issue, that state cast a single negative vote in Congress. A majority of states carried most questions but not the one most important to all government: Every proposal in Congress to levy a tax required the approval of all thirteen states!

Congress was not powerless. The Articles authorized it to maintain an army and navy, to declare war and make peace, and to maintain diplomatic relations with foreign countries and the Indian tribes, which were defined as "nations." Congress was entrusted with the maintenance of the post office system inherited (in pretty good shape) from the colonial era and it was empowered to establish a system of uniform weights and measures. Congress could mint coins, issue paper money, and borrow money.

However, the Articles also permitted the individual states to maintain navies (nine states had one), issue money (seven states did), and to ignore the Confederation's standards of measurement. Indeed, states could levy tariffs on goods imported from other states and individually negotiate commercial treaties with other countries. A state could even, "with

the consent of Congress," declare war on a foreign nation. Under the Articles, it would have been impeccably constitutional if New Jersey went to war with Holland while neighboring Pennsylvania agreed by treaty to sell gunpowder to the Dutch. (It never happened.)

The weakness of the ties binding the states to one another was not the fruit of incompetence or inexperience (although the confusion of granting the same powers to Congress and the states was certainly short-sighted). The weakness of the Confederation Congress was consciously written into the Articles because the majority of the revolutionaries who approved it were hostile to powerful government. From the start, some Americans thought that the nature of the Articles' government was a big mistake. Not long after the peace treaty with Great Britain, John Jay of New York wrote that "I am uneasy and apprehensive, more so than during the war.... We are going and doing wrong ... I look forward to evils and calamities." With each year, increasing numbers of people came to agree with him. But there was nothing thoughtless or accidental in the design of the government the Continental Congress created.

The Western Lands

The Confederation Congress had its achievements. The war was, if sometimes fitfully, prosecuted. Congress created a bureaucracy in Philadelphia (then the capital) that administered the government's day-to-day business well enough. States did contribute to the Confederation treasury. And Congress solved one conflict of interest big enough to have torn apart many a stronger federal government.

The issue was the land between the Appalachians and the Mississippi River. Who owned it? The Treaty of Paris said that the United States did. But seven colonial charters said that seven of the thirteen states were the owners. Their claims overlappped. The charters, which were still lawful, had been drafted between 1606 and 1732 by British officials with little knowledge of North American geography and less regard for what their predecessors in drawing boundaries had already given away.

So, Virginia's colonial charter (the oldest) gave that state boundaries that flared north at the crest of the Appalachians, encompassing the northern half of the western lands. New York claimed the same territory and land farther south than Virginia's. Connecticut conceded that New York's and Pennsylvania's charters, both drafted later than Connecticut's, had removed the area within New York and Pennsylvania from Connecticut's colonial land grant. However, Connecticut claimed that a "western reserve" in what is now northern Ohio, Indiana, and Illinois was still its property. Massachusetts, North Carolina, South Carolina, and Georgia also had charter-based claims on the West.

The snarl was complicated further by fears in the six states having no western claims: New Hampshire, Rhode Island, New Jersey, Pennsylvania, Delaware, and Maryland. Understandably, citizens of those states worried that the landed states would finance their governments indefinitely by selling their western lands, reducing state taxes to next to nothing,

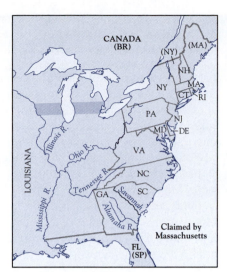

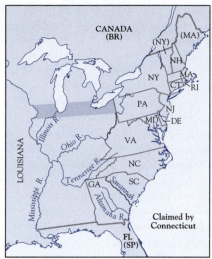

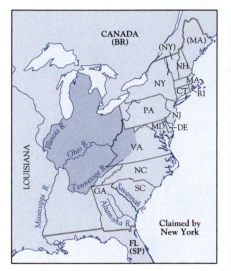

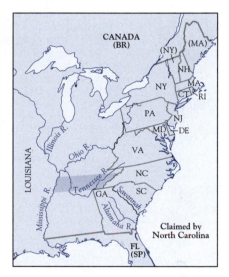

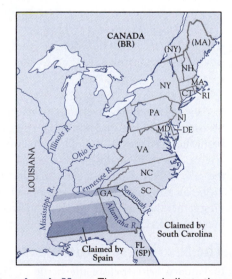

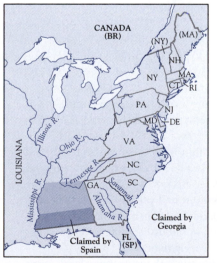

MAP 10:1 **The Western Lands Mess.** These maps indicate the mess of conflicts in state claims to western lands. Thus, the charters of the Massachusetts and Connecticut colonies set their western boundaries at the Pacific. Both states conceded that royal grants to New York and Pennsylvania took precedence over their charters but insisted that their claims resumed at those states' western boundaries. Virginia's grant of land from the king in 1606 predated every other colony's claim and was never explicitly superseded.

It would have been politically impossible to untangle the snarl to the satisfaction of all. The dispute—and the prize was a rich one—could be resolved only by force (Connecticut and Pennsylvania settlers came close to a battle in Pennsylvania's Wyoming Valley) or by what was actually done: All states with western claims gave them up to the Confederation.

Laying Out the Land

A traveler flying across the United States will notice that, once west of the Appalachians, the country is laid out geometrically. Except when the terrain is defiantly uncooperative, as in the Rocky Mountains—property lines and the highways that follow them are straight lines; farms and ranches are squared, neatly aligned north and south and east and west. This regimented landscape is a legacy of the Northwest Ordinances.

Using lines of latitude as boundaries dated back to the 1630s. Many east to west borders between colonies, beginning with the Massachusetts-Connecticut, were straight lines because the officials in London who drafted colonial charters were ignorant of American geography. In Ireland where, during the same years, they were laying out properties, they could employ well-mapped rivers, ridge lines, and other natural features as boundaries. Of the North American lands they knew next to nothing.

By the late 1600s, colonials were adopting geometric political and property lines for the sake of tidiness and convenience. The streets of Charleston, Philadelphia, and Savannah intersected at right angles. Massachusetts Bay colony, Connecticut, and New Hampshire laid out townships founded after about 1650 using straight lines so as to keep western settlement orderly, each new township

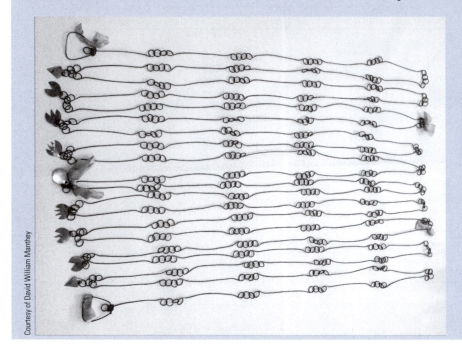

Courtesy of David William Manthey

A Gunter's chain, a unique surveyor's tool. The chain was 22 yards (66 feet) long; 80 chains equaled a mile. Twenty-five links equaled a "perch," a surveyor's term for a rod or pole (16.5 feet), then a common measure of length. On some Gunter's chains, every twenty fifth link was marked; on this one, every tenth link is marked.

thus attracting people of the landless states to emigrate. On these grounds, Maryland refused to sign the Articles of Confederation until 1781.

There was an obvious solution to the problem, suggested by John Dickinson as early as 1776. However, it called on human beings to give up wealth for the sake of an ideal, the union of the states. Dickinson had proposed that the states with claims to western lands cede them to the Confederation (as the Treaty of Paris would do) so that all of the states shared in the benefits of owning them.

Remarkably, Virginia, the state with the strongest legal claims to the western lands, was willing to give them up. Virginia's political leaders had good reasons to sacrifice in order to keep the Confederation together. It was the largest and richest state with a third of the country's population and a third of its commerce. Its first citizen, George Washington, was the first citizen of the United States. Other Virginians played prominent roles

in the Confederation government even though the state cast the same single vote that other states did. Finally, it was commonly believed that free republican institutions could not survive in countries—states—that were the size of empires. For the sake of hard-won independence and the Confederation, Virginia's leaders preferred to see new states carved out of the West rather than endless bickering and likely interstate conflict in defense of a colonial land grant 160 years old.

The Northwest Ordinances

In January 1781 (before the battle of Yorktown), Virginia ceded the northern part of its claims to what would come to be called the national domain. Within a few years, all the states with western claims except Georgia followed suit. (Georgia held out long after it had become absurd to do so, until 1802.) In 1792, Virginia added what became the state of Kentucky to its cession.

abutting a township already established. (Some townships in New Hampshire, oddly, were parallelograms.)

The Northwest Ordinance of 1785 virtually ignored natural features in surveying the Northwest Territory. It called for crisscrossing the Territory north to south and east to west with straight lines forming squares. In 1785, Thomas Hutchins was commissioned to survey the "first seven ranges" of the Territory in what is now eastern Ohio in squares. (A "range" was a north–south stack of 36 square mile townships.) His starting point was the high water mark of the Ohio River opposite the border between Pennsylvania and Virginia (now West Virginia). Arriving at what was then wilderness in August, Hutchins used a navigational instrument, either a Davis Quadrant or a sextant (invented in Philadelphia in 1731), to identify this point as north latitude 40 degrees, 38 minutes, 27 seconds, written 40°, 38', 27". (Hutchins's calculation later proved to be slightly off, but not so much that, had he been captaining a ship at sea, he would have missed even a tiny island.)

After marking the spot, Hutchins returned in September with eight of the thirteen surveyors Congress had authorized for the job. (Each state was supposed to send one.) He hired about thirty men to fell trees so as to have clear sight lines and to handle the heavy and cumbersome "Gunter Chains" that, along with compasses and theodolites, were the surveyor's peculiar tools.

A theodolite was a telescope with a plumb line for positioning it and cross hairs for precise sighting. A Gunter's chain consisted of 100 links each just under 8 inches in length so that it was 22 yards (66 feet) long. To us, the "chain" is an awkward, even absurd standard of measure. In fact, it was ingeniously suited to measuring land.

Twenty-two yards was equal to 4 rods (surveyors called them "perches") of 16.5 feet. The "rod" has just about vanished as a measure today, but it was an everyday term in the eighteenth-century; 25 "links" was a much more convenient measure for calculation than 16.5 feet.

Eighty chains (320 perches) was a mile on the button. A square mile—called a "section" by the Northwest Ordinances, a term still in use today—equaled 640 acres. An acre equaled 40 square perches. Once you got the hang of it, the dimensions of the Gunter chain made excellent sense.

Hutchins's crew made little progress in 1785. The had run one line for only 4 miles when they disbanded for fear that Indians, who understood very well what the survey meant, were about to attack them. Hutchins returned to Ohio only in August 1786 with twelve surveyors (Delaware never did send one) and a larger crew of axemen and chainmen, all of them armed. They surveyed four of the seven ranges when, again, Indians scared them off. They finished the job in 1787 at a cost to the government of $14,876.43.

The "first seven ranges"—minimum parcel a section at a minimum cost of $1 per acre—went on sale immediately in New York, which had replaced Philadelphia as the capital. Speculators hoping to make a fortune in real estate (an eternal dream) purchased 108,431 acres for a total of $176,000; the more desirable land sold for more than $1 per acre. The first recorded buyer of a piece of what would be called the national domain was one John Martin who paid the minimum for 640 acres: Section 20 of Township 7, in Range 4. The historic site is about 10 miles west of Wheeling, West Virginia.

This remarkably generous act—European princes went to war to grab parcels of land the size of a few football fields from their neighbors—was followed by a series of congressional acts that were equally novel: the Northwest Ordinances of 1784, 1785, and 1787. These laws created procedures by which five future states—equal in all ways to the thirteen original states—would, once they were settled, be carved from the "Northwest Territory" north of the Ohio River and east of the Mississippi. (Those states are Ohio, Indiana, Michigan, Illinois, and Wisconsin.) The Ordinance of 1785 provided for the survey of the Territory and the orderly sale of the lands.

In the Northwest Ordinances, the United States asserted that the country would have no colonies subordinate to the states as the thirteen colonies had been subordinate to Great Britain. When the population of a "territory" equaled the population of the smallest existing state (Delaware in 1787) and fulfilled a few other requirements, that territory would be admitted to the Confederation as a state. No new states were admitted during the Confederation period, but the principles laid down in the Northwest Ordinances were adopted by the government established by the Constitution of 1787.

Although he was absent as Minister to France, Thomas Jefferson was one of the early architects of the Northwest Ordinances. He claimed that it had been his idea to forbid slavery in the Northwest Territory, which was enacted in the Ordinance of 1787, reserving the land for independent family farmers, by protecting them from the impossibility of competing with slaveowners. In fact, Timothy Pickering of Massachusetts, later Jefferson's bitterest critic, authored the absolute prohibition of slavery in the Northwest. Jefferson's proposal banned slavery in the Territory *after 1800*. Had his plan been adopted, slavery might have been too firmly established north of the Ohio River to be abolished.

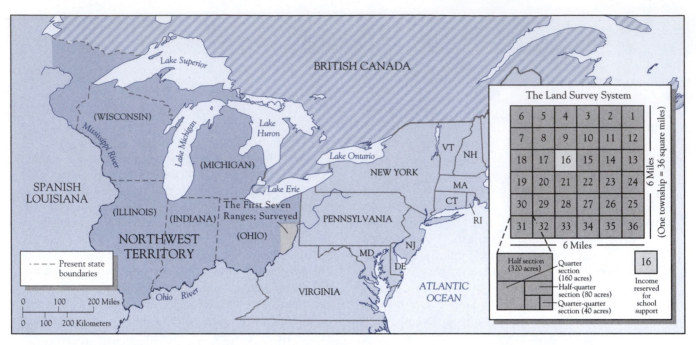

MAP 10:2 **The Northwest Terrritory and the Rectangular Survey.** The "rectangular survey" system. An American innovation, it provided for orderly disposition of Confederation-owned land to settlers. By dividing the western domain geometrically, all the land, and not just prize parcels, was sold in square sections (square miles) to speculators who subdivided the land into smaller squares for sale to settlers. The rectangular survey was later applied to the Louisiana Purchase and the Mexican Acquisition except where land claims under French and Mexican rule were judged valid.

Metes and Bounds

Yet another novelty of the Ordinances was a methodical system of surveying and selling the western lands. During the colonial period, and after independence in territory not regulated by the Northwest Ordinance, property lines were described by metes and bounds. That is, a settler located the land he wanted; then, at the land office, he described it by referring to boundaries to adjacent properties that were already deeded. and to natural features: creeks, outcroppings of rock, and even trees as in this legal description of a 140-acre parcel in Kentucky:

> Beginning at the mouth of a branch at an ash stump thence up the creek south 20 poles to 2 beach, two beech trees thence east 41 poles to a small walnut in Arnett's line, thence north 50 east 80 poles to a linn hickory dogwood in said line, thence north 38 poles to an ash, thence west 296 poles with Potts's line till it intersects with Tolly's line, thence south 30 west 80 poles to a whiteoak and sugar [maple], thence east 223 poles to beginning.

(*Branch* was another word for a creek. *Pole* was a synonym for a rod, 16.5 feet, a measure now rarely used but an everyday term in the eighteenth century.)

A problem with describing a parcel of land by metes and bounds was that settlers left on their own selected only prime farmland and excluded steep hillsides, rocky ground, marshes, and other wasteland from their property. Once established, they did not really waste the wasteland. They quarried rock and gravel from it, cut timber and firewood there, and grazed livestock on it. But no one had paid for it, and no one paid taxes on it.

The Rectangular Survey

To avoid this in the Northwest Territory, Congress adopted the rectangular survey. Before land was made available for purchase, surveyors crisscrossed it with straight lines creating townships six miles square, which, in turn, were subdivided (also in squares) into thirty-six "sections" of one square mile (640 acres). Buyers located the tract they wanted, but they had to purchase an entire square section, hillsides and swamps as well as fertile, level farmland. The government was not left holding pockets of unsellable, untaxable land.

A section, the smallest tract that could be purchased under the Northwest Ordinance at a minimum of a dollar an acre, was far more land than a family needed or could make use of. And, in most cases, $640 was more than pioneering farmers, poor almost by definition, could afford to spend. Congress was, in effect, selling to developers, speculators who could afford to buy land in sections and subdivide them into farm-size parcels for resale at a profit. This was not necessarily a law intended to enrich speculators. Congress simply did not want to involve the government in the headaches of retail sales. Congress did remember the educational needs of the communities that would emerge in the Territory. Section 16, right in the middle of each township, was withheld from sale. Income from renting out the land in that section was to be used to fund schools.

DIFFICULTIES AND ANXIETIES

Despite its achievements, disillusionment with the Confederation grew steadily. Prominent Americans like Alexander Hamilton of New York and George Washington of Virginia no longer thought of New York and Virginia as their country. (Hamilton, born and raised in the West Indies, never did.) They vested their pride, loyalties, and hopes in the United States and, in their eyes, the provincialism and pettiness of the individual states were close to pulling the country apart. They believed that only a stronger central government could save the country.

Money Problems

Finance was a tenacious problem thanks to petty politics. Even during the war, when defeat might well ruin them, delegates in Congress bickered and connived, denying or delaying the funds the Continental army needed. Congress even dithered for hours as to whether a man who claimed a meager $222.60 for ferrying troops should be paid in full. Complicating the chronic shortage of funds was the fact that all thirteen states had to approve all taxation measures. In 1781, alone of the thirteen states, Rhode Island, home to just 2 percent of the country's population, refused to approve a very low tariff of 5 percent on imports. On another occasion, New York killed a tax bill that the other twelve states approved.

Because Congress was unable to levy taxes, it resorted to a mischievous means of paying the bills: printing ever larger amounts of paper money popularly known as "Continentals." In 1775, some $6 million in paper money was in circulation. Congress printed $63 million in 1778 and $90 million in 1779. Virtually no one (except soldiers who had no choice) accepted the bills at face value, even when they were still crisp from the printer. By 1783, $167 in Continentals were needed to purchase what one silver Spanish dollar bought. "Not worth a Continental" was a catch-phrase that long survived the Articles of Confederation.

Seven states also printed paper money. The assembly of Rhode Island, controlled by farmers in debt, churned it out in bulk. The state's money was worthless beyond its boundaries. Tales were told of creditors fleeing Rhode Island so that those who owed money to them could not pay their debts in the state's legal tender. Merchants—including Rhode Island's—needed a sound currency valid in every state and accepted abroad. Such a currency, they believed with good reason, needed a strong, sound central government backing it.

Getting No Respect

Britain refused to turn over a string of Great Lakes forts as the Treaty of Paris required. Nor did the British send a minister (ambassador) to America. A British diplomat joked that it was too expensive to outfit thirteen men with homes and the other accoutrements of office in the thirteen sovereign states. In London, the American minister, John Adams, was openly mocked when he acted with the dignity of a legate.

There were insults elsewhere. A world-traveling American sea captain said that the United States was regarded "in the same light, by foreign nations, as a well-behaved negro is in a gentleman's family," that is, as an inferior scarcely to be noticed. The Barbary states of northern Africa seized American ships and seamen with impunity. These Muslim principalities—Tunis, Algiers, Tripoli, and Morocco—lived by seizing the cargos and enslaving the crews of countries with which they were "at war"—all Christian nations by Barbary definitions—unless a treaty had been neotiar negotiated, that is, money paid to the Barbary states.

The Barbary pirates were no problem for Americans as long as they were part of the British Empire. Great Britain paid annual tribute in return for "protection" from the African corsairs. With independence, Americans lost their immunities; indeed, Britain encouraged the Barbary states to seize American ships. There was a flurry of patriotic indignation when, in October 1785, a Moroccan pirate seized the *Betsey*, enslaving ten seamen, and a short time later, when Algiers

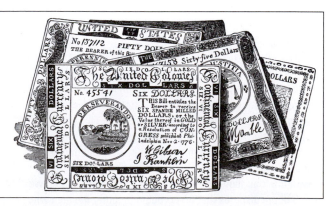

North Wind Picture Archives

Confederation era currency. The bills were known as "continentals." "Dollar" as a denomination was borrowed from the Spanish. However, the Spanish unit was subdivided into eighths, the famous "pieces of eight." The division of the continental dollar into sixths was a British survival as reflected in the famous British six pence coin and the division of its shilling into twelve pence (twice six). The dollar was decimalized (100 cents to the dollar) in 1791.

seized the *Dauphin* and *Maria* with twenty-one passengers and crew.

Naval action was out of the question; the United States had no navy. So, in 1785, Congress appropriated $80,000 to negotiate treaties with the Barbary states, instructing diplomats to keep the payments "as much below that sum as you possibly can." This was a delusion. France paid just one Barbary state, Morocco, $1.5 million (in today's money) for protection, Sweden $500,000 a year. It was a sorry state of affairs for the young men of the Revolution who had crowed of national greatness.

Meddling Foreigners

Squabbles among the states invited foreign meddling. In 1784, a Spanish diplomat, Diego de Gardoqui, played on the commercial interests of the northern states in the hopes of dividing the United States on geographic lines. He proposed to open Spanish ports to American ships if Congress gave up its treaty rights to export goods via the Mississippi River.

New Englanders and New Yorkers cared little about trade on the Mississippi. Their delegations tried to ram de Gardoqui's treaty through Congress. Had they succeeded, the southern states would have been under great pressure to go their own way. The Mississippi and Ohio River system was vital to the tens of thousands of southerners who had moved to what are now the states of Kentucky and Tennessee.

Britain schemed to detach Vermont from the United States. Claimed by both New York and New Hampshire, the isolated Green Mountain country functioned as an independent commonwealth during the 1780s, dominated by Ethan and Levi Allen, two Revolutionary War veterans. The Allens tried to negotiate a treaty with the British that would have tied Vermont more closely to Canada. The Green Mountains were thinly populated, but an independent Vermont protected by Great Britain would drive a salient more than 100 miles into the United States. Congress was powerless to stop the Allens; the Continental Army had shrunk to 700 soldiers, fewer men than Allen could have mobilized within a month. Only because the British failed to act decisively did the project fall through.

The Oyster War

When a waterway is a boundary, the actual dividing line is drawn at the *thalweg*, the deepest part of a creek, river, or bay. However, the boundary between Maryland and Virginia in the Chesapeake Bay and Potomac River was set as the high tide line on the Virginia side. This peculiar specification gave Marylanders the right to harvest oysters on Virginia shores. Virginia oystermen were not happy with the arrangement. They engaged in several shooting wars with the Marylander watermen. One such "oyster war" was one of the disputes that first brought together the men who would eventually write the Constitution. Over the years, at least fifty oystermen were killed in the wars; the last known fatality was in 1959. Even today, Chesapeake watermen are forbidden to have firearms on their boats.

Calls for Change

A trivial conflict in domestic waters triggered the movement to overhaul the government. In March 1785, a small group of Marylanders and Virginians gathered at Mount Vernon, George Washington's home on the Potomac, to discuss the conflicting claims of Maryland's and Virginia's fishermen in the Chesapeake Bay. They were unable to come up with a boundary acceptable to the two states. They did, however, conclude that the problem was only one in a morass of disputes among the states and between the states and the Confederation. They invited all thirteen states to send delegates to a meeting the next year in Annapolis, Maryland, to discuss what might be done.

Five states responded, so decisive action was out of the question. Only Alexander Hamilton of New York was undiscouraged. He persuaded the other men who had wasted their time traveling to Annapolis to try again in more centrally located Philadelphia. They should prepare, Hamilton told them, to discuss all the "defects in the System of the Federal Government."

Hamilton and a few others, notably James Madison of Virginia, who was scarcely older than Hamilton, had more than jawing in mind. They intended a bloodless coup d'état, peacefully replacing the Articles of Confederation with a completely new frame of government. Rumors of their intentions spread and met less than universal approval. Virginia's Governor Patrick Henry, Madison's rival in state politics, said that he "smelled a rat" and refused to endorse the proposal. Rhode Island officially declared that the state would not participate. Hamilton's Philadelphia convention would likely have fizzled like the Annapolis meeting had it not been for a wave of protests in western Massachusetts that turned into armed rebellion.

The Shays Rebellion

Farmers in western Massachusetts resented the fact that the state's tax laws favored trade at the expense of agriculture. In 1786, hundreds of them held meetings at which they demanded that their property taxes be reduced. To make up for the loss of revenue, they called for the abolition of "aristocratic" public offices in the state government in Boston.

In several towns, angry crowds surrounded courthouses, harassed lawyers and judges, whom they considered parasites, and forcibly prevented the collection of debts. In September, a Revolutionary War veteran, Daniel Shays, led 2,000 armed men toward the state arsenal in Springfield.

Shays and his followers did not regard themselves as revolutionaries. They believed they were carrying on the spirit and struggle of the War for Independence against a privileged elite. Then minister in France, Thomas Jefferson agreed with them. "A little rebellion now and then is a good thing," he wrote to a friend. "The tree of liberty must be refreshed from time to time with the blood of patriots and tyrants." (So long as he was far from the scene, Jefferson was titillated by social disorder.)

The Shays Rebellion began as riotous behavior, beating up Massachusetts state officials, for example. But it evolved into an armed insurrection on a scale large enough to panic social conservatives all over the colonies.

North Wind Picture Archives.

The Shays Rebellion collapsed in December. But the men who were preparing to gather in Philadelphia the next summer, and some who were just considering it, determined not to risk another such crisis. To them, it was not Jefferson's pine tree of liberty that needed attention; it was the ailing oak of social stability and order. Washington, Hamilton, and conservative men like them believed that disorders like the uprising in Massachusetts were the inevitable consequence of weak government.

THE CONSTITUTION

The American Constitution has been hailed with a reverence that is sometimes religious. It "was intended to endure for ages to come," said John Marshall, the great Chief Justice of the Supreme Court. The Constitution, said Henry Clay, "was not made merely for the generation that then existed but for posterity—unlimited, undefined, and endless, perpetual posterity." British Prime Minister, William Gladstone called the Constitution "the most wonderful work ever struck off at a given time by the brain and purpose of man." Jefferson called the men who write it "demigods." Indeed, with all its anachronisms (which all have too many powerful defenders

to be eliminated) the Constitution has been a remarkably successful frame of government.

The Founding Fathers who designed, debated, and wrote the Constitution were infinitely richer in talents than any cohort of American politicians since. But they were not demigods. They were well-to-do, privileged, conservative, and plenty fallible human beings of their times who happened to find a good deal about their times alarming.

The Convention

The convention began on May 25, 1787. The fifty-five delegates almost immediately agreed that the Articles of Confederation could not, realistically, be revised. Ironically, it was

Social Butterfly

George Washington, the "star" of the Constitutional Convention, got his exercise by, almost all of the 128 days he was in Philadelphia, riding out for several hours at five o'clock each morning. He dined out 110 times, attended 69 afternoon teas, stepped out in the evening on 20 occasions to lectures, concerts, and plays, had four portraits painted, and went fishing at least once.

The National Archives

The Founding Fathers at Philadelphia. It is an imagined reconstruction of the scene painted after the Convention. No one who was not a delegate was admitted to the meeting room in Independence Hall. George Washington is presiding. Seated second from left is Benjamin Franklin. Neither of them played much of a role in the historic debates, Washington because he was uncomfortable with heady discussions, Franklin because he was old and fading. At 81, he had to be carried from his home in a sedan chair.

much easier to effect a coup d'état, to create a government from scratch, than it was to amend the Articles. Amendment required that all thirteen states concur. Rhode Island had already made it quite clear that it opposed change by refusing to send delegates to Philadelphia.

The Constitutional Convention met in secret first to last. For four months the delegates bolted the doors and sealed the windows of the Pennsylvania State House (Independence Hall)—which was a demigod-like sacrifice in Philadelphia's hot and humid summer. Every delegate swore not to discuss the proceedings with outsiders. George Washington, who presided, was furious when a page of a delegate's notes was found where anyone could have picked it up.

There was nothing sinister about the secrecy. The goal of the convention—a new frame of government—was common knowledge. The delegates sequestered themselves because they were conscious of the gravity of their work. As James Wilson of Pennsylvania said, "America now presents the first instance of a people assembled to weigh deliberately and calmly, and to decide leisurely and peaceably, upon the form of government by which they will bind themselves, and their posterity." No small business that: Never before had a nation been invented. There was also a practical reason for secrecy. The delegates were politicans. Successful politicians calculate their public utterances

so as to please or, at least, so as not to displease the people who elect them to office. The delegates to the convention, to their credit, wanted to voice their most candid opinions rather than, as politicians must do in public, truckle to popular prejudice.

Moreover, the delegates knew that there would be opposition to the constitution they wrote. Wilson said that "the people" were assembled in Independence Hall. The Constitution begins with the words "We the People of the United States." In fact, most of the Founding Fathers represented just one of several American political tendencies, and they knew it. They wanted their program complete before they had to debate its merits.

And a Partridge in a Pear Tree

Two days before the Founding Fathers signed the Constitution, they gathered at Philadelphia's City Tavern at a party honoring George Washington. They consumed seven bowls of punch (not a pineapple juice concoction but mostly alcohol), eight bottles of cider, eight bottles of whiskey, twelve bottles of beer, twenty-two bottles of port wine, fifty-four bottles of madeira, and sixty bottles of claret (what we would call Cabernet Sauvignon).

The Delegates

They finished in September 1787 whence most of the delegates scattered north and south to lobby for their states' approval. (A few delegates did not sign the document.) They were a formidable lot, all of them influential at home by virtue of their wealth, education, and political prominence. Of the fifty-five, only three—Benjamin Franklin; Roger Sherman of Connecticut, who had been a cobbler as a young man; and Alexander Hamilton, the illegitimate son of a ne'er-do-well merchant in the West Indies—had been weaned on anything less glittering than a silver spoon.

Careers devoted to justifying independence and creating state governments meant that many of the delegates were keen students of political philosophy. During the years just preceding the convention, James Madison augmented his library with 200 books on the subject. Just as important was the delegates' practical experience: seven had been governors; thirty-nine had sat in the Continental Congress.

Most of the Founding Fathers were quite young. Only nine signers of the Declaration of Independence were present (and three of them refused to sign the Constitution). Only Benjamin Franklin at 81 was antique. The other delegates averaged 40 years of age; ten were not yet 35 years; one was 26. Such youngsters had been barely old enough in 1776 to play minor roles in the war. They had been children during the Stamp Act crisis. They were heirs of the Revolution, not makers of it.

The youth of the Founding Fathers is of some importance in understanding the nature of the Constitution they wrote. Most of the delegates had not thought of themselves as colonials. By 1787, most wanted to think of themselves not as New Hampshiremen or South Carolinians, but as Americans. Unlike their more provincial forebears, they had moved freely and often from one state to another. In the Continental Army (a third of the delegates had been soldiers, mostly junior officers) and in the Confederation Congress, they met and formed relationships with men from other states. They thought in terms of a continent rather than of coastal enclaves looking back to a mother country for an identity.

Conservatives

Youth does not, as we are often told, equate with radicalism. The men who drew up the Constitution were conservatives in the classic (not the contemporary) meaning of the word. They did not believe with Thomas Jefferson (then in France) that human nature was essentially good and eternally malleable, that people and society were perfectible if left free. Most of the Founding Fathers feared the darker side of human nature that Jefferson refused to acknowledge. They believed that, without powerful institutional restraints, self-seeking individuals were quick to trample on the rights of others. To such conservatives, democracy and liberty did not go hand in hand. On the contrary, if "the people" were unchecked, they would destroy liberty, and a good deal more. Rufus King of New York defined democracy as "madness." John Adams who was also serving in Europe during the Convention,

© Copyright Yale University Art Gallery, "Alexander Hamilton" by John Trumbull

Alexander Hamilton was one of the youngest Founding Fathers. He thought the Constitution allowed the states too much power and the president too little. But he accepted the document in the spirit of give-and-take compromise that Benjamin Franklin asked of the delegates. And, for Hamilton, the imperfect Constitution was an infinite improvement on the Articles of Confederation, which he despised.

called rule by the masses of people "the most ignoble, unjust, and detestable form of government."

The most pessimistic of the lot was Alexander Hamilton. Sent by men who recognized his genius to King's College in New York (now Columbia University), Hamilton never returned to the West Indies. He quit college to serve Washington as an aide-de-camp during the war, impressing the general with his intelligence and, no doubt, with his political principles, for Washington too looked on democracy with distaste. Hamilton may never have actually said that the "people are a great beast," but the remark comes close to his feelings on the subject.

Had Hamilton been English, he would have defended those institutions that British conservatives believed helped to control the passions of the masses: the monarchy, the aristocracy, the established church, and the centuries-old accretion of law and custom that is the British constitution. In fact, Hamilton admired British culture and government. Like Edmund Burke, he thought of the American Revolution as a conservative movement. In rebelling, the Americans had defended traditional liberties against a reckless, innovative Parliament.

In the Constitution, Hamilton wanted to recapture some of what had been lost with independence. He suggested that the president and senators be elected for life, thus creating a kind of monarch and aristocracy. He was unable to sway his fellow delegates in this. Many of them shared Hamilton's sentiments, but they understood better than he ever would that Americans would not tolerate institutions that even hinted of aristocracy. What the majority of delegates did approve, and Hamilton accepted as preferable to "anarchy and convulsion," was a system of government that was partly democratic (by eighteenth-century standards) but in which democracy was limited. The government they created was, in John Adams's word, "mixed," a balance of the "democratical" principle (power in the hands of the many); the "aristocratical" (power in the hands of a few); and the "monocratical" (power in the hands of one).

Reading Assignment
Students asssigned to read the Constitution often complain that it is "too long." It is actually quite short, fewer than 10 pages in this book, including all the amendments. Oklahoma's state constitution runs on and on and on for 158 pages without amendments. Does anyone care to argue that it is the superior document?

Checks, Limits, Balances

The House of Representatives was "democratical." Representatives were elected frequently (every two years) by a broad electorate—most free, white, adult males. The Senate and the Supreme Court reflected the "aristocratical" principle. Senators were elected infrequently (every six years) and by state legislatures, not by popular vote. They were thus somewhat insulated from the fickleness of the crowd.

The Supreme Court was almost totally insulated from popular opinion. Justices were appointed by the president, but, once confirmed by the Senate, they were immune to his or the Senate's or the people's influence. Justices served for life. They could be removed from the bench only by a difficult impeachment process.

The "monocratical" principle was established in the presidency and was, therefore, the most dramatic break with the Confederation government. The president alone represented the whole nation, but he owed his power neither directly to the people nor to Congress. He was put into office by an electoral college that selected the president and then dissolved. How electors were chosen was left to each state.

An intricate web of checks and balances tied together the three branches of government. Only Congress could enact a law, and both democratic House and aristocratical Senate had to agree to every syllable. The president could veto an act of Congress if he judged it unconstitutional or adverse to the national interest. However, to check the president's power, Congress could override a veto by a two-thirds majority of both houses.

The judiciary was independent of both the executive and legislative branches of government, a significant innovation meant to insulate judges from political pressure. The Supreme Court was the final court of appeal. In time (this was not written into the Constitution), the Supreme Court established a quasi-legislative role of its own in the principle of judicial review; that is, in judging according to the law, the Supreme Court also interpreted the law. Implicit in this process was the power to declare a law unconstitutional and, therefore, void.

Finally, the Constitution could be amended, although the process of making changes was deliberately made difficult. An amendment may be proposed in one of two ways: Two-thirds of the states' legislatures can petition Congress to summon a national constitutional convention. Or, and this is the only method by which the Constitution has in fact been amended, Congress can submit proposals to the states. If three-fourths of the states ratify a proposed amendment, it becomes part of the Constitution.

The Federal Relationship

Another web of checks and balances defined the relationship between the central government and the states. Under the Articles, the United States was a confederation of independent states that retained virtually all the powers possessed by sovereign nations. Under the Constitution, the balance shifted, with preponderant powers going to the federal government. The states were not reduced to administrative districts, as Hamilton would have liked. Nationalistic sentiments may have been high in 1787, but local interests and jealousies were a long way from dead. If the Constitution were to win popular support, the states had to be accommodated.

Small states like Delaware, New Jersey, and Connecticut were particularly sensitive in this matter. If they were not to be bullied or even absorbed by larger, wealthier neighbors, delegates from the small states insisted, they must be accorded fundamental protections. These they received in the decision that states rather than population would be represented in the Senate. That is, each state elected two senators, no matter what its population. Virginia, the largest, was ten times as populous as Delaware but had the same number of senators. Without this "great compromise," which was accomplished only after intense debate in July 1787, the delegates from the small states would have gone home. As it was (again excepting Rhode Island), the small states enthusiastically backed the Constitution.

The Constitution and Slavery

The question of slavery necessitated another compromise. Virtually none of the delegates from the northern states were sympathetic to the institution. Some, including Benjamin Franklin, Hamilton, John Jay, and Gouverneur Morris, were declared abolitionists. Jay actually purchased slaves in order to free them. Some Virginians like Washington regarded slavery as a curse on the country; a dozen years later, Washington freed all his slaves in his will. But with the African American population of the South so large, antislavery southerners feared that any gesture in the direction of emancipation

Three-Fifths

Defining a slave as three-fifths of a free person, as the Constitution does, is often described as racist, but it was not. A slave was accounted as three-fifths of a free black too, and the curious fraction originated in an economic and financial debate during the Confederation period, not the proportion of a slave's humanity. The question was: How much wealth did a slave produce as compared to a free worker? Northerners said "almost as much." Southerners said "very little; slaves were not productive workers." After bandying about figures varying from one-third to two-thirds, the debaters compromised on three-fifths (whence the bill under consideration failed to pass).

The three-fifths clause in the Constitution was to poison North–South relations because it gave southern voters much more representation in Congress and the electoral college than it gave northerners. (A master of 100 slaves cast, in effect, sixty-one votes.) When the fraction originated, however, representation was not an issue. Under the Articles of Confederation, each state, no matter the size of its population, had one vote in Congress.

would mean social disorder far worse than Shays's Rebellion. Only the South Carolinians and Georgians, as a group, can be described as *pro*slavery.

Even their sensibilities had been jarred by a decade talking about liberty. Tellingly, the word *slave* does not appear in the Constitution (although that nicety was the work of the outspoken abolitionist, Gouverneur Morris, who wrote the final draft of the document). But slavery, unnamed, was basic to it. In Article I, Section 9, which guaranteed the importation of slaves for twenty years, they are referred to obliquely as "such Persons as any of the States now existing find proper to admit." Elsewhere, slaves are identified as "all other persons."

This was the term employed in the "three-fifths compromise" by which a North–South conflict was averted. The northern delegates wanted to count slaves for purposes of apportioning taxation among the states on the grounds that their labor produced taxable wealth, but not when apportioning seats in the House of Representatives. Slaves, after all, did not vote and their interests could not be said to be represented, like the interests of white women, by fathers, husbands, and sons. Some southern delegates, with nothing resembling a comparable argument except a threat to oppose the Constitution without a concession, wanted to count slaves when apportioning representatives but not when apportioning taxes.

For the northern delegates, it was a matter of forgetting about the new Constitution or making a distasteful deal. Each slave in a state was counted as three-fifths of a person in apportioning that state's tax burden and its representation in the House. Politically, this gave southern white voters considerably more power than northern voters, a fact fraught with undesirable consequences.

RATIFICATION

The Constitution was to go into effect when conventions in nine states ratified it. Three did so immediately, Delaware and Connecticut almost unanimously, thanks to the "great compromise." Pennsylvania's ratification also came quickly, but in a manner that dramatized the widespread opposition to the new government and the determination of the supporters of the Constitution, who called themselves "federalists," to have their way.

Federalist Shenanigans

"Federalist" was something of a misnomer since they proposed to replace a genuinely federated government with a more centralized one. In Pennsylvania, the federalists secured ratification only by physically forcing two anti-federalist members of the state convention to remain in their seats when they tried to leave the hall. This irregular maneuver—not that the anti-federalist strategy of paralyzing the convention was admirable—was necessary to guarantee a quorum so that the federalist majority could legally register a pro-Constitution vote.

In Massachusetts, anti-federalists claimed that scheduling the election of delegates to the ratification convention in mid-winter prevented many snowbound anti-federalist farmers from getting to the polls. Even then, ratification was approved in Massachusetts by the narrow margin of 187 to 168 only because several delegates pledged to vote against the Constitution changed their minds and voted for it.

In Virginia in June 1788, Edmund Randolph, an announced anti-federalist, changed his vote and took a coterie of followers with him; the federalist victory in Virginia was by a vote of only 89 to 79. A switch of six votes would have reversed the verdict in the largest state, and that, in turn, would have kept New York in the anti-federalist camp.

Unpredictable Critic

Mercy Otis Warren, sister of hell-raiser James Otis and wife of another prominent patriot, was of a type familiar today. In the vanguard of many radical causes, her blood was the bluest Massachusetts produced and she knew it. She condescended even to those just a notch below her in social status like her friends, John and Abigail Adams. Her condescensions were subtle because her pen was among the deftest of the era. Warren wrote several plays reviling loyalists and a history of the Revolution.

Mercy Otis Warren was not happy with America under the Articles of Confederation. She called the country a "restless, vigorous youth, prematurely emancipated from the authority of a parent, but without the experience necessary to direct him to act with dignity or discretion."

That sounds like a federalist in the making, but Warren was no federalist. She regarded the Constitution as a plot, sinister in ways she (untypically) never quite defined in writing.

In New York, a large anti-federalist majority was elected to the ratifying convention. After voting to reject the Constitution, the convention reversed its decision when news of Virginia's approval reached the state. Still, the vote was closer than it was in Massachusetts and Virginia, a razor-thin 30 to 27.

There is good reason to believe that if an open, democratic, countrywide referendum had been held in 1787, the Constitution would have been rejected.

The Anti-Federalists

North Carolina was decisively anti-federalist. Only in November 1789, eight months after the new government began to function, did the state reluctantly join the Union. Rhode Island held out longer, until May 1790. Rhode Island became the thirteenth state only when Congress threatened to pass a tariff that would have shut its produce out of the United States.

Today, when the Constitution has worked successfully for 200 years, it can appear that the anti-federalists of 1787 were cranks. In fact, their reasons for favoring the Articles of Confederation were firmly within the tradition of the Revolution. Among the anti-federalists were fiery old patriots who feared that any centralized power was an invitation to tyranny. Samuel Adams, still padding about Boston shaking his head at moral decadence, opposed the Constitution until Massachusetts federalists, needing the old lion's support, agreed to press for a national bill of rights. In Virginia, Patrick Henry battled James Madison around the state. Some of Henry's arguments against the Constitution were rather bizarre. At one point he concluded that the Constitution was an invitation to the pope to set up court in the United States. Henry had his peculiarities.

But he and other anti-federalists also argued, with plenty of evidence behind them, that free republican institutions could survive only in small countries such as Switzerland (itself a federation), the city-states of ancient Greece, and, of course, an independent and sovereign Virginia. When the Roman republic became an empire, they pointed out, Rome became despotic. The same thing would happen, anti-federalists warned, to a large, centrally governed United States.

Answering such arguments was the federalists' most difficult task. Madison, Hamilton, and John Jay of New York took it upon themselves to do so in eighty-five essays later collected under the name the *Federalist Papers*—which is still a basic textbook of political philosophy. They argued that a powerful United States would guarantee liberty. These ingenious essays, however, were probably less important to the federalist victory than their agreement, quite reluctant in Hamilton's case, to add a bill of rights to the Constitution.

The Bill of Rights

The Constitutional Convention paid little attention to the rights of citizens. The Founding Fathers were by no means hostile to individual rights, but their preoccupation in 1787 was strengthening the government. They assumed that the rights of individuals were protected in the state constitutions.

Because the Constitution created a national government superior to the states, however, anti-federalists like Samuel Adams and Edmund Randolph agreed to scrap their opposition to ratification only when the rights that had been adopted by the states since 1776 were guaranteed on the federal level. The Bill of Rights, the first ten amendments to the Constitution, was ratified in 1791 but tacitly agreed upon during the ratification process. The First Amendment guaranteed freedom of religion, speech, the press, and peaceable assembly. The Second Amendment guaranteed the right to bear arms. The Third and Fourth Amendments guaranteed security against the quartering of troops in private homes (still a sore point with older Americans) and against unreasonable search and seizure.

The famous Fifth Amendment is a guarantee against being tried twice for the same crime and, in effect, against torture. It is the basis of a citizen's right to refuse to testify in a trial in which he or she is a defendant. (British practice did not permit a defendant to testify.) The Sixth Amendment also pertains to criminal trials. It guarantees the right to a speedy trial and the right to face accusers: no secret witnesses. The Seventh and Eighth Amendments likewise protect the rights of a person who is accused of committing a crime.

The Ninth and Tenth Amendments are catchalls. They state that the omission of a right from the Constitution does not mean that the right does not exist, and that any powers not explicitly granted to the federal government are reserved to the states.

FURTHER READING

Classics Charles A. Beard, *An Economic History of the Constitution*, 1913; Merrill Jensen, *The Articles of Confederation: An Interpretation of the Social-Constitutional History of the American Revolution*, 1948, and *The New Nation: A History of the United States During the Confederation*, 1950.

General Gordon S. Wood, *The Creation of the American Republic, 1776–1787*, 1969, and *The Radicalism of the American Revolution*, 1991.

The Confederation Period Jackson T. Main, *The Sovereign States, 1775–1783*, 1973; Kenneth Silverman, *A Cultural History of the American Revolution*, 1976; Richard B. Morris, *The Forging of the Union, 1781–1789*, 1987; Willi P. Adams, *The First American Constitution*, 1988; Larry E. Tise, *The American Counterrevolution: A Retreat from Liberty, 1783–1800*, 1998; David Szarmary, *Shay's Rebellion*, 1980; Leonard L. Richards, *Shay's Rebellion: The American Revolution's Final Battle*, 2002; Richard H. Kohn, *Eagle and Sword: The Federalists and the Creation of the Military Establishment in America, 1783–1802*, 1975. On surveying, see Andro Linklater, *Measuring America: How the United States Was Shaped by the Greatest Land Sale in History*, 2002.

The West Gregory E. Dowd, *A Spirited Resistance: The North American Indian Struggle for Unity, 1745–1815*, 1992; R. Douglas Hurt, *The Ohio Frontier: Crucible of the Old Northwest, 1720–1830*,

1996; Peter S. Onus, *Statehood and Union A History of the Northwest Ordinance,* 1987.

The Constitution Richard Beeman, Stephen Botein, and Edward C. Carter, *Beyond Confederation: Origins of the Constitution and American National Identity,* 1987; Herbert J. Storing, *What the Anti-Federalists Were For,* 1981; Richard B. Bernstein, *Are We to Be a Nation?: The Making of the Constitution,* 1987; Morton White, *Philosophy, the Federalist, and the Constitution,* 1987; Gary Nash, *Race and Revolution,* 1990; Thornton Anderson, *Creating the Constitution,* 1993; Jack N. Rakove, *Original Meanings: Politics and Ideas in the Making of the Constitution,* 1996; Akhil Reed Amar, *The Bill of Rights: Creation and Reconstruction,* 1998; Saul Cornell, *The Other Founders: Anti-Federalism and the Dissenting Tradition in America, 1788–1828,* 1999; Michael Kammen, *A Machine That Would Go by Itself: The Constitution in American Culture,* 1986; Robert A. Rutland, *The Ordeal of the Constitution: The Anti-Federalists and the Ratification Struggle of 1787–1788,* 1966; Garry Wills, *Explaining America, The Federalist,* 1981, and *"Negro President": Jefferson and the Slave Power,* 2003.

Biographies Lance Banning, *The Sacred Fire of Liberty: James Madison and the Founding of the Federal Republic,* 1995; Stuart Leibiger, *Founding Friendship: George Washington, James Madison, and the Creation of the American Republic,* 1999; Richard Brookhiser, *Founding Father: Rediscoverng George Washington,* 1996; Joseph J. Ellis, *Founding Brothers: The Revolutionary Generation,* 2000, and *His Excellency, George Washington,* 2004; Ron Chernow, *Alexander Hamilton,* 2004; Walter Stahr, *John Jay: Founding Father,* 2005.

KEY TERMS

Use the following listing of key terms to review important figures, events, locations, and concepts covered in this chapter. A glossary of these terms is available on *The American Past* companion Web site: www.cengage.com/history/conlin/tap9e

Northwest Ordinances, p. 166   **The Shays Rebellion, p. 179**

ONLINE RESOURCES

Find additional resources, including primary source documents, images, interactive maps, simulations, chapter review exercises, and Internet links at

***The American Past* companion Web site**
www.cengage.com/history/conlin/tap9e

American History Resource Center
http://ushistory.wadsworth.com/

Chapter 11

We the People

Putting the Constitution to Work
1789–1800

Reproduced from the Collections of the Library of Congress

The father of his country.

—*Francis Bailey*

First in war, first in peace, first in the hearts of his countrymen.

—*Henry Lee*

America has furnished to the world the character of Washington. And if our American institutions had done nothing else, that alone would have entitled them to the respect of mankind.

—*Daniel Webster*

Everyone knew who would be elected to the presidency, an office unlike any under the Articles of Confederation. George Washington towered in prestige so far above every other American that all sixty-nine members of the electoral college chose him. After a slow, triumphal procession from Virginia to New York City, then the capital, Washington took the presidential oath on April 30, 1789.

As originally written, the Constitution provided that each member of the electoral college voted for two candidates *for president,* at least one of whom was from a state other than the elector's. There was no election for the vice presidency. The presidential candidate who finished second in the electoral college stepped into that position. John Adams believed that his services to the country entitled him to the honor; 34 electors, almost half of the total, agreed. Adams was miffed that the total was so low; he was always vain, this time he had a right to feel insulted.

THE FIRST PRESIDENCY

Washington was more than first in the hearts of his countrymen. He was possessed of qualities perhaps indispensable to overseeing the launch of a government designed from scratch. He was committed to the republican ideal. His sense of duty was the very core of his personality. He was aware that events had made him one of Western civilization's most revered figures, which increased his obligation to act wisely and prudently. He knew that, as first president, he would set a precedent with every deed, from signing an act of Congress into law to the manner in which he greeted a guest at dinner.

Setting Precedents

It is fortunate that Washington was a dedicated republican, and it was by no means a given that he should have been. The advisor he trusted most, Alexander Hamilton, was not so dedicated. Nor were some members of the Order of Cincinnatus, a society of Revolutionary War officers. Hamilton had wanted the president to serve for life, an elected monarch in fact if not in name. Some Cincinnati wanted to make him a military dictator. When the new government was mustering itself in New York in 1789, it was proposed that Washington be addressed as "Your Elective Majesty." He toyed with "His High Mightiness" but settled for "Mr. President."

Washington was not, however, "just one of the boys," as recent presidents strive to be. He was fussy about the trappings of office. He dressed his servants in livery (clothing identifying them as servants) and powdered wigs. He was driven about

Washington was feted all the way from Mount Vernon to his inauguration in New York City, then the nation's capital. He crossed the Hudson in a splendidly decorated barge and took the presidential oath on a balcony cheered by thousands in the street below.

New York in a splendid carriage drawn by matched cream-colored horses. When he toured the country—Washington visited every state while he was president—he stopped his unattractive overland coach before entering towns and mounted a fine, large charger that he sat on "straight as an Indian." He consciously affected the appearance and manners of a European prince. On a bet that he would not dare do it, Gouverneur Morris chummily slapped Washington on the back at a public function. The president stared him down with such iciness that Morris retreated stammering from the room. They were never again quite as cordial with one another as they had been. Morris said it was the costliest bet he ever won.

In being as much monument as man, Washington won an even greater respect than his generalship had earned him. No European nations feared the United States, but neither did they mistake George Washington for a head-scratching bumpkin.

The Cabinet

Washington was accustomed to wielding authority. Rarer qualities among men raised high by history were his awareness of his personal limitations and his receptivity to advice, even when it contradicted his own impulses. He did not resent brighter people as, for instance, George III did. Washington sought out intelligent and learned men and listened to them. When advisors disagreed, he insisted they hash out their arguments in his presence.

Political considerations entered into his appointments of the men who headed the five executive departments, who were soon collectively known as the cabinet. (The word does not appear in the Constitution.) He chose Edmund Randolph to be attorney general because Randolph had been an

The Federalist Presidents 1789–1801

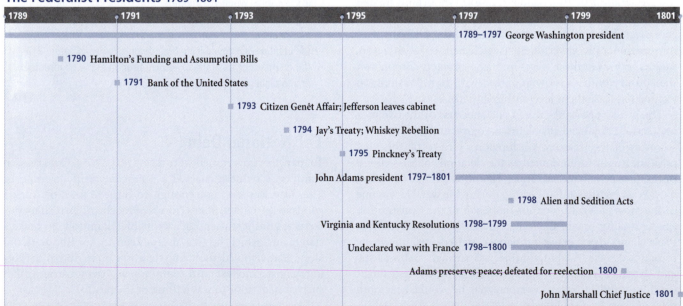

1789	1791	1793	1795	1797	1799	1801	

1789–1797 George Washington president

1790 Hamilton's Funding and Assumption Bills

1791 Bank of the United States

1793 Citizen Genêt Affair; Jefferson leaves cabinet

1794 Jay's Treaty; Whiskey Rebellion

1795 Pinckney's Treaty

John Adams president 1797–1801

1798 Alien and Sedition Acts

Virginia and Kentucky Resolutions 1798–1799

Undeclared war with France 1798–1800

Adams preserves peace; defeated for reelection 1800

John Marshall Chief Justice 1801

North Wind Picture Archives

The Cincinnati

Lucius Quinctius Cincinnatus was a Roman farmer who was twice made dictator for six months when enemies threatened the republic. Both times Cincinnatus was quickly victorious. Instead of exploiting the rest of his dictatorship remaining to enrich himself, he resigned and went back to his plow. Americans familiar with Roman history likened the selfless patriot George Washington to Cincinnatus.

At the end of the war, Continental Army officers organized the Society of the Cincinnati (the plural of Cincinnatus in Latin). The club was controversial from the start. The Cincinnati met secretly and membership was hereditary: only the first-born sons of members were eligible to join. Thomas Jefferson called the society "a nascent nobility."

Some of the Cincinnati discussed—no one knows how many or how seriously—setting George Washington up as a dictator. Washington quashed the idea as soon as he heard of it and the other Cincinnati grew long in the teeth without biting. They abandoned primogeniture, opening membership to all male descendants of Revolutionary officers. The society evolved into an organization "devoted to the principles of the Revolution, the preservation of history and the diffusion of historical knowledge," as which it exists today.

Military men wear medals. The old soldiers of the Order of the Cincinnati wore this one to identify themselves. The inscription reads: "All sacrificed to serve the republic."

anti-federalist, and Washington wanted to win anti-federalist support for the government. He named Samuel Osgood to be postmaster general so that Massachusetts, the only state to rival Virginia in importance, would have two cabinet members, as his own state of Virginia did.

But the other three men in the first cabinet Washington chose mainly because he respected their advice. Secretary of War Henry Knox (from Massachusetts) had been one of Washington's favorite generals and remained a friend. Secretary of State Thomas Jefferson (Virginia) was the author of the Declaration of Independence. More important, he had lived six years in France, America's ally, four years as minister. Moreover, Jefferson was widely considered a proponent of more democratic government (which neither Washington, Adams, nor Hamilton were) and had contacts throughout the country with those who agreed with him. Washington wanted to please them too (within limits).

The most important cabinet post, because of the complex and serious financial problems the government faced, was secretary of the treasury. Washington's pick to fill this vital position was as foreordained as the electoral college's choice of the first president. Alexander Hamilton of New York had been Washington's aide-de-camp during the war. He was one of the most energetic workers on behalf of the Constitution (he wrote fifty-one of the long and closely argued Federalist Papers) and his expertise in financial matters was universally recognized. Like Washington, he was strongly nationalistic and conservative. Did Washington know, when he brought Hamilton and Jefferson together, that he would hear both sides of every basic political question argued as articulately as they could possibly be argued? If not, he was soon to learn it.

Government on the Cheap

Hamilton's 5 percent tariff provided enough revenue to finance the federal government in normal times because the government was so small. Farmer George Washington presided over a larger staff at Mount Vernon than President George Washington did in Philadelphia. The Treasury Department had 39 employees, the State Department five. Secretary of War Henry Knox made do with one clerk and one secretary.

The government grew slowly. State had only two employees in the capital when Washington retired and War employed just twelve civilians. Treasury had several hundred employees, but most were customs agents scattered in seaports. When, in 1799, the capital was moved from Philadelphia to Washington, DC, the entire archives of the executive branch of the government fit into eight packing crates.

The National Debt

To pay the government's running expenses, Congress, at Hamilton's request, enacted a 5 percent tariff on imports. The duty was low, not enough to impede sales of foreign goods in the United States (mostly French and British manufactures) but it was enough to enable Hamilton "to make a statement," which he was always keen to do. Rhode Island alone had crippled the Confederation government by voting against a modest tariff. Hamilton was demonstrating that such obstructionism was a thing of the past.

Revenue from the tariff was not enough to sustain the government in a crisis, an Indian war, for example. The

Reproduced from the Collections of the Library of Congress

The first cabinet in a rather inept drawing. From left to right: the president, Secretary of War Henry Knox (depicted at less than his usual 300 pounds), Attorney General Edmund Randolph, Secretary of State Thomas Jefferson, and Secretary of the Treasury Alexander Hamilton. There was a postmaster general but he was not then considered a member of the cabinet.

government, like all governments, would need to borrow money now and then—often! For that, the government had to have sound credit. Foreign governments, banks at home and abroad, and even individuals who could afford to buy low denomination government bonds, had to be confident that the United States was a good risk, that it could raise the money to repay their loans.

In 1789, the United States was a terrible financial risk. The Confederation Congress had been badly delinquent in repaying the money it had borrowed. The United States owed $12 million to foreigners and $44 million to Americans. Creditors were, with good reason, wary. Would the new government repudiate the old government's obligations? It had happened often enough in the past, kings refusing to honor the debts of the kings they ousted.

In January 1790, Hamilton reassured the government's creditors by asking Congress to fund the entire Confederation debt at face value. That is, the government would retire Confederation bonds by exchanging new federal bonds, dollar for dollar (restructuring the debt, we might say) for them. The government would assert, with no immediate expenditure, its financial reliability. As for launching the new government with a large national debt, Hamilton said it would

be a blessing. He believed that the British government's perpetual indebtedness—and its steady payment of interest to creditors—explained the extraordinary economic growth of Great Britain during the eighteenth century. The treasury's constant repayment of loans plus interest had financed private investment in Great Britain and would do the same in the United States.

Few in Congress objected to funding the debt owed abroad at face value. Americans were cash poor. Big future loans would have to be floated in Europe. The Dutch and the French governments (and British bankers) must have confidence in the new government.

The First Debate: Funding

However, Hamilton's proposal to pay American creditors the face value of the Confederation paper they held met stiff resistance in Congress. The sticking point was speculation. Most of the domestic debt dated to the war years when, moved by patriotism among other things, thousands of Americans bought government bonds. Continental Army soldiers had been given promissory notes when there was no cash with which to pay them. As the years passed and the Confederation failed to redeem these obligations, many (perhaps most) lenders and veterans lost hope. They sold their claims on the government at big discounts to speculators willing to take a chance that, eventually, they would collect full value on the paper. For ordinary people strapped for cash, getting 20% or 30% on the dollar was better than getting nothing from a government bankrupt. By 1790, most Confederation obligations were in the strongboxes of financial adventurers.

Nor had all of them been so very adventurous. As James Madison explained in the House of Representatives in opposing the funding bill, some speculators, learning that Hamilton would propose payment of the debt at face value, had fanned out in the countryside, scouring villages and buying up dirt cheap—the war had been over for seven years, nine if dated from Yorktown—all the old bonds and soldiers' notes they could find. In our parlance, they had traded on "insider information."

Congress should not reward such parasitical profiteers, Madison said. He proposed to fund debts at face value (plus 4 percent annual interest) only when the people who presented them for redemption had themselves loaned the money to the government or fought in the army. Speculators who had bought the paper from the original creditors would get half face value.

Morally, Madison's argument was appealing. It rewarded those who had stepped forward during the times that tried men's souls and put financial manipulators on notice that the government would not reward them. Hamilton replied that morality was beside the point. At issue was the government's credit. By rewarding people with money—capitalists—which, unfortunate as it was, included speculators, his funding bill would encourage them to be lenders in the future. Hamilton believed that the support of the monied classes was key to the success of the new government.

However compelling Hamilton's realism was, it did not hurt that several dozen members of Congress stood to profit personally from his funding bill. Critics grumbled that Hamilton had tipped speculators off, but the evidence is that he did not. If he was indifferent to the integrity of financial manipulators, he guarded his own fastidiously. Funding was approved.

Bucks and Quarters

Buck was slang for a dollar before there was a United States. A Spanish dollar was the usual price paid to hunters for a buckskin.

In 1793, Congress adopted decimal coinage—100 cents to the dollar—to replace the eighths into which Spanish dollars were divided. Nevertheless, old habits died hard. Congress also instructed the U.S. Mint to coin quarter dollars. Quarters made little sense decimally, but they reflected the partition of a Spanish dollar into eight *reales,* the Hollywood pirate's "pieces of eight." Americans commonly referred to quarters as "two bits." ("Two bits, four bits, six bits, a dollar, all for our history professor stand up and holler.") The mint never coined a "bit," but stubborn traditionalists persisted in calling the dime a "short bit" (2½ ¢ short) to the end of the nineteenth century.

Assumption

Hamilton's second program had tougher sledding in Congress. He proposed that the federal government assume responsibility for and fund the debts that the states had contracted since independence, a total of $25 million. Hamilton's political motive was obvious: Assumption would demonstrate that the new Constitutional government was serious about its credit as many of the states had not been. Hamilton the nationalist meant to reduce the prestige of the states relative to the federal government.

What looked on the face of it to be a bonanza for all the states, however, was not. Virginia, with almost twice as many congressmen as the second largest state, had been religiously paying off its war debt. James Madison pointed out that Virginians, having been taxed by the state to retire Virginia's debt, would, if the federal government assumed all states' debts, be taxed by the federal government to pay off the debts of states that had shirked their responsibilities. His arithmetic showed that while assumption would relieve Virginia of $3 million in debt, Virginians would pay $5 million in federal taxes to retire the assumed debt of the other states.

Just enough congressmen from other states joined Virginia's large delegation in the House of Representatives to defeat assumption by a vote of 31 to 29. That was too narrow a margin to send Hamilton home to bed, particularly because he had a horse to trade that Virginians wanted. Madison, Secretary of State Thomas Jefferson, George Washington, and many other southerners wanted the permanent capital of the United States to be located in the South.

Horse Trade: Assumption for the Capital

In 1790, New York, Hamilton's home town, was the nation's capital. However, everyone except some New Yorkers agreed that it was not going to stay there. New York was not central. It was too far to the north, just 300 miles from Boston, the northernmost city of any size, but 800 miles from Charleston, 900 from Savannah. Moreover, New York was not the national metropolis it is today. The city was a poor second to Philadelphia in size, sophistication, and amenities. As president, Washington had a fine, centrally located home, but Vice President John Adams had to go out of town to find a suitable house to rent. Secretary of State Jefferson roomed at a tavern; Speaker of the House James Madison lived at a boarding house.

Some twenty-five cities and towns, including tiny Trenton, New Jersey, and Frederick, Maryland, had put in bids to be the permanent capital. Philadelphia's bid was, of course, the best. It had been the capital during most of the Confederation period and was 100 miles south of New York, an easy trip by land or water from populous Virginia. But there was a problem—for southerners: Pennsylvania's hostility to the institution of slavery. Pennsylvania's gradual abolition program was well along. Manumissions were numerous. Many southern congressmen, whose domestic servants were slaves, were uneasy about bringing them to a city where almost all blacks were free.

In 1790, in part to mollify the southerners, the Pennsylvania legislature enacted a law providing that slaves accompanying their masters to the state would remain slaves. After six months in the state, a slave was legally free, but Congress did not sit for this long.

It was not enough to ease southern anxieties. If congressmen came and went, southerners serving in the executive branch did not. Moreover, the slaves congressmen brought to Philadelphia would, if only for months be living in a place where most blacks, with whom they could socialize, were free. They would learn of the six months' law and make contacts who would hide them when the day of their emancipation neared and their masters began to pack their suitcases. Some Philadelphia Quakers were already offering assistance in court to slaves with a legal claim to freedom. Indeed, during the 1790s, President Washington resorted to subterfuge to get several of his personal servants who knew the law back to Virginia. Had they walked off on their date of emancipation, he would have faced an embarrassment worse than Gouverneur Morris's slap on the back.

According to Thomas Jefferson, he hosted a dinner for Hamilton and Madison so that Hamilton could propose a deal to the Speaker of the House. Hamilton would deliver the votes of enough northern congressmen to locate the permanent capital on an undeveloped site on the Potomac River where slavery was legal. In return, while Madison himself would not vote for assumption—he had spoken against it vehemently—he would quietly inform other southern congressmen that the fix was in. Pennsylvania was compensated by the provision that, until the permanent capital was ready for occupancy, Philadelphia would have the honor. (Many Pennsylvanians believed that "Federal City" would never exist—the chosen site was hotter and more humid than Philadelphia and much of it was malarial marsh.)

The Granger Collection, New York

The First Bank of the United States in Philadelphia. Imposing in size, its classical design, was then avant-garde and deliberate. Size conveyed power and reliability. The classical facade hearkened to the republics of antiquity, with which Americans liked to identify

A National Bank

Hamilton had been an ardent patriot during the Revolution. He was also, however, a lifelong Anglophile. He admired British institutions including the monarchy and, even more, the Bank of England. Almost unique in Europe, it was a powerful central bank that handled the Crown's revenues, issued paper money, acted as a watchdog on other banks, and—for the asking—loaned the government whatever money it needed at interest rates far lower than other European governments had to pay.

The Bank of England's financial services to the Crown increased Britain's military power to far beyond what the nation's modest size warranted. For a century, Great Britain, with a population a fraction of the population of France and a much more modest agricultural base, fought the vaunted armies of France as an equal. Loans from the Bank of England paid for Prussia's pinning down France's armies in Europe during the French and Indian War and paid for the Hessian mercenaries during the Revolution. The Crown and the Bank of England had a mutually satisfactory relationship.

Hamilton envisioned a powerful United States based on a similar symbiosis. In 1791, he proposed that Congress charter, for twenty years, a Bank of the United States (BUS) patterned on the Bank of England. While it would be the repository of all the government's money, it was a private institution, financed by private investors. The president would name five of the bank's directors; twenty were to be elected by shareholders, men of Hamilton's monied classes again.

Hamilton pushed the bank through Congress without Jefferson's help. Indeed, Jefferson urged Washington to veto the bill. He argued that, in chartering the BUS, Congress had exceeded the powers granted it by the Constitution. Nothing in the document gave Congress and the president the authority to create such an institution.

Washington had presided at the Constitutional convention where, indeed, nothing had been said about national banks. He found Jefferson's reasoning convincing. But Hamilton won the day. The point, he argued in his response to Jefferson's argument, was that nothing in the Constitution *prohibited* Congress from chartering a national bank. The BUS, he said, was justified under Article I, Section 8, which authorized Congress "to make all laws which shall be necessary and proper for carrying into execution," among other things, the regulation of commerce, and to "provide for . . . the general welfare." Which, to Hamilton, the bank would do by using its powers to maintain a dependable currency beneficial to all. Washington was uneasy; neither argument had swept the board. But he signed the bank bill.

In the bank debate, Jefferson and Hamilton formulated fundamentally different theories of what the Constitution permitted the federal government to do and what it forbade. Hamilton's "broad construction" of the Constitution permitted Congress to legislate on any matter that was not specifically prohibited by the Constitution. Jefferson's "strict construction" held that if the Constitution did not clearly spell out a governmental power, Congress and the president could not exercise it. Which interpretation prevailed would depend on the political party in power at a given time and the rulings of the Supreme Court.

Hamilton Rebuffed

The BUS was Hamilton's last victory. Congress rejected the fourth pillar of his financial edifice, the protective tariff he called for in his "Report on Manufactures" in December 1791. Hamilton observed that the United States was blessed with a rich agricultural base and a flourishing mercantile economy. (There were as many American merchantmen as British engaged in overseas trade.)

However, Hamilton continued, the country imported almost all its manufactured goods, mostly from Great Britain, draining money abroad. In order to encourage American investors to put their money into manufacturing, the government had to protect infant industries from competition with British manufacturers who, in their established position, would easily undersell American competitors, and therefore, destroy them. A substantial import duty on, for example, British cloth, shoes, and iron products, would increase their selling price in the United States to a level with which American textile mills, shoe, and iron mills could compete.

Consumers—all farmers!—opposed Hamilton's protective tariff. They were not interested in paying higher prices for goods they needed in order to subsidize manufacturers. Southern planters led the opposition. They purchased shoes and cloth for their gangs of slaves, not a pair and a yard at a time, but in large quantities. Raising the retail price of textiles and shoes by 40 or 50 percent (or more!) to benefit would-be mill owners in New England was unacceptable.

Family farmers in the middle colonies, who grew grain and raised livestock for export without slaves, were concerned that Britain and France would retaliate against high American import duties by excluding their products from lucrative markets in the West Indies. Even some New England merchants, staunch Hamiltonians in other matters, disliked the protective tariff. Their business was transporting goods; the more cargos that needed moving about the better. Already British mercantilist laws restricted their activities within the empire. They could not afford to have their own government shutting down yet more trade.

Hamilton's plan to promote manufacturing in the United States may have been his most far-sighted program. And, because the big loser if America manufactured its own goods would be Great Britain, it gave the lie to accusations, beginning to be heard in 1792 and encouraged by Thomas Jefferson, that Hamilton was a stooge for the British, little more than an agent. This was too much opposition, even for Hamilton. Import duties remained low; they provided revenue, but no protection for manufacturers.

TROUBLES ABROAD

By 1792, Hamilton's and Jefferson's differences on policy had turned into an ugly personal animosity. Even in their letters to Washington begging him to agree to a second term—

Washington seriously considered retirement—they sniped at one another. Jefferson wanted to resign from the cabinet. In part, he vacillated his entire life between intense political ambition and a longing to retire to his beloved home, Monticello, in the Virginia foothills. In part, except for the tariff, he wanted out because he had lost every contest for Washington's approval to Hamilton.

Washington was aware of the fact that his and Hamilton's ambitions for the United States did not accord with Jefferson's. However, his appreciation of Jefferson's talents was genuine; he never closed his ears to the secretary of state. In 1792 (when Washington was unanimously reelected), he persuaded Jefferson to remain at his post. In 1793, after foreign policy further divided and embittered Jefferson and Hamilton, on the last day of the year, Jefferson resigned and went home.

The French Revolution

In 1789, the year of Washington's first inauguration, France exploded in revolution. Just about every American rejoiced. Had not the Declaration of Independence spoken of the inalienable rights of all people? Was not Lafayette one of the leaders of the movement to expand the liberties of the French people on the American model? Lafayette sent Washington the key to the Bastille, a royal prison that, in the first act of the Revolution, a Parisian mob had stormed. Washington did not much like mobs. Nevertheless, he prized the gift and displayed it prominently in his home. It became fashionable among Americans to festoon their hats with cockades of red, white, and blue ribbon—the badge of the revolutionaries.

Aside from Lafayette and a few others, the French revolutionaries were not imitating the Americans of 1776. The Revolution moved rapidly beyond a demand for liberty to the ideals of social equality and fraternity. Conservatives like Washington and Hamilton recoiled at the thought of wiping out social distinctions. As for *fraternity,* it soon came to mean more than national brotherhood. The idea of the nation as a morally bound community became a rationale for ensuring that no one disagreed with, or merely displeased, the national brotherhood's guardians.

Moderates like Lafayette, who had envisioned a liberal, democratic constitutional monarchy, were undercut on one side by the resistance of most of the nobility to any change and King Louis XVI's clumsy scheming with foreign powers to restore him to power. On the other side, they were sabotaged by radicals who proclaimed France a republic, imprisoned Louis XVI, and, in January 1793, beheaded him. During the "Reign of Terror" that followed, radicals known as Jacobins guillotined thousands of nobles, their political rivals, and even ordinary people who ran afoul of a low-level Jacobin bully. The virtual dictator of France during the Terror, Maximilien Robespierre, tried to purify the country by wiping out religion—in France, Roman Catholicism. He converted Paris's cathedral of Notre Dame into a "Temple of Reason" where paunchy politicians and actresses performed contrived rituals that struck some as blasphemous, others as ridiculous.

Reproduced from the Collections of the Library of Congress, Prints and Photographs Division, Washington, D.C. [LC-USZ62-124552]

MORT DE LOUIS XVI, LE 21 JANVIER 1793

Place de la Concorde : on voit à gauche le socle de la statue de Louis XV déboulonnée

(Extrait des *Révolutions de Paris*)

Just about every American with political interests greeted the early stages of the French Revolution with joy—even conservatives like Washington, Hamilton, and Timothy Pickering, later the most ultra of ultra-Federalists. The French, as Americans had done, were establishing a constitutional government of the people. As the Revolution turned violent with mass murders of nobles and then the king (shown here), and finally revolutionaries who disagreed with those in power, more and more Americans, both prominent and ordinary, grew disillusioned.

Despite the bloodshed and horrors, many Americans remained avid pro-French "Francomen." William Cobbett, an Englishman then living in the United States, observed with distaste that crowds in the streets guillotined dummies of Louis XVI "twenty or thirty times every day during one whole winter and part of the summer."

Jefferson, Adams, and France

When it came to France, Jefferson was blind (perhaps, in part, because he was a gourmet and seduced by *la cuisine*). In Paris for six years during the 1780s, he hobnobbed happily with aristocrats; he had an artist paint his portrait as a French noble. Back home in 1789, he zealously supported the French Revolution. Almost everyone did in 1789. But Jefferson never faltered in his enthusiasm through all the crimes committed in the name of "liberty, equality, and fraternity," including the murders of several of his friends.

Jefferson was consistently wrong on the subject. In 1789, just months before the revolutionary spiral of violence began, he predicted that France "will within two or three years be in the enjoiment of a tolerable free constitution and without its having cost them a drop of blood." In 1792, with the French slaughtering one another wholesale, Jefferson discounted the news of mass executions; they were exaggerated if not entirely false, he insisted with no grounds for thinking so except faith. When denial was no longer possible, he wrote that rather than see the revolution fail, "I would rather have seen half the earth desolated, were there but an Adam and Eve left in every country, and left free, it would be better than it is now." Which was pretty much how Robespierre justified the Reign of Terror.

John Adams was almost alone among American political leaders in being skeptical of the French Revolution from the start. Even *before* the start, in 1787, he told Jefferson that any revolution in France would be taken over by irresponsible fanatics and would lead to "confusion and carnage."

Turning Forests into Farms

Before the rectangular survey opened the Northwest Territory to settlement, the frontier was in western Pennsylvania (where the Whiskey Rebellion erupted in 1794). By the 1790s, there were few Indian problems in the region. The tribes that had dwelled there had been pushed west or had relocated there in disgust. During the 1790s, the northern frontier moved to Ohio where the experience of pioneering in the hardwood and conifer forests was much the same as it had been in Pennsylvania, except with plenty of conflict with Indians.

The first settlers tried to arrive in April. Winter's snow had melted, but the trees were just beginning to leaf. The pioneers' first job was to kill the hardwoods Indian style—by girdling their trunks—and to build cabins so as to have shelter by mid-May when a crop of corn, beans, and squash could be planted. Pines, spruce, and firs–softwoods with long, straight trunks—were felled for the logs with which cabins and barns were built. Crops were planted among the dead hardwoods. Only later—sometimes years—were they felled. Frontier "fields" were far from pretty, but the virgin soil was rich. Even the first year, farmers harvested 40 to 50 bushels of corn, wheat, or rye per acre.

A log cabin could be built with just one tool, an axe, and little skill—just the muscle power to move the logs into position. If a man owned an adze, he hewed (squared) the logs on two sides for a tighter fit when they were stacked, but that could also be done awkwardly with an axe. The ends of each log were notched so that, by locking them perpendicularly, it was possible to construct walls without uprights. The only task of cabin building requiring more than a man's and woman's labor was raising the roof beam. For this, neighbors were summoned and entertained as thanks for their help. Even the author of an article in the *Columbian* magazine in 1786, who described the pioneers as the dregs of society, admired the fact that roofs were raised "without any other pay than the pleasures which usually attend a country frolic."

Log cabins were tight, strong buildings. The walls, chinked with moss and mud, provided better insulation from cold and heat than clapboards sawn at a mill did.

The logs were plenty of protection from arrowhead, musket ball, and even fire. To burn a log cabin, it was necessary to ignite the shingled or thatched roof.

A yoke of oxen (a pair), maybe a few horses, perhaps a milk cow, were usually hobbled the first year, not fenced. Fences came later. The animals' forelegs were bound loosely enough that they could walk, but too tightly for them to run away. Hogs, the chief source of meat, were cheap and more than a match for any predator. They ran loose in the woods and were hunted rather than rounded up for slaughter in October. Salt was a necessity—the pork was heavily salted in barrels to preserve it—and often difficult to obtain. Thus, the priority given to finding a deer's salt lick. Deer were abundant at first. Fresh venison supplemented the salt pork and beef from worn-out milk cows and oxen. Meat shortages were less of a problem on the frontier than keeping deer and domestic animals out of the fields and garden.

For this, during the winter or second spring, the pioneers built zigzag fences. Logs split into rails—again, only an axe and self-made wooden wedges were needed—were stacked alternately, at angles a little more than 90°—*zigzag*. No postholes needed digging. They were not very good fences. Deer could leap them, of course, and the largest hogs could push them over. But they were a first line of defense.

According to the *Columbian*, "the first settler in the woods" rarely stayed more than a year or two. He was "generally a man who has outlived his credit of fortune in the cultivated parts of the State." Not a very good citizen, he was an anarchic, irreligious, and hard-drinking individual who "cannot bear to surrender up a single natural right for all the benefits of government." (The Whiskey Rebellion again!) Soon restless, he sold out to a newcomer who improved the farm, felling and burning the dead hardwoods and adding to the cabin. The people of the second wave of settlement, often enough, were in the business of turning a profit by improving the land and selling it. Only the "the *third* and last species of settler," a solid citizen whose habits were a relief to the author of the article, was "commonly a man of property and good character."

Citizen Genêt

Well before the Terror, conservatives like Washington, Hamilton, and John Adams were dismayed by the direction the French were taking. Worse, France's declaration of war on Great Britain early in 1793 presented them with a touchy diplomatic problem. The United States had a mutual assistance treaty with France which the French government called on Washington to honor by going to war with Britain.

Luckily, there were two loopholes through which Washington immediately scrambled. The 1778 treaty obligated the United States to join France in a war against Great

Britain only when Britain was the aggressor, which was clearly not the case in 1793. Moreover, the trusty Hamilton argued, the treaty had been contracted with the French monarchy which—to put it delicately—no longer existed. (Louis XVI was executed ten days before France declared war.) Washington announced that the United States would be neutral, "impartial toward the belligerent powers."

Then, in April 1793, a new French minister, Edmond Genêt, arrived in Charleston. Genêt was young (30), brilliant (he spoke seven languages), and as subtle as fireworks. Within days of stepping ashore, he began commissioning Americans as French privateers, sending them to sea to seize British ships. The raiders soon brought eighty British "prizes" into American ports where "Citizen Genêt" presided over prize courts and awarded a share of the loot to the captors. This was all standard procedure except that the United States was a proclaimed neutral and Genêt was commissioning privateers, an act of war. Indeed, in his numerous speeches, Genêt spoke as if he were the governor of a French colony.

By the time the minister called on the president, Washington was livid. He received the minister coldly, commanding him to cease commissioning privateers and bringing captured British vessels into American ports. Genêt bowed, retired, and almost immediately commissioned a captured British vessel, the *Little Sarah*, as a privateer. Washington ordered him to return to France.

This was not good news. Back in France, Genêt's party had been ousted from power and the Reign of Terror was in full swing. Going home meant a rendezvous with Madame la Guillotine. Suddenly abject, Genêt apologized to Washington and requested political asylum. The president granted it. Genêt married into the wealthy Clinton family of New York and lived a long, quiet life as a country gentleman.

Citizens

In Revolutionary France, it was illegal to address a person using a form that smacked of social inequality. Titles of nobility were forbidden, of course, but also *Madame* and *Monsieur,* terms that had been reserved for ladies and gentlemen. Everyone was *Citoyen* or *Citoyenne,* "Citizen" and "Citizeness." When France's minister in the United States called himself Citizen Genêt, pro-French Jeffersonians adopted the practice, addressing one another as "Citizen." (The Russian revolutionaries of 1917 did much the same thing when they replaced traditional forms of address with *Tovarich,* or "Comrade.")

In the United States, the problem of according people social status when addressing them was resolved differently. Instead of abolishing honorifics, American society upgraded everybody to "Mr." and "Mrs.," which previously had been inappropriate to people at the low end of the social scale.

British Provocations

Now it was Britain's turn to test Washington's determination to stay out of the war. The British proclaimed that they would fight the war with France at sea under the Rule of 1756. This policy, defined during the French and Indian War, stated that ships of neutral countries could not trade in ports from which they had been excluded before the war.

The proclamation was aimed at American merchants who were carrying grain and livestock to the French West Indies—Martinique, Guadeloupe, and Haiti. These colonies had been closed to American trade before 1793 but thrown open when the war started. American merchants did not want to give up the newfound business. It was immensely profitable.

The British did not want war with the United States, but they were concerned about more than the ability of French sugar planters to feed their slaves. Concerned about the vitality of the American merchant marine, they feared that, after the war, they would have lost much of the West Indies business to upstart Yankees. They rigorously enforced the Rule of 1756. In 1793 and 1794, British warships and privateers seized 600 American vessels, half of them in West Indian waters.

The seagoing merchants of Philadelphia, New York, and Boston protested, but few demanded war. Most traders in the Indies got through; profits exceeded losses. The complaints of common seamen were more bellicose. When the ships on which they were sailing were seized, they were, at best, interned by the British for months, losing income. Some were impressed into the Royal Navy.

Impressment was a British practice made necessary by the vast numbers of men the Royal Navy needed to sail its warships. To make up for the constant shortage of crewmen, naval commanders were authorized to replace sailors who died or deserted by forcing—pressing—able-bodied British subjects into service. If a warship needing men was in port, press-gangs roamed the streets collaring young men who looked like seamen or, there being none of them, young men who were "idle," without employment. At sea, short-handed warships hailed merchant vessels flying the Union Jack to heave to—the proverbial shot across the bow—whence press-gangs boarded them and took their pick of the crew.

The United States became involved in impressment because British seamen also boarded American vessels and seized sailors whom they identified—by their seamen's papers or accents—as British-born. The rub was that many of the British-born seamen on American ships had taken out American citizenship. But British law did not recognize naturalization; if a man was born in Great Britain, he was British for life. And then, mistakes were made. Some American-born seamen were forced into the Royal Navy.

Pro-French Americans set up a clamor: protest meetings, torchlight parades, and vituperative attacks in newspapers on the president's forbearing neutrality policy, although not yet on the president himself. Thomas Jefferson, living in retirement in Virginia, was himself silent. In confidential letters, however, he egged on political allies like James Madison and newspaper editors like the intemperate Philip Freneau. The nation's honor was being insulted, they said, and Washington did nothing.

Jay's Treaty

By April 1794, war fever was so heated that, in a last ditch effort to cool it down, Washington rushed Chief Justice John Jay across the Atlantic to appeal to the British for a settlement. Just sending Jay to beg (as the Anglophobes saw it) further agitated the fury. When the news trickled back that Jay was gaily hobnobbing in London society and had kissed the queen's hand, the anti-administration press had a field day. Many opposition newspapers reprinted this anonymous ditty:

> May it please your highness, I John Jay
> Have traveled all this mighty way,
> To enquire if you, good Lord will please
> To suffer me while on my knees,
> To show all others, I surpass,
> In love, by kissing of your ___.

The British wanted peace too. They agreed to compensate Americans whose ships had been seized in the West Indies and opened some trade in India to Americans from which, previously, they had been excluded. Finally, the British agreed to evacuate the western forts they should have surrendered to the United States in 1783. This was not as meaningless a concession as it may sound. The British had retained the forts because the Americans had not, as promised, paid money owed to British subjects.

Nothing was said of impressment, the most emotional point of conflict, nor about British aid to Indians who were warring against settlers in the Northwest Territory, nor about slaves who had escaped to Canada. All were matters that had aroused anti-British feelings in the West.

Jay was less than delighted with his treaty. It was the best he could do, he said, from his weak position. Washington was unhappier yet. He had hoped to placate the anti-British westerners. Washington seriously considered trashing Jay's Treaty himself. He kept its terms secret for a week. But the demands to see it increased and Washington concluded that the only alternative to ratifying the agreement was war with Britain.

As expected, the publication of Jay's Treaty set off an uproar. To westerners and southerners and other Anglophobes hot to fight Great Britain, the only beneficiaries of the treaty were the selfsame northeastern commercial interests that had reaped the rewards of Hamilton's financial program at their expense. The attacks on Jay were so violent—"Damn John Jay! Damn everyone that won't put lights in his windows and sit up all night damning John Jay!"—that the New Yorker resigned from the Supreme Court and retired to private life.

Political Parties

The furor over Jay's Treaty exhibited the first signs that two political parties were beginning to organize in the United States. Newspapers calling themselves "Republicans" roundly attacked the "Federalist" administration and, for the first time, attacked Washington personally for his policies. The two parties had, in fact, been in the cards since Hamilton and Jefferson clashed in 1790 and 1791. Nationalists like Hamilton, social conservatives, committed to clear-cut social inequalities as essential to stability and horrified by the French Revolution (men like John Adams, Jay, and Gouverneur Morris), and mercantile and financial interests recognized, gradually, that they were agreed on a broad range of policies the Washington administration was pursuing. By 1794, most were calling themselves Federalists. They were strongest in the northeastern states, but many southerners were Federalists too, notably the Pinckneys of South Carolina and, not notably at the

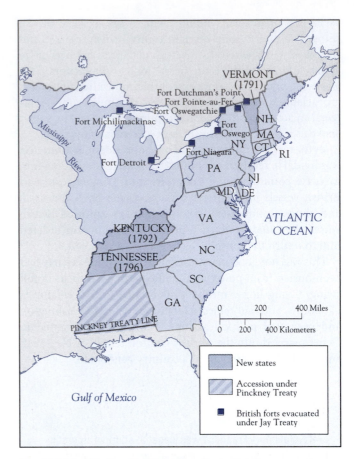

MAP 11:1 **The Federalist Treaties.** Great Britain reneged on its agreement to turn over seven frontier forts to the United States. Because American acquisition of the forts was the only significant British concession in Jay's Treaty, Thomas Jefferson's followers denounced it as humiliating. Pinckney's Treaty with Spain, by way of contrast, was popular. War was averted when Spain surrendered its claims to what are now the states of Mississippi and Alabama (except the Gulf Coast).

time, a young Virginia lawyer, John Marshall. A majority of southern planters, small farmers in every section, ideological Democrats, and those who were still enthused by the French Revolution called themselves Republicans. Quietly—in his innumerable letters—then, in 1796, openly, Thomas Jefferson assumed leadership of the party.

Neither the early Federalists nor the early Jefferson Republicans believed they were creating permanent institutions. Both sides continued to pay lip service to the ideal of a government without organized parties. But there was a multifaceted crisis—each party regarded the other as dangerous—that called for mobilization and political cooperation.

Pinckney's Treaty

Indirectly—although few Republicans admitted it—Jay's Treaty led to major benefits for westerners. Spain was negotiating a peace treaty with France. However, Spanish diplomats feared that when Spain left the anti-French camp, the British would retaliate, in league with the Americans with whom, in Jay's Treaty, they had reconciled, and seize Spanish Louisiana. The sprawling colony was poorly defended. Except around

New Orleans, it was hardly populated. Louisiana would fall easily to a combined attack of Americans by land and the British by sea.

Spanish anxieties were not far-fetched. Some Kentuckians had—unauthorized—begun to prepare an attack on New Orleans on their own.

In order to head off the loss of Louisiana, Spanish diplomats reversed a decade of trying to close the Mississippi to American trade. Out of the blue, they offered the American minister in Spain, Thomas Pinckney (whom they had recently threatened with expulsion) to open the Mississippi River to American navigation and to grant Americans the "right of deposit" in New Orleans. That is, Americans were given the privilege of storing and selling their exports (mostly food-stuffs and timber from the Northwest) in the great port.

The Treaty of San Lorenzo (or Pinckney's Treaty) was a major triumph for the Washington administration. If the United States had been the weaker party in the Jay Treaty negotiations, Spain was the conciliatory party in dealing with Pinckney. And the 100,000 Americans living in Kentucky, Tennessee, and the Northwest Territory—most of them Jefferson Republicans—had reason to calm down.

THE TUMULTUOUS NORTHWEST

Washington had already appealed to westerners for support by crushing the military power of the Indians in the Northwest Territory. It had not been easy. The tribes living in Ohio and Indiana—Shawnee, Miami, Potawatomi, Ojibwas, even Iroquois refugees after the disintegration of the Confederacy and defeats during the Revolution—were numerous, well organized, armed by the British in Canada, and determined to hold the line against white expansion.

The Dark and Bloody Ground

The Northwest Ordinance of 1787 had stated that "the utmost good faith shall always be observed towards the Indians; their lands and property shall never be taken from them without their Consent; and in their property, rights

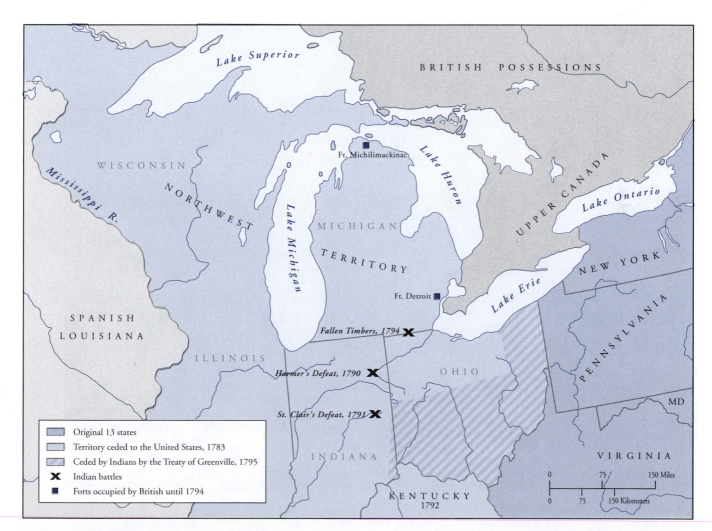

MAP 11:2 **Indian Wars in the Northwest Territory.** After victories over American militia in 1790 and 1791, the Indians of the Northwest Territory met their match in an army led by General "Mad Anthony" Wayne in the Battle of Fallen Timbers. In the Treaty of Greenville signed after Fallen Timbers, the defeated Indians gave up their claims to most of Ohio. However, Wayne did not destroy the tribes' capacity to resist. The Indians of the Northwest were still powerful twenty years later.

and liberty they shall never be invaded or disturbed." The frontiersmen who were moving into the Territory (and Kentucky and Tennessee) did not read such fine sentiments and laughed at them if they did. They were tough, rugged people; if cultured Easterners who observed them are to be allowed to describe them, they were "depraved." "Like dogs and bears, they use their teeth and feet, with the most savage ferocity, upon one another."

They used their rifles on Indians who got in their way. War, in the form of skirmishes, was pretty much constant. Both Indians and whites were responsible for massacres. Privately, Washington blamed the whites. Nothing but "a Chinese Wall or a line of troops" could stop their illegal "encroachment" on Indian lands, he said. However, when the tribes of the region threatened all-out war, he did not hesitate to send armies west to battle them. This was to be the story of the Indian wars for a century. Frontiersmen hungry for land (or gold) started them, not usually a disapproving and even disgusted government. When the Indians retaliated, however, the government sent in troops.

Most Americans' image of Indian wars is set on the Great Plains in the late nineteenth century: the Seventh Cavalry versus the mounted Sioux, Cheyenne, and Comanche in eagle feather war bonnets. In fact, the Indians wars on the Great Plains involved far fewer soldiers and Indians than the wars in the Northwest Territory during the 1790s, and they were far less bloody. George Armstrong Custer's column at the endlessly celebrated battle of the Little Big Horn in 1876 numbered 265 men. In Ohio in 1794, General Anthony Wayne commanded an army ten times that number. Deaths in Kentucky were so numerous that both Indians and whites called Kentucky "the dark and bloody ground."

In 1790, Washington sent General Josiah Harmer to subdue the Miamis and Shawnees who, under the command of Little Turtle, were harassing white settlers. Poorly supplied, wracked by dysentery and malaria, and handicapped by unfamiliarity with the country, Harmer and his men were decimated near the site of present-day Fort Wayne, Indiana. The next year, a better-prepared expedition under Arthur St. Clair met the same fate; 600 militiamen were killed.

The Whiskey Rebellion began with assaults on federal tax collectors like this man, stripped, tarred, and feathered. Washington tried to calm the rebels by promising a reduction in the tax on whiskey. They resisted, forcing the president to mobilize an armed force. Washington, perhaps just to insult the rebels, commuted the death sentences handed out to a few leaders on the grounds that they were mental defectives.

Brown Brothers

Washington blamed both defeats on the fact that the soldiers were militiamen, for whom he never had a good word. In 1794, he gave General Anthony "Mad Anthony" Wayne command of troops from the regular army. Wayne defeated Indians from several tribes at the Battle of Fallen Timbers near present-day Toledo. (The fallen trees on the battlefield had been leveled by a tornado.) In the Treaty of Greenville that followed, the battered tribes ceded the southern half of Ohio and a sliver of Indiana to the United States. Another line was drawn—until the southern half of Ohio was populated.

The Whiskey Rebellion

The men and women of the frontier were heavy drinkers. They launched their days with an "eye-opener" or "flem-cutter": raw, homemade whiskey. A jug sat on shop counters like a dish of mints today; general stores doubled as saloons. Westerners swigged whiskey like wine with their meals and like water when they worked. Preachers refreshed themselves with "the creature" during their sermons. William Henry Harrison, appointed governor of Indiana Territory in 1800, said that he "saw more drunk men in forty-eight hours succeeding my arrival in Cincinnati than I had in my previous life."

Endemic illness explains some of the drinking. Frontier settlers suffered chronically from the alternating chills and fevers of malaria. (They called it the "ague".) The medicine for which they reached was alcohol. Isolation contributed. Travelers in the Ohio valley invariably described conversations with men, and especially women, who commented mournfully on the lack of company. Whiskey was a companion.

Finally, whiskey was cheap. The corn and rye from which it was made were easy to grow. The technology was simple: ferment a mash of grain and water; boil it in an enclosed "kettle"; condense the steam that escaped and, presto, white lightning. (Alcohol vaporizes at a lower temperature than water requires.) Fuel was free: the wood from endless land clearing that had to be burned anyway. Many family farmers kept a small still percolating day and night. And whiskey was a cash crop. Before Pinckney's Treaty opened the Mississippi to American trade, the westerners' only market lay back East, by land over the Appalachians. The cost of transporting a low-value bulk commodity like grain was prohibitive. A pack horse could carry about 200 pounds: 4 bushels of corn. Four bushels of corn, in the food-rich United States, sold for pennies. However, a horse could carry the equivalent of 24 bushels of grain when it was converted into liquor. A gallon of whiskey sold for 25¢, which provided just enough profit to make the trek over the mountains plausible.

In 1791, to augment federal revenues, Hamilton slapped an excise tax of 7¢ per gallon on distilled liquor. It was almost enough to wipe out the western distillers' profits. Like Daniel Shays's followers in Massachusetts a few years earlier, farmers in western Pennsylvania kidnapped a federal marshal and terrorized tax collectors. When one tax collector summoned twelve soldiers to protect his house, 500 rebels attacked and burned the man's barn, stables, and crops, roughed up federal tax collectors, and rioted. Other mobs destroyed the stills of neighbors who had paid the tax.

Conciliatory as ever, Washington tried to negotiate a peaceful end to the violence. Hamilton expressed his willingness to make "any reasonable alterations" in the tax to make it more palatable. But the Whiskey Rebels had been carried away by the excitement and a regimen of pro-French rhetoric calling for the erection of guillotines. So Washington himself set out at the head of 15,000 troops. Just the news an army was on the way was enough to scatter the rebels. When the news of their dispersal reached Washington, he left the column and returned to Philadelphia. Hamilton, whose yen for military glory had not been sated by the Revolution, pushed on. He was denied a battle but managed to arrest a few rebels who were promptly convicted of treason and sentenced to death. Washington pardoned them, calling them mental defectives.

In one sense, the suppression of the Whiskey Rebellion was a farce. An army as large as the one at Yorktown—and much larger than Wayne's army at Fallen Timbers—was mobilized to crush a rebellion it could not find. But the political significance of the episode was profound. The Federalist Hamilton was delighted to assert the national government's power to enforce order entirely within one state with troops raised in other states. The resentment of the western Pennsylvanians, however, ensured that when they got the chance, they would vote for the emerging Jefferson Republican party against Washington's and Hamilton's Federalists.

THE PRESIDENCY OF JOHN ADAMS

The Republicans got their chance in 1796 when Washington rejected plenty of pleas that he once again stand for reelection. In retiring (quite happily) after two terms, he not only set a precedent that would not be broken for 144 years, he also astonished both Americans and Europeans: He was indeed a Cincinnatus, voluntarily walking away from power to be a farmer. Even George III said that Washington's act made him "the most distinguished of any man living . . . the greatest character of the age." (A few years later, when Napoleon clung to power at the cost of tens of thousands of lives, he dismissed those who urged him to retire with the scornful remark: "They wanted me to be another Washington.")

The Election of 1796

Because Washington made his retirement official only with his Farewell Address of September 1796, the official presidential campaign was the shortest in history. (Twenty-first century Americans cannot help but look back at it wistfully.) Privately, however, in letters and conversation, politicians had been assuming Washington would retire for months and their machinations were frenzied. Vice President John Adams stood for the Federalists; if he had been the "second best man" for eight years, who else? James Madison persuaded Thomas Jefferson, after a little foot-dragging, to oppose him. Only Jefferson had a chance to defeat a Federalist party in the sinister hands of Alexander Hamilton with his pro-British

The Vice Presidency: Not a Crime

The vice president's only constitutional functions are to preside over the Senate (casting the deciding vote when there is a tie) and to step in if the president dies, resigns, or is removed from office.

John Adams called the vice presidency "the most insignificant office that ever the invention of man contrived." John Nance Garner, vice president between 1933 and 1941, said the job wasn't "worth a pitcher of warm spit." (Some insist that the profane old codger said that the pitcher was filled with "warm piss.") Finley Peter Dunne, who wrote a popular newspaper column in Irish-American dialect at the turn of the twentieth century, summed it up as: "Th' prisidency is th' highest office in th' gift iv th' people. Th' vice-presidincy is th' next highest an' the lowest. It isn't a crime exactly. Ye can't be sint to jail f'r it, but it's a kind iv a disgrace."

Indeed, the vice presidency ceased to be an honor after the adoption of the Twelfth Amendment to the Constitution in 1804. Before 1804, the runner-up in the *presidential* election—the country's "second best man"—became vice president. But the Twelfth Amendment called for nominations specifically for the vice presidency. Parties selected them not for the nominees' abilities but because they were from states (or regions) where the presidential nominee needed help winning electoral votes. Political parties *preferred* mediocrity in the vice presidency so that vice presidents did not compete for prestige with the president.

foreign policy, his anti-democratic sympathies, his banker and speculator friends, and his resolve to increase the power of the federal government at the expense of the states. In fact, Adams was not Hamilton's stooge. Neither man trusted the other, but Madison and Jefferson could talk themselves into a kind of political hysteria.

The Republicans' chief second candidate—there were still no nominations for vice president—was Aaron Burr of New York, Hamilton's chief rival in the state. The Federalists's second-best man was Thomas Pinckney of South Carolina. And his name prompted Hamilton into one of the devious under-the-table schemes for which he had a tragic weakness. Quietly, but not quite secretly, Hamilton tried to put Pinckney rather than Adams into the presidential chair. Pinckney, Hamilton believed, would listen to him as the vain and suspicious Adams was unlikely to do. Hamilton believed that he would easily be persuaded to carry out Hamilton's wishes.

Hamilton's scheme involved persuading South Carolina's eight electors to cast one vote for Pinckney but to "throw away" their second vote on someone other than Adams. This might indeed have made Pinckney a surprise victor except for two developments Hamilton did not anticipate. (Most of his devious schemes went awry.) All eight South Carolinians did Hamilton's bidding. However, all eight gave their second votes not to throwaway candidates but to Thomas Jefferson. In the meantime, New England Federalist electors, all Adams

men, got wind of the conspiracy; twenty-two of them voted for Adams but not, as they had intended, for Pinckney. The result was that Adams won, but just barely. Needing 70 electoral votes to have a majority, Adams won 71. And Pinckney did not finish second. Thanks to South Carolina's votes, Thomas Jefferson won 68 votes. (Pinckney was third with 59.) The president and vice president represented the two opposing parties. Hamilton succeeded in electing a Federalist he opposed as president, and a Republican he loathed as vice president.

"His Rotundity"

After 200 years, it is easy to admire John Adams. When he was dispassionate, he was a moderate man who acted according to admirable principles. He could be humorous. (Neither George Washington nor Jefferson had a sense of humor.) When scandalmongers said absurdly that Adams sent Charles Cotesworth Pinckney to London to procure four loose women for his and Adams's pleasure, he responded, "I do declare upon my honor, General Pinckney has cheated me out of my two." His relationship with his wife, Abigail, was unique. He discussed public issues with her in detail, sought her advice, and often took it. "The President would not dare to make a nomination without her approbation," an opponent said.

Benjamin Franklin said that Adams was "always honest and often great." He then added, however, that Adams was "sometimes mad." Neurotically insecure, Adams was peevish even when his actions were constructively criticized. He had a raging temper that was quick to erupt, and it incinerated his judgment. All work and duty, he was socially inept. A friend commented, "he cannot dance, drink, game, flatter, promise, dress, swear with the gentlemen . . . or flirt with the ladies."

Adams's pomposity was laughable. Wits poked fun at his short, dumpy physique, a sharp contrast to Washington's height and military bearing by calling him "His Rotundity." Rather than ignore it or laugh it off, Adams reacted as if the dignity of the presidency had been attacked. He isolated himself, even from well-wishers. He spent less time in the capital than any other president. For four years, he was one day in four at his home in Quincy, Massachusetts. Washington was absent from his post only one day in eight.

Still, Adams's presidency might have gone better had it not been for James Madison's political partisanship and astuteness. Adams and Jefferson had once been close personal friends. Just before they were inaugurated, Adams told Jefferson that he hoped they could be reconciled and put the interests of good government above their political differences. Jefferson wrote a reply in which he went even farther in pledging Adams his cooperation and support. However, he showed the letter to Madison, who was horrified. He pointed out that the first time Jefferson openly differed from Adams on an issue, as was inevitable given their philosophical differences, Adams would publish Jefferson's letter and embarrass, if not discredit him. Jefferson got the point and did not send the letter.

Adams did himself in finally by retaining Washington's final cabinet intact. Two secretaries were incompetent. They reported the confidential proceedings of cabinet meetings

North Wind Picture Archives

President John Adams was richly talented, able, and principled but (in Benjamin Franklin's words) "sometimes mad." He was as intelligent as any of his contemporaries. His personal integrity was equal to Washington's and far superior to Jefferson's and Hamilton's. He was often good-humored and witty. Unfortunately, he was as vain and pompous as human beings come, and he lacked tact and social graces.

to Hamilton and, when told to do so, actively obstructed Adams's policies. Adams never had more than half of the Federalist Party behind him, and he did not discover his cabinet problems for several years.

War Scare with France

Like Washington, Adams faced the threat of war, but with France rather than Britain. Worried by the Anglo-American rapprochement Jay's Treaty seemed to mean, the French government ordered its navy and privateers to regard American ships as fair game. Even before Adams was inaugurated in March 1797, they had seized 300 American vessels. Moreover, the French defined American sailors captured off British ships (many of whom had been pressed involuntarily into the Royal Navy) as pirates who could legally be hanged. The American minister in Paris, Charles Cotesworth Pinckney, was threatened with arrest. The French minister in

the United States, Pierre Adet, railed against Adams almost as intemperately as Genêt had assailed Washington.

Hamilton's "High Federalists," who had shrugged off British seizures of American ships, demanded war with France. Determined to keep the peace, Adams dispatched John Marshall of Virginia and Elbridge Gerry of Massachusetts to join Pinckney in Paris to negotiate an end to the "quasi-war."

They were shunned for weeks, a calculated insult by the French foreign minister, the charming but deceitful and corrupt Charles Maurice de Talleyrand. Finally, Talleyrand sent word through three aides, identified in the Americans' code as X, Y, and Z, that he would speak with Pinckney, Marshall, and Gerry if they made a personal gift to Talleyrand of $250,000 and agreed in advance of negotiations to lend France $12 million.

Bribes were routine in diplomacy, but the sum Talleyrand demanded was excessive and the tempers of the Americans had worn thin from waiting. "Not a sixpence," Pinckney snapped to X, Y, and Z. In the United States, Pinckney's reply was dressed up (and converted into American currency) as "millions for defense but not one cent for tribute."

The High Federalists were delighted. Hamilton pressured Adams to create an army of 10,000 men to be commanded by the national hero, George Washington. Aged as he was, Washington agreed to the commission, but only if Adams named Hamilton as second in command. With good reason, Adams resisted. It offended his principles that Washington, a private citizen, should, in effect, issue an order to the president. It would demoralize the officer corps to jump Hamilton, a former colonel, over a raft of Revolutionary War generals. And Adams, quite as deeply as Jefferson and Madison, believed that Hamilton, with an army, was quite capable of a military coup. Unhappily, with the whole business public knowledge, Adams felt he had no choice but to agree. No one, not even the president, rejected George Washington. Adams was apt to think himself humiliated when he was not. In the affair of the army, the humiliation was total.

Adams was more comfortable with the navy. Sea power posed no threat to civil government; a people cannot be subdued by ships. Moreover, while it was difficult to say where France and America might battle on land, an undeclared war already raged madly on the seas. Adams and Congress authorized the construction of forty frigates and lesser warships, a huge jump from the three vessels the president had inherited from Washington.

The Alien and Sedition Acts

The Jefferson Republicans, many still pro-France despite its corruption and dictatorial government, loudly opposed preparations for war. As always, the furtive Jefferson—he was as fond of covert operations as Hamilton—was silent. On his instructions, however, his catspaws, both politicians and journalists, attacked the army and heaped abuse on Adams. The Federalist Congress responded to the criticism with a series of laws called the Alien and Sedition Acts.

The first Alien Act extended the period of residence required for American citizenship from five to fourteen years.

A second act authorized the president to deport any foreigner whom he deemed "dangerous to the peace and safety of the United States." The two laws were blatantly partisan, aimed at anti-British French and Irish immigrants. Leaving no doubt of their political purpose, the Alien Acts were to expire shortly after Adams's term ended in 1801.

The Alien Acts had few consequences. The Sedition Act did. It provided stiff fines and prison sentences for persons who published statements that held the United States government in "contempt or disrepute." The government brought twenty-five cases to trial; ten defendants were convicted. Most were journalists, but when Adams visited Newark, New Jersey, and was saluted with a volley of gunfire and a Republican said, "There goes the president and they are shooting at his ass," another responding, "I don't care if they fire through his ass," the court ruled that the words were seditious.

The Virginia and Kentucky Resolutions

Jefferson and Madison believed that the Sedition Act violated the Bill of Rights and was therefore unconstitutional.

A Death in the Family

In December 1799, 67-year-old George Washington took to his bed with a sore throat and fever. Modern physicians have diagnosed his illness as a bacterial infection, probably strep throat. Bacteria were unknown in 1799, but Washington's doctors could only have hastened his death with their well-meaning treatments. The gargles (tea and vinegar) and syrups (molasses, vinegar, and butter) to ease the pain in his throat did not hurt. And the emetics (tartar and calomel) might have helped reduce his fever. But the bloodlettings, applying leeches to Washington, a therapy doctors seem to have prescribed whenever they were confused, surely weakened the old man. The doctors took 82 ounces of Washington's blood in about a week, 5 pints! Blood donors today rest after being relieved of a single pint.

But who was to declare that an act of Congress signed by the president was invalid? The Constitution did not say. It was one of the important questions the Founding Fathers had left unresolved. The answer Jefferson and Madison gave was to haunt American history for half a century.

The Virginia Resolutions, written by Madison and adopted by the Virginia legislature, and the Kentucky Resolutions, which Jefferson wrote, proclaimed that the federal government was a compact of sovereign states. Congress was, therefore, the creation of the states. If Congress enacted a law that a state deemed unconstitutional, that state had the right and the power to forbid its enforcement within the state's boundaries.

It is difficult to understand how Madison, the most nationalistic of Americans in 1787 and a nationalist again when he was president, could espouse such a doctrine. He betrayed his own uneasiness when, after reading Jefferson's first draft of the Kentucky Resolutions, he persuaded him to delete the word *nullify* to describe a state's right to reject a federal law. The word was too strong; it gave Madison the shivers, although the principle of nullification remained implicit in both Virginia's and Kentucky's resolves. Perhaps the explanation of Madison's willingness to define a state's power as superior to the federal governments is nothing more than his sometimes supine worship of Jefferson. When the two men disagreed, Madison could sometimes sway Jefferson. But he never in his life differed openly with him.

There was logic in the Virginia and Kentucky Resolutions, but their implications were ominous. Had the principle on which they were based been accepted, the United States would have reverted halfway to the state sovereignty of the Articles of Confederation. As it was, they remained expressions of a political abstraction. No other state legislature adopted them. The death of George Washington in December 1799 briefly calmed political tempers and, as the election of 1800 drew nearer, it became obvious to the Jefferson Republicans that the unpopularity of the Alien and Sedition Acts was winning voters to their party.

FURTHER READING

Classics Edmund S. Morgan, *The Meaning of Independence: John Adams, George Washington, Thomas Jefferson*, 1976.

General Joyce Appleby, *Capitalism and the New Social Order: The Republican Vision of the 1790s*, 1984; Gordon S. Wood, *The Radicalism of the American Revolution*, 1991; Stanley Elkins and Eric McKitrick, *The Age of Federalism: The Early American Republic, 1788–1800*, 1993; Jack Larkin, *The Reshaping of Everyday Life 1790–1840*, 1988; Garry Wills, *A Necessary Evil: A History of American Distrust of Government*, 1999; Joanne B. Freeman, *Affairs of Honor: National Politics in the New Republic*, 2001; Cynthia A. Kierner, *Scandal at Bizarre: Rumor and Reputation in Jefferson's America*, 2004.

Founding Fathers Joseph J. Ellis, *Founding Brothers: The Revolutionary Generation*, 2000; Joyce Appleby, *Inheriting the Revolution: The First Generation of Americans*, 2000; Gore Vidal, *Inventing a Nation: Washington, Adams, Jefferson*, 2003; Frank Lambert, *The Founding Fathers and the Place of Religion in America*, 2003; Brooke Allen, *Moral Minority: Our Skeptical Founding Fathers*, 2006; John Meacham, *American Gospel: God, the Founding Fathers, and the Making of a Nation*, 2006; David L. Holmes, *The Faiths of the Founding Fathers*, 2006; Richard Brookhiser, *What Would the Founders Do?: Our Questions, Their Answers*, 2006.

Washington: Garry Wills, *Cincinnatus: George Washington and the Enlightenment*, 1984; Richard Brookhiser, *Founding Father: Rediscovering George Washington*, 1996; Joseph J. Ellis, *His Excellency, George Washington*, 2004; Peter R. Henriques, *Realistic Visionary: A Portrait of George Washington*, 2006. **Adams** Lynne Withey, *Dearest Friend: A Life of Abigail Adams*, 1981; David McCullough, *John Adams*, 2001; Richard Brookhiser, *America's First Dynasty: The Adamses, 1735–1918*, 2002. **Hamilton** Richard Brookhiser, *Alexander Hamilton, American*, 1999; Stephen K.

Knott, *Alexander Hamilton and the Persistence of Myth*, 2002; Ron Chernow, *Alexander Hamilton*, 2004. **Jefferson** Joseph J. Ellis, *American Sphinx: The Character of Thomas Jefferson*, 1996; Garry Wills, *"Negro President": Jefferson and the Slave Power*, 2003. Christopher Hitchens, *Thomas Jefferson: Author of America*, 2005. **Others** Walter Starr, *John Jay, Founding Father*, 2005; Richard Brookhiser, *Gentleman Revolutionary: Gouverneur Morris, the Rake Who Wrote the Constitution*, 2003.

Foreign Policy Jerald Combs, *The Jay Treaty*, 1970; Daniel G. Lang, *Foreign Policy in the Early Republic: The Law of Nations and the Balance of Power*, 1985; Albert Bowman, *The Struggle for Neutrality: Franco-American Diplomacy During the Federalist Era*, 1974.

Party Politics Richard Buel, Jr., *Securing the Revolution: Ideology in American Politics, 1789–1815*, 1972; John Hoadley, *Origins of American Political Parties, 1789–1803*, 1986; Lance Bannon, *The Jeffersonian Persuasion: Evolution of a Party Ideology*, 1980; James Roger Sharp, *American Politics in the Early Republic: The New Nation in Crisis*, 1995; Joanne B. Freeman, *Affairs of Honor: National Politics in the New Republic*, 2001; Robert V. Remini, *The House: The History of the House of Representatives*, 2006.

The West Gregory Evans Dowd, *A Spirited Resistance: The North American Indian Struggle for Unity, 1745–1785*, 1992; Robert V. Hine and John Mack Faragher, *The American West: A New Interpretive History*, 2000; Reginald Horsman, *Expansion and American Indian Policy, 1783–1812*, 1992; Stephen Aron, *How the West Was Lost: The Transformation of Kentucky from Daniel Boone to Henry Clay*, 1996; Thomas G. Slaughter, *The Whiskey Rebellion: Frontier Epilogue to the American Revolution*, 1986.

KEY TERMS

Use the following listing of key terms to review important figures, events, locations, and concepts covered in this chapter. A glossary of these terms is available on *The American Past* companion Web site: www.cengage.com/history/conlin/tap9e

funding, p. 181

assumption, p. 182

broad construction, p. 183

strict construction, p. 183

Genêt, Edmond Charles, p. 186

Treaty of San Lorenzo (Pinckney's Treaty), p. 188

Wayne, Anthony, p. 190

Whiskey Rebellion, p. 191

XYZ Affair, p. 193

ONLINE RESOURCES

Find additional resources, including primary source documents, images, interactive maps, simulations, chapter review exercises, and Internet links at

***The American Past* companion Web site**
www.cengage.com/history/conlin/tap9e

American History Resource Center
http://ushistory.wadsworth.com/

Chapter 12

The Age of Jefferson

Frustration Abroad 1800–1815

Stapleton Collection HIP/The Image Works

The immortality of Thomas Jefferson does not lie in any one of his achievements, or in the series of his achievements, but in his attitude toward mankind.

—*Woodrow Wilson*

Once again in 1800, Thomas Jefferson challenged John Adams in the presidential election. Most of the states were expected to vote as they had in 1796. The count in the electoral college would again be close. The Federalists were dominant in the New England states (although the Jefferson Republicans were becoming a genuine opposition party there). Except for Delaware, Charleston in the South, and a few districts in Virginia, the other states were Republican or leaned in that direction. New York was the big question mark.

Popular opinion had been wrenched in both directions during Adams's presidency. The Federalists' Alien and Sedition Acts were unpopular, but a decade of Republican cheerleading for the French Revolutionaries had come back to haunt Jefferson because of the quasi-war, the X, Y, Z Affair, and Napoleon Bonaparte's creation of the military dictatorship that Federalists like Adams and Gouverneur Morris had predicted. Had Adams nurtured the call for war with France, as he was advised to do, he would likely have been reelected by a wave of Francophobic patriotism. But Adams, to his credit (historically anyway) valued peace above politics. In a last ditch effort, he risked yet another French insult by dispatching a new team of negotiators to Paris. On the very eve of the election, news arrived that they had secured a settlement. The quasi-war was over and the anti-French sentiment that favored Adams politically evaporated. But it was too late. New York's vote had already been committed—to Jefferson.

THE ELECTION OF 1800

The "will of the people" had little to do with the election of 1800. Only five of the sixteen states chose presidential electors by popular vote. State legislatures made the selection in the others. It is worth noting that the Founding Fathers intended that presidential elections *not* be democratic. Today, when presidential campaigns go on for two and a half years, it is not difficult to be nostalgic for their wisdom. On the other hand, they did not eliminate unattractive political maneuvering by reserving the selection of the president to a presumably educated elite.

Crunching Numbers

In 1796, Adams defeated Jefferson in the electoral college 71 votes to 68. In 1800, Jefferson won by roughly the same margin, 73 to 65. Ruefully, Adams believed—and he was right—flukish political events in New York and South Carolina cost him the election.

New York's electors were the most important part of the reversal. In 1796, New York voted for Adams and looked to do so again. However, in April 1800, after an ugly partisan battle for control of the state legislature between Alexander Hamilton's Federalists and the Jefferson Republicans, led by Aaron Burr, the Republicans won. The issues in the contest were local and personal (Hamilton and Burr loathed one another), not national. But the national consequences of

The Negro Vote

There was yet another twist in electoral college votes of 1800. As Timothy Pickering of Massachusetts and other New Englanders pointed out, Jefferson and Burr defeated John Adams only because of the Constitution's "three-fifths compromise," which provided that, in apportioning representatives and electoral votes to a state, slaves in the state counted as three-fifths of a free citizen.

Of Jefferson's 73 electoral votes, a bare majority, 53 were from slave states. If slaves had not been "represented" in the electoral college, Adams would have been reelected. Fourteen Jefferson electors represented slaves. Pickering (a lifelong and outspoken abolitionist) called Jefferson the "Negro President."

Burr's victory were immediately obvious for, in New York, the legislature chose the state's presidential electors.

Alexander Hamilton, always quick with a scheme, even when it meant abandoning his principles, tried to repair the damage by proposing that New York select electors that year by popular vote, something he had consistently opposed. "In times like these in which we live," Hamilton commented privately, "it will not do to be over-scrupulous." The Republicans, proponents of popular elections, were equally cynical. Their legislature voted Hamilton's democratic reform down. Months before the presidential election, poor Adams knew he had lost New York's votes. The state's switch from 1796 subtracted 12 electors from Adams's column and added them to Jefferson's.

Even then, Adams would have won the election had the Federalists' choice for vice president, Charles Cotesworth Pinckney of South Carolina, been better served by his own state's Federalists. Pinckney urged South Carolina's eight electors to vote for Adams as well as for himself. Had they done as he asked, Adams would have been president and Pinckney vice president. But the South Carolinians, abhorring New England and New Englanders, told Pinckney that, as in 1796, they would vote for him and Jefferson. That formula would have elected Jefferson president with Pinckney vice president. However, an angry Pinckney would have none of it; he took his name off the ballot. South Carolina's eight electoral votes, and the election, went to Jefferson and Burr.

Failures to Communicate

It went literally to Jefferson *and* Burr. No Republican elector "threw away" one of his two votes on a man who was not a candidate so that Jefferson would finish one vote ahead of vice presidential candidate Burr. (Not that it mattered, but the losing Federalists did not make the same mistake; one Rhode Island elector voted for Adams and John Jay.)

When the votes were counted in the Senate (by Vice President Jefferson), Jefferson and Burr each had 73 electoral votes—a majority but a tie. The Constitution provided that, in such a case, the House of Representatives choose the president, voting not as individuals but as states, one vote per state. Republicans had a majority in half of the sixteen state delegations in the House, one short of the majority needed to seat Jefferson. Two state delegations were evenly divided between Republicans and Federalists. The rest were Federalist delegations.

Most Federalists preferred Burr, not because he was brilliant, which he was, but because he was an opportunist, a man who would deal. Jefferson the Federalists regarded as

The Jefferson Republicans Triumphant 1801–1815

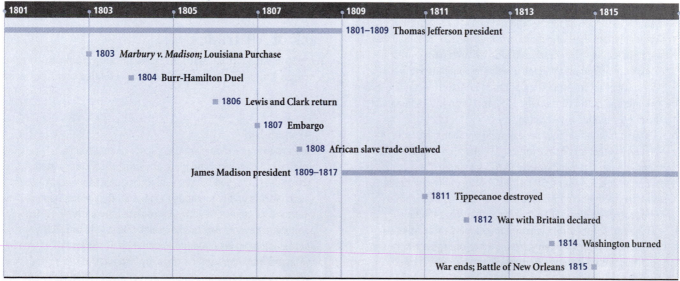

| 1801 | 1803 | 1805 | 1807 | 1809 | 1811 | 1813 | 1815 |

1801–1809 Thomas Jefferson president

1803 *Marbury v. Madison;* Louisiana Purchase

1804 Burr-Hamilton Duel

1806 Lewis and Clark return

1807 Embargo

1808 African slave trade outlawed

James Madison president 1809–1817

1811 Tippecanoe destroyed

1812 War with Britain declared

1814 Washington burned

War ends; Battle of New Orleans 1815

dangerous, immoral, an atheist, and a demagogue. Some said (seriously?) that, if he had his way, blood would run in the streets of American cities as, indeed, it had in France.

For thirty-five ballots, the tally in the House was unchanged: Jefferson eight states, Burr six states, two states abstaining because their representatives were divided. James Bayard, Delaware's only congressman, a Federalist who was voting for Burr, took the initiative in breaking the impasse. He secretly sent intermediaries to both Burr and Jefferson, asking each if he would agree not to molest the Bank of the United States and Federalist judges and other federal appointees, Bayard would do his best to throw the election the agreeable candidate's way.

Burr's only public statement favoring Jefferson had been weak and ambivalent. He wanted to be president. However, and uncharacteristically, for Burr was a man for backroom bargains, Burr refused to deal with Bayard's emissary. It is not certain just what Jefferson told Bayard's man—Federalists said he agreed to the conditions, Jefferson that he was noncommittal—but it was enough to persuade Bayard to announce that he would change his vote from Burr to Jefferson. In the end, neither he nor any other Federalist had to do so. But enough Federalists abstained to allow Jefferson to carry ten states. Burr ended up with four.

Jefferson's *bête noire*, Alexander Hamilton, had a hand in Jefferson's election. Still smarting from Burr's personal attacks on him the previous year, Hamilton wrote to several House Federalists urging them to prefer Jefferson. Hamilton disliked Jefferson; he detested Burr. Burr, he said, would surround himself with rogues from both parties; "his private character is not defended by his most partial friends. He is bankrupt beyond redemption." Jefferson, he wrote (it was not saying much) had "pretensions to character."

The Twelfth Amendment

So that the fiasco of 1800 would not be repeated, the Twelfth Amendment to the Constitution, ratified in 1804, provided that electors would vote not for two men for president, but for a "ticket," a president and vice president nominated together. An unforeseen consequence of the change was a decline in the prestige of the vice presidency and, indeed, the quality of those nominated for the office.

That is, in the first four presidential elections, electors cast two votes, ostensibly for the two men best qualified to be president. The candidate with the second highest count became vice president. Since 1804, parties have generally selected as their vice presidential candidates mediocrities who would not diminish the luster of their presidential candidate. The criterion was not the nominee's abilities, but whether or not he came from a state or region where the presidential nominee was weak and he—the vice presidential candidate—might attract votes because he was a local boy (or, more recently, local girl).

The Sage of Monticello

Jefferson one day reflected that once a man "cast a longing eye" on public office, "a rottenness begins in his conduct." It would have been on a day when he was happy living at Monticello, a gentleman planter reading and tinkering, as he loved to do. On other days, also at Monticello, Jefferson was obsessed with politics and devoured by his ambitions for office. He devoted hours daily to writing letters to his political supporters in which he schemed, conspired, and manipulated in a manner that might reasonably be described as "rotten." The politician Jefferson was as devious as Burr and Hamilton.

Before he was elected president, however, with the exception of writing the Declaration of Independence, his public career had not been distinguished. The vice presidency was a job that made no demands. (Jefferson, who had many interests, was perhaps the only talented vice president who enjoyed the position.) As Washington's secretary of state, Jefferson had been eclipsed by Hamilton. His four years as minister in France were as much holiday as work. His stint as governor of Virginia during the Revolution was nearly a career-ending disaster. He was an ineffective executive and was accused of cowardice in the state assembly for fleeing when the British invaded the state.

This was unfair. It was true enough that Jefferson was not personally brave. His enemy Hamilton liked to crack that he was "womanish." (Jefferson was not immune to such jibes or above the gospel of manliness. A superb horseman, he delighted in describing Hamilton's "timidity" in the saddle.) But Jefferson fled Richmond only when he learned that a British detachment had been specifically assigned to capture him as a trophy (and came close to succeeding). Was he to deliver himself to the redcoats on the steps of his residence? Correctly, the legislature exonerated him of the charges.

Jefferson's lackluster record in public office was not the point, as Woodrow Wilson said. Jefferson has been remembered because he put into noble words and perfect sentences a vision of human nature and liberty that have become our civilization's ideals.

Jack of All Trades

Jefferson was a scholar with interests ranging from philosophy through linguistics to natural science. His library numbered

Wine Snob

Jefferson was a moderate drinker. He did not touch spirits, but he insisted on wine at dinner, rarely more than two glasses. He sometimes subjected guests to lengthy disquisitions on the nuances of the wine they were sipping, perhaps lengthier than they appreciated. As early as 1773, Jefferson gave an Italian immigrant, Filippo Mazzei, 200 acres adjoining his plantation so that he could plant a vineyard from imported cuttings. Unfortunately, just as the vineyard was beginning to produce, Mazzei enlisted to fight the British and never returned.

Monticello, Jefferson's home in Charlottesville, Virginia, on one of several plantations he owned. Here he studied and carried on a correspondence that consumed many hours daily. He took little interest in agriculture but regularly checked up on a slave-operated shop in which nails were manufactured. Monticello was the love of his life, but his debts were so great that his daughter had to sell it.

6,000 books; it became the core of the Library of Congress which continued to employ Jefferson's classification system for eighty-two years. He was a musician; he played the violin, quite well according to those who heard him. He was a talented architect. He designed and built and redesigned and rebuilt Monticello several times. He designed the buildings of the University of Virginia, which he founded, then wrote its curriculum. He was an inventor: The dumbwaiter and the swivel chair are attributed to him.

He wrote better than any other president has. His English was precise in vocabulary and mellifluous in its rhythms. He authored only one short book, *Notes on Virginia*, but it is a gem. Mostly, he wrote letters, lots of them; 18,000 survive. When it is remembered that most were responses to letters he had just received—his topic was assigned to him; in other words, he replied "off the top of his head" with no time for rewrites—the quality of his language is astonishing.

As a thinker Jefferson was neither original nor profound. His mind was compartmentalized, unlike Hamilton's or Adams's or Madison's. One historian has called him a "fragmentarian," which is a good reason to take care when using the term "Jeffersonian" to describe anything more systematic than inclinations.

Inevitably, he was inconsistent and self-contradictory. He pontificated endlessly about the virtues of the "common man" but, a Virginia aristocrat to the core, was no more a democrat than Hamilton was. Jefferson praised farming above all other ways of life, but the nitty-gritty of agriculture bored him. (John

Adams, when at home in Quincy, Massachusetts, pitched in with the chores from sowing to haying to shoveling manure and made no fuss about it, philosophical or otherwise.) Jefferson called cities "pestilential to the morals, the health, and the liberties of man" and was particularly harsh on New York and Philadelphia. But he lived ecstatically in Paris at a time when the misery of the Parisian poor—a large majority of the city's population—made New York and Philadelphia look heavenly.

Jefferson unambivalently denounced slavery in his younger years and, his entire life, when pressed on the subject, he replied that the institution was a curse on everyone involved in it. Then he changed the subject. For he owned hundreds of slaves each of the last fifty years of his life and he allowed only two to go free (both, probably, his own children). When sorely pressed for money, he sold slaves in order to raise it, 160 on one occasion. (Washington refused to sell slaves to a fate that was necessarily uncertain.) When northerners began openly to criticize southerners for clinging to slavery, Jefferson was all but explicit in saying that if the critics seriously threatened the institution, Virginia would be justified in leaving the Union in order to preserve it.

Jefferson could be juvenile, as when he said that every generation should write its own constitution and that, given a choice between government without newspapers and newspapers without government, he would opt for the latter. It takes some searching, but he even wrote a few sentences that, on a freshman's term paper, would by circled in red ink: "The President is fortunate to get off as the bubble is bursting, leaving others to hold the bag."

A Few Continuities

Jefferson was a fascinating conversationalist, but he hated giving speeches and avoided them whenever possible. He

Shop 'Til You Drop

Jefferson is the patron saint of economical government, an honor he deserves. He insisted that his secretary of the treasury count by the penny when he drafted federal budgets. Personally, however, Jefferson was a spendthrift. He spent as much as $2,800 a year on wine, up to $50 a day on groceries at a time when a turkey cost 50¢. Twice when he had a new architectural idea, he had large parts of Monticello torn down and rebuilt. In Paris during the 1780s, he lived as extravagantly as the French nobles with whom he hobnobbed; when he visited John and Abigail Adams in London, the frenzy of his shopping spree appalled the thrifty New Englanders.

Already rich in land and slaves, Jefferson inherited more acreage and slaves from his wife when she died in 1782—also a huge debt her father had bequeathed her. Jefferson was never again out of debt and he never made what can be called a serious attempt at belt-tightening to reduce it. He sold slaves, land, and even his beloved library when his creditors threatened to take legal action. When he died in 1826, he saddled his daughter with so much debt that she had to sell Monticello, Republican shrine though it had become.

Courtesy of the Thomas Jefferson Memorial Foundation

Stapleton Collection HIP/The Image Works

Thomas Jefferson, author of the Declaration of Independence, second vice president and third president of the United States. The co-founder (with James Madison) of the Jefferson Republican party, he was a man of broad intellectual interests, a talented architect, a gourmet, and the best writer of any president. As a politician he was skilled but devious, scheming from behind the scenes while his disciples (who were numerous) did the dirty work. Jefferson's presidency was not successful except for his acquisition of Louisiana in 1803. Although the purchase violated his own principles, Jefferson went ahead because it doubled the size of the United States, avoided a was with France, and frustrated British designs on the mouth of the Mississippi river.

mumbled his inaugural address which was conciliatory and almost nonpartisan. "Every difference of opinion is not a difference in principle," he said, "We have called by different names brethren of the same principle. We are all republicans, we are all federalists."

Jefferson did quietly shelve some of his prepresidential positions, and he left some Federalist programs in place. (The "deal" with Senator Bayard?) Nothing more was heard of the right of states to nullify federal laws within their borders. He allowed Hamilton's financial edifice to stand; like Washington and Adams, he deposited federal revenues in the Bank of the United States that he had called unconstitutional and a servant of speculators. He appointed as secretary of the treasury a Swiss-born Pennsylvanian, Albert Gallatin, who was a responsible money manager.

And Some Departures

However, Jefferson rejected the Hamiltonian shibboleth that a national debt was a blessing. Gallatin devised a schedule for eliminating the government's debt by 1817. Jefferson slashed expenditures that had been high under Washington and Adams. The army's appropriation was reduced from $4 million to $2 million, the navy's from $3.5 million to $1 million. Jefferson pardoned everyone convicted under the Sedition Act, all of them his supporters, of course. He restored the five-year residency for citizenship and replaced many Federalists drawing government salaries with Republicans. He did not have much patronage to hand out. The federal government employed 3,000, but most were postal employees and customs collectors who were paid little for doing hard work. Jefferson had only about 300 more or less desirable jobs at his disposal.

Jefferson brought a dramatically new style to the presidency. He disliked the pomp and protocol of the Federalist administrations. Instead of bowing, he shook hands. He abolished presidential levées (regularly scheduled, highly formal receptions) and, much to the annoyance of high-ranking officials and diplomats, he paid scant attention to protocol assigning a rank of precedence—a chair at the dinner table, a position in a procession—to every senator, representative, judge, cabinet member, and minister from abroad. Even at state dinners, guests had to scramble for the places they believed appropriate to their dignity. At the small dinner parties he preferred, Jefferson served his guests himself.

Jefferson's "republican simplicity" was made easier by the move of the capital, the summer before his inauguration, from sophisticated Philadelphia to Washington. Washington was not really a city in 1801. It was a hodgepodge of partly constructed public buildings and ramshackle boardinghouses isolated from one another by dense woods and swamps in which strangers routinely got lost. There were few private homes. For decades to come, there would be no houses suitable for congressmen's families. Wives and children stayed home. Capital social life was masculine and on the raw side: smoky card games, heavy drinking, even brawls.

These departures hardly constituted the "Revolution of 1800" that Jefferson called his election. The only fundamental innovation in government during Jefferson's presidency was effected by the Federalist Chief Justice of the Supreme Court, John Marshall, who was appointed days before Jefferson was inaugurated.

Marshall, Marbury, and Madison

During his final weeks as president, John Adams appointed forty-two Federalists to various federal courts. Federal judges served (on good behavior) for life, so Adams's "midnight judges," all good Federalists, of course, were securing long-term employment and Adams was ensuring that the judiciary would enforce Federalist principles. (The Jefferson Republicans had won majorities in both Houses of Congress as well as the presidency.)

The most important of Adams's appointments was 45-year-old John Marshall of Virginia, the fourth Chief Justice of the Supreme Court. Marshall was related to Jefferson, but their political principles were diametrically opposed and, for good measure, they disliked one another. Marshall is the major figure of the era with whom we of the twenty-first century would be most comfortable. As careless of protocol and his dress as Jefferson, he was good-humored and personable. Always, excepting Jefferson, he got along personally with political opponents; he remained good friends with many of them. He liked his Madeira wine, poured it generously, and was reputed in both Virginia and Washington to serve the best there was.

The first important case to come before the Marshall Court involved another midnight judge, William Marbury. Adams appointed him to a judgeship literally hours before he left office but, somehow, Adams's secretary of state (none other than John Marshall!) failed to deliver Marbury's commission to him. When Jefferson's secretary of state, James Madison, sat down at his desk, he found the document that put Marbury on the bench sitting on top. Madison filed it away; Marbury never received it.

Marbury sued for a writ of *mandamus*, a court order that commands a government official to perform a duty he has neglected. In 1803, *Marbury* v. *Madison* reached the Supreme Court. Already, Marshall had created a cooperative and personal spirit among the justices—they even boarded together—whom he gracefully dominated. He encouraged single unanimous opinions—no dissents—and was willing to do the lion's share of the Court's work; he wrote most of the Court's opinions and would do so for thirty years.

In the *Marbury* v. *Madison* decision, Marshall scolded Madison for his inappropriate behavior. However, instead of commanding Madison to deliver Marbury's commission (which would probably have precipitated a grave constitutional crisis), Marshall ruled that the section of the Judiciary Act of 1790 that Marbury cited was unconstitutional (for reasons unrelated to the dispute with Madison). Congress did not have the power, under the Constitution, to enact the law it had.

Judicial Review

Marbury v. *Madison* may not have been flawless constitutional law. It was, however, a political masterstroke with profound implications. By sacrificing the paycheck of one Federalist politico and negating part of one Federalist law, Marshall asserted the Supreme Court's power to decide whether or not acts of Congress signed by the president were constitutional, voiding federal laws the Court decided were not. The Supreme Court, Marshall said, not only judged cases according to law; it also judged the validity of the law itself.

The principle of judicial review was nothing new. Any number of people had suggested that it was the soundest way of determining the validity of federal laws. But the Founding Fathers had dodged the issue. Nothing in the Constitution vested the Supreme Court with this substantial power. Judicial review enabled the Supreme Court to trump both the executive and legislative branches of the government. Only a constitutional amendment (or the Court itself) could reverse a decision. Implicitly, *Marbury* v. *Madison* condemned the contention of the Kentucky and Virginia Resolutions that state legislatures had the power to find federal laws unconstitutional within a state. (Marshall could not have then known that Jefferson and Madison had written the resolutions, but he knew that Jefferson Republicans were responsible.)

Unable to fight Marshall on high ground, Jefferson launched a campaign of machination and low blows against the Federalist judiciary. He got rid of some Federalist judges by abolishing their jobs. Then the Republicans impeached and removed from office a Federalist judge in New Hampshire, John Pickering. Pickering was easy pickings; he was given to drunken tirades in court and was probably insane.

But Jefferson, who wanted to inch closer to Marshall himself, was stymied when his followers impeached Supreme Court Justice Samuel Chase. Chase was grossly prejudiced, overtly partisan, sometimes asinine. But the Senate, despite a Republican majority, refused to find him guilty of the "high crimes and misdemeanors" that the Constitution defines as grounds for impeachment. Like other presidents unhappy with the Supreme Court, Jefferson had no choice but to wait until seats fell vacant in order to change its complexion. He was to appoint three justices, but they too were captivated by Marshall's mind, personality, and will.

THE LOUISIANA PURCHASE

Jefferson believed that, in *Marbury*, Marshall, like Hamilton ten years earlier, had tweaked the Constitution. Almost simultaneously, however, Jefferson gave the document a real shaking in what turned out to be the most significant achievement of his presidency, the purchase of Louisiana from France for $15 million. This was not just our state of Louisiana but included the better part of the thirteen states that lie between the Mississippi River and the Rocky Mountains, 828,000 square miles. The United States paid less than 3¢ an acre for the colony. It was the greatest real estate bargain of all time. The seller was France.

Sugar and Foodstuffs

Which nation, officially in 1801, did not own it. Since 1763, Louisiana had been a Spanish colony. However, Napoleon

Bonaparte had reduced Spain into France's client state and quietly, but not all that secretly, he forced the Spanish government to agree to a return of the province to France. Louisiana was still mostly wilderness, a splotch of color on maps. Only about 50,000 Europeans lived in the colony. Louisiana's agricultural potential, however, was obvious. Napoleon wanted its fertile lands as the breadbasket for France's lucrative sugar-producing islands in the West Indies, tiny Martinique and Guadaloupe and, most of all, large and fabulously profitable Saint-Domingue—Haiti. Haiti produced more sugar than the rest of the West Indies combined.

The crop was grown, of course, by African slaves, more than 500,000. They were worked with less regard for their humanity than any other slaves in the Americas, In 1790, Haitian slave owners had to import fully 48,000 Africans to maintain the labor force. Much of the slaves' food was imported and, during the Anglo-French wars of the 1790s, American merchants provided it. Even during America's quasi-war with France, American merchants fed the population because much of Haiti was then under the control not of the French colonial government but of "people of color," people of mixed race—mulattos to Americans—who, in 1791, had staged a French Revolution of their own and abolished slavery.

Americans, especially slave owners, were shocked by the former slaves' wholesale massacres of whites. Some 10,000 slave owners (and their slaves) fled the island in one year, most to Louisiana. Even when the carnage ceased, blacks battled "people of color" who owned a quarter of the land and slaves. But everyone—the blacks, mulattos, and French beleaguered in a few enclaves—paid premium prices for American grain and livestock.

Napoleon intended to crush the revolution, restore slavery, and cut the Americans out of their bonanza market by provisioning Haiti from Louisiana. He sent a crack, battle-tested army of 20,000 to Haiti, but it was soon reduced to an ineffective remnant by malaria and yellow fever (thousands of soldiers died before disembarking) and battle with the blacks. Thomas Jefferson offered to assist the French, but he soon backed off when, on Napoleon's orders, Spain revoked the American right of deposit in New Orleans, that is, the right to warehouse goods and do business in the city. This was bad news for the 400,000 Americans living in the Mississippi Valley. Annually, they had been shipping 20,000 tons of provisions and lumber through New Orleans. To westerners, in James Madison's words, the Mississippi was "the Hudson, the Delaware, the Potomac, and all the navigable rivers of the Atlantic formed into one stream." Jefferson added, "there is on the globe one single spot, the possessor of which is our natural and habitual enemy. It is New Orleans."

All-out war with France, so recently averted, seemed inevitable. Congress voted to call up 80,000 state militiamen. But an overland attack on New Orleans would have to be backed up by a naval blockade which Jefferson's evisceration of the navy made impossible. Jefferson, like John Adams, turned to diplomacy.

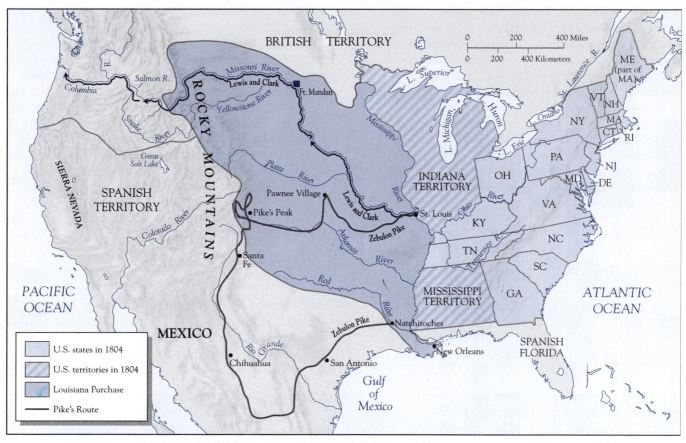

MAP 12:1 **Louisiana and the Expeditions of Discovery, 1804–1807.** The Louisiana Purchase doubled the area of the United States. Except for the banks of the Mississippi and Missouri Rivers, little was known about the country and its native peoples until the federally sponsored explorations of the Lewis and Clark expedition through the northern parts of Louisiana and the semi-official Zebulon Pike party in the south.

An Offer Not to Be Refused

Jefferson instructed his minister in France, Robert Livingston, to offer Napoleon $2 million (voted him by Congress) for a tract of undeveloped land on the lower Mississippi where the Americans could build their own entrepôt for the westerners' exports. In January 1803, uneasy because there had been no message from Livingston, Jefferson sent James Monroe to Paris to offer France up to $10 million (a sum that had appeared in no congressional appropriation) for the city of New Orleans and West Florida, the gulf coast of Mississippi and Alabama.

Monroe was stunned to learn that, just a few days before his arrival in Paris, the French foreign minister (Talleyrand again) had offered to sell the whole of Louisiana for $15 million. This remarkable turnabout in Napoleon's plans for Louisiana came about because Haiti's black and colored rebels, assisted by malaria and yellow fever, had utterly destroyed the French army that Napoleon had sent to put an end to the rebellion. Haiti was lost to France, and Louisiana, therefore, worthless. Napoleon intended to resume his war with Great Britain and he reasoned, correctly, that one of Britain's first responses would be to send the Royal Navy to seize New Orleans. The Americans had the money; better to take it rather than to lose Louisiana in battle.

Livingston and Monroe jumped at the offer and Jefferson sealed the deal despite the fact that Congress had authorized spending $2 million, not $15 million. Much more embarrassing, for the Republican Congress would cough up the money, the Constitution made no provision for such acquisitions of territory, nor did it provide for conferring immediate American citizenship on the French and Spanish residents of Louisiana as the agreement with Napoleon required. According to the "strict construction" of the Constitution that Jefferson had propounded, the Louisiana Purchase was unconstitutional.

Jefferson—sheepishly—wrote that "what is practicable must often control what is pure theory." Confidentially, he instructed Republicans in Congress that "the less we say about constitutional difficulties respecting Louisiana the better." The Louisiana Purchase was too incredible a stroke of good fortune to reject. Even Republicans far more extreme in their Jeffersonian principles than the president, notably Congressman John Randolph of Roanoke, a loose cannon his entire life, held their tongues. The Federalists gleefully made hay of Jefferson's "hypocrisy," but they did not oppose an act of nationalistic exuberance bolder than anything Alexander Hamilton had dared.

African American Explorer

In the informality wilderness demands, William Clark's slave, York, participated in the great expedition as an equal. Meriwether Lewis recorded that Indians thought York was a white man wearing paint and rubbed him, trying to remove the makeup. Lewis noted that "instead of inspiring any prejudice, his color served to procure him additional advantages from the Indians," a polite way of saying that a number of Indian ladies wanted to have a black child. Clark freed York after the expedition, but rather gracelessly. Despite York's invaluable services, Clark had to be pressured by Lewis and others to do the decent thing.

Pike's Expedition

Shortly before Lewis and Clark arrived back in St. Louis in 1806, Zebulon Pike, an army officer commanding seventeen men, left the city to explore the southern part of the Louisiana Purchase. At the Rockies ("Pike's Peak") he headed south to Santa Fe and deep into Mexico, returning to Louisiana the next year. His exploits were not as celebrated as those of the Lewis and Clark Expedition, in part because Jefferson suspected him of scouting for Aaron Burr. Unknowingly, he may have been doing just that. He was sent west not by the president, but on the orders of Louisiana Governor Wilkinson, who testified against Burr but may have been in cahoots with him.

The Magnificent Journey

Louisiana could be drawn on a map but it was, in fact, a mystery. Only a few grubby trappers and traders had wandered far from the Mississippi and Missouri Rivers. Congress appropriated a modest $2,500 to finance an expedition of exploration of the country to gather scientific information about it and to search for a feasible overland route to the Pacific.

Jefferson appointed a Virginia neighbor, Meriwether Lewis, to head the expedition. Lewis persuaded William Clark, his friend and former commanding officer, to be a co-commander (officially, Lewis was in charge). Jefferson, himself no wilder-

Montana Historical Society, Helena

York was a valuable member of the Lewis and Clark expedition, strong, rarely ill, resourceful in the wilderness, decisive in crises. He was William Clark's slave but, despite York's services, Clark had to be pressured to reward him with his freedom.

ness traveler, attended to the most picayune details of preparation, listing in his own hand the equipment and provisions the explorers would take with them.

The journey of Lewis and Clark exceeded anything ventured by conquistadors or voyageurs. A party of forty men (and, for most of the way, an Indian girl and her baby) plus one Newfoundland dog rowed, poled, and pulled their skiffs up the Missouri to the spectacular falls now the site of Great Falls, Montana. Learning from the Mandan, Shoshone, and Nez Percé Indians that a portage of 16 miles would bring them to a river flowing westerly, they deduced that it was a tributary of the Columbia River. (The mouth of the Columbia had been discovered only in 1792.) They reached the Pacific on November 15, 1805. There they lived four and a half months—it rained every day but twelve—and returned to St. Louis in September 1806.

Lewis and Clark were among the last Americans to contact Indians untouched by white civilization. Their experience is instructive. While they had a few uneasy moments with the Sioux and Shoshone, the explorers were involved in nothing resembling conflict with the many tribes with whom they dealt. (There was a skirmish with Blackfoot Indians on the return trip.) The native peoples of the interior were not only friendly, they were also hospitable and generous once they learned that Lewis and Clark were not members of enemy tribes. When Lewis needed to prove this, he exposed his arm, which was not burned brown by the sun, to show that his skin was white. York, Clark's slave, was a source of endless fascination because of his color. Indians rubbed him raw, thinking he had painted himself black.

The touchiest moment on the westbound trip was with the Shoshone, who, at first, were not friendly. In the single most astonishing moment of the journey, Sacajawea, a Shoshone teenager carrying her infant son on her back, recognized her brother among the Shoshone warriors. Sacajawea had been kidnapped by another tribe years earlier and been purchased as a wife by a Frenchman whom Lewis and Clark hired as a guide.

The tribes of the Pacific coast were familiar with whites. Spanish, American, and British seamen, whalers, and fur traders had camped among them. One woman had the name "Jonathan Bowman" tattooed on her leg. Among the words the coastal Indians had adopted into their language were "misquito, powder, shot, nife, file, damned rascal, son of a bitch."

The Burr-Hamilton Duel

Louisiana also attracted the attention of Vice President Aaron Burr. His political fortunes tumbled with the election of 1800. Jefferson snubbed him; he believed that Burr had connived to steal the election from him. And the restless Burr found the vice presidency's obscurity and impotence stultifying.

Burr was involved in a scheme with a few embittered Federalists called the Essex Junto to detach New England and New York from the United States. The plan—if it got far enough beyond fantasy to be called a plan— depended on Burr winning the governorship of New York. But he was defeated, in part because of campaign propaganda authored by Alexander Hamilton. The propaganda was nasty, but that was routine in New York politics. When the two old enemies exchanged insults, however, Burr challenged Hamilton to a duel.

Hamilton repeatedly said he disapproved of dueling, and his son had been killed in one shortly before Burr's challenge. In fact, while he had never faced a man, both armed with pistols, Hamilton had been involved in ten "affairs of honor," the ritualized exchange of accusations and grievances of which the duel was the final act—unless the offending party apologized or a peaceful resolution was negotiated. All of Hamilton's affairs of honor were resolved without gunfire.

Not the affair with Burr. On July 11, 1804, Burr, Hamilton, their seconds, surgeons, and two .54-caliber dueling pistols were rowed across the Hudson to Weehawken, high on the New Jersey Palisades. They fired at one another from 20 paces. Hamilton's bullet went astray; his seconds said he deliberately shot high, as reluctant duelists sometimes did. Burr aimed; his bullet pierced Hamilton's liver and lodged in his spine. He died the next day.

Hamilton was never beloved. He was too adept at offending people for that. But the death of so eminent a man in a duel was shocking. Burr was indicted for murder in New York and New Jersey. He fled to the South while friends ironed out his legal difficulties. His name mud among both Jeffersonians and Federalists and not yet 50 years of age, what was Burr to do?

The Burr Conspiracy

Burr went west. He linked up with one Harman Blennerhasset, an Irish exile who lived opulently, on wealth never explained, on an island in the Ohio River. Blennerhasset financed the construction of thirteen flatboats, including a barge for Burr outfitted with glass windows, a fireplace, a promenade deck, and a wine "cellar." With sixty men, the flotilla meandered slowly down the Ohio, then the Mississippi.

Burr met secretly with Andrew Jackson, Tennessee's most prominent politician and Indian fighter. In New Orleans, he huddled with the head of the French Ursuline Convent, perhaps a polite gesture, perhaps something more. Mostly, he talked with James Wilkinson, the territorial governor of Louisiana who was well along in earning a reputation for chicanery, personal treachery, and corruption.

Wilkinson and Burr (and Jackson?) were plotting something or, at least, discussing the possibility of a plot. Exactly what it was remains mysterious. Neither Burr nor Wilkinson was the type to put anything on paper. Some said Burr planned to invade Texas, the northeastern corner of Spanish Mexico, and set Burr up as its dictator. Others accused him of planning to detach the Louisiana Territory and even some western states from the Union. (Andrew Jackson was visibly shaken when he was told that Burr had been arrested.)

Which he soon was. Jefferson believed the worst of Burr; Wilkinson, possibly to save his own skin, accused Burr of treason. Jefferson determined to hang his former vice president; it was not the president's finest hour what with the little evidence against Burr being from very impeachable sources. Worse, Burr's defense attorney was Luther Martin, known in equal parts as a prodigious drinker and the country's best criminal lawyer. And then, because Burr's alleged treason

White Americans in Slavery

North African Muslims had crossed the Sahara to enslave blacks for centuries before the trans-Atlantic slave trade began. But slavery was not linked with race in Islamic lands as it was in America. Indeed, the Arabs preferred white slaves. So, during the 1600s, raiders from the Barbary states (Morocco, Algeria, Tunis, and Tripoli) ranged far to the north to capture Europeans for enslavement. Entire villages in Ireland were carried off. In a single Barbary raid in Iceland, 800 people were enslaved. Fisherman off Newfoundland were seized.

By the mid-1700s, there were few slave-catching raids in northern Europe although the Mediterranean coasts of Italy, France, and Spain remained vulnerable. The North Africans increasingly depended on trade with black Africa for slaves put to heavy labor, household servants, military units, concubines, and eunuchs to attend the concubines. However, Barbary corsairs—pirates—continued to seize merchant ships of every nation. Their cargos were less important than their crewmen, who were enslaved.

Reports as to how well Europeans (and a few colonials) were treated as slaves differed radically. Most narratives written by white slaves who were freed and reports by consuls and Catholic priests who went to the Barbary States to aid them emphasized their wretchedness: minimal food, lodgings in dungeons, killing labor with a 50-pound chain on their ankles. Women and men were forced into "revolting sexual practices." In stark contrast to this picture, William Eaton, the American consul in Tunis, said that "the Christian slaves among the barbarians of Africa are treated with more humanity than the Africans among the professing Christians of civilized America." This was certainly true of those who "turned Turk"—converted to Islam. Indeed, a few talented "renegades" rose to high positions in the rulers courts; others commanded slave-hunting voyages.

During the 1700s, the Barbary states suffered an economic decline. The population of Algiers, 100,000 in 1650, was 30,000 a century later. The once formidable Barbary fleets shrunk so that, in some years, Tripoli, Algiers, and Tunis each had as few as a dozen vessels and many of them were obsolete. Long after Europeans had abandoned oar-driven vessels in favor of sailing ships carrying tons of powerful cannon, many Barbary warships were galleys carrying a hundred or more fighting men armed with cutlasses and small arms. The Barbary navies were not battle fleets. When they sighted a European frigate, they fled. By 1750, their major function was piracy or, more properly, privateering, for they were authorized in their work by the pasha of Tripoli, the dey of Algiers, the bey of Tunis, and the emperor of Morocco. Their corsairs preyed on European and American merchant vessels in the Mediterranean not primarily for their cargos but to capture their crews.

While enslaved seamen were still put to work on the bey's, dey's, or pasha's construction projects, fewer were sold into private ownership. By 1750 they were less valuable as laborers than as hostages held for ransom and as inducements to maritime nations to negotiate treaties with the Barbary rulers so as to exempt ships flying their flags from seizure. In return for substantial annual payments of tribute in money and commodities, the Barbary rulers granted immunity—as long as the payments were made on time—to Venice, Spain, France, Denmark, Britain, and other states. It was a protection racket and very expensive. Just in 1785, buying seamen immunity from seizure cost Spain a million silver dollars, 50 cannon and 10,000 cannonballs, 20,000 kegs of gunpowder, and 500,000 musketballs.

Great Britain paid tribute most years so that, during the colonial period, American vessels were usually safe. Only about 130 American seamen were enslaved between 1650 and 1783.

After independence, of course, the United States lost imperial protection. Indeed, some British officials encouraged the Barbary pirates to seek out American merchantmen. In 1784, a Moroccan corsair seized the *Betsey* and its crew of ten. The next year, Algerine pirates captured the *Dauphin* and *Maria,* enslaving twenty-one. Thomas Jefferson, then minister in France, was enraged. He met with diplomats from Portugal, Sicily, Venice, Malta, Denmark, and Sweden and sketched the outline of a joint naval expedition to end the kidnapping by bombarding the Barbary cities. John Jay and John Adams overruled him, pointing out to Jefferson the unpleasant fact that the United States had no navy. In 1785, Congress sold off the last frigate built during the Revolution.

In 1793, during Washington's presidency, Barbary pirates seized eleven American ships, enslaving 104 men. Presidents Washington and Adams opted for paying ransom and tribute. However, when Jefferson became president in 1801 and the annual payoff to the pasha of Tripoli was due, Jefferson dispatched a squadron to Tripoli—ships Adams had built with Jefferson opposing their construction. But when the frigate *Philadelphia* went aground in Tripoli harbor and fell into the pasha's hands, Jefferson and James Madison swallowed their pride and paid tribute until, during the War of 1812, all the Barbary states except Morocco hit American shipping hard. In 1815, the war concluded, Stephen Decatur sailed with ten warships to Algiers, Tunis, and Tripoli and, with the help of cannon, largely ended the threat to Americans. Barbary piracy was not finally destroyed until the 1830s when France began to establish its colonial domination of North Africa.

The Rhode Island Historical Society #Rhix3 3035, All Rights Reserved

President Jefferson dispatched several punitive expeditions against the Barbary states. In this painting the fleet is bombarding Tripoli in present-day Libya. The attacks were popular in the United States and effective—briefly. The Barbary states remained a threat to commerce in the Mediterranean until France began to seize North Africa as colonies.

occurred in Virginia, the presiding judge of the circuit court in Richmond was Jefferson's longtime enemy, Chief Justice John Marshall. Ironically, Marshall and other justices rode circuit because Jefferson's Republicans had repealed a Federalist law that spared them the onerous duty.

Marshall was too conscious of his and the Supreme Court's integrity to preside at the Burr trial with less than total impartiality. However, when he ruled that the crime of treason be defined strictly as an overt act—talk, no matter how loose, would not do—the case against Burr was doomed. He had *done* nothing. Burr was acquitted, lived abroad for a few years, then returned to New York where he prospered as a lawyer.

FOREIGN WOES

Like Washington and Adams, Jefferson was bedeviled by problems overseas. Unlike his predecessors, Jefferson contributed to his problems by reducing the size of the navy Adams and the Federalists had created during the quasi-war. Before the cost-cutting began, however, Jefferson put the little American navy to work on a pet project. Indeed, in virtually the first important act of his presidency—three weeks after he was sworn in—Jefferson dispatched a naval squadron to punish the Barbary pirates of North Africa, whom he had passionately loathed for twenty years.

The Barbary Pirates

The Barbary states were four Muslim principalities on the Mediterranean sea: Tripoli (Libya today), Tunis, Algiers, and Morocco. They were poor and backward. The common people survived by fishing, farming, and trading by caravan across the Sahara. The elite lived in decadent luxury by sending out privateers to seize European merchant ships. Their cargos were less valuable than the crews. Captured seamen were enslaved and held for ransom. Even more lucrative, the Barbary states negotiated treaties with seafaring nations. In

A Present for the Pasha

The annual payment to the pasha of Tripoli, which Jefferson tried to terminate in 1801, consisted of $40,000 in gold and silver, $12,000 in Spanish money, and an assortment of diamond rings, watches, and brocade. The rulers of the Barbary states considered the loot as gifts from a friend rather than as extortion. Thus, in 1806, the bey of Tunis, who also received tribute, sent Jefferson a gift of four Arabian horses.

return for annual payments of money and goods, the pasha, bey, dey, and "emperor" (of Morocco) granted freedom of passage to merchantmen flying a friendly flag and carrying the proper papers. They justified what westerners called piracy on the grounds that Muslims were at war with all Christians unless a treaty of friendship was signed. We would call Barbary policy a protection racket.

During the 1790s, the United States had paid the tribute, something between $1 million and $2 million. Jefferson consistently condemned the payoffs (while, paradoxically, he opposed the proposal, in 1794, to build a navy). When he became president and found on his desk a reminder from Tripoli that the 1801 installment was due, Jefferson dispatched a squadron of warships to the Mediterranean to bombard Tripoli until the piracy ceased. Unfortunately, the frigate *Philadelphia* ran aground in Tripoli and the Pasha had a fine ship for his navy and 309 captives, the crew of the *Philadelphia,* to ransom, more Americans than had been enslaved by the Barbary states since independence.

Marines, in a daring raid led by Stephen Decatur ("to the shores of Tripoli" in the Marine Corps hymn), denied the pasha his frigate. They boarded and burned it, making a national hero of Decatur. Only in 1805, however, was a settlement negotiated that freed the last prisoners at a cost of $60,000. Jefferson had discovered that the cheapest Barbary policy was to pay up.

Caught in the Middle

A more serious problem was the Anglo-French war that began shortly after the Louisiana Purchase. Jefferson declared neutrality and, as during the 1790s, American shipowners reaped bonanza profits trading with both sides. Particularly lucrative was the re-export trade: Sugar and molasses were carried to the United States, then shipped—re-exported—to Europe. Because the ships flew the neutral American flag and their voyages originated in the United States, the trade did not, ostensibly, violate the rules of war. In two years, America's re-export business quadrupled in value from $13 million to $60 million.

Then, in 1806, the Anglo-French war stalemated. The Royal Navy was supreme at sea after the famous battle of Trafalgar when the British virtually destroyed the navies of France and its ally, Spain. On the continent, however, in rapid succession, Napoleon's armies soundly defeated Britain's allies, Austria, Russia, and Prussia, dictating the terms of the peace treaties.

Britain and France dug in for a protracted economic war, each aiming to ruin the other by crippling its trade. The British issued the Orders in Council which forbade neutrals (meaning, most of all, the United States) to trade in Europe unless their ships first called at a British port to purchase a license. New England merchants, who inclined to be pro-British anyway, did not find the Orders intolerable; Britain was on the way to northern European ports anyway. However, Napoleon retaliated with the Berlin and Milan decrees of 1806 and 1807. They enacted what Napoleon called the Continental System: Neutral vessels that observed the Orders in Council would be seized by the French.

The Granger Collection, New York

A British press-gang forces a crewman from an American ship into service in the Royal Navy. The British insisted that they pressed only British subjects, but many men born under the British flag considered themselves Americans and mistakes were made. If a pressed seaman survived and later proved he was American born, he was released but not compensated for the injustice done him.

American merchants were caught in the middle. Within a year the British seized 1,000 American ships and the French about 500. Even then, the wartime trade was profitable. A Massachusetts senator calculated that if a merchant sent three ships out and two were dead losses, the profits from the third made up for them and returned a dandy profit. Statistics bear him out. In 1807, at the height of the seizures, Massachusetts merchants earned $15 million in freight charges.

Impressment Again

There was more at stake than confiscated ships. During the wars with France, Britain launched a massive naval construction program that more than doubled the size of the Royal Navy. The navy had a manpower shortage far more serious than in the 1790s. By 1810, the navy consisted of more than 600 warships; 175 were ships of the line, larger than any American vessel. The shortage of seamen to man them became critical.

Crews reduced to ineffectiveness by disease, battle, and desertion were routine. Impressment of replacements, from American as well as British vessels, became more aggressive. The British insisted that their captains pressed only British subjects. There were plenty of them on American vessels. Between 10,000 and 20,000 seamen in the American merchant marine were born in Britain or British colonies. (A seaman on an American ship was paid up to three times what British merchant seamen were.)

But many were naturalized American citizens, a transfer of allegiance the British did not recognize. And there were

The Two-Term Tradition

When Washington decided against a third term as president, he made no point of principle about it. He was old and tired, he said. When Jefferson said he would retire after two terms, he understood that his decision was historically significant. "A few more precedents," he wrote, "will oppose the obstacle of habit to anyone after a while who shall endeavor to extend his term. Perhaps it may beget a disposition to establish it by an amendment to the Constitution."

Madison, Monroe, and Andrew Jackson all retired after two terms. So did Ulysses S. Grant although he later tried to run again. Theodore Roosevelt retired after nearly eight years in office although, having been elected only once, he could have run again without violating the tradition. Like Grant, Roosevelt tried to get the White House back four years after leaving it. Woodrow Wilson and Calvin Coolidge both wanted a third term but dared not say it, so powerful had the tradition become. Only in 1940, with Europe at war, did Franklin D. Roosevelt

(FDR) seek and win a third term (and four years later, a fourth).

Republican hatred for FDR was so intense that, in 1947, two years after Roosevelt died, they had a kick at his corpse by proposing the Twenty-Second Amendment to the Constitution. Ratified, it forbids a president more than two terms. Ironically, the two presidents since who could have easily won a third term had it been constitutional, were Republicans: Dwight D. Eisenhower and Ronald Reagan.

---

plenty of "mistakes,"—American-born sailors impressed into the Royal Navy by a cynical or desperate commander. Between 1803 and 1812, about 6,000 United States citizens were forced into service by British press gangs. (British courts were more scrupulous about the rules of impressment than naval commanders were; about 4,000 pressed Americans were released when they reached a British port.)

The impressment crisis came to a head in June 1807. When HMS *Leopard,* with fifty guns, was resupplying in the Chesapeake Bay, four sailors deserted. Safely on American soil, they taunted their officers and made the mistake of telling them they had signed up in the American navy, aboard a frigate, the *Chesapeake.* The *Leopard* sailed off and waited. When the *Chesapeake* left port and refused to allow a British press gang to board, the *Leopard* fired three broadsides, killing eighteen sailors. The press gang then boarded and seized the four deserters.

Three of the four were blacks, two of them American born. Newspapers and politicians made little of their race (which would have diluted the impact of their propaganda), but much of Britain's arrogant insult of the nation's honor. The *Chesapeake* was not a merchantman making a dollar for a Boston merchant; it was a ship of the American navy. The patriotic uproar was deafening. Jefferson, who had hoped to resolve the impressment crisis by negotiation, had to act. Still, he meant to avoid war with Great Britain. He chose what he called "peaceable coercion," the Embargo Act of 1807.

The Embargo

The Embargo Act forbade American ships in port to set sail for foreign ports. Foreign vessels in American ports had to depart in ballast (carrying boulders or other worthless bulk in their hulls; no cargos). All imports and exports were prohibited. Jefferson was applying the same economic pressure on Great Britain that had been so successful in his youth in winning the repeal of the Townshend Acts. "Our commerce," Jefferson wrote, "is so valuable to them, that they will be glad to purchase it, when the only price we ask is to do us justice."

The embargo reduced American exports from $108 million to $22 million. The British found enough other sources

of foodstuffs to survive. Some 6,000 American merchant vessels slipped out of port with cargos legally designated for other American ports—the coastal trade—and sailed instead to the West Indies or Britain. Smugglers hauling exports across the border into Canada was so numerous and brazen that Jefferson's customs officers could only watch.

And the embargo caused grave hardships in American ports. Idle ships by the hundred rotted at anchor. The streets of ports were filled with tens of thousands of unemployed seamen and dock workers. Small businesses dependent on seamen's and stevedores' wages closed their doors. The Federalist party, badly maimed when Jefferson was reelected in 1804, began to make a comeback in New England and New York. Farmers in Pennsylvania and the western states remained good Republicans, but they complained vociferously when their crops could not be sold.

Jefferson wanted to hang on. He was sure that, in time, the embargo would bring Britain around. But he could not dictate to Republican congressmen as he once had. In the final days of his administration, the Embargo was repealed. On March 15, 1809, shortly after James Madison was inaugurated the fourth president, it was replaced by the Non-Intercourse Act. It opened trade with all nations except Britain and France, providing that the president could reopen trade with either of those two warring nations if it agreed to respect American shipping.

JEMMY APPLEJOHN AND THE WAR OF 1812

James Madison was a political philosopher of the first rank whose writings are still studied. But he was less suited to be a head of a government than Jefferson was. His only executive experience was as Jefferson's secretary of state and he lacked his idol's prestige. Jefferson's enemies vilified him; Madison's enemies (the same crowd) ridiculed him. They mocked his short stature—his famous wife, Dolley, towered over him—his pinched face, deeply furrowed even at age 50. The writer, Washington Irving quipped that "Little Jemmy" looked like a "withered applejohn," a dried apple. Madison was "too timid," Federalist Fisher Ames said. He was "wholly unfit for the Storms of War," according to a young Jefferson Republican, Henry Clay.

Madison Hornswoggled

He was humiliated almost immediately by the British. David Erskine, the British minister in Washington, signed a treaty with Madison agreeing to terms which entitled Madison to resume trade with Britain. In April, Madison did so and hundreds of American ships left port with cargos destined for Britain and the West Indies. Many had loaded up with British manufactures and were headed home when the British foreign office repudiated Erskine's treaty. An angry Madison reinstated Non-Intercourse while customs officials tried to clean up the mess: Which cargos coming into port were legal, which not?

In May 1810, Congress modified non-intercourse with Macon's Bill No. 2. It *opened* commerce with both Britain and France with the proviso that if either of the two ceased to molest American shipping, the United States would cut off trade with the other. Macon's Bill No. 2 was an invitation to mischief. Rather than avoiding war, it pledged the United States to become the economic ally of France or Britain, whichever of the two belligerents acted first.

Napoleon was the quicker. He revoked those parts of the Continental System that concerned American shipping. His purpose was to embroil the Americans and British in a shooting war and he succeeded, despite the fact that Britain, in response, revoked the Orders in Council. Once again, the slowness of trans-Atlantic communications played a fatal part in events. The British agreed to American demands on June 16, 1812. Two days later, across the ocean, under pressure from mostly young, super-patriotic westerners and southerners in Congress, Madison asked for a formal declaration of war. Napoleon's trickery had worked.

Opposition to the War

Madison asked for war on behalf of American commerce and the American seamen who were being impressed into the Royal Navy. However, opposition to the war, which was considerable, was centered in the Northeast, the section of the country most deeply dependent on overseas trade. In the House of Representatives, New England, New York, and New Jersey voted 34 to 14 against the War of 1812. Not a single Federalist voted for war. Connecticut's governor forbade the state militia to leave the state, a challenge to presidential authority.

In December 1814, Federalist leaders from Massachusetts, Connecticut, and Rhode Island assembled in Hartford, Connecticut, to discuss their grievances with "Mr. Madison's War." Hotheads at the Hartford Convention called openly for New England to secede from the United States rather than accept dictation from the South and West. However, moderate Federalists were in the majority. The Convention's resolutions included no threats but called strongly for reforms that would reduce the political power of the states where slavery was legal. There was no mention of the morality of slavery in the resolutions. The target of the Hartford Convention was the Constitution's three-fifths compromise that allotted the southern states extra seats in the House "representing" their slaves.

A few southern congressmen denounced the war for different reasons. Their chief spokesman was the erratic, eloquent, and usually vitriolic John Randolph of Roanoke, Virginia. Pompously or, perhaps whimsically, they called themselves "Tertium Quids," Latin for the "third somethings." They were not Federalists, but neither were they quite Republicans. They were the true Jeffersonians, they said, cleaving to the Republican principles that Madison and Jefferson himself had abandoned as early as 1806. Randolph listed those principles as

> love of peace, hatred of offensive war, jealousy of the State Governments toward the General Government; a dread of standing armies; a loathing of public debt, taxes, and excises; tenderness for the liberty of the citizen, jealous, Argus-eyed jealousy of the patronage of the President.

In 1812, Randolph accused Madison of embracing Hamiltonian militarism. Not one to mince words, he said that the president's army was an assembly of "mercenaries picked up from brothels and tippling houses."

The War Hawks

Who wanted war? Most Republicans representing agricultural regions voted for it. The Pennsylvania, southern, and western delegations in the House voted 65 to 15 to go to war. They were led by a young and exuberant gaggle of congressmen, many elected for the first time in 1810, known as "War Hawks." They brimmed with the cocky belligerence of youth and they were super-nationalists. They had been conditioned by Jefferson and his followers to regard Great Britain as the national enemy. They dreamed of completing the work of the Revolution by conquering Canada and annexing it to the United States.

The notion of conquering Canada was not far-fetched. Many Americans had settled in Upper Canada, present-day Ontario. Some openly called for making the region an American state. Militarily, the prospects for an American war of expansion were pretty good. Locked in mortal battle with Napoleon, Great Britain had reduced its professional army in Canada to a few thousand soldiers. There were large Canadian militias, but their reputations were no better than those of their American counterparts.

Canada's only formidable defenders were the Indian tribes of the Northwest Territory. They were bitterly anti-American; they were numerous and well armed by the British; and they had been revitalized by a religious revival and the emergence of the greatest of Native American leaders. Had the Indians' power been intact in 1812, the War Hawks might have been less cocky. But it was not. In November 1811, it had been shattered.

Revival

Canada's defense depended on the Delawares, Pottawottamies, Miamis, Shawnees, and some refugee Iroquois living south of the Great Lakes. Demoralized after their defeat at Fallen Timbers in 1794, the Indians of present-day Indiana and

Tecumseh, a Shawnee, was born about 1768. No other Indian leader quite measures up to him. He was well educated (self-educated) and understood the culture of the white settlers from having lived among them. He was devoted to preserving Indian cultures but did not share the mischievous mysticism of his brother, "The Prophet." Had he been at his capital, Tippecanoe, in 1811, it is unlikely the Indians would have suffered their crushing defeat there. Tecumseh was killed in battle in 1813.

Illinois were revitalized in the early 1800s by a reformed Shawnee drunk turned visionary, Tenskwatawa. Americans called him "The Prophet."

Tenskwatawa preached pan-tribalism. That is, he said that Indians must give up their ancient tribal animosities and recognize that all of them together had a common enemy in the relentlessly advancing white settlers. In order to stop the loss of their lands, the Prophet said, Indians must cease adopting white ways. They must move out of American-style houses, discard clothing made of purchased cloth, and stop using the white man's tools. The Prophet even preached that Indians should extinguish all their fires, for they had been ignited using the white man's flint and steel, and start new ones using Indian methods. Most important of all, Indians must give up the white man's alcohol, which, obvious to all, was the major element in the moral decay of the native peoples.

White settlers in the Northwest Territory paid little attention to the Indian religious revival until, in 1808, Tenskwatawa's followers expelled Christian Indians from their lands and founded a town, Tippecanoe (or Prophetstown) which was soon quite large. There, the Prophet's brother, Tecumseh ("Panther Lying in Wait'), by force of his intelligence and charismatic personality, made himself the chief of a confederation of virtually all the tribes of the Northwest Territory.

Tecumseh and Tippecanoe

Tenskwatawa was an inspired preacher, a mystic who was sometimes cockeyed. Unlike Tecumseh, however, he was no warrior. Tecumseh's reputation for bravery in battle dated back to the Indian victory over General St. Clair in 1792 when he was a teenager. Most important than bravery, Tecumseh understood the Americans' culture and strengths. For ten years, he had lived among whites, developing a strong personal friendship with a prominent Ohioan, James Galloway. Galloway owned 300 books with which Tecumseh educated himself. In 1808, he proposed marriage to Galloway's daughter, Rebecca. She consented on the condition that Tecumseh abandon Indian ways; they must live like Americans.

Tecumseh was torn. In the end, more sensible than most people in love, he concluded that his culture was too important to him. He left Rebecca and Ohio to join his brother at Tippecanoe. The sensible Tecumseh modified the Prophet's commandments. He exempted the white man's firearms from the Prophet's list of taboos and he ended the persecution of Christian Indians. He embarked on long journeys to convert more tribes to the Prophet's revitalization movement or, at least, to Tecumseh's pan-Indian military alliance. His effectiveness—even the nobility of his character—was

The Star-Spangled Banner
On the evening of September 13, 1814, Francis Scott Key, a lawyer, was detained on a British ship where he was arranging for the release of a prisoner. That night, the British shelled Fort McHenry, the chief defense for the city of Baltimore. The fort held out and the sight of the American flag waving atop its ramparts next morning inspired Key to write a verse, "The Star-Spangled Banner."

Key did the nation no favor by choosing as music an English song, "To Anacreon in Heaven." Perhaps because "Anacreon" was a bar-room drinking song, sung by people who, at the moment, did not care what they sounded like, "The Star Spangled Banner" resists attractive vocalization by all but the most gifted professional singers. This unfortunate reality has not discouraged the assignment of important renditions of the song to teenage rock and roll guitarists, actresses from television comedies, and mayors' nephews.

"The Star-Spangled Banner" has not been the national anthem for very long. Although unofficially sung as one since Key published it in 1814, it was not officially adopted by Congress until 1931 after a century's worth of evidence that the tune, at least, should have been scrapped.

universally recognized. The British knew that Tecumseh and his confederation were Canada's only dependable defense against the Americans. His enemy, William Henry Harrison, the territorial governor of Indiana, called him "one of those uncommon geniuses who spring up occasionally to produce revolutions and overturn the established order of things."

In 1811, Tecumseh traveled south to enlist the large Cherokee, Creek, Choctaw, and Chickasaw tribes in his confederacy. Had he succeeded and launched a coordinated attack on the frontier from Lake Michigan to the Gulf of Mexico, the white westerners would have suffered a serious defeat.

It was not to be. Allowing blood relationship to rule his better judgment, Tecumseh had left the Prophet in control of Tippecanoe during his absence. He emphatically instructed Tenskwatawa to keep the peace with the whites until he

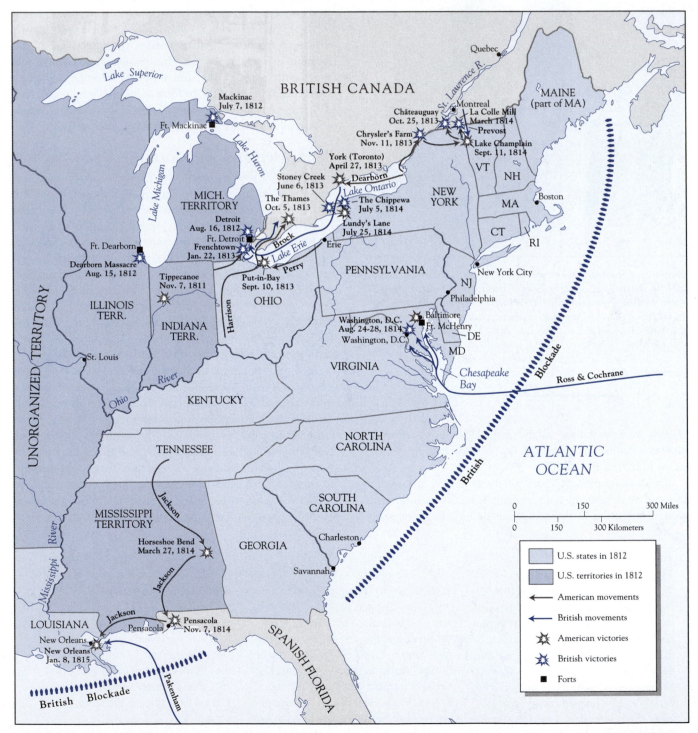

MAP 12:2 **The War of 1812.** Until the final battle of New Orleans, the War of 1812 was fought at sea and on the Canadian-American border. The capitals of both belligerents were burned by the enemy, York (now Toronto) in April 1813, Washington in August 1814.

returned. But a man who believed in visions was not a man to whom to entrust such a task.

In November 1811, Governor Harrison arrived at Tippecanoe, camping about a mile away from the town with 1,000 soldiers. He had come to fight but was alarmed to discover that he was badly outnumbered by well-armed Indian warriors, possibly as many as 3,000. He was leaning toward withdrawing when The Prophet ordered an attack on the American camp. The Indians came within an ace of overrunning Harrison's army, but his line held and the Americans counterattacked, winning the day. Tippecanoe's inhabitants scattered, most fleeing to Canada. Harrison leveled the town. He was an instant hero to the War Hawks who took their seats in Congress unrestrained by fear of Tecumseh's Confederacy.

Bunglers

Nevertheless, the American assault on Canada was a fiasco. New York militia refused to cross the Niagara River. They delayed a mass desertion only long enough to watch a duel between two bickering American officers (which Canadians across the river also enjoyed). Surprised at American ineffec-

tiveness, the British, Canadians, and Indians counterattacked and captured Detroit. An Indian force destroyed the stockade at Chicago, then called Fort Dearborn.

A Canadian-Indian offensive—in five of the seven land battles of the war, Indians outnumbered white soldiers on the British side—was stymied when, in September 1813, Captain Oliver Hazard Perry secured control of Lake Erie for the Americans. Receiving his famous message, "We have met the enemy and they are ours," William Henry Harrison led 4,500 men toward York (now Toronto), the capital of upper Canada.

There, the British and Canadians proved as inept as the Americans. According to Tecumseh, who was with them, they were cowards. He told the British commander, "We must compare our father's conduct to a fat dog that carries its tail upon its back, but when afrightened drops it between its legs and runs off." Harrison defeated the combined force at the Battle of the Thames and burned the public buildings in the city. Tecumseh was killed.

In the meantime, Canadian forces invaded New York via Burgoyne's route and were stopped at Lake Champlain,

The Battle of New Orleans. Like many other patriotic paintings, this one was concerned more with arousing national pride (and celebrating Andrew Jackson) than in accuracy. The British troops never got closer than a hundred yards of the American position. General Jackson did not direct the battle from a position in which he could have easily been killed.

The Granger Collection, New York

again by a freshwater navy commanded by Captain Thomas Macdonough. Ironically, while Americans won few victories on land, American naval forces on both the lakes and the ocean won most of their encounters.

The British revenged the burning of York in August 1814 when they launched an amphibious raid on Washington, D.C. The troops burned the Capitol and the White House. British officers claimed that they ate a dinner, still warm, that had been set for James and Dolley Madison. Dolley Madison saved the Gilbert Stuart portrait of George Washington and several valuable documents. President Madison, braver than he, his supporters, and his critics ever acknowledged, narrowly escaped capture when he rode out of Washington to rally the city's American defenders. (They fled, abandoning him.)

The Battle of New Orleans

Napoleon abdicated in the spring of 1814, freeing British troops for American service. Some 8,000 experienced soldiers under General Sir Edward Pakenham sailed to the Gulf of Mexico with orders to occupy New Orleans. The city was undefended. It augured to be an American disaster. Instead, Packenham was humiliated by a Tennessean who hurriedly organized a defense of the city, Andrew Jackson.

Jackson was a self taught lawyer, a slave owner, a land-speculator, an Indian fighter, and notorious as a duelist. At New Orleans, he cobbled together an army of 2,000 Kentucky and Tennessee riflemen, New Orleans merchants, two battalions of free blacks, some Choctaw Indians, and artillerymen in the employ of a pirate-businessman, Jean Lafitte. Jackson's men threw up earthworks 5 miles south of New Orleans, the

Mississippi River on their right, swamp on the left. Jackson created a wide-open battlefield with his own army well protected.

Packenham should have paid closer attention to the battlefield Jackson had designed. But, like so many British generals, he disdained American soldiers too reflexively to take notice of how unfavorable his situation was. He sent his army through a morning mist in a straightforward frontal assault. Lafitte's cannoneers raked the British with grapeshot. When the redcoats were 200 yards from Jackson's earthworks, the riflemen opened up with "a leaden torrent no man on earth could face." More than 2,000 British soldiers fell dead—one in four on the expedition! They never got close to the American lines. In the mist and gunpowder smoke, few ever saw the fortifications. Only seven Americans were killed, four of them when they mindlessly pursued the fleeing British. After the battle, Jackson hanged as many American soldiers for desertion as were killed during it.

Ironically, the Treaty of Ghent, which restored British-American relations to what they had been before the war, had already been signed. Nevertheless, the news of Jackson's astonishing victory had an electrifying effect on the country. So glorious a conclusion to an unnecessary and mostly calamitous war seemed to many a divine reaffirmation of the nation's destiny. When, within three years, Jackson crushed the Creeks in the southeast and Stephen Decatur returned to the Barbary Coast to sting the Algerians, Americans could imagine they had won respect in a world where armed might was the measure of greatness. According to another of those measures, a nation's sway over vast territory, the United States had already captured European attention.

FURTHER READING

Classics Henry Adams, *History of the United States from 1801 to 1817,* 9 volumes, 1889–1891; Dumas Malone, *Jefferson and His Time,* 6 volumes, 1948–1974; Fawn Brodie, *Thomas Jefferson: An Intimate History,* 1974.

General Marshall Smelser, *The Democratic Republic, 1801–1815,* 1992; Sean Wilentz, *The Rise of American Democracy: Jefferson to Lincoln,* 2005; Joanne B. Freeman, *Affairs of Honor: National Politics in the New Republic,* 2001; Joseph J. Ellis, *Founding Brothers: The Revolutionary Generation,* 2000; Joyce Appleby, *Inheriting the Revolution: The First Generation of Americans,* 2000; Peter Onuf, *Jefferson's Empire: The Language of American Nationhood,* 2001; R. Kent Newmeyer, *The Supreme Court under Marshall and Taney,* 1986; Garry Wills, *A Necessary Evil: A History of American Distrust of Government,* 1999; James F. Simons, *What Kind of Nation: Thomas Jefferson, John Marshall and the Epic Struggle to Create a United States,* 2002; Bruce A. Ackerman, *The Failure of the Founding Fathers: Jefferson, Marshall, and the Rise of Presidential Democracy,* 2005; Gordon S. Wood, *Revolutionary Characters: What Made the Founders Different,* 2006.

Thomas Jefferson John C. Miller, *The Wolf By the Ears: Thomas Jefferson and Slavery,* 1977; Robert Tucker and David Hendrickson, *Empire of Liberty: The Statecraft of Thomas Jefferson,* 1990; John Ferling, *Adams vs. Jefferson: The Tumultuous Election of 1800,* 2004;

Edward J. Larson, *The Magnificent Catastrophe: The Tumultuous Election of 1800,* 2007; Joseph J. Ellis, *American Sphinx: The Character of Thomas Jefferson,* 1996; Andrew Burstein, *Jefferson's Secrets: Death and Desire at Monticello,* 2005; Roger Kennedy, *Burr, Hamilton, and Jefferson: A Study in Character,* 2000; Christopher Hitchins, *Thomas Jefferson: Author of America,* 2005; Conor Cruise O'Brien, *The Long Affair: Thomas Jefferson and the French Revolution, 1785–1800,* 1996; Annette Gordon-Reid, *Thomas Jefferson and Sally Hemmings: An American Controversy,* 1997; Garry Wills, *"Negro President": Jefferson and the Slave Power,* 2003; Damon Lee Fuller, ed., *Dining at Monticello: In Good Taste and Abundance,* 2005.

Contemporaries Leonard Baker, *John Marshall: A Life in Law,* 1974;. Jean Edward Smith, *John Marshall: Definer of a Nation,* 1996; Nancy Isenberg, *Fallen Founder: The Life of Aaron Burr,* 2007; Ron Chernow, *Alexander Hamilton,* 2004; Stephen K. Knott, *Alexander Hamilton and the Persistence of Myth,* 2002; Thomas J. Fleming, *Duels: Alexander Hamilton, Aaron Burr, and the Future of America,*1999; Robert Dawidoff, *The Education of John Randolph,* 1979.

The Barbary Pirates Joseph Whelan, *Mr. Jefferson's War: America's First War on Terror 1801–1805,* 2003; Frank Lambert, *The Barbary Wars: American Independence in the Atlantic World,* 2005; Ian W. Toll, *Six Frigates: The Epic History of the Founding of the U.S. Navy,*

2006; Frederick C. Leiner, *The End of Barbary Terror: America's 1815 War Against the Pirates of North Africa*, 2006.

Haiti and Louisiana Alfred N. Hunt, *Haiti's Influence on Antebellum America*, 1988; Philippe R. Girard, *Paradise Lost: Haiti's Tumultuous Journey from Pearl of the Caribbean to Third World Hot Spot*, 2005; Gordon S. Brown, *Toussaint's Clause: The Founding Fathers and the Haitian Revolution*, 2005; Alexander Deconde, *This Affair of Louisiana*, 1976; Roger G. Kennedy, *Mr. Jefferson's Lost Cause: Land, Farmers, Slavery, and the Louisiana Purchase*, 2003; Stephen Ambrose, *Undaunted Courage: Meriwether Lewis, Thomas Jefferson, and the Opening of the American West*, 1996; James Ronda, *Lewis and Clark Among the Indians*, 1984 and *Finding the West: Explorations with Lewis and Clark*, 2001; Carolyn Gilman, *Lewis and Clark: Across the Great Divide*, 2003.

Madison and His Presidency Jack M. Rakove, *James Madison and the Creation of the American Republic*, 1990; Drew McCoy, *The Last of the Fathers: James Madison and the Republican Legacy*, 1989; Robert A. Rutland, *The Presidency of James Madison*, 1990; Lawrence

Kaplan, *"Entangling Alliances With None": American Foreign Policy in the Age of Jefferson*, 1987.

War with the Indians and Great Britain Edward M. Coffman, *The Old Army: A Portrait of the American Army in Peacetime, 1784–1898*, 1986; Gregory E. Dowd, *A Spirited Resistance: The North American Indian Struggle for Unity, 1745–1815*, 1992; R. David Edmunds, *The Shawnee Prophet*, 1983 and *Tecumseh and the Quest for Indian Leadership*, 1984; John Sugden, *Tecumseh: A Life*, 1998; Jeffrey Bolster, *Black Jacks: African American Seamen in the Age of Sail*, 1997; Donald R. Hickey, *The War of 1812: A Forgotten Conflict*, 1989; J. C. A. Stagg, *Mr. Madison's War: Politics, Diplomacy, and Warfare in the Early American Republic*, 1983; Steven Watts, *The Republic Reborn: War and the Making of Liberal America 1790–1820*, 1987; Richard Buel Jr., *America on the Brink: How the Political Struggle Over the War of 1812 Almost Destroyed the Young Republic*, 2005; Robert V. Remini, *The Battle of New Orleans*, 1999; John Lehman, *On Seas of Glory: Heroic Men, Great Ships, and Epic Battles of the American Navy*, 2001.

KEY TERMS

Use the following listing of key terms to review important figures, events, locations, and concepts covered in this chapter. A glossary of these terms is available on *The American Past* companion Web site: www.cengage.com/history/conlin/tap9e

midnight judges, p. 201

judicial review, p. 201

Pike Zebulon, p. 204

"Burr Conspiracy," p. 205

Barbary Pirates, p. 207

impressment, p. 208

"War Hawks," p. 210

Tenskwatawa, p. 211

Perry, Oliver Hazard, p. 213

Treaty of Ghent, p. 214

ONLINE RESOURCES

Find additional resources, including primary source documents, images, interactive maps, simulations, chapter review exercises, and Internet links at

The American Past **companion Web site**
www.cengage.com/history/conlin/tap9e

American History Resource Center
http://ushistory.wadsworth.com/

DISCOVERY

The Treaty of Paris of 1783 confirmed the independence of the thirteen former colonies. During the war, almost all of the new states extended the vote to many who had been denied it under British rule. Some states liberalized property and inheritance laws. But some groups of Americans gained no new benefits from Independence. Who were they? Why, do you think, they were ignored?

Culture and Society: When the Second Continental Congress was debating independence in the spring of 1776, John Adams received the following letter from his wife (and only trusted advisor), Abigail. To what extent, do you think, she was joking with her husband? To what extent was she serious? How did the patriots of the Revolutionary era respond to suggestions like those Abigail Adams made? The image, "New Jersey Gives the Vote to all 'Free Inhabitants,'" depicts women voting. Does this mean that woman suffrage was a consequence of independence?

North Wind Picture Archives

New Jersey Gives the Vote to All

Abigail Adams to John Adams, Braintree, 31 March 1776

I long to hear that you have declared an independancy-and by the way in the new Code of Laws which I suppose it will be necessary for you to make I desire you would Remember the Ladies, and be more generous and favourable to them than your ancestors. Do not put such unlimited power into the hands of the Husbands. Remember all Men would be tyrants if they could. If perticuliar care and attention is not paid to the Ladies we are determined to foment a Rebelion, and will not hold ourselves bound by any Laws in which we have no voice, or Representation.

That your Sex are Naturally Tyrannical is a Truth so thoroughly established as to admit of no dispute, but such of you as wish to be happy willingly give up the harsh title of Master for the more tender and endearing one of Friend. Why then, not put it out of the power of the vicious and the Lawless to use us with cruelty and indignity with impunity. Men of Sense in all Ages abhor those customs which treat us only as the vassals of your Sex. Regard us then as Beings placed by providence under your protection and in immitation of the Supreem Being make use of that power only for our happiness.

What precedents—examples for future presidents—did George Washington try to establish during his eight years in the office?

Politics and Foreign Relations: The engraving, "Mort de Louis XVI," showing the execution of the king by French revolutionaries in 1793, was circulated throughout the United States. How did President Washington respond to the news? How did the American people in general react? Also in 1793, France and Great Britain went to war. Did Louis XVI's execution have any bearing on Washington's proclamation of neutrality in that war despite continuing animosity toward Britain and the American alliance with France? Washington did not mention the king in his proclamation. What reasons did he give for neutrality?

Reproduced from the Collections of the Library of Congress, Prints and Photographs Division, Washington, D.C. [LC-USZ62-124552]

MORT DE LOUIS XVI, LE 21 JANVIER 1793

Place de la Concorde : on voit à gauche le socle de la statue de Louis XV déboulonnée

(Extrait des *Révolutions de Paris*)

Mort de Louis XVI

"George Washington on Foreign Affairs"

. . . After deliberate examination, with the aid of the best lights I could obtain, I was well satisfied that our country, under all the circumstances of the case, had a right to take, and was bound in duty and interest to take, a neutral position. Having taken it, I determined, as far as should depend upon me, to maintain it, with moderation, perseverance, and firmness. . . .

The duty of holding a neutral conduct may be inferred, without any thing more, from the obligation which justice and humanity impose on every nation, in cases in which it is free to act, to maintain inviolate the relations of peace and amity towards other nations.

The inducements of interest for observing that conduct will best be referred to your own reflections and experience. With me, a predominant motive has been to endeavour to gain time to our country to settle and mature its yet recent institutions, and to progress without interruption to that degree of strength and consistency, which is necessary to give it, humanly speaking, the command of its own fortunes. . . .

To read extended versions of selected documents, visit the companion Web site www.cengage.com/history/conlin/tap9e; click on "Discovery Sources"

Chapter 13

Nationalism: Culture, Politics, Diplomacy

1815–1824

Reproduced from the Collections of the Library of Congress

A national language is a bond of national union. Every engine should be employed to render the people of this country national; to call their attachments home to their own country; and to inspire them with the pride of national character.

—*Noah Webster*

I have heard something said about allegiance to the South. I know no South, no North, no West, to which I owe any allegiance.

—*Henry Clay*

Evidence of northern dislike of southerners and vice versa dates to the first years of the English settlements in North America. Puritan preachers in New England warned their congregations about the irreligion and immorality into which the people of the tobacco colonies had fallen. Marylanders and Virginians responded that New Englanders were self-righteous hypocrites.

The societies of the northern and southern colonies developed so differently that few European visitors failed to comment upon the contrast. The South was almost entirely rural and agricultural with few towns. The South was dominated socially and politically by great tobacco planters who, at the top, owned acres by the thousand and slaves by the hundred.

Most northerners were farmers too, of course, but on small holdings worked by members of the family and, among the most prosperous, maybe three or four servants or slaves. And there were three large cities in the North—Philadelphia, New York, and Boston—and dozens of vibrant towns larger than any town in the South except Charleston. From Pennsylvania north, the social and cultural norms were defined by businessmen ranging from merchant princes engaged in seaborne trade to retailers, artisans, and hustling middlemen who bought and sold agricultural produce and wholesale goods manufactured in the cities or abroad.

TWO SECTIONS, ONE COUNTRY

The North was capitalistic; its economy was based on the fact that everything had a money value, its culture was increasingly centered on acquiring wealth. To the planters of the South, who saw themselves as aristocrats entrusted with the responsibility of looking after a society based on personal relationships, northerners were narrow-minded money-grubbers. In northern eyes, southerners were indolent, unprogressive, and, depending on their social class, either parasites or toadies.

Thomas Jefferson (who thought of himself as a *Virginian!*) drew up a list of contrasting character traits that distinguished northerners from southerners. Northerners were cool and sober, southerners fiery and "voluptuary." Northerners were hard-working, self-interested, and devious; southerners were lazy, generous, and candid. Northerners were "jealous of their own liberties, and just to those of others." Southerners were "zealous for their own liberties, but trampling on those of others."

Sectionalism

The most conspicuous distinction between North and South was the enduring vitality of African slavery below the Mason-Dixon line. After the War for Independence, the northern states abolished slavery. It was a painless experience in almost every state because slaves were few in the North; slavery was incidental to the northern economy. In the South, however, African Americans were numerous, a majority of the population in some counties of Virginia and South Carolina. Slavery was the bedrock on which the southern economy was built.

Slavery was a troublesome sectional issue at the Constitutional Convention of 1787 and was put to rest only by the contrived "three-fifths compromise." But it was put to rest. Only South Carolinians and Georgians aggressively defended slavery. The people of the upper south, even planters who owned hundreds of slaves, inclined to the belief that the institution was dying. Given time, it would disappear, and good riddance to it.

The issues of the 1790s that led to the formation of the Federalist and Jefferson Republican parties reflected American sectionalism. The core of Federalist support was in New England and New York. The Republicans depended on comfortable majorities in the southern states for their strength. Jefferson's trade policies and the War of 1812 aggravated North–South animosities. Southerners wanted the war and overwhelmingly supported it. Most New Englanders were opposed to it first to last. Federalist extremists proposed that the northeastern states, including New York, secede from the Union and form a nation free of southern domination.

Even before the war, however, there were indications of a resurgence of the patriotism of the Revolutionary era and the nationalism that had animated the men who wrote the Constitution. In 1815, when the War of 1812 ended with Andrew Jackson's miraculous victory at the battle of New

Orleans and Stephen Decatur returned to the Barbary Coast to decisively punish Algiers, a wave of exuberant national patriotism seemed to drown sectional feelings everywhere. The mood swing was so obvious that, in welcoming the southern president James Monroe to Boston, an editor wrote that Monroe presided over an "Era of Good Feelings."

Patriotic Culture

During the postwar years, the Fourth of July became a major popular holiday of sometimes raucous patriotic celebration. Formerly, Independence Day had been observed with religious services, long, scholarly addresses that were more lectures than speeches, and decorous promenades by the social elite in city squares. Ordinary people who were not churchgoers, paid little attention to the observances. After 1815, the Glorious Fourth combusted into a day when everyone laid

Cleaning up the Good Book

Not all of Noah Webster's spelling reforms caught on, although some may be found in student essays to this day: *karacter, wimmen, definit, fether, tung, bred* (bread). Indeed, Webster himself traveled to England in 1828 and was so swept off his feet by the sophistication and praises of English literary figures that he recanted his spellings of *gaol, kerb,* and soon, but it was too late. Americans liked *jail* and *curb.*

Webster was brilliant; he taught himself twenty languages. He was also humorless, socially awkward, and excruciatingly pious. He prepared an edition of the Bible in which he left out words "offensive to delicacy."

> Many words are offensive, especially for females, as to create a reluctance in young persons to attend Bible classes and schools, in which they are required to read passages which cannot be repeated without a blush; and containing words which on other occasions a child ought not to utter without rebuke.

Nationalism and Expansion

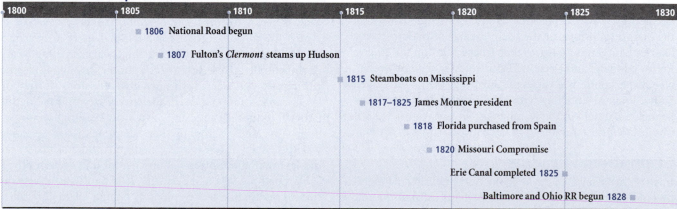

| 1800 | 1805 | 1810 | 1815 | 1820 | 1825 | 1830 |

- 1806 National Road begun
- 1807 Fulton's *Clermont* steams up Hudson
- 1815 Steamboats on Mississippi
- 1817–1825 James Monroe president
- 1818 Florida purchased from Spain
- 1820 Missouri Compromise
- Erie Canal completed 1825
- Baltimore and Ohio RR begun 1828

The Fourth of July, 1818. Twenty years earlier, The Fourth was a holiday to which only the genteel paid much attention, promenading in their best clothing. After the widespread patriotism aroused by the War of 1812, Independence Day became a raucous, popular holiday, lubricated by free-flowing liquor.

down their tools and locked the doors of their shops to pay homage to "the greatest country on earth" with mass picnics, excessive drink, and boisterous gaiety.

Patriotism permeated popular art. Woodcarvers and painters trimmed canal boats, sailing ships, stagecoaches, and private homes with screaming eagles clutching braces of arrows; the idealized vigilant female figure who personified liberty; and the flag, "Old Glory," the only national ensign that had progress sewn into it. Between 1816 and 1821, six new stars were added to the flag as six new states entered the Union.

The samplers that girls made to display their mastery of needlecraft now had patriotic as often as religious themes: the Stars and Stripes, or the brave sayings of national heros like Nathan Hale's "I regret that I have but one life to give for my country" and Decatur's "Our country right or wrong." Newspapers published verses touting the glories of the United States. Francis Scott Key wrote the instantly popular "Star-Spangled Banner" in the waning days of the War of 1812; it was just the most durable of many patriotic songs of the era.

Inspirational Reading

In 1817, Attorney General William Wirt published a biography of Patrick Henry in which he perhaps inflated the role of the Virginian in the War for Indpendence. The book's success inspired patriots from other states to write overblown celebrations of the virtues of their homegrown heros. Massachusetts revived the memory of Paul Revere. In 1825,

100,000 people attended the laying of the cornerstone of a monument on Bunker Hill. The master of ceremonies, Massachusetts congressman and peerless orator, Daniel Webster, told the audience, "Let our object be our country, our whole country, and nothing but our country."

Rhode Islanders touted Nathaniel Greene even though he moved to South Carolina after the British were defeated. South Carolina had its own Revolutionary hero, the "Swamp Fox," Francis Marion, who, with scant resources, harassed a British army to frustration.

Less controversial because of its singular subject was Mason Locke Weems's *The Life and Memorable Actions of George Washington.* Originally published in 1800, Weems's unblushing exercise in hero worship peaked in popularity during the 1810s and early 1820s, running through fifty-nine editions. It was Weems who invented the story of the boy Washington chopping down the cherry tree and telling his father "I cannot tell a lie" and of an older Washington throwing a silver dollar across the Rappahannock River. So noble was the father of his country that he could not fib; so far did he tower above other nations' heroes that even in physical strength he was a superman: "It is hardly an exaggeration to say that he was as pious as Numa; just as Aristides; temperate as Epictetes; patriotic as Regulus; impartial as Severus," Weems wrote, challenging readers' recollection of the ancient history that all boys in grammar schools ("college prep" schools) had studied.

Another influential author was Noah Webster, whose *American Spelling Book,* first published in 1783, sold more than 60 million copies in perhaps 300 editions. Webster did not get rich from the astronomical sales; in 1808 he sold the rights to his book for $2,365. However, he unknowingly won immortatlity as the father of that unique American institution, the spelling bee. Webster was a stickler for correct, uniform spelling. It saddened him that even so prominent a figure as the explorer, William Clark, in his journal of the transcontinental expedition, spelled *mosquito* nineteen different ways.

From Webster's "blue-backed speller," schoolchildren learned that the American tongue was unique, different from British English and destined to grow yet more distinct. Webster himself tried to strip English of decadent Old World affectations and proposed many spelling reforms, the least radical of which caught on and survive today: American *labor, theater, curb,* and *jail* for British *labour, theatre, kerb,* and *gaol.* Webster's *American Dictionary of the English Language,* published in 1828, also distinguished American English from British English by including hundreds of words Americans had adopted from Indian languages.

For their literature, Americans continued to look to England. The first generation of self-consciously American writers came of age during the Era of Good Feelings but had not yet made their mark. Still, Washington Irving's *Sketch Book,* published in 1820, was popular and praised on both sides of the ocean. Another New Yorker, James Fenimore Cooper, wrote on American themes, most famously the all-American frontiersman Natty Bumppo, who was the superior of Indians thanks to civilization and more virtuous than Europeans because he lived close to nature.

Nationalism in the Courtroom

The Supreme Court under Chief Justice John Marshall remained a bastion of Federalist nationalism through sixteen years dominated by a Jeffersonian presidency and Congress. Then and after the War of 1812, the Virginian dominated the Court. (He was Chief Justice for thirty-four years, the record.) Most of the Court's decisions were unanimous; a majority of them—all of the landmark decisions—were written by Marshall himself. Marshall strove for unanimity. He believed

Library of Congress Prints and Photographs Division Washington, D.C. [LC-US262-8499]

John Marshall was 46 years old when, in 1801, during his final days as president, John Adams named him Chief Justice of the United States. Marshall remained head of the Supreme Court until his death in 1835. No other Chief Justice has served longer. Nor has any shaped American development as profoundly as Marshall did. He established the Court's power to rule on the constitutionality of state and federal laws, the supremacy of federal over state law, and–not so lastingly– the inviolability of contracts.

that if the Court was to be respected as the ultimate word on the meaning of the law, it should speak with one voice. Dissents encouraged doubts about the Court's wisdom.

Sanctity of Contracts

Scarcely less important to John Marshall than nationalism was his dedication to the inviolability of contracts. Even when he found the terms of a contract morally repellent, as he did in *Fletcher* v. *Peck* (1810), he insisted that it be honored. In 1794, a corrupt Georgia legislature—just about every member was bribed—sold 35 million acres of what is now Alabama and Mississippi to speculators for 1.5 ¢ an acre. Two years later, an entirely new legislature elected

in protest rescinded the sale and voided the deeds of those who had purchased land from the speculators. One such buyer, Robert Fletcher, sued to have the recision invalidated as a violation of the Constitution's "contract clause" (Article 1, Section 10). Reprehensible as the justices found the corruption, the Court held that the original sale was nonetheless a legal contract and could not be rescinded.

In *Dartmouth College* v. *Woodward* (1819), Marshall ruled that a royal charter of 1769 granting self-governance to

Dartmouth College, a private corporation, was a contract. It could not, therefore, be invalidated by the New Hampshire state legislature, no matter that invalidation might be more in the public interest than the private status of Dartmouth.

In *Ogden* v. *Saunders* (1827), Marshall found himself in dissent in a contract case. All those years of Republican presidents appointing justices had caught up with him. In a 4 to 3 decision, the Court ruled that contract rights were not absolute.

Marshall was likable, generous, and accommodating. He remained friendly with the fiercest critics of his politics and philosophy—Thomas Jefferson excepted, but not James Monroe—and close personal friends with some. His manner when not on the bench was informal and unguarded. We of the twenty-first century would be more comfortable in his company than with any other public figure of the era. In order to avoid dissents, he was willing to modify his own opinions and wording to win over justices who expressed reservations with which Marshall could come to terms.

Thanks to his affable and sociable personality—for as long as he could do so, Marshall arranged that the justices all roomed at the same boardinghouse—he converted most of Jefferson's and Madison's Republican appointees to the Court to his nationalism. In chambers by day, in the evening at their boardinghouse, over law books and tumblers brimming with Marshall's beloved Madeira wine, his court whittled away at state power and strengthened the federal government.

In *Martin* v. *Hunter's Lessee* (1816), Marshall established the Court's authority to reverse the decision of a state court. In *McCulloch* v. *Maryland* (1819), a unanimous decision, Marshall told Maryland and other states that their legislatures could not tax the Bank of the United States because, although it was privately owned, the bank had been chartered by Congress to serve a public purpose. "The power to tax involves the power to destroy," Marshall wrote. In words deliberately selected to reflect Alexander Hamilton's in arguing the constitutonality of the first Bank of the United States with Jefferson, Marshall made Hamilton's broad construction of the constitution a principle of the Court.

Gibbons v. *Ogden* (1824) denied the states a voice in regulating any commerce that was interstate, that is, involving more than one state. Aaron Ogden held a monopoly on steamboat navigation on the Hudson River granted by the New York state legislature. Thomas Gibbons had a federal license to run steamboats across the Hudson between New York and New Jersey. Ogden tried to stop him. Marshall ruled that Gibbons's federal license trumped Ogden's state-granted monopoly.

Henry Clay

Henry Clay was a dyed in the wool nationalist, a latter-day Alexander Hamilton in some ways. He was elected to Congress in 1810 as a War Hawk and, at the age of 33, was named Speaker of the House by the War Hawk Congress. Clay remained Speaker until 1821 except for a year when he was appointed as a peace commissioner to negotiate a treaty to end the War of 1812. The Speakership was a powerful position, more powerful than the president in so far as legislation was concerned. The president could veto an act of Congress, but he could not initiate one. A shrewd Speaker had an immense, even decisive say, in how bills were worded, which ones got to the floor of the House for consideration, and which way the final tally went. Clay was very shrewd.

The Speaker's key power lay in the fact that, at the outset of each Congress, he assigned representatives to the committees where the real work of the House was done. (The House floor was for oratory and voting.) Clay could ensure that his allies

North Wind Picture Archives

Young Henry Clay when he was Speaker of the House of Representatives. He had known nothing but success in politics; he was popular with his colleagues and already something of a hero to many westerners. He had no doubt that he would one day be elected president, perhaps in 1824 when James Monroe's second term ended. As an old man, Clay would look back on his life astonished (and bitter) that he never was elected.

and supporters had a majority on the committees important to him, his opponents powerless to shape a bill, and his sworn enemies banished to committees concerned with trivial issues.

But Clay did not make enemies easily. He rarely used committee assignments as punishments. He was, by nature, a compromiser and builder of majorities who understood that a Congressman who voted against him on one bill might be persuaded to vote with him on another issue if they remained on friendly or at least civil terms. And he was a most popular man, in Congress and out. He was keenly intelligent and a dazzling orator who attracted crowds to the Capitol when he was scheduled to speak. His manners were gracious; he was witty and sociable. He charmed women and won the loyalty of men. He was equally comfortable sipping claret with an elegant lady and playing faro with "the boys" until all the whiskey and tobacco were gone.

The American System

Clay was ambitious. He wanted very badly to be president. He meant to make himself the man who could not be denied the White House by promoting a comprehensive program that would bind northeasterners, southerners, and westerners together economically as the Constitution had united them politically.

He called his program the "American System." Its centerpiece was a national bank patterned on Hamilton's Bank of the United States. The BUS was the sole depository of the government's money, much of it in the form of bank notes issued by local state banks that had been paid into the Treasury as taxes and by purchasers of federal land in the West. Its huge cash reserves enabled the Bank to control just how much paper money each state bank printed. That is, if a bank ignored BUS guidelines and printed too much paper in order to make loans, the BUS shut it down by presenting the bank's notes in its possession (inevitably a lot of them) and demanding gold and silver coin in return. No bank kept enough gold and silver in its vaults to redeem, at one time, more than a fraction of the notes it had issued. The financial power of the BUS looming over local banks was to ensure that their practices were conservative.

There was no Bank of the United States between 1811 and 1816. When the charter of Hamilton's BUS came up for renewal in 1811, the Jeffersonian Congress refused. The consequences were dire. Without regulation, many state banks, especially in the West, loosed a torrent of bank notes to lend to land speculators. The most reckless—crooked, actually—were called wildcat banks because, it was said, in order to avoid people demanding coin, they were located nearer to where the wildcats prowled than to human population centers. Bank failures were numerous, each one wiping out the savings of honest depositors. By 1816, enough of the same Congressmen who killed the first BUS had repented and chartered the Second Bank of the United States for a period of twenty years.

THE TRANSPORTATION REVOLUTION

As a westerner, Henry Clay appreciated the need beyond the Appalachians for internal improvements: good roads, canals, bridges, docks in riverfront cities. The problem was that the

young western states (and territories) lacked a sufficient tax base to finance such costly projects. As the second part of the American System, Clay proposed that the federal government pay the bills.

That made for a tougher fight than the BUS charter. Many legislators from the old states saw no reason to increase their tax burden to pay for distant building projects from which they would reap no benefit.

Clay won some supporters in the Northeast by tying internal improvements projects with his support for a protective tariff, the third element of his system. During the years of the Embargo and the War of 1812, northeastern investment capital had shifted significantly from overseas trade into manufacturing. (See Chapter 14.) Clay pointed out that a populous West would provide an ever-growing market for

The Granger Collection, New York

A stagecoach collapses at the end of a corduroy road. Although the cause of this accident is not clear, such mishaps, often resulting in serious injuries and deaths, not to mention horses that had to be shot, were common on dirt, corduroy, and plank roads. Note that there are no springs on the coach. Riding on a such a vehicle was an ordeal even when it completed its journey without mishap.

Turnpikes

Privately owned turnpike companies built more roads in the United States between 1800 and 1830 than the federal and state governments combined, 10,000 miles of them according to the best estimate. Turnpikes were toll roads, built and managed by investors who had been granted a charter by the state legislature. The name derived from the fact that at toll stations in medieval England, a pike blocked the roadway until the fee was paid whence it was swiveled—"turned."

Most early American turnpikes were corduroy roads. However, the most ambitious and profitable, the sixty-two-mile-long Philadelphia-Lancaster Pike (present-day U.S. 30) was designed by John MacAdam and had a macadam surface.

Tolls were cheap; 25 ¢ every 10 miles or so for a wagon, a dime for a traveler on horseback, variable rates for a herd of cattle or flock of sheep. Some charters required turnpike companies to allow locals to use them free over short hauls; others forbade collecting tolls on Sunday.

It was well known that few turnpikes made much money, but there were enough willing investors that several thousand companies were organized to build them during the first half of the century. Local merchants were happy to break even on their investments because good roads to and from town increased business. When a turnpike was a big loser—many were—the owners turned the road over to the state or county which usually converted it into a free public highway.

the products of Eastern mills and factories *if* the goods could be gotten to the westerners.

Clay was least successful in winning southern support for the American System. The market for cotton—now the South's most important crop—was in Europe, chiefly Great Britain. The American System offered little to cotton planters but the higher prices—thanks to higher import duties—that they would have to pay to clothe, shoe, and put tools into the hands of their slaves.

Roads

Most southern roads were no better than the narrow tracks through forests. Dirt roads everywhere were churned into impassable quagmires within days of a heavy rain. In the Northeast, maintaining highways was the responsibility of the people who lived along them. Connecticut, for example, required "every teeme and person fitt for labour" living along a road to devote two days each year to repairing it. Over most of the South, travelers simply skirted the mud as best they could and waited for the road to dry. Philadelphia was only a hundred miles from New York and one of the country's best highways

connected them. Nonetheless, better-off travelers made the trip by rounding New Jersey on a schooner or sloop.

In heavily forested areas such as upper New England, roads were surfaced with logs laid crosswise. The ride in a wagon over these "corduroy roads" was uncomfortable although preferable to digging a wagon out of muck. Westerners adopted corduroy roads but, as in New England, they deteriorated quickly.

In the early nineteenth-century, a Scots engineer, John McAdam, developed the first "all-weather" road since the Romans had built their highways of large stone blocks. On a base of angular stones three or so inches across, laid down in layers each of which was rolled to lock the stones into one another, McAdam surfaced the road with several layers of pulverized stone which was repeatedly soaked and rolled to harden it.

Americans took to macadam immediately. The first great nationally financed internal improvement project, the National Road, was built with a macadam surface. Begun in 1806 and completed in 1818, the National Road connected Cumberland, Maryland, at the head of navigation on the Potomac River, with Wheeling on the Ohio River. It was

Collection of The New-York Historical Society, #1918.45

The Erie Canal where a village has grown up next to a pair of locks. There would be taverns, inns, provisioners, and residences for canal employees. Long stretches of the Erie were indeed idyllic, as the artist has presented this scene. Other canal towns were raucous, rough-and-tumble places where navigators congregated, as wild as the cowtowns and mining camps of a later era. Genteel lady passengers on a canal boat would likely have fled into the cabin upon approaching one.

expensive, $13,000 per mile. But it was a godsend for emigrants bound West and to farmers who lived along the right-of-way.

Henry Clay appointed himself the National Road's godfather. He took the lead in persuading Congress to finance its extension from Wheeling through southern Ohio and Indiana to Vandalia, Illinois. By veering northwesterly, the road brought the benefits of through transportation to farmers who lived too far from the Ohio River to get their crops to Wheeling. Not incidentally, Clay's promotion of the National Road won him a political following in Ohio, Indiana, and Illinois.

The Erie Canal

Even on the smooth surface of the National Road, moving freight by wagon was too expensive over long hauls to be profitable. It cost $30 to $35 per hundred miles to transport a ton of grain worth $40. The revolution in transportation that slashed the cost of such a shipment to less than $2 per

MAP 13:1 **Rivers, Roads, and Canals 1820–1860.** During the early nineteenth century, the United States boasted two of the world's longest continuous highways. When it was completed, the National Road (today, U.S. 40/I-70 follows its route) had a macadam surface. Most of the north–south highway that is now U.S. 1/I-95 was built earlier in sections. Its oldest parts are the Boston Post Road in New England and the highway crossing New Jersey between Philadelphia and New York.

Funding and Digging the Erie Canal

Any number of people who crossed New York state to the Great Lakes via the Mohawk River Valley observed that it was an excellent route for a canal connecting the Northwest to the Hudson River and, therefore, to New York City. Except in a few places, the terrain was flat or gently undulating. The distance from Albany to Lake Erie, more than 300 miles, was daunting. But the Grand Canal of China was then 1,000 miles long and much of it had been dug before the year 1000.

The problem was not terrain or distance, but capital. The cost of so massive a project was far beyond what any imaginable consortium of American capitalists could raise. The longest canal in the United States at the time ran just 27 miles and all but three American canals were less than 2 miles long. Most were bypasses around waterfalls or shallow rapids in otherwise navigable rivers. Short canals were cheap and quickly profitable. But 300 miles and years of construction before a cent of investment was returned?

DeWitt Clinton, of a disinguished New York family and an energetic and accomplished politician, realized that only government could finance the enterprise. To him, it was clear that the federal government had a compelling reason to do so. The canal would link the entire Great Lakes basin to the Eastern states, conquering the Appalachians. Clinton had the route surveyed and commissioned engineers to explain how the natural obstacles on the route could be overcome. He then petitioned President Jefferson to ask Congress for federal aid, but the president declined, calling Clinton's project "little short of madness." He meant the immense cost, not the feasibility of the canal; Jefferson was frugal with the government's money. In 1816, President Madison also turned Clinton down.

If the federal government would not recognize the national interest in the Erie Canal, New York state alone had a particular interest in it. A canal across the state would funnel the commerce of the explosively growing upper West to New York City, decisively ending the city's competition for the West's business with Philadelphia and Baltimore. In 1816, Clinton was elected governor of New York and quickly persuaded the state legislature to fund what critics were calling "Clinton's Folly." The digging began almost immediately at several points along the route—Clinton's idea so as to create jobs and win popular support across the state. It was muscle, pick, and shovel work. The 40-foot-wide ditch was excavated by hand to a depth of four feet with no help except from the oxen, mules, horses, and wagons that hauled the earth away.

At first, laborers were drawn from the local population, including farmers during idle spells. They were paid $1 a day if they provided their own meals, $13 a month with meals and a half pint of whiskey daily. It was the going rate for unskilled labor. But local labor was not up to the task. On long stretches of the route, through forests and where the soil was rocky, there were no farms and, therefore, no population. Clinton turned to New York's growing but largely impoverished Irish population. He was popular with the Irish because he had sponsored the law that ended restrictions on Catholics' right to vote in the state. Immigrants scraping by in New York City and even Irishmen in the old country who heard of the "big ditch" flocked upstate. They were soon the bulk of a workforce that was 3,000 at one time.

The durable stereotype of the Irish as drunken brawlers dates, in America, from the digging of the Erie Canal. The workers were young men, all but a few without wives and children to support and to moderate their behavior. They spent their wages in the grog shops and brothels that popped up wherever the work gangs were.

The Erie Canal was the greatest construction project of the era, its progress chronicled in European as well as American newspapers. Plenty of engineering problems arose to spare journalists a monotonous recounting of the week's construction mileage and the weekends' ructions. In several places, the soil was so porous that it sucked the ditch dry and collapsed the banks of the canal. The workers solved the problem by "puddling" the sodden clay, turning it again and again—kneading it—until it was transformed into an impermeable surfacing.

Hills that could not be dug around were traversed by slicing through them. The cut through one put the canal 30 feet below ground level, every shovelful removed by hand! Even more dirt had to be moved when the canal crossed a valley on a man-made embankment 70 feet high. The Genesee River, which flooded destructively almost annually, was neutralized by building an 800-foot long aqueduct over it. Another aqueduct ran for 3,000 feet and was as high as 30 feet above the surface. In heavily populated areas, bridges over the canal to accomodate local traffic were constructed every quarter mile.

The route bypassed Lake Ontario in favor of Lake Erie because Erie was above Niagara Falls, Ontario below. The route skirted the highest cliffs of the Niagara escarpment but still had to make a significant climb at the western end, 60 feet in elevation within a mile. The builders negotiated the climb with five pairs of locks—"step locks," one after another like stairs. The town already started there by Quaker investors awaiting the construction crews was, appropriately, named Lockport.

Dissenting Opinion

Not everyone who lived along the route of the Erie Canal welcomed the big ditch. One man complained, "I'm sickening of the damned canal. There's nothing but worry in it. What does it bring to any locality that it invaded? Fever and disease. Lawlessness and rapine and immorality. Conflict between respectable people and the wild Irish. Corruption of the lower classes and unsettlement of trade."

His neighbor nodded but slyly expressed the majority opinion: "And money . . . . Don't forget the money, Squire."

hundred miles was the Erie Canal, built not with federal money but by the state of New York. Begun in 1817, the 364-mile-long, 40-foot-wide "big ditch" connected the Hudson River (thereby New York City) with Lake Erie and the entire Great Lakes basin above Niagara Falls.

It was a monumental undertaking, even more expensive to build than the National Road, $7 million or almost $20,000 per mile. But the canal was so successful that, in a single year of operation after it was opened in 1825, the state paid the interest on its bonds and completely retired its debt in twelve.

The canal displaced the National Road as the emigrants' preferred route west. (In twenty years, 100,000 people relocated to the west on Erie Canal boats. Towed by mules, the boats were no faster than wagons on a good road, two or three miles an hour. But they moved around the clock! A trip from Albany on the Hudson River to Buffalo on Lake Erie (a city the canal created) took six to eight days without a lick of physical exertion on the part of passengers.

Canal boats were little more than flat-bottomed platforms owned and operated by licensed towing companies. The law required they be no longer than 78 feet in order to fit into the 84 locks that raised and lowered them over the undulating terrain. The maximum beam (width) of a canal boat was 14 to 15 feet so that there was sufficient clearance between boats moving in opposite directions. The number of boats in service at any one time was about 3,400.

Low Bridge, Everybody Down

The "navigators," as canal boat workers good-humoredly called themselves, worked two six-hour shifts each day, two crews alternating twice in twenty-four hours. The mules that towed the boats, two or three of them on each boat, had it a little easier; they worked five-hour shifts. An expert crew could unharness a mule, get her to her stall in the boat, and harness her relief in fifteen minutes. In practice, the job was usually performed at a more leisurely pace.

Accomodations on passenger boats ranged from depressing to nearly luxurious. (Going first class cost a traveler 5¢ a mile.) Aft—in the rear of the boat—was the passenger cabin, about ten feet by twelve. Travelers sat and ate there during the day and slept there at night, two to a drop-down bunk three-feet wide. Luggage was stowed in a hold below the cabin.

The stalls for the mules were fore (in the front), their hay and grain in a center compartment. In good weather, many passengers got off and walked along the towpath for exercise, or they sat on the roof of the cabin to see the sights. A chair on the roof, however, was not relaxing in populated areas where numerous bridges spanned the canal. Passengers on the roof had to lie flat or be knocked on the head. One verse in the canalers' anthem, "Fifteen Years on the Erie Canal," had it

> Low bridge, everybody down,
> Low bridge, for we're coming to a town

Fastidious ladies and gentlemen could not have been enthusiastic about leaping up from a chair and flopping down prone on a deck that could not have been too clean. Then again, some may have found such out of character behavior to be great fun.

The navigators, many of them Irishmen who had dug the big ditch, were a rough lot, both the boat-owning entrepreneurs and the "hoggies," teenaged boys who walked with the mules. A canal song less genteel than "Fifteen Years" poked fun at those menial workers:

> Hoggie on the towpath,
> Five cents a day,
> Picking up horseballs
> To eat along the way.

Towns at toll booths and locks were notorious for their whorehouses and drunken firstfights. In 1835, the Bethel Society—evangelical Protestants trying and generally failing to improve navigator morals—counted 1,500 grog shops along the Erie, an average of four per mile. (They were, of course, in clusters.)

By the 1840s, 30,000 people made their living on the Erie Canal: lock tenders, toll house workers and repairmen (all state employees) and the navigators, saloon keepers, innkeepers, farriers, and hay and feed merchants who catered to the needs of workers and travelers.

Boom and Bust

When construction of the Erie began, there were about 100 miles of canal in the United States; the longest ran only 27 miles. When it was finished, many who had ridiculed it went fairly berserk in their rush to duplicate the bonanza the Erie had created for New York.

The most ambitious project was the Mainline Canal in Pennsylvania, intended by Philadelphians to put their city back into competition with New York for the business of the West. The Mainline was shorter than the Erie. However, while the New York canal rose to 650 feet above sea level at its highest point, and required 84 locks, the Mainline Canal climbed to 2,200 feet and needed 174 locks.

And not just locks. At the Allegheny ridge, the highest in Pennsylvania's Appalachians, boats had to be hauled out of the water and winched up and over the mountain on fantastic inclined planes. It was a horrendous bottleneck. Miraculously, the Mainline Canal was actually completed and more or less functioned. Indeed, at the height of the canal craze, the state of Pennsylvania operated 608 miles of artificial waterway. But the Mainline was not the gold mine the Erie was. There were too many bottlenecks crowded with swearing boatmen in the mountains where no boatman belonged.

All in all, some 4,000 miles of canal were dug in imitation of the Erie. Another 7,000 miles were on the drawing boards when the bubble burst. Only a few made enough money to cover the investment in them. So many states saddled themselves with debt to fund poorly conceived projects—the Great Lakes states gave away 4 million acres of land to construction companies—that many politicians swore never again to finance any internal improvements with public money. In 1848, the constitution of the new state of Wisconsin forbade the expenditure of tax money on public works. The bitter reaction to the canal bust ensured that railroads (which helped to end the canal age) would not be built and owned by governments but by private entrepreneurs.

Early Railroads

Canals were destined to be superceded by a machine that first proved workable in England in 1825, the steam locomotive that could pull dozens of heavily laden cars on iron rails. Railroads had decisive advantages over canals. Canals were plausible only where the terrain was not theatrical—reasonably flat country—and where the water supply (at the highest point on the canal) was plentiful and constant. Canals shut down during the winter when they froze over. Railroads could be built almost anywhere; trains were many times faster than canal boats; and, barring catastrophic blizzards, they operated every day and night.

The first two American railroads were built in 1827. Both were just a few miles long; they replaced long used wagon routes. One connected the granite quarries of Quincy, Massachusetts, with the Neponset River. The other carried coal from Carbondale, Pennsylvania, to the Lehigh River. They were built by quarrying and mining companies for their exclusive use.

Elsewhere, entrepreneurs built railroads that would haul any kind of freight a customer would pay to have moved, and passengers too. The earliest connected cities with their hinterlands or other cities nearby. In 1833, with 136 miles of track, the Charleston and Hamburg was the longest railroad in the world.

Shipping by rail was more expensive than by canal. Start-up costs were greater. Right-of-way had to be secured on private property by hook or crook. Construction costs were about the same as the costs of digging a canal because of

Reproduced from the Collections of the Library of Congress

It cost more to ship by rail than by canal, but canals could not be dug across mountains and they froze into uselessness in winter. This locomotive was one of the first to cross the Appalachians. The men and women posing on the cowcatcher are probably company officials and their wives. Unless the engine had been scoured for the festive occasion, they were dirty when they climbed down.

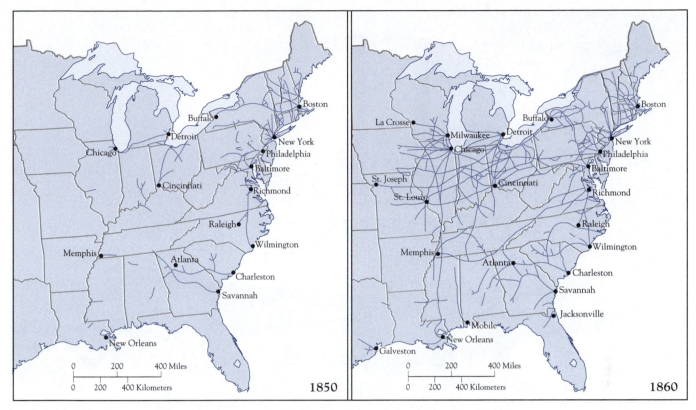

Map 13:2 **Railroads 1850–1860.** In 1850, railroads were short. They served only local regions; there was no system. By 1860, several east–west trunk lines were complete and one running north–south, the Illinois Central.

the many trestles on a railroad. However, unlike canals (and turnpikes) which collected tolls from users who owned their boats and mules or wagons and teams, railroad companies had to purchase locomotives and rolling stock. Investors were reluctant to risk their money anywhere but in country where plenty of paying customers already lived.

The railroad's full potential lay in using it, like the National Road and the Erie Canal, over long distances, connecting distant regions. The first entrepreneurs to recognize this were Baltimoreans hoping to get their city back into the competition for the trade of the West. In 1828, work began on America's first trunk line, the Baltimore and Ohio (B&O).

The B&O was plagued by financial difficulties. On several occasions, construction was suspended for years while the company hunted for more capital. Finally, in 1853, the line was completed to Wheeling. In the meantime, another trunk line, the Erie Railroad, had been built. It extended 441 miles across New York state and was the longest railroad in the world. Indeed, the United States was the world's premier railroad country from the start. When American railroad mileage reached 6,000 in 1848, there were fewer than 3,000 miles of track in the rest of the world.

Old Man River

With its two great tributaries, the Ohio and Missouri Rivers, and dozens of smaller but navigable feeders, the Mississippi River drains the central third of the North American continent. Westerners who lived in the Mississippi Valley traditionally shipped their corn and livestock to New Orleans on log rafts that, broken up and sawed into lumber, supplemented their income. A young Abraham Lincoln shipped aboard a Mississippi raft.

The catch was getting goods upstream. Despite the width of the lower Mississippi, sailing ships were of little use. The current was too powerful for the strongest winds and channels deep enough to float ocean-going vessels too narrow for tacking.

Some cargo was moved upstream in 50-foot-long shallow-draft "keelboats" by a procedure so laborious that one can feel faint reading about it. When the river bottom was deep enough to allow movement close to the banks, ropes were secured to trees upstream and the crew heaved the keelboat forward. Away from the riverbanks, the work was even harder. Bracing a long, sturdy pole in the muddy bottom, crewmen in a line walked bow to stern, poling the boat forward, then returned to the bow, and on and on. A keelboat could move only fifteen miles a day. Hauling a cargo from New Orleans to Louisville took between three and four months.

Because crews had to be large, shipping by keelboat was very expensive. It was feasible to ship only the costliest cargos upriver: cloth, leather products, iron and steel tools, furniture. Even then, it cost less to move a ton of anything from Europe to New Orleans than from New Orleans to St. Louis.

© Bettmann/Corbis

The flat bottoms and shallow drafts of Mississippi river steamboats allowed them to tie up at river banks in order to take aboard cotton directly from a plantation, as shown here. Steamboats also pulled over to the banks when they needed cord wood, which was often; steamboats devoured fuel. Locals, sometimes slaves who were permitted to work for money on their own time, piled up mountains of firewood they had cut and stacked to attract the boats.

Queens of the Mississippi

The marvel that solved the problem of upstream transportation on the Mississippi was the flat-bottomed steamboat. A Connecticut Yankee named John Fitch, living in Philadelphia, ran a practical 45-foot steamboat down *and up* the Delaware River in 1787. (Several delegates to the Constitutional Convention witnessed the spectacle.) But Fitch, a star-crossed genius, never exploited his invention. The steamboat had to be reinvented in 1807 by Robert Fulton, this time in New York. Fulton's *Clermont* wheezed, chugged, and clanked up the Hudson to Albany at five miles per hour. The *Clermont* was three times as long as Fitch's boat, but the dimension that thoughtful people noticed was that it drew only seven feet of water. The boat was able to clear shallows and underwater obstacles such as snags (fallen trees) that would ground or sink a sailing ship.

Steamboats more than paid their way on eastern rivers. But it was on the Mississippi, Missouri, and Ohio that they were indispensable. Fulton understood this; just a few years after his success with the *Clermont* he went west and built the first Mississippi paddle-wheeler. It was not sufficiently powerful enough to buck the river's current, but a competitor's boat was. In 1815, it made the first steam-powered upstream

voyage from New Orleans to Louisville. By 1817, there were 17 steamboats on the Mississippi. By 1830, there were 187 with new ones being constructed more quickly than the old ones blew up.

Boiler explosions were no small problem. In order to minimize the weight of the boats, boilers were constructed more flimsily than good sense prescribed. Nonetheless, after the *Tecumseh* set a record of eight days and two hours from New Orleans to Louisville in 1827, rival riverboat captains found it difficult to resist a race. Speed sold tickets and attracted shippers. So, despite the opulence of some steamboats, traveling on one was a bit of a gamble. At the peak of the steamboat age, 500 people died in accidents each year. In the explosion of the *Moselle* in 1838, 150 people were lost.

Steamboats drew very little water. Sandbars piled up to just feet below the surface and they shifted location constantly; the Missouri River was shallower than the Mississippi. If the competition to design boats with ever shallower drafts was less dramatic than the competition to set speed records, it was also less dangerous, and much more important. The champion was the *Orphan Boy,* launched in 1841. Loaded with forty tons of freight plus passengers, it skimmed atop water only 2 feet deep. Dozens of paddle wheelers carrying much heavier cargos drew just 3 or 4 feet. The steamboats' shallow drafts not only solved the problems of shifting sandbars and snags, it also enabled the boats to tie up at river banks anywhere to take on the cordwood the boats burned in prodigious quantities.

THE HAPPY PRESIDENCY OF JAMES MONROE

The gentleman who presided over the Era of Good Feelings and the beginnings of the transportation revolution was, like three of the four presidents who preceded him, a Virginian. James Monroe of Westmoreland County is a blurred figure in the history books. His personality, like his face in maturity, had no hard edges. His achievements before he was elected president were not spectacular but neither were they negligible. He had been an able diplomat and secretary of state, a good administrator as governor of Virginia, and—though he lacked the wealth of Washington, Jefferson, and Madison, utterly incorruptible. "Turn his soul wrong side outwards," Jefferson said, "and there is not a speck on it." It can be noted that his wife was considered one of the country's most beautiful women. Portraits of Monroe reveal that, even in his dotage, he dressed in the old-fashioned knee breeches of the Revolutionary era while his contemporaries had long since given theirs to their servants and were pulling on the trousers of the nineteenth century.

Monroe was a lifelong Jeffersonian, one of his most radical disciples during the 1790s. Unlike Madison, however, he was capable of disobeying the old man. Unlike Jefferson's and Madison's, his intelligence was ordinary and his intellectual interests few. "No man," a contemporary said of Monroe, "ever succeeded so well with powers so moderate."

Looking back at him, he is two-dimensional, even inanimate: an oil painting. This is due in part, no doubt, to the fact that his two-term presidency was an effortless success. Presidents confronted by crises come alive to us easily because of their struggle in grappling with them. Monroe was confronted by no crisis and only a few problems that were promptly dispatched. Happy presidencies, like Leo Tolstoy's happy families, are all the same and, therefore, not so interesting. In his second inaugural address in 1821, Monroe could intone the bromide that United States "will soon attain the highest degree of perfection of which human institutions are capable," and get away with it.

The Politics of Calm

The Founding Fathers expected that the United States would be governed without political parties. Something like their ideal came to pass during Monroe's presidency: There was only one political party. The Federalists, hostile to the War of 1812, collapsed when the war was concluded with the spectacular victory at New Orleans. After 1815, Federalist opposition to the war seemed more like disloyalty than good sense, even in New England, where the opposition had centered.

The number of Federalist congressmen declined from 68 during the war to 42 in 1817 and 25 in 1821 (compared with 158 Jefferson Republicans). By 1821, there were only 4 Federalists in a Senate of 48 members. Old John Adams, in retirement in Quincy, took little interest in the evaporation of the party he had helped to found. His son, John Quincy Adams, had already joined the party of Thomas Jefferson, serving it as a diplomat and then, under Monroe, as secretary of state.

In 1816, Monroe easily defeated Federalist Rufus King, who won the electoral votes of only Delaware, Connecticut, and Massachusetts. By 1820, the few Federalists left had given up; Monroe ran for reelection unopposed. (One member of the electoral college cast his vote for John Quincy Adams so that no president but George Washington would have the distinction of being a unanimous choice.)

Politicians were almost indifferent to presidential politics. In 1816, William Crawford of Georgia would have won the Republican nomination over Monroe if he had thought the prize worth a contest. He did not; his supporters did not bother to attend the caucus at which the candidate was named.

Nor was there much interest at the polls. In 1816, only six of nineteen states chose presidential electors by popular vote. In 1820, only seven of twenty-four states did. Voter participation in the popular election states ranged from lukewarm to cold. In Richmond, Virginia, a city of 12,000, in 1820, only seventeen men bothered to vote. In states in which the legislatures named the electors, they treated the task casually, as they might have considered a motion to buy a watch for a retiring doorkeeper.

There is nothing intrinsically wrong in a subdued presidency and popular indifference to politics, particularly according to the Jeffersonian faith. Jefferson said that the government that governed least governed best. If Monroe was neither mover nor shaker, history's movers and shakers have done a good deal of mischief along with any legacies with which they are credited. Monroe left little legacy; he did no mischief. He was competent and conscientious. As for the lack of popular enthusiasm for presidential politicking, it is difficult to disdain it in a day when we select our president on an interactive television show that runs for more than two years long.

The Year Without a Summer

For those who lived through it, 1816 was less memorable for James Monroe's election to the presidency than for the fact that there was no summer. On June 6, between one and two feet of snow fell over much of the Northeast. Temperatures were twenty or thirty degress cooler than usual and almost every day was cloudy. It snowed again in both July and August.

Only in the twentieth century was the summerless year explained. Mount Tamboura in Java had erupted, filling the atmosphere with a cloud of dust dense enough to filter the sun over much of the world. Europe had even less of a summer than North America.

Oregon

The noteworthy achievements of the Monroe administration were in foreign affairs, which were adroitly managed by Secretary of State John Quincy Adams. In the Rush-Bagot Agreement of 1817, just two years after the War of 1812 was concluded, Adams arranged with Great Britain virtually to demilitarize the Great Lakes that separated Canada from the United States. This remarkable agreement saved both countries a good deal of money and freed the inhabitants of lakefront cities and towns from the fear of a naval bombardment. Rush-Bagot also set the Canadian-American border west of the Lakes at 49° north latitude, where it remains today. Finally, the two nations agreed to a unique "joint occupation" of the Oregon Country (present-day Oregon, Washington, and British Columbia). Citizens of both countries were to enjoy equal access to Oregon and equal rights there whether the local authority was British or American.

In reality, neither the British nor the Americans had much of a presence in the Oregon country. A few trappers trundled about waiting for ships to buy their pelts and bring in liquor; that was about it. The Russians (whose trappers had already taken all the furs they wanted and moved on) had a better legal claim to Oregon than either. Joint occupation was, therefore, a quiet triumph for Quincy Adams. He won the implicit promise of British cooperation, if push came to shove with Russia, in a far-off region where it would have been difficult to bring any American power to bear.

Florida

To the south, Quincy Adams's expansionism had more immediate consequences at the expense of the once mighty Spanish Empire. It was falling to pieces. "Liberators" José de San Martín, Bernardo O'Higgins, and Simon Bolivar had ended Spanish rule in South America. Mexican independence, proclaimed in 1810 by a village priest, Miguel Hidalgo y Castillo, was virtually assured in 1819 by an army commmanded by Agostin de Iturbide. (Officially, Mexican independence dates from 1821.) Only in Cuba, Puerto Rico, the eastern half of Santo Domingo, and Florida was Spain still in charge.

And Spanish rule in Florida was largely theoretical. Four-fifths of the peninsula was unexplored. The swamps and forests were firmly in the possession of Indians, including the warlike Seminoles, a branch of the Creek nation that had incorporated many blacks who had escaped from masters in Florida and Georgia. Except for sleepy communities like Pensacola and St. Augustine and a string of tiny missions across the north of the colony, all of Florida's European population lived on the island, *Cayo Hueso* (now Key West), which was closer to Cuba than to St. Augustine. And as many of the whites on Key West were French, British, and American as were Spanish.

In 1818, Andrew Jackson demonstrated how weak Spain's hold on Florida was. Pursuing Creek warriors, his militia pushed brazenly across the border. In the village of Suwanee, he arrested two British subjects whom he accused of arming the Creeks. Jackson tried and convicted them of treason and hanged them.

This was preposterous. The two men were British subjects. They could not, by definition, commit treason against the United States. Moreover, Jackson tried and hanged them on foreign soil where his judicial powers extended only to his own troops. To compound his high-handedness, Jackson entered Pensacola without President Monroe's approval and deposed the Spanish governor.

When the Spanish minister, Luis de Oñis, protested, as well he might, Quincy Adams replied that trouble between the United States and Spain in Florida would continue until, inevitably, the United States seized the colony by force. Instead, he offered to buy Florida amicably for $5 million.

Spain had good reason to take the money. Some of Jackson's troops were still in Pensacola. Planters from Georgia and Alabama were, at will, foraying across the border scouting possible cotton lands. With Spanish hopes of holding on to Mexico still alive, there were no troops available to defend Florida against American seizure. In the Adams-Oñis

---

Russian California

In 1784, Russian fur trappers and missionaries founded a trading station and village in Alaska. The Russia America Company, to which the Czar entrusted the colony, aggressively expanded its operations to the south. Early in the nineteenth century, Russians and Alaskan Indians harvested furs on the Oregon Coast—sea otter was most treasured—but they built no permanent settlements until 1812 when twenty-five Russians and eighty native Alaskans constructed farms, a village, and a sturdy stockade, complete with blockhouses and cannon, at Fort Ross in Spanish Californa, less than 80 miles from Spain's northernmost port of Yerba Buena (San Francisco).

By 1821, the sea otters around Fort Ross were hunted out. However, the company decided to stay at Fort Ross to raise grain, cattle, and sheep to feed the settlements in Alaska. The United States had no grievance with the outpost. The Russians were trespassing on Spanish, then Mexican, not American territory. Indeed, the few American ships that cruised the California coast were delighted that Fort Ross existed. It was a welcome anchorage and a speck of civilization at the end of the world.

Then the Czar protested British and American claims to Oregon by banning all foreign ships within 100 miles of Russian America. The lonely Russians at Fort Ross ignored the ban. They were as delighted when seamen came to call as the visitors were to knock on the door. In 1841, the Russia America company decided it could buy provisions for Alaska from the British in Canada more cheaply than to maintain the fort where, although livestock flourished, crops did not. They abandoned Fort Ross and all Russian claims in North America below 54° 40′ north latitude, the southern boundary of Alaska today.

Treaty of 1819, Florida sold Florida to the United States and agreed to receive American traders in isolated Santa Fe, New Mexico. More to save face than anything else, Oñís insisted that Adams recognize Spain's version of the boundary between Texas part of Mexico and Louisiana.

The Monroe Doctrine

The Czar of Russia protested the Anglo-American occupation of Oregon by announcing that foreign ships were no longer welcome at Fort Ross, a Russian outpost on the northern California coast. It was a trivial matter, but it provided Adams with a pretext for making a momentous proclamation through President Monroe.

The true motivation for the announcement of what, seventy years later, was called the Monroe Doctrine, was the agreement of Russia, Austria, and France to coperate in restoring the world to what it had been before the French Revolution. They had already drawn the map of Europe to their liking and enforced reactionary policies wherever they had the power to do so. Among their other projects was a proposal to dispatch a joint military expedition to the Americas that would restore Spain's empire. Neither John Quincy Adams nor the British foreign minister, George Canning, took the Austrian and Russian threats seriously. But France was another matter.

Canning quietly proposed to Adams that Britain and the United States jointly issue a statement that the Western Hemisphere was closed to colonization, including the restoration of former colonies. Adams was all for the doctrine but decided that the United States should proclaim it alone. The United States itself did not have the military power to resist a serious French expedition to Mexico, let alone to South America. Only Britain's Royal Navy, that really did rule the waves, could do that.

However, a joint proclamation with Great Britain would make the United States look like "a cock-boat in the wake of the British man-of-war," the me-too junior partner in an alliance. By announcing the Monroe Doctrine as an American policy, Adams would implicitly state that the United States was the preeminent power in the Western Hemisphere. Moreover, Canning's doctrine included an American pledge not to "colonize" beyond its borders, a promise the expansionist Adams was certainly not prepared to make.

The occasion for the proclamation was President Monroe's annual message to Congress in December 1823. In an otherwise dull statement, Monroe mentioned "the respective rights and interests" of Russia and the United States on the Pacific coast. He informed Congress that he had asked the Czar to join in "amicable negotiations" to resolve any conflicts before they materialized.

From this nonissue, Monroe moved abruptly—dramatically—to the subject of the "American continents." North and South America, he declared, were "henceforth not to be considered as subjects for future colonization by any European powers." The United States would never intervene in the affairs of the European nations "relating to themselves." But the independence of the Spanish-speaking republics of Central and South America was final. A "system" in the Americas had been created that was "essentially different" from the "system" of Europe.

With existing colonies in the Americas—Canada, Russian America, numerous islands in the West Indies—the United States had no quarrel. (Seven European nations then had American colonies.) However, Monroe concluded, "We should consider any attempt on [Europe's] part to extend their system to any portion of this hemisphere as dangerous to our peace and safety." The United States would regard any attempt to reestablish Spain's authority in the Americas as a "manifestation of an unfriendly disposition *toward the United States.*" This was diplomatese for, If France intervened in the Western Hemisphere, it would mean war.

MISSOURI

If President Monroe did not have to deal with a major crisis, the Sixteenth Congress did and it came out of nowhere, like a lightning strike on a sunny day. In 1819, a part of Missouri Territory applied for admission to the Union. The would-be state of Missouri's constitution provided that slavery was to be legal there.

This came as no surprise. Slavery had a continuous history in Missouri under French and Spanish law since 1719 and after the United States acquired it in 1803 as part of the Louisiana Purchase. Most of Missouri's settlers had come from slave states. There were fully 10,000 slaves in Missouri's population of 60,000. The shock came when a New York congressman, James Tallmadge, proposed an amendment to the statehood bill forbidding Missourians to import additional slaves and providing that all children in Missouri were free at birth and that slave children already in the state be freed when they reached the age of 25.

In other words, Missouri would become a free state by the same process adopted by most of the northern states: gradual emancipation.

An Angry Debate

There were good reasons for insisiting that Missouri should be a free state. The land was unsuitable to plantation agriculture. Would-be cotton growers owning large gangs of slaves knew it and were emigrating to farther south: to Alabama, Mississippi, Louisiana, and Arkansas Territory. Missouri was clearly destined to be a family farmers' country, producing foodstuffs on small acreages. Moreover, Missouri was geographically "northern." All but a sliver of the proposed state lay north of the point at which the Ohio River—the border between slave states and free states—flowed into the Mississippi.

But Tallmadge and other northern congressmen added the argument that slavery was a social evil and morally wrong. If the southern states faced profound difficulties in abolishing the institution, Congress could, at least, ensure that slavery did not spread into the thinly settled West.

Thirty years earlier, there had been no significant objections in the South when the Northwest Ordinance forbade slavery north of the Ohio River. Twenty years earlier, many southern congressmen would still have agreed that slavery was a socially and even morally undesirable institution that was, fortunately, slowly dying because it was uneconomical everywhere but in the rice-growing regions of South Carolina and Georgia.

But that was before the bonanza profits in growing cotton had reinvigorated plantation agriculture economically and made southern whites less inclined to apologize for slavery. Northern attacks on the morality of the institution were implicit and sometimes, in the heat of the debate in Congress, there were explicit attacks on the personal morality of every slave owner. Southern congressmen responded to the name-calling in kind. Thomas Jefferson, in retirement at Monticello, was still saying privately to visitors that he thought slavery undesirable and hoped it would die out. But the news of the angry, ugly debate in Congress was, to him, "like a firebell in the night," a terrifying way to be awakened. He feared that if northerners and southerners divided on a question of morality, the Union was in grave danger.

The Missouri Compromise

The Talmadge Amendment passed in the House of Representatives when almost every northern congressman voted for it. There were 105 representatives from free states, 81 from the South. In the upper house, however, there were 22 slave state senators and 22 from free states. When a few northern senators, alarmed by the temper of the debate, joined with every slave state senator, the amendment was defeated.

The equal number of slave states and free states provided moderates in Congress with an opening wedge for a compromise. For several years, the people of the "Maine District" of Massachusetts had favored separating from the state. (Maine and Massachusetts were not contiguous.) Compromise-minded congressmen proposed that the equality of free states and slave states be preserved by admitting Missouri with no restrictions on slavery and Maine as a free state. Pro-slavery southerners were mollified because there were, on the horizon, as many future slave states as free states.

In return for this concession, antislavery northern congressmen were rewarded with an act that extended the southern boundary of Missouri—36° 30' north latitude—through the reminder of the Louisiana Purchase lands and forbade slavery north of that line. Slavery's further expansion was, therefore, restricted to Arkansas, where slavery was already established and present-day Oklahoma to which the federal government was already resettling Eastern Indians on the assumption that it would never be a state.

The Second Missouri Compromise

That should have been the end of it. Most senators and congressmen had been alarmed by the antagonistic debate. Unfortunately, Missouri's political leaders insisted on a defiant last word. They prohibited free blacks and mulattos from emigrating into Missouri. This was a blatant violation of Article IV, Section 2 of the Constitution, which guaranteed citizens the rights they enjoyed in their own state in every other state. Free African Americans were citizens in several northern states and, in 1820, in North Carolina and Tennessee too.

Missouri's exclusionary rule would have been overturned by John Marshall's Supreme Court as soon as a case was brought before it. However, Henry Clay and others feared that, in the meantime, the North–South shouting match in Congress would resume and do further damage. In the *second* Missouri Compromise, they prevailed on Missouri to declare that in no way should its state constitution be construed as conflicting with Article IV, Section 2.

That, of course, is precisely what it did. But Missouri's hotheads had a semblance of a "last word" and Congress had peace and, once again, good feelings.

FURTHER READINGS

Classics Mark Twain, *Life on the Mississippi*, several editions; George R. Taylor, *The Transportation Revolution, 1815–1860*, 1951; Philip D. Jordan, *The National Road*, 1948.

General D. W. Meinig, *The Shaping of America: A Geographical Perspective on 500 Years of History*, vol. 2, *Continental America, 1800–1867*, 1993; Charles G. Sellers, *The Market Revolution: Jacksonian America, 1815–1846*, 1991; Jack Larkin, *The Reshaping of Everyday Life, 1790–1940*, 1988; Henry L. Watson, *Liberty and Power*, 1990; Jean Mathews, *Toward a New Society: American Thought and Culture, 1800–1830*, 1990.

Nationalism Jill Lepore, *A Is for America; Letters and Other Characters in the Early United States*, 2002; Richard J. Moss, *Noah Webster*, 1984; E. Jennifer Monaghan, *A Common Heritage: Noah Webster's Blue Back Speller*, 1983; David Mickelthwait, *Noah Webster and the American Dictionary*, 2000; Morton J. Horwitz, *The Transformation of American Law, 1780–1860*, 1977; Jean Edward Smith, *John Marshall*, 1995; Robert V. Remini, *Henry Clay: Statesman for the Union*, 1991; Merrill D. Peterson, *The Great Triumvirate: Webster, Clay, and Calhoun*, 1987.

Canals, Railroads, Steamboats John L. Larson, *Internal Improvement: National Public Works and the Promise of National Government in the Early United States*, 2001; Ronald E. Shaw, *Erie Water West: A History of the Erie Canal, 1792–1854*, 1966; Carol Sheriff, *The Artificial River: The Erie Canal and the Paradox of Progress, 1817–1863*, 1996; Dan Murphy, *The Erie Canal: The Ditch that Opened a Nation*, 2001; Peter L. Bernstein, *The Wedding of the Waters: The Erie Canal and the Making of a Great Nation*, 2005; Ronald E. Shaw, *Canals for a Nation: The Canal Era in the United States, 1790–1860*, 1990; Albert Fishlow, *American Railroads and the Transition of the Ante-Bellum Economy*, 1965; James A. Ward, *Railroads and the Character of America, 1820–1887*, 1986; David F. Hawke, *Nuts and Bolts of the Past: A History of American Technology, 1776–1860*, 1988; David Nye, *Consuming Power: A Social History of American Energies*, 1998; Kirkpatrick Sale, *The Fire of His Genius: Robert Fulton and the American Dream*, 2001.

The Monroe Presidency William P. Cresson, *James Monroe*, 1971; Harry Ammon James, *James Monroe: The Quest for National Identity*, 1971; Noble E. Cunningham, *The Presidency of James Monroe*, 1996; Ernest R. May, *The Making of the Monroe Doctrine*, 1976; Donald J. Weber, *The Spanish Frontier in North America*, 1992; James E, Lewis, *The American Union and the Problem of Neighborhood: The United States and the Collapse of the Spanish Empire, 1783–1829*, 1998; William E. Week, *John Quincy Adams and American Global Empire*, 1992; Greg Russell, *John Quincy Adams and the Public Virtues of*

Diplomacy, 1995; Gary V. Wood, *John Quincy Adams and the Spirit of Constitutional Government*, 2004.

The Missouri Compromise Glover Moore, *The Missouri Controversy*, 1953; Donald L. Robinson, *Slavery in the Structure of American Politics, 1765–1820*, 1979; Don E. Fehrenbacher, *The Slaveholding Republic: An Account of the United States Government's Relationship to Slavery*, 2001.

KEY TERMS

Use the following listing of key terms to review important figures, events, locations, and concepts covered in this chapter. A glossary of these terms is available on *The American Past* companion Web site: www.cengage.com/history/conlin/tap9e

Wirt, William, p. 218	**Clinton, DeWitt**, p. 224	**Adams-Oñis Treaty**, p. 230
American System, p. 221	**Mainline Canal**, p. 225	**Fort Ross**, p. 231
wildcat bank, p. 221	***Orphan Boy***, p. 228	**Monroe Doctrine**, p. 231
internal improvements, p. 221	**caucus**, p. 229	**Missouri Compromise**, p. 232
National Road, p. 222	**joint occupation**, p. 230	

ONLINE RESOURCES

Find additional resources, including primary source documents, images, interactive maps, simulations, chapter review exercises, and Internet links at

***The American Past* companion Web site**
www.cengage.com/history/conlin/tap9e

American History Resource Center
http://ushistory.wadsworth.com

© Bettmann/Corbis

Chapter 14

Machines, Cotton, Land

Economy and Society 1790–1824

Sir, A few days ago I was informed that you wanted a manager of cotton spinning, &c. in which business I flatter myself that I can give the greatest satisfaction, in making machinery, making good yarn, either for Stockings or twist, as any that is made in England; as I have had opportunity, and an oversight, of Sir Richard Arkwright's works, and in Mr. Strutt's mill upwards of eight years....My intention is to erect a perpetual card and spinning [mill.] If you please to drop a line respecting the amount of encouragement you wish to give, by favour of Captain Brown, you will much oblige, sir, your most obedient humble servant,

—Samuel Slater

In 1792, Alexander Hamilton submitted a "Report on Manufactures" to Congress. He observed that the American economy was overwhelmingly agricultural. Sixteen years after the Declaration of Independence, Americans were still dependent on Great Britain for most of the manufactured goods they consumed.

To remedy this undesirable situation, Hamilton asked Congress to enact an aggressive program to promote manufacturing at home. He proposed that the federal government pay bounties to inventors of useful machines and to capitalists who would invest in key industries. He called for duties on imported goods high enough to protect American manufacturers from being undersold in their own country.

Hamilton's proposals went nowhere. Southern congressmen saw them as another device to enrich Hamilton's capitalist cronies in the North with public money. Many of them shared Thomas Jefferson's aversion to the squalid towns and cities that had already grown up around British factories to house poorly paid factory workers. "While we have land to labor," Jefferson had written, "let us never wish to see our citizens occupied at a workbench or twirling a distaff. . . . For the general operations of manufacture, let our workshops remain in Europe. It is better to carry provisions and materials to workmen there than bring them to

the provision and materials and with them their manners and principles."

The kind of bounties Hamilton proposed would likely have encouraged wholesale corruption. In fits and starts, without federal subsidies and very little tariff protection for twenty years, private investors built factories throughout the northeastern states, bringing the Industrial Revolution to America.

THE INDUSTRIAL REVOLUTION

There was, of course, plenty of industry in the United States in 1792, plenty of people making things. There were shipyards in just about every harbor from New Hampshire to the Chesapeake. While Americans had been forbidden to export iron goods when they were colonials, forges and foundries had been permitted to produce for the home market. Blacksmiths were not just horseshoers. They made wrought-iron tools, utensils, and decorative gewgaws to order. Foundries turned out cast-iron goods. Entrepreneurs organized networks of spinners and weavers to make woolens, albeit of the plainest kind. (Wearing "homespun" instead of fine British fabrics was a badge of patriotism during the Revolution.) Every town had artisans; cities had a fairly complete complement of the crafts: distillers, brewers, potters, coopers, tanners, rope makers, glass blowers, furniture makers, pewterers, silversmiths and goldsmiths, even makers of luxuries like perfumes. In farm towns were blacksmiths, of course, and carpenters, wheelwrights, wagon makers, flour mills, and sawmills.

All of them, however, were small businesses dependent on the skills of their owners, employing very few people, and serving only local markets. What was lacking—what Hamilton was talking about—was factories in which goods—cotton cloth being the most important—were turned out cheaply and quickly in massive quantities by unskilled workers whose jobs involved little more than tending the complex machines that were revolutionizing manufacturing in Great Britain.

Lady CEOs

Few women headed manufacturing companies, but there were some. Rebecca Lukens owned and managed the Lukens Steel Company for twenty-five years. Her father had turned the company over to her husband, Charles Lukens. When Charles died in 1825, Rebecca was 30 with three young children. Rather than sell out, she took over management of the factory and won the respect of other ironmasters.

Some goods resisted machine manufacture and continued to be produced by cottage industry. Abby Condon of Penobscot, Maine, became a jobber during the Civil War when she won a government contract to provide mittens for the army at 25¢ a pair. She recruited women to knit from all over northern New England, collected the mittens, and delivered them to the army. When the war ended, the wholesale price of mittens collapsed to 6¢ a pair. Had Mrs. Condon's mittens been made on expensive machinery in a factory, she would have been bankrupt. But because there was little overhead in the putting-out system, she stayed in business with as many as 250 knitters in her network. In 1882, when a mitten-knitting machine was perfected, Mrs. Condon did not miss a beat. She purchased four of the devices and built a factory to house them. When she died in 1906, she owned 150 knitting machines. Her business consumed six tons of woolen yarn a year and annually produced 96,000 pairs of mittens.

How Cloth was Made

Today, clothing is so cheap that even college students have closets stuffed with it. It takes a well-focused imagination to appreciate how many hours of tedious hand labor it took before the age of mass production to make just a few yards of fabric.

Cloth began as natural fiber from the cocoons of silkworms, the stems of flax (for linen), the bolls (seed pods) of the cotton plant, and sheep's wool. All four textiles were manufactured in Great Britain before 1700, but most silks and cottons were imported already woven from China and India. In Great Britain, wool was king.

Transforming fleeces into cloth involved innumerable men, women, and children performing one or two steps of the process. The sheep had to be shorn. The wool was "scoured": cleaned of oils, dirt, twigs, and other solids the animals had collected. The clean wool was then carded, brushed with carding boards that looked much like the brushes with which we groom dogs today. Carding thinned the wool, aligned the fibers in the same direction, and evenly distributed them in a fluffy spiral called a rove.

The roves were spun into yarn by being twisted around one another on spinning wheels. The operator powered the wheel with a foot treadle while she firmly drew the yarn or thread to keep it uniform, winding the finished product on a spindle. Spinning was women's work. The wives and older daughters of farmers and artisans spun part-time in their homes to earn money for the household. Unmarried female relatives often worked at the wheel full-time. Thus, the legal term *spinster* meaning an unmarried woman. Spinning required a deft touch, but it was a skill that most women could master with practice. Even in the nineteenth century, after machinery in factories had taken over spinning in the United States, the spinning wheel remained a fixture on many farms.

Weaving yarn or thread into cloth required looms that were too expensive to be operated only part-time. Weavers (usually men) worked dawn to dusk six days a week at the trade. Entire villages and neighborhoods in towns were populated exclusively by weavers and their families.

The woven cloth—the textile—was fulled, washed in fuller's earth, an absorbent clay, and pounded to flatten out

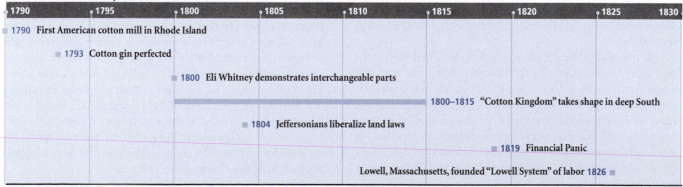

Economic Development 1790–1830

1790 First American cotton mill in Rhode Island

1793 Cotton gin perfected

1800 Eli Whitney demonstrates interchangeable parts

1800–1815 "Cotton Kingdom" takes shape in deep South

1804 Jeffersonians liberalize land laws

1819 Financial Panic

Lowell, Massachusetts, founded "Lowell System" of labor 1826

imperfections. Then the cloth was bleached and usually dyed. Finally, cloth dealers, often prosperous weavers, carried a week's or a month's production to regularly scheduled fairs in market towns to sell it to retailers, tailors, seamstresses, and exporters.

Woolens versus Cottons

Woolens manufacture had been central to England's economy since the Middle Ages. The only people who got rich in the business were the large landowners who raised sheep at the beginning of the process and clothiers and exporters at the end of it. There were plenty of them; no combination of individuals dominated the industry. Collectively, however, the "woolens interest" was politically powerful. When, during the 1700s, landowners flooded Parliament with requests for permission to take farmland out of cultivation, sow grasses, and convert their estates into pasture for sheep, they were quickly obliged. When the East India Company began to sell calico, India's gaily colored high-quality cotton cloth in England, thus competing with woolens, Parliament banned the import of Indian cloth. When the company imported raw cotton to be spun and woven in Britain, Parliament tried several expedients to hinder the industry. It was all for naught. Cotton cloth was in demand and the new industry thrived.

Like woolens manufacture, cotton production was organized in what was called "cottage industry" or the "putting-out system." Weavers "put out" the fiber to the cottages of women who spun, buying the finished yarn from them at a price on which both parties had agreed. Traditionally, a weaver (of wool or cotton) needed about six spinners working as many hours as he did to keep his loom supplied.

In the mid-1700s, however, with the near universal adoption of John Kay's flying shuttle, an improvement of the hand loom that dramatically stepped up a weaver's productivity, the spinner to weaver ratio increased to the point that there were not enough spinners available. The cotton fiber was abundant. The demand for cotton cloth at home and abroad kept increasing. But weavers could not get enough yarn, and the young industry faced a serious depression.

Machines

"Necessity is the mother of invention." What England's weavers needed was a more productive way of spinning yarn. It was this necessity that launched the Industrial Revolution in textiles.

It is not always clear if the individuals credited with technological breakthroughs like the spinning jenny and the water frame really deserve their places in history. It was not clear at the time they were invented. James Hargreaves was involved in so many lawsuits with men he accused of stealing his spinning jenny that he died poor despite the fact that his jenny was revolutionary; one of the machines spun as much cotton fiber as eight hand-spinners could. The spinning jenny was a small machine powered by the operator. It could be put into homes, replacing spinning wheels, and many

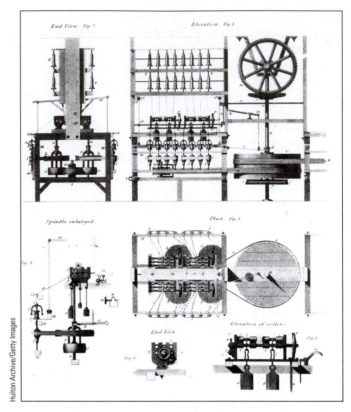

Hulton Archive/Getty Images

Diagram of an early nineteenth century water frame, a water-powered machine for spinning cotton yarn. The technology was British. In an attempt to preserve Britain's monopoly of textile manufacture, Parliament forbade the export of plans like these. Men like Samuel Slater who brought spinning and weaving technology to the United States had to commit designs, including precise numerical specifications, to memory.

were. By the end of the 1700s, however, there were 20,000 of the machines in Great Britain, more than testing the limits of cottage industry.

Richard Arkwright's water frame, an even more productive spinning machine, was introduced in 1768. It produced more and better cotton yarn than a jenny did because it was driven not by muscle power but by a water mill. The energy generated by fast-flowing water made even faster spinning possible. A water mill did not tire and it was possible to link several—numerous!—water frames to a single mill by means of drive shafts and leather belts and pulleys.

Arkwright may not have been the seminal inventor he claimed to be. He had been a barber who seems to have known little or nothing about cloth making. If Arkwright borrowed his technology from others, however, he was indisputably the creator of the factory system. The water frame killed off spinning as a cottage industry. Instead of putting out fiber to spinners' homes, the workers who tended water frames had to come each day to a factory. Instead of working as skilled contractors making the best deal they could for their labors, the workers in an Arkwright mill were employees paid fixed take-it-or-leave-it wages.

The spinning machines of the late 1700s (and, soon enough, mechanized looms) were revolutionary. Unlike tools, which are passive, useless without the skills of the person using them, machines do their job without human input. The factory workers who attended spinning machines merely watched them. Their only function was to keep moving parts lubricated, tie together the loose ends of threads that broke, and stop the machine if there was a serious malfunction. No skill was involved; anyone could do it. And so, spinning mill hands were paid a fraction of what hand spinners had earned for the same hours of work. And one mill-hand tending machines turned out more yarn than dozens of hand spinners in cottages had produced.

THE INDUSTRIAL NORTHEAST

The Industrial Revolution found its American home in the northeastern states. There, water power was abundant. Shipping, to bring in raw materials and carry finished goods to buyers, was centered in the Northeast. Capital for investment in mills was available. And in New England, with too many people for its poor soil to support as farmers, provided a pool of labor from which factories could draw their workers. The industrialization of the Northeast, however, began with an act of technological thievery.

The Granger Collection, New York

The Slater Mill, the first carding and spinning mill in America, considerably expanded from its beginnings in 1790. It was on the Blackstone River in Pawtucket, Rhode Island. Note the dam spanning the river. It was necessary to divert some of the river's flow (upstream, to the right) into a reservoir, the "mill pond" that plays so prominent a part in nostalgia for a bucolic past. From the pond, the water was funneled into a mill race that descended sharply so as to create a fast-running torrent. The water in the race powered the waterwheel that, in turn, powered the machinery inside. The tail race returned the water to the river, to the left of this picture.

The Great Defector

The British recognized the role of government in developing carding, spinning, and weaving machines. Parliament forbade the export of machinery and the plans for making them were kept in vaults. Engineers who knew how the build the new machines and mechanics who repaired them were forbidden to leave the country. The latter was a difficult law to enforce, of course. However, the pains that Samuel Slater had to take to break it indicate that the authorities did their best.

Slater had been apprenticed to a partner of Richard Arkwright and, in 1789, worked as a mechanic in an Arkwright mill. The pay was good, but Slater knew that, having no capital, he would never be more than an employee. Learning that American investors were offering bounties and partnerships to anyone who would come to the United States and build a cotton mill, Slater memorized the intricate drawings of spinning and carding machines and long lists of specifications. (The machines were so complex that tolerances were minuscule; there was no room for even slight errors.) Just 19 years of age, he slipped away when his absence would not be noticed for several days. Disguised as a farm laborer, he shipped off to the United States. There he struck a bargain with a rich Quaker merchant in Rhode Island, Moses Brown. Brown had experimented with spinning machines but could not make one that worked.

Brown put up the money. Slater contributed the know-how. In 1790, they opened a water-powered cotton mill in Pawtucket. It was tiny by English standards, housing only seventy-two spindles. But it worked! The Slater Mill turned out yarn at a far faster rate than seventy-two women sitting at seventy-two spinning wheels in seventy-two cottages could have done. And at a fraction of the cost: Slater ran the mill with nine children between the ages of 7 and 12. Their wages ranged from 33¢ to 60¢ a week. Slater pumped his profits into more and bigger mills. He became one of New England's leading industrialists, owning mills in three states.

There were other acts of technological piracy. In 1793, two brothers from Yorkshire, John and Arthur Schofield, emigrated illegally to Byfield, Massachusetts, where they established the first American woolens mill. Just before the War of 1812, Francis Cabot Lowell of Massachusetts smuggled plans for a power loom out of England. Throughout the nineteenth century, Englishmen would bring valuable technological knowledge to America in their sea trunks or in their heads.

Power and Capital

Textile production centered in the northeastern states because of its abundance of water power. The Blackstone River (which powered Slater's first mill) became virtually a fifty-mile-long mill race between Worcester, Massachusetts, and Providence, Rhode Island. One factory after another lined both banks. There were dozens of fast-running streams like the Blackstone throughout New England. The Merrimack River, which winds through New Hampshire and Massachusetts, powered mills and created major textile centers at Manchester and Lowell. A single Manchester firm, the Amoskeag

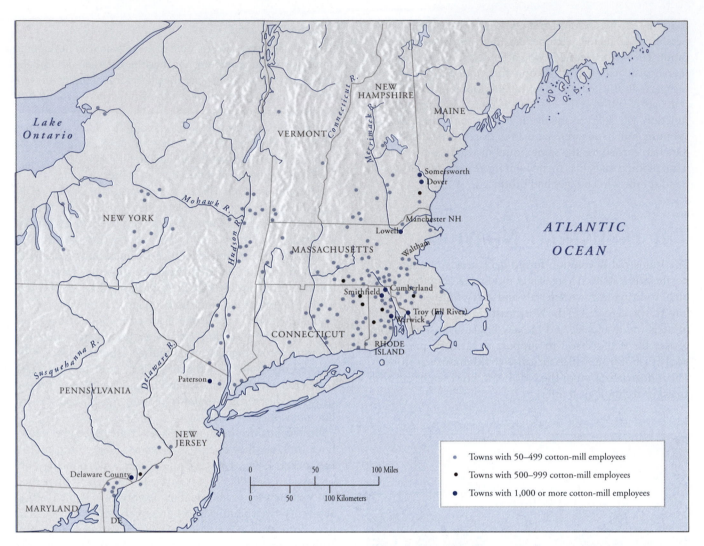

MAP 14:1 **Cotton Mills, 1820.** Milltowns were built where creeks and rivers dropped sharply in waterfalls or rapids. The stream was dammed above the fall line to create a reservoir. A mill race channeled the flow from this mill pond in a torrent to the waterwheel that turned the machinery. The tail race returned the water to the river. Lowell, Massachusetts, was built at the 32-foot falls of the Merrimack River. Farther up the Merrimack, at Manchester, New Hampshire, a "hideous rapids" dropped 85 feet. Paterson, New Jersey, was built where the Passaic River, searching for the Hudson, found a shortcut by creating a dramatic falls. Note that there were few mills on the broad and mostly slow-flowing Connecticut River.

Manufacturing Company, eventually operated thirty mills on the Merrimack. Mill towns sprung up where creeks emptied into New York's Hudson River. The Passaic river in northern New Jersey falls almost eighty feet at Paterson (where Alexander Hamilton hoped to build mills). In Pennsylvania, the Schuylkill, the principal tributary of the Delaware River, ran in rapids even within Philadelphia's city limits.

The Northeast was also rich in capital that was diverted to manufacturing when the Embargo, Non-Intercourse Acts, and the War of 1812—all of which the Northeast opposed—disrupted overseas trade. With ships an unwise investment, merchant princes put their money into textile mills. In 1800, ten years after Slater's Mill, but before the long war between France and Britain, there were only seven spinning mills with a total of 290 spindles in all of New England. After fifteen years of maritime war and Jefferson's restrictions on

trade, there were 130,000 spindles in 213 factories just in Massachusetts, Connecticut, and Rhode Island.

Inventors

If Americans imported their textile technology, they soon numbered among the pioneer innovators in other industries. Hamilton had observed "a peculiar aptitude for mechanical improvements" in the American people. In the 1820s, a foreign observer marveled that "everything new is quickly introduced here. There is no clinging to old ways; the moment an American hears the word 'invention' he pricks up his ears."

Oliver Evans of Philadelphia earned international fame when he contrived a continuous-operation flour mill. Previously, to make flour, laborers had hauled grain in sacks or wheelbarrows from wagons up ramps to the water powered grindstones and dumped it in. Other men working below shoveled the flour into barrels or sacks and carried or wheeled them out of the building. It was backbreaking labor and the handling at every turn made for dirty flour.

Evans designed a belt and bucket conveyor that could carry 300 bushels of grain per hour to the top of his multistory mill where it was dumped automatically into hoppers that funneled it to the grindstones. Another conveyor removed the flour and loaded it into barrels. With just four to six men—whose principal task was to hammer lids on the barrels—an Evans mill could grind 100,000 bushels of grain in a year. By 1840, there were 1,200 Evans mills in the western states producing an astronomical 2 million barrels of flour each year.

Eli Whitney, already famous as an inventor, designed a rotary metal-cutting machine with which, he believed, he could mass produce an item with a much bigger profit margin than flour or yarn: muskets. In 1798, in the midst of a war scare and unable to import muskets, the federal government invited bids from gunsmiths to supply the army. The government expected to contract with a great many gunsmiths, each of whom could make only small numbers of the guns. Gunsmithing was slow, highly skilled work. The time-consuming part of the manufacture was the making and assembly of the lock—the firing mechanism—trigger and hammer and the parts that linked them. Each part had to be fashioned by a skilled gunsmith using hand tools. Each musket was "custom made." If a part of the lock broke, only a skilled gunsmith could make a replacement that fit perfectly, a procedure more difficult than manufacture.

Whitney believed that his machine would finish the parts of the lock so precisely that they would be identical—"interchangeable." The muskets would go together quickly and no longer would a skilled gunsmith be needed to repair a broken lock. A soldier in the field could disassemble it, insert the needed part, and put the mechanism back together.

Whitney appeared before a congressional committee with a dramatic presentation. He disassembled ten functioning muskets and jumbled the pieces together on a table. Picking out parts at random, he reassembled ten locks and they all worked. The congressmen were impressed, as they should have been. Whitney was awarded a contract to manufacture 10,000 muskets at $13.40 each. It was a bargain for the army and potentially very profitable to Whitney.

The American System of Manufacture

Unfortunately, Whitney had faked the show. His interchangeable parts were what he was sure his cutting machine was capable of doing, but he had not yet done it. His ten sets of parts were identical because they had been painstakingly finished off by hand. Whitney could not quite perfect his tool. He delivered only 500 muskets in 1801 when the 10,000 were due; the last of the order was ready only in 1809.

The vision of interchangeable parts and mass production intrigued manufacturers of many kinds. A successful maker of expensive clocks he sold to institutions and the rich, Chauncey Jerome, developed a machine that stamped the gears and other parts of a clock out of sheets of brass. They were genuinely interchangeable and were made in quantity by unskilled workers guided by a template. In 1856, Jerome was able to sell a handsome clock (they are collector's items today) for just $6. In less than a year, he increased production so that he cut the price to $4. All but the poor could afford what had been a luxury.

Jerome's stamping machines were machine tools, highly specialized devices that removed one part of the skilled artisan's craftsmanship from human hands and put it into the workbench. Unskilled or semiskilled workers, guided by jigs and precision gauges, could run the lathes, drill presses, planers, grinders, gear shapers, and other machine tools that rapidly performed a single step in the complex process of manufacture and pass the result along to another worker tending a machine tool that performed the next procedure.

The mass production of firearms—Eli Whitney's dream—was perfected at the federal arsenal at Springfield, Massachusetts. Everything from the irregularly shaped wooden stocks of muskets to the tiny parts of the locks that had foiled Whitney were made, step-by-step, by easily trained machine tenders. When the process was explained at the Crystal Palace Exposition in London in 1851 (the first great world's fair), the British, in a rare expression of admiration for their former colonies, dubbed it the "American System of Manufacture."

The First Factory Workers

Slater and Brown hired children to tend the machinery in their mill. Because they could be paid minimal wages, young children continued to fill factory jobs that were not dangerous and called for no great strength. In cotton mills well into the twentieth century, "bobbin boys" carried boxes of wooden bobbins (spools) wound with newly spun yarn to the weaving room and the empty bobbins back to the spinning machines.

However, as machinery grew larger and faster, bobbins whirling at hundreds of revolutions each minute, operators had to take care lest hair, clothing, or a hand be caught in the works. Children at their freshest are not attentive, and they tire quickly when set to monotonous tasks.

Some factory owners, notably at Fall River, Massachusetts, hired entire families to work their mills. Their reasoning was rooted in the way of life all preindustrial people: Families ran farms, adult males shouldering the heavy work, women the jobs requiring skill but less physical strength, children saving adults time by fetching water and firewood, feeding chickens, and so on. Why not, then, hire families to divide up millwork similarly? The "Fall River system" was a failure. The pace of factory work was entirely different from the rhythms of life on a farm. The head of the family's traditional authority over and his concern for his wife and children clashed with the millowner's authority over all of them. First in Rhode Island, then elsewhere, including Fall River, mill owners left the man of the house on a small farm and put his wife and children to work in the mills.

New England Mill Girls

When Francis Cabot Lowell advertised all over New England for female workers, other mill owners quickly followed suit. They had to overcome an aversion to allowing young women to leave home because "mill girls" in England and France had a reputation for moral laxity. But they overcame it by promising to supervise their employees as strictly as the Puritan Fathers would have done.

Most of the women who answered the call were between 15 and 25 years of age, but there were older women tending carding and spinning machines and power looms from the start: impoverished widows, some with small children whom they cared for at their posts. There were not many ways a woman without a husband or grown son could support herself in rural New England. The mills had put an end to spinning at home. A woman could become a domestic servant, but Americans who had known independence found that life humiliating. Every township maintained a primary school, and the pay was so meager that most teachers were female. But if the teacher was from out of town, she could barely make ends meet on the pay and, as an outsider in a close-knit community, she was likely to be lonely.

Factory work paid more than teaching. It was laborious, twelve to thirteen hours a day, six days a week. "Enter with us into the large rooms," an investigator wrote of Manchester, New Hampshire's Amoskeag Mill in 1846:

> It is four hundred feet long, and about seventy broad; there are five hundred looms, and twenty-one thousand spindles in it. The din and clatter . . . struck us on first entering as something frightful and infernal, for it seemed such an atrocious violation of one of the faculties of the human soul, the sense of hearing. After a while we became somewhat inured to it, and by speaking quite close to the ear of an operative and quite loud, we could hold a conversation, and make the inquiries we wished. . . .

The atmosphere of such a room cannot of course be pure; on the contrary it is charged with cotton filaments and dust, which, we were told, are very injurious to the lungs. On entering the room, although the day was warm, we remarked that the windows were down; we asked the reason, and a young woman answered very naively, and without seeming to be in the least aware that this privation of fresh air was anything else than perfectly natural, that "when the wind blew, the threads did not work so well." After we had been in the room for fifteen or twenty minutes, we found ourselves, as did the persons who accompanied us, in quite a perspiration, produced by a certain moisture which we observed in the air, as well as by the heat.

Living conditions were equally dismal.

> The young women sleep upon an average six in room; three beds to a room. There is no privacy, no retirement here; it is almost impossible to read or write alone, as the parlor is full and so many sleep in the same chamber. A young woman remarked to us that if she had a letter to write, she did it on the head of a band-box, sitting on a trunk, as there was not space for a table. So live and toil the young women of our country in the boarding-houses and manufactories, which the rich and influential of our land have built for them.

Orestes Brownson, a prominent literary figure in New England, denounced the moral effects of the life. After working for three years, he asked, " What becomes of them then? Few of them ever marry; fewer still ever return to their native places with reputations unimpaired. 'She has worked in a factory' is almost enough to damn to infamy the most worthy and virtuous girl." Harriet Farley, a mill

The Lowell Girls

More successful was the "Waltham System" or "Lowell System." The brainchild of Francis Cabot Lowell, who owned several mills at Waltham, Massachusetts, in 1813; in 1826, he founded Lowell as a town that was nothing but textile mills. By 1850, its population was 33,000, making it the second biggest city in Massachusetts and the largest industrial town in the United States. Lowell and his associates elected to hire only young women and girls for all but supervisory jobs. Making cloth was traditionally women's work. Tending machines was not strenuous work. Single women—so Lowell thought—were more docile than men and with few ways to earn money, they would accept lower wages.

Finally, rural New England was overpopulated. Infant mortality had declined and farm families were large; there were too many people for the stony soil of New England to support as farmers. Grown daughters were often an economic burden. They could no longer contribute to the household income by spinning and it was still customary that, when there was a marriage, the bride bring a dowry to it. A struggling New Hampshire farmer with three or four daughters approaching marrying age must have had frequent nightmares.

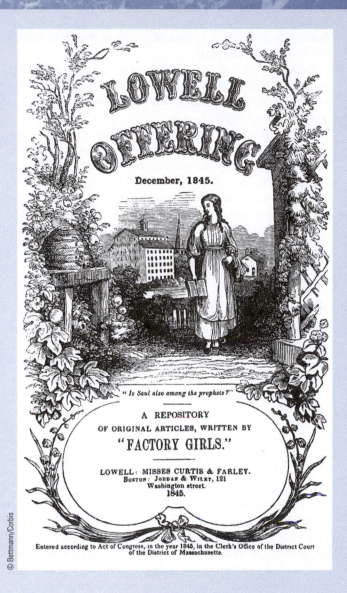

In 1840, a Universalist minister in Lowell suggested that mill girls who attended his church found and publish a literary magazine. The result was the Lowell Offering, *which was issued regularly for five years. All the poetry, stories, and essays (both serious and humorous) were written and edited by mill workers in their spare time. Some of the writing was highly sentimental in the fashion of the era. Some of the essays were hardheaded and intelligent, although always civil. The quality of the* Offering *was at least equal to that of other New England magazines of its kind.*

girl in Lowell, was infuriated by his article. In the *Lowell Offering,* she denounced Brownson as a slanderer of

> a class of girls who in this city alone are numbered by thousands, and who collect in many of our smaller towns by hundreds; girls who generally come from quiet country homes, where their minds and manners have been formed under the eyes of the worthy sons of the Pilgrims, and their virtuous partners, and who return again to become the wives of the free intelligent yeomanry of New England and the mothers of quite a portion of our future republicans. Think, for a moment, how many of the next generation are to spring from mothers doomed to infamy! "Ah," it may be replied, "Mr. Brownson acknowledges that you may still be worthy and virtuous." Then we must be a set of worthy and virtuous idiots, for no virtuous girl of common sense would choose for an occupation one that would consign her to infamy....

Brownson was a leading light in New England intellectual circles, but Harriet Farley bested him on this one.

Enter the Lowell System: Farmers were urged to send their grown girls to work in Lowell's mills for six days a week, about twelve hours a day, for weekly wages of $3. They would pay their employer $1.50 a week for room and board at company-owned dormitories closely supervised by company-employed "keepers," older women, spinsters, or widows. A few companies offered cultural and educational programs in the evenings. Most mills required that the factory girls attend church services every Sunday (at "the church of their choice") and prove it by presenting their overseer (shop foreman) a certification they had done so signed by a minister. Factory work was not a career. As firmly as any Calvinist

farmer, Lowell believed that a woman's role in society was to be a wife and mother. After two, three, four years, "Lowell Girls" would return home to marry.

New England farmers were not difficult to persuade. Simply subtracting one or two daughters from the supper table each evening was financially inviting for many of them. The girls' wages were handy as the makings of their dowries or to pay for the higher education of a bright brother. The strict moral discipline the Lowell System promised allayed the anxieties of sternly religious families.

Early, Waltham and Lowell seem to have been, on balance, fairly benign places. The pace of the machines was far more

University of Massachusetts, Lowell

New England mill girls in smocks that protected their clothing from dirt, lint, and tears in the mill. Most mill girls were in their late teens or early twenties and worked in the mills for only a few years. Some of the girls found the experience of getting away from home exhilarating or, at least, liberating, with so many friends their own age. Others hated the long hours, the relentless pace, the noise of factory life, and the lack of privacy. There were well supported strikes in 1836 and 1838.

frantic than farm work but not as relentless as working on an assembly line today. Visitors from England, including the great novelist, Charles Dickens, commented that Lowell's mills were idyllic compared to the "dark, satanic mills" at home. After Francis Cabot Lowell's death, however, the mill owners gradually lost interest in the paternalistic side of the system. Some Lowell girls compared themselves to southern slaves. In 1836 and 1838, most of the workers in Lowell went on strike demanding a reduction of hours in the killing twelve-hour workday.

THE SOUTH AT THE CROSSROADS

The mills of the Northeast competed with British mills to buy cotton grown in the South. During the 1810s, a few prominent southerners like the young congressman John C.

Calhoun of South Carolina asked themselves: Why let the English and New Englanders pocket the lion's share of the money to be made in the manufacture of cotton cloth? Calhoun proposed that cotton mills be built at the "fall line" in South Carolina where Appalachian streams tumbled rapidly down to the coastal plain.

Calhoun was well ahead of the times. Seventy years later, increased labor costs in the northern states would drive the cotton industry to the Carolinas, albeit to steam rather than water-powered mills.

But the idea of "factories in the fields" went nowhere during the 1810s. Thanks to the Industrial Revolution and, in particular, thanks to the mechanical ingenuity of a Yankee visiting in Georgia, cotton cultivation became the way to wealth in the lower South. The agrarian mindset that the seventeenth-century tobacco boom had imprinted on the South was revived by the cotton boom of the early nineteenth century. The money to be made growing cotton also reinvigorated the institution of slavery.

Slavery in Decline

When John C. Calhoun was born in 1782, African American slavery appeared to be dying out. The northern states abolished the institution when Calhoun was a child. Many southern slave owners, influenced by the Revolution's ideology of individual freedom as a natural right, manumitted their slaves. Others, in the tobacco states, found the costs of feeding, clothing, and housing large numbers of slaves too great when the exhausted soil of their plantations would no longer produce a good crop and the world price of tobacco declined. George Washington stopped growing tobacco at Mount Vernon; wheat was his principal crop. Wheat was not as labor intensive as tobacco. It could be and was grown by slaves but left them so much free time that land owners realized they would be better off hiring free labor seasonally. Even South Carolina's rice and indigo lost luster when British subsidies ceased following independence and, taking turns during the 1790s, the French and the British refused to buy American rice. In 1808, Congress forbade the further importation of slaves, an act which many regarded as a first step toward ridding the country of the institution.

By 1808, however, cotton culture was returning bonanza profits. Like rice and tobacco, it lent itself to large-scale cultivation by gangs of slaves. The "cotton kingdom" extended from upland South Carolina and Georgia to western Tennessee, including the future states of Alabama, Mississippi, and Louisiana. The demand for slaves to serve the "King," coupled with the end of the slave trade with Africa and the West Indies, caused the price of slaves to increase radically. Slaves that had been a financial burden on their owners in the upper South were now commodities that could be sold profitably in the cotton states.

The cause of this sudden reversal of fortunes for the future of slavery was an "absurdly simple contrivance" invented in 1793 by Eli Whitney.

Cotton and the Cotton Gin

The cotton plant was well known in the South. The first colonists at Jamestown domesticated cotton plants native to North America, but they abandoned the crop when tobacco proved to be the big moneymaker. Very little cotton was cultivated anywhere until 1769 when a "long staple" cotton (so called because of the length of the fibers) was introduced from the Bahamas to the sea islands of South Carolina and Georgia. The sandy soil and mild climate of the offshore islands suited the plant perfectly. Slaves prepared it for export to England by pushing and pulling the cotton bolls through rollers set slightly closer together than the diameter of the slick and slippery black seeds. This spit the seeds out of the bolls while the fiber came through clean. (The seeds were pressed to extract a useful oil.)

However, sea island cotton did not do well on the mainland and the roller device crushed the sticky green seeds of native American plants; they had a Velcrolike texture that clung to the fiber and fouled the fiber with cottonseed oil when they were crushed.

In 1793, seven years before his historic demonstration of interchangeable parts before Congress, Whitney was visiting a friend who lived on a plantation near Savannah.

There he saw his first cotton plants and learned that they flourished wild all over the upland South. There was plenty of rain for the thirsty plant and more than the 210 frost-free days that cotton demanded. Cotton fiber was then selling in Britain for 30¢ to 40¢ a pound—a fabulous price. The trouble was that no one knew how to separate the fiber from the seeds economically. By hand, the seeds had to be removed one by one. The nimblest fingers could not process much more than a pound of the fluff a day, not even enough to pay for a slave's meager diet and rough clothing.

After only a few days of thinking about the problem, Whitney put together a small machine (he called it an "engine")—thus the name "cotton 'gin"—that worked miraculously well. Whitney dumped cotton bolls into an open wooden box. At the bottom of the box were slots too narrow for the seeds to pass through. A drum studded with wire hooks revolved so that the hooks snagged the fibers and pulled them through the slots, leaving the seeds behind. A second drum on which brushes were mounted revolved in the opposite direction, brushing the fiber from the wire hooks.

It was a magnificent device—for planters. A single slave cranking a gin little larger than Whitney's model could clean

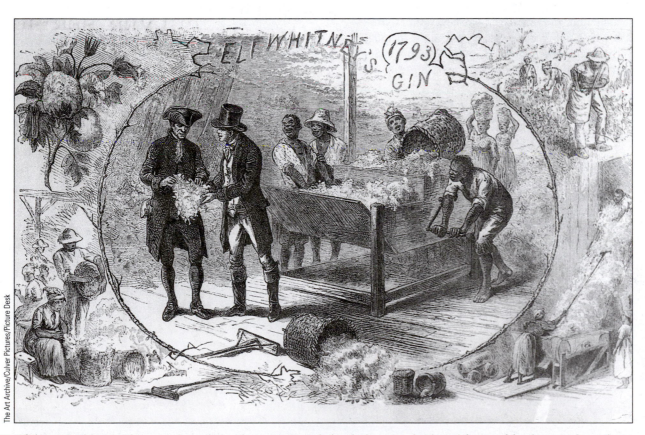

The Art Archive/Culver Pictures/Picture Desk

A lithograph celebrating the economic revolution the cotton gin worked in the lower South. The satisfaction of the planter in the top hat as he shows seed-free cotton fiber to a visitor in an old-fashioned tricorn topper is easy to understand. Cotton was making him rich very quickly. It is more difficult to accept the delight his slaves seem to take cranking the gin from sunup to sundown and packing and hauling the cotton in hot late summer weather.

ten pounds of cotton a day ($3 to $4 at 1793 prices). A larger gin turned by a horse on a windlass could clean 50 pounds a day ($15 to $20!). When steam-powered gins were developed, the capacity for producing cotton was limited not by the gin's capacity, but by the number of acres that a planter's slaves could cultivate.

Whitney's invention should have made him as rich as Richard Arkwright. But the cotton gin was so splendidly simple a machine that pirates were able to make gins that, with trivial modifications, dodged Whitney's patents. He was no longer manufacturing gins in 1798 and nearly broke.

Slavery Revived

Technology had come to the South, but not industry. Eli Whitney's machine revived the one-crop economy that planters of Washington's generation had considered the South's curse. Cotton, like tobacco and rice, was well adapted to gang cultivation. Cotton culture required plenty of unskilled labor: plowing, planting, "chopping" (killing weeds, an endless task in the hot, fertile South), ditch digging and maintenance, picking, ginning, pressing, baling, and getting the bales to buyers.

The fertile upland black belt that extends from South Carolina and Georgia to eastern Texas was natural cotton country. Southerners streamed into the "Old Southwest" (Alabama, Mississippi, and northern Louisiana) and eventually across the Mississippi into Texas and Arkansas. In 1800, excluding Indians, there were about 1,000 people in what is now Alabama. In 1810, there were 9,000; in 1820, 128,000!

The growth of Mississippi was less dramatic but not lethargic: 1800, 8,000; 1810, 31,000; 1820, 75,000.

The emigration included not only poor families seeking a better life, but also wealthy planters who sold their land in the old states and made the trek with their slaves in tow. In 1800, there were 4,000 blacks in Alabama and Mississippi. In 1810, there were 17,000, virtually all of them slaves. In 1820, the African American population was 75,000. Almost half the people of Mississippi were slaves.

The demand for "prime field hands"—young, healthy men—to toil in the cotton fields caused the price of slaves to soar. The average purchase price of a slave doubled between 1795 and 1804. In Louisiana by 1810, slaves cost twice what they cost in Virginia. Blacks who had been financial burdens in Maryland and Virginia were easily sold in the cotton South. The most humane masters found it difficult to resist the temptation of the high prices offered for their slaves. Although it was illegal to sell Delaware and New Jersey slaves out of state, a few slave owners there smuggled their property into Maryland and Virginia and, from there, shipped them to the cotton kingdom.

THE TRANS-APPALACHIAN FRONTIER

The Appalachians are not high as mountains go. But they were long an impediment to settlement because they form a series of ridges that extend northeast to southwest into

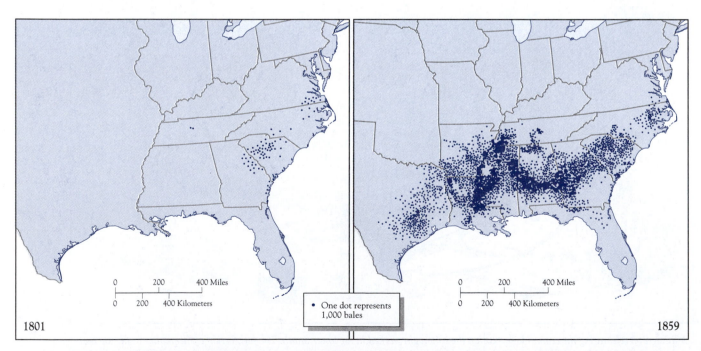

1801

• One dot represents 1,000 bales

1859

MAP 14:2 **The Spread of Cotton Cultivation.** Green-seed cotton grew "like a weed" on the uplands of the lower south. It was too difficult to retrieve its fibers until Eli Whitney's cotton gin extracted the oily seeds without fouling the precious fiber. Then, commercial cotton cultivation spread "like a weed."

northern Alabama and there are very few passes through them. South of the route of the Erie Canal, the easiest crossings were from Cumberland, Maryland, to the Monongahela River (a route scouted by George Washington) and the Cumberland Gap between Virginia and Kentucky. But the Potomac River from Cumberland, Maryland, to the Chesapeake Bay was not navigable for long stretches and Daniel Boone's Cumberland Gap pass climbed to 1,600 feet above sea level. In addition to Vermont, which was mostly mountainous, the only states west of the Appalachians in 1800 were Kentucky and Tennessee.

Population Explosion

The population explosion west of the mountains in the early 1800s was not restricted to the cotton belt. Kentucky continued to grow and the states north of the Ohio

River grew even more dramatically than Alabama and Mississippi. In 1800, there were 45,000 white people in Ohio and a few African Americans, all of them free because the Northwest Ordinance had prohibited slavery. Ten years later, the state's population was 230,000. By 1820, trans-Appalachian Ohio was the fifth largest state in the Union. By 1840, with 1.5 million people, it was fourth; only New York, Pennsylvania, and Virginia had larger populations. Ohio, little more than a generation from wilderness (and still wild in the center) was home to more people than Finland, Norway, or Denmark.

Between 1800 and 1840, the mostly white population of Indiana grew from a few hundred to 685,856, Illinois from next to nil to 476,183. In 1800, Michigan amounted to one wretched fort inherited from the French and British: Detroit. In the 1830s, New Englanders flocked to

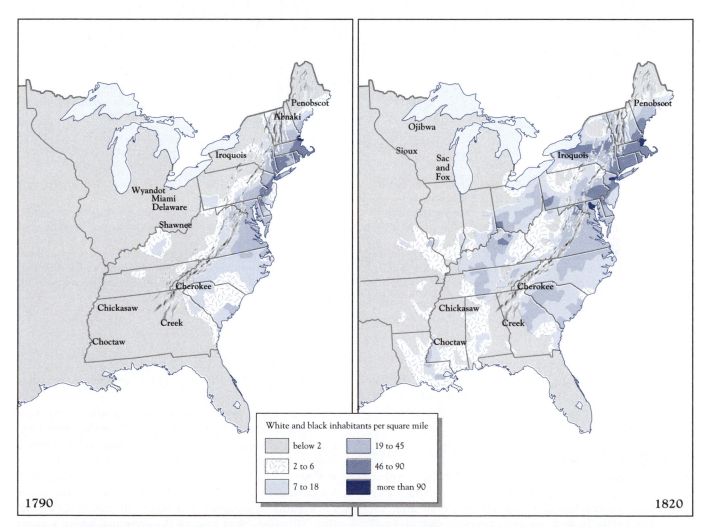

White and black inhabitants per square mile

below 2		19 to 45
2 to 6		46 to 90
7 to 18		more than 90

MAP 14:3 **Population Density, 1790–1820.** A comparison of these two maps shows a dramatic increase in population density in the northeastern states during the early years of the nineteenth century. In part, this was a consequence of industrialization. Maryland, Virginia, and North Carolina show little change. They remained rural and grew crops of declining value. From upland South Carolina west, cotton cultivation transformed near wilderness into a booming farm belt. Population growth in Tennessee, Kentucky, Ohio, Indiana, and Illinois was due to heavy western migration.

The conestoga wagon was big and rugged. An early model was 19 feet long at the top of the four feet deep bucket, 14 feet long in the bed. It could carry 6 tons. Conestoga wagons were as tightly caulked as boats. If it was emptied, it could be floated across a river.

The front wheels were four feet in diameter, providing enough clearance for pretty big rocks. The rear wheels were six feet across so that, when the wagon needed a push, the spokes provided handholds with good leverage. The famous canvas bonnet was stretched on iron hoops and kept possessions and sleeping emigrants dry when it rained.

Conestogas crossing the Appalachians were drawn by one or two yokes (pairs) of oxen. The plodding powerful beasts were kept moving by a drover who poked their flanks with a stick and constantly repeated command to walk. (Oxen have short memories.) Dogs were trained to run alongside and bark, both to keep the oxen moving and to prevent local dogs from harassing them. If you lived near an emigrant road, you heard a conestoga wagon coming from as far as sound carried.

Michigan's "oak openings," fertile prairies amidst the forests. By that time, the Mississippi River itself had ceased to be a frontier. Missouri, on the west bank, had been a state for ten years.

People on the Move

The abundance of cheap land does not by itself explain the torrent of people that flooded west. Russia had even more land for the taking in Siberia but, even after the czar freed the serfs, few peasants migrated to "the East." They had to be dragooned into settling Siberia (or exiled there as punishment for crime). But Americans were not peasants, wary of the unfamiliar. Always excluding slaves, Americans were free to live where they chose and it made them inherently restless, as nervous and agitated as the

"painters" (panthers) they chased away when they pushed ever deeper into the woods.

To Europeans, and sometimes to themselves, Americans were incapable of putting down roots. The young couple saying their marriage vows and promptly clambering aboard a wagon to head west was as familiar a scene in New England as stone fences. During the first decades of the century, white Virginians, some with their slaves in tow, headed across the mountains as rapidly as a high birth rate could replace them. In central and western Pennsylvania, where a major wagon road ran west, the regional economy was closely tied to emigration. Inns and the stables of horse and oxen traders (teams needed constantly to be replaced) dotted the highway. Pennsylvania's Conestoga Valley gave its name to a type of wagon manufactured there. It was a high-slung, heavy-wheeled vehicle that could roll where there was no road, with a deep bed for possessions and sleeping dry. (A cheap cigar that many Conestoga wagon drivers clenched between their teeth was dubbed the "stogie.")

"In the United States," marveled Alexis de Tocqueville, "a man builds a house in which to spend his old age, and he sells it before the roof is on." An Englishman looking over lands near the Ohio River reported that if, to be polite, he admired the improvements a recent settler had made on his land, the man was likely to propose selling him everything on the spot so that he could start improving again farther west. A joke of

the era had it that, every spring, American chickens crossed their legs so they could be tied up for the next push west.

Patterns of Settlement

A few of these eternal pilgrims were simply antisocial, the "eye-gougers" and "frontier scum" of legend and reality. Others were as respectable as the King James Bible they read regularly and wanted as much company on the frontier as they could persuade to join them. They meant to re-create the way of life they had known back east but better, because, out west, they could own much more land than they could afford east of the mountains.

Yet other pioneers were speculators and developers—a profession still with us and sometimes accepted in polite society—dreamers, schemers, and promoters of new Edens, Romes, and Lexingtons. Poor men like Abraham Lincoln's father, Thomas, who made a career of clearing a few acres of forest and building a cabin to sell to a newcomer were small-time developers. More important to western development were men with some capital (or credit) who purchased large tracts of land—a section or two or even more—trumpeted its glorious fertility and future, and sold, at a profit, farm-sized parcels—"quarter sections" (160 acres) or "quarter quarter-sections" (40 acres), which was about right for a family in well-watered areas.

Some boosters laid out what they called cities divided into building lots suitable to a blacksmith, grocer, printer, or lawyer. They named streets before trees growing in imagined intersections had been felled. Some of these town fathers were merchants or even manufacturers who intended to stay in the settlements they often named for themselves, and prosper as the country grew. Others were promoters who moved on as soon as they made their bundle—or lost it. They were quite as rootless as the hunters and trappers whom farmers displaced.

The Kentucky Long Rifle

The gun that won the trans-Appalachian West was the Kentucky long rifle. It had a 44 inch barrel and enough maple stock to make it the height of an average man. However, it weighed only eight pounds, a considerable recommendation to those who had to carry one all day.

The long rifle was a muzzle loader. With the butt on the ground, a charge of coarse black powder (measured by dead reckoning) was poured from a "powder horn" (the horn of an ox sealed against moisture) down the muzzle into the breech. Then a ball, wrapped in greased linen or a leather patch to seal the explosion, was rammed home, then a wad of paper to keep the ball in place.

In even the most practiced hands, the long rifle failed to fire one time in four. The phrase "flash in the pan" derives from the all too common, aggravating phenomenon of a charge that flashed when the trigger was pulled but failed to send the ball on its way.

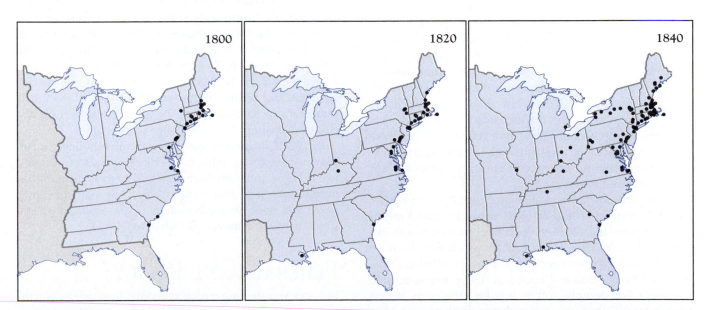

MAP 14:4 **Cities of at Least 5000 Inhabitants, 1800–1840.** The northeastern states were highly urbanized (by nineteenth-century standards) between 1800 and 1840, a phenomenon that would continue. By comparison, the slave states remained thoroughly rural. North Carolina, Florida, and Mississippi lacked a single sizable town. In the more northerly trans-Appalachian West, however, genuine cities have made their appearance.

SOUTH WATER STREET.　　　　CHICAGO. 1834.

Chicago Historical Society

In 1834, Chicago was a cluster of rude one- and two-room buildings on a mud flat barely higher than Lake Michigan. The town grew slowly until it became the northern terminus of the Illinois Central Railroad and, later, the western terminus of several eastern trunk lines. Chicago's population exploded when the transcontinental railroads were built, bringing through the "Windy City" the produce of the last great American West, most famously hogs and cattle.

Frontier Cities

The army was the cutting edge on some frontiers. Soldiers posted in the West to keep an eye on Indians had to be fed, clothed, and entertained. Shopkeepers, saloon keepers, and log-cabin prostitutes clustered around military installations. The security the fort provided encouraged trappers, hunters, and others who tramped the woods to congregate within or near them during times of Indian trouble. Indians hooked by civilization's goods—alcohol all too prominently—abandoned tribal life to make a sort of life on the fringes of the army towns. Tribal Indians also showed up periodically to trade. The wants of this diverse assortment of westerners stimulated the growth of a mercantile economy before there was much tillage in the neighborhood. Urbanization actually preceded agriculture. Vincennes, Detroit, and other western towns developed in this manner.

Cities preceded farms along major rivers too. Only after a fairly advanced (if not refined) urban life had evolved did the hinterland fill in with farmers to feed places like Cincinnati, Louisville, and Nashville, which were built on sites at which river travelers could conveniently beach canoes and tie up rafts and keelboats. These towns became rest stops and jumping-off points for emigrants bound farther west. When the cotton lands of the lower Mississippi boomed, sending out calls for provisions for the slaves who raised the lucrative crop, the river ports became entrepôts of grain and livestock. Cincinnati, "the Queen City of the West," was famous for its slaughterhouses and packing plants when, a few miles away, great hardwood forests blocked the sun from the earth and lonely men and women battled malaria.

Most astonishing is how quickly some western cities became manufacturing centers. In 1815, when there were no more than fifteen steam engines in all of France (a nation of 20 million people), half-wild Kentucky, population 500,000, boasted six steam mills turning out cloth and even paper. Before the War of 1812, St. Louis had a steam mill six stories high. Like medieval burghers determined to erect their cathedral's spires higher than the spires in the next nearest city, Cincinnatians built a mill nine stories high.

By 1828, Cincinnati boasted nine factories building steam engines, nine cotton mills, twelve newspapers, forty schools, two colleges, and a medical school. It was a metropolis but unmistakably raw and western too: Only one street was paved and hogs were everywhere. (Then, again, hogs still freely roamed the streets of Washington, D.C.)

FEDERAL LAND POLICY

Industry was the motivating economic force in the Northeastern states, cotton in the South. In the trans-Appalachian West, including the southwest, the way to wealth was the land itself. Many people went to Illinois or Michigan or Alabama neither to farm, run a shop, nor pack pork. They were speculators dreaming of getting rich by the eternal, risky game of buying land cheap, subdividing it, and selling it dear to people who wanted to live on it (or to other speculators). Some were sharpers by any era's standards, out to line their pockets without a nod for the law, ethics, or common decency.

Settlers and Speculators

Speculators were intensely interested in the price at which the federal government disposed of its land and the terms of purchase. Originally, in the Northwest Ordinances, the federal government sold its land for a minimum of $1 per acre (the price of specific tracts could be bid higher at auction) in parcels no smaller than a section, 640 acres. Actual settlers neither needed so much land nor could an ordinary farmer afford to part with $640. The buyers were men who intended to make a profit by selling it in farm-sized pieces. The Confederation government was not so much catering to speculators as it was sparing itself, with its tiny bureaucracy, the prodigious costs and complex record keeping that selling millions of acres in forty-acre parcels meant. (Recording deeds was a county, not a federal function.)

However, during the Federalist decade, land law was revised to favor big-time speculators. In 1796, the minimum price of federal land was doubled to $2 per acre payable within one year of purchase. The law also provided that only half the land put up for sale could be purchased in sections; the other half was sold in eight-section units: 5,120 acres, for a minimum price of $10,240. That was a fortune. But the Federalist Congress badly overestimated how many rich plungers there were. Land sales collapsed. In four years, the government disposed of fewer than 50,000 acres. In 1800, land policy was revised again. While the minimum price remained $2 per acre, buyers could purchase as little as a half-section (320 acres) and extend their payments over four years. And there was an 8 percent discount for those who paid cash.

Good Intentions, Bad Consequences

In 1804, Jefferson's Republicans were firmly in power. Anti-speculator, they reduced the size of the smallest parcel available to 160 acres and the minimum price per acre to $1.64. To encourage cash-poor settlers to buy, the land office required only a small down payment.

The well-intentioned law encouraged reckless speculation. For very little cash outlay—and that could be borrowed from newly chartered state banks that churned out paper money—shoestring speculators could gain title to numerous 160-acre parcels which they intended to sell at a profit before too many installment payments came due. Many a lucky gambler got rich quickly by shuffling deeds and loans. Each fabulous success story, bragged about at inns and taverns, encouraged others to have a go at the game. After the War of 1812, values soared as speculators grasping wads of bank notes bid prices up at federal auctions and bought properties from one another. Hysterical paper-rich speculators bid one tract of prime cotton acreage in Alabama up to $100 an acre!

It was, in the language of the era, a bubble. The ostensible values of land bore no rational relationship to the wealth that the land could actually produce. Asking prices were inflated with air. Sales were transacted in borrowed bank notes supposedly redeemable in gold and silver but which often were nothing more than elegantly printed paper. Like all bubbles, the land bubble was inflated by the delusion that no matter how absurd the price one man paid for land, someone else was willing to buy it for more. In 1815, the government sold a million acres, in 1819 more than 5 million. Nor was it just the price of land that rose. With so much paper money circulating, the prices of all commodities rose. Cotton, tobacco, and grain prices climbed. Back East, even groceries and rents rose.

The Panic of 1819

The bubble had to burst and it did, in 1819. Speculators found no buyers for parcels of their landed empires at the prices they needed to meet their own obligations and retain title. They defaulted at both the land office and at banks. Acreage the government had marked "Sold" reverted to the public domain. Wildcat banks, with little coin in their vaults and few loans being repaid, closed their doors by the dozens every week; the paper money they had issued was worthless. The price of cotton collapsed, causing bonafide planters to default on their loans. Nationwide, about half a million wage workers lost their jobs,.

What Caused the Panic of 1819?

At bottom, like all booms that bust, it was caused by the human capacity for greed and an even more marvelous capacity for self-delusion. Crazed speculations, whether in land, gold, silver, diamonds, dot.com stocks, or even tulip bulbs as happened in seventeenth-century Holland, are based on the principle of "the greater fool." People pay absurd prices for a commodity in the belief that a "greater fool," willing to pay even more for it, is just around the corner. When the supply of greater fools runs out, however, or the money fueling the speculation loses value, the bubble bursts and paper fortunes disappear.

The Panic of 1819 had specific causes too. British buyers of cotton looked elsewhere in the world for fiber when inflation drove the price of American cotton too high. The western banks that combusted like mushrooms to exploit the speculation were poorly capitalized and irresponsibly managed. They printed and loaned out far more paper money than, given their tiny gold and silver reserves, they could redeem if more than a few people demanded coin. The Second Bank of the United States, chartered in 1816 to monitor and restrain state banks, failed to do its job. In 1817, after encouraging the purchase of federal land with borrowed paper money, the federal government abruptly ordered the land office to accept only specie (gold and silver coin) as payment. There was, simply, not enough gold and silver circulating and the commerce in land (and a good deal else) came to a halt.

Squatters and Their Hero

In the trans-Appalachian West, the word *squatter* lacked the disagreeable odor it has today. Squatters were just settlers who,

Western Eloquence

The following statement was made before a land auction in Missouri by Simeon Cragin who was, it would seem, himself a speculator.

> I own fourteen claims, and if any man jump one of them, I will shoot him down at once, sir. I am a gentleman, sir, and a scholar. I was educated at Bangor, have been in the United States Army, and served my country faithfully. I am the discoverer of the Wopsey, can ride a grizzly bear, or whip any human that ever crossed the Mississippi, and if you dare to jump one of my claims, die you must.

out of orneriness, innocence, or ignorance of the law, developed farms on public land before the government offered it for sale. They cleared trees and plowed fields and built cabins and barns. The created a home on land to which they did not hold legal title. Such improved land was particularly attractive to speculators because the squatters had substantially increased the property's value. When the Land Office held its auction, many squatters saw their claims "jumped." They were outbid for their own homes by speculators rich in bank notes.

Some squatters responded with vigilante action. They banded together in "land clubs," threatening physical reprisals against anyone who bid on a member's land. Not infrequently, they made good on their threats. But speculators determined to jump squatter claims could and did hire toughs, never hard to find on the frontier, who were more than a match for farmers. And the law was on the speculators' side; the squatters had no legal right to the land they had improved.

Squatters and their sympathizers turned to Congress for help. After 1820, they found a tireless spokesman in Senator Thomas Hart Benton of Missouri. Born in North Carolina,

Benton was building a political career in Tennessee when he was involved in a gunfight with a group pf men including Andrew Jackson, the most powerful man in the state. Sensibly, Benton moved again—to Missouri.

Although he was well read in the classics and liked to sprinkle his oratory with allusions to Greek and Roman history, Benton knew how to turn on the bluster that amused rough-hewn westerners. "I never quarrel, sir," he told an opponent in a political debate. "But sometimes I fight, sir; and when I fight, sir, a funeral follows, sir."

Benton was a populist. That is, he trumpeted the interests of the common people against the rich, bankers, paper money, land speculators, anyone and anything else he defined as inimical to the common man. Throughout his long career—thirty years in the Senate—he fought for an ever more liberal land policy favoring settlers over speculators. His pet project was "squatters' rights," or preemption. The principle of preemption provided that people who settled on and improved land before the government offered it for sale were permitted to purchase the land at the government's minimum price. They were not required to bid against others at auction.

Another Benton program was graduation: Land that remained unsold after government auction—the least desirable—would be offered for sale at half the minimum price and, after a passage of time, at a quarter. The price of the land would be graduated downward so as to increase the number of people able to afford it. Eventually, Benton hoped, long unsold land would be given away to people willing to settle it.

Benton's sentiments were more Jeffersonian than anything Jefferson ever proposed. Land was for use; it was not a commodity whose value could be manipulated by speculators for their own enrichment. Benton favored those who tilled the soil, "the bone and sinew of the republic" in Jefferson's phrase, over financial interests once associated with the Federalists and, during Benton's career, with the Whig party.

FURTHER READING

Classics Arnold Toynbee, *Lectures on the Industrial Revolution in England*, 1884 (reprint 2004); Paul Mantoux, *The Industrial Revolution*, English language edition 1961.

General D. W. Meinig, *The Shaping of America: A Geographical Perspective on 500 Years of History*, vol. 2, *Continental America, 1800–1867*, 1993; Charles G. Sellers, *The Market Revolution: Jacksonian America, 1815–1846*, 1991; Jack Larkin, *The Reshaping of Everyday Life, 1790–1940*, 1988; Henry L. Watson, *Liberty and Power*, 1990; Jean Mathews, *Toward a New Society: American Thought and Culture, 1800–1830*, 1990.

Technology and Industry Thomas C. Cochran, *Frontiers of Change: Early Industrialists in America*, 1981; David J. Jeremy, *Transatlantic Industrial Revolution: The Diffusion of Textile Technologies between Britain and America*, 1981; David F. Hawke, *Nuts and Bolts of the Past: A History of American Technology, 1776–1860*, 1988; Walter Licht, *Industrial America: The Nineteenth Century*, 1995; Arand R. Mayr and Robert C. Post, eds., *Yankee Enterprise: The Rise of the American System of Manufactures*, 1981; David A. Hounshell, *From the American System to Mass Production, 1800–1932*, 1984; Carroll

Pursell, *The Machine in America: A Social History of Technology*, 1995; David Nye, *Consuming Power: A Social History of American Energies*, 1998.

Factory Workers Cynthia Shelton, *The Mills of Manayunk: Industrialization and Social Conflict in the Philadelphia Region, 1787–1837*, 1986; Bruce Laurie, *The Working People of Philadelphia, 1800–1850*, 1980 and *Artisans and Workers: Labor in Nineteenth Century America*, 1989; Jeanne Boydston, *Home and Work: Housework, Wages, and the Ideology of Labor in the Early Republic*, 1990; Thomas Dublin, *Women at Work: The Transformation of Work and Community in Lowell, Massachusetts, 1810–1860*, 1979 and *Transforming Women's Work: New England Lives in the Industrial Revolution*, 1994.

Cotton and Slavery Angela Lakwete, *Inventing the Cotton Gin: Machine and Myth in Antebellum America*, 2003; Bruce Collins, *White Society in the Antebellum South*, 1985; James Oates, *The Ruling Race: A History of American Slaveholders*, 1982, and *Slavery and Freedom: An Interpretation of the Old South*, 1990; Gavin Wright, *The Political Economy of the Cotton South*, 1998.

Land Policy Malcolm J. Rohrbaugh, *The Trans-Appalachian Frontier: People, Societies, Institutions,* 1978; Daniel Feller, *The Public Lands in Jacksonian Politics,* 1984; Stephen Aron, *How the West Was Lost: The Transformation of Kentucky from Daniel Boone to Henry* *Clay,* 1996; Joan E. Cashin, *A Family Venture: Men and Women on the Southern Frontier,* 1991; John Mack Faragher, *Sugar Creek: Life on the Illinois Prairies,* 1986.

KEY TERMS

Use the following listing of key terms to review important figures, events, locations, and concepts covered in this chapter. A glossary of these terms is available on *The American* *Past* companion Web site: www.cengage.com/history/conlin/tap9e

putting-out system, p. 236

factory system, p. 236

interchangeable parts, p. 239

cotton gin, p. 243

specie, p. 250

Benton, Thomas Hart, p. 250

preemption p. 250

graduation, p. 250

ONLINE RESOURCES

Find additional resources, including primary source documents, images, interactive maps, simulations, chapter review exercises, and Internet links at

The American Past **companion Web site**
www.cengage.com/history/conlin/tap9e

American History Resource Center
http://ushistory.wadsworth.com/

Chapter 15

The People's Hero

Andrew Jackson and a New Era
1824–1830

General Andrew Jackson (colour litho), Sully, Thomas (1783-1872) (after)/ Private Collection, Peter Newark American Pictures/Bridgeman Art Library

Thou great democratic God!, ... who didst pick up Andrew Jackson from the pebbles; who didst hurl him upon a warhorse; who didst thunder him higher than a throne! Thou who, in all Thy mighty, earthly marchings, ever cullest Thy selected champions from the kingly commons.

—Herman Melville

Except an enormous fabric of executive power, the President has built up nothing.... He goes for destruction, universal destruction.

—Henry Clay

The single-party political world of the Monroe years had its virtues. Americans were spared appeals to party loyalty, at its best an ignoble loyalty. Holding high office was an honorable profession; it could be viewed, and was, as fulfilling a gentleman's duty to perform public service, as the Founding Fathers, at their best, intended. The same four men headed the four most important cabinet departments—State, Treasury, Justice, and War—throughout Monroe's presidency. They were all of the first rank, arguably the best men in the country for their jobs. Little bothered by pressures to find salaried jobs for party hacks, they ran their departments efficiently and honestly. Attorney-General William Wirt took over a Justice Department that was a mess because of his predecessors' neglect and (over twelve years) put its procedures, record keeping, and ethics into order. Cabinet discussions of issues facing the government were, possibly, never more intelligent and disinterested.

THE ELECTION OF 1824

But it could not last. There were too many prominent men around (including three cabinet officers) who had presidential ambitions, who, indeed, believed they had each earned the right to succeed Monroe. The Jefferson Republican party

had traditions and a procedure for nominating its candidate for the presidency but, in 1824, they so heavily favored one of the aspirants that the others were inclined to think them out-of-date.

An Orderly Succession

Before 1824, the Jefferson Republicans chose their presidential candidate in a caucus of the party's senators and representatives. Even it was a formality because, except in 1808, there was always only one contender for the honor, either the incumbent or his hand-picked successor. (In 1808, James Monroe challenged Jefferson's choice, James Madison, and lost.)

In 1824, now himself the retiring president, Monroe hoped that his designation of a successor, ratified by the caucus, would be enough. He asked the party to nominate his Secretary of the Treasury, William Crawford. Crawford had another tradition on his side. He was the crown prince of the "Virginia Dynasty." Four of the first five presidents were Virginians. Crawford was from Georgia, but he had been born in Virginia.

The caucus met and nominated Crawford, but only Crawford men attended. "King Caucus" was dead. Long before it met in 1824, the legislatures of their home states had put forward the names of three other candidates: General Andrew Jackson of Tennessee, Secretary of State John Quincy Adams of Massachusetts, and Speaker of the House Henry Clay of Kentucky.

252

Virginia Dynasty

Four of the first five presidents were from Virginia. Virginians were president for thirty-two of the republic's first thirty-six years.

This seems a bit grotesque today. Indeed, the term "Virginia Dynasty" was pejorative, coined by a contemporary who was not at all happy with all those Virginians. On closer examination, however, the political prominence of Virginians at the top made sense statistically and was, in part, accidental.

Virginia was the most populous state until about 1820. When Washington and Thomas Jefferson were nominated to head the country, fully one American in five lived in Virginia. The state's population was just a few thousand less than the combined populations of the six smallest states!

Nevertheless, the only dynast who would not have been elected without Virginia's electoral votes was Jefferson in 1800. George Washington would have been president for life had he been born and bred in Delaware, the smallest state. And the other three Virginia presidents—Jefferson, Madison, and Monroe—were hardly Washington's heirs. They opposed his policies during his second term and Washington came to despise Jefferson.

Jefferson did pick Madison to succeed him and Madison picked Monroe, but not because they were Virginians. Madison had been Jefferson's most intimate and obeisant advisor since 1790. He would have gotten Jefferson's nod in 1808 had he been a Delawarean. Madison selected Monroe because he had served Madison as secretary of state.

Madison's and Monroe's four lopsided election victories had nothing to do with the state from which they hailed. It was because of the collapse of the Federalist party including, after Hamilton's death, a collapse in the quality of the party's leaders.

DeWitt Clinton had considered running but decided to seek the governorship of New York instead. South Carolina's legislature was poised to nominate the state's favorite son, Secretary of War John C. Calhoun. Calhoun had traveled in the North trying to recruit supporters there. But the signs there were not good, and not much better in the South where Crawford was the favorite. When Calhoun was nominated for vice president on both the Jackson and Adams tickets, he opted out of the presidential contest in favor of the sure thing. He was only 42, younger than anyone yet elected president. Calhoun could reasonably conclude that his turn would come.

The Candidates

The election was more about personalities and sectional loyalties than about issues. Adams and Clay, for example, were both nationalists. Both advocated a high protective tariff and favored a nationally financed and coordinated internal improvements program. Had the election been about competing principles, either Clay or Adams would have been under great pressure to step aside in order to unite the nationalist vote behind one candidate. But it was not, and it probably did not matter. Clay and Quincy Adams disliked one another personally. When they were both peace commissioners in Ghent, negotiating a treaty to end the War of 1812, Clay had thrown himself into the high life during off-hours, drinking, gambling, and chasing women. To Adams, who was personally fastidious and a workaholic, there were no off-hours. He thought Clay frivolous and dissolute. Clay thought Quincy Adams was a yankee prig.

Clay conceded that Adams would win the electoral votes of New England. However, he expected that his long labors in Congress working for internal improvements would carry most of the western states, and that his leadership in

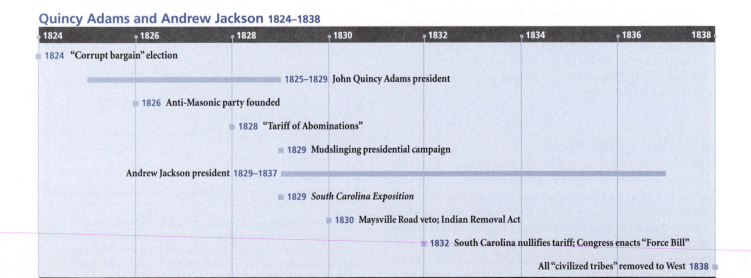

Quincy Adams and Andrew Jackson 1824–1838

1824   1826   1828   1830   1832   1834   1836   1838

1824 "Corrupt bargain" election

1825–1829 John Quincy Adams president

1826 Anti-Masonic party founded

1828 "Tariff of Abominations"

1829 Mudslinging presidential campaign

Andrew Jackson president 1829–1837

1829 *South Carolina Exposition*

1830 Maysville Road veto; Indian Removal Act

1832 South Carolina nullifies tariff; Congress enacts "Force Bill"

All "civilized tribes" removed to West 1838

compromising the ugly Missouri dispute would win enough electoral votes in the upper South, which had been pro-compromise, to put him over. Clay was himself a slave owner. Had there not been another westerner in the contest, the "Great Compromiser" might well have won the election.

But another westerner there was, and he was a formidable rival. Clay was famous and loved; Andrew Jackson of Tennessee was celebrated and adored. He was the hero of New Orleans and the conqueror of the Creek nation. So magical was his name that his supporters did not much care that Jackson's views on every political issue of the day were something of a mystery. As one admirer put it, "he has slain the Indians and flogged the British, and therefore is the wisest and greatest man in the nation."

William Crawford was the only old-time Jeffersonian in the contest and even he, like Monroe, had accommodated with the nationalistic mood of the era and trimmed his Jeffersonian suspicion of the federal government to mouthing the occasional piety. Crawford expected to win the electoral votes of the slave states (except Clay's Kentucky and Jackson's Tennessee) and he had enough support in New Jersey, Pennsylvania, and New York to encourage his illusions.

President Calhoun

John C. Calhoun came closer to being president in 1824 than he ever again would. He was elected vice president by the electoral college, but no presidential candidate had a majority of electoral votes. The Twelfth Amendment provided, in that case, that the House of Representatives chose the president. If the House failed to do so by inauguration day—it almost did just that in 1800—"then the Vice-President shall act as President, as in the case of the death or other constitutional disability of the President."

It is fortunate that this provision has never been called upon because its sloppy wording would have invited a constitutional crisis. What would happen if, after the vice president-elect had been sworn in as president, the House got its act together and announced it had made its choice? Would the "acting president" have stepped down? Or would he have insisted that, having been sworn in, he had been constitutionally installed for four years and was not going anywhere? The Amendment can be read either way and surely would have been.

And the Winner is...?

When the votes were counted, the importance of regional loyalties was obvious, but so was the nationalism of the wake of the War of 1812. General Jackson, alone of the four candidates, was a hero nationwide, and the count in the electoral college showed it. Clay won only four electoral votes outside of the West; he even lost Indiana and Illinois, major beneficiaries of the National Road, to Jackson. Crawford won just five votes outside of the South; indeed, Jackson defeated him in every southern state except Georgia and Virginia. Adams

won only seven electors outside the Northeast. Only Jackson carried states in all three sections.

The General won more popular votes and electoral votes than any of his opponents. However, his 99 electoral votes fell 32 short of the majority the Constitution required. As in 1800, the job of choosing the president fell to the House of Representatives casting one vote per state. The Twelfth Amendment restricted the House to choosing from among the top three vote-getters in the electoral college. So Clay, who finished fourth, was eliminated from contention. (A nasty blow; as the popular Speaker of the House and a master of patching together alliances of congressmen, he should have been able to eke out a majority of states.) Crawford was out of the running too. He had been felled by a stroke that left him bedridden and unable to speak.

So, it was Jackson versus Adams. Jacksonians argued that it was no contest; it was the duty of the House to ratify the General's election. He had won a plurality of both popular and electoral votes. He was the choice of three western states, five southern states, and Pennsylvania. The House of Representatives was morally bound to ratify the people's choice.

It was a good argument—the democratic argument—but it did not carry the day. Instead, largely because of the political principles, personal ambitions, and influence of Henry Clay and, some would say, the doddering impulse of an elderly New York congressman, the prize went to John Quincy Adams.

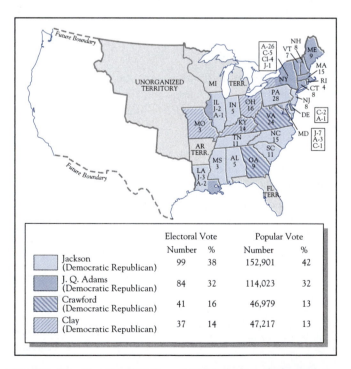

	Electoral Vote		Popular Vote	
	Number	%	Number	%
Jackson (Democratic Republican)	99	38	152,901	42
J. Q. Adams (Democratic Republican)	84	32	114,023	32
Crawford (Democratic Republican)	41	16	46,979	13
Clay (Democratic Republican)	37	14	47,217	13

MAP 15:1 **Presidential Election of 1824.** Andrew Jackson won more electoral votes in the southern states than William Crawford, the "southern candidate," did. He carried Indiana, which Henry Clay expected to win and Pennsylvania, the second biggest state, in John Quincy Adams's Northeast. He was the only truly national candidate, winning states in the North, the South, and the West.

Reproduced from the Collections of The Library of Congress Prints and Photographs Division, Washington, D.C. [LC-US262-1563].

An overly optimistic cartoon by a Henry Clay supporter. Clay is sewing closed the mouth of Andrew Jackson to silence his false accusations of a "corrupt bargain" between Clay and President John Quincy Adams. Actually, Jackson did not speak publicly about the alleged bargain; he left that to his henchmen. And Clay's lengthy rebuttal of the charge, published in 1827, did not silence them. The corrupt bargain issue contributed to Adams's defeat in the election of 1828 and shadowed Clay for the rest of his life.

Losers Who Won

John Quincy Adams is the only president who won fewer electoral votes than an opponent and still took office. But he is not the only president to be elected with fewer popular votes than another candidate. In 1876, Republican Rutherford B. Hayes won fewer votes than Democrat Samuel J. Tilden, but Hayes was inaugurated. In 1888, Republican Benjamin Harrison lost the popular vote to Democrat Grover Cleveland but won handily in the electoral college. In 2000, the Democratic party candidate, Albert Gore, had a popular majority but lost in the electoral college to Republican George W. Bush.

New York Elects Quincy Adams

The state delegations in the House were divided cleanly down the middle between Jackson and Quincy Adams. New York was the swing state. New York had given 26 of its 36 electoral votes to Adams, only 1 to Jackson. However, its representatives were torn evenly between the two candidates. Some had been persuaded by the Jacksonian appeal to democracy. Others had ties to the Albany Regency, a faction that leaned toward Jackson. The New Yorkers might well have given Jackson the presidency had not Henry Clay gone to work. If Clay disliked Adams, he detested and feared Jackson. Jackson was his rival for the political leadership of the West. Clay thought Jackson unfit for the job. Winning battles was not a qualification for national leadership. And, as a general, Jackson had a reputation for the ruthless exercise of power. He had disobeyed orders in his actions in Florida and he had been—Clay believed—too liberal with the firing squad in disciplining his soldiers.

The importance of retaining the Speaker's favor prevented a Jackson stampede in the New York delegation. The deadlock that resulted was broken by Stephen Van Rensselaer. He later explained that, just before the roll call, he bowed his head to pray for divine guidance and saw on the floor a piece of paper on which was written "Adams." Taking it as a sign, he voted for Quincy Adams, giving him New York's vote and the presidency.

Jackson's backers were enraged. God had not selected Adams; Henry Clay had. When, a short time later, the new president named Clay to be his secretary of the state, they claimed that the two men had negotiated a "corrupt bargain": the presidency for Adams in return for the position of heir-apparent for Clay.

John Randolph's Slaves

John Randolph was what today is called "emotionally unstable" and was several times laid low with temporary insanity. It affected his treatment of the 300 slaves he owned and almost determined their fate after his death.

The rational Randolph consistently maintained that he hated slavery, and he meant it. He inherited his slaves; he never bought one and he never sold one. He was usually a kind master. An abolitionist from Massachusetts who visited Randolph's plantation, Josiah Quincy, admitted that Randolph's slaves loved him. However, Randolph's neighbors said that when he was out of his mind, he was an abusive master.

Randolph wrote three wills. In two of them he freed his slaves and bequeathed each of them enough money to establish themselves. In a third will, he ordered his slaves sold at auction and the proceeds divided among his heirs. Much to the chagrin of those heirs, the court ruled that Randolph had not been "of sound mind" when he wrote the third will and ordered his slaves freed.

"Corrupt Bargain!"

It is difficult to believe that there was an explicit "bargain." Adams and Clay did not, as the Jacksonians claimed, sit down at a table—or have intermediaries meet—and work out a trade-off. Clay was not above such an arrangement. How else did a "Great Compromiser" operate except by political horse-trading? But John Quincy Adams would have bristled at so unsavory a proposition. He valued his haughty New England integrity to the extent that it incapacitated him for public life in the emerging age of democratic politics and slavish partisanship.

He was, no doubt, thanking Clay for his support when he named him secretary of state, but there was no deal. Indeed, it was a politically stupid act of stubborn rectitude of which Adams was quite capable. It was inevitable that the charge of a corrupt bargain would follow and haunt the rest of his political career. Why the canny Clay accepted the appointment is more difficult to understand. As Speaker of the House, he was the second most powerful official in government. He could advance the programs both he and Adams espoused as Speaker, which he could not do as secretary of state. He was not yet 50. He had plenty of career ahead of him to risk being tainted by the charge of corruption, but he did it.

Reproduced from the Collections of The Library of Congress Prints and Photographs Division, Washington, D.C. [LC-USZ62-12470].

Few presidents have come to the White House with John Quincy Adams's experience in government. He was the American minister in several European countries, a senator, and, for eight years, secretary of state. He was also aloof to the point of arrogance, not a desirable trait for a politician in an increasingly democratic era.

THE AGE OF THE COMMON MAN

Like his father, John Quincy Adams brought impressive credentials to the presidency. He had almost literally spent his entire adult life in public service. Jacksonians made much of the fact that when Jackson was 14, a British officer slashed his face when the boy refused to clean his boots. When John Quincy Adams was 14, he was serving as secretary and personal assistant to an American minister abroad in France and the Netherlands (his father). As a young man, Jackson had been "the most roaring, game-cocking, horse-racing, card-playing, mischievous fellow that ever lived in Salisbury," North Carolina. Quincy Adams was himself minister in the Netherlands and Prussia during his twenties.

Another Unhappy Adams

Unfortunately, Adams was not in tune with his times. His pride in his heritage and achievements made him hyper-dignified, formal. He was temperamentally incapable of providing what more and more voters were demanding of their leaders: easy informality, the "common touch," glad-handing. Indeed, with government at every level becoming more democratic, John Quincy Adams remained as suspicious of the power of the people as any Federalist had been. He spoke contemptuously of being "palsied by the will of our constituents."

Ironically, given the corrupt bargain charge, Quincy Adams was not only above corruption, he found bargains—political horsetrading—distasteful. He tried to stand above partisan politics just at the time when the first political machine, based on rewarding party workers with government jobs, was

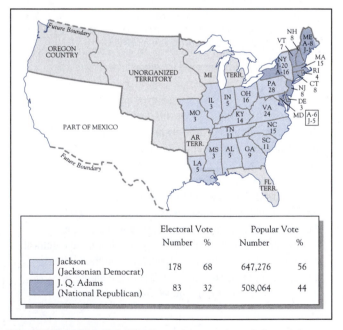

		Electoral Vote		Popular Vote	
		Number	%	Number	%
	Jackson (Jacksonian Democrat)	178	68	647,276	56
	J. Q. Adams (National Republican)	83	32	508,064	44

MAP 15:2 **Presidential Election of 1828.** John Quincy Adams held his ground in his electoral college rematch with Andrew Jackson in 1828. Indeed, he won a majority in New Jersey, which had voted for Jackson in 1824. But Jackson swept the West and the South, winning the states that had voted for Crawford or Clay four years earlier, including Henry Clay's Kentucky.

taking shape in New York state. Like his father, who retained cabinet members disloyal to him, Quincy Adams allowed open enemies—Jacksonians—whom it was his prerogative to fire to stay in office. To have removed them and filled their posts with his own supporters, Adams felt, was unworthy.

Adams had supporters but, perhaps, no friends. By the end of his term, he had a smaller political base in Washington that was unreservedly devoted to him than any previous president.

A Democratic Upheaval

Adams's view of himself as a member of a natural elite of talent, education, and culture was a characteristic of his father's generation. During the 1820s, and obvious to those who would see even before 1824, politics was ceasing to be the almost exclusive concern of the gentlemen, men with the leisure and financial independence to think of holding office as a public service. Increasingly, politics (and highly partisan newspapers) preoccupied the white male population. The great French commentator on American attitudes and folkways, Alexis de Tocqueville, wrote that "almost the only pleasure which an American knows is to take part in government." A visitor to the United States less sympathetic to Americans than de Tocqueville, Mrs. Frances Trollope, was appalled that American men would rather talk politics than mend their fences and tend their crops.

In part, this great democratic upheaval was the fruit of half a century of Jeffersonian rhetoric that flirted with democracy. The Jeffersonians never ceased saying that "the people should rule." They transformed *democracy* from something of a dirty word (which it was in the 1790s) into an ideal. Jefferson himself did not believe that "the common man" was "as good as" he was. In their correspondence, he and John Adams agreed on the term "natural aristocracy" to define the men (like themselves) who should rule. But the Jefferson party's endlessly repeated paeans to democratic government could not fail to have effect.

The expansion of democracy in the 1820s and 1830s was also the consequence of the extraordinary growth and energy of the young republic. An increasingly ambitious and prosperous people needed to struggle less in order to survive and, therefore, had more time to think about public affairs (without neglecting their fences and crops). With issues like the tariff, land policy, and internal improvements bearing heavily on them, ordinary men had good reason to take an interest in politics and demand a greater say in government.

Finally, the wave of democratic reform had a peculiarly western source. In order to attract population, western territories and young states extended the right to vote to all free adult white males. All five western states admitted to the Union between 1816 and 1821—Indiana, Mississippi, Illinois, Alabama, and Missouri—required no property ownership of voters. Western states enacted other laws designed to appeal to people of modest station. Kentucky abolished imprisonment for debt in 1821. No longer could a man (or the occasional woman) be jailed for financial misfortune (or calculated dereliction).

The older states had no alternative but to copy the western example. Fearful of losing too many people to the West, most eastern states adopted universal white manhood suffrage and the popular election of presidential electors. In 1824, about half the states retained some property qualifications in order to qualify to vote. By 1830, only North Carolina, Virginia, Rhode Island, and Louisiana did, and Rhode Island's conservatism in the matter can be misleading. Still governed under the state's colonial charter, which could not easily be amended, Rhode Island was rocked by a brief but violent uprising in 1842, Dorr's Rebellion, which resulted in an extension of the vote to all adult white males.

In 1800, only two of sixteen states named presidential electors by popular vote. In 1824, eighteen of twenty-four states did. By 1832, only planter-dominated South Carolina still named electors in the legislature.

Given the right to vote, white males did. In 1824, the first presidential election in which there was widespread popular participation, about one-quarter of the country's eligible voters cast ballots. In 1828, one-half of the eligible voters voted, in 1840, more than three-quarters. If a similar proportion of eligible voters voted in a presidential election today, it would be accounted a revolution.

The "Workies"

Newly enfranchised voters sometimes built parties around specific issues. During the 1820s, "workingmen's parties" sprang up in several eastern cities. Called the "Workies," they pushed in city and state elections for a variety of reforms to protect themselves: abolition of imprisonment for debt, which hit independent artisans hard; mechanics' lien laws, which prevented creditors from seizing an indebted carpenter's or blacksmith's tools to satisfy their claims; laws giving unpaid employees, rather than creditors, first crack at the assets of a bankrupt employer; and free public education open to all children. To the workingmen of the Northeast, education was the equivalent of the westerner's free land, the key to moving up in the world.

The Workies had their victories, especially in New York. But the party's support dwindled when middle-class visionaries joined the parties and tried to commit them to more cosmic reforms. Scotland-born Frances "Fanny" Wright, a feminist before feminism's time, spoke to Workie rallies advocating equal rights for women and "free love"—the freedom of all, unmarried and married, to enjoy any sexual partner they chose.

Fanny's embrace was the kiss of death. Workingmen had no more interest in modifying the legal status of women than merchant princes did. And they were quite as committed to traditional sexual morality as their ministers and priests. No doubt as likely to dally individually as people of the middle and upper classes, skilled workers were sensitive to the fact that their social status was superior to that of the urban underclass in part because of the blatant promiscuity of the lower orders. Once most of the Workies' bread-and-butter reforms were enacted, they lost interest in the Workingmen's parties and drifted into the Jacksonian camp.

The Anti-Masonic Party

The Anti-Masonic party was an expression of the democratic upheaval of the 1820s and 1830s. It was founded in upstate New York when a bricklayer named William Morgan

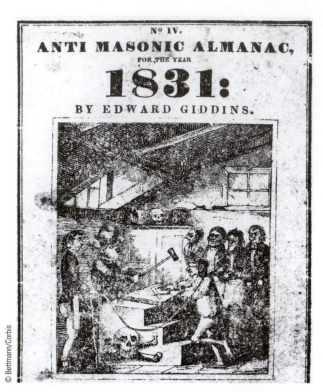

© Bettmann/Corbis

Founded in 1826, the Anti-Masonic Party had astonishing success in the Northeast—for a few years. In 1832, it elected fifty-three Congressmen, about as many as the National Republicans, soon to be known as Whigs. In part, the party reflected the cult of the common man. Its supporters regarded the Masons as a conspiracy that discriminated against non-Masons in business and government. As shown in this illustration, however, the most effective anti-Masonic propaganda was emotional, emphasizing what was widely believed to be the Masons' lurid, even obscene secret rituals.

published an exposé of the Society of Freemasons and, shortly thereafter, was taken away by several Masons, disappeared, and was probably murdered.

Founded in London in 1717 by gentlemen who believed in God but not necessarily in Christianity, the Masonic Order devised secret rituals drawn in part from what was known about ancient Egypt in the time of the building of the pyramids. Thus, the stonemason regalia (and the pyramid topped by an all-seeing eye) still on the back of the dollar bill. (Benjamin Franklin and George Washington were both Masons).

By the 1820s, the order was quite large in the United States and membership mainly consisted of middle- and upper-class businessmen, professionals, and, in the South, well-to-do planters. In small towns, invitations to join were usually snapped up; being a Mason was a sign that a man had "arrived." The increasingly elaborate hocus-pocus of lodge meetings and handshakes and passwords by which Masons could identify one another were considered sacred secrets. Much of Morgan's book dealt with Masonic rituals and regalia. He quoted the initiation ceremony during which a new member swore "to keep all Masonic secrets under the

penalty of having his throat cut, his tongue torn out, and his body buried in the ocean." When Morgan disappeared and a corpse apparently mutilated according to regulations was dragged out of the Niagara River, outrage swept the state.

Politicians made much of the fact that Morgan was a workingman. The Order, they said, was a conspiracy aimed at keeping Masons on top and the common man down. The handshakes and passwords, they pointed out, quoting from Morgan's book, were to identify Brother Masons so as to do business with them rather than with "any other person in the same circumstances."

In part, then, the Anti-Masonic party was a common man's rebellion against the establishment. Every governor of New York between 1804 and 1828 had been a Mason. No more, the Anti-Masons said. Secret societies and preferential treatment for members had no place in the United States. Indeed, if a man was required to keep secrets from his own wife, he was violating the sanctity of marriage as surely as if he practiced free love.

A brace of political leaders who would later play important roles in national politics were Anti-Masons during the 1820s and 1830s: Thaddeus Stevens, Thurlow Weed, William H. Seward, and a future president, Millard Fillmore. In 1832, the party's presidential candidate, former Attorney General William Wirt, won 33,000 votes and carried the state of Vermont; the party elected 53 candidates to Congress.

The Anti-Masons had difficulty with the fact that the universal hero, George Washington, had been a Mason. They had none with the fact that Andrew Jackson was active in the Order. They were staunch anti-Jacksonians. When, in 1834, the anti-Jackson Whig party was organized, most Anti-Masons drifted into it. (Although Henry Clay too was a Mason.)

THE REVOLUTION OF 1828

Thomas Jefferson had called his election in 1800 the "Revolution of 1800," but the election of 1828 marked as great a break with what had gone before as 1800 had. Andrew Jackson's overwhelming victory in 1828 was a more decisive repudiation of the incumbent administration than Jefferson's tiny margin of victory in 1800. And Jackson was the first president to come from a western state. (He was the first president not from Virginia or Massachusetts.) The 1828 election campaign was as "dirty" as the Federalist versus Jefferson Republican campaigns of 1800 and 1804, and because most white men could vote in 1828, it was noisier and more intrusive in daily life than any election campaign that had preceded it.

Slinging Mud

Jackson followed precedent by taking no part in the campaign of 1828. Indeed, he was uncharacteristically restrained in his public remarks and letters between his "corrupt bargain" defeat in 1824 and 1828. He remained in his plantation home, the Hermitage, while his supporters, calling themselves Democratic-Republicans, fired insulting salvos at President Adams. They depicted Quincy Adams as a usurper

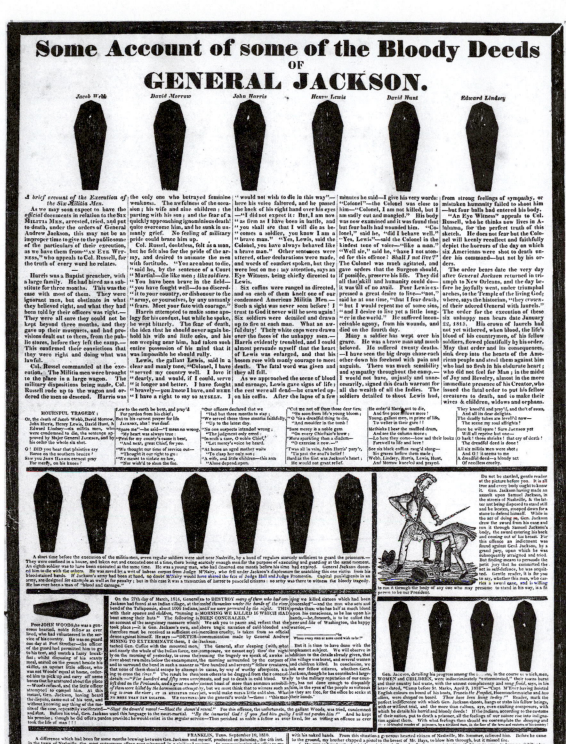

Collection of The New-York Historical Society. #44655

The notorious "coffin handbill," a widely distributed anti-Jackson advertisement describing in detail the men Jackson had "murdered." Most of Jackson's "victims" were, in fact, militiamen under his command executed for desertion or mutiny, which were legitimate capital crimes. Jackson was, however, much freer in his use of firing squads than other generals of the time.

Pistols at Twenty Paces

A duel is a prearranged combat in cold blood between two gentlemen in front of witnesses. The issue was the honor of a man who believed he had been insulted, or the honor of a woman under his protection. It was not necessary that duelists fight to the death. Merely observing the intricate rules of the duel confirmed the honor of both men. Many American duels—fought with a pair of identical pistols— ended when each party discharged his weapon in the general direction of the other. The point was the display of courage. That was why only gentlemen dueled; the vulgar multitude brawled.

Although Edward Doty and Edward Leicester fought something like a duel in Virginia in 1621, the custom was almost unknown in colonial America. Scholars have found records of only a dozen before 1776. Then, during the Revolutionary War, French officers introduced the *Code Duello*, the European rules of etiquette, to their American friends. American officers took so zealously to the institution that, even before the war was over, a Frenchman wrote, "the rage for dueling here has reached an incredible and scandalous point." A decade later, when some aristocrats fled the French Revolution to Louisiana, they made New Orleans the dueling capital of North America. On one Sunday in 1839, ten duels were fought in the city. A woman wrote that the young men of her acquaintance kept score of their duels as young ladies kept count of marriage proposals.

Dueling spread rapidly as sudden wealth created men in a hurry to prove their gentility. Timothy Flint wrote of Mississippi: "Many people without education and character, who were not gentlemen in the circles where they used to move, get accommodated here from the tailor with something of the externals of a gentleman, and at once set up in this newly assumed character. The shortest road to settle their pretensions is to fight a duel."

Button Gwinnet, a signer of the Declaration of Independence from Georgia, was killed in a duel in 1777. James Madison fought a duel in 1797. Commodore Stephen Decatur fought a duel in 1801 and was killed in another in 1820. Of the four presidential candidates in 1824, three were duelists. Henry Clay had several duels despite the fact that he was a notoriously bad shot. Andrew Jackson's enemies tried (without success) to blacken his character because he had killed men in duels.

Duels were illegal almost everywhere, but only in New England were they unrespectable. In 1802, two Massachusetts congressmen, Josiah Quincy and Timothy Pickering, let it be known they would neither challenge anyone to a duel nor accept a challenge. They paid a price for their principles; Republicans did not restrain their language in debating them.

In 1828, Andrew Jackson's political enemies said that he had been involved in a hundred duels. Not likely; not even Old Hickory was lucky enough to beat those odds. But he fought several and the written terms of one of them have survived. In 1806, Jackson faced Charles Dickinson, a Nashville lawyer:

It is agreed that the distance shall be 24 feet, the parties to stand facing each other, with their pistols drawn perpendicularly. When they are ready, the single word fire is to be given at which they are to fire as soon as they please. Should either fire before the word is given, we [the seconds of both parties] pledge ourselves to shoot him down instantly. The person to give the word to be determined by lot, as also the choice of position.

Dickinson fired first, wounding Jackson. "Back to the mark, sir," Jackson said when Dickinson staggered in fear of what was to come. Then, according to Jackson's enemies, Jackson's pistol misfired, and in violation of the *Code Duello*, he pulled the hammer back and fired again. This breach of honor haunted Jackson for the rest of his life, for Dickinson died.

Thomas Hart Benton fought a grotesque duel with a man named Charles Lucas. They fired at one another at a distance of ten feet! Or, rather, Benton fired at a distance of ten feet and put a ball in Lucas's heart. To Benton's credit, he was ashamed of the affair. He burned all the documents pertaining to the duel and never spoke of it. Another episode that mocked the duelists' pretensions to gentlemanly honor involved Col. William Cumming and a prominent Jeffersonian Congressman, George McDuffie of South Carolina. President Monroe and John C. Calhoun tried to stop it. Calhoun believed that Cumming was insane and subsequent events confirmed his diagnosis. Cumming wounded McDuffie. When told McDuffie had repeated his insult to Cumming's honor, Cumming demanded a rematch. Cumming's shot missed; he then stooped into a crouch. McDuffie, disgusted, walked away. Cumming had the brass to demand they meet again. At the third duel, Cumming's ball broke McDuffie's arm.

By the 1820s, dueling was a crime almost everywhere. South Carolina imposed a fine of $2,000 and a year in prison for seconds as well as for duelists. Alabama's anti-dueling law indicates that the institution had lost its gentlemanly luster by the time it was enacted in 1837; among prohibited weapons were those instruments "known as Bowie knives or Arkansas Tooth-picks." (Fannie Kemble told of a duel in Georgia in which one of the terms was that the winner could cut the loser's head off and impale it on a stake on the property line the two gentlemen were disputing.)

Authorities could and did prevent duels—if they got wind of them before they occurred. But it was difficult to prosecute duelists after the fact even if one of the men was killed. How to convince a jury that a man had committed murder—as most states defined a death in a duel—when the dead man had a loaded pistol in his hand, or one he had just fired at the man at the alleged murderer? The survivor was not going to testify. Nor were the only eye-witnesses, the seconds; they were also accessories to the crime, whatever it was. People who knew all about the affair in advance could provide only hearsay evidence. Even the most famous of American duels, the Burr-Hamilton affair, was not prosecuted.

(the corrupt bargain), an elitist, a man with effete European tastes who squandered money filling the White House with elegant furniture and its cellar with European wines. The Jacksonians made a great fuss over Adams's purchase of a billiard table; billiards, because of the high cost of the table, was an aristocrat's game. (Adams had bought a billiard table, but he paid for it out of his own pocket, not from White House funds.)

Alarmed by the positive response to the attacks, Adams partisans replied that Jackson was a savage, indeed, no better than a murderer. Calling themselves National-Republicans, they reminded voters that Jackson had disobeyed presidential orders in 1818 when he invaded Florida. (Neither they nor Jackson knew at the time that, within the Monroe cabinet, Quincy Adams had defended Jackson and Jackson's vice presidential running mate, John C. Calhoun, had demanded the general be disciplined. Neither Adams nor Calhoun was talking.) The National-Republicans printed broadsides that listed the men whom Jackson had killed in duels and the soldiers whom he had executed.

The assault that enraged Jackson was the accusation that he and his beloved wife, Rachel, had lived in sin. "Ought a convicted adulteress and her paramour husband," wrote a Cincinnati editor, "be placed in the highest offices in this free and Christian land?" The circumstances surrounding the Jacksons' first years together remain murky. On the record, however, was the fact that Rachel Jackson's divorce from her first husband was not legally final when she and Andrew, believing that it was, were wed; several years later, they had to go through a mortifying second ceremony to legalize their union.

Laxity in observing marriage customs was common on the frontier. When Daniel Boone returned home after a two-year's absence to find he had a son a few months old who had been fathered by Boone's brother, he shrugged. But whatever Rachel Jackson's sexual code may have been when she was young, in 1828 she was a dowdy, prim old lady married to Tennessee's most prominent citizen. When the story of the marriage snafu was printed in every anti-Jackson newspaper in the country (with plenty of creative embellishments), she was mortified. When she died shortly after the election, Jackson blamed Adams for his deeply felt loss.

In the meantime, the Jacksonians had responded in kind. They dug up a preposterous tale that, when he was minister to Russia, Adams had procured the sexual favors of a young American girl for the dissolute czar. Then there were whispers of bizarre perversions in the Adams White House. "Negative campaigning" had come to American politics.

The Symbol of His Age

Mudslinging did not decide the election of 1828. John Quincy Adams's failure to capture the popular imagination, the taint of the corrupt bargain, and a cross-sectional coalition put together by Jackson, Vice President Calhoun, and Martin Van Buren of New York, turned that trick. Jackson swept to victory with 56 percent of a total vote that was three times larger than the popular vote in 1824. In the electoral college, Jackson won 178 votes to 83 for Adams.

OK

"OK," an expression now found in most of the world's languages, originated in Andrew Jackson's day. But no one knows where it came from. There are theories. One holds that it was borrowed from the Choctaw Indians whose *okeh* had a similar although not identical meaning. Another says that it was an abbreviation of "Old Kinderhook," one of Martin Van Buren's nicknames, or of an obscure shipping agent, Obadiah Kelly, who chalked it on trunks and boxes he passed on, or even that it came from the box of "Orrins-Kendall Crackers," well known at the time. But where is the tie-in with "OK" as a word of approval?

An anti-Jackson smear from 1839 may be close to the mark. The president was such an ignoramus, a Whig journalist wrote, that he approved papers crossing his desk by marking them "OK" for "oll korrect." Jackson's spelling was not good, but it was not that bad. However, it is plausible that someone whose identity is lost to history did spell "all correct" just so; people who knew him were amused and, as with catch-phrases today, they spread it.

We shall never know. The origins of OK were a matter of conjecture as early as 1839 and an army of linguistic scholars have since tried to solve the mystery and failed.

On Inauguration Day in March 1829, about 10,000 people crowded into Washington, shocking what the capital had of genteel society with their drinking, coarse language, and boisterous behavior in the White House. Invited in by the new president, the mob muddied the carpets, broke crystal stemware, and stood on upholstered sofas and chairs to catch a glimpse of their gaunt, white-haired hero.

The adoring mob was so unruly that Jackson's friends feared he might be injured. They spirited the president away through a window; he spent his first night as president in a hotel. Back at the executive mansion, servants lured the mob outside by setting up bowls of lemonade, whiskey punch, and tables heaped with food on the lawn.

An Uncommon Man

The man whom these people idolized was by no definition a "common man." He was a successful land speculator, planter, and, of course, soldier. He was probably the richest man in Tennessee. He was certainly not the desperado the Adams camp depicted. Jackson was "erect and dignified in his carriage" in the words of Fanny Kemble, an English woman who met him. Josiah Quincy Jr., a patrician New Englander, described him as "a knightly personage." His manners were on the courtly side.

Jackson thought well enough of himself, but he also believed that his success—he was the first log-cabin-born president—was due to the openness of American society. All people were not equally talented, but American society provided everyone with the opportunity to exploit his abilities and enjoy the fruits of his efforts unimpeded by artificial social and economic obstacles. The government's task, as

General Andrew Jackson (colour litho), Sully, Thomas (1783-1872) (after)/Private Collection, Peter Newark American Pictures/Bridgeman Art Library

Andrew Jackson. Artist Thomas Sully's portrait captures Jackson's majesty. He looks more like a European nobleman than an Indian fighter or hero of the common man. Sully did not create this Jackson. Visitors to the White House expecting to find a rough-hewn, tobacco-spitting frontiersman were surprised by Jackson's gracious manners.

Jackson saw it, was to preserve opportunity by striking down obstacles to it, such as laws that benefited some and, therefore, handicapped others.

Jackson's concept of government was essentially negative, the polar opposite of Adams's and Clay's conviction that government was and should be an active force for progress. Jackson believed that government should, as far as possible, leave people, society, and the economy alone so that natural social and economic forces and human initiative could operate freely.

Attitudes of the Hero: Women

Jackson's concept of equal, unimpeded opportunity extended only to white males. In this too, however, as in his attitudes toward women, children, blacks, and Indians, he represented the general opinion of his times.

Jackson believed that women lived—and should live—in a "sphere" entirely apart from the competitive world of men.

It was men's destiny to struggle in an often brutal world. Women's role was to guard home and hearth from the world's nastiness so as to provide a haven for their menfolk. In their religious and moral sensibilities, women were superior to men. Indeed, so that men could find moral and spiritual refreshment at home, they had to shelter women from a public life that would harden or corrupt them.

Jackson and most Americans (women certainly included) agreed with the clergymen, increasingly dependent on female congregants, who preached the "Gospel of Pure Womanhood." Woman's "chastity is her tower of strength," one wrote, "her modesty and gentleness are her charm, and her ability to meet the high claims of her family and dependents the noblest power she can exhibit to the world." The Rev. Edward Kirk of Albany, New York, preached that "the hopes of human society are to be found in the character, in the views, and in the conduct of mothers."

The reward due women for accepting a private and submissive role in society was the right to be treated with deference and delicacy. Jackson was famous for his chivalry. He was gracious and prim in the company of women. Even in the absence of the ladies, he habitually referred to them as "the fair" and disliked salacious gossip about them. "Female virtue is like a tender and delicate flower," he said. "Let but the breath of suspicion rest upon it, and it withers and perhaps perishes forever."

Attitudes of the Hero: Children

Toward children, foreign visitors were shocked (and sometimes appalled) to discover, the old soldier was a pussycat. The man who aroused armies to bloodlust and slaughtered enemies without wincing, and the president who periodically exploded in rages that left him and everyone else trembling, beamed happily as young children destroyed rooms in the White House before his eyes. The British minister wrote that he could not hear the president's conversation because the two men were surrounded by caterwauling children. Jackson smiled absentmindedly and nodded all the while. At the table, the president fed children first, saying that they had the best appetites and the least patience.

A visitor to the Hermitage found him sitting before a fire with a child and a lamb sleeping between his knees. Embarrassed, he had a slave remove both and explained that the child had cried because the lamb was out in the cold. So Jackson had brought the animal in.

Indulgence of children was not universal in the United States. Calvinists in New England and elsewhere still raised their children with the "Good Book" and the strap. But too many Europeans commented in horror that American children had the manners of "wild Indians" to say that their observations were unfounded. Some foreigners also noticed that American children were independent and self-reliant at a younger age than European children because of the freedom allowed them. It was this quality—"standing on your own two feet"—that Jackson and his countrymen valued in their heirs.

Attitudes of the Hero: Race

Toward Indians and blacks, Jackson also shared the prejudices of his age. Blacks were doomed to be subject to whites by the Bible or nature or both. Blacks *were* slaves; they were intended to be slaves; American blacks were fortunate to be the slaves of enlightened, Christian masters. Jackson never troubled himself with the implications of owning slaves while believing in equal rights because, to him, the values of the Declaration of Independence were never intended to apply to Africans. After fifty years of the Declaration and human bondage coexisting, all but a small minority of Americans felt the same.

As a westerner, Jackson had thought a great deal about Indians. He spent many years at war with them. He was the conqueror of the Creeks, the largest and most aggressive of the southeastern tribes.

Although he was ruthless in the Indian wars, Jackson was not the simple "Indian-hater" his enemies portrayed. He found much to admire in Native Americans (as he did not in African Americans). He admired their closeness to nature, a view promoted during the 1820s by the popular novelist and Jackson supporter, James Fenimore Cooper, and their courage in resisting their conquerors. There was a tinge of regret, a sense of tragedy, in Jackson's statement to Congress that the white and red races simply could not live side by side. Left in that situation, the Indians would simply die out. He rescued, adopted and raised a Creek orphan he found in the ashes of a town his soldiers had burned.

Government by Party

Attitudes are not policies, but President Jackson soon cleared up the uncertainties as to what he would do. As the first president to represent a political party without apologies, he made it clear that he would not hesitate to replace federal officeholders who had conspicuously opposed his election.

There were about 20,000 federal jobs in 1829; Jackson eventually dismissed about a fifth of the employees he inherited from the Adams administration. Even acknowledging that some federal officeholders had supported Jackson, that was by no means a clean sweep. John Quincy Adams, who never dismissed anyone, privately admitted that many of the people Jackson fired were incompetent.

As for those who were able and lost their jobs, Jackson said that every government job should be designed so that any reasonably intelligent American citizen could perform it adequately. If that were so, it was perfectly legitimate to say, as New York Jacksonian William Marcy said, "To the victor belongs the spoils."

Attacks on the "spoils system" were noisy but short-lived. When Jackson's political enemies won power in 1840, they carved up the spoils of office far more lustily than Jackson's lieutenants had done. The "patronage," a polite way to say "spoils," became an established feature of American party politics.

ISSUES OF JACKSON'S FIRST TERM

When he became president, Jackson did not have particularly strong opinions on the questions of the tariff or internal improvements. In his first address to Congress, he called for a protective tariff, but he later drifted (again without passion) to the southern position of a low tariff solely for the purpose of earning revenue.

Constitutional Inconsistencies

As a pioneer in Nashville, Jackson was aware of the need in the West for good roads and navigable rivers. As a senator, he had lobbied for federally financed internal improvements that would benefit Tennessee. By 1829, however, he had developed constitutional scruples about the federal government financing internal improvements that directly benefited the citizens of only one state. Or so he said in 1830 when he vetoed a bill to construct a road between Maysville and Lexington, Kentucky, a distance of about 20 miles. He told Congress that it was the responsibility of the state of Kentucky to pay for a road that lay entirely within it borders. If the Constitution was amended to authorize projects like the Maysville Road, he would approve them.

Jackson's reasoning was not new. James Madison had vetoed similar projects on the same grounds. In his Maysville Road veto, however, Jackson was also taking a slap at Henry Clay. Clay's hometown was Lexington. Later in his presidency, Jackson approved without comment local internal improvement projects much like Maysville that had been introduced by and benefited members of his own party.

On a much more basic issue—the relative constitutional powers of the federal government versus the powers of the states—Jackson was also inconsistent. He shrugged when the state of Georgia ignored federal treaties with the Cherokee Indians even after the Supreme Court ruled that the treaties were binding. But when South Carolina attempted to defy an act of Congress that he had signed, he moved quickly and decisively to crush the challenge. He came close to cleaning and pressing his old uniform, polishing his sword, and personally leading an army south.

Indian Removal

The destruction of Tecumseh's tribal alliance in the War of 1812 and Jackson's defeat of the Creeks destroyed the last major Indian military powers east of the Mississippi. The federal government tried to avoid skirmishing between white settlers and the surviving tribes by negotiating treaties, at almost the rate of one a year. One tribe after another ceded its lands and moved into the Louisiana acquisition to find new homelands.

A few tribes resisted. In the Southeast, the Seminoles of Florida harassed outlying American settlements; the Seminoles were never decisively defeated, just worn down. In 1831, Black Hawk, a chief of the Sauk and Fox tribes of Illinois and Wisconsin, led a last-ditch attempt to drive frontier farmers back. His warriors were cornered and hundreds of Sauks and Foxes slaughtered. The remnant of the tribes were forced to relocate west of the Mississippi.

Thomas Jefferson had believed that if the Indians gave up the seminomadic life, stayed in one place and farmed as whites did, they would be amalgamated peacefully into American society. However, Presidents Monroe, John Quincy Adams, and Jackson, believed the Indians' tenacity in clinging to their traditional cultures made it impossible for whites and Indians to live side by side. The only alternative to wars in which the Indians would be exterminated was Indian Removal, the "removal" of the tribes from settled areas to permanent Indian territories, the largest of which is now eastern Oklahoma. There the federal government would prohibit white incursions.

Four large tribes of the southeast—the Cherokee, Creeks, Choctaws, and Chickasaws—resisted removal by consciously undercutting the rationale on which the policy was based: the incompatibility of Indian and white cultures. Beginning in the 1790s in the case of the Cherokee, the tribe closest to large white populations, they gave up wandering and began to farm commercially, even growing cotton with slave labor. Whites called them "the civilized tribes."

Courtesy of the Edward E. Ayer Collection, Newberry Library, Chicago

Sequoyah with the syllabary he created so that the Cherokee language could be written and printed in phonetic characters. Sequoyah understood that the letters in books shown to him recorded the sounds of spoken English. But he could not read English and never bothered to learn. In effect, he invented a means of writing Cherokee from scratch, knowing nothing but the principle of written language.

But being civilized was not enough to save them. The Creeks were too weak and demoralized after their defeat by Jackson's soldiers to resist removal. The Choctaw and Chickasaws were defrauded. Federal agents bribed renegade chiefs to sign removal treaties that were then enforced on the entire people. Between 1830 and 1833, the Choctaws were forced to march west under army supervision. The Cherokee, the most "civilized" of all, fought removal by going to the courts.

Writing Down Words

Most of the world's written languages are alphabetical. The symbols, the letters, represent basic sounds that, combined, make words. The number of letters in an alphabet varies from one language to another. English uses twenty-six of them, of course. The sounds of Russian require several more. Italians, which is almost perfectly phonetic, gets along with twenty-one. Hawai'ian is written with just thirteen letters.

The symbols in a syllabary such as Sequoyah invented represent not basic sounds but syllables, combinations of a consonant sound and a vowel sound. Syllabaries are well suited to spoken languages having relatively few syllables. Thus, Sequoyah's Cherokee syllabary had 86 characters, easy enough to learn. Had the Hawai'ian language been written as a syllabary, it would have been even easier, with just 40 characters. An English syllabary, however, would not work very well. It would require roughly 500 characters.

Sequoyah and the Cherokee

The Cherokee had traded with Americans as soon as there was an established colony in Charleston. During the 1700s, they were the largest tribe in the South, ranging over about 70,000 square miles in northern Georgia and Alabama. By 1800, their numbers had been reduced, mostly by disease, to about 16,000 and their range to 20,000 square miles. However, they resolved almost entirely the internal conflicts that had weakened the nation. Their leaders concluded that to avoid being overrun by the whites, they must make peace with them and become more like them.

So, the Cherokee were Jackson's allies in his war against the Creeks. They intermarried with whites and blacks, farmed intensively, and founded permanent towns undistinguishable in appearance and function from towns in South Carolina and Georgia. Many were Christians. They taxed themselves, funded schools, and built mills. They had a more efficient police force than neighboring whites did. They elected their leaders according to a tribal constitution based in part on the American Constitution. They sent their brightest young men to the United States to be educated. And a most remarkable uneducated individual, Sequoyah, also known as George Guess, devised a means by which the Cherokee could read, write, and publish in their own Iroquoian language.

Sequoyah was a silversmith who neither spoke nor read English. However, he grasped the principle of written language when it was explained to him that the individual characters on the pages of books represented sounds. Had Sequoyah been literate, he would have done what other Indians would do later—adapt the letters of the Latin alphabet to the tribe's language. Instead, beginning in 1809, Sequoyah started from scratch and created not an alphabet but a syllabary: eighty-six symbols that represented the eighty-six syllables (a consonant sound plus a vowel sound) that Sequoyah counted in Cherokee speech. It was the same method of writing that had been developed in Minoan Crete two thousand years earlier and in several other cultures. The Cherokee Nation immediately adopted Sequoyah's creation, teaching it in schools and publishing books using it. A newspaper, the *Cherokee Phoenix,* was published in both English and Cherokee.

The Cherokee Go to Court

By the late 1820s, however, white Georgians wanted the land the Cherokees held by right of their treaty with the United States. In 1828, the state legislature asserted its authority over Cherokee territory. The Cherokee asked the Supreme Court to invalidate Georgia's claims on the grounds the Cherokee

people comprised an independent nation. The Court rejected the Indians' argument. Writing for the majority in *Cherokee Nation* v. *Georgia* (1831), John Marshall denied Cherokee independence, but he left the tribe a significant opening in his decision. The Cherokee Nation was, Marshall wrote, a "domestic, dependent nation" within the United States, like the "ward" of a guardian.

In the meantime, the state of Georgia arrested Samuel Worcester, a Congregationalist minister, for violating a Georgia law requiring "white persons" to apply for a license before they entered Indian lands. Financed by the Cherokee, Worcester sued for his release on the grounds that Georgia was violating Cherokee treaties with the United States and congressional acts regulating Indian affairs. In other words: A state was usurping federal power, an issue on which Marshall had made his nationalist sympathies clear. The treaties between the United States and a "domestic dependent nation," the Cherokee argued, were inviolable contracts.

With only one dissenting vote, the Supreme Court ruled in *Worcester* v. *Georgia* that the Cherokee nation was a "distinct community, occupying its own territory, with boundaries

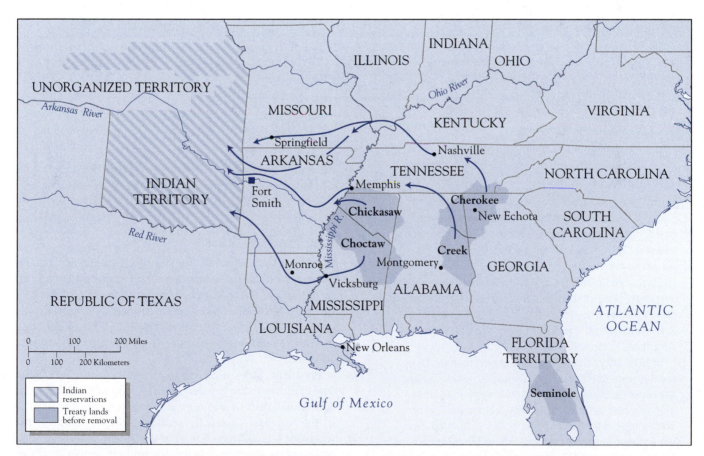

MAP 15:3 **Removal of the Southeastern Tribes 1820–1840.** "Removing" the people of the Civilized Tribes from their homeland in the Southeast was a cynical land grab. The Cherokee, Creek, Choctaw, and Chickasaw had discredited the pious cultural argument that Indians could not function and prosper living side by side with whites. Intermarriage was common and successful. The four nations were thriving by incorporating elements of the whites' culture into their own. Their leaders had negotiated firm treaties with the United States confirming their rights to their lands. The Cherokee won a case in the Supreme Court that affirmed their rights. Still they were forced to leave.

Woolaroc Museum, Bartlesville, Oklahoma

This famous painting depiction of the Cherokee on their "Trail of Tears" from Georgia to Oklahoma only hints at the horrors of the trek. The procession looks almost triumphant. Cherokee emigrants and sympathetic army officers who accompanied them—and the number of deaths on the journey, a fourth of those who started—describe a horror not hinted at here.

Jackson and Eisenhower

In 1957, the governor of Arkansas activated the state's National Guard to prevent several African American pupils from enrolling at all-white Little Rock High School. In doing so, he defied a Supreme Court order that the school be racially integrated. Personally, President Dwight D. Eisenhower disapproved of the Supreme Court ruling that segregated schools were unconstitutional. But he had been a soldier who did his duty. He took command of the Arkansas National Guard and used it to protect African Americans at the school.

In 1832, Georgia's legislature and governor defied the Supreme Court's ruling in *Worcester* v. *Georgia* and set about dispossessing the Cherokee nation of lands guaranteed it by treaty. President Jackson had been a soldier too but one who obeyed orders or ignored them depending on his personal inclinations. He ignored Georgia's defiance of federal authority because he had no sympathy for the rights of Indians no matter what the Supreme Court said.

accurately described . . . which the citizens of Georgia have no right to enter." The law under which Worcester had been arrested was invalid.

The Trail of Tears

The Cherokee celebrated, but Georgia gambled or, perhaps, secured confidential assurances from Jackson through intermediaries. The state defied the Supreme Court and held on to its prisoner. State commissioners engineered purchases of lands from Cherokees who could be bought and began preparations to remove by force the Indians who resisted.

President Jackson may not actually have said, "John Marshall has made his decision, let him enforce it," as he was quoted. But he did nothing to stop Georgia's defiance of the Supreme Court. By 1838, the dispossession of the Cherokee was complete. On what the Indians called the "Trail of Tears," they were marched 1,200 miles to Indian Territory, accompanied by federal troops. An officer sent to supervise one march, General John E. Wool, was disgusted by his assignment: "The whole scene since I have been in this country has been nothing but a heart-rending one." The Indians were forced from their homes under the gaze of "vultures ready to pounce on their prey and strip them of everything they have."

Two thousand died in camps waiting for the migration to begin, another 2,000 on the trail. About 15,000 Cherokees made it to Oklahoma along with smaller numbers of Choctaws, Chicksaws, and Creeks.

The South and the Tariff

South Carolina had less luck defying the federal government. The issue that brought the state (and Vice President Calhoun) into conflict with Jackson was the tariff. In 1828, before Jackson's election, Congress enacted an extremely high protective tariff. Southern planters hated what they called the "Tariff of Abominations." Cotton growers believed that their crop was paying the country's bills and underwriting industrial development in the North.

They had a point. Cotton accounted for fully half of American income from abroad. Some of this wealth was effectively diverted into the hands of northern manufacturers by the tariff that, by raising the price of imported products, permitted American millowners to charge more for the goods they produced. As long as a majority of congressmen favored high tariffs, however, what could be done?

As a young man, Vice President Calhoun had favored protective tariffs. He had hoped to see South Carolina develop mills to spin and weave its cotton—factories in the fields. Those hopes came to nothing. The cotton industry and most other manufacturing were centered in New England and the middle states. South Carolina's economy was almost exclusively agricultural; the state grew and exported rice and cotton and imported its manufactures.

The price of cotton depended on a world market under no one's control. The price of manufactures was artificially propped up by a tariff enacted, in effect, by northern congressmen with a few southern allies. When the Tariff of Abominations was enacted, the heavily industrialized northeastern states had eighty-seven representatives in Congress. The cotton states of the South had thirty-one. Even adding Virginia's votes, the core of the anti-tariff faction in the House numbered just fifty-three.

Nullification

Compromise was impossible, Calhoun concluded. Northern and southern positions were irreconcilable. The only political solution was "surrender, on one side or the other."

In 1829, secretly, Calhoun wrote *The South Carolina Exposition and Protest.* It was an ingenious, but mischievous interpretation of the relationship of the states to the federal union that provided South Carolina and other southern states a rationale for defying the federal tariff. The *Exposition* took up where Madison's and Jefferson's Virginia and Kentucky Resolutions left off. Calhoun stated that the United

States had not been created by the people of America (John Marshall's premise), but by the people acting through the states of which they were citizens. This was not splitting hairs. Calhoun was saying that the states were sovereign, not the federal government. The United States was a voluntary compact of the states.

If, therefore, the United States Congress enacted and the president signed a law that a sovereign state found intolerable, that state had the right to nullify the law (to prevent its enforcement) within its borders. Such a nullification could be overridden only by three-quarters of the other states. (Calhoun was here referring to the Constitution's amendment procedure, which requires the ratification of an amendment by three-fourths of the states.) In that event, Calhoun concluded, the nullifying state could choose between "surrender" to the will of the other states or leaving the Union of which it was a voluntary member: secession.

South Carolina Acts, the President Responds

Calhoun and his supporters were content to leave the *South Carolina Exposition* in the abstract in the hope that the large Jacksonian majority elected to Congress in 1830 would repeal the Tariff of Abominations and enact a low tariff. However, in 1832, while slightly lowering rates, Congress adopted a tariff that was still protective, and Jackson signed it. South Carolinians elected a convention that declared the Tariff of 1832 "null and void" within the borders of the state. State officials were ordered not to collect tariff payments, and federal officials in the state were warned that collection of the duties was "inconsistent with the longer continuance of South Carolina in the Union."

Jackson exploded in one of his frightening rages. South Carolinians would rather rule in hell, he said, than be subordinate in heaven. They could promulgate a dozen expositions, but if "a single drop of blood shall be shed there" in interfering with the collection of the tariff, "I will hang the first man I can lay my hand on engaged in such treasonable conduct, upon the first tree I can find."

Congress supported him with a "Force Bill." It authorized the army to collect duties in South Carolina. The bloodshed for which Jackson was waiting seemed inevitable. It was avoided because the nullifiers lost heart when no other southern state nullified the tariff act. Calhoun met with Henry Clay, and they put together a tariff bill with duties just low enough that the nullifiers could save face but not so low as to arouse a fury in the industrial states. In 1833, the state rescinded its nullification of the tariff. However, it pointedly did not repudiate the principle of nullification.

Jackson let it ride. It was just paper like *Worcester* v. *Georgia.* He had had his way and he had identified a new enemy, his own vice president.

FURTHER READING

Classics James Parton, *Life of Andrew Jackson*, 3 vols, 1859–1860; Arthur M. Schlesinger Jr., *The Age of Jackson*, 1946; John William Ward, *Andrew Jackson: Symbol for an Age*, 1962.

Politics Richard McCormick, *The Party Period and Public Policy: American Politics from the Age of Jackson to the Progressive Era*, 1986, and *The Second American Party System: Party Formation in the Jacksonian Era*, 1966; Daniel Feller, *The Public Lands in American Politics*, 1984; Harry L. Watson, *Liberty and Power: The Politics of Jacksonian America*, 1990; Lawrence F. Kohl, *The Politics of Individualism: Parties and the American Character in the Jacksonian Era*, 1989.

Jackson Robert V. Remini, *Andrew Jackson and the Course of American Freedom*, 3 vols., 1981, and *Andrew Jackson and the Course of American Democracy*, 1984, and *Andrew Jackson and His Indian Wars*, 2001; M. P. Rogin, *Fathers and Children: Andrew Jackson and the Destruction of American Indians*, 1975; Bertram Wyatt-Brown, *Honor and Violence in the Old South*, 1986; Joanne B. Freeman, *Affairs of Honor: National Politics in the New Republic*, 2001.

Indian Removal William G. McLaughlin, *Cherokee Renascence in the New Republic*, 1986; Theda Perdue, *Slavery and the Evolution of Cherokee Society, 1540–1866*; Anthony Wallace, *The Long Bitter Trail: Andrew Jackson and the Indians*, 1993; John Ehle, *Trail of Tears*, 1988; Michael D. Green, *The Politics of Indian Removal: Creek Government and Society in Crisis*, 1982; Ronald Satz, *American Indian Policy in the Jacksonian Era*, 1974.

Nullification William W. Freehling, *Prelude to Civil War: The Nullification Controversy in South Carolina, 1816–1836*, 1966; Richard E. Ellis, *The Union at Risk: Jacksonian Democracy, States' Rights, and the Nullification Crisis*, 1987; John Niven, *John C. Calhoun and the Price of Union*, 1988.

Biographies Merrill D. Peterson, *The Great Triumvirate: Webster, Clay, and Calhoun*, 1987; Robert V. Remini, *Henry Clay: Statesman for the Union*, 1991; John Niven, *Martin Van Buren: The Romantic Age of American Politics*, 1983; Donald B. Cole, *Martin Van Buren and the American Political System*, 1984.

KEY TERMS

Use the following listing of key terms to review important figures, events, locations, and concepts covered in this chapter. A glossary of these terms is available on *The American Past* companion Web site: www.cengage.com/history/conlin/tap9e

Virginia Dynasty, p. 252

Crawford, William, p. 252

King Caucus, p. 252

"corrupt bargain", p. 255

Anti-Masonic party, p. 257

Masons (Freemasons), p. 258

Democratic-Republicans, p. 258

"spoils system", p. 263

Indian Removal, p. 263

civilized tribes, p. 264

Worcester v. *Georgia*, p. 265

nullification, p. 267

ONLINE RESOURCES

Find additional resources, including primary source documents, images, interactive maps, simulations, chapter review exercises, and Internet links at

The American Past **companion Web site**
www.cengage.com/history/conlin/tap9e

American History Resource Center
http://ushistory.wadsworth.com/

Reproduced from the Collections of The Library of Congress Prints and Photographs Division Washington, D.C. [LC-USZ62-3576]

Chapter 16

In the Shadow of Old Hickory

Personalities and Politics 1830–1842

He prefers the specious to the solid, and the plausible to the true.... I don't like Henry Clay. He is a bad man, an impostor, a creator of wicked schemes. I wouldn't speak to him, but by God, I love him.

—*John C. Calhoun*

[Calhoun is] a smart fellow, one of the first among second-rate men, but of lax political principles and a disordinate ambition not over-delicate in the means of satisfying itself.

—*Albert Gallatin*

Such is human nature in the gigantic intellect, the envious temper, the ravenous ambition, and the rotten heart of Daniel Webster.

—*John Quincy Adams*

Thank God. I—I also—am an American.

—*Daniel Webster*

To those who revered him, Andrew Jackson was "Old Hickory," a tough, timeless frontiersman as straight as a long rifle. In the flesh, however, Jackson was a frail, elderly wisp of a man who, on many days, looked to be hours from death. More than 6 feet in height, Jackson weighed only 145 pounds. His posture was indeed soldierly, but he was frequently ill. He suffered from chronic lead poisoning (he carried two bullets in his body), headaches, diarrhea, kidney disease, and edema, a painful swelling of the legs. He was beleaguered by coughing fits. When he was sworn in as president in March 1829, many who knew him wondered if he would live to finish his term.

VAN BUREN VERSUS CALHOUN

Vice President John C. Calhoun had a more than academic interest in Jackson's health. When Jackson accepted Calhoun as his vice president in 1828, he was not merely pocketing South Carolina's electoral votes. He was also naming his heir apparent as the next presidential candidate of what was now called the Democratic-Republican party and, possibly, for Jackson was not oblivious to his age and health, president within four years.

JOHN C. CALHOUN

Like Jackson, Calhoun was Scotch-Irish, a descendant of those eighteenth-century emigrants invariably described as hot tempered and pugnacious. Calhoun was passionate and willful. Several portraits capture a burning in his eyes that seems just short of rage, but never the hint of a smile. Photographers, coming along late in Calhoun's life, confirmed the painters' impressions. "There is no recreation in him," a woman friend said, "I never heard him utter a jest." Did he

High Praise

Calhoun's integrity was unassailed (except by Andrew Jackson). Two of the nation's leading abolitionists, men sworn to destroy the institution Calhoun swore to preserve, slavery, respected him. William Lloyd Garrison, who vilified virtually every other slaveowner, called Calhoun "a man who means what he says and never blusters. He is no demagogue." Wendell Phillips spoke of "the pure, manly and uncompromising advocate of slavery; the Hector of a Troy fated to fall."

ever enjoy a moment's peace of mind? A perceptive Englishwoman who wrote a book about the United States called him "the cast-iron man, who looks as if he had never been born, and never could be extinguished."

As a young man, Calhoun was a nationalist who encouraged South Carolina planters to build spinning mills amidst their cotton fields. In 1815, as earnestly as Henry Clay, he wanted to "bind the nation together with a perfect system of roads and canals." In 1816, he introduced the bill that chartered the Second Bank of the United States. John Quincy Adams said that Calhoun was "above all sectional and factious prejudices," that he had a "fair and candid mind," that is, he was of the same mind as Adams.

Fair-minded Calhoun remained until the very end of his life. And he was certainly more candid in expressing his views than many of his illustrious contemporaries. But several slips into prevarication when he was Jackson's vice president cost him dearly.

By 1828, when South Carolina had not, as Calhoun hoped, industrialized, and its elite embraced agrarian opposition to protective tariffs and large federal expenditures, Calhoun abandoned his youthful nationalism. He opposed the protective tariffs of 1828 and 1832 and voted against most internal improvements bills. He wrote the *South Carolina Exposition*

and Protest that defined and justified a state's right to nullify a federal law. Still, hoping that he would be the next president, he kept his authorship of the doctrine secret. Had Jackson known it to be Calhoun's work, he would have openly repudiated his vice president. However, it was a triviality—an etiquette issue—and Jackson's discovery of an opinion Calhoun had expressed ten years earlier, that made enemies of the two men.

Peggy O'Neill Eaton

Peggy O'Neill was the attractive daughter of a Washington innkeeper who catered to congressmen. Jackson boarded with the O'Neills when he was a senator between 1823 and 1825. Peggy married a seaman named Timberlake who was, as seamen are wont to be, rarely at home. In her husband's absence, so it was whispered, she found solace in the arms of other men, including Tennessee congressman John Eaton who, in 1829, Jackson named secretary of war.

Less than proper affairs were not unusual in Washington. With a population of 30,000, the capital was no longer the rude all-male outpost it had been when Jefferson was president. Given the uncertainty of electoral politics, however, most congressmen left their families back home and lived in boarding houses. Inevitably, some of them—the bachelors, certainly—found lady friends. As long as they were discreet, little was made of it. Henry Clay was reputed to have been a roué during the 1810s; if so, it did not hinder his career. Richard M. Johnson of Kentucky was not even discreet—he cohabited with a black woman who was also his slave—and he would be vice president in 1837.

But Johnson's common law wife did not accompany him to social functions. Peggy O'Neill became an affair of state when, after husband Timberlake died at sea, she married Eaton. The couple assumed that, as cabinet member and wife, they would mix in Washington society.

The wives of Eaton's cabinet colleagues, perhaps led by Floride Calhoun, the vice president's wife, did not think so.

Democrats versus Whigs 1828–1845

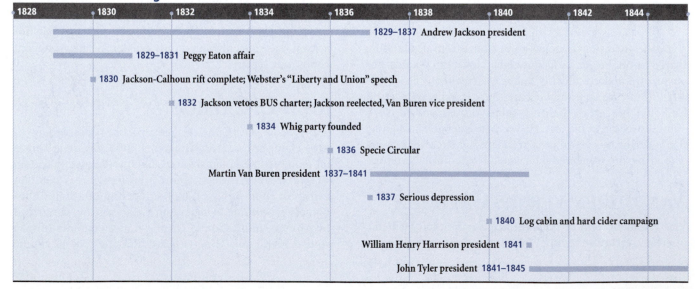

1829–1837 Andrew Jackson president

1829–1831 Peggy Eaton affair

1830 Jackson-Calhoun rift complete; Webster's "Liberty and Union" speech

1832 Jackson vetoes BUS charter; Jackson reelected, Van Buren vice president

1834 Whig party founded

1836 Specie Circular

Martin Van Buren president 1837–1841

1837 Serious depression

1840 Log cabin and hard cider campaign

William Henry Harrison president 1841

John Tyler president 1841–1845

Collection of The New-York Historical Society #28542

President Jackson did not really have Peggy O'Neill Eaton cavort for the members of his cabinet. The cartoon (almost salacious for the period) was drawn for the amusement of Jackson's political enemies. But the president defended Mrs. Eaton's chastity at great length in cabinet meetings and demanded that the wives of cabinet members receive her socially. Secretary of State Martin Van Buren, the beneficiary of the hubbub, is at the right studying Mrs. Eaton through a lorgnette, hand-held eye glasses associated with pretentious women and effeminate men.

They cut Mrs. Eaton cold. They refused to call on her at her home, mandatory good manners at the time, and they ignored her at official receptions and dinners.

Jackson was furious. He was still mourning his wife, whose death he blamed on attacks on her chastity. He found Peggy charming. Her only mistake, if such it was, was being a little "too forward in her manner." At a cabinet meeting, he pronounced her "as chaste as a virgin." He commanded his niece (his official hostess) to receive her socially and instructed the men in his cabinet to do the same with their wives. His niece refused, and he threw her out of the White House. The cabinet wives refused (if their husbands dared ask them), and he was helpless. If women were excluded from public life, the rules of morality and society were squarely within their sphere. Within that sphere, husbands did as they were told to do. At official functions, only Secretary of State Martin Van Buren dared to be seen admiring Peggy's gowns and fetching refreshments for her. Van Buren was a widower; he had no wife to oblige.

The Rise of the Sly Fox

Charm and chitchat came easily to Martin Van Buren. His worst enemies conceded his grace and wit. His portraits, in contrast to Calhoun's, show a twinkling eye and an easy smile. But Van Buren was more than a jolly Dutchman. He was a devilishly clever politician, almost always several moves ahead of his rivals. Van Buren's wiles in New York politics had earned him the nickname "the Sly Fox of Kinderhook"

Love is a Many-Splendored Thing

John and Peggy Eaton had a long and apparently happy marriage. After Eaton died in 1856, however, Peggy's life turned tragic for reasons recalling her reputation as a young woman for defying social conventions. As a well-fixed widow of 59, she married a 19-year-old dancing teacher, Antonio Buchignani. She was momentarily sensible enough to protect her fortune with a prenuptial agreement. But Antonio knew Peggy better than Peggy knew herself. He signed the agreement cheerfully and, soon after the wedding, began chipping away at her money. Peggy gave him a $14,000 house ($350,000 in today's dollars). Her husband stole and pawned her silver. When he threatened to leave her, she turned over almost everything she still owned to him. Buchignani then ran off with Peggy's granddaughter. She died nearly destitute.

(his hometown). He was a more successful political organizer in New York than either Hamilton or Burr had been. He owed his high position in Jackson's cabinet to the fact that he delivered a majority of New York's electoral votes to the Democratic-Republican ticket in 1828 just four years after the state had voted for John Quincy Adams.

Van Buren was in tune with the country's new democratic mood. He understood that before a political party could be anything else, it had to be a vote-gathering machine—to win elections. Therefore, a party had to reward the activists who rounded up the voters by appointing them to government jobs.

Van Buren's sensitivity to Peggy Eaton's feelings may have been quite sincere, but his courtesy to her also won Jackson's friendship where, previously, they had merely been political allies. Then, with the Eaton mess paralyzing the administration (it consumed more of Jackson's time during his first two years as president than any other matter), Van Buren suggested a way out of it to the perplexed president.

Van Buren proposed that he resign as secretary of state and Eaton as secretary of war. The other members of the cabinet, whose wives were causing the president so much anxiety, would have to follow their example and depart. Jackson would be rid of the social tempest, but no particular wing of the Democratic-Republican party could claim to have been wronged. Jackson appreciated both the strategy and Van Buren's willingness to sacrifice his prestigious office. He appointed a new cabinet and rewarded Van Buren by naming him minister to England, then, as now, the plum of the diplomatic service.

Calhoun Blunders

The Sly Fox was lucky too. While he calculated each turning with an eye on a distant destination, Calhoun bumped into posts and walls like a blind horse. Jackson was shown some old papers revealing that, ten years earlier, Calhoun (then

Courtesy Chicago Historical Society

Martin Van Buren was a dapper dresser, a good-humored bon vivant, and a shrewd politician. He was also very lucky until he was elected president and the country was rattled by a serious depression that no political career could have survived. Van Buren's did not.

secretary of war) wanted Jackson punished for invading Florida. Calhoun tried to wriggle out of the fix with a long, convoluted, and unconvincing explanation. The president cut him off by writing, "Understanding you now, no further communication with you on this subject is necessary."

(In the same papers, Jackson discovered to his surprise that John Quincy Adams had been his chief defender in the Florida business. To Jackson's credit, he tried to reconcile personally with Adams. Adams, to his discredit, publicly snubbed the president.)

There was not much further communication between Jackson and Calhoun on any subject except when, in April 1830, they attended a formal Democratic dinner. Some twenty of Calhoun's cronies offered toasts to states' rights and nullification. When it was the president's turn to lift his glass, he rose, stared at Calhoun, and toasted, "Our Union: It must be preserved." Calhoun got in the last word. He replied, "The Union, next to our liberty, the most dear." But Jackson took satisfaction in the fact that, as he told the story, Calhoun trembled as he spoke.

The old duelist delighted in such confrontations. Van Buren took pleasure in his enduring good luck, for he was abroad during the nastiest squabbling between Jackson and Calhoun when an even slyer fox than he might easily have stumbled across a hound.

Then Calhoun blundered, ensuring that Van Buren would be Jackson's successor. For no better reason than personal animosity, he cast the deciding vote in the Senate's refusal to confirm Van Buren's diplomatic appointment. This brought the New Yorker back to the United States, but hardly in disgrace. Jackson was yet more deeply obligated to him. He named Van Buren as his vice presidential candidate in 1832, as he might not have done had Calhoun left Van Buren in London.

THE WAR WITH THE BANK

Jackson's health did not improve. He suffered two serious hemorrhages of the lungs as president. But he was still alive in 1832 and, apparently, never thought of retiring after one term. Unlike the personalities and smears of the campaign of 1828, the presidential election of 1832 centered on a serious issue, the Second Bank of the United States. It need not have been an issue; the bank's charter had four years to run. Jackson was on record as disliking the bank but, like his predecessors, he had entrusted the government's money to it. The bank became an issue in 1832—*the* issue of the campaign—because Henry Clay, now a senator, believed he could defeat Jackson in the presidential election if the future of the BUS was at stake.

A Powerful Institution

The Second BUS was a large and rich institution. Its twenty-nine branches controlled about a third of all bank deposits in the United States, and did some $70 million in transactions each year. Such vast resources gave the bank immense power over the nation's money supply and, therefore, the economy.

A satirical 6 ¢ bill ostensibly issued by one of Jackson's irresponsible pet banks, the Humbug Glory. It is festooned with Democratic party symbols: Jackson's head on the penny, a leaf from a hickory tree, a hat and pipe associated with Irish immigrants—Jackson voters—and, curiously, a donkey. The donkey became a symbol of the Democratic symbol only a generation later.

In an impolitic but revealing moment, the head of the bank, Nicholas Biddle, told Congress that the BUS was capable of destroying any bank in the country.

What he meant was that the BUS was likely to have in its possession more paper money issued by a state bank than the bank had gold and silver in its vaults. If the BUS presented this paper for redemption in coin, the bank that issued the notes would have to close its doors.

On a day he was more tactful, Biddle said that, in fact, the BUS exercised only "a mild and gentle but efficient control" of other banks. Because state banks were aware of the sword the BUS held over them, they maintained larger reserves of gold and silver than they might otherwise have done. Rather than ruining banks, the BUS ensured that they operated more responsibly.

Biddle was as proud of the public service the bank rendered as of its considerable profits. Nevertheless, the fact remained that the bank was powerful because it controlled the nation's money supply, a matter of profound public interest, while it remained a private institution. BUS policy was made not by elected officials, nor by bureaucrats responsible to elected officials, but by a board of directors chosen by and responsible to shareholders.

This was enough in itself to merit the suspicion of a president who abhorred special interests. Therefore, Biddle had attempted to make a friend of the president by making generous loans to key Jackson supporters, and he presented the president with a plan to retire the national debt—a goal dear to Jackson's heart—with the final installments coinciding with the anniversary of the Battle of New Orleans. Jackson did not bite. He told Biddle that it was not a matter of disliking the BUS more than he disliked other banks; he did not like any of them.

The Bank's Enemies

The president was not the bank's only enemy. Aside from their hostility to the BUS, they had little in common with one another. Indeed, their aspirations were contradictory.

First was the growing financial community of New York City, the bankers and money manipulators who would soon be known collectively as "Wall Street." Grown wealthy from the Erie Canal and New York's role as the nation's leading port, they were keen to challenge the financial powerhouse that dominated them, the Philadelphia-based BUS.

Second, the freewheeling bankers of the West resented Biddle's restraints, "mild and gentle" as they were. Just as during the 1810s, they were caught up in the financial opportunities of land speculation and the rapid growth of western cities. Thus, some of the most avid allies of the president who hated all banks were themselves bankers and, in general, not the most virtuous of their profession.

A third group anxious to see the BUS declawed was the fraternity of hard-money men like Jackson and Thomas Hart Benton. To them, real money made a clinking sound, it did not fold. They disapproved of the very concept of an institution that issued paper money in quantities greater than it had gold and silver on hand. Thirty years earlier, John Adams, who was far from simple-minded, had condemned the principle of banking. Mechanics, especially in the East, were hard-money men. They had too often been paid in bank notes that, when they presented them to landlords and shopkeepers, found that they were discounted because the banks that had issued them were considered shaky. They wanted to be paid in coin that did not decline in value between payday and rent day.

Collection of The New-York Historical Society, #44812

The Battle Joined

Biddle's plan was to prepare for 1836, when the bank's charter expired, by making loans to key congressmen and senators at very favorable rates. He put several on the payroll as legal advisors and created jobs for their cronies. In another of his tactless moments—Biddle was a poor politician—he said that he could "remove all the Constitutional Scruples in the District of Columbia" by handing out "a dozen cashierships and fifty clerkships to worthy friends [of congressmen] who have no character and no money."

Henry Clay did not want to wait four years to see if Biddle's favors would save the bank. He proposed to a very reluctant Biddle to apply for a new charter immediately. National-Republicans and pro-Bank Democrats were a majority in both houses; Clay had counted heads. If Jackson gritted his teeth and signed the bill, all well and good. If, which was more likely, Jackson vetoed the recharter, Clay would have the issue of the bank on which to oppose the president in the election of 1832. Clay believed that the bank had proved its value to the voters; that they had not forgotten the ruinous panic of 1819. He persuaded Biddle that if he waited until 1836 to apply for his charter, Jackson's veto would not easily be reversed because, by the time a new president was inaugurated, the BUS would be dead.

Clay's scenario proceeded exactly as he wrote it except for the final act. Congress voted the bank a new charter. Jackson vetoed the bill. Clay ran for president promising to save the bank. And he lost—big. Jackson won 55 percent of the popular vote and 219 electoral votes. Clay won only 49 electoral votes. (Anti-Masonic candidate William Wirt won 7 electoral votes, and South Carolina gave its 11 votes to another stand-in for Calhoun, John Floyd.)

Financial Chaos

Now it was Jackson's turn not to wait until 1836. "The Bank is trying to destroy me," he said from his bed during a serious illness, "but I will destroy the Bank." He already hated Henry Clay. Now his hatred extended to the "Monster Bank!" In September 1833, six months after his second inauguration, Jackson ceased depositing the government's revenues in the Bank. Instead, he scattered the government's deposits among eighty-nine state banks. His defeated enemies called them Jackson's "pet banks" because he selected them not because they had good reputations, but because they were recommended by Democratic party leaders.

The BUS, as its charter required, continued to pay the government's bills. But with no new federal money coming in, the government's account sank from the $10 million it had averaged for ten years to $4 million in just three months. Biddle had no choice but to reduce the scope of the Bank's operations. He also chose, at least in part, to retaliate against Jackson, to call in debts owed the Bank by other financial institutions. The result was a wave of bank failures that wiped out the deposits of tens of thousands of people, just what Jackson had feared BUS power might mean.

Under pressure from the business community, Biddle relented. He let other banks' obligations ride and actually reversed direction, increasing the money supply by making loans to state banks. The result was a speculative mania such as, before 1832, the BUS had prevented. Many of the eighty-nine pet banks to which Jackson had entrusted federal money proved to be among the least responsible in feeding the frenzy.

In 1836, Henry Clay made his contribution to what would be the most serious economic depression since Jefferson's embargo. He convinced Congress to pass a distribution bill that apportioned $37 million among the states to spend on internal improvements. The politicians reacted as politicians presented with a windfall always do: They spent recklessly on the least worthy of projects. Values in land, both in the undeveloped West and in eastern cities, soared. Federal land sales rose to $25 million in 1836. Seeking to get a share of the freely circulating cash, new banks were chartered at a dizzying rate. There had been 330 state banks in 1830; there were almost 800 in 1836.

And there was, of course, no Bank of the United States to cool things down. Its charter expired on schedule, and Biddle transformed what was left of it into a Pennsylvania-chartered state bank. Jackson tried to end the speculative frenzy in the only way within his powers. In July 1836, he issued the Specie

Reproduced from the Collections of The Library of Congress Prints and Photographs Division Washington, D.C. [LC-US262-3576]

Jackson in old age. He was 70 when he retired from the White House to the Hermitage, his plantation near Nashville, in 1837. The man who suffered so many ailments that many believed he would die in office survived until 1845, watching Democrats and Whigs politicking in his shadow.

Circular requiring that all purchases of government lands be paid in gold and silver coin. No paper money would be accepted.

The Specie Circular stopped the runaway speculation, as a stone wall stops a runaway horse. Land sales collapsed overnight. Neither land speculators nor would-be settlers could make their installment payments in gold and silver. Banks that had fueled the speculation by churning out paper money that the government would not accept collapsed. The financial disaster spread to the East when gold and silver flowed westward and Eastern bank notes lost value. Unable to pay their workers in anything resembling money, employers laid them off.

The Giant of His Age

Clay's political gamble and Jackson's determination to have his revenge on the Bank, whatever the consequences, combined to wreak a financial disaster. Had Jackson still been president when depression descended in 1837, he would have been cursed by many a "common man" who had idolized him. Instead, by the time the economy hit bottom, Jackson had retired to Tennessee and his successor, Martin Van Buren, took the fall for Jackson's victory in the Bank War.

Old Hickory had slashed and chopped his way through eight pivotal years in the history of the nation. Though aching and coughing daily and refusing to mellow—he said his greatest regret was not shooting Henry Clay and hanging John C. Calhoun—Jackson would live for nine more years to observe from Nashville an era that unfolded in his shadow. Jackson was never wise. His intelligence was ordinary; his learning beyond land law and military command was spotty. He was too easily ruled by his temper, confusing his passions with the interests of the country. He reduced all disagreements and disputes, personal and political, to the corrupt character of his opponents. His vision of America was pocked with more flaws than the visions of many of his contemporaries, including the not unflawed Henry Clay.

For all that, Andrew Jackson personified his times. He was the personification and symbol of a popular upheaval that democratized American government. Indeed, he presided over a time of ferment in nearly every facet of American life. He established a new pattern of presidential leadership by seizing the initiative in making policy. Jackson impressed his personality on American politics, and not only the Democratic party.

THE SECOND PARTY SYSTEM

In 1828, John Quincy Adams and Andrew Jackson ran for president under the half-fiction that they were both Jefferson Republicans. In fact, Adams's National-Republicans and Jackson's Democratic-Republicans were not organized political parties. They were names adopted by loose coalitions of those who supported a number of anti-Jackson regional leaders, notably Henry Clay and John Quincy Adams and, on the other side, Jackson legalists.

During Jackson's presidency, Martin Van Buren, Amos Kendall of Kentucky, and others mobilized Jackson's supporters into a well-organized national party, the Democratic party. Most of the Democrats' opponents, who lacked

Collection of The New-York Historical Society. #35603

The Whigs took their name from the British political party that dated its origins to the battle to defend the powers and prerogatives of Parliament against the authority of the monarchy. The American Whigs tried to identify Jackson with monarchy—they called him "King Andrew I." Perhaps the only principle on which all of the diverse Whigs agreed was the primacy of Congress, that the president was an executive who should enforce policies legislated by Congress, not go his own way, as Jackson was inclined to do.

anything resembling a national organization, clung to the name National-Republican until Jackson's second term. Then they adopted the name "Whig," and the second American party system was born.

What of John C. Calhoun, senator from South Carolina in 1836, and his disciples, southerners who believed that defending (and promoting) the institution of slavery took priority over all other questions? Most remained Democrats. A few, like John Tyler of Virginia, were so embittered by Jackson that they became Whigs. Calhoun, in everything but his hatred for Jackson and resentment of Van Buren, was a Democrat. However, with his unbreakable political lock on South Carolina and his once glowing presidential prospects dashed, he refused to accept the party label. No other prominent politician of the era could think of standing alone.

The Whigs

The name Whig was borrowed from Great Britain. Historically, the British Whigs had stood for the supremacy of

President Veto

Jackson's veto of the Bank Bill was just another day's work for him. No previous president used the veto so often. Indeed, the first six presidents altogether vetoed a total of ten acts of Congress. Jackson vetoed twelve.

Parliament and for restraining and reducing the power of the king. The American Whigs borrowed the name because, they said, with his many vetoes of congressional acts—twelve of them in eight years—"King Andrew I" was attempting to destroy representative government.

Beyond their emphasis on the supremacy of Congress, the Whigs were a diverse group. In the Northeast, the Whig party included most people of education, means, and high social status. Four out of five merchants were Whigs. Alexis deTocqueville, the great French commentator on Jacksonian America, wrote that "all the enlightened classes" opposed Jacksonian democracy. In their social composition, the Whigs were the heirs of the Federalists.

Most northern Whigs were also latter-day Federalists in their support of Henry Clay's American System. Most Whigs believed that the federal government (Congress!) should play an active role in promoting national progress. A Whig editor nicely summed it up: "The government is not merely a machine for making wars and punishing felons, but is bound to do all that is within its power to promote the welfare of the people. Its legitimate scope is not merely negative, representative, defensive, but also affirmative, creative, constructive, beneficent." This ideology attracted moral and social reformers of all kinds. They wanted to enlist the affirmative, creative, constructive, and beneficent powers of government in the causes of strict observance of the sabbath, temperance in the use of alcohol, helping the physically and mentally

Courtesy Boston Art Commission

Daniel Webster has the floor in the celebrated Webster-Hayne debate of January 1830. Senator Robert Hayne of South Carolina is seated dead center. In an artistic masterstroke, the painter shows John C. Calhoun in shadows at the left. As vice president, Calhoun could not speak, but he was the co-author of Hayne's eloquent defense of the South and nullification. Daniel Webster stole the show. Parts of his speech exalting the Union as inseparable from American liberty were memorized by northern schoolchildren for generations.

handicapped, and a welter of other reforms. Northern Whigs, at least, thought of their party as "the party of hope," the Democrats as "the party of fear"—fear of change, fear of progress.

Southern and western Whigs were less likely to be interested in reform. Many Louisiana sugar planters and Kentucky hemp growers were Whigs for little more reason than the fact that their crops required tariff protection if they were to be profitable. Other southern and western Whigs had been appalled by Jackson's high-handedness and the narrow sectionalism of southern Democrats. David Crockett of Tennessee, remembered today as a frontiersman and martyr for Texas independence, was best known in the 1830s as a Whig congressman who wrote lampoons of Jackson and Van Buren.

The party was instantly successful. In 1834, Whigs won ninety-eight seats in the House of Representatives and almost half the Senate, twenty-five seats to the Democrats' twenty-seven. For twenty years, while unlucky in presidential politics, the Whigs would battle the Democrats as equals in House, Senate, and in the states.

Unlikely Democrat

James Fenimore Cooper, author of *The Last of the Mohicans*, was a rich, cultivated, and cosmopolitan Hudson Valley patrician. His family had been Federalist, and Cooper had a Federalist's scant regard for "the people." He sued his neighbors near Cooperstown, New York, to stop them from swimming in a lake he owned, as they had been doing for generations. The dispute inspired him to write a book indignant about the pushiness of the lower orders.

And yet, Cooper was an active supporter of the Democratic party, which promoted the cult of the common man. How to explain it? By the fact that Cooper deplored "Wall Street Whiggery . . . a race of cheating, lying, money-getting blockheads" more than he deplored farmers cooling off in his lake. The Wall Street crowd would speculate in anything, he wrote, "in the general delusion of growing rich by pushing a fancied value to a point still higher." In those sentiments, he was indeed a true-blue Jacksonian.

The Godlike Daniel

Next to Henry Clay, the best-known Whig was Daniel Webster of Massachusetts. At the peak of his powers in the 1830s, Webster was idolized in New England as the "Godlike Daniel." The adoration owed to Webster's personal presence and his peerless oratory. With a great face that glowered darkly when he spoke, his eyes burned like "anthracite furnaces." A look from him, it was said, was enough to win most debates. Webster was described as "a steam engine in trousers" and "a small cathedral in himself." An admirer said he was "a living lie because no man on earth could be so great as he looked."

Webster was not a fraction as great as he looked. He was an able administrator and an effective diplomat. But Webster's character was less than shining. Of humble origin, he took too zestfully to the high life that his success as a lawyer opened up to him. He dressed grandly, savored good food, and basked in the company of the wealthy. He was also an alcoholic and he invested his money as foolishly as he spent it. He should have been quite rich, but he never was. He was constantly in debt and effectively sold his services to manufacturers and bankers who regularly bailed him out of his financial difficulties by sending him gifts of money, no visible strings attached. During Jackson's war on the BUS, Webster not too subtly threatened to cancel his contract as the Bank's legal counsel unless Nicholas Biddle paid him off. Biddle did. Webster came to expect money in the mail after every speech on behalf of the tariff or even the ideal of the Union. All of this was more or less common knowledge. So, while he remained popular in New England, his not-so-secret vices provided an easy target for the Democrats.

And yet, it was this corrupted man who gave voice to the ideal that was to sustain the indisputably great Abraham Lincoln during the Civil War. In 1830, when Calhoun and Jackson were toasting the relative values of union versus liberty, Webster rose in the Senate to tell the nation that "Liberty and Union, now and for ever," were "one and inseparable."

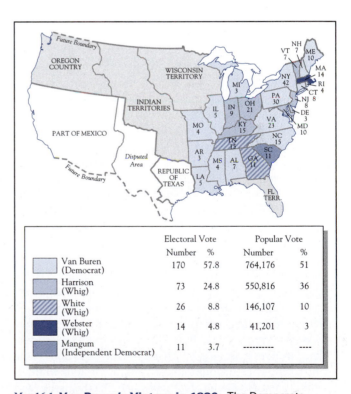

MAP 16:1 **Van Buren's Victory in 1836.** The Democrats and Whigs were both national parties. Both carried states in North, South, and West. (A Whig carried the retiring president Jackson's Tennessee.) But the Whig strategy of running three candidates popular in the section where they lived in order to send the election to the House of Representatives was a failure. The three plus South Carolina's Willie Mangum, who was no Whig, won almost as many popular votes as Van Buren, but nowhere near a majority of electoral votes.

Alma Mater

Students today would find little that was familiar if they were transported to a college of the Jackson era. Student life then more closely resembled student life in the Middle Ages than student life in the twenty-first century.

Almost all colleges were private institutions. As late as 1860, only 17 of America's 246 colleges and universities were state funded. With a few exceptions, the others were funded and closely administered by Protestant denominations to train ministers and to maintain the loyalty of other young men to their creeds. This was particularly true of the colleges founded during the Jackson years when dozens of new colleges were founded by evangelical Protestants committed to reforming society as well as to saving souls.

All but a handful of colleges were male institutions. What was a woman's need for higher learning when her divinely ordained role was in the home as a wife and mother? There were dissenters. In 1833, Ohio's Oberlin College, a hotbed of evangelical reform, began to admit women as students. A few other colleges followed suit. In 1837, two women's colleges were founded, Georgia Female College in Macon (now Wesleyan College) and Mount Holyoke in South Hadley, Massachusetts.

Higher education was not career oriented. Students were not taught the specifics involved in an occupation or profession (except the ministry). The young man who wanted to be an engineer, an architect, or a businessman apprenticed himself to someone in those callings; he learned "on the job." Although some universities had established medical and law schools, apprenticeship was also the most common means of preparing for those professions, too.

The heart of college curricula was the same as it had been for centuries. The sequence of courses was strictly prescribed. Everyone studied the liberal arts. Colleges taught Latin, Greek, sometimes Hebrew; classical literature; natural science; mathematics, and political and moral philosophy. Rhetoric, both theory and a great deal of public speaking, was an important subject.

Colleges were small. Except at the very oldest institutions such as Harvard and Yale and public institutions like the University of Virginia, the typical student body rarely numbered more than a few dozen, the typical faculty perhaps three or four professors and an equal number of tutors ("assistant professors"). In so small a community, everyone knew everyone else at least by sight. But there was none of the instructor–student chumminess so common today. Professors erected a high wall of formality between themselves and those they taught, both because they believed in hierarchy and out of the fear that friendliness would lead to a breakdown in discipline. Instructors' stiff-necked behavior also owed to the fact that they were little older and sometimes younger than their students. Joseph Caldwell became president of the University of North Carolina when he was 24.

Ostensibly, student behavior was governed by detailed rules. Students were to toe the line not only in class but also in their private lives. Attendance at religious services was mandatory at church institutions. Strict curfews determined when students living in dormitories extinguished their lamps. Even impoliteness was to be punished by a fine or suspension.

The long lists of rules had more to do with reassuring parents than with students' actual behavior. College students were at least as rambunctious as they are today. They defied their professors by day—the distinguished political philosopher Francis Lieber had to tackle students he intended to discipline—and they taunted them by night. A common prank was stealing into the college chapel and ringing the bell until dawn or, better, an enraged professor emerged in his nightshirt. Students threw snowballs and rocks through tutors' windows. They led the president's horse to the roof of three- and four-story buildings. Students at Dickinson College in Pennsylvania sent a note to authorities at Staunton, Virginia, where Dickinson's president was visiting, informing them that an escaped lunatic was headed that way and would claim to be a college president. He should be returned under guard.

Some rebellions were more violent, if on a smaller scale, than the student uprisings of the 1960s. Professors were assaulted: stoned, horsewhipped, and fired on with shotguns. At the University of Virginia in 1840, Professor Nathaniel Davis was murdered. Writing to his own son at college in 1843, Princeton professor Samuel Miller warned against sympathizing with rebels. Miller lived in fear of student uprisings, perhaps because one rebellion at Princeton was so serious that the faculty had to call in club-wielding townspeople to put it down.

What caused student rebelliousness in the Jackson era? One explanation is that college rules were written at an earlier time when students were 14 to 18 years old. By the 1820s, however, many college students were in their mid-20s and, in that tougher world, much more mature than people in their 20s today. They were simply not inclined to conform to behavior appropriate to adolescents.

Moreover, many students lived not in closely supervised dormitories but in private lodgings in town. They fraternized largely with other students and developed a defiant camaraderie directed against outsiders. Enjoying broad freedoms, they were unlikely to conform to strict rules of behavior when they were on campus.

Finally, while the rules were strict, enforcement was erratic. "There were too many colleges," historian Joseph F. Kett wrote, "and they needed students more than students needed them." Faculty members, ever nervous for their jobs, overlooked minor offenses which inevitably led to greater ones. Several colleges suspended the entire student body for "great rebellion." However, financial pressures usually resulted in their readmission for the price of a written apology. Professor Miller described student rebels as "unworthy, profligate, degraded, and miserable villains." But if they could pay the tuition, there was a place for them, if not at alma mater, then at another college up the road.

He was replying to Robert Hayne of South Carolina, himself a fine orator who, when Calhoun was vice president, spoke Calhoun's lines on the floor of the Senate. Hayne identified the doctrine of nullification with American liberty. Then, in a brilliantly crafted speech that kept every senator in his seat for two days, Webster dissected Calhoun's doctrine legally, constitutionally, and historically. In a ringing rhetorical climax, he declared that it was not state sovereignty, but the Constitution that was the wellspring of American liberty, and the indissoluble union that was liberty's protector. "It is, Sir, the people's Constitution, the people's government, made for the people, made by the people, and answerable to the people."

The liberty and union speech transformed a political abstraction, the Union, into an object for which people were willing to die thirty years later.

1836: Three Whigs versus a Democrat

In 1836, the Whigs could not agree on a presidential candidate to run against Martin Van Buren. Henry Clay was the party's most distinguished leader. But the Whigs wanted to win, and Clay had been trounced in 1832 on an issue of his own choosing. Van Buren was not the gigantic national figure Jackson was. Therefore, the Whigs decided to run different candidates against him in states where each was popular. If they could deny Van Buren a majority in the electoral college, the election would be decided in the House of Representatives where the Whigs were likely to control a majority of state delegations. They would then unite behind whichever of their candidates qualified for the runoff.

Webster was the candidate in lower New England and New York (although Van Buren was bound to carry his home state). Hugh Lawson White of Tennessee was the candidate in the southern states. In the Northwest and rural upper New England, the Whigs' man was William Henry Harrison, the hero of the Battle of Tippecanoe. The Whig strategy got a boost when South Carolina refused to give its votes to Calhoun's enemy, Van Buren, and nominated a Calhoun henchman, Willie P. Magnum.

The popular vote was close. Van Buren won just 26,000 votes more than the Whigs. And, as they expected to do, the Whigs increased their representation in the House. But Van Buren won a comfortable 170 to 124 majority in the electoral college. Daniel Webster failed to carry even Massachusetts neighbors Connecticut and Rhode Island. Harrison lost in Michigan and Illinois. In the South, White carried only Tennessee and Georgia. Martin Van Buren was president.

Depression

Election to the presidency was just about the last good thing that ever happened to Martin Van Buren. When his administration was just a few months old, the country reaped the whirlwind of Jackson's Specie Circular. Drained of their gold and silver, several big New York banks announced in May that they would no longer redeem their notes in specie. Speculators and honest workingmen alike found themselves holding paper money that even the institutions that issued it would not accept.

In 1838, the depression worsened. In 1841 alone, 28,000 businesses declared bankruptcy. Factories closed. Several cities were unsettled by riots of unemployed workers. Eight western state governments defaulted on their debts.

Van Buren tried to meet the fiscal part of the crisis. He attempted to divorce the government from the banks which Jackson, for all his talk about all banks being bad, had not done. Van Buren established the subtreasury system by which, in effect, the government kept its money in its own vaults. The Whigs protested that what was needed was an infusion of money into the economy, not burying it. But they could not influence what was an executive decision.

Van Buren also maintained the Democratic faith in refusing to take any measures to alleviate popular suffering. The Founding Fathers, he said (in fact voicing Jefferson's and Jackson's sentiments), had "wisely judged that the less government interfered with private pursuits the better for the general prosperity."

Whatever the virtues of Van Buren's position—whatever the convictions of most Americans on the question of government intervention in the economy—it is difficult for any administration to survive a serious depression. The president, who reaps the credit for blessings that are none of his doing, gets the blame when things go badly, blameless as he may be. By early 1840, the Whigs were sure that hard times would put their candidate into the White House.

Pop Art

In 1834, with the hero of the common man in the White House, Nathaniel Currier of New York democratized art in America. He began to sell lithographs depicting natural wonders, marvels of technology such as locomotives, battles (New Orleans, of course), portraits of prominent people, and scenes of everyday life, both sentimental and comical.

Currier and Ives (the partner arrived in 1852) sold their prints for as little as 25¢ for a small black and white to $4 for a hand-colored engraving 28 by 40 inches. They were affordable to just about all but just expensive enough to be acceptable as a wall hanging in a self-consciously middle-class household.

More than 7,000 different Currier and Ives prints were produced by a process that can only be called industrial. Some artists specialized in backgrounds, others in machinery, others in faces, yet others in crowd scenes. By the late nineteenth century, it was a rare American who could not have identified Currier & Ives to an enquirer.

"Tippecanoe and Tyler Too"

But who was to be the sure-thing candidate? Clay believed that he deserved the nomination. For twenty-five years, he had promoted a coherent national economic policy that, for the most part, the Whigs had adopted. For half that time he

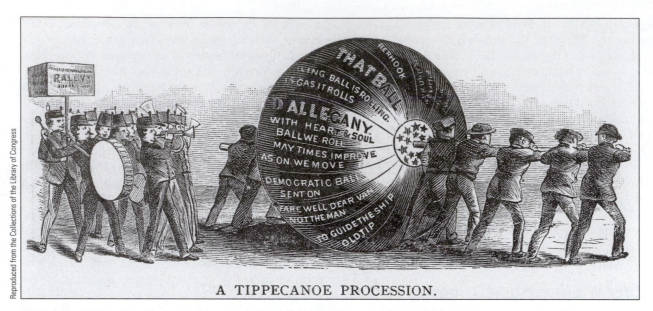

Reproduced from the Collections of the Library of Congress

In 1840, the Whigs built mock-up log cabins for rallies in support of William Henry Harrison's candidacy. Another gimmick new to electioneering was a great ball covered with party slogans and rolled to and through towns on an axle pushed by younger party workers. The phrase "keep the ball rolling," still common parlance, dates from the landmark campaign of 1840.

led the fight against Jackson. However, so thought calculating Whig politicos like Thurlow Weed of New York, Clay's distinguished career was also his weakness. In standing in the vanguard for so long, in brokering so many deals, Clay inevitably made enemies. Another Whig, Edmund Quincy, wrote (in dreadfully purple prose) of "the ineffable meanness of the lion turned spaniel in his fawnings on the masters whose hands he was licking for the sake of the dirty puddings they might have to toss him."

Victory-hungry Whigs led by Weed called for choosing a candidate who had little or no political record but who, like Jackson, could be packaged as a national symbol. The first and foremost object of a political party, Weed said (echoing Martin Van Buren) was to win elections. Then it could talk about its principles and pursue its goals.

Weed's candidate was William Henry Harrison. He had done better than either Webster or White in 1836. He was the scion of a distinguished Virginia family; his father signed the Declaration of Independence. He was identified with no controversial political position. Best of all, like Jackson, he was both a westerner and a military hero, the victor of Tippecanoe. When the Whigs nominated him, his "handlers" admonished one another, "let him say not one single word about his principles or his creed, let him say nothing, promise nothing. Let no [one] extract from him a single word about what he thinks. . . . Let use of pen and ink be wholly forbidden as if he were a mad poet in Bedlam."

To appeal to voters in the South, where the Whigs were weak, John Tyler of Virginia was nominated for vice president: "Tippecanoe and Tyler Too!"

Politics as Marketing

The Whigs intended to campaign simply by talking about Harrison's military record. Then a Democratic newspaper editor made a slip that opened up a whole new world in American politics. Implying that Harrison was incompetent, the journalist sneered that the elderly, Harrison would be quite happy with an annual pension of $2,000, a jug of hard cider, and a bench on which to sit and doze at the door of his log cabin.

Such snobbery was ill-suited to a party that had come to power as the champion of the common man. The Whigs, who suffered Democratic taunts that they were elitists, charged into the breach. They hauled out miniature log cabins at city rallies and country bonfires. They tapped thousands of barrels of hard cider. They sang raucous songs like

> Farewell, dear Van,
> You're not our man,
> To guide our ship,
> We'll try old Tip.

Stealing another leaf from the Jacksonian book, the Whigs depicted Van Buren as an effeminate fop who sipped champagne, ate fancy French food, perfumed his whiskers, and flounced about in silks and satins. Before he departed for Texas, death, and immortality at the Alamo, Davy Crockett said that Van Buren was "laced up in corsets such as women in a town wear, and if possible tighter than the best of them. It would be difficult to say from his personal appearance whether he was man or woman, but for his large red and gray whiskers."

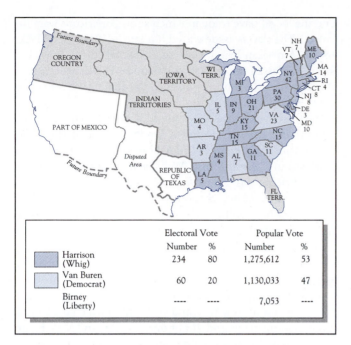

MAP 16:2 **The Whig Victory of 1840** In 1840, the Whigs demonstrated to generations of politicians yet to come that a non-issue, all hoopla campaign is sometimes the way to go. Whig strategists persuaded candidate William Henry Harrison to say nothing of substance. But Van Buren was doomed even if the pompous Harrison had stumped the country delivering his notorious dull speeches. The country was in the midst of a serious economic depression. That, far more than the Whigs' "fun" campaign, defeated Van Buren.

It was all nonsense. Harrison lived in no log cabin but in a mansion. He was no simple country bumpkin, but rather the opposite, a pedant given to tedious academic discourse on subjects of little interest to ordinary people. Van Buren, while indeed a dandy, was of modest origins; his father had kept a tavern. He was earthy, and he subscribed to much more democratic ideals than did old Tippecanoe.

But nonsense worked, as it often has since. Although Van Buren won 47 percent of the popular vote, he was trounced in the electoral college 60 to 234. Jacksonian chickens had come home to roost. Rarely again would a presidential election be contested without great fussing about symbols and images.

With their successful appeal to the common man, the Whigs of 1840 demonstrated that the democratic upheaval of the Age of Jackson was complete. Never again in the egalitarian United States would there be political profit in appealing to the superior qualifications of the better sort. Perhaps what is most noteworthy about the election of 1840 is that a political candidate was marketed as a commodity—Harrison was "packaged"—long before the techniques of modern advertising were formulated.

Fate's Cruel Joke

Wherever William Henry Harrison stood on specific issues, he was fully in accord with one fundamental Whig principle—that Congress should make the laws and the president execute them. He was quite willing to defer to the party professionals, particularly Clay, whom he admired, in making policy. With Whig majorities in both houses of Congress, the Great Compromiser had every reason to believe that, if not president in name, he would direct the nation's affairs. Old Tip dutifully named four of Clay's lieutenants to his cabinet.

Harrison would have done well to defer to Daniel Webster in his area of expertise—oratory. Webster wrote an inaugural address for Harrison, but the president politely turned it down, having prepared his own. It is the longest, dullest inaugural address in the archives, a turgid treatise on Roman history and its relevance to the United States of America circa March 1841. Harrison delivered it out of doors on a frigid, windy day. He caught a cold that turned into pneumonia. For weeks he suffered, half the time in bed, half the time receiving Whig office seekers as greedy for jobs as the Democrats of 1828. Then he ceased to rise and dress. On April 4, 1841, exactly one month after lecturing the country on republican virtue, he passed away.

At first the Whigs did not miss a stride. Clay lectured "Tyler Too" that he was an "acting president." He would preside over the formalities of government while a committee of Whigs chaired by Henry Clay made policy decisions. John Quincy Adams, now a Whig congressman from Massachusetts, concurred. Tyler would have none of it. He insisted that the Constitution authorized him to exercise the same presidential powers that he would exercise if he had been elected.

A President without a Party

Tyler tried to get along with Clay. He went along with the abolition of the subtreasury system, and, although a low-tariff man, he agreed to an increase of rates in 1842 as long as the rise was tied to ending federal finance of internal improvements. Tyler also supported Clay's attempt to woo western voters from the Democrats with his Preemption Act of 1841. This law provided that a family that squatted on up to 160 acres of public land could purchase it at the minimum price of $1.25 per acre without having to bid against others.

But Tyler was no Henry Clay Whig. He had split with Jackson over King Andrew's arrogant use of presidential power. His views on other issues were closer to those of John C. Calhoun than to those of the nationalistic Whigs. Most notably, Tyler wanted no new BUS. He told Clay not to try to force one on him.

Clay tried anyway, and Tyler vetoed one bank bill after another. Furious, the Whigs expelled the president from the party, and Tyler's entire cabinet, inherited from Harrison, resigned. (Except Secretary of State Webster, who wanted to complete some touchy negotiations with Great Britain). Clay left the Senate in order to devote all his time to winning the presidential election of 1844.

Tyler's new cabinet was made up mostly of nominal southern Whigs who shared his views. The president's plan was to piece together a new party of such states' rights Whigs and some Democrats. Toward this end, he named John C. Calhoun secretary of state.

The Webster–Ashburton Treaty

The major accomplishments of the Tyler administration were in the area of foreign affairs: resolving a series of potentially dangerous disputes with Great Britain, and paving the way for the annexation of the Republic of Texas.

Relations with Great Britain were eased by Secretary of State Webster. One problem was a boundary dispute between Maine and the Canadian province of New Brunswick. According to the Treaty of 1783, the line ran between the watersheds of the Atlantic and the St. Lawrence River. Both sides agreed that Benjamin Franklin had drawn the boundary in red ink on a map used at the negotiations.

However, the map had disappeared and, in 1838, Canadian lumberjacks began cutting timber in the Aroostook Valley, which the United States claimed. A brief "war" between the Maine and New Brunswick militias ended with no deaths, and Van Buren managed to cool things down. But he could not resolve the boundary dispute.

The Canadian–American line west of Lake Superior was also in question, and there were two more points of friction because of unofficial American assistance to Canadian rebels and the illegal slave trade in which some Americans were involved. The slavery issue waxed hot late in 1841 when blacks on the American brig *Creole* mutinied, killed the crew, and sailed to Nassau in the British Bahamas. The British hanged the leaders of the mutiny but freed the other slaves, enraging southerners.

Neither Britain nor the United States wanted war. And, fortuitously, Webster found a kindred spirit in the high-living British negotiator, Lord Ashburton. Over brandy, they worked out a compromise. Webster made a big concession to the British, too big as far as Maine's loggers were concerned. Never above chicanery, Webster forged Franklin's map to show a red line that gave Maine less territory than he "won" from Ashburton. He warned that the United States had better take what it could get. (The real Franklin map surfaced some years later and showed that the United States was shorted.)

Ashburton was generous, too. He ceded a strip of territory in northern New York and Vermont to which the United States had no claim and about 6,500 square miles at the tip of Lake Superior. It was wilderness at the time. Later, known as the Mesabi Range, it held one of the world's richest iron ore deposits.

When the Senate ratified the Webster–Ashburton Treaty in 1842, every outstanding difference between the United States and Britain was resolved. Webster had good reason to be pleased with himself, and he joined his fellow Whigs in leaving Tyler's cabinet.

FURTHER READING

Classics James Parton, *Life of Andrew Jackson*, 3 vols, 1859–1860; Arthur M. Schlesinger Jr., *The Age of Jackson*, 1946; John William Ward, *Andrew Jackson: Symbol for an Age*, 1962.

The Jackson Presidency Robert V. Remini, *Andrew Jackson and the Course of American Freedom*, 3 vols., 1981; *Andrew Jackson and the Course of American Democracy*, 1984, *The Revolutionary Age of Andrew Jackson*, 1985; Robert E. Wright, *The First Wall Street: Chestnut Street, Philadelphia, and the Birth of American Finance*, 2005; Edward Pessen, *Jacksonian America: Society, Personality, and Politics*, 1978; Andrew Burstein, *The Passions of Andrew Jackson*, 2005; John F. Marszallek, *The Petticoat Affairs: Manners, Mutiny, and Sex in Andrew Jackson's White House*, 1997; John R. Bumgarner, *The Health of the Presidents*, 1994; H. W. Brands, *Andrew Jackson: His Life and Times*, 2005.

Party Politics Richard McCormick, *The Party Period and Public Policy: American Politics from the Age of Jackson to the Progressive Era*, 1986; Harry L. Watson, *Liberty and Power: The Politics of Jacksonian America*, 1990; Lawrence F. Kohl, *The Politics of Individualism: Parties and the American Character in the Jacksonian Era*, 1989.

Democrats D. B. Cole, *Martin Van Buren and the American Political System*, 1984; John Niven, *Martin Van Buren: The Romantic Age of American Politics*, 1983; M. L. Wilson, *The Presidency of Martin Van Buren*, 1984; John Niven, *John C. Calhoun and the Price of Union*, 1988.

Whigs D. W. Howe, *The Political Culture of the American Whigs*, 1979; Merrill D. Peterson, *The Great Triumvirate: Webster, Clay, and Calhoun*, 1987; Robert V. Remini, *Henry Clay: Statesman for the Union*, 1991; Sydney Nathan, *Daniel Webster and Jacksonian Democracy*, 1973; M. G. Baxter, *One and Inseparable: Daniel Webster and the Union*, 1984; Mark Derr, *The Frontiersman: The Real Life and the Many Legends of Davy Crockett*, 1993; Edward P. Crapol, *John Tyler: The Accidental President*, 2006; Michael F. Holt, *The Rise and Fall of the American Whig Party*, 1999.

KEY TERMS

Use the following listing of key terms to review important figures, events, locations, and concepts covered in this chapter. A glossary of these terms is available on *The American*

Past companion Web site: www.cengage.com/history/conlin/tap9e

Eaton, Peggy (O'Neill), p. 270

Biddle, Nicholas, p. 273

pet banks, p. 274

Specie Circular, p. 275

Second American Party System, p. 276

Webster, Daniel, p. 277

subtreasury system, p. 279

"Tippecanoe and Tyler too!", p. 279

ONLINE RESOURCES

Find additional resources, including primary source documents, images, interactive maps, simulations, chapter review exercises, and Internet links at

The American Past **companion Web site**
www.cengage.com/history/conlin/tap9e

American History Resource Center
http://ushistory.wadsworth.com/

DISCOVERY

How did new means of transporting people and goods about affect the societies and economies of Northeast, South, and West?

Economics and Technology: Excerpts from two articles of the early industrial age, "*The Harbinger*, Female Workers of Lowell" and "Morality of Manufactures" present two sharply different pictures of the effects of cotton mills on the lives of New Englanders. Which assessment do you find more convincing? Why? Is the debate here relevant to factory work today?

The Harbinger, Female Workers of Lowell (1836)

. . . In Lowell live between seven and eight thousand young women, who are generally daughters of farmers of the different states of New England. Some of them are members of families that were rich in the generation before. . . .

The operatives work thirteen hours a day in the summer time, and from daylight to dark in the winter. At half past four in the morning the factory bell rings, and at five the girls must be in the mills. A clerk, placed as a watch, observes those who are a few minutes behind the time, and effectual means are taken to stimulate to punctuality. This is the morning commencement of the industrial discipline (should we not rather say industrial tyranny?) which is established in these associations of this moral and Christian community.

At seven the girls are allowed thirty minutes for breakfast, and at noon thirty minutes more for dinner, except during the first quarter of the year, when the time is extended to forty-five minutes. But within this time they must hurry to their boardinghouses and return to the factory, and that through the hot sun or the rain or the cold. A meal eaten under such circumstances must be quite unfavorable to digestion and health, as any medical man will inform us. After seven o'clock in the evening the factory bell sounds the close of the day's work.

Thus thirteen hours per day of close attention and monotonous labor are extracted from the young women in these manufactories. . . . So fatigued-we should say, exhausted and worn out, but we wish to speak of the system in the simplest language-are numbers of girls that they go to bed soon after their evening meal, and endeavor by a comparatively long sleep to resuscitate their weakened frames for the toil of the coming day.

Morality of Manufactures, 1823

. . . "Before I commenced the erection of these works, said Mr. S. and established in this place the branch of cotton manufacture, the process of which you have been just examining, the man who built, and now owns that neat little tenement, had no place to shelter himself and his numerous family, but the wretched hovel which you may observe at a few rods distance from his present abode. At that time, continued my informant, his only occupation was that of fishing or rambling in the mountains in pursuit of such game as chance might throw in his way. Of the little he obtained by this occasional and precarious mode of subsistence, a large proportion was expended in the purchase of rum; in the use of which he indulged to such an extent as to brutalize his faculties, and render him a pest to society, as well as a curse to his family; which he kept in a state of the most deplorable and squalid poverty. Of his children three of four were daughters, of various ages, from seven or eight to fourteen years; these, said Mr. S. on commencing my establishment, I took into the factory; where, from that period to the present time, they have always had constant and regular employment. The proceeds of their first week's labor, amounting to six or seven dollars, when paid and taken home to their parents, was an amount which, it is probable, they never before at any one time possessed. The almost immediate effect on the mind of the father appears to have been a conviction that his children, instead of being a burden which he despaired of supporting, and, therefore, never before made an effort to accomplish, would, on the contrary, by the steady employment now provided for them, be able, by their industry, not only to sustain themselves, but also contribute to the maintenance and support of the other members of the family. From that moment, it would appear, as if he had determined to reform his vicious habits, and to emerge from that state of degradation and wretchedness into which he had plunged himself and family. He has done so, said Mr. S. and, instead of being a pest, he has become a useful member of society; instead of being a curse to his family, and occupying with them that wretched hovel yonder, fit only for swine to wallow in, he has, by his own exertions, aided the industry and good conduct of his children, lately purchased the soil, and erected the comfortable cottage, which said Mr. S. smiling, appears so powerfully to attract your notice."

What role did Andrew Jackson's personality play in shaping politics and government policy during the 1820s and 1830s?

Government and Law: Based on only the imagery in "Daniel Webster has the floor" and "King Andrew," what were the painter's and the cartoonist's opinions of the two politicians? To which political party does the artwork imply the creator of each belonged? What is the painter's implied view of Congress? The cartoonist's view of the presidency?

Daniel Webster has the floor

King Andrew

To read extended versions of selected documents, visit the companion Web site www.cengage.com/history/conlin/tap9e; click on "Discovery Sources"

© Bettmann/Corbis

Chapter 17

Religion and Reform

Evangelicals and Enthusiasts 1800-1850

God has found it necessary to take advantage of the excitability there is in mankind, to produce powerful excitements among them, before he can lead them to obey. Men are so spiritually sluggish, there are so many things to lead their minds off from religion, and to oppose the influence of the Gospel, that it is necessary to raise an excitement among them, till the tide rises so high as to sweep away the opposing obstacles.

—*Charles G. Finney*

Religious Insanity is very common in the United States

—*Alexis de Tocqueville*

Before 1800, most American churchgoers were Congregationalists, Anglicans, Presbyterians, or Quakers. There were other denominations: Baptists, Lutherans; Dutch Reformed; German Mennonites and Amish in southeastern Pennsylvania (the "Pennsylvania Dutch"). Indeed, there was still an old Roman Catholic community in Maryland and a few Catholic missions elsewhere; and synagogues in the major seaports. But none of these groups had nearly as many houses of worship as the Congregationalists (almost 500), the Anglicans (400), or the Quakers and Presbyterians (about 250 each).

AGE OF REASON, AGE OF FAITH

Churchgoing declined during the Revolution and the Confederation years. The philosophers of the Enlightenment had convinced many Americans that human reason was enough to understand and shape the world. There was wisdom in the Bible, the philosophers said, but there was mythology too, and irrational nonsense of obviously human origin.

Ordinary workaday men and women did not read the books of European philosophers. Their drift away from church reflected their unhappiness with doctrines that were

hard to understand—too much theology in sermons—and, in the case of the Anglicans, the fact that virtually all their ministers had been loyalists during the Revolution. Emigrants to the West ceased to belong to churches because there were no churches on the raw frontier, in some places not for years after the first settlers.

With such different reasons for their discontent with traditional beliefs and practices, Americans influenced by the Enlightenment and ordinary folk took very different paths in their religious lives.

Deists

Any Americans who were atheists kept their disbelief to themselves. Known atheists were not permitted to vote. By the time of the Revolution, however, many educated people were deists.

Deists believed in a supreme being, but not in a God who was constantly at work in human affairs, listening to prayers and shaping events. They compared God to a watchmaker who created the complex mechanism that was the world and then let it run by itself according to natural laws that were rational and could be understood, just as Sir Isaac Newton, a century earlier, had explained the mysteries of gravity and the movement of the planets using mathematics.

The President Goes to Church

Nine of the first ten presidents were members of "mainstream" denominations. (Jefferson belonged to no church.) Washington, Madison, Monroe, Harrison, and Tyler were Episcopalians. John Adams and John Quincy Adams were Unitarians. Martin Van Buren was a member of the Dutch Reformed Church. Late in life, at his wife's urging, Jackson joined the Presbyterian church.

Deists rejected the belief that the Bible and the detailed creeds of the various denominations were divinely inspired. To deists, the Bible and creeds were human creations subject to the same critical scrutiny as monarchy. Thomas Jefferson prepared a "rational" New Testament by crossing out the miracles and other supernatural events and retaining only the moral teachings of Jesus.

Like Jefferson, Benjamin Franklin, George Washington, and many other Founding Fathers were deists. Washington remained an Anglican church member, but he attended services only when ceremonial obligations or good manners required him to do so; he never knelt when prayers were said. In his public statements and private letters, he never used the words "Jesus," "Christ," "savior," and "redeemer" and "God" very rarely. He preferred deist terms like "Great Architect" and "Almighty Ruler of the Universe."

During the 1790s, Thomas Paine published *The Age of Reason,* which included a scorching denunciation of Christianity. But most deists were not hostile to the churches—for others. Social conservatives among them believed that the traditional faiths imbued the uneducated and superstitious with morality and ethics.

Deists advocated religious toleration and equal rights for all, regardless of their religious beliefs or lack of them. When, at New York state's constitutional convention, John Jay (who was not a deist) proposed to deny the vote to Catholics, Gouverneur Morris (a deist) opposed his resolution and won the debate.

Unitarians and Universalists

Deism shook up the Congregationalists of New England and sharply reduced the number of their churches. Orthodox Congregationalists, latter-day Puritans, clung to the harsh and inflexible Calvinist doctrines of the innate depravity of humanity and the predestination of souls. By the late 1700s, however, fewer Congregational ministers and church members were orthodox.

Each Congregational church was self-governing. Therefore, a majority of members of the church could redefine their congregation's creed. In 1785, a prestigious Boston congregation voted to eliminate all references to the Trinity from its services. The doctrine of the Trinity—that in God there were three persons, the Father, the Son, and the Holy Spirit—was, they said, "idolatrous" and irrational. God was one, unitary; thus the name the breakaway churches took—Unitarian.

The Unitarians' rejection of the Trinity led to other doctrinal innovations. If God was one, then Jesus was not divine. He was a saintly teacher, to be sure, but a human being.

Unitarianism spread rapidly in New England after 1800. When, in 1819, William Ellery Channing, the most respected of Congregational ministers, declared himself a Unitarian, dozens of local churches followed him into the new denomination. Channing rejected the angry and vengeful Calvinist God. God had a father's concern for his creatures, a father's desire for their improvement, a father's equity in

Religion and Reform 1800–1850

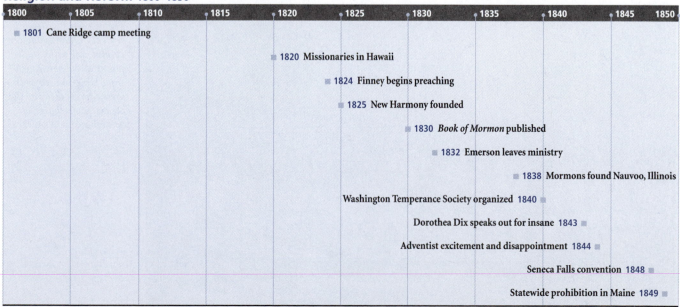

1800	1805	1810	1815	1820	1825	1830	1835	1840	1845	1850

1801 Cane Ridge camp meeting

1820 Missionaries in Hawaii

1824 Finney begins preaching

1825 New Harmony founded

1830 *Book of Mormon* published

1832 Emerson leaves ministry

1838 Mormons found Nauvoo, Illinois

Washington Temperance Society organized 1840

Dorothea Dix speaks out for insane 1843

Adventist excitement and disappointment 1844

Seneca Falls convention 1848

Statewide prohibition in Maine 1849

proportioning his commands to their powers, a father's joy in their progress, a father's readiness to receive the penitent, and a father's justice for the incorrigible.

Some Congregational churches that rejected the doctrine of predestination—that God saved some and marked others for eternal damnation—became Universalists. How could an all-good, loving God damn some of his children to hell from the instant of their conception? It made no sense. Salvation was accessible to all; it was "universal."

Unitarian and Universalist beliefs were much the same. Both denominations shunned convoluted doctrines. They sought to be godly by being moral, by following the precepts of Jesus without (Jefferson's words) "hocus-pocus phantasms."

The early Universalists and Unitarians had different social bases. Universalist congregations were generally made up of plain farmers and, in the towns, men and women of the humbler sort. Unitarianism attracted New England's elite and middle classes. Presidents John and John Quincy Adams were Unitarians. By 1805, so was Harvard's president. A few years later, a visitor in Boston observed that all the literary men of Massachusetts were Unitarians; all the trustees and professors of Harvard College were Unitarians; all the elite of wealth and fashion crowded Unitarian churches. Even Thomas Jefferson, who did not like much that came out of New England, thought that Unitarianism was "the pure and uncompounded" religion of "the early ages of Christianity."

Cane Ridge

Where the Unitarians and Universalists were cerebral, the religious phenomenon that combusted in August 1801 at Cane Ridge, Kentucky, was unbridled emotion. Hardly concerned with reconciling Christianity and the Age of Reason, the local Presbyterian minister, Barton W. Stone, sent out a call for a camp meeting, an open air revival for the purpose of recapturing—*reviving*—the religious zeal that frontier settlers seemed to have left back East.

The response indicated that a good many trans-Appalachian pioneers felt that something was missing from their lives. Between 10,000 and 30,000 people gathered at a hastily cleared campground near Stone's log church. For a few days, Cane Ridge was larger than just about every American city not on tidal waters.

The labor-hardened pioneers, many of them first and second generation Scotch-Irish, listened to sermons by ministers of several denominations and some of no denomination who believed that God commanded them personally to be there. A few preachers had built roofed platforms so they could speak rain or shine. Most clambered atop wagons or stumps. There was nothing resembling a program. As many as a dozen revivalists spoke simultaneously.

The preachers' messages were much the same, however: Every man and woman at Cane Ridge was a sinner. They were going to burn in hell for eternity unless they repented of their sins, prayed for God's grace, and accepted Christ as their

© Bettmann/Corbis

A camp meeting. The preacher has most of the crowd writhing, which is how he wants them. To the right, a few well-dressed visitors are unmoved and perhaps amused. They have come for the show, not the religion. Skeptics were welcome at revivals. Often enough to confirm the belief in the power of the holy spirit, some who came to scoff were carried away by the electric atmosphere (or something) and converted.

personal savior when that grace was freely bestowed. If there were any old-time Calvinists there preaching predestination, they were few. The whole point of the revival was that salvation was available for all. Shortly after Cane Ridge, Barton Stone severed his Presbyterian ties, saying, "Calvinism is among the heaviest clogs on Christianity. It is a dark mountain between heaven and earth."

Conversions were numerous and passionate. One preacher wrote that "at one time I saw at least *five hundred* swept down in a moment as if a barrage of a thousand guns had been opened upon them." Repentant sinners fell to their knees, weeping uncontrollably. Some scampered about on all fours, barking like dogs. The most talked about manifestation of God's presence was what the unpretentious pioneers called "the jerks." People who resisted God's grace lurched about, their heads and limbs snapping uncontrollably. A rumor spread that a man who cursed God was seized by the jerks and broke his neck.

There were plenty of skeptics and scoffers at Cane Ridge, as there would be at the hundreds of revivals called in imitation of it. So concentrated a mass of humanity in the middle of the woods was exhilarating; who could pass on it? Young men and women with little interest in religion came for the socializing, for the showmanship, and to exploit the occasion with thievery, heckling, drinking, and the sexual opportunities that religious excitement often provides. An oft-repeated saying had it that more souls were begotten at camp meetings than were saved. Opportunists had plenty of opportunities for the next thirty years. Camp meetings were frequent events in the southwestern states, and revivals held under a roof were common in the East.

Growth Industries

In 1804, Barton Stone founded the Disciples of Christ for other Presbyterians who had rejected Calvinism. In 1832, the Disciples merged with another Presbyterian offshoot, the "Campbellites," and were soon a major denomination. Doctrines were of minor importance to the Disciples. What counted was an individual's personal relationship with God. This was the key to the evangelicals of the early nineteenth century: a personal conversion experience.

The Baptists dated their origins to the early years of the Reformation. Their signature belief (and thus their name) was their repudiation of infant baptism, which most Christians practiced. For Baptists, only those who were capable of choosing to be a Christian could be baptized—by complete immersion, as in the Bible, not by a symbolic sprinkling of water. (They were originally called "anabaptists," *re*-baptisers, because, in the 1500s, converts had already been baptized as babies.)

The Baptists believed in the literal truth of every word in the Bible. Ironically, these fundamentalists provided much of the popular support for the deist Jefferson in his battle to dis-establish the Anglican church in Virginia. Except for adult immersion baptism, the Baptists differed little from other evangelicals. They took minimal interest in formal creeds.

Reproduced from the Collections of the Library of Congress, Prints and Photographs Division, Washington, D.C. [LC-USZ62-120350]

A Methodist circuit rider making his way from one frontier settlement to another to preach the gospel, counsel the faithful, marry couples, and baptize newborns. Circuit riders were the Methodists' response to the fact that, on the frontier, there were usually too few people in any one place to support a full time preacher. The ministers survived on the meals provided them on the circuit and whatever money those they visited could afford to give them.

The Methodists

Both the Disciples and the Baptists grew rapidly. But neither's growth came close to rivaling the astonishing success of the Methodists in making converts. In 1770, no more than 1,000 Americans called themselves Methodists. Fifty years later, the Methodist Episcopal Church counted 250,000 members, and there were many more "adherents" who attended Methodist services but had not joined the church. By 1850, one American church member in three was a Methodist.

Methodism was founded in Great Britain by a Church of England minister, John Wesley. Wesley did not found a new denomination. His Methodism was an unsanctioned movement within the Church of England. Wesley criticized the church for its frigid formalism and for relying on ritual and formulaic sermons that did not touch the hearts of parishioners. Denied access to Anglican churches, Wesley set up his pulpit in the street or in chapels that were usually no more than a room. He was unusually successful in luring the poor and uneducated from the pews in the parish churches.

Wesley condemned the American Revolution, but his hostility caused hardly a blip in the growth of Methodism in the United States. Immediately after the War for Independence, Francis Asbury, himself a missionary from England, declared the independence of the Methodist Episcopal Church in America.

The Methodists differed from the Baptists and Disciples in several ways. Because of their Anglican roots, they retained bishops to administer the denomination. Although they too de-emphasized doctrine—Wesley even deleted the Credo from the prayerbooks he sent to America—the Methodists demanded strict moral behavior of church members. Both Wesley and Asbury condemned "enthusiasm," the "religious madness arising from some falsely imagined influence or inspiration of God." However, at the peak of the revival craze, they tacitly encouraged "sudden Agonies, Roarings and Screamings, Tremblings, Droppings-down, Ravings and Madnesses."

Methodist leaders soon soured on camp meetings because of the unedifying activities that accompanied them. They sought converts by sending out itinerant preachers to preach the message door-to-door, swapping their words for dinner and a place to sleep. In areas where there were too few Methodists to support a local minister, "circuit riders"—intensely devoted, poorly paid, usually unmarried men—unendingly rode a circuit of ten or twenty little settlements. They forded swollen creeks in all weather, carrying little on their nags but a Bible. They preached, gave lessons, performed marriages and baptisms, took their rest and meals in the cabins of the faithful, and rode on. In old age, Francis Asbury, who owned no home of his own, estimated that he had sat a horse for more than 300,000 miles. For three decades, Finis Ewing and Peter Cartwright were rarely off their horses for more than three days at a time.

THE BURNED-OVER DISTRICT

The "Second Great Awakening" of the early nineteenth century was immensely successful. Before the 1800s, about one American in six belonged to a church. In 1850, one in three was a church member. At first, the Disciples, Baptists, and Methodists converted many Presbyterians and Congregationalists to their denominations. But when some Presbyterian and Congregationalist ministers embraced evangelicalism, sidling away from Calvinism, their numbers also increased.

Indeed, the most famous preacher of the Second Great Awakening was a Presbyterian, Charles Grandison Finney. Finney preached wherever he could borrow a church or rent a hall. Well educated as he was, Finney was not averse to camp meeting antics. He writhed during sermons and invented the "anxious bench." Members of the audience who sensed they felt a divine presence were ushered to a seat directly in front of Finney where he could bring them along personally. When he sensed a breakthrough, he shouted, "Do it! Get saved."

Finney's favorite tramping ground was central and western New York, a region of substandard farmland settled by emigrants from the substandard farmland of northern New England. They had been tossed about socially and psychologically by the commercial revolution worked by the Erie Canal. Finney called it the "burned-over" district because the fires of religious enthusiasm blazed in the country so frequently.

Superstition and belief in magic flourished in the burned-over district. Farmers hired "water witchers" with dousing sticks to locate the best location for a well (it was called "scrying") and conjurors with peep stones to find the treasure they were positive was buried somewhere on their property. A Vermont editor estimated that, at one time, 500 people were digging up the Green Mountains searching for buried gold; there must have been as many in New York's burned-over district. Prophets and seers preaching bizarre panaceas for solving one problem or another, some of them charlatans, some merely disturbed, wandered from town to town.

During the 1830s, two religious sects destined to become major denominations emerged from the region plus a third, beginning as a kind of prank, that evolved into a sect that is still around although far from major.

The Millerites

In 1831, after a decade of pouring over biblical prophecies and making mathematical calculations, William Miller announced that the Second Coming of Christ—the end of the world, when those who were saved would be transported to heaven—was imminent. He could not name the day but,

William Miller's prediction of the end of the world in 1843 or 1844 was based on his study of biblical prophecies. This Adventist chart traced the rise and fall of earthly kingdoms from Babylon through the "Mahometans" and beyond.

Jehovah's Witnesses

The Jehovah's Witnesses were an offshoot of the Millerites. Like the Adventists, they looked (and look) forward to the end of the world. Their founder, Charles Taze Russell, was a denomination hopper, in turn a Presbyterian, Congregationalist, and Adventist. He and his successors, claiming papal-like authority to explain the meaning of the scriptures, predicted the end of the world for 1878, then for 1881, 1914, 1925, and 1975. After the end, 144,000 of God's elect will live in heaven; faithful Witnesses will dwell in a paradise on earth; everyone else will be destroyed.

when pressed, said that it would occur sometime between March 21, 1843 and March 21, 1844.

For a decade, Miller wandered the Northeast preaching. The number of his converts increased slowly but steadily until, at the beginning of the fateful year, an omen appeared in the sky. (It was Halley's Comet.) In the burned-over district and parts of New England, Millerites hurriedly wrapped up their affairs, many selling their possessions, some contributing the proceeds to Miller. On March 21, 1844, several thousand people in New York climbed trees and hills in "Ascension Robes" so as to be first in line for the flight to heaven. When midnight arrived without incident—the "Great Disappointment"—the miserable Miller went back to his computations, found an error, and rescheduled the Second Coming for October 22.

Fewer people climbed hills in October. After the "Second Disappointment," Miller's most devoted followers somehow held on until, in 1863, James and Ellen G. "Mother" White revitalized them as the Seventh Day Adventists. (Their day of worship was the sabbath, Saturday, as in the Bible, not Sunday, the Lord's Day.) They steered clear of dates, saying only that the faithful should be prepared for the advent (the coming) every day.

The Book of Mormon

Joseph Smith Jr. was the handsome, charming, day-dreaming son of a wretchedly poor family that had settled in Palmyra, New York. Smith preferred treasure hunting to working. He grew up hearing the wondrous stories of the region and listened to any number of revivalists who passed through. Apparently he had a conversion experience in 1820. (Later, he said it had been a vision.) On one of his rambles—again he told the story only much later—he was accosted by an angel named Moroni. After several meetings, Moroni directed him to buried gold plates bearing mysterious inscriptions. With the help of peep stones, Smith translated the plates into English which he published as *The Book of Mormon*, a "Bible of the New World." It told the story of the Nephites, descendants of the lost tribes of Israel who had come to America, of Christ's visit to them, and of their wars with the Lamanites (the Indians) who were victorious, killing all of the Nephites except the author of Smith's book, Mormon.

The Book of Mormon lacked the diversity and poetry of the Bible. Mark Twain called it "chloroform in print," observing that the phrase "and it came to pass" appeared 2,000 times. But it was a sensational success. When he published *The Book of Mormon*, Smith's Church of Jesus Christ of the Latter Day Saints had fifty members. Within a year, there were a thousand Mormons, as Smith's followers were dubbed, and thousands more the next.

It was not hard to accept the belief that the Indians were descendants of the lost tribes of Israel. Since Columbus, many people, including the Puritans, believed it. (Thomas Jefferson instructed Lewis and Clark to determine if any Indian religious ceremonies resembled Jewish services.) Nor did the magical aspects of Smith's teaching put off the impoverished and superstitious people of the burned-over district. Josiah Quincy Jr., an educated New Englander, described the early Mormons as "feeble or confused souls who are looking for guidance." The Quaker poet, John Greenleaf Whittier, was kinder. He wrote that the Mormons "speak a language of hope and promise to weak, heavy hearts, tossed and troubled, who have wandered from sect to sect, seeking in vain for the primal manifestation of divine power."

A Singular Man

The *Book* was not, like the Bible for evangelical Protestants, the sole source of God's word and a comprehensive guide to right living and salvation; it was a story. God's teachings, the Mormons believed, were revealed directly to Joseph Smith. Between 1830 and 1834, Smith had more than 100 revelations.

At the start, Mormonism looked like another variant of evangelical Protestantism. However, Smith's revelations carried the Mormons far beyond the boundaries of Christianity. His doctrine of "proxy baptism," for example—Mormons saving those who had lived before Smith's revelations by being baptized in their place—was an original idea. "Plural marriage," polygamy, a revelation Smith shared with only a few close associates and the ladies he secretly "wed", was a practice long forbidden by Christians.

And yet, the Mormons followed Smith into this strange territory. He was so extraordinarily charismatic, and the comforts of belonging to the tight-knit Mormon community were so reassuring that the Church grew steadily despite harassment by gentiles (as Mormons called nonbelievers) and Mormons whom Smith alienated.

Palmyra was so hostile that the Mormons moved to Kirtland, Ohio. There Smith founded a bank with freely given capital and was prospering when the bank failed in the Panic of 1837. Smith was accused of stealing from it, then accused of adultery, which was a criminal offense in Ohio. Hurriedly, he went to western Missouri where a number of Mormons had already settled. There the hostility was more than verbal. Hard-bitten frontier gentiles burned Mormon houses and shops and killed several. The Mormons responded in kind. There were plenty of thugs among them willing to do whatever Joseph Smith asked. But the Mormons were outgunned and moved yet again.

Joseph Mustering the Nauvoo Legion, C.C.A. Christensen. © Courtesy Museum of Art, Brigham Young University. All rights reserved.
Photographer: David W. Hawkinson, Joseph Smith & Nauvoo Legion

Joseph Smith reviews the "Mormon Legion" at Nauvoo, Illinois. Smith's militiamen were not quite the disciplined, spit-and-polish parade ground soldiers depicted here. No state militia unit was. However, the Nauvoo Legion was the largest and best armed militia in Illinois; its unquestioning personal allegiance to Smith alarmed non-Mormons.

Nauvoo

They settled in Nauvoo, Illinois, on the banks of the Mississippi. By 1844, it was the largest city in the state. Because Smith could deliver the votes of Nauvoo as a bloc, the Democrats and Whigs both vied for his favor. The legislature authorized him to organize the Nauvoo Legion. Officially, it was a unit of the state militia; in fact, it was Joseph Smith's private army and was half the size of the United States army.

Again, however, Smith's sexual appetites nearly destroyed him. He continued to contract plural marriages with women he found attractive; it was easy enough to send their husbands out of town on errands and at least one devoted Mormon willingly married his teenage daughter to the "Prophet, Seer, and Revelator." Smith's wife, however, did not buy his plural marriage revelation and chased two of his wives down the street with a broom, which encouraged gossip. When an unwilling bride and her husband exposed Smith, a crowd of angry Mormons gathered outside his home. Smith denied he had committed adultery and denounced polygamy as a sin. A good many Mormons were unconvinced of his sincerity and left Nauvoo. But most remained.

Their collective wealth (few were rich individually), their undisguised dislike of outsiders, and fear of the Nauvoo Legion had already aroused local gentiles when Smith let his power obliterate what little good judgment he possessed. In sermons reported in newspapers which anyone could read, he said such things as "I will consecrate the riches of the gentiles unto my people which are the House of Israel." Then, in 1844, he declared that he was a candidate for the presidency of the United States. This inexplicably foolish decision put an end to his ability to play the state's Whigs and Democrats against one another. When he sent a mob to destroy the office of a hostile newspaper, he was arrested and jailed in nearby Carthage. With the collusion of state militia assigned to guard him, he was murdered.

Utah: The Mormon Zion

Internal dissension might have split the Mormons into a number of small sects but for the emergence of Brigham Young, a leader as singular as Smith but, fortuitously, quite different. Smith was tall and good-looking; Young was short, stout, and homely. Where Smith occasionally hinted that he looked on his religion as a scam, Young was a true believer. Most important, Smith's brain swirled constantly with nebulae; Brigham Young was a hard-headed and calculating realist. As head of the church for fourteen years, Smith had more than 100 divine revelations; in thirty-three years as his successor, Brigham Young had 1 and it had nothing to do with religion. It concerned the logistics of removing the Mormons from the United States to the Great Salt Lake Basin, then, nominally, in Mexican territory.

Young chose the desolate alkaline desert precisely because it was so forbidding a place that "no other well-informed people can covet its possession." There, thanks to Mormon industriousness, Young supervised the construction of Salt Lake City's broad avenues and blooming gardens, nourished by irrigation ditches that brought water from the Wasatch Mountains. Within a few years more than 10,000 people lived in what is now northern Utah. Mormon missionaries provided a constant influx of converts, especially from Britain and Scandinavia.

The Latter-Day Saints did not, however, escape from the United States. Even while Salt Lake City was being surveyed, the American victory in the Mexican War brought the Mormon Zion into the United States. But Young handled threats from the federal government, including military intervention, with a shrewdness of which Joseph Smith would not have been capable. Later, when President Abraham Lincoln was asked why he did not assert more federal authority in Utah, he recalled how, when clearing land, settlers ran across a log that was too hard to split, too wet to burn, and too heavy to move, they plowed around it.

Oneida

John Humphrey Noyes was a theology student in 1831 when he was converted at a revival. A few years later, he broke with mainstream evangelicalism almost as radically as Joseph Smith did. That is, most evangelicals believed that they were preparing for the millennium, the second coming of Christ. Noyes was a "post-millennialist." He said that the millennium had come and gone in A.D. 70 Therefore, it was possible—indeed, it was a Christian's right and duty—to approximate on earth what life was like for those already in heaven. There was no sin in heaven so Noyes proclaimed that he was sinless—perfect—and that everyone could be. He attracted some followers—few if any preachers of the day failed to attract some followers—whom Noyes called "perfectionists."

Like the Shakers, a religious sect that had founded about twenty utopian communities from Maine to Kentucky, the perfectionists withdrew to a farm on the outskirts of Putney, Vermont, where, as in heaven, there was no private property. Everything was owned in common; everyone shared equally in the labor of maintaining the place. Newcomers were welcome, but they were carefully screened to keep out freeloaders.

Where the Shakers resolved the problems of marriage and sex by forbidding both—everyone was celibate—Noyes determined that there was no monogamous marriage, itself a form of exploitation, in heaven. At Putney, all men were married to all women. If a man and woman chose to have sexual relations for pleasure, they were free to do so. Noyes called this "complex marriage."

When Noyes was arrested for adultery, he and his followers moved to Oneida, New York. Like the Shakers (and unlike other utopians), the perfectionists prospered. They manufactured an improved trap for fur trappers; when the fur trade declined, they turned to making silverware. Oneida's

American Utopias

Poets Samuel Taylor Coleridge and Johann Wolfgang von Goethe both considered emigrating to the United States to live in one of the many utopian communities that bloomed during the early nineteenth century. Robert Owen, a Scottish manufacturer famous for his concern for the welfare of his employees, founded New Harmony in Indiana in 1825. Owen believed that private property and acquisitiveness were at the root of social ills, a view other utopians shared. If property were held in common, life need not consist of drudgery but be morally and intellectually fulfilling. Unfortunately, New Harmony attracted too many parasites who avoided doing their share of the labor. Believing deeply in the goodness of human nature, Owen was incapable of throwing the freeloaders out. In 1827, somewhat poorer, he returned to Scotland.

Another star-crossed utopia was Fruitlands in Massachusetts. It was the brainstorm of Bronson Alcott, best-known today as the father of the author Louisa May Alcott. He, like many other intellectuals, did not cope well with workaday life. He inaugurated Fruitlands by planting several apple tree seedlings within a few feet of the front door, dropped his shovel, and returned to his meditations, ramblings, and long conversations with everyone he met.

Brook Farm in Massachusetts was founded by some of the less productive members of New England's literary elite. Like several other utopias, Brook Farm was based on the speculations of a French writer, Charles Fourier, but stopped short of adopting Fourier's kinky sexual prescriptions. (He approved of all sexual practices, including homosexuality and sado-masochism, which he called "amorous mania.")

The most successful utopians were the Shakers who had about twenty tidy and prosperous communities going by the 1830s. Shakers were celibate; they believed that there was no need to perpetuate the human race by the disgusting means required. Men and women lived separately, coming together for meals, conversation, and religious services that included dancing (in men's lines and women's lines, not in couples). Their gyrations when they danced were the source of the name "Shakers."

Unlike other utopians, the Shakers were popular. Celibacy was peculiar, but it offended no one. Unlike the Mormons, the Shakers were hospitable to outsiders. And they performed a valuable social service. They took in and raised orphaned children, giving them the choice when they reached adulthood to remain as a Shaker or to return to "the world."

population rose to 300 people who, thanks to Noyes's watchful eye, were industrious and productive. Again, however, the Oneida community's neighbors were outraged by its sexual practices. Noyes was tipped off that he was going to be arrested for statutory rape. He fled to Canada and, chastened by his humiliation—he was an old man—he instructed the perfectionists to abandon complex marriage. They did so and, in 1881, divided up the real estate at Oneida into private homes and reorganized the profitable silverware business as a corporation in which the former communists (a name they themselves used) held stock.

Spiritualism

Margaret Fox, age 15 in 1848, and her sister Kate, 12, were "strange" girls (although that word may not have been employed loosely in their home town of Hydesville, New York, in the heart of the burned-over district). They told neighbors that they were communicating with the ghost of a man who had been murdered and buried in the house in which they were living.

For a fee, they began to host séances for people who wanted to contact dead relatives. In a darkened room, clients asked yes-or-no questions which were answered by eerie rappings, one rap for yes, two for no. When anxious men and women from miles around began coming to Hydesville, the Fox girls became famous, interviewed and written up by newspaper reporters. In 1851, they moved to New York City where the eccentric editor, Horace Greeley, endorsed them and provided lodgings. Their popularity was apparently unabated when a medical school in Buffalo declared that one or both of the girls had trick knees or ankles and created the rappings by dislocating them. Instead, their séances became more elaborate with levitating tables and messages from the dead written on slates.

Mediums—mediating between the living and the dead—popped up all over the country. After the Civil War, with so many parents and wives mourning dead sons and husbands, spiritualism was organized as a church with regular services. In 1888, Margaret Fox told the New York *World* that the whole thing was a fraud, that the sisters had indeed made the rapping sounds by snapping abnormal joints in their legs. She almost immediately recanted, saying that she had lied to the *World* to earn a $1,500 fee. The spiritualists refused to repudiate the Fox sisters and maintain their graves to this day at a town in southwestern New York where one must be a spiritualist in order to reside.

EVANGELICAL REFORM

The evangelicals' war against sin was fought in society as well as within souls. The era of the Second Great Awakening was not only a time of increased church going and new religious denominations, but also America's first great era of social reform. Reform societies proliferated as rapidly as religions.

Some evangelical reformers called on society to reform itself. Others mobilized the fortunate to attend to the needs of the disabled, the misguided, and the oppressed. Thomas Gallaudet, for example, was troubled by Americans' indifference to the deaf. Deafness was not simply a personal misfortune, he said; the unique isolation the deaf suffered was a social evil to be remedied. Gallaudet was disgusted when he learned that some Britons who had developed techniques for teaching lipreading and sign language to the deaf viewed their knowledge as a means of making money to be guarded as a trade secret. He pieced together his own method and, in 1817, founded the American Asylum, a free school for the deaf in Hartford, Connecticut. Gallaudet shared his techniques with anyone interested in doing the same work.

Samuel Gridley Howe dramatized his success in educating the severely disabled by touring the country with a girl, Laura Bridgman, who was both deaf and blind. Howe had established communication with her, laying to rest the universal assumption that nothing could be done for such people but to see that they were fed.

Prisons

Prisons attracted evangelicals because its residents were, by definition, sinners to be saved. Penitentiaries and long prison terms were fairly new institutions in the early 1800s. Previously, the most serious crimes were punished by hanging; there were as many as sixteen capital offenses in some

The whipping post at New Castle, Delaware. Corporal punishments of offenders, including executions, were public in most states during the antebellum period. Delaware was the last state—by many decades—to employ the whipping post. Wife beaters were flogged as late as the 1950s, although not in public.

North Wind Picture Archives

states. Other felonies merited a flogging or physical mutilation. Thomas Jefferson advocated the castration of rapists and homosexuals, and boring a half-inch hole through the noses of lesbians. In Massachusetts until 1805, counterfeiters, arsonists, and wife beaters were whipped and had their ears cropped or their cheeks branded with a hot iron so that they could be identified at sight.

Influenced by an Italian criminologist, Cesare Beccaria, most states reduced the number of capital offenses, abolished mutilation as a punishment, and reduced the use of whipping. They turned to prison terms to punish criminals and to protect society from them. Conditions of confinement were execrable. Connecticut's state prison was an abandoned mine shaft.

Evangelicals introduced the idea of the prison as a correctional institution, a place for moral and social rehabilitation as well as for punishment. Theories as to how best to reform convicts varied. The "Pennsylvania System" kept every prisoner in solitary confinement day and night except when a minister came to call. The idea was that, with this guidance and plenty of time on their hands, inmates would meditate on their sins, pray, and leave the prison saved. The flaws in the Pennsylvania System were apparent immediately: Individual cells, no matter how tiny, with guards delivering meals, were extremely expensive. And total isolation resulted in a lot of mental breakdowns. The "Auburn System," evolved in New York, addressed these problems by marching prisoners to workrooms and the dining hall several times a day. Conversation was forbidden, not for evangelical reasons but to ensure order.

Dorothea Dix

The severely insane were housed in prisons separate from convicts but with dangerous lunatics bunched together with harmless idiots. In 1841, Dorothea Dix, a Massachusetts schoolteacher, visited the Cambridge House of Correction where the room for the insane was unheated even in the New England winter. At the age of 39, Dix's shy and retiring personality was transformed by the experience. From living the sheltered life of a middle-class spinster, she became an aggressive and eloquent reformer.

In 1843, Dix scolded the Massachusetts legislature for housing the helpless insane "in *cages, closets, cellars, stalls, pens!*" where they were "*chained, naked, beaten with rods, and lashed* into obedience." Her revelations of the state's sin, for that is how she viewed it, spurred the legislators to immediate action. They constructed a state asylum where the insane were cared for physically and morally. Dix then carried her message throughout the nation. She persuaded Congress to establish St. Elizabeth's Hospital for the Insane in Washington and fifteen states to build humane asylums.

Blue Hawai'i

The most far-reaching evangelical project was the mission to rescue the people of the Hawai'ian islands, almost halfway around the world. Hawai'i was unknown to the outside world until 1778. Once discovered, the islands became an irresistible attraction to New England whalers. They needed up to two years to fill their holds with whale oil, and they had hunted out the Atlantic. Without Hawai'i, there would have been no whaling in the Pacific because the islands sit quite alone in the middle of the ocean far from any other landmass. There alone could whalers refit their battered vessels, recover their health, take on provisions, and hire "Kanakas" (as Hawai'ians were called) to replace crewmen who had died.

Hawai'i's isolation also meant that the native Polynesians lacked immunities to virtually every infectious disease known in America and Europe. Between 1778 and 1804, the population of the islands was halved, from about 300,000 to 150,000. Hawai'ian culture was devastated by the demographic disaster, the introduction of western goods which were traded for the provisions, and alcohol and the other debaucheries introduced by the whalers.

Missionaries

In 1819, a young Hawai'ian who worked his way to New England aboard a whaling ship told the students of Andover Theological Seminary of the harm done to his homeland by Americans. The evangelical students were galvanized by the opportunity to set right the sins of their own countrymen. The next year, well financed by willing contributors, several newly ordained ministers and their wives and sisters shipped out to the islands. Their letters home, widely published in newspapers, encouraged others to follow by the dozens each year.

Like John Eliot, "the Apostle to the Indians," two centuries earlier, many missionaries failed to distinguish between religious essentials and morally neutral customs. They insisted that Hawai'ians adopt proper New England clothing and manners as well as the gospel. The best known example of their tunnel vision was their insistence that Christian Hawai'ian girls cover their breasts and legs in full-length "Mother Hubbard" dresses that were ill-suited to Hawai'i's warm, humid climate.

On balance, however, the evangelical missions were beneficial to the native population. The missionaries, a large majority of them women, fought against the depredations of visiting seamen and founded hospitals and schools. As early as 1830, missionary schools enrolled 52,000 Hawai'ians, 40 percent of the population. In addition to proper religion, they taught other subjects in the Hawai'ian language, which a missionary put into writing.

Demon Rum

Americans were heavy drinkers. Per capita consumption of alcohol peaked in the 1820s at more than 7.5 gallons of alcohol a year for each American man, woman, and child. And, compared to today, little of it was ingested in beer, ale, and wine. Rum was an everyday beverage in New England. Elsewhere, the daily tonic was whiskey.

Drunkenness was considered sinful, of course. But there was more. Even before 1800, Dr. Benjamin Rush of Philadelphia described the physically destructive effects of excessive drinking.

Secular Sensations

Americans who were not evangelicals tended to look on religious enthusiasm with scorn or amusement. Unitarians, Episcopalians, many Presbyterians, Congregationalists, and those who attended no church were put off by theatrical preaching and busybodies attempting to bring everyone to their truth. And yet, many of the nation's most stolid citizens had great awakenings of their own during the 1830s and 1840s. Their enthusiasms, however, were for new ideas that were (so they believed) scientific.

Hydropathy—the "water cure"—was one such mania. The belief that certain mineral springs—usually hot springs—had curative properties was ancient. The nineteenth-century twist on "taking the waters" originated during the 1820s when an Austrian, Vincent Priessnitz of Grefenburg, observed a deer heal a bullet wound quickly by bathing in a spring-fed pool in the forest. When Priessnitz broke his own rib, he bound the injury with cold wet compresses and had the same results.

News of his success got around and, after an ailing countess visited Grefenburg and was cured, the news got around in the right circles. In 1839 Priessnitz hosted 1,700 paying patients in a hotel he had built. He boasted that among his clients were an archduchess and a hundred odd countesses and barons. Already accustomed to vacationing with their own kind at ancient hot springs like the original Spa (Belgium), Vichy (France), Marienburg (Czech Republic), and Bath (England), European nobles saw to it that Priessnitz's hydropathic treatments be added to the amenities there. Priessnitz made no claims for the unique qualities of the water he used, and he was a cold water man. His scientific explanation of hydrotherapy was that pure water applied to the body was exchanged in the bloodstream for the impure water than was causing the illness or pain. It could be done anywhere.

A few American spas—Saratoga Springs, New York; White Sulphur Springs, Virginia (now West Virginia); and Warm Springs, Georgia—added hydrotherapy clinics. However, visiting such places was too expensive for all but the wealthy. So, disciples of Priessnitz opened clinics in cities for the commuter trade and "economy" hydropathy hotels in converted farmhouses. Guests chose among the "rubbing wet sheet bath," a "sponge bath," an "affusion bath," a "plunge bath," a "wave bath," a "half bath," a "nasal bath," or to stand under a stream of water an inch in diameter dropped on them from ten to twenty feet above them. There were no race tracks at the hardcore hydropathy resorts, no casinos, ballrooms, broad verandahs, no French chefs. Indeed, photographs of them show buildings and grounds so dismal that (unless the water cure actually worked!) patrons must have departed in a profound depression.

Far more popular than hydropathy was phrenology, "the only true science of the mind." A German, Franz Josef Gall, hatched his theory in his imagination, but he explained it in scientific terms: mental processes were material, not spiritual phenomena; the mind was not unitary but made up of thirty-seven "brain organs", such as benevolence, amativeness, combativeness, cautiousness, destructiveness. Because the shape of the brain determined the shape of the cranium, an individual's character and potential could be determined by touch, a phrenologist feeling the skull—"bumps" in the skull—and determining which, in each individual, were well developed.

Gall and an associate, Johann Gaspar Spurzheim, toured Europe, lecturing and, for a modest fee, fondling skulls. They had a falling out when Spurzheim, obviously the better marketer, wanted to play down their negative findings and even eliminate other bump sites from the phrenological chart (such as "likelihood to commit murder"). Spurzheim came to the United States but died soon after arriving. Two brothers, Orson Fowler and Lorenzo Fowler, picked up the fallen standard and opened an office in New York City where a walk-in could, for $3, buy a lengthy handwritten analysis of his character and talents or, for a dollar, get a quickie—an oral report.

The Fowlers were tireless propagandists. Their publications covered most of the bases: mesmerism, hydropathy, and temperance as well as phrenology. Their *American Phrenological Journal* was published for seventy-three years. They lectured endlessly and profitably: a twenty-lecture course in Philadelphia for a class of 500; forty lectures in Boston for audiences of up to 3,000. They knew how to please a crowd. Lorenzo inaugurated his lectures in Boston by exclaiming "my eyes never rested on such a collection of excellent brains . . . big headed, moral, intellectual and energetic."

Flattery got them everywhere. Among the tens of thousands of ordinary Americans they phrenologized were Supreme Court Justice Joseph Story, dozens of senators, President John Tyler, and future presidents U.S. Grant and James Garfield; celebrated ministers Lyman Beecher and Henry Ward Beecher; banker Nicholas Biddle (an early convert); educator Horace Mann (a fanatical disciple); feminist Susan B. Anthony; the father of Mormonism, Joseph Smith Jr. (who published his report); and the then unknown but soon to be notorious John Brown.

Editor Horace Greeley wrote in the New York *Tribune* that railroad companies could cut down on accidents if would-be locomotive engineers were phrenologized before they were hired. Many an ambitious young man included a phrenologist's report in his job applications.

Not everyone was carried away by the mania. At the height of the craze, John Quincy Adams wondered how two phrenologists could look one another in the face without bursting into laughter. The popularity of phrenology declined after the Civil War—or rather, evolved into sideshow entertainment—not because it was refuted scientifically. It never had a scientific basis. It died because, as with religious enthusiasms, the novelty wore off.

With the blossoming of the evangelical spirit, anti-alcohol reformers added two more arrows to the quiver.

First, they published statistics showing that a substantial number of crimes were committed by people who were drunk. Second, they drew a connection between poverty and drinking. Some said that the miseries of poverty led to drunkenness. Others believed that drink was a major cause of poverty.

In either case, it was an evil to be attacked. By 1835, there were 5,000 temperance societies in the United States with a membership of more than a million. In 1840, six reformed sots founded a national organization, the Washington Temperance Society. Two years later, a more militant association, the Sons of Temperance, began to promote sobriety as a basic religious duty. One of the Sons' most effective lecturers was John B. Gough, an ex-drunk who rallied audiences with the lurid language of the camp meeting revivalist: "Crawl from the slimy ooze, ye drowned drunkards, and with suffocation's blue and livid lips speak out against the drink."

The Granger Collection, New York

Temperance society propaganda: a reformed drunkard, impoverished, no doubt, because of "demon rum," commits himself to abstinence while his wife thanks God for the grace that made his conversion possible. Middle-class women were the backbone of evangelical reform movements. The one reform for which poor women could be grateful was temperance for they and their children were the chief victims of drunken husbands.

The Pledge

Temperance was an evangelical Protestant movement, but not exclusively. In 1840, an Irish priest, Theobald Mathew of the Teetotal Abstinence Society, toured the United States and administered "The Pledge" to, he claimed, half a million Irish Catholics. The "pledge" was never to touch another drop of liquor. It is not known how many kept their promises. It is, however, safe to say that Father Mathew's campaign did not perceptibly alter the popular stereotype of Irish Americans as hard drinkers.

Prohibition

Temperance reformers quarreled and parted ways as promiscuously as drunks and churches did. One cleavage ran between advocates of moderation in the use of alcohol and complete abstainers. The former argued that drunkenness was the evil, not alcohol itself. They saw no harm in the occasional sip of wine or restorative dram. The abstainers, observing that alcohol was addictive, concluded that it was inherently sinful. Moderation was asking for trouble. It was necessary to swear off drink "Tee-totally."

The teetotalers divided between "moral suasionists" who said abstinence was an individual responsibility and "legal suasionists" who called for the prohibition of the manufacture and sale of liquor. People would be *prevented* from sinning. In 1838, Massachusetts experimented with a law designed to reduce alcohol consumption among the poor, who were its most obvious victims. The "Fifteen Gallon Law" prohibited the sale of whiskey or rum in quantities smaller than fifteen gallons. The democratic temper of age ran against any law privileging the rich. The Fifteen Gallon Law was repealed within two years.

In 1845, New York state enacted an emphatically democratic anti-liquor law. It authorized local governments to forbid the sale of alcohol within their jurisdictions. Within a few years, five-sixths of the state was "dry." In 1846, the state of Maine, led by Neal Dow, a Portland businessman, adopted the first statewide prohibition law. By 1860, thirteen states had followed suit. But alcohol was too ingrained in the culture to be abolished by ordinance. Prohibition laws were flagrantly violated and, by 1868, they were repealed in every state but Maine.

A Woman's World

More women than men experienced evangelical conversions. Women were a majority of church members in the evangelical denominations (and others too). Evangelical women were the backbone of the temperance movement. The sisters and wives of the New England ministers who went to Hawai'i outnumbered the male missionaries and were the secret of their success.

The prominence of New England women in evangelical reform movements owes in part to the fact that there was a surplus of women in the Northeast. Opportunities out west drained away so many unmarried young men that, great as the pressure on young women to marry and have children was, there were simply not enough husbands to go around. In Catholic countries, single women became nuns. In New England, a good many single women channeled their energies into church work and reform.

Many women who were devoting their lives to the improvement of others sooner or later paused to reflect on and discuss the disabilities society imposed on them because they were female. They were the workhorses of every reform movement but, with a few remarkable exceptions like Dorothea Dix, they were subject to men within reform societies. In 1839, they organized the American Female Moral Reform Society so that, in at least one organization, women would make policy. The next year, several women who were to become the founding mothers of American feminism were set on that path when, having accompanied their husbands to an international antislavery conference in London, they were denied admission because of their sex.

Seneca Falls

In the summer of 1848, a small group of women (and a few men) called for a convention at Seneca Falls, New York, to consider a "Declaration of Sentiments and Resolutions" they had drafted. It was a deadly serious parody of the Declaration of Independence:

> When in the course of human events it becomes necessary for one portion of the family of man to assume among the people of the earth a position different from that which they have hitherto occupied, but one to which the laws of nature and nature's God entitle them, a decent respect to the opinions of mankind requires that they should declare the causes that impel them to such a course. . . .

The injustices suffered by women that they listed included the denial of the right to vote even when it was extended to "the most ignorant and degraded men"; the forfeiture by a married woman of control over her own property; a husband's considerable authority over his wife, which "made her, morally, an irresponsible being"; and the exclusion of women from the professions and other gainful employment. The organizers of the Seneca Falls convention and those who attended were Quakers or members of evangelical churches. Most were already active in other reform movements.

The Declaration was signed by only sixty-eight women and thirty-two men. However, in questioning almost universally held assumptions about women's place in society, the convention was discussed avidly in newspapers. Lucretia Coffin Mott and Elizabeth Cady Stanton, two of the organizers, continued to play an important part in the fight for women's rights for a generation. Among the attendees was Amelia Jenks Bloomer, a temperance reformer who was soon famous as the advocate of a new kind of dress for women that bore her name.

Evangelical reformers were generally (but not unanimously) sympathetic to the cause of women's rights. However, they almost unanimously urged feminists like Mott, Stanton, and Susan B. Anthony, a Quaker schoolteacher who soon became Stanton's lifelong collaborator, to defer their campaign until the most important evangelical reform had succeeded. This was the abolition of slavery, a cause entering its final phase when the Seneca Falls convention was called.

"I do not see how anyone can pretend that there is the same urgency," the African American abolitionist Frederick Douglass, said, "in giving the ballot to the woman as freedom to the Negro." Stanton, Mott, and Anthony, who had been abolitionists before they were feminists, reluctantly agreed.

THE ABOLITIONISTS

The first abolitionists were Quakers. Anthony Benezet of Philadelphia, a teacher of African American children, condemned slavery as evil around 1750. About the same time, John Woolman of New Jersey told his Meeting that those Friends who owned slaves were sinning. Woolman made a career of visiting Quaker Meetings throughout Pennsylvania and the upper South with the same message. He admonished the slave-owning Quakers who put him up to free their slaves at once. A Philadelphia Quaker, Isaac Harris (after a solid Quaker antislavery vote had been the key to abolishing slavery in Pennsylvania) assisted runaway slaves from Maryland and Virginia in winning permanent freedom in court. By 1800, few if any Quakers in good standing still owned slaves.

Gentle Persuaders

Benezet and Woolman were concerned almost exclusively with fellow Quakers. When Isaac Harris could not win a fugitive slave's freedom legally, he took them to Quaker farmers outside Philadelphia to conceal them. The Quakers were emphatically not evangelical. They did not attempt to convert others to their faith. A runaway slave who, for more than a year, fled from one Quaker household to another, marveled that no one said a word to him about joining the Society of Friends. Only after they observed and were influenced by the crusading activism of evangelical abolitionists did Quakers cooperate and even take the lead on the movement to end slavery throughout the United States.

Benjamin Lundy was a key figure in the transformation. A Quaker born in New Jersey, he was inspired to devote his life to fighting slavery after witnessing outside his workshop in the South the ugliest face of the institution, the business of buying and selling slaves. He described "droves of a dozen to twenty ragged men, chained together and driven through the streets, bareheaded and barefooted, through mud and snow, by the remorseless sellers with horsewhips and bludgeons in their hands."

Lundy founded one of the first abolitionist organizations in Baltimore in 1815 and, in 1821, began publishing one of the first abolitionist newspapers, *The Genius of Emancipation*. He carried his message personally through Ohio, Pennsylvania, Kentucky, Virginia, and Maryland—walking! On one trip, he covered 700 miles. His life was threatened in Kentucky and he was beaten senseless on the streets of Baltimore.

But he retained his Quaker belief in nonviolence and brotherly love. He aimed at persuading slave owners of their erring ways, not vilifying them as personally evil. When, during one of his absences, a young man he had taken on at *The Genius of Emancipation*, William Lloyd Garrison, wrote and published an intemperate article, Lundy suggested that Garrison resign.

Lundy also differed from evangelical militants like Garrison in his belief that abolitionists had to concern themselves with the fact that the immediate abolition of slavery in a state would result in serious economic and social problems. For this reason, he advocated gradual emancipation programs such as those that had worked so well in Pennsylvania and New Jersey. Quite aware of the racism of most white people, he looked for places to which emancipated blacks could move. He twice went to Haiti and once to Mexico looking for such a refuge.

Garrison on the Constitution

William Lloyd Garrison's opinion of the Constitution was less than patriotic. He called it "a covenant with death and an agreement with hell" because it sanctioned slavery.

Garrison did not hesitate to oversimplify and overstate in the cause. "A sacred compact, forsooth!" he wrote in *The Liberator,* "We pronounce it the most heaven-daring arrangement ever made for the continuance and protection of a system of the most atrocious villainy ever exhibited on earth."

David Walker's *Appeal*

Antislavery Unitarians and Univeralists were also inclined to be moderate and conciliatory. William Ellery Channing told southerners, "We consider slavery your calamity and not your curse."

Not so the evangelicals. To them, slavery was the most horrid of sins and slaveowners were sinners. It was a simple as that. Slavery must, like all sins, be ended. Those who continued to sin and those who defended them were enemies to be battled and vanquished. The economic disruption and interracial violence likely to follow emancipation were regrettable, but slavery and slave owners were responsible for what happened, not abolitionists.

By the late 1820s, evangelical abolitionism was a national phenomenon of which anyone who read a newspaper was aware. In 1829, an African American cloth dealer in Boston, David Walker, published a pamphlet called *The Appeal.* Walker reviewed the arguments about the immorality and injustice of slavery and described instances of cruelty slaves suffered. Walker then concluded that if whites did not abolish slavery, black people had a moral right—a moral duty—to rise up and destroy slavery violently. Walker was an evangelical; he backed up almost every point he made, including his call for violence, with quotations from the Bible.

William Lloyd Garrison

William Lloyd Garrison, who moved to Boston after leaving Lundy, rejected Walker's call to arms. Among the many evangelical causes Garrison advocated (just about all of them), he was a pacifist. He had no trouble, however, with Walker's sometimes intemperate language. Indeed, in *The Liberator,* the antislavery newspaper Garrison founded in 1831, his rhetoric was incendiary and personal as often as not. In the first issue of the paper, Garrison wrote:

> I am aware that many object to the severity of my language; but is there not cause for severity? I will be as harsh as truth, and as uncompromising as justice. On this subject I do not wish to think, or speak, or write, with moderation. No! No! Tell a man whose house is on fire to give a moderate alarm; tell him to moderately rescue his wife from the hands of the ravisher; tell the mother to gradually extricate her babe from the fire into which it has fallen;—but urge me not to use moderation in a cause like the present.

Garrison described the slave-owner's life as "one of unbridled lust, of filthy amalgamation, of swaggering braggadocio, of haughty domination, of cowardly ruffianism, of

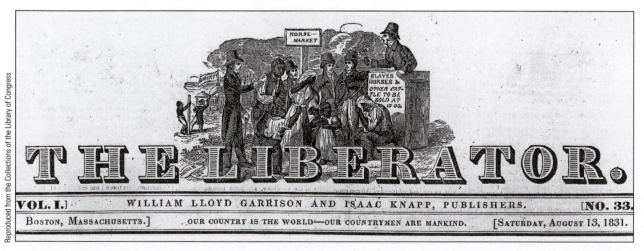

Reproduced from the Collections of the Library of Congress

The masthead of William Lloyd Garrison's The Liberator *when it first appeared in 1831. It was a weekly and the most uncompromising of the many abolitionist newspapers. Garrison's writings were often intemperate, for which he made no apologies: slavery was sinful; God had not admonished Christians to be well mannered in confronting sin. Many abolitionists disapproved of Garrison's rhetoric, but* The Liberator *had many readers, perhaps in part because Garrison published sensational accounts of cruelty to slaves that others considered indelicate.*

boundless dissipation, of matchless insolence, of infinite self-conceit, of unequaled oppression, of more than savage cruelty."

Garrison was never a "popular" man. Even in Boston, a center of antislavery sentiment, he was hooted and pelted with stones when he spoke in public. On one occasion, a mob threw a noose around his neck and dragged him through the streets. They might have hanged him had a group of abolitionist women not stunned the mob by wading into it and rescuing him. (Garrison was also a supporter of women's rights.)

Orators, Financiers, and Politicians

In 1833, with Garrison the prime mover, the American Anti-Slavery Society was organized. Its statement of purpose reflected Garrison's radicalism. However, abolitionists who differed from Garrison on one issue or another flocked to it. By 1835, there were more than 600 local chapters, by 1838 more than 1,300 and 250,000 members.

The Society funded speaking tours by dozens of abolitionists. Among the most popular was Wendell Phillips who, like Garrison, cursed the Constitution because it sanctioned slavery. A well-to-do Boston lawyer, Phillips forbade sugar and cotton clothing in his home because they were made from crops grown by slave labor.

An even more eloquent speaker than Phillips was Theodore Dwight Weld, "as eloquent as an angel and as powerful as thunder." He was equally persuasive in person. Weld convinced two brothers, wealthy merchants Arthur and Lewis Tappan, to devote large chunks of their fortunes to the Anti-Slavery Society; Kenyon and Oberlin, abolitionist colleges in Ohio; and the "Underground Railroad," an informal series of networks that aided runaway slaves.

Weld was also influential in making an antislavery activist of James G. Birney who had destroyed a promising political career in both Kentucky and Alabama by proposing legislation that regulated the buying and selling of slaves, perhaps to lay groundwork for eventual abolition. Birney came from a family that had not been entirely comfortable owning slaves. (An aunt insisted on paying wages to hers.) But, Birney included, they did not manumit them, classic exemplars of slave owners who, whatever their moral principles, understood what made them rich. In 1840 and 1844, Birney ran for president as the candidate of the abolitionist Liberty party. It was a bust; Birney won only 2 to 3 percent of the popular vote.

Weld's wife, Angelina Grimké, and her sister Sarah also lectured against slavery. They too were southerners, from a distinguished, wealthy, and slave-owning South Carolina family. They had fled the state in fear of their lives because of their abolitionist views.

Black Abolitionists

The abolitionist movement owed a great deal to Garrison, Weld, and the Tappans. Its indispensable rank-and-file, however, was the free black community of the North. Although all but a few were poor, African Americans contributed a disproportionate part of the money that financed antislavery newspapers and sent antislavery lecturers on their tours.

Several prominent abolitionists were black. Sojourner Truth was the name adopted by Isabella Van Wagenen, a physical giant of a woman born a slave in New York in 1797. Freed in 1827, she worked as a domestic servant, was briefly a Millerite, then burst on the abolitionist scene as a popular orator. She was illiterate to the end—she died in 1893, age 96, but she transfixed audiences by accompanying her speeches with songs she had herself composed.

The most distinguished African American abolitionist was Frederick Douglass. Born a slave in Maryland, he escaped to Massachusetts, educated himself, and, in 1845, wrote his autobiography. As an indictment of slavery it was more effective than Garrison's journalism because Douglass had experienced slavery firsthand. When his book made him famous, his former master set out to re-enslave him and Douglass fled to England. There, he furthered his education

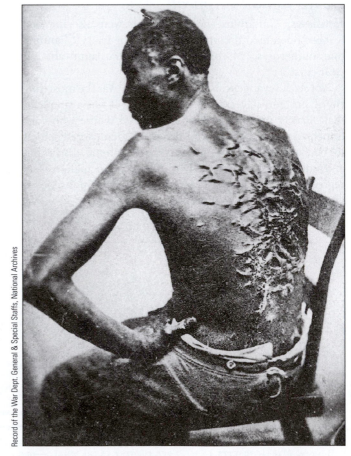

Record of the War Dept. General & Special Staffs, National Archives

Southerners (and many northerners) accused abolitionists of inventing horrifying stories about the abuse of slaves. In fact, they did not have to resort to imagined cruelties. They proved it by taking men who had been viciously whipped on speaking tours or, if the victim was a fugitive, photographs like this one.

and earned enough money from writing and lecturing to pay his old master off.

Mrs. Stowe and Uncle Tom

The single most effective abolitionist propaganda was a novel of 1852, *Uncle Tom's Cabin, or Life among the Lowly,* written by Harriet Beecher Stowe, a member of a distinguished family. Not only did Stowe's book sell an astonishing 300,000 copies within a year of publication (the equivalent of more than 3 million books today), but it was adapted into plays performed by professional and amateur troupes in small towns and cities alike. So influential was Mrs. Stowe's tale of Uncle Tom, a submissive and loyal old slave, that when Abraham Lincoln met her during the Civil War, he remarked, "So you are the little woman who wrote the book that made this great war."

The underlying theme of *Uncle Tom's Cabin* was that no matter how well intentioned an individual slave owner was, he cannot help but do wrong by living with an inherently evil institution. Uncle Tom's first owner is the epitome of the kind, paternalistic planter. He genuinely loves Uncle Tom. Nevertheless, when financial troubles require him to raise money, he sells Tom. Heartbroken, he promises that, as soon as he is able, he will find Tom and buy him back. The point was: The noblest of white men sells the best of black men when the law allows him to do so.

It was not this insight, however, that made *Uncle Tom's Cabin* so popular. The book owed its success to the lurid cruelties that Tom witnesses and suffers. Mrs. Stowe herself thought that this was the book's contribution. When southerners complained that she had distorted the realities of slave life, she responded in 1853 with *A Key to Uncle Tom's Cabin,* which set out the documentary basis of her allegations in quotations from southern newspapers.

FURTHER READING

Classics Fawn M. Brodie, *No Man Knows My History: The Life of Joseph Smith, the Mormon Prophet,* 1945, 1971.

General Martin E. Marty, *Pilgrims in Their Own Land: 500 Years of Religion in America,* 1984; Jon Butler, *Awash in a Sea of Faith: Christianizing the American People,* 1990; Christine L. Heyrman, *Southern Cross: The Beginnings of the Bible Belt,* 1997; Paul Johnson, *A Shopkeeper's Millennium: Society and Revivals in Rochester, New York, 1815–1837,* 1978; Nathan D. Hatch, *The Democratization of American Christianity,* 1989; Paul Boyer, *When Time Shall Be No More: Prophecy Belief in Modern American Culture,* 1992; Frederic J. Baumgartner, *Longing for the End: A History of Millennialism in Western Civilization,* 1999; Charles Hambrick-Stowe, *Charles Grandison Finney and the Spirit of American Evangelism,* 1996.

Denominations Ann Lee Bressler, *The Universalist Movement in America, 1770–1880,* 2001; Frederick Dreyer, *The Genesis of Methodism,* 1999; David Hempton, *The Religion of the People: Methodism and Popular Religion, 1750–1900,* 1996, and *Methodism: Empire of the Spirit,* 2005; Richard L. Bushman, *Joseph Smith and the Beginnings of Mormonism,* 1984, and *Joseph Smith: Rough Stone Rolling,* 2005; Leonard J. Arrington, *Brigham Young: American Moses,* 1984; John Shipps, *Mormonism: The Story of a New Religious Tradition,* 1985; Will Bagley, *Blood of the Prophets: Brigham Young and the Mountain Meadows Massacre,* 2002.

Reform Stuart M. Blumin, *The Emergence of the Middle Class,* 1989; Lori D. Ginzberg, *Women and the Work of Benevolence: Morality, Politics, and Class in the Nineteenth Century United States,* 1990; Steven Mintz, *Moralists and Modernizers: America's Pre-Civil War Reformers,* 1995; Robert H. Abzug, *Cosmos Crumbling: American Reform and the Religious Imagination,* 1994; Richard J. Cawardine, *Evangelicals and Politics in Ante-Bellum America,* 1993.

Evangelicals at Work Patricia Grimshaw, *Paths of Duty: American Missionary Wives in Nineteenth Century Hawaii,* 1989; Mary Zwiep, *Pilgrim Path: The First Company of Women Missionaries to Hawaii,* 1991; W. G. Rorabaugh, *The Alcoholic Republic: An American Tradition,* 1979; M. E. Lender and J. K. Martin, *Drinking in America: A History,* 1982; Ruth Bordin, *Women and Temperance,* 1981; David J. Rothman, *The Discovery of the Asylum,* 1970; Gerald M. Grob, *The Mad Among Us: A History of the Care of America's Mentally Ill,* 1994; David Gallagher, *Voice for the Mad: The Life of Dorothea Dix,* 1995; Michael Meranze, *Laboratories of Virtue: Punishment, Revolution, and Christianity in Philadelphia, 1760-1835,* 1996.

The Woman's Movement Carl M. Degler, *At Odds: Women and the Family in America from the Revolution to the Present,* 1980; Gerda Lerner, *The Woman in American History,* 1970; William L. O'Neill, *Everyone Was Brave: The Rise and Fall of Feminism in America,* 1970; Mary P. Ryan, *Womanhood in America,* 1975; Eleanor Flexner, *Century of Struggle: The Women's Rights Movement in the United States,* 1975; Lois Banner, *Elizabeth Cady Stanton,* 1980; Alma Lutz, *Susan B. Anthony,* 1979.

Abolitionists Thomas Bender, *The Anti-Slavery Debate,* 1992; Ronald Abzug, *Passionate Liberator: Theodore Dwight Weld and the Dilemma of Reform,* 1980; M. L. Dillon, *The Abolitionists: The Growth of a Dissenting Minority,* 1974; Aileen S. Kraditor, *Means and Ends in American Abolitionism: Garrison and His Critics on Strategy and Tactics,* 1967; Gerda Lerner, *The Grimké Sisters from South Carolina: Rebels against Slavery,* 1967; Benjamin Quarles, *Black Abolitionists,* 1969; J. B. Stewart, *Holy Warriors: The Abolitionists and American Slavery,* 1976; Julie Ray Jeffery, *The Great Silent Army of Abolitionism: Ordinary Women in the Antislavery Movement,* 1998; Shirley Yee, *Black Women Abolitionists: A Study in Activism, 1828–1860,* 1992; Nell Irvin Painter, *Sojourner Truth: A Life, a Symbol,* 1996; Waldo C. Martin, *The Mind of Frederick Douglass,* 1984; William S. McFeely, *Frederick Douglass,* 1990; Henry Mayer, *All on Fire: William Lloyd Garrison and the Abolition of Slavery,* 1998.

Secular Fads Harry B. Weiss and Howard R. Kemble, *The Great American Water-Cure Craze: A History of Hydropathy in the United States,* 1967; John D. Davies, *Phrenology Fad and Science: A 19th Century American Crusade,* 1955; Stephen Tomlinson, *Head Masters: Phrenology, Secular Education, and Nineteenth Century Social Thought,* 2005.

KEY TERMS

Use the following listing of key terms to review important figures, events, locations, and concepts covered in this chapter. A glossary of these terms is available on *The American*

Past companion Web site: www.cengage.com/history/conlin/tap9e

deists, p. 284

Channing, Wiliam Ellery, p. 285

camp meeting, p. 286

burned-over district, p. 288

"Great Disappointment", p. 289

"moral suasionist", p. 295

Stanton, Elizabeth Cady, p. 296

Uncle Tom's Cabin p. 299

ONLINE RESOURCES

Find additional resources, including primary source documents, images, interactive maps, simulations, chapter review exercises, and Internet links at

The American Past **companion Web site**
www.cengage.com/history/conlin/tap9e

American History Resource Center
http://ushistory.wadsworth.com/

Chapter 18

The Peculiar Institution

Southern Slavery

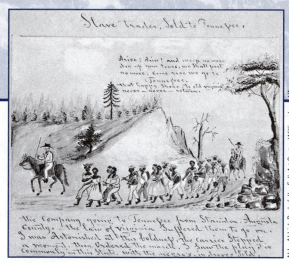

Abby Aldrich Rockefeller Folk Art Center, Williamsburg, VA

Oppression has, at one stroke, deprived the descendants of the Africans of almost all the privileges of humanity. The Negro of the United States has lost all remembrance of his country; the language which his forefathers spoke is never heard around him; he abjured their religion and forgot their customs when he ceased to belong to Africa, without acquiring any European privileges. But he remains halfway between the two communities; sold by the one, repulsed by the other; finding not a spot in the universe to call by the name of country, except the faint image of a home which the shelter of his master's roof affords.

—Alexis de Tocqueville

There were still slaves in New York and New Jersey in 1830, people who had fallen through the cracks of those states' gradual emancipation laws. (There would be a few elderly slaves in New Jersey at the outbreak of the Civil War in 1861.) As a going institution, however, slavery was a sectional institution, the South's "peculiar institution," when the evangelical abolitionists burst on the national scene.

SOUTHERN ANTISLAVERY

The possibility of abolishing slavery was still openly discussed in the states of the upper South—Delaware, Maryland, Virginia, Kentucky. Economically, slave labor was no longer vital to prosperity there; in the eyes of many, it was a drag on the economy, tying up too much capital that would be far more productive if invested elsewhere. Manumissions were not as numerous as they had been. Since 1800, owners of slaves who were costing them money to feed and clothe could sell them profitably "down the river," down the Mississippi, to the booming cotton lands of Louisiana, Mississippi, Alabama, and western Tennessee.

Still, manumissions occasionally made the national news. A former Virginia governor, James Wood, took his slaves to Ohio, freed them, and set them up with small farms. The largest single manumission in American history—of about 300 slaves—occurred as late as 1833 when the famous John Randolph of Roanoke died. He wrote in his will that "I give and bequeath my slaves their freedom, heartily regretting that I have ever been the owner of them." Randolph also provided money so that his former slaves could get a fresh start in a free state.

Numbers and Race

Two great impediments stood in the way of southern whites who favored state emancipation by law: the sheer numbers of African Americans in the south and the virtually universal assumptions among whites that black people were, as a race, intellectually and morally inferior.

It had been no problem, southerners pointed out, for the northern states to abolish slavery. The black population of the North was numerically insignificant. In 1830, there were 125,000 African Americans in the northeastern states with a combined population of 5.54 million; blacks were 2 percent of the whole. In the states of the old Northwest Territory there were 42,000 blacks among 1.6 million people, about the same percentage as back East.

So tiny a minority posed no threat to society. Blacks could be ignored, patronized or disdained, taken on as domestic servants, or shunted aside into their own communities at the

Monrovia (named for James Monroe) was built on a thinly inhabited stretch of coast beginning in 1822. This engraving shows the town about 1847 when Liberia declared its independence of the American Colonization Society, which had managed the affairs of the transplanted African Americans for twenty-five years.

edge of town, which was, indeed, the lot of African Americans in the North.

In the South, however, African Americans were a substantial proportion of the population: 2.16 million in 1830 alongside 3.54 million whites or 38 percent. Slaves were nearly half the population of Virginia, more than half in Louisiana and in South Carolina—90 percent in the coastal districts! Even in Maryland and Kentucky in the upper South, blacks were a quarter of the population.

A South in which so many African Americans were free was unimaginable. It was not just the assumption that African Americans could not successfully hold their own as farmers or in other occupations. It was the fact that struggling white farmers and shopkeepers would not tolerate competition from people whom so many of them had come to despise

Where Is Home?

In 1822, James Forten responded sarcastically to the American Colonization Society's proposal that free blacks like him "return" to Africa: "My great-grandfather was brought to this country a slave from Africa. My grandfather obtained his own freedom. My father never wore the yoke. He rendered valuable service to his country in the war of our Revolution; and I, though then a boy, was a drummer in that war. I have since lived and labored in a useful employment, have acquired property, and have paid taxes. . . . Yet some ingenious gentlemen have recently discovered that I am still an African; that a continent three thousand miles away—and more—from the place where I was born is my native country."

The South Closes Ranks 1800–1857

1800	1805	1810	1815	1820	1825	1830	1835	1840	1845	1850	1855

1800 Gabriel's slave rebellion

1822 Vesey's rebellion

1824 Monrovia founded in Liberia

1831 Turner's rebellion

1832 Virginia Assembly debates future of slavery

1836 Anti-abolitionist "gag rule" in Congress

National antislavery campaign by Liberty party 1840

Minstrel shows and Stephen Foster songs at peak of popularity 1850s

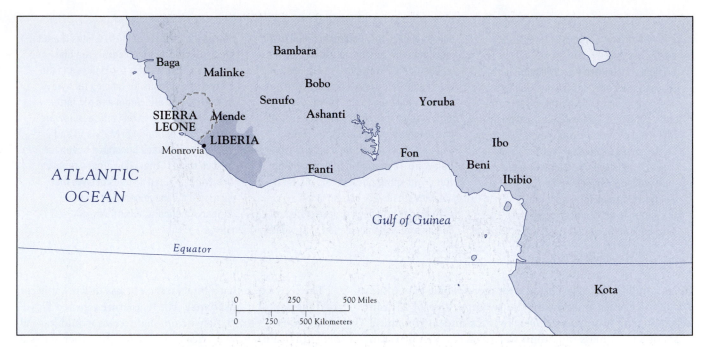

MAP 18:1 **Liberia.** As early as 1787, British abolitionists settled freed West Indian slaves in Sierra Leone. An African American sea captain scouted the coast to the south for a site to which free American blacks might move. In 1822, Monrovia was founded there by the American Colonization Society. In 1847, Liberia, dominated by Americans, declared its independence.

because they associated the African race with slavery, the one degradation poor southern whites were spared. If the slaves were freed, thus losing the protection of their owners, the South would be plunged into chronic racial warfare that could bring the entire society down.

The Colonization Movement

Beginning in the late 1810s, some antislavery southerners hit on "colonization" as the answer to the interrelated problems of black numbers and racist white violence. In 1817, with the endorsement of President Monroe, former President Madison, Chief Justice John Marshall, Henry Clay—all southerners—and many other luminaries, the American Colonization Society was founded. Its object was to raise money to assist free blacks in "returning" to Africa where the society would assist them in creating a viable economy and government. Slave owners were urged to free their slaves on condition they agree go to Africa under the society's auspices. In time—the hope was—the success of colonization in reducing the free Negro population would persuade southern legislatures to emancipate slaves without fear of social chaos.

In 1821, the society financed the emigration of a few free blacks to Sierra Leone, a colony the British had founded on the Guinea coast as a refuge for former West Indian slaves. The next year, with the help of some federal funds, the society purchased a stretch of coast south of Sierra Leone and established Liberia, "land of freedom." In 1824, construction of a capital, named Monrovia after President Monroe, was begun.

Liberia

About 11,000 African Americans emigrated to Liberia. For twenty years, the country functioned as a colony of the American Colonization Society, which appointed the governor and subsidized economic development. In 1847, prominent Liberians—all former Americans—declared the nation's independence.

There were other colonization schemes. Benjamin Lundy had hopes for lightly populated northern Mexico. Lundy and others looked to Haiti, a black nation, as a destination for free African Americans. But the Republic of Mexico took no interest in the proposal and Haiti was crowded, French-speaking, unstable, and governed by dictators. African Americans did not find it attractive as a home.

The fact is: "Colonization" was a pipedream from the start. The black population of the United States was 1.5 million in

The Discoverer of Liberia

Paul Cuffee, an African American, was a master mariner who plied the Atlantic trade routes. During the 1810s, he called at Freetown in Sierra Leone, a British colony created as a home for West Indian blacks who had been freed. Cuffee scouted the coast south of Freetown to locate a site where free American blacks might settle. It is not clear if it was Cuffee who picked the site of Monrovia in Liberia and informed the American Colonization Society. But he was the first American to think of the region as a refuge for African Americans who wanted out of (and who were free to leave) the United States.

The Strange Case of the State of Delaware

Originally, Delaware was William Penn's property, part of Pennsylvania. Quakers were numerous in the northern part of the state. Southern Delaware was settled by Marylanders who brought slaves with them. So there was a geographical dimension to pro- and antislavery sentiments in the state.

Slave labor was never critical to Delaware's small farm economy, even in the south. In 1830, slaves were only 3 percent of the state's population. Several bills to abolish the institution failed in the legislature by very narrow margins. The legislature did, however, enact several laws regulating slave owners not to be found in any other state. It was illegal to import additional slaves into Delaware and to sell slaves out of state. (Both were violated but not on a large scale.) Delaware's congressman and senators voted with other border state moderates, not with proslavery extremists.

Delaware remained a slave state less because its white population approved of the institution than because whites feared being overrun by free blacks. Free blacks were 15 percent of the population and the state was notorious for helping runaways from Maryland and Virginia to get farther north. Whites feared that a free Delaware, with its long border with Maryland and Virginia, would itself become a haven for fugitive slaves. After Nat Turner's rebellion, Delaware enacted a series of laws that restricted the movement of the state's African Americans, all of them, not just slaves.

1820, 2 million in 1830. That was far more people than could survive, let alone prosper, on the swampy strip of African seacoast that was Liberia. The logistics and astronomical costs of such a mass migration were well outside the realm of reason.

Few slave owners manumitted their slaves to the society for colonization. Most of the people who went were free blacks who preferred the risks of West Africa to the harsh discrimination they suffered at home. (Many were northerners.) The 11,000 who actually went to Liberia added up to less than a drop in the bucket, just 7 percent of the South's free black population. There were 37,000 free blacks just in Virginia in 1820.

Few of them were interested in the society's propositions. Unless they or their parents had been born and raised in Africa—and that described few free blacks—they were, simply, not African. They felt no more connection with Liberia than President Monroe felt toward Scotland.

The Last Debate

In December 1831, Governor John Floyd presented the Virginia legislature with a plan for the gradual abolition of slavery in the state. In addition to the northern state formula of permitting slave owners to work adult slaves they already owned long enough to recover their investments, Floyd's scheme proposed to hasten the emancipation process by compensating slave owners for lost investment out of state funds. For three weeks in January 1832, the legislators discussed the plan, for the most part moderately and intelligently.

The morality of slavery played little part in Virginia's debate, but even the staunchest proslavery men were defensive. Typically, they introduced their speeches by regretting the fact that Africans ever been brought to Virginia, and by saying that the state would be a better place if it had been developed by free white labor. However, what had been done was done. In 1832, African Americans constituted well over a third of Virginia's population. That they should all be set free, however gradually, was out of the question. Virginia law already required slaves who were manumitted to move out of state. Colonization was obviously a failure.

The conviction that a biracial society was unworkable carried the day—but just barely. The legislature rejected Floyd's proposal by 73 to 58. A switch of eight votes would have altered the course of American history for the other states of the upper South would likely have followed Virginia's example had its legislature voted yes. Had those states phased out slavery, the institution would have no longer split the Union down the middle. It would have been the very peculiar institution of the few cotton states, no more able to threaten the Union than the regularly rambunctious New England states. Once Virginia's debate was resolved in favor of slavery, no significant body of southern whites ever again considered the possibility of ridding themselves of the institution.

THREATS TO THE SOUTHERN ORDER

Virginia's debate took place in the shadow of two events that unsettled the peace of mind of southern slave owners: the bloodiest slave rebellion in the history of North America and the emergence in the North of articulate and aggressive evangelical abolitionists who assailed the common decency of slave owners and seemed, to many, to be encouraging slave rebellions.

Rebellions

There were a number of slave uprisings and scares during the colonial era, but a serious fear of rebellion became a part of the southern white mentality only after 1791 when many of Haiti's slaves erupted in fury and murdered thousands of their masters, both whites and *gens de couleur,* (mulattos who owned a quarter of the real estate and slaves on the island). Haitian slavery was crueler than slavery in the United States; more than one slave in twenty died each year; Haiti imported 20,000 to 30,000 Africans annually just to maintain the population. Nevertheless, American slave owners were alarmed. For several years, South Carolina actually forbade the importation of slaves from abroad to keep out Haitian blacks "infected" with revolutionary ideas.

The Granger Collection, New York

The Gabriel and Vesey rebellions were exposed before they began. Nat Turner's was not because he informed very few trusted friends of his plans. Turner may have been familiar with the fact that Vesey was betrayed by a slave who knew of his plans. It had been only nine years since Vesey and thirty-four other rebels had been hanged. The slave grapevine could and did convey news hundreds of miles in a week or two.

Then, in 1800, two years after a second wave of massacres in Haiti, the state capital of Virginia, Richmond, narrowly escaped a rebellion led by a slave blacksmith, Gabriel. Gabriel, white Virginians observed when the scare was over, was literate, as were many of his cronies, both black and white, who were, also like him, skilled tradesmen. Presumably, they read the newspapers; they admitted discussing politics in their off hours.

Gabriel was neither racist nor bloodthirsty. He expected poor whites to join his struggle against the planter elite that ran Virginia. His followers had strict instructions not to molest Quakers and Methodists who were known to be antislavery and to kill others only if they resisted. With a core of about 150 rebels, Gabriel expected hundreds of slaves to join his army once the rebellion was underway on August 30, 1800. The objectives were to make a hostage of Governor James Monroe and to occupy key points in the city whence Gabriel and others would negotiate a settlement. Gabriel was realistic about the limits of what his little band could actually accomplish but was deluded to think that Richmond's whites would honor any agreement once Monroe was safe.

In any event, there was no rising. Torrential rains on August 30 prevented the rebels from assembling. A few slaves acting suspiciously were arrested, questioned, and the plot was exposed. Twenty-seven of the ringleaders were hanged; others were sold out of state.

In 1822, a free black carpenter and Methodist preacher in Charleston, South Carolina, Denmark Vesey, hatched a plan for a slave uprising that had a clear Haitian connection. Vesey's idea was for slaves to sack the city for arms and provisions, seize ships in the harbor, and sail for Haiti where, he believed, they would be welcomed. Vesey talked the plot up among Charleston's slaves. His chief lieutenant, Gullah Jack, was an Angola-born plantation slave. He recruited rebels on plantations outside Charleston. Many were, like Jack, African-born. South Carolina had imported 40,000 Africans in 1807, the last year it was legal to purchase slaves from abroad, and illegal slave traders had continued to sneak into the port.

The rising was scheduled for June 16. Two days earlier, an informer revealed the plan. Vesey, Gullah Jack, and thirty-three others were hanged. No one knew (or knows) how many slaves were involved, which was enough in itself to unnerve white South Carolinians. Worse, many house slaves, whose owners trusted them, knew of the planned uprising. They refused to participate, but none of them exposed Vesey.

Nat Turner

Gabriel's and Vesey's plans were more or less rational, their objectives were precise and limited. Neither fantasized that rebel slaves could turn the world upside down. Nat Turner's rebellion in August 1831, which was not nipped before it started, was altogether different. A field hand in southern Virginia whose first owner had taught him to read, Turner was a pious Baptist who pored endlessly over the Bible and may have seen abolitionist propaganda. A packet containing fifty copies of David Walker's *Call* had been confiscated at the Savannah post office the previous year. It is reasonable to suppose that others got through and were circulated.

But Turner admitted to no inspiration except the Bible and "his voices." He was mentally disturbed, even psychotic, seeing visions and hearing divine instructions. When there was a solar eclipse in February 1831, he took it to be God's go-ahead to slaves to rise up and kill all whites. Unlike Gabriel and Vesey, Turner's objective was an Armageddon, a holy battle between God's people and God's enemies. That

Fugitive Slaves

The underground railroad was an improvised and changing network of "lines" over which runaway slaves, accompanied by "conductors," traveled secretly north. "Stationmasters" concealed the fugitives in their homes from their masters, law officers, and professional slave catchers.

The underground railroad existed before the real railroad did. About 1800, a Philadelphia Quaker, Isaac Harper, concealed a slave who was being pursued by his Maryland master and, by night, snuck him out of the city to a Quaker farmer who gave him a job and kept him hidden. They were violating the Fugitive Slave Act of 1793 that enabled masters to repossess slaves who had escaped to states where slavery had been abolished. Harris and other Quakers believed they had a moral duty to help African Americans to escape from slavery, whatever the consequences. "We might as well look for a needle in a haystack as for a nigger among Quakers," a frustrated slave owner complained. Another said, "There is no use in trying to capture a runaway slave in Philadelphia."

In 1820, the Pennsylvania assembly came close to nullifying the federal fugitive slave law. It provided that only a constable with a warrant could legally take custody of an alleged runaway. Anyone else who did so (including the owner or a hired slave catcher) could be fined $2,000 and imprisoned up to twenty-one years. In court, an owner's claim that he owned a certain person was not admitted into evidence. He had to bring someone else to court to swear that he owned the slave in order to prove his claim. It was so expensive a procedure that many owners of runaway slaves just gave up trying to retrieve them.

Not all of them, however. So, to give runaways a reasonable chance to stay free, antislavery Pennsylvanians established a network of houses across the state and in New Jersey—about twenty miles apart—at which runaways were welcome to hide and rest during the day while, at night, they made their way to the next station and north to New York or New England. Similar lines were developed in Ohio and Indiana for slaves who managed to get across the Ohio River, the boundary between slave states and free states.

There was an underground railroad in Kentucky, Virginia, and Maryland too. Some slaves helped others get to a free state. A few southern whites did too although usually, Quaker stationmaster Levi Coffin said, in the South "it was done for money."

A white man got Jarm Logue started on his escape by selling him food, a revolver, and interesting advice. As long as he was in a slave state, the man told Logue, "If you go dodging and shying through the country, you will be suspected." Logue, he said, should move about boldly and confidently, as if he were a free black. He should stop only at "big houses" to ask for food, as a free black would. Alfred T. Jones also traveled through Kentucky openly. He used a pass from his owner that he had forged. Looking back on his escape years later, Jones remembered, "I could hardly put two syllables together, but in fact, one half the white men there were not much better."

Southern congressmen tried repeatedly to strengthen federal laws providing for the return of slaves who escaped to free states. By the 1840s, between 1,000 and 1,500 were making it each year. The Fugitive Slave Act of 1850 bypassed antislavery state judges in the North by creating special federal commissioners to assist and rule on the claims of slave owners and professional slave catchers.

he convinced anyone to join him indicates how charismatic he must have been.

Turner was shrewd enough to divulge his plans to a very few trusted friends. (He may have known that Vesey's rebellion was squelched because of an informer.) On the night of August 21, 1831, armed with little more than farm tools, his band swept across Southampton county, killing sixty whites and recruiting supporters from among their slaves. The murders were over in a couple of days although it was six weeks before the last of seventy rebels were rounded up. Turner and thirty-nine others were hanged. Rebels who were not killed whites were sold out of the state.

Turner's rebellion terrified slave owners, particularly those who lived in parts of Louisiana, Mississippi, and South Carolina where blacks outnumbered whites by as many as twenty to one. Mary Boykin Chesnut, the wife of a planter, was not mentioning a demographic curiosity when she described her plantation home, Mulberry, as "half a dozen whites and sixty or seventy Negroes, miles away from the rest of the world."

White belief in African American inferiority made it difficult for some southerners to believe that slaves, on their own devices, could mount a rebellion like Turner's. It was no coincidence, they said, that the massacre in Southampton County coincided with the flood of abolitionist literature coming out of the North.

THE SOUTH CLOSES RANKS

The South was not quite alone in the western world in clinging to slavery, but almost. The Spanish-speaking republics of the Americas abolished the institution as soon as they won independence. Great Britain abolished slavery in her West Indian colonies in 1833. In the entire Christian world, slavery survived only in Spain's colonies of Cuba and Puerto Rico

Anyone who helped a fugitive slave "directly or indirectly" was fined and jailed. The commissioners were empowered to "compel" bystanders to assist them in capturing a fugitive. The law jeopardized the freedom of African Americans who had lived in a free state for years. One of the first persons arrested under the 1850 act—and returned to slavery!—was a man who had lived in Indiana for nineteen years.

Rather than shutting down after 1850, the underground railroad extended its "track." It was now necessary to spirit runaways out of the United States into Canada. During the first three months the 1850 law was in effect, 3,000 African Americans crossed the international border. Between 1848 and 1853, the black population of Upper Canada (Ontario) increased from 20,000 to 35,000.

Eighty percent of the blacks in Canada were from Virginia, Maryland, and Kentucky. Getting from the deep South to the underground railroad was not a realistic possibility although at least one Georgia slave, Charles Ball, did it. Ball planned carefully and saved money to buy food. He "followed the North Star" by night although, on several cloudy nights, Ball discovered he had walked in circles. Once, the presence of slave catchers nearby so frightened him that he hid in the woods for eleven days. It took him nine months to reach Pennsylvania.

A few slaves from the deep South escaped by getting to seaports like Mobile and Savannah where they located a sailor from a vessel bound for a northern port who, for a price, would hide them aboard. Some southern ports forbade free black seamen to come ashore in order to prevent such transactions, and suspect ships were thoroughly searched. The penalties for helping a slave to escape were severe: ten years in prison in Louisiana, hanging in North Carolina. No one was hanged for the offense, but Florida branded SS for "slave stealer" on a convicted white sailor's cheek.

Men outnumbered women and children on the underground railroad for good reason. The risk of capture (and severe punishment) was high. Josiah Henson had to threaten his wife that he would go without her to persuade her to accompany him. "We should die in the wilderness," she told him, "we should be hunted down with bloodhounds, we should be brought back and whipped to death." In truth, the Hensons had a harrowing experience. In 1830, when they made their flight, central Ohio was still virtual wilderness. Only friendly Indians saved them from starvation. Sandusky, on Lake Erie, was crawling with slave catchers who collected fees of up to $100 for each runaway they caught that far north.

The Hensons got lucky. The captain of a ship headed for Buffalo on the Canadian border agreed to take the family even though it meant, after leaving Sandusky by day, he had to return after dark so the Hensons could board unseen. In Buffalo, the captain paid the Hensons' fare on a ferry that crossed the Niagara River to Ontario. As Henson and his family boarded the ferry, his benefactor told him, "Clap your wings and crow like a rooster; you're a free nigger as sure as the devil."

How many slaves escaped to freedom on the underground railroad or by their own devices? No one really knows; estimates range between 70,000 and 100,000. Between a fourth and a third of them went all the way to Canada although, after emancipation in 1865, many returned to the United States.

(until 1873 and 1886, respectively), the tiny French islands of Martinique and Guadaloupe (until 1848), and in Brazil (until 1888). Slavery was universal in Muslim lands and widespread in black Africa, but white southerners did not care to look for comrades in those places.

After Turner's Rebellion and the appearance of *The Liberator,* white southerners, recognizing that their slavery was a "peculiar institution," moved on three fronts to preserve it. They suppressed criticism of the institution at home and attempted to insulate their slaves from antislavery propaganda from the North. Slave owners ceased to regret the existence of slavery as a historical burden or a necessary evil in their dealings with outsiders. They adopted the line that slavery was a positive good that was a blessing on slaves, masters, and southern society as a whole. Finally, they reformed the states' slave codes—the laws that governed the peculiar institution—to improve the material conditions under which slaves lived and instituted stricter controls over the black population.

Suppressing Discussion

Most southern states forbade the distribution of abolitionist literature. The post office authorized southern postmasters to examine suspicious mail and to destroy material that was objectionable. Innumerable copies of *The Liberator* and other antislavery newspapers were burned.

Georgia's legislature offered a reward of $5,000 to any person who would bring William Lloyd Garrison into the state to stand trial for inciting rebellion. The fact that a state legislature was willing to encourage an abduction—Garrison had no intention of taking a vacation in Georgia—indicates the depth of the South's hatred of him. Only in border states like Maryland and Kentucky could native son abolitionists like John Gregg Fee and Cassius Marcellus Clay continue to speak openly against slavery without fear of anything worse than heckling and harassment. Elsewhere in the South, the expression of antislavery opinions was not acceptable.

In the House of Representatives, beginning in 1836, southern congressmen, with the support of some northern Democrats, annually adopted a procedural rule that petitions to the House calling for the abolition of slavery in the District of Columbia be tabled without discussion. That is, the petitions were simply set aside. There were a lot of them. By March 1838, the tabled petitions filled a room 20 feet by 30 feet. Former President John Quincy Adams, now a Massachusetts congressman, argued that the "gag rule" violated the right to free speech. Adams did not approve of intemperate zealots like Garrison, but he insisted that every citizen had a constitutional right to petition Congress on any subject. In 1838, Robert Rhett of South Carolina conceded his point by proposing that the Constitution be amended to exempt discussion of slavery from the First Amendment's guarantee of free speech.

A "Positive Good"

Shortly after Virginia's debate, a professor at the College of William and Mary, Thomas Roderick Dew, published a systematic defense of slavery. He said that as a means of organizing and controlling labor, the slavery system was superior to the free wage-worker system. By 1837, southern preachers and politicians were parroting and embroidering on Dew's theories. In the Senate, John C. Calhoun declared that compared with other systems by which racial and class relationships were governed, "the relation now existing in the slave holding states is, instead of an evil, a good—a positive-good"—better for everyone concerned, slaves included, than other systems.

In *A Sociology for the South,* published in 1854, George Fitzhugh of Virginia amassed statistics and other evidence with which he argued that the southern slave lived a better life than did the northern wage worker or the European peasant.

In every society, Fitzhugh wrote, someone had to perform the drudgery. In the South, menial work was done by slaves who were cared for from cradle to grave. Not only did the slave owner feed, clothe, and house his workers, but he also supported slave children, the injured, disabled, and elderly— all of whom were nonproductive. By comparison, the northern wage worker was paid only as long as there was work for him and the worker was fit to do it. The wage worker who was injured was cut loose to fend for himself. His children, the elderly, and the incompetent were no responsibility of capitalist employers and the "free labor" system in which they took pride.

Consequently, Fitzhugh continued, the North was plagued by social problems unknown in the South. The North teemed with obnoxious, nattering demagogues trying to stir up the working class. The lower classes were irreligious and, in their misery, drunken and tumultuous. By comparison, Fitzhugh claimed, southern slaves were contented, indeed, happy. "A merrier being does not exist on the face of the globe," Fitzhugh wrote, "than the Negro slave of the United States."

Even John Randolph, who hated slavery, told of touring Ireland attended by his valet, a slave. Both men were shocked by the squalor in which the Irish lived. Randolph's slave told him that he "was never so proud of being a *Virginia slave.* He looked with horror upon the mud hovels and miserable food of the *white slaves."*

The Bible, the Ancients, and Culture

The "positive good" line was new. Before Nat Turner and the evangelical abolitionists, only the odd South Carolinian and Georgia had suggested that slavery was a desirable institution. The new southern ideology incorporated religious and cultural justifications into Dew's and Fitzhugh's social and economic arguments.

Thus, hitting the evangelicals head on, southerners said that Bible sanctioned slavery. The ancient Hebrews—the patriarchs Abraham, Isaac, Jacob, and their successors—owned slaves with God's blessing. In the New Testament, when a slave approached Christ saying he wished to follow him, Christ replied that he should return to and serve his master, practicing Christ's teachings as a slave.

John Randolph and Slavery
Randolph despised slavery. He never bought a slave or any of those he inherited. He voted to abolish the slave trade in the District of Columbia, calling it "infamous." He never passed up an opportunity for an antislavery witticism. In the early 1830s, when the Greeks were fighting for independence from the Turkish empire, things Greek were a rage among trendy Americans. After listening to a southern lady gushing about "the noble Greeks" and their fight for freedom, Randolph pointed with his riding crop to some slave children playing outside. "Madam," he said, "the Greeks are at your door."

Dew and others pointed out that the great civilizations of antiquity, Greece and Rome, were slave-holding societies. Hardly a barbaric institution, slavery had made possible the classical cultures studied in colleges and universities for their art, literature, and wisdom. Slavery made possible the leisured, gracious, and cultured upper classes who preserved the highest refinements of human achievement. It was possible to put a racial spin on Aristotle's justification of slavery and southerners like Dew did: "Just as some are by nature free, so others are by nature slaves, and for these latter the condition of slavery is both beneficial and just."

Southerners pointed out that more of them than northerners were college-educated. Even as late as 1860, there were more than 6,000 college students in Georgia, Alabama, and Mississippi, compared to fewer than 4,000 in the more populous (and intellectually pretentious) New England states.

As an aristocracy, southern planters were closer to the tradition of the gentlemanly founding fathers than were the money-grubbing capitalists of the North. Because gentlemen dominated politics in the South, the southern states were better governed than the northern states were. In the North, demagogues won elections to high position by playing to the passions of the dregs of society. Some planters liked to think of themselves as descendants of the cavaliers of seventeenth-century England. The South's favorite author was Sir Walter Scott, who spun enchanting tales of knighthood and chivalry.

Race: The Trump Card

But did all these "proofs" justify denying personal freedom to human beings? Yes, Fitzhugh said in a second book, *Cannibals All!*, published in 1857. The Negro race was incapable of civilization's higher callings. In return for enjoying the fruits of their labor, the owners of slaves did African Americans a favor by providing their necessities and protecting them against competition (and from poor whites).

Here and there, a southerner argued that African Americans could be enslaved because they were not quite human. One quack, on the subject, Josiah Nott, collected skulls from all over the country and the world. He measured brain cavities by drilling a hole in his skulls, filling them with buckshot, and then measuring the shot. He concluded that blacks had significantly smaller brains than whites.

Few southerners bought Nott's theories. Different species do not produce fertile offspring and the number of mulattos in the southern "black" population was overwhelming evidence that blacks and whites were both *Homo sapiens*. White southerners, most of them religious—many of them members of the evangelical Baptist and Methodist churches—preferred to argue that by bringing blacks from savage Africa and exposing them to Christianity, whites had done them the greatest service of all.

Management

Blind to higher faculties among African Americans, positive good southerners equated happiness with the material conditions of slave life—housing, clothing, diet. They compared the slaves' lot favorably with the conditions under which the poorest wage workers of the North lived. By the 1850s, when Fitzhugh wrote, most southern state legislatures had, in fact, defined minimum living standards as part of their slave codes. Magazines like the *Southern Agriculturalist* featured exchanges among slave owners about how well they treated their people.

The most obvious reason for keeping slaves adequately housed, clothed, and fed was, of course, practical: A healthy slave worked more efficiently than one weak from deprivation. Also underlying the trend toward improvement in the conditions of slave life after the 1830s was the South's determination to give the lie to the abolitionists' depiction of slavery as a life of unrelenting misery. Planters who provided decent accommodations for their slaves took pleasure in showing "the quarters" to northern and foreign visitors. They reassured themselves that they were indeed kindly patriarchs.

Control

Visitors were less likely to be apprised of the new measures of slave control that were introduced after the Turner conspiracy. By 1840, the states of the deep South had adopted laws that made it extremely difficult for a slave owner to manumit his slaves. (Virginia had long required manumitted blacks to leave the state.) It was a crime in most southern states to teach a slave to read. Gabriel, Vesey, and Turner had all been literate, a fact lost on no one.

County governments were required to maintain slave patrols to cruise the countryside at night looking for wandering slaves. Some counties required all fit white males to take turns on the patrols. Most counties, however, because few wealthy planters were interested in the dismal duty, hired paid "paddyrollers," as slaves called them. These mounted posses of armed, lower-class whites had the legal right to break into slave cabins or demand at gunpoint that all blacks (and whites) account for themselves. Hard-bitten men, the "paddyrollers" were inclined to be rough even with slaves carrying written passes granting them permission to be off their master's property.

Muslim Slaves

The West Africans who supplied British and American slavers with captives sometimes raided Islamic peoples in the interior. Several Muslim slaves in the United States distinguished themselves by virtue of their literacy and personal qualities. About 1730, Job Ben Salomon Jallo took two slaves to sell in the Mandingo country along the Gambia River. He was himself enslaved by the Mandingos and ended up in Annapolis, Maryland. There he astonished his owner when he asked to write a letter to his father in Senegal to arrange his ransom. He was freed, returned to the Gambia via England where he was hired as an agent for the Royal African Company to provide slaves for the transatlantic trade.

Omar ibn Said, a slave in South Carolina, impressed his owner because he was literate in Arabic. He was not freed, but he was exempted from labor. Salil Bilali (called "Tom") managed a 450-slave plantation in Georgia that the *Southern Agriculturalist* singled out as a model operation. Ibrahim Abd ar-Rahman was a plantation manager in Natchez, Tennessee. He became a national celebrity when, astonishingly, he met a white man whom he had known in Africa. With his help, Ibrahim was introduced to Henry Clay and John Quincy Adams who assisted him in raising the money to buy his freedom and the freedom of his American-born wife and their grandchildren. They went to Liberia in 1829.

Free blacks—there were about 250,000 in the South by 1860, one to every fifteen slaves—carefully protected the documentary evidence of their status. Kidnappings of free blacks, and the sale of them as slaves elsewhere in the South, were far from unknown.

The mere existence of a free African American population among slaves was a bothersome problem for slave owners. It was as important to the institution that blacks be convinced that God and nature intended them to be slaves as it was to persuade northerners that slavery was a positive good. If slaves saw free blacks prospering, the argument disintegrated. Slave owners also believed that free blacks were likely to stir up discontent among slaves, and they were probably right. Thus, the laws requiring masters who freed their slaves to take them out of state.

Free blacks who had no land to farm needed little persuasion to congregate in towns. Only there could they find work and a social life; and, living in numbers among other free African Americans provided some security. A free black family living in a remote rural area was vulnerable to abuse and worse—re-enslavement.

Religion: A Threat to Control

Probably less than a half of southern slaves were Christians at the time of the Revolution. Neither masters, slaves, nor ministers took much interest in conversion. This changed with the rise of the Methodists and the revitalization of the Baptists, both of which groups preached to slaves; the purchase of Louisiana (where most slaves were Roman Catholics); and, after 1807, the end of large-scale importation of Africans bringing their African religions with them. Within a few decades after 1800, almost all slaves embraced one or another kind of Christianity, usually, like their masters, the evangelical varieties. Indeed, religious observance—almost always highly personal and emotional—became an important part of slave culture.

All southern states had laws, inherited from colonial times, specifying that conversion to Christianity did not affect a slave's status. Nevertheless, religious zeal in the quarters presented a problem of control. Denmark Vesey had been a Methodist minister; Nat Turner had been led to rebellion by Bible reading; David Walker's *Appeal* was laced with biblical quotations.

Some masters took their slaves to their own churches where the minister was expected, now and then, to deliver a sermon based on biblical stories such as that of Hagar: "The angel of the Lord said unto her, return to Thy mistress, and submit thyself under her hands." Other masters permitted their slaves to have their own preachers. These often literate and more often eloquent men were instructed to steer clear of lessons that might cast doubt on the rightness of slavery. Some toed the line; it was an African American minister in Savannah who informed the authorities that Walker's *Appeal* had been mailed to him. Others conveyed an antislavery message by placing heavy emphasis on the ancient Israelites' bondage in Babylon and Egypt—and their ultimate deliverance.

WHAT WAS SLAVERY LIKE?

While slavery existed and long afterwards, two sharply contradictory visions of the institution contended for popular acceptance. Abolitionist and, after emancipation, those who honored the abolitionist for their crusade, emphasized the forced labor of slavery, the squalid living conditions, the ever-present blacksnake whip (and atrocities much worse than floggings), children torn from their mothers' arms to be sold, the sadism of masters and overseers (and slave drivers, fellow slaves), and, most of all, the dehumanizing fact of being "owned," of being subject to someone else's decisions in even the minutiae of life.

The other side, beginning with Dew and Fitzhugh and impressed on popular culture by minstrel shows, romantic authors, and, in the twentieth century, movies depicting "de ol' plantation" as a paternalistic, easy-going place where simple-minded slaves lived worry-free, contented, and devoted to "ol' massa."

The Minstrels

In Louisville, Kentucky, in 1830, a performer in a traveling variety show, Thomas D. "Daddy" Rice, saw an African American dancing on the street for the pennies of passersby. Rice copied

The Granger Collection, New York

Publicity for a minstrel show. The stereotypical characters are simpleminded and exuberantly happy. The players were whites in blackface, often grotesque. Minstrels were very popular during the 1850s. At one time or another during the decade, a hundred different troupes were touring the country.

the man's dance on stage and, blacking his face (with soot from an oil lamp or scorched cork), he called his act "Jumpin' Jim Crow." He was a sensation and soon had imitators.

A song writer, Daniel D. Emmett, and an impresario, Edwin P. Christy, broadened "blackface" entertainment beyond Jumpin' Jim Crow when they created the "minstrel show." The minstrels (a medieval word meaning traveling musicians) sat in a line of chairs across the stage. In the center was the master of ceremonies, "Mr. Interlocutor," a white man who spoke in a stilted, pretentious accent. The rest of the cast was white too, but in blackface. They sang or danced (always Jumpin' Jim Crow) or juggled when called upon by Mr. Interlocutor.

What made the minstrels unique were the two "end men" at either side of the stage: "Brother Tambo" (he played a tambourine) and "Brother Bones," whose instrument was "the bones," two hog's ribs which, in fact, slaves used for rhythm in their music. Brother Tambo was a dim-witted plantation slave. The other was a black city slicker, dandy, and confidence man sometimes called Zip Coon. Between songs and dances, they insulted one another and Mr. Interlocutor with broad comedy.

The makeup and dialect were grotesque stereotypes, but minstrel shows were not vicious. The end men were good-natured, even lovable. The city slicker's schemes to bilk Mr. Tambo were usually foiled by his own bumbling, sometimes by Mr. Tambo's disguised down home shrewdness. If the blackface characters were not menacing, however, they were stupid, lazy, and childlike. They confirmed white convictions that African Americans were inferior. Minstrel show slaves enjoyed their life on the plantation.

Neither Emmett nor Christy was conscious of being proslavery propagandist. Both were northerners; Emmett's father was a prominent abolitionist. They and their many imitators were interested in making money in show business, which minstrel shows did. Christy's Minstrels packed a large New York theater for 2,500 performances. But the minstrels served to calm any anxieties about slavery among ordinary white people that the abolitionists struggled to arouse.

Stephen Foster

Stephen Foster, who wrote "Ethiopian songs" for minstrel shows, was the first great American composer of "pop music." His first hit, a nonsense song of 1848 called "Oh! Susannah," became the anthem of the Forty-Niners, the men who rushed to California the next year to mine for gold. In fact, it was a song sung by a black man to his lover written for the minstrel shows.

Few of Foster's lyrics were condescending to African Americans. He publicly regretted writing one early song that he later found patronizing, and he deleted a questionable verse from "Oh! Susannah." Foster's intention was to humanize the characters of his songs and to dignify relations between African Americans and between whites and blacks, including master and slave.

"Massa's in de Cold, Cold Ground" and "Old Black Joe," which were not written in dialect, were later criticized for depicting slaves devoted to "Ol' Massa," but there is no hint of an apology for slavery in them. They gush with sentimentality, but the warmth of a human relationship was Foster's theme.

Indeed, Foster may have been an abolitionist. His best friend was one of Pittsburgh's most prominent antislavery leaders. In "Old Folks at Home" (1851), in which a slave far from "de old plantation" longs for familiar surroundings, there is an implication that the singer is a runaway. "Ring, Ring de Banjo," written the same year, is explicitly about a slave fleeing his master.

When Foster realized that his songs were being used to justify the simple-minded darky version of slavery, he instructed singers not to mock black people in their presentations. He stopped writing in dialect and told Edwin P. Christy that he detested the "trashy and really offensive words" of other writers' minstrel show songs. He refused to call his verses "Ethiopian songs," insisting they be called "plantation songs" and, later, "American melodies."

Washington the Slave Owner

George Washington owned 300 slaves. His record as a master was mixed. On the one hand, according to a visitor from Poland, the slaves' houses at Washington's River Farm were "more miserable than the most miserable cottages of our peasants." And he once had several of a slave's healthy teeth pulled to make dentures for himself.

On the other hand, Washington respected his slaves' family and marriage relationships more than most slave owners did. When husbands and wives were temporarily separated, Washington meticulously recorded who was tied to whom. He refused to sell slaves "because they could not be disposed of in families . . . and to disperse the families I have an aversion."

Structure of the Institution: White Perspective

There were elements of truth in the abolitionists' and the minstrels' vision of slavery, but neither was an accurate portrayal. Slavery was not the same institution everywhere in the South. Slavery in Texas was not the same institution as slavery in Virginia. Life for slave and slave owner was not the same on a big plantation as it was on a family homestead just a decade from raw frontier. In the law—the classification of human beings as property—slavery was one thing. The experience of slavery, however, was as diverse as the South.

The census of 1860, the last taken when slavery was legal, reveals that nearly 4 million people lived in bondage in the fifteen states south of the Mason-Dixon line and the Ohio River. West of the Mississippi River, Missouri, Arkansas, Louisiana, and Texas were slave states. Some tribes in Indian Territory (Oklahoma) owned African Americans.

One white southern family in four owned slaves. Even when those whose living depended directly on the existence of the institution—overseers, slave traders, patrollers—are added in, however, only a minority of white southerners had a material stake in slavery.

The great planter class (the only slave owners in the world of the minstrel shows) was quite small. In 1860, only 2,200 people, less than 1 percent of the southern population, owned 100 or more slaves. Only 254 owned 200 slaves or more. Nathaniel Heyward of South Carolina was at the top of the pyramid, owning 2,000 slaves on seventeen plantations.

A more typical slave owner was Jacob Eaton of North Carolina. On his 160-acre farm he worked side by side with the slave family he owned. Eaton's class of small independent farmers—owning from none to nine slaves—was the backbone of the southern economy and the slavery system. About 74 percent of slave owners fell into that category. Another 16 percent of slave owners owned between ten and twenty people. Just 10 percent of slave owners owned more than twenty slaves.

Structure of the Institution: Black Perspective

If few slave owners lived on large plantations, life in the shadow of the "big house" was the experience of most slaves.

In 1860, more than half the South's slaves lived on what we would think of as a plantation rather than a farm. Half a million African Americans, one slave in eight, belonged to members of the great planter class.

There were black slave owners. The census of 1830 counted 3,775 free African Americans in possession of 12,760 slaves. A few, most in Louisiana, qualified as "great planters." Andrew Durnford of New Orleans had seventy-seven slaves. When questioned, Durnford said that owning slaves was the only way to wealth in the South. Although he contributed to the American Colonization Society, Durnford freed only four slaves during his lifetime, one in his will.

More typical of black slave owners was Dilsey Pope, a free black woman in Georgia, who owned her husband. Like Virginia, Georgia required slave owners who manumitted their slaves to send them to another state. Therefore, free African Americans who bought their spouses out of slavery were able to stay together only by owning them (and their children) as slaves. Dilsey Pope's story was unusual only in that, after she and her husband had a nasty quarrel, Mrs. Pope sold him to a white neighbor. When the couple reconciled, the new owner refused to sell Mr. Pope back to his wife.

A cotton field at picking time. "Chopping cotton," hoeing the weeds in the rows and between plants, was hard work, but the harvest was frantic. The cotton had to be out of the fields and under cover before autumn rains. On all but the largest plantations, every slave was sent to the fields, including house servants and children able to walk.

© UPI-Bettmann/Corbis

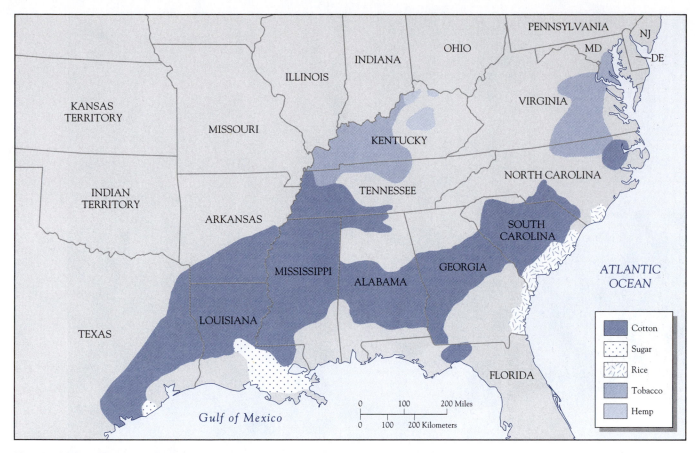

MAP 18:2 **Major Southern Crops, 1860.** Cotton was king. Almost two-thirds of African American slaves raised cotton. Growing and processing sugarcane in Louisiana was even harder work, but localized. The rice fields of South Carolina and Georgia were unhealthier than either and also a crop of limited extent as was the "hemp belt" of Kentucky.

First Light to Sundown

A few slaves enjoyed the relative advantages of living as domestic servants: better food, clothing, beds. Cooks, maids, butlers, valets, carriage drivers, and footmen made life pleasanter for the great planters who could afford them, but they did not make money for their masters. So, "house slaves" were few. The vast majority of slaves were field hands who raised a cash crop by means of heavy labor from first light to sundown almost year-round. For a slave owner to justify investing capital in a labor force rather than hiring free laborers, it was necessary to keep the property hopping.

Cotton was by far the most important southern product (the most important American product!). During the 1850s, an average annual crop of 4 million bales brought more than $190 million into the American economy from abroad. Cotton represented two-thirds of the nation's total exports and (in 1850) employed 1.8 million slaves out of 3.2 million. In 1860, the twelve richest counties in the United States were cotton counties. Other cash crops dependent on slave labor were tobacco (350,000 slaves), sugar (150,000), rice (125,000), and hemp (60,000).

Southern farmers and planters strived for self-sufficiency. Therefore, slaves raised corn, vegetables, and hogs for food, and hay for fodder, as well as the cash crop. There was plenty of work to be done. Thomas Jefferson heated Monticello with 10 cords of wood a month in winter: a lot of chopping. The calendar of a cotton plantation was packed with jobs, major and odd, except for a short period around Christmas. Slaves looked forward to their brief vacation as "laying-by time."

Slaves were expensive. By the 1850s, it cost as much as $1,500 (about $25,000–$30,000 today) to buy a prime field hand, a healthy male in his twenties. Consequently, planters preferred to hire free blacks or Irish immigrants for unhealthy and dangerous work. It made little economic sense

The Health of Slaves

In an age when nothing was known of scientific nutrition, the slaves' diet was comparable to that of poor southern whites and free blacks, and better on plantations where slaves were permitted to keep gardens. The life expectancy of slaves was about the same as that of free blacks and poor southern whites. Statistical surveys done about 1860 showed southern slaves averaging 3 inches more in height than the West Africans from whom they were descended. They were 2 inches taller than Trinidadians, who had been free since 1830, and an inch taller than British marines.

Missouri Historical Society

A slave auction in St. Louis. There is more decorum in this representation than in any of the written descriptions of slave auctions that have survived. If some buyers were, no doubt, as well dressed and gentlemanly as the white men here, there were plenty of baser types not pictured here, some buyers, some just there for the show, sometimes drunk and making coarse comments, particularly when, as here, an attractive woman was on the block.

to risk costly human property draining malarial swamps or working at the bottom of chutes down which 600-pound bales of cotton came hurtling at high speeds.

The Rhythms of Labor

By the 1850s, a slave produced from $80 to $120 in wealth each year and cost between $30 and $50 to feed, clothe, and shelter. The margin of profit was not large enough to allow the small-scale slave owner to get by unless he worked in the fields side by side with his slaves.

Planters owning ten to twenty slaves could avoid manual labor. However, because few slaves worked any harder than they were forced to do (their share of the fruits of their labor was fixed), they had to be supervised closely and constantly: variously bribed, cajoled, threatened, or whipped. A man with twenty or more slaves hired a white overseer or assigned one of his slaves to be a driver, paying him or, at least, granting him privileges. On large plantations, masters had little contact with their field hands.

Slaves on large plantations worked according to the task system or the gang system. Under the task system, a specific job was assigned each day to every slave. When the task was complete, the slave's time was his or her own. Some planters insisted that the task system was the most productive form of slave management because, provided with an incentive, the slaves worked harder. Other planters complained that the task system resulted in slipshod work as the slaves rushed so as to get to their own chores or recreation.

Under the gang system, slaves worked from sunrise to sundown in groups under an overseer or driver. Who knows how frequently they felt the sting of the blacksnake? The lash was always in evidence, in black hands as well as white. Frederick Douglass remarked that "everybody in the South wants the privilege of whipping someone else." But some masters refused to let overseers whip slaves except as formal punishment and only with the master's specific permission.

Slave Traders

Slaves were defined in law as chattel property: personal possessions legally the same as cattle, hogs, a necklace, or a

Slave-trader, Sold to Tennessee,

Arise! Arise! and weep no more dry up your tears, we Shall part no more. Come rose we go to Tennessee, that happy Shore. to old virginia never — never — return.

the Company going to Tennessee from Staunton. Augusta County, the law of virginia Suffered them to go on. I was Astonished at this boldness, the Carrier Stopped a moment. then Ordered the march. I Saw the play it is Commonly in this State, with the negro's in droves Sold,

Abby Aldrich Rockefeller Folk Art Center, Williamsburg, VA

A familiar sight on southern roads: slaves from the upper south (in this case, Virginia) being marched to the cotton lands of western Tennessee. Slaves dreaded being "sold down the river" where work was harder and escape almost impossible. The unfortunates in this watercolor by an eyewitness are, at least, not hobbled, probably because they are in family groups and, therefore, unlikely to run. Had they been mostly "prime field hands," young men, they would have been in a coffle, tied or chained together neck to neck.

share of stock. They could be bought, sold, given away, or passed on to heirs. The commerce in slaves was brisk and profitable.

Even slavery's defenders conceded that the slave trade was an ugly business. The slave auction was a livestock auction. Prospective buyers clustered around the auction block, determining the age of the merchandise by examining their teeth, as they would vet a horse. Slaves were forced to run to test their wind. Buyers wiped their bodies with rags to determine if the auctioneer had dyed gray hair black or rubbed oil into aged skin. If adolescent girls were for sale, sexual innuendos floated around the crowd. Foreigners, northerners, and many southerners were simultaneously disgusted and fascinated by slave auctions, much as American tourists in Mexico today react to bullfights.

Masters aspiring to be patriarchs disapproved of the slave trade, describing traders as base, crude, unworthy men. Nevertheless, without the slave trade there could have been no slavery. If some humans were property, owners had to be free to buy and sell them. Where there is trade, there are brokers.

The general flow of the commerce was "down the river"— the Mississippi—from the older, declining tobacco states to the cotton states of the Deep South. Professional slave traders purchased African Americans in Virginia, Maryland, and Kentucky and marched them, like their African ancestors, in coffles to Memphis or New Orleans, where as many as 200 companies were in the business.

LIFE IN THE QUARTERS

The slave codes of the southern states specified that slaves had no civil rights. They could not own property under the law; therefore, they could not legally buy and sell anything. They could not make contracts. Their marriages were not legally recognized lest a slave owner face complications if he wanted to sell a woman but not her husband. Slaves could not testify in court against a white person. (Nor could free blacks in some southern states.) They could not leave the plantation without written permission.

It was a crime for a slave to strike a white person, even to save his own life. Slaves could not carry firearms. They could not congregate in more than small groups except at religious services under white supervision. They could not be abroad at night.

Humans without Human Rights

The actual experience of slave life sometimes deviated from the letter of the slave codes. For example, a master could not legally kill his slave, but it was not accounted murder when a slave died during "moderate correction," a debatable term in court. Whipping was the most common form of corporal punishment, and fifty lashes—quite enough to kill a man—was not an uncommon sentence. In the end, the slaves' only guarantees against brutality at the hands of their masters were the gospel of paternalism, social expectations of the master by his peers, religious scruples, and the slaves' cash value.

There are few better guarantees of a man's good behavior than the knowledge that bad behavior will cost him money. But that applies to men who are thinking. Slave owners and their overseers flew into uncontrolled rages and unintentionally maimed and killed slaves. Because their property rights in their slaves almost always took precedence in court over the slaves' human rights, owners were rarely punished for such crimes. After an incident of hideous torture in Virginia in 1858, with a slave dying after twenty-four hours of torture, the court imprisoned the sadistic master. But he did not forfeit ownership of the other blacks he owned.

A Diverse Institution

Many slave owners were impelled by their religion, their personal sense of decency, and by their aspirations to be seen as benevolent patriarchs to care generously for their slaves, sometimes even in violation of the slave codes.

A family that owned only one or two slaves occasionally developed a relationship much like partnership with them. Such white owners and their slaves ate the same food, slept in the same cabin, and worked together. However, the slave on a large plantation was likelier to be better off because of the poverty of the struggling small farmer.

After about 1840, large-scale slave owners generally provided adequate rations of corn meal, salt pork, and molasses. It was common to allow slaves to keep their own vegetable gardens and chicken coops. Some masters purchased vegetables and eggs from their slaves, reasoning that if both they and their slaves were in the vegetables and chicken businesses, they could not determine if the makings of a slave's dinner was stolen. For the same reason, few slave owners allowed slaves to raise hogs for their own use. Pork was one of the staples; the planter needed to control its production and distribution.

Some slaves were permitted to buy and sell beyond the boundaries of the plantation and to keep the money they earned. Along the Mississippi, task system slaves working on their own time cut wood for steamboats. Some sold chickens and eggs in towns, and here and there a slave had a shotgun for hunting small game. One remarkable slave entrepreneur was Simon Gray, a skilled flatboatman whose owner paid him $8 a month to haul lumber to New Orleans. Gray commanded crews of up to twenty men, including free whites, and kept detailed accounts. He eventually bought his freedom.

A few masters permitted their slaves to save money in order to purchase their freedom, their spouse's, or their children's, but the deal depended on the owner's decency. No contract with a slave was enforceable in most southern states. (Kentucky was an exception.)

A well-known example of open violation of a slave code was the model plantation of Joseph Davis, brother of Jefferson Davis, the future president of the Confederacy. Joseph Davis ignored a Mississippi law forbidding the education of blacks; he maintained a school and teacher for the children of the quarters.

It is important to recall, however, that for every master like Joseph Davis, there were a dozen who kept their slaves just sound enough to work and a dozen more who, out of stupidity, ignorance, or malevolence, treated them worse than they treated their mules. The editor of a southern magazine made no comment when a subscriber wrote, "Africans are nothing but brutes, and they will love you better for whipping, whether they deserve it or not."

RESISTANCE

Adherents of the positive good gospel were dead wrong to insist that most slaves were content with their lot in life. Many were fondly attached to kind masters, but the vast majority hated slavery, protesting and resisting both indirectly and by running away. When freedom became a realistic possibility during the Civil War, slaves deserted their homes by the tens of thousands to flee to Union lines. After the war, a South Carolina planter wrote candidly: "I believed these people were content, happy, and attached to their masters." That, he concluded sadly, had been "a delusion."

Running Away

The clearest evidence of slave discontent was the prevalence of runaways. Only blacks who lived in the states bordering the free states—Delaware, Maryland, Virginia, Kentucky, Missouri—had a reasonable chance of escaping to permanent freedom. Some "rode" the "underground railway," rushing at night from hiding places in one abolitionist's home, most often a black abolitionist's, to another.

Harriet Tubman, who escaped from her master in 1849, returned to the South nineteen times to lead other slaves to

Harriett Tubman (far left) with a "cargo" she has led from bondage in Maryland to relative safety in Pennsylvania. To guarantee freedom after 1850, when Tubman was a conductor on the "underground railroad," runaway slaves (especially those from nearby Maryland) had to make their way to Canada with the help of other conductors and station masters. Tubman made nineteen trips into the South at great risk. Legally she was herself still a slave and the penalties for helping slaves escape were harsh.

Pennsylvania. The "Black Moses" was a brave, shrewd, hands-on, and no-nonsense liberator. Tubman went south only in winter when the nights were longer and fewer people were out of doors. She herself never set foot on a plantation; she selected a rendezvous spot several miles away and sent locals to tell the slaves where she was.

Departure was almost always on Saturday night. The runaways, whom Tubman called her "cargo," would be missed Monday morning, but their master would not be alarmed until Monday evening. It was common for slaves to disappear for a few days even if their vacation meant a whipping. With her two day head start, Tubman moved only by night, depending on African American families known to her, free and slave, for food and shelter. If Tubman had to go into a town for some reason, she always approached from the north and left in a southerly direction. In appearance and manners, she was "a very respectable Negro, not at all a poor fugitive."

In a dangerous business—if caught she faced serious penalties—Tubman was no sunshine and sugar social worker. She screened would-be runaways with a jaundiced eye: "if he was weak enough to give out, he'd be weak enough to betray us all." She told her cargo she would shoot anyone who gave up.

The Slave Community

The culture of the quarters will never be fully understood because the slaves kept no written records. However, some reliable conjectures can be ventured based on what is known of African American religion and folklore.

By the 1850s, most slaves were Baptists or Methodists. Their religious services centered on animated sermons by unlettered, but eloquent preachers, some free, some slaves, and exuberant rhythmic singing.

In both sermons and song, the slaves identified with the ancient Hebrews. While in bondage in Babylon and Egypt, the Hebrews had been, nevertheless, God's chosen people. The protest—for God delivered the Hebrews from both of their captivities—was too obvious to be lost on whites. But as long as they were convinced—and the slaves obliged them—that blacks associated freedom with the afterlife, "crossing over Jordan," their religion was not stifled.

Slaves presented a face to whites quite different from their face among their own people. Some consciously played to white beliefs in their inferiority by playing the lazy, dimwitted, comical "Sambo," patently incapable of taking care of himself. However, a few observant whites noticed that Sambo was quick-witted enough when they surprised him while he was talking to other slaves, or that he literally slaved in his garden and slept only when in the fields of cotton.

Although marriage between slaves had no legal standing, family was more vital among slaves than it is among poor African Americans, poor whites, and, for that matter, the middle classes today. Both parents were present in two-thirds of slave families, the same proportion as among European peasants at that time. Perhaps the most striking demonstration of the resiliency of African Americans, even when oppressed by slavery, is the fact that, in 1865, when slavery was abolished, there were ten times more blacks in the United States than had been imported from Africa and the West Indies between 1619 and 1807. The American slave population was the only slave population in the Western Hemisphere to increase as a result of natural reproduction.

FURTHER READING

Classics Ulrich B. Phillips, *American Negro Slavery*, 1918, and *Life and Labor in the Old South*, 1929; Frank Tannenbaum, *Slave and Citizen*, 1947; Kenneth M. Stampp, *The Peculiar Institution*, 1956; Stanley Elkins, *Slavery: A Problem in American Institutional and Intellectual Life*, 1959; Eugene Genovese. *The Political Economy of Slavery*, 1965.

General D. W. Meinig, *The Shaping of America: A Geographical Perspective on 500 Years of American History*, Vol. 2, *Continental America, 1800–1867*, 1993; Don E. Fehrenbacher, *The Slave-Holding Republic: An Account of the United States Government's Relations to Slavery*, 2001; Peter J. Parish, *Slavery: History and Historians*, 1989; James Oates, *Slavery and Freedom: An Interpretation of the Old South*, 1990; Gavin Wright, *The Political Economy of the Cotton South*, 1998.

Slave Owners Eugene D. Genovese, *The World the Slaveholders Made*, 1988; William J. Cooper, *The South and the Politics of Slavery, 1828–1856*, 1978; James Oates, *The Ruling Race: A History of American Slaveholders*, 1982; Bruce Collins, *White Society in the Antebellum South*, 1985; Bertram Wyatt-Brown, *Honor and Violence in the Old South*, 1986, and *Southern Honor: Ethics and Behavior in the Old South*, 1988, and *The Shaping of Southern Culture: Honor, Grace, and War, 1760s–1890s*, 2001; Elizabeth Fox-Genovese, *Within the Plantation Household: Black and White Women of the Old South*, 1988; Brenda L. Stevenson, *Life in Black and White: Family and Community in the Old South*, 1996; Ira Berlin, *Many Thousands Gone: The First Two Centuries of Slavery in North America*, 1998; Thomas Bender, *The Anti-Slavery Debate*, 1992; Allison G. Freehling, *Drift Toward Dissolution: The Virginia Slavery Debate of 1831–1832*, 1982;

Eric Burin, *Slavery and the Peculiar Solution: A History of the American Colonization Society*, 2005.

Rebellions Douglas R. Egerton, *Gabriel's Rebellion: The Virginia Slave Conspiracies of 1800 and 1802*, 1993, and *He Shall Go Free: The Lives of Denmark Vesey*, 1999; James Sidbury, *Ploughshares into Swords: Race, Rebellion, and Identity in Gabriel's Virginia, 1730–1810*, 1997; David Robertson, *Denmark Vesey*, 1999; Scot French, *The Rebellious Slave: Nat Turner in American Memory*, 2004; James T. Baker, *Nat Turner: Cry Freedom in America*, 1998.

Slave Culture John Blassingame, *The Slave Community*, 1972, and *Slave Testimony*, 1977; Eugene Genovese, *Roll Jordan Roll*, 1975; Herbert G. Gutman, *The Black Family in Slavery and Freedom, 1750–1925*, 1976; Lawrence W. Levine, *Black Culture and Black Consciousness: Afro-American Folk Thought from Slavery to Freedom*, 1977; Albert J. Raboteau, *Slave Religion: The "Invisible Institution" in the Ante-Bellum South*, 1978; Vincent Harding, *There Is a River: The Black Struggle for Freedom in America*, 1981; Sterling Stuckey, *Slave Culture: Nationalist Theory and the Foundation of Black America*, 1987; Mia Bay, *The White Image in the Black Mind: African-American Ideas about White People, 1838–1925*, 2000; Deborah Gray White, *Ar'n't I a Woman?: Female Slaves in the Plantation South*, 1985.

Fugitives Albert J. Van Frank, *The Trials of Anthony Burns: Freedom and Slavery in Emerson's Boston*, 1996; Kate Clifford Larson, *Bound for the Promised Land: Harriett Tubman, Picture of an American Hero*, 2003; Fergus M. Bordewich, *Bound for Canaan: The Underground Railroad and the War for the Soul of America*, 2005.

KEY TERMS

Use the following listing of key terms to review important figures, events, locations, and concepts covered in this chapter. A glossary of these terms is available on *The American Past* companion Web site: www.cengage.com/history/conlin/tap9e

Liberia, p. 303

underground railroad, p. 306

Fugitive Slave Act of 1850, p. 306

"gag rule", p. 308

"positive good", p. 308

Fitzhugh, George, p. 308

Foster, Stephen Collins, p. 311

ONLINE RESOURCES

Find additional resources, including primary source documents, images, interactive maps, simulations, chapter review exercises, and Internet links at

The American Past companion Web site
www.cengage.com/history/conlin/tap9e

American History Resource Center
http://ushistory.wadsworth.com/

Chapter 19

From Sea to Shining Sea

Expansion 1820–1848

Denver Public Library, Western History Collection, [X11929].

Our manifest destiny is to overspread the continent allotted by Providence for the free development of our yearly multiplying millions.

—John Louis O'Sullivan

Poor Mexico, so far from God, so close to the United States.

—Porfiro Díaz

The Louisiana Purchase and the Adams-Oñis Treaty seemed to establish a permanent western boundary for the United States. The Rocky Mountains were a formidable natural barrier and beyond them was (so most people believed) forbidding desert that could be crossed only by heroic efforts. With the Atlantic to the east and the demilitarized Great Lakes to the north, Americans were secure.

But not necessarily satisfied. The Adams-Oñis agreement established the Sabine River as the boundary between the United States and Mexico, but would-be cotton barons could see that the land on the west bank was as fertile and well watered as the cotton lands in Louisiana. By 1821, with the consent of newly independent Mexico, Americans began to cross the Sabine.

MEXICO'S BORDERLANDS

New Spain—Mexico—was the jewel of the Spanish Empire for three centuries. A small elite of Spanish-born *gachupines* and Mexican-born but Caucasian *criollos* monopolized the best lands, living well off the labor of some slaves but, mostly, *péons*, Indians and the people who were the large majority of the population, the *mestizos* of European and Native American blood blended over centuries.

Expansion to the North

Just as Americans migrated westward, Mexicans expanded from the heart of New Spain to the north but, because of the government's tight controls on them, more slowly. Common people were rarely in the vanguard. They followed the military who established posts in the lands of warlike Indians and missionaries where the tribes had been pacified.

In 1609, contemporary with the founding of Jamestown, Santa Fe was established near the headwaters of the Rio Bravo del Norte (the Rio Grande), about 75 miles from the Indian pueblo of Taos, where Franciscan missionaries built a mission. Beginning later in the century, Franciscan priests founded more than twenty-five missions for the Indians on several Texas rivers. They were surrounded by sturdy walls to defend against the Comanches, a ferocious tribe of raiders feared by other Indians. (Sometimes the mission chapel was fortified as a kind of castle keep, a final refuge.)

Much later, beginning in 1769, another Franciscan friar, Junípero Serra, laid out a string of missions in Alta California ("Upper California," now the state of California). Serra was motivated by the missionary impulse to save souls. The viceroy of Mexico financed his project in order to establish an actual Spanish presence in the distant coastal province which navigators from other European nations were visiting. Serra's design, more or less completed in 1823, long after his death, was to establish a mission every 30 miles along the *camino real* ("royal highway," then a trail, now U.S. 101) so that a traveler on horseback could find dinner and shelter every night, and a foot traveler every second night. *Presidios* (military posts) near each mission would provide security. The Mexicans followed the friars and soldiers who

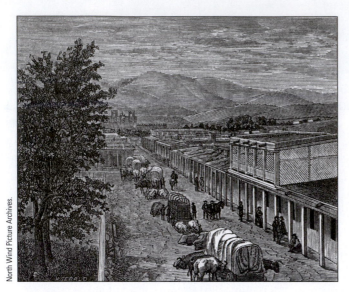

North Wind Picture Archives.

A wagon train loaded with trade goods enters Santa Fe after an 800 mile trip from Missouri across the plains of what is now Kansas, the Oklahoma panhandle, and Texas. Just about anything manufactured in the United States could be in the wagons, including some luxuries for the small New Mexican elite. The traders returned to Missouri with furs, gold, and silver.

supported themselves by raising cattle, exporting hides and tallow (animal fat that has been rendered, melted down, and clarified).

The Santa Fe Trade

New Mexico's products—furs and silver—were high in value and potentially profitable. But they could be exported only by mule train down the Rio Grande. The cost of overland transportation 300 miles from Santa Fe through rugged, arid country to El Paso and 1,000 more miles to the Gulf of Mexico (1,300 miles to a seaport on the Gulf of California) was prohibitive. There were few of life's amenities in Santa Fe.

Missouri was just 800 miles away and the terrain was mostly gentle. Until 1819, however, Americans were banned

from Spanish territory. The odd trespasser was arrested, sometimes roughly treated, and deported.

In 1821, with traders welcome, William Becknell of Franklin, Missouri, set off cross country in a wagon packed with cloth, shoes, tools, and some luxury items. Finding his way by compass and dead reckoning across what is now Kansas, he blazed a workable trail to Santa Fe. The 7,000 inhabitants of the town were so delighted to see him that they paid Becknell many times what his merchandise was worth in furs, gold, and silver.

Annually for fourteen years, a convoy of wagons rolled down the Santa Fe Trail. A few Missourians, such as horse handler and scout Christopher "Kit" Carson, settled in New Mexico, adapting easily to the Spanish-Indian culture. The presence of even a few *sassones* (Saxons) in Santa Fe and the vital overland trade forged a link between New Mexico and the United States that was—no matter the flag that flew, the religion practiced, and the language spoken—more substantial than the link between Santa Fe and Mexico City.

The Great American Desert

Most Americans, including the Santa Fe traders, believed that the territory the trail crossed was worthless except as a highway. At about 100° longitude (central Kansas), the land gradually rises from an elevation of 2,000 feet to, at the base of the Rockies, 5,000 to 7,000 feet. These high plains lie in the rain shadow of the Rockies. Before the westerly winds reach the plains, the moisture in them is scooped out by the great mountains.

Save for cottonwoods along the rivers, few trees grew on the plains. The vastness of the landscape unnerved Americans accustomed to dense forests and vistas interrupted by woods. When they gazed over the windblown buffalo grass, they thought not of farmland, but of the ocean. Indeed, the Santa Fe traders called their wagons "prairie schooners." Less poetic military mapmakers labeled the plains "the Great American Desert."

It was a mistake to believe, as Americans did, that only land that grew trees naturally would support crops. However, it was true enough that the tough sod of the plains, formed by centuries of grasses growing, dying, and thatching, was more than a blunt cast-iron plowshare pulled by a yoke of oxen or

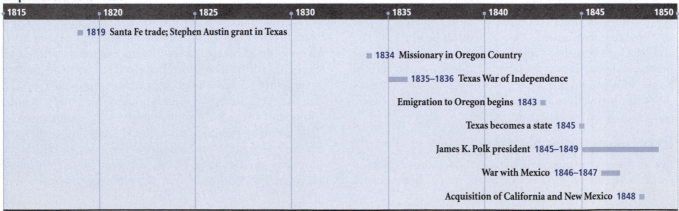

Expansion 1815–1850

1815	1820	1825	1830	1835	1840	1845	1850

■ 1819 Santa Fe trade; Stephen Austin grant in Texas

■ 1834 **Missionary in Oregon Country**

■ 1835–1836 **Texas War of Independence**

Emigration to Oregon begins 1843 ■

Texas becomes a state 1845 ■

James K. Polk president 1845–1849

War with Mexico 1846–1847 ■

Acquisition of California and New Mexico 1848 ■

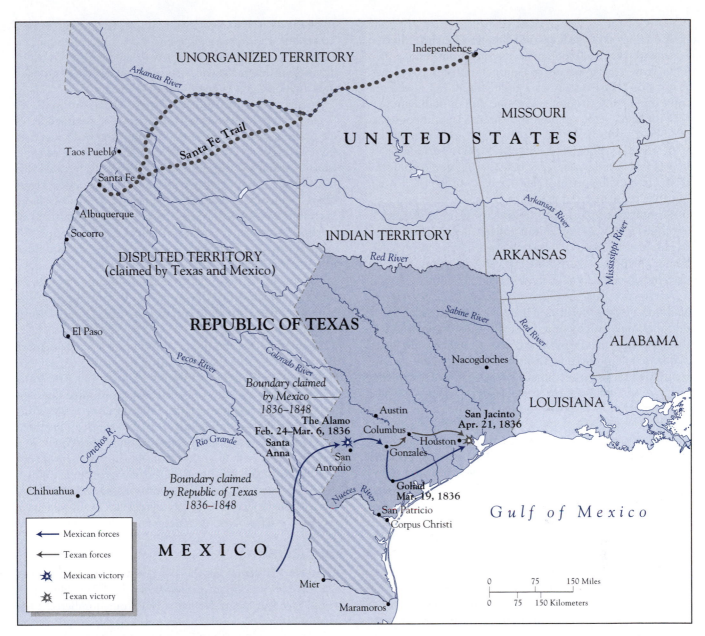

MAP 19:1 **Americans in the Mexican Borderlands, 1819–1848.** The Santa Fe Trail, which annually brought traders hauling American manufactures to New Mexico, was welcomed by the isolated population there. At first, American settlers in Texas were welcomed by the Mexican government. However, when they ignored Mexico's requirement they convert to Catholicism and Mexico's abolition of slavery, the stage was set for a violent confrontation that led to Texan independence.

a pair of horses could turn over. And there was not enough rainfall west of 100° longitude to sustain a grain crop. Travelers through the region observed that the grass that supported 10 million bison would fatten cattle too. But how could the hypothetical steers be gotten back East where the butcher shops were?

The Texians

The Great Plains extended into Texas, the northernmost part of the Mexican state of Coahuila. There, cattle could be grazed within driving distance of the Gulf of Mexico and transported by boat to New Orleans. In 1819, a Connecticut Yankee named Moses Austin was attracted by the economic possibilities of grazing and even more by the suitability

of eastern Texas to cotton cultivation. He proposed to the Mexicans that, in return for land grants, American settlers would settle the country and provide a counterforce to the Comanche, whose ferocity had discouraged Mexican settlers.

Moses Austin died but, in 1821, his son Stephen concluded the negotiations. He was licensed to bring 300 American families to Texas, each to receive 177 acres of farmland and 13,000 acres of grassland, an extraordinary giveaway. The contract required American immigrants to abide by Mexican law, to adopt the Spanish language, and to conform to the Roman Catholic religion. But for any government to expect the people of an alien culture living adjacent to their native land to alter their ways so radically was foolish (or the fruit of corruption in Mexico City).

Many of the earliest Texians (the name they originally gave themselves) were baptized Catholic, including Stephen Austin, who banned Protestant clergymen from Texas and, in 1826, drove a ragtag force from Louisiana out of Nacogdoches, just inside Texas. Austin was a good citizen. But he did not force immigrants to become Catholic, and most did not.

With land a tenth of the cost of similar land in Louisiana (and land grants much larger), Texas was soon overwhelmingly "Anglo" in population. By 1834, 15,000 of Texas's 20,000 whites were from the United States. They never did bridle the Comanche (who remained free agents until the Civil War), but they prospered and paid their taxes. There was no serious conflict with Mexican authorities until, in 1829, Mexico abolished slavery. Texian cotton growers depended on slaves to raise their crop and some grazers had slave *vaqueros* (cowboys). There were about 2,000 African Americans in a total non-Indian population of about 22,000.

For several years, the Texians got away with ignoring the abolition of slavery. Then, in 1833, General Antonio Lopez de Santa Anna seized power in Mexico City. In order to end the squabbling that had plagued Mexican politics since independence and promoting a sense of Mexican nationality, he centralized the government and cancelled American trading privileges in Santa Fe. Anglo-Texans feared for the considerable autonomy they had enjoyed and their economic connections with the United States, to say nothing of their illegal slaves.

Several hundred Anglo and a few Hispanic Texans seized the only military post in Texas, at San Antonio. Like the American rebels before 1776, they insisted they were fighting for the rights they had traditionally exercised as Mexican citizens. However, some spoke of independence and annexation to the United States from the start.

The Alamo

Like George III, Santa Anna had no intention of parleying with rebels. Indeed, he welcomed the uprising in Texas as an opportunity to rally the Mexican people around a national cause. In 1836, he led an army of 6,000 to San Antonio, assuming that the 200 Texans and a few newly arrived Americans who were holed up in an old mission compound called the Alamo (cottonwood tree) would, sensibly, surrender without a fight. Thence he would establish the authority of the national government in the province.

Among the men in the Alamo were several who were well known in the United States—celebrities. The commander of the garrison was William Travis, a Texan who had taken over from James Bowie, inventor of the famous double-edged knife, who was unable to rise from a sickbed. Even better known in the United States was the Whig politician from Tennessee, David "Davy" Crockett, a political opponent of Andrew Jackson. Recruiting rebels east of San Antonio was a good friend of Jackson and former governor of Tennessee, Sam Houston.

When the tiny force in the Alamo refused to surrender, Santa Anna had to choose between besieging the fort or containing it with part of his army and moving on to nip Houston's recruitment efforts before they bore fruit. Houston was having problems. Many Texans were uneasy about confronting professional soldiers.

Santa Anna chose to sit in San Antonio for ten days, more infuriated daily that the defenders of the Alamo (whose position was indeed hopeless) would not surrender. The "rules of war" said that when a hopelessly besieged force does not surrender, thus costing the attacking army unnecessary casualties, those defenders who survive the battle are not entitled to quarter. So, when Santa Anna captured the Alamo, at a terrible cost in men, his orders that all male prisoners be shot was not really the atrocity that Texans represented. (When, two weeks later at Golead, Santa Anna massacred 365 Texans who had surrendered, it was a different story but, somehow, the Alamo victims were the ones remembered as martyrs.)

San Jacinto

The delaying action of the defenders of the Alamo and Santa Anna's execution of prisoners solved Sam Houston's recruitment problems. He had a real if out-numbered army behind him when, on the banks of the San Jacinto River on

Santa Anna: A Curse Upon Mexico

Antonio López de Santa Anna was a courageous, even reckless soldier. He was also among the worst things that happened to Mexico during the nineteenth century. Juan O'Donoju, the last Spanish colonial governor of Mexico whom Santa Anna fought to overthrow, predicted his future as he prepared the return to Spain: "That young man will live to make his country weep."

Santa Anna was president of Mexico eleven times, a major contributor to the nation's political instability. He stole on a colossal scale from both the nation and (with forged documents) his neighbors. Just between Vera Cruz and Jalapa, a distance of miles, he owned nearly 500,000 acres, much of the land ill-gotten, 40,000 head of cattle, and thousands of horses. His military decisions at the Alamo, San Jacinto, and Buena Vista contributed vitally to Mexico's defeats. Yet with each of the disasters to which he contributed, he grew more egocentric, pathologically so at the end.

He even managed to inflict a new addiction on Americans. Between 1841 and 1844, exiled from Mexico, he lived in New York where he indulged his habit of chewing chicle, sap from the sapodilla tree. When he hurried back to Mexico to have another go at the presidency, he left his stash behind. It fell into the hands of Thomas Adams who marketed it as an alternative to chewing tobacco, a ubiquitous habit thought filthy in polite society. Adams made a decent living from "chewing gum." Fifty years later, it made William Wrigley very, very rich when he hit on the idea of sweetening and flavoring the chicle, calling it "Juicy Fruit."

© Bettmann/Corbis

A fanciful depiction of the final moments at the Alamo. The ailing Jim Bowie is in the archway at the left lying on a cot but still fighting away. (Who knows?) The heroic figure in fringed buckskin and coonskin cap is Davy Crockett. (If he ever wore a coon tail on a fur hat, it was unlikely he was wearing one at the battle at the Alamo.) Some accounts of the battle have Crockett fighting to the end, as in this picture; others say he was shot from a distance by a sniper; yet others have him surrendering only to be executed.

April 21, he routed the Mexicans and captured Santa Anna. In order to secure his release, Santa Anna agreed to the independence of Texas with its southern boundary at the Rio Grande rather than the Rio Nueces, which had been the boundary of Texas under Mexican authority. As soon as he was free, Santa Anna repudiated the agreement and the government that succeeded him (he was promptly overthrown) refused to recognize the Republic of Texas, let alone the Rio Grande border. Nonetheless, so as not to push their luck and provoke an invasion, few Texans moved south of the Nueces.

The Lone Star Republic

In October 1836, Sam Houston was inaugurated president of a republic patterned on the United States and dispatched

a minister to Washington. Houston hoped that his friend Jackson would push for an annexation bill in Congress before he left the presidency the next year. Jackson liked the idea of sewing the "Lone Star" of the Texas republic on the American flag. However, Congress was embroiled in a debate in which the topic of slavery was being bandied about and the Texas constitution protected slavery. Jackson recognized Texas independence on his last day in office in order to spare his northern successor, Martin Van Buren, political problems on that score, but he avoided recommending statehood.

Van Buren opposed annexation and was able to dodge a controversy because he had worse troubles, the Panic of 1837. The disappointed Texans, worried about facing a Mexican invasion better commanded than Santa Anna's, looked to Europe for an ally. They sent out feelers to Leopold I, king of the Belgians, offering him a huge grant of land in return for a loan and a military presence that, with a war against the Netherlands coming to an end, he had available. But the United States warned Leopold off. (The king occupied himself by encouraging a marriage between his niece, Queen Victoria, and another member of his family, Prince Albert.)

Texas then turned to Great Britain. British mills were already making deals to buy Texas cotton, and both political parties were favorable to the idea of an independent Texas under British protection as a barrier to further American expansion to the southwest. The hang-up was slavery. Parliament had recently abolished slavery throughout the empire (Britain had her militant evangelicals too), and the Royal Navy's ongoing campaign to wipe out the trans-Atlantic slave trade was popular. A British government committed to protecting a state run by slaveholders ran the risk of being voted out of office.

THE OREGON COUNTRY

The American government was uneasy about British influence in Texas. The joint occupation of Oregon, so good an idea when next to no Canadians or Americans lived there, had become an irritant when American missionaries and farmers began to settle in numbers in the Willamette River Valley.

Trappers and Indians

The mountain men needed the friendship of at least one Indian tribe, a second reason to take an Indian wife. With tribal enmities in the Northwest strong, however, identification with one people meant that others were enemies. In confrontations, the trappers' rifles gave them little edge. The large-bore Hawkens they favored for their stopping power were accurate to a hundred yards, 20 or 30 yards more than an Indian archer's arrow. But it took half a minute to reload a Hawken. A good Indian bowman could shoot ten arrows in that time.

The tribe most respected was the Blackfoot. So great was the fear of them that when, by 1840, overtrapping had destroyed the beaver population all over the West, the species remained numerous in Blackfoot country.

Mountain Men

Spain's claim to Oregon was never more than nominal. Spanish influence ended at the northernmost mission at Sonoma, just north of San Francisco, and it was nebulous there. So, after 1819, the northern boundary of Mexico was set at 42° north latitude (the present California-Oregon line) and Russia withdrew to Alaska above 54° 40' north latitude. The jointly occupied Oregon Country lay between the two parallels.

Harvesting the Beaver

Trapping beaver was not a Sierra Club wilderness adventure. It was hard work—and cold work, because the best pelts were taken when the animals were wearing their winter coats. The entrance to a beaver burrow was several feet below the surface of a river or pond. A trap weighing 5 pounds was anchored near the entryway and baited with the beaver's marking scent. The beaver died by drowning.

After cleaning, the pelt of an adult weighed about 2 pounds. At the annual rendezvous, trappers were paid $3 per pound, more if they took their pay in merchandise. So, in order to earn enough income for a year, a trapper had to harvest hundreds of animals. To move their cargos, they needed pack horses, which were expensive. Jedediah Smith bought broken-down nags by the dozen in California and sold them in the mountains for $50 each ($150 on one occasion) to mountain men whose horses had been stolen or killed by abuse.

American emigrants to Oregon were guided by the only people who knew the way, fur trappers popularly called "mountain men," Americans and Canadians who disappeared into the Rockies for eleven months each year to trap beaver. Some were freelancers, forming groups of a dozen or so for protection and company. The majority were employees of Canada's Hudson's Bay Company and John Jacob Astor's American Fur Company. At the peak of the fur trade, after

A mountain man and his equipage, drawn by the celebrated illustrator of western subjects, Frederic Remington. Remington never knew a real mountain man; he was born in 1861. But his research was solid and this portrayal rings true.

The Patricios

Half of the American soldiers who fought in the Mexican War were foreign-born. Half of them were immigrants from Ireland. Twenty-five percent of the army was Irish; yet others were the sons of Irish immigrants.

Like other recruits, some enlisted for patriotic reasons. Irish-Americans were famous for their patriotic observances. And for their Democratic party and proslavery politics. If northeastern Whigs called the Mexican War a slave-owners' land grab, that was no deterrent to Irish immigrants in Philadelphia, New York, and Boston.

Other Irish enlistees were destitute young men for whom the army meant shelter, good clothing, and three meals a day. The mid-1840s were the years of Ireland's Great Famine when desperate half-starved emigrants crammed into "famine ships" where the mortality rate on the Atlantic crossing was worse than it had been on the slave ships out of Africa. Army recruiters met immigrant ships at the docks. Many hundreds of hungry men enlisted as their first act on American soil.

Whatever an individual's reasons for signing up, army life lost many of its charms in Mexico. The death rate from disease in the camps for all soldiers was worse than in any other American war. Most of the Irish troops were Roman Catholic and many junior officers were both nativists (anti-immigrant) and anti-Catholic. The evidence that Irish Catholic soldiers were discriminated against, bullied, and prevented from attending mass or confessing to a priest before battles is anecdotal but persuasive. Every soldier heard anti-Mexican propaganda that often included reminders that the Mexicans were superstitious Catholic idolators. It went down well enough with Protestant soldiers who had heard about the evils of the Roman Church all their lives. It did not please Catholic Irishmen who, for one reason or another, were disenchanted with the army.

Soldiers of all backgrounds began to desert Zachary Taylor's army as soon as it crossed into Mexican territory. (Total desertions ranged between 15 percent and 20 percent each year of the war.) Most tried to get back to the United States where they could disappear. Others, the

Irish most conspicuously, deserted to Mexican lines. Some chose to fight on the "Catholic side." Others were lured by printed promises or whispers by Mexican infiltrators in the American camps that Americans who enlisted in the Mexican army would be paid better (an American private was paid a meager $7 a month) and, when the war was over, be given 300 acres of land.

Most deserters who joined the Mexican army were kept together in the *Batalion de San Patricio*, the Saint Patrick's Battalion, where they were augmented by a few prisoners of war whom the Mexicans recruited and Irishmen living in Mexico before the war began. Mexicans fondly called them *colorados* (the red-haired ones) and Patricios (the Patricks). At Buena Vista, they manned artillery and, according to American troops, fought better than anyone else in the Mexican lines.

Joining the retreat to Mexico City, the Saint Patrick's Battalion fought in every battle against Winfield Scott's army, but as infantrymen. At Churubusco, assigned to a position where retreat was next to impossible, and knowing that if captured they would be shot, 260 Patricios almost alone delayed the American advance for a full day.

By the end of the fighting, eighty-five alleged Patricios were American prisoners. Thirteen were released when it was determined that they had not fought in the battalion or had never been United States soldiers. Of the seventy-two who were tried in court martials, seventy were sentenced to death. General Scott pardoned five (he thought the evidence against them faulty) and reduced the sentences of fifteen. Fifty were executed, thirty at Chapultepec.

The Patricios were (and are) remembered as national heroes in Mexico, and they are commemorated annually in County Galway in Ireland. Ironically, historians who have identified 103 individuals who fought in the Saint Patrick's Battalion, discovered that only 40 of them were Irish, although another 22 who were born in the United States may have been Irish-American. Several nationalities were represented, but most of the non-Irish Patricios were German. Rather more surprising, while most of the Patricios were Roman Catholic, a significant minority was not.

---

the War of 1812, there may have been 500 mountain men in the wilderness. About half of them took Indian wives.

Before 1825, they took their pelts to the companies' headquarters on the Columbia River. Beginning in 1825, with the beaver population drastically reduced except in the most isolated mountain valleys, they met buyers at a prearranged site for "rendezvous" on the Platte, Sweetwater, or Big Horn Rivers. For a few weeks, buyers, mountain men, and Indians traded, drank, generally enjoyed a riotous orgy, and now and then bit off the ear of an old pal.

Geography Teachers

A few mountain men were legends during their lifetimes. Jedediah Smith identified South Pass in Wyoming, where most overland emigrants crossed the continental divide. Smith should also have been singled out because he was pious and abstemious; he neither drank alcohol nor slept with Indian women. (Other mountain men, who were none of the above, certainly noticed.) Jim Beckwourth, the son of an African American woman and a white man, discovered the lowest (therefore, the least snowy) pass through the

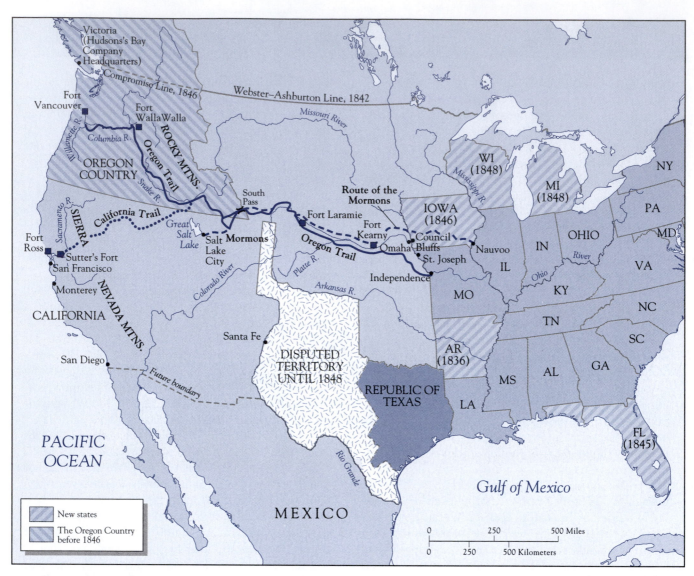

MAP 19:2 **Americans in the West to 1849.** In 1846, Britain and the United States divided the Oregon Country at the 49th parallel. Northern Utah was still Mexican territory when the Mormons began to settle it. By the time of the discovery of gold in California, however, Mexico had ceded the entire southwest to the United States.

Sierra Nevada. His cronies valued him for his toughness and bravery but, even in a society in which the tall tale was king, they said that it was wise not to believe a word Beckwourth said. There was little race consciousness in the mountains. Polette Labross was an African American who traveled with Jedediah Smith. Many of the French Canadian trappers were *metís,* "half-breeds."

Jim Bridger, perhaps the greatest mountain man of them all, was a walking, talking atlas of the West. He explored almost every nook of the Rockies. He was the first non-Indian to lay eyes on the Great Salt Lake. The geographic knowledge of the mountain men was their great legacy. Along with a young army officer sent west, John C. Frémont, a better self-publicist than wilderness explorer (he was guided by a mountain man, Kit Carson, who saved his skin on several occasions), they taught the folks back home that while it would be a long, hard journey, it was possible to cross the continent—with wagons.

The Oregon Trail

Among the first to make the six-month journey for the purpose of settling in the Oregon Country were missionaries. In 1834, eight years before Frémont's first expedition, the Methodists sent Jason Lee, a longtime circuit rider, to the Indians. In 1835, four Nez Percés visited the American Board of Foreign Missions and, so the board reported, persuaded them that the gospel their tribe wanted to hear was the Presbyterian. In 1836, Marcus and Narcissa Whitman carried it to them on foot. (The Whitmans converted a Scot, a French Canadian, and a Hawai'ian, but not a single Indian; in 1847, Indians blamed a measles epidemic on the Whitmans and murdered them.) The Catholic University at St. Louis sent Father Pierre-Jean de Smet to Oregon.

The wagon trains on Frémont's Oregon Trail, the first ones in 1843, usually set out from Independence, Missouri, a city that had specialized in outfitting overland travelers since the

The overland trail forked near the Snake River. The Oregon Trail followed the Snake to the northwest; the California trail branched southwest into what is now Nevada. This extraordinary photograph, with two wagon trains side by side, indicates how crowded the trail could be during the 1850s.

Santa Fe trail had opened. The first great "Oregon or Busters," a thousand in 1843, took oaths to observe strict rules of behavior and to cooperate for the duration of the crossing.

Guided by hired mountain men, the emigrants crossed Kansas to the Platte River and followed that broad, shallow stream to Fort Laramie, the army's westernmost outpost. They crossed the continental divide over South Pass and struggled to near the Snake River, which flows into the Columbia and the Pacific. A wagon train covered up to 20 miles a day or as few as none at all, depending on the terrain and the weather. At night, exhausted by the killing labor of moving dozens of wagons and several hundred head of oxen, horses, mules, and cattle (Kit Carson crossed the continent with a huge flock of sheep), the emigrants drew their prairie schooners into a hollow square or circle as a precaution against Indian attack.

In fact, Indians threatened but knew better than to attack large, well-organized expeditions armed with rifles. While hardly delighted to see hordes of white strangers crossing their ancestral hunting lands (3,000 in 1845), these whites were, at least, passing through. Theft, however, was a constant problem for the emigrants. Indians made a game of stealing horses that strayed too far from the caravans. They also traded with the travelers and picked up the discarded gewgaws that soon littered the trail. Long before the annual river of wagons wore ruts into the sod and rock (some can be seen today), professional guides were no longer necessary. The Oregon Trail was marked with broken furniture, discarded barrels, broken-down wagons, the skeletons of animals, and simple grave markers. Death from accidents or disease, particularly cholera, was part of the adventure. But it was impossible to lose the way.

Manifest Destiny

By 1845, the American population of the Columbia and Willamette Valleys had grown to 7,000. The Hudson's Bay Company prudently moved its headquarters from the mouth of the Columbia to Vancouver Island. What is now the state of Washington was a buffer zone between British and American population centers. There were occasional clashes—brawls, not battles—but the possibility of worse was obvious.

The Americans in Oregon wanted an end to joint occupation. In July 1843, a group met at Champoeg and established a provisional territorial government under the American flag. Some Democratic party politicians back East called for unilateral annexation of the Oregon Country. They were as interested in "twisting the lion's tail," taunting the British, a nonissue popular with demagogues with nothing else to say, as in affecting policy.

Weary, sunburned, dusty, tough-looking emigrants bound overland. It is probably Sunday when many wagon trains, for religious reasons or just to give their livestock a break, stayed where they were.

But the idea of aggressive territorial expansion was taking on an unprecedented life at the grass roots. (The annexations of Louisiana and Florida had been quietly initiated at the top and sprung as a surprise on the nation.) To some, territorial expansion was a sacred national duty. Democratic party propagandists claimed that the United States had an obligation to increase the domain in which democracy and liberty held sway. It remained for a New York journalist, John O'Sullivan, to coin a catchphrase. It was, he wrote, the "manifest destiny" of the United States—clearly God's will—to expand from sea to sea.

The Texas Debate

Some southerners added slavery to the list of American institutions to be carried across the continent. In 1843, then Secretary of State John C. Calhoun asked the Senate to annex

"Dark Horse"

The term "dark horse," which Americans applied to surprise presidential candidates (a species now extinct) came from a novel, *The Young Duke,* published in 1832 by future British prime minister Benjamin Disraeli: "A dark horse which never had been thought of, and which the careless St. James had never even observed in the list, rushed past the grandstand in sweeping triumph." The phrase was part of race track lingo when the Democrats nominated James K. Polk to run for president in 1844. Other dark horse presidential candidates were James A. Garfield (1880), William Jennings Bryan (1896), and Wendell Willkie (1940).

Texas lest growing British influence result in the abolition of slavery there. He won the support of some northern Democrats such as Lewis Cass of Michigan and James Buchanan of Pennsylvania. But not enough of them. In 1844, the Senate rejected Calhoun's proposal by a 2 to 1 vote. Every Whig but one voted nay.

Most northern Whigs opposed the addition of new slave states to the Union except for Florida (which became a state the next year). Except for the Indian Territory (Oklahoma) slavery was illegal in all the western lands. Moreover, the Whigs argued that annexing Texas would lead to a war with Mexico in which the Mexicans, not the Americans, would be in the right.

Neither of the likely presidential nominees of 1844 was happy to see Texas annexation shaping up as the principal issue of the campaign. Henry Clay knew that his Whig party, already strained by slavery issues, might split in two over Texas. Martin Van Buren, who commanded a majority of delegates to the Democratic nominating convention, had the same problem. The Democrats were torn between proslavery and antislavery factions. If the two candidates took opposite stands on the question, both of their parties would be disarrayed as voters voted on Texas rather than on party lines. Neither partisan old rogue wanted that. They met quietly and agreed that both would oppose annexation and compete on more comfortable issues.

Their unusual bargain presented lame-duck President Tyler with an opportunity. He would be a third candidate favoring annexation. Tyler had no party behind him, so his announcement did not disturb Clay and Van Buren. Then

Reproduced from the Collections of The Library of Congress Prints and Photographs Division, Washington, D.C. [LC-USZC4-668]

Amusing in the extravagance of its symbolism, this is a splendid representation of the exuberance of American expansion: Indians and bison flee before emigrants— miners and farmers— followed by the telegraph, the overland stagecoach, and the railroad. The rider to the left of the giantess symbolizing civilization is a pony express rider.

occurred one of those unlikely events that unexpectedly changes the course of history. Manifest Destiny Democrats revived a neglected party rule that a presidential nominee win the support of two-thirds of the delegates to the convention, not just a simple majority. Having declared against annexation, Van Buren was stymied. Pro-Texas Democrats numbered far more than a third of the delegates.

After eight ballots, the convention turned to a dark-horse candidate, that is, a man who was not a contender for the nomination. He was James Knox Polk of Tennessee, a protégé of Jackson not yet 50 years old. (Supporters called him "Young Hickory.") Polk was a Van Buren man but, personally, he favored annexation of Texas; he was a perfect compromise candidate.

The Election of 1844

"Who is Polk?" the Whigs asked scornfully. The sarcasm was misplaced. Polk had not been seeking the nomination, but he was well-known. He had been governor of Tennessee and served in Congress for fourteen years, several of them as Speaker. Nevertheless, he lacked the stature of Henry Clay. A frail, small man with a look of melancholy about him, Polk was priggish, disapproving of alcohol, dancing, and playing cards.

At first, Henry Clay was delighted to have Polk as his opponent. After three attempts, he would be president at last. The partyless Tyler and the colorless Polk would divide the pro-Texas vote. The anti-Texas vote, including the antislavery Democrats who would have voted for Van Buren, was his.

Then another piece of sky fell. Tyler withdrew from the contest and every wind brought Clay news that Manifest Destiny was carrying the day. He began to waffle on expansion. His equivocation on Texas may have cost Clay the election by angering anti-annexation Whigs in New York State which, as so often in the nineteenth century, was the key to the election. Polk carried New York by a scant 5,000 votes. Counties that had voted Whig for ten years gave 16,000 votes to James G. Birney, the candidate of the abolitionist Liberty party.

Encouraged by the election results and egged on by the Secretary of State Calhoun, Tyler moved on the Texas question. He could not muster the two-thirds vote in the Senate that ratification of a treaty requires, but he had a majority of both houses of Congress behind him. Three days before Polk's inauguration, Congress approved a joint resolution with the Texas Congress making the Lone Star Republic the twenty-eighth state.

A Successful President

In terms of defining his goals clearly and, in the four years he allotted himself, accomplishing each of them, he must be considered one of the most successful of presidents. Shortly before he was inaugurated, Polk declared he would serve only one term. In that time he would secure Texas to the Union; acquire New Mexico and California from Mexico; and annex the Oregon Country.

General John E. Wool and his staff in Saltillo, shortly before or after the battle of Buena Vista in 1846. This is believed to be the earliest surviving photograph of American soldiers.

Polk was a hardworking president, an *over*worker, a confessed micromanager. "I prefer to supervise the whole operations of the government myself," he said, "rather than entrust the public business to subordinates." With Texas already in the bag, he turned to Oregon, publically embracing a chauvinistic slogan of the day: "Fifty-four Forty or Fight!" That is, if the British did not agree to cede the entire Oregon Country to the United States (up to the boundary of Russian America at 54° 40' north latitude), he would ask Congress for a declaration of war.

Polk's saber rattling was all for show. The Democrats were comfortably in control of Congress, but Polk could never have persuaded all of them to vote for a war of aggression to abrogate an agreement (joint occupation) to which both countries had freely agreed. Polk himself, expecting war with Mexico, had no intention of fighting the British too. He let it be known that he would "settle" for an extension of the Webster-Ashburton line, 49° north latitude, through the Oregon country with Britain retaining all of Vancouver Island. The 49th parallel suited the British fine; they had few interests south of it. Except for a minor adjustment of the border in the Strait of Juan de Fuca in 1872, the American-Canadian boundary was final in 1846.

Polk was equally cynical in his designs on California and New Mexico, but less devious. The United States had no legal claim on either Mexican province. Nor could Polk claim, as he could about Texas and Oregon, that California and New Mexico were peopled largely by Americans. Unassimilated gringos were few in New Mexico, and there were only about 700 Americans in California among 6,000 *californios*. Two years before Polk's election, an American naval officer, Thomas Catesby Jones, somehow got it into his head that the United States was at war with Mexico and he seized Monterey, California's provincial capital. When he learned that he was mistaken, he had to run down the flag and sail off, rather the fool. Jones was merely a few years ahead of the game. When Mexico turned down Polk's offer

Gringos

The origin of the word *gringo,* once a pejorative Mexican term for Americans, now inoffensive, is obscure. One theory is that it originated during the American occupation of Mexico City when a song popular with American troops began, "Green grows the grass . . ." To Mexicans, it was gobbledygook, but they caught the first two syllables and used them to refer to the *norteamericanos.* Another theory is that the word was a corruption of *griego,* "Greek," which Mexicans applied to people speaking a foreign language in the same sense that Americans say, "it's Greek to me."

to buy California and New Mexico for $30 million, he set out to take them by force.

War with Mexico

The luckless Santa Anna was back in power in Mexico City. This time, however, he was uncharacteristically cautious. He ordered Mexican troops in Coahuila not to provoke the Americans in Texas. It was no use. Polk was determined to have war. He drew up an address asking Congress for a declaration of war on the grounds that the Mexican government owed $3 million to American banks. It was pretty weak stuff, and he did not have to use it. When, on Polk's orders, General Zachary Taylor of Louisiana took 1,500 soldiers across the Nueces River into disputed territory, there was a skirmish with a Mexican patrol in which sixteen American soldiers were killed.

Affecting outrage, Polk declared that because of Mexican aggression, a state of war between the two nations already existed. Constitutionally, this was nonsense. Congress alone had the authority to declare war. (And it was not clear if the skirmish had been north of the Rio Grande.) But patriotic danders were up; Congress rubber-stamped Polk's presidential declaration.

The Mexican army was much larger than the American and there were several regiments the equal of any in the world. But a majority of troops were conscripts, debtors, and petty criminals given the choice between the army and prison. They were poorly equipped: many muskets were European castoffs and Mexican artillery was antiquated. Generals owed their rank not to merit, but to social connections; many junior officers were social climbers who had bought their commissions. The army was demoralized by political instability. And Mexico was divided and flat broke. Only seven of Mexico's nineteen states contributed men and money to the war effort. When, in September 1846, Santa Army marched north to confront Zachary Taylor, there were precisely 1,839 pesos in the national treasury.

The Campaigns

There were two American advances into California. To the south, after occupying Santa Fe in the summer of 1846, Stephen W. Kearny marched his troops to California where he fought a few minor engagements against hastily organized *californio* militia and small Mexican garrisons. In the north, John C. Frémont arrived in Sacramento to discover that a ragtag bunch of American civilians had, in a ludicrous imitation of Texas, proclaimed the Bear Flag Republic.

In September, 1846, General Taylor advanced into northern Mexico and defeated Mexican armies at Matamoros and Nuevo León (also known as the Battle of Monterey). Although "Old Rough and Ready," as his men called him, showed shrewd tactical judgment, the Nuevo León garrison escaped. Polk, a man ruled by his prejudices, disliked Taylor and used his mistake as an excuse to divert many of Taylor's troops to General Winfield Scott's command. In February 1847, Taylor's depleted army of about 4,000 was attacked by

MAP 19:3 Campaigns of the Mexican War, 1846–1847. Frémont's and Kearny's invasions of California met little armed resistance. Zachary Taylor won the decisive battle of Buena Vista near Saltillo against the odds, but President Polk, in part to deny Taylor any more glory, reduced the size of his army so that he could not march on Mexico City. That campaign, commanded by Winfield Scott, followed the route of Cortes from Vera Cruz.

about 15,000 Mexicans commanded by Santa Anna at Buena Vista. Miraculously, Taylor defeated the president (then, again, Santa Anna specialized in losing battles to inferior numbers) and Old Rough and Ready was, justifiably, an instant national hero.

The next month, March 1847, Scott landed at Vera Cruz and fought his way toward Mexico City along the ancient route of Cortés. He won a big victory at Cerro Gordo and an even bigger one at Chapultepec, where he captured 3,000 men and eight generals. On September 14, 1847, Scott donned one of the gaudy uniforms he loved (his men called him "Old Fuss and Feathers") and occupied Mexico City, "the Halls of Montezuma."

By the Treaty of Guadalupe-Hidalgo, pretty much dictated by Nicholas Trist and signed in February 1848, Mexico agreed to Texas's Rio Grande boundary and ceded California and New Mexico, (including the present states of Arizona, Nevada, and Utah) to the United States. Mexico was paid $15 million and relieved of its American debts.

Mexico was dismembered like a carcass of beef. One-third of Mexican territory—an area larger than France and Spain combined—was detached because the Polk administration wanted it and the United States was strong enough to take it. While the failings of the Mexican military played a part in the national disaster, the reduction of the country to a rump could not but leave bitterness in the historical memory of the Mexican people.

The Opposition

Despite the president's cynicism, the war was popular at home. The regular army could accept only a fraction of the young men who tried to enlist. When the governor of Tennessee called for 3,000 volunteers for the state militia, 30,000 showed up. Almost every battle was an American victory: Buena Vista was a near miracle and Chapultepec and Cerro Gordo were brilliantly commanded major confrontations. Only 1,700 Americans died in battle (although 11,000 soldiers succumbed to disease, making for the worst casualty rate in the nation's history). About 50,000 Mexican soldiers lost their lives.

There were dissenters, some openly critical of "Mr. Polk's War," many more people quietly unhappy. Although the two great commanders, Taylor and Scott, were both Whigs, some Whig congressmen, including a freshman representative from Illinois, Abraham Lincoln, voted against the declaration and were never reconciled to what they considered a war to expand slavery. In the Senate, Thomas Corwin of Ohio warned his jingo colleagues, "If I were a Mexican, I would tell you, 'Have you not room in your own country to bury your dead men? If you come into mine, we will greet you with bloody hands, and welcome you to hospitable graves.'" (Two decades later, President Abraham Lincoln named Corwin minister to Mexico, hoping that his sympathies in 1846 would be remembered.)

In New England, Whig politicians and clergymen condemned the war from platform and pulpit. Ralph Waldo Emerson and much of the Massachusetts cultural establishment opposed it. Henry David Thoreau went to jail rather than pay a tax that, he said, would help pay for adding new slave states to the Union.

Not even the officer corps of the regular army was unanimous in favor of war. Years later in his autobiography, Ulysses S. Grant, whose performance in Mexico was outstanding, remembered that he had been "bitterly opposed," regarding the war "as one of the most unjust ever waged by a stronger against a weaker nation.... Even if the annexation itself could be justified, the manner in which the ... war was forced upon Mexico cannot."

Nicholas Trist, who negotiated the Treaty of Guadalupe-Hidalgo for the United States, wrote of the day he signed the agreement, "Could those Mexicans have seen into my heart at that moment, they would have known that my feeling of shame as an American was strong." The treaty was something "for every right-minded American to be ashamed of, and I was ashamed of it, most cordially and intensely ashamed of it."

The vote in the Senate to ratify Guadalupe-Hidalgo was 38 to 14. Had four senators changed their votes, the treaty would not have been approved.

Expansion Run Amok

Cynical as the treaty was, the Mexican acquisition was moderate compared to the demands of some expansionists. Trist had to rush the negotiations because Polk had decided to seize even more of Mexico. Just about the time Trist's treaty arrived in Washington, there was a rebellion in the Yucatan Peninsula, and the president asked Congress to authorize the army, which was still in Mexico, to take over the tropical province.

Polk also had designs on Spanish Cuba where the island's 350,000 slaves had long excited the imaginations of proslavery southerners. Polk wanted to present Spain with a choice between selling Cuba and running the risk of a rebellion fomented by the United States and followed by American military intervention.

Even more bizarre was J. D. B. De Bow, an influential southern editor. He wrote that it was the American destiny to absorb not only *all* of Mexico, but also the entire West Indies, Canada, and Hawai'i. And that was for appetizers. De Bow continued:

> The gates of the Chinese empire must be thrown down by the men from the Sacramento and the Oregon, and the haughty Japanese tramplers upon the cross be enlightened in the doctrines of republicanism and the ballot box. The eagle of the republic shall poise itself over the field of Waterloo, after tracing its flight among the gorges of the Himalaya or the Ural mountains, and a successor of Washington ascend the chair of universal empire.

FURTHER READING

General John Mack Faragher and Robert V. Hine, *The American West: A New Interpretive History,* 2000; Don E. Fehrenbacher, *The Slaveholding Republic: An Account of the United States Government's Relationship to Slavery,* 2001; Reginald Horsman, *Race and Manifest Destiny: The Origins of American Racial Anglo-Saxonism,* 1981; Patricia Limerick, *Legacy of Conquest: The Unbroken Past of the American West,* 1987; Richard D. White, *"It's Your Misfortune and None of My Own": A History of the American West,* 1992; Paul H. Bergeron, *The Presidency of James K. Polk,* 1987.

The Southwest Donald J. Weber, *The Spanish Frontier in North America,* 1992; David J. Beber, *The Mexican Frontier: The American Southwest Under Mexico,* 1982; Gregory M. Franzwa, *The Santa Fe Trail Revisited,* 1989; William Y. Chalfant, *Dangerous Passage: The Santa Fe Trail and the Mexican War,* 1994; Cheryl J. Foote, *Women of the New Mexico Frontier, 1846–1912,* 2005; Michael A. Morrison, *Slavery and the American Southwest: The Eclipse of Manifest Destiny,* 1997; Timothy Matovina, *Tejano Religion and Ethnicity: San Antonio, 1821–1860,* 1995; Paul D. Lack, *The Texas Revolutionary Experience: A Political and Social History, 1835–1836,* 1992; Mark Derr, *The Frontiersman: The Real Life and Many Legends of Davy Crockett,* 1993; Edward P. Crapol, *John Tyler: The Accidental President,* 2006.

Oregon Laura Parker, *Jim Bridger, Mountain Man,* 1981; D. J. Wishart, *The Fur Trade of the American West, 1807–1840,* 1979; Theodore J. Karamanski, *Fur Trade and Exploration: Opening the Far Northwest, 1821–1852,* 1983; Jennifer S. Brown, *Strangers in Blood: Fur Trade Company Families in Indian Country,* 1980; John D. Unruh, *The Plains Across: The Overland Emigrants and the Trans-Mississippi West, 1840–1860,* 1979; John Mack Faragher, *Women and Men on the Oregon Trail,* 1979; David Dary, *The Oregon Trail: An American Saga,* 2004; David A. Johnson, *Founding the Far West: California, Oregon, and Nevada, 1840–1890,* 1992; Albert L. Hurtado, *Intimate Frontiers: Sex, Culture, and Gender in California,* 1999; Malcolm Clark, Jr., *The Eden-Seekers: The Settlement of Oregon, 1812–1862,* 1981; Glenda Riley, *The Female Frontier,* 1988.

The War with Mexico K. Jack Bauer, *The Mexican–American War, 1846–1848,* 1974; Robert W. Johansen, *To the Halls of Montezuma: The Mexican War in the American Imagination,* 1985; John S. D. Eisenhower, *So Far From God: The U.S. War with Mexico, 1846–1849,* 1989; Paul Foos, *A Short, Offhand, Killing Affair: Soldiers and Social Conflict During the Mexican-American War,* 2002; Timothy J. Henderson, *A Glorious Defeat: Mexico and the War with the United States,* 2007; James McCaffrey, *Army of Manifest Destiny: The American Soldier in the Mexican War,* 1992; Iris Engstrand et al., *Culture y Cultura: Consequences of the U.S.-Mexican War, 1846–1848,* 1998; K. Jack Bauer, *Zachary Taylor: Soldier, Planter, Statesman of the Old Southwest,* 1985; Timothy D. Johnson, *Winfield Scott: The Quest for Military Glory,* 1998; Allan Peskin, *Winfield Scott and the Profession of Arms,* 2003; Robert L. Scheina, *Santa Anna: A Curse Upon Mexico,* 2002; Robert R. Miller, *Shamrock and Sword: The Saint Patrick's Battalion in the U.S.-Mexican War,* 1989.

KEY TERMS

Use the following listing of key terms to review important figures, events, locations, and concepts covered in this chapter. A glossary of these terms is available on *The American Past* companion Web site: www.cengage.com/history/conlin/tap9e

Junipero Serra, p. 319

Alamo, p. 322

Whitman, Marcus, p. 326

Santa Fe Trail, p. 327

Manifest Destiny, p. 327

dark horse candidate, p. 329

"Fifty-Four Forty or Fight", p. 330

ONLINE RESOURCES

Find additional resources, including primary source documents, images, interactive maps, simulations, chapter review exercises, and Internet links at

***The American Past* companion Web site**
www.cengage.com/history/conlin/tap9e

American History Resource Center
http://ushistory.wadsworth.com/

Chapter 20

Apples of Discord

Western Lands and Immigration 1844–1856

North Wind Picture Archives

The United States will conquer Mexico, but it will be as the man who swallows the arsenic which brings him down in turn

—Ralph Waldo Emerson

The defeat of the Mexican army and the huge acquisition of land in the Treaty of Guadalupe-Hidalgo did not usher in even a few years of concord in the United States. The treaty was ratified in March 1848. Two months earlier, an American carpenter already living in California discovered gold. President Polk confirmed the discovery in December. The next year, a deluge of gold seekers populated the state, setting in motion a series of events that made the question of slavery in the new western territories the subject of a sectional debate that almost led to the break-up of the Union. In 1854, the question of slavery in the Louisiana Purchase lands, thought to be resolved for all time in the Missouri Compromise of 1820, was reopened.

The immigration of destitute Irish Catholics, annually increasing since the 1820s, became a flood in 1845, arousing fears and resentments so powerful that an anti-immigrant, anti-Catholic political party was, briefly, the second largest party in the United States.

SLAVERY AND THE WEST

Slavery had been the subject of acrimonious conflict since the early 1830s. Abolitionists and slavery's defenders had hurled anathemas at one another. But the debate had been between zealots, evangelical abolitionists on the one side and on the other, hyper-agitated southerners who called slavery a positive good. Mainstream politicians, both northerners and southerners, tried to stay out of it; they were appalled that fanatics should be playing an ever-increasing role in political discourse.

John Quincy Adams, who fought for the right of antislavery petitioners to be heard in Congress, regarded the rhetoric of extremist abolitionists like William Lloyd Garrison as reprehensible. Thomas Hart Benton of Missouri, himself a slave owner, was disgusted by southerners who were obsessed with the question of slavery. It was like the biblical visitation of the plague of frogs in Pharaoh's Egypt: "You could not look on the table but there were frogs. You could not sit down at the banquet table but there were frogs, you could not go to the bridal couch and lift the sheets but there were frogs! We can see nothing, touch nothing, have no measures proposed, without having this pestilence thrust before us."

Congress and Slavery

Democrats like Benton and Martin Van Buren and Whigs like Adams and Henry Clay were practical politicians. To them, the invective exchanged by abolitionists and proslavery extremists had no place in government where it could have no constructive end. Slavery had come to be defined as a "domestic institution" within each state. Whether or not the institution was to be legal was for each state to decide.

Slavery could be abolished nationally by amending the Constitution, but that amendment was beyond the realm of reality. Amendments must be ratified by three-fourths of the states; in 1850, half the states protected slavery within their borders; none of them was going to ratify an abolition amendment. When William Lloyd Garrison cursed the Constitution and called on the free states to secede from the Union, it was because the abolition of slavery was politically impossible.

Congress had the power "to exercise exclusive legislation in all cases whatsoever" within the District of Columbia at that time; a congressional committee governed Washington.

Reproduced from the Collections of The Library of Congress Prints and Photographs Division, Washington, D.C. [LC-B811 - 2299]

A slave trader's "holding pens" —cells, actually. Here slaves were confined until a buyer walked into the office or there was an auction. It was the ugliness of the auction block and these "warehouses" for human beings in Washington that persuaded even some pro-slavery southern congressmen to agree to the abolition of the slave trade—the buying and selling of slaves—in the national capital. Who needed that kind of publicity?

Antislavery congressmen could and did call for banning the buying and selling of slaves in the capital. Northerners (and even some politicians from the border states) were open to the idea if only for cosmetic reasons. Slave auctions were ugly affairs at their best. The headquarters of professional slave traders were jails where the merchandise was displayed in cells. Why put what even the proslavery forces admitted was slavery's worst face on view in the American city which almost all foreigners visited?

A Dead Letter

Congress had the authority to legislate concerning slaves who fled across a state line. Because they were property, slaves who ran away from their masters were, in effect, stealing themselves. The Fugitive Slave Act of 1793 required that state authorities return runaway slaves to their owners, but several free states, led by Pennsylvania, found ways to obstruct enforcement of the act without running afoul of the Constitution. By the end of the 1840s, the states of the upper South faced a serious runaway problem. Each year, between 1,000 and 1,500 slaves in Maryland, Virginia, and Kentucky were getting away to free states. Southerners demanded a new fugitive slave law that northerners could not easily evade.

A few southern hotheads proposed legalizing the importation of slaves from abroad. No one with any sense expected a resumption of the African slave trade. That would bring the United States into a head-on conflict with Great Britain which, in peacetime, assigned ships of its navy to cruise the West African coast and seize vessels with slaves aboard. But it was a short voyage from Savannah and Charleston to Cuba through waters the American navy patrolled, and there were plenty of slaves for sale in Cuba at the prices Americans would pay.

In the Missouri Compromise of 1820, Congress had exercised its authority to permit or prohibit slavery in territories. Until the acquisition of Mexico's land, however, the expansion of slavery beyond the slave states was a dead letter. The only federal territory where the ownership of slaves was legal was Indian Territory (most of present-day Oklahoma). A few southern tribes which had relocated there, most notably the Cherokees, owned African Americans and were staunchly proslavery. But as long as Oklahoma was reserved for Indians, it was not a candidate for statehood.

The Wilmot Proviso and Free Soil Party

The Mexican War changed all that. Proslavery southerners were particularly keen on the war in order to annex land into

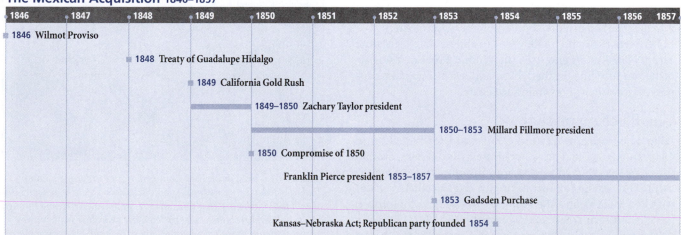

The Mexican Acquisition 1846–1857

| 1846 | 1847 | 1848 | 1849 | 1850 | 1851 | 1852 | 1853 | 1854 | 1855 | 1856 | 1857 |

1846 Wilmot Proviso

1848 Treaty of Guadalupe Hidalgo

1849 California Gold Rush

1849–1850 Zachary Taylor president

1850–1853 Millard Fillmore president

1850 Compromise of 1850

Franklin Pierce president 1853–1857

1853 Gadsden Purchase

Kansas–Nebraska Act; Republican party founded 1854

which slavery could expand. Some antislavery northerners responded that Mexico had abolished slavery in the new territories, and it should not be restored. But that was a moral statement, not an argument. The Roman Catholic Church was the established church in Mexico and nobody—least of all evangelical abolitionists—believed that would continue to be so in territory taken from Mexico.

So, in the first year of the war, Congressman David Wilmot of Pennsylvania attached a rider to a bill appropriating money for the army. The Wilmot Proviso stated that "neither slavery nor involuntary servitude shall ever exist" in lands taken from Mexico after the war. Every northern Whig and all but four northern Democrats in the House of Representatives voted for it.

The proviso was killed in the Senate. Whereas, in the House, northern congressmen outnumbered those from the South, each state has two senators and in 1846 there were fifteen slave states and thirteen free states. John C. Calhoun held the southerners held together by arguing that the Constitution guaranteed citizens who emigrated to territories the same rights they enjoyed in the states from which they came. Citizens of the southern states could own slaves. Therefore, they had the right to take their slaves with them if they moved to the former Mexican lands.

Northern Democrats replied with the argument Thomas Jefferson had made for banning slavery in the Northwest Territory. The West, they said, should be reserved for family farmers, the "bone and sinew of the republic." In almost every state where slavery was legal, a slave-owning elite dominated government in their own interests and to the detriment of the small farmer. The "slavocrats" had to be kept out of the West in the interests of the common man.

When President Polk endorsed Calhoun's reasoning, a substantial number of northern Democrats bolted the party and organized the Free Soil party. A few of them were abolitionists, but not many. The Free Soil party went to great pains to endorse the constitutional right of southerners to protect slavery in the states. Most Free Soilers cared little about the suffering of African Americans that the abolitionists emphasized. Indeed, some Free Soilers were vociferous racists who wanted to exclude not only slaves from the West, but free blacks too. (As late as 1857, Oregon prohibited the emigration of African Americans into the state and expelled those who were already there.)

Between 1846 and 1850, every northern state legislature except New Jersey's endorsed the Wilmot Proviso. It was attached to fifty bills in the House and, each time it was approved, it was voted down in the Senate.

The Election of 1848

Polk, as he had promised, did not stand for reelection in 1848. In fact, he had so worn himself out working around the clock that he died, age 54, four months after leaving the White House. The Democrats nominated a northern senator who had voted against the Wilmot Proviso, the accomplished but gloriously dull Lewis Cass of Michigan.

The Whigs, having lost again with Clay in 1844, returned to the winning formula of 1840—a military hero whose political views were little known, the victor of Buena Vista,

Junk Mail

Had the leaders of the Whig party been up to date, they might have spared themselves embarrassment when Zachary Taylor refused to pay the postage due on the letter from the party notifying him he was the Whigs' nominee for president. The previous year, 1847, the U.S. Post Office had begun to issue adhesive-backed paper stamps that permitted the sender to pay the postage.

When someone else paid the postage due on Taylor's letters, he remained diffident. He replied, "I will not say I will not serve if the good people were imprudent enough to elect me."

Zachary Taylor of Louisiana. (Indeed. the 64-year-old Taylor had never been sufficiently interested in politics to vote in a presidential election.) Taylor owned about 130 slaves and believed he had every right to own them, but he was no proslavery zealot. Whig strategists gambled that, because he was a slave owner Taylor would carry southern states that would otherwise be lost to the Democrats.

California State Library, negative #918.

Placer miners at Spanish Flat, California. They are using a Long Tom, a wooden sluice with riffles on the bottom where heavy particles of gold collect when, with a constant stream of water running through the sluice, the dirt in the gravel the men are shoveling washes away. Larger stones in the gravel were picked out by hand. There is a pile of them at the feet of the miner on the right.

"He really is a most simple-minded old man," said Whig educator Horace Mann. "Few men have ever had more contempt for learning," wrote Winfield Scott, who had expected to win the Whig nomination. "He doesn't know himself from a side of sole leather in the way of statesmanship," wrote Whig editor Horace Greeley.

The Free Soil party named a more distinguished and able candidate than either the Democrats or Whigs, former president Martin Van Buren. Along in years, he had announced his opposition to the expansion of slavery into the territories. But Little Van's day had come and gone. He did not have a chance, but he may have cost the Democrats the election. The electoral college cast 163 votes for Taylor, 127 for Cass. Van Buren won more votes in New York state than Lewis Cass, throwing the state's thirty-six electoral votes to Taylor. Had Cass won New York, he would have been president. (On the other hand, Van Buren may have won enough Whig voters in Ohio, a Whig state in 1844, to give Cass that state's twenty-three electoral votes.)

THE CRISIS OF 1850

Congressional Whigs hoped that the apolitical Taylor would be content to be a ceremonial president, allowing veteran Whigs like Clay and Daniel Webster to make policy. But

Taylor was a lifelong professional soldier, accustomed to giving orders since the War of 1812. When the California Gold Rush of 1849 set in motion an unforeseeable chain of events leading to a grave sectional crisis (and raising Taylor's hackles!), his presidency was anything but ceremonial.

Gold!

On the evening of January 24, 1848, a carpenter from New Jersey, James Marshall, took a walk along the American River where it tumbles through the foothills of the Sierra Nevada. Marshall was working for John Augustus Sutter, a colorful Swiss adventurer who had turned a Mexican land grant into

The Gold Rush That Wasn't

In 1844, four years before Marshall's discovery, Pablo Gutiérrez discovered gold in the bed of the Bear River. He immediately obtained a land grant of 22,000 acres that included what he hoped would be a rich mine. When he went to Sutter's Fort to buy mining equipment, Sutter asked him to go to Monterey and investigate rumors of a social tumult there. Gutiérrez was killed on his journey and knowledge of his gold discovery died with him. No matter: The Bear was overrun in 1849 and 1850 by miners and the deposit was rediscovered.

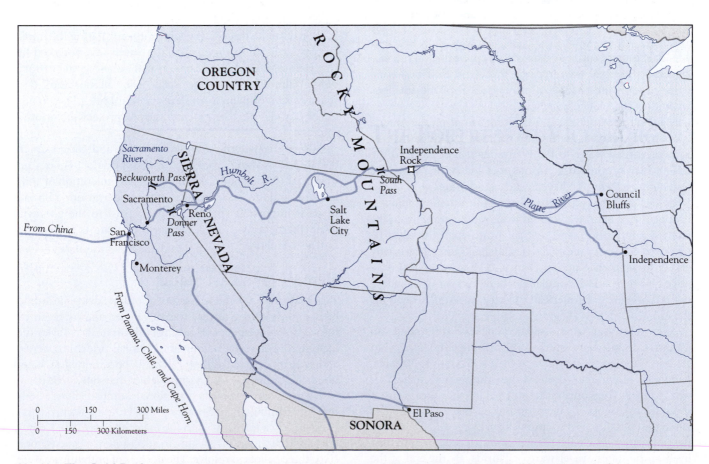

MAP 20:1 **The Gold Rush.** The Forty-Niners' principal overland route was long known by Mountain Men and, most of the way, to the Oregon emigrants. It was virtually a highway during the Gold Rush. Mexicans from Sonora were among the first in the gold fields, but they were brutally treated and driven out of the "diggings" by American miners.

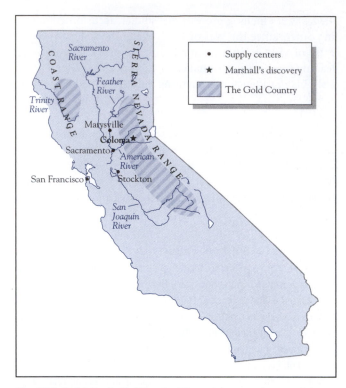

MAP 20:2 **Gold Rush California.** The gold camps (some of them sizable towns built of brick) were located in the western foothills of the Sierra Nevada. They were supplied through San Francisco via river towns like Marysville, Sacramento, and Stockton.

a feudal domain. Sutter's castle was an adobe fort on the Sacramento River. He was prepared to defend it, if necessary, with several cannon he had purchased from the Russians when they abandoned Fort Ross.

Marshall was building a sawmill for Sutter on the American river. He was inspecting the tail race (the ditch that returned rushing water to the river after it had powered the mill) when he noticed a curious metallic stone. "Boys," he told his crew, "I think I have found a gold mine."

He had, and that was it for the sawmill. Sutter's employees dropped their hammers and set to shoveling gravel from the river, separating the sand and silt from what proved to be plenty of gold dust and nuggets. Marshall's discovery briefly ended the existence of San Francisco. A town of 500 on a huge harbor, it was depopulated when "everyone," including the recently arrived American military garrison, headed for the hills.

The next year—1849—80,000 people descended on California. Some came overland. Some sailed by clipper ship around Cape Horn. Yet others took a steamship to Panama, paddled, rode, and hiked across the isthmus, and made their way to the diggings on another steamer. Mexicans came from the state of Sonora. Chileans found berths on the clippers when they put into port for provisions. By the end of the year, the population of California was about 100,000, more than lived in the states of Delaware or Florida. By the end of the year, the Forty-Niners produced $10 million in gold. They said, plausibly enough, that their numbers and their value to the nation merited immediate statehood. When Congress

convened in December 1849, California's provisional constitution was already on the table. It prohibited slavery in the "golden state."

Political Trauma

It all happened so fast. The first vague news of the discovery reached Washington in December 1848, a month after Taylor's election. The astonishing gold rush began immediately. It was still underway in October when California's constitution was delivered to Congress. In December, President Taylor recommended that Congress grant statehood immediately.

The southern senators and congressmen were in a panic. They had assumed, reasonably, that California, the cream of the Mexican acquisition, would be populated very slowly: it was a long way from the United States. They also assumed, again reasonably, that a good many southerners (and their slaves) would be among those who populated the territory. When, some years down the line, it was time to create a state or two on the Pacific, at least part of California would apply for admission as a slave state.

Now, even before Congress had created a territorial government in California, proslavery southerners saw their expectations pulverized. The worst of it was that California statehood meant the end of free state–slave state equality in the Senate with two more embryonic free states about to hatch in Oregon and Minnesota.

Even with the three-fifths compromise inflating the number of slave state congressmen, the South was outvoted by free state representatives on sectional issues, as the history of the Wilmot Proviso demonstrated. Southerners looked to senators, half of them from slave states in 1849, plus a handful of friendly northern Democrats, to protect the South's interests.

A large majority of southern senators and congressmen declared they would vote against California statehood, no matter its 100,000 population. The North's toleration of abolitionists and the "slave stealers" of the underground railroad made it impossible for the South to trust to the goodwill of northerners. The South needed the Senate as a check on northern fanatics.

Henry Clay's Last Stand

Taylor was infuriated. He was on record as saying he would take up his sword if slavery was threatened and he regarded the free soil movement as a passing enthusiasm. But Taylor the lifelong soldier was a nationalist. National pride, prosperity, and security demanded that California be admitted to statehood; if Californians said it must be as a free state, so be it.

When Congress convened, sectional animosities were boiling. The naming of the Speaker of the House of Representatives, usually a formality with the majority party (the Democrats by a slim margin) making the decision in a caucus, took sixty-three ballots to resolve. The dockets of both houses were chockablock with bills that further inflamed North–South animosities. In addition to the California statehood bill, there was a proposal to abolish the slave trade in Washington; a

The great debate of 1850. Henry Clay is making his plea for compromise in the cause of the Union. John C. Calhoun, the third senator from the right (standing), was ill and near death. His speech had to be read for him. Daniel Webster, seated to the left with his head in his hand, would soon speak magnificently in support of Clay and compromise.

fugitive slave bill designed to end evasion throughout the North; and a bill creating the New Mexico Territory.

The New Mexico bill made no reference to the status of slavery in the territories (which meant another southern fight with Free Soil Democrats) and it angered southern Democrats (and some southern Whigs) because, in their eyes, it detached land that the slave state, Texas, had claimed since 1835. (Texas claimed that its western boundary was the Rio Grande all the way to its source, even beyond Santa Fe, the only conceivable capital of New Mexico.)

Henry Clay, frail and weary at 72, beyond all hope of being president, saw in the mess of bills the possibility of a great compromise that might put an end to sectional bitterness. His "Omnibus Bill" was comprehensive and complicated. It addressed all the divisive problems then facing Congress, requiring proslavery and antislavery men to back off some of their demands in the interests of the Union, while winning others.

California would be admitted as a free state. The rest of the Mexican acquisition, notably New Mexico, would be organized into territories with no reference to the status of slavery. New Mexico's eastern border was drawn at 103° west longitude (where it is today); Texas was compensated for its loss of land by the federal government's assumption of the state's $10 million debt, which was pushing Texas close to bankruptcy. Its big concession to slavery was a procedure for returning runaways who made it to the North that had been designed by southerners. A final proposal, not part of the Omnibus, abolished the slave trade in the national capital.

Reproduced from the Collections of The Library of Congress Prints and Photographs Division Washington, D.C. [LC-USZ62-5127]

Millard Fillmore, who succeeded to the presidency when Zachary Taylor died in office. History has unfairly ridiculed Fillmore. He was a moderate, responsible president whose support of the Compromise of 1850 helped to avert a secession crisis.

How They Mined for Gold

Few of the Americans who rushed to California in 1849 were familiar with even the rudiments of mining. Fortunately, their ignorance and lack of capital did not much matter in California's placer mines. The gold they were seeking was pure—in nuggets or dust (tiny flakes, actually), not chemically bonded with other elements—and it was on the surface in the sand and gravel of creek and river beds, not deep within the earth.

Placer mining was laborious, but the process was simple. To determine if there was gold in a creek, a miner "panned" it. He scooped up a pound or two of river silt, sand, and pebbles in a sturdy, shallow pan; removed the stones by hand; and then agitated the finer contents, constantly replenishing the water in the pan so that the lighter mud and sand washed over the sides while the heavier gold dust remained.

When there was enough "color" in a pan to warrant mining the placer, a group of partners staked a claim and built a "rocker" or a "Long Tom" out of rough-sawn boards. The rocker was a simple watertight wooden box, 3 to 5 feet long and a foot or so across. It was mounted on a base like that of a rocking chair so that it could be tipped from side to side. In the bottom of the box were wooden riffles or a sheet of corrugated metal, and sometimes a fine wire mesh. These simulated the crevices in a creekbed, where the gold naturally collected. Into the rocker, by means of a sluice easily built of two planks, ran a stream of water. While one partner shoveled gravel and sand into the box, another rocked it and agitated the contents with a spade or a pitchfork. The lightweight dross washed out of the rocker (stones were manually removed) and the gold remained at the bottom. It was collected at the end of the day, weighed, divided among the partners, and cached.

The Long Tom took more time to build, but it was more productive. In effect, the water-bearing sluice was extended into a long, high-sided, watertight channel with riffles in the bottom. With a Long Tom and a steady flow of water, all the miners in a partnership could shovel gravel: no rocking required.

Placer mines were known as the "poor man's diggings" because mining them required little money, just a strong back and a grubstake. Indeed, a man with capital had no advantage in the diggings. With just about everyone hoping to strike it rich, few men were willing to work for wages, no matter how high they were. The discoverer of a rich gold deposit had to take on equal partners if he wanted to work it efficiently.

As long as the "poor man's diggings" held out, life in the mining camps was egalitarian and democratic. By custom and then by state law, no one was permitted to stake a claim larger than he and his partners could mine within a season or two. Order in the earliest mining camps was maintained by the informal common consent of the men who lived in them. Except for small military units that were plagued by desertions, there was no formal legal authority in California until late 1850, and no significant government presence in the gold fields for several years.

Not all the fruits of this grass-roots democracy were edifying. A man with the majority of a camp behind him could "get away with murder." Nor did miner equality extend to other than native-born Americans and western Europeans. The Forty-Niners learned how to mine from the Sonorans who were among the first in the gold fields. But the Americans, still imbued with the anti-Mexican prejudice of the recent war, expelled the Mexicans (and Spanish-speaking Chileans) from all but the southernmost diggings.

Worst treated of all were the Chinese. Because their culture was so alien and because they worked in large groups, thus spending less in order to live, the Chinese frightened the Forty-Niners. They feared that the "Celestials," as they called the Chinese, would drag down everyone's standard of living. In fact, Chinese miners did not compete with Americans. Aware of the contempt in which they were held, they restricted themselves to "leftovers," streams that had been abandoned by white and the few African American miners as yielding too little gold to be worth the work. Other Chinese who came to the "Golden Mountain" to mine drifted into California's towns and cities and settled for other jobs or founded small businesses, most famously laundries and cheap restaurants.

Impasse

Two decades earlier, Clay's Omnibus Bill would likely have sailed through Congress amidst cheers, tossed hats, and invitations to share a bottle after work. Not in 1850; the rise of the abolitionists, the epidemic of runaway slaves, the devious annexation of Texas, and the unimaginable growth of California's population in one year had hardened sectional animosities. Extremists from both sections, and more than a few moderates, refused to support Clay's compromise because they found one or another of its provisions unacceptable.

To many northerners, and not just abolitionists, the Fugitive Slave Act, which allowed federal officials to arrest people who had committed no crime under their state laws, made slavery quasi-legal in states where it had long been abolished. Southern extremists, called fire-eaters because of their scorching rhetoric, refused to accept the abolition of the slave trade in Washington, meaningless as it was to slave owners in the capital. (If they wished to buy or sell slaves, they needed only to cross the Potomac to Alexandria, Virginia.)

The *spirit* of compromise seemed to be dead. New York's William H. Seward called the idea of compromise with the slavocrats "radically wrong and essentially vicious." The fire-eaters swore to yield nothing to northerners they saw as bent on the destruction of the South. John C. Calhoun, the master of cold logic and constitutionalism, was reduced to the sophistry of a county-seat lawyer. Obsessed with preserving a southern veto on any federal act, he devised a preposterous scheme in which there would be two presidents, one from the North and one from the South, each with the power of veto over acts of Congress and one another. The old man was dying painfully of throat cancer, surrounded by a gaggle of romantic young disciples with, among them, half the brain he had once had in his head.

Henry Clay plugged away, mustering his eloquence one last time. "I have heard something said about allegiance to the South," he told the Senate, "I know no South, no North, no East, no West to which I owe any allegiance. The Union, sir, is my country."

Because his terminal disease left him almost voiceless, Calhoun's response had to be read for him. Where Clay appealed to ideals that were dying, the dying Calhoun realistically assessed the mood of 1850: "The cry of 'Union, Union, the glorious Union!' can no more prevent disunion than the cry of 'Health, health, glorious health!' . . . can save a patient lying dangerously ill."

Daniel Webster, the last of the Senate's "Great Triumvirate," then delivered one of his finest orations. Webster supported the Omnibus Bill. To save the Union, he said, he would swallow even the fugitive slave law. His speech shocked and infuriated moralists. Seward called Webster "a traitor to the cause of freedom." "The word 'honor' in the mouth of Mr. Webster," wrote Ralph Waldo Emerson, "is like the word 'love' in the mouth of a whore."

THE COMPROMISE

The Omnibus Bill failed and it probably did not matter. President Taylor said he would veto the whole thing rather than compensate Texas a dollar. The only possible explanation of the old coot's intensity of his feelings on the subject

Border Dispute

The federal government set the eastern border of New Mexico Territory at 103° west longitude. Texans protested that the border should be farther west of the Rio Grande. They argued that, in the treaty ending the Texas war for independence, Mexico agreed to the Rio Grande as the line between Texas and its territory of New Mexico. This was true. However, the agreement by which the United States granted Texas statehood in 1845 clearly reserved to the federal government the authority to adjust "all questions of boundary that may arise with other governments."

So, Texas ended up smaller than Texans wanted. However, if the old Mexican boundary of Texas (the Nueces River) had been adopted as the New Mexico line, Texas today would have been half the size that is.

is that, like just about every other army officer who was stationed in Texas, he hated the place.

Death of a Soldier

On July 4, 1850, the president attended a ceremony on the Capitol mall where, for two hours, he sat hatless in the sun listening to patriotic oratory. Back at the White House, he wolfed down cherries and cucumbers and several quarts of iced milk and water. A few hours later the old man took to bed with stomach cramps. Instead of leaving him alone, his doctors bled him and administered one powerful medicine after another—ipecac to make him vomit, quinine for his fever, calomel as a laxative, and opium for the pain to which they had contributed. Old Rough and Ready was murder on Indians, Mexicans, and Texans, but he could not handle the pharmacopoeia of the nineteenth century. He died on July 9.

He was succeeded by Millard Fillmore, who has often been mocked as the least memorable of American presidents. A New

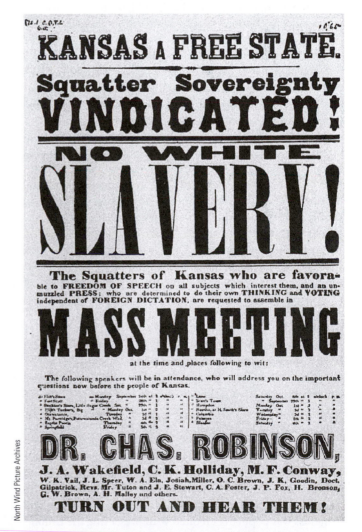

A poster announcing an anti-Kansas-Nebraska Act rally. There were many such meetings all over the North within weeks of Congress's enactment of the law. Rarely has there been so widespread a spontaneous protest.

Yorker born in poverty, he educated himself to be a lawyer. As a young man, he flirted with third-party politics, winning his first election as an Anti-Mason. Like most other Anti-Masons, he became a Whig when the short-lived excitement evaporated. He served in Congress as a Clay-Webster man, neither proslavery nor antislavery, which made him a wiser choice for the Whigs as their vice presidential candidate than the states rights southerner Tyler had been in 1840. Suddenly president in July 1850, he called the Omnibus Bill "a final settlement of sectional discord," but it was not enough to save it.

The "Little Giant"

Compromise was, however, saved by a Democrat from Illinois, just three years in the senate and not yet 40 years of age. Stephen A. Douglas revived Clay's design for compromise, but not in the form of one comprehensive bill. Douglas was barely 5 feet in height and already portly. But he was known in Illinois as the "Little Giant" because of his oratorical powers and his political finesse as a political tactician. Douglas wanted to be president; he had devoted his three years in the senate to ingratiating himself with both northern and southern Democrats, and with Whigs too. He was on the verge of being considered a "national figure" when the sectional crisis made him one in a month.

Douglas tirelessly explained his plan for shimming Clay's collection of compromises through Congress. Rather than introduce them in a single bill, Douglas carved the Omnibus Bill into five bills. Tirelessly buttonholing senators and congressmen one-on-one and in small groups, he patched together different coalitions—but each one a majority—for all five. Douglas could count on northern senators and representatives of both parties to vote for California statehood and end the slave trade in the capital. Both sailed through the House. In the Senate, Douglas won the votes of enough Whigs from the border states to slip the bills through with slim majorities.

For the Fugitive Slave and the Texas compensation bills, Douglas started with a solid southern bloc. Northern Whigs were opposed to both but, arguing for the necessity of preserving the Democratic party in both sections, Douglas added enough Democratic party senators and representatives to build majorities for both.

Douglas's manipulations were dazzling, but the five-part "Compromise of 1850" was, to a great degree, not a give-some–take-some agreement. Except on Texas compensation, most congressmen yielded nothing on their sectionalist positions. Only four of sixty senators voted for all of Douglas's bills. Only 11 voted for five of six. (Even Douglas was absent for the vote on the Fugitive Slave Act.) Only 28 of 240 Representatives voted for all six bills. The Omnibus Bill was a compromise. Douglas's was sleight of hand. In Congress, sectional animosities were as intense after Douglas's trick as before. In the country, however, there was a great sense of relief, and Congress was popularly credited with preserving the Union.

Changing of the Guard

The Congress of 1849–1851 saw the nation's second generation of political leaders—the men of the age of Andrew Jackson—pass the torch to a third. Jackson was already gone,

dead in 1845. Calhoun died in March 1850, croaking to his young disciples, "the South, the poor South." Henry Clay and Daniel Webster passed on two years later. Thomas Hart Benton survived until 1858 and Martin Van Buren until 1862. Van Buren returned to the Democratic party, but as an "elder statesman." After thirty years in the Senate, Benton lost his seat in 1850 because he had plumped for sectional compromise. He was defeated in a race for a House seat in 1856 and lost again when he ran for governor of Missouri.

The Whig party dwindled after 1850. Some younger southern Whigs outdid the Calhounites in their obsession with defending slavery. Robert Toombs of Georgia supported the Compromise of 1850 but within a few years he was himself a fire-eater. Only in the border states did a few old Henry Clay Whigs continue to win elections because they were respected as individuals and compromisers. Most notable was John J. Crittenden of Kentucky.

In the North, the Whigs were weakened by tensions between "Cotton Whigs" and "Conscience Whigs." Cotton Whigs tried to downplay the slavery issue because of the importance of southern cotton to the northern textile industry. Conscience Whigs were abolitionists and, like the southern Democratic fire-eaters, they were younger, members of a new generation. Among the ablest was William H. Seward of New York, a former Anti-Mason. Charles Sumner of Massachusetts, who succeeded Webster as New England's most prominent Senator, was as obnoxious personally as any southern fire-eater.

With the Free Soilers gone from the Democratic party, most northern Democrats were friendly to the South and slavery, but to different degrees. A few northern Democrats preached positive, good propaganda with the best of them. Others, notably Stephen A. Douglas, did not look on slavery as a desirable institution, but their sensibilities were not outraged by its existence in the South. For the sake of Democratic party unity, they were willing (in vain) to make concessions to southern Democrats.

Franklin Pierce

At the Democratic convention in 1852, Franklin Pierce was New Hampshire's favorite son candidate. His supporters kept his name before the delegates in the hope they would deadlock and need a compromise candidate acceptable to all. Deadlock was always a danger at Democratic party conventions because the party required that its presidential nominee win the votes of two-thirds of the delegates rather than a simple majority. In 1852, a deadlock was assured by the fact that there were three strong and personally irreconcilable candidates: Lewis Cass, Stephen A. Douglas, and James Buchanan of Pennsylvania.

After forty-eight wearying ballots, the Democrats did indeed turn to Pierce. Handsome, charming, and sociable—perhaps too sociable; a colleague called him the "hero of many a well-fought bottle"—Pierce had been popular in the Senate until he quit politics to fight in the Mexican War. The Whigs, despite Millard Fillmore's success as president, dumped him and nominated yet another military hero, General Winfield Scott.

Pierce won just over 50 percent of the popular vote, but he eked out pluralities in all but a few states, winning 254 electoral votes to Winfield Scott's 42.

American voters had made one of their worst mistakes. Scott, for all his pomposity, was an able, compelling leader who had, since 1841, superbly administered the army in war and peace as general-in-chief. He was a southerner—a Virginian—but also a nationalist who abhorred both abolitionists and fire-eaters. He was the kind of president the country needed after the traumas of 1850.

Pierce was ambivalent about returning to politics and unsuited to be an executive. As a fellow New Hampshireman commented, "Up here, where everybody knows Frank Pierce, he's a pretty considerable fellow. But come to spread him out over the whole country, I'm afraid he'll be dreadful thin in some places."

Personal tragedy ended any possibility that Pierce would flourish in the White House. Just before his inauguration, his young son was killed in a railroad accident. Pierce was stunned; his wife, an emotionally fragile woman already, was shattered. Preoccupied with his wife's distraction, Pierce leaned heavily on his friend, Jefferson Davis of Mississippi, whom he named secretary of war. Davis was not quite a fire-eater; he had presidential ambitions. But he had not succeeded in the slavocratic politics of Mississippi by urging moderation on sectional issues. Davis was the dominating intellect and will of the Pierce administration, like Dick Cheney during the presidency of George W. Bush.

THE KANSAS-NEBRASKA ACT

A Railroad to California

Davis looked like an aristocrat, spare and military in bearing. But he was born in a log cabin in Kentucky. He was one of the Mexican War's genuine battlefield heroes, having distinguished himself for bravery in several battles, including Buena Vista. (His first wife was Zachary Taylor's daughter.) He was the baby in a family of ten children—his middle name was "Finis" (Latin for "the end," undoubtedly bestowed by his mother) and the beneficiary of an older brother's rise to be one of the richest planters in Mississippi.

With Pierce's approval, Davis tried to revive the expansionism of the 1840s with unsuccessful attempts to annex Hawai'i and Cuba. He tacitly supported American filibusters, freelance adventurers, mostly southerners, who led private armies into unstable Central America in the hopes of creating personal empires.

Davis's most important ambition was to encourage the construction of a transcontinental railroad to California that funneled its trade to the southern states. He had geography going for him. Of the transcontinental routes on the table, the best from an engineer's perspective was through Texas and along the southern boundary of New Mexico territory. There were no mountains of any consequence to be crossed except above the Gila River in present-day Arizona. There, in order to keep the projected railroad on the flat, it would be necessary to build in Mexico, which was unacceptable.

To remedy the problem, Davis sent James Gadsden, a railroad man, to Mexico City. For $10 million, the United States purchased a 30,000-square-mile triangle of arid but level land. With the Gadsden Purchase (the Treaty of Mesilla in Mexico), Davis appeared to have plucked a plum for the South that was also a great national enterprise. He further advanced his cause by inflating the estimate of constructing the "central route," beginning in Chicago, from $117 million to $141 million and decreasing the figures for his route from $169 million to $95 million.

Re-enter Stephen A. Douglas

None of this deterred Senator Stephen A. Douglas. He wanted the transcontinental railroad's eastern terminus in Chicago. Chicago had better railroad connections with the populous Northeast than any southern city. However, the "central route" west had serious drawbacks. It had to negotiate both the Rockies and the Sierra Nevada. Moreover, beyond Missouri, it ran through "unorganized territory," those parts of the Louisiana Purchase that had been left to the Indians. The only federal presence there was small military installations at distant intervals along the overland trail. There was no territorial government. Southern senators could kill off the central route and win the transcontinental for the South

---

Filibusters

"Filibuster" is a corruption of the Dutch *vrijbuiter,* "freebooter." The filibusters of the 1850s were mostly southern Mexican War veterans who saw greater opportunities as freebooters in Central America and the Caribbean than back home on a farm.

The first filibuster was a Cuban rebel, Narciso Lopez, although most of his soldiers, were American adventurers. In 1850, with financial support from southerners, he tried to overthrow the Spanish regime in Cuba. The plan was to annex Cuba, where slavery was legal, to the United States. The Spanish executed fifty of Lopez's Americans. Chastened, the federal government arrested Mississippi governor John A. Quitman before he could lead a filibustering expedition to resume the fight.

Secretary of War Jefferson Davis actively supported the most famous of the filibusters, William Walker. More interested in personal glory than in adding slave states to the Union, Walker invaded Baja California in 1853 but was driven out within weeks. Reorganizing his ragtag army, he went to Nicaragua, then in an anarchic state. With the support of Nicaraguan rebels as well as American mercenaries, Walker proclaimed himself president and actually ran Nicaragua (insofar as it was "run" at all) for two years. When things turned sour, an American warship rescued him. Walker tried again, this time in Honduras, where he was executed by a firing squad in 1860.

Reproduced from the Collections of the Library of Congress

A destructive and murderous anti-Irish riot in Philadelphia in 1844. At the left, Pennsylvania militia are trying to subdue Protestant rioters, who are fighting back. The rioters burned two Irish Catholic churches to the ground (one burns in the rear, far right) but, curiously, left two German Catholic Churches in the area untouched. It was as much an anti-Irish riot as it was anti-Catholic.

Slavery in Maine?

The Missouri Compromise provided that slavery was "forever forbidden" in the *territories* of the Louisiana Purchase north of 36° 30′. Did that mean that the *states* that emerged in those lands were forbidden to legalize slavery? Legally, no. Before he signed the Missouri act, President Monroe consulted with his cabinet. All, including John Quincy Adams and John C. Calhoun, said that once a territory had become a state, its "domestic institutions" were its own business. In other words, had the legislature of Maine, a state after 1820, amended its constitution to allow slavery, it was constitutionally free to do so.

In practice, prohibiting slavery in a territory meant that states that emerged there would be free states. There would be no slave owners at the state's constitutional convention.

simply by refusing to organize territorial governments west of Missouri.

Douglas hatched a scheme to seduce southern senators by playing on their obsession: slavery. In May 1854, he introduced a bill to establish the Kansas and Nebraska territories. The bill explicitly repealed the section of the Missouri Compromise that prohibited slavery in both. Instead, borrowing from Lewis Cass, Douglas said that the people who settled Kansas and Nebraska would decide in their territorial legislatures whether they would permit or prohibit the institution. "Popular sovereignty," Douglas said, was the democratic solution to the divisive problem of slavery in the territories.

Southern congressmen and senators jumped at the bait. None had illusions about the Nebraska Territory, through which the central route ran. It bordered on the free state of Iowa and would be populated by northerners. Kansas, however, abutted on Missouri, where slavery was an emotionally passionate issue, even with poor whites who owned no slaves.

Douglas's popularity soared in the South. (He planned to exploit it when he again sought the Democratic presidential nomination in 1856.) As in 1850, he presented himself as an honest broker between the sections. To southerners, he was the man who opened Kansas to slavery. To northerners, he was the man who got them the transcontinental railroad.

Douglas would not, however, win the nomination in 1856 because his Kansas-Nebraska Act did not, as it turned out, work in favor of the proslavery cause. The Whigs would not exist as a national party, largely because the Kansas-Nebraska Act split them wide open on sectional lines, and also because of the astonishing rise, largely at Whig expense, of the nativist and anti-Catholic American party.

Stresses of Immigration

A wary aversion to Roman Catholicism had been widespread among Americans since the founding of the colonies. It was a highly hypothetical prejudice until the 1830s. There were, simply, very few Catholics in the United States. As late as

1820, there were only about 120 Catholic churches in the entire country, and many of them were Indian missions.

After 1830, the Catholic population steadily increased due to massive immigration from Ireland and the Catholic states of Germany. Between 1830 and 1860, the population of the United States doubled. The Catholic population increased tenfold, from 300,000 to 3 million. All but a few of the immigrants were dirt poor, seeking economic opportunities rather than religious freedom. Many of the Irish were penniless. The Emerald Isle, ruled roughly by Great Britain, was dangerously overpopulated. With about 1.5 million people in 1750, Ireland was a kind of home to nearly 6 million in 1840, more than live in Ireland today. Catholics, 80 percent of the population, had few civil rights until 1829. Most were landless, living on tiny plots allotted them to grow potatoes. Local famines were common, hunger practically the rule.

Then, in 1845, the inevitable catastrophe: Ireland's potato crops was hit by a then mysterious potato blight that virtually destroyed the sole food source of the poor. (The potato blight also helps account for a sudden increase of German immigrants.) The disease returned almost annually. About a million people, more than a tenth of the population, starved to death. Millions more emigrated, most to the United States.

Those who did not die on the voyage (mortality on the "famine ships" was worse than it had been on slavers) were willing to accept wages for unskilled labor lower than Protestant workingmen would. The competition aroused resentment that exploded in riots in Boston and Philadelphia. The apparent predilection of the Irish for drinking and brawling and the flocking of the Germans to beer gardens on Sundays shocked evangelicals. In the cities where Catholics were concentrated, they were successfully wooed by Democratic politicians, many of them corrupt, enhancing anti-Irish sentiments among Whigs.

The Know-Nothings

Angry native-born Protestants formed anti-immigrant, anti-Catholic lodges. The largest was the Order of the Star-Spangled Banner, founded in New York City in 1849, which was soon recruiting members in almost every state. It was a highly secret organization. Members were instructed to respond to questions about the Order by saying, "I Know Nothing." When the lodge (with, possibly, a million members and supporters) came above ground in 1854 as the American Party, their critics continued to call them Know-Nothings.

Uninvolved in the Kansas-Nebraska debate, their candidates were able to appeal to voters in both North and South by claiming that the furor over slavery was a distraction from the important issues: jobs for native Americans, political corruption, and the flood of immigrants. They demanded restrictions on immigration, especially from Catholic countries; that the residency requirement for citizenship be increased from five to twenty-one years; that even citizens who had been born abroad be prohibited from holding public office; and that only Protestants be hired as teachers. The Know-Nothings, partly because of their large evangelical component, partly as a rebuke of the bibulous Irish and Germans, were prohibitionists.

Their success at the polls was due to their appeal to working people, but they had middle-class supporters too. Those who followed the news were appalled by Pope Pius IX, elected in 1846. He was an unbending opponent of religious toleration, democracy, and civil rights and liberties. John J. Hughes, the Catholic bishop of New York, did not help the Church's public relations when he wrote that "Protestantism is effete, powerless, dying out . . . and conscious that its last moment is come when it is fairly set, face to face, with Catholic truth." The Catholic church meant, Hughes said, "to convert the world—including the inhabitants of the United States . . . , the president and all."

Successful the Know-Nothings were. In 1854 and 1855, their candidates were elected mayors in dozens of cities, including New York, governors in several states, practically the entire Massachusetts legislature and control of legislatures elsewhere, and forty congressmen. In 1856, their candidate for president, Millard Fillmore, won 40 percent of the vote in most southern states.

Fillmore would have done much better if the slavery issue had not caught up with the Know-Nothings. At their national convention early in 1856, southern delegates pushed through a platform sympathetic to slavery. The northerners walked out and, in the fall, many of them voted for the candidate of yet another new party, the Republicans. When the election was over, the Republicans had replaced the Know-Nothings or remnants of the Whigs as the chief opposition party in every northern state.

The Republican Party

What happened to the Whigs? To a degree, they had flirted with disintegration from the day the party was founded. It was a ménage of politicians frightened by Andrew Jackson on one count or another. But the Whigs never agreed on much except their aversion to Old Hickory Democrats. Such a delicate coalition could not survive the sectional bitterness caused by the debate over slavery in the territories. The Kansas-Nebraska Act killed the party off.

Southern Whigs voted for the American party for a few years, then either drifted into the Democratic party or dropped out of politics.

Some northern Whigs became Know-Nothings. Others, like William Seward of New York and Abraham Lincoln of Illinois, joined with Free Soil Democrats, abolitionists who did not scorn politics, and, after 1856, with most northern Know Nothings to form the Republican party. Amos A. Lawrence, a rich textile manufacturer and a moderate Whig, described what Kansas-Nebraska meant for him: "we went to bed one night, old-fashioned, conservative compromise Union Whigs, and we woke up stark mad Abolitionists."

Unlike the Democrats, Whigs, and Know-Nothings, the Republicans were a purely sectional party. Republicans did not—they could not—exist in the South. While they made it clear they had no intentions of interfering with slavery where it existed, they demanded the repeal of the Kansas-Nebraska Act and the exclusion of slavery from all the western territories.

Beyond this first principle borrowed from the Free Soilers, the Republicans tried to steal Douglas's thunder on the railroad issue by insisting that the transcontinental be built on the central route. They appealed to farmers by advocating a Homestead Act giving western land free to families who would settle and farm it.

From the Whigs, the Republicans inherited the demand for a high protective tariff, thus winning manufacturing interests to the party. They also appealed to industrial capitalists by advocating a liberal immigration policy to keep the costs of labor down. This plank risked alienating Know Nothings just as the call for a protective tariff risked losing the support of farmers. However, the Republican position on slavery in the territories was so powerful an appeal in the North that Republican gambles on the tariff and immigration did not cost them many votes.

FURTHER READING

Classics David Potter, *The Impending Crisis, 1848–1861*, 1974; *The Growth of Southern Nationalism 1848–1861*, 1953; Oscar Handlin, *The Uprooted*, 1951; John Higham, *Strangers in the Land*. 1955.

General Leonard Richards, *The Slave Power: The Free North and Southern Domination, 1780–1860*, 2000; James M. McPherson, *Battle Cry of Freedom: The Civil War Era*, 1988; Richard A. Sewell, *A House Divided: Sectionalism and Civil War, 1848–1860*, 1988; Kenneth S. Greenberg, *Masters and Statesmen: The Political Culture of American Slavery*, 1985; Bruce Levine, *Half Slave and Half Free: The Roots of the Civil War*, 1992; Michael F. Holt, *The Political Crisis of the 1850s*, 1978; William W. Freehling, *The Road to Disunion*, 1990; Sean Wilentz, *The Rise of American Democracy: Jefferson to Lincoln*, 2005.

The Gold Rush Malcolm J. Rohrbaugh, *Days of Gold: The California Gold Rush and the American Nation*, 1997; H. W. Brands, *The Age of Gold: The California Gold Rush and the New American Dream*, 2002.

1850 and Kansas-Nebraska John Mayfield, *Rehearsal for Republicanism: Free Soil and the Politics of Anti-Slavery*, 1980; Holman Hamilton, *Prologue to Conflict: The Crisis and Compromise of 1850*, 1964; K. J. Bauer, *Zachary Taylor: Soldier, Planter, Statesman of the Old Southwest*, 1985; Robert J. Scarry, *Millard Fillmore*, 2001; Robert Remini, *Henry Clay: Statesman for the Union*, 1991; Merrill Peterson, *The Great Triumvirate: Webster, Clay, and Calhoun*, 1987; John R. Baumgarner, *The Health of the Presidents*, 1944; Gerlad W. Wolff, *The Kansas-Nebraska Bill: Party, Section, and the Coming of the Civil War*, 1977; Robert G. Angevine, *The Railroad and the State: War, Politics and Technology in Nineteenth Century America*, 2004; Robert W. Johannsen, *The Frontier, the Union, and Stephen A. Douglas*, 1989; Larry Gara, *The Presidency of Franklin Pierce*, 1991; Felicity Allen, *Jefferson Davis: Unconquerable Heart*, 1999.

Catholic Immigrants John Bodnar, *The Transplanted: A History of Immigration*, 1985; Charles R. Morris, *American Catholic: The Saints and Sinners Who Built America's Most Powerful Church*, 1997; Roger Daniels, *Coming to America: A History of Immigration and Ethnicity in American Life*, 2002; Steven P. Eric, *Rainbow's End: Irish Americans and the Dilemmas of Urban Machine Politics, 1840–1945*, 1988; Kerby A. Miller, *Emigrants and Exiles: Ireland and the Irish Exodus to North America*, 1985; Dale T. Knobel, *Paddy and the Republic: Ethnicity and Nationality in Ante-Bellum America*, 1980; Daniel R. Roediger, *Working Toward Whiteness: How America's Immigrants Became White*, 2005.

Political Parties Darrell W. Howe, *The Political Culture of the American Whigs*, 1980; Thomas Brown, *Politics and Statesmanship: Essays on the American Whig Party*, 1985; Michael F. Holt, *The Rise and Fall of the American Whig Party*, 1999; Dale T. Knobel, *America for the Americans: The Nativist Movement in the United States*, 1996; Thomas J. Curran, *Xenophobia and Immigration, 1820–1930*, 1975; William E. Gienapp, *The Origins of the Republican Party, 1852–1856*, 1987; Kenneth Winkle, *The Young Eagle: The Rise of Abraham Lincoln*, 2003.

KEY TERMS

Use the following listing of key terms to review important figures, events, locations, and concepts covered in this chapter. A glossary of these terms is available on *The American Past* companion Web site: www.cengage.com/history/conlin/tap9e

rider, p. 336

Wilmot Proviso, p. 336

Omnibus Bill, p. 339

placer mining, p. 340

fire-eaters, p. 340

Douglas, Stephen A., p. 342

Cotton Whigs, p. 342

favorite son, p. 342

ONLINE RESOURCES

Find additional resources, including primary source documents, images, interactive maps, simulations, chapter review exercises, and Internet links at

The American Past **companion Web site**
www.cengage.com/history/conlin/tap9e

American History Resource Center
http://ushistory.wadsworth.com/

DISCOVERY

To what extent (if any) can the social and religious ferment of the early nineteenth century be attributed to the rapid economic changes of the era?

Culture and Society: The authors of "Observations on the Real Rights of Women" and "Declaration of Sentiments" have two sharply contrasting views of the role women should play in American society. Define and describe their differences. How would Elizabeth Cady Stanton have likely responded to "The Real Rights of Women"? How would the author of that essay have reacted to Stanton's "Declaration"?

Observations on the Real Rights of Women, 1818

It must be the appropriate duty and privilege of females to convince by reason and persuasion. It must be their peculiar province to sooth the turbulent passions of men, when almost sinking in the sea of care, without even an anchor of hope to support them. Under such circumstances women should display their talents by taking the helm, and steer them safe to the haven of rest and peace, and that should be their own happy mansion, where they may always retire and find safe asylum from the rigid cares of business. It is women's peculiar right to keep calm and serene under every circumstance in life, as it is undoubtedly her appropriate duty, to sooth and alleviate the anxious cares of man, and her friendly and sympathetic breast should be found the best solace for him, as she ahs an equal right to partake with him the cares, as well as the pleasures of life.

It was evidently the design of heaven by the mode of our first formation, that they should walk side by side as mutual supports in all times of trial. There can be no doubt, that, in most cases, their judgement may be equal with the other sex; perhaps even on the subject of law, politics, or religion, they may form good judgement, but it would be improper, and physically very incorrect, for the female character to claim the statesman's birth or ascend the rostrum to gain the loud applause of men, although their powers of industry may be equal to the task. . . .

Elizabeth Cady Stanton, Declaration of Sentiments (1848)

When, in the course of human events, it becomes necessary for one portion of the family of man to assume among the people of the earth a position different from that which they have hitherto occupied, but one to which the laws of nature and of nature's God entitle them, a decent respect to the opinions of mankind requires that they should declare the causes that impel them to such a course.

We hold these truths to be self-evident: that all men and women are created equal; that they are endowed by their Creator with certain inalienable rights; that among these are life, liberty, and the pursuit of happiness; that to secure these rights governments are instituted, deriving their just powers from the consent of the governed. Whenever any form of government becomes destructive of these ends, it is the right of those who suffer from it to refuse allegiance to it, and to insist upon the institution of a new government, laying its foundation on such principles, and organizing its powers in such form, as to them shall seem most likely to effect their safety and happiness. Prudence, indeed, will dictate that governments long established should not be changed for light and transient causes; and accordingly all experience has shown that mankind are more disposed to suffer, while evils are sufferable, than to right themselves by abolishing the forms to which they are accustomed. But when a long train of abuses and usurpations, pursuing invariably the same object, evinces a design to reduce them under absolute despotism, it is their duty to throw off such government, and to provide new guards for their future security. Such has been the patient sufferance of the women under this government, and such is now the necessity which constrains them to demand the equal station to which they are entitled.

What were the reasons why some Americans became abolitionists favoring (demanding!) the extinction of slavery in the United States? How did they express their disapproval of the institution?

Culture and Society: Peter Osborne, a free black man, and the people who circulated this photograph of a slave grotesquely scarred from whippings were all abolitionists. However, Osborne in his speech takes a different tack in condemning slavery than the critique implied in the photograph. How do the messages differ? Why? Which approach was more likely to win support for the abolitionist movement?

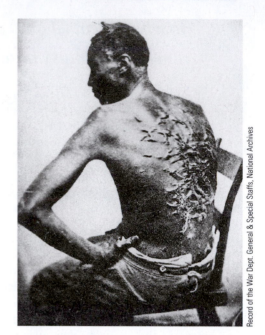

Record of the War Dept. General & Special Staffs, National Archives

Former Slave

Peter Osborne Speaks to a Crowd Celebrating American Independence, 5 July 1832 *Delivered to the people of color in the African Church in the city of New-Haven, Connecticut.*

Fellow Citizens—On account of the misfortune of our color, our fourth of July comes on the fifth; but I hope and trust that when the Declaration of Independence is fully executed which declares that all men, without respect to person, were born free and equal, we may then have our fourth of July on the fourth. It is thought by many that this is as impossible to take place, as it is for the leopard to change his spots; but I anticipate that the time is approaching very fast. The signs in the north, the signs in the south, in the east and west, are all favorable to our cause. Why, then, should we forbear contending for the civil rights of free countrymen: What man of rational feeling would slumber in content under the yoke of slavery and oppression, in his own country? Not the most degraded barberian in the interior of Africa.

If we desire to see our brethren relieved from the tyrannical yoke of slavery and oppression in the south, if we would enjoy the civil rights of free countrymen, it is high time for us to be up and doing. It has been said that we have already done well, but we can do better. What more can we do? Why, we must unite with our brethren in the north, in the south, and in the east and west, and then with the Declaration of Independence in one hand, and the Holy Bible in the other, I think we might courageously give battle to the most powerful enemy to this cause. The

Declaration of Independence has declared to man, without speaking of color, that all men are born free and equal. Has it not declared this freedom and equality to us too?

What man would content himself, and say nothing of the rights of man, with two millions of his brethren in bondage? Let us contend for the prize. Let us all unite, and with one accord declare that we will not leave our own country to emigrate to Liberia, nor elsewhere, to be civilized nor christianized. Let us make it known to America that we are not barbarians; that we are not inhuman beings; that this is our native country; that our forefathers have planted trees in America for us, and we intend to stay and eat the fruit. Our forefathers fought, bled and died to achieve the independence of the United States. Why should we forbear contending for the prize? It becomes every colored citizen in the United States to step forward boldly and gallantly defend his rights. What has there been done within a few years, since the union of the colored people? Are not the times more favourable to us now, than they were ten years ago? Are we not gaining ground? Yes—and had we begun this work forty years ago, I do not hesitate to say that there would not have been, at this day, a slave in the United States. Take courage, then, ye African-Americans! Don't give up the conflict, for the glorious prize can be won.

To read extended versions apf selected documents, visit the companion Web site www.cengage.com/history/conlin/tap9e; click on "Discovery Sources"

Reproduced from the Collections of the Library of Congress [LC-US262-120309]

Chapter 21

The Collapse of the Union

From Debate to Violence 1854–1861

Shall I tell you what this collision means? They who think it is accidental, unnecessary, the work of interested or fanatical agitators, and therefore ephemeral, mistake the case altogether. It is an irrepressible conflict between opposing and enduring forces.

—William H. Seward

"A house divided against itself cannot stand." I believe this government cannot endure permanently half-slave and half-free. I do not expect the Union to be dissolved—I do not expect the house to fall—but I do expect it will cease to be divided.

—Abraham Lincoln

Stephen A. Douglas believed that the Kansas-Nebraska Act would make him president. Already popular among northern Democrats, he expected that by sponsoring the bill opening the Kansas Territory to slavery, he would win the support of the party's southern wing. The vote on the act in Congress told him he was right. Practically every southerner voted for it.

BLEEDING KANSAS

What Douglas did not anticipate was the conflagration of anti-Kansas feelings across the North. Of the forty-four northern Democrats who voted in favor of the bill, thirty-seven were defeated in the 1854 election by Know-Nothings and Whigs, some calling themselves Republicans too. The Democrats lost control of the House of Representatives and so many state legislatures that the Republican party elected fifteen senators.

Free Soilers and Border Ruffians

Also dismaying was the fact that antislavery forces in New England and the Midwest mobilized to ensure that Kansas would enter the Union as a free state under the rules of

A Hard Country

The western tier of counties in Missouri was a particularly violent frontier before (and after) the slavery issue aroused tempers there. During the 1840s, western Missourians drove Mormon settlers out with arson, beatings, and even killings. After the Kansas-Nebraska Act, proslavery western Missourians were denounced as "border ruffians" for their mounted raids in eastern Kansas. A disproportionate number of dubious characters of the Civil War era had roots there. Western Missouri was prime recruiting ground for Quantrill's Raiders, notorious Confederate irregulars responsible for terroristic attacks on civilians. William Quantrill's right-hand man, Bloody Bill Anderson, scalped the northerners he killed. The postwar outlaws Jesse and Frank James and the Younger brothers came from western Missouri, as did the "bandit queen," Myra Belle Shirley, or Belle Starr. Today, however, things are calm and western Missouri is a nice place for the timid to stay overnight, or even longer.

popular sovereignty. Organizations such as Eli Thayer's New England Emigrant Aid Company urged farmers thinking of going west to make Kansas their destination. They sweetened

The Granger Collection, New York

"Border ruffians" leaving for a raid of free state settlers in Kansas. The portrayal of them is, obviously, hostile but, perhaps, not a distortion. The men who lived in the far west of Missouri were mostly poor struggling farmers, and many of them were pretty tough characters. Not every Missourian who harassed free staters in Kansas, however, was frontier scum of this caliber.

the pot by contributing toward the costs of emigration and setting up a farm. Within two years, Thayer's group alone helped to send two thousand people to Kansas. Their propaganda boosting Kansas—abolitionists praised the soil and climate as if they were real estate agents—encouraged other northerners to head for Kansas instead of Nebraska or Minnesota.

Proslavery southerners could not compete with the northern propaganda and subsidy campaign. No part of the

antebellum South was so densely populated with whites as most of New England was. Southerners thinking about emigration were still drawn more to potential cotton lands in Arkansas and Texas than to the prairies of Kansas. With the future of slavery in the territory uncertain, southerners owning even just a few slaves were unwilling to risk losing them and their capital in Kansas. Not even western Missourians, for whom relocating in Kansas was a short wagon ride, went in any great numbers. Except for the city of Independence,

The Breakup of the Union 1856–1861

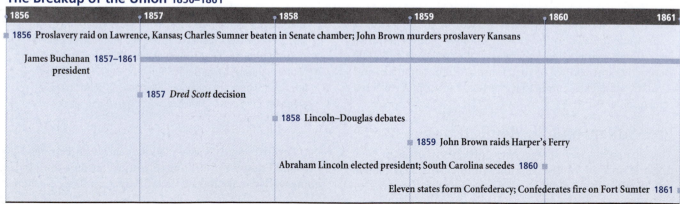

1856	1857	1858	1859	1860	1861

1856 Proslavery raid on Lawrence, Kansas; Charles Sumner beaten in Senate chamber; John Brown murders proslavery Kansans

James Buchanan 1857–1861 president

1857 *Dred Scott* decision

1858 Lincoln–Douglas debates

1859 John Brown raids Harper's Ferry

Abraham Lincoln elected president; South Carolina secedes 1860

Eleven states form Confederacy; Confederates fire on Fort Sumter 1861

SOUTHERN CHIVALRY — ARGUMENT versus CLUB'S.

The Granger Collection, New York

Preston Brooks clubbing Charles Sumner on the Senate floor. The incident readily lent itself to the antislavery movement's portrayal of proslavery southerners as barbarians and Sumner as a man of the pen. Note the laughing senators in the background, southerners, of course (although few of Sumner's northern colleagues liked him very much).

western Missouri was still nearly naked frontier. The western counties wanted emigrants; they had no surplus to send west in the interest of a cause.

However, a good many of western Missouri's rougher lot were willing to vote fraudulently in Kansas elections and even to harass free staters who had settled in the territory. About 5,000 Missourians voted in the election of a territorial legislature in March 1855. In one county in which there were only eleven cabins, 1,828 proslavery votes were recorded. "Border ruffians," mounted and armed, intimidated settlers they believed to be free staters, roughing them up and even burning barns and cabins.

The violence had more to do with racism and adolescent hormonal upheaval than with promoting slavery. Most western Missourians were struggling farmers; only a minority owned slaves. Most border ruffians were, of course, teenagers and young men who owned nothing but, as they have since time began, found bullying others and generally raising hell an appealing recreation.

The Lawrence Raid

It is impossible to say how many of the innumerable beatings, robberies, arsons, and murders of free staters (six in 1855 and early 1856) should be attributed to the slavery controversy and how many would have occurred had slavery not been an issue. Frontiers were socially unstable places with rudimentary law enforcement; they were attractive to ne'er-do-well petty criminals, "frontier scum" as Americans called them long before and long after the Kansas-Nebraska Act. But many northern newspapers put a sectional twist on the sustained violence of the summer of 1856. "Bleeding Kansas" was clearly a miniature civil war fought over slavery. Nor were the free staters in Kansas all passive victims. Some

organized paramilitary cavalries as nasty as the border ruffians. The "jayhawkers" beat and robbed proslavery Kansans and raided into Missouri.

On May 21, 1856, a large gang of border ruffians rode into the antislavery town of Lawrence, Kansas. They shot it up and set several buildings afire. Only one person was killed (a Missourian crushed by a falling wall), but in other incidents, probably the work of the same gang, several free-state settlers were murdered.

Bully Brooks

In Washington at about the same time, Massachusetts Senator Charles Sumner delivered a speech he called the "Crime Against Kansas." Like Garrison, Sumner was a pacifist; also like Garrison, he was given to vituperative language that pacifists ought to avoid. During his review of the proslavery violence in Kansas, Sumner threw in a gratuitous personal insult of an elderly senator from South Carolina, Andrew Butler, who was sitting nearby. Butler suffered from a physical defect that caused him to salivate when he spoke. Sumner coarsely alluded to his slobbering as emblematic of the bestiality of slave owners.

Two days later, Butler's nephew, a congressman named Preston Brooks, entered the Senate chamber, approached Sumner from behind, and beat him senseless with a heavy cane—more a club than a walking stick. Brooks explained his action by citing the *Code Duello*, which held that a gentleman avenged another gentleman's insult by challenging him to a duel. But a gentleman horsewhipped or caned a social inferior who insulted him or his family.

Actually, Brooks mocked "the code of honor." He did not humiliate Sumner with a few sharp raps, which was what the *Code Duello* prescribed; he bludgeoned him until Sumner was close to death. Rather than disown or ignore Brooks as no gentleman, southerners feted him at banquets, making him gifts of gold-headed canes to replace the one he had broken. When Brooks resigned his seat in the House, his district reelected him resoundingly. Sumner, who had overstepped the bounds of Senate etiquette and common decency, became a martyr in the North. His injuries were so severe he was unable to return to work for several years, but Massachusetts reelected him so that his empty desk would stand as a rebuke to southern barbarity.

Pottawatomie Brown

Back in Kansas, John Brown, a zealous abolitionist who had helped the underground railroad in Ohio and then joined five of his sons who had moved to Kansas to vote free state, snapped when he heard of Lawrence and Sumner. On the night of May 24, with four sons and two other men, he descended on the cabins of five proslavery Kansans on Pottawatomie Creek carrying bladed farm tools. When one of the party hesitated, Brown said, "I have no choice. It has been ordained by the Almighty God, ordained from eternity, that I should make an example of these men." He called them outside whence they were hacked to death.

Southern politicians who had joked about the border ruffians as if they were pranksters, and who continued to fete Preston Brooks, howled in humanitarian anguish. Abolitionists who had wrung their hands over the clubbing of Senator Sumner were silent about Brown's cold-blooded ritual murders. That such an act should be excused and such a man idolized by cultivated New Englanders who liked to parade their moral rectitude indicates the extent to which sectional hatreds had grown. Extremists on both sides justified anything done in the name of "the South, the poor South" or "ordained by the Almighty God" in the cause of striking the chains from the bondsman.

Fugitive Slaves

To proslavery militants, the Kansas-Nebraska Act, a great victory in 1854, looked to be at best hollow in 1856. The expansion of slavery apparently won in Congress was facing defeat at the polls in Kansas. Another so-called concession to the South, the Fugitive Slave Act of 1850, was having fewer results than slave owners anticipated. Although not a dead letter, it had not solved the problem of runaway slaves.

Before 1850, between 1,000 and 1,500 slaves had escaped to northern states each year. Only a few were returned to their owners. Once in Indiana, Ohio, or Pennsylvania, many were helped by the underground railroad to escape farther north where, further aided by antislavery blacks and whites, they found jobs and disappeared into the population. Even when a slave owner or a professional slave catcher identified and arrested a runaway, antislavery state and county judges often found technicalities that prevented them from returning the fugitive to the South, or made it their return too expensive to be worthwhile.

The Fugitive Slave act of 1850 took northern law officers and courts out of the loop. It created officials concerned exclusively with fugitive slaves. Special federal commissioners were authorized to arrest, judge, and return runaways independent of state officials. The act levied harsh punishments on any person helping a runaway slave "directly or indirectly." The commissioners could "compel" a bystander to assist in restraining a fugitive who was resisting. To refuse meant being punished. The law jeopardized the freedom of African Americans who had lived as free men and women in the North for years. One of the first persons arrested by a federal commissioner had lived in the North for nineteen years. (Why his master wanted a runaway long past his best working years is anyone's guess.)

Another Hollow Victory

At first, the 1850 act lived up to southern expectations. During the first three months the law was in effect, hundreds of fugitives were returned to their masters. Where professional slave catchers had rarely operated more than a few dozen miles north of the Mason-Dixon line or Ohio River, they now ranged as far north as Boston and the Great Lakes, grabbing blacks long known to be runaways. About 3,000 African Americans who had lived securely in the North fled to Canada to be beyond the reach of the 1850 law.

Antislavery northerners reacted with the same fury with which they responded to the Kansas-Nebraska Act. If a man or woman could be snatched from the streets and returned to slavery without recourse to the courts, they said, slavery was de facto legal in Wisconsin and New Hampshire as well as in Alabama—no matter that the people of the state had abolished the institution.

By 1856, the underground railroad had adjusted to the new circumstances and expanded its "track" so that runaways who managed to get aboard would be hidden, fed, and guided all the way to Canada. Arrests by the federal commissioners declined. In a few cases, mobs forcefully freed fugitive slaves whom commissioners had taken into custody. Northerners saw the federal law as the arrogance of the slave power. Southerners saw northern resistance to the law as acts of war against their institutions.

A HARDENING OF LINES

In normal times, politicians who argue emotionally with one another in the halls of Congress socialize outside the Capitol. John Randolph and Josiah Quincy, on opposite sides of almost every issue, were warm personal friends. Calhoun and John Quincy Adams liked one another. Webster and Clay, unequal rivals for the Whig presidential nomination, conversed pleasantly at receptions. Even Andrew Jackson and Nicholas Biddle managed a civil chat when they met socially. By 1856, this was no longer so. Some congressmen, both northerners and southerners, carried firearms on the floor. They withdrew into their own tribes for social occasions. Against such a backdrop was held the presidential election of 1856.

1856: James Buchanan

The Democrats had no choice but to nominate a doughface. A southern slave owner could not win. However, southern Democrats would accept no northerner who had not established his friendship to the South. Had Kansas not become a battleground, the Democrats would surely have picked Stephen A. Douglas. But the Little Giant, a hero in the South in 1854, had lost much of his southern following when the opening of Kansas to slavery proved to be largely theoretical.

Theoretical even to Douglas: Surprised and alarmed by the widespread opposition to Kansas-Nebraska in the North, Douglas assured his Illinois constituents and northern Democrats generally that they need not worry about Kansas becoming a slave state. His concession to slavery was a symbolic gesture of goodwill to southerners. Kansas would be a free state, Douglas said, because of the unsuitability of the territory to plantation agriculture. Douglas was probably right. Alas, for every northern Democrat he reassured, he alienated a southerner.

The Democrats turned to James Buchanan of Pennsylvania, a stolid and dependable party regular since the Monroe administration. Buchanan excited no one, but he was offensive to few. He was lucky too. He had been out of the country serving as minister to Great Britain between 1853 and 1856 so he had played no role in the passage of the Kansas-Nebraska Act. Still, his southern sympathies were well known. In 1854, he and two other diplomats had written a secret memorandum, the "Ostend Manifesto" (soon leaked to the public) in which he advocated pressuring Spain into selling Cuba to the United States (then admitting the island to the Union as a slave state).

1856: Frémont and Fillmore

The Republican party nominated John C. Frémont, celebrated as "the Pathfinder" for his books describing his explorations in the West. Frémont was no giant of character or intellect. Indeed, his greatest asset was his wife, Jessie Benton, the beautiful, intelligent, willful, and energetic daughter of Old Bullion Benton. In 1856, Frémont was a logical pick for the Republicans. The young party had, as yet, little cohesion. Frémont was a military man like the only Whig presidents, and he was a Free Soiler.

The southern rump of the American party nominated former president Millard Fillmore. But the Know-Nothings had committed political suicide when, early in 1856, their southern wing forced a proslavery statement into the party platform. The northerners walked out of the convention, most to vote Republican. In effect, the Know-Nothings were, in 1856, like the Republicans, a sectional party.

They did well in the slave states, winning more than 40 percent of the vote, and carrying Maryland's electoral votes. Frémont won a third of the popular vote and the electoral votes of New England and New York. Buchanan swept the South and won the electoral votes of New Jersey, Pennsylvania, Indiana, and Illinois.

The Granger Collection, New York

Dred Scott, his wife, and (above them) their daughters. This sympathetic presentation of the beleaguered family indicates how anger in the north toward "the slavocrat conspiracy" had spread far beyond the abolitionists. Frank Leslie's was no antislavery newspaper, but a general-interest periodical that usually avoided taking stands on controversial issues in order to attract the largest possible readership.

Dred Scott

Buchanan's presidency began with a bang. In his inaugural address he hinted that the question of slavery in the territories would shortly be answered for all time. Two days later, March 6, 1857, Americans learned what he meant when the Supreme Court handed down a decision in the case of *Dred Scott* v. *Sandford*.

Dred Scott was a slave in Missouri. For much of his life he was the valet of an army officer, in 1834 accompanying his master to Illinois, where slavery was prohibited under the Northwest Ordinance. Briefly, Scott lived in a part of the Louisiana Purchase where slavery was illegal under the Missouri Compromise.

In 1844, Scott's owner died, bequeathing him to his widow. With the help of abolitionists, Scott sued his owner (eventually a man named Sandford) for his freedom on the grounds that for four years he was held as a slave in territory where Congress had prohibited slavery.

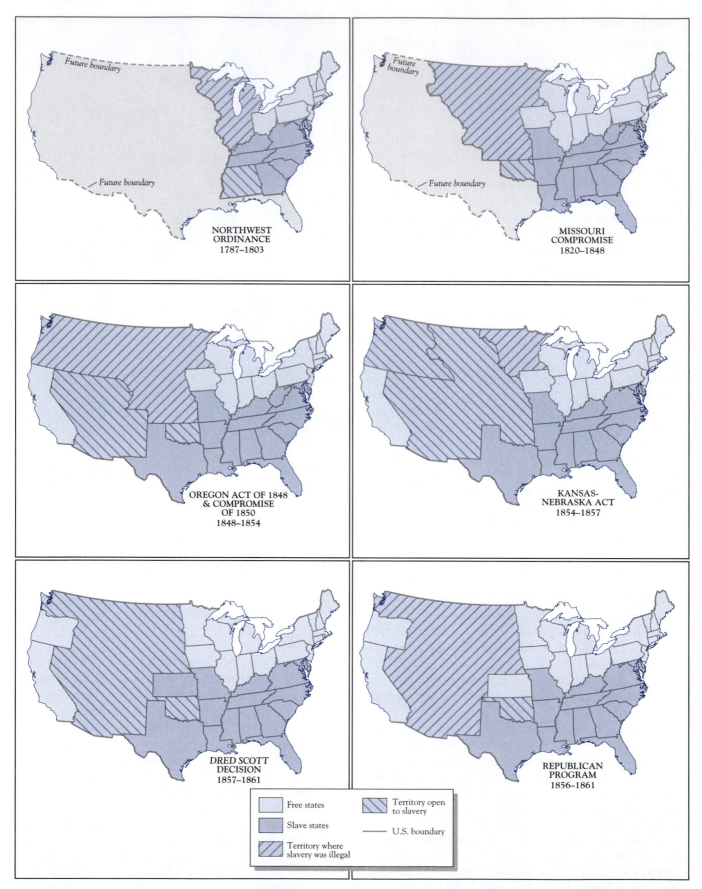

NORTHWEST
ORDINANCE
1787–1803

MISSOURI
COMPROMISE
1820–1848

OREGON ACT OF 1848
& COMPROMISE
OF 1850
1848–1854

KANSAS-
NEBRASKA ACT
1854–1857

DRED SCOTT
DECISION
1857–1861

REPUBLICAN
PROGRAM
1856–1861

Free states

Slave states

Territory where
slavery was illegal

Territory open
to slavery

U.S. boundary

MAP 21:1 **The Legal Status of Slavery 1787–1861.** This series of maps illustrates why ever-increasing numbers of northerners were frustrated during the 1850s. While a majority of Americans wanted to keep slavery out of the territories, every change in the status of the institution after 1820 increased the area in which slavery was legal.

Missouri courts had released slaves with cases similar to Scott's, but that was before sectional animosity had become so strident. Scott lost his case in state court on the grounds that whatever his legal status may have been when he was in Illinois twenty years earlier, he became a slave again when he returned to Missouri. By 1856, Scott's appeal had reached the Supreme Court.

Chief Justice Taney's Final Solution

Every justice commented individually on the case, unusual for the Supreme Court. However, Chief Justice Roger B. Taney, an old Jackson henchman from Maryland, spoke for the majority when he declared that because Scott was black, he could not be a citizen of Missouri, which restricted citizenship to white people. Therefore, Scott could not legally bring his suit in Missouri courts.

The Court could have let the decision go at that; several justices had the good sense to do so. The legal reasoning was

Chief Justice Roger B. Taney is remembered only for his disastrous decision in the Dred Scott *case. Supreme Court scholars almost unanimously regret this because, during Taney's twenty-eight years on the Court, he was a thoughtful, constructive jurist. Taney was of an old Maryland planter family—the Taneys were Catholic, dating back to Maryland's brief spell as a refuge for English Catholics. His weakness as a judge was in cases involving slavery.* Dred Scott v. Sandford *was not the first case in which Taney's proslavery sentiments overcame his usual judiciousness. Taney was a nationalist and remained as chief justice until he died in 1864. Still, it is impossible to say if he would have remained if his native state, Maryland, had seceded.*

Library of Congress, Prints and Photographs Division, Washington, DC (LC-USZ62-107508)

sound and a strictly legalistic decision would have raised few hackles. (Not even Scott's; he had been assured he would be freed when the case was concluded.)

Unfortunately, Taney continued. He believed he had the ultimate constitutional solution to the question of slavery in the territories that was convulsing the nation. Unfortunately, he failed to recognize that northern public opinion, infuriated by the Kansas-Nebraska Act, would hardly accept his formula passively.

In fact, Taney's formula had been propounded years before by John C. Calhoun. Taney declared that the Missouri Compromise had been unconstitutional in prohibiting slavery north of 36°30' because the Constitution forbade Congress to discriminate against the rights of the citizens of every state. A state legislature could abolish slavery; the states were sovereign. However, neither Congress nor a territorial legislature (a dependency of Congress; a territory was not sovereign) could do so because that would deny the right of the citizens of states where slavery was legal to take their property into the territories.

The Republican Panic

The Republicans were floored. The essence of their program was to win a majority in Congress so as to forbid slavery in the western territories. Taney had told them in advance that they could not do so. Antislavery northerners saw their political intentions, based on democracy, frustrated by proslavery justices.

To Republicans, the history of the status of slavery in the territories was a step-by-step whittling away of the will of the majority to prevent the expansion of slavery. Between 1820 and 1854, under the Missouri Compromise, slavery was illegal in all territories north of 36° 30'. The Kansas-Nebraska Act of 1854 legalized slavery in territories where it had been forbidden—if a majority of citizens in that territory voted to do so. Now, the Dred Scott decision of 1857 *prevented* a majority of a territory's population from keeping slavery out.

Their fury was fanned in October 1857 when President Buchanan endorsed the "Lecompton Constitution," a constitution for Kansas that declared it a slave state. The Lecompton Constitution was, in fact, a dubious proposition. It had been drafted by one of two rival legislatures in Kansas. Proslavery Kansans met at Lecompton, free staters at Topeka. Nevertheless, Congress might have accepted it at Buchanan's behest—Democrats had a majority in both houses—had not Stephen A. Douglas, the author of the Kansas-Nebraska Act, insisted that the Lecompton document be approved in a referendum of all Kansans before Congress considered it.

Douglas's Freeport Doctrine

Douglas, so recently a shoo-in for the presidency, now feared that he might lose his senate seat in 1858. The Republicans painted him as a proslavery doughface. Few Democrats in Illinois were antislavery; many of them, however, opposed the expansion of slavery into the territories. Having presented himself as friendly to the South in 1854, in 1858 Douglas had to explain to Illinois that popular sovereignty could ensure that the territories would be reserved for free men and women.

Race Mixing

Few whites, including abolitionists, believed in racial equality. Thus, it was in the political interest of northern Democrats to accuse the Republicans of advocating miscegenation, race mixture. "I am opposed to Negro equality," Stephen A. Douglas said in a debate with Abraham Lincoln, "I am in favor of preserving not only the purity of the blood but the purity of the government from any mixture or amalgamation with inferior races."

This kind of attack worried Republicans. They had to assure voters that their party's opposition to slavery did not mean they believed in the equality of the races or even equal civil rights for African Americans. Lincoln replied to Douglas: "I protest, now and forever, against that counterfeit logic which presumes that because I do not want a Negro woman for a slave, I necessarily want her for a wife. . . . As God made us separate, we can leave one another alone, and do one another much good thereby."

Lincoln shrewdly took the debate back to the territorial question by quipping directly to Douglas, "Why, Judge, if we do not let them get together in the Territories, they won't mix there."

John Brown's Mountains

The Appalachians where John Brown planned to base his slave rebellion contained many corners that were nearly impenetrable. During the Civil War, Confederate draft dodgers and deserters roamed the mountains with little fear of being caught. Some folklorists believe that Elizabethan speech patterns and seventeenth-century ballads that survived nowhere else were found in remote Appalachian hollows into the twentieth century, so isolated were the people there. "Moonshining" is still associated with Appalachian "hillbillies" because it was (and is) easy to conceal an illegal still (and, today, a methamphetamine lab) in the mountains.

So, as crackbrained as John Brown may have been in other matters, he was probably correct to maintain that a guerrilla band could function in the Appalachians.

His task was complicated by the *Dred Scott* decision for it denied territorial legislatures the power to keep slavery out. In a debate with his Republican opponent at Freeport, Illinois, Douglas explained how the voters in a territory could keep slavery out without violating the Supreme Court's ruling. The Freeport Doctrine was ingenious—Douglas had not been a successful lawyer because he had been lucky.

The Freeport Doctrine held that a territorial legislature could ensure that no slave owners brought their slaves into that territory simply by failing to enact a slave code: the laws in every slave state protected a master's property rights in his slaves. No slave owner, Douglas continued, would be so foolish as to take his valuable property to a place where there were no laws protecting his rights, no law enforcement officers required to arrest and return slaves who ran away. Therefore, when the day came for a territory to apply for statehood, there would be no slave owners in the convention that wrote the state constitution to ensure that slavery was legal. The Supreme Court could overturn an act of Congress or of a territorial or state legislature; the Court could not compel a legislative body to enact a law it did not choose to enact.

Douglas was reelected to his seat in the Senate. But the Freeport Doctrine no more solved the slavery in the territories problem than the *Dred Scott* decision did. Southern extremists merely shifted their position, demanding that Congress enact a *national* slave code to protect slave owners in the territories.

John Brown Returns

John Brown went into hiding after the Pottawatomie murders, but not for long. Although he was wanted for murder in Kansas, he discovered that he could move around openly in northern New York and New England. Prominent New England abolitionists and their wives were titillated rather than appalled by the Kansas murders. They invited him to dinners where he showed off the bowie knife and revolver he kept tucked into his boots and excited his hosts with repartee such as "Talk! talk! talk! That will never free the slaves. What is needed is action—action" and "Caution, caution . . . I am

Public Domain

A curiously unbiased nineteenth-century drawing of John Brown during the final minutes of his rebellion in the roundhouse at Harper's Ferry. Southerners depicted Brown as a devil, northern abolitionists as a godly crusader. The man in Brown's arms is his son, who was already dying when Marines stormed the ill-chosen fortress. Brown himself was seriously wounded when he was captured. He lay on a stretcher at his trial.

Defying the Law: Importers of Slaves

In 1807, Congress prohibited the importation of slaves from abroad. In part, the act represented a revulsion to the horrors of the trans-Atlantic slave trade. In part, the ban on imported slaves was seen as a step toward abolition in the southern states.

At first, compliance with the law was virtually universal (although South Carolinians went on a slave-buying orgy in anticipation of the ban). However, the cotton boom in the deep South and the end of the foreign slave trade caused a steady rise in the cost of slaves that inevitably attracted the attention of the kind of men willing to break the law when the price is right. Those who sailed to the old slaver ports in West Africa found the markets still open. The Ashanti king had been bewildered when he was told he was losing his American customers. Other African chiefs had condemned the American action as an insult to Islam. They and others were delighted that at least some Americans were back. They had plenty of slaves for sale. King Gezo of Dahomey (whose bodyguard was a platoon of tall, fierce, strong women) sold 9,000 slaves annually between 1809 and 1850. The major vendors at Sangha were an American, Paul Faber, and his African wife, Mary, who kept meticulous books, as if they were grocers.

But the transatlantic slave trade was a risky business. Great Britain, which abolished the African slave trade about the same time as the United States, patrolled the African coast looking for violators. By the 1840s, the British were stationing thirty naval ships in African waters. They returned captives they rescued to Africa and harshly punished illegal slave traders; it was a hanging offense. (The United States Navy kept a squadron of eight ships in Caribbean waters to search suspicious vessels. Between May 1818 and November 1821, the navy freed 573 Africans from American-owned ships.)

The Portuguese and Spanish continued to buy Africans for enslavement in their American colonies. So, the abundance of slaves for sale in Brazil and Cuba, including recently imported Africans, made the shorter voyages from there to Savannah or Charleston more inviting to Americans.

Northern shipyards continued to build vessels for the slave trade. Of 170 slaving expeditions between 1859 and 1862 that the British intercepted, seventy-four of the vessels involved had been outfitted in New York. The schooner *Wanderer* ostensibly a yacht built for John Johnston of New Orleans in 1856 was, with its oversize water tanks, obviously designed for the slave trade. Still, authorities could do nothing until the vessel was caught in the act—after the *Wanderer* had landed 325 slaves at Jekyll Island, South Carolina, in December 1858,

By the 1850s, it was difficult to get a conviction for slave trading from a southern jury. In 1859, a U.S. warship brought the bark *Emily,* obviously a slaver, into port. The case was dismissed. In 1860, the owner of the *Wanderer* was acquitted in Savannah and permitted to buy his ship back for a quarter of its value. Under the law, crewmen on a slaver were liable to be prosecuted along with the ship's owner, but they rarely suffered more than a slap on the wrist. With so little deterrence, seamen found it difficult to ignore the fact that wages on an illegal slave ship running from Cuba were as high as $10 a day, astronomical pay.

---

eternally tired of hearing that word caution. It is nothing but the word of cowardice."

Such bravado is often effective among people who like to talk up "sacred causes" as long as they have to risk nothing. Brown persuaded six well-to-do abolitionists to give him money to launch a slave rebellion. He divulged few details of his plans; the "Secret Six" who financed him did not want to know too much. He did tell Frederick Douglass what he planned to do: With a small disciplined cadre of whites and blacks, he would seize the federal arsenal in Harper's Ferry, Virginia (now West Virginia), capture guns and ammunition, arouse slaves in the area to join him, and escape into the Appalachians, which rise steeply all around Harper's Ferry. From their mountain sanctuary, Brown's guerrilla band would swoop down on plantations, free a few slaves at a time, and enlarge the army. Before long, Brown predicted, slave rebellions would erupt all over the South, destroying the peculiar institution.

Douglass was no pacifist; he was not opposed to employing force to destroy slavery. But he wanted no part of Brown's scheme. It was doomed to failure, Douglass said; Harper's Ferry was "a perfect steel trap." He urged Brown to call his project off.

Many critics of John Brown's Raid after the fact have echoed Douglass. The impossibility of his scheme proved that either the old man was out of his mind or that he all along intended to fail, offering himself as a martyr to the cause of abolition. It is possible that Brown was thinking martyrdom all along.

Shortly before his execution, he wrote to his wife that "I have been whipped but am sure I can recover all the lost capital . . . by only hanging a few minutes by the neck." However, he never mentioned martyrdom as his purpose to Douglass or any of the "Secret Six."

Brown was no rock of emotional stability; he may well have been insane. The Pottawatomie murders were the act of a psychopath. But there was nothing crazy about the idea of a small guerrilla force operating from a remote and shifting base, avoiding big battles in which conventional military forces have an overwhelming advantage, and winning the support of ordinary people, in Brown's instance the slaves. Such tactics led to several successful revolutions in the twentieth century. The odds were never with Brown, but they were not prohibitive.

Harper's Ferry

On October 16, 1859, Brown and eighteen others, including several African Americans, captured the arsenal. Then, Brown either lost his nerve or deluded himself into believing that the slaves in the area were going to join him. Instead of making for the hills, he holed up in the roundhouse where he was surrounded by United States Marines under the command of Colonel Robert E. Lee. In two days Lee's professionals killed ten of Brown's followers and captured the others, including Brown. He was immediately tried for treason by the state of Virginia and found guilty. He was hanged in December.

Most northerners grimly approved the speedy trial and execution. "It was not a slave insurrection," Abraham Lincoln said. "It was an attempt by white men to get up a revolt among slaves. . . . It was so absurd that the slaves saw plainly enough it could not succeed." Southerners, for whom fears of slave rebellion were, if rarely spoken of, frequently in mind, saw only an attempt by abolitionists to instigate an uprising that would leave them, their wives, and children dead in their beds. Virginia governor, Henry A. Wise, who interviewed Brown and was impressed by him, dismissed the suggestion that he was a lone lunatic. Brown was "fanatic, vain, and garrulous," Wise said, but also "cool, collected, and indomitable . . . firm, truthful, and intelligent." By implication, Brown was like a great many northern abolitionists.

Southern hysteria was confirmed by the fact that most abolitionists remained silent, and a few openly praised Brown as a hero and a martyr. Ralph Waldo Emerson said that Brown's death made the gallows as holy as the Christian cross. Brown was hanged in December 1859; 1860 was an election year. Could the South trust a Republican president to protect southern whites against other John Browns?

THE ELECTION OF 1860

Southern fire-eaters declared that if the Republicans won the presidency, the southern states would secede from the Union. Then, having threatened northern voters, the extremists not only failed to work against a Republican victory, they also guaranteed it. They destroyed the Democratic party that had served southern interests so well.

The Democrats Split

In 1860, the Democratic party was almost the last national institution in the United States. The Methodist church had split into northern and southern churches in 1844, the Baptists in 1845, the Presbyterians during the 1850s. Fraternal lodges broke in two. The Whig party, the nation's nationalist party, was a fading memory. The Republican party was exclusively a northern institution. Only within the Democratic party did men from both sections still come together in the hope of settling sectional differences.

In April 1860, with the smell of John Brown's gunpowder still in the air, the Democratic convention met in Charleston.

The majority of the delegates wanted to nominate Stephen A. Douglas as the Democrat most likely to defeat the Republicans. This was sound reasoning. With the electoral votes of the South in his pocket, Douglas could expect to win enough northern states to have a decisive majority.

However, the delegations of eight southern states had come to the convention primed. They would agree to Douglas only if he repudiated the Freeport Doctrine and called for a federal slave code in the territories. It was a senseless ultimatum. If Douglas agreed, he would provide the Republicans with the argument that he was the willing stooge of the slavocracy. Northern Democrats would vote Republican by the thousands. If all the free states voted Republican, the Republican candidate would win in the electoral college.

Southerners, Douglas's men argued, should be satisfied with a lifelong friend of the South who was the one candidate who could keep the Republicans out of the White House. Unmoved, the eight hard-line states walked out of the convention. The Douglas forces recessed without nominating him, hoping to talk sense into the fire-eaters and reunify the party.

The Democrats reassembled in Baltimore in June. Again extremists refused to budge. Disgusted, the regular Democrats, a few southerners among them, nominated Douglas and a southern moderate, Herschel V. Johnson of Georgia, as his running mate. The southern Democrats nominated John C. Breckinridge of Kentucky; to give the ticket a semblance of national support, they chose an Oregon doughface, Joseph Lane, as their vice presidential candidate.

Republican Opportunity

The Republicans met in Chicago, optimistic but cautious. With the Democrats split, victory was likely. But if they picked too strident an antislavery candidate, worried northern voters might back Douglas as the voice of moderation. Many delegates believed that the most prominent Republican, William H. Seward of New York, had been too avid in his attacks on slavery. Seward had spoken of "a higher law than the Constitution" and, worse, of an "irrepressible conflict" between North and South. Former Know-Nothings could not forgive Seward for opposing anti-Catholic legislation in New York.

So the Republicans turned to the less-known Abraham Lincoln. Lincoln was rock solid on the fundamental Republican principle that slavery must be banned in the territories, but he was no abolitionist. He had opposed Know Nothingism and was popular with German voters in Illinois, but he was not on record as "pro-Catholic." In manner he was modest, moderate, humane, and ingratiating. In a speech introducing himself to eastern Republicans in New York City in February 1860, he struck a note of humility, prudence, and caution. Not only was slavery protected by the Constitution in those states where it existed, Lincoln said, but northerners ought to sympathize with slave owners rather than vilify them. Lincoln himself had been born in Kentucky, a slave state. He knew that a quirk of fate might have made him a slave owner. By choosing him, the Republicans accommodated southern sensitivities as far as they could do so without giving up their basic principles.

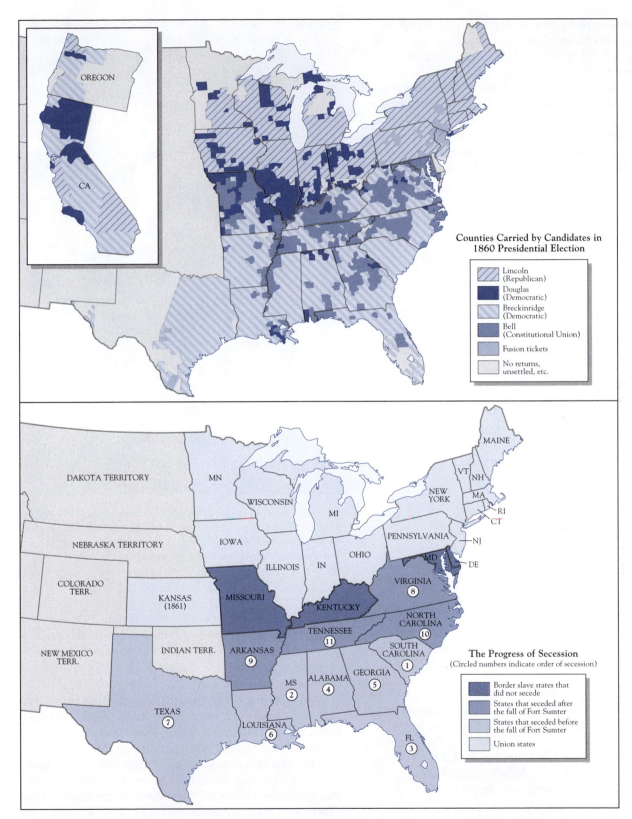

Counties Carried by Candidates in 1860 Presidential Election

- Lincoln (Republican)
- Douglas (Democratic)
- Breckinridge (Democratic)
- Bell (Constitutional Union)
- Fusion tickets
- No returns, unsettled, etc.

The Progress of Secession
(Circled numbers indicate order of secession)

- Border slave states that did not secede
- States that seceded after the fall of Fort Sumter
- States that seceded before the fall of Fort Sumter
- Union states

MAP 21:2 **Presidential Election of 1860 and Southern Secession.** Note in the upper map, Lincoln's sweep in the North and Breckinridge's in the South. Bell won the border states and did well in the deep South but won few votes in the free states. There, Know-Nothings and former Whigs like Bell had thrown in with the Republicans. Except in the Midwest and New Jersey, few counties, North and South, voted for Douglas. But he finished second almost everywhere to Lincoln, Bell, or Breckinridge. He was the true national candidate. His popular vote total was second to Lincoln's and closer to Lincoln's vote than third-place finisher, Breckinridge, was to him.

The lower map indicates the order in which the eleven Confederate states seceded from the Union. Virginia, North Carolina, Arkansas, and Tennessee resisted secession until Lincoln's call for troops after the fall of Fort Sumter. Four slave states (Delaware, Maryland, Kentucky, and Missouri) did not secede.

The Republican platform was comprehensive: a high protective tariff; a liberal immigration policy; the construction of a transcontinental railway; and a homestead act. The platform was designed to win the votes of disparate economic groups often at odds with one another: eastern industrial capitalists, workers, and midwestern farmers. Moreover, by avoiding a single-issue campaign, the Republicans hoped to signal the South that they were not, as a party, antislavery fanatics. They even named a vice presidential candidate who had been a Democrat as late as 1857, Hannibal Hamlin of Maine.

The Old Man's Party

A fourth party entered the contest, the Constitutional Union party, representing Henry Clay's brand of nationalism: sectional forbearance and compromise. The platform of the party was, in effect, to stall, reconcile, and hope. It was a mistake, its leaders said, to force a sectional confrontation while tempers were up; put off the problem of slavery in the territories to a later day when tempers had cooled.

For president the Constitutional Unionists nominated John Bell of Tennessee, a protégé of Clay. For vice president they chose the distinguished Whig orator Edward Everett of Massachusetts. Republicans and Democrats alike dismissed them as "the old man's party," but they had a base. The remnants of the Whigs and Know-Nothings in the South, voters who could not stomach the idea of voting for a Democrat, supported Bell. The party was strongest in the states of the upper South: Maryland, Virginia, Kentucky, and Tennessee.

Republican Victory

Abraham Lincoln's name was not even on the ballot in ten of fifteen slave states; he won only 4 percent of the vote in those slave states where he was listed. But he won 54 percent of the popular vote in the North. He carried every free state except New Jersey, just as the Douglas Democrats had warned was possible. The sweep gave him a clear majority in the electoral college. Breckinridge won 45 percent of the vote in the slave states (only 5 percent in the North). It was a sectional vote.

Douglas, one of two candidates appealing to voters nationwide, won only 12 electoral votes (in Missouri and New Jersey). He ran second to Lincoln in the North and second to John Bell in the upper South. Bell carried three border states and did well throughout the South. But even if the Douglas and the Bell votes had been combined—which was out of the question—Lincoln would have been elected.

South Carolina Leads the Way

Having already announced that Lincoln's election meant secession, the fire-eaters of South Carolina (where there was no popular vote for presidential electors) called a convention that, on December 20, 1860, unanimously declared that "the union now subsisting between South Carolina and the other States, under the name of the 'United States of America,' is

Library of Congress, Prints and Photographs Division, Washington, DC (LC-USZ62-5803)

Abraham Lincoln about the time he was elected president in 1860. He grew his trademark beard between election day and his inauguration because, so he said, a little girl had written to him that he was so homely, a beard could only help his appearance.

hereby dissolved." Winfield Scott, a Unionist of southern birth, wrote to the wife of one of the secessionist delegates: "I know your little South Carolina. I lived there once. It is about as big as Long Island and two-thirds of the population are negroes. Are you mad?"

South Carolina did not expect to go it alone. In January 1861, six states of the Deep South followed suit, declaring that a Republican administration threatened their "domestic institutions." Then came a glimmer of hope. The secession movement stalled when none of the other slave states approved secession ordinances. At the same time they rejected secession, however, conventions in the border states plus North Carolina, Tennessee, and Arkansas declared their opposition to any attempt by the federal government to use force against the states that had seceded. By rebuffing the big talkers on both sides, the leaders of the border states hoped to force a compromise.

The outgoing president, James Buchanan, was not the man to engineer such a compromise. Few still respected Old Buck. His secretary of war, John Floyd of Virginia, betrayed him by transferring tons of war matériel to southern states before he resigned. Other friends and allies resigned and left Washington, few pausing to call on the president who had worked on behalf of the South. The first bachelor to occupy the White House was quite alone and he knew it. After a hand-wringing message sent to Congress in which he declared that while secession was illegal, he was powerless to do anything about it, Buchanan sat back to wait for the day he could go home to Pennsylvania.

THE CONFEDERACY

As Buchanan slumped, Senator John J. Crittenden stood up. Like many Kentuckians, Crittenden had made a career of trying to mediate between northerners and southerners. Like John Bell, he was a Henry Clay Whig. Now he proposed that rather than break up the Union, divide the territories between North and South; extend the Missouri Compromise line to the California border; guarantee slavery to the south of it, forbid slavery to the north.

The Compromisers Fail

Because of the *Dred Scott* decision, Crittenden's plan could not be put into effect without a constitutional amendment. Crittenden hoped that the specter of civil war, now chillingly real with militias drilling in both North and South, would prompt both northern and southern state legislatures to act in haste.

With some encouragement they might have done so. There was a flurry of enthusiasm for Crittenden's compromise on both sides of the Mason-Dixon line. But before the seceded states were forced to take a stand, President-elect Lincoln quashed the plan. His reasons were political but nonetheless compelling. His Republican party was a diverse alliance of people who disagreed with one another on many issues. The one adhesive that bound them together was the principle that slavery must not expand. If Lincoln gave in on this point, he would take office with at least half his party in opposition.

Lincoln also discouraged a second attempt at compromise, a peace conference held in Washington in February 1861. It was a distinguished assembly, chaired by former president John Tyler. Tyler had been a southern extremist and, a few months later, he would support the secession of Virginia. But he worked hard for a settlement in February, proposing a series of constitutional amendments along the same lines as Crittenden's plan.

Once again, Lincoln drew the line on allowing slavery in the southern territories. Instead, he endorsed an amendment (immediately passed by both houses of Congress) that would "forever guarantee" slavery in the states where it already existed. As he well knew, this was a symbolic gesture. A constitutional amendment can be repealed by another constitutional amendment. But the question was moot by February 1861. Heady with the excitement of creating a new nation, the secessionists had lost any interest in restoring the Union.

The Confederate States of America

According to secessionist theory, the seven states that left the Union were now independent republics. However, no southern leader intended his state to go it alone. Although they were disappointed that eight of the fifteen slave states refused to join them, they met in Montgomery, Alabama, shortly before Lincoln's inauguration and established the Confederate States of America.

The government of the Confederacy differed little from the one the secessionists had abandoned. The Montgomery convention adopted the Constitution of 1787 plus amendments almost word for word. All federal laws were to remain in effect until repealed. The changes the Confederates made reflected the South's obsession with slavery and with Calhoun's political theories, and resulted in several curious contradictions.

Thus, the Confederates defined the states as sovereign and independent but called their new government permanent. Even more oddly, they declared that individual states might

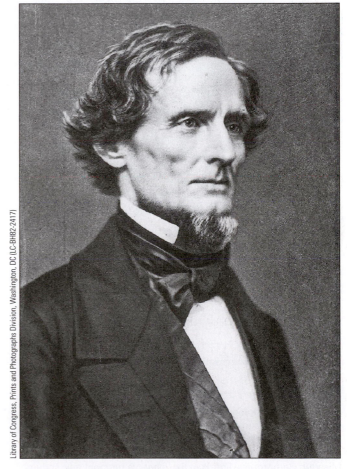

Library of Congress, Prints and Photographs Division, Washington, DC (LC-BH82-2417)

Jefferson Davis, first and only president of the Confederacy. Davis was zealously proslavery and supported every measure to expand it to the territories. Still, he tried to delay Mississippi's secession, arguing that the state should wait until Lincoln was inaugurated and given the opportunity to make concessions to the South. His last-minute conversion to moderation ensured that he would be elected president. The infant Confederacy was hoping for a peaceful secession.

not interfere with slavery, a restriction on states' rights that no prominent Republican had ever suggested.

The Confederates also modified the presidency. The chief executive was to be elected for a term of six years rather than four, but he was not permitted to run for a second term. While this seemed to weaken the office, the Confederates allowed the president to veto parts of congressional bills rather than, as in the Union, requiring the president to accept all or nothing.

Jeff Davis

As their first president, the Confederates selected Jefferson Davis. On the face of it, he was a good choice. His bearing was regal and he was a model slave owner, the sort that southerners liked to pretend was typical of the institution. Davis seemed to be a wise choice because he had kept his distance from secessionist extremists. Indeed, Davis asked his fellow Mississippians to delay secession until Lincoln had a chance to prove himself. When his state overruled him, Davis delivered a moderate, eloquent, and affectionate farewell speech in the Senate. By choosing such a man, rather than

a fire-eater, the Confederates demonstrated their willingness to work with southerners who opposed secession, and there were plenty of them, both Douglas Democrats and Whigs.

In other ways, the choice of Jefferson Davis was ill-advised. It was not so much the coldness of his personality; George Washington had been icy. Davis's weakness was that despite his bearing, he lacked self-confidence and was, consequently, easily irritated and inflexible. He proved incapable of cooperating with critics, even those who differed with him on minor points. He seemed to need yes-men in order to function. As a result, he denied his administration the services of some of the South's ablest statesmen.

Worse, Davis was a dabbler. Instead of delegating authority and presiding over the government, he repeatedly interfered in the pettiest details of administration—peering over his subordinates' shoulders, arousing personal resentments among even those who were devoted to him. He had been a good senator and secretary of war; he was not up to being the "Father of His Country."

Abe Lincoln

By comparison, Abraham Lincoln knew the value of unity and competent help. Rather than shun his rivals within the Republican party, he named them to his cabinet. Seward became secretary of state; Salmon P. Chase of Ohio was Lincoln's secretary of treasury. After a brief misadventure with an incompetent secretary of war, Simon Cameron, Lincoln appointed a Democrat, Edwin Stanton, to that post because his talents were obvious. Lincoln wanted able aides, not pals or toadies. Within their departments, Lincoln's cabinet officers were free to do anything that did not conflict with general policy. As a result, a cantankerous and headstrong group of men never challenged his control of fundamentals.

Lincoln differed from Davis in other ways. Far from regal, he was an awkward, plain, even ugly man. Tall and gangling, with oversize hands and feet, he impressed those who met him for the first time as a frontier oaf. His enemies called him "the baboon." Some of his supporters snickered at his clumsiness and were appalled by his fondness for dirty jokes.

But both friends and enemies soon discovered that the president was no yokel. Lincoln had honed a sharp native intelligence on a stone of lifelong study and proved to be one of the three or four most eloquent chief executives. And yet, behind his brilliance was a humility born of modest background that can be found in no other American president.

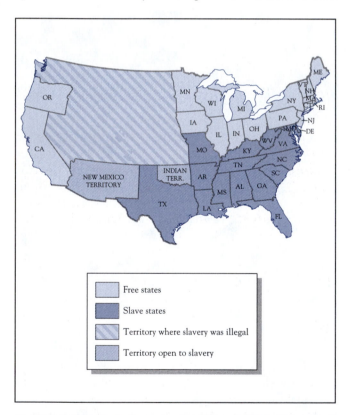

Free states

Slave states

Territory where slavery was illegal

Territory open to slavery

MAP 21:3 **Crittenden's Compromise Plan of 1861.** Crittenden's Compromise recognized the justice of northern anger over the Kansas-Nebraska Act and the *Dred Scott* decision. Crittenden, one of the last Whigs, called for the restoration and extension of the Missouri Compromise line. Had there been a national referendum on it, it might well have won. But, there was no more nation— seven states had seceded—and Lincoln and the Republicans could not accept even the theoretical possibility of a slave state emerging in New Mexico Territory. (Unlikely as that was: New Mexico was mostly desert; there were more slaves in Mormon Utah than in all of New Mexico.) "Absolutely no slavery in the territories" was the single principle that held the Republican party together.

First Blood
The first blood of the Civil War was not shed at Fort Sumter. No one was killed there. The first deaths of the Civil War occurred in Baltimore a week after the fall of Sumter. A prosecession mob attacked soldiers from Massachusetts as they marched from one railroad terminal to another. The soldiers fired back. Twelve members of the mob and four soldiers were killed.

Reproduced from the Collections of the Library of Congress [LC-USZ62-120309]

Fort Sumter, the day after it was surrendered to the Confederacy. The commander of the fort was expected to make only a symbolic resistance; Sumter was at the mercy of the batteries in Charleston. Nevertheless, the fort took a terrific battering as this photograph shows.

Lincoln needed all his native resources. On March 4, 1861, when he was sworn in before a glum Washington crowd, the Union was in tatters. During the previous two months, the Stars and Stripes had been hauled down from every flag staff in the South except for one at Fort Pickens in Pensacola, Florida, and another at Fort Sumter, on an island in the harbor of Charleston, South Carolina.

A War of Nerves

Neither of the forts threatened the security of the Confederacy. They were old installations designed for defense and were manned by token garrisons. But symbols take on profound importance in edgy times, and the southern fire-eaters, itching for a fight, ranted about the insulting occupation of their country by a "foreign power."

Davis was willing to live with the Union forts for the time being. He understood that the Confederacy could not survive as long as it consisted of seven of the least populated states. His hope was to delay a confrontation with the North until he could make a foreign alliance or induce the eight slave states that remained in the Union to join the Confederacy. He feared that if he fired the first shot, the states of the upper South might support the Union.

The fire-eaters disagreed. They believed that a battle, no matter who started it, would bring the other slave states to their side. Nevertheless, when the commander at Fort Sumter made it known that he would soon have to surrender the fort for lack of provisions, Davis had his way.

Within limits, Lincoln also favored delaying confrontation. He believed that the longer the states of the upper South did not secede, the less likely they were to go. Moreover, the leaders of Virginia, Kentucky, Tennessee, and

Arkansas formally warned him against using force against the Confederacy. If the Union fired the first shot, they would secede.

Finally, Lincoln did not have the people of the North solidly behind him. Northern Democrats would not support an act of aggression and Winfield Scott, Lincoln's chief military adviser, told him that the army was not up to a war of conquest. Some abolitionists who were pacifists, such as Horace Greeley and William Lloyd Garrison, urged the president to "let the wayward sisters depart in peace."

The First Shot

Lincoln had no intention of doing that. He was determined to save the Union by peaceful means if possible, by force if necessary. He reasoned that if the Confederates fired the first shot, the border states might secede anyway, but at least the act of rebellion would unite northerners. If he delayed a confrontation indefinitely, he still might lose the border states and still have a divided, uncertain North.

This was the reasoning behind Lincoln's decision to resupply Fort Sumter. He announced that he would not use force against the state of South Carolina. (Lincoln would not communicate with the Confederate government.) There would be no arms in the relief ship, only food, medicine, and other nonmilitary supplies. He repeated his wish that the crisis be resolved peacefully. But he insisted on his presidential obligation to maintain the government's authority in Charleston harbor.

And so the war came. When the relief ship approached the sandbar that guarded Charleston harbor, the Confederate artillery opened fire. On the morning of April 12, 1861, cannon under the command of General P. G. T. Beauregard of

Louisiana slowly reduced Sumter to rubble. The following day, the fort surrendered. Davis was reluctant to the end. In a way, he lost control of South Carolina.

The Border States Take Sides

The Battle of Fort Sumter served both Confederate and Union purposes. Lincoln was able to call for 75,000 volunteers and to get them within days. However, his call for troops pushed four more states into the Confederacy: Virginia,

---

Lee's Loyalties

Robert E. Lee was the most respected officer in the army in 1861. When he was asked if he would support the Union or the South in the event of a civil war, Lee replied that he would support neither; he would support his native state, Virginia. "If Virginia stands by the old Union, so will I. But if she secedes (though I do not believe in secession as a constitutional right, nor that there is sufficient cause for revolution) then I will follow my native state with my sword and, if need be, with my life."

It was because Lee's unionism and opposition to slavery were well known that he was not immediately put in command of a Confederate army. Many Confederates did not trust him.

North Carolina, Tennessee, and Arkansas. In deference to Virginia's prestige, the capital of the new nation was moved from Montgomery to Richmond.

Secessionist feeling was strong in the slave states of Maryland, Kentucky, and Missouri, but far from overwhelming. Lincoln was able to prevent all three from seceding by a combination of shrewd political maneuvers and the tactful deployment of troops. Delaware, the fifteenth slave state, never considered secession.

Then, in the contest for the border states, the North won a bonus. The mountainous western part of Virginia was peopled by farmers who owned few slaves. They traditionally resented the planter aristocracy that dominated Virginia politics. The westerners had no interest in fighting and dying to protect the human property of the rich flatlanders. In effect, the fifty western counties of Virginia seceded from the Old Dominion. By an irregular constitutional process, the Republicans provided the means for West Virginia to become a Union state in June 1863.

For the border states, the Civil War was literally a war between brothers. Henry Clay's grandsons fought on both sides. Several of President Lincoln's brothers-in-law fought for the South, and Jefferson Davis had cousins in the Union Army. The most poignant case was that of Senator Crittenden of Kentucky, who had tried to head off war with a compromise. One of his sons became a general in the Union Army, another a general in the Confederate Army.

FURTHER READING

Classics John G. Randall, *The Civil War and Reconstruction*, 1937; David Potter, *The Impending Crisis, 1848–1861*, 1974, *The Growth of Southern Nationalism 1848–1861*, 1953; Bruce Catton, *The Coming Fury*, 1961; Kenneth M. Stampp, *And the War Came: The North and the Secession Crisis 1860–1861*, 1950; Richard N. Current, *Lincoln and the First Shot*, 1963.

General Kenneth M. Stampp, *The Imperfect Union: Essays on the Background of the Civil War*, 1980; Leonard Richards, *The Slave Power: The Free North and Southern Domination, 1780–1860*, 2000; James M. McPherson, *Battle Cry of Freedom: The Civil War Era*, 1988; Richard A. Sewell, *A House Divided: Sectionalism and Civil War, 1848–1860*, 1988; Bruce Levine, *Half Slave and Half Free: The Roots of the Civil War*, 1992; Michael F. Holt, *The Political Crisis of the 1850s*, 1978; William W. Freehling, *The Road to Disunion*, 1990; Gabor Boritt, *Why the Civil War Came*, 1996.

Kansas and Dred Scott Richard H. Sewell, *Ballots for Freedom: Antislavery Politics in the United States, 1837–1860*, 1976; Gerald W. Wolff, *The Kansas-Nebraska Bill: Party, Section, and the Coming of the Civil War*, 1977; James A. Rawley, *Race and Politics: "Bleeding Kansas" and the Coming of the Civil War*, 1969; Nicole Etcheson, *Bleeding Kansas: Contested Liberty in the Civil War Era*, 2004; Don E. Fehrenbacher, *The Dred Scott Case: Its Significance in American Law*

and Politics, 1981; Kenneth M. Stampp, *America in 1857: A Nation on the Brink*, 1990; David Zarefsky, *Lincoln, Douglas, and Slavery: In the Crucible of Debate*, 1990; Kenneth Winkle, *The Young Eagle: The Rise of Abraham Lincoln*, 2003; David Donald, *Abraham Lincoln*, 1995.

John Brown Stephen Oates, *To Purge This Land With Blood: A Biography of John Brown*, 1984; Truman Nelson, *The Old Man John Brown at Harpers Ferry*, 1973; Paul Finkelman, *His Soul Goes Marching On: Responses to John Brown's Harper's Ferry Raid*, 1995; John Stauffer, *The Black Hearts of Men*, 2002; Franny Nudelman, *John Brown's Body*, 2004; David S. Reynolds, *John Brown, Abolitionist: The Man Who Killed Slavery, Sparked the Civil War, and Seeded Civil Rights*, 2005; Merrill D. Peterson, *John Brown: The Legend Revisited*, 2005.

Secession W. L. Barney, *The Road to Secession*, 1972; Stephen A. Channing, *Crisis of Fear: Secession in South Carolina*, 1970; R. A. Wooster, *The Secession Conventions of the South*, 1962; Charles B. Dew, *Apostles of Disunion: Southern Secession Commissioners and the Causes of the Civil War*, 2001; Maury Klein, *Days of Defiance: Sumter, Secession, and the Coming of the Civil War*, 1997; Daniel W. Crofts, *Reluctant Confederates: Upper South Unionists in the Secession Crisis*, 1989.

KEY TERMS

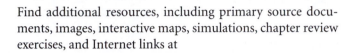

Use the following listing of key terms to review important figures, events, locations, and concepts covered in this chapter. A glossary of these terms is available on *The American*

Past companion Web site: www.cengage.com/history/conlin/tap9e

popular sovereignty, p. 347	**jayhawkers**, p. 349	**Lecompton Constitution**, p. 353
"Bleeding Kansas", p. 349	**doughface**, p. 351	**Freeport Doctrine**, p. 354
border ruffians, p. 349	**Know-Nothing Party**, p. 351	**John Brown's Raid**, p. 355

ONLINE RESOURCES

Find additional resources, including primary source documents, images, interactive maps, simulations, chapter review exercises, and Internet links at

The American Past companion Web site
www.cengage.com/history/conlin/tap9e

American History Resource Center
http://ushistory.wadsworth.com/

Chapter 22

Tidy Plans, Ugly Realities

The Civil War through 1862

The Cooper Union Museum, New York

Our new Government is founded upon ... the great truth that the Negro is not the equal to the white man; that slavery, subordination to the superior race, is his natural and moral condition. This, our new Government, is the first, in the history of the world, based upon this great physical, philosophical, and moral truth.

—Alexander H. Stephens

The first blast of civil war is the death warrant of your institution.

—Benjamin Wade

The bombardment of Fort Sumter answered the big question: There would be a war. When Lincoln called for 75,000 volunteers to suppress the rebellion, he was flooded with recruits. (The Confederacy already had 60,000 under arms in mobilized militias.) By the fall of 1861, the Union had 186,000 soldiers in uniform, the Confederacy 112,000.

What would battle be like? Armies so large had not clashed since the Napoleonic Wars in Europe half a century earlier. During the Mexican War, the United States never had more than 10,000 men on a battlefield. Now, just fifteen years later, two American governments were faced with the challenge of feeding, clothing, sheltering, transporting, training, and directing a mass of humanity ten and twenty times that size.

THE ART OF WAR

The Civil War took up where Napoleon and the Duke of Wellington had left off in 1815. What schooling West Pointers had in making war—their education was basically in engineering—derived largely from the ruminations of a Swiss officer of the Napoleonic era, Antoine-Henri Jomini. Jomini's *Art of War* had not been translated into English, but a textbook based on his ideas was available.

Position, Maneuver, and Concentration

Jomini emphasized position and maneuver as the keys to winning battles. The first goal of a commander was to occupy the most favorable position on a battlefield, usually high ground, then to ascertain the weakest point in the enemy's lines, and concentrate his power there. The general who better exploited the terrain and moved his troops more skillfully would throw back or break through the opposing army.

Jomini reduced battle situations to twelve models. Therefore, officers trained in his school (and with a brain in their heads) knew in general what their adversaries had in mind. Unlike European generals before the French Revolution, commanders were willing to sustain high casualties if the objective of a battle was important enough. As in the eighteenth century, however, the general who realized that he had been outfoxed was duty bound to disengage so that his army could fight another day. Retreat, far from shameful, was among the most important of military maneuvers because it preserved an army as a functioning machine. "Fighting to the last man" was insanity.

The Armies

Civil War armies were comprised of cavalry, artillery, and infantry with support units such as the Corps of Engineers (which constructed bridges, fortifications, and the like) and the Quartermaster Corps (entrusted with supply).

364

Photo by Timothy O'Sullivan, Chicago Historical Society

Wagons of a Union supply unit in Virginia. The North's advantage in resources and greater efficiency in getting them to troops were immense advantages over the Confederacy.

The cavalry's principal job was reconnaissance. Horse soldiers were an army's eyes (although there was some experimentation with anchored balloons during the Civil War). Battle plans were based on the information the cavalry brought back from sometimes spectacular rides that circled the enemy force. Because of its mobility and speed, cavalry was also used for raids, plunging deep into hostile territory, burning and destroying what they found, seizing what useful booty they could transport, and hightailing it out before they ran into masses of enemy infantry.

In a pitched battle, cavalry rushed to weak points in the line, dismounted, and served as reinforcements. If enemy troops fled in disorder, the horse soldiers pursued and harassed them. But cavalrymen were lightly armed by definition. For all the dash and flash, cavalry played a subsidiary role in Civil War battles. Early in the war, the generals learned that, with the improvements in artillery, the gallant old cavalry charge was not a good idea.

Artillery was organized into batteries attached to infantry regiments. A Union battery consisted of six field cannon,

Military Stalemate 1861–1863

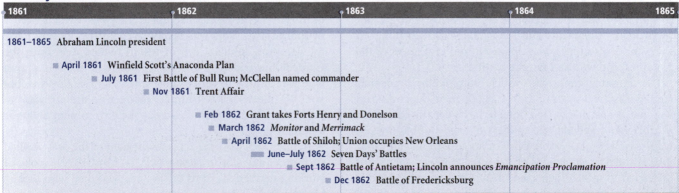

1861	1862	1863	1864	1865

1861–1865 Abraham Lincoln president

■ **April 1861** Winfield Scott's Anaconda Plan
■ **July 1861** First Battle of Bull Run; McClellan named commander
■ **Nov 1861** Trent Affair

■ **Feb 1862** Grant takes Forts Henry and Donelson
■ **March 1862** *Monitor* and *Merrimack*
■ **April 1862** Battle of Shiloh; Union occupies New Orleans
■ **June–July 1862** Seven Days' Battles
■ **Sept 1862** Battle of Antietam; Lincoln announces *Emancipation Proclamation*
■ **Dec 1862** Battle of Fredericksburg

> **Organizational Chart**
> The smallest unit in the two armies was the company of 100 men, officered by a captain and two lieutenants. On paper, ten infantry companies made up a regiment commanded by a colonel. (Regiments were almost always undermanned because of casualties and disease.) A brigade consisted of four or more regiments under a brigadier general. Three brigades were a division. Two to four divisions were a corps. At one time or another during the war, the Union army consisted of twenty-five corps but, by 1865, many had been liquidated because of losses, the survivors in them assigned elsewhere.

a Confederate battery four. About ten men were assigned to each gun, and others tended the horses that moved the guns and caissons (two-wheeled carts carrying powder and projectiles) into position. A fully loaded caisson weighed almost 2 tons, requiring a team of six horses. A battery was officered by a captain and at least three lieutenants. Laborious, noisy, and grimy, the artillery was decidedly unglamorous. However, as Napoleon had shown, big guns were critical to both attack and defense. In several battles, the Confederates' shortage of horses to move artillery into position contributed to their defeat.

Before an attacking army moved, its artillery slugged away at enemy positions with exploding shells, "softening them up." When in a defensive position, artillery greeted attacking infantry with grapeshot or canister. A canister was a tin cylindrical projectile filled with small lead or iron balls packed in sawdust. The can disintegrated upon firing and was devastating at 100 to 200 yards. Grapeshot consisted of somewhat larger balls in canvas bags. It was used on a charging army at longer ranges. Examinations of dead soldiers after several Civil War battles revealed that the attacking armies suffered more from artillery than from small arms. (In other battles, five soldiers were killed by minié balls fired from muskets for every one killed by grapeshot and canister.) Soldiers joked that they fired a man's weight in lead and iron for each enemy they killed. A Union expert learned that their estimate was conservative; he calculated that 240 pounds of gunpowder and 900 pounds of lead were expended for every Confederate soldier who was felled.

The Infantry

The infantry was the backbone of the army. The cavalry might worry the enemy and the artillery weaken him, but it was the foot soldiers who slogged it out, took most of the casualties, and won and lost the battles.

The infantry unit with which commanding generals worked was the brigade of 2,000 to 4,000 men, depending on what battle and disease had done to it. Under the command of a brigadier general, the soldiers formed double lines in defense or advanced over a front of about a thousand yards. During the first campaigns of the war, captains in the front lines tried to march their men in step, as had been done in the Mexican War. With the increased firepower of the 1860s, however, such formal advances were sensibly abandoned.

It was enough that the men continued to trot or walk into grapeshot, minié balls, thunderous noise, and a haze of black, sulfurous smoke. Junior officers led the charges; thus the high casualty rate among lieutenants and captains. Majors walked behind the lines to discourage stragglers. They carried revolvers and were authorized to shoot men who panicked and broke ranks, and they did.

If an advancing army was not turned back, the final phase of battle was hand-to-hand combat. The attackers clambered over the enemy's fortifications of earth and lumber. Attackers and defenders swung their muskets at one another like the baseball bats they played with in camp until the defenders broke and ran or the attackers were killed or captured. The men had bayonets, but neither side succeeded in training the soldiers to use them very well. The importance of infantrymen mastering this difficult, deadly skill was one lesson that European military observers (who were numerous) took home with them.

Except for special units of sharpshooters, there was not much aiming. Foot soldiers were not trained to be marksmen. There was little sense in taking on the big and expensive job of training large numbers of men in the refined skill of hitting small targets at great distances. With a few important exceptions (Antietam, Gettysburg), Civil War battles were not fought in open country. The men confronted one another in dense woods on terrain broken by hills, creeks, stone fences, and ditches. In several battles, attackers had to clamber up Appalachian cliffs on all fours. Often, opposing soldiers could not see one another until they were on the verge of touching.

Even in open country, up to hundred cannon and tens of thousands of muskets filled the air with a dense, acrid smog that, on a windless day, shrouded the battlefield. (Smokeless powder was decades in the future.) Even if a soldier was a good shot, there was little he could see to aim at.

Billy Yank and Johnny Reb

As always, the men who fought the Civil War were young, most between the ages of 17 and 25 with drummer boys as young as 12. They came from every state and social class although when both sides adopted draft laws (the Confederacy in April 1862, the Union in March 1863), the burden fell more heavily on poorer farmers and workingmen than on the middle and upper classes.

This was because there were legal ways to dodge the draft. The Confederates exempted men who owned twenty or more slaves. This was sorely resented by "Johnny Reb," the common soldiers, few of whom owned one. Both the Confederate and Union conscription laws allowed a man who was drafted to hire a substitute at a price that was beyond the means of the ordinary fellow who did not want to go. In the North, a man could pay the government $300 for an exemption.

In July 1863, working-class resentment of the draft law led to a week-long riot in New York City. Mostly Irish mobs of workingmen sacked draft offices, attacked men who looked wealthy, and lynched blacks, whom they considered the cause of the war and a threat to their jobs. Some 60,000 people were involved; at least 400 were killed; some $5 million in property was destroyed.

In the South, resistance to conscription took the form of thousands of draft dodgers and deserters heading west or into the Appalachians and Ozarks where some organized outlaw gangs raided farms and occasionally skirmished with Confederate troops. Most southern opposition to the war centered in the poorer mountain counties of western Virginia and North Carolina, eastern Tennessee, and northeastern Mississippi.

Both Union and Confederate armies were plagued by a high desertion rate, about 10 percent through most of the war. Bounty jumpers were professional deserters. Because some units paid cash bounties to men who signed up, they made a lucrative but risky business of enlisting, skipping out at the first opportunity, and looking for another unit paying a bounty. In March 1865, Union military police arrested one John O'Connor, who was surely the champion. He confessed to enlisting, collecting a bounty, and deserting thirty-two times.

The penalty for desertion was death; about 200, a small proportion of the whole, were actually shot. Most were branded with a "D" on buttock, wrist, or cheek, put back in the army in none too desirable situations, and watched.

Shirking was not typical of either army. Over the course of the war, 1.5 million young men served in the Union Army, more than 1 million from a much smaller population with the Confederacy. Whatever their resentments, ordinary people thought they had something at stake in the conflict. Despite their exemption, southern slave owners served in proportion to their numbers.

It's a Woman's War

A few women worked as spies. The most famous Confederate agent was Rose O'Neal Greenhow, a Washington widow with entreé into Washington society. During 1861, she forwarded

The Cooper Union Museum, New York

A soldier's sketch of troops on the march. Exhausting treks, heavy labor, and training (or languishing) in camp occupied far more of a soldier's days than preparing for a battle, fighting, and recovering afterward.

Wilhelmina Yank and Joanna Reb

Women posing as men fought in the Civil War. Official records list 127 female soldiers who were discovered (6 because they got pregnant). One historian suggests the number was closer to 400. Among them were Jennie Hodges, who fought for an Illinois regiment as Albert Cashier; her sex was not discovered until "Albert" died in 1911. Sarah Lemma Edmonds was Franklin Thompson in the Second Michigan. Passing as Lyons Wakeman in the 153rd Regiment of the New York State volunteers, Sarah Rosetta Wakeman rose to the rank of major.

information that she had charmed out of Union officers to Richmond. She was caught before the end of the year but, rather than cause a fuss by trying her for treason, Union authorities deported her through southern lines. There were, no doubt, dozens of less respectable pro-Confederate ladies in Washington, their names unknown for obvious reasons, who wheedled information from officers by sleeping with them. There were plenty of Confederate sympathizers of both sexes in the capital.

Harriet Tubman continued to penetrate into Virginia in her role of harmless "mammy," reporting back to the Union army the disposition of rebel troops and locations of fortifications. Mary Elizabeth Bowser, a domestic slave in Jefferson Davis's household in Richmond, could read, unbeknownst to her master, and passed whatever information she could to Union forces. Slaves were sources of information for the Union armies everywhere although their information was often unreliable. An abolitionist Union officer was not surprised by slave spying: "After all, they had been spies all their lives."

Most women who wanted to serve became nurses. Shortly after Fort Sumter, Elizabeth Blackwell, the first American woman to become a medical doctor, organized what became the United States Sanitary Commission, which put 3,000 nurses in army hospitals. At first, the army did not want them. Closeness to the front lines, the gore, and the male nakedness of the hospitals did not accord with the ideals of the gospel of true womanhood. But women like Clara Barton (later founder of the American Red Cross) and Dorothea Dix, both women of impeccable propriety and powerful wills, wore the generals down. The fiercest opponents of female nurses were forced to admit that they were infinitely superior to the disabled soldiers who had previously assisted in army hospitals.

A shortage of male workers due to the size of the armies and full employment in industry, opened jobs in the federal bureaucracy for women at the lower levels. After the war, the taboo broken, the number of female civil servants steadily increased until, by the end of the century, they were a majority of federal employees in Washington. In the South more than the North, for there the manpower shortage was far more serious, women took heavy and dirty factory jobs. And dangerous: an estimated 100 southern women were killed in explosions in munitions plants.

THE SOBERING CAMPAIGN OF 1861

Those who rallied to the colors in the spring of 1861 thought of the war as a great adventure, a vacation from the plow and hog trough that would be over too soon. They trimmed themselves in gaudy uniforms. Some, influenced by pictures of Turkish soldiers in the recently concluded Crimean War, called themselves "Zouaves," donning fezzes and baggy pantaloons. Other units adopted names that seem more appropriate to a boys' club. One Confederate regiment called itself "the Lincoln Killers."

On to Richmond

Abraham Lincoln shared the illusion that the war would be short and almost painless. He waved off General Winfield

Scott's somber warnings that it would take three years and 300,000 men to crush the rebellion (itself an underestimate). Lincoln asked the first volunteers to enlist for ninety days. That would be long enough, he thought. Southerners too spoke of "our battle summer." The soldiers and civilians on the two sides disagreed only as to who would be celebrating when the leaves fell in the autumn of 1861.

These pleasant visions were blown away on a fine July day about 20 miles outside Washington. Believing that his volunteers could take Richmond before their enlistments expired, Lincoln sent General Irvin McDowell marching directly toward the Confederate capital with 30,000 troops but without a single reliable map of the country. Laughing and joking as they went, sometimes shooting at targets, the boys from Ohio and Massachusetts were accompanied by a parade of carriages filled with congressmen, socialites, newspaper reporters, and curiosity seekers. The crowd carried picnic lunches and discussed where in Richmond they would enjoy a late supper.

They were met by a Confederate force of 22,000 under the command of General Beauregard, recently arrived from Charleston. The rebels had hastily dug in on high ground behind a creek called Bull Run, near a railroad crossing named Manassas Junction. McDowell attacked immediately, guessing that the Confederate left flank to be the weakest point in the line. He was right about that. Although his troops were shocked by the ferocity of the musket fire that greeted them, they almost cracked the southern line.

Had it cracked, the war might have been over in the upper South. To the rear of Beauregard's line the road to Richmond was wide open. At the critical moment, however, 9,000 Virginians commanded by Joseph E. Johnston arrived on the field after a frantic train ride from the Shenandoah Valley.

> **Manassas or Bull Run?**
>
> Early in the war, the Confederacy named battles after the nearest town. So, they called the first battle, on July 21, 1861, Manassas. The Union army, although not consistently, named battles after the nearest waterway; thus, Manassas was the Battle of Bull Run. The Union's Antietam (a creek) was the South's Sharpsburg (a town in Maryland).
>
> The Confederacy named armies after the states they were initially assigned to defend, or part of a state in the case of Robert E. Lee's Army of Northern Virginia. The Union named its armies after rivers: McClellan's Army of the Potomac. There was a Confederate Army of Tennessee and a Union Army of *the* Tennessee, after the river of that name.

Library of Congress, Prints and Photographs Division, Washington, DC (LC-USZ62-62758)

A clash at close quarters between Union and Confederate cavalries. Skirmishes of this kind lent an aura of romance to the cavalry, but they were rare. The cavalry's chief function was reconnaissance and lightning raids behind enemy lines. Battles like this one occurred only when a scouting party or raiders were surprised by enemy cavalry as when the Union general Philip Sheridan caught Confederate General Jubal Early in the Shenandoah Valley in 1864.

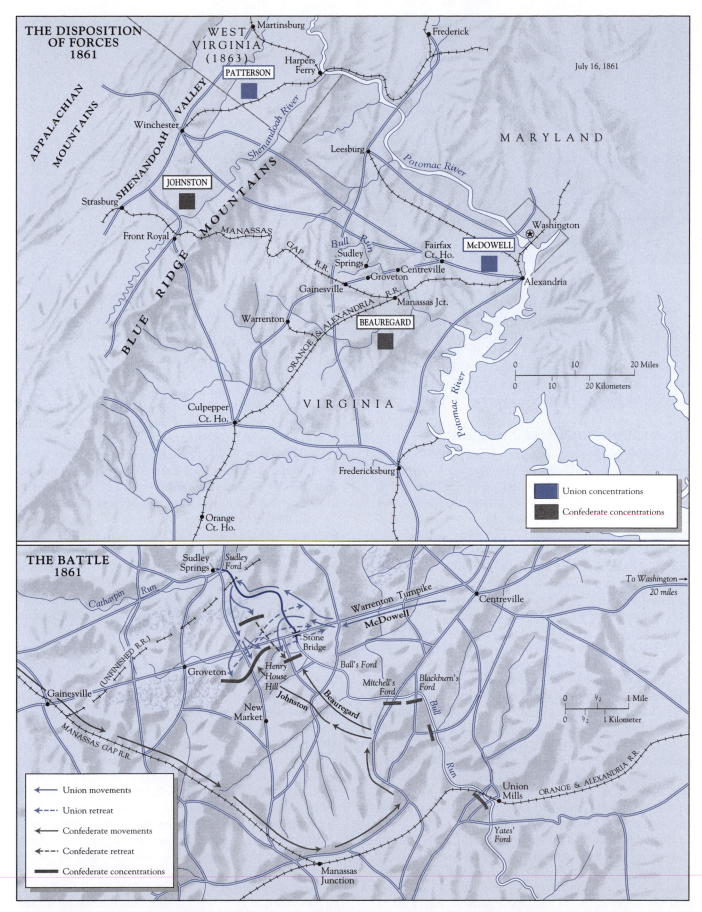

THE DISPOSITION OF FORCES 1861

WEST VIRGINIA (1863)

Martinsburg

Frederick

July 16, 1861

PATTERSON

Harpers Ferry

Shenandoah River

M A R Y L A N D

Winchester

SHENANDOAH VALLEY

APPALACHIAN MOUNTAINS

Leesburg

Potomac River

Strasburg

JOHNSTON

BLUE RIDGE MOUNTAINS

MANASSAS

Washington

Front Royal

GAP R.R.

Bull Run

Sudley Springs

Fairfax Ct. Ho.

McDOWELL

Alexandria

Gainesville

Centreville

Groveton

Manassas Jct.

Warrenton

ORANGE & ALEXANDRIA R.R.

BEAUREGARD

| 0 | 10 | 20 Miles |
| 0 | 10 | 20 Kilometers |

V I R G I N I A

Culpepper Ct. Ho.

Potomac River

Fredericksburg

Orange Ct. Ho.

Union concentrations
Confederate concentrations

THE BATTLE 1861

Sudley Springs

Sudley Ford

Catharpin Run

Warrenton Turnpike

Centreville

To Washington →
20 miles

(UNFINISHED R.R.)

Stone Bridge

McDowell

Groveton

Henry House Hill

Ball's Ford

Mitchell's Ford

Blackburn's Ford

Gainesville

New Market

Johnston

Beauregard

Bull Run

MANASSAS GAP R.R.

| 0 | ½ | 1 Mile |
| 0 | ½ | 1 Kilometer |

Union Mills

ORANGE & ALEXANDRIA R.R.

Yates' Ford

→ Union movements
⇠ Union retreat
← Confederate movements
⇠ Confederate retreat
▬ Confederate concentrations

Manassas Junction

MAP 22:1 **The Battle of Bull Run, July 21, 1861.** McDowell's army advanced from Washington along the highway that led to Winchester in the Shenandoah Valley. The battle lines stretched along Bull Run, a creek, straddling the Warrenton turnpike. Confederate generals Johnston and Jackson rushed reinforcements to the scene on the Manassas Gap railroad.

Battle of First Bull Run, 1861 (litho) by American School (19th century) Private Collection/Peter Newark Military Pictures/The Bridgeman Art Library.

The defeat of the Union Army at Manassas/Bull Run. At the end of the day it was a rout, but the Confederate army had itself come so close to disintegration that a follow-up march on Washington was out of the question.

A brigade under the command of Thomas J. Jackson, a 37-year-old mathematics instructor at Virginia Military Academy, shored up the sagging Confederate left. The Union soldiers fell back and then broke in hysteria, fleeing for Washington along with the panicked spectators.

Celebrations and Recriminations

The South had a victory and a hero. At the peak of the battle, a South Carolinian rallied his men by shouting, "There stands Jackson like a stone wall." The name stuck, for it seemed appropriate to more than Thomas J. Jackson's performance on the battlefield. He was introspective and humorless; his dullness as a lecturer was legendary among his students at Virginia Military Institute. Jackson was a stern Presbyterian who took long cold showers to kill his sexual impulses and constantly sucked on lemons (reason unknown). Southern civilians canonized him although his troops never loved him as they loved some generals.

Jackson was an awesome soldier; he came to life when the bullets whistled. He never yielded a line to the enemy, and he was a genius at maneuvering troops. For two years Jackson would do what the South needed done, inserting his men into critical positions and standing like a stone wall.

By way of contrast, General Beauregard's reputation collapsed after Bull Run because, his critics said, he failed to follow up his victory by marching on Washington. This was unfair: His army had come within an ace of defeat; it was in no condition to march anywhere. Nonetheless, Beauregard was replaced as Confederate commander in Virginia by Joseph E. Johnston, who had brought the troops that saved the day from the Shenandoah Valley.

Neither Johnston, Jefferson Davis, nor the president's military advisor, Robert E. Lee, faulted Beauregard. "The Confederate Army," Johnston said, "was more disorganized by victory than that of the United States by defeat." He, Davis, and Lee emphasized the need for a pause in action for the purpose of intensively training the troops.

The Summer Lull

Davis cautioned Richmond society that there was hard fighting to come, a lot of it. Few seemed to listen. The casualties at Manassas had not been excessive. Once rested, the Confederate soldiers were cocky. Southern politicians spoke as though the war were over. Volunteer officers who had not been near the battlefield nagged their tailors to finish sewing gold braid on their dress uniforms so that they could show them off once or twice before the Union capitulated. And they bickered. At an endless round of gala parties in Richmond, old personal jealousies revived as blustering colonels and generals blamed one another for blunders real and imaginary.

In the North, the defeat at Manassas taught the lesson so many southerners tried to ignore. The spectacle of McDowell's men throwing down their guns and trotting wild-eyed into Washington, where they slept in doorways and on the sidewalks, alarmed Lincoln and brought him closer to Winfield Scott's way of thinking. The war would be no summer's diversion, but a long, hard fight. Now when Lincoln asked Congress for troops, he wanted 300,000 men for three years.

Lincoln relieved Irvin McDowell from command of what was named the Army of the Potomac, replacing him with George B. McClellan. After distinguishing himself in Mexico, McClellan had been stationed at West Point where he was an innovator with an eye for self-promotion. He introduced a bayonet drill he called the "McClellan Bayonet Drill" and modified a Hungarian saddle for the cavalry which he called the "McClellan Saddle." (It remained the army's standard until 1920.) As president of the Illinois Central Railroad (for which Lincoln had been a lawyer), McClellan had been a superb organizer and administrator, just what the Union needed. In November 1861, when the 75-year-old Winfield Scott retired, McClellan took overall command of the Union armies that were being drilled throughout the Midwest.

Northern Strategy

A three-part strategy Winfield Scott had recommended became, with modifications, Union policy. First and obvious, Washington had to be defended by the Army of the Potomac; if Washington was lost, Lincoln could not very well have continued the war. However, the Army of the Potomac was conceived as being an offensive weapon with the goal of capturing Richmond. Richmond, just 100 miles from Washington, was important not only because it was the Confederate capital, but also because it was a railroad hub and an industrial center. It was the home of the Tredegar Iron Works, which was to sustain the Confederacy's fighting machine throughout the war. The rebellion might have continued had Richmond fallen early in the war, but not for long.

Second—and Lincoln the westerner needed no tutoring on this—because the Ohio-Mississippi waterway was vital to the economic life of the Midwestern states, Union armies would strike down the rivers and their tributaries. The ultimate object was to win complete control of the Mississippi. That would permit western farmers to export their crops, as they had down the river. And control of the river would isolate Texas, Arkansas, and Louisiana from the heart of the Confederacy and left to small Union armies (including Texas Unionists led by Sam Houston) while the large armies concentrated their force in the East.

Third, the Union would exploit its overwhelming naval superiority to blockade the South, strangling its import-export economy. If the Confederates were unable to sell cotton abroad, they could not buy the manufactures, particularly the munitions, that were essential in a lengthy war. Critics of Scott called the blockade the "Anaconda Plan" after the South American snake that slowly crushes its prey.

On the face of it, an effective blockade was out of the question. The navy had only forty-two vessels and the Confederate coastlines were labyrinths of inlets, sheltered channels, coves, bays, bayous, salt marshes, and lonely broad beaches. It was impossible to prevent every vessel from reaching shore or from making a break for the high seas. Nevertheless, a national commerce could not be rowed through the surf or unloaded in swamps. The commanders of the Union Navy felt confident that with time and enough ships, they could seal the Confederate ports that counted.

Mismatched Adversaries

Southern chances of victory were, on the face of it, pretty thin. The disparity between the Union's and the Confederacy's material resources was a yawning gulf. The population of the Union states was 22 million (and immigration continued during the war). About 9 million people lived in the eleven Confederate states and 3.5 million of them were slaves. Slaves produced, of course. They were the backbone of southern agriculture and could be pressed into military labor that, otherwise, would occupy soldiers. But the white population pool from which the Confederate armies could draw soldiers was 5.5 million, just a fourth the size of the Union's.

The gap between the northern and southern industrial economies was even wider. There was literally a factory in the Union devoted to manufacturing for every factory worker in the Confederacy. Almost all the nation's munitions makers were in the North. The arsenal at Harper's Ferry, Virginia, was effectively closed as possession of the town changed hands several times. The arsenal at Springfield, Massachusetts, produced more arms than the entire Confederacy. The South had to import most of its gunpowder and small arms (thus the importance of the Union blockade) and capture much of its artillery. As the war progressed, many Confederate batteries were makeshift combinations of different caliber cannon, gravely affecting their efficiency.

Southern railroads were a hodgepodge. There was no line to compare to northern trunk lines like the Erie, the Pennsylvania Railroad, and the Baltimore and Ohio (which, however, was vulnerable to Confederate raids). About 80 percent of the nation's banking was in the North, 75 percent of taxable wealth.

Southern Hopes

Nevertheless, the southern cause was far from hopeless. The Confederacy was fighting an easier war than the Union was. Like the patriots in the War for Independence (with whom southerners identified), the Confederacy did not have to conquer, subdue, and pacify their enemy's territory—which is precisely what the Union had to do. The southerners' war was defensive—the defense of their homes against invaders they thought of as foreigners.

Southern generals were familiar with the ground on which the battles would be fought, intimately so on the Virginia front. Northern generals were fighting in what was, at least at the beginning, to them, a foreign land. Indeed, the Union army's maps in 1861 were next to useless. Irvin McDowell knew the direction in which Richmond lay when he set out on the campaign that ended at Bull Run. But he did not have a good map of the roads and waterways of the country—and this was country within a hundred miles of Washington. The western army's maps of Tennessee were worse.

Fighting a defensive war meant that the Confederacy had interior lines. That is, shunting armies from one front to another meant covering far fewer miles than Union troops, looping around the lines, had to cover. This advantage was somewhat neutralized by the North's better railroads but interior lines help to explain why General Robert E. Lee was able, throughout the war, to outmaneuver every Union general who faced him.

It was an article of southern faith that their generals and their soldiers were superior to the commanders and soldiers of the North. Southerners had accorded higher status to military education than northerners had. There was stiff competition among the southern elite for appointments to West Point. In the North, congressional appointments to the academy sometimes remained unfilled for so long that congressmen and senators awarded them to anyone who asked. All but one American military college was located in the South. In 1861, Confederate officers had, at the higher ranks,

Facing Battle

The battle experience was much the same whether a soldier wore blue or gray—except that Union troops were almost always better supplied with shelter, food, clothing, and shoes. It is difficult to say how much this meant to the outcome of the war. Cold, wet, tired, and ill soldiers are surely less effective than well-equipped ones. Confederate troops without shoes—not uncommon—were usually, but not always, exempt from charging enemy lines. As early as the second Battle of Bull Run in 1862, the commander of a unit called Toombs's Georgians told of leading so many barefoot men that they "left bloody footprints among the thorns and briars." Nevertheless, "Johnny Reb," the Confederate foot soldier, won the respect of both his officers and his enemies as a fighting man.

Johnny Reb and his Union counterpart, Billy Yank, knew when they were going to fight. In only a few large battles was an army caught by surprise. Preparations for massive attack were so extensive that getting caught napping, as Grant's men were at Shiloh, was rare. In fact, the men who would be defending a position were generally prepared for battle with extra rations and ammunition earlier than the attackers. The men on the attack knew when they would be moving; defenders did not.

Each infantryman was given 40 to 60 rounds of ammunition for the cartridge box he wore on a strap slung over a shoulder. Springfield repeating rifles took a round that looked like a modern cartridge but they were introduced late in the war and only in the Union army. The muzzle-loading musket—which was used by the Confederates and most Yankees—took a round that consisted of a ball and a properly measured charge of powder wrapped together in paper that was twisted closed at the powder end. To load the musket, a soldier bit off the twist so that the powder was exposed, pushed the cartridge into the muzzle of his gun, inserted the paper he held in his teeth to keep the ball from rolling out, and rammed a rod (attached to his gun) into the barrel to the breech. Each time he fired, he had to fall to one knee in order to reload. That moment, and when men were retreating, were far more dangerous than when troops were advancing.

On the eve or morning of a battle, the commanding general addressed his troops either personally or in written orations read by line officers. Confederate General Albert Sidney Johnston took the high road in his speech before Shiloh:

> The eyes and the hope of eight millions of people rest upon you. You are expected to show yourselves worthy of your race and lineage; worthy of the women of the South, whose noble devotion in this war has never been exceeded in any time. With such incentives to brave deeds and with the trust that God is with us, your general will lead you confidently to the combat, assured of success.

Others, like, General T. C. Hindman in December 1862, were demagogues:

> Remember that the enemy you engage has no feeling of mercy. His ranks are made up of Pin Indians, Free Negroes, Southern Tories, Kansas Jayhawkers, and hired Dutch cutthroats. These bloody ruffians have invaded your country, stolen and destroyed your property, murdered your neighbors, outraged your women, driven your children from their homes, and defiled the graves of your kindred.

As the war ground on, veterans of battle tended to grow quiet and reflective before a fight. Many read their Bibles. The American Bible Society printed 370,000 more Bibles in 1861 than in 1860. Five million in various formats, most "pocket size," were given to soldiers by the end of the war. When, in the war's final months the Confederacy could devote no resources to printing Bibles, Union generals sent them between the lines under a flag of truce.

Some soldiers took a few quick pulls of whiskey before battle. Friends made promises to look for one another at the end of the day and if one of them was dead, to send his personal belongings to his family. During the brutal battles before Richmond, soldiers wrote their names and addresses on pieces of paper pinned to their clothing on the assumption that there would be no friends alive to identify them.

---

five or six years more military experience than their northern counterparts.

The belief in the superiority of the southern soldier was based on the fact that they were country boys, accustomed to the rigors of living in the out-of-doors. This was true enough and Johnny Reb proved to be a very tough customer. But by no means were all northern boys dissipated city dwellers, as southern stereotype had it. If soldiers from Philadelphia and New York found and sleeping in tents (or outside in the rain) to be disagreeable at first, most Union soldiers were from the country like their southern counterparts (and accustomed to harsher winters at that).

The Quest for an Ally

Thinking of themselves as latter-day American patriots fighting latter-day British tyrants, Confederate leaders looked for a foreign ally to help them as France had intervened in the first War for Independence. They believed that if they proved their rebellion viable by winning a battle the equivalent of Saratoga, France or Britain or both would recognize Confederate independence and aid them.

Both British and French governments looked favorably on the Confederate cause in 1861. The French emperor, Napoleon III, was an adventurer, always on the lookout for opportunities to win the glory his illustrious uncle had brought to France. The idea of creating a French dependency in North America appealed to him. He encouraged Confederate diplomats in Paris but informed them that he would not intervene without British cooperation or, at least, acquiescence.

Then a far more enticing invitation: While Napoleon was waiting for the Confederate Saratoga, Mexican conservatives—landlords and the Catholic Church—who were faced with a massive mestizo and Indian rebellion, offered to make Napoleon's nephew, Maximilian of Austria, emperor of Mexico in return for the help of French troops in defeating the revolutionaries. The beleaguered Union was in no position to oppose a French intervention. What self-respecting emperor could take an interest in a quasi-dependency of headstrong cotton planters when he could tread in the footsteps of Cortés? Not Napoleon III. By mid-1862, he was dodging the Confederate lobbyists in Paris.

British Ambivalence

The pro-Confederate sentiments of some ministers in Lord Palmerston's Liberal party cabinet had a solid economic foundation. The South was the chief source of the fiber that fed Britain's textile industry, the foundation of the nation's wealth and power. The great English lords (members of the Tory opposition) looked upon southern planters as rough-cut kinsmen, flattering in their Anglophilia and imitation of the manners and paternalism of the British upper classes. Far-seeing British statesmen saw what might be their last opportunity to arrest the growing economic power of the United States; otherwise, they knew, it was destined to eclipse Great Britain's.

The hang-up was slavery. British public opinion was staunchly antislavery. It had prevented British friendship with Texas. By 1861, having nearly destroyed the trans-Atlantic slave trade, the government was committed to ending the much greater flow of black slaves to the Muslim lands of North Africa and the Middle East. Lord Palmerston, the prime minister, was unwilling to risk the wrath of antislavery voters unless the Confederates demonstrated that they had a real chance of winning the war. But Britain would not help them to fight the open-ended defensive war that was Confederate policy.

A combination of Confederate blunders, bad luck, Union diplomatic finesse, and a great Union victory on the battlefield put an end to British thoughts of drawing a new map of North America.

Diplomacy

The blunder was Jefferson Davis's belief that Britain could be blackmailed into coming to the aid of the South. In the excited solidarity of the Confederacy's first days, he prevailed on cotton shippers to put the 1860 crop in storage rather than export it to Britain. The idea was to put the pinch on British mill owners, the Liberal party's money men, so that they would set up a cry for a war to liberate southern fiber.

"Cotton diplomacy" failed. English mill owners had seen the war coming and stockpiled huge reserves of cotton. By the time their inventory was exhausted in 1862, the world price of cotton had tripled, inducing farmers in Egypt, the Middle East, and India to devote more land to the crop. In one year, they had filled the gap in supply caused by the American war. To make matters worse, Union troops captured enough cotton in Tennessee in 1861 and 1862 to keep the mills of New England humming and even to sell some to Britain.

Two successive failures of the grain crop in Western Europe put the finishing touches on cotton diplomacy. Fearing food shortages, monarchical Britain discovered that Union wheat was more royal than King Cotton. Blessed with bumper crops, the northern states increased grain exports by forty times between 1860 and 1863.

In November 1861, a zealous Union naval officer almost sabotaged northern efforts to keep Britain out of the war. The captain of the U.S.S. *San Jacinto* boarded a British steamer, the *Trent,* and seized two Confederate diplomats who were aboard, James M. Mason and John Slidell. Northern public opinion was delighted; Lincoln was not. The British minister in Washington came close to threatening war. Mason and Slidell were two hot potatoes of no value in captivity. Lincoln took advantage of the first lull in the celebrations to hasten them aboard a British warship. "One war at a time," he remarked to his cabinet.

No harm was done. In France, Slidell was frustrated by Napoleon III's preoccupation with Mexico. In Britain, Mason proved no match for the Union minister, Charles Francis Adams, who moved with great skill and energy through London's salons. (It ran in the family.) Adams was unable to prevent the *Alabama,* a commerce-raider built in Britain, from putting to sea, but he cajoled and threatened the British government into preventing other raiders and several Confederate rams from leaving port.

1862 AND STALEMATE

As hopes of foreign intervention dimmed, the South looked increasingly to northern sympathizers and defeatism to win the day for them. A small but noisy minority of northern Democrats were frankly pro-Confederate. Former President Franklin Pierce was one. Pro-southern sentiment was strong in the Union slave states of Maryland, Kentucky, and Missouri, but also significant in the Ohio River counties of the midwest, a region with a strong southern heritage. However, these "copperheads" as Republicans called pro-southern Democrats (and, unfairly, any Democrats who criticized government policies) never mounted a decisive threat to the Union war effort. They were a minority and Lincoln played free with the civil liberties of dissenters.

Lincoln and the Copperheads

One of the president's most controversial acts was his suspension of the ancient legal right of *habeas corpus,* a protection against arbitrary imprisonment basic to English and American law. At one time or another, about 13,000 people were jailed without being charged with a crime, most of them within a few miles of the front lines and all but a few released within a short time. Lincoln also used his control of the post office to even suppress hostile newspapers.

The most prominent copperhead was Clement L. Vallandigham, a Democratic congressman from Ohio. His attacks on the war were so unsettling that, after General Ambrose Burnside jailed him, Lincoln feared he would be honored as a martyr. The president solved the problem with his usual ingenuity. He handed Vallandigham over to the Confederates as if he were a southern agent. In 1863, Vallandigham was forced to run for governor of Ohio from exile in Canada. At home, even in prison, he might have won; he was popular in Ohio. *In absentia*, and unable to campaign, he was defeated. When he returned to the United States in 1864, the thrill was gone and Lincoln was able to ignore him.

More worrisome than the copperheads was defeatism, the widespread (although never dominant) conviction that, at best, the war was not worth the expense in blood and money. Each time the Army of the Potomac lost a battle, which happened frequently, more and more northerners wondered if it would not be wiser just to let the southern states go. Others asked if it was really impossible to negotiate a settlement. Was Lincoln's Republican administration, rather than the southern states, the obstacle to a compromise peace?

It was in fact impossible for Lincoln to secure reunion on any other basis than victory. Even at the bitter end of the war, when the Confederacy was not only defeated, but devastated, Jefferson Davis insisted that recognition of southern independence be a condition of peace talks.

In 1861 and most of 1862, the Confederates won all the battles in Virginia. The show belonged to Stonewall Jackson and Robert E. Lee, who succeeded Joseph Johnston as commander of the Army of Northern Virginia when, at the Battle of the Seven Pines in May 1862, Johnston was seriously wounded. Time after time, Lee and Jackson halted or drubbed the Army of the Potomac.

But Lee's and Jackson's cause was less the Confederacy than the defense of "Old Virginny." Lee had long disliked slavery, and he had opposed secession. He told the emissary from Lincoln who offered him the command of the Union army, "I look upon secession as anarchy. If I owned four millions of slaves in the South I would sacrifice them all to the Union. But how can I draw my sword upon Virginia, my native state?"

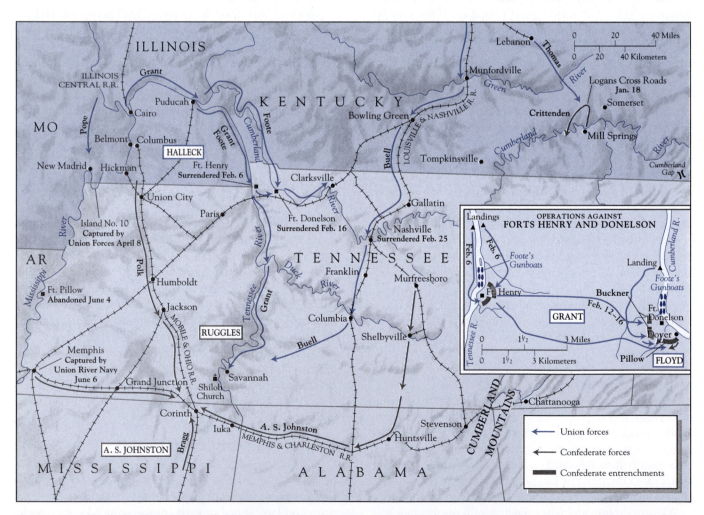

MAP 22:2 **The War in the West, 1862.** The importance of the Tennessee and Cumberland Rivers for communication and transportation can be clearly seen in this map. Thus, the importance of the surrender of Forts Henry and Donelson to General Grant in February 1862. Grant's advance through Tennessee was without incident. Then came bloody Shiloh on the Mississippi border.

Lee's love of home and his somewhat snobbish distaste for parvenus of the cotton states was noble, but also the source of his strategic weakness. He never fully appreciated the fact that while he was defending the Old Dominion with such mastery, the southern cause was slowly being throttled in the Mississippi valley and at sea.

The War in the West

Lincoln was no soldier, but he understood better than Lee the importance of the war in the West. "We must have Kentucky," he told his cabinet. Without Kentucky—the southern bank of the Ohio River—Lincoln feared the war would be lost. Before the army in the East recovered from the defeat at Manassas, Lincoln approved moving a large force into Kentucky under the command of Generals Henry Halleck and Ulysses S. Grant. Early in 1862, Grant thrust into Tennessee, capturing two important forts, Henry and Donelson. They guarded the Tennessee and Cumberland Rivers, two waterways of infinitely greater value than muddy Bull Run.

Moving through Tennessee to the Mississippi lines, however, General Grant stumbled into a battle that taught both sides that they were not playing chess. Grant intended to attack Corinth, Mississippi, where, he thought, Confederate General Albert Sidney Johnston was holed up. Despite evidence that Johnson was able and willing to go on the offensive, Grant and his subordinates camped at Shiloh Church, Tennessee, and took no defensive precautions. On April 6, 1862, Grant's soldiers were surprised, some still in their bedrolls, by 40,000 rebels. Grant rode frantically to the front and the army held on, but just barely. Only when, late in the day, a fresh army under General Don Carlos Buell arrived, did the Confederates withdraw.

Albert Sydney Johnston was killed at Shiloh. Other southern casualties numbered 11,000 of 40,000 troops engaged. The Union lost 13,000 of 60,000 men. Bodies were stacked like cordwood while mass graves were dug. Acres of ground were reddened with blood; the stench of death sickened the survivors assigned to the grisly task of cleaning up.

Grant was nearly disgraced, accused of being drunk on the night before the attack (not true). Before Shiloh, soldiers of the two armies in the West had fraternized, conversing in the night and trading southern tobacco for northern coffee. Not after Shiloh. Manassas had shown that the war would be long. Shiloh showed that it would be bloody.

The War at Sea

Confederate seamen on the *Alabama* saw the world. The commerce raider logged about 75,000 miles looking for northern merchantmen, burning something between 50 and 200 of them—the claims differed wildly—and defeating one warship in an evenly matched battle for which the *Alabama* had not been designed. Sailors on the ship experienced naval warfare at its most exhilarating.

For the Union sailors assigned to the blockade, days were long and boring. They passed slowly as their ships bobbed in the waves outside southern seaports in scorching sun and winter winds. In 1861 and 1862, blockade duty was pure frustration. Four out of five Confederate blockade runners, ships designed for speed and a low profile in the ocean, successfully made it in and out of port. The blockade runners did not cross the Atlantic. European shippers brought the goods the Confederates wanted—everything from munitions to cloth—to Bermuda or to the West Indies. There blockade runners collected the goods, paying for them with cotton or bills of exchange issued as loans by British banks. Blockade running was ferrying, with quick turnarounds and big profits.

The Confederacy came close to breaking the blockade of the Chesapeake Bay in March 1862. An old warship, newly named the *Merrimack,* had been armored with iron plates so that she had the shape of a tent. Cannonballs fired at the ship ricocheted harmlessly off the slanting superstructure. The *Merrimack* was primarily a ram; its prow was a heavy iron blade like a plowshare that could slice through a wooden hull. Within a few hours of her debut, the *Merrimack* sank several Union warships.

Left unopposed for a few weeks, this single ship might have opened the Chesapeake to a busy commerce. But the

The Granger Collection, New York

Thomas J. "Stonewall" Jackson was the hero of Manassas (and of several subsequent battles). He was polite at celebrations in his honor, but he probably did not enjoy himself very much. Jackson was all soldier, eccentric, and the morally strictest and most disciplined of Presbyterians. When, in camp, another officer asked him why he did not drink—did he dislike whiskey?—Jackson replied that he did not drink because he liked whiskey too much.

Williamson Art Gallery & Museum, Birkenhead, England

Confederate commerce raiders under construction in Liverpool. Three put to sea, the most effective being the Alabama, *which savaged Union shipping. American minister Charles Francis Adams persuaded the British not to release additional raiders to the Confederacy after it became likely the Union would win the war. Adams was the son of John Quincy Adams and the grandson of John Adams. Effective diplomacy ran in the family.*

Merrimack did not have even a few days. The Union navy also had an experimental ironclad ready to go. The *Monitor* resembled a cake tin on a platter skimming the waves. The cake tin was a turret containing two big guns; it was not necessary to turn the vessel in order to fire; the turret rotated, an innovation soon copied by designers of ships that looked like ships. The *Monitor's* round shape deflected projectiles as effectively as the *Merrimack's* sloping walls. Its hull, barely above the level of the water, provided no target.

For five hours on March 9, 1862, the two ships had at one another, then disengaged. The battle was a draw but strategically a Union victory. The *Merrimack* had to retreat for repairs. In May, the Confederates destroyed it so that it would not fall into Union hands and never built another ship like it. The *Monitor* was a prototype for a flotilla of others like it.

McClellan and the "Slows"

In creating the Army of the Potomac, George McClellan made an invaluable contribution to the Union cause. Not only were his men better trained than most southern troops, they were also better armed. While the Confederates had to import or capture most of their arms, McClellan (and his successors) had a limitless supply of munitions and constantly improved firearms. The Springfield repeating rifle, introduced late in the war, allowed Union soldiers to fire six times as fast as musket-armed Confederates.

McClellan was one of the best desk generals either army produced. He knew how to create an edge in numbers, training, and equipment—and his soldiers were devoted to him. McClellan thought of himself as a battlefield commander too, a Napoleon. He posed, strutted, and issued bombastic proclamations to his troops. But a fighter he was not. Confronted with an enemy army, he lost confidence. Time after time he refused to advance, telling Lincoln that he needed more troops even when his army outnumbered Lee's by two to one.

His lack of aggressiveness was partly a personality issue. In addition, McClellan was a Democrat and held Lincoln in contempt. His conception of the war was at odds with the president's. He did not want to crush the South. He believed that by creating a terrifying military machine, he could persuade the Confederates to negotiate a peace that would return the southern states to the Union. But his army was never terrifying enough for himself. He constantly

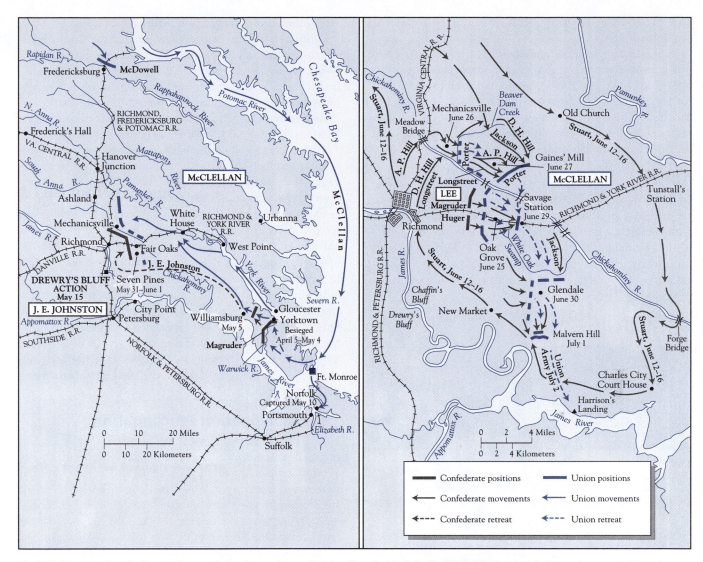

MAP 22:3 The Peninsula Campaign and the Seven Days Battle, March 17–July 2, 1862. The Peninsula Campaign was brilliant in conception. By approaching Richmond from the southeast, virtually all the fortifications built to defend the city to the north were rendered irrelevant. But McClellan dawdled. Although his numerical advantage was overwhelming, he wanted more troops before he moved. Brilliant improvised maneuvers by Johnston, Jackson, and Lee fought McClellan to a standstill practically within sight of the Confederate capital.

overestimated Confederate strength and lied to Lincoln about his own.

The Peninsula Campaign

When McClellan finally moved in April 1862, he did not drive directly toward Richmond as McDowell had. Instead, he moved his army by sea to the peninsula between the York and James Rivers. In a month he had 110,000 troops poised to take Richmond from the south, bypassing the city's fortifications.

The plan was ingenious; it may well have worked had McClellan not been afflicted with a dose of what Lincoln called "the slows." The Confederate Army of Northern Virginia was outnumbered and surprised by McClellan's maneuver. However, McClellan squandered his advantage by besieging a fort that could easily have been bypassed, then assuming a defensive position on the peninsula.

He grossly overestimated the size of the Confederate army facing him and demanded reinforcements from Lincoln. Lincoln refused to send them for good reason. McClellan had left fewer troops to defend Washington than Lincoln had requested. Robert E. Lee, who took command of the Army of Northern Virginia when Johnston was wounded, fooled Lincoln into thinking that the capital was in danger by sending Stonewall Jackson and a small force on a diversionary mission. (Jackson did not have the numbers to make a genuine assault on the city.)

The ruse was successful and Jackson rushed back to the peninsula to reinforce the army that McClellan could easily have crushed. By the time McClellan moved, Lee had 85,000 men dug in.

Seven days of battle followed between June 26 and July 2, 1862, and McClellan was fought to a standstill. Lincoln called off the Peninsula Campaign and replaced McClellan as commander of the army before Washington with General John Pope.

Pope had won several impressive victories in the West and was a favorite with abolitionists in Congress because of his opposition to slavery. But he was no match on the battlefield for Lee. At the end of August, with the peninsula secure, Lee met him on the same ground as the first Battle of Manassas and beat him back more easily than Beauregard had repulsed McDowell the previous year.

Antietam

In part because of criticism in the Republican press, Lincoln recalled McClellan to command the Army of the Potomac. Unfortunately, his reinstatement only confirmed the general's low opinion of the president. Several officers on his staff went so far as to say that McClellan should march the army on Washington and depose the president. (Lincoln was aware of this talk.)

The Granger Collection, New York

General George McClellan was a superb organizer; he had been an efficient president of the Illinois Central Railroad. He was popular with his troops, in part because he tried to avoid battles in which casualties were likely to be high. (Ironically, he was in command at the battle of Antietam, the bloodiest single day of the war.) He was a failure as general-in-chief because, a Democrat, McClellan did not want to crush the rebellion; he hoped there would be a negotiated peace. Unfortunately for his political goals, the Confederates would accept nothing but recognition of their independence.

The Richmond-Washington battlefront bogged down into a fortified stalemate. This was favorable to the Confederacy which needed only to preserve the rebellion. But Jefferson Davis too was under pressure to "do something." Dissatisfied with Lee's brilliance in repelling Union advances, critics wanted the war carried into the North. The chances of British intervention were fading. Only a major victory on Union soil, critics said, could bring Britain into the war.

Unfortunately, while Lee worked defensive miracles with inferior numbers, his army of 40,000 was not up to an advance when the enemy was 70,000 strong. Then, the Confederates suffered an appalling stroke of bad luck when a copy of Lee's plans, wrapped around a pack of cigars, fell into Union hands. McClellan caught Lee before he was prepared for a battle at Sharpsburg in Maryland near Antietam Creek.

The fighting was as vicious and gory as it had been at Shiloh. Antietam was the worst single day of the war. Lee lost a quarter of his men. His army was in such disarray that it was in no condition to retreat efficaciously into Virginia. Stoically, Lee waited on the Maryland side of the Potomac for the counterattack that would destroy the Army of Northern Virginia. To his amazement and Lincoln's fury, McClellan did not move. On the second night after the battle, Lee slipped back into Virginia.

The Emancipation Proclamation

During the first year of the war, Lincoln insisted that his aim was not the destruction of slavery but the preservation of the Union. He constantly reassured uneasy political leaders from the loyal slave states, especially in Maryland. When General Frémont freed captured slaves as contraband, Lincoln countermanded his order and wrote to Jesse Frémont, "the General should never have dragged the Negro into the war. It is a war for a great national object and the Negro has nothing to do with it."

His insistence on keeping "the Negro" out of it faced considerable opposition in Congress where Republicans who had not been abolitionists began to side with abolitionists who argued that, in a war brought on by slave owners, destroying the peculiar institution should be a war aim alongside the restoration of the Union. Lincoln looked at the issue from a different perspective: What policy was most likely to win the war. In August 1862, shortly before Antietam, Horace Greeley, an editor with influence nationally, demanded that Lincoln move against slavery. The president replied: "If I could save the Union without freeing any slave, I would do it; and if I could save it by freeing all the slaves, I would do it; and if I could do it by freeing some and leaving others alone, I would also do it."

In fact, Lincoln had already decided to free some of the slaves. In the summer of 1862 he read to his cabinet a proclamation that, as of a date to be determined, all slaves held in territory still in rebellion were henceforth free. It was a longshot gamble that at least some southern leaders would calculate that the only realistic hope to save slavery was to come to make peace before Lincoln's deadline. At the least, it would mollify the "Radical Republicans" in Congress and be popular in Great Britain.

Secretary of State William Seward, who had become Lincoln's close friend (the president often walked unannounced to Seward's home in the evenings to discuss affairs privately) advised caution. He persuaded Lincoln to keep the Emancipation Proclamation secret until after the North won a major battle. Otherwise, Seward argued—and it was a good point—the Proclamation would look like an act of desperation to the Confederates and abroad. Despite McClellan's failure to exploit it, Antietam was that major victory. On September 22, 1862, five days after the battle, Lincoln issued his ultimatum, to go into effect on January 1, 1863.

Slavery: The Beginning of the End

Abolitionists were not appeased. They pointed out that not a single slave would be emancipated on January 1. The Proclamation did not apply in the loyal slave states nor to those parts of the Confederacy occupied by Union troops: parts of Virginia and Texas, most of Tennessee, and several coastal enclaves elsewhere.

This was true enough but, assuming the Confederates did not come to terms before the new year, which everyone knew was unlikely, the complaint had no substance; it was numbskulled. The Emancipation Proclamation was a political master stroke. It reassured Unionist slave owners by allowing them to keep their slaves. But it permitted northern generals to make use of African Americans who, once Union armies were nearby, fled to them in the thousands. They could not enlist in the army, which did not accept even free blacks. They could, however, be hired to dig fortifications and perform other labor. And they were no longer producing for the Confederate economy.

With Union troops slowly advancing everywhere except Virginia, the Emancipation Proclamation was the first step in the abolition of slavery that could never be accomplished by constitutional amendment, only by a military proclamation like Lincoln's.

The Emancipation Proclamation allowed Lincoln, without committing himself, to test northern opinion on the subject of abolition. When Union soldiers adopted Julia Ward Howe's abolitionist "Battle Hymn of the Republic" as their anthem—"let us fight to make men free"—Lincoln learned that by striking at slavery, he had improved morale.

African Americans in Uniform

Lincoln was dead set against enlisting northern free blacks because, among other things, he thought them incapable of being soldiers. By steps, he changed his mind. Thousands of free African Americans had begun to train as militias in Massachusetts

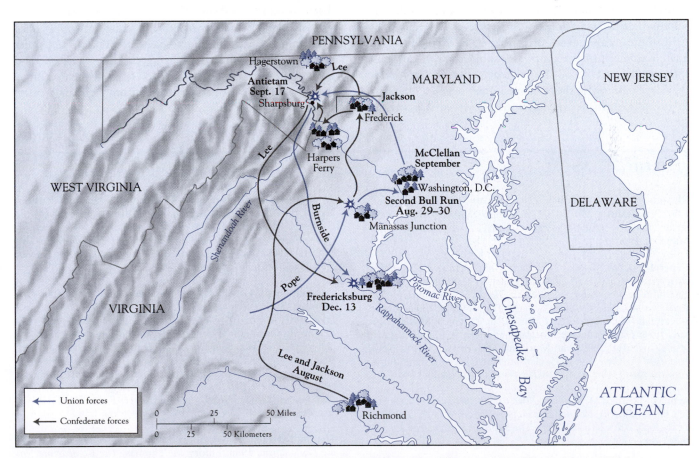

MAP 22:4 **Stalemate in the East, 1862.** Lee and Jackson displayed their mastery of tactics at Second Bull Run in August 1862, but, in September, their army was almost destroyed at Antietam on the Maryland side of the Potomac, in part because Lee's plans fell by a fluke into McClellan's hands. Lee's reputation was restored when Union troops made an ill-advised attempt to cross the Rappahannock at Fredericksburg at the end of 1862.

Prisoners and Race

During the first years of the war, Union and Confederate armies routinely exchanged prisoners. This ended in 1864 for two reasons. First, General Grant opposed exchanges; his intention was to reduce the Confederate armies to ineffectiveness. He did not want to return captured rebels so that they could fight again: "We would have to fight on until the whole South is exterminated." Second, the Confederates refused to exchange captured African American soldiers. In this, at least, Lincoln insisted that black soldiers be treated according to the same rules that white soldiers were.

and several other states. Abolitionists, most notably Frederick Douglass, nagged Lincoln into accepting them into the army.

With his generals constantly demanding more recruits, Lincoln eventually relented. By the end of the war, fully 150,000 blacks—both free blacks and slaves freed by the Emancipation Proclamation—served in Union blue, one Billy Yank in eight. (Only eight African Americans were commissioned officers; five of them were chaplains.)

African American units were usually assigned the dirtiest duty and, when sent into combat, the most dangerous tasks. Many white officers looked upon them as cannon fodder to soften up the enemy. Some officers, however, were moved by African American bravery. Black soldiers were paid only half a white soldier's wages, about $7 a month. When captured, they were treated brutally by Confederates. And yet, because they were fighting for the freedom of their people rather than for an abstraction, black soldiers were observed to bicker and gripe far less than whites did: Their desertion rate was a fraction of the army average.

Stalemate Resumed

Terminally disgusted with McClellan after Antietam, Lincoln named an antislavery general, Ambrose E. Burnside, to command the Army of the Potomac. Burnside did not want the job. An excellent corps commander, he believed the complexities and responsibilities of directing an entire army were beyond his capabilities. His self-assessment proved tragically on target. He blundered so egregiously that Lee and his generals were astonished. On December 13, 1862, with several options available, Burnside ordered a frontal assault on an impregnable southern position on high ground near Fredericksburg, Virginia.

Union soldiers were slaughtered. General Darius Crouch exclaimed, "Oh, great God! See how our men, our poor fellows are falling!" Robert E. Lee remarked to an aide that "it is well that war is so terrible or we would grow too fond of it." Burnside retreated, in tears and broken. And the Union and Confederate armies settled down to winter quarters on either side of the Rappahannock River.

The war in the West also bogged down. After Shiloh, Confederates under General Braxton Bragg moved through eastern Tennessee into Kentucky in an attempt to capture that state. At Perryville on October 8, Bragg fought to a draw against General Don Carlos Buell, decided his supply lines were overextended, and moved back into Tennessee. On the last day of 1862, Bragg fought another standoff with the Union Army at Murfreesboro. Both sides went into winter quarters—neither beaten, neither within sight of victory, stalemated.

FURTHER READING

Classics James G. Randall, *The Civil War and Reconstruction*, 1937; Bruce Catton, *Mr. Lincoln's Army*, 1951, and *Glory Road*, 1952; Shelby Foote, *Fort Sumter to Perryville*, 1958, and *Fredericksburg to Meridian*, 1963.

General D. W. Meinig, *The Shaping of America: A Geographic Perspective on 500 Years of History*, Vol. 2, *Continental America, 1800–1867*, 1993; James McPherson, *Battle Cry of Freedom: The Civil War Era*, 1988; Geoffrey C, Ward, *The Civil War*, 1999; Edward Hagerman, *The American Civil War and the Origins of Modern Warfare*, 1988; David J. Eicher, *The Longest Night: A Military History of the Civil War*, 2001; Ivan Musicant, *Divided Waters: The Naval History of the Civil War*, 1995; Herman Hattaway and Archer Jones, *How the North Won: A Military History of the Civil War*, 1980.

Armies Richard M. McMurry, *Two Great Rebel Armies*, 1989; Steven E. Woodworth, *Nothing But Victory: The Army of the Tennessee 1861–1865*, 2005; Jeffry D. Wert, *The Sword of Lincoln: The Army of the Potomac*, 2005.

Soldiers Reid Mitchell, *The Vacant Chair: The Northern Soldier Leaves Home*, 1993; James M. McPherson, *For Cause and Comrades: Why Men Fought in the Civil War*, 1997; James W. Geary, *We Need Men: The Union Draft in the Civil War*, 1991; Gerald E. Linderman,

The Experience of Combat in the Civil War, 1987; Joseph Glatthaar, *Forged in Battle: The Civil War Alliance of Black Soldiers and White Officers*, 1990; Dudley T. Comish, *The Sable Arm*, 1966; Lauren M. Cook, *They Fought Like Demons: Women Soldiers in the American Civil War*, 2002; Elizabeth Leonard, *All the Daring of the Soldier: Women in the Civil War Armies*, 1999.

Commanders Joseph G. Glatthaar, *Partners in Command: The Relationships Between Leaders in the Civil War*, 1993; Gabor Boritt, *Lincoln's Generals*, 1994; Ethan F. Rafuse, *McClellan's War: The Failure of Moderation in the Struggle for the Union*, 2005; Brooks D. Simpson, *Ulysses S. Grant*, 2000; Jean Edward Smith, *Grant*, 2001; Edward G. Longacre, *General Ulysses S. Grant: The Soldier and the Man*, 2006; Joseph L. Harsh, *Confederate Tide Rising: Robert E. Lee and the Making of Southern Strategy, 1861–1862*, 1998; Alan Nolan, *Lee Considered: General Robert E. Lee and Civil War History*, 1991.

The Confederacy Drew Gilpin Faust, *The Creation of Confederate Nationalism*, 1988; Emory M. Thomas, *The Confederate Nation, 1861–1865*, 1979; Richard E. Beringer et al., *Why the South Lost the Civil War*, 1991; Gary W. Gallagher, *The Confederate War*, 1997; William Blair, *Virginia's Private War: Feeding Body and Soul in the Confederacy, 1861–1865*, 1998; Drew Gilpin Faust, *Mothers of*

Invention: Women of the Slaveholding South in the American Civil War, 1996.

The Union Eric Foner, *Politics and Ideology in the Age of the Civil War*, 1980; J. Matthew Gallman, *The North Fights the War: The Home Front*, 1994; Philip S. Palaudan, *"A People's Contest": The Union and the Civil War, 1861–1865*, 1988, and *The Presidency of Abraham Lincoln*, 1994; Lawanda Cox, *Lincoln and Black*

Freedom, 1981; Michael Lind, *What Lincoln Believed: The Values and Convictions of America's Greatest President*, 2004; Doris Kearns Goodwin, *Team of Rivals: The Political Genius of Abraham Lincoln*, 2005; Joel Silber, *A Respectable Minority: The Democratic Party in the Civil War Era*, 1977; Jean Baker, *Affairs of Party: The Political Culture of the Northern Democrats in the Mid-Nineteenth Century*, 1983; Elizabeth D. Leonard, *Yankee Women: Gender Battles in the Civil War*, 1994.

KEY TERMS

Use the following listing of key terms to review important figures, events, locations, and concepts covered in this chapter. A glossary of these terms is available on *The American*

Past companion Web site: www.cengage.com/history/conlin/tap9e

minié ball, p. 366

bounty jumpers, p. 367

Anaconda Plan, p. 371

cotton diplomacy, p. 373

copperheads, p. 373

***Monitor*, p. 376**

Emancipation Proclamation, p. 378

ONLINE RESOURCES

Find additional resources, including primary source documents, images, interactive maps, simulations, chapter review exercises, and Internet links at

The American Past **companion Web site**
www.cengage.com/history/conlin/tap9e

American History Resource Center
http://ushistory.wadsworth.com/

National Park Service, Harpers Ferry Center

Chapter 23

Driving Dixie Down

General Grant's War of Attrition
1863–1865

The rebels now have in their ranks their last man. The little boys and old men are guarding prisoners and railroad bridges, and forming a good part of their forces, manning forts and positions, and any man lost by them cannot be replaced. They have robbed the cradle and the grave.

—*Ulysses S. Grant*

By the spring of 1863, the Confederacy was suffering severe shortages and a rapid inflation of its paper currency. In the Union, the chief problem was frustration. Lincoln had men, matériel, and money, but he could not find a general who would fight and win. In the East, Robert E Lee had defeated or confounded four commanders. In the West, the situation was more encouraging. Southern Louisiana and western Tennessee were occupied although not secure. Kentucky was still wide open to Confederate cavalry raids.

THE CAMPAIGNS OF 1863

The third summer of the war began with more bad news for the Union. By the end of the year, however, the tide had unmistakably turned against the South. A second Confederate invasion of the North ended in a disaster far worse than Antietam. In the West, Union armies broke the two-year stalemate and Lincoln found there a general in whom he could place full confidence. He was the man who had flirted with disgrace at Shiloh, Ulysses S. Grant.

Chancellorsville

After the debacle at Fredericksburg, Ambrose Burnside's most abusive critic was General Joseph Hooker. "Fighting Joe" had distinguished himself in the Seven Days Battles and was a key commander in the great victory at Antietam. Later in the war he would perform indispensable service at Chattanooga and Lookout Mountain, and he would ride with William Tecumseh Sherman on the March from Atlanta to the sea.

Hookers

It is a common misconception that the term *hookers* to refer to prostitutes was a kind of tribute to General "Fighting Joe" Hooker because he was not sufficiently spirited in keeping whores away from the Army of the Potomac. Not true: *Hooker* in its colloquial sense was included in the second edition of John R. Bartlett's *Dictionary of Americanisms,* published in 1859. Apparently, the term originated in North Carolina and refers to the obvious, an aggressive prostitute's practice of hooking her arm around the arm of a potential client.

Hooker had a history of indiscretion. He had resigned from the army in 1853 when Winfield Scott chastised him for badmouthing fellow officers. Publicly faulting Burnside after Fredericksburg was bad enough, but he also criticized Lincoln. The country needed a dictator for the duration of the war, he said, broadly implying that Lincoln was not up to the task. In one of the most unusual commissions ever given a military commander, Lincoln wrote Hooker that only victorious generals could set up dictatorships. If Hooker would win the victory that the North badly needed, Lincoln would run the risk that Hooker was a Napoleon.

Hooker restored the morale of the Army of the Potomac. (He was as good an administrator as McClellan) and drew up the Union's best battle plan since the Peninsula. He crossed the Rappahannock River with more than twice as many soldiers as Lee's 60,000 and, unlike McClellan, he knew it. Once again Lee gambled. He threw away the book and *divided* his

382

Reproduced from the Collections of the Library of Congress, Prints and Photographs Division, Washington, DC [LC-B8155-1]

Robert E. Lee took great pride in his family heritage. He was a patrician, always soberly dignified, "the marble man." He owned no slaves, opposed secession, and looked down upon newly rich cotton planters from the deep South. Lee did not so much join the Confederacy as he defended Virginia.

army; Jomini must have turned over in his grave. His men left their fortifications, another "don't" when badly outnumbered, and hit Hooker from two directions near the town of Chancellorsville.

According to the book, Lee should have been badly defeated. But luck, in the shape of the opposing general, was with him again. At the very moment the outnumbered Confederates were wobbling on the brink of disintegration, Hooker, utterly out of character, ordered a withdrawal. His field commanders were incredulous. One general told the courier who delivered the order to pull back, "You are a damned liar. Nobody but a crazy man would give such an order when we have victory in sight!" General Henry Slocum was so sure the order was a hoax that he personally galloped his horse to Hooker's headquarters to hear it with his own ears.

What happened? Did Lee's bizarre division of his army scuttle Hooker's confidence? No one can say. The battle was lost inside Hooker's mind; he had humiliated himself and was soon relieved of command and sent to the western armies.

The Army of the Potomac suffered 11,000 casualties at Chancellorsville. However, the summary of the battle exposed a weakness in the South's fighting capacity that could only grow more serious. Lee's losses were worse than Hooker's. If the two armies continued to suffer more or less equally in battle, the Confederacy would simply run out of soldiers no matter how long Lee's string of victories.

The casualty Lee felt most grievously was the loss of his "strong right arm," Stonewall Jackson. To make things worse, Jackson's death was a fluke; he was felled by "friendly fire." The General was returning from a reconnaissance mission between the lines when Confederate pickets opened fire before they identified their targets. Jackson's arm was amputated in an effort to save him, but he died several days after the operation. Lee tactlessly but honestly said that he could never replace Jackson. He was never as confident in any other subordinate as he was in Jackson.

THE FORTRESS AT VICKSBURG

In the West, the Union's primary objective remained what it had been for two years: winning control of the Mississippi. By holding fast to a 150-mile stretch of the river between Vicksburg, Mississippi, and Port Hudson, Louisiana, the rebels were able to shuttle goods and men from one end of the

The North's War of Attrition 1863–1865

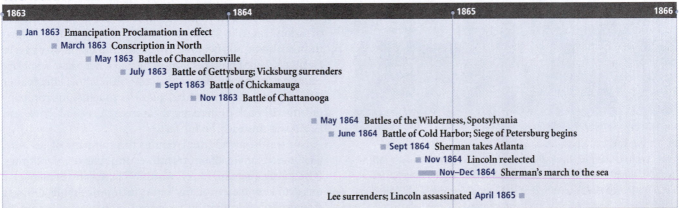

1863	1864	1865	1866

■ **Jan 1863** Emancipation Proclamation in effect
■ **March 1863** Conscription in North
■ **May 1863** Battle of Chancellorsville
■ **July 1863** Battle of Gettysburg; Vicksburg surrenders
■ **Sept 1863** Battle of Chickamauga
■ **Nov 1863** Battle of Chattanooga

■ **May 1864** Battles of the Wilderness, Spotsylvania
■ **June 1864** Battle of Cold Harbor; Siege of Petersburg begins
■ **Sept 1864** Sherman takes Atlanta
■ **Nov 1864** Lincoln reelected
■ **Nov–Dec 1864** Sherman's march to the sea

Lee surrenders; Lincoln assassinated **April 1865** ■

Confederacy to the other. Midwestern farmers were unable to export their crops down the Mississippi because Vicksburg sat on a sweeping bend of the river on bluffs up to 200 feet high. Confederate artillery, extending for 7 miles, could blow any heavily laden steamboat or drifting raft carrying freight out of the water, as the gunners several times demonstrated.

The Confederate army in Vicksburg was commanded by a most unlikely southern general. John C. Pemberton was a Pennsylvanian, born and raised a Quaker, who had married into a southern slave-owning family. He was a competent commander but was made uneasy by southerners who called him a Yankee traitor. When Joseph Johnston told him to abandon Vicksburg and save his army, Pemberton refused rather than listen to more abuse.

Reproduced from the Collections of the Library of Congress, Prints and Photographs Division, Washington, DC [LC-US261-903]

As a soldier, Grant took little interest in his appearance. Only his epaulets indicated his rank. But his subordinates soon learned that he sized up battle situations calmly and almost always accurately. He had his share of luck, but he was, in the end, the best general of the war.

Actually, the topography was on Pemberton's side. Naval assault proved impossible in the face of Pemberton's 200 big guns atop the cliffs. Union infantry could not approach the city from the north where Vicksburg was protected by rugged woodland laced by bayous and creeks running in deep ravines. It was a tangle of woods, earth, brush, and water that the Confederates knew but which was, around every tree, a surprise to Union soldiers. Each time they tried to struggle through the morass, the Confederate garrison sallied out and repelled them. Vicksburg was as near and as far from the Union's western armies as Richmond was from the Army of the Potomac.

U. S. Grant

Then, in March 1863, commanding the Army of the Tennessee, Ulysses S. Grant, just 41 years old, hatched a plan to take Vicksburg that was as daring and as risky as Lee's maneuver at Chancellorsville.

A West Point graduate, Grant had been cited for bravery in the Mexican War but then was shunted off to duty at a lonely desert fort and subsequently to a cold, wet, and lonelier outpost on the northern California coast. Far from his wife, to whom he was devoted, Grant took to whiskey and, after several dressings down by his superior, he resigned from the army. In business and trying to farm back in Illinois and Missouri, he failed at everything. When the Civil War broke out, he was a clerk in a relative's store—a charity job.

The Civil War was a godsend for men like Grant. Critically short of officers, the army did not quibble because Joe Hooker had been obnoxious and Grant a drunk. Grant was in command at the first notable Union victory of the war, the capture of Forts Henry and Donelson. Then came Shiloh which, while a Union victory in the end, caught Grant by surprise and revived suspicions of his friendship with the bottle.

He usually looked as if he was hungover. His figure was dumpy, his posture unmilitary. His beard was carelessly trimmed; his uniform—without regalia—was perpetually rumpled and soiled. He napped under trees with his hat over his face. During a battle he sat on a stump whittling a stick into shavings. Grant struck some people as listless, even stupid, but he was neither.

Nor was he a drunk. Like most other Civil War officers, he whiled away the evenings with whiskey and conversation. On occasion—no one knows how often—he had to be helped to his cot, but not necessarily because he drank excessively. Grant could not hold his liquor; he had what today would be called a very low tolerance of alcohol. He felt its effects after "two fingers" of the creature, about as much as his companions tossed back to moisten their teeth. A second drink and Grant was unsteady on his feet.

Nor was he an addict. When in the company of his wife, who joined him in all but frontline camps, he drank nothing. (Obviously, there had been words.) There is no evidence he was drunk on the eve of any battle, including Shiloh. Officers close to him said that he recovered from an evening under the weather with just an hour's sleep.

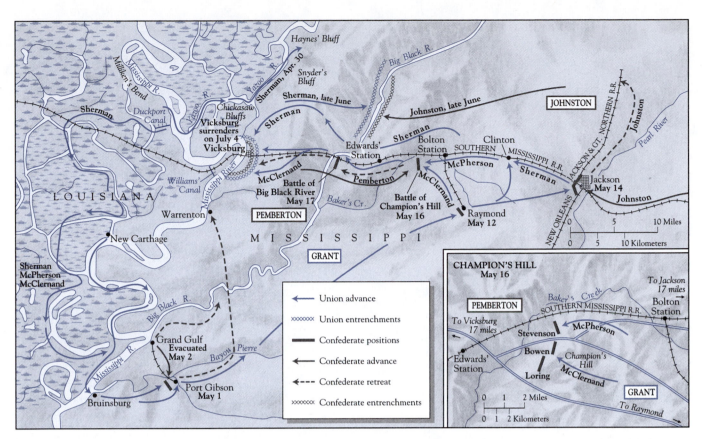

MAP 23:1 **Grant's Vicksburg Campaign.** The campaign that made Ulysses S. Grant's reputation: It was a combination of daring, risky maneuvers that bewildered the Confederates and a classic siege, isolating fortress Vicksburg, bombarding the city into rubble, and starving its defenders and civilian population.

The Siege

Grant understood battles; he would soon demonstrate that he also understood war. He was capable of boldness equal to Stonewall Jackson's and he had Lee's confidence with large commands. His written instructions to his subordinates would have allayed the worries of those who doubted him, had they seen them. Dashed off on his knee, they were invariably clear, precise, even literary. At Vicksburg, Grant scored a feat of old-fashioned military derring-do and then sat down to a model exercise in siege warfare, literally starving his enemy into surrender. In March 1863, unbeknownst to Pemberton, Grant transferred most of his army to the west bank of the Mississippi. He marched the men swiftly to a few miles below Vicksburg, recrossed the river, ferried by gunboats that had raced by night under the Confederate guns.

Having bypassed the rugged country where Pemberton had been unbeatable, Grant abandoned his supply lines, a risky maneuver in hostile territory that confused the Confederates. What did Grant know that they did not? Was there another Union army moving in from another direction? There was not. Grant charged to the east and frightened a small Confederate force under Joseph Johnston to withdraw into Jackson, the capital of Mississippi. Grant feigned an all-out assault on the town. When its defenders were holed up, he left a rear guard behind to contain them and reversed direction, turning back west to Vicksburg (and his supply line!).

The befuddled Pemberton was trounced in a series of brief battles. In a little more than two weeks, Grant won half a dozen confrontations; 8,000 Confederates were prisoners. On May 19, with Pemberton unable to escape, Grant sat his weary army down before Vicksburg while artillery bombarded the city. Nothing was settled. Vicksburg was a natural fortress and still commanded the river below. But Union forces had broken through where they had been helpless for more than a year.

Loaded Guns

Some 24,000 of 37,000 muskets collected from the battlefield at Gettysburg were still loaded; they had not been fired. About 6,000 of them had between three and ten charges in them. The soldiers were so excited that they continued to reload without discharging their weapons.

The Gettysburg Campaign

Richmond was alarmed. Jefferson Davis urged Lee to dispatch part of the Army of Northern Virginia to hit Grant from the rear and lift the siege. Lee refused. He reasoned that he could raise the siege by invading Pennsylvania, threatening Washington from the north, and frightening Lincoln into calling on Grant to send men East.

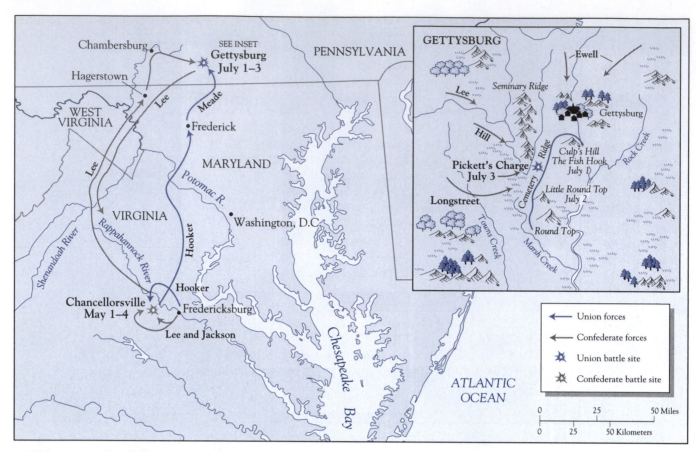

MAP 23:2 **Chancellorsville and Gettysburg.** Had General Joseph Hooker been aggressive at Chancellorsville as he had been earlier in the war, and afterwards, he would likely have been the hero of the war. But he withdrew when victory was within his grasp. His defeat made Lee's immediate offensive into Pennsylvania possible but, at Gettysburg, the Confederacy's offensive capability was destroyed.

It was a good plan. It had worked during the Peninsula Campaign when Stonewall Jackson feigned a move on Washington. Had Lee succeeded in 1863, his reputation as a strategist would equal his reputation as a tactician. But he failed because, ironically, in the most famous battle of the Civil War, Lee made the most serious tactical mistake of his career.

At first, all went well. Lee's thrust into Pennsylvania surprised the Army of the Potomac, now commanded by General George Meade. Lee's whereabouts were a mystery; his army moved faster than anyone who saw it could inform Washington. Meade drifted to the northwest on several roads, hoping he would find Lee on ground favorable to his army. On July 1, 1863, forward units of both armies bumped into each other near Gettysburg, Pennsylvania. The Union troops were looking for Confederates. The Confederates were looking for shoes.

The two armies descended on rolling farmland south of Gettysburg. The Confederates occupied the battlefield from the north, the Yankees from the south. Both established good positions on parallel ridges about half a mile apart, the rebels on Seminary Ridge, the Union troops on Cemetery Ridge.

Deciding to move before Meade's entrenchments were complete, Lee attacked with his left flank (Meade's right) and almost won the battle on the first day. As Lee calculated,

his men pushed Meade's line back until it was curled into the shape of a fish hook. Then, however, the Union soldiers held and Lee did not have the resources with which to turn Meade's flank without exposing the rest of his army to counterattack that might split his army in two.

On July 2, Lee attacked with his right wing, at the opposite end of the Union line (the eye of the fishhook). Once again, the rebels came within a few yards and a few hundred men of breaking through. But when the sun set, Union troops under Joshua Lawrence Chamberlain of Maine had survived hideous casualties but still held a steep, rocky 150-foot-high hill called Little Round Top. It was a critical position, perhaps the most important single position on the battlefield. The army that occupied Little Round Top—and Chamberlain was flooded with reinforcements overnight—could enfilade the open fields that separated the two ridges. That is, they could shoot into an advancing army from the side, vastly increasing the odds of balls finding targets.

That night, Lee's imagination failed him. (If, indeed, there was anything he could do.) Badly outnumbered now, he guessed correctly that Little Round Top had been reinforced. He rejected a second attack on the fish hook for the same reason he left off there on day one. He ordered a massive frontal assault on the Union center. General James Longstreet argued

The Anti-Draft Riots

In 1861, the United States army had no trouble recruiting troops. By activating state militias and signing up ninety-day enlistees, Lincoln had 187,000 men in the ranks within a few months. When the defeat at Bull Run in July demonstrated that winning the war would require a much larger force, patriotic recruitment rallies all over the country swelled the number of soldiers to 630,000 by the end of winter 1862.

Then came the carnage at Shiloh and the even higher casualties at Antietam in September. Enlistments sagged and desertions increased. Civic leaders hoping to raise a regiment and be commissioned colonels found they had to pay bounties to fill the ranks. Even then, with 900,000 in arms at the beginning of 1863, it was clear that the pool of willing volunteers was close to dry. Just to maintain the size of the armies in the face of deaths and disabilities (more from disease than from battle), conscription was a must. (The Confederacy already had a draft.)

The Conscription Act of March 1863 applied to all men between the ages of 20 and 45. However, it was far from equitable. By paying a "commutation fee" of $300, a man could have his name removed from the list from which draftees would be picked. If a man was drafted and did not want to go, he could still pay a man who was not selected to substitute for him.

The Conscription Act was, quite baldly, a rich man's law. In 1863, $300 was a munificent sum, $4,500–$5,000 in today's dollars. Only a wealthy man could hand over such a sum with a shrug. Most Democratic party politicians denounced the draft, organizing demonstrations in several cities. There was little violence, however, before July, 1863 when the first draw of names was scheduled. Then, in New York City, there was a riot on the scale that astonished everyone.

On July 12, New York's newspapers published the names of the city's draftees. A large number of them were Irish immigrants. A quarter of New York's population was Irish-born; among the lower classes that the draft hit hardest, the percentage was much higher. Spontaneously on July 13, about 500 mostly Irish workingmen stormed and destroyed the Provost-Marshall's office where draftees were to report.

News of the action spread rapidly in the slums; within hours, tens of thousands were on a rampage. Federal offices were the first targets, but the rioters also roughed up men who looked rich and every black man unlucky enough to be on the streets. By the end of the day, the rioters had taken control of large parts of the city. Shortly before midnight, the army telegraphed Secretary of War Edwin Stanton:

SIR: The situation is not improved since dark. The programme is diversified by small mobs chasing isolated negroes as hounds would chase a fox. I mention this to indicate to you that the spirit of mob is loose, and all parts of the city pervaded. The Tribune office has been attacked by a reconnoitering party, and partially sacked.

A strong body of police repulsed the assailants, but another attack in force is threatened. The telegraph is especially sought for destruction. One office has been burned by the rioters, and several others compelled to close.

In brief, the city of New York is to-night at the mercy of a mob, whether organized or improvised, I am unable to say. As far as I can learn, the firemen and military companies sympathize too closely with the draft resistance movement to be relied upon for the extinguishment of fires or the restoration of order. It is to be hoped that to-morrow will open upon a brighter prospect than is promised to-night.

The next day was worse. Mobs burned black residences, churches, dance halls, and brothels known to accommodate both black and white patrons. They even destroyed the Colored Orphan Asylum that was home to 237 children under the age of 12. (The children were evacuated and sent on their way before the building was torched.)

By afternoon of the 14th, several regiments from the Army of the Potomac arrived in the city. Small detachments had to retreat when confronted by large mobs but, when the troops advanced en masse, the rioters were "beaten and dispersed." Estimates of the number of rioters ranged up to 50,000 (too high) and no one knew how many people were killed, but, surprisingly, given the scale of the violence, the total did not exceed a hundred.

Why was it a largely Irish riot? Why were African Americans prime targets? Irish immigrants had enlisted in the Union army in large numbers. There were fully thirty-eight "Irish regiments" in the army in the summer of 1863, including the famous "Fighting 69th" of New York. Many more Irish immigrants were serving in units with no ethnic identification. By the end of the war, more than 150,000 Irish immigrants had served in Union blue, plus an unknown number of first-generation Irish-Americans. There was no racial prejudice in Ireland, as Frederick Douglass had been astonished to discover. Irish Americans were famous, even notorious, for their red, white, and blue patriotic observances.

The explanation lies in the Emancipation Proclamation, which had been in effect for six months in July 1863. To Irish workingmen, the war was no longer just a war to preserve the Union, but a war to free the slaves. Patriotic as they were, Irish immigrants were Democrats almost to the man. Northern Democrats had long-standing ties with the almost solidly Democratic South; they were opposed to emancipating the slaves. Irish workingmen were already hostile toward their African American neighbors because blacks competed with them for jobs as unskilled laborers. They feared (and were egged on by Democratic politicians) that if slavery were abolished, hundreds of thousands of southern blacks would migrate north to overwhelm them.

loudly, intemperately, almost insubordinately, and most of the night against the assault. He compared it to Burnside's charge into the powerful Confederate position at Fredericksburg. Longstreet pointed out that with two days in which to dig in on Cemetery Ridge, the Union line would be invulnerable. Longstreet urged Lee to sit tight the next day, improve the Confederate fortifications, and force Meade to attack across the wide-open country that separated the two armies.

"Dixie" and "The Battle Hymn"

The unofficial anthems of the Confederate and Union soldiers, "Dixie" and "The Battle Hymn of the Republic," were both stolen from the other side. "Dixie" was a minstrel show song written by Dan Emmett of New York. The music to "The Battle Hymn of the Republic" (and its predecessor, "John Brown's Body") was southern gospel. Its composer is unknown, but it was first noted in Charleston during the 1850s. Julia Ward Howe wrote the words of the "Battle Hymn."

Pickett's Charge

Stonewall Jackson might have persuaded Lee. James Longstreet could not. But his assessment of the situation was dead right. General Meade was betting on an attack on his center, and he concentrated his forces there. On the afternoon of July 3, he had the satisfaction of seeing his reasoning confirmed. Shortly after one o'clock, howling the eerie rebel yell, 15,000 men in gray began to trot across the no man's land. This was Pickett's Charge, a misnomer because the angry Longstreet was in overall command, George Pickett overseeing only part of the line. The charge was a nightmare from the moment the rebels left

their trenches. They were hit first with exploding shells, then grapeshot, then canister and minié balls from 30,000 muskets. The most destructive fire came from Little Round Top.

Although it boggles the imagination to understand how they did it, about a hundred Virginians and North Carolinians actually reached Union lines. There were far too few of them. They were immediately surrounded by a thousand Union soldiers and killed or captured.

Pickett's Charge lasted less than an hour. When the survivors dragged themselves back to Seminary Ridge, 10,000 men were dead, wounded, or missing. Five of twenty regimental commanders were wounded; the other fifteen were dead. So were two brigadier generals. Robert E. Lee rode among the survivors, barely restraining tears, apologizing over and over.

On July 4, with 28,000 fewer soldiers than he had led into Pennsylvania, Lee waited for the Union counterattack. It never came. Meade was still ruminating over the horrors of Pickett's Charge. He could see the thousands of bodies lying in the open fields. He would not expose his men to the same experience. By nightfall, a drizzle became a downpour, making the Potomac impassable and setting up Lee's army for a plucking. Defeated and huddled together, the Confederates were in a worse position than they had been after Antietam. But Lee, his wits collected, designed a complex, brilliant retreat and the pouring rain discouraged Meade. He did not attack. "We had them within our grasp," Lincoln fumed in his first display of temper since he had gotten rid of McClellan. "We had only to stretch forth our hands and they were ours. And nothing I could say or do could make the Army move."

High Tide

Gettysburg was an important victory. It ravaged southern morale. Confederate desertions broke all records. Thoughtful

National Park Service, Harpers Ferry Center

Pickett's Charge at the battle of Gettysburg, the high water mark of the Confederacy. When about a hundred Virginians and North Carolinians reached the Union line, the South came close to making the breakthrough for which Lee was hoping. But there were too few of them. They were killed or captured in hand-to-hand fighting. Pickett's charge turned out to be the worst tactical decision General Lee ever made. He sent his army over open country at the strongest part of the Union line.

southerners understood that their armies would never again be capable of an offensive campaign.

Lincoln was still without the decisive, relentless general who would exploit the Union's advantages. Meade had done well, but Lincoln was right to think him a man who needed a superior. Then, news from the West. The victory at Gettysburg had not yet been digested in Washington when a spate of telegrams informed the president that the siege of Vicksburg had ended on July 4, 1863, the same day Lee withdrew from Gettysburg.

Literally starving after having stripped the streets of pets and the cellars of rats, Pemberton, the soldiers, and the people of Vicksburg faced up to the fact that they were finished. Five days later, Port Hudson, Louisiana, the last Confederate stronghold on the Mississippi, gave up without a fight. Union General Nathaniel Banks took 30,000 prisoners. Within a week, the Confederacy lost several times more men than the rebels had put into the field at the first Battle of Bull Run.

Tennessee

Worse news followed. In September, a previously cautious Union general, William S. Rosecrans, attacked the remaining Confederate Army in the West. Rosecrans pushed Braxton Bragg out of Tennessee and into northern Georgia. Union troops occupied Chattanooga, a major railroad center on the Tennessee River.

Like Grant at Shiloh, however, Rosecrans was surprised by a counterattack. On September 19, reinforced by grim Confederate veterans of Gettysburg, Bragg hit him at Chickamauga Creek. It was one of the few battles of the war in which the Confederates had the larger army, 70,000 to Rosecrans's 56,000, and numbers told. The rebels smashed through the Union right flank, scattering the defenders and making Chickamauga among the bloodiest battles of the war. It would have been a total rout but for the stand on the Union left flank commanded by a Virginian who had remained loyal to the Union, George H. Thomas. The "Rock of Chickamauga," as Thomas was soon nicknamed, had suffered from the same snide questioning of his loyalties as Pemberton had. Thanks to him, the Union army was able to retire in something like good order to the fortifications of Chattanooga.

Wisely, Bragg decided to besiege rather than attack the city. Unlike Grant at Vicksburg, however, Bragg had enemies to his rear. On learning that Rosecrans's army was bottled up, Grant himself marched his men to Chattanooga and, by rail, brought an additional 23,000 troops from the East, many of them Gettysburg veterans. Late in November, he drove Bragg's Confederates from strongholds on Missionary Ridge and Lookout Mountain and back into Georgia.

The long campaign for Tennessee was over. It took two years longer than Lincoln had scheduled for it, but at last the Confederacy was severed. After Vicksburg and Chattanooga, there was no doubt about the man who was to lead the Union army in the end game. Early in 1864, Lincoln promoted U. S. Grant to the rank of lieutenant general—the highest rank in the army—and gave him command of all Union forces. Grant gave the western theater to his strong right arm, William Tecumseh Sherman.

TOTAL WAR

Grant had shown that he could be a daring tactician of the old school. At Vicksburg, with dash and flash, he outsmarted and outmaneuvered the enemy. Now he informed Lincoln that his object was not the capture of Confederate flags, commanders, cities, and territory, but the total destruction of the enemy's ability to fight. Richmond mattered to Grant not because Jefferson Davis lived there, but because it was an industrial center. He would "hammer continuously against the armed force of the enemy and his resources until by mere attrition, if in no other way, there should be nothing left to him but . . . submission."

The Union's numerical and material superiority was greater than it had been in 1861. Grant intended to put it to work. He would force the Confederates to fight constant battles on all fronts simultaneously. Unlike in the past, when Union forces "acted independently and without concert, like a balky team, no two ever pulling together," Grant would coordinate every army's offensives. Unlike McClellan, Grant was willing to sustain high casualties on the cold-blooded but rational grounds that the North could bear the losses and the South could not. Grant supported the naval blockade with more enthusiasm than his predecessors at the head of the army. He appreciated that, by 1864, the blockade was strangling the southern economy.

Grant's brand of warfare was not chivalrous. It involved wreaking devastation not only on soldiers, but also on a society. Philip Sheridan, Grant's cavalry commander, first put "total war" into practice when his soldiers stripped the

A Union supply depot in Virginia. Grant's army was abundantly equipped, fed, and sheltered. The troops at Petersburg were treated to a grand Thanksgiving dinner in 1864. The Confederates facing them ate corn meal mush. By the end of winter, thousands of the rebel soldiers were shoeless.

© Bettmann/Corbis

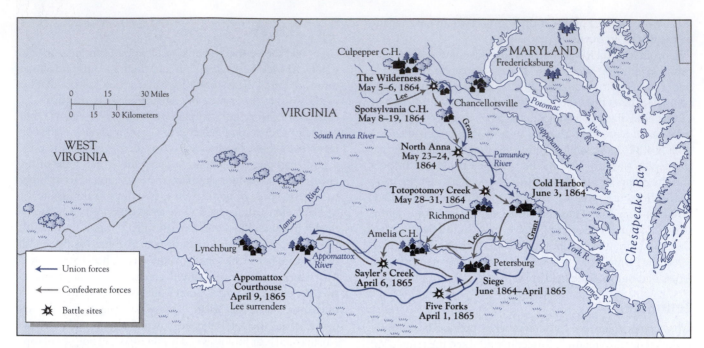

MAP 23:3　**Grant Before Richmond, 1864–1865.** Grant was a kind of general Lee had not seen in Virginia. When his assaults were rebuffed, he moved south and attacked again. The casualties at each battle were horrendous. Grant was determined to reduce Lee's army by attrition. Lee was fighting a war of attrition too. He hoped by inflicting even greater casualties on the North, he would persuade northern voters to defeat Lincoln in the fall of 1864 and negotiate a peace.

Shenandoah Valley, which had fed Richmond and Lee's army for three years. As Sheridan put it, a crow flying over the valley would have to carry his provisions with him. It was left to Grant's favorite commander, William Tecumseh Sherman, to give it a name. "War is hell," Sherman said. He was a no-nonsense man, even unpleasant in his refusal to dress up dirty work with fuss, feathers, and pretty words.

Sherman's assignment was to move from his base in Chattanooga toward Atlanta, the railroad center of the lower south that was defended by the Army of Tennessee under Joseph E. Johnston. Grant, with General Meade as his field commander, would personally direct the assault on Richmond.

Grant before Richmond

The war of attrition—grinding down the Confederacy—began in May 1864. With 100,000 men, Grant marched into The Wilderness, dense scrub forest near Chancellorsville. There he discovered that Lee was several cuts above the Confederate commanders he had faced in the West. Badly outnumbered, Lee took advantage of the thick woods and neutralized Grant's greater numbers, surprising Grant by attacking. Although the Union suffered 18,000 casualties to Lee's 12,000, replacements were rushed to Grant from Washington. Lee counted his dead and deserters and sent his wounded men home.

Now it was Lee's turn to discover that he was up against a new kind of adversary. Instead of withdrawing so that his men could lick their wounds and regroup, Grant shifted his army to the south and, two days later, attacked again, at Spotsylvania Court House. He calculated that Lee would have had no time to construct fortifications. Overnight, Lee's men did dig protective trenches. For five days, spearheaded in

places by African American troops, the Army of the Potomac attacked. Grant lost 12,000 men, almost twice Lee's casualties. Northern congressmen and editors, including a few Republicans, howled that Grant was a butcher. Lincoln was alarmed. But Grant was unmoved. He sent a curt message to the president that he intended "to fight it out on this line if it takes all summer."

Again, Grant swung to the south and Lee's men, miraculously, dug in. Lee rallied his shrinking army and somehow managed to scratch together enough munitions and provisions to keep his men in the field. In June, at Cold Harbor, 10 miles from Richmond, the two armies fought another gory battle. Before they charged, Union troops wrote their names on scraps of paper and pinned the tags to their uniforms. They expected to die. Even Grant was rattled by the casualty list. He later wrote that the attack at Cold Harbor was his worst mistake in the war.

Petersburg and the Shenandoah

At the time, however, he swung south again to Petersburg, a railroad center that was the key to Richmond's survival. He might have broken into the town, but for the failure of General Benjamin Butler, a political general in charge of 30,000 reinforcements, to join him in time. After four days, the summer only begun, Grant stopped and ordered a siege.

Grant had lost 65,000 men in a month and a half, more than Lee had in his army. (Lee lost almost 40,000.) One Maine regiment of 850 soldiers (already shorthanded; 1,000 was regulation) reported 218 survivors. Democratic party newspapers were infuriated by the gore and, preparing for the November election, began calling the entire war a "failure." The siege of

Wounded soldiers outside a makeshift hospital. Army surgeons were dedicated and inexhaustible. They learned a great deal during the war. After a battle, however, their daylong and nightlong work was mainly amputating shattered limbs. They were able to do little about infection.

Petersburg would last nine months, seven months longer than Vicksburg, through the harshest winter of the war.

In July, Lee tried a trick that, with Stonewall Jackson in charge, had worked in 1862. He sent General Jubal Early on a cavalry raid toward Washington, hoping to force Grant to weaken his lines in order to protect the capital. Early's raid was sensational. Early's men rode to within sight of the Capitol dome. But it was a last hurrah. Grant did not panic, and, this time, neither did Lincoln. (In fact, Lincoln nearly got himself shot by a sniper when he rode out to witness the battle and did not take cover until forced by soldiers to do so.) Grant's army stayed outside Petersburg. He countered Early's raid by sending cavalry under General Philip Sheridan—cavalry was of no use in a siege—to intercept Early, preventing him from rejoining Lee.

Sheridan chased Early into the Shenandoah Valley, the fertile country to the west of Richmond that had been a Confederate sanctuary and Richmond's breadbasket for three years. Sheridan defeated Early three times. More important, he laid waste to the land that had fed the Army of Northern Virginia, burning houses, barns, and crops, and slaughtering what livestock his men did not eat or drive away.

Sherman in Georgia

General Sherman was equally destructive in scouring Georgia. He moved into the state at the same time Grant attacked at The Wilderness. At first he met brilliant harassing action by Joseph E. Johnston. Then an impatient Jefferson Davis, unaware that Johnston's army was not up to a major battle, replaced him with courageous, but reckless John B. Hood, whom Sherman defeated. On September 2, 1864, with Grant beginning his third month outside Petersburg, Union troops occupied Atlanta. The loss of the city was a devastating blow to the economy of the lower South and to Confederate morale.

Perhaps more important, the capture of Atlanta took the sting out of Democratic attacks on continuing the war. At the end of August, the Democrats nominated George McClellan to oppose Lincoln in the presidential election. McClellan refused to agree to southern independence (as many Democrats were willing to do). He called for a truce and negotiations to end the war. To Lee and Davis, that meant that if the Confederate army could hold out until November, and McClellan won, they might win independence. In a way, Lee was fighting a war of attrition too; he was fighting to kill so

Reproduced from the Collections of the Library of Congress Prints and Photographs Division Washington, DC [LC-USZC2-1947]

Maj. Rathbone.   Miss Harris.   Mrs Lincoln.   President.   Assassin.

THE ASSASSINATION OF PRESIDENT LINCOLN,
AT FORD'S THEATRE WASHINGTON, D.C. APRIL 14TH 1865.

Published by Currier & Ives, 152 Nassau St. New York

Booth's murder of Lincoln as drawn soon after the assassination. Newspapers and magazines were not usually sticklers for accuracy in their pictorials. However, this representation is confirmed by eye-witness accounts gathered by investigators.

many northern soldiers that the people of the North cried "enough!"

In Atlanta, Sherman devised a plan that alarmed even Grant. After destroying the city's railroads and warehouses, he would abandon Atlanta and "march to the sea," across Georgia to Savannah. His 60,000 men would live off the land and then lay the countryside waste, "making Georgia howl." Both Grant and Lincoln opposed the plan. At Vicksburg, Grant had ventured fewer than 50 miles from his supplies and that was risky. By the time he got to Savannah, Sherman would be 350 miles from Chattanooga with no railroad behind him (his troops having destroyed it). Hood's Army of Tennessee, 40,000 strong, would have a big edge if he caught up to Sherman's army strung out for miles on several roads.

Sherman responded that, if Hood pursued him, George Thomas's Army of the Cumberland in Tennessee, with 60,000 soldiers, would attack Hood from the rear. With grave misgivings, Grant gave in. The depth of his confidence in Sherman rivaled Lee's confidence in the dead Stonewall Jackson. A far more anxious Lincoln agreed. He had been looking for Grant too long to overrule him.

Sherman ordered the people of Atlanta to evacuate whence he put everything of military value to the torch. (Much of the residential city was also destroyed although that was not Sherman's intention.) His army set out to the southeast in four columns, moving at top speed so as to outrun Hood. Hood, right, concluded he could not ignore Thomas to his rear. He attacked him in Tennessee and was defeated twice, reducing the Army of Tennessee nearly to uselessness.

Sherman's men destroyed everything of use to the Confederacy in a swath 60 miles wide. They not only tore up the railroad between Atlanta and Savannah, but they also burned the ties and twisted the iron rails around telegraph poles. "Sherman bow ties," they called them. Sherman's purpose in laying Georgia waste was to punish the people of Georgia. Those who caused and supported the war (and profited grandly from it, as Georgia had) would suffer for the suffering they had abetted. This was total war.

Sherman reached Savannah on December 10 and captured it two weeks later. Resupplied from the sea, he turned north, continuing to scorch the earth in South Carolina. He intended to join forces with Grant and fight the war's final battle with an irresistible numerical superiority.

The Sudden End

That battle was never fought. In February 1865, Jefferson Davis sent Confederate Vice President Alexander H. Stephens and two others to meet and try to make peace with Lincoln and Secretary of State Seward on a ship off Hampton Roads, Virginia. Another Confederate diplomat met with newspaper editor Horace Greeley in Canada. Absurdly, they insisted on Confederate independence as a condition of peace. Davis was out of touch.

Lee and Davis discussed solving their critical manpower problem by recruiting slaves. After the war, black soldiers would be freed. Lee, and probably Davis too, realized that even if southern independence was won, slavery was doomed. Such institutions do not survive the disruptions of war, whomever the victor. Desperate as the situation obviously was, the Confederate Congress resisted! The bill passed the Senate by only one vote. A few African Americans were enlisted. None saw action.

Late in March, Lee tried to draw Grant into a battle in open country. He had 54,000 men to Grant's 115,000, and

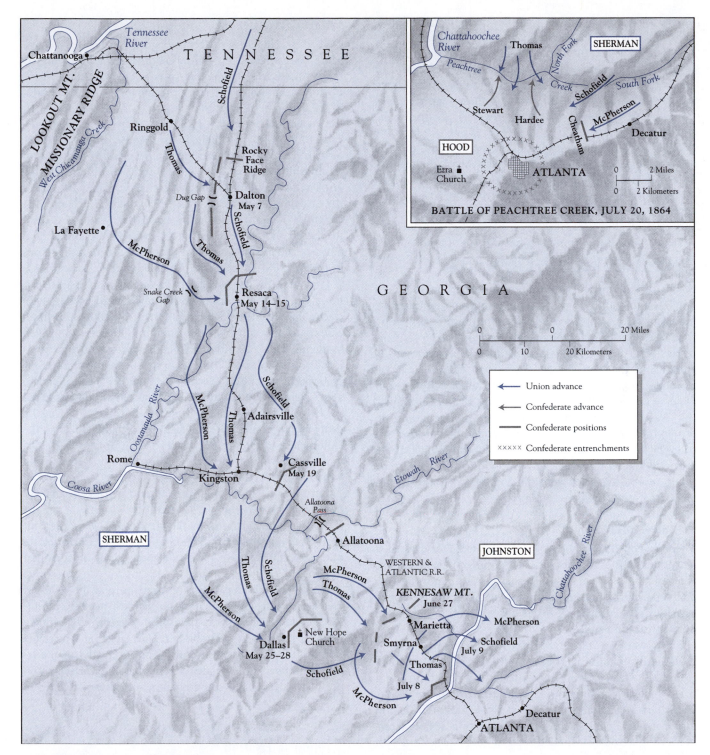

MAP 23:4 **The Campaign for Atlanta.** Sherman's advance from Chattanooga to Atlanta was timed to coincide with Grant's assault on Richmond; the Confederates would be unable to shift troops from front to front. President Lincoln owed his reelection in November 1864 to Sherman's capture of Atlanta rather than to Grant, whose bloody attacks were repeatedly stopped.

was easily pushed back into Richmond. On April 2, Lee concluded that he did not have the manpower to hold his 37 mile long line. The Union line lapped the Confederates at both ends. Rather than be surrounded, Lee abandoned Petersburg and therefore Richmond. He plan was to make a dash west, turn south, resupply in untouched North Carolina, and link up with Johnston (again in command of the Army

of Tennessee) for a last stand. Jefferson Davis, fleeing Richmond, was able to put a happy face on the loss of the capital. "Relieved of our obligation to defend cities, we . . . ."

Grant cut Lee off. Desertions had reduced the Army of Northern Virginia to 30,000 men and many men were shoeless. On April 9, Lee met Grant at Appomattox Court House in Virginia in, ironically, the home of a man who had moved there from Manassas after the first battle of Bull Run. Grant's terms were simple and generous. The Confederates surrendered all equipment and arms except for officers' revolvers and swords. Grant permitted both officers and enlisted men to keep their horses for plowing. After taking an oath of loyalty to the Union, the southern troops could go home. At Lee's request, Grant provided rations for the starving southerners.

Jefferson Davis ordered Joseph Johnston to fight on. The veteran soldier, who had not fared well by Davis's military decisions, knew better. On April 18, he surrendered to Sherman at Durham, North Carolina. The ragged remnants of two other Confederate armies gave up over the next several weeks.

THE AMERICAN TRAGEDY

More than a third of the men who served in the Civil War died in action or of disease, were wounded, maimed permanently, or captured. In some southern states, more than one-quarter of all the men of military age lay in cemeteries. The depth of the gore can best be understood by comparing the 620,000 dead (360,000 Union, 260,000 Confederate) with the population of the United States in 1860, about 30 million. Considering that half the population was female and 7 or 8 million males were either too old or too young for military service, more than one out of every 25 men "eligible" to die in the war did. Until the Vietnam War of the 1960s and 1970s added its dead to the totals, more Americans were killed in the Civil War than in all other American wars combined.

Assassination

There was one more casualty to be counted. On April 14, a few days after the fall of Richmond, President Lincoln and his wife attended a play at Ford's Theater in Washington. Shortly after ten o'clock, Lincoln was shot point-blank in the head by a zealous pro-Confederate, John Wilkes Booth. Lincoln died early the next morning.

Booth was one of those disturbed characters who pop up periodically to remind us of the significance of the irrational in history. An actor with romantic delusions, Booth organized a cabal including one mental defective to avenge the Confederacy by wiping out the leading officials of the Union government. Only he succeeded in his mission, although one of his gang seriously wounded Secretary of State Seward with a knife.

As he fled from the theater, Booth shouted, *"Sic semper tyrannis!"* which means "Thus always to tyrants" and was the motto of the state of Virginia. Booth fled into Virginia; on April 26, he was cornered and killed at a farm near Bowling Green. In July, four others were hanged for Lincoln's murder, including a woman, Mary Surratt, in whose boardinghouse the plot was hatched. (She may have been innocent of everything except a vague awareness of the scheme.) But vengeance did not bring the president back, and his loss proved to be inestimable, perhaps more for the South than for the North.

Father Abraham

To this day, Lincoln is the central figure of American history. More books have been written about him than about any other American. He was the American Dream made flesh. He rose from humble frontier origins to become the leader of the nation in its greatest crisis.

Lincoln was not always popular as a president. The Radicals of his own party assailed him because of his reluctance to make war on slavery early in the war, and his opposition to punishing the South when the war neared its end. Northern Democrats vilified him because the war dragged on and the casualties mounted. As late as September 1864, after the casualties of Grant's Richmond campaign, Lincoln expected to lose his bid for reelection to George McClellan. Several advisers said he should call the election off. With his religious devotion to the Constitution, Lincoln never considered it.

Lincoln weathered McClellan's threat thanks in part to political machinations; he made Nevada a state, gaining three electoral votes, although Nevada consisted of little more than a dozen mining camps of uncertain future. States controlled by Republicans permitted soldiers to vote by absentee ballots, the first ever used. Indiana, a state with a strong Democratic party, permitted Massachusetts soldiers posted there to vote—Republican, of course. Four out of five soldiers voted for Lincoln. Lincoln also appealed to prowar Democrats by dropping the name "Republican" and calling himself the Union party candidate. For vice president he chose a Democrat from Tennessee, Andrew Johnson, hoping that would win him votes in the border states.

But Lincoln did not win the election of 1864 because of political ploys. He won because, in the two months before the election, Sherman captured Atlanta, Admiral David Farragut took Mobile, Alabama, and Sheridan drove the Confederates out of the Shenandoah Valley for good. It was obvious that the Confederacy was doomed.

Lincoln had won the respect of the majority of the people of the North by the example of his dogged will, personal humility, and eloquent humanitarianism. In a speech dedicating a national cemetery at Gettysburg in November 1863, he stated American ideals more beautifully (and succinctly) than anyone had done since Jefferson's preamble to the Declaration of Independence). His second inaugural address, delivered in

---

Union and Nation

Before 1861, "United States" was grammatically a plural; since 1865, it has been a singular. That is, before the Civil War, one said, "The United States *are* . . ." Since, we have said, "The United States *is* . . . ."

Lincoln quietly charted the transformation in his speeches. In his first inaugural address (March 1861), he used the word *Union* twenty times, *nation* not once. In his first message to Congress (July 1861), he said *Union* forty-nine times and *nation* thrice. In the Gettysburg Address, Lincoln never said *Union* but referred to the *nation* five times.

Washington a month before Lee's surrender, was simultaneously a literary masterpiece, a signal to southerners that they could lay down their arms without fear of retribution, and a plea to northerners for a compassionate settlement of the national trauma. "With malice toward none," he concluded, "with charity for all; with firmness in the right, as God gives us to see the right, let us strive on to finish the work we are in."

CONSEQUENCES OF THE CIVIL WAR

The triumph of the Union guaranteed several fundamental changes in the nature of the American republic. Once and for all, the inseparability of the states was defined beyond argument. The theories of John C. Calhoun, compelling in the abstract, were buried without honor. If the United States was ever a federation of sovereign states, it was not so any longer. It was a nation, one and indivisible. Politicians (mostly southerners) have called themselves "states' righters" since the Civil War. But never after 1865 would anyone suggest that a state could leave the Union if its people disapproved of a national policy.

A New Political Majority

The South's political domination of the federal government was finished. Since the founding of the republic, southerners played a role in the government of the country out of all proportion to their numbers. Eight of the fifteen presidents who preceded Lincoln came from slave states. At least two of the seven northerners who held the office—Pierce and Buchanan—were blatantly proslavery. After Lincoln and Andrew Johnson, no citizen of a former Confederate state would occupy the White House until Lyndon B. Johnson in 1963, and he was as much a westerner as a southerner.

Since the Age of Jackson, southerners had dominated Congress through a combination of the three-fifths compromise, political skill, and an on-again–off-again agrarian alliance with western farmers. In making good on the threat to secede, the southern bloc lost everything but its leaders' political skills. The Democratic party remained a major force in New York and the Midwest. But the Republicans held the edge above the Mason-Dixon line; never again would an agrarian coalition dominate the federal government.

In its place, northeastern industrial and financial interests came to the fore. Businessmen had been late in joining the antislavery coalition. To bankers, great merchants, and factory owners, the Republican party was of interest more because of its economic policies than because of its hostility to slavery. With the war concluded, however, these forces held a strong position and exploited the emotional attachment of most northern voters to the "Grand Old Party."

New Economic Policies

During the war, the Republican Congress enacted a number of laws that would have been defeated had southerners been in their seats and voting. In July 1862, about the time of Antietam, both houses approved the Pacific Railways Act. As modified later in the war, this act gave 6,400 square miles of the public domain to two private companies, the Union Pacific and the Central Pacific railroads. These corporations were authorized to sell the land and use the proceeds to construct a transcontinental railway, the ultimate internal improvement. In 1864, while Grant slogged it out with Lee before Richmond, Congress gave the Northern Pacific Railroad an even more generous subsidy. These acts revolutionized the traditional relationship between private enterprise and the federal government.

The tariff was another issue on which southern interests had repeatedly frustrated the manufacturers of the Northeast. Since 1832, with few exceptions, the Democratic party drove the taxes on imported goods ever downward. The last tariff before the war, passed in 1857 with the support of southern congressmen, set rates lower than they had been since the War of 1812.

In March 1861, even before secession was complete, the Republican Congress rushed through the Morrill Tariff, which pushed up import duties. In 1862 and 1864, rates went even higher. By 1867, the average tax on imported goods stood at 47 percent, about the same as in the Tariff of 1828 that some southerners had called grounds for secession.

The South had long frustrated the desire of northern financial interests for a centralized banking system. Opposition to a national bank was one of the foundation stones of the old Democratic party. During the war, with no southern congressmen in Washington and with the necessity of financing the Union Army looming over Congress, New York's bankers had their way.

Financing the War

The Union financed the war in three ways: by heavy taxation, by printing paper money, and by borrowing, that is, selling bonds abroad and to private investors in the United States. The principal taxes were the tariff, an excise on luxury goods, and an income tax. By the end of the war, the income tax provided about 20 percent of the government's revenue.

The government authorized the printing of $450 million in paper money. These bills were not redeemable in gold. Popularly known as "greenbacks" because they were printed on the obverse in green ink (like our money), they had value (like our money), because the federal government declared they must be accepted in the payment of debts. When the fighting went badly for the North, the greenbacks were traded at a discount. By 1865, a greenback with a face value of $1 was worth only 67¢ in gold. This inflation was minuscule compared with inflation in the Confederacy, where government printing presses ran amok. By 1864, a citizen of Richmond paid $25 for a pound of butter and $50 for a breakfast. By 1865, prices were even higher; many southern merchants accepted only gold or Union currency, including greenbacks!

The banking interests of the North were uncomfortable with the greenbacks. However, they profited nicely from the government's large-scale borrowing. By the end of the war,

© Bettmann/Corbis

By the end of the war, 150,000 African Americans had donned Union uniforms, serving both in labor units (where many officers wanted to keep them) and in some of the fiercest assaults of 1864. In several instances, Confederate soldiers murdered black prisoners. In the last month of the war, the Confederacy began to train black soldiers, but it was too late to make up for the decimation of the southern armies.

the federal government owed its own citizens and some foreigners almost $3 billion, about $75 for every person in the country. Much of this debt was held by the banks. Moreover, big financial houses like Jay Cooke's in Philadelphia reaped huge profits in commissions for their part in selling the bonds.

Free Land

Another momentous innovation of the Civil War years was the Homestead Act. Before the war, southern fear of new free states in the territories restrained efforts to liberalize the means by which the federal government disposed of its western lands. In May 1862, the system was overhauled. The Homestead Act provided that every head of family who was a citizen or who intended to become a citizen could receive 160 acres of the public domain. There was a small filing fee, and homesteaders were required to live for five years on the land that the government gave them. Or, after six months on the land, they could buy it outright for $1.25 per acre.

A few months after approving the Homestead Act, Congress passed the Morrill Act. This law granted each loyal state 30,000 acres for each representative and senator that

state sent to Congress. The states were to use the money they made from the sale of these lands to found agricultural and mechanical colleges. In subsequent years, the founding of sixty-nine land-grant colleges greatly expanded educational opportunities, particularly in the West.

Again, it was a free-spending policy which parsimonious southern politicians would never have accepted, and the revolutionary infusion of government wealth into the economy spawned an age of unduplicated expansion—and corruption.

Family Circle

In Washington, slavery was abolished by congressional act, with slave owners compensated for their financial loss. One of the largest and surely the oddest payment was to Robert Gunnell, an African American who received $300 each for his wife, children, and grandchildren—18 people in all. Gunnell had owned them as slaves, believing it was the safest status for members of his family.

Free People

No consequence of the Civil War was as significant as the abolition of slavery. In a sense, the peculiar institution was doomed when the first shell exploded over Fort Sumter. As Congressman Ben Wade of Ohio told southerners in 1861, "the first blast of civil war is the death warrant of your institution." As an immoral institution, slavery might have survived indefinitely; immoral institutions do. By the middle of the nineteenth century, however, slavery was also hopelessly archaic. It is the ultimate irony of wars that are fought to preserve outdated institutions that war itself is the most powerful of revolutionary forces. Precariously founded institutions such as slavery rarely survive the disruptions of armed conflict.

Some 150,000 African Americans, some free northerners, most of them runaway slaves, served in the Union Army. They were less interested in preserving the Union than in freeing slaves. Their bravery won the admiration of many northerners. Lincoln confessed his surprise that blacks made such excellent soldiers, and he seems to have been revising the racist views that he shared with most white Americans.

For a time, at least, so did Union soldiers. Fighting to free human beings, a positive goal, was better for morale than fighting to prevent secession, a negative aim at best. By 1864, as they marched into battle, Union regiments sang "John Brown's Body," an abolitionist hymn, and Julia Ward Howe's more poetic "Battle Hymn of the Republic":

> As He died to make men holy,
> Let us die to make men free.

Because the Emancipation Proclamation did not free all slaves, in February 1865 radical Republicans in Congress proposed, with Lincoln's support, the Thirteenth Amendment to the Constitution. It provided that "neither slavery nor involuntary servitude, except as a punishment for crime . . . shall exist within the United States." Most of the northern states ratified it within a few months. Once the peculiar institution was destroyed in the United States, only Brazil, Cuba, Puerto Rico, Moslim lands, and sub-Saharan Africa continued to condone the holding of human beings in bondage.

FURTHER READING

Classics Ulysses S. Grant, *Personal Memoirs of U.S. Grant*, 1885–1886; James G. Randall, *The Civil War and Reconstruction*, 1937; Bruce Catton, *A Stillness at Appomattox*, 1952; Shelby Foote, *Red River to Appomattox*, 1974.

General James McPherson, *Battle Cry of Freedom: The Civil War Era*, 1988; Geoffrey C, Ward, *The Civil War*, 1999; Edward Hagerman, *The American Civil War and the Origins of Modern Warfare*, 1988; David J. Eicher, *The Longest Night: A Military History of the Civil War*, 2001; Ivan Musicant, *Divided Waters: The Naval History of the Civil War*, 1995; Herman Hattaway and Archer Jones, *How the North Won: A Military History of the Civil War*, 1980; Richard E. Beringer et al., *Why the South Lost the Civil War*, 1991; Charles B. Royster, *The Destructive War: William Tecumseh Sherman, Stonewall Jackson, and the Americans*, 1991; Charles B. Flood, *Grant and Sherman: The Friendship that Won the Civil War*, 2005.

Battles James M. McPherson, *For Cause and Comrades: Why Men Fought in the Civil War*, 1997; Gerald E. Linderman, *The Experience of Combat in the Civil War*, 1987; Joseph Glathaar, *Forged in Battle: The Civil War Alliance of Black Soldiers and White Officers*, 1990; Michael B. Ballard, *Vicksburg: The Campaign that Opened the Mississippi*, 2004; Kent Masterson Brown, *Retreat from Gettysburg: Lee, Logistics, and the Pennsylvania Campaign*, 2005; J. Tracy Power, *Lee's Miserables: Life in the Army of Northern Virginia from the Wilderness to Appomattox*, 1998; Lauren M. Cook, *They Fought Like Demons: Women Soldiers in the American Civil War*, 2002; Elizabeth Leonard, *All the Daring of the Soldier: Women in the Civil War Armies*, 1999.

Armies Richard M. McMurry, *Two Great Rebel Armies*, 1989; Steven E. Woodworth, *Nothing But Victory: The Army of the Tennessee 1861–1865*, 2005; Jeffry D. Wert, *The Sword of Lincoln: The Army of the Potomac*, 2005.

Generals Joseph G. Glathaar, *Partners in Command: The Relationships Between Leaders in the Civil War*, 1993; Gabor Boritt, *Lincoln's Generals*, 1994; Brooks D. Simpson, *Ulysses S. Grant*, 2000; Jean E. Smith, *Grant*, 2001; Charles B. Flood, *Grant and Sherman: The Friendship That Won the Civil War*, 2005; Alan Nolan, *Lee Considered:*

General Robert E. Lee and Civil War History, 1991; Charles B. Royster, *The Destructive War: William Tecumseh Sherman, Stonewall Jackson, and the Americans*, 1991; William Marvel, *Burnside*, 1991; Richard M. McMurry, *John Bell Hood and the War for Southern Independence*, 1982; Gilbert E. Govan and James Livingood, *General Joseph E. Johnston, CSA*, 1993; Craig L. Symonds, *Joseph E. Johnston: A Civil War Biography*, 1993.

Politics and Society North James A. Rawley, *The Politics of Union*, 1974; J. Matthew Gallman, *The North Fights the War: The Home Front*, 1994; Philip S. Palaudan, *"A People's Contest": The Union and the Civil War, 1861–1865*, 1988; James W. Geary, *We Need Men: The Union Draft in the Civil War*, 1991; E. D. Fite, *Social and Industrial Conditions in the North during the Civil War*, 1976; Joel Silber, *A Respectable Minority: The Democratic Party in the Civil War Era*, 1977; Jean Baker, *Affairs of Party: The Political Culture of the Northern Democrats in the Mid-Nineteenth Century*, 1983; Elizabeth D. Leonard, *Yankee Women: Gender Battles in the Civil War*, 1994; Iver Bernstein, *The New York City Draft Riots*, 1990.

Politics and Society South Emory M. Thomas, *The Confederate Nation, 1861–1865*, 1979, and *The Confederacy as a Revolutionary Experience*, 1991; William Blair, *Virginia's Private War: Feeding Body and Soul in the Confederacy, 1861–1865*, 1998; Stephen Ash, *When the Invaders Came: Conflict and Chaos in the Occupied South*, 1996; Drew Gilpin Faust, *Mothers of Invention: Women of the Slaveholding South in the American Civil War*, 1996; Gary W. Gallagher, *The Confederate War*, 1997; Michael B. Ballard, *A Long Shadow: Jefferson Davis and the Final Days of the Confederacy*, 1997; Bruce Levine, *Confederate Emancipation: Southern Plans to Free and Arm Slaves During the Civil War*, 2006.

Lincoln Philip S. Palaudan, *The Presidency of Abraham Lincoln*, 1994; Garry Wills, *Lincoln at Gettysburg: The Words that Remade America*, 1992; Lawanda Cox, *Lincoln and Black Freedom*, 1981; Michael Lind, *What Lincoln Believed: The Values and Convictions of America's Greatest President*, 2004; Doris Kearns Goodwin, *Team* *of Rivals: The Political Genius of Abraham Lincoln,* 2005; Joshua Wolf Shenk, *Lincoln's Melancholy: How Depression Challenged a President and Fueled His Greatness,* 2005; Michael W. Kauffman, *American Brutus: John Wilkes Booth and the Lincoln Conspiracies,* 2004; Thomas Goodrich, *The Darkest Dawn: Lincoln, Booth, and the Great American Tragedy,* 2005.

KEY TERMS

Use the following listing of key terms to review important figures, events, locations, and concepts covered in this chapter. A glossary of these terms is available on *The American* *Past* companion Web site: www.cengage.com/history/conlin/tap9e

Vicksburg, p. 383

Pickett's Charge, p. 388

Rock of Chickamauga, p. 389

Wilderness, Battle of the, p. 390

Booth, John Wilkes, p. 394

Homestead Act, p. 396

Wade, Benjamin F., p. 396

ONLINE RESOURCES

Find additional resources, including primary source documents, images, interactive maps, simulations, chapter review exercises, and Internet links at

***The American Past* companion Web site**
www.cengage.com/history/conlin/tap9e

American History Resource Center
http://ushistory.wadsworth.com/

Chapter 24

Aftermath

The Era of Reconstruction
1863–1877

National Archives

You say you have emancipated us. You have; and I thank you for it. But what is your emancipation? … When you turned us loose, you gave us no acres. You turned us loose to the skies, to the storm, to the whirlwind, and, worst of all, you turned us loose to the wrath of our infuriated masters.

—Frederick Douglass

When the guns fell silent in 1865, some southern cities were flattened. Vicksburg, Atlanta, Columbia, and Richmond were eerie wastelands of charred timbers, rubble, and freestanding chimneys. Few of the South's railroads were operating for more than a dozen miles. Bridges were gone wherever armies had passed. River commerce had dwindled to a trickle. The only new boats on the Mississippi were from the North. The South's commercial ties with Europe had been snapped. All the South's banks, having long since redeemed worthless paper money with gold and silver, were ruined.

Even the cultivation of the soil had been disrupted. By the thousands, the small farms of the men who served in the ranks were overgrown in weeds and brambles. Plantations were abandoned. An Indiana soldier, stationed in central Louisiana where there had been little fighting, wrote that "You could travel for miles and not see cotton, corn, or produce, except peaches. . . . A few of the inhabitants had returned from the rebel army, but the darkies were gone, and there was no one to work the farms."

THE RECONSTRUCTION CRISIS

Looking back at the desolation, *reconstruction* seems the appropriate word for the postwar era. However, as the term was used at the time, "Reconstruction" had nothing to do with laying bricks, rehabilitating railroads, or recovering fields. Reconstruction referred to the political process by which the eleven rebel states were restored to "a normal constitutional relationship" with the federal government. It was the Union, that great abstraction over which so many had died, that was rebuilt.

Blood was shed during the Reconstruction era too, but little glory was won. Few political reputations—northern, southern, white, black, Republican, Democratic—emerged from the era unstained. It may be that Abraham Lincoln is a sainted figure only because he did not survive the war. The reconstruction process Lincoln proposed in 1863 was rejected by Congress. Had he survived and pushed it, he would have had a nasty fight on his hands. His successor, Andrew Johnson, did just that, and Congress and the majority of northern voters repudiated him.

Lincoln's Plan

By December 1863, Union armies occupied large chunks of the Confederacy. Ultimate victory, while not yet in the bag, was a reasonable expectation. To provide for the rapid reconciliation of North and South—Lincoln's postwar priority—the president proclaimed that as soon as 10 percent of the eligible voters in a former Confederate state took an oath of allegiance to the Union, the people of that state could write a new state constitution, organize a state government, and elect representatives to Congress. Three southern states that were mostly occupied—Tennessee, Arkansas, and Louisiana—immediately complied.

Congressional Republicans refused to recognize them as states of the Union and restored them to military control.

Richmond in ruins, more from fire than from bombardment. Atlanta looked worse. The Shenandoah Valley and northeastern Georgia were laid waste. Even areas of the South untouched by war were impoverished, dwellings and fields neglected.

National Archives

Many Republicans (and, of course, Democrats) had long been alarmed by Lincoln's expansion of presidential powers. Not even Andrew Jackson had effected policies by executive proclamation or played free and easy with the ancient personal protection of *habeas corpus* to the extent Lincoln did.

With the survival of the Union at stake, Republican congressmen swallowed their anxieties. But reconstruction was a postwar issue, and Lincoln's plan did not involve Congress, except to call for the election of senators and representatives in reconstructed states. Congress was keenly sensitive to its

Reconstruction 1863–1877

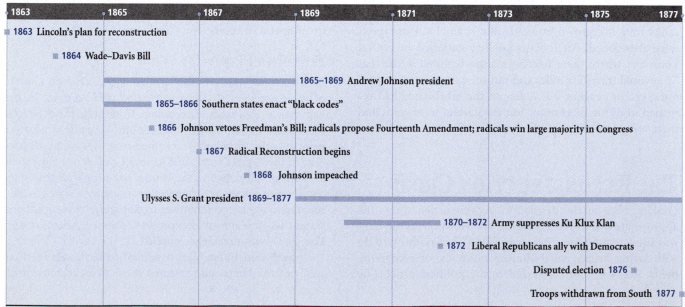

1863	1865	1867	1869	1871	1873	1875	1877

- 1863 Lincoln's plan for reconstruction
- 1864 Wade–Davis Bill
- 1865–1869 Andrew Johnson president
- 1865–1866 Southern states enact "black codes"
- 1866 Johnson vetoes Freedman's Bill; radicals propose Fourteenth Amendment; radicals win large majority in Congress
- 1867 Radical Reconstruction begins
- 1868 Johnson impeached
- Ulysses S. Grant president 1869–1877
- 1870–1872 Army suppresses Ku Klux Klan
- 1872 Liberal Republicans ally with Democrats
- Disputed election 1876
- Troops withdrawn from South 1877

right to assess the credentials of those who showed up at the capital claiming to have been duly elected. After four years when Alabama, Texas, and the other rebel states had sent no representatives to Congress, Congress had the authority to determine how and when they could do so.

The Wade-Davis Bill

Only a minority of the Republicans in Congress called themselves radicals. But the radicals were militant and persuasive with the others, and they had reasons in addition to the credentials issue to reject Lincoln's proposal. Many radicals were former abolitionists who blamed the slavocracy, the South's great planters, for causing the terrible war. They were determined that the slavocrats be punished and destroyed as a class so that the reconstructed states were free of their domination. The only way to ensure this, the radicals concluded, was to see to it that the freedmen, as the emancipated slaves were called, participated in southern state governments.

So, in July 1864, Congress enacted the Wade-Davis Bill as an alternative to Lincoln's plan. It provided that only after *50 percent* of the eligible voters of a former Confederate state swore the oath of loyalty could the reconstruction process begin. Congress—not the president—would supervise the oath taking and approve or disapprove of the state constitutions the southern states wrote. The Wade-Davis bill did not detail the reconstruction process beyond that point. Aware that Lincoln would veto it, the radicals enacted it in order to slow down things that Lincoln was trying to rush through.

Lincoln killed the Wade-Davis Bill with a pocket veto, which did not require him to explain his reasons for rejecting it in a veto message. During the final months of his life, he dropped hints that he was willing to work out a compromise with Congress. He even reached out to the radicals (whom he had never much liked) by saying that he had no objection to giving the vote to blacks who were "very intelligent and those who have fought gallantly in our ranks." He urged the military governor of Louisiana to extend the suffrage to some blacks. And there things stood when John Wilkes Booth sent events on an unforeseen course.

Lincoln's Goals

Why did Lincoln dodge radical demands that the freedmen be granted civil rights equal to those of whites? Mainly because his priority was the reconciliation of northern and southern whites. He made his intention eloquently clear in his second inaugural address a few weeks before he was shot. "With malice toward none, with charity for all, . . . let us strive on to finish the work we are in, to bind up the nation's wounds, . . . to do all which may achieve and cherish a just and lasting peace among ourselves."

For Lincoln, the interests of African Americans were at best secondary to the interests of whites. If white southern refusal to accept the freedmen as their equals stood in the way of reconciliation—and common sense said that it would— Lincoln was willing to give way. Radical Senator Ben Wade said that Lincoln's views on black people "could only come of one who was born of poor white trash and educated in a

Reproduced from the Collections of the Library of Congress, Prints and Photographs Division, Washington, DC [LC-BH83-171]

President Andrew Johnson. He was a man of integrity, but inflexible and, despite his hatred of secessionists, hostile to every suggestion that the freedmen be granted civil equality.

slave state." This was as unfair as it was ugly. Lincoln's racism was passive. In finding African Americans unacceptable company and morally and intellectually inferior to whites, he was expressing the views not just of southern white trash, but of a large majority of white northerners.

There is reason to believe that Lincoln's views on race had changed during the war. He admitted being surprised and impressed by the bravery and loyalty of African American soldiers. Lincoln had always been a flexible politician, willing to bargain. "Saying that reconstruction will be accepted if presented in a specified way," he announced, "it is not said that it will never be accepted in any other way." He was telling the radicals that nothing about the reconstruction procedure and the future status of the freedmen was final.

Stubborn Andrew Johnson

After April 15, 1865, it did not matter what Lincoln thought; and Andrew Johnson was not the flexible politician Lincoln had been. Nor had his "white trash" views on race undergone any changes during the war.

Johnson grew up in stultifying poverty in Tennessee. Unlike Lincoln, who taught himself to read as a boy, Johnson was an illiterate adult when he asked a schoolteacher in Greenville to teach him how to read and write. She did, then married him, and encouraged her husband to go into politics. Johnson won elective office on every level from town councilman to congressman to senator. He had owned a few slaves during his life, but he hated the secessionist cotton planters of western Tennessee. He was the only southerner to refuse to walk out of the Senate in 1861. He called for a ruthless war on the rebellion and harsh punishment of Confederate leaders, including the gallows for Jefferson Davis and other top officials. Lincoln appointed him governor of occupied Tennessee and chose him to run for vice president in 1864 in the hope of winning the votes of other southern Unionists.

Johnson's political experience was extensive, but his personality was ill-suited to Washington politics. Where Lincoln understood what he could do and what he could not accomplish, Johnson was principled, willful, and stubborn. It did him no good to have had virtually dictatorial powers as military governor of Tennessee. He got off to a bad start as vice president. Suffering from a bad cold on inauguration day, he bolted several glasses of brandy for a pick-me-up and was visibly drunk when he took the oath of office. Fortunately, only a few people were present and Lincoln told aides to keep Johnson under tight control at the public ceremony outside the Capitol.

Johnson was not, in fact, a "problem drinker." His behavior on inauguration day was a fluke and nothing was made of it at the time. The likeliest people to jump on the southern vice president, the radicals, rather liked Johnson for wanting to hang Jeff Davis and because as governor of Tennessee he had approved the confiscation of some rebel estates.

But the radicals misread Johnson's anti-Confederate ardor. Emancipation pleased him not because he thought slavery wicked—the well-being of African Americans did not interest him—but because emancipation destroyed the wealth and power of the slavocrats.

Johnson: They Are Already States

Johnson adopted Lincoln's reconstruction policy with minor changes. However, the chief point of friction with Congress—presidential supervision of the process of restoring the rebel states to the Union—remained unchanged.

Johnson had sound constitutional reasons for saying that the reconstruction of the Union was an administrative matter and, therefore, the responsibility of the executive branch of the government. Constitutionally, the Union *could not* be dissolved; states *could not* secede. There had indeed been a rebellion and an entity called the Confederate States of America. However, Johnson said, individuals had rebelled; people—traitors—had taken up arms against the United States and created the Confederacy. The *states* of Virginia, Alabama, and the rest had not seceded. The contention that the states were sovereign components of a federation was Calhounism, contradicted by the Preamble of the Constitution, the Marshall Court, Andrew Jackson, Henry Clay, and the eloquence of Daniel Webster in his famous debate with Robert Hayne. During the crisis of 1861, almost every northerner, Democrats as well as Republicans, not to mention southern Unionists, had rejected secession as unconstitutional.

What had been true in 1861 was true in 1865. Virginia, Alabama, and the rest had never ceased to be states. Therefore, there was no call for congressional legislation to return them to their normal place in the Union. Indeed, for Congress to interfere in any way would be an unconstitutional violation of the southern states' legitimate rights.

An Unpopular Policy

Lincoln had worried about the reconstruction debate centering on a "pernicious abstraction." "Pernicious" and "abstract" were precisely how congressional Republicans and most Republican newspaper editors saw Johnson's justification of his policy. The nation was just emerging from four years of a terrible war forced on the North by the slavocracy in which 360,000 northern boys had died in order to defeat them. Many more were maimed for life. When, under Johnson's rules, southern voters sent four Confederate generals, six members of Jefferson Davis's cabinet, and the Confederate vice president to Congress, it was as if nothing had happened between 1861 and 1865. The same old southern leaders—traitors all—were back.

They and a great many other military officers and civil officials had been pardoned for the asking. Before the end of 1865, President Johnson signed pardons for 13,000 Confederates, restoring their civil rights. (That was a rate of 2,000 per month!) What was Johnson thinking? Lincolnian reconciliation required the goodwill of northerners too.

Southern legislatures established under the Johnson plan enacted "black codes," comprehensive laws governing the freedmen that, to some northerners seemed to return them to slavery in all but name. Indeed, Mississippi refused to ratify the Thirteenth Amendment; Alabama rejected part of it. In South Carolina, Robert Rhett frankly said that blacks should "be kept as near to the condition of slavery as possible, and as far from the condition of the white man as is practicable."

Some states made it illegal for African Americans to live in towns and cities, a backhanded way of keeping them in the fields. In no southern state were blacks permitted to own firearms. South Carolina's code said that African Americans could not sell goods! Mississippi required freedmen to sign twelve-month labor contracts before January 10 of each year. Those who failed to do so could be arrested and their labor for the year sold to the highest bidder, the slave trade in annual installments. Blacks who reneged on labor contracts were not to be paid for the work that they had already performed. Mississippi made it a crime for an African American to "insult" a white person.

Not that northern whites believed in racial equality. They did not. When the war ended, only six of the loyal states allowed African American men to vote. Between 1865 and 1867, six more states held referenda on the question of black suffrage. The voters in all six rejected it. In 1866, the same Congress that approved a constitutional amendment granting equal civil rights to blacks segregated schools in the District of Columbia by race.

The Radicals: The States Have Forfeited Their Rights

The radical Republicans feared that, despite the widespread hostility in the North to southern actions, racial prejudice

North Wind Picture Archives

Congressman Thaddeus Stevens of Pennsylvania. He was in his seventies when this picture was made; the coal black hair was a wig. He had been an abolitionist before the war. Southerners hated him; during the war, Confederate cavalry raiders went out of their way to burn a factory he owned. During the first years of reconstruction, he led House radicals in calling for punishing leading rebels and in guaranteeing the right to vote of southern blacks.

would enable Johnson to have his way. They countered Johnson's compelling constitutional argument with several justifications to keeping the former rebel states out of the Union until some needed changes were made.

Thaddeus Stevens of Pennsylvania, the radical leader in the House of Representatives, said that the Confederate states had committed "state suicide" when they seceded. They were not, in 1865, alive. Therefore, it was within the purview of Congress to determine when they were satisfactorily reborn.

Charles Sumner, a prominent Senate radical, said that the former southern states were "conquered provinces." Their constitutional status was identical to that of the western territories. Congress (not the president) would admit them as states when Congress approved of the state constitutions they wrote. Another Republican, Samuel Shellabarger of Ohio, came up with language that was more agreeable to moderate Republicans who were sitting on the fence: When the rebel states seceded, they "forfeited" the rights reserved to the states by the Constitution.

Congress's Joint Committee on Reconstruction settled on a plausible formula: "The States lately in rebellion were, at the close of the war, disorganized communities, without civil government and without constitutions or other forms, by virtue of which political relations could legally exist between them and the federal government." This provided all but a few Republicans loyal to Johnson with grounds for

refusing to seat the southerners who came to Washington as the elected representatives of their states.

Radical Goals and Motives

The radicals were motivated by ideals, passions, and hard-headed politics. Many of them had been abolitionists, morally repelled by the institution of slavery. Thaddeus Stevens, Ben Wade, Charles Sumner, and others believed in racial equality and were determined that, if they could carry the day, African Americans would enjoy full civil rights. Stevens, Wade, and George W. Julian hated the slavocracy with a seething passion they did not conceal.

The planters' power had been maimed by the abolition of slavery, but they still owned the land. Julian proposed to confiscate the estates of planters who had been active Confederates, high ranking army officers, and government officials. He had a good precedent to which to point, the confiscation of Loyalist estates after the War for Independence. Not only would confiscation punish rebels and destroy their economic power, by dividing the plantations into 40-acre farms to be granted to the freedmen, the government would give southern blacks the economic independence that, in the Jeffersonian tradition, was essential to good citizenship.

The radicals had frankly partisan motives too. The Republican party was a sectional party. If the party did not establish itself in the South, it was doomed to be defeated at the polls. The party's political prospects going into the congressional elections of 1866 were worse than they had been in 1860. With slavery gone, the number of southern congressmen would actually increase. Where, formerly, slave states had counted three-fifths of the slaves in calculating the size of their congressional delegations, they were now entitled to count the entire population at face value. There would be more Democrats in Congress after 1866 than there had been in 1861, and the South would have more electoral votes, all destined to be Democratic, in the presidential election of 1868—if Johnson's reconstructed state governments were allowed to stand.

There were white southerners likely to vote Republican: old Whig nationalists who had sat out the war and farmers in the mountain counties of Kentucky, Tennessee, Virginia, and North Carolina. Many of them had fought in Union armies and they no more wanted to see the secessionist Democrats return to power than the radicals did. But white Republicans were a minority in every southern state, a tiny minority in the deep South. If the party was to compete with the Democrats in the former Confederacy, it was necessary to ensure that the freedmen voted. Thaddeus Stevens did not ask moderate Republicans to advocate African American suffrage in the North. But if southern blacks did not vote, he argued, the Republican party was a dead duck and all Republican policies, such as the protective tariff, things of the past. "I am for negro suffrage in every rebel state," he told Congress, "If it be just, it should not be denied; if it be necessary, it should be adopted; if it be a punishment to traitors, they deserve it."

1866: THE CRITICAL YEAR

Stevens and the radicals trod carefully with the moderate Republicans. The congressional radicals were a minority of the party. If they were to affect their programs, they had to win over those Republicans who hesitated about granting full citizenship to the freedmen.

President Johnson played into the radicals' hands. He pushed the Republican moderates into cooperating with the radicals when he tried to destroy a federal agency that had averted mass starvation in the South and was still, in 1866, helping to prevent social chaos there.

The Freedmen's Bureau

The former slaves responded to emancipation in different ways. Some, who were bewildered or who had been treated well by their masters, stayed where they were. Promised wages when their cash-strapped masters found money, they worked on in the fields as they always had (minus the blacksnake whip). Others took to the roads, testing their freedom by going where they pleased. They heard rumors that every freed family would be granted "40 acres and a mule," and searched for the Union officer who would give them their farm. The wanderers gathered in ramshackle camps that were often disorderly and inevitably short of food. Discharged Confederate soldiers, trudging sometimes hundreds of miles toward their homes, also had difficulty finding enough to eat.

Fortunately, Congress had foreseen both problems. In March 1865—before Appomattox and Lincoln's assassination—Congress established the Bureau of Refugees, Freedmen, and Abandoned Land. General O.O. Howard was named to head what was commonly called the Freedmen's Bureau.

Howard's most pressing task was relief: avoiding starvation. In 1865, the Freedman's Bureau distributed rations to 150,000 people each day, about a third of them whites, ex-soldiers and their families. When Congress decided against confiscating lands on a large scale, bureau employees

The Freedmen's Bureau was the federal government's response to the old proslavery argument that freeing the slaves in the South would cause serious social and economic problems. The bureau confronted many of those problems, from starvation to African American illiteracy, with remarkable success. Former slaves most gratefully remembered bureau schools, so great was the hunger to learn among the freedmen. Many Freedmen's Bureau schools were run by northern white women; this class has a black male teacher (far right), probably a northerner.

The Valentine Museum

negotiated labor contracts between destitute former slaves and land owners. Because there was little coin in the South and southern bank notes were worthless, the bureau resorted to sharecropping arrangements. In return for the use of a farm and a cabin, the sharecropper (white as well as black) gave his landlord a third of the crop at harvest time.

The Freedmen's Bureau also set up medical facilities for the inevitable health problems. (Again, whites were served as well as freedmen.) Ultimately the bureau built and staffed forty-six hospitals and treated more than 400,000 cases of illness and injury.

The most popular bureau program with the freedmen was its school system. Freedom released a craving for education among blacks, adults as well as children. Appleton and Company, a publishing house, sold a million copies annually of Noah Webster's *Elementary Spelling Book*—the "Blue-Backed Speller" from which American schoolchildren learned to read—for forty years. Except in 1866, when sales jumped to 1.5 million; the 50 percent increase was due to sales to the Freedmen's Bureau. Teachers from the North, mostly white and mostly women, opened multigrade "one-room schoolhouses" throughout the South. Many of them later reminisced that never before or after had they had such dedicated pupils.

Discouraging Rebellion

A now forgotten provision of the Fourteenth Amendment forbade the former Confederate states to repay "any debt or obligation incurred in aid of insurrection or rebellion against the United States." By punishing banks and individuals, including Europeans and European banks, that had loaned money to the rebel states, the amendment put potential underwriters of future rebellions on notice that such loans had consequences.

Open Conflict

In 1865, Congress had given the Freedmen's Bureau a year to do its job. The assumption was that, by then, reconstructed state governments would take over its schools, hospitals, and other functions. In February 1866, however, Reconstruction had not begun. Congress refused to recognize Johnson's state governments but had created none itself. The South was still occupied territory. So Congress extended the life of the Freedman's Bureau for two years.

Johnson vetoed the bill, insisting that the former rebel states had constitutional governments. A month later, he vetoed another bill that granted citizenship to the freedmen. The Constitution, he said, gave the states the power to decide on the terms of citizenship within their borders. Once again he had the better constitutional argument and he might have won the political contest had northerners not been appalled by mob attacks on freedmen in several southern cities, including New Orleans.

In June 1866, perceiving a shift in mood in their favor, radical Republicans, now joined by the moderates, drew up a constitutional amendment on which to base Congress's reconstruction plan (and to answer Johnson's point about citizenship). The long and complex Fourteenth Amendment banned from federal and state office all high-ranking Confederates unless they were pardoned *by Congress*. The amendment also established, for the first time, *national* citizenship which states could not modify. It guaranteed that all "citizens of the United States and of the State wherein they reside" were to be treated equally. If ratified, the Fourteenth Amendment would prevent the southern states from passing laws applicable only to African Americans—like the black codes.

The Republicans were taking a big chance. The Fourteenth Amendment would also cancel northern state laws that discriminated against blacks. In that, Johnson saw his opportunity. He calculated that a majority of northern voters, particularly in the Midwest, would rather have ex-Confederates in Washington than accept African American equality at home. He decided to campaign personally in the midterm elections of 1866 for congressional candidates who supported him and opposed the radicals.

The Radical Triumph

Northern Democrats supported Johnson's reconstruction policy, but the Democratic party had withered to near impotence by the end of the war; in 1866, only 42 of 191 representatives were Democratic, only 10 of 52 Senators. Johnson's hopes of success depended on the support of anti-radical Republicans like Secretary of State Seward and an uncertain number of fence-sitting senators, representatives, and governors. They persuaded friendly Democrats to join them in the "National Union party," the name under which Lincoln had been elected in 1864.

The message of the "party"—actually a makeshift coalition—was sectional reconciliation. To symbolize its ideal, the National Union convention opened with a procession of pairs, a northerner and southerner in each, marching arm in arm into the auditorium. Things went wrong from the start. The first couple in the procession was South Carolina Governor James L. Orr, a huge, fleshy man, and Massachusetts Governor, John A. Andrew, a little fellow with a way of looking intimidated. When Orr seemed to drag the mousy Andrew along, Radical newspapers had a field day: the National Union party was a front for the rebels Johnson had pardoned wholesale.

Johnson's speaking tour in the Midwest, his "swing around the circle," consummated the disaster. One after another, he delivered blistering speeches denouncing the radicals, some in halls, others where a crowd had gathered near the railroad. No president had ever politicked personally in such a manner. Republican newspapers shook their heads sadly at Johnson's lack of dignity. To make things worse, Johnson had learned his oratorical technique in the rough-and-tumble, grass-roots politics of eastern Tennessee where mountaineers liked to hear

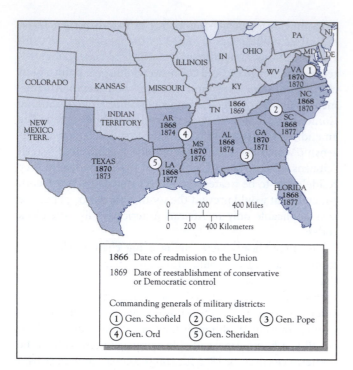

MAP 24:1 **Radical Reconstruction.** The radicals partitioned the Confederacy into five military districts of manageable size. The Union army supervised the establishment of state governments that guaranteed equal civil rights to freedmen whence each state was readmitted to the Union (with Republican governments). Tennessee was not included in the program. Occupied for much of the war by the Union army, Tennessee had a reconstructed state government by 1866 thanks, ironically, to its wartime governor, Andrew Johnson who, as president, opposed radical Reconstruction in the other southern states.

candidates scorching each other and trading gibes with hecklers. When it was the president of the United States snapping vulgarly at the bait radicals waved in front of him, the saltiest farmers were taken aback. Drunk again, radical editors surmised, rehashing the story of Johnson's inauguration as vice president.

The result was a radical landslide. Most of Johnson's candidates were defeated. The Republican party, now led by the radicals, won nearly three-fourths of the seats in the House, a dozen more than the two-thirds needed to override every veto Johnson threw at them. (Four out of five senators were Republican.)

RADICAL RECONSTRUCTION

The lopsided Fortieth Congress dissolved the southern state governments Johnson had recognized. Except for Tennessee, which had already been readmitted to the Union (with a Republican government), the former Confederacy was divided into five military provinces, each commanded by a major general. The army would maintain order and register voters from among blacks and those whites who

had not been disenfranchised. The state conventions these voters elected were required to ratify the Thirteenth and Fourteenth Amendments and to guarantee the vote to adult black males. After Congress approved their constitutions, the reconstructed states would be admitted to the Union and elect representatives to Congress.

Radicals in Control

In 1868, as a result of a large freedman vote, six more states were readmitted. Alabama, Arkansas, Florida, Louisiana, North Carolina, and South Carolina all sent Republican delegations, including some black congressmen, to Washington. In the remaining four states—Georgia, Mississippi, Texas, and Virginia—whites obstructed every attempt to set up a government in which blacks participated. The army continued to govern them until 1870.

Johnson vetoed every radical reconstruction bill, repeating his constitutional objections in every message, then watched helplessly as his veto was overridden.

Congress even took partial control of the army away from him and struck at the president's control of his own cabinet officers. The Tenure of Office Act forbade the president to remove any appointed official who had been confirmed by the Senate without the Senate's approval of his dismissal.

It was obvious what was coming. The radicals wanted Johnson to violate the Tenure of Office Act so that they could impeach him. In part because of his constitutional scruples, in part because Secretary of War Stanton had openly thrown in with the radicals—an intolerable disloyalty—he fired Stanton in February 1868. Although Johnson's term had only a year to run, the now vindictive radicals in the House of Representatives drew up articles of impeachment. As provided in the Constitution, the Senate sat as the jury in the case; Chief Justice Salmon B. Chase presided as judge. Conviction, removal of Johnson from office, required two-thirds of the senators.

The Impeachment Trial

All but two of the eleven articles of impeachment dealt with the Tenure of Office Act. Johnson's attorneys argued that

Impeached Presidents

Andrew Johnson was impeached, that is, he was "indicted" by the House of Representatives for offenses grave enough (in the opinion of the radicals) to warrant his removal from office. However, at his trial—the Senate is the "jury" in impeachment cases—Johnson was acquitted and remained in office.

President William Clinton was impeached for perjury and obstruction of justice in 1999. He too, was acquitted. In 1974, articles of impeachment were drawn up against President Richard M. Nixon for lying to Congress. With impeachment a certainty and conviction likely, he resigned the presidency before the House voted.

Forgotten Achievements

Andrew Johnson is remembered only for his battles with the radicals and his impeachment trial, but he did not neglect other issues. Soon after being sworn in, he informed the French minister in Washington that the United States looked on the 34,000 French troops in Mexico "with considerable impatience." The implicit threat of military action contributed to Napoleon III's withdrawal of the garrison.

In March 1867, Secretary of State Seward negotiated a treaty with Russia to purchase Alaska for $7,200,000. Critics called Alaska "Seward's Icebox" and "Seward's Folly." But the fact was that there was little opposition to the bargain. The Senate promptly ratified the treaty and the House appropriated the money to finalize it.

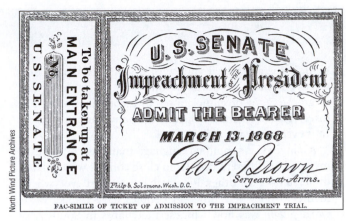

A ticket to the impeachment trial of President Johnson. It was the high point of Washington's social season with the chief justice presiding, the entire Senate sitting as jury, and leading House radicals as prosecutors. The president, however, did not attend; he was acquitted by one vote.

even if the law was constitutional, which was dubious, it did not apply to Johnson's dismissal of Stanton because Johnson had not appointed him to office. Lincoln had. It was a good argument, quite enough to carry the day had the issue been legal rather than political.

The other two articles condemned Johnson for disrespect of Congress, which was silly. Johnson had disrespected Congress alright but, as the president's defenders pointed out, intemperate language did not constitute one of the "high crimes and misdemeanors" stipulated as grounds for impeachment.

The radicals needed thirty-six votes to oust Johnson; if more than eighteen senators voted to acquit him, the impeachment failed. The tally was 35 to 19. Johnson remained president by a single vote.

Actually, it was not that close. The radicals' case was so flimsy that at least six Republican senators who voted to convict in order to save their political careers had said that if their vote was needed to acquit the president, they would vote for him. Events proved they were prudent to vote their careers rather than their consciences. The Republican senator from Kansas who provided Johnson's margin of victory was read out of the party and defeated when he ran for reelection.

The Fifteenth Amendment

In November 1868, the Democratic presidential candidate was New York Governor Horatio Seymour, who had supported the war but been harshly critical of Lincoln. The Republican candidate was Ulysses S. Grant. Grant won easily in the electoral college, 214 to 80. However, close examination of the popular vote indicated that Grant had won several states by a hair. In fact, it appeared that a majority of white voters preferred Seymour; Grant's national plurality was 300,000; he won 500,000 black votes in the southern states.

Grant lost New York by a slender margin. Had all blacks been able to vote in New York (some could, under special circumstances), Grant would have carried the state easily. Grant won Indiana by a handful of votes; had African Americans been able to vote in Indiana (they were not), Grant would have won the state in a landslide.

Thaddeus Stevens had argued in 1865 that the Republican party's future depended on the freedmen voting in the southern states. The election of 1868 indicated that the party's edge in some northern states depended on black men voting there.

Consequently, the Republicans drafted a third "Civil War Amendment." The Fifteenth Amendment forbade states to deny the vote to any person on the basis of "race, color, or previous condition of servitude." Because Republican governments favorable to blacks still controlled most of the southern states, the amendment was easily ratified.

Grant, Race, and the South

U. S. Grant was a close-mouthed man. He was sociable; he liked company and chatting. Except on subjects in which he was expert, however, he expressed few opinions that have survived. His politics before the Civil War were Democratic, but he was clearly not very interested in them. During his interlude as a farmer in Missouri during the 1850s, he several times borrowed his father-in-law's slaves to help him. But, if

Birth of a Legend

The legend of a South "prostrate in the dust" during Reconstruction had its origins during the Reconstruction era. In 1874, journalist James S. Pike wrote of "the spectacle of a society suddenly turned bottomside up. . . . In the place of this old aristocratic society stands the rude form of the most ignorant democracy that mankind ever saw, invested with the functions of government. It is the dregs of the population habilitated in the robes of their intelligent predecessors, and asserting over them the rule of ignorance and corruption, through the inexorable machinery of a majority of numbers. It is barbarism overwhelming civilization by physical force."

Gullah

A *dialect* is a regional variety of a language that is distinctive because of words unique to it, or variant rules of grammar, or pronunciation—or a combination of the three. The nonstandard speech of many African Americans even today is a dialect.

A *pidgin* is a simplified language that was consciously invented by different peoples in close contact who did not understand each other. Pidgins have evolved everywhere in the world where different peoples have traded. (The word *pidgin* was how Chinese merchants in South Asia pronounced "business.") Pidgins are usually based on one dominant language, but they reduce its grammar to bare basics for easy learning and instant communication. Several English-based, French-based, and Portuguese-based pidgins are spoken by hundreds of thousands of people today. The "Hawai'ian accent" is a remnant of what was once a pidgin.

When people elaborate on a pidgin so that it serves as their language, in which they can speak about a broad range of subjects, linguists call the result a *creole*.

Numerous creoles developed among the first Africans in America. Their masters spoke English. The other slaves with whom they worked and lived spoke mutually incomprehensible languages. So, the first generation of slaves created a pidgin so they could understand overseers and fellow slaves. Their children—second generation African Americans—had no use for their parents' mother tongues and they knew more English than their parents had. They transformed the pidgin into a creole.

Almost all slave creoles died out after emancipation. African Americans began to move around during Reconstruction and found their localized creoles useless. However, on the "sea islands" off the coast of South Carolina and Georgia, Gullah, sometimes called Geechee, survives to this day. It is still the language of home, church, and social occasions for thousands of people. At last count, between 5,000 and 8,000 mostly elderly sea islanders spoke only Gullah.

Because Gullah is not a written language, its history is something of a mystery. Even the origin of the name is disputed. The most obvious explanation is that Gullah is a corruption of Angola, which makes sense. During the final years of the legal African slave trade, 1803–1807, sea island planters imported 24,000 Africans, 60 percent of them from Angola (including present-day Congo). However, there is some evidence that the word "Gullah" was in use by 1750. Some linguists think it derives from Gola, a tribe that lived on the border of modern Liberia and Sierra Leone. Sea island planters favored Africans from that region because they were skilled rice growers. Similarities shared by Gullah and a creole still spoken in Sierra Leone, Krio, are so striking that Gullah may have first emerged not on the sea islands but in Africa.

Gullah is not the "southern accent" or "African American dialect." Its sounds are soft and it is spoken rapidly, not drawled. More than 90 percent of its vocabulary is English, but pronunciation differs so radically from American English pronunciation that visitors to the sea islands cannot understand more than the shortest, simplest statements. Spelled out phonetically, however, Gullah is easily deciphered. The first sentence of the Lord's Prayer in Gullah:

> Ow'urr Farruh, hu aht in Heh'um, hallowed be dy name, dy kingdom come, dy wil be done on ut as it done in heh'um.

How did Gullah thrive when other slave creoles died out? Cultural continuity is part of the reason. Before 1800, when the Angolans began to arrive, most sea island slaves' African roots were in a rather limited area of Sierra Leone. The isolation of the sea islands prevented the Gullahs from mixing with mainland slaves, reinforcing their sense of cohesion. Their creole was quite adequate for all their communications. Whites were few on the islands. Work was supervised by black slave drivers and even, at the top, black plantation managers. When the Civil War began, there were more than 33,000 blacks in the Beaufort district of South Carolina, and 6,700 whites. When Union troops occupied the islands early in the war, virtually every white southerner had fled. By 1870, 90 percent of St. Helena island's population was black.

Because of their isolation, the Gullahs were generally more self-sufficient than most mainland slaves. When the Union army put up confiscated sea island plantations for sale, an astonishing number of Gullahs had enough money to buy farms albeit in small parcels. By 1870, seven of ten Gullah families owned their homes and farms.

African religious practices survived after the Gullahs became Methodists or Baptists in the early nineteenth century. White missionaries were frustrated to distraction when islanders explained that while a dead person's "soul" went to live with God in heaven, his "spirit" or ghost continued to roam the islands, sometimes helping descendants, sometimes doing them mischief. Only a century later was it learned that Gullah spirits had West African origins. The word *voodoo* entered the American language through the Gullahs, although, on the sea islands, it simply meant magic with none of the sinister connotations of West Indian voodoo as sensationalized in movies.

African folk tales survived longer and closer to the originals on the sea islands. Joel Chandler Harris, the white journalist who collected the B'rer Rabbit and other slave stories (now known to have African origins) found the sea islands his most productive hunting grounds. In 1925, DuBose Heyward wrote a play, *Porgy*, better known as the opera based on it, *Porgy and Bess.* It was set among Gullahs who, after the Civil War, moved to Charleston.

no abolitionist, he was not comfortable with the institution. The single slave he briefly owned he freed rather than sold, although he was virtually penniless at the time.

His racial attitudes were undoubtedly those of his kind and times. His closest friend in the Civil War army, William Tecumseh Sherman, was an outspoken racist with whom Grant probably agreed, but with none of Sherman's passion. Now president in 1869 at 46 years of age (to that time the youngest president), he immediately understood that he owed his election and the Republican party its dominance to African American voters. Moreover, Grant was unswervingly loyal to those who were loyal to him. The radicals made him president and he turned to them when he needed advice. And his champion in the Senate and chief senatorial adviser was Roscoe Conkling of New York, who believed in African American equality as an ideal as well as an expedient.

During most of Grant's presidency, the Republican party was dominant because, when first admitted to statehood, the southern states sent mostly Republicans to Congress. In some states, where blacks were a majority of the population or nearly so—South Carolina, Mississippi, Louisiana—Republican control was likely as long as African Americans voted. In other southern states, there were enough white Republicans who, combined with a bloc African American vote, comprised a majority.

If blacks were the backbone of the southern party, providing 80 percent of Republican votes, white men ran the party. No African American was elected governor in any state. There were only two black senators, Blanche K. Bruce and Hiram Revels, both from Mississippi. There were fewer than twenty black Republican congressmen. Indeed, blacks filled only a fifth of federal jobs in the South, most in low-level positions. The tyrannical "Black Rule" of which Democrats spoke was a myth.

Corruption

Who were the white Republicans in the South? Some were former Whigs who had opposed secession. In the mountain counties, particularly in Tennessee, a majority of ordinary whites voted Republican. Some Confederates decided that their political future lay with the Republicans and joined the party. Democrats called them "scalawags"—scoundrels, reprobates—who betrayed their neighbors to ignorant, savage former slaves. Northern Republicans who moved South after the war for political purposes or to invest in the development of the shattered economy were known as "carpetbaggers." The message was that they had arrived in the South so poor they could carry everything they owned in a carpetbag, the cheapest sort of suitcase, but were soon rich from looting southern state treasuries along with their scalawag friends and their black stooges.

Lowlife carpetbaggers could be found on the lower levels of the Republican party. But the dozen or so carpetbaggers who rose to high political office were men with money the South sorely needed. The real "crime" of Reconstruction which the Democrats hammered on was the fact that African Americans had a say in government.

There was plenty of corruption, as there inevitably is when governments spend a lot of money in a short time. The Republican legislatures voted huge appropriations for legitimate, even essential programs that the prewar southern legislatures had ignored. There was not a single statewide public school system in any former Confederate state until Reconstruction. The first free schools in the South for white as well as black children were established by the Republican legislatures. Programs for the relief of the destitute and institutions for the handicapped and the insane were few in the prewar South.

The start-up costs were immense. Politicians, all the way at the top, dipped into the flow of money to fill their own purses. The Republican governor of Louisiana, Henry C. Warmoth, banked $100,000 during a year when his salary was $8,000. Favored state contractors padded their bills and bribed state officials not to examine their invoices closely. In 1869, the state of Florida spent as much on its printing bill as had been spent on the entire state government in 1860.

There was nothing uniquely southern in the thievery. The 1860s and 1870s were an era of corruption throughout American society. Civil War contractors had cheated the government. The "Tweed Ring" that looted New York City was Democratic. And the champion crooks in the South were not Reconstruction Republicans but post-Reconstruction Democrats. After a "Black Republican" administration in Mississippi ran a largely corruption-free regime for six years, the first Democratic treasurer of the state absconded with $415,000. This paled compared to the swag E. A. Burke, the first post-Reconstruction treasurer of Louisiana, took with him to Honduras in 1890: $1,777,000.

Redeemers and the Klan

Nevertheless, political corruption was an effective issue for Democrats out to defeat the Republicans at the polls. They persuaded whites who had voted Republican to switch to the Democrats as the only way to avoid ruinous taxes to pay the crooks' bills. Race was an even more effective issue. The spectacle of former slaves who had once said "yes sir" and "no sir" to every white man dressing in frock coats and cravats, making laws, and drinking in hotel bars infuriated whites. Democratic politicians called themselves "Redeemers." They would redeem the captive South from thieving carpetbaggers and scalawags and redeem the white race from the degradation the Yankees had forced on them.

In states where a more-or-less solid white vote could be mobilized to vote Democratic, the solidly Republican black vote could be overcome. Virginia was "redeemed" quickly, North Carolina and Georgia after a short campaign. Elsewhere, Redeemers brought economic pressure on blacks to stay home on election day. Most African Americans were tenants with a family to support. They were inclined to value their leased cabins and acreage more highly than the vote when their landlords told them it was one or the other.

Ku Klux Klan night riders shoot up the house of an African American who voted or, possibly, merely offended whites by insisting on being treated as a free man. At the peak of Klan violence in 1868 and 1869, it is estimated that Klan-like terrorists murdered an average of two people a day, almost all of them blacks.

The Granger Collection, New York

Blacks determined to exercise their rights were met with violence. In 1866, General Nathan Bedford Forrest of Tennessee founded the Ku Klux Klan as a social club for Confederate veterans. Like other men's lodges, the Klan was replete with hocus-pocus, including the wearing of white robes and titles like Kleagle and Grand Wizard.

In 1868, the Klan turned political. The Klan and copycat organizations like the Knights of the White Camelia, masked and riding only at night to avoid Union army detachments, harassed, terrorized, whipped, and murdered carpetbaggers, scalawags, and politically active African Americans. Soon enough the night riders turned on blacks accused of being "impudent." The Klan hit the South like a tornado. The federal government estimated that the Klan murdered 700 in 1868, all but a few of them blacks. The next year was worse. Violence worked. In ever-increasing numbers, African Americans stopped voting.

In 1870 and 1871, Congress passed two Ku Klux Acts which made it a federal offense "to go in disguise upon the public highway . . . with intent to . . . injure, oppress, threaten, or intimidate [citizens] and to prevent them from enjoying their constitutional rights." The laws were effective. The Union army harassed known or suspected Klansmen and wiped out many "Klaverns." Between 1870 and 1872, Texas arrested 6,000 Klansmen. Still, the greatest Klan atrocity occurred in April 1873 when 100 blacks were killed.

By then, five of the former rebel states were in Redeemer hands and the Republicans were facing powerful Democratic opposition in the others. Just as important, northern support for radical Reconstruction was in rapid decline.

GRANT'S TROUBLED ADMINISTRATION

Grant had been lionized after Appomattox. He was showered with gifts, including cold cash. New York City's present to him of $100,000 was just the biggest. Wealthy businessmen and bankers, knowing well he would soon be president, treated him at their clubs and on their yachts. The soldier in a dusty, rumpled uniform was dumbstruck. He took zestfully to the high life, from dining on caviar and *tournedos sauce béarnaise* to wearing silk top hats and well-tailored suits of the best worsteds.

Celebrity and money came too fast to a man who had struggled to pay the bills for thirty years—and for Mrs. Julia Grant, who had struggled to keep her family together. The Grants never quite grasped the fact that their benefactors were not so much appreciating what they had done as they were paying in advance for future favors. There is no evidence that a scintilla of corruption tainted Grant personally. But his administration was shot through with crookery, and Grant's sense of loyalty was so strong that he never punished or even shunned those of his "friends" who disgraced him.

Jim Fisk and Jay Gould

Most of the corruption of the Grant administration was exposed only late in his eight years as president. But there was an odor of corruption in Washington from the start. Henry Adams, the fourth-generation scion of the distinguished Massachusetts family, smelled it in 1869 when he visited the

The Grant Scandals

Only one of the scandals of the Grant years came close to tarring the president himself. Secretary of War William W. Belknap pocketed bribes from a federal contractor who supplied Indian tribes with goods due them under the terms of treaties with the government. Belknap then averted his eyes when the company delivered less than the contract required. He was caught red-handed and resigned, but Grant refused to prosecute him. Officials in the Treasury Department, in cahoots with the president's personal secretary, Orville Babcock, provided excise tax stamps to whiskey distillers at a discount. In effect, they stole the stamps as a clerk in a store might steal cigars. No one was punished.

city. Adams fairly fled Washington, writing that the capital was filled with men of shady character chasing the fast buck and, to all appearances, catching it. Another writer described the Grant years as "the great barbecue" with the government "supplying the beef."

During his first year as president, Grant made the mistake of hitching a ride on the yacht of James "Jubilee Jim" Fisk, a notorious and unabashed financial schemer. Also aboard was Jay Gould who, the previous year, along with Fisk, had bilked the railroader Cornelius Vanderbilt in a stock fraud. The final acts of the drama were played out in public, lovingly chronicled in the newspapers. Gould and Fisk were infamous when Grant accepted their hospitality.

Their purpose in entertaining Grant on a yacht was to be seen with the president. Fisk and Gould created the illusion that they had a privileged relationship with the president. Indeed, they were already scheming with Grant's brother-in-law, Abel R. Corbin. Their plan was to corner the nation's privately owned gold supply, dumping it on the market when the shortage of gold had driven its price to absurd levels. Success depended on the federal government keeping its gold holdings—the largest in the country—in its vaults, off the gold market. Corbin assured Gould and Fisk that, as a trusted relative, he would see to it that Grant would do just that. The party on the yacht was staged to fool the people Gould and Fisk planned to fleece that the president was in cahoots with them.

Black Friday

The two pirates conspicuously snapped up every gold future (a commitment to buy gold at an agreed price at a specified future date) they could. The price of gold soared because of their purchases until, in September 1869, it was selling for $162 an ounce. By taking delivery of gold futures they had purchased at $40 less per ounce, they would make a killing in an instant.

Corbin did his job persuading Grant that by selling government gold, he would cause an agricultural depression. However, Treasury officials, realizing what was happening, persuaded Grant that he would look very bad if he did not

foil Fisk and Gould. On their advice, the president dumped $4 million of the government's gold on the market on Friday, September 24.

The price collapsed. New York's financial community called the day "Black Friday." Businessmen who had purchased gold at bloated prices to pay debts and wages were ruined; thousands of employees of bankrupt companies lost their jobs. And the luster of a great general's reputation was tarnished before he had been president for eight months. Jay Gould did not make as much money as he had hoped he would, but he made plenty. Without informing his partner, he had already sold most of his holdings. Nor did Jim Fisk lose; he simply refused to honor his futures commitments and hired thugs to intimidate those with whom he had signed contracts.

The Election of 1872

By 1872, some Republicans like Henry Adams's father, Charles Francis Adams; Senators Carl Schurz of Missouri, Lyman Trumbull of Illinois, and Charles Sumner of Massachusetts;

Culver Pictures, Inc.

Horace Greeley was one of the country's most influential editors and its best known eccentric. During his long career he had not only supported dozens of reform movements, he had also dabbled at least briefly in as many quack fads: vegetarianism, phrenology, spiritualism, others. He was, therefore, a popular object of ridicule, a terrible pick as a presidential nominee. He was so roundly abused during the presidential campaign of 1872 that it may have contributed to his death shortly after the election.

and crusading editors Horace Greeley of the New York *Tribune* and E.L. Godkin of *The Nation* concluded that, with Grant's acquiescence, thieves were taking over the Republican party.

They were also disgusted by corruption in the southern state governments that, they believed, remained in power only because of Grant's support. Most of the reformers—Sumner was an exception—concluded that the whole idea of entrusting poor and ignorant blacks with the vote was a mistake. Better to allow the Redeemers, Democrats that they were, to take over and run the southern state governments. The dissidents formed the Liberal Republican party and said they would oppose Grant in the presidential election of 1872. Their convention nominated Horace Greeley to run against him.

It was an unwise choice. Greeley was a lifelong eccentric, and he looked it. During his 61 years, he had clambered at least briefly aboard every nutty fad that rolled down the road. His appearance invited ridicule. He looked like a crackpot with his round, pink face, close-set, beady eyes, and a wispy white fringe of chin whiskers. He wore an ankle-length white overcoat on the hottest days, and carried a brightly colored umbrella on the driest. Pro-Grant cartoonists had an easy time making fun of him.

Greeley also was a poor choice because, on their own, the Liberal Republicans had no chance of winning the election. They needed the support of both northern and southern Democrats. The Horace Greeley of 1872 might call for North and South to "clasp hands across the bloody chasm" and denounce carpetbaggers as "as stealing and plucking, many of them with both arms around negroes, and their hands in their rear pockets." The Horace Greeley of 1841–1869 had roasted northern Democrats daily in the *Tribune* and vilified southern Democrats for their espousal of slavery and rebellion.

Nevertheless, the Democrats nominated Greeley. If the liberal Republicans could not hope to win without the Democrats, the Democrats could not hope to win without the liberals. The ratification of the Fifteenth Amendment in 1870 had added tens of thousands of blacks—all Republicans—to the voters' lists.

In fact, the mismatched two-party coalition could not win. With half the southern states still governed by Republicans, and Grant still a hero despite the rumors of scandals, the president won 56 percent of the popular vote and a crushing 286 to 66 victory in the electoral college.

The Twilight of Reconstruction

Poor Greeley died weeks after the election. One by one, dragging their feet, the other liberals returned to the Republican party. Grant would be gone after the election of 1876. Perhaps the party had learned its lesson and would nominate a reformer? In fact, the exposure of several scandals during Grant's second term did just that.

Except for Sumner, who was pushing for a federal civil rights law when he died in 1874 (it was enacted in 1875, thanks to the Grant Republicans in Congress), the liberals of 1872 were not unhappy when, at the end of 1874, Redeemers in Texas, Arkansas, and Mississippi wrestled those states into the Democratic party. By 1876, southern Republicans remained in power only in South Carolina, Florida, and Louisiana.

The Disputed Election

The Democratic candidate in 1876, New York Governor Samuel J. Tilden, said he would withdraw the troops from these three states, which would mean a further reduction in the numbers of black voters and the end of Reconstruction. The Republican candidate, Governor Rutherford B. Hayes of Ohio, ran on a platform pledged to protect African American rights in the South, but Hayes was well known to be skeptical of black capabilities and a personal friend of several southern

Last Gasps

In 1875, in the twilight of the reconstruction era, Congress enacted the Civil Rights Act. It outlawed racial discrimination in public facilities such as hotels and theaters and forbade the exclusion of blacks from juries. Another provision forbidding racially segregated schools was not included. Although the law was not as thoroughgoing as the historic Civil Rights Act of 1964, its purposes were identical.

The 1875 law had no effect on racial discrimination. Rutherford B. Hayes, president in 1877 because he acquiesced to white Democratic control of the South, did not enforce it. In 1883, a number of lawsuits demanding enforcement reached the Supreme Court. In the civil rights cases, with only one dissenting vote, the Court ruled the act unconstitutional because it outlawed social discrimination, which was beyond the authority of Congress. The lone dissenting Justice was John Marshall Harlan, who would also stand alone in defending equal rights for blacks in the famous case *Plessy* v. *Ferguson* case of 1896. (Harlan was a southerner. Indeed, he had briefly been a slave owner.)

In Congress, the last gasp of Republican support for African American rights was the Force Bill of 1890, designed to guarantee southern blacks the right to vote. (It was the equivalent of the Voting Rights Act of 1965.) The House approved the Force Bill, but it failed passage in the Senate when Republican senators from silver-producing states voted against it in return for southern Democratic support of a law propping up the price of silver. That was the end of significant civil rights legislation for more than seventy years.

Democratic politicians. Both candidates were "honest government" men. Tilden had helped destroy a corrupt political ring in New York. As governor of Ohio, Hayes had run a squeaky clean administration.

When the votes were counted, Hayes's personal opinions about the wisdom of Reconstruction seemed beside the point. Tilden won the popular vote narrowly, and he appeared to have won the electoral college 204 to 165. However, Tilden's count included the electoral votes of South Carolina, Florida, and Louisiana, where Republicans still controlled the state governments. On telegraphed instructions from Republican leaders in New York, officials in those three states declared that Hayes had carried their states. According to this set of returns, Hayes eked out a 185 to 184 electoral vote victory.

So, two sets of returns for South Carolina, Florida, and Louisiana reached Washington, one set electing Tilden, the other Hayes. The Constitution provided no guidelines for resolving such a problem. So, Congress created a commission to decide which returns were valid. Five members from each house of Congress and five members of the Supreme Court sat on the panel. Seven of them were Republicans; seven were Democrats. One, David Davis of Illinois, a Supreme Court justice, was known as an independent. No one else was interested in determining the cases on their merits. Each commissioner intended to vote for his party's candidate, no matter what documents were set before him. The burden of naming the next president of the United States fell on David Davis.

He did not like it. No matter how conscientious he was—and Davis had a good reputation—half the country would call for his scalp. Davis prevailed on friends in Illinois to get him off the hook by naming him to a Senate seat that had fallen vacant. He resigned from the court and, thereby, from the commission. His replacement was a Republican justice, and the stage was set for the Republicans to steal the election.

The Compromise of 1877

The commission voted 8 to 7 to accept the Hayes's returns from Louisiana, Florida, and South Carolina—giving Rutherford B. Hayes the presidency by a single electoral vote. Had that been all there was to it, there might well have been violence. At a series of meetings, however, prominent northern and southern politicians and businessmen came to an informal agreement with highly placed southern Republicans who had Redeemer connections.

The "Compromise of 1877" involved several commitments, not all of them honored, by northern capitalists to invest in the South. Also not honored in the end was a vague agreement by conservative southerners to build a white Republican party in the South based on the economic and social views that they shared with northern conservatives.

As to the disputed election, Hayes would move into the White House without Democratic resistance. In return, he would withdraw the remaining troops from South Carolina, Florida, and Louisiana, thus allowing the Democratic party in these states to oust the Republicans and eliminate African American political power. Those parts of the compromise were honored.

FURTHER READING

Classics William A. Dunning, *Reconstruction Political and Economic, 1865–1877*, 1907; John Burgess, *Reconstruction and the Constitution, 1866–1876*, 1908; W. E. B. DuBois, *Black Reconstruction, 1866–1880*, 1935.

General Michael Perman, *Emancipation and Reconstruction, 1862–1879*, 2003; James McPherson, *Ordeal by Fire: The Civil War and Reconstruction*, 1982; Eric Foner, *Reconstruction: America's Unfinished Revolution*, 1988, and *A Short History of Reconstruction*, 1990.

The Southern Economy Michael Goray, *A Ruined Land: The End of the Civil War*, 1999; Roger L. Ransom and Richard Sutch, *One Kind of Freedom: The Economic Consequences of Emancipation*, 1977; James Roark, *Masters Without Slaves: Southern Planters in the Civil War and Reconstruction*, 1977; Lawrence Powell, *New Masters: Northern Planters During the Civil War and Reconstruction*, 1980; Richard N. Current, *Those Terrible Carpetbaggers*, 1988; Gavin Wright, *Old South, New South: Revolutions in the Southern Economy Since the Civil War*, 1986.

Politics LaWanda Cox, *Lincoln and Black Freedom: A Study in Presidential Leadership*, 1981; Peyton McCrary, *Abraham Lincoln and Reconstruction*, 1978; Dan Carter, *When the War Was Over: The Failure of Self-Reconstruction in the South, 1865–1867*, 1985; Michael L. Benedict, *The Impeachment and Trial of Andrew Johnson*, 1973; Brooks D. Simpson, *The Reconstruction Presidents*, 1998; Jean

E. Smith, *Grant*, 2001; Xi Wang, *The Trial of Democracy: Black Suffrage and Northern Republicans, 1860–1910*, 1997; George C. Rable, *But There Was No Peace: The Role of Violence in the Politics of Reconstruction*, 1984; Laura F. Edwards, *Gendered Strife and Confusions: The Political Culture of Reconstruction*, 1997; Otto H. Olson, *Reconstruction and Redemption in the South*, 1980; Michael Perman, *The Road to Redemption: Southern Politics 1868–1879*, 1984; L. Seip, *The South Returns to Congress*, 1983; Dewey Grantham, *Life and Death of the Solid South*, 1988.

African Americans Leon F. Litwack, *Been in the Storm So Long*, 1979; Eric Foner, *Nothing But Freedom*, 1983; James McPherson, *The Struggle for Equality*, 1964; Herman Belz, *Emancipation and Equal Rights*, 1978; Joel Williamson, *The Crucible: Black-White Relations in the American South Since Emancipation*, 1984; Harold O. Rabinowitz, *Southern Black Leaders of the Reconstruction Era*, 1982; William McFeeley, *Frederick Douglass*, 1991; Daniel Stowell, *Rebuilding Zion: The Religious Reconstruction of the South, 1863–1877*, 1998.

The Freedmen's Bureau Robert C. Morris, *Reading, 'Riting, and Reconstruction: The Education of Freedmen in the South, 1861–1870*, 1981; Jacqueline Jones, *Soldiers of Light and Love: Northern Teachers and Georgia Blacks*, 1980; Barry A. Craven *The Freedman's Bureau and Black Texas*, 1992; Donald Nieman, *To Set the Law in Motion: The Freedman's Bureau and the Legal Rights of Blacks, 1865–1868*, 1979; Peter Kolchin, *First Freedom*, 1972.

KEY TERMS

Use the following listing of key terms to review important figures, events, locations, and concepts covered in this chapter. A glossary of these terms is available on *The American* *Past* companion Web site: www.cengage.com/history/conlin/tap9e

freedmen, p. 401

Wade-Davis Bill, p. 401

pocket veto, p. 401

black codes, p. 402

Freedmen's Bureau, p. 404

carpetbaggers and scalawags, p. 409

"Black Friday," p. 411

Greeley, Horace, p. 412

ONLINE RESOURCES

Find additional resources, including primary source documents, images, interactive maps, simulations, chapter review exercises, and Internet links at

***The American Past* companion Web site**
www.cengage.com/history/conlin/tap9e

American History Resource Center
http://ushistory.wadsworth.com/

DISCOVERY

How did the experience of battle temper the fervor with which both northern and southern boys looked at war in the spring of 1861?

Warfare: In his diary, Union Army Private Ephraim A. Wood described conversations with a miller and a young woman in northern Virginia, rebel country occupied by northern troops. What opinion of slavery is expressed? What opinions of the war? How does Wood's report relate to northerners' conventional image of southerners at the time (and the views of some historians since).

Diary of Private Ephraim A. Wood Monday July 7, 1862 (near Warrenton, VA)

"I was supernumery of the Guard this morning. After Guard mounting I went to the brook and had a bath. I then went and got all the cherries that I wanted to eat. I took a walk around the Country. On my travels I came to a mill, the owner of which was close by sitting, on a stone wall talking with a couple of Soldiers. He seemed anxious to have our forces whip the Rebels at Richmond, and that the War would end as soon as possible. The opinion I formed of him was, that he sympathized with the South, but that he thought it was useless for them to hold out any longer and was in hope our forces would conquer as soon as possible. He denounced the Rebel Leaders. The next house I came to I stopped and took dinner, as it was after two O'clock. I had been away from Camp ever since eight O'clock. I found the people here very pleasant and kind. There was two persons in the House, one a Lady of about the age of Fifty, and her daughter, who was about twenty five or six years of age. Here I met two Soldiers, one from this Regt and one from the New York Ninth.

The Youngest Lady entertained us for nearly three hours. She said that she had three brothers in the Rebel Army, whose time of enlistment had expired some time ago, but the Conscript law that was passed, held them in Service over their time. She thought that the Law very unjust, and denounced the Rebel Leaders more severely, then the Miller did. She tried to prevent her brothers from joining the Army in the first place. When the Rebel forces were at Manassas, she said that Gen. Johnsons wife boarded in Warrenton. The slavery question was brought up. She thought that they were better off with their Masters, then they would be if free. She said she did not approve of selling them. She had cried many a time at seeing an infant separated from its Mother and sold to the highest bidder. I got back to Camp a little before six O'clock, just in time to escape a heavy shower. It was said that the thermometer yesterday in the shade stood at a hundred and ten degrees. To day one hundred and three. Very Warm Weather."

Richmond in Ruins

National Archives

In what ways was American society affected more profoundly by the Civil War than by the Mexican War and the War of 1812?

Warfare: This newspaper report from the summer of 1864 and the photograph of Richmond in the spring of 1865 on the preceding page both depict the devastation of parts of the South. In the twenty-first century, such total destruction is familiar. It was not so common in the 1860s. What was new in the Civil War that made such devastation possible? Was the leveling of Richmond (and Atlanta, Georgia) necessary? Why or why not?

The Aftermath of Destruction at a Town Near Washington, D.C., 1864

THE REBEL INVASION
A Visit to the Front lines of Battlefield.
[From the Washington Chronicle, July 14, 1864]

I proceeded north of Fort Stevens on the seventh street road half-a-mile, when I came to the ruins of the residence of Mr. Lay of the city post office, which was destroyed day before yesterday by shell from Fort Stevens to prevent the sharp shooters from occupying it. A little north of this depleted stop are the ruins of the residence of Mr. Carberry, which was also destroyed by our cannonball. Near this place I came upon the new made grave of an unknown cavalry man. Still further north and a mile from Fort Stevens, I came to a fence thrown across the road, and occupied as a breastwork by the rebels the day previous. Here were marks of hard fighting; Union and rebel muskets, broken and unbroken, and thrown aside by their owners, hay piled in a heap by the way; while hats, caps, haversacks, pouches, and thousands of cartridge sand bullets were scattered here and there on both sides of the rebel breastworks and among the rifle pits dug by the Union soldiers in a field near by. Every rail on the fence and the tree show well the work which has been done the last few hours in that vicinity. While I was looking on the scene a squad of Union Calvary passed on the way from the front, escorting [?] rebel captures, covered with dust and apparently worn out with constant traveling and hard service. I proceeded on my way, and visited the residences of Dr. S. Heath and Captain Richardson-Here was a scary

picture. Hearing of the approach of the rebels on Monday morning, they removed the female members of their families to the fort, and before they could return the rebels had possession of the premises. Everything about the place is scattered in great confusion. What clothing could be made use if the rebels exchanged for their less attractive suits. The building is badly shattered by our artillery fire. Eight common balls or shells had passed through one side to the other and the doors, windows, and side boards are filled with bullet marks. In the field south of this house are the graves of eleven rebel dead, and in a corn field on the opposite side in [?] the way fifteen other rebel soldiers rest from their destructive work. In a grove on the opposite from Mr. Blair's residence, was found a book (the eighth volume Byron's works) tacked by a rebels, which I have brought with me, and transcribes the following inscription, while which is written on a fly-leaf:

NEAR WASHINGTON, JULY 12, 1864

Now, Uncle Abe, you had better be quiet the balance of your administration. We only come near your town this time just to show what we could do-but if you go on in your mad career we will come again soon, and then you had better stand from under.

Yours, respectfully,
The Worst Reb you ever saw.
FIFTY-EIGHT VIRGINIA INFANTRY.

To read extended versions of selected documents, visit the companion Web site
www.cengage.com/history/conlin/tap9e; click on "Discovery Sources"

Appendix

The Declaration of Independence

The Constitution of the United States of America

Admission of States

Population of the United States

Presidential Elections

Justices of the U.S. Supreme Court

Political Party Affiliations in Congress and the Presidency

The Declaration of Independence
The Unanimous Declaration of the Thirteen United States of America

When in the Course of human events it becomes necessary for one people to dissolve the political bands which have connected them with another, and to assume among the Powers of the earth, the separate and equal station to which the Laws of Nature and of Nature's God entitle them, a decent respect to the opinions of mankind requires that they should declare the causes which impel them to the separation.

We hold these truths to be self-evident, that all men are created equal, that they are endowed by their Creator with certain unalienable Rights, that among these are Life, Liberty and the pursuit of Happiness. That to secure these rights, Governments are instituted among Men, deriving their just Powers from the consent of the governed. That whenever any Form of Government becomes destructive of these ends, it is the Right of the People to alter or to abolish it, and to institute new Government, laying its foundation on such principles and organizing its Powers in such form, as to them shall seem most likely to effect their Safety and Happiness. Prudence, indeed, will dictate that Governments long established should not be changed for light and transient causes; and accordingly all experience hath shewn, that mankind are more disposed to suffer, while evils are sufferable, than to right themselves by abolishing the forms to which they are accustomed. But when a long train of abuses and usurpations, pursuing invariably the same Object evinces a design to reduce them under absolute Despotism, it is their right, it is their duty, to throw off such Government, and to provide new Guards for their future security. Such has been the patient sufferance of these Colonies; and such is now the necessity which constrains them to alter their former Systems of Government. The history of the present King of Great Britain is a history of repeated injuries and usurpations, all having in direct object the establishment of an absolute Tyranny over these States. To prove this, let Facts be submitted to a candid world.

He has refused his Assent to Laws, the most wholesome and necessary for the public good.

He has forbidden his Governors to pass Laws of immediate and pressing importance, unless suspended in their operation till his Assent should be obtained; and when so suspended, he has utterly neglected to attend to them.

He has refused to pass other Laws for the accommodation of large districts of people, unless those people would relinquish the right of Representation in the Legislature, a right inestimable to them and formidable to tyrants only.

He has called together legislative bodies at places unusual, uncomfortable, and distant from the depository of their Public Records, for the sole Purpose of fatiguing them into compliance with his measures.

He has dissolved Representative Houses repeatedly, for opposing with manly firmness his invasions on the rights of the People.

He has refused for a long time, after such dissolutions, to cause others to be elected; whereby the Legislative Powers, incapable of Annihilation, have returned to the People at large for their exercise; the State remaining in the mean time exposed to all the dangers of invasion from without, and convulsions within.

He has endeavoured to prevent the Population of these States; for that purpose obstructing the Laws for Naturalization of Foreigners; refusing to pass others to encourage their migrations hither, and raising the conditions of new Appropriations of Lands.

He has obstructed the Administration of Justice, by refusing his Assent to Laws for establishing Judiciary Powers.

He has made Judges dependent on his Will alone, for the tenure of their offices, and the amount and payment of their salaries.

He has erected a multitude of New Offices, and sent hither swarms of Officers to harass our People, and eat out their substance.

He has kept among us, in times of peace, Standing Armies without the Consent of our legislatures.

He has affected to render the Military independent of and superior to the Civil Power.

He has combined with others to subject us to a jurisdiction foreign to our constitution, and unacknowledged by our laws; giving his Assent to their Acts of pretended Legislation:

For Quartering large bodies of armed troops among us:

For protecting them, by a mock Trial, from Punishment for any Murders which they should commit on the Inhabitants of these States:

For cutting off our Trade with all parts of the world:

For imposing Taxes on us without our Consent:

For depriving us in many cases, of the benefits of Trial by Jury:

For transporting us beyond Seas to be tried for pretended offences:

For abolishing the free System of English Laws in a neighbouring Province, establishing therein an Arbitrary government, and enlarging its Boundaries so as to render it at once an example and fit instrument for introducing the same absolute rule into these Colonies:

Text is reprinted from the facsimile of the engrossed copy in the National Archives. The original spelling, capitalization, and punctuation have been retained. Paragraphing has been added.

For taking away our Charters, abolishing our most valuable Laws, and altering fundamentally the Forms of our Governments:

For suspending our own Legislatures, and declaring themselves invested with Power to legislate for us in all cases whatsoever.

He has abdicated Government here, by declaring us out of his Protection, and waging War against us.

He has plundered our seas, ravaged our Coasts, burnt our towns, and destroyed the lives of our people.

He is at this time transporting large Armies of foreign Mercenaries to compleat the works of death, desolation and tyranny, already begun with circumstances of Cruelty and perfidy scarcely paralleled in the most barbarous ages, and totally unworthy the Head of a civilized nation.

He has constrained our fellow Citizens taken Captive on the high Seas to bear Arms against their Country, to become the executioners of their friends and Brethren, or to fall themselves by their Hands.

He has excited domestic insurrections amongst us, and has endeavoured to bring on the inhabitants of our frontiers, the merciless Indian Savages, whose known rule of warfare, is an undistinguished destruction of all ages, sexes and conditions.

In every stage of these Oppressions We have Petitioned for Redress in the most humble terms: Our repeated Petitions have been answered only by repeated injury. A Prince, whose character is thus marked by every act which may define a Tyrant, is unfit to be the ruler of a free People.

Nor have We been wanting in attentions to our British brethren. We have warned them from time to time of attempts by their legislature to extend an unwarrantable jurisdiction over us. We have reminded them of the circumstances of our emigration and settlement here. We have appealed to their native justice and magnanimity, and we have conjured them by the ties of our common kindred to disavow thee usurpations, which, would inevitably interrupt our connections and correspondence. They too have been deaf to the voice of justice and of consanguinity. We must, therefore, acquiesce in the necessity, which denounces our Separation, and hold them, as we hold the rest of mankind, Enemies in War, in Peace Friends.

WE, THEREFORE, the Representatives of the UNITED STATES OF AMERICA, in General Congress, Assembled, appealing to the Supreme Judge of the world for the rectitude of our intentions, do, in the Name, and by Authority of the good People of these Colonies, solemnly publish and declare, That these United Colonies are, and of Right ought to be FREE AND INDEPENDENT STATES; that they are Absolved from all Allegiance to the British Crown, and that all political connection between them and the State of Great Britain, is and ought to be totally dissolved; and that, as Free and Independent States, they have full Power to levy War, conclude Peace, contract Alliances, establish Commerce, and to do all other Acts and Things which Independent States may of right do. And for the support of this Declaration, with a firm reliance on the protection of divine Providence, we mutually pledge to each other our Lives, our Fortunes and our sacred Honor.

The Constitution of the United States of America

We the People of the United States, in Order to form a more perfect Union, establish Justice, insure domestic Tranquility, provide for the common defence, promote the general Welfare, and secure the Blessings of Liberty to ourselves and our Posterity, do ordain and establish this Constitution for the United States of America.

Article. I.

SECTION. 1. All legislative Powers herein granted shall be vested in a Congress of the United States, which shall consist of a Senate and House of Representatives.

SECTION. 2. The House of Representatives shall be composed of Members chosen every second Year by the People of the several States, and the Electors in each State shall have the Qualifications requisite for Electors of the most numerous Branch of the State Legislature.

No Person shall be a Representative who shall not have attained to the Age of twenty five Years, and been seven Years a Citizen of the United States, and who shall not, when elected, be an Inhabitant of that State in which he shall be chosen.

Representatives and direct Taxes[1] shall be apportioned among the several States which may be included within this Union, according to their respective Numbers, which shall be determined by adding to the whole Number of free Persons, including those bound to Service for a Term of Years, and excluding Indians not taxed, three fifths of all other Persons.[2] The actual Enumeration shall be made within three Years after the first Meeting of the Congress of the United States, and within every subsequent Term of ten Years, in such Manner as they shall by Law direct. The Number of Representatives shall not exceed one for every thirty Thousand, but each State shall have at Least one Representative; and until such enumeration shall be made, the State of New Hampshire shall be entitled to chuse three; Massachusetts eight; Rhode Island and Providence Plantations one; Connecticut five; New York six; New Jersey four; Pennsylvania eight; Delaware one; Maryland six; Virginia ten; North Carolina five; South Carolina five; and Georgia three.

When vacancies happen in the Representation from any State, the Executive Authority thereof shall issue Writs of Election to fill such Vacancies.

The House of Representatives shall chuse their Speaker and other Officers; and shall have the sole Power of Impeachment.

SECTION. 3. The Senate of the United States shall be composed of two Senators from each State, chosen by the Legislature thereof, for six Years; and each Senator shall have one Vote.[3]

Immediately after they shall be assembled in Consequence of the first Election, they shall be divided as equally as may be into three Classes. The Seats of the Senators of the first Class shall be vacated at the Expiration of the second Year, of the second Class at the Expiration of the fourth Year, and of the third Class at the Expiration of the sixth Year, so that one third may be chosen every second Year; and if Vacancies happen by Resignation, or otherwise, during the Recess of the Legislature of any State, the Executive thereof may make temporary Appointments until the next Meeting of the Legislature, which shall then fill such Vacancies.[4]

No Person shall be a Senator who shall not have attained to the Age of thirty Years, and been nine Years a Citizen of the United States, and who shall not, when elected, be an Inhabitant of that State for which he shall be chosen.

The Vice President of the United States shall be President of the Senate, but shall have no Vote, unless they be equally divided.

The Senate shall chuse their other Officers, and also a President pro tempore, in the Absence of the Vice President, or when he shall exercise the Office of President of the United States.

The Senate shall have the sole Power to try all Impeachments. When sitting for that Purpose, they shall be on Oath or Affirmation. When the President of the United States is tried, the Chief Justice shall preside: And no Person shall be convicted without the Concurrence of two thirds of the Members present.

Judgment in Cases of Impeachment shall not extend further than to removal from Office, and disqualification to hold and enjoy any Office of honor, Trust or Profit under the United States: but the Party convicted shall nevertheless be liable and subject to Indictment, Trial, Judgment and Punishment, according to Law.

SECTION. 4. The Times, Places and Manner of holding Elections for Senators and Representatives, shall be prescribed in each State by the Legislature thereof, but the Congress may at any time by Law make or alter such Regulation, except as to the Places of chusing Senators.

The Congress shall assemble at least once in every Year, and such Meeting shall be on the first Monday in December, unless they shall by Law appoint a different Day.[5]

SECTION. 5. Each House shall be the Judge of the Elections, Returns and Qualifications of its own Members, and a Majority of each shall constitute a Quorum to do Business; but a smaller Number may adjourn from day to day, and may be authorized to compel the Attendance of absent Members,

---

Text is from the engrossed copy in the National Archives. Original spelling, capitalization, and punctuation have been retained.

[1]Modified by the Sixteenth Amendment.

[2]Replaced by the Fourteenth Amendment.

[3]Superseded by the Seventeenth Amendment.

[4]Modified by the Seventeenth Amendment.

[5]Superseded by the Twentieth Amendment.

in such Manner, and under such Penalties as each House may provide.

Each House may determine the Rules of its Proceedings, punish its Members for disorderly Behaviour, and, with the Concurrence of two thirds, expel a Member.

Each House shall keep a Journal of its Proceedings, and from time to time publish the same, excepting such Parts as may in their Judgment require Secrecy; and the Yeas and Nays of the Members of either House on any question shall, at the Desire of one fifth of those Present, be entered on the Journal.

Neither House, during the Session of Congress, shall, without the Consent of the other, adjourn for more than three days, nor to any other Place than that in which the two Houses shall be sitting.

SECTION. 6. The Senators and Representatives shall receive a Compensation for their Services, to be ascertained by Law, and paid out of the Treasury of the United States. They shall in all Cases, except Treason, Felony and Breach of the Peace, be privileged from Arrest during their Attendance at the Session of their respective Houses, and in going to and returning from the same; and for any Speech or Debate in either House, they shall not be questioned in any other Place.

No Senator or Representative shall, during the Time for which he was elected, be appointed to any civil Office under the Authority of the United States, which shall have been created, or the Emoluments whereof shall have been encreased during such time; and no Person holding any Office under the United States, shall be a Member of either House during his Continuance in Office.

SECTION. 7. All Bills for raising Revenue shall originate in the House of Representatives; but the Senate may propose or concur with Amendments as on other Bills.

Every Bill which shall have passed the House of Representatives and the Senate shall, before it become a Law, be presented to the President of the United States; If he approve he shall sign it, but if not he shall return it, with his Objections to that House in which it shall have originated, who shall enter the Objections at large on their Journal, and proceed to reconsider it. If after such Reconsideration two thirds of that House shall agree to pass the Bill, it shall be sent, together with the Objections, to the other House, by which it shall likewise be reconsidered, and if approved by two thirds of that House, it shall become a Law. But in all such Cases the Votes of both Houses shall be determined by yeas and Nays, and the Names of the Persons voting for and against the Bill shall be entered on the Journal of each House respectively. If any Bill shall not be returned by the President within ten Days (Sundays excepted) after it shall have been presented to him, the Same shall be a Law, in like Manner as if he had signed it, unless the Congress by their Adjournment prevent its Return, in which Case it shall not be a Law.

Every Order, Resolution, or Vote to which the Concurrence of the Senate and House of Representatives may be necessary (except on a question of Adjournment) shall be presented to the President of the United States; and before the Same shall take Effect, shall be approved by him, or being disapproved by him shall be repassed by two thirds of the Senate and House of Representatives, according to the Rules and Limitations prescribed in the Case of a Bill.

SECTION. 8. The Congress shall have power To lay and collect Taxes, Duties, Imposts and Excises, to pay the Debts and provide for the common Defence and general Welfare of the United States; but all Duties, Imposts and Excises shall be uniform throughout the United States;

To borrow Money on the credit of the United States;

To regulate Commerce with foreign Nations, and among the several States, and with the Indian Tribes;

To establish an uniform Rule of Naturalization, and uniform Laws on the subject of Bankruptcies throughout the United States;

To coin Money, regulate the Value thereof, and of foreign Coin, and fix the Standard of Weights and Measures;

To provide for the Punishment of counterfeiting the Securities and current Coin of the United States;

To establish Post Offices and post Roads;

To promote the Progress of Science and useful Arts, by securing for limited Times to Authors and Inventors the exclusive Right to their respective Writings and Discoveries;

To constitute Tribunals inferior to the Supreme Court;

To define and punish Piracies and Felonies committed on the high Seas, and Offences against the Law of Nations;

To declare War, grant Letters of Marque and Reprisal, and make Rules concerning Captures on Land and Water;

To raise and support Armies, but no Appropriation of Money to that Use shall be for a longer Term than two Years;

To provide and maintain a Navy;

To make Rules for the Government and Regulation of the land and naval Forces;

To provide for calling forth the Militia to execute the Laws of the Union, suppress Insurrections and repel Invasions;

To provide for organizing, arming, and disciplining, the Militia, and for governing such Part of them as may be employed in the Service of the United States, reserving to the States respectively, the Appointment of the Officers, and the Authority of training the Militia according to the discipline prescribed by Congress;

To exercise exclusive Legislation in all Cases whatsoever, over such District (not exceeding ten Miles square) as may, by Cession of particular States, and the Acceptance of Congress, become the Seat of the Government of the United States, and to exercise like Authority over all Places purchased by the Consent of the Legislature of the State in which the Same shall be, for the Erection of Forts, Magazines, Arsenals, dock-Yards, and other needful Buildings;—And

To make all Laws which shall be necessary and proper for carrying into Execution the foregoing Powers, and all other Powers vested by this Constitution in the Government of the United States, or in any Department or Officer thereof.

SECTION. 9. The Migration or Importation of such Persons as any of the States now existing shall think proper to admit, shall not be prohibited by the Congress prior to the Year one thousand eight hundred and eight, but a Tax or duty may be imposed on such Importation, not exceeding ten dollars for each Person.

The Privilege of the Writ of Habeas Corpus shall not be suspended, unless when in Cases of Rebellion or Invasion the public Safety may require it.

No Bill of Attainder or ex post facto Law shall be passed.

No Capitation, or other direct, Tax shall be laid, unless in Proportion to the Census or Enumeration herein before directed to be taken.

No Tax or Duty shall be laid on Articles exported from any State.

No Preference shall be given by any Regulation of Commerce or Revenue to the Ports of one State over those of another: nor shall Vessels bound to, or from, one State, be obliged to enter, clear, or pay Duties in another.

No Money shall be drawn from the Treasury, but in Consequence of Appropriations made by Law, and a regular Statement and Account of the Receipts and Expenditures of all public Money shall be published from time to time.

No Title of Nobility shall be granted by the United States: And no Person holding any Office of Profit or Trust under them, shall, without the Consent of the Congress, accept of any present, Emolument, Office, or Title, of any kind whatever, from any King, Prince, or foreign State.

SECTION. 10. No State shall enter into any Treaty, Alliance, or Confederation; grant Letters of Marque and Reprisal; coin Money; emit Bills of Credit; make any Thing but gold and silver Coin a Tender in Payment of Debts; pass any Bill of Attainder, ex post facto Law, or Law impairing the Obligation of Contracts, or grant any Title of Nobility.

No State shall, without the Consent of the Congress, lay any Imposts or Duties on Imports or Exports, except what may be absolutely necessary for executing its inspection Laws: and the net Produce of all Duties and Imposts, laid by any State on Imports or Exports, shall be for the Use of the Treasury of the United States; and all such Laws shall be subject to the Revision and Controul of the Congress.

No State shall, without the Consent of Congress, lay any Duty of Tonnage, keep Troops, or Ships of War in time of Peace, enter into any Agreement or Compact with another State, or with a foreign Power, or engage in War, unless actually invaded, or in such imminent Danger as will not admit of delay.

Article. II.

SECTION. 1. The executive Power shall be vested in a President of the United States of America. He shall hold his Office during the Term of four Years, and, together with the Vice President, chosen for the same Term, be elected, as follows:

Each State shall appoint, in such Manner as the Legislature thereof may direct, a Number of Electors, equal to the whole Number of Senators and Representatives to which the State may be entitled in the Congress: but no Senator or Representative, or Person holding an Office of Trust or Profit under the United States, shall be appointed an Elector.

The Electors shall meet in their respective States, and vote by Ballot for two Persons, of whom one at least shall not be an Inhabitant of the same State with themselves. And they shall make a List of all the Persons voted for, and of the Number of Votes for each; which List they shall sign and certify, and transmit sealed to the Seat of the Government of the United States, directed to the President of the Senate. The President of the Senate shall, in the Presence of the Senate and House of Representatives, open all the Certificates, and the Votes shall then be counted. The Person having the greatest Number of Votes shall be the President, if such Number be a Majority of the whole Number of Electors appointed; and if there be more than one who have such Majority, and have an equal Number of Votes, then the House of Representatives shall immediately chuse by Ballot one of them for President; and if no Person have a Majority, then from the five highest on the List the said House shall in like Manner chuse the President. But in chusing the President, the Votes shall be taken by States, the Representation from each State having one Vote; A quorum for this Purpose shall consist of a Member or Members from two thirds of the States, and a Majority of all the States shall be necessary to a Choice. In every Case, after the Choice of the President, the Person having the greatest Number of Votes of the Electors shall be the Vice President. But if there should remain two or more who have equal Votes, the Senate shall chuse from them by Ballot the Vice President.[6]

The Congress may determine the Time of chusing the Electors, and the Day on which they shall give their Votes; which Day shall be the same throughout the United States.

No Person except a natural born Citizen, or a Citizen of the United States, at the time of the Adoption of this Constitution, shall be eligible to the Office of President, neither shall any Person be eligible to that Office who shall not have attained to the Age of thirty five Years, and been fourteen Years a Resident within the United States.

In Case of the Removal of the President from Office, or of his Death, Resignation, or Inability to discharge the Powers and Duties of the said Office, the Same shall devolve on the Vice President, and the Congress may by Law provide for the Case of Removal, Death, Resignation or Inability, both of the President and Vice President, declaring what Officer shall then act as President, and such Officer shall act accordingly, until the Disability be removed, or a President shall be elected.[7]

The President shall, at stated Times, receive for his Services, a Compensation, which shall neither be encreased nor diminished during the Period for which he shall have been elected, and he shall not receive within that Period any other Emolument from the United States, or any of them.

Before he enter on the Execution of his Office, he shall take the following Oath or Affirmation:—"I do solemnly swear (or affirm) that I will faithfully execute the Office of President of the United States, and will to the best of my Ability, preserve, protect and defend the Constitution of the United States."

SECTION. 2. The President shall be Commander in Chief of the Army and Navy of the United States, and of the Militia of the several States, when called into the actual Service of the

---

[6]Superseded by the Twelfth Amendment.

[7]Modified by the Twenty-fifth Amendment.

United States; he may require the Opinion, in writing, of the principal Officer in each of the executive Departments, upon any Subject relating to the Duties of their respective Offices, and he shall have Power to grant Reprieves and Pardons for Offences against the United States, except in Cases of Impeachment.

He shall have Power, by and with the Advice and Consent of the Senate, to make Treaties, provided two thirds of the Senators present concur; and he shall nominate, and by and with the Advice and Consent of the Senate, shall appoint Ambassadors, other public Ministers and Consuls, Judges of the supreme Court, and all other Officers of the United States, whose Appointments are not herein otherwise provided for, and which shall be established by Law; but the Congress may by Law vest the Appointment of such inferior Officers, as they think proper, in the President alone, in the Courts of Law, or in the Heads of Departments.

The President shall have Power to fill up all Vacancies that may happen during the Recess of the Senate, by granting Commissions which shall expire at the End of their next Session.

SECTION. 3. He shall from time to time give the Congress Information of the State of the Union, and recommend to their Consideration such Measures as he shall judge necessary and expedient; he may, on extraordinary Occasions, convene both Houses, or either of them, and in Case of Disagreement between them, with Respect to the Time of Adjournment, he may adjourn them to such Time as he shall think proper; he shall receive Ambassadors and other public Ministers; he shall take Care that the Laws be faithfully executed, and shall Commission all the Officers of the United States.

SECTION. 4. The President, Vice President and all civil Officers of the United States, shall be removed from Office on Impeachment for, and Conviction of, Treason, Bribery, or other high Crimes and Misdemeanors.

Article. III.

SECTION. 1. The judicial Power of the United States, shall be vested in one supreme Court, and in such inferior Courts as the Congress may from time to time ordain and establish. The Judges, both of the supreme and inferior Courts, shall hold their Offices during good Behaviour, and shall, at stated Times, receive for their Services, a Compensation, which shall not be diminished during their Continuance in Office.

SECTION. 2. The judicial Power shall extend to all Cases, in Law and Equity, arising under this Constitution, the Laws of the United States, and Treaties made, or which shall be made, under their Authority;-to all Cases affecting Ambassadors, other public Ministers and Consuls;—to all Cases of admiralty and maritime Jurisdiction;—to Controversies to which the United States shall be a Party;—to Controversies between two or more States;—between a State and Citizens of another State;[8]—between Citizens of different States,— between Citizens of the same State claiming Lands under

Grants of different States, and between a State, or the Citizens thereof, and foreign States, Citizens or Subjects.

In all Cases affecting Ambassadors, other public Ministers and Consuls, and those in which a State shall be Party, the supreme Court shall have original Jurisdiction. In all the other Cases before mentioned, the supreme Court shall have appellate Jurisdiction, both as to Law and Fact, with such Exceptions, and under such Regulations as the Congress shall make.

The Trial of all Crimes, except in Cases of Impeachment, shall be by Jury; and such Trial shall be held in the State where the said Crimes shall have been committed; but when not committed within any State, the Trial shall be at such Place or Places as the Congress may by Law have directed.

SECTION. 3. Treason against the United States, shall consist only in levying War against them, or in adhering to their Enemies, giving them Aid and Comfort. No Person shall be convicted of Treason unless on the Testimony of two Witnesses to the same overt Act, or on Confession in open Court.

The Congress shall have Power to declare the Punishment of Treason, but no Attainder of Treason shall work Corruption of Blood, or Forfeiture except during the Life of the Person attainted.

Article. IV.

SECTION. 1. Full Faith and Credit shall be given in each State to the public Acts, Records, and judicial Proceedings of every other State. And the Congress may by general Laws prescribe the Manner in which such Acts, Records and Proceedings shall be proved, and the Effect thereof.

SECTION. 2. The Citizens of each State shall be entitled to all Privileges and Immunities of Citizens in the several States.

A Person charged in any State with Treason, Felony, or other Crime, who shall flee from Justice, and be found in another State, shall on Demand of the executive Authority of the State from which he fled, be delivered up, to be removed to the State having Jurisdiction of the Crime.

No Person held to Service or Labour in one State, under the Laws thereof, escaping into another, shall, in Consequence of any Law or Regulation therein, be discharged from such Service or Labour, but shall be delivered up on Claim of the Party to whom such Service or Labour may be due.

SECTION. 3. New States may be admitted by the Congress into this Union; but no new State shall be formed or erected within the Jurisdiction of any other State, nor any State be formed by the Junction of two or more States, or Parts of States, without the Consent of the Legislatures of the States concerned as well as of the Congress.

The Congress shall have Power to dispose of and make all needful Rules and Regulations respecting the Territory or other Property belonging to the United States; and nothing in this Constitution shall be so construed as to Prejudice any Claims of the United States, or of any particular State.

SECTION. 4. The United States shall guarantee to every State in this Union a Republican Form of Government, and shall protect each of them against Invasion; and on Application

---

[8]Modified by the Eleventh Amendment.

of the Legislature, or of the Executive (when the Legislature cannot be convened) against domestic Violence.

Article. V.

The Congress, whenever two thirds of both Houses shall deem it necessary, shall propose Amendments to this Constitution, or, on the Application of the Legislatures of two thirds of the several States, shall call a Convention for proposing Amendments, which, in either Case, shall be valid to all Intents and Purposes, as Part of this Constitution, when ratified by the Legislatures of three fourths of the several States, or by Conventions in three fourths thereof, as the one or the other Mode of Ratification may be proposed by the Congress; Provided that no Amendment which may be made prior to the Year One thousand eight hundred and eight shall in any Manner affect the first and fourth Clauses in the Ninth Section of the first Article; and that no State, without its Consent, shall be deprived of its equal Suffrage in the Senate.

Article. VI.

All Debts contracted and Engagements entered into, before the Adoption of this Constitution, shall be as valid against the United States under this Constitution, as under the Confederation.

This Constitution, and the Laws of the United States which shall be made in Pursuance thereof; and all Treaties made, or which shall be made, under the Authority of the United States, shall be the supreme Law of the Land; and the Judges in every State shall be bound thereby, any Thing in the Constitution or Laws of any State to the Contrary notwithstanding.

The Senators and Representatives before mentioned, and the Members of the several State Legislatures, and all executive and judicial Officers, both of the United States and of the several States, shall be bound by Oath or Affirmation, to support this Constitution; but no religious Test shall ever be required as a Qualification to any Office or public Trust under the United States.

Article. VII.

The Ratification of the Conventions of nine States, shall be sufficient for the Establishment of this Constitution between the States so ratifying the Same.

Done in Convention by the Unanimous Consent of the States present the Seventeenth Day of September in the Year of our Lord one thousand seven hundred and Eighty seven and of the Independence of the United States of America the Twelfth. **In witness** whereof We have hereunto subscribed our Names,
Articles in Addition to, and Amendment of, the Constitution of the United States of America, Proposed by Congress, and Ratified by the Legislatures of the Several States, Pursuant to the Fifth Article of the Original Constitution.

Amendment I[9]

Congress shall make no law respecting an establishment of religion, or prohibiting the free exercise thereof; or abridging the freedom of speech, or of the press; or the right of the people peaceably to assemble, and to petition the Government for a redress of grievances.

Amendment II

A well regulated Militia, being necessary to the security of a free State, the right of the people to keep and bear Arms shall not be infringed.

Amendment III

No Soldier shall, in time of peace, be quartered in any house, without the consent of the Owner, nor in time of war, but in a manner to be prescribed by law.

Amendment IV

The right of the people to be secure in their persons, houses, papers, and effects, against unreasonable searches and seizures, shall not be violated, and no Warrants shall issue, but upon probable cause, supported by Oath or affirmation, and particularly describing the place to be searched, and the persons or things to be seized.

Amendment V

No person shall be held to answer for a capital or otherwise infamous crime, unless on a presentment or indictment of a Grand Jury, except in cases arising in the land or naval forces, or in the Militia, when in actual service in time of War or public danger; nor shall any person be subject for the same offence to be twice put in jeopardy of life or limb; nor shall be compelled in any criminal case to be a witness against himself, nor be deprived of life, liberty, or property, without due process of law; nor shall private property be taken for public use, without just compensation.

Amendment VI

In all criminal prosecutions, the accused shall enjoy the right to a speedy and public trial, by an impartial jury of the State and district wherein the crime shall have been committed, which district shall have been previously ascertained by law, and to be informed of the nature and cause of the accusation; to be confronted with the witnesses against him; to have compulsory process for obtaining witnesses in his favor, and to have the Assistance of Counsel for his defence.

Amendment VII

In suits at common law, where the value in controversy shall exceed twenty dollars, the right of trial by jury shall be preserved, and no fact tried by a jury, shall be otherwise reexamined in any Court of the United States, than according to the rules of the common law.

Amendment VIII

Excessive bail shall not be required, nor excessive fines imposed, nor cruel and unusual punishments inflicted.

Amendment IX

The enumeration in the Constitution, of certain rights, shall not be construed to deny or disparage others retained by the people.

---

[9]The first ten amendments were passed by Congress September 25, 1789. They were ratified by three-fourths of the states December 15, 1791.

Amendment X

The powers not delegated to the United States by the Constitution; nor prohibited by it to the States, are reserved to the States respectively, or to the people.

Amendment XI[10]

The Judicial power of the United States shall not be construed to extend to any suit in law or equity, commenced or prosecuted against one of the United States by Citizens of another State, or by Citizens or Subjects of any Foreign State.

Amendment XII[11]

The Electors shall meet in their respective States and vote by ballot for President and Vice-President, one of whom, at least, shall not be an inhabitant of the same State with themselves; they shall name in their ballots the person voted for as President, and in distinct ballots the person voted for as Vice-President, and they shall make distinct lists of all persons voted for as President, and of all persons voted for as Vice-President, and of the number of votes for each, which lists they shall sign and certify, and transmit sealed to the seat of the government of the United States, directed to the President of the Senate;—The President of the Senate shall, in the presence of the Senate and House of Representatives, open all the certificates and the votes shall then be counted;—The person having the greatest number of votes for President, shall be the President, if such number be a majority of the whole number of Electors appointed; and if no person have such majority, then from the persons having the highest numbers not exceeding three on the list of those voted for as President, the House of Representatives shall choose immediately, by ballot, the President. But in choosing the President, the votes shall be taken by states, the representation from each state having one vote; a quorum for this purpose shall consist of a member or members from two-thirds of the states, and a majority of all the states shall be necessary to a choice. And if the House of Representatives shall not choose a President whenever the right of choice shall devolve upon them, before the fourth day of March next following, then the Vice-President shall act as President, as in the case of the death or other constitutional disability of the President.—The person having the greatest number of votes as Vice-President, shall be the Vice-President, if such number be a majority of the whole number of Electors appointed, and if no person have a majority, then from the two highest numbers on the list, the Senate shall choose the Vice-President; a quorum for the purpose shall consist of two-thirds of the whole number of Senators, and a majority of the whole number shall be necessary to a choice. But no person constitutionally ineligible to the office of President shall be eligible to that of Vice-President of the United States.

Amendment XIII[12]

SECTION. 1. Neither slavery nor involuntary servitude, except as a punishment for crime whereof the party shall have been duly convicted, shall exist within the United States, or any place subject to their jurisdiction.

SECTION. 2. Congress shall have power to enforce this article by appropriate legislation.

Amendment XIV[13]

SECTION. 1. All persons born or naturalized in the United States, and subject to the jurisdiction thereof, are citizens of the United States and of the State wherein they reside. No State shall make or enforce any law which shall abridge the privileges or immunities of citizens of the United States; nor shall any State deprive any person of life, liberty, or property, without due process of law; nor deny to any person within its jurisdiction the equal protection of the laws.

SECTION. 2. Representatives shall be apportioned among the several States according to their respective numbers, counting the whole number of persons in each State, excluding Indians not taxed. But when the right to vote at any election for the choice of electors for President and Vice-President of the United States, Representatives in Congress, the Executive and Judicial officers of a State, or the members of the Legislature thereof, is denied to any of the male inhabitants of such State, being twenty-one years of age, and citizens of the United States, or in any way abridged, except for participation in rebellion, or other crime, the basis of representation therein shall be reduced in the proportion which the number of such male citizens shall bear to the whole number of male citizens twenty-one years of age in such State.

SECTION. 3. No person shall be a Senator or Representative in Congress, or elector of President and Vice-President, or hold any office, civil or military, under the United States, or under any State, who, having previously taken an oath, as a member of Congress, or as an officer of the United States, or as a member of any State legislature, or as an executive or judicial officer of any State, to support the Constitution of the United States, shall have engaged in insurrection or rebellion against the same, or given aid or comfort to the enemies thereof. But Congress may by a vote of two-thirds of each House, remove such disability.

SECTION. 4. The validity of the public debt of the United States, authorized by law, including debts incurred for payment of pensions and bounties for services in suppressing insurrection or rebellion, shall not be questioned. But neither the United States nor any State shall assume or pay any debt or obligation incurred in aid of insurrection or rebellion against the United States, or any claim for the loss or emancipation of any slave; but all such debts, obligations, and claims shall be held illegal and void.

SECTION. 5. The Congress shall have the power to enforce, by appropriate legislation, the provisions of this article.

---

[10]Passed March 4, 1794. Ratified January 23, 1795.

[11]Passed December 9, 1803. Ratified June 15, 1804.

[12]Passed January 31, 1865. Ratified December 6, 1865.

[13]Passed June 13, 1866. Ratified July 9, 1868.

Amendment XV[14]

SECTION. 1. The right of citizens of the United States to vote shall not be denied or abridged by the United States or by any State on account of race, color, or previous conditions of servitude—

SECTION. 2. The Congress shall have power to enforce this article by appropriate legislation.

Amendment XVI

The Congress shall have power to lay and collect taxes on incomes, from whatever source derived, without apportionment among the several States, and without regard to any census or enumeration.

Amendment XVII[15]

The Senate of the United States shall be composed of two Senators from each State, elected by the people thereof, for six years; and each Senator shall have one vote. The electors in each State shall have the qualifications requisite for electors of the most numerous branch of the State legislatures.

When vacancies happen in the representation of any State in the Senate, the executive authority of such State shall issue writs of election to fill such vacancies: Provided, That the legislature of any State may empower the executive thereof to make temporary appointments until the people fill the vacancies by election as the legislature may direct.

This amendment shall not be so construed as to affect the election or term of any Senator chosen before it becomes valid as part of the Constitution.

Amendment XVIII[16]

SECTION. 1. After one year from the ratification of this article the manufacture, sale, or transportation of intoxicating liquors within, the importation thereof into, or the exportation thereof from the United States and all territory subject to the jurisdiction thereof for beverage purposes is hereby prohibited.

SECTION. 2. The Congress and the several States shall have concurrent power to enforce this article by appropriate legislation.

SECTION. 3. This article shall be inoperative unless it shall have been ratified as an amendment to the Constitution by the legislatures of the several States, as provided in the Constitution, within seven years from the date of the submission hereof to the States by the Congress.

Amendment XIX[17]

The right of citizens of the United States to vote shall not be denied or abridged by the United States or by any State on account of sex.

Congress shall have power to enforce this article by appropriate legislation.

Amendment XX[18]

SECTION. 1. The terms of the President and Vice-President shall end at noon on the 20th day of January, and the terms of Senators and Representatives at noon on the 3d day of January, of the years in which such terms would have ended if this article had not been ratified; and the terms of their successors shall then begin.

SECTION. 2. The Congress shall assemble at least once in every year, and such meeting shall begin at noon on the 3d day of January, unless they shall by law appoint a different day.

SECTION. 3. If, at the time fixed for the beginning of the term of the President, the President elect shall have died the Vice-President elect shall become President. If a President shall not have been chosen before the time fixed for the beginning of his term, or if the President elect shall have failed to qualify, then the Vice-President elect shall act as President until a President shall have qualified; and the Congress may by law provide for the case wherein neither a President elect nor a Vice-President elect shall have qualified, declaring who shall then act as President, or the manner in which one who is to act shall be selected, and such person shall act accordingly until a President or Vice-President shall have qualified.

SECTION. 4. The Congress may by law provide for the case of the death of any of the persons from whom the House of Representatives may choose a President whenever the right of choice shall have devolved upon them, and for the case of the death of any of the persons from whom the Senate may choose a Vice-President whenever the right of choice shall have devolved upon them.

SECTION. 5. Sections 1 and 2 shall take effect on the 15th day of October following the ratification of this article.

SECTION. 6. This article shall be inoperative unless it shall have been ratified as an amendment to the Constitution by the legislatures of three-fourths of the several States within seven years from the date of its submission.

Amendment XXI[19]

SECTION. 1. The eighteenth article of amendment to the Constitution of the United States is hereby repealed.

SECTION. 2. The transportation or importation into any State, Territory, or possession of the United States for delivery or use therein of intoxicating liquors, in violation of the laws thereof, is hereby prohibited.

SECTION. 3. This article shall be inoperative unless it shall have been ratified as an amendment to the Constitution by conventions in the several States, as provided in the Constitution, within seven years from the date of the submission hereof to the States by the Congress.

Amendment XXII[20]

No person shall be elected to the office of the President more than twice, and no person who has held the office of

---

[14]Passed February 26, 1869. Ratified February 2, 1870.

[15]Passed May 13, 1912. Ratified April 8, 1913.

[16]Passed December 18, 1917. Ratified January 16, 1919.

[17]Passed June 4, 1919. Ratified August 18, 1920.

[18]Passed March 2, 1932. Ratified January 23, 1933.

[19]Passed February 20, 1933. Ratified December 5, 1933.

[20]Passed March 12, 1947. Ratified March 1, 1951.

President, or acted as President, for more than two years of a term to which some other person was elected President shall be elected to the office of the President more than once.

But this Article shall not apply to any person holding the office of President when this Article was proposed by the Congress, and shall not prevent any person who may be holding the office of President, or acting as President, during the term within which this Article becomes operative from holding the office of President or acting as President during the remainder of such term.

Amendment XXIII[21]

SECTION. 1. The District constituting the seat of Government of the United States shall appoint in such manner as the Congress may direct:

A number of electors of President and Vice President equal to the whole number of Senators and Representatives in Congress to which the District would be entitled if it were a State, but in no event more than the least populous State; they shall be in addition to those appointed by the States, but they shall be considered, for the purposes of the election of President and Vice President, to be electors appointed by the State; and they shall meet in the District and perform such duties as provided by the twelfth article of amendment.

SECTION. 2. The Congress shall have power to enforce this article by appropriate legislation.

Amendment XXIV[22]

SECTION. 1. The right of citizens of the United States to vote in any primary or other election for President or Vice President, or for Senator or Representative in Congress, shall not be denied or abridged by the United States or any State by reason of failure to pay any poll tax or other tax.

SECTION. 2. The Congress shall have power to enforce this article by appropriate legislation.

Amendment XXV[23]

SECTION. 1. In case of the removal of the President from office or of his death or resignation, the Vice President shall become President.

SECTION. 2. Whenever there is a vacancy in the office of the Vice President, the President shall nominate a Vice President who shall take office upon confirmation by a majority vote of both Houses of Congress.

SECTION. 3. Whenever the President transmits to the President pro tempore of the Senate and the Speaker of the House of Representatives his written declaration that he is unable to discharge the powers and duties of his office, and until he transmits them a written declaration to the contrary, such powers and duties shall be discharged by the Vice President as Acting President.

SECTION. 4. Whenever the Vice President and a majority of either the principal officers of the executive department or of such other body as Congress may by law provide, transmit to the President pro tempore of the Senate and the Speaker of the House of Representatives their written declaration that the President is unable to discharge the powers and duties of his office, the Vice President shall immediately assume the powers and duties of the office of Acting President.

Thereafter, when the President transmits to the President pro tempore of the Senate and the Speaker of the House of Representatives his written declaration that no inability exists, he shall resume the powers and duties of his office unless the Vice President and a majority of either the principal officers of the executive department or of such other body as Congress may by law provide, transmit within four days to the President pro tempore of the Senate and the Speaker of the House of Representatives their written declaration that the President is unable to discharge the powers and duties of his office. Thereupon Congress shall decide the issue, assembling within forty-eight hours for that purpose if not in session. If the Congress, within twenty-one days after receipt of the latter written declaration, or, if Congress is not in session, within twenty-one days after Congress is required to assemble, determines by two-thirds vote of both Houses that the President is unable to discharge the powers and duties of his office, the Vice President shall continue to discharge the same as Acting President; otherwise, the President shall resume the powers and duties of his office.

Amendment XXVI[24]

SECTION. 1. The right of citizens of the United States, who are eighteen years of age or older, to vote shall not be denied or abridged by the United States or by any State on account of age.

SECTION. 2. The Congress shall have power to enforce this article by appropriate legislation.

Amendment XXVII[25]

No law, varying the compensation for the service of the Senators and Representatives, shall take effect, until an election of Representatives shall have intervened.

---

[21]Passed June 16, 1960. Ratified April 3, 1961.

[22]Passed August 27, 1962. Ratified January 23, 1964.

[23]Passed July 6, 1965. Ratified February 11, 1967.

[24]Passed March 23, 1971. Ratified July 5, 1971.

[25]Passed September 25, 1989. Ratified May 7, 1992.

ADMISSION OF STATES

Order of admission	State	Date of admission	Order of admission	State	Date of admission
1	Delaware	December 7, 1787	26	Michigan	January 26, 1837
2	Pennsylvania	December 12, 1787	27	Florida	March 3, 1845
3	New Jersey	December 18, 1787	28	Texas	December 29, 1845
4	Georgia	January 2, 1788	29	Iowa	December 28, 1846
5	Connecticut	January 9, 1788	30	Wisconsin	May 29, 1848
6	Massachusetts	February 6, 1788	31	California	September 9, 1850
7	Maryland	April 28, 1788	32	Minnesota	May 11, 1858
8	South Carolina	May 23, 1788	33	Oregon	February 14, 1859
9	New Hampshire	June 21, 1788	34	Kansas	January 29, 1861
10	Virginia	June 25, 1788	35	West Virginia	June 20, 1863
11	New York	July 26, 1788	36	Nevada	October 31, 1864
12	North Carolina	November 21, 1789	37	Nebraska	March 1, 1867
13	Rhode Island	May 29, 1790	38	Colorado	August 1, 1876
14	Vermont	March 4, 1791	39	North Dakota	November 2, 1889
15	Kentucky	June 1, 1792	40	South Dakota	November 2, 1889
16	Tennessee	June 1, 1796	41	Montana	November 8, 1889
17	Ohio	March 1, 1803	42	Washington	November 11, 1889
18	Louisiana	April 30, 1812	43	Idaho	July 3, 1890
19	Indiana	December 11, 1816	44	Wyoming	July 10, 1890
20	Mississippi	December 10, 1817	45	Utah	January 4, 1896
21	Illinois	December 3, 1818	46	Oklahoma	November 16, 1907
22	Alabama	December 14, 1819	47	New Mexico	January 6, 1912
23	Maine	March 15, 1820	48	Arizona	February 14, 1912
24	Missouri	August 10, 1821	49	Alaska	January 3, 1959
25	Arkansas	June 15, 1836	50	Hawaii	August 21, 1959

POPULATION OF THE UNITED STATES
(1790–2000)

Year	Total population (in thousands)	Population density: People per square mile	Year	Total population (in thousands)	Population density: People per square mile
1790	3,929	4.5	1900	76,094	25.6
1800	5,297	6.1	1910	92,407	31.0
1810	7,224	4.3	1920	106,466	35.6
1820	9,618	5.6	1930	122,775	41.2
1830	12,901	7.4	1940	131,669	44.2
1840	17,120	9.8	1950	150,697	50.7
1850	23,261	7.9	1960	180,671	60.1
1860	31,513	10.6	1970	205,052	57.52
1870	39,905	13.4	1980	227,225	64.0
1880	50,262	16.9	1990	250,122	70.3
1890	63,056	21.2	2000	281,400	79.1

Figures are from *Historical Statistics of the United States, Colonial Times to 1957* (1961), pp. 7, 8; *Statistical Abstract of the United States: 1974*, p. 5, Census Bureau for 1974 and 1975; and *Statistical Abstract of the United States: 1988*, p. 7.

PRESIDENTIAL ELECTIONS
(1789–1832)

Year	Number of states	Candidates[1]	Parties	Popular vote	Electoral vote	Percentage of popular vote[2]
1789	11	**George Washington***	**No party designations**		69	
		John Adams			34	
		Minor Candidates			35	
1792	15	**George Washington**	**No party designations**		132	
		John Adams			77	
		George Clinton			50	
		Minor Candidates			5	
1796	16	**John Adams**	**Federalist**		71	
		Thomas Jefferson	Democratic-Republican		68	
		Thomas Pinckney	Federalist		59	
		Aaron Burr	Democratic-Republican		30	
		Minor Candidates			48	
1800	16	**Thomas Jefferson**	**Democratic-Republican**		73	
		Aaron Burr	Democratic-Republican		73	
		John Adams	Federalist		65	
		Charles C. Pinckney	Federalist		64	
		John Jay	Federalist		1	
1804	17	**Thomas Jefferson**	**Democratic-Republican**		162	
		Charles C. Pinckney	Federalist		14	
1808	17	**James Madison**	**Democratic-Republican**		122	
		Charles C. Pinckney	Federalist		47	
		George Clinton	Democratic-Republican		6	
1812	18	**James Madison**	**Democratic-Republican**		128	
		DeWitt Clinton	Federalist		89	
1816	19	**James Monroe**	**Democratic-Republican**		183	
		Rufus King	Federalist		34	
1820	24	**James Monroe**	**Democratic-Republican**		231	
		John Quincy Adams	Independent Republican		1	
1824	24	**John Quincy Adams**	**National-Republican**	**108,740**	**84**	**30.5**
		Andrew Jackson	National-Republican	153,544	99	43.1
		William H. Crawford	National-Republican	46,618	41	13.1
		Henry Clay	National-Republican	47,136	37	13.2
1828	24	**Andrew Jackson**	**Democratic**	**647,286**	**178**	**56.0**
		John Quincy Adams	National Republican	508,064	83	44.0
1832	24	**Andrew Jackson**	**Democratic**	**687,502**	**219**	**55.0**
		Henry Clay	National Republican	530,189	49	42.4
		William Wirt	Anti-Masonic	}	7	
		John Floyd	South Carolina Democratic	33,108	11	2.6

[1]Before the passage of the Twelfth Amendment in 1804, the Electoral College voted for two presidential candidates; the runner-up became vice president. Figures are from *Historical Statistics of the United States, Colonial Times to 1957* (1961), pp. 682–83; and the U.S. Department of Justice.

[2]Candidates receiving less than 1 percent of the popular vote have been omitted. For that reason the percentage of popular vote given for any election year may not total 100 percent.

*Note: Boldface indicates the winner of each election.

PRESIDENTIAL ELECTIONS
(1836–1888)

Year	Number of states	Candidates	Parties	Popular vote	Electoral vote	Percentage of popular vote[1]
1836	26	**Martin Van Buren**	Democratic	765,483	170	50.9
		William H. Harrison	Whig		73	
		Hugh L. White	Whig		26	
		Daniel Webster	Whig	739,795	14	
		W. P. Mangum	Independent		11	
1840	26	**William H. Harrison**	Whig	1,274,624	234	53.1
		Martin Van Buren	Democratic	1,127,781	60	46.9
1844	26	**James K. Polk**	Democratic	1,338,464	170	49.6
		Henry Clay	Whig	1,300,097	105	48.1
		James G. Birney	Liberty	62,300		2.3
1848	30	**Zachary Taylor**	Whig	1,360,967	163	47.4
		Lewis Cass	Democratic	1,222,342	127	42.5
		Martin Van Buren	Free Soil	291,263		10.1
1852	31	**Franklin Pierce**	Democratic	1,601,117	254	50.9
		Winfield Scott	Whig	1,385,453	42	44.1
		John P. Hale	Free Soil	155,825		5.0
1856	31	**James Buchanan**	Democratic	1,832,955	174	45.3
		John C. Frémont	Republican	1,339,932	114	33.1
		Millard Fillmore	American	871,731	8	21.6
1860	33	**Abraham Lincoln**	Republican	1,865,593	180	39.8
		Stephen A. Douglas	Democratic (Northern)	1,382,713	12	29.5
		John C. Breckinridge	Democratic (Southern)	848,356	72	18.1
		John Bell	Constitutional Union	592,906	39	12.6
1864	36	**Abraham Lincoln**	Republican	2,206,938	212	55.0
		George B. McClellan	Democratic	1,803,787	21	45.0
1868	37	**Ulysses S. Grant**	Republican	3,013,421	214	52.7
		Horatio Seymour	Democratic	2,706,829	80	47.3
1872	37	**Ulysses S. Grant**	Republican	3,596,745	286	55.6
		Horace Greeley	Democratic	2,843,446	[2]	43.9
1876	38	**Rutherford B. Hayes**	Republican	4,036,572	185	48.0
		Samuel J. Tilden	Democratic	4,284,020	184	51.0
1880	38	**James A. Garfield**	Republican	4,453,295	214	48.5
		Winfield S. Hancock	Democratic	4,414,082	155	48.1
		James B. Weaver	Greenback-Labor	308,578		3.4
1884	38	**Grover Cleveland**	Democratic	4,879,507	219	48.5
		James G. Blaine	Republican	4,850,293	182	48.2
		Benjamin F. Butler	Greenback-Labor	175,370		1.8
		John P. St. John	Prohibition	150,369		1.5
1888	38	**Benjamin Harrison**	Republican	5,477,129	233	47.9
		Grover Cleveland	Democratic	5,537,857	168	48.6
		Clinton B. Fisk	Prohibition	249,506		2.2
		Anson J. Streeter	Union Labor	146,935		1.3

[1]Candidates receiving less than 1 percent of the popular vote have been omitted. For that reason the percentage of popular vote given for any election year may not total 100 percent.

[2]Greeley died shortly after the election; the electors supporting him then divided their votes among minor candidates.

PRESIDENTIAL ELECTIONS
(1892–1932)

Year	Number of states	Candidates	Parties	Popular vote	Electoral vote	Percentage of popular vote[1]
1892	44	Grover Cleveland	Democratic	5,555,426	277	46.1
		Benjamin Harrison	Republican	5,182,690	145	43.0
		James B. Weaver	People's	1,029,846	22	8.5
		John Bidwell	Prohibition	264,133		2.2
1896	45	William McKinley	Republican	7,102,246	271	51.1
		William J. Bryan	Democratic	6,492,559	176	47.7
1900	45	William McKinley	Republican	7,218,491	292	51.7
		William J. Bryan	Democratic; Populist	6,356,734	155	45.5
		John C. Wooley	Prohibition	208,914		1.5
1904	45	Theodore Roosevelt	Republican	7,628,461	336	57.4
		Alton B. Parker	Democratic	5,084,223	140	37.6
		Eugene V. Debs	Socialist	402,283		3.0
		Silas C. Swallow	Prohibition	258,536		1.9
1908	46	William H. Taft	Republican	7,675,320	321	51.6
	–	William J. Bryan	Democratic	6,412,294	162	43.1
		Eugene V. Debs	Socialist	420,793		2.8
		Eugene W. Chafin	Prohibition	253,840		1.7
1912	48	Woodrow Wilson	Democratic	6,296,547	435	41.9
		Theodore Roosevelt	Progressive	4,118,571	88	27.4
		William H. Taft	Republican	3,486,720	8	23.2
		Eugene V. Debs	Socialist	900,672		6.0
		Eugene W. Chafin	Prohibition	206,275		1.4
1916	48	Woodrow Wilson	Democratic	9,127,695	277	49.4
		Charles E. Hughes	Republican	8,533,507	254	46.2
		A. L. Benson	Socialist	585,113		3.2
		J. Frank Hanly	Prohibition	220,506		1.2
1920	48	Warren G. Harding	Republican	16,143,407	404	60.4
		James N. Cox	Democratic	9,130,328	127	34.2
		Eugene V. Debs	Socialist	919,799		3.4
		P. P. Christensen	Farmer-Labor	265,411		1.0
1924	48	Calvin Coolidge	Republican	15,718,211	382	54.0
		John W. Davis	Democratic	8,385,283	136	28.8
		Robert M. La Follette	Progressive	4,831,289	13	16.6
1928	48	Herbert C. Hoover	Republican	21,391,993	444	58.2
		Alfred E. Smith	Democratic	15,016,169	87	40.9
1932	48	Franklin D. Roosevelt	Democratic	22,809,638	472	57.4
		Herbert C. Hoover	Republican	15,758,901	59	39.7
		Norman Thomas	Socialist	881,951		2.2

[1]Candidates receiving less than 1 percent of the popular vote have been omitted. For that reason the percentage of popular vote given for any election year may not total 100 percent.

PRESIDENTIAL ELECTIONS
(1936–2008)

Year	Number of states	Candidates	Parties	Popular vote	Electoral vote	Percentage of popular vote[1]
1936	48	**Franklin D. Roosevelt**	**Democratic**	**27,752,869**	523	**60.8**
		Alfred M. Landon	Republican	16,674,665	8	36.5
		William Lemke	Union	882,479		1.9
1940	48	**Franklin D. Roosevelt**	**Democratic**	**27,307,819**	449	**54.8**
		Wendell L. Willkie	Republican	22,321,018	82	44.8
1944	48	**Franklin D. Roosevelt**	**Democratic**	**25,606,585**	432	**53.5**
		Thomas E. Dewey	Republican	22,014,745	99	46.0
1948	48	**Harry S Truman**	**Democratic**	**24,105,812**	303	**49.5**
		Thomas E. Dewey	Republican	21,970,065	189	45.1
		J. Strom Thurmond	States' Rights	1,169,063	39	2.4
		Henry A. Wallace	Progressive	1,157,172		2.4
1952	48	**Dwight D. Eisenhower**	**Republican**	**33,936,234**	442	**55.1**
		Adlai E. Stevenson	Democratic	27,314,992	89	44.4
1956	48	**Dwight D. Eisenhower**	**Republican**	**35,590,472**	457	**57.6**
		Adlai E. Stevenson	Democratic	26,022,752	73	42.1
1960	50	**John F. Kennedy**	**Democratic**	**34,227,096**	303	**49.9**
		Richard M. Nixon	Republican	34,108,546	219	49.6
1964	50	**Lyndon B. Johnson**	**Democratic**	**43,126,506**	486	**61.1**
		Barry M. Goldwater	Republican	27,176,799	52	38.5
1968	50	**Richard M. Nixon**	**Republican**	**31,785,480**	301	**43.4**
		Hubert H. Humphrey	Democratic	31,275,165	191	42.7
		George C. Wallace	American Independent	9,906,473	46	13.5
1972	50	**Richard M. Nixon**	**Republican**	**47,169,911**	520	**60.7**
		George S. McGovern	Democratic	29,170,383	17	37.5
1976	50	**Jimmy Carter**	**Democratic**	**40,827,394**	297	**50.0**
		Gerald R. Ford	Republican	39,145,977	240	47.9
1980	50	**Ronald W. Reagan**	**Republican**	**43,899,248**	489	**50.8**
		Jimmy Carter	Democratic	35,481,435	49	41.0
		John B. Anderson	Independent	5,719,437		6.6
		Ed Clark	Libertarian	920,859		1.0
1984	50	**Ronald W. Reagan**	**Republican**	**54,281,858**	525	**59.2**
		Walter F. Mondale	Democratic	37,457,215	13	40.8
1988	50	**George H. Bush**	**Republican**	**47,917,341**	426	**54**
		Michael Dukakis	Democratic	41,013,030	112	46
1992	50	**William Clinton**	**Democratic**	**44,908,254**	370	**43.0**
		George H. Bush	Republican	39,102,343	168	37.4
		Ross Perot	Independent	19,741,065		18.9
1996	50	**William Clinton**	**Democratic**	**47,402,357**	379	**49**
		Robert J. Dole	Republican	39,198,755	159	41
		H. Ross Perot	Reform	8,085,402		8
2000	50	**George W. Bush**	**Republican**	**50,456,062**	271	**47.9**
		Albert Gore	Democratic	50,996,582	266	48.4
		Ralph Nader	Green	2,858,843		2.7
2004	50	**George W. Bush**	**Republican**	**60,693,281**	286	**52**
		John F. Kenry	Democratic	57,355,978	251	47
		Ralph Nader	Green	240,896		
2008	50	**Barack Obama**	**Democratic**	**66,679,680**	356	**52.7**
		John McCain	Republican	58,227,508	162	46.1

[1]Candidates receiving less than 1 percent of the popular vote have been omitted. For that reason the percentage of popular vote given for any election year may not total 100 percent.

JUSTICES OF THE U.S. SUPREME COURT

Chief Justices appear in bold type

	Term of Service	Years of Service	Appointed by
John Jay	1789–1795	5	Washington
John Rutledge	1789–1791	1	Washington
William Cushing	1789–1810	20	Washington
James Wilson	1789–1798	8	Washington
John Blair	1789–1796	6	Washington
Robert H. Harrison	1789–1790	—	Washington
James Iredell	1790–1799	9	Washington
Thomas Johnson	1791–1793	1	Washington
William Paterson	1793–1806	13	Washington
John Rutledge[1]	1795	—	Washington
Samuel Chase	1796–1811	15	Washington
Oliver Ellsworth	1796–1800	4	Washington
Bushrod Washington	1798–1829	31	J. Adams
Alfred Moore	1799–1804	4	J. Adams
John Marshall	1801–1835	34	J. Adams
William Johnson	1804–1834	30	Jefferson
H. Brockholst Livingston	1806–1823	16	Jefferson
Thomas Todd	1807–1826	18	Jefferson
Joseph Story	1811–1845	33	Madison
Gabriel Duval	1811–1835	24	Madison
Smith Thompson	1823–1843	20	Monroe
Robert Trimble	1826–1828	2	J. Q. Adams
John McLean	1829–1861	32	Jackson
Henry Baldwin	1830–1844	14	Jackson
James M. Wayne	1835–1867	32	Jackson
Roger B. Taney	1836–1864	28	Jackson
Philip P. Barbour	1836–1841	4	Jackson
John Catron	1837–1865	28	Van Buren
John McKinley	1837–1852	15	Van Buren
Peter V. Daniel	1841–1860	19	Van Buren
Samuel Nelson	1845–1872	27	Tyler
Levi Woodbury	1845–1851	5	Polk
Robert C. Grier	1846–1870	23	Polk
Benjamin R. Curtis	1851–1857	6	Fillmore
John A. Campbell	1853–1861	8	Pierce
Nathan Clifford	1858–1881	23	Buchanan
Noah H. Swayne	1862–1881	18	Lincoln
Samuel F. Miller	1862–1890	28	Lincoln
David Davis	1862–1877	14	Lincoln
Stephen J. Field	1863–1897	34	Lincoln
Salmon P. Chase	1864–1873	8	Lincoln
William Strong	1870–1880	10	Grant
Joseph P. Bradley	1870–1892	22	Grant
Ward Hunt	1873–1882	9	Grant

[1]Acting Chief Justice; Senate refused to confirm appointment.

(continued)

JUSTICES OF THE U.S. SUPREME COURT *(continued)*

Chief Justices appear in bold type

	Term of Service	Years of Service	Appointed by
Morrison R. Waite	1874–1888	14	Grant
John M. Harlan	1877–1911	34	Hayes
William B. Woods	1880–1887	7	Hayes
Stanley Matthews	1881–1889	7	Garfield
Horace Gray	1882–1902	20	Arthur
Samuel Blatchford	1882–1893	11	Arthur
Lucius Q. C. Lamar	1888–1893	5	Cleveland
Melville W. Fuller	1888–1910	21	Cleveland
David J. Brewer	1890–1910	20	B. Harrison
Henry B. Brown	1890–1906	16	B. Harrison
George Shiras, Jr.	1892–1903	10	B. Harrison
Howell E. Jackson	1893–1895	2	B. Harrison
Edward D. White	1894–1910	16	Cleveland
Rufus W. Peckham	1895–1909	14	Cleveland
Joseph McKenna	1898–1925	26	McKinley
Oliver W. Holmes, Jr.	1902–1932	30	T. Roosevelt
William R. Day	1903–1922	19	T. Roosevelt
William H. Moody	1906–1910	3	T. Roosevelt
Horace H. Lurton	1910–1914	4	Taft
Charles E. Hughes	1910–1916	5	Taft
Willis Van Devanter	1911–1937	26	Taft
Joseph R. Lamar	1911–1916	5	Taft
Edward D. White	1910–1921	11	Taft
Mahlon Pitney	1912–1922	10	Taft
James C. McReynolds	1914–1941	26	Wilson
Louis D. Brandeis	1916–1939	22	Wilson
John H. Clarke	1916–1922	6	Wilson
William H. Taft	1921–1930	8	Harding
George Sutherland	1922–1938	15	Harding
Pierce Butler	1922–1939	16	Harding
Edward T. Sanford	1923–1930	7	Harding
Harlan F. Stone	1925–1941	16	Coolidge
Charles E. Hughes	1930–1941	11	Hoover
Owen J. Roberts	1930–1945	15	Hoover
Benjamin N. Cardozo	1932–1938	6	Hoover
Hugo L. Black	1937–1971	34	F. Roosevelt
Stanley F. Reed	1938–1957	19	F. Roosevelt
Felix Frankfurter	1939–1962	23	F. Roosevelt
William O. Douglas	1939–1975	36	F. Roosevelt
Frank Murphy	1940–1949	9	F. Roosevelt
Harlan F. Stone	1941–1946	5	F. Roosevelt
James F. Byrnes	1941–1942	1	F. Roosevelt
Robert H. Jackson	1941–1954	13	F. Roosevelt
Wiley B. Rutledge	1943–1949	6	F. Roosevelt

(continued)

JUSTICES OF THE U.S. SUPREME COURT (continued)

Chief Justices appear in bold type

	Term of Service	Years of Service	Appointed by
Harold H. Burton	1945–1958	13	Truman
Fred M. Vinson	1946–1953	7	Truman
Tom C. Clark	1949–1967	18	Truman
Sherman Minton	1949–1956	7	Truman
Earl Warren	1953–1969	16	Eisenhower
John Marshall Harlan	1955–1971	16	Eisenhower
William J. Brennan, Jr.	1956–1990	34	Eisenhower
Charles E. Whittaker	1957–1962	5	Eisenhower
Potter Stewart	1958–1981	23	Eisenhower
Byron R. White	1962–1993	31	Kennedy
Arthur J. Goldberg	1962–1965	3	Kennedy
Abe Fortas	1965–1969	4	Johnson
Thurgood Marshall	1967–1994	24	Johnson
Warren E. Burger	1969–1986	18	Nixon
Harry A. Blackmun	1970–1994	24	Nixon
Lewis F. Powell, Jr.	1971–1987	15	Nixon
William H. Rehnquist[2]	1971–2006	35	Nixon
John P. Stevens III	1975–	—	Ford
Sandra Day O'Connor	1981–2006	26	Reagan
Antonin Scalia	1986–	—	Reagan
Anthony M. Kennedy	1988–	—	Reagan
David Souter	1990–	—	Bush
Clarence Thomas	1991–	—	Bush
Ruth Bader Ginsburg	1993–	—	Clinton
Stephen G. Breyer	1994–	—	Clinton
John G. Roberts, Jr.	2006–	—	G. W. Bush
Samuel Alito	2006–	—	G. W. Bush

[2]Chief Justice from 1986 (Reagan administration).

POLITICAL PARTY AFFILIATIONS IN CONGRESS AND THE PRESIDENCY, 1789–2011*

Congress	Year	House* Majority Party	House* Principal Minority Party	House* Other (except Vacancies)	Senate* Majority Party	Senate* Principal Minority Party	Senate* Other (except Vacancies)	President and Party
1st	1789–1791	Ad-38	Op-26	—	Ad-17	Op-9	—	F (Washington)
2nd	1791–1793	F-37	DR-33	—	F-16	DR-13	—	F (Washington)
3rd	1793–1795	DR-57	F-48	—	F-17	DR-13	—	F (Washington)
4th	1795–1797	F-54	DR-52	—	F-19	DR-13	—	F (Washington)
5th	1797–1799	F-58	DR-48	—	F-20	DR-12	—	F (John Adams)
6th	1799–1801	F-64	DR-42	—	F-19	DR-13	—	F (John Adams)
7th	1801–1803	DR-69	F-36	—	DR-18	F-13	—	DR (Jefferson)
8th	1803–1805	DR-102	F-39	—	DR-25	F-9	—	DR (Jefferson)
9th	1805–1807	DR-116	F-25	—	DR-27	F-7	—	DR (Jefferson)
10th	1807–1809	DR-118	F-24	—	DR-28	F-6	—	DR (Jefferson)
11th	1809–1811	DR-94	F-48	—	DR-28	F-6	—	DR (Madison)
12th	1811–1813	DR-108	F-36	—	DR-30	F-6	—	DR (Madison)
13th	1813–1815	DR-112	F-68	—	DR-27	F-9	—	DR (Madison)
14th	1815–1817	DR-117	F-65	—	DR-25	F-11	—	DR (Madison)
15th	1817–1819	DR-141	F-42	—	DR-34	F-10	—	DR (Monroe)
16th	1819–1821	DR-156	F-27	—	DR-35	F-7	—	DR (Monroe)
17th	1821–1823	DR-158	F-25	—	DR-44	F-4	—	DR (Monroe)
18th	1823–1825	DR-187	F-26	—	DR-44	F-4	—	DR (Monroe)
19th	1825–1827	Ad-105	J-97	—	Ad-26	J-20	—	C (J. Q. Adams)
20th	1827–1829	J-119	Ad-94	—	J-28	Ad-20	—	C (J. Q. Adams)
21st	1829–1831	D-139	NR-74	—	D-26	NR-22	—	D (Jackson)
22nd	1831–1833	D-141	NR-58	14	D-25	NR-21	2	D (Jackson)
23rd	1833–1835	D-147	AM-53	60	D-20	NR-20	8	D (Jackson)
24th	1835–1837	D-145	W-98	—	D-27	W-25	—	D (Jackson)
25th	1837–1839	D-108	W-107	24	D-30	W-18	4	D (Van Buren)
26th	1839–1841	D-124	W-118	—	D-28	W-22	—	D (Van Buren)
27th	1841–1843	W-133	D-102	6	W-28	D-22	2	W (Harrison) W (Tyler)
28th	1843–1845	D-142	W-79	1	W-28	D-25	1	W (Tyler)
29th	1845–1847	D-143	W-77	6	D-31	W-25	—	D (Polk)
30th	1847–1849	W-115	D-108	4	D-36	W-21	1	D (Polk)
31st	1849–1851	D-112	W-109	9	D-35	W-25	2	W (Taylor) W (Fillmore)
32nd	1851–1853	D-140	W-88	5	D-35	W-24	3	W (Fillmore)
33rd	1853–1855	D-159	W-71	4	D-38	W-22	2	D (Pierce)
34th	1855–1857	R-108	D-83	43	D-40	R-15	5	D (Pierce)
35th	1857–1859	D-118	R-92	26	D-36	R-20	8	D (Buchanan)
36th	1859–1861	R-114	D-92	31	D-36	R-26	4	D (Buchanan)
37th	1861–1863	R-105	D-43	30	R-31	D-10	8	R (Lincoln)
38th	1863–1865	R-102	D-75	9	R-36	D-9	5	R (Lincoln)
39th	1865–1867	U-149	D-42	—	U-42	D-10	—	R (Lincoln) R (Johnson)
40th	1867–1869	R-143	D-49	—	R-42	D-11	—	R (Johnson)
41st	1869–1871	R-149	D-63	—	R-56	D-11	—	R (Grant)
42nd	1871–1873	R-134	D-104	5	R-52	D-17	5	R (Grant)
43rd	1873–1875	R-194	D-92	14	R-49	D-19	5	R (Grant)
44th	1875–1877	D-169	R-109	14	R-45	D-29	2	R (Grant)
45th	1877–1879	D-153	R-140	—	R-39	D-36	1	R (Hayes)
46th	1879–1881	D-149	R-130	14	D-42	R-33	1	R (Hayes)
47th	1881–1883	R-147	D-135	11	R-37	D-37	1	R (Garfield) R (Arthur)
48th	1883–1885	D-197	R-118	10	R-38	D-36	2	R (Arthur)

*Letter symbols for political parties. Ad—Administration; AM—Anti-Masonic; C—Coalition; D—Democratic; DR—Democratic-Republican; F—Federalist; J—Jacksonian; NR—National-Republican; Op—Opposition; R—Republican; U—Unionist; W—Whig.

Source: *Historical Statistics of the United States: Colonial Times to the Present*, Various eds. Washington, D.C.: GOP.

(continued)

POLITICAL PARTY AFFILIATIONS IN CONGRESS
AND THE PRESIDENCY, 1789–2011 *(continued)*

Congress	Year	House* Majority Party	House* Principal Minority Party	House* Other (except Vacancies)	Senate* Majority Party	Senate* Principal Minority Party	Senate* Other (except Vacancies)	President and Party
49th	1885–1887	D-183	R-140	2	R-43	D-34	—	D (Cleveland)
50th	1887–1889	D-169	R-152	4	R-39	D-37	—	D (Cleveland)
51st	1889–1891	R-166	D-159	—	R-39	D-37	—	R (B. Harrison)
52nd	1891–1893	D-235	R-88	9	R-47	D-39	2	R (B. Harrison)
53rd	1893–1895	D-218	R-127	11	D-44	R-38	3	D (Cleveland)
54th	1895–1897	R-244	D-105	7	R-43	D-39	6	D (Cleveland)
55th	1897–1899	R-204	D-113	40	R-47	D-34	7	R (McKinley)
56th	1899–1901	R-185	D-163	9	R-53	D-26	8	R (McKinley)
57th	1901–1903	R-197	D-151	9	R-55	D-31	4	R (McKinley) R (T. Roosevelt)
58th	1903–1905	R-208	D-178	—	R-57	D-33	—	R (T. Roosevelt)
59th	1905–1907	R-250	D-136	—	R-57	D-33	—	R (T. Roosevelt)
60th	1907–1909	R-222	D-164	—	R-61	D-31	—	R (T. Roosevelt)
61st	1909–1911	R-219	D-172	—	R-61	D-32	—	R (Taft)
62nd	1911–1913	D-228	R-161	1	R-51	D-41	—	R (Taft)
63rd	1913–1915	D-291	R-127	17	D-51	R-44	1	D (Wilson)
64th	1915–1917	D-230	R-196	9	D-56	R-40	—	D (Wilson)
65th	1917–1919	D-216	R-210	6	D-53	R-42	—	D (Wilson)
66th	1919–1921	R-240	D-190	3	R-49	D-47	—	D (Wilson)
67th	1921–1923	R-301	D-131	1	R-59	D-37	—	R (Harding)
68th	1923–1925	R-225	D-205	5	R-51	D-43	2	R (Coolidge)
69th	1925–1927	R-247	D-183	4	R-56	D-39	1	R (Coolidge)
70th	1927–1929	R-237	D-195	3	R-49	D-46	1	R (Coolidge)
71st	1929–1931	R-267	D-167	1	R-56	D-39	1	R (Hoover)
72nd	1931–1933	D-220	R-214	1	R-48	D-47	1	R (Hoover)
73rd	1933–1935	D-310	R-117	5	D-60	R-35	1	D (F. Roosevelt)
74th	1935–1937	D-319	R-103	10	D-69	R-25	2	D (F. Roosevelt)
75th	1937–1939	D-331	R-89	13	D-76	R-16	4	D (F. Roosevelt)
76th	1939–1941	D-261	R-164	4	D-69	R-23	4	D (F. Roosevelt)
77th	1941–1943	D-268	R-162	5	D-66	R-28	2	D (F. Roosevelt)
78th	1943–1945	D-218	R-208	4	D-58	R-37	1	D (F. Roosevelt)
79th	1945–1947	D-242	R-190	2	D-56	R-38	1	D (Truman)
80th	1947–1949	R-245	D-188	1	R-51	D-45	—	D (Truman)
81st	1949–1951	D-263	R-171	1	D-54	R-42	—	D (Truman)
82nd	1951–1953	D-243	R-199	1	D-49	R-47	—	D (Truman)
83rd	1953–1955	R-221	D-211	1	R-48	D-47	1	R (Eisenhower)
84th	1955–1957	D-232	R-203	—	D-48	R-47	1	R (Eisenhower)
85th	1957–1959	D-233	R-200	—	D-49	R-47	—	R (Eisenhower)
86th	1959–1961	D-283	R-153	—	D-64	R-34	—	R (Eisenhower)
87th	1961–1963	D-263	R-174	—	D-65	R-35	—	D (Kennedy)
88th	1963–1965	D-258	R-177	—	D-67	R-33	—	D (Kennedy) D (Johnson)
89th	1965–1967	D-295	R-140	—	D-68	R-32	—	D (Johnson)
90th	1967–1969	D-247	R-187	1	D-64	R-36	—	D (Johnson)
91st	1969–1971	D-243	R-192	—	D-58	R-42	—	R (Nixon)
92nd	1971–1973	D-255	R-180	—	D-54	R-44	2	R (Nixon)
93rd	1973–1975	D-242	R-192	1	D-56	R-42	2	R (Nixon, Ford)
94th	1975–1977	D-291	R-144	—	D-61	R-37	2	R (Ford)
95th	1977–1979	D-292	R-143	—	D-61	R-38	1	D (Carter)
96th	1979–1981	D-277	R-158	—	D-58	R-41	1	D (Carter)
97th	1981–1983	D-242	R-192	—	R-54	D-45	1	R (Reagan)
98th	1983–1985	D-266	R-167	2	R-55	D-45	—	R (Reagan)
99th	1985–1987	D-252	R-183	—	R-53	D-47	—	R (Reagan)
100th	1987–1989	D-258	R-177	—	D-55	R-45	—	R (Reagan)
101st	1989–1991	D-262	R-173	—	D-57	R-43	—	R (Bush)
102nd	1991–1993	D-267	R-167	1	D-57	R-43	—	R (Bush)
103rd	1993–1995	D-256	R-178	1	D-56	R-44	—	D (Clinton)

(continued)

POLITICAL PARTY AFFILIATIONS IN CONGRESS AND THE PRESIDENCY, 1789–2011 *(continued)*

Congress	Year	House*			Senate*			President and Party
		Majority Party	Principal Minority Party	Other (except Vacancies)	Majority Party	Principal Minority Party	Other (except Vacancies)	
104th	1995–1997	R-230	D-204	1	R-52	D-48	—	D (Clinton)
105th	1997–1999	R-228	D-206	1	R-55	D-45	—	D (Clinton)
106th	1999–2001	R-223	D-211	1	R-55	D-45	—	D (Clinton)
107th	2001–2003	R-221	D-212	1	D-50	R-49	2	R (Bush)
108th	2003–2005	R-229	D-205	1	R-51	D-48	2	R (Bush)
109th	2005–2007	R-232	D-202	1	R-55	D-44	1	R (Bush)
110th	2007–2009	R-202	D-233	1	R-49	D-49*	2	R (Bush)
111th	2009–2011	D-256	R-175	0	D-55	R-40	2	D (Obama)

*The two independents caucused with the Democrats giving them a majority in the Senate.

Credits

These pages constitute an extension of the copyright page. We have made every effort to trace the ownership of all copyrighted material and to secure permission from copyright holders. In the event of any question arising as to the use of any material, we will be pleased to make the necessary corrections in future printings. Thanks are due to the following authors, publishers, and agents for permission to use the material indicated.

Photo Credits

Chapter 1

1 The Art Archive/Picture Desk; **3** Mark Karrass/CORBIS; **5** © Copyright The British Museum/British Museum Photography & Imaging; **7** Reproduced from the Collections of the Library of Congress, Prints and Photographs Division, Washington, D.C.; **9** Ariadne Van Zandbergen/africanpictures. net/Image Works; **11** The Art Archive/Picture Desk; **12** Sketch of the coast of Espanola, drawn by Columbus on the first voyage, from the original in the possession of the Duque de Barwick y de Alba, 1492 (ink on paper), Columbus, Christopher (1451-1506) (attr.to)/Private Collection/The Bridgeman Art Library; **14** Bibliotheque Nationale, Paris/Biblioteca Internacional de Fotographia; **17** Leonard de Selva/CORBIS; **18** Reproduced from the Collections of the Library of Congress, Prints and Photographs Division, Washington, D.C.

Chapter 2

20 Collection of The New-York Historical Society. #1049 C; **21** Bettmann/CORBIS; **23** Queen Elizabeth I (1530-1603) knighting Francis Drake (1540-96) from 'Illustrations of English and Scottish History' Volume I (engraving), Gilbert, Sir John (1817-97) (after)/Private Collection, Ken Welsh/Bridgeman Art Library; **25** Reproduced from the Collections of the Library of Congress, Prints and Photographs Division, Washington, D.C.; **26** Portrait of Sir Walter Raleigh (1554-1618) 1588 (oil on panel), English School, (16th century)/Private Collection/Bridgeman Art Library; **28** North America published by Hakluyt in 1582. The British Library C.21.b.35.; **29** Public domain; **31** North Wind Picture Archives; **33** Courtesy of John Carter Brown Library at Brown University; **34** Photo courtesy of Maryland Department, Enoch Pratt Free Library, Baltimore; **37** Collection of The New-York Historical Society. #1049 C.

Chapter 3

39 The Art Archive/Picture Desk; **40** Plimouth Plantation, Inc., Photographer, Gary Andrashko.; **42** The Art Archive/Picture Desk; **44** Public domain; **45** Photograph by Wilfred French. Courtesy of the Historic New England; **47** North Wind Picture Archives; **50** The Colonial Williamsburg Foundation; **52** Reproduced from the Collections of the Library of Congress [LC-USZC4-7157]; **53** Public domain; **54-A** Leonard de Selva/CORBIS.

Chapter 4

55 Reproduced from the Collections of the Library of Congress, Prints and Photographs Division, Washington, D.C.; **56** Victoria and Albert Museum, V & A Picture Library; **57** Courtesy, Murray Harbour, Prince Edward Island, Canada; **59** The Colonial Williamsburg Foundation; **62** Reproduced from the Collections of the Library of Congress, Prints and Photographs Division, Washington, D.C.; **63** Reproduced from the Collections of the Library of Congress [LC-USF34-045219-D]; **67** Courtesy Peabody Essex Museum, Salem, Massachusetts .neg.#14,272.; **68** Library of Congress Prints and Photographs Division Washington, D.C. [LC-USZC4-12538]; **69** Public domain.

Chapter 5

71 Roberta Wilson, New York State Museum; **73** Reproduced from the Collections of the Library of Congress, Prints and Photographs Division, Washington, D.C.; **75** Roberta Wilson, New York State Museum; **77** North Wind Picture Archives; **79** Culver Pictures, Inc.; **82** Mary Evans Picture Library/Arthur Rackman/Image Works; **85** North Wind Picture Archives; **87** Courtesy, American Antiquarian Society, Worcester, Massachusetts.

Chapter 6

91 North Wind Picture Archives; **93** Public domain; **94** Brown Brothers; **95** North Wind Picture Archives; **97** North Wind Picture Archives; **98** Reproduced from the Collections of the Library of Congress, Prints and Photographs Division, Washington, D.C. [LC-D416-43720]; **100** Reproduced from the Collections of the Library of Congress, Prints and Photographs Division, Washington, D.C.;

104 Collection of The New-York Historical Society. #1952.80; **105** North Wind Picture Archives; **109** North Wind Picture Archives; **111-A** Courtesy, American Antiquarian Society, Worcester, Massachusetts.

Chapter 7

112 The Metropolitan Museum of Art, Bequest of Charles Allen Munn, 1924. (24.90.1566a) © The Metropolitan Museum of Art; **113** Public domain; **116** *A View of the House of Commons*, engraved by B. Cole (fl.1748-75) (engraving), English School, (18th century)/Stapleton Collection, UK,/Bridgeman Art Library; **117** The Colonial Williamsburg Foundation; **118** Harcourt Picture Collection; **120** Culver Pictures, Inc.; **121** The Metropolitan Museum of Art, Bequest of Charles Allen Munn, 1924. (24.90.1566a) © The Metropolitan Museum of Art; **123** Courtesy Peabody Essex Museum, Salem, Massachusetts. neg.#16,507; **124** Rare Books Division, The New York Public Library. Astor, Lenox and Tilden Foundations.

Chapter 8

126 Reproduced from the Collections of the Library of Congress, Prints and Photographs Division, Washington, D.C.; **127** Reproduced from the Collections of the Library of Congress, Prints and Photographs Division, Washington, D.C. [LC-USZ62-35522]; **128** Bettmann/CORBIS; **129** Reproduced from the Collections of the Library of Congress, Prints and Photographs Division, Washington, D.C.; **130** Historical Picture Archive/CORBIS; **132** Reproduced from the Collections of the Library of Congress, Prints and Photographs Division, Washington, D.C. [LC-D416-256]; **134** CORBIS; **136** Courtesy of John Carter Brown Library at Brown University; **140** The Art Archive/Picture Desk.

Chapter 9

143 North Wind Picture Archives; **144** Culver Pictures, Inc.; **145** Fenimore Art Museum, New York State Historical Association, Cooperstown, New York; **146** Reproduced from the Collections of the Library of Congress, Prints and Photographs Division, Washington, D.C.; **151** The Continental Insurance Companies; **153** North Wind Picture Archives; **155** Anne S.K. Brown Military Collection, Brown University; **157** Reproduced from the Collections of the Library of Congress, Prints and Photographs Division, Washington, D.C. [LC-D43-T01-50236]; **159-A** *left* CORBIS; *right* Reproduced from the Collections of the Library of Congress, Prints and Photographs Division, Washington, D.C. [LC-USZ62-35522]; **159-B** Courtesy of John Carter Brown Library at Brown University.

Chapter 10

160 The National Archives; **162** North Wind Picture Archives; **166** Courtesy of David WIlliam Manthey; **169** *both* North Wind Picture Archives; **171** North Wind Picture Archives; **172** The National Archives; **173** Yale University Art Gallery/Art Resource, NY.

Chapter 11

178 Reproduced from the Collections of the Library of Congress, Prints and Photographs Division, Washington, D.C.; **179** North Wind Picture Archives; **180** Reproduced from the Collections of the Library of Congress, Prints and Photographs Division, Washington, D.C.; **181** Reproduced from the Collections of the Library of Congress, Prints and Photographs Division, Washington, D.C.; **183** The Granger Collection, New York; **185** Reproduced from the Collections of the Library of Congress, Prints and Photographs Division, Washington, D.C. [LC-USZ62-124552]; **190** Brown Brothers; **193** North Wind Picture Archives.

Chapter 12

196 Stapleton Collection HIP/Image Works; **199** Courtesy of the Thomas Jefferson Memorial Foundation; **200** Stapleton Collection HIP/Image Works; **204** Montana Historical Society, Helena.; **207** The Rhode Island Historical Society. #Rhix3 3035, All Rights Reserved.; **208** The Granger Collection, New York; **211** World History/Topham/Image Works; **213** The Granger Collection, New York; **215-A** North Wind Picture Archives; **215-B** Reproduced from the Collections of the Library of Congress, Prints and Photographs Division, Washington, D.C. [LC-USZ62-124552].

Chapter 13

216 Reproduced from the Collections of the Library of Congress, Prints and Photographs Division, Washington, D.C.; **218** Historical Society of Western Pennsylvania; **219** Library of Congress Prints and Photographs Division Washington, D.C. [LC-USZ62-8499]; **220** North Wind Picture Archives; **221** The Granger Collection, New York; **222** Collection of The New-York Historical Society. #1918.45; **226** Reproduced from the Collections of the Library of Congress, Prints and Photographs Division, Washington, D.C.; **228** Bettmann/CORBIS.

Chapter 14

234 Bettmann/CORBIS; **236** Hulton Archive/Getty Images; **237** The Granger Collection, New York; **241** Bettmann/CORBIS; **242** University of Massachusetts, Lowell; **243** The Art Archive/Culver Pictures/Picture Desk; **246** Public domain; **248** Chicago Historical Society, ICHI-04701.

Chapter 15

252 General Andrew Jackson (colour litho), Sully, Thomas (1783-1872) (after)/Private Collection, Peter Newark American Pictures/Bridgeman Art Library; **255** Reproduced from the Collections of the Library of Congress, Prints and Photographs Division, Washington, D.C. [LC-USZ62-1563]; **256** Reproduced from the Collections of the Library of Congress, Prints and Photographs Division, Washington, D.C. [LC-USZ62-12470]; **258** Bettmann/CORBIS; **259** Collection of The New-York Historical Society. #44655; **262** General Andrew Jackson (colour litho), Sully, Thomas (1783-1872) (after)/Private Collection, Peter Newark American Pictures/Bridgeman Art Library; **264** Courtesy of the Edward E. Ayer Collection, Newberry Library, Chicago; **266** Woolaroc Museum, Bartlesville, Oklahoma.

Chapter 16

269 Reproduced from the Collections of the Library of Congress, Prints and Photographs Division, Washington, D.C. [LC-USZ62-3576]; **271** Collection of The New York Historical Society, #28542; **272** Chicago Historical Society; **273** Collection of The New-York Historical Society. #44812; **274** Reproduced from the Collections of the Library of Congress, Prints and Photographs Division, Washington, D.C. [LC-USZ62-3576]; **275** Collection of The New-York Historical Society. #35603; **276** Courtesy, Boston Art Commission 2003; **280** Reproduced from the Collections of the Library of Congress, Prints and Photographs Division, Washington, D.C.; **283-B** *left* Courtesy, Boston Art Commission 2003; *right* Collection of The New-York Historical Society. #35603.

Chapter 17

284, 286 Bettmann/CORBIS; **287** Reproduced from the Collections of the Library of Congress, Prints and Photographs Division, Washington, D.C. [LC-USZ62-120350]; **288** Courtesy, American Antiquarian Society, Worcester, Massachusetts; **290** Joseph Mustering the Nauvoo Legion, C.C.A. Christensen. © Courtesy Museum of Art, Brigham Young University. All Rights reserved. Photographer: David W. Hawkinson; **292** North Wind Picture Archives; **295** The Granger Collection, New York; **297** Reproduced from the Collections of the Library of Congress, Prints and Photographs Division, Washington, D.C.; **298** Record of the War Dept. General & Special Staffs, National Archives.

Chapter 18

301 Abby Aldrich Rockefeller Folk Art Museum, The Colonial Williamsburg Foundation, Williamsburg, Va.; **302** Culver Pictures, Inc.; **305** The Granger Collection, New York; **310** The Granger Collection, New York; **312** UPI-Bettmann/CORBIS; **314** Missouri Historical Society. MHS art acc# 1939.3.1; **315** Abby Aldrich Rockefeller Folk Art Museum, The Colonial Williamsburg Foundation, Williamsburg, Va.; **317** Bettmann/CORBIS.

Chapter 19

319 Denver Public Library, Western History Collection, [X11929]; **320** North Wind Picture Archives; **323** Bettmann/CORBIS; **324** Public domain; **327** #1940. Association of American Railroads; **328** Denver Public Library, Western History Collection, [X11929]; **329** Reproduced from the Collections of the Library of Congress, Prints and Photographs Division, Washington, D.C. [LC-USZC4-668]; **330** Yale Collection of Western Americana/Beinecke Rare Book and Manuscript Library.

Chapter 20

334 North Wind Picture Archives; **335** Reproduced from the Collections of the Library of Congress, Prints and Photographs Division, Washington, D.C. [LC-B811- 2299]; **336** California State Library; **339** *top* The Granger Collection, New York; *bottom* Reproduced from the Collections of the Library of Congress, Prints and Photographs Division, Washington, D.C. [LC-USZ62-5127];

341 North Wind Picture Archives; **344** Reproduced from the Collections of the Library of Congress, Prints and Photographs Division, Washington, D.C.; **346-B** Record of the War Dept. General & Special Staffs, National Archives.

Chapter 21

347 Library of Congress, Prints and Photographs Division, Washington, D.C. [LC-USZ62-120309]; **348** The Granger Collection, New York; **349, 351** The Granger Collection, New York; **353** Reproduced from the Collections of the Library of Congress, Prints and Photographs Division, Washington, D.C. [LC-USZ62-107588]; **354** Harper's Ferry Historical Society **358** Reproduced from the Collections of the Library of Congress, Prints and Photographs Division, Washington, D.C. (LC-USZ62-5803); **359** Reproduced from the Collections of the Library of Congress, Prints and Photographs Division, Washington, D.C. (LC-BH82-2417);

361 Reproduced from the Collections of the Library of Congress, Prints and Photographs Division, Washington, D.C. [LC-USZ62-120309].

Chapter 22

364 Cooper Hewitt National Design Museum; **365** Photo by Timothy O'Sullivan, Chicago Historical Society, ICHi-08091; **367** Cooper Hewitt National Design Museum; **368** Reproduced from the Collections of the Library of Congress, Prints and Photographs Division, Washington, D.C. [LC-USZ62-62758]; **370** *Battle of First Bull Run*, 1861 (litho) by American School (19th century) Private Collection/Peter Newark Military Pictures/The Bridgeman Art Library; **375** The Granger Collection, New York; **376** Williamson Art Gallery & Museum, Birkenhead, England; **378** The Granger Collection, New York.

Chapter 23

382 National Park Service, Harper's Ferry Center; **383** Reproduced from the Collections of the Library of Congress, Prints and Photographs Division, Washington, D.C. (LC-B8155-1); **384** Reproduced from the Collections of the Library of Congress, Prints and Photographs Division, Washington, D.C. [LC-USZ61-903]; **388** National Park Service, Harper's Ferry Center; **389** Bettmann/CORBIS; **391** Bettmann/CORBIS; **392** Reproduced from the Collections of the Library of Congress, Prints and Photographs Division, Washington, D.C. [LC-USZC2-1947]; **396** Bettmann/CORBIS.

Chapter 24

399, 400 The National Archives; **401** Reproduced from the Collections of the Library of Congress, Prints and Photographs Division, Washington, D.C. [LC-BH83-171]; **403** North Wind Picture Archives; **404** The Valentine Museum; **407** North Wind Picture Archives; **410** The Granger Collection, New York; **411** Culver Pictures, Inc.; **414-A** National Archives.

Index

Note: *Italic* page numbers indicate illustrations, maps, and photographs.

A

Abolition and abolitionists, 174–175, 296–299, 397; black abolitionists, 298–299; Compromise of 1850 and, 342, *352*; at end of Civil War, 397; in England, 324; Garrison, Lloyd, 296–298, 307, 361; in the North, 163–164; southern movement for, 301–304; Virginia debate on, 304. *See also* Slaves and slavery; Underground railway

Act of Toleration (Maryland), 34, 35

Adams, Abigail, 135, 139; on liberties for women, 162–163, 215-A

Adams, Charles Francis, 373, 411

Adams, Henry, 410–411

Adams, John, 127, 133, 191–194, *193*; cabinet of, 192–193; Declaration of Independence and, 139; federalist party and, 229; French Revolution and, 185; July 4th holiday and, 139; midnight judges of, 201; on natural rights of man, 140; in Peace of Paris negotiations, 156; on people ignoring the War for Independence, 156; personal life and qualities of, 192–193; presidency of, 191–194, *193*; on Washington, George, 157; wife Abigail and, 135, 139, 162–163

Adams, John Quincy, 229, *256*, 350; election of 1824 ("corrupt bargain") and, 252–256, *254*, *255*; on gag rule, 308; Oregon and, 230; presidency of, *253*, 256–258, *256*; Rush-Bagot Agreement and, 230

Adams-Oñis Treaty, 230–231, 319

Adams, Samuel, 132–133, *132*; as anti-federalist, 176; Boston Massacre and, 127

Adams, Thomas, 322

Adet, Pierre, 193

Adultery, punishments for (colonial), 44

Adventists, *288*, 289

Africa: Liberia, *302*, 303–304, *303*; slave trade and, 80, 85–89, *89*, 355

African Americans: as abolitionists, 298–299; black codes and, 402; in Civil War, 379–380, *396*, 397; Communist party and, 66; school segregation and, 266; as slave owners, 312; voting rights of, 161–162, 403, 412; workplace prohibitions and discrimination, 365. *See also* Africans in the Americas; Race and racism; Slaves and slavery

African slave trade, 80, 85, 87–89, *89*, 355

Africans in the Americas: in Carolinas, 49; change in status to slaves, 84; in the colonies, 80–89; diseases and, 85; free/freed, 82–83, 310; "half-freedom", 83; as loyalists, 145–146; population of, 98, 103, 301–302, 318; race, role of, 84; as servants, 32, 83–84; voting rights of, 161–162. *See also* Slaves and slavery

Age of Exploration (1400-1550), *2*

Age of Reason (Paine), 285

Agriculture, 2–3; frontier methods of, 186; methods of, 186; slash-and-burn, 72. *See also specific crops*

Ahuitzotl, 6

Ailly, Pierre D', 11

Aix-la-Chapelle, Treaty of, 107

Alabama (ship), 373, 375, *376*

Alamo, battle at, 322, *323*

Alaska: Bering land bridge to, 1–2; purchase from Russia, 407

Albany, New York, 79

Alcohol: bootleggers and moonshiners and, 354; demon rum, 293–295; Prohibition and, 295; temperance movement, 295, *295*; temperance pledge, 295

Alden, John, 39

Algonkian (Algonquin) Indians, 79, 93; language of, 74

Alien Act, 193–194, 196

Alien and Sedition Acts (1798), 193–194, 196

Allen, Ethan, 138

Amendments to Constitution: first ten (Bill of Rights), 176; process for, 174, 334. *See also specific amendments*

America, naming of, 12

American Dictionary of the English Language (Webster), 219

American fighting men: opinions on, 108, 143; weapons/arms of, 135

American Indians. *See* Indians

American party. *See* Know-Nothings

American Red Cross, 367

"American Style" of war, 96

American System, 220–221, 276

American System of Manufacture, 239

Amherst, Jeffery, 109–110, 115

Amish, 284

Anabaptists, 68

Anaconda Plan, 371

Anasazi, housing of, 3

Andrew, John A., 405

Andros, Edmund, 65, 66

Anghiera, Peter Mabry d', 1

Anglicans, 284, 285

Animals, Columbian Exchange and, 16–18

Annexation: of Mexican territories, 330–332, *335*; of Texas, 328–329

Annulment, 22

Anthony, Susan B., 296

Anti-Catholicism: Know-Nothings and, 345; presidential elections and, 134

Anti-draft riots, 387

Anti-federalists, 176. *See also* Jefferson Republicans

Anti-Masonic Party, 257–258, *258*

Antietam, Battle of, 378

Antinomianism, 46

Appalachian region, 354; as frontier, 244–248; trans-Appalachian frontier, 244–248

Appeal (Walker), 310

Appomattox, Lee's surrender at, 393–394

Apprentices, 81, 101

Arab explorers, 10

Arawak Indians, 6–7, *7*

Arizona, 332

Arkansas, school desegregation decision in, 266

Arkwright, Richard, 236

Armada. *See* Spanish Armada

Armed forces: mercenaries and, 143, 152–153; in War for Independence, 108, 143–145. *See also* Army; Navy; *And specific wars*

Army: British, 143; in Civil War, 364–367, 372; Continental, 143–145, 152–153; Continental, payment of, 181–182; mercenaries and, 143, 152–153

Arnold, Benedict: service in War for Independence, 138, 151; as traitor, 154

Art of War (Jomini), 364

Articles of Confederation, 160, *161*, 164–168

Artillery: in Civil War, 365–366. *See also* Firearms

Ashburton, Lord (Webster-Ashburton Treaty), 282

Assassinations, of Lincoln, *392*, 394

Assiento, 57

Assumption, of state debts, 182

Athaulpa, 16

Atlanta: campaign for, *393*; occupation and burning of, 392

Atrocities, 108, 150

Attucks, Crispus, 127, 129

Auburn system, 293

Austin, Moses, 321

Austin, Stephen, 321–322

Aztecs, 3, 5–6, *6*, *14*; city life of, 15; conquest of, 13–14

B

Babcock, Orville, 411

Backstaff, 69

Bacon, Nathaniel, 61, *62*

Bacon's Rebellion, 56, 61, *62*, 84

Bahamas, Columbus' landing in, 6–7

Bailey, Nathan, 81

Baja California, Walker's invasion of, 343

Balboa, Vasco Núñez de, 12

Bank of England, 183

Bank of the United States (BUS), 183–184, 221; First, 183–184, *183*, 221; Second, 221, 272–273

Bank War, 272–275

Banks and banking: Bank of the United States (BUS), 183–184, 272–273; national bank, 183–184, *183*; pet banks, 274; war with the BUS, Jackson, Andrew, and, 272–275; wildcat banks, 221. *See also* Money

Baptiste, Jean, Comte de Rochambeau, 153, 155, 157

Baptists, 287, 356

Barbados, 49

Barbary pirates, 169–170, 206, 207–208

Barbary states, 206, 207–208, *207*

Barnard, Thomas, 112

Barry, John, 152

Barton, Clara, 367

Battle at Lexington and Concord, 136–137, *136*, *137*, 159-B

"Battle Hymn of the Republic, The" (song), 379, 388, 397

Battle of Bunker Hill, 137–138, *137*

Battle of Golden Hill, 127

Battle of New Orleans, *212*, *213*, 214, 217

Battle of Saratoga, 151–152, *151*

Battle of Yorktown, *154*, 155–156, *155*

Battles. *See* War(s) and warfare; *specific battles and wars*

Bay Colony, 66

Bayard, James, 198

Bayonet, 96

Beans, 73

Bear Flag Republic, 331

Beaumarchais, Pierre de, 147

Beauregard, P. G. T., 361–362, 370

Beaver, 324

Becknell, William, 320

Beckwourth, Jim, 325–326

Belknap, William W., 411

Bell, John, 358

Belle Starr, 347

Benezet, Anthony, 296

Benton, Thomas Hart, 250, 334; duel of, 260; slavery and, 334

Bering Strait, 1–2

Beringia, 1–3

Berkeley, Lord John, 50–51

Berkeley, William, 49, 60–61; Bacon, Nathaniel and, 61, *62*

Bible: pocket size, in Civil War, 372; slavery defense and, 308–309

Biddle, Nicholas, 273–274, 277, 350

Bill of Rights, 176

Billy Yank (northern soldiers in Civil War), 366–367

Birney, James G., 298, 329

Black Bart (pirate), 99

Black codes, 402

Black Friday (1869), 411

"Black legend", 16

Blackbeard (pirate), 99

Blacks. *See* African Americans

Blackwell, Elizabeth, 367

Bleeding Kansas, 347–349

Blennerhasset, Harman, 205

Blind people, reforms for, 292

Blockade: in Civil War, 371, 375–376; War for Independence and, 152, 153; in War of 1812, *212*

Blood sacrifice (Mayan), 4, *5*

Bloody Mary, *21*, 24

Blue laws, 43–44, 47

Blythe, William Jefferson. *See* Clinton, William Jefferson

Boleyn, Anne, 22

Bonaparte. *See* Napoleon

Bonds, government: Civil War, 395–396; Confederation and, 181

Book of Common Prayer, 24

Book of Mormon, The, 289

Boone, Daniel, 156; marriage laxity of, 261

Booth, John Wilkes, *392*, 394

Border ruffians, 347–349, *348*

Borders. *See* Expansion and expansionism; Frontier; *And specific border disputes*

Borrowing: in Civil War, 395–396. *See also* Debt

Boston: Bunker Hill, 137–138, *137*; Dorchester Heights, 147–148, *148*; War for Independence and, 147–148, *148*

Boston Massacre, 126–127, *127*, 159-A

Boston Tea Party, 129, 133, *134*, 159-A

Boulders, breaking up, 63, 64

Bounty jumpers, 367

Bowie, James, 322, *323*

Boycotts, Townshend Duties and, 124–125

Braddock, Edward, 108–109

Bradford, William, 39; Merrymount and, 42

Bragg, Braxton, 380, 389

Brant, Joseph (Thayendanega), *145*, 146, 150, 151

Breckinridge, John C., 356, 358

Breed's Hill, 137–138

Bridger, Jim, 326

Bridgman, Laura, 292

Brief Relation of the Destruction of the Indians, A (De las Casas), 16

Britain. *See* England (Great Britain)

Broad construction (of Constitution), 183, 220

Brooks, Preston, clubbing of Sumner by, 349–350, *349*

Brown, John: Harpers Ferry's raid by, 354–356, *354*; Pottawatomie Creek massacre and, 350, 355

Brownson, Orestes, 240–241

Bryan, William Jennings, as dark horse candidate, 328

Buccaneers. *See* Pirates and piracy

Buchanan, James, 328, 351–356, 395; Dred Scott case and, 351–353; election of 1856 and, 351; secession and, 358–359

Buck (slang for dollar), 182

Buell, Don Carlos, 375, 380

Buena Vista, battle at, *330*, *331*, 332

Bull Run: First Battle of, 368–370, *369*, *370*; Second Battle of, *379*

Bunker Hill, Battle of, 137–138, *137*

Bureau of Refugees, Freedmen, and Abandoned Lands. *See* Freedmen's Bureau

Burgoyne, John ("Gentleman Johnny"), 137, 138, 150–151; surrender at Saratoga, *151*

Burke, Edmund, 112, 123, 146, 147

Burned-over district, 288–292

Burnside, Ambrose, 374

Burr, Aaron: "conspiracy" of, 205–207; duel with Hamilton, 205; election of 1796, 192; election of 1800, 196–198

BUS. *See* Bank of the United States

Butler, Andrew, 349

Byles, Mather, 145

Byrd, William, 62, 105

C

Cabinet: of Adams, 192–193; department of, 252; of Jackson, 270–271, *271*; of Lincoln, 360; of Tyler, 281–282; of Washington, 179–180, *181*

Cabot, John, 20, *21*

Cabral, Pedro, 10

Calhoun, John C., 242, 253, 269–270, 350; blunders of, 272; Clay's Omnibus Bill and, 339–341, *339*; death of, 342; Jackson, Andrew, rift with, 269–270, *270*, 272; as Secretary of State, 282, 328; slavery and, 308; *South Carolina Exposition and Protest* by, 267, 270; Tariff of Abominations and, 267; Texas annexation and, 328; two presidents idea of, 341; as vice president, 254, 269–270; Wilmot Proviso and, 336

California: Alta California, 319; as Bear Flag Republic, 331; *camino real* in, 319; ceded from Mexico, 332; Chinese immigrants/ laborers in, 340; gold rush in, 337–338, *337*, *338*, 340; as Mexican territory, 319–320; missions in, 319; Russian claim to, 230, 231; statehood process of, 338–342

California trail, *327*

Californios, 330

Calvert, Cecilius, 34, *34*

Calvert, George, 34

Calvin, John, 21

Calvinists, 39, 42, 105

Camino real, 319

Camp meetings, 286–287, *286*, 288

Canada: American "assault" on (1812), 210–214; border disputes, definition, and treaties, 230, 282; British debate on return to France, 112–114; British take possession of (1763), 110, 115;

Catholic population in, 112; Catholic status in (Quebec Act), 134; Catholics forbidden in, 92; encouragement of settlement in, 92–93; French in, 91–95; habitants of, 115; indentured servitude in, 3 year length of, 92; "joint occupation" of Oregon, 230; as New France (1608–1763), 91–95; population, lack of, 92; Quebec Act and, 134; Rush-Bagot Agreement and, 230; slaves in, 93

Canals, 223–226; Erie Canal, *222*, 223–226, *223*; Mainline Canal, 225–226

Cane Ridge, Kentucky, 286–287, *286*

Cannibals All! (Fitzhugh), 309

Cannibalism (Aztec), 6

Canning, George, 231

Capital (city), decisions on location of, 182–183

Captain Kidd, 98

Carolina Grant (1663), 48–49

Carolinas, 48–50; Carolina Grant, 48–49; Charleston, 49, *50*; Fundamental Constitutions in, 49. *See also* North Carolina; South Carolina

Carpetbaggers, 409

Carson, Christopher ("Kit"), 320, 325, 327

Carter, Robert, 163

Carteret, George, 50–51

Cass, Lewis, 328, 336

Casualties. *See specific wars*

Catherine of Aragon, 22, 24

Catholicism, 16; anti-Catholics (Know-Nothings), 344–345; in Canada, 92, 112, 134; in French Canada, 112, 134; Indians and, 77–78; Jesuit priests, 93–94, *93*; Maryland as refuge for, 34–35, 48; One True Church of, 77; Quebec Act and, 134; in Texas, 321, *321*. *See also* Religion

Caucus, 229, 252; "King Caucus", 252

Cavaliers, 60

Cavalry, in Civil War, 365, *365*, 368

Cavelier, Robert, 94

Cayuga Indians, 75, 79

Central America, filibusters (adventurers) in, 343

Central Pacific Railroad, 395

Cerro Gordo, battle at, *331*, 332

Chamberlain, Joshua Lawrence, 386

Champlain, Samuel de, 35, 91; on intermarriage, 93

Chancellorsville, Battle of, 382–383, *386*

Channing, William Ellery, 285–286, 297

Chapultepec, battle at, 325, *331*, 332

Charles I, king of England, 31

Charles II, king of England, 48, 55; Berkeley, William, and, 61; Penn, William, and, 51, 52, *52*

Charles V, emperor, 14, 21, 22

Charlesfort, 35

Charleston Harbor, Fort Sumter in, 361–362, *361*

Charleston, South Carolina, 49, *50*, 63

Chase, Samuel, 202

Chatham, Lord, 133–134

Chauncy, Charles, 106–107

Checks and balances, in U.S. government, 174

Cheng Ho (Zheng He, China), 10

Cherokee Indians, 264–267; Sequoyah and, 264–265, *264*; spelling/syllabary of, 264–265, *264*; Trail of Tears and, 266–267, *266*

Cherokee Nation v. Georgia (1831), 265

Chesapeake (ship), 209

Chesapeake Bay region, 30, 59–60, *60*; Oyster War and, 170; Tidewater and, 59–60, *60*

Chewing gum, 323

Chicago, as frontier city (1843), *248*

Chichén Itzá, 4, *4*

Chickamauga, Battle of, 389

Child labor, 239–242, *242*

Children: American attitudes toward, 262; child labor, 239–242; Jackson's attitude toward, 262; as mill workers, 239–242, *242*; Pilgrim beliefs on, 45

Chili peppers, 17–18

Chinese immigrants, in California, 340

Christianity: Indians and, 77–78. *See also* Religion

Christy, Edwin P., 311

Chronometer, 69

Church: Church of England, 105–106, 161; Protestant Reformation and, 21–24; Roman Catholic, 16, 77; state separation from, 45–46. *See also* Religion; *specific religions*

Church of England. *See* Anglicans

Church of Jesus Christ of Latter-Day Saints. *See* Mormons and mormonism

Cincinnati (city), as frontier city, 248

Cincinnati, Order of, 178, 180, *180*

Cities: frontier, 248, *248*; settlement patterns (1800s), 247, *247*. *See also specific cities*

Citizen (French term)/Citizen Genêt, 186–187

Citizenship, period of residence for, Alien Act and, 193–194

Civil Rights Act (1875), 412

Civil War (U.S.), 364–398; from 1861-1862, 364–381, *365*; abolition of slavery and, 397; African Americans in Union army, 379–380, *396*, 397; aftermath of (Reconstruction), 399–414; Antietam and, 378; armies in, 364–367, 372; artillery in, 365–366; attrition, war of (1863–1865), 382–394, *383*; Billy Yank and Johnny Reb in, 366–367; Bull Run, Battles of, 368–370, *369*, *370*, *379*; campaign of 1861, 368–373; campaigns of 1863, 382–389, *383*; casualties in, *391*, 394; cavalry in, 365, *365*, *368*; Chancellorsville and, 382–383, *386*; Confederacy formation and, 359–360; consequences of, 395–397; desertions in, 367, 388, 393; draft in, 366–367, 387; economic policies and, 395; Emancipation Proclamation and, 378–379, end of, 392–394; experiences in (diaries and letters), 414-A-B; financing of, 395–396; first blood in, 360; Fort Sumter and, 361–362, *361*; Gettysburg and, 385–389, *386*; Grant and, 384–385, *385*, 389–394, *390*; infantry in, 366, 372; land policies and, 396; *Merrimack* and *Monitor* battle in, 375–376; musical anthems in, 379, 388; naming of battles in, 368; naval blockade in, 371, 375–376; navies in, 371, 375–376; northern strategy (Anaconda Plan) and, 371; Peninsula Campaign and, 377–378, *377*; Petersburg and Shenandoah in, 390–391; Pickett's Charge and, 388, *388*; politics after, 395; prisoner exchanges in, 380; Reconstruction after, 399–414, *400*; Seven Days' Battle and, 377–378, *377*; Sherman in Georgia, 391–392; Shiloh, Battle of, 372, *374*, 375; soldiers in, 366–367, *367*; southern strategy and, 371–373; stalemate in 1861–1863, *374*; stalemate in 1862, 373–380, *379*; Tennessee campaigns in, *374*, 375, 380, 389; "total war" in, 389–394, *390*; Vicksburg and, 383–384, *385*, 389; in West, *374*, 375, 380; women as soldiers in, 367; "Zouave" regiments in, 368. *See also* Reconstruction

"Civilized tribes", 268

Clarendon, earl of. *See* Cornbury, Lord (Edward Hyde)

Clark, William, 204–205

Class status, 100–103; lower orders, 102–103; mobility of, 101; property ownership and, 100–101; of women, 101–102

Clay, Henry, 220, *220*, 334; American System of, 220–221, 276; Bank War and, 274; California statehood debate and, 338–342, *339*; on the Constitution, 171; "corrupt bargain" election and, 255–256, *255*; election of 1824 and, 253–254, *254*, *255*; election of 1844 and, 329; Missouri Compromise and, 334, 335; National Road and, 222–223; Omnibus Bill and, 339–341, *339*; Second Bank of the United States and, 272–273; as Secretary of State, 256; as Speaker of the House, 220, *220*; transportation improvements and, 221–229

Clement VII (pope), 22

Clermont (steamboat), 228

Clinton, DeWitt, 224, 253

Clinton, Henry, 53, 137, 138, 151

Clinton, William Jefferson ("Bill"), impeachment of, 406

Cloth manufacturing, 57, 235–238, *236*; children and girls in, 239–242, *242*; wool vs. cotton, 236. *See also* Cotton and cotton industry; Textile industry; Wool and wool industry

Cobbett, William, 185

Code Duello, 349

Code of Honor, The, 349

Coercive Acts (1774), 133–134

Coffin handbill, *259*

Coinage, in Massachusetts, 65–66

Colleges. *See* Universities and colleges

Colón, Cristóbal. *See* Columbus, Christopher

Colonies (initial, in U.S.), 39–57, *40*, *56*; African Americans in, 80–89; Continental Congresses, 135; corporate, 47; culture in, 105–107; economy in, 41, 55–60, *56*, 62–65, 67–68; English background and, *21*, 26–30; English culture in, 105; family in, 98, 100–101; first colonization, 2–3; "Great Migration" and, 42, 43; Indians in/ interactions with, 71–80, *72*, *74*; life and society in 1600s, 55–70, *56*; life expectancy in, 60, 85, 97–98; mercantilism and, 55–63, *58*–63; moneymaking in, 48; Piedmont conflicts, 60; population in, 28–29, *29*, 39, 97–98, 108; private enterprise/trading companies and, 29–30; promoters of, 27; proprietary, 47–52; punishments in, 44, *44*; Puritans and, 42–45, 53; royal, 47, 48, 50; self-government in, 41–42; societal changes in (1700–1776), 97–103; trade and, 55–63, *56*; women's status in, 101–102. *See also* Colonial dissension; Colonial incidents and protests; Colonies, specific; Settlements; States

Colonies, specific: Carolinas, 48–50; Connecticut, 47; Georgia, 52; Maine, 47; Massachusetts Bay, 41–42; middle colonies, *49*, 67–68; New England, 39–45, *40*, *46*, 63–67; New Hampshire, 47; New Jersey, 50–52; Pennsylvania, 52; Plymouth Plantation, 40–41; Rhode Island, 45–47; Roanoke, 25–26; southern colonies, *51*, 58–63; Tidewater area, 59–60, *60*

Colonial assemblies and governors, 104–105

Colonial dissension (1763–1770), 112–125, *113*; boycott and, 124–125; British economy and, 115–116; British garrison established, 115–116; British soldiers, presence and, 127–128; Canada vs. sugar debate and, 112–114; Declaratory Act and, 124; Pontiac's rebellion and, *113*, 115; Proclamation of 1763 and, *114*, 115; Quartering Act of 1765 and, 116, 128; Sons of Liberty and, 121, 129, 133, 136; taxation acts and, *113*, 118–125, *121*. *See also* Taxes and taxation

Colonial incidents and protests (1770–1776), 126–142, *127*; alcohol, role in, 129; Boston Massacre, 126–127, *127*, 159-A; Boston Tea Party, 129, 133, *134*, 159-A; Bunker Hill, 137–138, *137*; *Common Sense* (Paine), 139; cutting the tie, 139–141; Declaration of Independence, 139–141; "Declaration of the Cause and Nature of Taking up Arms", 138–139; first battles, *127*; First Continental Congress, 135; friction with British soldiers (redcoats), 126–128, 130–131; *Gaspée*, burning of, *129*, 131–132; Intolerable Acts, 133–134; Lexington and Concord, 136–137, *136*, *137*, 159-B; protest leaders, 132–133, *132*; rebellion, 134–139, *137*; Regulators, 129–131; Second Continental Congress, 138–139; Sons of Liberty, 121, 129, 133, 136; Tea Act, 133. *See also* War for independence

Colonial militias, 96, 135, 143; opinions on, 108, 143

Colonial politicians, 122

Colonial tavern, *128*

Colonial wars, 92, 95–97, 107–110; "American Style" of war, 96; European warfare, 95–96, *95*

Colonization movement, for African Americans, 303–304

Columbian Exchange, 16–18

Columbus, Christopher, 6–8, *7*, 11–12; cost of expeditions of, 12; as mapmaker, 11, *12*; misjudgments of, 11; motives of, 7–8; ships of, 12; start as common sailor, 36; title of, 12, 20

Comanche Indians, 319, 322

Commerce. *See* Trade

Committees of Correspondence, 134–135

Common Sense (Paine), 139

Communities: of Puritans, 43; slave, 317–318; utopian, 291

Compass, 69

Compromise of 1850, 342, *352*

Compromise of 1877, 413

Concord, battle at, 136–137, *137*

Condon, Abby, 235

Conestoga wagons, *236*, 246–247

Confederacy, 359–360; army of, 364–367; Fourteenth Amendment, 405; government of, 359–360; pardons for Confederates, 402; Radical Reconstruction, 406–410, *406*; readmission of former states of, 401–403. *See also* Civil War (U.S.); Reconstruction

Confederate States of America. *See* Confederacy

Confederation, Articles of, 160, *161*, 164–168; divided authority under, 164; Northwest Ordinances, 166–167, *168*; western lands under, 164–166, *165*

Congregationalist Church, 47, 106, 161

Congress, Continental, 135, 138–139

Congress (U.S.), 174, Appendix A-4 to A-5; political party affiliations in, Appendix A-21 to A-23; slavery and, 334–335. *See also* House of Representatives; Senate

Connecticut (colony), 47. *See also* New England colonies

Conquistadores, 14–15, 16

Conscription Act (1873), 387

Consent of governed, for taxation, 104, 118–119, 122–123

Constitution(s): Articles of Confederation and, 160, *161*, 164–168; British equivalent of, 160; Fundamental Constitutions of Carolina, 49; Lecompton Constitution, 353; state, 160–164

Constitution (U.S.), 171–176, Appendix A-4 to A-11; admirability/reputation of, 171; alcohol consumed during party for, 172; amendment process, 174, 334; amendments to, 176, Appendix A-8 to A-11; Bill of Rights, 176; broad construction of, 183, 220; checks, limits, and balances in, 174; conservatives at convention for, 173–174; convention for, 171–173, *172*; delegates at convention for, *172*, 173, *173*; federal relationship in, 174; federalists and anti-federalists and, 175–176; Founding Fathers and, 171–173, *172*; interpretation of, 183–184, 194; judicial review of, 201–202; length of, relative, 174; ratification of, 175–176; slavery and, 174–175, 334; strict construction of, 183–184; "three-fifths compromise" and, 175, 197. *See also specific amendments*

Constitutional Convention, 171–173, *172*

Constitutional era (1781–1789), 160–177, *161*; Articles of Confederation and, 160, *161*, 164–168; authority of states vs. Congress and, 164; change, calls for, 170; Constitution and, 171–176; difficulties and anxieties in, 169–171; foreign meddling and, 170; lack of respect and insults in, 169–170; monetary system and problems in, 161, 169, *169*; Northwest Ordinances and, 166–167, *168*; ratification and, 175–176; religion in, 161; Shays Rebellion and, 170–171, *171*; slaves, manumission in the South and, 163; state constitutions and, 160–164; voting rights and, 161–162, *162*; western lands and, 164–166, *165*; women's place and rights and, 162–163

Constitutional Union party, 358

Construction of constitution: broad construction, 183, 220; strict construction, 183–184

Continental Army, 143–145, 152–153

Continental Congress: First (1774), 135; Second (1775), 138–139. *See also* Constitutional era

Contracts, sanctity of, 219

Convention, Constitutional, 171–173, *172*

Coode, John, 35, 66

Cooper, James Fenimore, 219, 277

Copperheads, 373–375

Corbin, Abel R., 411

Corbin, Margaret, 152

Corduroy roads, *221*

Corn, maize (American corn), 17

Cornbury, Lord (Edward Hyde), *104*

Cornwallis, Charles, 150, 154–155, *154*; surrender at Yorktown, 155

Coronado, Francisco, 16

Corporate colonies, 47

"Corrupt bargain" election (1824), 255–256, *255*

Corruption: Black Friday (1869) and, 411; Grant administration and, 409; Reconstruction governments and, 410–413

Cortés, Hernán, 13–14, *14*

Corwin, Thomas, 332

Cottage industry, 236

Cotton, John, 43, 45, 77

Cotton and cotton industry, 49, 242–244; cloth manufacture in, 236; cottage industry (putting-out system) and, 236; cotton gin and, 242–244, *243*; expansion of, 244, *244*, *313*;

mills and, 237–238, *237*, *238*; naval blockade (Civil War) and, 373; slave labor and, 244, *312*, 313, *313*; spinning machines and, 236–237, *236*; tariffs and, 267

Cotton diplomacy, 373

Cotton gin, 242–244, *243*

Coureurs de bois, 94

Coverture, 101–102

Cowboys, *vaqueros*, 322

Cragin, Simeon, 250

Crawford, William, 229, 254, *254*

Crime: "lower orders" and, 102–103; punishments in the colonies, 44, *44*

Crittenden, John J., 359

Crittenden's Compromise Plan (1861), 359, *360*

Croatoan Island and "CROATOAN" inscription, 25, 26

Crockett, David ("Davy"): at Alamo, 322, *323*; on Van Buren, 280

Cromwell, Oliver, 55, 65, 95

Crops. *See* Agriculture; *specific crops*

Cross-dressing, *104*

Cross-staff, 69

Crouch, Darius, 380

Cuba, 12; filibusters in, 343; Polk's expansionism and, 332

Cuffee, Paul, 303

Cuitláhuac, 13

Cultivation. *See* Agriculture

Cumberland Gap, 245

Cumberland River, in Civil War, *374*, 375

Cumberland Road, 222, *223*

Currency. *See* Money

Currier, Nathaniel, 279

Currier and Ives prints, 279

Custer, George Armstrong, 190

Custis, Martha, 101

Cutler, Timothy, 105

D

Daily life. *See* Lifestyles

Dale, Thomas, 30, 31

Dark horse candidates, 328

Dartmouth College v. Woodward (1819), 219

Davenport, James, 106

Davis, David, 413

Davis, Jefferson, *359*; in Civil War, 385, 392–394; as president of Confederacy, 359, 360, 361–362; Taylor, Zachary, and, 343; transcontinental railroad and, 343

Davis, Joseph, 316

De Bow, J. D. B., on U.S. expansion, 332

De las Casas, Bartolomé, 15, 16, 54-A

De Sille, Nicholas, 48

Deaf people, schools and reforms for, 292

Debates: Lincoln-Douglas, *360*; Webster-Hayne, 276

Debt, assumption of state debt, 182–183

Debt, national, 180–181; Civil War and, 395–396; Confederation debt, 181; Jefferson, Thomas and, 201; War for Independence and, 181–182

Decatur, Stephen, 208, 217

Declaration of Independence, 139–141; borrowed statements in, 140; depiction of George III in, 139–140; "inalienable rights" and, 141; quotations from, 126, 141, 159-A; signing of (painting), *140*; text of, Appendix A-2 to A-3; universal human rights in, 141

"Declaration of Sentiments and Resolutions", 296

"Declaration of the Cause and Necessity of Taking Up Arms", 138–139

Declaratory Act (1766), 124

Deerfield, Massachusetts, 97, *97*

Defoe, Daniel, 96

Deists, 284–285

Delaware: annexed to Pennsylvania, 52; Continental Congress and, 139; economy in, 67–68; population diversity in, 68; slaves in, 304

Delaware Indians, 115

Delaware River, Washington's crossing of, 150

Democracy, Pilgrims' view of, 41

Democratic party: Civil War and, 395, 405; as Democratic-Republicans, 258–261, 269, 275; election of 1860 and, 356, *357*; ideology of, 276–277; Mexican War, sentiments on, 332; slave states and, 328; in South, 395; split in 1860, 356; symbols of, *273*; "Whigs", 275–281. *See also* Elections

Democratic-Republicans, 258–261, 269, 275

Depression, of 1830s–1840s, 275, 279

Desegregation, 266

Desert, Great American, 320–321

Desertion, in Civil War, 367, 388, 393

Dew, Thomas Roderick, 308

Dialect, 408

Díaz, Bartholomeu, 10, 11

Dickinson, John, 121, 139, 166

Dictionary of the English Language (Webster), 219

Dinwiddie, Robert, 108

Disciples of Christ, 287

Discoveries, 1–19; exchange of plants, animals, and disease and, 16–18; first colonization of Americas and, 2–3; Mesoamerican civilization and, 2–6, *3–5*; other discoverers in, 7; Portugal and Spain and, 10–16; of United States, 14; Western European expansion and, 6–10

Disease, 18; Columbian Exchange and, 18; smallpox, 18, *18*, 76; veneral disease, 18

Disraeli, Benjamin, 328

Dix, Dorothea, 293

"Dixie" (song), 388

Doctors, women as, 367

Dollar, 161; Confederation era, 169, *169*; division into quarters, 182

Domesticated mammals, 16–17

Dominion of New England, 56, 66–67

Dorchester Heights, 147–148, *148*

Dorr's Rebellion, 257

Doughface, 351, 353, 356

Douglas, Stephen A.: Compromise of 1850 and, 342; debates with Lincoln, *360*; election of 1860 and, 356, 358; Freeport Doctrine of, 353–354; Kansas-Nebraska Act and, 343–344, 347; Lecompton Constitution and, 353; on radial equality, 354; transcontinental railroad and, 343–344

Douglass, Frederick, 296, 298–299, 314

Dousing, 288

Draft (military): anti-draft riots, 387; Civil War and, 366–367, 387

Drake, Francis, *23*, 24–25, 80

Dred Scott case (*Dred Scott v. Sandford*), 351–353, *351*; legal status of slavery and, *352*

Drinking. *See* Alcohol; Prohibition

Drums, snare, 148

Duels and dueling, 205, 260

Dulany, Daniel, 119

Durante vita, 84

Dutch: New Netherland/New Amsterdam settlement, 35–36, *37*; Pennsylvania Dutch, 68, 99; women's rights and, 101

Dutch language, insulting uses of, 48
Dutch Reformed Church, 48, 106
Dutch settlements. *See* New York
Dutch West India Company, 35, 48
Duties. *See* Tariffs

E

Early, Jubal, 391
East India Company, 29, 30; Tea Act and, 133
Eastern Woodlands Indians, 71–76, *74*
Eaton, Peggy O'Neill, 270–271, *271*
Eaton, William, 206
Economy: Bank War and, 272–275; Civil War and, 395; in colonial period, 41, 55–60, *56*, 62–65, 67–68; cotton economy in the South, 242–244; depressions in, 275, 279; development in 1790–1830, 234–242, *235*; financial chaos in (1833), 274–275; land and, 244–250; manufacturing and the Northeast, 234–242, 283-A; Panic of 1819 and, 249. *See also* Depression
Edmonds, Sarah Lemma, 367
Education. *See* Schools; Universities and colleges
Edward VI, king of England, *21*, 24
Edwards, John, 106, 113
Eighth Amendment, 176, Appendix A-8
El Dorado, 16
Elcaño, Juan Sebastián de, 13
Elections: of 1796 (Jefferson elected), 191–192; of 1800 (Jefferson elected), 196–202; of 1824 (Quincy Adams elected), 252–256; of 1828 (Jackson elected), 258–263; of 1832 (Jackson elected), 272; of 1836 (Van Buren elected), *277*, 279; of 1840 (Harrison elected), 279–281, *281*; of 1844 (Polk elected), 329; of 1848 (Taylor elected), 336–337; of 1852 (Pierce elected), 342–343; of 1856 (Buchanan elected), 350–351; of 1860 (Lincoln elected), 356–359, *357*; of 1868 (Grant elected), 407; of 1872 (Grant elected), 411–412; of 1876 (Hayes elected), 412–413; complete details on, Appendix A-14 to A-17; "corrupt bargain" election (1824), 255–256, *255*; dark horse candidates in, 328; lame duck period and, 328–329; parties and candidates in, Appendix A-14 to A-17; popular and electoral votes in, Appendix A-14 to A-17; two-term tradition for presidents and, 209. *See also* Electoral college
Electoral college, 178, 196, Appendix A-9; "corrupt bargain" election and, 255–256, *255*; tie resolution in, 197
Eliot, John, 77
Elizabeth I, queen of England, 23, *23*, 24–26; reign of, *21*, 24–27; sea dogs and, 24–25; Virginia named for, *26*
Emancipation Proclamation, 378–379
Embargo Act (1807), 209
Emerson, Ralph Waldo, 356; on Mexican War, 332, 334; on Webster, Daniel, 341
Emmett, Daniel D., 311, 388
Empires: English (British), in North America, 26–30, 107–110, *107*; French, in North America, 35, 91–95, *107*; Spanish, in the Americas, 13–16, 35
Enclosure movement (England), 28
Encomiendas, 15, 16
England (Great Britain): age of consent for sex in, 102; Britain vs. England, terminology, 55; Civil War (U.S.) and, 373; "constitution" of, 160; Elizabethan reign in, 24–26;

empire in North America, 26–30, 107–110, *107*; France, wars with, 95–97, 187; House of Commons and, 116–117, *116*; House of Lords and, 116–117, *116*; impressment of sailors by, 187, 208–209, *208*; instability in, 22–24; King (monarch), Parliament and, 116–117, *116*, 161; mercantilism and, 55–57, 112; monetary system, 115–116, 161; Navigation Acts, 58; Parliament and, 116–117, *116*, 161; promoters of colonization in, 27; Protestant Reformation in, 21–24; salutary neglect, 103–104, 112; Scotland and, 55; sea dogs of, 24–25; soldiers of (*See* Redcoats); Spanish Armada and, *21*, 26–27; surplus population of, 28–29, *29*; taxation by, 104, 118–121; trade and, 55–63, *119*; War of 1812 and, 209–213, *212*
England's Treasure by Foreign Trade (Mun), 55, 112
English colonies in the Americas, 30–35, 39–57, *40*; background for colonization, 21, 26–30; colonial incidents and protests, 112–142, *113*, *127*; colonial wars and, *92*, 95–97; dependence on colonial economies, 57–58; economic competition with, 64; private enterprise and, 29–30; promoters of, 27; surplus population for, 28–29; trade with, 27, 55–57
English Navy, 24–25, 144–145, 156, 187, 208
Entail, laws of, 101
Enumerated articles, 58
Epidemics: Columbian Exchange and, 16–18; smallpox, 18, *18*, 76. *See also* Disease
Era of Good Feelings, 217, 229–231
Erie Canal, *222*, 223–226
Erie Indians, 79
Europe: expansionism in the Americas, 6–10; exploration by, motivations for, 7–9; political instability in, 20–24. *See also* Colonies; Discoveries; Settlements
European warfare, 95–96, *95*
Evangelical reform, 292–296
Evangelicalism, 288–292
Evans, Oliver, 238–239
Everett, Edward, 358
Exchange of plants, animals, and disease (Columbian Exchange), 16–18
Executions, in the colonies, 44
Expansion and expansionism, *217*, 230–232, 319–333; from 1815–1850, 319–333, *320*, *326*; extreme designs for, 332; Florida and, 230–231; Manifest destiny and, *326*, 327–328; Mexican War and, 330–332, *331*; Mexico Borderlands, Americans in, 319–324, *321*; Missouri and, 231–232; Oregon Country and, 230, 324–328; symbol of, *329*; Texas and, 321–324, 328–329. *See also* Discoveries; Empires
Expedition by Lewis and Clark, *203*, 204–205
Exploration. *See* Discoveries

F

Factors, tobacco, *59*, 60
Fall River system, 239
Fallen Timbers, Battle of, *189*, 191
Families: colonial law and, 100–101; size of, 64, 98
Farley, Harriet, 240–241
Farming. *See* Agriculture
"Father of his country", Washington as, 157–158, *157*
Favorite son, 342
Federal deficit. *See* Debt, national
Federal government, assumption of state debts by, 182

Federal relationship, 174
Federalist Papers, 176
Federalists, 175–176, 188; Alien and Sedition Acts and, 193–194, 196; anti-federalists, 176; Federalist party, 188, 191, 217; land law and policies of, 249; presidents (1789–1801), *179*; treaties of (Jay's and Pinckney's), 187–189, *188*; Whigs and, 276
Fences, stone (New England), *63*
Ferdinand, king of Aragon, 7, 12
Fife music, 148
Fifteen Gallon Law (1838), 295
Fifteenth Amendment, 407, Appendix A-10
Fifth Amendment, 176, Appendix A-8
"54-40 or fight", 340
Filibusters (adventurers), 343
Fillmore, Millard, *339*, 341–342, 345; election of 1856 and, 351
Financing, of roads and highways, 221–222
Finney, Charles Grandison, 288
Fire-eaters, 340
Firearms: Kentucky long rifle, 247; manufacture/ mass production of, 239; muskets, 96, 135; muskets retrieved from Gettysburg, 385
First Amendment, 176, Appendix A-8
First Bank of the United States, 183–184, *183*, 221
First Continental Congress (1774), 135
First Great Awakening, 106, 107, 113
Fishing, in colonial times, 64
Fisk, James ("Jubilee Jim"), 410–411
Fitch, John, 228
Fitzhugh, George, 308, 309
Five Nations of the Iroquois Confederacy, *72*, 75–76
Flag ("Old Glory"), 218
Fletcher v. Peck (1810), 219
Florida, 230–231; British possession of (1763), 110; Ponce de León in, 14; Spain and, 16, 35, 94–95, 230
Flour mills, 238–239
Floyd, John, 358–359
Flu (influenza), 18
Foods, New World contributions, 17–18
Forbes, John, 135
Force Bill: of 1832, 267; of 1890, 412
Foreign policy, Monroe Doctrine and, 231
Fort Orange (Albany, New York), 79
Fort Ross, 230, 231
Fort St. George, 30
Foster, Stephen, 311
Founding Fathers, 171–173, *172*
Fourteenth Amendment, 405, Appendix A-9
Fourth Amendment, 176, Appendix A-8
Fourth of July, 139, 217–218, *218*
Fox, Charles, 123–124, 147
Fox, Margaret, 292
France: aid to American War for Independence, 147, 152, 155; American colonies of, 35; in the Americas, 91–95; "citizen" title and Citizen Genêt, 186–187; early settlements, 35; empire in North America, 35, 91–95, *107*; explorers in the Americas, 94; Franklin, Benjamin, in, *146*, 147, 157; Indians as friends and allies of, 93–94, 95, 108; Louisiana Purchase from, 202–207; New France (Canada) and, 91–95; privateers of, 186–187; Queen Anne's War and, *92*, 96–97; revolution and Reign of Terror in, 184–187, *185*; U.S. Civil War and, 372–373; U.S. ships seized by, 193; war scare with (1797), 193, 196; wars with Great Britain, 95–97; XYZ Affair and, 193, 196
Francis I, king of France, 20–21

Franklin, Benjamin, 80; as abolitionist, 174; Anglophilia of, 105; on Canada, potential of, 114; at Constitutional Convention, 171, *172*, 173; Declaration of Independence and, 139; family size of, 98; First Continental Congress and, 135; in France during War of Independence, *146*, 147, 157; on German immigrants, 99; illegitimate son of, 103; Stamp Act collection, application for, 119; on Whitefield, George, 106; "wife" of (Deborah Read), 103

Free Soil party, 336, 337, 347–349

Free speech, First Amendment and, 176, Appendix A-8

Freedmen, 401, 404–405; black codes and, 402

Freedmen's Bureau, 404–405, *404*

Freemasons. *See* Masonic Order

Freeport Doctrine, 353–354

Frémont, John C., 326–327, *331*, 378; election of 1856 and, 351

French America, 91–95

French and Indian War, *92*, 108

French Revolution, 184–187, *185*

Freneau, Philip, 187

Frethorne, Richard, 20

Friends, Society of. *See* Quakers

Frobisher, Martin, 24–25

Frontier: border ruffians in, 347–349, *348*; cities in, 248, *248*; federalist treaties and, *188*; Indian Wars in, 189–191, *189*; life in, 186, 349; population in (1790–1820), 245–246, *245*; Regulators and, 129–131; trans-Appalachian, 244–248; unrest in, 129–131; Whiskey Rebellion and, *190*, 191. *See also* West

Fugitive Slave Act: of 1793, 306, 335; of 1850, 342, 350

Fugitive slaves, 306–307

Fulton, Robert, 228

Funding debate (1790), 181–182

Fur trade, 57, 78–79, 324

G

Gadsden, James, 343

Gadsden Purchase, 343

Gag rule, 308

Gage, Thomas, 133–134, 138

Gallatin, Albert, 201

Gallaudet, Thomas, 292

Galloway, James, 211

Galloway, Joseph, 135, 138, 151

Gálvez, Bernardo de, 147, 152

Gama, Vasco da, 10

Gardoqui, Diego de, 170

Garfield, James A., as dark horse candidate, 328

Garrison, William Lloyd, 296–298, 307, 361

Gaspée (ship), burning of, *129*, 131–132

Gates, Horatio, *151*, 152

Gauntlet, running the, 75

Gender, male-female ratio of colonists, 42

Genêt, Edmond (Citizen Genêt), 186–187

George III, king of England, 117, *117*; crowning of, *113*; depiction by Thomas Paine, 139; depiction in Declaration of Independence, 139–140; desires for his colonial subjects, 126; equestrian statue in New York, *144*; eyeglasses of, 141; First Continental Congress and, 135; the "king's friends", 117, 124; personal style of, 117; preference for Tory ministers, 116; Tea Act and, 133; on Washington, George, retirement of, 191

Georgia: Cherokee removal and lawsuits in, 265–266; colony, 52; Sherman's march across, 391–392. *See also* Southern colonies

German immigrants, 83, 98–99; German language newspaper, *100*

Germany, immigrants from, 83, 98–99

Gerry, Elbridge, 193

Gettysburg, campaign and Battle of, 385–389, *386*

Gettysburg Address, 394–395

Ghent, Treaty of, 214

Gibbons v. Ogden (1824), 220

Gilbert, Humphrey, *21*, 25

Gilbert, Raleigh, 30

Girls: Lowell Girls, 240–242, *242*, 283-A. *See also* Child labor; Children; Women

Gladstone, William, 171

God(s). *See* Religion; specific gods

Gold: Black Friday scandal and (1869), 411; early exploration and, 5, 13, 16, 27; *siglo de oro*, 21, 26–27; in Spanish America, 16

Gold Coast, 87, 89

Gold rush, 337–338, *337*, *338*, 340

Golden Hind (ship), 24, 25

Goose girl, *82*

Gorges, Fernando, 47

Gould, Jay, 410–411

Government (U.S.): checks and balances in, 174; Congress and, 174, Appendix A-4 to A-5; executive branch of, Appendix A-7 to A-8; judicial branch of, 174, Appendix A-7. *See also* Congress (U.S.); Federal government; Supreme Court

Governors, royal (colonial), 104–105

Graduation (land policy), 250

Grains, Old and New World, 17

Grant, Ulysses S., 375, *384*; before Richmond (1864–1865), 390, *390*; characteristics of, 384–385, *384*; in Civil War, 385, 389–394; corruption and, 409; election of 1868 and, 407; election of 1872 and, 411–412; on Mexican War, 332; presidency of, 409–412; racial attitudes of, 407–409; Vicksburg campaign of, 385, *385*

Great American Desert, 320–321

Great Awakening, 106, 107, 113; Second Great Awakening, 288

Great Britain. *See* England (Great Britain)

"Great Migration" (1630–1640), 42, 43

Greeley, Horace, 361, 392, *411*, 412

Green Mountain Boys, 138

Greenbacks, 395–396

Greene, Nathaniel, 147, 218

Greenhow, Rose O'Neal, 367

Greenville, Treaty of, *189*, 191

Grenville, George, 117–118, *118*, 119

Grotius, Hugo, 55, 95

Guadalupe-Hidalgo, Treaty of, 332, 334

Guadeloupe. *See* Martinique and Guadaloupe

Guerrero, Gonzalo, 13

Gullah, 408

Guns. *See* Firearms

Gunter's chain, 166, 167

Gutiérrez, Pablo, 337

H

Habeas corpus, suspension by Lincoln, 373–374, 400

Haiti, 202–203

Hakluyt, Richard, *21*, 27; map of, *28*

Hale, Nathan, 218

Halleck, Henry, 375

Hamilton, Alexander, 145, 169; as abolitionist, 174; Annapolis meeting and, 170; assumption and, 182; broad constructionism of, 183; Burr duel with, 205; capital location and, 182–183; at Constitutional Convention, 173–174, *173*; death of, 205; election of 1800 and, 197, 198; as federalist, 176, 191; tariff of, 180, 184; as treasury secretary, 180–184, *181*; whiskey tax of, 191

Hamlin, Hannibal, 358

Hancock, John: house of, *105*; signature on Declaration of Independence, *105*, 141; smuggling by, 118

Hard-money men, 274

Hargreaves, James, 236

Harlan, John Marshall, 412

Harmer, Josiah, 190

Harpers Ferry, Brown's raid on, 354–356, *354*

Harriot, Thomas, 32

Harris, Isaac, 296

Harris, Joel Chandler, 408

Harrison, William Henry, 191, 279–281; death of, 281; election of 1840 and, 279–281, *281*; at Tippecanoe, 212–213; "Tippecanoe and Tyler Too" slogan and, 279–280, *280*

Hartford Convention, 210

Harvard College, 105, 278

Harvey, William, 106

Hawai'i, missionaries in, 293

Hayes, Rutherford B., election of 1876 and, 412–413

Hayne, Robert, Webster-Hayne debate, *276*, 279

Hays, Molly, 152

Headright system, 32, 48

Henry, Patrick, 77, 132; as anti-federalist, 176; biography of, 218; "Caesar and Brutus" speech of, 122, 132; family size of, 98; "Give me liberty" speech of, 132; proposal for Indian-white marriages, 162; on proposed Constitutional change, 170; on Stamp Act, 122

Henry the Navigator (Portugal), 10

Henry VII, king of England, 20, 55

Henry VIII, king of England, 22; annulment and marriages of, 22; reformation and, 22–24; religious practices of, 22

Herkimer, Nicholas, 151

Hessian troops, 143, 152

Heyward, Nathaniel, 312

Hiawatha, 75–76

Higher education. *See* Universities and colleges

Highways. *See* Roads and highways

Hillbillies, 354; accent of, 100

Hindman, T. C., 372

Hispanic settlements, 35

Hispaniola, 7, 12, 16, 54-A. *See also* Haiti

Hodges, Jennie, 367

Holidays, Fourth of July, 139, 217–218, *218*

Holland, Pilgrims in, 39–40

Homestead Act (1862), 396

Homesteads, 396

Hooker, Joseph ("Fighting Joe"), 382–383, *386*

Hooker, Thomas, 47

Hookers (term use), 383

Hopkinson, Francis, 156

Hopper, Isaac, 163–164

Hore, Richard, 21

House of Burgesses, 34, 60, 84

House of Commons (England), 116–117, *116*

House of Lords (England), 116–117, *116*

House of Representatives (U.S.), 174; composition of, Appendix A-4; gag rule in, 308. *See also* Impeachment

Housing: log cabins, 186. *See also* Cities
Houston, Sam, 322, 323
Howard, O. O., 404
Howe, Julia Ward, 379, 388, 397
Howe, Samuel Gridley, 292
Howe, William, 139–140, 147, 151; Loring, Elizabeth and, 147
Howland, John and Eliza, 39
Hudson, Henry, 27
Hudson's Bay Company, *326*, 327
Hughes, John J., 345
Huguenots, 35, 92
Huitzilopochtli, 6
Human rights, in Declaration of Independence, 141
Human sacrifice, Aztecs and, 5
Huron Indians, 79, *79*, 93
Hutchins, Thomas, 167
Hutchinson, Anne, 46–47, *47*
Hutchinson, Thomas, 133
Hyde, Edward, Lord Cornbury, *104*

I
Illegitimate births, 103
Imago Mundi (d'Ailly), 11
Immigrants and immigration: Chinese, 340; German, 83, 98–99; Irish, 100, 325, 334; Scotch-Irish, 100, 130; stresses of, 344–345; westward expansion (1844–1856), 334–346, *335*
Immigration Restriction League
Impeachment, 406; of Clinton, Bill, 406; of Johnson, Andrew, 406–407; Nixon and, 406
Import duties. *See* Tariffs
Impressment, 187, 208–209, *208*
Inalienable rights, 141
Incas, conquest of, 15–16
Indentured servitude, 81–83; numbers and cost of immigrants, 98–99; seven years of, 81; three year term (in Canada), 92
Independence: Declaration of, 126, 139–141, *140*; first battles for, *127*; First Continental Congress, 135; protests and incidents leading to, 126–142, *127*; War for. *See* War for Independence. *See also* Colonial incidents and protests
Independence Day (July 2, 1776), 139. *See also* Fourth of July
India, East India Company and, 29, 30
Indian wars: French and Indian War, 92, 108; in Northwest Territory, 189–191, *189*
Indians, 71–80; bow and arrow of, 72; Cherokee, 264–267, *264*; Christianity and, 77–78; "civilized tribes", 268; colonial interactions with, 76–80; colonial women captured by, 76; costumes used in Boston Tea Party, 133; culture in transition, 76–80, *77*; diseases and, 71, 76, *79*; in early colonial history, 11, 71–80, *72*; of eastern woodlands, 71–76, *74*; as farmers, 72–73; Five Nations and, *72*, 75–76; as French friends/allies, 93–94, 95, 108; fur trade and, 78–79; gauntlet, running the, 75; Hiawatha and, 75–76; horses and, 17; as hunters, 72; Huron warrior, *79*; Iroquois Confederacy and, *72*, 75–76; Iroquois longhouse, *75*; Jackson, Andrew, and, 263; King Philip's War and, 79–80; land purchases and misunderstandings about, 78; languages of, 74; marriages, interracial, and, 76–77, 93, 162; names of and used by, 73, 74, 92; naming of (by explorers), 7; Northwest Territory, wars in, 189–191, *189*;

population decline of, 16; portrayal of, *17*, 54-A; "praying" Indians, 77, 79, 80; racial concepts and, 76–77, 80; removal of Southeastern tribes and, 263–267, *265*, *266*; Sacajawea, 205; as "les sauvages", 92; scalping by, 78; scalps of, bounty for, 96; scurvy among, 73; Secotan village and, *73*; segregation and, 76–77; seminomadic lifestyle of, 73; separate sphere for, 76–77; "starving times" of, 73; Tecumseh and, 211–213, *211*; Tenskwatawa ("The Prophet") and, 211–213; tobacco use by, 32; Trail of Tears and, 266–267, *266*; in War for Independence, *145*, 146, 150, 151; in War of 1812, 210–213, *212*; as warriors, 74–75; women among, empowerment and status of, 76; women captured by, fate of, 76. *See also* Indian wars
Indigo, 62, 101
Individual rights, 176
Industrial Revolution, 234–237; in Northeast, 237–242; technological piracy and, 237
Industrialization, cotton and, 242–244
Infanticide, 102–103
Infantry, in Civil War, 366, 372
Influenza, 18
Inheritance, laws concerning, 101
Insane asylums, reform of, 293
Inter Caetera, 13
Interchangeable parts, 239
Interracial marriages, of Indians and whites, 76–77, 93
Intolerable Acts, 133–134
Inventors and inventions, 238–239; cotton gin, 242–244, *243*. *See also specific inventors and inventions*
Irish Americans: anti-draft riot (1863), 387; Catholicism of, anti-Catholic sentiments, 345, 350; immigration of, 100, 325, 334; Know-Nothings and, 345, 350; in Mexican War, 325; as Patricios (in Mexico), 325; Scotch-Irish, 100, 130
Irish immigrants, 100, 325, 334
Iroquois Confederacy, *72*, 75–76; in War for Independence, 146
Iroquois Indians. *See* Iroquois Confederacy
Iroquois longhouse, *75*
Irving, Washington, 209, 219
Isabella, queen of Castille, 7, 11, 12
Iturbide, Agostin de, 230
Ivory Coast, 87, *89*

J
Jackson, Andrew, *262*, *274*; attitudes on women, children, race, and governance, 261–263; Bank War and, 272–275, 276; at Battle of New Orleans, 214, 217; Burr conspiracy and, 205; Calhoun, rift with, 269–270, *270*, 272, 275; constitutional inconsistencies of, 263; duels of, 260; Eaton affair and, 270–271, *271*; election of 1824 and, 254, *254*; election of 1828 and, *256*, 258–263; election of 1832 and, 272; in Florida, 230; health of, 269, 272; inauguration celebrations and mob for, 261; Indian removal and, 263–267, *265*; as "King Andrew", *275*, 276; Masonic membership of, 258; mudslinging and attacks on, 258–261, *259*; nullification crisis and, 267, 270; in old age, *274*; Peggy O'Neill Eaton affair and, 270–271, *271*; pet banks of, 274; presidency of, 258, 263–275; regrets of, 275; road bills and, 263; spoils system and, 263;

as symbol/giant of his age, 261, 275; Tariff of Abominations and, 267; Texas and, 322, 323; vetoes of, 276
Jackson, Thomas J. ("Stonewall"), 370, 374, *375*, 383
Jaeger rifle, 135
James I, king of England, 27, 29–30, 55, 100; control of Virginia by, 34, 47; Pilgrims and, 40, 41; on smoking, 32
James II (Duke of York, England), 48
James, Jesse and Frank, 347
Jamestown, 30–34; Massacre of 1622, *33*, 34; Powhatans and, 31, 33–34; survival in, 30–31; tobacco and, *31*, 32. *See also* Virginia
Japan, distance from Europe, 11
Jay, John, 164; as abolitionist, 174; as federalist, 176; Jay's Treaty, 187–188; resignation of, 188
Jayhawkers, 349
Jay's Treaty, 187–188, *188*
Jefferson, Thomas, 196–209, *197*; on constitutions, 160; Declaration of Independence and, 139–140, 141; election of 1796 and, 191–192; election of 1800 and, 196–202; Francophilia of, 185; Kentucky Resolutions, 194; Louisiana Purchase, 202–207; *Marbury v. Madison* and, 201; Monticello and, *199*; on northerners vs. southerners, 216–217; Northwest Ordinances and, 167, *168*; personal qualities of, 198–199; presidency of, 196–209, *197*, *200*; Republican party of, 188; Second Continental Congress and, 138; as Secretary of State, 180, *181*; slaves of, 145, 199; as vice president, 192; Washington, George and, 157, 158, 184; wife of, 101
Jefferson Republicans, 188, 193, *197*, 217, 252–253
Jehovah's Witnesses, 289
Jenkins, Robert, ear of, 107
Jerome, Chauncey, 239
Jesuit priests, 93–94, *93*
Johnny Reb, 366–367
Johnson, Andrew, 401–403, *401*; achievements of, 407; background of, 401–402; Fourteenth Amendment and, 405; impeachment of, 406–407, *407*; National Union party and, 405–406; reconstruction and, 402, 404, 405–407
Johnson, Robert G., 18
Johnston, Albert Sidney, 372, 375
Johnston, Joseph E., 368, *369*, 394
Joliet, Louis, 93, *93*
Jomini, Henri de, 364
Jones, John Paul, 152
Judicial review, 201–202
Judiciary Act (1790), 201
Judiciary branch of government, 174, Appendix A-7
Julian, George W., 403
Jumpin' Jim Crow, 311

K
Kalb, Johann, 153
Kansas-Nebraska Act (1854), *341*, 343–346, *352*
Kansas Territory: Bleeding Kansas, 347–349; border ruffians in, 347–349, *348*; Lecompton Constitution in, 353
Kay, John, 236
Kearny, Stephen W., 330–331, *331*
Keelhauling, 36
Kelpius, Johannes, 51
Kentucky: Boone in, 156; in Civil War, *374*, *375*, 380

Kentucky long rifle, 247
Kentucky Resolutions, 194, 202
Key, Frances Scott, 211, 218
Kidnapping, 81–82
Kieft, Willem, 36
King George's War, *92*, 96, 107–108
King Philip's War, 79–80
King, Rufus, 229
King William's War, *92*, 95, 96
Kings and kingdoms. *See specific countries and rulers*
King's Friends (England), 117, 124
Klan. *See* Ku Klux Klan (KKK)
Know-Nothings, 345, 350
Knox, Henry, 147; as Secretary of War, 180, *181*
Kosciusko, Thaddeus, 153
Ku Klux Klan (KKK), 410, *410*

L

La Flesche, Susette, 78
La Salle, Sieur de (René-Robert Cavelier), 94
Labor: apprentices and, 81, 101; Lowell girls and, 240–242, *242*; servants and, 81–85. *See also* Machines; Slaves and slavery
Labrador, 21
Lafayette, Marie Joseph, Marquis de, 152–153, *153*, 155, 157, 184
Lafitte, Jean, 214
Lame duck presidency period, of Tyler, 328–329
Land: Articles of Confederation and, 164–166, *165*; Civil War policies and, 396; federal land policy (1800s), 248–250; free land, 396; graduation and, 250; Homestead Act and, 396; Morrill Act and, 396; ownership, voting rights and, 100–101, 161–162, 257; Panic of 1819 and, 249; preemption ("squatters' rights") and, 250; speculation in, 248–250; squatters and, 249–250; surveying of, 166–168, *168*; trans-Appalachian frontier and, 244–248; waterway boundaries and, 170; western lands and, 164–166, *165*. *See also* Property; West
Land bridge, Siberian, 1–2
Landa, Diego de, 3, 5
Lane, Joseph, 356
Las Casas, Bartolomé de, 15, 16, 54-A
Last of the Mohicans (Cooper), 277
Latitude, determination of, 69
Laudonnière, René Goulaine de, 35
Lawrence, Kansas, raid of, 349
Law(s). *See specific laws*
Lawyers, 120
Lecompton Constitution, 353
Lee, Richard Henry, 119, 139
Lee, Robert E., *383*; in Civil War, 368, 370, 374, 378, 382–383, 390–394; Gettysburg campaign and, 385–389, *386*; loyalties of, 362, 374; surrender at Appomattox, 393–394
Legislative branch of government, 174
Leisler, Jacob, 66
Leo X (Pope), 22
Lèse-majesté, crime of, 121–122
Letter of Prester John, 8
Lewis, Meriwether, 204–205
Lewis and Clark expedition, *203*, 204–205
Lexington, Battle of, 136–137, *136*, *137*, 159-B
Li, Hee, 7
Liberator, The (Garrison), 297, *297*, 307
Liberia, *302*, 303–304, *303*
"Liberty and Union speech" (Webster), 277–279
Liberty party, 329

Life expectancy: in colonies, 60, 85, 97–98; in eighteenth century, 97–98; in New England, 97; of slaves, 313
Lifestyles: along frontier, 156, 186; dueling and, 260; of gold miners, 340; in Mesoamerica (Tenochitlán), 15; of mill girls, 240–241; in Northwest Territory, 186; of pirates, 98–99; Puritan Sundays, 53; of sailors, 36; slave stations and, 88
Lincoln, Abraham, *358*; "A house divided" statement of, 347; assassination of, *392*, 394; cabinet of, 360; characteristics of, 360–361; during Civil War, 368, 369, 373–375, 388–389; election of 1860 and, 356–359; Emancipation Proclamation and, 378–379; Gettysburg Address of, 394–395; *habeas corpus*, suspension of, 373–374, 400; leadership of, 394; on Mexican War, 332; Reconstruction plan of, 399–401; Republican party and, 345
Lincoln, Benjamin, 155
Lincoln-Douglas debates, *360*
Liquor. *See* Alcohol
Little Giant. *See* Douglas, Stephen A.
Little Rock, Arkansas, school desegregation in, 266
Livingston, Robert, 139, 203
Locke, John, 140
Locomotives. *See* Railroads
Log cabins, 186
Logan, James, 100
Logging. *See* Timber industry
London Company, 30, *30*
The Long Peace, *92*, 97, 103, 107
Longitude, determination of, 69
Longstreet, James, 386–388
Loring, Elizabeth, 147
Loring, Israel, 43
Louis XIV, king of France, 92, 93
Louis XVI, king of France, 185, 186, 215-B
Louisbourg, 107
Louisiana, 94–95; France and, 94; Spain and, 94–95; surrendered to British, 110
Louisiana Purchase, 202–207
Lowell, Francis Cabot, 240
Lowell System/Lowell Girls, 240–242, *242*, 283-A
Lower orders, 102–103
Loyalists, 145–146
Lucas, Eliza, 101
Lukens, Rebecca, 235
Lundy, Benjamin, 296–297
Luther, Martin, 21
Lutheranism, 21–22

M

Macadam roads, 222–223
Machines, 234–242; spinning machines, 236–237, *236*. *See also* Manufacturing
Macon's Bill No. 2, 210
Madison, Dolley, 209, 214
Madison, James, 170; as federalist, 176; *Marbury v. Madison* and, 201–202; national debt position of, 182; presidency of, 209–214; Virginia Resolutions, 194; War of 1812 and, 209–213
Magazines, for slave owners, 309
Magellan, Ferdinand, 13
Magna Carta, 160
Maine: border dispute with Canada, 282; colony of, 47. *See also* New England colonies
Mainline Canal, 225–226
Maize ("Indian corn"), 17, 73

Malaria, 85
Manassas, Battles of. *See* Bull Run
Mandamus, 201
Manhattan Island, purchase of, 36, 78
Manifest destiny, *326*, 327–328
Manioc (tapioca), 17
Mann, Horace, 337
Manufacturing, 234–242, 283-A; American System of, 239; child labor in, 239–242, *242*; cloth manufacturing, 235–236, *236*; colonial, 57; Industrial Revolution and, 234–242; interchangeable parts and, 239; inventors and, 238–239; mass production and, 239; in Northeast, 237–242; protective tariffs and, 180, 184, 221; spinning/cotton mills and, 237–238, *237*, *238*; technological piracy and, 237
Manumission, 163, 301
Marbury, William, 201
Marbury v. Madison, 201–202
Marcos de Niza, Fray, 16
Marine Corps Hymn: "Halls of Montezuma" (source for phrase), 332; "Shores of Tripoli" (source for phrase), 208
Marquette, Jacques, 93
Marriage: Indian-white, 76–77, 93; interracial, 76–77, 93
Marshall, James, 337–338
Marshall, John, 162, 193, *219*; on American Constitution, 171; contracts, sanctity of, and, 219; family size and, 98; judicial review principle and, 201–202; as Supreme Court Justice, 201, 219, *219*
Martin v. Hunter's Lessee (1816), 220
Martinique and Guadaloupe, 112–113, 202, 307
Mary Tudor, queen of England ("Bloody Mary"), *21*, 24
Maryland: boundary dispute of, 56; early settlement in, 34–35, 48; Oyster War and, 170; religious toleration in, 34; spending and lifestyle in, 61–62. *See also* Southern colonies
Mason-Dixon Line, 56, 217, 311
Mason, James M., 373
Mason, John, 47
Masonic Order, 258; Anti-Masonic Party, 257–258, *258*
Massachusetts: Boston Massacre, 126–127, *127*, 159-A; Boston Tea Party, 129, 133, *134*; Bunker Hill, 137–138, *137*; Coercive Acts and, 133–134; colony in, 41–42; Deerfield Massacre in, 97, *97*; land title in, 65; mint of own coin, 65–66; Minutemen, 135; as royal colony, 66; Shays Rebellion in, 170–171, *171*; voting rights in, 161; witchcraft and, 56, 66–67, *67*. *See also* Massachusetts Bay colony; New England colonies
Massachusetts Bay colony, 41–42; acquisition of Maine by, 47; blue laws in, 43–44; education in, 45; payment for land in, 46
Massacres. *See* Atrocities
Mastodons, 1–2
Matamoros, battle at, 331
Mather, Cotton, 43, 105; on "riotous young men", 102; on Scotch-Irish, 100
Mather, Increase, 105
Matoaka. *See* Pocahontas
Maya, 3–5; blood sacrifice, 4, *5*; cities, *4*, 5; pyramids, *3*, 4
Mayer, Tobias, 69
Mayflower Compact, 41, 54-B
Mayflower (ship), 40–41

Maysville Road, 263
McAdam, John, 222
McClellan, George B., *378*, 391; in Civil War, 369, 376–377
McCulloch v. Maryland (1819), 220
McDowell, Irvin, 368, 369, 371
Meade, George, 386
Measles, 76
Menéndez de Avilés, Pedro, 35
Mennonites, 68, 99
Mercantilism, 55–63, 112; colonies and, 57–58; southern colonies and, 58–63
Mercenaries, in War for Independence, 143, 152–153
Merchants-adventurers companies, 29
Merrimack (ship), 375–376
Merrymount, 42
Mesoamerica, 2–6; Aztecs in, 5–6, *6*; blood sacrifice in, 4, *5*; cities in, *4*, 15; farming and agriculture in, 2–3; pyramids in, *3*, 4; war and religion in, 4–5
Mestizos, 319
Metacomet, 79
Metes and bounds, 168
Methodists, 287–288, *287*, 356
Mexican-American War, 325, 331–332, *331*
Mexican cowboys (*vaqueros*), 322
Mexican territories, annexation of, 330–332, *335*
Mexican War (1846–1847), 330–332, *331*
Mexico: Aztec culture in, 3, 5–6, *6*, *14*; borderlands of, Americans in (1820–1850), 319–324; boundary with U.S., 230–231, 319; "conquest" of, 13–16; Cortés in, 13–14; expansion northward of, 319–320; Mesoamerican culture in, 2–6; Tenochtitlán and, 5, *6*, 15; Texas as district of, 321–322, *321*; Treaty of Guadalupe-Hidalgo and, 332, 334; U.S. acquisition of territory from (1846–1857), 330–332, *335*; war with U.S. (1846–1847), 330–332, *331*
Mexico City: Battle of Chapultepec and, 325, *331*, 332; U.S. occupation of, 332
Middle colonies, *49*, 67–68
Midnight judges, 201
Migration, *See also* Immigrants and immigration
Military draft. *See* Draft (military)
Military music, 148
Militias, colonial, 96, 108, 135, 143; arming of, 135; snipers in, 137
Miller, William, 288–289, *288*
Millerites, 288–289, *288*
Mills: flour mills, 238–239; Lowell system and, 240–242; mill girls and, 240–242, *242*; spinning and cotton mills, 237–238, *237*, *238*
Minié ball, 366
Mining, gold and silver rushes and, 337–338, *337*, *338*, 340
Minstrels/minstrel shows, 310–311, *310*
Minuit, Peter, 36, 41
Minutemen, 135, *136*
Missions and missionaries, 293; in California, 319; in Hawaii, 293
Mississippi River, 227; steamboats, 228–229, *229*
Missouri, 231–232, 347; border ruffians and, 347–349, *348*; Lawrence raid and, 349; Missouri Compromise and, 232, 334; Second Missouri Compromise, 232; slavery and, 231–232
Missouri Compromise (1820), 232, 334, 335, 344; repeal of, 344; slave states and, *352*
Moctezuma II (Aztec ruler), *6*, 13, *14*

Mohawk Indians, 47, 75, *76*, 79, 80; arming/weapons of, 91; Thayendanega (Joseph Brant), *145*, 146; in War for Independence, *145*, 146
Mohican Indians, 72, *74*, 79–80
Molasses, sugar industry and, 64, 103–104
Molasses Act (1733), 103–104, 118, 119
Monarchs. *See specific countries and rulers*
Money: British, 115–116, 161; bucks and quarters, 182; Confederation era, 169, *169*; dollar, 161, 169, *169*; financial chaos and, 274–275; funding debate (1790) and, 181–182; greenbacks, 395–396; hard-money men and, 274; Specie Circular, 274–275, 279; United States currency, 161, 169, *169*. *See also* Banks and banking; Paper money
Money supply, Bank of the United States and, 221, 272–273
Monitor (ship), 376
Monroe Doctrine, 231
Monroe, James, 217, 229–231; Missouri Compromise and, 232; Monroe Doctrine of, 231; presidency of, 217, 229–231
Monrovia, Liberia, *302*, *303*
Montcalm, Louis de, 108, 109, 110
Montgomery, Richard, 138
Monticello, *199*
Moody, Lady Deborah, 100
Moonshining, 354
"Moral suasionists", 295
Morgan, William, 257–258
Mormons and Mormonism, 289–291, *290*
Morrill Act (1862), 396
Morrill Tariff (1861), 395
Morris, Gouverneur, 174, 183, 188, 196
Morris, John, 139
Morris, Robert, 139
Morton, Thomas, 39, 42
Mott, Lucretia Coffin, 296
Mound Builders, 3
Mount Vernon, 170, 180
Mountain men, 324–326, *324*
Mr./Mrs., as titles of address, 187
Mullins, Priscilla, 39
Mun, Thomas, 55, 112
Muscovy Company, 29
Music: "Battle Hymn of the Republic", 379; Civil War anthems and, 379, 388; of Foster, Stephen, 311; Marine Corps Hymn, 208, 332; military, 148; patriotic, 218; "Star-Spangled Banner", 211, 218
Muskets, 96, 135; manufacture/mass production of, 239; retrieved from Gettysburg, 385
Muskohegan Indians, 49
Muslim slaves, 309

N

Napoleon Bonaparte (France), 191, 196, 214; Louisiana Purchase and, 202, 203
Napoleon III, Civil War (U.S.) and, 372–373, 407
Narragansett Indians, 47, 78, 79
National anthem, "Star-Spangled Banner, The", 211, 218
National bank, 183–184, *183*
National debt. *See* Debt, national
National-Republicans, 251, 275
National Road, 222–223, *223*
National Union party, 405–406
Nationalism, 216–221, *217*; American System, 220–221, 276; expansionism and, *217*, 230–232; patriotic culture, books, and readings, 217–218, *218*; Supreme Court decisions and, 219–220

Native Americans. *See* Indians
Nauvoo, Illinois, 290, *290*
Navigation: methods and instruments, 69. *See also* Trade
Navigation Acts (1660–1663), 55, *56*, 58; evasion of, 59
Navy: English, 144–145, 156, 187, 208; French, 152, 193; impressment and, 187, 208–209, *208*. *See also* Sailors
Navy (U.S.): in Civil War, 371; *Monitor* and *Merrimac* and, 376; ships seized by France, 193; in War for Independence, 152
Nebraska Territory, 344; Kansas-Nebraska Act, *341*, 343–346, *352*
Netherlands, New Netherland and New Amsterdam, 35–36, *37*
Nevada, 332
New Amsterdam. *See* New York City
New England colonies, 39–45, *40*, *46*, 63–67; accent in, 63; blue law in, 43–44, 47; competition with England, 64; Connecticut, 47; Dominion of New England, *56*, 66–67; economy of, 64; family size and population in, 64, 97–98; geography and society in, 63–64; health and life span in, 64; healthy food of, 64; housing in, *45*; independent spirit in, 65–66; life expectancy in, 97; Maine, 47; Massachusetts Bay Colony, 41–42; New Hampshire, 47; New Jersey, 50–52; Plymouth Plantation, 40–41; Puritans in, 42–45, 63; Rhode Island, 45–47; soil in, 64; stones/stone fences in, 63, *63*, 64; witchcraft and, *56*, 66–67, *67*; Yankee traders, 64–65
New France (Canada), 91–95. *See also* Canada
New Hampshire: colony of, 47; voting rights in, 161. *See also* New England colonies
New Haven, Connecticut, 47
New Jersey: colony of, 50–52; during Revolution, *149*, 150–155; economy in, 67–68; population diversity in, 68; Quakers and, 51–52; toleration in, 68; voting rights in, 161
New Lights, 106–107
New Mexico: boundary disputes with Texas, 321–324, *321*, 341; ceded from Mexico, 332
New Netherlands. *See* New York
New Orleans: battle of, *212*, 213, 214, 217; Mississippi River and, 227
New Spain, 14, 319. *See also* Mexico
New Sweden, 36, 48
New World of Worlds (Philips), 81
New York: Battle of Golden Hill, 127; as capital of nation, 182; as colony, 35–36, *37*; economy in, 67–68; Manhattan purchase and, 36, 78; as New Netherlands, 35–36, *37*, *40*, 48; population diversity in, 68; Quincy Adams election and, 255; as royal colony, 48; transition of New Netherlands to, 48; War for Independence, actions in, 149–152, *149*, *151*. *See also* New England colonies; New York City
New York City, 67, 68; antidraft riot in (1863), 387; as New Amsterdam, 35–36, *37*; purchase of (from Indians), 36, 78
Newfoundland, 20, 24–25
Newport, Christopher, 30
Newport, Rhode Island, slave trade and, 64, 98
Newton, Isaac, 106
Nez Percé Indians, 326
Nichols, James, 48
Niña (ship), 12
Ninth Amendment, 176, Appendix A-8
Nixon, Richard M., impeachment and, 406
"Noche triste", 13

Non-Intercourse Act (1809), 209
North, Lord Frederick: battles and, 137; Intolerable Acts and, 133–134; Tea Act and, 133
North: Civil War draft in, 366–367. *See also* Civil War (U.S.)
North, differences from South, 216–221; economic differences, 216–217; slave states vs. free states (Missouri Compromise), 232; slavery issues, 217
North Carolina: colony of, 49–50. *See also* Southern colonies
Northeast Passage, 27
Northern Pacific Railroad, 395
Northwest Ordinances (1784, 1787), 166–167, *168*, 189–190, 249; slavery and, *352*
Northwest Passage, 24–25, 27
Northwest Territory, *168*, 189–191; Indian Wars in, 189–191, *189*
Nova Scotia, 20; Treaty of Utrecht and, 97
Nuevo León, battle at, 331, *331*
Nullification, 267, 270
Nursing, during Civil War, 367

O

Ogden v. Saunders (1827), 219
Oglethorpe, James, 52, 103
"Oh! Susannah" (Foster), 311
Ohio Valley, 115; Catholicism and, 134; in Civil War, *374*, 375; Northwest Ordinances and, 167, *168*
OK (expression), 261
Oklahoma, slavery and, 335
"Old Folks at Home" (Foster), 311
Old Lights, 106–107
Olive Branch Petition, 141
Olmecs, 3, *4*, 5, 7
Omnibus Bill, of Clay, 339–341, *339*
Onandaga Indians, 75
Oneida Indians, 75
Oneida, New York (utopian community), 291–292
O'Neill, Peggy. *See* Eaton, Peggy O'Neill
Opechancanough, 33, 34
Order of Cincinnati, 178, 180
Order of the Star-Spangled Banner. *See* Know-Nothings
Oregon, *See also* Oregon Country
Oregon Act (1848), slavery and, *352*
Oregon Country, 230, 324–328; "54-40 or fight" and, 340; African American emigration prohibited in, 336; mountain men in, 324–326, *324*; Russia and, 230
Oregon Trail, 326–327, *326*
Orellana, Francisco, 16
Orphan Boy (steamboat), 228
Orphans, 81, *82*, 92
Orr, James L., 405
Osgood, Samuel, 180
Ostend Manifesto, 351
O'Sullivan, John Louis, 328
Otis, James, 122–123, 132
Oyster War, 170

P

Pacific Railways Act (1862), 395
Pacifism, Quakers and, 51
Paddyrollers, 309
Paine, Thomas, 139; *The Age of Reason*, 285; *Common Sense*, 139; "times that try men's souls", 150
Pakenham, Edward, 214
Paleo-Indians, 2–3

Palmerston, Lord, 373
Panama, Isthmus of, 12–13
Panic of 1819, 249
Paper money: during Civil War, 395–396; greenbacks, 395–396
Pardons, for Civil War Confederates, 402
Paris: Peace of (1763), *92*, 110, 112; Treaty of (1783), 156–157, 164, 215-A
Parliament (England), 116–117, *116*
Parties, political. *See* Political parties
Party system. *See* Political parties
Patricios, 325
Patriotism: books and readings in, 218–219; culture of, 217–218, *218*. *See also* Nationalism
Pawtuxet Indians, 41, 71
"Paxton Boys", 130
Payne, John, 163
Peace of Paris (1763), *92*, 110, 112
Pemberton, John C., 384, 385
Penn, William, 51, 52, *52*, 56
Pennsylvania, 52, 67–68; boundary dispute with Maryland, 56; bounty for Indian scalps in, 96; colony, 52; eccentrics in, 51; economy in, 67–68; Germans in, 83, 99, *100*; land purchased from Indians, 78; "Paxton Boys", 130; Philadelphia, 52, *68*; population diversity in, 68; population in, 68; Quakers and, 50–52, 67; Scotch-Irish in, 130; slaves/slavery in, 163–164, 183; toleration in, 51, 67; women's status in, 102
Pennsylvania Dutch, 68, 99
Pennsylvania system, for correctional institutions, 293
Penny (British), 115
Pequot Indians, 47
Pequot War, *72*, 79
Perry, Oliver Hazard, 213
Peru, Incas in, 15–16
Pet banks, 274
Petersburg, siege of, 390–391
Petite guerre, 96, 97, 107
Philadelphia, 52, *68*; Bank of United States in, 183; as capital of nation (temporary), 183; Constitutional Convention in, 171–173, *172*; First Continental Congress in, 135
Philadelphia Convention. *See* Constitutional Convention
Philadelphia (ship), 208
Philip II, king of Spain, 24, 26
Philippines, Treaty of Tordesillas and, 13
Philips, Edward, 81
Phillips, Wendell, 298
Phipps, William, 98
Pickering, John, 202
Pickering, Timothy, 167, 197
Pickett's Charge, 388, *388*
Pidgin, 408
Pierce, Franklin, 342–343, 373, 395
Pike, Zebulon, 204
Pilgrims: goals of, 54-B; in Leiden, Holland, 39–40; Mayflower Compact and, 41, 54-B; in Plymouth Plantation, 40–41; view of Church of England, 42. *See also* Puritans
Pinckney, Charles, 101
Pinckney, Charles Cotesworth, 192, 193, 196
Pinckney, Thomas, 192
Pinckney's Treaty, 188–189, *188*
Piñta (ship), 12
Pirates and piracy, 98–99; Barbary pirates, 169–170, 206, 207–208; French definition of Americans as, 193; French privateers, 186–187

Pitcairn, John, 136–137
Pitt, William (the elder), 109, 116; Stamp Act and Declaratory Act and, 123, 124
Pius IX (pope), 345
Pizarro, Francisco, 15–16
Placer mining, *336*, 340
Plants, Columbian Exchange and, 16–18
Plessy v. Ferguson, 412
Plymouth, 39, 40–41, *40*; combined with Massachusetts, 66
Plymouth Company, 30, *30*, 40
Plymouth Harbor, England, 40
Pocahontas, 32, 33
Pocket veto, 401
Political campaigns. *See* Elections
Political parties, 188, 217, 229; Anti-Masonic Party, 257–258, *258*; caucus and, 229, 252; Democratic Party, 275–276; Democratic-Republicans, 258–261, 269, 275; in England (Whigs and Tories), 116, 276; Federalist Party, 188, 191, 217; Free Soil party, 336, 337, 347–349; Jefferson Republicans, 188, 193, *197*, 217, 252–253; National-Republicans, 251, 275; National Union party, 405–406; Republican party, 345–346; Second Party System, 275–282; single (years with only one), 229; spoils system and, 263; Whigs (Democrats), 275–281; "Workies"/ workingmen's parties, 257. *See also* Democratic party; Federalists; Republican party; *And other specific parties*
Politicians, colonial, 122
Polk, James K., 329–330; as dark horse candidate, 328; death of, 336; election of 1844 and, 329; election of 1848 and, 336; expansionism of, 329–332; Mexican War and, 330–332, *331*; presidency of, 329–330
Polo, Marco, 8, 9
Ponce de León, Juan, 14
Pontiac, 115
Pontiac's rebellion, *113*, 115
Poor people and poverty, 102–103; street people, 128–129; in Virginia, 60
Pope, Dilsey, 312
Popé's Rebellion, 35
Popular sovereignty, 344, 347, 353
Population: in colonies, 97–101; movement of, 246–247; settlement patterns, 247, *247*; in trans-Appalachian frontier (1790–1820), 245–246, *245*
Populism and populists, 250
Pore, Tryal, 43
Porgy and Bess, 408
Port Royal, 97, 99
Porter, Joseph, 44
Portugal, discoveries and exploration by, 10–13
Positive good, slavery as, 308, 316
Potatoes, 17, 18
Pottawatomie Creek massacre, 350
Pound sterling, 115
Poverty. *See* Poor people and poverty
Power of the purse, 104
Powhatan Indians, 33; Chief Powhatan and, 33, 71, *74*; converted by Spanish, 25; Jamestown Massacre by, *33*, 34; Jamestown settlement and, 31, 33–34; Pocahontas and, 32; tobacco use by, 32
Prairie schooners, 320. *See also* Conestoga wagons
Preemption ("squatters' rights"), 250
Prejudice. *See* Race and racism; Segregation; *And specific groups*

Presbyterians, 326, 356
Prescott, Samuel, 136
President of Confederacy (Jefferson Davis), 359, 360, 361–362
President of United States: dark horse candidates for, 328; electoral college selection of, 178, 196; lame duck period and, 328–329; nomination process for, 252; Twelfth Amendment and, 192, 198, 254, Appendix A-9; two-term tradition for, 209; Virginia Dynasty of, 252, 253. *See also specific presidents*
Presidential elections. *See* Elections
Presidios, 319
Press gangs. *See* Impressment
Prester John, 8
Primogeniture, 101
Princeton, battle at, *149*, 150
Principal Navigations (Hakluyt), *21*, 27
Prison reform, 292–293, *292*
Privateering. *See* Pirates and piracy
Proclamation of 1763, *114*, 115
Prohibition, 295
Promoters of colonization, 27
Property: laws (colonial), 101; lines, 166–167; ownership, voting rights and, 100–101, 161–162, 257
Prophet. *See* Tenskwatawa (The Prophet)
Proprietary colonies, 47–52
Protective tariffs. *See* Tariffs
Protestant Reformation, 21–24
Protests. *See* Colonial incidents and protests; Revolts and rebellions
Psalms, Puritan translation of, 53
Pueblo Indians, 35
Pulaski, Casimir, 153
Punishments, in the colonies, 44, *44*
Purgatory, 22
Puritans, 42–45, 63; assumptions of, 45; beliefs of, 42–43; blue laws of, 43–44; community and, 43; 'health food' of, 64; names of, 44; psalms, translation of, 53; Sunday practices of, 53
Purse, power of, 104
Putnam, Israel, 158
Pyramids, Aztec and Mayan, *3*, 4

Q
Quakers, 50–52, 67, 106; anti-slavery stance of, 163, 296, 306; in colonial militias, 135; pacifism of, 51; Penn, William as, 52; slave trade by, 98; use of *thou, thy,* and *thee* by, 51; women's status, 102
Quantrill, William, 347
Quartering Act of 1765, 116, 128, 134
Quarters, dollar divided into, 182
Quebec, 35, 92, 139; battle for, 109–110, *109*, 139; British occupation of ("fall of"), 110; Catholic status in, 134; Fort Ticonderoga and, 138
Quebec Act of 1774, 134
Queen Anne's War, *92*, 96–97
Quincy Adams. *See* Adams, John Quincy
Quitrent, 48

R
Race and racism: interracial marriages and, 76–77; segregation by, 76–77; slavery and, 84, 309. *See also* Abolition and abolitionists; Segregation; Slaves and slavery; And *specific groups*
Radical Reconstruction, 406–410, *406*

Railroads, 226–227; during Civil War, 395; early, 226–227, *226*, *227*; Pacific Railways Act, 395; transcontinental, 343–344, 346. *See also* Transcontinental railroads; *specific railroads*
Raleigh, Walter, *21*, 23, 25–26, *26*; promotion of colonization by, 27
Ramsden, Joseph, 53
Randolph, Edmund, 175, 176; as attorney general, 179–180, *181*
Randolph, John, 203, 301, 308, 350; slaves of, 255, 301
Randolph, Richard, 163
Randolph, William, 60
Rape, 102
Rebellions. *See* Revolts and rebellions
Reconstruction, 399–414, *400*; black codes and, 402; carpetbaggers and scalawags, 409; Civil Rights Act (1875) and, 412; corruption and, 410–413; end of, 412–413; Fifteenth Amendment and, 407; Fourteenth Amendment and, 405; Johnson and, 401–403, 404, 405–407; Lincoln's plan for, 399–401; pardons for Confederates and, 402; Radical program for, 402–403, 406–410, *406*; readmission of Confederate states, 401–403; twilight of, 412–413; Wade-Davis Bill and, 401
Rectangular survey, 168, *168*
Red Cross, American, 367
Redcoats: Boston Massacre and, 126–127, *127*; friction with, in colonial cities, 126–128, 130–131; garrisoned in the Americas, 115–116; Paul Revere's ride and, 135, 136; Quartering Act of 1765, 116, 128, 134
Redeemers, 409–410, 413
Redemptioners, 83, 99
Reed, Esther, 159-B
Reform and reform movements, 292–296; for blind, 292; for deaf, 294; early, 292–296; of insane asylums, 293; for prisons, 292–293, *292*; Prohibition, 295; temperance movement, 295, *295*
Reformation, Protestant, 21–24
Regulators, 129–131
Religion, 16, 105–107, 284–300; abolitionists and, 296–299; Act of Toleration and, 34, 35; Adventists and, *288*, 289; burned-over district and, 288–292; Calvinism and, 39, 42, 105; Cane Ridge and camp meetings and, 286–287, *286*; Catholicism and, 16; in Constitutional era, 161; cures and treatments and, 294; Deists and, 284–285; Disciples of Christ and, 287; evangelical reform and, 292–296; evangelicalism and, 288–292; freedom of, in colonies, 39; Great Awakening and, 106, 107, 113; growth and new sects in, 287; Indians and, 77–78; Jehovah's Witnesses and, 289; Jesuit priests and, 93–94, *93*; Maryland settlement and, 34–35, 48; mellowing of churches and, 105–106; Methodists and, 287–288, *287*; Millerites and, 288–289, *288*; missionaries and, 293; Mormonism and, 289–291; New Lights vs. Old Lights and, 106–107; Oneida community and, 291–292; Pilgrims and, 39–40; Protestant Reformation and, 21–24; Puritans and, 42–43; Quakers and, 50–52, 67, 106; reform and, 284–300, *285*; revival of, 106, 113; Second Great Awakening and, 288; separation of government and, 45–46; slaves, in control of, 308–309, 310; spiritualism and, 292; Unitarians and Universalists and, 285–286. *See also* Catholicism; Church; *specific religious denominations*

Religious toleration: in Maryland, 34; in Middle Colonies, 68
Rendezvous, of mountain men, 325
Rent. *See* Quitrent
Representation: required for taxation ("no taxation without representation"), 104, 118–120, 122–123; residence not required for, 123; virtual, 123
Republican party, 345–346; caucus of, 229, 252; election of 1860 (Lincoln) and, 356–358; formation of, 345–346; ideology of, 346, 358; nomination procedures of, 252; in North, 356; slavery and, 345–346, 353; in South, 217. *See also* Jefferson Republicans
Revere, Paul: Boston Massacre depicted by, 127, *127*; as hero, 218; "ride of", 135, 136
Revolts and rebellions: Bacon's Rebellion, *56*, 61, *62*, 84; Dorr's Rebellion, 257; Pontiac's rebellion, *113*, 115; Shays Rebellion, 170–171, *171*; slave rebellions, 103, 304–306; Turner's Rebellion, 305–306; Vesey's Rebellion, 305, *305*, 310; Whiskey Rebellion, *190*, 191. *See also* Colonial incidents and protests
Revolutionary War. *See* War for Independence
Revolutions: American (*See* War for Independence); French, 184–187, *185*
Rhode Island: colony, 45–47; dissenters banished to, 46–47; Dorr's Rebellion, 257; *Gaspée*, burning of, *129*, 131–132; purchase of land from Narragansetts, 78; as "Sewer of New England", 46; slave trade and, 64, 98; voting rights in, 257. *See also* New England colonies
Ribault, Jean, 24, 35
Rice, Thomas D. ("Daddy"), 310–311
Rice, 49, 50; slave labor and, 313, *313*
Rider, in lawmaking process, 336
Rifles. *See* Firearms
Rights: individual (Bill of Rights), 176; to levy taxes, 118–120, 122–123, 220
Rights, voting. *See* Voting
Rio Grande, as U.S./Mexico boundary, 332
Riot(s): against Stamp Act, 121, *121*; anti-draft (1863), 387
Rivers, 227–229; Mississippi, 227; transportation and (1820–1860), *223*, 227–229. *See also* specific rivers and regions
Roads and highways, 221–223; *camino real*, 319; corduroy roads, *221*; development of, 221–223; federal financing for, 221–222; macadam and, 222; Maysville Road, 263; National Road, 222–223, *223*; toll roads, 221; turnpikes, 221
Roanoke, 25–26, *25*
Roberts, Bartholomew ("Black Bart"), 99
Robespierre, Maximilien, 184, 185
Rochambeau, Jean-Baptiste, comte de, 153, 155, 157
Rockingham, Marquis of, 157
Rodney, Caesar, 139
Rolfe, John, 32, 33, 34
Roman Catholic Church. *See* Catholicism
Rosecrans, William S., 389
Rotten boroughs, 123
Royal colonies, 47, 48, 50; assemblies and governors in, 104–105
Rule of 1756, neutral shipping and, 187
Rum, 64; demon rum, 293–295
Runaway slaves, 84, 103, 296, 306–307
Rush-Bagot Agreement, 230

Russia: Alaska purchased from, 407; Oregon Country and, 230

Russian California, 230

S

"S" (letter), typesetting and, 139

Sacajawea, 205

Sailors: common, 36; impressment of, 187, 208–209, *208*; lifestyles of, 36; navigation methods of, 69; pirates, 98–99. *See also* Navy; Navy (U.S.)

Saint-Domingue. *See* Haiti

St. Augustine, Florida, 35

St. John's River, Florida, 35

Salem witchcraft hysteria, *56*, 66–67, *67*

Salutary neglect, 103–104, 112

Sampson, Deborah, 152

San Antonio, Texas, Alamo and, 322, *323*

San Jacinto, battle at, 322–323

San Salvador, Columbus and, 6, 7, *7*

Sandys, Edwin, 40

Santa Anna, Antonio López de, 322–323

Santa Fe, 35, 319, *321*; trade and, 320, *320*

Santa Fe Trail, *321*

Santa Maria (ship), 12

Saratoga, Battle of, 151–152, *151*

Sassones ("Saxons"), 320

Savannah, Georgia, 52

Scalawags, 409

Scalping, 78; bounty for scalps, 96; in War for Independence, 150, 152

Scandals. *See specific scandals*

Schools: desegregation of, 266; of Freedmen's Bureau, *404*, 405; segregation in, 266. *See also* Universities and colleges

Schurz, Carl, 411

Schuyler, Philip, 138

Scotch-Irish, 100, 130

Scotland, government of, 55

Scott, Dred. *See* Dred Scott case

Scott, Winfield, 325, 331–332, *331*; in Civil War, 368, 369; election of 1852 and, 342–343; on secession, 358, 361

Scrooby villages, England, 39

Scurvy, 36; in Indians, 73

Sea dogs, *21*, 24–25

Seamen. *See* Sailors

Searle, Andrew, 44

Secession, *357*, 358–359

Second Amendment, 176, Appendix A-8

Second Bank of the United States, 221, 272–273

Second Continental Congress (1775), 138–139

Second Great Awakening, 288

Second Party System, 275–282

"Second sons", 101

Secotan village, *73*

Sectionalism, 217–221

Sedition Act (1798), 193–194, 196

Segregation, 76–77; of Indians, 76–77; *Plessy v. Ferguson* case and, 412; of schools, 266; of schools, desegregation and, 266. *See also* Race and racism

Self-government: in Massachusetts Bay, 41–42; in Plymouth Plantation, 41

Seminole Indians, 263–264

Senate (U.S.), 174; clubbing of Sumner in, 349–350, *349*. *See also* Congress (U.S.)

Seneca Falls "Declaration", 296

Seneca Indians, 75, 79

Separation of church and state, 45–46

Separatists. *See* Pilgrims

Sequoyah, 264–265, *264*

Serfs, 80

Serra, Junípero, 319

Servants: black, 32, 83–84; cheaper than slaves, 84–85; indentured servitude, 81–83; kidnapping and, 81–82; mortality rate for, 85; rights of, 84; seven years term of service for, 81

Settlement patterns (1800s), 247, *247*

Settlements, 20–38; economic facts of, 28; Elizabethan England and, 24–26; English empire, beginnings and, 26–30; English Reformation and, 21–24; French, 35; Hispanic, 35; Jamestown, 30–34; Maryland, 34–35; New Netherlands and New Sweden, 35–36, *37*; private enterprise (trading companies) and, 29–30; promoters of, 27; source of labor for, 32; surplus population and, 28–29, *29*. *See also* Colonies

"Seven Cities of Cíbola", 16

Seven Days' Battle, 377–378, *377*

Seventh Amendment, 176, Appendix A-8

Seventh-Day Adventists, 289

Seward, William H., 340–341, 342, 345, 356; Alaska purchase and ("Seward's Folly"), 407; Civil War and, 392; Emancipation Proclamation and, 379; National Union party and, 405

"Sewer of New England", 46

Sexual intercourse: English age of consent for, 102; forbidden on Sunday, 43; rape, 102

Shakers, 291

Shays Rebellion, 170–171, *171*, 175

Shenandoah Valley, in Civil War, 390–391

Sheridan, Philip, 389–400

Sherman, Roger, 139, 173

Sherman, William Tecumseh, 391–392, 409; burning of Atlanta and, 392; campaign for Atlanta and, *393*; march across Georgia by, 391–392

Shillings, 115

Shiloh, Battle of, 372, *374*, 375

Shirley, Myra Belle (Belle Starr), 347

Shirley, William, 114

Siberian land bridge, 1–2

Siglo de oro, 21, 26–27

Sign language, 292

"Silk Road", *8*, 9

Sixth Amendment, 176, Appendix A-8

Slash-and-burn agriculture, 72

Slater, Samuel, 237, 239

Slave patrols, 266–267, 271

Slave rebellions, 103, 304–306

Slave trade, 10, 85–89, 314–315, 355; abolition of, 163–164; African role in, 85–89, *89*, 355; in Rhode Island, 64, 98; routes for, 86–87, *86, 89*; "seasoning" of slaves and, *87*, 88–89; slave stations and, 88, *89*; "sold down the river" fears and, *315*

Slaves and slavery, 301–318, *302*; abolition and abolitionists and, 174–175, 296–299; abolition of (at end of Civil War), 397; abolition of (in England), 324; abolition of (in the North), 163–164; abolitionists, black, 298–299; auction advertisements for, *87*; auctions and, *314*, 315, 335; black perspective on, 312; black slave owners, 312; in Canada, *93*; in Carolinas, 49; coffles and, 86–87; colonization movement and, 303–304; community of, 317–318; Congressional powers and, 334–335; Constitution and, 174–175, 334; control over, 309–310; cost of, 84–85, 87, 242, 313–314;

cotton and, 244, *312, 313, 313*; cotton gin and, 242–244; Crittenden's Compromise Plan (1861) and, 359, *360*; daily life of, 317–318; defense of, 308–309; diversity in treatment of, 316; *Dred Scott* case and, 351–353, *352*; *durante vita* term for, 84; Emancipation Proclamation and, 378–379; emergence of, 84; in English colonies, 80–81; freedmen, 401, 404–405; Freeport Doctrine and, 353–354; Fugitive Slave Acts, 306, 335, 342, 350; gag rule and, 308; gang system and, 314; health of, 313; "holding pens" for, *335*; horrifying images of, *298*; indentured servitude and, 81–83; legal status/free vs. slave states (1787–1861), *352*; Liberia and, *302*, 303–304, *303*; life expectancy and, 313; living conditions of, 310–315, 316, 317–318; as loyalists, 145–146; manumission and, 163, 301; marriage and family and, 317–318; Mason-Dixon line and, 56, 217, 311; minstrels and, 310–311, *310*; in Missouri, 231–232; Missouri Compromise and, 232, 334, 335, 344; mortality in colonies, 85; mortality in transport, 87, 88; Muslim slaves, 309; Northwest Ordinances and, *352*; population of, 98, 103, 217, 301–302, 311; "positive good" defense of, 308; punishment of, *298*, 310, 314; Quakers and, 98, 163, 296, 306; rebellions and, 103, 304–306; religion and, 308–309, 310; religious services of, 317; resistance of, 316–318; rights, lack of, 316; runaways, 84, 103, 296, 306–307, 316–317, *317*, 335; slave codes, 354; slave labor, 49, 313–314, *313*; in South Carolina, 62–63; southern antislavery sentiments and, 301–304; southern support for, 306–310; task system and, 314; in Texas, 322, 324; Thirteenth Amendment and, 397; "three-fifths" definition/compromise and, 175, 197; tied by necks, *85*; *Uncle Tom's Cabin*, 299; underground railway and, 306–307, 316–317, *317*, 350; in Virginia, 304; in West, 334–337; West African role in, 80, 85, 87–89, *89*; whippings and, *298*, 314, 316; white slaves in Africa, 206; white southern perspective on, 311–312. *See also* Abolition and abolitionists; Freedmen; Servants

Slavocrats, 336, 341, 343, 401–402

Slavocrats conspiracy, *351*

Slidell, John, 373

Smallpox, 18, *18*, 76

Smith, Jedediah, 325

Smith, John, 30, 31, 33; Pocahontas and, 32

Smith, Joseph, 289–290, *290*

Smoking. *See* Tobacco

Smuggling, 59

Social class. *See* Class status

Social mobility, 101

Society of Freemasons. *See* Masonic Order

Society of Friends. *See* Quakers

Sociology for the South, A (Fitzhugh), 308

Soldiers. *See* Army; Redcoats; *And specific wars*

Songs. *See* Music; *specific songs*

Sons of Liberty, 121, 129, 133, 136

Soto, Hernando de, 16

South: antislavery movement in, 301–304; cotton and, 242–244, 244, *244, 313*; Democratic party in, 395; economy in, 242–244; life expectancy in, 97–98; mercantilism in, 58–63; politics after Civil War and, 395;

Radical Reconstruction in, 402–403; Republican party in, 345; secession of, *357*, 358–359; slavery in, 301–318; tariffs and, 267; tobacco and, 18, 34, 58–59, 61, 242. *See also* Civil War (U.S.); Confederacy; Reconstruction

South, differences from North. *See* North, differences from South

South Carolina: Charleston, 49, *50*, 63; colony, 49–50, *50*; crops of, 62–63; Force Bill of 1832 and, 267; nullification and, 267; secession of, 358–359; slaves in, 62–63; social structure in, 62–63; *South Carolina Exposition and Protest*, 267, 270; tariff and, 267. *See also* Southern colonies

Southern Agriculturalist (magazine), 309

Southern colonies, *51*; life expectancy in, 97–98; mercantilism in, 58–63; Piedmont conflicts and, 60; Tidewater region and, 59–60, *60*; tobacco in, 58–59, *59*

Spain: American empire of, 13–16, 35; "black legend" of, 16; Columbus and, 7, 12; *conquistadores* of, 14–15; dollar of, 182; explorations and discoveries of, 11–13, 15–16; Florida and, 16, 35, 94–95, 230; New Spain (Mexico), 14, 319

Spanish Armada, *21*, 26–27

Spanish empire, in the Americas, 13–16, 35

Specie Circular (1836), 274–275, 279

Speculation: in land, 248–250; Panic of 1819 and, 249

"Speech codes", 34

Speedwell (ship), 40

Spelling/spelling books, 217, 218, 405

Spice Islands, 7

Spice trade, 8, *8*, 10

Spies, female, in Civil War, 367

Spinning and cotton mills, 237–238, *237*, *238*

Spinning machines, 236–237, *236*

Spiritualism, 292

Spoils system, 263

Spotsylvania, Battle of, *383*, 390

Squanto, 41

Squash, 73

Squatters, 249–250

Stamp Act Congress, 121, 121–122, 123

Stamp Act of 1765, *113*, 119–121, *121*; repeal of, 123–124, *123*, 157

Stamps, 120

Standish, Miles, 41

Stanton, Edwin, 406

Stanton, Elizabeth Cady, 296

"Star-Spangled Banner, The" (Key), 211, 218

State(s): Articles of Confederation, 160, *161*, 164–168; authority of, vs. Congress, 164, 174; constitutions of, 160–164; federal relationship of, 174; taxation powers of, 220

States' rights, 194, 202, 263; nullification and, 267; slavery and, 334–335; taxation and, 220; Virginia and Kentucky Resolutions and, 194, 202

Steamboats, 228–229, *229*

Stephens, Alexander H., 392

Stereotypes, in minstrel shows, 310–311

Steuben, Friedrich Wilhelm von, 153, 155

Stevens, Thaddeus, 403–404, *403*, 407

Stocks, as colonial punishment, *44*

Stone Age nomads, 1–2

Stone fence (New England), *63*

Stones, breaking boulders, method for, 63, 64

Stowe, Harriet Beecher, 299

Street people, 128–129

Strict construction (of Constitution), 183–184

Stuart, Mary, 26

Stuyvesant, Peter, 48

Suffolk Resolves, 135

Suffrage: Fifteenth Amendment and, 407, Appendix A-10. *See also* Voting

Sugar, 57, 202–203; economics of, 113; slave labor and, 313, *313*; "sugar islands", 112–113, 202–203

Sugar Act of 1764, *113*, 118, 119

Summerless year (1816), 229

Sumner, Charles, 342, 403, 411–412; clubbing of, 349–350, *349*

Sumter, Fort, 361–362, *361*

Sunday: blue laws and, 43–44; practices forbidden on, 43

Supreme Court (U.S.), 174; *Dred Scott* case and, 353, *353*; judicial review powers of, 201–202; Marshall, John, nationalism in decisions of, 219–220

Surveys and survey techniques, 166–168; metes and bounds, 168; rectangular survey, 168, *168*

Sutter, John Augustus, 337–338

Sutter's Fort, gold discovery at, 337–338

Sweden, New Sweden and, 36, 48

Sweet potato, 17

Syphilis, 18

T

Talleyrand, Charles Maurice de, 193, 203

Tallmadge, James, 231, 232

Tallmadge Amendment, 232

Taney, Roger B., 353, *353*

Tappan, Arthus and Lewis, 298

Tariffs, 253; of Abominations, 267; Clay's, 221; Hamilton's, 180, 184; Jackson's, 267; Morrill, 395. *See also* Taxes and taxation

Taxes and taxation: in colonies, 118; consent required for, 104, 118–120, 122–123; during Civil War, 395–396; in England, 117–118; Hamilton's, 180, 184, 191; Molasses Act and, 103–104, 118, 119; "no taxation without representation", 119–120, 122–123; Stamp Act and, 119–121, *121*; Stamp Act repeal, 123–124, *123*; state power and, 220; Sugar Act and, *113*, 118, 119; tea, tax on, 124–125, *124*; Townshend Duties and, 124–125, *124*. *See also* Tariffs

Taylor, Zachary, 337–341; death of, 341; election of 1844 and, 336–337; in Mexican War, 325, 331–332, *331*; as "Old Rough and Ready", 331, 341; Omnibus Bill and, 341; opinions on, 337; presidency of, 337–341

Tea: tax on (Townshend Duties), 124–125, *124*; Tea Act (1773), 133; Tea Parties, 133, *134*

Teach, Edward ("Blackbeard"), 99

Technology: cotton gin and, 242–244, *243*; inventions and, 238–239; piracy of, 237. *See also specific inventions*

Tecumseh (Indian chief), 211–213, *211*

Teetotalers, 293

Temperance movement, 295, *295*; temperence pledge ("The Pledge"), 295

Tennessee, Civil War and, *374*, 375, 380, 389

Tenochtitlán, 5, 6, 15

Tenskwatawa ("The Prophet"), 211–213

Tenth Amendment, 176, Appendix A-9

Tenure of Office Act (1867), 406

Teotihuacan, 4

Texas, 321–324; Alamo, battle at, 322, *323*; annexation debate on, 328–329; border disputes with New Mexico, 321–324, *321*, 341;

Catholicism in, 321, *321*; compensation bill, 339, 341, 342; Lone Star Republic of, 323–324; as Mexican territory, 321–322, *321*; Mexican War (1846–1847) and, 330–332, *331*; Rio Grande as border of, 332, 341; San Jacinto, battle at, 322–323; slavery in, 322, 324; statehood of, 329; Texians (U.S. settlers in), 321–322

Textile industry, 235–238; children and girls in, 239–242, *242*. *See also* Cotton and cotton industry; Wool and wool industry

Thayer, Eli, 347–348

Theodolite, 167

Third Amendment, 176, Appendix A-8

Third parties. *See* Political parties; *specific parties*

Thirteenth Amendment, 397, Appendix A-9

Thirty Years' War (1618–1648), 95

Thomas, George H. ("Rock of Chickamauga"), 389

Thoreau, Henry David, 332

Thou, thy, and *thee*, 51

Three-fifths compromise, 175, 197, 217

Ticonderoga, Fort, 138, 147, 151; artillery from, 147, 148

Tidewater region, 59–60, *60*; Piedmont conflict and, 60

Tilden, Samuel J., 412–413

Timber industry, 57, *57*

Tippecanoe, 211–213, *211*

"Tippecanoe and Tyler Too", 279–280, *280*

Tobacco, 18, 34, 40; anti-smoking ordinances and, 32; decline of cultivation and industry, 58–59, 61, 242; as God, 58; Indian use of, 32; Jamestown settlement and, *31*, 32; servants/indentured servitude and, 81, 84–85; slave labor and, 313, *313*; tobacco factor and, *59*, 60

Tocqueville, Alexis de, 257

Toll roads, 221

Tomatoes, 17, 18

Tordesillas, Treaty of, 13

Tories, 116. *See also* Loyalists

Townshend, Charles ("Champagne Charley"), 124

Townshend Duties, *113*, 124–125, *124*

Trade, 55–63, *56*; competition of colonies with England, 64; Embargo Act (1807) and, 209; with England, 55–58, 64–66; in furs and hides, 57, 78–79, 324; Jay's Treaty and, 187–188, *188*; mercantilism and, 55–57; Navigation Acts and, 55, 58; Rule of 1756 and, 187; Sugar Act and, *113*, 118, 119; trading companies, 29–30; value of colonial trade with England, *119*; Yankee traders, 64–65. *See also* Slave trade

Trade routes, 8, 64–65, *65*; before the 1500s, 7–10, *8*; triangular, *65*; of Yankee traders, 64–65. *See also* Slave trade

Trail of Tears, 266–267, *266*

Trains. *See* Railroads

Trans-Appalachian frontier, 244–248

Transcontinental railroads, 343–344; Davis, Jefferson, and, 343; Douglas, Stephen, and, 343–344; route(s) of, 343–344, 346. *See also* Railroads

Transportation, 221–229; canals and, *222*, 223–226, *223*; Erie Canal and, *222*, 223–226; railroads and, 226–227, *226*, *227*; revolution in (1800s), 226–229; rivers and, 227–229; roads and, 221–223, *223*; turnpikes and, 221. *See also specific topics and modes of transportation*

Transubstantiation, 22

Trappers (mountain men), 324–326, *324*

Travis, William, 322

Treasury, Hamilton, Alexander and, 180–184, *181*

Treaties. See specific treaties by place name
Treaty of Aix-la-Chapelle, 107
Treaty of Ghent, 214
Treaty of Guadalupe-Hidalgo, 332, 334
Treaty of Paris, 156–157, 164, 215-A
Treaty of San Lorenzo. See Pinckney's Treaty
Treaty of Tordesillas, 13
Treaty of Utrecht, 97
Trent incident, 373
Trenton, battle at, 149, 150
Tripoli, 207–208
Trist, Nicholas, 332
Trollope, Frances, 257
Trumbull, John, 140
Tubman, Harriet, 316–317, 317, 367
Tudor, Mary ("Bloody Mary"), 21, 24
Turner, Nat, 305–306, 310
Turner's Rebellion, 305–306
Turnpikes, 221
Tuscarora Indians, 49
"Tweed Ring", 409
Twelfth Amendment, 192, 198, 254, Appendix A-9
Twenty-Second Amendment, 209, Appendix A-10
"Two bits", use of term, 182
Tyler, James, 276
Tyler, John, 281–282; cabinet of, 281–282;
    election of 1840 and, 280; election of 1844
    and, 328–329; as lame duck president,
    328–329; presidency of, 281–282; secession
    compromise attempts and, 359; Texas
    annexation and, 328–329; "Tippecanoe and
    Tyler Too", 279–280, 280

U

Uncle Tom's Cabin (Stowe), 299
Underground railway, 306–307, 316–317,
    317, 350
Uniforms, military, 95
Union: collapse of, 347–363, 348; vs. "United
    States", 394. See also Civil War (U.S.)
Union Pacific Railroad, 395
Unitarians and Universalists, 285–286
United States: discovery of, 14; term usage
    (singular vs. plural), 394
Universalists, Unitarians and, 285–286
Universities and colleges, 105, 278; Morrill Act
    and, 396. See also specific institutions
Urban areas. See Cities
U.S. Supreme Court. See Supreme Court (U.S.)
Usher, John, 47
Utah: ceded from Mexico, 332; Mormons and
    Mormonism in, 290–291
Utopian communities, 291
Utrecht, Treaty of, 97

V

Vallandigham, Clement L., 374
Valley Forge, 149, 150, 151, 153, 153
Van Buren, Martin, 271–272, 342; annexation of
    Texas and, 323–324, 328; Eaton affair and,
    271, 271; election of 1836 and, 277, 279;
    election of 1848 and, 337; presidency of,
    279; "Sly Fox" nickname, 271–272
Van Rensselaerswyck, 36
Vanarsdalen, Simon, 163
Vanderbilt, Cornelius ("Commodore"), 411
Vaqueros, 322
Vaudrouil, Pierre de Rigaud de, 96
Vegetables: New World, 17–18; Old World, 17
Veneral disease (VD), Columbian exchange
    and, 18
Vera Cruz, 13

Vergennes, Charles, comte de, 147, 152
Vermont, Green Mountain Boys, 138
Verrazano, Giovanni, 20
"Verrazano's Sea", 20, 27, 28
Vesey, Denmark, and Vesey's Rebellion, 305,
    305, 310
Vespucci, Amerigo, 12
Vetoes: by Jackson, 276; by Lincoln, 401; pocket
    veto, 401
Vice presidency, 192; opinions on position of,
    192; Twelfth Amendment and, 192, 198, 254
Vicksburg, siege of, 383–384, 385, 389
Vikings, 7
Vinland, 7
Virginia: Bacon's Rebellion in, 56, 61, 62, 84;
    Berkeley in, 60–61; colonial elections in, 122;
    colony in, 30–34; direct control by James I, 34,
    47; first families of, 60–61; headright system
    of, 32; House of Burgesses in, 84; Jamestown
    settlement in, 30–34; naming of, 26; Oyster
    War and, 170; Piedmont conflicts and, 60;
    poor in, 60; residence and representation
    in, 123; as royal colony, 47; slavery in, 304;
    Spanish settlement in, 25; spending and
    lifestyle in, 61–62; stockade system in, 61;
    Tidewater area and, 59–60, 60; tobacco
    and, 31, 32, 34, 40, 61; Virginia Dynasty (of
    presidents), 252, 253; western lands/border of,
    164–166, 165; women barred from voting in,
    100. See also Southern colonies
Virginia and Kentucky Resolutions, 194, 202
Virginia Company, 30, 30, 34
Virginia Dynasty (of presidents), 252, 253
Virtual representation, 123
Voting: African Americans and, 403, 412; African
    Americans, voting rights of, 161–162, 403, 412;
    extension of voting rights (1820s–30s), 257;
    Fifteenth Amendment and, 407, Appendix A-10;
    property ownership requirements, 100–101,
    161–162; property ownership, western states
    not requiring, 257; rights for blacks, 161–162;
    state constitutions and, 161–162, 162; women
    denied right of, 41, 100; women's suffrage, 100,
    161–162, 162
Voyages. See specific explorers
Voyages of Ser Marco Polo (Polo), 8, 9

W

Wade, Ben, 397, 401, 403
Wade-Davis Bill (1864), 401
Wagenen, Isabella Van, 298
Wagon trains, 320, 326–327, 327, 328
Wakeman, Sarah Rosetta, 367
Walker, William, 343
Walpole, Robert, 103, 104
Waltham System. See Lowell System
Wampanoag Indians, 41, 71, 79
War(s) and warfare: American fighting men,
    opinions on, 108; "American Style" of, 96;
    Art of War (Jomini) and, 364; atrocities and,
    108; battle line in, 95; colonial (1688–1763),
    92, 95–97, 107–110; colonial militias and,
    96, 108, 135; European (1689–1763), 95–96,
    96; petite guerre, 96, 97, 107; "rules" of, 95,
    108; uniforms, military, and, 95. See also
    Draft (military); specific wars
War for Independence (1776–1781), 143–161;
    American fighting men, opinions on, 108,
    143; American hopes for, 146–147; atrocities
    in, 150; Boston and Dorchester Heights in,
    147–148, 148; British strategy in, 150–151;
    colonial militias and, 96, 108, 135, 143;

Continental Army and, 143–145; Franklin,
    Benjamin, in France during, 146, 147; French
    aid during, 147, 152, 155; ignoring of, 156;
    imbalance of power in, 143–147; loyalists
    and, 145–146; mercenaries in, 143, 152–153;
    miliary music during, 148; New York, defeats
    in, 149–150, 149; New York, victory in
    (Saratoga), 151–152, 151; protests leading
    to, 126–142; risk to participants in, 143; tide
    turns toward Americans in, 152–158; timeline
    of, 144; Treaty of Paris and, 156–157; Valley
    Forge and, 149, 150, 151, 153, 153; women
    warriors in, 152, 159-B; Yorktown, Battle of,
    154, 155–156, 155
"War Hawks", 210
War of 1812, 209–213, 212; "Star-Spangled
    Banner" and, 211, 218
War of Jenkin's Ear, 107
Warmoth, Henry C., 409
Warren, James, 133
Warren, Joseph, 127
Warren, Mercy Otis, 175
Washington, George, 108; actions and strategies
    in War for Independence, 147, 148, 149,
    154, 154; biography and stories on, 218;
    cabinet of, 179–180, 181; at Constitutional
    Convention, 171, 172; death of, 194; defeat
    at Fort Necessity, 108; Delaware River
    crossing of, 150; dentures of, 158; during
    First Continental Congress, 135; family
    and personal attributes of, 158; as "father
    of his country", 157–158, 157; fox hunting
    rides of, 105, 158; Jefferson, Thomas and,
    157, 158, 184; Lafayette, friendship with,
    153, 153; Masonic membership of, 258;
    non-residence in county he represents, 123;
    precedents of, 178–179, 215-B; presidency
    of, 178–191, 179, 215-B; pride in soldiers
    of, 108; retirement of, 191; as second son,
    101; slaves of, 145, 174, 311; social skills of,
    135; at Valley Forge, 149, 150, 151, 153, 153;
    Whiskey Rebellion and, 190, 191; wife of
    (Martha), 101
Washington, Martha, 101
Washington, D.C., capital in, 183
Waterways. See Canals; specific river regions
Wayne, Anthony ("Mad Anthony"), 189,
    190–191
Weapons. See Firearms
Webster-Ashburton line, 326
Webster-Ashburton Treaty, 282
Webster, Daniel, 218, 277–279; Clay's Omnibus
    Bill and, 339, 341; "Godlike Daniel"
    designation for, 277; inaugural address
    for Harrison by, 281; "Liberty and Union"
    speech of, 277–279; Webster-Ashburton
    Treaty and, 282; Webster-Hayne debate, 276
Webster, Noah, 217, 219; Elementary Spelling Book
    by, 405
Weed, Thurlow, 280
Weems, Mason Locke, 218
Weld, Theodore Dwight, 298
West, Thomas, 31
West: bleeding Kansas, 347–350; Civil War in,
    374, 375; immigration and (1844–1856),
    334–346, 335; Mexican acquisition (1846–
    1857), 335; mining and gold rushes in, 337–
    338, 337; slavery and, 334–337, 352, 354
West Point, Benedict Arnold's "sale" of, 154
Western lands: Articles of Confederation and,
    164–166, 165. See also West
Western states, democratic reform in, 257

Wheelwright, Esther, 76
Wheelwright, John, 45
Whig party (U.S.), 275–281; decline of, 342, 344, 345; division of, 342; election of 1840 and, 279–281, 281; Kansas-Nebraska Act and, 341, 343–346; Mexican War and, 332; "Tippecanoe and Tyler Too" slogan and, 279–280, 280
Whigs and Tories (English Parliament), 116, 276
Whiskey Rebellion, 190, 191
White, John, 25–26, 25; watercolor by, 73
Whitefield, George, 106
Whitman, Marcus and Narcissa, 326
Whitney, Eli, 239; cotton gin of, 242–244, 243; musket manufacture and, 239
Whittier, John Greenleaf, 289
Wigglesworth, Michael, 43
Wildcat banks, 221
Wilderness, Battle of, 390
Wilkes, John, 123, 147
Wilkinson, James, 205
William and Mary, College of, 105
William and Mary, monarchs of England, 48, 66
William III, king of England, 95
Williams, Roger, 45–47, 78; peace with the Indians of, 79
Willkie, Wendell, 328
Wilmot, David, 336

Wilmot Proviso, 335–336
Wilson, James, 172
Wilson, John, 46
Winthrop, John, 39, 43, 45; Hutchinson, Anne and, 46, 47; Williams, Roger and, 46
Wirt, William, 218, 252
Wise, Henry A., 356
Witches and witchcraft, 56, 66–67, 67
Wives, Pilgrim beliefs on, 45
Wolcott, Oliver, 112
Wolfe, James, 91, 109–110, 109, 112
Wollman, John, 296
Wollstencroft, Mary, 163
"Woman in the Wilderness", 51
Women: Adams, Abigail, on rights for, 162–163, 215-A; attitudes toward (1820s), 262; captured by Indians, fate of, 76; colleges, 278; Constitutional era laws and, 162–163; coverture and, 101–102; Dutch women's rights, 101; as early CEOs, 235; gender ratio of colonists and, 42; Indian (Iroquois), status of, 76; Lowell girls, 240–242, 242, 283-A; Puritan religious practice and, 53; Quaker practices and, 51; reform movements and, 295–296; religion and, 107; Seneca Falls "Declaration of Sentiments", 296; voting denied to, 41, 100; voting rights of (suffrage), 100, 161–162, 162;

as warriors in Civil War, 367; as warriors in War for Independence, 152, 159-B; women's rights movement, 257, 296
Wood, timber industry and, 57, 57
Wool, John E., 266–267
Wool and wool industry: export controls on, 57; putting-out system in, 236; wool manufacturing and, 236; wool vs. cotton, 236. See also Cotton and cotton industry
Worcester v. Georgia, 265–266
Workers, child labor and, 239–242, 242
Workingmen's parties ("Workies"), 257
Wrigley, William, 323

X
XYZ affair, 193, 196

Y
Yale College/Yale University, 105, 278
Yankees: origin of term, 48; Yankee traders, 64–65
Yellow fever, 85
York, Duke of (James II, England), 48
Yorktown, Battle of, 154, 155–156, 155
Young, Brigham, 290–291

Z
Zouaves, 368